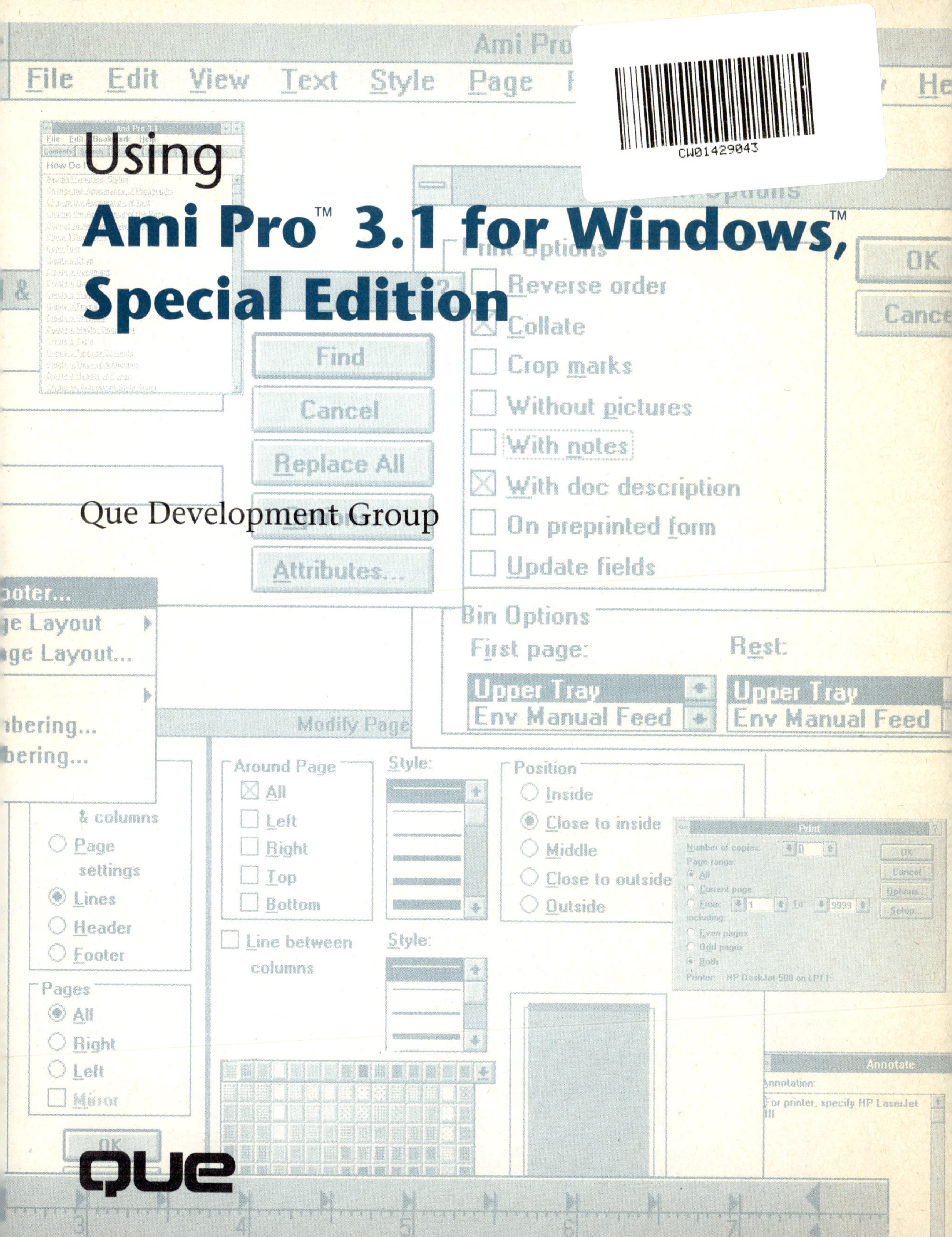

Using
Ami Pro™ 3.1 for Windows™, Special Edition

Que Development Group

que

Using Ami Pro 3.1 for Windows, Special Edition

Library of Congress Catalog No: 94-67946

ISBN: 1-56529-653-2

97 96 95 5 4

Interpretation of the printing code: the rightmost double-digit number is the year of the book's printing; the rightmost single-digit number, the number of the book's printing. For example, a printing code of 94-1 shows that the first printing of the book occurred in 1994.

Screen reproductions in this book were created with Collage Complete from Inner Media, Inc., Hollis, NH.

Using Ami Pro 3.1 for Windows, Special Edition is based on Lotus Ami Pro Version 3.1. Commands and functions detailed in this book may work with other versions in which the pertinent features are available.

Publisher: David P. Ewing

Associate Publisher: Don Roche, Jr.

Managing Editor: Michael Cunningham

Product Marketing Manager: Greg Wiegand

Associate Product Marketing Manager: Stacy Collins

Credits

Publishing Manager
Nancy Stevenson

Acquisitions Editor
Jenny Watson

Product Director
Kathie-Jo Arnoff
Steven M. Schafer

Production Editors
Elsa Bethanis
Nicole Rodandello

Copy Editors
JoAnna Arnott
Bill Barton
Jill Bond
Barb Colter
Lisa Gebken
Lorna Gentry
Julie A. McNamee
Cindy Morrow
Joy M. Preacher
Kathy Simpson

Technical Editors
Nancy Dykstra
John W. Khoury
Lisa Warner
Michael Watson
Michael Wentz

Technical Specialist
Cari Ohm

Acquistions Coordinator
Deborah Abshier

Editorial Assistants
Julia Blount
Sandra Naito
Jill Stanley

Book Designer
Amy Peppler-Adams

Cover Designer
Dan Armstrong

Imprint Manager
Kelli Widdifield

Production Team
Steve Adams
Amanda Byus
Stephen Carlin
Amy Cornwell
Chad Dressler
DiMonique Ford
Bob LaRoche
Elizabeth Lewis
G. Alan Palmore
Nanci Sears Perry
Kaylene Riemen
Clair Schweinler
Kris Simmons
Michael Thomas
Donna Winter

Composed in *Stone Serif* and *MCPdigital* by Que Corporation.

About the Authors

Stuart Bloom is a principal of Learning Associates, Inc., a Chicago consulting group that designs training for clients in technical, financial, and other fields. He also is a beta tester for WordPerfect and an active member of the WordPerfect Support Group Forum on CompuServe.

John Khoury is a software support specialist and has been involved in the PC computer industry since 1982. A native of Lake Charles, Louisiana, John resides with his wife and son in the Atlanta area.

Carolyn Kraut is a Boston-based consultant and author. She provides training, software development, testing, and documentation. She can be reached through CompuServe at 73537,472.

Elaine Marmel is president of Marmel Enterprises, Inc., an organization that provides PC software training and support and specializes in assisting small- to medium-sized businesses to computerize their accounting systems. She also is the author of *Word for Windows 2 Quick Start.*

Tish Nye is presently the Human Resource Information System Manager for the City of Indianapolis, currently implementing a new windows-based HRMS. She has technically edited over a dozen books for Que and enjoys keeping current on new software releases.

Sue Plumley is the owner of Humble Opinions, an independent consulting firm that offers training and seminars in popular software programs. She also is the author of *Look Your Best with Word for Windows* and *Look Your Best with Ami Pro.*

Trudi Reisner is a computer consultant specializing in training users of IBM PCs, PC compatibles, and Apple Macintoshes in the use of applications software. She is president of Computer Training Solutions, a Boston, Massachusetts company that provides PC training, writing, and consulting services. Ms. Reisner wrote and illustrated the *Bitstream FaceLift for WordPerfect* software documentation manual for Bitstream, Inc. She also is the author of Que's *Allways Quick Reference, Harvard Graphics 3 Quick Reference, Quattro Pro Quick Reference, Quattro Pro 4 Quick Reference, Word for Windows 2 Quick Reference,* and *Using PC-Write.*

Don Roche Jr. is the Associate Publisher at Que Corporation. Formerly an independent personal computer consultant, and a senior trainer and curriculum developer, he is the author of *Quattro Pro 4 QuickStart* and *Excel 4 for Windows Quick Reference*; and is a contributing author to *1-2-3 Power Macros*, *Using 1-2-3 for Windows*, and *Using 1-2-3 Release 2.4*, Special Edition. Roche also has performed technical edits of more than 15 computer books, including *Using Symphony*, Special Edition. He has a degree in English from Boston College.

Acknowledgments

As with any book published by Que Corporation, *Using Ami Pro 3.1 for Windows*, Special Edition was a team effort from start to finish. Que wants to thank the following people for their hard work and dedication during the development of this book:

The acquisitions team of Chris Katsaropoulos, Tim Ryan, and Jenny Watson for assembling an excellent team of authors. Product Director Steven M. Schafer, who kept the project together and on track.

The editing team of Elsa Bethanis and Nicole Rodandello who painstakingly maintained the consistency, accuracy, and readability of the text. Thanks also to the editing team from the last edition of this book: JoAnna Arnott, Bill Barton, Jill Bond, Barb Colter, Lorna Gentry, Cindy Morrow, Anne Owen, Joy Preacher, Kathy Simpson, and Robin Drake.

Patty Brooks, Que's Vendor Contact Coordinator, who ensured that everyone received and worked with the latest software release. Becky Beheler, Stacey Beheler, Julia Blount, Betsy Brown, Melissa Keegan, and Sandra Naito, who handled the details and much of the author review.

The technical editing team of Nancy Dykstra, John Khoury, Lisa Warner, Michael Watson, and Michael Wentz, whose outstanding and timely proofing helped maintain the accuracy of the text from cover to cover.

The authors, who worked to integrate the material into this final form.

Publisher David P. Ewing and Associate Publisher Don Roche, Jr., who made this project possible.

The production staff, who turned the final draft on disk into this printed copy in record time—a monumental task.

Lotus Development Corporation, who developed and produced a fine Windows word processing program.

Trademark Acknowledgments

Contents at a Glance

Contents

8 Changing Your Setup 215

II Automating Your Word Processing 243

9 Quick Start: Using a Style Sheet 245

10 Working with Style Sheets 261

11 Outlining a Document 297

III Producing Professional Ouput with Ami Pro 475

15 Quick Start: Creating Frames 477

16 Using Frames 497

17 Using the Draw Feature 533

18 Creating Charts 575

Introduction

Ami Pro 3 is a fully-featured WYSIWYG (what you see is what you get) word processing package that runs under Microsoft Windows. To summarize this software quickly, you can say appropriately that Ami Pro is all about *personality*.

Ami, of course, means *friend* in French. The package also is professional software, as suggested by *Pro*—you cannot mistake its powerful capabilities. But first and foremost Ami Pro is a friend.

Suppose that you want to place lines around the page; how do you indicate where you want them? To the professional artist you say, "Place the lines .73 inches outside the edge of the document." To a friend, however, you can say, "Place the lines close to the inside part of the margin." In Ami Pro, *close to inside* actually is an option you can choose.

Ami Pro is WYSIWYG word processing; that is, if you use italics, you see italics on the screen. If you add to your italic text a picture of a frustrated man breaking a pencil, you see the man on-screen, with the italic text. If you insert three or four drawings, you see each of them and the text as well. If you are creating three columns, you see three columns. If you have a footnote in the bottom margin, you see the footnote in the bottom margin.

In most respects, Ami Pro is friendly and professional at the same time. The Ami Pro SmartIcons, for example, are easy to use-but they also are an efficient shortcut. Instead of choosing a command from a menu, you simply click a SmartIcon. You even can implement a macro by clicking a SmartIcon.

Style sheets, too, are both easy to use and exceptionally powerful. *Templates* (basic documents with certain formats already set up) existed in other software before Ami Pro-but Ami Pro's style sheets create a whole new dimension for templates. In the style sheets, professional artists have drawn on advanced knowledge of the product to set up example documents with complete formatting. Want to add a line around the page but don't know how to do it? Choose a style sheet to do it for you. Want to create a newsletter but don't feel comfortable setting up columns, estimating headline sizes, and planning for pictures? Choose an appropriate style sheet to handle the work.

Frames, too, implement the spirit of Ami Pro—easy but powerful. If your document is basically just one text column, how do you create text in three columns for part of a page? How do you insert a pull-out quote or a picture of a Mack truck and make the text flow around it? How do you handle a chart? For all of these questions, the answer is the same: use a frame. You even can use a frame within a frame within a frame, as far as your computer memory allows.

SmartIcons, style sheets, and frames are just three examples of how the word processing package called "Friendly Professional" lives up to its name.

What Is New in Version 3?

Ami Pro was a powerful software product in earlier versions, such as version 1.2, but it only became a powerful market presence with version 2.0. Version 2.0 was released after Lotus Development Corporation—makers of Lotus 1-2-3, and one of the world's largest software companies—purchased Samna Corporation, a small Atlanta-based start-up company that staked its future on developing one product (Ami Pro) when no one else was thinking seriously about Windows word processing. Version 3 adds even more user-friendly capabilities and features.

Ami Pro 3 adds a Fast Format feature to apply consistent formatting quickly throughout a document. You can use the mouse to copy the formatting used in one structure and apply it to another. Text also can be interactively copied or moved with the mouse, using the new drag-and-drop feature. Editing functions have been added to the right mouse button.

The SmartIcons feature also has grown considerably. An easy way to determine the function of a SmartIcon is to move the mouse pointer over the desired icon and wait a second. A bubble will display with a brief description of what the SmartIcon will accomplish. Users now can save and recall sets of task-oriented SmartIcons. One set can be used for frames, another for equations, a third for editing, and so on. Each set is fully customizable to suit individual needs.

Ami Pro's SmartMerge feature uses a familiar cardfile approach to help the user with common merge applications. An easy-to-use, step-by-step guide can lead even the most inexperienced users through complex merge operations.

A revised Spell Checker, new Grammar Checker, and several document and style template features also have been added. WordPerfect users will appreciate the new WordPerfect SwitchKit feature that helps make the transition to Ami Pro easier.

Ami Pro now provides a mail front end to cc:Mail and Lotus Notes with capabilities to attach a document. When a mail item is received, Ami Pro displays a Mail button in the status bar and you just click the Mail button.

What Is Covered in This Book?

Like Ami Pro itself, this book attempts to be both friendly (easy to read and understand) and professional (comprehensive and in-depth). You might say that this book was written by *"Des Amis"* (some friends). Several authors, skilled with various aspects of the program, collaborated to bring you a comprehensive learning text.

The book begins with basic features and moves to more advanced features. Start by learning the basics; when you feel at home with the fundamentals, you can move to advanced features.

Three Quick Start chapters get you started using Ami Pro. Other chapters provide detailed explanations and additional tips so that you not only use the features, but also understand them and their relationship to each other and to the whole program.

Part I: Getting To Know Ami Pro

Part I introduces you to the basics of creating, editing, and printing a document.

Chapter 1, "Getting Acquainted with Ami Pro," tells you what you need to know to use the program. You learn about the screen display, discover how to use commands and dialog boxes, and explore Windows features and the Ami Pro SmartIcons. You also find out what to do when all else fails—how to get Help.

Chapter 2, "Quick Start: Creating a Document," enables you to use the basics right away. You open a document, choose a style sheet, type text, copy and delete text, and save the document.

Chapter 3, "Editing Techniques," provides details about some of what you learn in Chapter 2. You explore Ami Pro's basic document capabilities as you open, close, create, and save documents in the chapter. You learn how to select, cut, copy, move, and protect text. You also discover how to undo actions when necessary.

Chapter 4, "Formatting a Document," shows you how to modify text with a method familiar to DOS word processing users—by selecting text and using menu choices to format the text in boldface, italics, and so on. The chapter then introduces you to an approach Ami Pro has refined—modifying text by working with styles. When you modify a style (such as Body Text or Title), your changes apply to all text using that style in the document.

Chapter 5, "Working with Page Layout," accomplishes for the total page what the preceding chapter does for the text on the page. You learn how to work with margins, tabs, columns, and lines around the page or between columns.

Chapter 6, "Tools for Marking and Searching Text," shows you how to use a bookmark to mark text, a frame, a table cell, or a specific location in the document. You learn how to use the Go To command to move anywhere in the document—from a specific page to a frame. You also find out how to use Ami Pro's versatile Find & Replace capability.

Chapter 7, "Proofreading and Printing a Document," shows you how to complete a document by using Spell Check to make corrections, how to improve the language in the document with the Thesaurus, how to set up the printer, and how to print the document.

Chapter 8, "Changing Your Setup," completes the section on Ami Pro basics by showing you how to set defaults—for everything from the default mode for a new document to the default style sheet. You learn how to indicate view preferences, such as whether margins appear in color.

Part II: Automating Your Word Processing

Part II familiarizes you with powerful Ami Pro tools, many of which save time for the activities covered in Part I.

Chapter 9, "Quick Start: Using a Style Sheet," provides you with hands-on experience in choosing a style sheet, assigning styles to a document, and modifying those styles.

Chapter 10, "Working with Style Sheets," shows you how to create and modify your own styles and how to manage styles by moving them from a document to a permanent home in a style sheet.

Chapter 11, "Outlining a Document," discusses how to create an outline, how to promote and demote text, and how to collapse and expand an outline.

Chapter 12, "Using Reference Tools," teaches you how to create footnotes, a glossary, a table of contents, an index, and a table of authorities.

Chapter 13, "Working with Tables," covers how to create tables, navigate within them, select cells, edit cells, modify tables after you create them, and merge and sort table data.

Chapter 14, "Merging and Sorting Data," explains how to merge a data document and a standard document in Ami Pro, how to merge an Ami Pro standard document with data from an external file, and how to sort data.

Part III: Producing Professional Output with Ami Pro

Part III provides detailed information on the features of Ami Pro that you can use to improve the appearance of your Ami Pro documents.

Chapter 15, "Quick Start: Creating Frames," like the other quick starts, provides hands-on experience. This chapter covers the basic steps for creating and editing an Ami Pro frame.

Chapter 16, "Using Frames," shows how to create a frame with the mouse or automatically and how to modify such frame characteristics as type, size, position, lines, and shadows.

Chapter 17, "Using the Draw Feature," introduces you to the Ami Pro drawing tools and shows you how to use them to create or delete a drawing, select objects, and edit and size objects.

Chapter 18, "Creating Charts," covers Ami Pro's charting capability. You learn how to create a chart, type the data for the chart, choose a chart type, edit chart data, change the chart type, and use symbols in the chart.

Chapter 19, "Desktop Publishing with Ami Pro," provides a detailed look at important desktop publishing concerns for today's publications and examines Ami Pro's unique solutions for addressing these problems.

Part IV: Using Advanced Capabilities

Part IV provides a guide to Ami Pro's advanced features for readers whose word processing needs include importing or exporting text and graphics, detailed document management, equation capabilities, macros, and customizing the document with power fields.

Chapter 20, "Importing, Exporting, and Linking Files," shows how to import and export text files or graphics, how to edit imported graphics (including image processing), and how to link Ami Pro to another program.

Chapter 21, "Managing Files and Documents," introduces Ami Pro's File Manager for moving, copying, and manipulating entire documents.

Chapter 22, "Working with Equations," shows how to create, edit, and otherwise work with equations in Ami Pro's comprehensive equation editor.

Chapter 23, "Using Macros," discusses how to create, record, and modify Ami Pro macros to save time and keystrokes by automating repetitive tasks.

Chapter 24, "Creating Smart Documents with Power Fields," covers how to insert, display, create, and edit power fields.

Part V: Reference

Part V covers the most basic part of Ami Pro—selecting the appropriate style sheets to use with a document.

The Appendix, "A Guide to Style Sheets," lists all the style sheets that come with the program and provides a sample of each.

Who Should Use This Book?

If a program is a friend, like Ami Pro, why read a book about it? You can accomplish much in Ami Pro—with the exception of power fields and the macro language, perhaps—by browsing through menus and dialog boxes and making choices. The software has made even advanced features available and understandable. In addition, the Help files are excellent.

Nevertheless, at times nothing is as good as a book. You can read this book in the beginning just to canvass the many possibilities in Ami Pro. Take some time to discover notes or master documents or revision marking just by browsing through the chapter and the program. Even if a feature is easy to use, you must know it exists before you can use it. This book acquaints you with the many features that exist in the program.

Being familiar with the software's features is one challenge—being proficient is another. Ami Pro's designers may be friendly about the way they design certain capabilities, but you need to learn how to use those capabilities well. If you need to create a letter and perform a merge operation, for example, a handbook like this can guide you through the process. You may need help in editing an equation, modifying a style sheet, creating a drawing, importing a file from another program, building a table—a little step-by-step guidance can ensure that this friendly, professional program lives up to its name.

Using Ami Pro 3.1, Special Edition is written for everyday users; the book shows you how to use the program in a business context, but the same instructions apply to personal users. Simple guidelines and explanations keep you steadily on course and help you get the most out of Ami Pro in the least amount of time.

How To Use This Book

You need not read this book like a novel, from beginning to end. Keep it available as a reference when you use the program. You may use some features often—this book can help you get to know those features better.

Some Ami Pro features you may use rarely. (Not everybody performs a merge every day or has to manage a long document.) *Using Ami Pro 3.1,* Special Edition can serve as a reference for those capabilities you remember only partially.

Even if you use a feature often and know it well, check this book for shortcuts and special tips. A feature-rich program, no matter how easy to use, deserves a feature-rich book to help you get the most from it.

Other Suggested Reading

Using Ami Pro 3.1, Special Edition is a comprehensive guide to Ami Pro through version 3.1, but no single book can fill all your personal computing needs. Que Corporation publishes a full line of microcomputer books that complement *Using Ami Pro 3.1,* Special Edition.

Several Que books can help you master Windows. *Using Microsoft Windows 3.1,* Special Edition, Third Edition, an excellent guide to and reference for the Windows environment, helps you to understand the many features and capabilities of Windows. If you prefer an introductory text, try Que's *Windows 3.11 QuickStart.* This basic guide to Windows can give you a fast overall understanding, using step-by-step instructions and figures. You can also review *Windows 3.1 VisiRef.*

If you need information on spreadsheet software that works with Windows and Ami Pro, see *Using 1-2-3 Release 4 for Windows,* Special Edition and *Using Excel Version 5 for Windows,* Special Edition. Additional Que QuickStart and Quick Reference books are available for each of these excellent packages.

Conventions Used in This Book

Certain conventions are used in *Using Ami Pro 3.1,* Special Edition to help you understand the techniques and features described in the text.

Words printed in uppercase include file names (TEXT), DOS commands (COPY), and file extensions (SAM).

In most cases, keys are represented as they appear on the keyboard. The arrow keys are represented by name (for example, "the up-arrow key"). The Print Screen key is abbreviated PrtSc, Page Down is PgDn, Insert is Ins, and so on; on your keyboard, these key names may be spelled out or abbreviated differently. Note that, throughout the text, the term *Enter* is used instead of *Return* for the Enter key.

Ctrl+End indicates that you press and hold down the Ctrl key while you press the End key. Other key combinations (such as Alt+T) are performed in the same manner. If key combinations aren't indicated with a plus, don't hold down any of the keys; press each key once in the order listed (for example, End End).

Words or phrases defined for the first time appear in *italics*. Characters that you are to type appear in **boldface**. Words and prompts appearing on-screen and text quoted from a figure are printed in a special typeface. In the text, the underlined letter of each menu selection or option from Ami Pro appears in boldface; for example, **F**ile **S**ave.

Tip
This paragraph format suggests easier or alternate methods of executing a procedure, or shortcuts to simplify or speed the processes described in the text.

Caution

This paragraph format warns the reader of hazardous procedures (for example, activities that delete files).

Note

This paragraph format indicates additional information that may help you to avoid problems or that should be considered in using the described features.

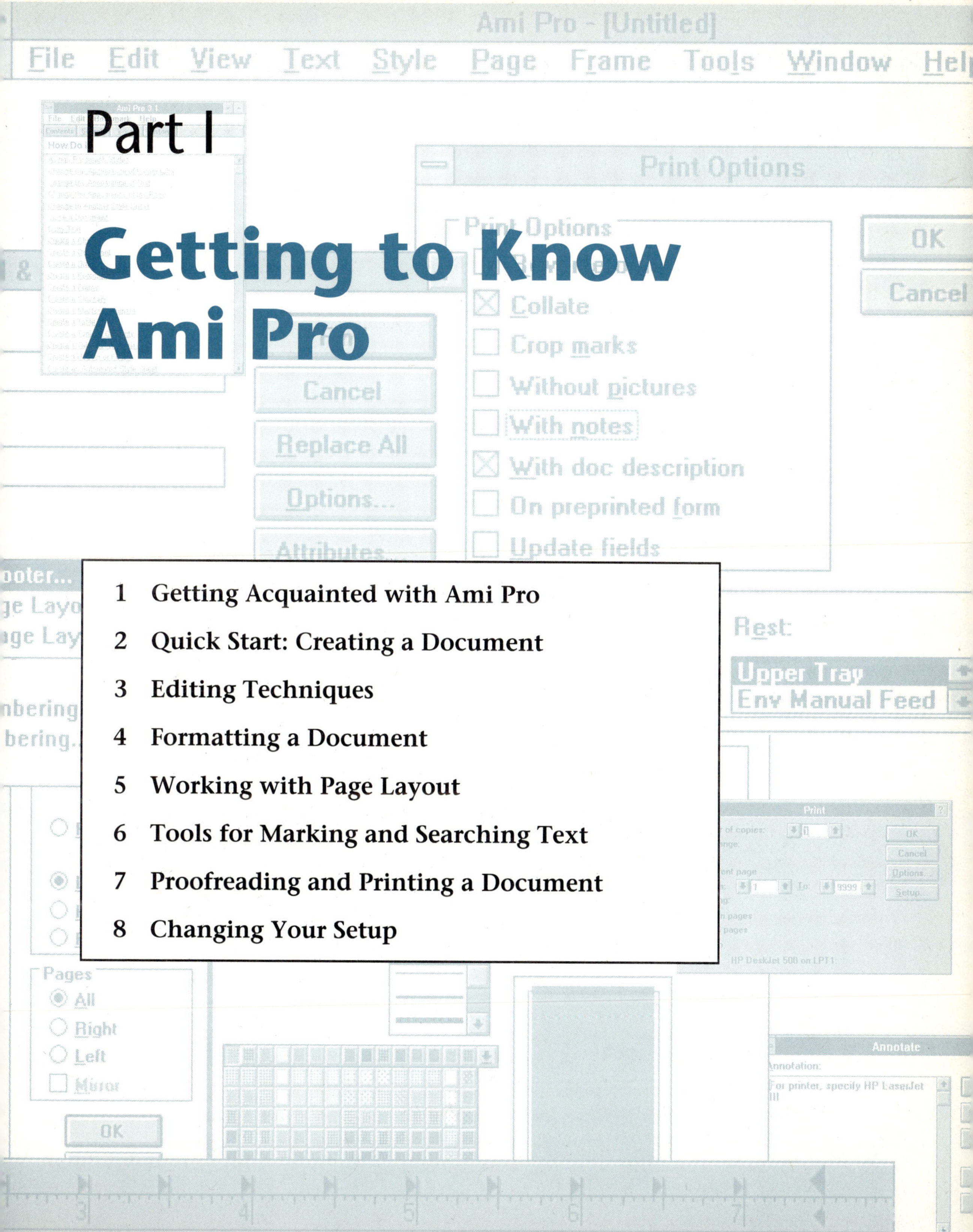

Ami Pro - [Untitled]
File Edit View Text Style Page Frame Tools Window Help
Print Options
Print Options
OK
Cancel
Collate
Crop marks
Without pictures
With notes
With doc description
On preprinted form
Update fields
Cancel
Replace All
Options...
Attributes...
Rest:
Upper Tray
Env Manual Feed
Print
OK
Cancel
Options...
Setup...
HP DeskJet 500 on LPT1
Pages
All
Right
Left
Mirror
OK
Annotate
Annotation:
For printer, specify HP LaserJet III
Clear Tabs

Part I

Getting to Know Ami Pro

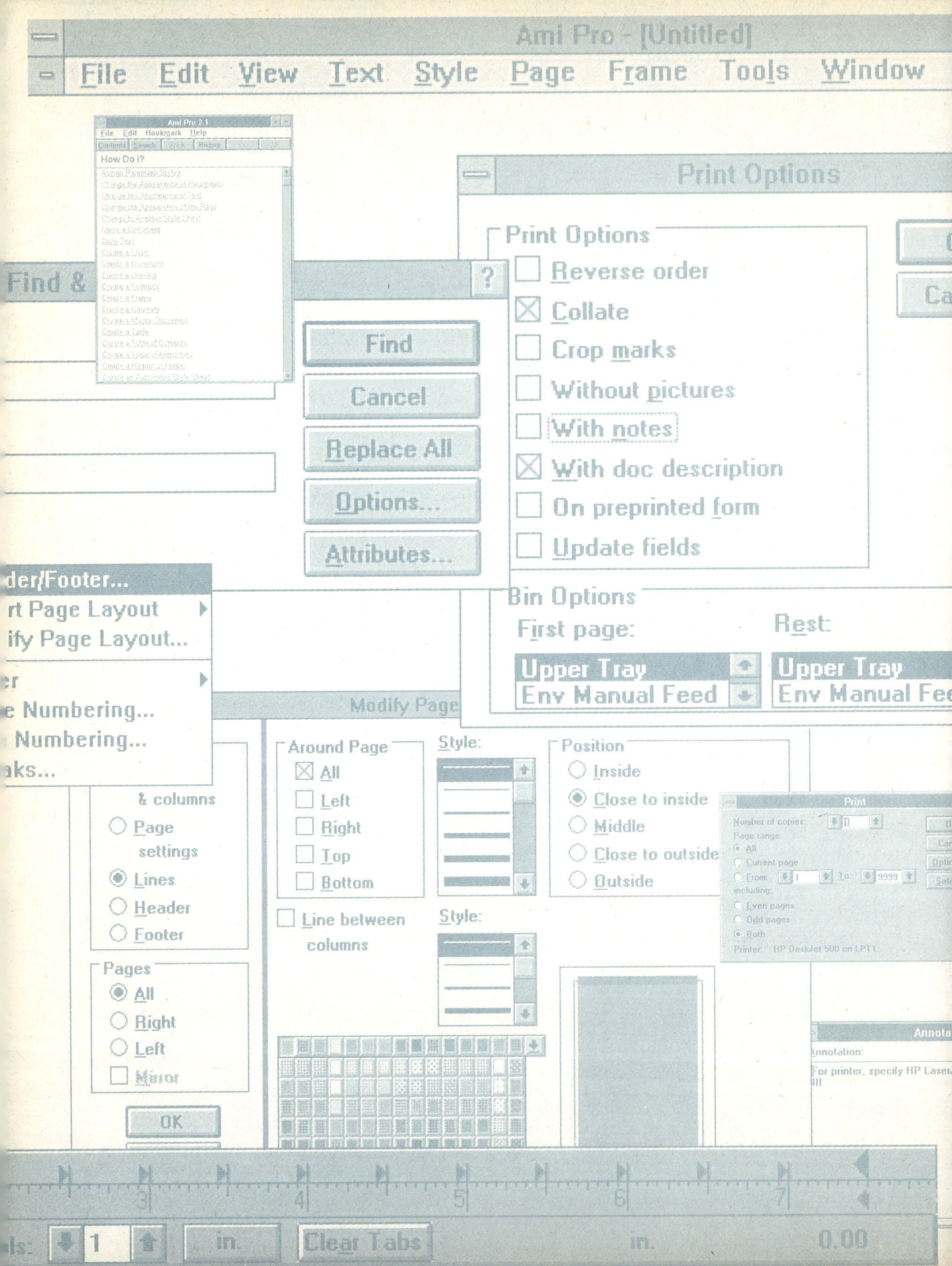
Ami Pro - [Untitled]
File
Edit
View
Text
Style
Page
Frame
Tools
Window
Print Options
Print Options
Reverse order
Collate
Crop marks
Without pictures
With notes
With doc description
On preprinted form
Update fields
Bin Options
First page:
Rest:
Upper Tray
Env Manual Feed
Upper Tray
Find &
Find
Cancel
Replace All
Options...
Attributes...
der/Footer...
rt Page Layout
ify Page Layout...
e Numbering...
Numbering...
aks...
Modify Page
& columns
Page
settings
Lines
Header
Footer
Pages
All
Right
Left
Mirror
OK
Around Page
All
Left
Right
Top
Bottom
Line between
columns
Style:
Style:
Position
Inside
Close to inside
Middle
Close to outside
Outside
Print
Annotation:
Clear Tabs
in.
in.
0.00

Chapter 1

Getting Acquainted with Ami Pro

Ami Pro 3 is one of the most powerful word processing software packages available for the Windows environment. This program provides all the basic features you expect from a word processing program, as well as advanced features for more complicated operations.

Ami Pro's numerous shortcuts enable you to perform operations quickly and efficiently. The designers of Ami Pro took great pains to create efficiencies for users; for any operation likely to be repeated often, Ami Pro seems to offer a shortcut.

Ami Pro rewards you for the time you spend getting acquainted. The shortcuts are a great boon, but only if you know how to use them. Otherwise, the Ami Pro screen can seem a mysterious clutter of icons, buttons, and options.

This chapter discusses the basics: how to navigate in Windows by using a keyboard or the mouse, starting Ami Pro, understanding the Ami Pro screen, making choices, and getting help.

Before you learn these basic skills, the chapter gives you a brief overview of Ami Pro features.

An Overview of Ami Pro Features

Ami Pro 3 is a word processing program that meets the needs of a variety of professionals in different industries. Ami Pro easily can support basic word processing features such as enhancing text with underlined, boldface, or italic type; checking for spelling errors; and checking basic grammar. Ami Pro also supports far more sophisticated features such as creating, editing, and publishing documents; automating work by using macros and glossaries; building tables and outlines; and merging text with graphics.

If you are upgrading from an earlier version of Ami Pro, you can learn about the features that are new in Ami Pro by using the **F**or Upgraders command on the **H**elp menu. Both the **F**or Upgraders command and the **H**elp menu are discussed later in this chapter.

Following are just a few of the features available in Ami Pro:

- Ami Pro 3 supports the capability to type in WYSIWYG (what you see is what you get) mode, as well as several different views of a document.
- You can get context-sensitive help anywhere in the program. To get help, press F1 or use the question mark (?) that appears in the upper right corner of a dialog box.
- You can format characters in different fonts and sizes and add emphasis by using underlined, boldface, or italic type. You can use Ami Pro's new Fast Format feature to quickly repeat text formatting with the mouse.
- You can move or copy text by dragging it with the mouse.
- With the SmartIcon Bar, you can execute many Ami Pro menu commands without opening the menus. If you want to see the function of a particular SmartIcon, just move the mouse pointer over the icon and a bubble will display with a brief description. From the SmartIcon Bar, you can apply boldfacing and italics to text, cut and paste text, open or save existing documents, and undo an action. You can customize the SmartIcon palette so that it provides the commands you use most often and you can save sets of SmartIcons and use them under different editing conditions. Ami Pro comes with nine predefined sets of SmartIcons.
- You can define paragraph styles and apply them throughout a document.
- The Status Bar not only provides status information; this interactive feature provides quick access to paragraph styles, font types and sizes, and SmartIcon sets.
- In addition to spell checking and the thesaurus, Ami Pro 3 provides a grammar checker.
- You can use any of the style sheets supplied with Ami Pro, or you can create your own style sheets to store text and formatting you use regularly, such as a layout for a monthly report. A new style sheet preview

feature enables you to view a style sheet before you attach it to a new document. Because many of the style sheets supplied with Ami Pro are automated, Ami Pro prompts you through actions such as creating a memo or a newsletter.

- With the new interactive Document Viewer, you can check the contents of a document before you open it. You also can print, copy, or find information in a document without opening it.
- You can automate repetitive work with macros and glossaries. Ami Pro comes with more than 65 macros.
- You easily can print envelopes and labels.
- You can create tables of contents and indexes, and you can use the Master Document feature to print multiple documents and create one table of contents and index for multiple documents.
- Legal users easily can mark citations and generate a Table of Authorities.
- You can use the group editing features of Ami Pro to indicate edited passages and to comment and ask questions within the document. You also can identify who made each comment or number the lines of a long document so that reviewers can refer to the line numbers when commenting. If more than one person edited a document and you want to incorporate all the changes, you can use the Document Compare feature to compare the files and combine the changes.
- You can create newspaper-style columns or use tables to create columnar text.
- You can add rows or columns anywhere in a table and change column sizes in a table by dragging. You also can use the drag-and-drop feature to move or copy columns and rows.

In the pages that follow, you find step-by-step instructions for using these features and others. This version of Ami Pro has made the software a versatile document generator; its capabilities enable you to achieve professional and useful—results. Read the next section to identify and interpret terms that appear throughout this book.

Understanding the Terminology

Before you review navigation in Windows and learn how to start Ami Pro, review the terms in table 1.1, which are introduced in this chapter for the first time. Learning these terms will help you understand concepts you read about later in this book.

Table 1.1 Terms in This Chapter

Term	Definition
Mouse	A device that enables you to move the insertion point or pointer when working in a Windows program.
Pointer or mouse pointer	Various shapes on-screen that represent the physical location of the mouse pointer.
Insertion point	A flashing vertical bar on-screen that indicates where Ami Pro will place text when you begin to type.
Pointing	Positioning the mouse pointer directly on top of an object on-screen. To click, double-click, or drag an item, you first point to that item.
Clicking	Pressing and releasing the mouse button one time. Unless otherwise specified, click the left mouse button.
Double-clicking	Pressing and releasing the mouse button two times in rapid succession.
Dragging	Pressing and holding down the mouse button while moving the mouse. Unless otherwise specified, press and hold down the left mouse button.
Choosing	Executing a command from a menu, the SmartIcon Bar, the rulers, or a dialog box by using the mouse or the keyboard.
Dialog box	A box that appears on-screen when Ami Pro needs additional information to complete an action.

The following section reviews navigation in Windows using a keyboard or a mouse.

Navigating in Windows

Although you can use Windows and Ami Pro with only a keyboard, both products are easier to use with both a mouse *and* a keyboard.

When you use DOS programs, you typically navigate by using the arrow keys to move the *cursor* (usually a flashing underscore or a highlight). Moving the cursor is often called *pointing* or *highlighting*. In DOS programs, you generally don't need to "open" a menu; generally, programs display the choices on the menus when you point to the menu name. To choose a command from a menu, for example, you point to that command and press Enter.

In Windows programs, the cursor usually is called the *pointer* and can have many different shapes. When you use Windows programs, you can use both the keyboard and the mouse to "point."

Most Windows programs have the same general appearance. When you start a Windows program, the name of the program appears in a bar at the top of the screen.

You can start Windows by typing **WIN** at the DOS prompt.

Note

If you have trouble starting Windows, be sure that you're in the directory that contains the Windows program or that the Windows directory is in the path set up in your AUTOEXEC.BAT file. Consult your DOS or Windows documentation for more detail.

When you start Windows, the Program Manager appears. If the Program Manager does not appear, open it by double-clicking the Program Manager icon. The Program Manager window opens on-screen (see fig. 1.1).

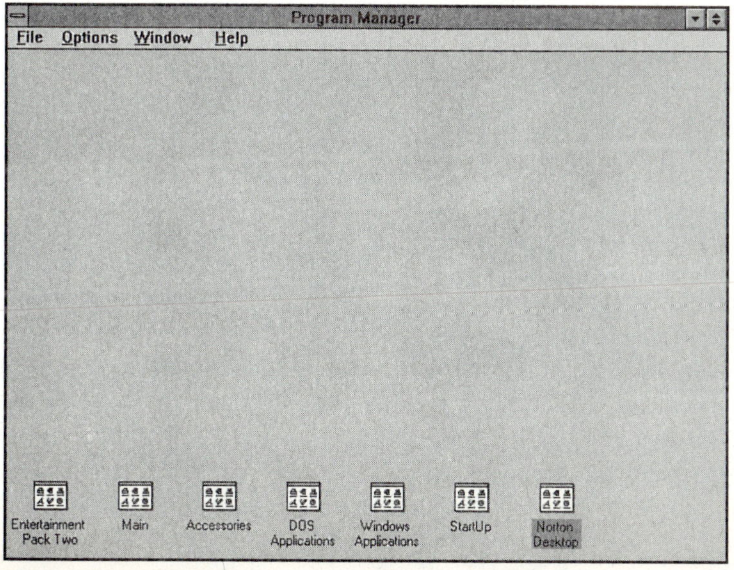

Fig. 1.1
At the top of the screen, you see the name of the program that is currently running (Program Manager).

Just below the program name, you see a *Menu Bar* that contains the names of the Windows menus: **F**ile, **O**ptions, **W**indow, and **H**elp. In Windows programs, you open a menu to see and choose commands.

Using the Keyboard

To activate the Menu Bar by using the keyboard, press the Alt key. Notice that a bar highlights the **F**ile menu's name.

After you activate the Menu Bar, you can open a menu in two ways:

- Move to the menu by pressing the right- or left-arrow key until Windows highlights the name of the menu, and then press Enter.

- Press the underlined letter in the menu name. Note that you do not need to move to the menu before you type the letter.

Windows opens the menu and highlights the first command on that menu. To choose a menu command, use the up- and down-arrow keys to "point to" the command and then press Enter, or press the underlined letter in the command name. Throughout this book, the underlined letters appear in boldface type.

Using the Mouse

The mouse provides an alternate way to navigate in Windows. Using the mouse to navigate in Windows programs reduces the number of keystrokes significantly. The mouse has two or three buttons. In Windows and Ami Pro, you use the left mouse button primarily, but you occasionally use the right mouse button.

The words *pointer* and *mouse pointer* refer to the cursor shape that represents the position of the mouse on-screen. The shape of the mouse pointer depends on its position. These shapes are discussed in detail later in this chapter. Usually the mouse pointer appears as an arrow that points up and slightly to the left.

To move the mouse pointer on-screen, slide the mouse on your desk top. As you move the mouse, the mouse pointer moves accordingly. To point with the mouse, move the mouse until the mouse pointer on-screen is in the position you want. To *choose* a menu command, a SmartIcon, or a dialog box option by using the mouse, press the left mouse button once. To open a menu by using the mouse, for example, point to the name of the menu and press the left mouse button. Windows opens the menu and highlights the first command on that menu. To choose a menu command, point to the menu command you want, and then press the left mouse button once.

Starting Ami Pro

Ami Pro must operate in the Windows environment. You can start the program in three ways:

- From the DOS command prompt
- From the **F**ile menu of the Windows Program Manager
- From the Ami Pro icon in a Windows program group

Note

The Ami Pro installation routine installs the program in the Lotus Applications program group.

The last method is the easiest way to start Ami Pro; however, this book provides instructions for all three methods. Starting Ami Pro by using one of the other methods is easier if you include the directory where you installed Ami Pro in the PATH statement set up in the AUTOEXEC.BAT file. If you installed Ami Pro with its defaults, you installed the program in the AMIPRO directory. The following examples assume you installed Ami Pro in the AMIPRO directory on drive C, and that you included the AMIPRO directory in the PATH statement in your AUTOEXEC.BAT file.

To start Ami Pro from the DOS prompt, follow these steps:

1. Type **WIN AMIPRO** at the DOS command prompt.
2. Press Enter.

   If the computer displays a message that indicates this command failed, the directory that contains Ami Pro is not included in the PATH statement in the AUTOEXEC.BAT file. Change to the directory that contains Ami Pro and try the steps again.

To start Ami Pro from the **F**ile menu of the Windows Program Manager, follow these steps:

1. Type **WIN** and press Enter at the command prompt to start Windows.
2. If necessary, open the Windows Program Manager by double-clicking its icon.
3. Open the **F**ile menu.

4. Choose **R**un. The Run dialog box appears.

   Note that the *insertion point*—a slowly flashing vertical bar—appears in the **C**ommand Line text box.

5. Type **amipro** and press Enter. If the directory that contains Ami Pro is not included in the PATH statement in your AUTOEXEC.BAT file, type the complete path, such as **C:\AMIPRO**, and then press Enter.

Note

By using either of the preceding methods, you can start Ami Pro and open a document at the same time by adding the document name to the end of the command. For example, if you type **AMIPRO SAMPLE**, Ami Pro starts and opens the document named SAMPLE.

Tip
These tips work only for documents in the Ami Pro DOCS subdirectory or the subdirectory specified with Too**l**s **U**ser Setup as the document directory.

To start Ami Pro from its Windows group icon, follow these steps:

1. Type **WIN** at the command prompt and press Enter to start Windows.
2. If necessary, open the Windows Program Manager by double-clicking its icon.
3. To open Ami Pro, double-click to open the Windows program group that contains the icon for Ami Pro.
4. Double-click the Ami Pro icon.

Program Manager starts Ami Pro and the opening Ami Pro screen appears.

Tip
To print a document immediately on starting Ami Pro from the DOS prompt, add **/P** and the file name to the command.

Understanding the Ami Pro Screen

If you chose to install the QuickStart Tutorial during installation, it automatically appears the first time you start Ami Pro. You can exit the QuickStart Tutorial without viewing it; during the installation process, Ami Pro placed a command on the **H**elp menu that enables you to start the QuickStart Tutorial whenever you want. For more information on the **H**elp menu and the QuickStart Tutorial, see later sections of this chapter.

Regardless of the method you use to start Ami Pro, the opening Ami Pro screen appears (see fig. 1.2).

When you start Ami Pro, the program opens a new document named [Untitled], where you can start typing.

You can open a maximum of nine Ami Pro documents at a time, each in its own window. When you open a new document, Ami Pro changes the title of the first document to [Untitled:1], and numbers additional new documents sequentially—[Untitled:2], [Untitled:3], and so on. When you exit and restart Ami Pro again, the program starts with [Untitled].

▶ See "Working with Multiple Document Windows," p. 86

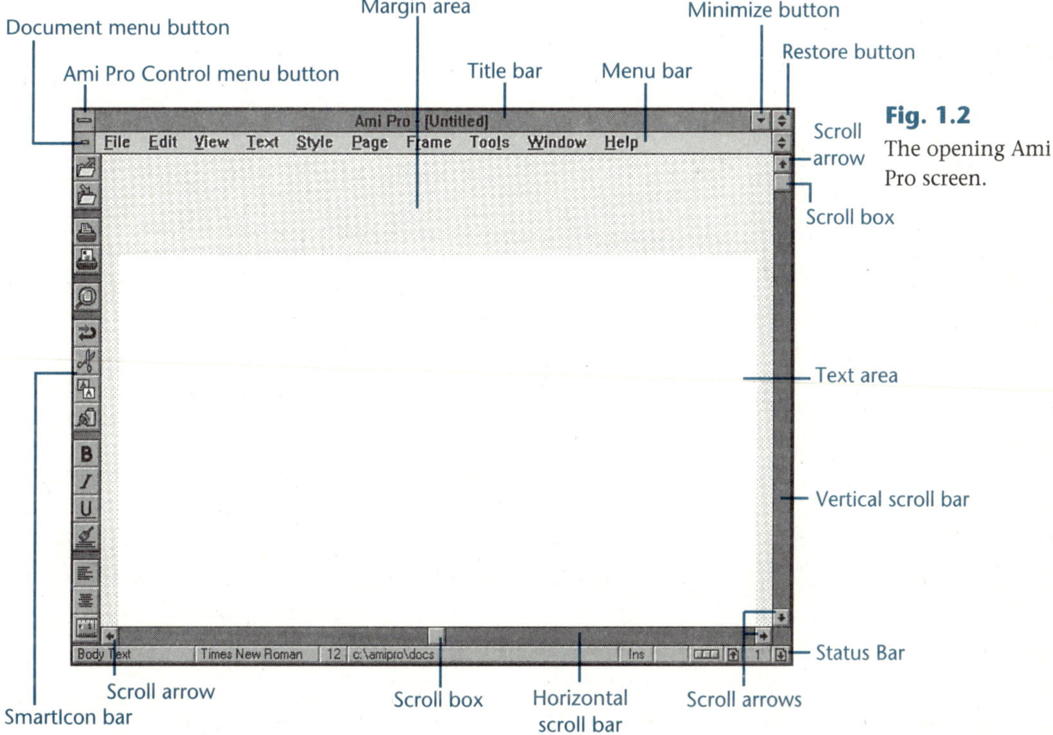

Fig. 1.2
The opening Ami Pro screen.

Identifying Screen Parts

In this section, you learn about the parts of the Ami Pro screen and how to use them. The first part of this section discusses the Title Bar.

Title Bar

The Title Bar appears at the top of the screen and displays the program name and the name of the document in which you are working.

When you start Ami Pro, the program and [Untitled] document are *maximized*, which means that they fill all the available work space on-screen. You can tell that Ami Pro and [Untitled] are maximized because they share the Title Bar. Working in a maximized window is not essential, but usually is easiest. You can change the size of either the document window or the Ami

Pro application window by using the Control Menu or the Minimize or Maximize button, described later in this chapter.

Ami Pro Control Menu

The button that opens the Ami Pro Control Menu looks like a handle on a file drawer and appears at the left end of the Title Bar, in the upper left corner of the screen (see fig. 1.3).

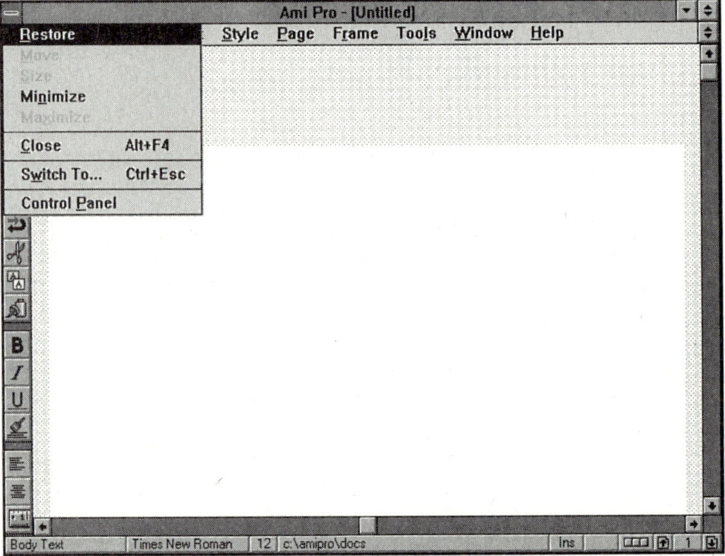

Fig. 1.3
The Ami Pro Control Menu includes commands for changing the size of the Ami Pro application window.

Note that if you reduce the size of the Ami Pro application window, you automatically reduce the size of the document in which you are working. The Ami Pro Control Menu also includes a command for switching to other programs.

Document Control Menu

When a document is open, two Control Menus appear on-screen. The top Control Menu controls the Ami Pro application. The bottom Control Menu controls the document.

The commands on the document Control Menu enable you to close the current document, switch to the next open document, and change the size of the document window (see fig. 1.4).

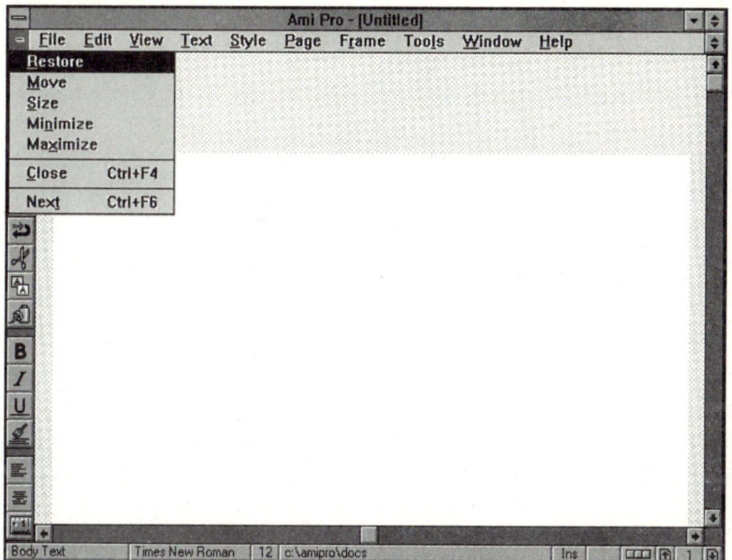

Fig. 1.4
The document Control Menu.

Maximize, Minimize, and Restore Buttons

Also at the top of the screen, but on the right side, are the Minimize button and the Restore button or Maximize button (refer to fig. 1.2). These buttons provide a quick way to change the size of the Ami Pro application window or the document window as detailed in the following list:

- Minimize button. Contains a small arrow that points down. If you click the Minimize button, Windows reduces the program window to its Windows icon. The program is still running but no longer fills the screen. To return to Ami Pro, double-click the Ami Pro Windows icon.

- Restore button. Contains small arrows that point up and down. If you click the Restore button, Windows reduces the window to a size between maximum (full screen) and minimum (icon) size, and the Restore button changes to the Maximize button.

- Maximize button. Appears only if you chose the Restore button previously and contains a small arrow that points up. If you click the Maximize button, Windows maximizes the window and the Maximize button changes to the Restore button.

Menu Bar

The Menu Bar, which contains the names of the Ami Pro menus, appears next to the document Control Menu button. The menus contain Ami Pro commands that are grouped by function. The **F**ile menu, for example, contains commands that open, close, save, and print documents and find information in document files. Ami Pro executes some commands, such as the **S**ave command, as soon as you choose that command. For other commands, the program requires additional information to execute the command. Choosing Ami Pro menu commands and supplying additional information are discussed in detail later in this chapter. Table 1.2 shows a short description of each main menu option.

Table 1.2 Main Menu Options

Option	Function
File	Provides access to the disk, creates new or opens existing documents, closes documents, saves documents, interacts with other applications, and prints documents.
Edit	Provides options that enable you to manipulate text.
View	Changes the display of the page to draft, layout, outline, full page, and other modes.
Text	Manipulates the appearance of text (enables you to change fonts, add italics, and other options).
Style	Creates and modifies paragraph styles and style sheets.
Page	Sets up and alters page layout.
F**r**ame	Creates and modifies frames.
Too**l**s	Provides access to spell checking, grammar checking, drawing, equations, and other powerful tools.
Window	Moves the insertion point between document windows and arranges document windows.
Help	Accesses Ami Pro help.

SmartIcon Bar

▶ See "Positioning the Palette," p. 216

By default, the SmartIcon Bar appears just below the Menu Bar. In this book, however, the SmartIcon Bar appears along the left side of the screen. You can change the placement of the SmartIcon Bar on-screen from the Too**l**s menu. The SmartIcon Bar contains a row of icons that provide shortcuts to Ami Pro menu commands. Choosing a command from the SmartIcon Bar enables you to save keystrokes by executing menu commands without opening menus. To execute the spell check command, for example, you can open the Too**l**s menu and choose the **S**pell Check command, or you can click the SmartIcon that represents the Spell Check command. The SmartIcon Bar also is discussed in more detail later in this chapter.

Text Area

The text area, located below the SmartIcon Bar, is where you type text and insert tables and graphics. In layout mode, the text area is surrounded by shading that represents the margins of the paper. The *insertion point* (a flashing vertical bar) appears in the upper left corner of the text area. The insertion point indicates where text will appear when you begin to type.

Scroll Bars

The scroll bars are located at the bottom and the right side of the screen (refer to fig. 1.2). You use the horizontal scroll bar to move the view of the text onscreen from side to side within the window. You use the vertical scroll bar to move forward and backward in the document.

Often, an entire document does not fit on one screen. To scroll through the document, use the mouse in conjunction with the vertical scroll bar. To move one line at a time, click one of the scroll arrows. To move in a particular direction continuously, press and hold down the mouse button while you point to the scroll arrow. To move up or down one window at a time, click above or below the scroll box, respectively. To move to a particular place in a document, drag the scroll box to that location (for example, to move to the middle of the document, drag the scroll box to the center point of the scroll bar).

Status Bar

In Ami Pro, the Status Bar is not a passive line on-screen that describes your document; it is an interactive tool you can use to implement commands (see fig. 1.5). The appearance of the Status Bar changes, depending on the function you are using. The buttons provide information about the current document and shortcuts to execute commands. If you have a mouse, you can click the buttons to see additional information and options.

Table 1.3 summarizes the buttons on the Status Bar.

Table 1.3 Status Bar Buttons

Button	Function
Style	Indicates the paragraph style for the current paragraph (such as Body Text). Click to choose from a list of available styles.
Font	Displays the name of the current typeface at the insertion point. Click to choose from a list of available typefaces.
Point size	Indicates the point size at the insertion point. Click to choose from a list of available point sizes.
Document path	Toggles between the path name for the current document; the current system date and time; and the line, column, and page position of the insertion point.
Typing mode	Toggles between insert mode (`Ins`), typeover mode (`Type`), and revision marking mode (`Rev`). Use the Ins key on the keyboard to toggle between insert mode and typeover mode. Use the mouse to toggle between insert mode, typeover mode, and revision marking mode. Insert mode inserts new text to the left of the insertion point. Typeover mode replaces old text with new text as you type, and pressing Enter doesn't move the insertion point to the next line. Revision marking mode enables Ami Pro to track insertions and deletions you make.
Caps lock	Indicates Caps Lock mode. This button appears blank if Caps Lock is off.
SmartIcons	Displays a list of available SmartIcon palettes. You can choose a palette from the list or choose to hide the SmartIcon Bar.
Page arrows	Moves the insertion point up one page (click the up arrow) or down one page (click the down arrow).
Page status	Displays the current page number. Click to display the Go To dialog box to move to a different page.

Tip

In draft mode, the Document Path button does not display the position of the insertion point, and the Page Status button is blank.

In figure 1.5, the Status Bar indicates that the style is Body Text, the font type is Times New Roman, the point size is 12, the current document directory is C:\AMIPRO\DOCS, Ami Pro is operating in insert mode, and the insertion point is on page 1.

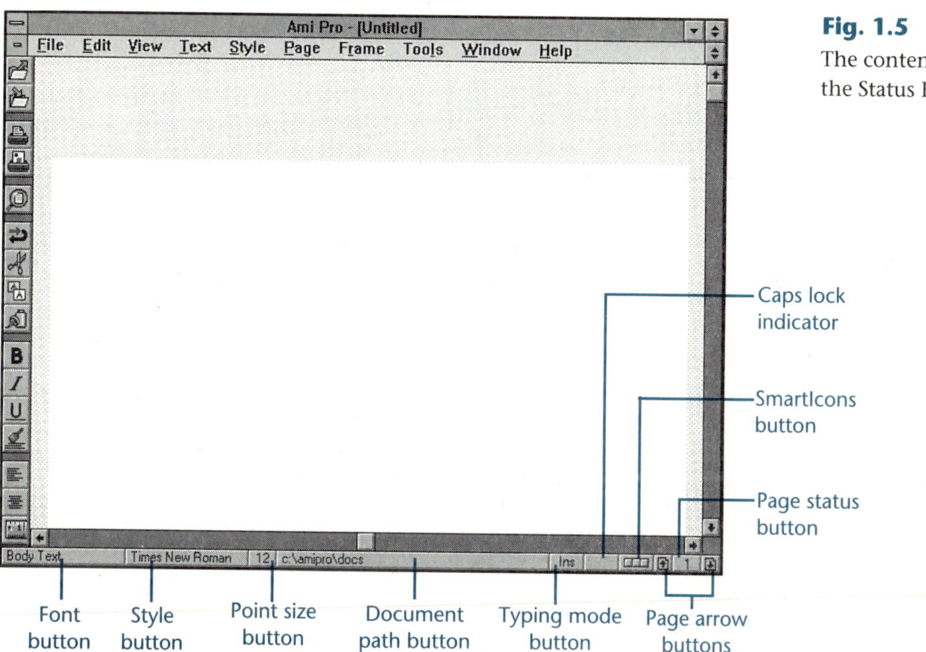

Fig. 1.5 The contents of the Status Bar.

Recognizing Mouse Pointer Shapes

You can use the keyboard or the mouse for most Ami Pro activities. Sometimes the keyboard method is faster because you can press a combination of keys more quickly than you can click a series of commands with the mouse. At other times, however, the mouse method is faster because you can move the mouse pointer across the screen more quickly than you can move the insertion point with a series of tabs or other keystrokes.

▶ See "Understanding the Insertion Point," p. 54

Most users become familiar with both methods of moving the insertion point and employ the fastest or most comfortable method in each situation. While you are learning the program, for example, the mouse enables you to point and click; thus, you can take the time to look over each command in a sequence of commands.

The shape of the mouse pointer changes, depending on the operation. When you type text, for example, the mouse pointer is an I-beam when it appears in the text area. The pointer is an arrow outside the text area and any time you are pointing (for example, at a menu item). The mouse pointer also can take a number of other shapes.

Table 1.4 summarizes the mouse pointer shapes in Ami Pro.

Table 1.4 Mouse Pointer Shapes

Name	Icon	Appears when
Menu Pointer		The mouse pointer is pointing at a menu, a command, a scroll bar, the SmartIcon Bar, a ruler, the Status Bar, or a frame.
I-beam		The mouse pointer is in the text area.
Hourglass		The computer is working on a task. Please wait until the hourglass disappears.
Move Text Pointer		Indicates that you are dragging text from one location to another. Place the vertical bar of the pointer where you want the text to appear.
Copy Text Pointer		You are copying text from one location to another. Place the vertical bar of the pointer where you want the copy of the text to appear.
Help Pointer		You requested command help. When the mouse pointer is this shape and you choose a command, Ami Pro displays help information about the command rather than executing the command.
Help Hand		The mouse pointer is pointing to a help topic for which more information is available.
Move/Size Arrow		You are changing the size or position of a window but have not yet moved the mouse pointer to one of the boundaries of the window. In a table, you are changing the size of a column.
Fast Format Pointer		You have extracted text attributes or paragraph styles and are applying them.
Frame Hand		The mouse pointer is inside a picture or drawing frame and is being used to position the object.
Frame Icon		When you click the Add a Frame SmartIcon (or choose manual frame creation), the cursor assumes this shape which you use to position and create the frame.

Making Choices

When you are working in Ami Pro, you *choose* items from menus, the SmartIcon Bar, and dialog boxes. This section describes how to choose items and how to undo your action if you change your mind.

Choosing from Menus with the Mouse

To open a menu with the mouse, follow these steps:

1. Move the mouse pointer into the Menu Bar.
2. Point to the name of the menu you want to open.
3. Click the menu name.

Ami Pro opens the menu and displays the commands. To choose a command from the menu, follow these steps:

1. Move the mouse pointer to the menu.
2. Point to the name of the command you want to choose.
3. Click the command.

If the command is followed by an arrow, Ami Pro displays another menu with additional commands. If the command is followed by an ellipsis (...), Ami Pro displays a dialog box to request more information. Otherwise, Ami Pro executes the command immediately. A *grayed* or *dimmed* command indicates that command is not available currently. When the insertion point is not in a frame, for example, most of the commands on the F**r**ame menu appear grayed or dimmed (see fig. 1.6). If the insertion point were in a frame, these commands would be available.

If you open a menu and then change your mind, you can close the menu by clicking the mouse anywhere in the text area, or you can open a different menu by clicking the name of that menu.

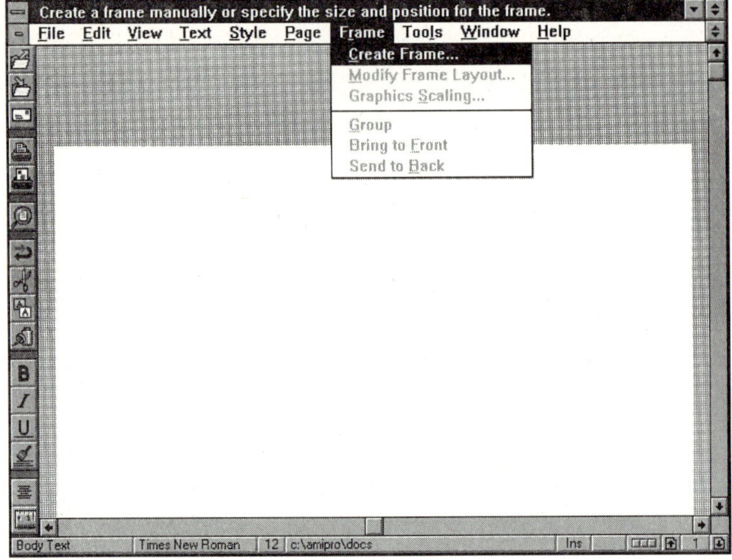

Fig. 1.6
When the insertion point is not in a frame, the only available choice on the **Frame** menu is **C**reate Frame.

Using the Keyboard To Choose from Menus

To open a menu and choose a command with the keyboard, follow these steps:

1. Press the Alt key; the document Control Menu button becomes darker.
2. Press the underlined letter in the name of the menu you want to open. In this book, the underlined letter appears in boldface type. To open the Too**l**s menu, for example, press **l**.

Ami Pro opens the menu and displays the commands of that menu. To choose a command from the menu, press the underlined letter in the command, or press the up- and down-arrow keys to point to (highlight) the command and then press Enter.

If you open a menu and then change your mind, you can do any of the following:

- Close the menu by pressing Esc two times.
- Open a different menu by pressing Esc one time and then pressing the underlined letter in another menu name.
- Open a different menu by pressing the arrow keys to point to (highlight) the menu name.

Ami Pro also provides keyboard shortcuts. Many keyboard shortcuts perform the same operations as options on the Status Bar or SmartIcon Bar; however, you may find using the keyboard faster than using the mouse. Table 1.5 summarizes the Ami Pro keyboard shortcuts.

Table 1.5 Ami Pro Keyboard Combinations

Command	Keyboard Combination
Bold	Ctrl+B
Center align	Ctrl+E
Copy	Ctrl+Ins or Ctrl+C
Cut	Shift+Del or Ctrl+X
Delete the next word	Ctrl+Del
Delete the preceding word	Ctrl+Backspace
Exchange the selected paragraph with the preceding paragraph	Alt+up arrow
Exchange the selected paragraph with the following paragraph	Alt+down arrow
Fast Format	Ctrl+T
Find & Replace	Ctrl+F
Glossary	Ctrl+K
Go To dialog box	Ctrl+G
Go To selected Next Item	Ctrl+H
Italics	Ctrl+I
Justify	Ctrl+J
Left align	Ctrl+L
Modify style	Ctrl+A
Normal	Ctrl+N
Open	Ctrl+O

(continues)

Table 1.5 Continued

Command	Keyboard Combination
Paste	Shift+Ins or Ctrl+V
Print	Ctrl+P
Right align	Ctrl+R
Save	Ctrl+S
Select a Style	Ctrl+Y
Show/hide SmartIcons	Ctrl+Q
Toggle draft/layout mode	Ctrl+M
Toggle full-page/current view	Ctrl+D
Underline	Ctrl+U
Undo	Alt+Backspace or Ctrl+Z
Word Underline	Ctrl+W

Choosing from the SmartIcon Bar

The SmartIcons enable you to execute many Ami Pro menu commands without opening menus. You can choose to display SmartIcons on the left, right, top, or bottom of the screen, or you can leave the SmartIcons floating and move them around as desired. For information on changing the SmartIcon Bar display, see Chapter 8, "Changing Your Setup." In this book, the SmartIcons appear on the left side of the screen in the same order as they would if they appeared in the default position across the top of the screen.

Tip
To take advantage of the shortcuts provided by the SmartIcon Bar, you must use the mouse.

To use the SmartIcons, position the mouse pointer on the SmartIcon and click. Suppose that you want to open an existing document without opening the **F**ile menu. Position the mouse pointer over the File Open SmartIcon and click. The Open dialog box appears, as if you had chosen the **O**pen command from the **F**ile menu.

To learn the purpose of any SmartIcon, position the mouse pointer on the SmartIcon and a bubble will appear with a brief description. Table 1.6 shows the default palette of SmartIcons that comes with Ami Pro.

Table 1.6 Default SmartIcons

Name	SmartIcon	Effect
Open		Opens an existing document.
Save		Saves the current document.
Print		Prints the current document.
Envelope		Prints an envelope.
View		Toggles between full-page and layout view.
Undo		Reverses the last action taken. (You cannot reverse some actions.)
Cut		Deletes the highlighted text and copies it to the Windows Clipboard.
Copy		Copies the highlighted text to the Windows Clipboard.
Paste		Inserts the contents of the Windows Clipboard into the current document at the insertion point.
Bold	B	Applies boldface type to selected text or begins boldface for next text typed.
Italics	I	Applies italics to selected text or begins italics for next text typed.
Underline	U	Applies underlining to selected text or begins underline for next text typed.
Fast Format		Toggles fast formatting on and off.
Left Align		Aligns text at the left margin.
Center Align		Centers text between the left and right margins.

(continues)

Tip
To hide the SmartIcons and provide a wider work area on-screen, choose **V**iew and then choose Hide Smart**I**cons. To quickly toggle between hiding and showing the SmartIcons, click the SmartIcons button on the Status Bar.

Table 1.6 Continued

Name	SmartIcon	Effect
Horizontal Ruler		Toggles between displaying and hiding the horizontal ruler.
Frame		Creates a frame on the current page in the position you specify.
Table		Creates a table at the insertion point.
Spell Check		Checks the spelling in the document.
Thesaurus		Opens the Thesaurus.
Grammar Check		Checks grammar in the current document.
Draw		Inserts a frame at the location of the insertion point and toggles draw mode on and off.
Chart		Inserts a frame at the location of the insertion point and toggles chart mode on and off.
Next SmartIcon Set		Calls the next SmartIcon set.

Choosing Options from Dialog Boxes

Whenever you choose a menu command followed by an ellipsis (...), Ami Pro displays a dialog box in which you supply additional information. Each dialog box may contain any or all of the following types of options:

- A *list box* contains a list of options. Ami Pro has two kinds of list boxes. The **R**esolution list box in the HP LaserJet Series II dialog box shown in figure 1.7 is an example of a "pull-down" list box and is closed when the dialog box first appears. To open a pull-down list box, click the down arrow at the right end of the box or press and hold down the Alt key and then press the underlined letter of the list box name. The Car**t**ridges box is an example of the other type of list box; this type of list box is open when the dialog box first appears. To choose an option from either type of list box, click the option or press the down-arrow key to point to the option, and then press Enter. If the list box is not long enough to display all available options, press and hold down the down-arrow key to move beyond the options that appear in the box.

- An *option button* is a small round button you use to choose one option from a group of related options. In figure 1.7, the **P**ortrait and **L**andscape buttons in the Orientation box are examples of option buttons. A black dot appears in the button of the currently selected option. To choose an option button, click the option button, or press and hold down the Alt key and then press the underlined letter in the option name. (Option buttons also are called *radio buttons*.)

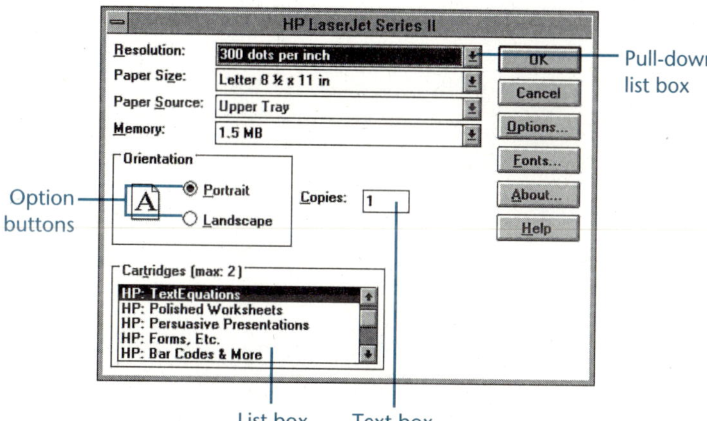

Fig. 1.7
The HP LaserJet Series II dialog box.

- A *text box* is a rectangular box in which you enter text. When a dialog box opens, the current text usually is selected. Ami Pro contains two kinds of text boxes. In figure 1.7, the **C**opies box is an example of a text box in which you just type the new information to replace the selected text. In the other kind of text box, Ami Pro predicts what you will type and offers you the opportunity to type the text or increment or decrement the current selection. In the Print dialog box that appears in figure 1.8, the **N**umber of Copies box is an example of this second type of text box.

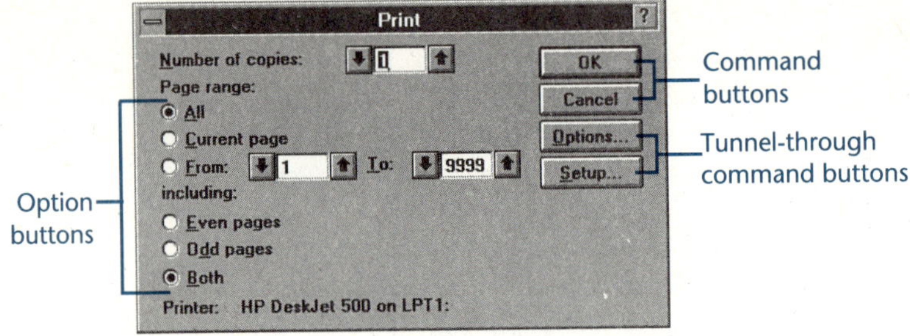

Fig. 1.8
The Print dialog box.

- A *command button* is an oblong button that performs an action. The OK button accepts the settings in the dialog box, closes the dialog box, and performs the command. The Cancel button cancels your changes to the settings in the dialog box and closes the dialog box without performing the command. To choose a command button, click the button, or press Tab until the button is highlighted and then press Enter.

- A *tunnel-through command button* is a command button that opens another dialog box. To choose a tunnel-through command button, click the button by using the mouse, or highlight the button by using the Tab key and press Enter. You also can press and hold down the Alt key and then press the underlined letter in the command button. In figure 1.8, the **S**etup button and the **O**ptions button are tunnel-through command buttons.

- A *check box* is a small square box you use to choose an option. You can choose more than one check box from a group of related options. An X appears in the check boxes of activated options. To choose a check box, click the check box, or press and hold down the Alt key and then press the underlined letter in the option name. To deactivate the option and remove the X from the box, choose the check box again. In the Print Options dialog box shown in fig. 1.9, the **C**ollate check box and the **W**ith Doc Description check box are activated because they each contain an X.

You also may notice a dotted box surrounding an option, like the With Notes option in figure 1.9. This dotted line highlights the current pointer location. To choose dialog box options by using the mouse, click the button or box. To choose dialog box options by using the keyboard, press and hold down the Alt key and then press the underlined letter in the option name. To choose either the OK button or the Cancel button, press the Tab key to highlight the button, and then press Enter.

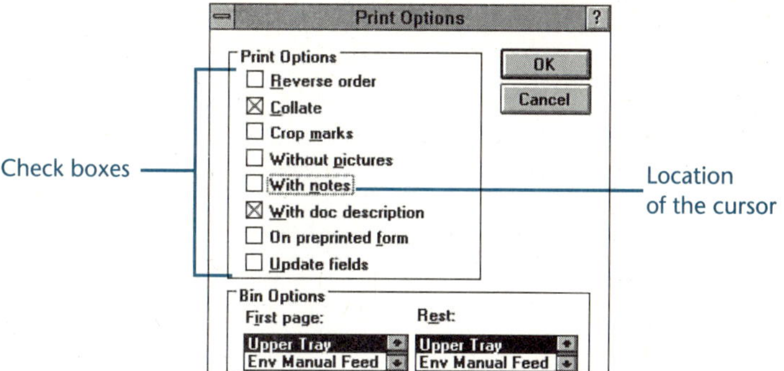

Fig. 1.9
The Print Options dialog box.

Using Help

Ami Pro Help enables you to move through lists of topics to find information or to search for keywords. You can scroll the Help window by using the scroll bars and change the size of the Help window as necessary. You can display definitions or move through cross-references. You also can print Help information, add comments to Help topics, place bookmarks in the Help file, and copy Help contents to the Clipboard (and later paste from the Clipboard to the text area).

Because you can resize and use the Help window when working in Ami Pro, you can place Help and your Ami Pro document side-by-side on-screen, referring to the Help information as needed. To get Help when an Ami Pro dialog box appears, press F1 or use the mouse pointer to click the question mark (?) that appears in the upper right corner of a dialog box.

You can use the extensive Help feature to do the following:

- Activate general Help
- Use context-sensitive Help
- Get Help before you choose a command

Activating General Help

Most users access the **H**elp **H**ow Do I? list of topics and use it to search for information. To activate general Help, open the **H**elp menu and choose the **C**ontents command. Then navigate through the screens to find the information you want. With the other forms of Help, you point to an item and then activate Help for information on that topic. The following sections explain context-sensitive Help and getting Help before you choose a command. To activate general Help, follow these steps:

1. Open the **H**elp menu (see fig. 1.10).

2. Choose **H**ow Do I? A list of subjects for Help appears (see fig. 1.11).

3. To use the list of topics for Help, click the desired topic to see more information, or choose one of the Help buttons at the top of the screen.

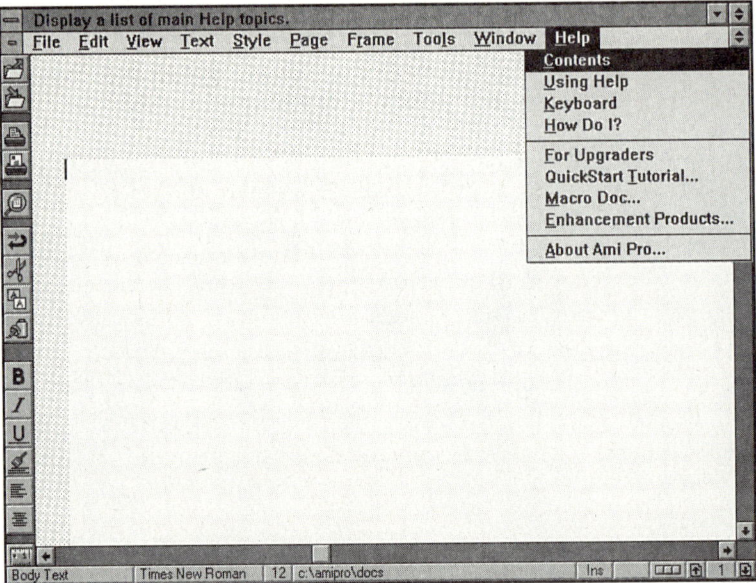

Fig. 1.10
The **H**elp menu.

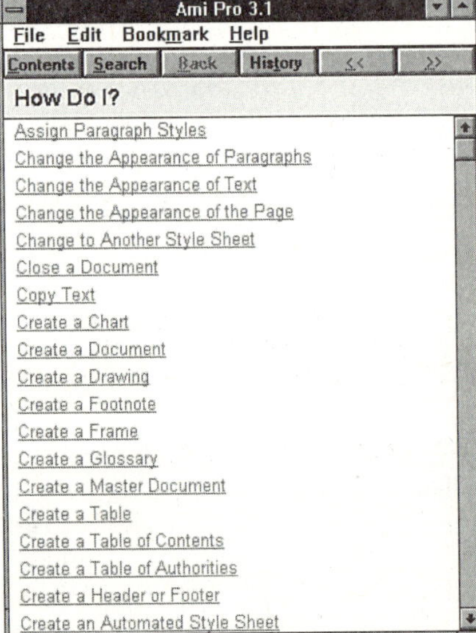

Fig. 1.11
Ami Pro displays a list of Help topics.

From left to right at the top of the Ami Pro Help window are the Control Menu button, the window's Title Bar, and the Minimize and Maximize buttons. Just below the Title Bar is the Help Menu Bar. The boxes below the Help Menu Bar are Help buttons. Help information appears below the Help buttons.

When you view topics, you see topics that have solid underlines. If you choose a topic with a solid underline, Ami Pro Help jumps to the Help information on that topic. Table 1.7 lists the Help buttons and their functions.

Table 1.7 Help Buttons

Button	Function
Contents	Displays a list of main Help topics.
Search	Displays a list of all Ami Pro keywords. Type or choose the keyword to go to the Help screen for that keyword.
Back	Moves to the preceding topic viewed. The button appears dimmed when you move back to the first topic viewed.
His**t**ory	Displays a list of previous Help topics viewed. Choose any topic from the list to move to that particular topic.
<<	Moves to the preceding topic in a series of topics (defined by Ami Pro).
>>	Moves to the next topic in a series of topics (defined by Ami Pro).

Looking Through Help Topics

The forward (>>) and backward (<<) buttons are available when Ami Pro Help has topics before or after the current topic. If the forward and backward buttons are available, you can use these buttons to view topics in the order in which they appear in Ami Pro Help. The forward button displays the next screen. The backward button displays the preceding screen.

Searching for Topics

You can use the **S**earch button to search for Ami Pro Help by using *keywords*. When you choose the **S**earch Help button, Ami Pro displays the Search dialog box (see fig. 1.12).

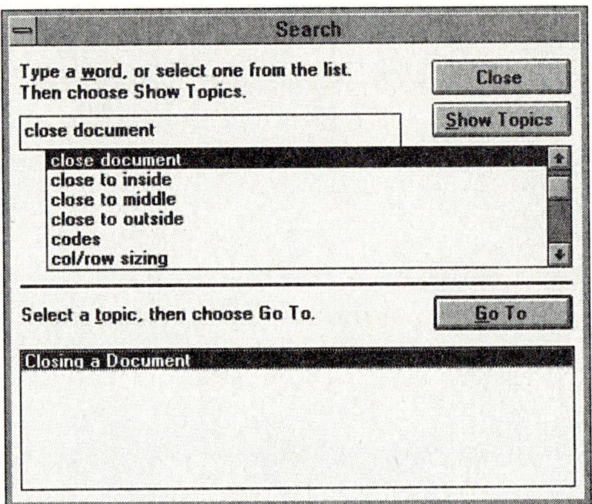

Fig. 1.12 The Search dialog box.

You can type the keyword you want Ami Pro to find in the text box, or choose a keyword from the list box. After you type or choose a keyword, choose the **S**how Topics command button. In the lower portion of the Search dialog box, Ami Pro identifies any related topics it finds. To view the topic directly, click that topic, and then choose the **G**o To button.

Marking Topics with Bookmarks

With bookmarks, you can mark a specific point in the text so that you can move to it quickly later. You can create multiple bookmarks and use them to move quickly between different points in the text.

Ami Pro enables you to use bookmarks in the Help text. Perhaps you use certain Help topics often, such as the steps for recording a macro. You can create a bookmark that pinpoints the Help section so that you can find it quickly. To define a Help bookmark, follow these steps:

1. Move to the help topic for which you want to define a bookmark. For this example, choose the How Do I list and then open the Book**m**ark menu.

2. Choose **D**efine. Ami Pro displays the Bookmark Define dialog box (see fig. 1.13). The topic name appears in the **B**ookmark Name text box.

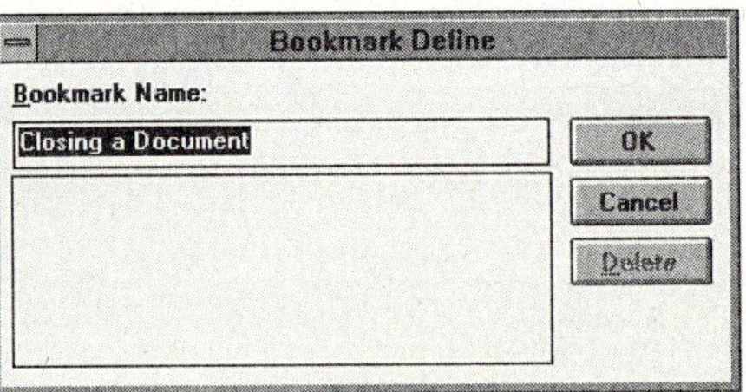

Fig. 1.13 The Bookmark Define dialog box.

3. To accept the suggested bookmark name, choose OK or press Enter. To enter a different name, type the name before choosing OK or pressing Enter.

The bookmarks you define appear on the Book**m**ark menu (see fig. 1.14). To use one of the bookmarks you defined, choose Book**m**ark and then choose the bookmark for the topic you want to view.

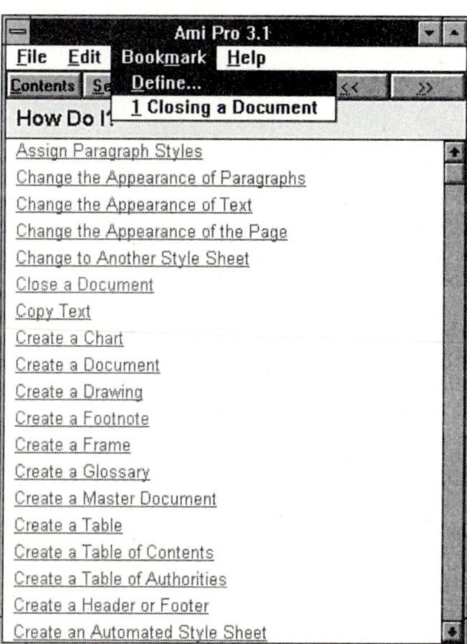

Fig. 1.14
The Book**m**ark menu with defined bookmarks.

Book**m**ark is on the Menu Bar after you choose **C**ontents from the Help menu.

To delete a bookmark, follow these steps:

1. Choose Book**m**ark.
2. Choose the **D**efine command. The Bookmark Define dialog box appears.
3. Choose the bookmark you want to delete.
4. Choose the **D**elete button.
5. Choose OK or press Enter. Ami Pro deletes the bookmark.

Adding Comments to Help

Ami Pro also enables you to add comments to the Help files. For example, in the topic "Printing the Current Document," the Help information tells you, `You can change the printer for the current document Using File/Printer Setup`. You can add your own note that reads, `For printer, specify HP LaserJet III.`

To annotate a Help topic, follow these steps:

1. Open the **H**elp menu and choose **H**ow Do I?
2. From the list, choose Print a document. Ami Pro Help displays `Printing the Current Document.`
3. Choose **E**dit.
4. Choose **A**nnotate. The **H**elp **A**nnotation dialog box appears (see fig. 1.15).
5. Type your comment in the **A**nnotation text box. In this example, type **For printer, specify HP LaserJet III**.
6. Choose **S**ave.

Ami Pro adds the comment to the current topic. Notice that a small green paper clip appears to the left of the topic to indicate that an annotation exists for this Help topic. If you click the paper clip, Ami Pro displays the annotation.

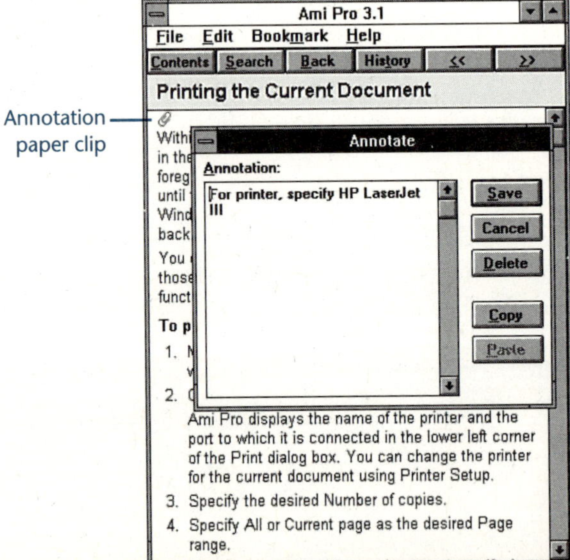

Fig. 1.15
Annotating a Help topic.

After you create an annotation, you can edit it by following these steps:

1. Display the topic that contains the annotation you want to edit. In this example, display the topic "Printing the Current Document."

2. Click the paper clip icon or open the **E**dit menu and then choose the **A**nnotate command. The Help Annotation dialog box appears.

3. Edit the text as desired.

4. Choose **S**ave.

To delete a Help annotation, follow these steps:

1. Display the Help topic that contains the annotation you want to delete.

2. Click the paper clip icon or open the **E**dit menu. Choose **A**nnotate. The Help Annotation dialog box appears.

3. Choose the **D**elete button. Ami Pro deletes the annotation and removes the paper clip icon from the Help text.

Copying Help to the Clipboard

Copying Help text into your document as you learn Ami Pro can make the learning process easier. For example, you can paste Help passages into your document, apply the information, and delete the Help text when you no longer need it. To copy a Help topic to the Clipboard, follow these steps:

1. Display the **H**elp topic you want to copy.

2. Open the **E**dit menu and choose the **C**opy command. Ami Pro opens the Copy dialog box.

3. Choose the **C**opy command button. Ami Pro copies the active Help topic to the Clipboard.

   By default, Ami Pro copies the entire Help topic. You can remove text you don't want to copy by selecting it in the Copy dialog box and deleting it before you choose the Copy command button. You will not delete text from Help; you will remove it from the copy that Ami Pro places on the Windows Clipboard.

4. To paste the copied topic into the document, return to the document, position the insertion point in the location where you want the topic to appear, and then choose **E**dit **P**aste, press Ctrl+V, or choose the Paste SmartIcon.

Tip
When you print from Help, you cannot change the format; Ami Pro always prints in a defined style to the printer you specify.

Printing a Help Topic

Rather than using the Help screen as you work with a command, you may want to use a printout of the Help information on that command. To print a Help topic, follow these steps:

1. Display the Help topic you want to print.
2. Open the **F**ile menu.
3. If you want to print to a specific printer, choose the P**r**int Setup command.
4. Choose **P**rint Topic. Ami Pro prints the Help topic to your printer.

Exiting from the Help Window

You can exit from the Help window in the following three ways:

- Choose E**x**it from the Help **F**ile menu.
- Click the Control Menu icon in the upper left corner of the screen, and then choose the Close command.
- Double-click the Control Menu icon.
- Press Alt+F4.

Note

If you click the mouse pointer anywhere outside the Help window, the Help window disappears, but you do not exit from Help. You can use the Task List to return to Help. Open the application Control Menu and choose S**w**itch To or press Ctrl+Esc. The Task List appears and Ami Pro Help is one of the choices on the Task List. Choose it and the Help window reappears.

Understanding Other Help Menu Commands

The Help menu contains several other commands you may not use as often as the **H**ow Do I command. To get information about how Ami Pro Help works, for example, choose **U**sing Help from the Help menu.

Use the **K**eyboard command to display the list of keyboard shortcuts for Ami Pro functions. Use the **C**ontents command to display a list of common Ami Pro functions and information about them. Choose the **F**or Upgraders command if you are upgrading from Ami Pro 2.0 and want information about the differences between Ami Pro 2.0 and Ami Pro 3.

If you installed the QuickStart Tutorial, you see a command for it on the **H**elp menu. The QuickStart Tutorial provides an overview for new users. If you installed the SwitchKit for WordPerfect Users, you may see the **For WordPerfect Users** command on the **H**elp menu. This utility helps convert other word processing files to Ami Pro format. In addition, it helps WordPerfect users learn how to use Ami Pro. The **M**acro Doc command provides an on-line reference for the Ami Pro macro language. Use this documentation to help you create and customize your own macros.

The **E**nhancement Products command provides information about other Windows products you can use with Ami Pro. The **A**bout Ami Pro command displays version, copyright, and memory availability information about Ami Pro.

Using Context-Sensitive Help

Rather than moving through the Help index topic-by-topic, you can get Help about any Ami Pro dialog box by opening that dialog box and pressing F1, or by using the mouse to choose the question mark (?) in the upper right corner of the dialog box.

To demonstrate getting context-sensitive Help in a dialog box, the following steps use the Find & Replace dialog box:

1. Open the **E**dit menu.

2. Choose Find and **R**eplace. The Find and Replace dialog box appears (see fig. 1.16). Note the question mark (?) in the upper right corner of the dialog box.

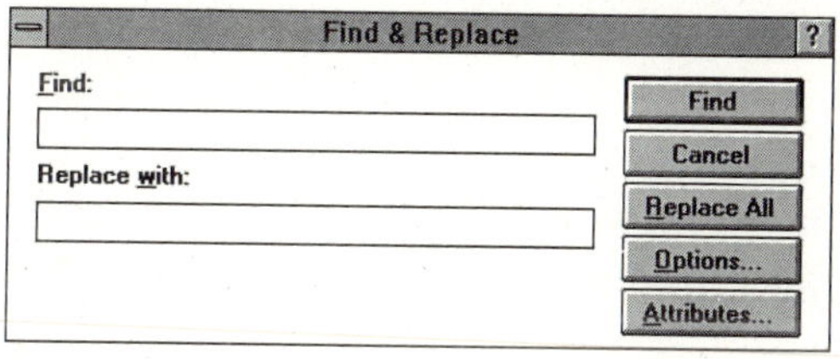

Fig. 1.16
The Find & Replace dialog box.

3. Press F1 or use the mouse pointer to click the question mark. The specific Help topic appears for that dialog box.

You can use this method with commands as well as dialog boxes, but you cannot choose the command from the menu by using the mouse. You must use the keyboard to point at it. As an alternative, see the following section.

Getting Help before Choosing a Command

You can turn the mouse pointer into a "help requester." When operating in this mode, you do not actually choose commands, but choose to view the Help topic related to the command or the area of the screen to which you pointed.

To get Help about the area or command to which you are pointing, follow these steps:

1. Press Shift+F1. The mouse pointer changes shape until you make a Help request (see fig. 1.17).

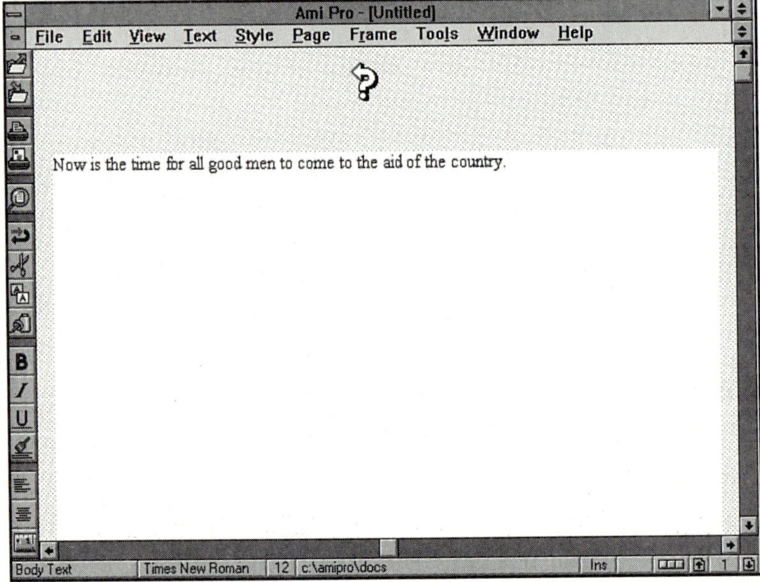

Fig. 1.17 The mouse pointer after you press Shift+F1.

2. Point to an area of the screen about which you want Help (the SmartIcon Bar, for example), or open a menu and choose a command. Ami Pro displays Help information on the command you chose.

Tip If you choose a command that contains intermediate menus, the mouse pointer retains the "help requester" shape until you choose a command.

You can make one Help request each time you press Shift+F1. When you exit Help, the mouse pointer returns to normal operation.

Exiting from Ami Pro

You can exit from Ami Pro in the following three ways:

- Choose **F**ile, and then choose E**x**it.
- Open the application Control Menu and choose the **C**lose command.
- Double-click the application Control Menu icon.

Regardless of the method you use, if you have made changes to the document you see a message asking whether you want to save the document. Choose **Y**es, **N**o, or Cancel.

Summary

In this chapter, you learned the basics of starting Ami Pro and using the mouse and the keyboard. This chapter also describes the parts of the Ami Pro screen and the mouse pointer shapes. You learned how to start Ami Pro, identify the parts of the screen, use dialog boxes, and access Help.

In the next chapter, you create an Ami Pro document.

Chapter 2

Quick Start: Creating a Document

This quick start chapter is designed to get you up and running quickly with Ami Pro. In this chapter, you learn how to create a new document, type text and correct simple mistakes, display different views of the document, and how to save and print the document.

As part of creating a document, you also learn how to choose a style sheet and assign styles to paragraphs in the document. When you understand how to choose a style sheet and assign styles, creating an Ami Pro document is largely a matter of typing what you want to say.

Understanding Style Sheets

Ami Pro uses *style sheets* to store formatting information about the paragraphs and pages of a document. The style sheet acts as a template to determine the document's initial appearance; you choose a style sheet for each document you create in Ami Pro.

Each style sheet contains multiple *paragraph styles* and one *page layout style.* As you type text, you use the paragraph styles in the style sheet to assign formatting to your document. The page layout style provides margins, tab settings, page size, orientation, and other elements.

You can override paragraph styles and the page layout style as needed; changes you make affect only the current document. You maintain complete control over the final appearance of your document, no matter which style sheet you choose. Formatting your document is easiest, however, when you choose a style sheet that closely matches the type of document you want to create.

You can use the style sheets you receive with Ami Pro, or you can create your own style sheets. Because you base your documents on style sheets, you don't need to create basic settings each time you start a new document; Ami Pro uses the settings in the style sheet as a guideline for formatting the document. You can change the settings before you start typing or at any time while you are typing. Figures 2.1 and 2.2 show the same sample document, using two different style sheets.

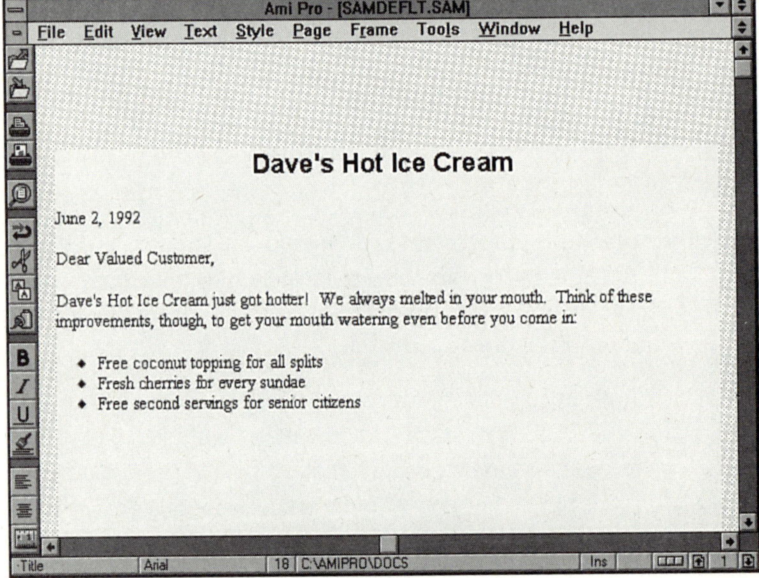
Ami Pro - [SAMDEFLT.SAM]
File Edit View Text Style Page Frame Tools Window Help
Dave's Hot Ice Cream
June 2, 1992
Dear Valued Customer,
Dave's Hot Ice Cream just got hotter! We always melted in your mouth. Think of these improvements, though, to get your mouth watering even before you come in:
Free coconut topping for all splits
Fresh cherries for every sundae
Free second servings for senior citizens
Title
Arial
18 C:\AMIPRO\DOCS
Ins

Fig. 2.1
This sample document uses the paragraph styles in the default style sheet.

Both of these documents use the "same" paragraph styles; the heading `Dave's Hot Ice Cream` appears in the Title paragraph style from each style sheet, and the list appears in the Bullet 1 paragraph style. The body of both letters appears in the Body Text paragraph style. In this case, the names of the paragraph styles happen to be the same. Because the paragraph styles have different definitions within their respective style sheets, however, the appearance of the text differs in the two examples. While the two style sheets share some paragraph style names, they also contain paragraph style names that differ, as you can see from the lists of styles in figures 2.3 and 2.4.

Some style sheets contain text; you can use a style sheet with or without its contents. (You can preview the style sheets before using them so that you can see what kinds of information they contain.)

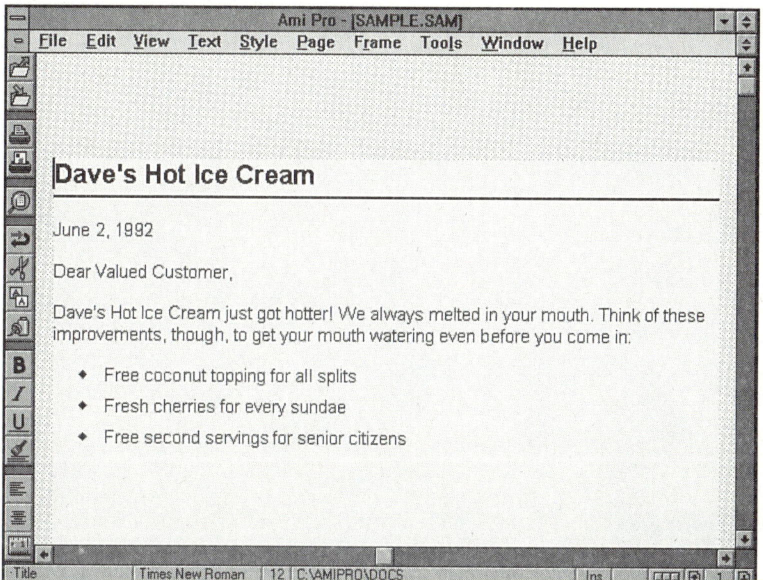
Ami Pro - [SAMPLE.SAM]
File Edit View Text Style Page Frame Tools Window Help
Dave's Hot Ice Cream
June 2, 1992
Dear Valued Customer,
Dave's Hot Ice Cream just got hotter! We always melted in your mouth. Think of these improvements, though, to get your mouth watering even before you come in:
Free coconut topping for all splits
Fresh cherries for every sundae
Free second servings for senior citizens
Title
Times New Roman
12
C:\AMIPRO\DOCS
Ins

Fig. 2.2
The same sample document, based on an informal business letter style sheet.

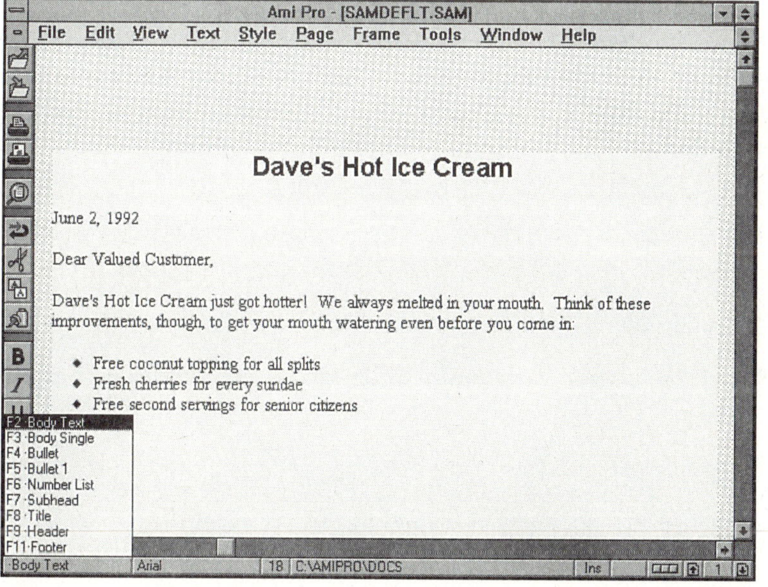
Ami Pro - [SAMDEFLT.SAM]
File Edit View Text Style Page Frame Tools Window Help
Dave's Hot Ice Cream
June 2, 1992
Dear Valued Customer,
Dave's Hot Ice Cream just got hotter! We always melted in your mouth. Think of these improvements, though, to get your mouth watering even before you come in:
Free coconut topping for all splits
Fresh cherries for every sundae
Free second servings for senior citizens
F2 Body Text
F3 Body Single
F4 Bullet
F5 Bullet 1
F6 Number List
F7 Subhead
F8 Title
F9 Header
F11 Footer
Body Text
Arial
18
C:\AMIPRO\DOCS
Ins

Fig. 2.3
The Styles list (bottom left corner of the screen) shows styles available in the default style sheet.

You learn more about style sheets, and about creating your own style sheets and paragraph styles, in Part II of this book. For a complete list of all Ami Pro standard style sheets, see the Appendix.

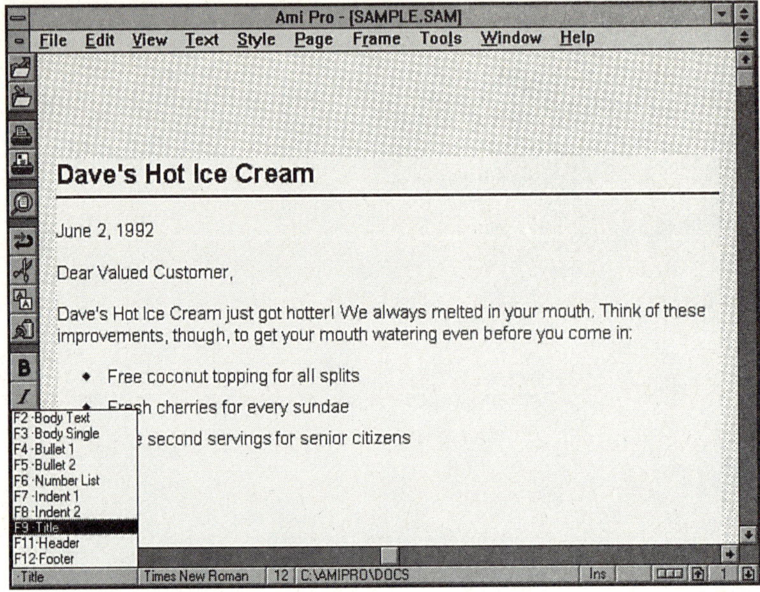
Ami Pro - [SAMPLE.SAM]
File Edit View Text Style Page Frame Tools Window Help
Dave's Hot Ice Cream
June 2, 1992
Dear Valued Customer,
Dave's Hot Ice Cream just got hotter! We always melted in your mouth. Think of these improvements, though, to get your mouth watering even before you come in:
Free coconut topping for all splits
Fresh cherries for every sundae
second servings for senior citizens
F2 Body Text
F3 Body Single
F4 Bullet 1
F5 Bullet 2
F6 Number List
F7 Indent 1
F8 Indent 2
F9 Title
F11 Header
F12 Footer
Title
Times New Roman
12
C:\AMIPRO\DOCS
Ins

Fig. 2.4
Styles available in the informal business letter style sheet.

Opening a New Document

You can begin typing text as soon as you start Ami Pro. The document that appears on-screen, `[Untitled]`, is based on a style sheet called _DEFAULT.STY. This style sheet provides basic settings established by Ami Pro. The _DEFAULT.STY style sheet includes the following settings:

- A general-use typeface (the specific typeface and point size depend on your printer)
- Margins of one inch all around
- Paragraph styles that produce single-spaced text, aligned with the left margin
- Tab stops set every half inch

Although you can use the [UNTITLED] document, for the example in this section you should use the following steps to create a new document.

Note

To choose options with the mouse, move the mouse pointer over the check box next to the option; then quickly press and release the left mouse button (*click*). To choose options with the keyboard, hold down the Alt key and press the highlighted letter in the option name, or use the Tab key to move the cursor to the option and then press the space bar to select the option.

1. Choose **F**ile.

2. Choose **N**ew. The New dialog box appears, as shown in figure 2.5. You use this dialog box to specify options for creating a new document—the desired style sheet, whether you want to use the text built into the style sheet, and so on.

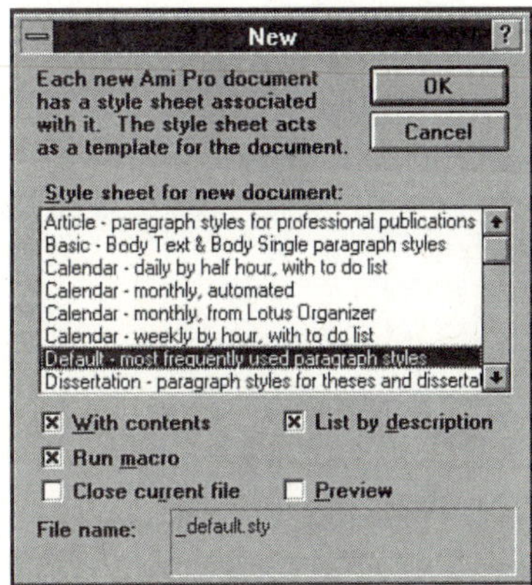

Fig. 2.5
The New dialog box.

In the **S**tyle Sheet for New Document list box, Ami Pro displays the available style sheets. With the next step, you begin the process of selecting a style sheet to use with your new document.

3. Select the List by **D**escription option to see a description of each style sheet.

4. In the **S**tyle Sheet for New Document list box, choose a style sheet. To choose with the keyboard, use the arrow keys to highlight the style sheet description. To choose with the mouse, click the style sheet description.

Optionally, you can choose to include the text that may be stored in the style sheet and to preview the style sheet (with or without its contents) on-screen. To include text stored in the style sheet, choose the **W**ith Contents option. To see the contents of the style sheet before you decide to use it, choose the **P**review option. Figure 2.6 shows a preview of the monthly calendar style sheet, shown with contents. (When the **W**ith Contents option is selected, you preview the style sheet with its contents. If you prefer to use the style sheet without contents, deselect the **W**ith Contents option after previewing the style sheet.)

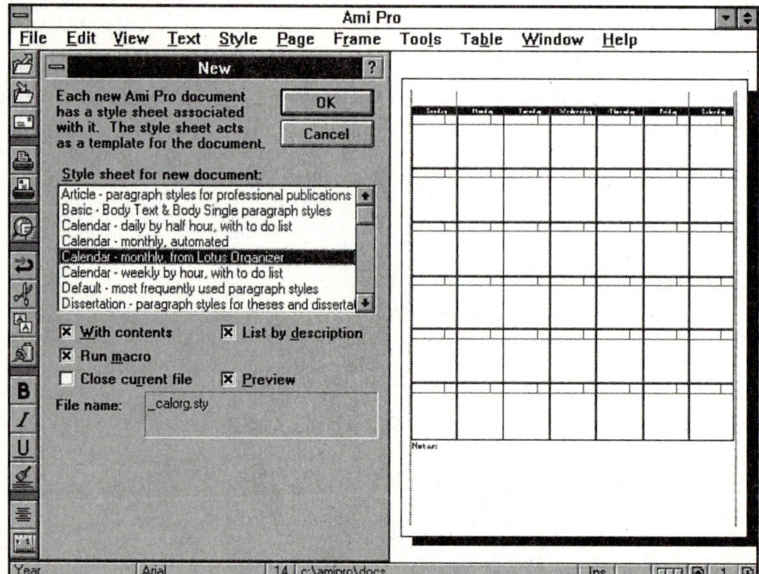

Fig. 2.6
The Monthly Calendar style sheet.

For this example, choose the default style sheet, _DEFAULT.STY, which contains no text.

5. Choose OK or press Enter. If you opened the new document with style sheet contents, Ami Pro displays the contents of the style sheet on-screen. If you opened the new document without style sheet contents, Ami Pro displays a blank editing window in which you can start typing. You then can use the styles available with the style sheet.

To see the paragraph styles contained in the style sheet, you use the Styles box (at the upper right corner of the screen) or the Styles list (at the bottom left corner of the screen), as shown in figure 2.7.

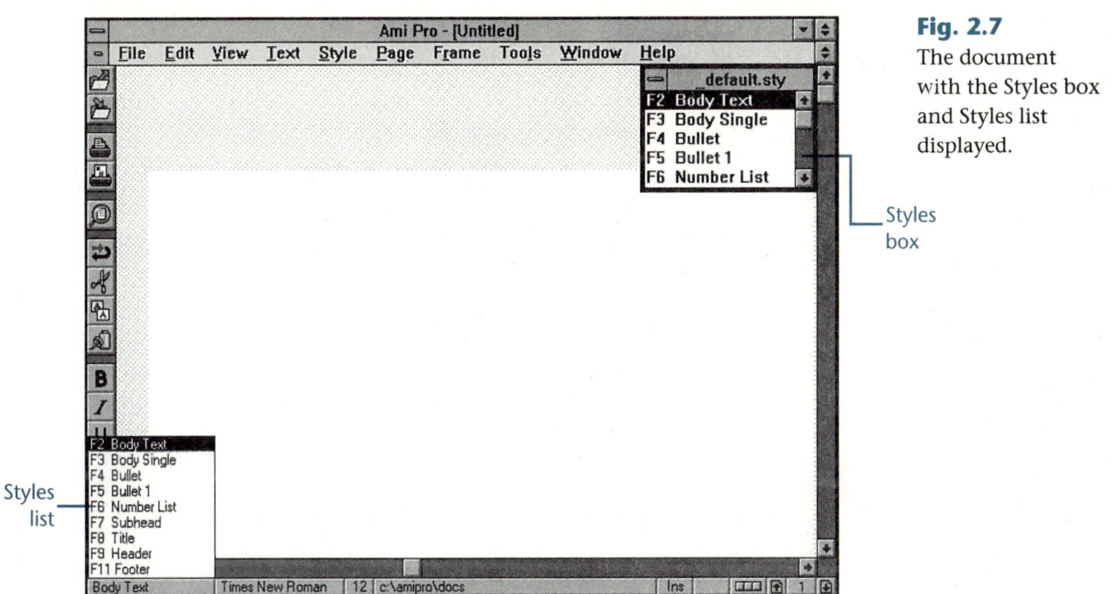

Fig. 2.7
The document with the Styles box and Styles list displayed.

To view the Styles box, follow these steps:

1. Open the **V**iew menu.

2. Select the Show Styles **B**ox command. The Styles box appears in the upper right corner of the screen, showing the name of the current style sheet and the paragraph styles it contains.

You can hide the Styles box by choosing Hide Styles **B**ox from the **V**iew menu, or by clicking the Control Menu on the Styles box and then choosing the Close command. (For details on using the Control Menu, see Chapter 1, "Getting Acquainted with Ami Pro.") You access the Styles list with the mouse by clicking the Style button on the Status Bar.

Entering Text in a Document

Typing text in a word processing program can be much faster and easier than writing on paper. You can make revisions quickly with word processing; if you change your mind about the structure of a sentence or the organization of a paragraph, you can insert words and sentences, delete phrases, move information from one location to another, and so on.

Understanding the Insertion Point

The *insertion point* is the flashing vertical bar in the text area of the document. The insertion point marks the place where Ami Pro inserts text into the document (see fig. 2.8). In a new document, the insertion point appears in the upper-left corner of the text area. As you type, text appears to the left of the insertion point, and the insertion point moves to the right. You can move the insertion point by using the keyboard or the mouse, but you cannot move the insertion point beyond the last character in the document.

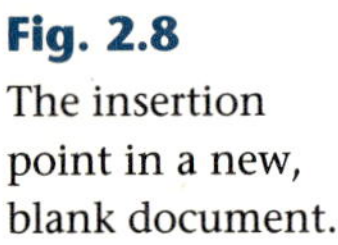

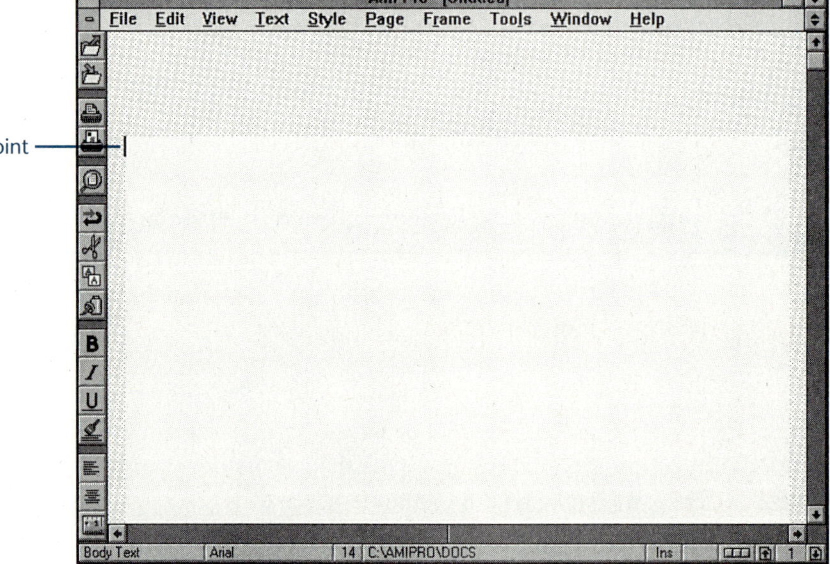

Fig. 2.8
The insertion point in a new, blank document.

Understanding Word Wrap

As you reach the end of a line when entering text in the document, the insertion point automatically moves to the next line. This action, known as *word wrap*, occurs because Ami Pro calculates when you reach the right margin and "returns the carriage" for you. When you want to start a new paragraph, press Enter.

Using the Backspace and Del Keys

When you type, you may make mistakes that you notice immediately and want to correct. You can use the Backspace key or the Del key to remove one character at a time. (Other editing keys are discussed later in this chapter.)

When you press Backspace, you delete the character immediately to the left of the insertion point. If you type the line shown in figure 2.9, for example, you can correct the mistake by pressing Backspace twice to remove the letters *t* and *y* (in that order). After you remove incorrect letters by pressing Backspace, you can type the correct letters immediately, without having to move the insertion point.

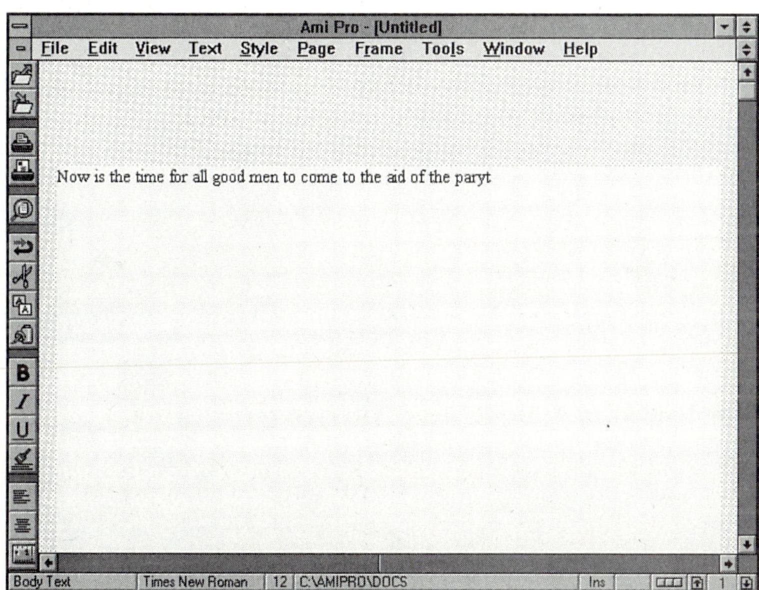

Fig. 2.9
Text that contains reversed letters (at the end of the sentence).

Whereas Backspace deletes the character to the left of the insertion point, Del deletes the character immediately to the right of the insertion point.

To use Del to correct the typed line shown in figure 2.9, you press the left arrow key twice to position the insertion point between the *r* and the *y* (see fig. 2.10), and then press Del twice to remove the letters *y* and *t* (in that order).

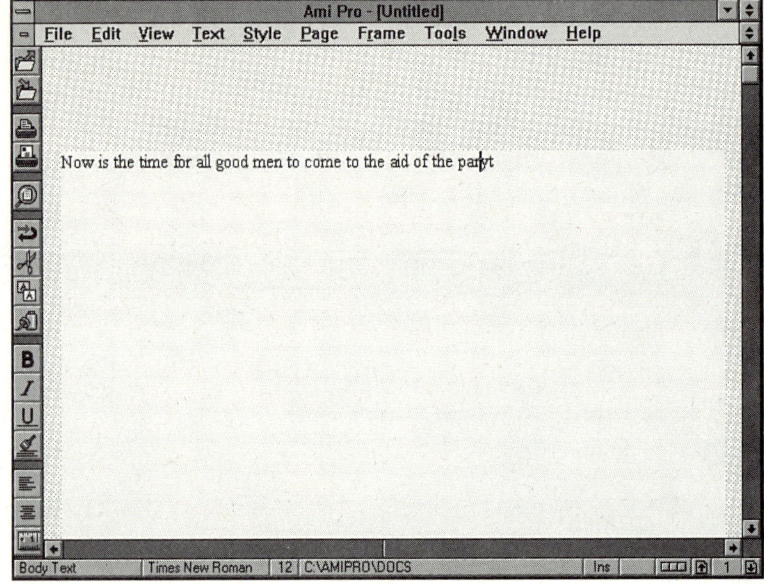

Fig. 2.10
You must reposition the insertion point before using the Del key to remove the incorrect characters.

Understanding Insert and Typeover Modes

Tip
You also can toggle between insert and typeover modes by clicking the Insert/Typeover button on the Status Bar.

When you open a document and start typing, you are using *insert mode*; Ami Pro inserts any typed characters at the insertion point, and any text already on-screen moves to the right as you type. If you want to replace text that appears on-screen, you can change to *typeover mode* by pressing the Ins key or by clicking the Ins button on the Status Bar at the bottom of the screen.

Three things happen when you change to typeover mode:

- The indicator `Type` replaces the indicator Ins at the right side of the Status Bar.
- Any characters you type replace existing text rather than move existing text to the right.
- The insertion point doesn't move to the next line when you press Enter; it just remains in the same position.

The Ins key is a *toggle* key. You press Ins once to change to typeover mode and press Ins again to change back to insert mode. `Type` appears on the Status Bar only when Ami Pro is operating in typeover mode. This indicator changes to `Ins` when you toggle back to insert mode.

Assigning Styles

Ami Pro uses style sheets to control formatting such as margins, spacing, paragraph indentation, and typefaces. Every paragraph in an Ami Pro document has a style. Unless you assign a different style, the paragraph uses the default style Body Text.

> **Note**
>
> You can choose styles from the Styles list or the Styles box. In this chapter, you choose styles from the Styles list. If you prefer to use the Styles box, display it by pressing Ctrl+Y, or open the **V**iew menu and choose the Show Styles **B**ox command. You can use the mouse or the keyboard to choose styles.

In the remaining portion of this section, you set up the sample document shown in figure 2.11. Later in this chapter, you learn how to save and print the sample document.

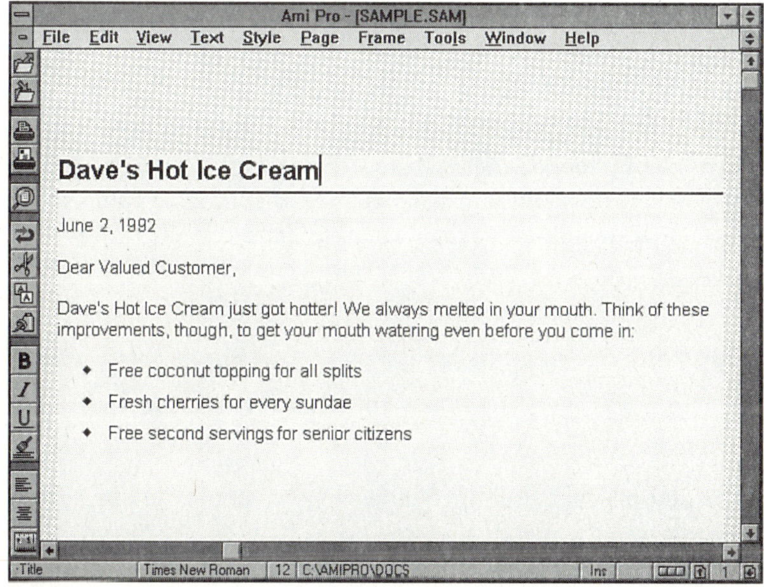
Ami Pro - [SAMPLE.SAM]
File Edit View Text Style Page Frame Tools Window Help
Dave's Hot Ice Cream
June 2, 1992
Dear Valued Customer,
Dave's Hot Ice Cream just got hotter! We always melted in your mouth. Think of these improvements, though, to get your mouth watering even before you come in:
Free coconut topping for all splits
Fresh cherries for every sundae
Free second servings for senior citizens
Title
Times New Roman
12
C:\AMIPRO\DOCS
Ins

Fig. 2.11
A sample document.

To create the sample document, follow these steps:

1. Open the **F**ile menu and choose the **N**ew command. The New dialog box appears.

Before you select a style sheet, make sure that the **W**ith Contents and Run **M**acro options are *deselected* (no X appears in the check box next to the option).

2. In the **S**tyle Sheet for New Document list box, highlight the style sheet you want to use for your document. For this example, select `_LETTER3.STY`. (If the List by **D**escription option is selected, highlight `Letter-business, informal with company name.`)

3. Make sure that the Close Cu**r**rent File check box contains a check (to close the window in which you've just been editing).

4. Choose OK. Ami Pro may ask if you want to save the changes for the document in which you were working. In general, you should choose **Y**es to save the changes you make to documents. Because this was a practice document, however, you can choose **N**o in this case.

5. Open the Styles list and choose the style you want. You can click the style with the mouse; press the function key listed before the style name; or use the arrow keys to move the highlight, and then press Enter or the space bar when the correct style is highlighted. For this example, use the F9 Title style.

6. Now type the title. For this example, type **Dave's Hot Ice Cream**.

   Ami Pro uses the specified style for the text as you type. In the sample document, the title text appears in Arial 18-point bold with a separator line under the title. Note that the Status Bar shows the current style name on the Style button, the typeface on the Font button, and the point size on the Point Size button.

7. Press Enter. The insertion point moves to the line below the title.

8. Choose the Body Text style from the Styles list to return to the normal text style.

9. To insert the date, open the **E**dit menu and choose the **I**nsert command. From the resulting menu, choose **D**ate/Time. The Insert Date/Time dialog box appears (see fig. 2.12).

10. In the Insert section, specify the date system you want to use. For this example, choose **T**oday's Date. Then choose a date format from the **S**tyle list box.

11. Choose OK.

The date text appears in Arial 12-point; this style uses the same typeface as the title, but in a smaller size and without boldfacing.

12. Press Enter to move to the line below the date.

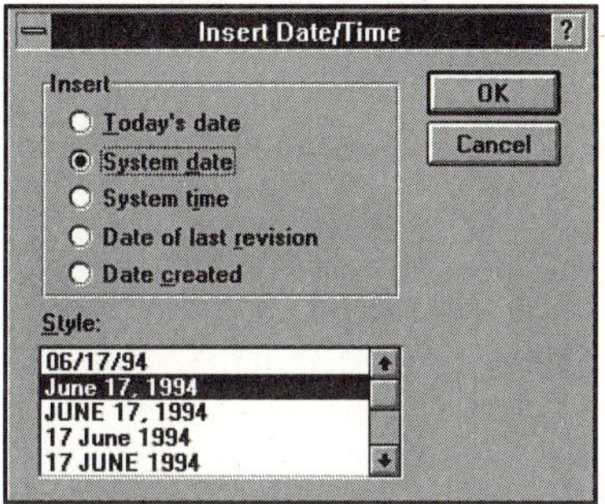

Fig. 2.12 The Insert Date/ Time dialog box.

To finish typing the sample document, follow these steps:

1. For the salutation, type **Dear Valued Customer,** and press Enter.
2. Type the following text and then press Enter:

   Dave's Hot Ice Cream just got hotter! We always melted in your mouth. Think of these improvements, though, to get your mouth watering even before you come in.

3. Choose the Bullet 2 style, and then type the following lines, pressing Enter after each line:

   Free coconut topping for all splits

   Fresh cherries for every sundae

   Free second servings for senior citizens

Ami Pro inserts bullets before each of the last three lines you typed, so your sample document should resemble the document shown in figure 2.11.

Tip
Try other styles in the sample document to see how the typeface changes with the style changes. Simply place the insertion point anywhere in the text and choose a style.

Saving the Active Document

You save the active document by choosing a command from a menu or by using the save SmartIcon (which looks like an arrow pointing into a folder). As figure 2.13 shows, the **F**ile menu provides two commands for saving documents: **S**ave and Save **A**s. You generally use **S**ave if the document already has been saved on disk, and you want to save the current version of the document with the same name. If you are saving a new document or saving a revised document under a new name, you use Save **A**s.

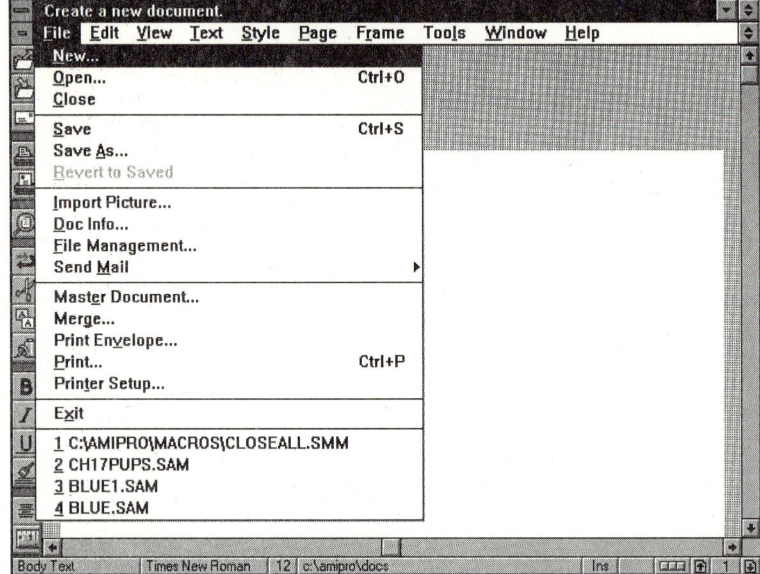

Fig. 2.13
The **F**ile menu.

To save a document (accepting as many default options as possible), follow these steps:

1. Choose **F**ile **S**ave or **F**ile Save **A**s, or click the save SmartIcon.

   If you are saving a previously saved document, and you chose **F**ile **S**ave or used the save SmartIcon, Ami Pro doesn't display any dialog boxes or ask you any questions. The mouse pointer changes to an hourglass shape while Ami Pro saves the document.

   If you haven't saved the document before, Ami Pro displays the Save As dialog box (see fig. 2.14).

2. In the File **N**ame text box, type a name for the document, following DOS naming conventions. You can use from one to eight characters; Ami Pro supplies the SAM extension. If you have saved the document before, Ami Pro suggests the existing name for the document. For this example, type **SAMPLE** for the name of the document.

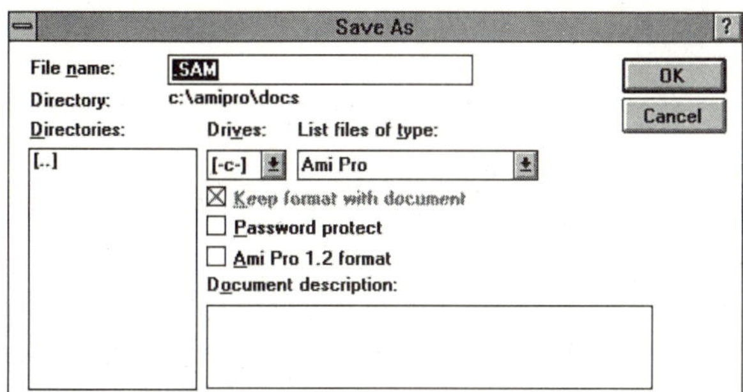

Fig. 2.14
The Save As dialog box.

3. To save the document to the current drive, directory, and file type, choose OK. (Other options are discussed at the end of these steps.)

The Save As dialog box provides the following options

- In the File **N**ame text box, you provide a name for the document. Ami Pro automatically assigns an extension that corresponds to the type of document you are saving. For this document, SAM is the mandatory extension.
- You can specify the drive and directory where Ami Pro is to save the document. Because Ami Pro can convert documents to other file formats, you also can save the document in another format by choosing an alternative format from the List Files of **T**ype list box.
- You can select the **K**eep Format With Document option to tell Ami Pro to store the document's formatting with the document and not with the style sheet. The document then maintains its formatting even if you change the style sheet. If you don't choose this option, the formatting of the document is overwritten if you change the style sheet.
- You select the **P**assword Protect option to assign a password to your document. If you assign a password to the document, no one else can open the document unless they supply the password.
- You can save the document to an earlier Ami Pro format by selecting the **A**mi Pro 1.2 Format option.
- You can supply a description of up to 199 characters in the D**o**cument Description text box.

Printing the Active Document

You can print the active document by using the print SmartIcon or by choosing **F**ile **P**rint. (Chapter 8, "Changing Your Setup," provides a more detailed discussion of other printing choices.)

Before you print, you may want to choose the **L**ayout Mode command and the **F**ull Page command from the **V**iew menu to see a reduced version of the document layout, complete with formatting information (see fig. 2.15).

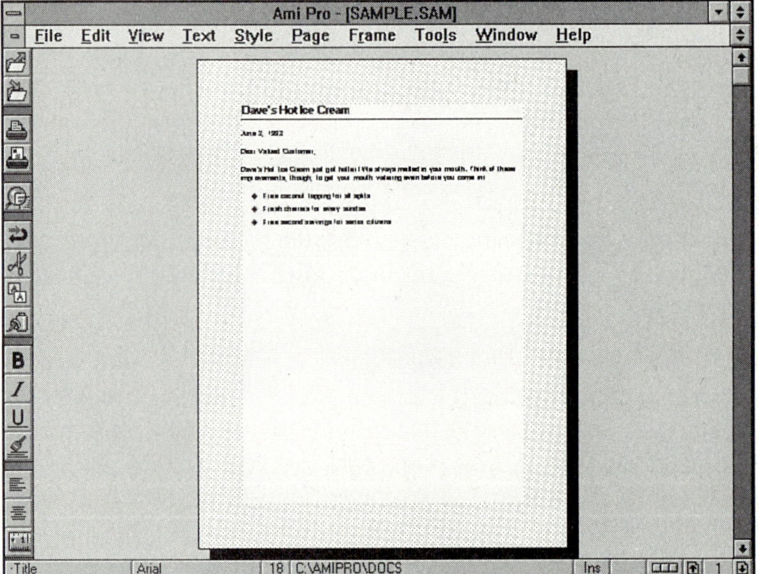

Fig. 2.15
The finished sample document in layout mode, full-page view.

After you check the layout and formatting, you are ready to print the active document (in this case, SAMPLE.SAM). Choose **F**ile **P**rint. The Print dialog box appears, as shown in figure 2.16. The following paragraphs describe the printing options.

In the Print dialog box, you can specify the **N**umber of Copies to print, the range of pages to print, and whether to include **E**ven pages, O**d**d pages, or **B**oth.

The **S**etup button opens a dialog box containing printer setup options. Ami Pro establishes the printer setup during installation; you usually don't need to change this setup. (Chapter 7, "Proofreading and Printing a Document," describes the options available in case you need to make some changes.)

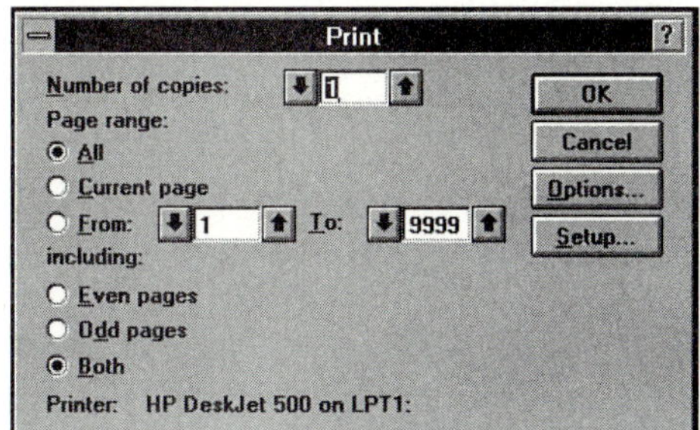

Fig. 2.16
The Print dialog box.

The **O**ptions command button opens the Print Options dialog box shown in figure 2.17. After you specify the options you want to use, choose OK or press Enter to close the Print Options dialog box.

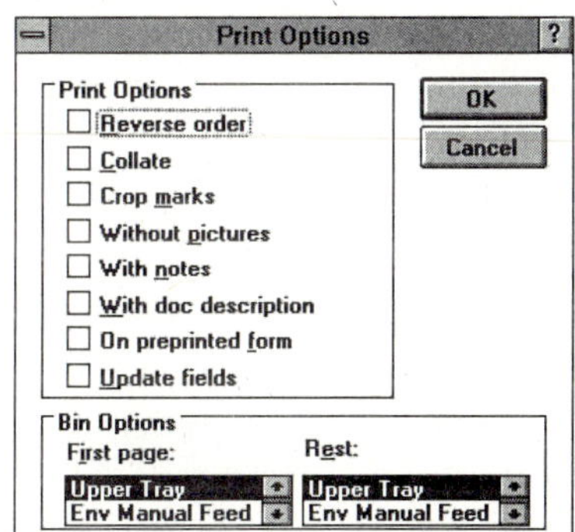

Fig. 2.17
The Print Options dialog box.

For this example, you don't need to choose any special printing options. To print the document by using the default options, choose OK or press Enter in the Print dialog box. Ami Pro prints the document and displays messages on-screen as necessary to indicate the progress of the current printing job. Figure 2.18 shows the printed sample document.

Fig. 2.18
The finished sample document.

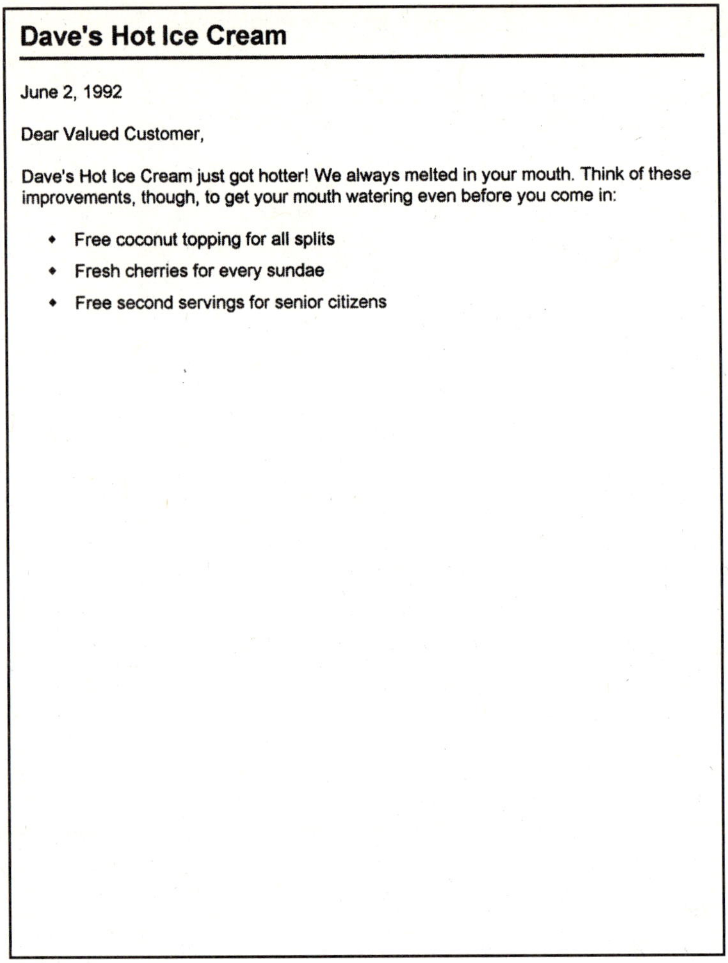

Dave's Hot Ice Cream

June 2, 1992

Dear Valued Customer,

Dave's Hot Ice Cream just got hotter! We always melted in your mouth. Think of these improvements, though, to get your mouth watering even before you come in:

- Free coconut topping for all splits
- Fresh cherries for every sundae
- Free second servings for senior citizens

Chapter 3

Editing Techniques

In Chapter 2, you learned how to open a new document, type text, assign paragraph styles, and save and print documents. Now that you know the basic techniques for creating a document, you are ready to learn the fundamentals of document editing. In this chapter, you learn how to open an existing document, move around in the document, and perform basic editing tasks. These tasks include inserting blank lines; selecting text; moving, copying, and deleting text; undoing actions; and working in multiple windows.

You also learn how to protect text and save documents. At the end of this chapter, you learn the difference between saving and closing documents.

Opening a New Document

In Chapter 2, you learned that you can begin typing as soon as you start Ami Pro, because the program automatically opens a new document based on the default style sheet. You also learned how to open a new document—by opening the **F**ile menu and choosing the **N**ew command. When you choose **F**ile **N**ew, Ami Pro displays the New dialog box shown in figure 3.1.

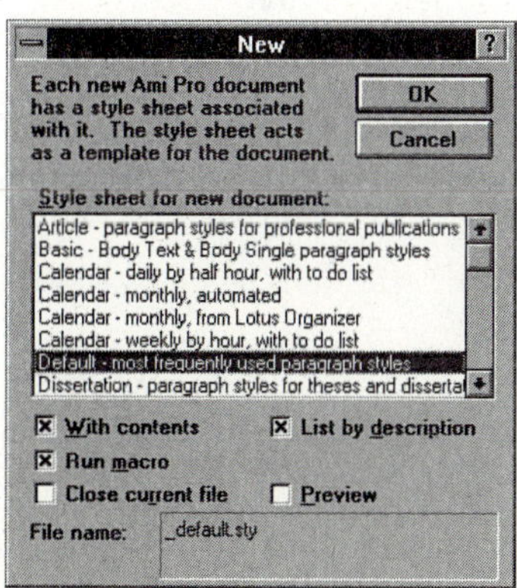

Fig. 3.1
The New dialog box.

In the New dialog box, you can select the style sheet you want to use. The style sheet contains information about margins, spacing, paragraph type (indented, numbered, bulleted, and so on), available typefaces, and special options such as headers and footers. (For more details on using style sheets, see Chapter 10, "Working with Style Sheets.")

The New dialog box offers a number of check box options, which work as described in the following list:

- *With Contents.* If you choose this option, Ami Pro uses, for the new document, any text stored in the style sheet. Ami Pro selects this option by default. Every time you open the New dialog box, the check mark appears in the **W**ith Contents check box, even if you deselected the option the last time you opened the dialog box.

- *Run Macro.* With this option selected, Ami Pro runs any macros stored in the style sheet. If you choose the _LETTER1.STY style sheet with the Run **M**acro option selected, for example, Ami Pro prompts you to provide name and address information. Like **W**ith Contents, the Run **M**acro option is selected by default when you start a new editing session.

- *Close Current File.* When this option is selected, Ami Pro replaces the text currently on-screen with the new document you are creating. If you haven't saved the file on-screen since making changes, Ami Pro displays a message that prompts you to save the document. This option is selected until you choose it again to turn off the option.

- *List by Description.* If you choose this option, Ami Pro displays style sheet descriptions rather than file names in the **S**tyle Sheet for New Document list box. This option remains selected until you choose it again.

- *Preview.* With this option, Ami Pro displays on-screen the contents of the style sheet. **P**review is not a default option; you must choose this option each time you want to use it.

After you choose the options you want, choose OK or press Enter. Ami Pro opens the new document.

Opening an Existing Document

You can open an existing document with a command from a menu or with a SmartIcon. To open an existing document, follow these steps:

1. To use the menu, open the **F**ile menu and choose the **O**pen command. To use the SmartIcons, click the Open SmartIcon (it shows an arrow coming out of a folder).

   Whether you use the **F**ile **O**pen command or the Open SmartIcon, the Open dialog box appears (see fig. 3.2).

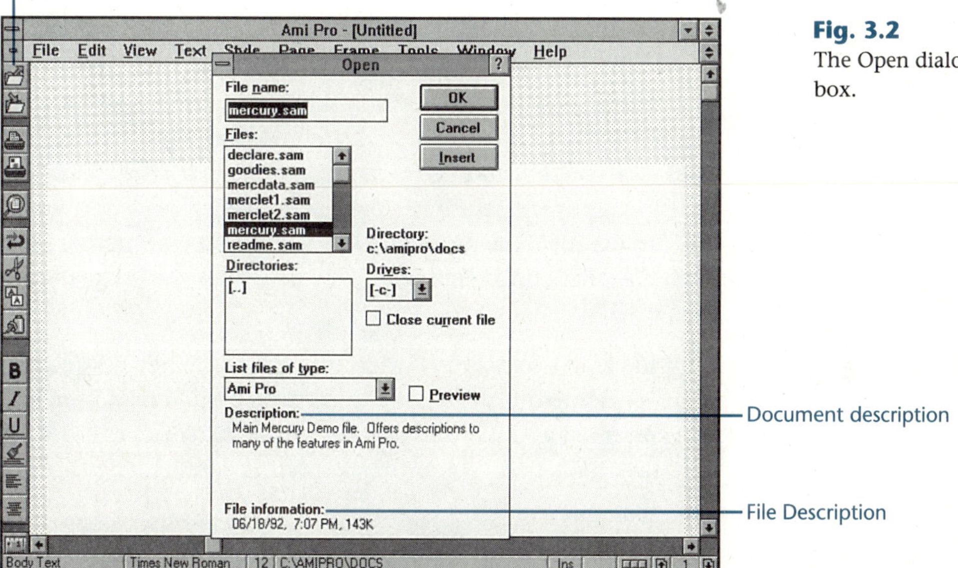

Fig. 3.2
The Open dialog box.

2. Use the Dri**v**es list box, **D**irectories list box, and **F**iles list box to choose the desired drive, directory, and file name, or type the name of the file you want to open in the File **N**ame text box.

3. Choose OK to open the document.

Tip
Rather than choosing the name of the document and then choosing OK or pressing Enter, you can open the document by double-clicking the name of the document in the **F**iles list box.

The options in the Open dialog box help you handle special situations, as described in the following list:

- The Close Cu**r**rent File option works like the option with the same name in the New dialog box; Ami Pro replaces the document currently on-screen with the one you open. (If you haven't saved the document on-screen, Ami Pro prompts you to save it.)

- The **P**review option works like its counterpart in the New dialog box. Choose the **P**review check box to view the document before opening it. Also, in the New dialog box, **P**review enables you to view the contents of the style sheet (if chosen in conjunction with **W**ith Contents). Here, **P**review enables you to see the document.
- To list files other than Ami Pro documents in the **F**iles list box, you can specify a different file type in the List Files of **T**ype list box.
- If you typed a description in the Document Description text box when you created the document, the description appears near the bottom of the Open dialog box.

The **I**nsert button serves several functions, as described in the following list:

Tip
Only documents opened from the hard disk (not from a floppy disk) are listed in the **F**ile menu.

- **I**nsert can combine multiple Ami Pro documents into one document. Open the first document, position the insertion point where you want to insert the next document, and choose **F**ile **O**pen. Select the file you want to insert, and choose **I**nsert rather than OK. Then reposition the insertion point and repeat the process until all documents are inserted. You can use the same procedure to combine data from other programs into an Ami Pro document (after choosing the appropriate file type from the List Files of **T**ype list box).
- With the **I**nsert command button, you can combine multiple Ami Pro documents into one document. You also can insert data from another program into an Ami Pro style sheet, table, or frame. For more information, see Chapter 20, "Importing, Exporting, and Linking Files."

Tip
Deleted documents continue to appear on the list until you open additional files.

Ami Pro "remembers" the documents you open. In the User Setup dialog box, you can instruct Ami Pro to remember up to the last four documents you opened. (See Chapter 8, "Changing Your Setup," for more information.) Ami Pro lists the documents at the bottom of the **F**ile menu (see fig. 3.3). You can open any of the documents that appear at the bottom of the **F**ile menu by clicking the mouse or pressing Alt and the number that appears in front of the name of the document you want to open.

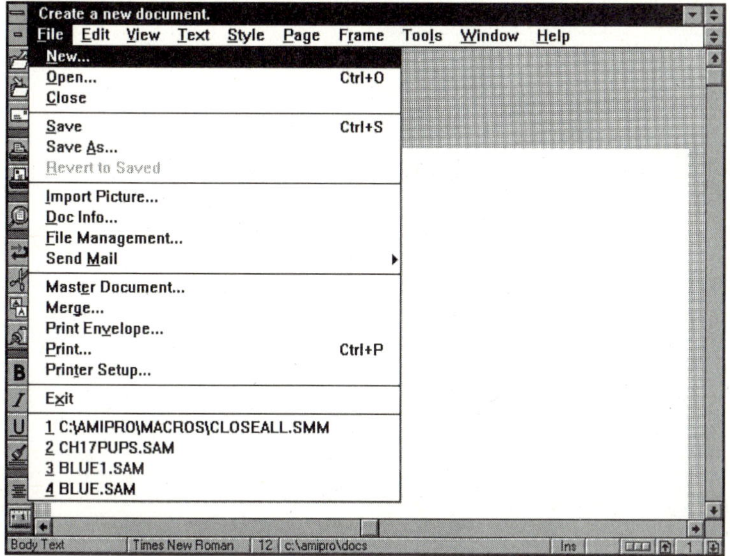

Fig. 3.3
The **F**ile menu lists the last four documents you opened.

Moving Around a Document

As you create longer documents, being able to move the insertion point around the document (*navigate*) efficiently becomes important. You can move the insertion point by using the mouse or the keyboard. This section describes the various methods you can use to navigate through an Ami Pro document.

Moving with the Mouse

To move the insertion point with the mouse, position the mouse pointer where you want the insertion point, and then click the left mouse button. If you want to move the insertion point to part of the document that doesn't appear in the window, you can display that part of the document by using the Page Up and Page Down buttons on the Status Bar or by using the vertical scroll bar (see fig. 3.4).

The position of the scroll box on the vertical scroll bar indicates the position of the text in the window relative to the beginning and the end of the document. If the scroll box is near the middle of the scroll bar, for example, the text that appears in the window is approximately in the middle of the document.

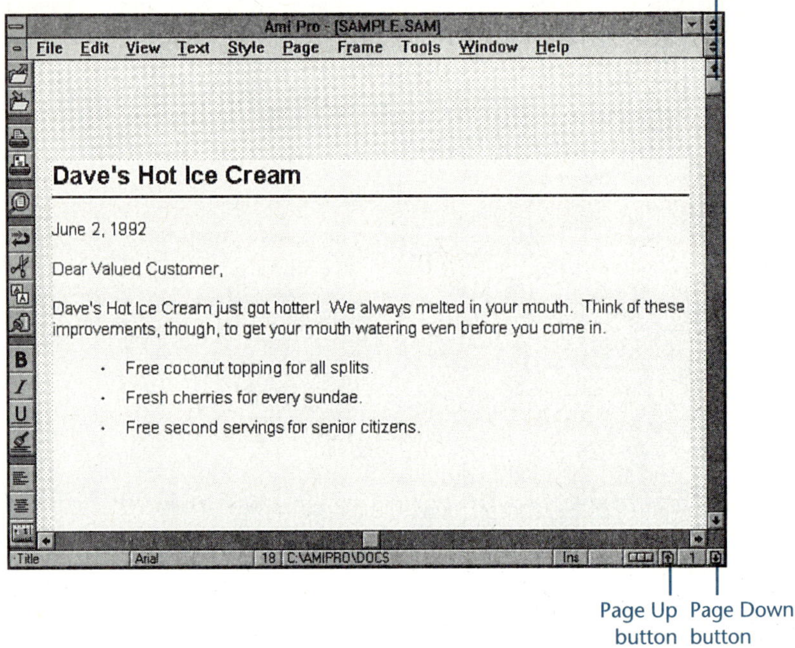
Vertical scroll bar
Ami Pro - [SAMPLE.SAM]
File Edit View Text Style Page Frame Tools Window Help
Dave's Hot Ice Cream
June 2, 1992
Dear Valued Customer,
Dave's Hot Ice Cream just got hotter! We always melted in your mouth. Think of these improvements, though, to get your mouth watering even before you come in.
Free coconut topping for all splits.
Fresh cherries for every sundae.
Free second servings for senior citizens.
Title
Arial
18 C:\AMIPRO\DOCS
Ins
Page Up button
Page Down button

Fig. 3.4
Use the vertical scroll bar or the Page Up and Page Down buttons to display different parts of the document.

To use the mouse and the scroll box to move to a different area of the document, follow these steps:

1. Position the mouse pointer on the vertical scroll box.
2. Press and hold down the left mouse button.
3. Drag the scroll box up to move toward the beginning of the document, or down to move toward the end of the document.
4. Release the mouse button when the scroll box indicates the approximate position of the text you want to view. The text in the corresponding position in the document appears in the window.
5. Move the mouse pointer into the text area. (When the mouse pointer is over the text area, it becomes an I-beam.)
6. Position the mouse pointer where you want the insertion point, and click the left mouse button.

The last step is very important—the insertion point doesn't move until you click the new location. If you start typing before you click the new location, Ami Pro inserts the text at the original insertion point location.

You also can use the arrows at the ends of the scroll bar (the *scroll arrows*) to move to a different area of the document. Follow these steps:

1. To scroll toward the beginning of the document, position the mouse pointer on the up arrow at the top of the vertical scroll bar. To scroll toward the end of the document, position the mouse pointer on the down arrow at the bottom of the vertical scroll bar.

2. Press and hold down the left mouse button. The text of the document scrolls toward the beginning or end of the document.

3. Release the mouse button when the text you want to view appears in the window.

4. Move the mouse pointer into the text area. The mouse pointer becomes an I-beam pointer.

5. Position the I-beam pointer where you want the insertion point, and then click the left mouse button.

Again, the insertion point doesn't move until you click the new location. If you start typing before you click the new location, Ami Pro inserts the text at the original insertion point location.

Moving with the Keyboard

Moving the insertion point with the keyboard can be very efficient. To move the insertion point, you use the direction keys individually or in combination with the Ctrl key.

Table 3.1 lists key combinations for moving the insertion point.

Table 3.1 Key Combinations for Moving the Insertion Point

Key or Key Combination	Effect
Left-arrow key	Moves the insertion point one character to the left.
Right-arrow key	Moves the insertion point one character to the right.
Up-arrow key	Moves the insertion point up one line.
Down-arrow key	Moves the insertion point down one line.
Ctrl+left-arrow key	Moves the insertion point one word to the left.

(continues)

Table 3.1 Continued

Key or Key Combination	Effect
Ctrl+right-arrow key	Moves the insertion point one word to the right.
Home	Moves the insertion point to the beginning of the line.
End	Moves the insertion point to the end of the line.
Ctrl+up-arrow key	Moves the insertion point to the beginning of the paragraph.
Ctrl+down-arrow key	Moves the insertion point to the end of the paragraph.
PgUp	Moves the insertion point up one screen.
PgDn	Moves the insertion point down one screen
Ctrl+PgUp	Moves the insertion point to the top of the preceding page.
Ctrl+PgDn	Moves the insertion point to the top of the next page.
Ctrl+Home	Moves the insertion point to the beginning of the document.
Ctrl+End	Moves the insertion point to the end of the document.
Ctrl+. (period)	Moves the insertion point to the beginning of the next sentence.
Ctrl+, (comma)	Moves the insertion point to the beginning of the preceding sentence.

You can go directly to a specific location in a document in three ways:

- Press Ctrl+G.
- Choose **E**dit **G**o To.
- Click the page number button near the right end of the Status Bar.

Regardless of the method you choose, Ami Pro displays the Go To dialog box (see fig. 3.5).

In the Go To dialog box, specify the page to which you want to move the insertion point (the first page, the last page, or a specific page number), or choose **N**ext Item and specify a location from the **N**ext Item list box. If your document contains bookmarks, footers, frames, and so on, you can choose them from the **N**ext Item list box.

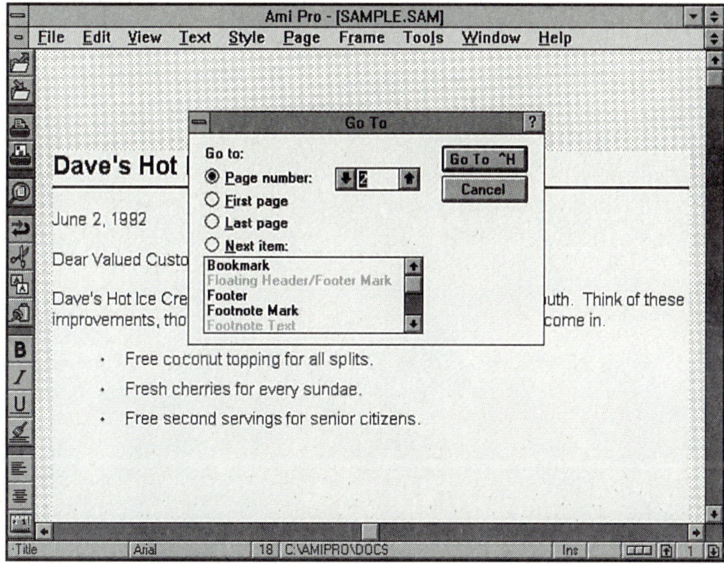

Fig. 3.5
The Go To dialog box.

After choosing a target location, choose the Go To ^H command button; the insertion point moves to that location. If you change your mind and don't want to move to another location, choose Cancel.

Basic Editing

In this section, you learn how to start new lines; how to select, copy, move, and delete text; and how to undo actions.

Starting a New Line

In Chapter 2, "Quick Start: Creating a Document," you learned that all documents are based on style sheets and each style sheet contains paragraph styles. As part of the paragraph style, Ami Pro assigns spacing (by default, in inches) above and below the paragraph. In the default style sheet, for example, the spacing above and below the body text style is 0. When you use this style and press Enter, Ami Pro "single spaces" the insertion point to the beginning of the next typing line. In figure 3.6, you can see the paragraph mark at the end of the first line; no extra white space separates the first and second lines. (See Chapter 8, "Changing Your Setup," for information on making paragraph marks visible on-screen.)

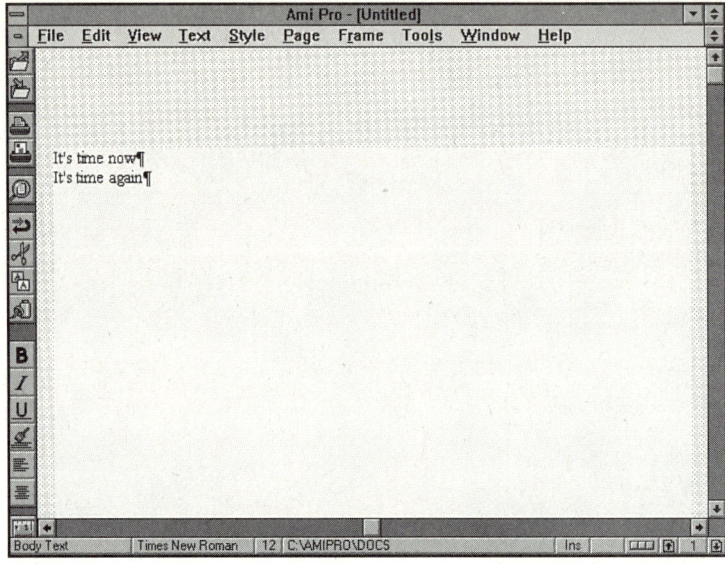

Fig. 3.6
When you use the Body Text style and press Enter, Ami Pro "single spaces" without inserting any extra white space.

In other cases, the spacing above and below a paragraph style may be set to another number other than 0. The spacing above and below the Subhead paragraph style in the default style sheet, for example, is .05 inches. When you use this style and press Enter, Ami Pro includes additional white space between lines as it moves the insertion point to the next typing line. In figure 3.7, note the two paragraph marks and the white space between the lines.

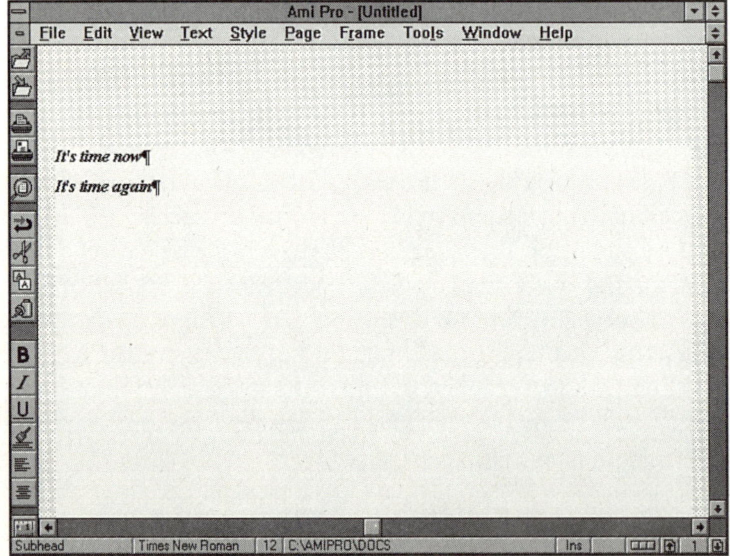

Fig. 3.7
Ami Pro inserts additional space between lines when you press Enter while using the Subhead paragraph style.

In Chapter 2, you also learned that you don't press Enter until you reach the end of a paragraph; Ami Pro's word wrap feature wraps text from line to line automatically. Unnecessary carriage returns cause problems if you edit or reformat the text or use style sheets to change styles; the paragraphs can end with extra lines.

Occasionally, however, you need to start a new line at a specific location. You also may want to insert a blank line to indicate the beginning of a new paragraph. You can start new lines in two ways: insert paragraph marks, or insert line breaks. You insert paragraph marks when you want Ami Pro to use the Spacing Above and Below settings specified for the paragraph style. You insert a line break when you want Ami Pro to ignore the Spacing Above and Below settings designated in the paragraph style.

When you work with a paragraph style, such as the Body Text style (whose Spacing Above and Below setting is 0), you start a new line by inserting a paragraph mark. Position the insertion point where you want to start a new line and press Enter. To insert a blank line, press Enter twice—once to end the paragraph and a second time to create a blank line before the next paragraph. The effect is similar to the one in figure 3.7, but with three paragraph marks (see fig. 3.8).

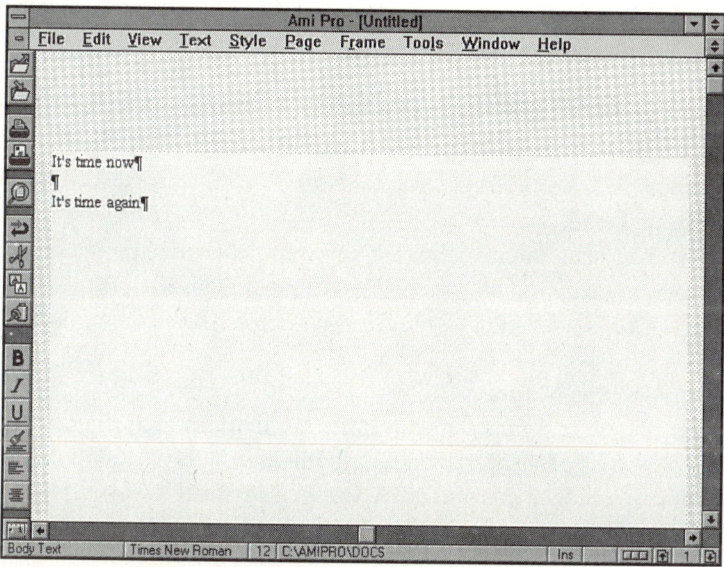

Fig. 3.8
An additional paragraph mark indicates a blank line.

When you work with a paragraph style such as the Subhead style, if you press Enter white space appears between the current location of the insertion point and the last line of text.

Occasionally, while working with paragraph styles, you don't want white space to appear when you press Enter. To eliminate the white space, insert a line break by positioning the insertion point where you want the current line to end and then pressing Ctrl+Enter. Because a line break tells Ami Pro to ignore the settings designated for spacing above and below the paragraph, Ami Pro "single spaces" the insertion point to the next typing line but does not insert a paragraph mark. The effect is similar to the one in figure 3.6 but, in figure 3.9, you see only one paragraph mark.

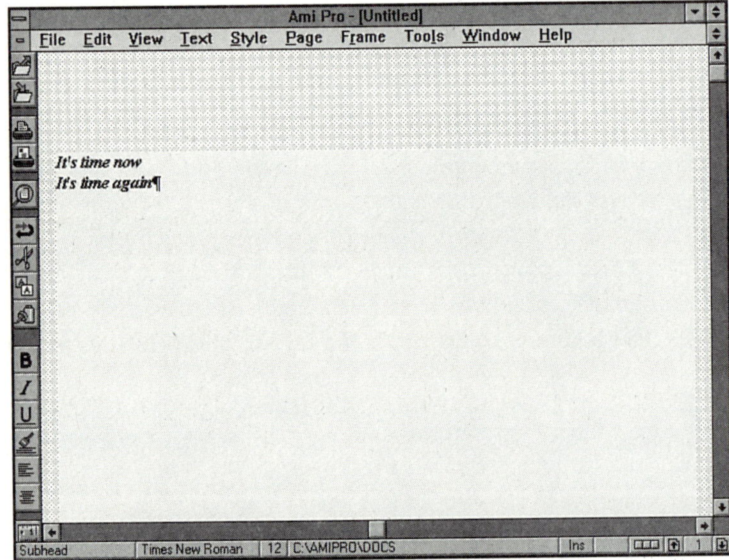

Fig. 3.9
In this case, Ami Pro doesn't insert a paragraph mark.

Selecting Text

In Ami Pro, you must identify the text you want to change before you can change it. To identify the text you want to change, you *select* it by using the mouse or the keyboard. In this section, you learn both selection methods.

Selecting with the Mouse

To select text with the mouse, position the mouse pointer at the beginning of the text you want to select, and then drag the mouse (press and hold down the left mouse button while you move the mouse) until the text is highlighted (see fig. 3.10).

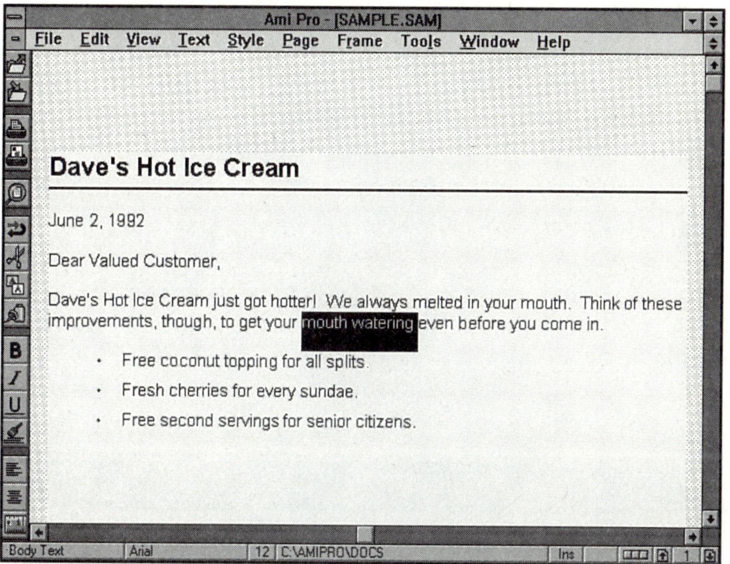
Ami Pro - [SAMPLE.SAM]
File Edit View Text Style Page Frame Tools Window Help
Dave's Hot Ice Cream
June 2, 1992
Dear Valued Customer,
Dave's Hot Ice Cream just got hotter! We always melted in your mouth. Think of these improvements, though, to get your mouth watering even before you come in.
Free coconut topping for all splits.
Fresh cherries for every sundae.
Free second servings for senior citizens.
Body Text
Arial
12
C:\AMIPRO\DOCS
Ins

Fig. 3.10
Selected text.

Table 3.2 lists techniques for selecting text with the mouse.

Table 3.2 Selecting Text with the Mouse

Selection	Technique
One word	Place the mouse pointer on the word and double-click.
Multiple words	Position the mouse pointer on the first word, double-click, and drag the mouse pointer across the other contiguous words.
One sentence	Place the mouse pointer in the sentence, press and hold down Ctrl, and click.
Multiple sentences	With the mouse pointer in the first sentence, press and hold down Ctrl, click, and drag the mouse pointer across the sentences you want to select.
One paragraph	Place the mouse pointer in the paragraph, press and hold down Ctrl, and double-click.
Multiple paragraphs	With the mouse pointer in the first paragraph, press and hold down Ctrl, double-click, and drag the mouse pointer across the paragraphs you want to select.

Selecting with the Keyboard

Table 3.1 (shown earlier in this chapter) provides information on moving the insertion point with the keyboard. To select text with the keyboard, you add the Shift key to the key combination used to move the insertion point. Table 3.3 lists key combinations for selecting text.

> **Caution**
>
> If you touch any key on the keyboard (or press Enter) while text is selected, Ami Pro deletes the highlighted text. You can "reverse" an accidental deletion by using Ami Pro's undo feature, covered later in this chapter.

Table 3.3 Selecting Text with the Keyboard

Key Combination	Effect
Shift+left-arrow key	Selects one character to the left
Shift+right-arrow key	Selects one character to the right
Shift+up-arrow key	Selects one line up
Shift+down-arrow key	Selects one line down
Ctrl+Shift+left-arrow key	Selects to the beginning of the next word
Ctrl+Shift+right-arrow key	Selects to the beginning of the preceding word
Shift+Home	Selects to the beginning of the line
Shift+End	Selects to the end of the line
Ctrl+Shift+up-arrow key	Selects to the beginning of the paragraph
Ctrl+Shift+down-arrow key	Selects to the end of the paragraph
Shift+PgUp	Selects up one screenful
Shift+PgDn	Selects down one screenful
Ctrl+Shift+PgUp	Selects all text from the insertion point to the beginning of the preceding page
Ctrl+Shift+PgDn	Selects all text from the insertion point to the end of the current page
Ctrl+Shift+Home	Selects text to the beginning of the document

Key Combination	Effect
Ctrl+Shift+End	Selects text to the end of the document
Ctrl+Shift+period	Selects text to the end of the sentence
Ctrl+Shift+comma	Selects text to the beginning of the sentence

Tip
To cancel selecting text, press any arrow key by itself (without Ctrl or Shift).

Moving Text

Moving text involves removing the text from its current location (*cutting*) and placing it in a new location (*pasting*). You can move text in three ways:

- Choose the Cu**t** and **P**aste commands from the **E**dit menu.
- Click the Cut and Paste SmartIcons.
- Use the mouse.

In the first two methods, when you cut text from the document, Ami Pro places the cut text on the *Windows Clipboard*. The Clipboard is a temporary holding area for the information you cut or copy. The text remains on the Clipboard until you exit Windows or place other text or graphics on the Clipboard. The Clipboard can hold only one entry at a time; each time you place information on the Clipboard, you replace any information previously stored there.

Moving Text with the Edit Menu

You can move text by choosing menu commands. Follow these steps to move text by using the **E**dit menu:

1. Select the text you want to move.
2. Choose **E**dit Cu**t**. Ami Pro removes the text from the document and stores the text on the Clipboard.
3. Position the insertion point where you want the text to appear. Don't forget to click the left mouse button to move the insertion point from its previous location.
4. Choose **E**dit **P**aste. The text appears in the new location.

Tip
You can place information on the Clipboard from many Windows programs and move or copy that information to other Windows programs.

Moving Text with the SmartIcons

You also can use the Cut and Paste SmartIcons to move text (see fig. 3.11).

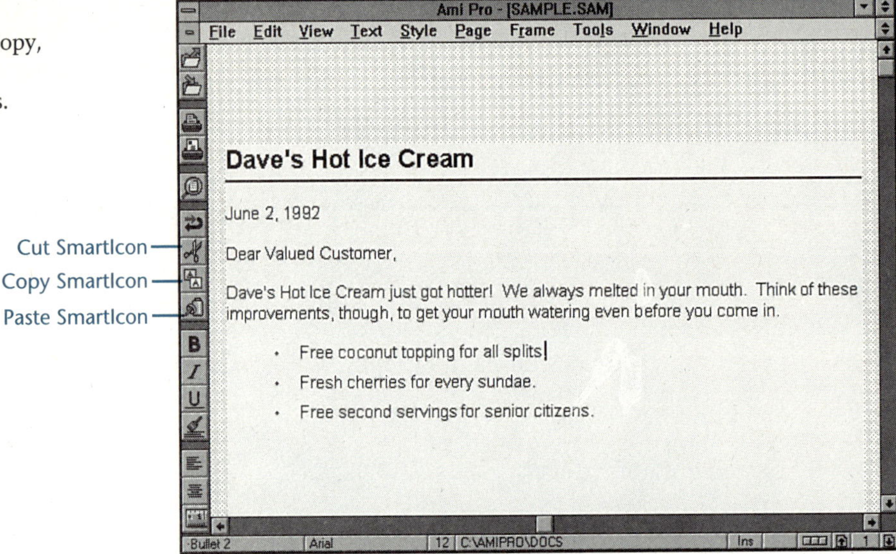

Ami Pro - [SAMPLE.SAM]
File Edit View Text Style Page Frame Tools Window Help
Cut SmartIcon
Copy SmartIcon
Paste SmartIcon
Dave's Hot Ice Cream
June 2, 1992
Dear Valued Customer,
Dave's Hot Ice Cream just got hotter! We always melted in your mouth. Think of these improvements, though, to get your mouth watering even before you come in.
Free coconut topping for all splits
Fresh cherries for every sundae.
Free second servings for senior citizens.
Bullet 2
Arial
12 C:\AMIPRO\DOCS
Ins

Fig. 3.11 The Cut, Copy, and Paste SmartIcons.

To move text by using the Cut and Paste SmartIcons, follow these steps:

1. Select the text you want to move.
2. Click the Cut SmartIcon. Ami Pro removes the text from the document and stores it on the Clipboard.
3. Position the insertion point where you want the text to appear. Don't forget to click the left mouse button to move the insertion point from its previous location.
4. Click the Paste SmartIcon. The text appears in the new location.

Moving Text with the Mouse

You also can use the mouse to move text, by dragging the text or by clicking the right mouse button.

To drag the text to a new location, follow these steps:

1. Select the text you want to move.
2. Position the mouse pointer anywhere in the selected text; then click and hold the left mouse button. The mouse pointer changes shape, showing an insertion point, an arrow pointing at the insertion point, and scissors attached to the pointer (see fig. 3.12).

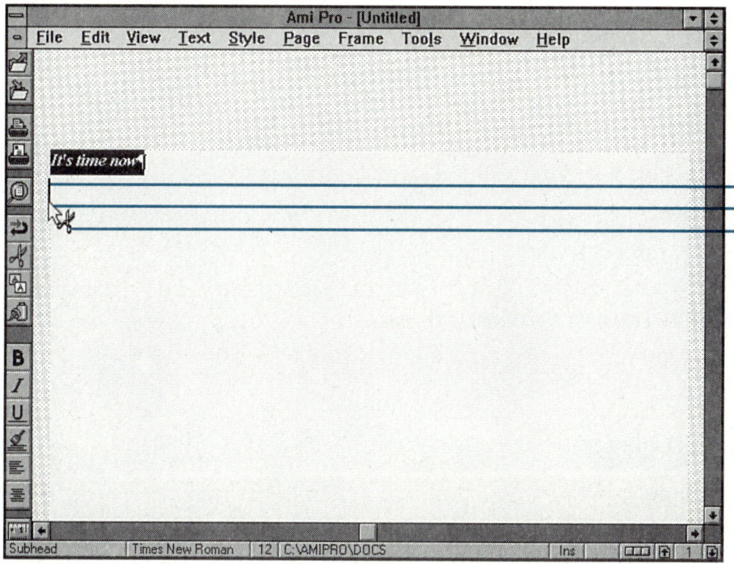

Fig. 3.12
The scissors are attached to the mouse pointer.

3. Drag the mouse pointer to the new location in which you want to insert text.

4. Release the mouse button. The text disappears from its original location and reappears in the new location.

To move text by using the right mouse button, follow these steps:

1. Select the text you want to move.

2. Position the mouse pointer at the new location for the text (but don't click).

3. Press and hold down the Ctrl key and click the right mouse button.

Note

If you want to use the right mouse button to copy or move selected text, and you plan to use any method other than the scroll bars to move through the document, press Ctrl *before* positioning the mouse pointer.

Copying Text

Copying text involves making a duplicate of the text (*copying*) and placing the duplicate in a new location (*pasting*). The original text remains in its original location. You can copy text in three ways:

- Choose the **C**opy and **P**aste commands from the **E**dit menu.
- Click the Copy and Paste SmartIcons.
- Use the mouse.

The first two methods use the Clipboard as a temporary storage area for the text you are copying. See the "Moving Text" section of this chapter for information on the Clipboard.

Copying Text with the Edit Menu

You can copy text by choosing menu commands. Follow these steps to copy text by using the **E**dit menu:

1. Select the text you want to copy.
2. Choose **E**dit **C**opy.
3. Position the insertion point where you want a duplicate of the text to appear. Click the left mouse button to move the insertion point from its previous location.
4. Choose **E**dit **P**aste. A duplicate of the text appears in the new location.

Copying Text with the SmartIcons

You also can use the Copy and Paste SmartIcons to copy text. To copy text by using the SmartIcons, follow these steps:

1. Select the text you want to copy.
2. Click the Copy SmartIcon.
3. Position the insertion point where you want a duplicate of the text to appear, and click the left mouse button.
4. Click the Paste SmartIcon. A duplicate of the text appears in the new location.

Copying Text with the Mouse

You can use the mouse to copy text in two ways: by dragging the text, or by using the right mouse button.

To copy text by dragging, follow these steps:

1. Select the text you want to copy.
2. Position the mouse pointer anywhere in the selected text and press and hold down the Ctrl key and the left mouse button. The pointer changes

shape, becoming the copy icon attached to a mouse pointer, pointing at an insertion point.

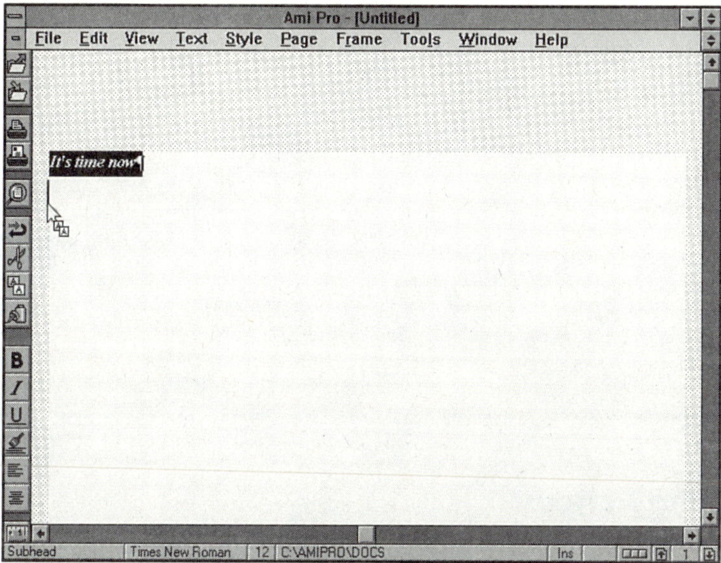

Fig. 3.13
The mouse pointer shape when you drag text to copy it.

3. Drag the mouse pointer to the new location for the text. Use the insertion point portion of the mouse pointer shape to align the text.

4. Release the left mouse button. The text remains at its original location and a copy appears in the new location.

Tip
If you plan to use any method other than the scroll bars to move though the document, press Ctrl or Ctrl+Shift before positioning the mouse pointer.

To copy text by using the right mouse button, follow these steps:

1. Select the text you want to copy.

2. Position the mouse pointer at the new location for the text, but don't click.

3. Hold down Ctrl+Shift and click the right mouse button.

Deleting Text

In Chapter 2, you learned how to delete characters by pressing Backspace or Del. When you need to delete more than a few characters at a time, you can select the text you want to delete and then press Enter, Backspace, or Del. Ami Pro also provides keyboard shortcuts for deleting blocks of text without selecting the text. Table 3.4 lists key combinations for deleting text.

Table 3.4 Keys for Deleting Text

Key or Key Combination	Effect
Backspace	Deletes the selected text or deletes one character to the left of the insertion point
Ctrl+Backspace	Deletes from the insertion point left to the end of the word
Del	Deletes the selected text or deletes one character to the right of the insertion point
Ctrl+Del	Deletes from the insertion point right to the end of the word, including the space after the word
Ctrl+X or Shift+Del	Deletes the selected text and stores the deleted text on the Clipboard
Ctrl+Z	Reverses the last action (also known as *undo*)

Undoing Actions

Occasionally, you may need to undo actions and commands. Perhaps you deleted text unintentionally, or made large-scale changes and want to restore the document to its original appearance. You can use the Undo SmartIcon or the **U**ndo command on the **E**dit menu to undo your last action or use the **R**evert to Saved command on the **F**ile menu to restore the earlier version of the document.

Caution

After you save a document, you cannot undo actions or revert to an earlier form of the document.

Using Edit Undo

In the User Setup dialog box, you can specify up to four undo levels; that is, you can tell Ami Pro to undo from one to four of the last four editing actions. If you deleted two words and pasted text twice in succession, for example, you can restore the two deleted words and undo the two pasting operations (see Chapter 8, "Changing Your Setup").

You can undo an action by clicking the Undo SmartIcon or by choosing **E**dit **U**ndo (see fig. 3.14). With either method, no prompt appears; Ami Pro immediately reverses the last action.

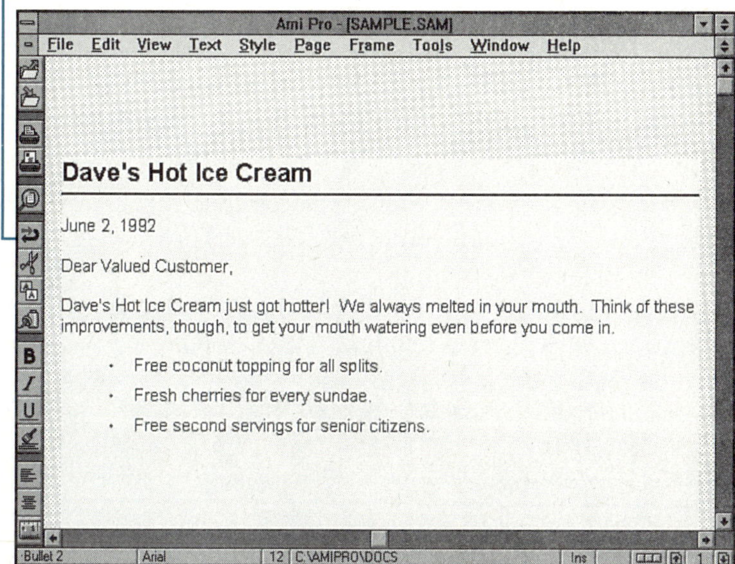
Undo SmartIcon
Ami Pro - [SAMPLE.SAM]
File Edit View Text Style Page Frame Tools Window Help
Dave's Hot Ice Cream
June 2, 1992
Dear Valued Customer,
Dave's Hot Ice Cream just got hotter! We always melted in your mouth. Think of these improvements, though, to get your mouth watering even before you come in.
Free coconut topping for all splits.
Fresh cherries for every sundae.
Free second servings for senior citizens.
Bullet 2
Arial
12 C:\AMIPRO\DOCS
Ins

Fig. 3.14 The Undo SmartIcon.

If the undo level is set above 1 in the User Setup dialog box, and you use the Undo SmartIcon or the **E**dit **U**ndo command again, Ami Pro undoes actions in reverse order. If you delete and then paste a word, for example, and click the Undo SmartIcon or choose **E**dit **U**ndo twice, Ami Pro first undoes the paste operation and then restores the deleted word.

Using File Revert to Saved

You can restore the last saved version of your document by choosing the **R**evert to Saved command from the **F**ile menu. Although you can undo up to the last four editing operations by using **E**dit **U**ndo or the Undo SmartIcon, the **R**evert to Saved command undoes all operations performed since the last time you saved the document. If you discover that you accidentally deleted an important passage, after which you performed enough editing changes to prevent **E**dit **U**ndo from restoring the material, **F**ile **R**evert to Saved may retrieve the appropriate version containing the lost text.

Tip
The **R**evert to Saved command appears on the menu only if you made changes to the document since the last time you saved.

If you choose the **R**evert to Saved command, Ami Pro warns you that you will lose all editing changes you made since the last time you saved.

Tip
Save your document frequently—at least once every 15 minutes.

If you plan to make a questionable major change in your document, save the document first so that you can use the **R**evert to Saved command if you don't like the results of the change.

Tip
You can use options in the User Setup dialog box to instruct Ami Pro to make backup files automatically at regular intervals.

To revert to the last saved version of your document, follow these steps:

1. Open the **F**ile menu.
2. Choose the **R**evert to Saved command. Ami Pro displays a dialog box; you must confirm that you want to undo all the changes made since the last time you saved.
3. To revert to the last saved version of the document, choose OK or press Enter. If you don't want to revert, choose Cancel or press Esc.

Working with Multiple Document Windows

One of the biggest advantages of Windows is the capability it gives you to work with multiple applications simultaneously. You can work with 1-2-3 for Windows in one window, Ami Pro in another, the Clipboard in another, and so on.

You also can use this multiple-windows capability within a program. In Ami Pro, for example, you can view and work on several documents in separate windows. You can open up to nine documents at a time (depending on the amount of memory available), and move from one document to another without closing any of the documents.

Working with multiple documents is useful in many situations. You may be working on more than one project, for example, and need immediate access to a monthly report, a letter to the sales force, and a special list of activities for a meeting. You can keep them all open in Ami Pro. If you are creating a new monthly report but want to copy portions from a previous version of the report, you can open the two documents in different windows and copy sections between the windows.

By default, Ami Pro maximizes the document window so that when you open a document it fills the entire window. When you open more than one document, only one of the open windows is visible at a time. The *active window* is the window containing the document on which you are currently working—and thus the insertion point. You can type and edit text in the active document only.

Ami Pro uses a Windows feature known as *Multiple Document Interface* (*MDI*). MDI enables you to do the following:

- Work with different documents in different full-sized windows.
- Split one window into smaller parts (called *panes*) and work with different documents in different panes.

- Work with one document in more than one full-sized window (by making multiple copies of the document).

The procedure for opening multiple documents is no more complicated than that for opening one document. With your existing document on-screen, choose **F**ile **N**ew or **F**ile **O**pen (depending on whether you are creating a new document or opening an existing document). If you choose **F**ile **N**ew, the New dialog box appears (refer to fig. 3.1); if you choose **F**ile **O**pen, the Open dialog box appears (refer to fig. 3.2). In either dialog box, make sure that the Close Cu**r**rent File check box is unselected. Select other options as desired to create or open the file. Continue opening or creating files as desired, using up to a maximum of nine open documents.

Tip
If you choose the E**x**it command from the **F**ile menu when you have multiple documents open, Ami Pro prompts you to save changes before you exit the program.

Using Maximized Windows

To make an open document active, you switch to its window by using the **W**indow menu (see fig. 3.15). In the **W**indow menu, a check mark appears next to the name of the active document. To make an open document active, open the **W**indow menu and choose the document you want to make active.

Each Ami Pro document is independent; you can work in any document without affecting other open documents.

Using Tiled and Cascading Windows

To see more than one document window on-screen, choose **W**indow **C**ascade or **W**indow **T**ile. When you use either command, Ami Pro displays each open document in a separate pane.

Tip
You also can open the Control Menu for the document and choose Next to cycle through the open documents.

If you choose the **C**ascade command, the panes containing each document are larger than the panes that appear when you choose the **T**ile command. With **C**ascade, however, the panes appear on top of each other and not all panes are immediately visible (see fig. 3.16). If you choose the **T**ile command, all panes are visible (see fig. 3.17).

Note

When you use the **T**ile command, Ami Pro divides the screen into as many panes as needed to display all open documents. If four documents are open, for example, Ami Pro divides the screen into four panes, and each open document occupies one pane. Because working in very small panes is difficult, don't choose the **T**ile command when many documents are open unless you need to see all the open documents on one screen.

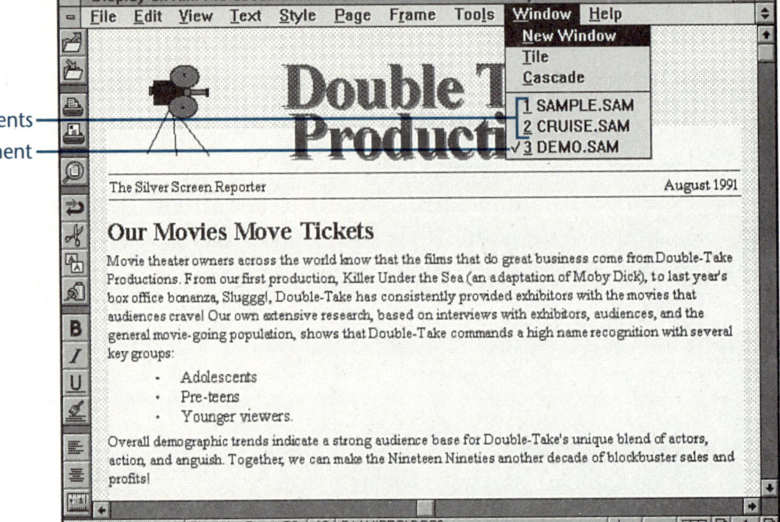

Fig. 3.15 The **W**indow menu.

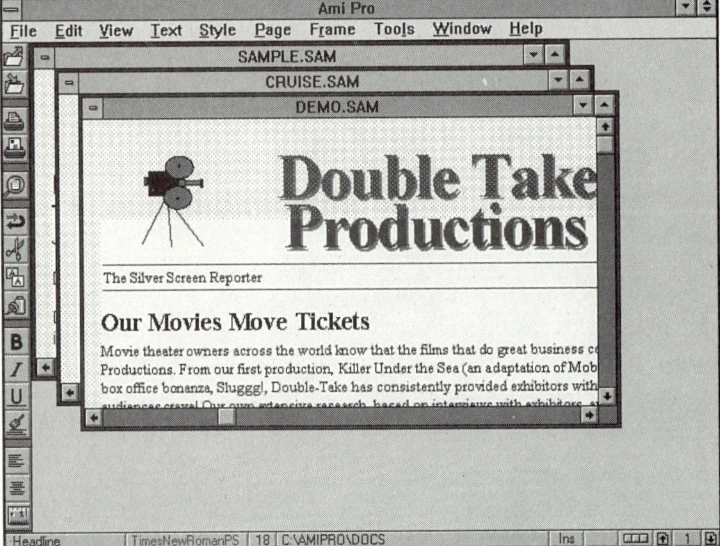

Fig. 3.16 Cascading windows.

To make a document active, click the mouse in the pane of that document, click the Title Bar of that document, or open the **W**indow menu and choose the document you want from the resulting list. Ami Pro remembers the location of the insertion point in each document; as you move from document to document, Ami Pro returns to the last location of the insertion point in the active document.

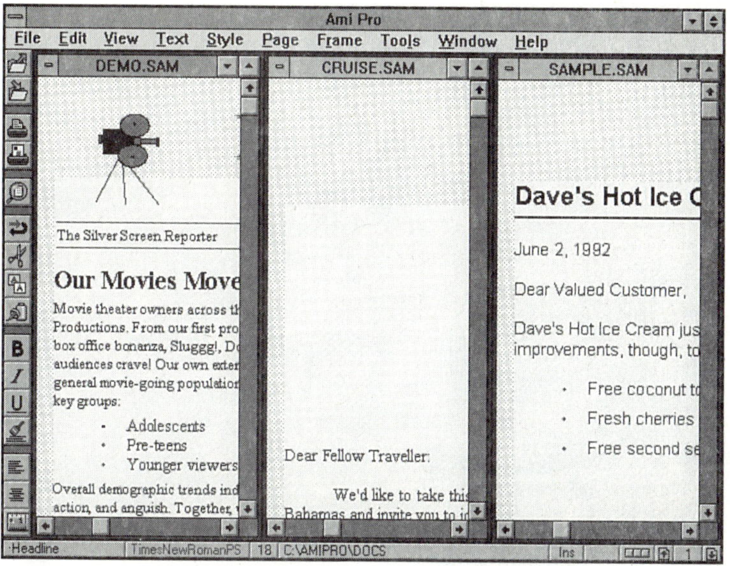

Fig. 3.17
Tiled windows.

To return to working in a full-sized window, you can close all the other open documents (see the section "Closing Documents," later in this chapter) or maximize any open document window.

To maximize a document window, activate the document you want to maximize. Then choose the Maximize command from the document Control Menu (at the left end of the document's Title Bar) or the Maximize icon (at the right end of the document's Title Bar). Ami Pro maximizes all open documents and displays the active document on-screen. You then can switch between the open documents by using the **W**indow menu.

Working with Multiple Copies of a Document

Although you can open multiple copies of a document in Ami Pro, you can only work in one copy of the document. Ami Pro labels the second copy *read-only*; you cannot save any changes made in the read-only copy. Working in two windows with the same document is useful when you need to see different parts of the document that are too large to fit together in a pane.

To create multiple full-size windows for the same document, make the document active and choose **W**indow **N**ew Window. Ami Pro displays a message indicating that you cannot save any changes you make in the second copy. After you choose OK to acknowledge the message, Ami Pro displays the second copy. As figure 3.18 shows, the read-only document's Title Bar (at the top of the document) displays the file name with a colon (:), a number, and the words `Read Only`.

Tip
Make changes in the copy of the document that you can save—not in the read-only copy.

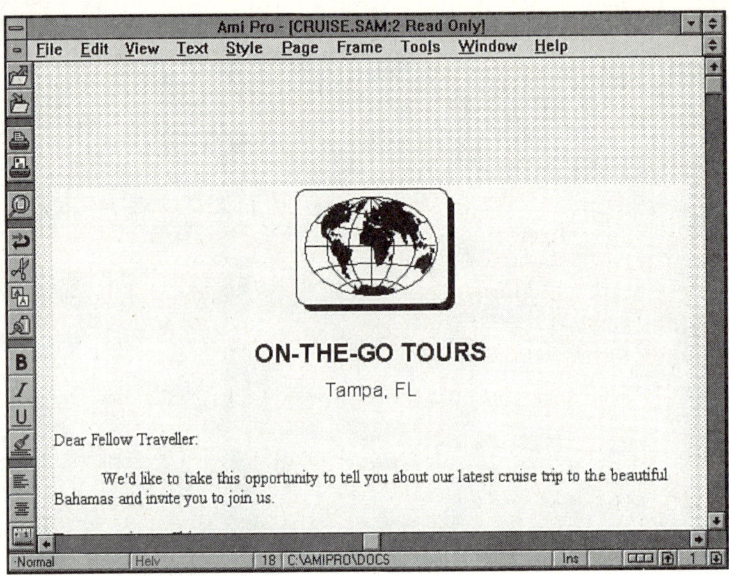

Fig. 3.18
The read-only copy of a document.

Tip
You also can use any of the previously discussed methods of opening a file to open a second copy of the document.

If you have multiple versions of a document open when you open the **W**indow menu, you see multiple versions of the same document listed, with numbers appended to the name (see fig. 3.19).

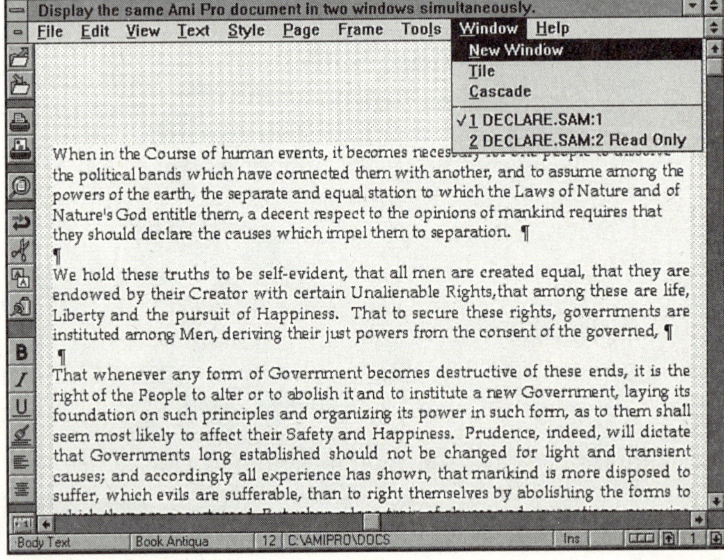

Fig. 3.19
The **W**indow menu, listing multiple copies of the same document.

To close each window, you can choose the Close command from the document Control Menu or choose **F**ile **C**lose (see the section "Closing Documents," later in this chapter, for more information).

Pasting Text between Ami Pro Documents

Working in multiple documents provides you with a great time-saving device: the ability to copy and move text between documents. As noted earlier, text placed on the Clipboard remains in place until you exit Windows, or cut or copy more text to the Clipboard. You can paste the text from the Clipboard into any Ami Pro document or Windows document. By opening multiple documents and using the Windows Clipboard, you can move and copy text between documents.

To move or copy text between documents, follow these steps:

1. Open the document that contains the text you want to copy or move.
2. Open the document to which you want to copy or move text.
3. Use the **W**indow menu to switch to the document that contains the text you want to move or copy.
4. Select the text.
5. Cut or copy the text by clicking the Cut or Copy SmartIcon, by choosing **E**dit Cu**t** or **E**dit **C**opy, or by using the keyboard shortcuts Ctrl+X or Ctrl+C.
6. Use the **W**indow menu to switch to the document where you want to place the cut or copied text.
7. Position the insertion point where you want the cut or copied text to appear.
8. Paste the text into the document by pressing Shift+Ins, clicking the Paste SmartIcon, or choosing **E**dit **P**aste. The text appears in the active document.

Pasting Ami Pro Text to Other Windows Applications

Because the Clipboard is a Windows feature instead of an Ami Pro feature, you can use the text you copy or cut to the Clipboard by pasting it into other Windows applications.

To copy Ami Pro text to another Windows application, follow these steps:

1. Select the text and cut or copy it to the Clipboard.

2. Open the document in another Windows application in which you want to paste the text.

3. Position the insertion point where you want the text to appear.

4. Choose the Paste command for that application.

Caution

Not all Windows applications accept text from the Clipboard (notably drawing applications).

Protecting Text

You may want to protect text from being modified or deleted. If someone else uses your files, for example, you may want to ensure that that person cannot inadvertently alter your text. You may have a document worded "just so" (perhaps even a legal document) that you want to protect from changes. You can protect the text by marking it.

To protect text, follow these steps:

1. Select the text you want to protect.

2. Choose **E**dit **M**ark Text. A cascading menu appears (see fig. 3.20).

3. Choose **P**rotected Text.

Tip
Because you can delete protected text, you may think that protecting text is pointless. But the text is protected from inadvertent changes, however, and indicates to others that you don't want changes.

You cannot place the insertion point in protected text with the mouse or arrow keys. You can delete protected text, however, by using the Backspace or Del keys or by selecting the text with Shift plus the arrow keys.

You can remove protection by repeating the steps for marking text. When you open the **E**dit menu, a check mark appears next to the **M**ark Text command. When you choose **M**ark Text, a check mark appears next to the **P**rotected Text option, indicating that Ami Pro is protecting the text. If you choose the option again, the check marks disappear and Ami Pro no longer protects the text.

You also can use password protection to protect an entire document. Select the Password **P**rotect option when you save the document (see Chapter 2, "Quick Start: Creating a Document," for information on saving documents).

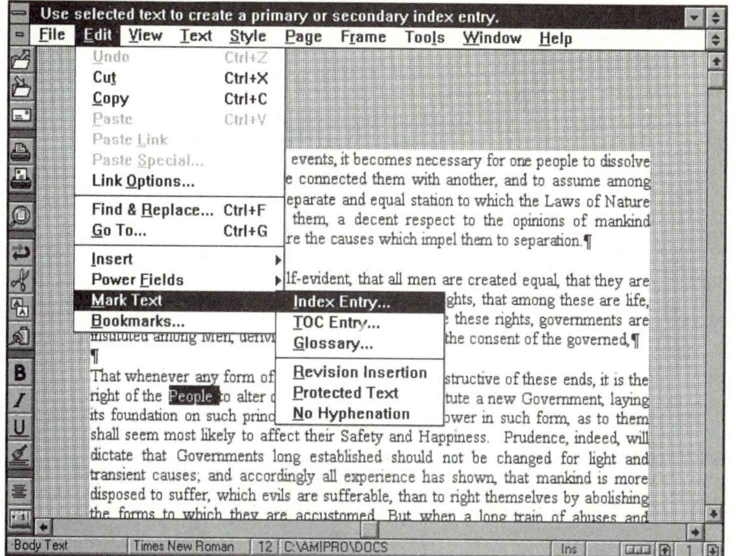

Fig. 3.20
The **Mark** Text menu.

> **Note**
>
> You can use protected text when you want to print text onto preprinted forms. You can type the entire form (including the preprinted fields) into Ami Pro. Then, if you protect the preprinted fields that appear on the form and set your print options properly (see Chapter 7 for more information), Ami Pro prints only the unprotected text.

Closing Documents

Saving documents transfers changes from the document on-screen to disk, but doesn't clear your screen. When you work in multiple documents, you may want to close some documents without opening any others.

Earlier in this chapter, you reviewed the procedures for opening a new document and learned how to open an existing document. In both discussions, you read about the Close Current File check box, which appears in the New dialog box and the Open dialog box. When you select this option, Ami Pro clears the screen before opening a new or existing document.

To close a document, follow these steps:

1. Make the file you want to close the active document.

2. Open the **F**ile menu or the document Control Menu.

3. Choose the **C**lose command. If the document is unnamed, Ami Pro displays a message asking if you want to save the document. If the document has a name but you have changed the document since the last time you saved it, Ami Pro displays a message asking if you want to save the changes.

4. Choose **Y**es, **N**o, or Cancel.

   If you choose **Y**es, you save the document with the changes and close it (if the document is new, Ami Pro prompts you for a name).

   If you choose **N**o, you close the document without saving the changes.

   If you choose Cancel, Ami Pro closes the dialog box but not the document.

After closing the document, Ami Pro displays another open document; if no other documents are open, Ami Pro displays the blank application screen.

You can close the active document and all other open Ami Pro documents by exiting from Ami Pro. Again, Ami Pro asks if you want to save documents in which you have made changes.

Summary

In this chapter, you learned important Ami Pro functions for creating and editing documents. You now know how to open a new or existing document, close the document, and mark text to protect it from revision. You learned how to move the insertion point around in a document, and discovered basic editing techniques for moving, copying, and deleting text. You learned how to undo actions and work with multiple documents and windows.

In the next chapter, you learn how to use formatting to change the appearance of text in Ami Pro.

Chapter 4

Formatting a Document

Often, you want to change the appearance of certain text in a document. You may want to enhance the appearance of a word, phrase, or paragraph, for example, by using underlining or boldface type.

Formatting is the process of specifying the appearance of text. Ami Pro divides formatting into three categories: character formatting, paragraph formatting, and page formatting. Within each category, you can format text in different ways. In this chapter, you learn about the available character and paragraph formats and how to use them. In Chapter 5, "Working with Page Layout," you learn about formatting document pages.

The first part of this chapter, "Character Formatting," discusses using Ami Pro to apply character formatting to enhance text. *Character formatting* includes modifying fonts and applying character attributes such as underlining or boldface type.

The second part of this chapter, "Paragraph Formatting," discusses using Ami Pro to apply paragraph formatting to enhance text. *Paragraph formatting* includes such enhancements as aligning and indenting text and setting line spacing. You can use both the **T**ext menu and the SmartIcon Bar to apply character and paragraph formatting.

Character Formatting

Characters are letters, numbers, and punctuation marks. When you format characters, you specify their appearance. In Ami Pro, you can change the font, point size, and placement of characters, as well as apply other character attributes such as boldface or underlining.

You can apply character formatting before you type the characters, or you can type the characters, select them, and then apply the formatting. Ami Pro enables you to apply character formatting by using the keyboard, the **T**ext menu, or the SmartIcon Bar. Table 4.1 lists the character attributes you can apply by using each of these methods.

Table 4.1 Character Formatting Methods

Method	Character Attributes
SmartIcon Bar	The default palette enables you to apply the bold, italic, and continuous single underline character attributes
Keyboard	Enables you to apply the continuous single underline, word underline, bold, and italic character attributes
Text menu	Enables you to specify the font, its point size, and color; the bold, italic, continuous single underline, word underline, double underline, and case character attributes; as well as special effects such as strikethrough, overstrike, superscript, or subscript

You can create a custom SmartIcon palette that includes all the character formatting SmartIcons (see fig. 4.1).

Although the **T**ext menu provides the most options, applying character formatting by using the SmartIcons or the keyboard often is faster than using the **T**ext menu and its dialog boxes.

Modifying Fonts

Fonts are collections of typefaces that share a common style. Each font has a distinctive look. Two common fonts are courier and script. Most fonts are available in a range of sizes. You measure the size of a font in points (one point is equal to 1/72 inch); smaller point sizes produce smaller text.

In Ami Pro, you can use preset point sizes from 6 to 48 points, or, for laser printers with adjustable or scalable fonts, you can specify the point size. To print documents, you can use the *hardware fonts* and point sizes available on your printer (the fonts supplied with your printer or fonts you added to your printer by using font cartridges), or you can use *software fonts* (also called *soft fonts*) if your printer supports them.

When you use fonts in Ami Pro, you must consider two aspects of fonts: the way they appear on-screen, and the way they print. To guarantee a true WYSIWYG environment, you want all your fonts to appear the same on-screen and in print. When you purchased Ami Pro, you also received the Adobe Type Manager (ATM) fonts. You can use the ATM fonts if you installed them with Ami Pro and if your printer supports them. Because ATM fonts provide matching screen and printer fonts, your document's appearance on-screen matches its printed appearance.

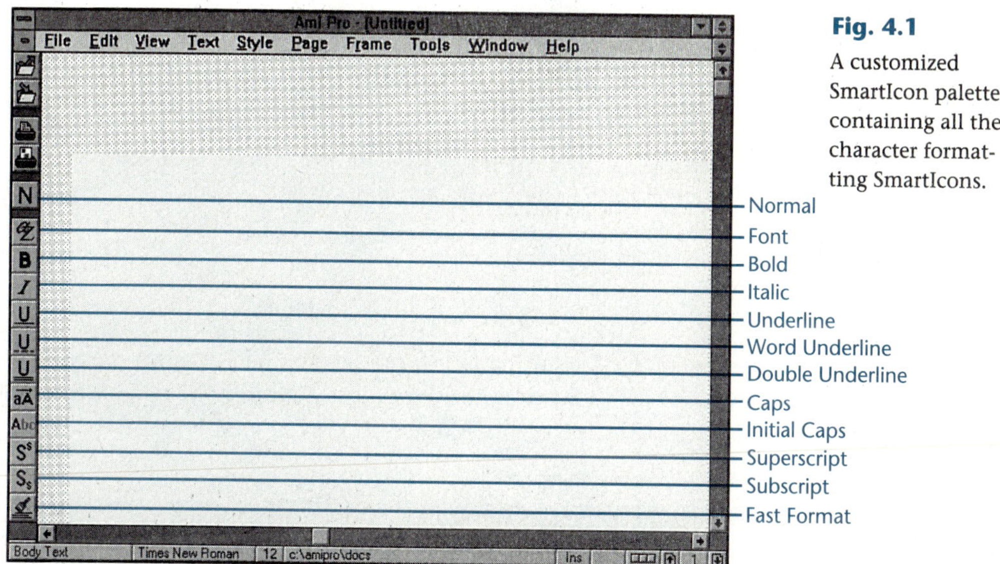

Fig. 4.1
A customized SmartIcon palette containing all the character formatting SmartIcons.

As you learn in Chapter 7, "Proofreading and Printing a Document," Ami Pro doesn't control printing or your display; Windows controls both. Screen fonts, printer fonts and the way they work in Windows are complex subjects. For more information, consult *Using Windows 3.1*, Special Edition (published by Que Corporation) or the *Windows User's Guide*. For more information on ATM fonts, see the *ATM User Guide*.

You can choose a font, point size, and color before you type the characters, or you can select existing characters and then make font choices. You choose the font, point size, and color by opening the Font dialog box.

To change the font of existing text, follow these steps:

1. Select the text you want to modify.
2. Choose **T**ext **F**ont. The Font dialog box appears (see fig. 4.2).
3. Choose the options you want to change. See table 4.2 for an explanation of each of the options. To see the potential effect before using the options in your text, watch the example box at the bottom of the Font dialog box. The example box shows sample text using the specified options.

4. Choose OK or press Enter to close the dialog box and apply the font changes to the selected text.

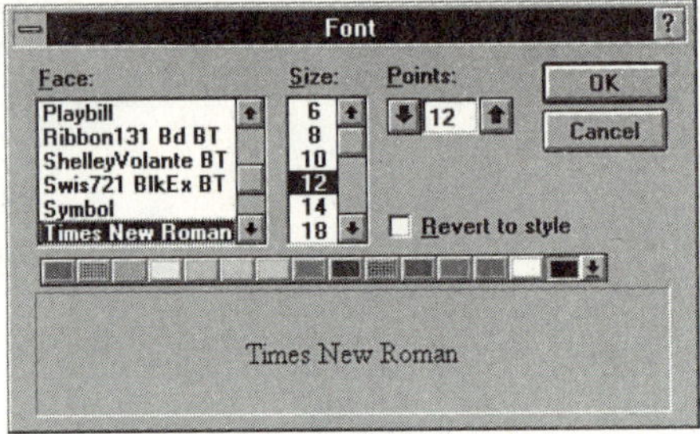

Fig. 4.2
The Font dialog box.

Table 4.2 briefly describes the options available in the Font dialog box.

After you change the font, you may want to modify other characteristics of the text. You can designate sections of text, for example, to appear in boldface or italics. The next section discusses how to modify these attributes.

Table 4.2 Font Dialog Box Options

Option	Action
Face	Controls the typeface used for the text
Size	Changes the point size for the typeface—the greater the point size, the larger the typeface
Points	Specifies an exact size for the typeface if you use a printer with scalable fonts
Revert to Style	Restores selected text to the font setting of the paragraph style
Color bar	Controls the color of the characters on color printers; on other printers, controls the shading of the characters

Modifying Character Attributes

You can use character attributes to enhance the appearance of text in many ways, as shown in table 4.3.

Figure 4.3 shows the striking differences you can achieve by applying character attributes to text.

You can choose a character attribute before you type the characters or you can type the characters, select them, and then choose a character attribute.

You can apply some character attributes by using the SmartIcon Bar or keyboard shortcuts.

Table 4.3 Character Styles

Character Attribute	Effect
Normal	Removes all character attributes and returns selected text to its original paragraph style settings
Bold	Characters appear in boldface type
Italic	Characters appear in italic type
Single continuous underline	Both words and spaces are underlined
Word underline	Words are underlined, but spaces are not
Uppercase	Characters are all uppercase
Lowercase	Characters are all lowercase
Initial caps	The first character of each word is uppercase
Small caps	Characters are all uppercase, but initial caps are in the assigned point size and the rest of the characters are in a slightly smaller point size
Superscript	Characters are raised above the regular line of type and in a smaller point size
Subscript	Characters are lower than the regular line of type and in a smaller point size
Double underline	Both words and spaces have a double underline
Strikethrough	Characters appear with a straight line through them
Overstrike	Characters appear with another character superimposed (you specify the overstrike character)

The following sections explain techniques for assigning character attributes by using SmartIcons, by using the keyboard shortcuts, and by using the **T**ext menu and its **C**aps submenu and Special **E**ffects dialog box. No matter which of these methods you use, you have the option of assigning character attributes before you type the characters, or assigning character attributes to selected typed characters.

> **Note**
>
> You remove character attributes by selecting the text and following the steps to apply the attribute, or by choosing the **N**ormal command from the **T**ext menu or SmartIcon Bar. When you open the **T**ext menu, a check mark appears next to the attributes applied to the selected text.

Applying Character Attributes with SmartIcons

An easy method of applying boldface, italic, or underline attributes is to use the Ami Pro SmartIcons and a mouse. To assign character attributes by using SmartIcons, follow these steps:

1. Before you type the text, click the SmartIcon for the character attribute you want to assign (see fig. 4.4).
2. Type the text that is to have the character attribute.
3. Click the character attribute SmartIcon or click the Normal SmartIcon.

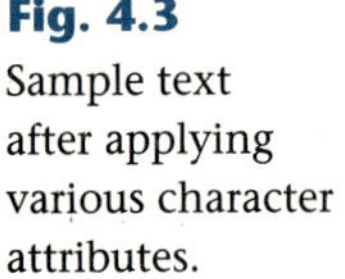

Fig. 4.3
Sample text after applying various character attributes.

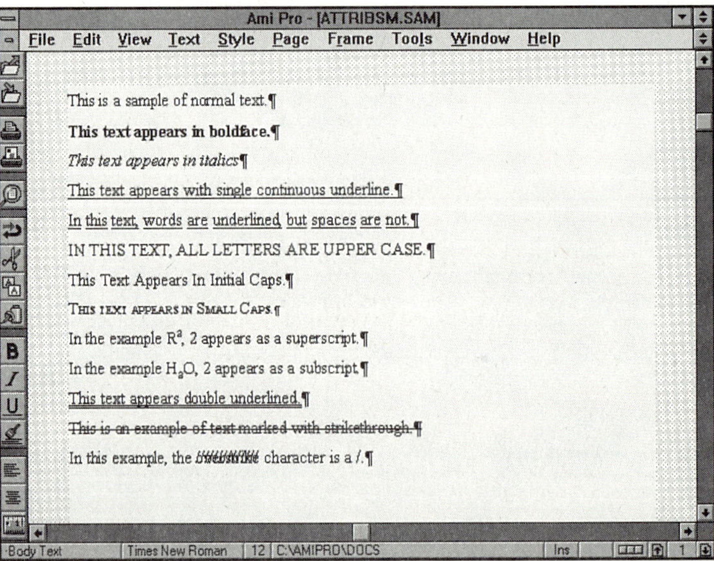

Alternatively, you can select typed text and then click the character attribute SmartIcon.

To remove the character attribute, select the text and follow step 3.

Applying Character Attributes with the Text Menu

You can choose a number of character attributes such as boldface, italics, and underlining directly from the Text menu. The Special Effects dialog box and Caps submenu (discussed later in this section), supply other attributes.

You can use the **T**ext menu to apply character attributes in two ways. For the first method, follow these steps:

1. Before you type the text, open the **T**ext menu and choose the command for the character attribute you want to assign. (After you apply an attribute, when you next open the menu a check mark appears next to that attribute.)

2. Type the text.

3. Open the **T**ext menu and choose the **N**ormal command or choose the selected attribute again to deselect it.

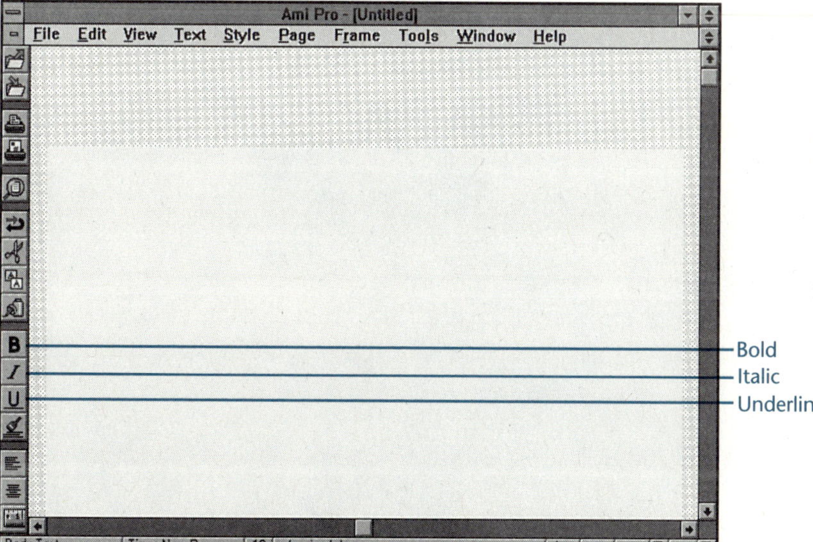

Fig. 4.4
The character-attribute SmartIcons on the default SmartIcon Bar.

Alternatively, you can use the following method:

1. Type the text to which you want to assign the character attribute.

2. Select the text.

3. Open the **T**ext menu and choose the attribute command.

You can remove character attributes by selecting the text and choosing the text attribute you want to remove or choosing **T**ext **N**ormal.

Using the Special Effects Dialog Box. The Special Effects dialog box enables you to assign the character attributes of Superscript, Subscript, Double Underline, Strikethrough, and Overstrike Characters to your text. Refer to table 4.3 for details on these character attributes.

You can use superscripts or subscripts for marking footnotes or for mathematical equations. Use strikethrough text primarily when proofreading to indicate text that should be removed from the document; Ami Pro places a straight line on top of existing text. You can use Ami Pro's overstrike character option to identify the character you want Ami Pro to use on top of existing text.

To assign character attributes by using the Special Effects dialog box, follow these steps:

1. Before you type the text, choose **T**ext Special **E**ffects. Ami Pro displays the Special Effects dialog box (see fig. 4.5).

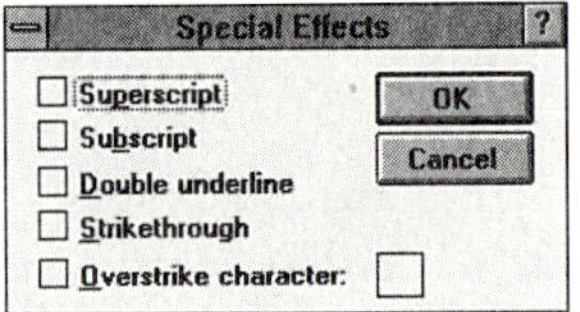

Fig. 4.5
The Special Effects dialog box.

2. Choose the character attribute you want to assign. (If you choose **O**verstrike Character, type the character you want Ami Pro to use in the text box next to the **O**verstrike Character check box.)
3. Choose OK.
4. Type the text.
5. When you finish typing the text to which you want to assign the character attribute, open the **T**ext menu and repeat steps 1 through 3 or choose the **N**ormal command.

Alternatively, you can type the text, select it, and then follow steps 1 through 3.

Using the Caps Submenu. To apply capitalization with the **C**aps submenu, follow these steps:

1. Before you type the text, choose **T**ext **C**aps. Ami Pro displays the **C**aps menu shown in figure 4.6.

2. From the menu, choose the kind of capitalization you want: **U**pper Case, **L**ower Case, **I**nitial Caps, or **S**mall Caps.

3. Type the text.

4. When you finish typing the text you want to capitalize, repeat steps 1 and 2 or choose **T**ext **N**ormal.

You also can assign capitalization by selecting typed text and then assigning the attribute of your choice. You remove capitalization by selecting the text and choosing the capitalization command again or choosing **T**ext **N**ormal.

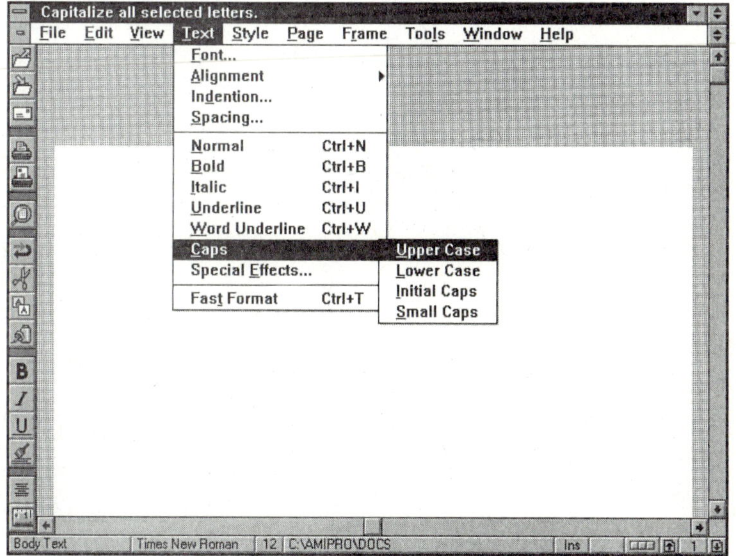

Fig. 4.6
The **T**ext **C**aps menu.

Using Keyboard Shortcuts To Assign Character Attributes

Five attributes in the **T**ext menu have shortcut key combinations. Table 4.4 lists these attributes and their keyboard shortcuts.

Table 4.4 Keyboard Shortcuts for Applying Character Attributes

Attribute	Shortcut
Normal	Ctrl+N
Boldface	Ctrl+B
Italics	Ctrl+I
Underline	Ctrl+U
Word underline	Ctrl+W

To assign character attributes by using keyboard shortcuts, follow these steps:

1. Press the shortcut key combination for the character attribute you want to assign.

2. Type the text that is to have the character attribute.

3. Press the same key combination or press Ctrl+N to return to normal text.

Alternatively, you can select typed text and then press the shortcut key combination for the character attribute you want to assign.

To remove character attributes by using the keyboard shortcuts, select the text and follow step 3.

Using the Fast Format Feature To Copy Character Formatting

You use the Fast Format command to copy character formatting. You must have a mouse to use the Fas**t** Format feature.

Suppose that you have italicized a few words in the first paragraph of the document. Then you decide to apply italics to the entire third paragraph. You can use the Fast Format command to copy the formatting of the italicized words in the first paragraph to the entire third paragraph.

To use the Fast Format feature, follow these steps.

1. Apply any kind of character formatting to text. You can apply the formatting by any of the methods mentioned in this chapter.

2. Select the text that contains the formatting you want to apply.

3. Click the Fast Format SmartIcon, choose **T**ext **F**ast Format, or use the keyboard shortcut by pressing Ctrl+T. Ami Pro opens and closes the **T**ext menu, and the mouse pointer shape becomes an I-beam with a paintbrush attached.

4. Use the mouse to select the text to which you want to apply the formatting. When you release the mouse button, Ami Pro applies the formatting. Fast formatting remains active, so you can continue selecting text and applying the formatting.

5. To turn off fast formatting, click the Fast Format SmartIcon again, press Ctrl+T, or open the **T**ext menu. If you use the **T**ext menu method, note that a check mark appears to the left of the Fas**t** Format command on the menu. Choose the command again to remove the check mark.

You can use fast formatting to apply any of the kinds of character formatting previously discussed in this chapter, including the fonts. Ami Pro can copy more than one type of character formatting at a time, but the text you select to copy must contain all the formats. In figure 4.7, for example, the phrase "for all good men" appears in boldface type and the phrase "to come to the aid" appears in both underlined and boldface type.

If you select both formatted phrases, turn on fast formatting, and then select the unformatted phrase "Now is the time," Ami Pro applies only boldface to "Now is the time." If you select only the phrase "to come to the aid," turn on fast formatting, and then select the phrase "Now is the time," Ami Pro applies both boldface and underlining to "Now is the time."

If you don't select text before choosing the Fas**t** Format command from the **T**ext menu, Ami Pro displays the Fast Format dialog box.

Paragraph Formatting

The traditional definition of the term *paragraph* is "a series of related sentences." In Ami Pro, the word *paragraph* has a special meaning: a paragraph is any amount of text or graphics followed by a paragraph mark (¶) (see fig. 4.8). If you have paragraph marks displayed, when you press Enter you insert a paragraph mark into your document.

► See "Customizing the Palette," p. 220

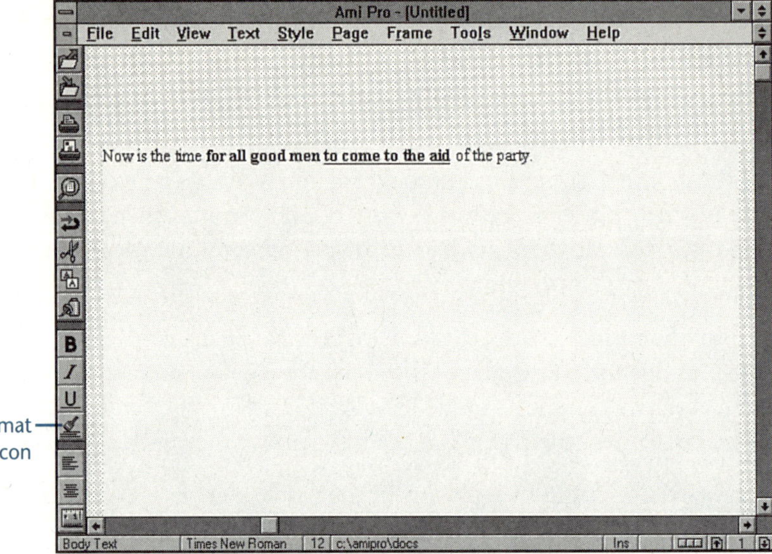

Fig. 4.7 Sample text containing mixed formats.

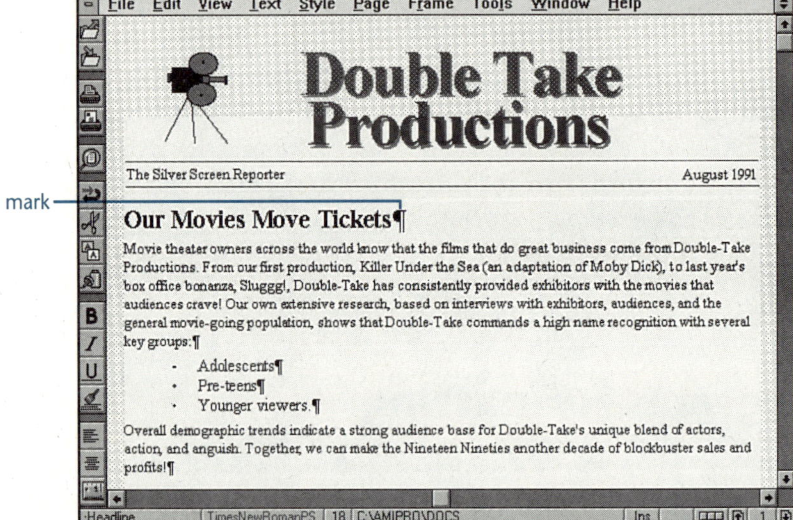

Fig. 4.8 Ami Pro paragraphs with paragraph marks displayed.

To display paragraph marks, choose **V**iew View **P**references. The View Preferences dialog box appears (see fig. 4.9).

If no X appears in the Tabs & **R**eturns check box, choose Tabs & **R**eturns to place an X in the check box, and then choose OK or press Enter.

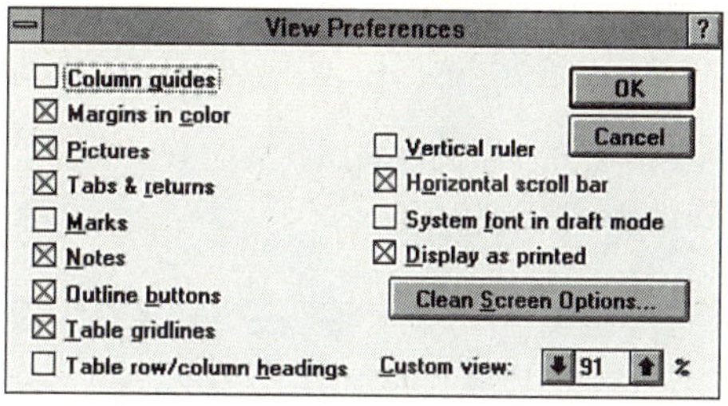

View Preferences

Column guides
Margins in color
Pictures
Tabs & returns
Marks
Notes
Outline buttons
Table gridlines
Table row/column headings
Vertical ruler
Horizontal scroll bar
System font in draft mode
Display as printed
OK
Cancel
Clean Screen Options...
Custom view: 91 %

Fig. 4.9
The View Preferences dialog box.

You can control the following attributes of paragraph formatting:

- Alignment
- Indention
- Line spacing

► See "Working with Page Layout," p. 119

Just as with character formatting, you can apply paragraph formatting before or after you type the text. To apply paragraph formatting after you type the text, place the insertion point in the paragraph you want to format and then apply the format. If you want to format more than one paragraph, select all the paragraphs you want to format and then apply the format.

Ami Pro enables you to apply paragraph formatting by using the keyboard, the mouse, or the SmartIcon Bar. Table 4.5 lists the paragraph attributes you can apply by using each of these methods.

Table 4.5 Paragraph Formatting Methods

Method	Paragraph Attributes
SmartIcon Bar	The default palette enables you to specify left and center paragraph alignment
Keyboard	Enables you to specify all paragraph alignment
Text menu	Enables you to specify all paragraph alignment, indention, and line spacing

Tip
You can change the SmartIcon Bar to include more paragraph alignment options than are available in the default palette.

The **T**ext menu provides the most complete way to format paragraphs; through it you can access all the paragraph formatting options. Although using the keyboard or the SmartIcons is faster than using the **T**ext menu, both of the former methods offer fewer paragraph formatting options.

Remember that to apply formatting by using the SmartIcons, you must display the SmartIcon Bar and then use the mouse to choose formatting options.

You can create a custom SmartIcon palette that includes all the paragraph-formatting SmartIcons (see fig. 4.10).

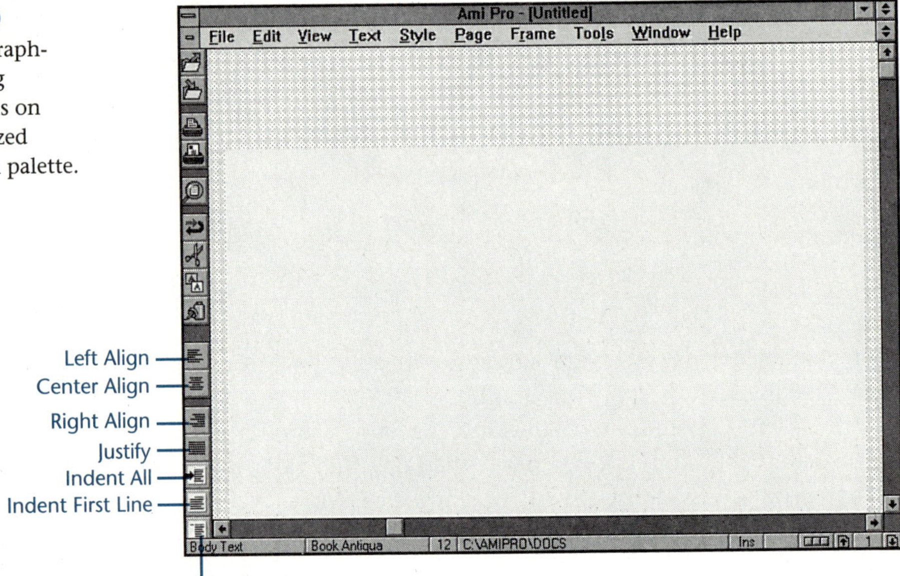

Fig. 4.10
The paragraph-formatting SmartIcons on a customized SmartIcon palette.

Setting Alignment

Alignment refers to the position of the main document text on the page. In tables or frames, Ami Pro measures alignment from the margins of the column, frame, or cell. In Ami Pro, you can align text to the left or right margins, center the text, or justify the text.

As figure 4.11 shows, left alignment aligns text at the left margin and produces a ragged right margin.

When you use center alignment (see fig. 4.12), the text is centered between the left and right margins, and both margins appear ragged.

Figure 4.13 shows right alignment. Aligning text at the right margin produces a ragged left margin.

If you justify text, Ami Pro aligns the text at both margins by expanding the spaces between words (see fig. 4.14).

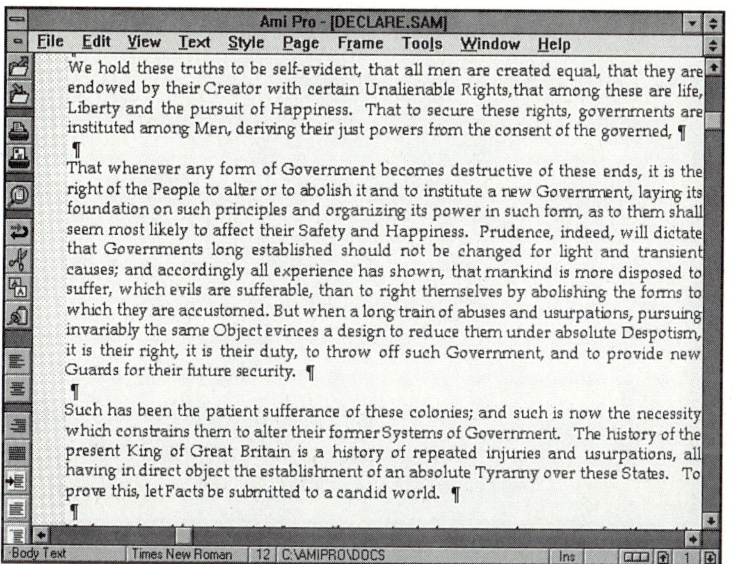

Fig. 4.11
Left-aligned text.

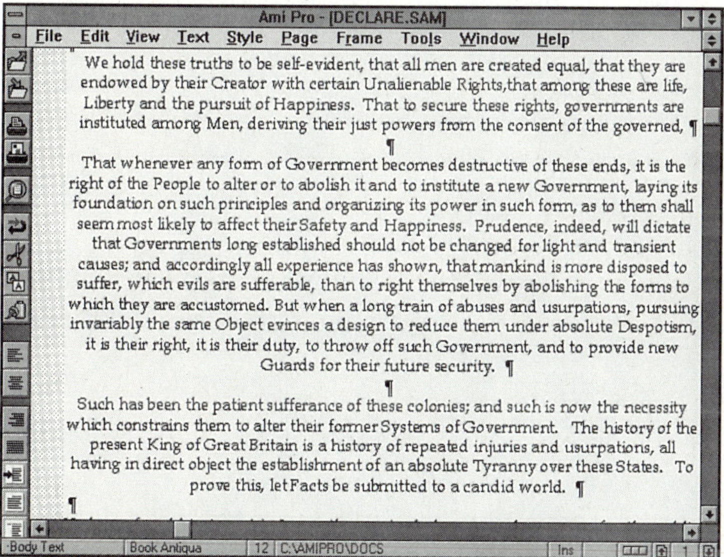

Fig. 4.12
Center-aligned text.

When you change the alignment, you don't need to select the entire paragraph. You can select any part of the paragraph, or just place the insertion point somewhere in the paragraph, because Ami Pro aligns only entire paragraphs. You can align text by using the keyboard, commands on the Text menu, or the SmartIcons.

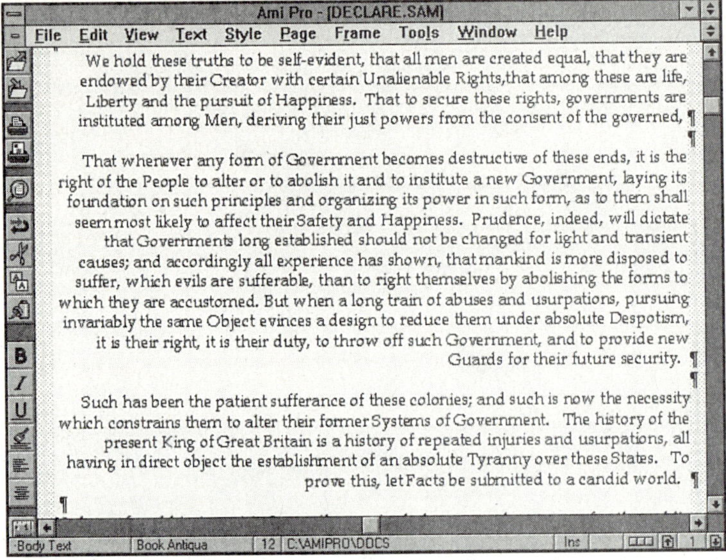

Fig. 4.13
Right alignment.

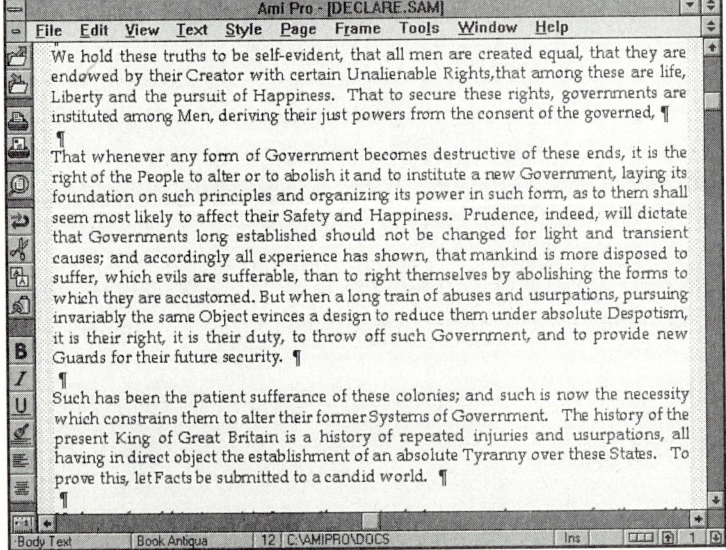

Fig. 4.14
Justified text.

To align text, follow these steps:

1. Place the insertion point anywhere in the paragraph you want to align, or select multiple paragraphs to align.

2. Choose **T**ext **A**lignment. Ami Pro displays the cascading **A**lignment menu shown in figure 4.15.

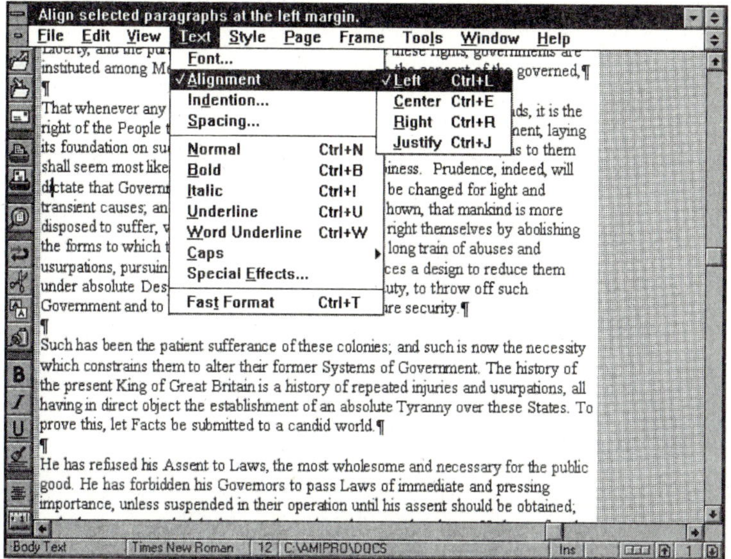

Fig. 4.15
The **Text Align**-ment menu.

3. From the **Alignment** menu, choose the desired alignment.

4. Choose OK or press Enter.

Table 4.6 shows the keyboard shortcuts you can use to align paragraphs. To use a keyboard shortcut, place the insertion point in the paragraph you want to align (or select text in that paragraph) and then press an alignment key-combination.

Table 4.6 Alignment Keyboard Shortcuts

Alignment	Shortcut
Left	Ctrl+L
Center	Ctrl+E
Right	Ctrl+R
Justify	Ctrl+J

You also can apply justification by using SmartIcons (see fig. 4.16).

Fig. 4.16
Alignment SmartIcons on the default palette.

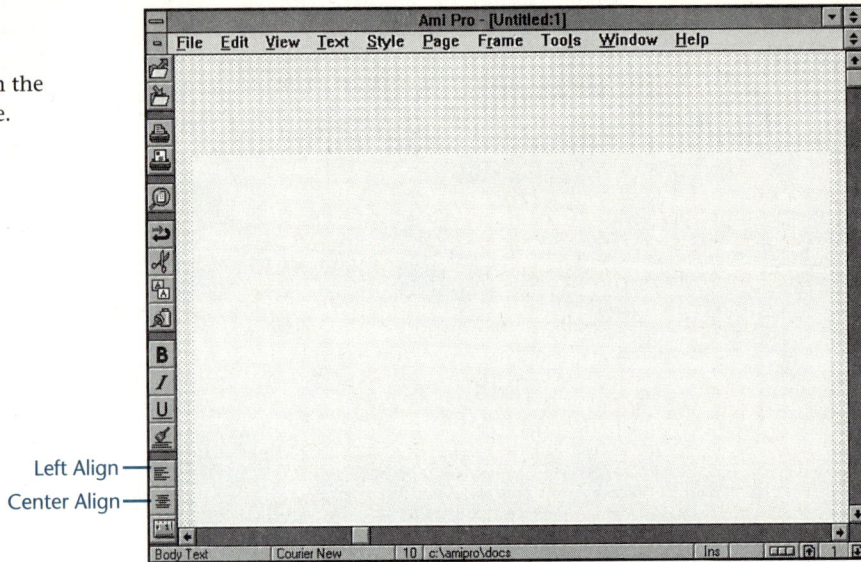

> **Note**
>
> To remove alignment, choose the alignment again. If you centered a paragraph, for example, place the insertion point in that paragraph and click the Center Align SmartIcon, press Ctrl+E, or choose **T**ext **N**ormal to return the paragraph to the default left alignment.

Indenting Text

Using *indention*, you can inset one line or an entire paragraph of text from the normal text margins. Ami Pro enables you to use a variety of indents to create special document effects. You can create bibliographies, for example, using *hanging indents*, which align the first line of the paragraph at the left margin and indent subsequent lines of the paragraph.

You can change indention by making changes to the contents of the Indention dialog box, shown in figure 4.17.

Ami Pro provides a variety of indention styles. Table 4.7 briefly describes the types of indention available in the Indention dialog box.

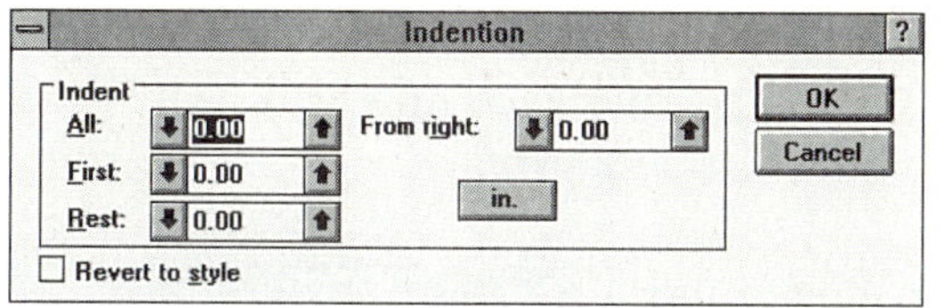

Fig. 4.17 The Indention dialog box.

Table 4.7 Indention Dialog Box Options

Option	Description
All	Indents all lines from the left margin, using the specified measurement
From Right	Indents all lines from the right margin, using the specified measurement
First	Indents only the first line of the paragraph
Rest	Indents all except the first line of the paragraph (hanging indent)
Revert to Style	Returns the paragraph to the indenting format in the existing paragraph style (for a full discussion of style sheets, see Chapter 10, "Working with Style Sheets")

Figure 4.18 shows examples of paragraphs using each form of indention:

- The first paragraph is indented 1/2 inch from both margins.
- In the second paragraph, the first line is indented one inch from the left margin.
- The third paragraph is not indented (*flush left*).
- The fourth paragraph uses a hanging indent (**R**est option set at one inch).
- The last paragraph is indented one inch from the right margin.

You also can use the Indention dialog box to specify the amount of each indention. You can type the exact amount in the text box following the indention style you have chosen, or click the up- and down-arrow buttons located at the ends of the text box. Each time you click the arrow button, you increase or decrease the amount by .05 inch.

The default unit of indention measurement is inches. By choosing the unit of measure button (labeled in.), you can change the unit of measurement to centimeters, picas (1/6 inch), or points (1/72 inch). Although some typesetting equipment requires points or picas, in general you can use inches for all Ami Pro activities involving measurement.

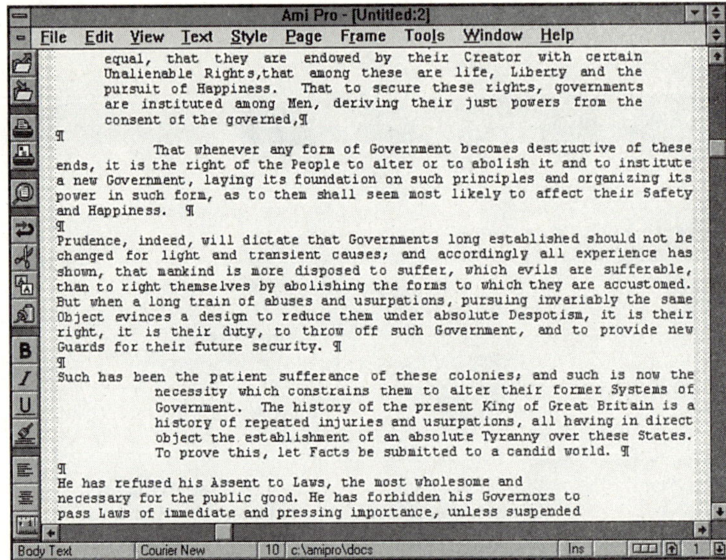

Fig. 4.18 Examples of indented text.

To indent a paragraph, follow these steps:

1. Place the insertion point anywhere in the paragraph or select the paragraphs you want to indent.

2. Choose **T**ext **I**ndention. The Indention dialog box appears (refer to fig. 4.17).

3. Use the unit of measure button (labeled in.) to specify the units you want to use.

4. Choose the type of indention you want to use (All, **F**irst, **R**est, or From Ri**g**ht) and specify the amount of indention you want.

5. When you are satisfied with your entries, choose OK or press Enter. Ami Pro returns to the document and indents the selected text as specified.

Note

Ami Pro adds the amount of indention for the **F**irst option and the **R**est option to the amount for the **A**ll option. For example, if you specify .5 inch for **A**ll, 1.0 for **F**irst, and .5 for **R**est, Ami Pro indents the first line 1.5 inches and the rest of the lines 1 inch.

Setting Line Spacing

Line spacing refers to the amount of space between lines in a document. For text in *single-space* format, no blank line appears between lines of text. In *double-space* format, a blank line (the height of one line of text) appears between lines of text. Ami Pro offers single, double, and 1 1/2-line spacing, and also enables you to specify custom spacing formats. Custom spacing is useful if you need to fit text into a preprinted form.

The Spacing dialog box enables you to select and change line spacing formats (see fig. 4.19).

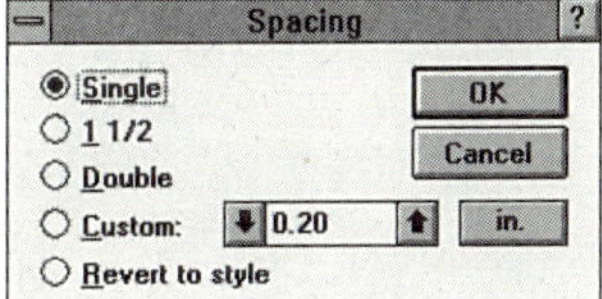

Fig. 4.19
The Spacing dialog box.

Table 4.8 briefly describes the options in the Spacing dialog box.

Table 4.8 Spacing Dialog Box Options

Option	Description
Single	Formats the text with single-spacing
1 1/2	Formats the text with 1 1/2-line spacing
Double	Formats the text with double-spacing
Custom	Formats the text with the spacing you specify in the text box
Revert to Style	Returns the paragraph to the spacing format in the existing style (for a full discussion of style sheets, see Chapter 10, "Working with Style Sheets")

If you select **C**ustom spacing, you can specify the spacing size by typing the number in the text box or clicking the arrow buttons until you see the size you want. If you want to change the measurement unit, click the unit of measure button until you see the appropriate measure (inches, picas, points, or centimeters).

To change line spacing, follow these steps:

1. Place the insertion point in the paragraph you want to modify, or select the paragraphs you want to modify.

2. Choose **T**ext **S**pacing. The Spacing dialog box appears (refer to fig. 4.19).

3. Select the spacing you want: **S**ingle, **1** 1/2, **D**ouble, **C**ustom, or **R**evert to Style.

4. Choose OK or press Enter.

Figure 4.20 shows a sample document using the various forms of line spacing:

- The first paragraph shows single-spacing.
- The second paragraph shows 1 1/2-spacing.
- The third paragraph is double-spaced.
- The fourth paragraph uses the **C**ustom spacing option; this sample uses .2 inch as the setting.

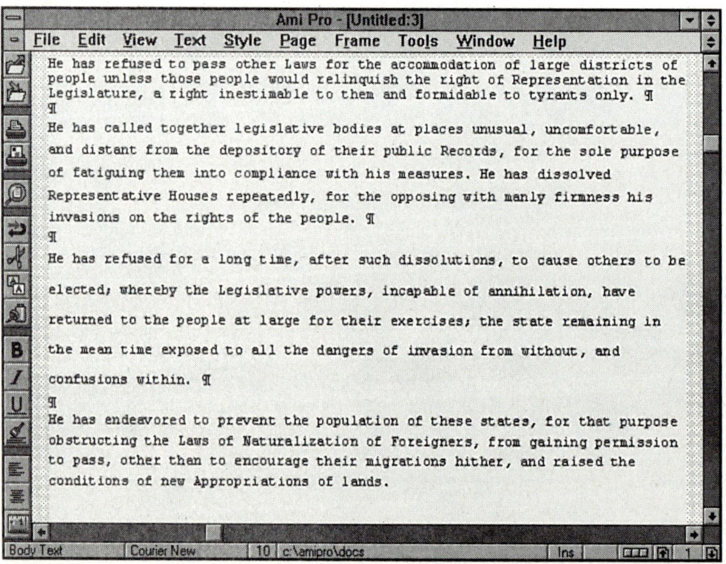

Ami Pro - [Untitled:3]
File Edit View Text Style Page Frame Tools Window Help
He has refused to pass other Laws for the accommodation of large districts of people unless those people would relinquish the right of Representation in the Legislature, a right inestimable to them and formidable to tyrants only. ¶
¶
He has called together legislative bodies at places unusual, uncomfortable, and distant from the depository of their public Records, for the sole purpose of fatiguing them into compliance with his measures. He has dissolved Representative Houses repeatedly, for the opposing with manly firmness his invasions on the rights of the people. ¶
¶
He has refused for a long time, after such dissolutions, to cause others to be elected; whereby the Legislative powers, incapable of annihilation, have returned to the people at large for their exercises; the state remaining in the mean time exposed to all the dangers of invasion from without, and confusions within. ¶
¶
He has endeavored to prevent the population of these states, for that purpose obstructing the Laws of Naturalization of Foreigners, from gaining permission to pass, other than to encourage their migrations hither, and raised the conditions of new Appropriations of lands.
Body Text
Courier New
10
c:\amipro\docs
Ins
1

Fig. 4.20
Examples of Ami Pro line spacing.

Paragraph Styles

Using the **T**ext menu to change the appearance of text serves well when you don't have much formatting to do, but often you need to apply the same formats to many paragraphs in the document.

▶ See "Setting Tabs," p. 123

▶ See "Setting Up SmartIcons," p. 216

Because Ami Pro enables you to store formatting information as a paragraph style, you can easily apply a set of formats to more than one block of text. When you want to make a change to the appearance of your entire document, therefore, you change the paragraph styles and Ami Pro applies the modifications globally to all paragraphs with that style.

A *paragraph style* consists of all elements discussed earlier in this chapter—font, alignment, indenting method, spacing, attributes, and special effects. Paragraph styles also can include additional elements such as hyphenation and bullets or numbers. Creating, using, and—when necessary—modifying paragraph styles ensures uniformity in a document.

Ami Pro stores paragraph styles in style sheets. A *style sheet* (or *template*) is a collection of paragraph styles and page layouts well-suited for a certain type of work. Ami Pro comes with many style sheets containing different collections of paragraph styles and page layout information.

When you open a new document, you generally work with the default style sheet. The default style sheet contains margin and tab defaults and a number of paragraph styles, including Body Text. The Body Text style, used for the majority of the text in most documents, contains information about the default font, point size, and text alignment.

You can change the Body Text style and the default style sheet if they don't meet your everyday work needs. You use the **S**tyle menu to set up and modify styles as well as to perform style management functions. Chapter 10, "Working with Style Sheets," covers creating and using paragraph styles and style sheets and describes the style sheets that come with Ami Pro.

Summary

In this chapter, you learned about the ways you can format characters and paragraphs in Ami Pro. You learned how to apply and remove character and paragraph formatting by using the SmartIcons, the keyboard, and the **T**ext menu, and how to use the fast formatting feature to repeat character formatting.

This chapter also introduced the concept of paragraph styles and style sheets as ways to store often-used formatting information.

In the next chapter, you learn how to set up documents and use page-related functions in Ami Pro.

Chapter 5

Working with Page Layout

In Chapter 4, "Formatting a Document," you learned about modifying fonts and character attributes and applying paragraph formatting as ways to change the style of a document.

Style also occurs within the larger context of *page layout*. Ami Pro page layout comprises margins, tabs, columns, page settings, lines, headers, footers, and page numbering.

Two main methods are available for changing page layout in Ami Pro. You can use the **P**age menu and the Modify Page Layout dialog box to change the standard settings, or you can insert a new page layout and specify the desired settings for that layout. (In a sense, a third method for changing page layout is to switch back from the inserted layout to the standard page layout.)

In this chapter, you learn how to use the Modify Page Layout dialog box to change the page layout settings for the document. You learn how to change margins, tabs, indents, and columns. You see how to set the page size (legal, letter, or a custom size), and how to specify the orientation (portrait or landscape).

In this chapter, you explore the use of page lines and boxes, header and footer formats, automatic page numbering, tabs, and indenting. You learn how to work with page and column breaks. Finally, you learn about Ami Pro display views and modes and the advantages and disadvantages of using the views and modes available.

Modifying the Standard Page Layout

When you open a document in Ami Pro, you associate a style sheet with the document. The style sheet contains instructions regarding page layout and specialized paragraph styles. Not only does Ami Pro provide you with a general-use default style sheet, it also provides over 50 specialized style sheets for memos, envelopes, letters, invoices, and other documents (see the appendix "A Guide to Style Sheets," for a complete listing). In addition, you can create your own style sheets.

▶ See "Working with Style Sheets," p. 261

▶ See "Design Strategies," p. 611

▶ See "Design Elements," p. 623

▶ See "Producing Style Sheets," p. 640

Although the style sheet is the source of the default values for page layout parameters, such as margin size, number of columns, tabs, and so on, the page layout in the style sheet may not meet all your needs for your document. In this section, you learn how to modify and customize the page layout to create a document that looks exactly as you want it to look.

The changes you make to the page layout apply only to the current document unless you save page layout changes as a style sheet by choosing **S**tyle Sa**v**e as a Style Sheet. The style sheet you used to open the document remains intact even if you change the page layout within that particular document.

Ami Pro must be in layout mode to change page layout. If you open the **P**age menu and see that the options for modifying page layout aren't available, check the **V**iew menu to ensure that Ami Pro is in layout mode. To change to layout mode, choose **V**iew **L**ayout Mode.

To access the page layout options, choose **P**age. The **P**age menu, which contains all the operations you use to change page layout, appears (see fig. 5.1).

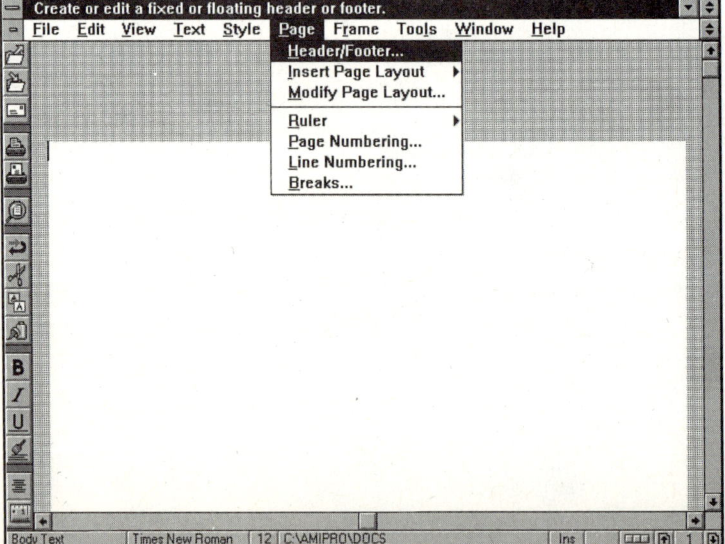

Fig. 5.1
The **P**age menu.

Using the Modify Page Layout Dialog Box

To change components in the page layout, you use the Modify Page Layout dialog box. To access the dialog box, choose **P**age **M**odify Page Layout. Ami Pro displays the Modify Page Layout dialog box, as shown in figure 5.2.

Note

If you cannot access the Modify Page Layout dialog box, Ami Pro isn't in layout mode. Choose **V**iew **L**ayout Mode and try again.

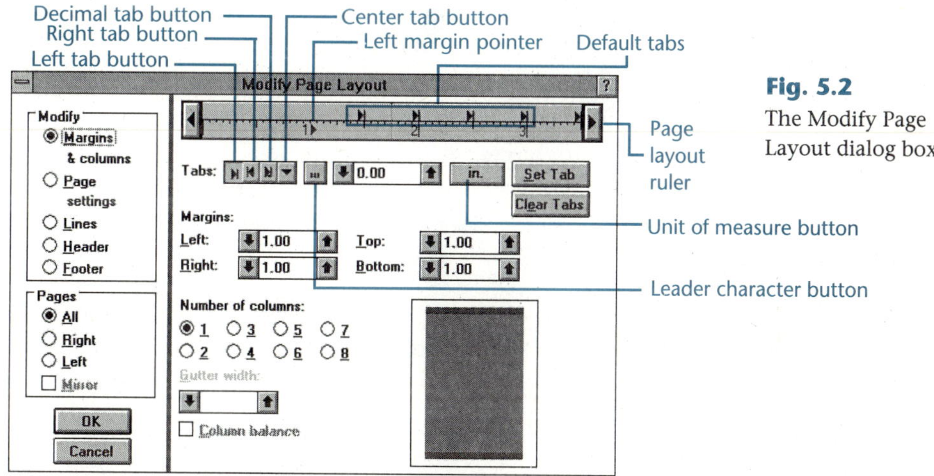

Fig. 5.2
The Modify Page Layout dialog box.

When you specify in the Modify section of the dialog box which type of options you want to see (**M**argins & Columns, **P**age Settings, **L**ines, **H**eader, or **F**ooter), Ami Pro displays the appropriate options for that selection in the right side of the dialog box. The default Modify selection is **M**argins & Columns; figure 5.2 shows the margins and columns options in the right side of the dialog box.

Tip
Position the mouse cursor in the margin and click the *right* mouse button to access the Modify Page Layout dialog box.

Note

The example box (in the lower right corner of the dialog box) shows a sample document that changes with the settings in the dialog box. You can use the example box to experiment—seeing the results of different settings for margins, columns, and so on, without actually modifying the document.

Setting Margins, Tabs, and Columns

▶ See "Creating and Modifying Styles," p. 273

With the **M**argins & Columns options showing in the Modify Page Layout dialog box, you can change tabs, columns, and margins for the entire document at one time. Regardless of where the insertion point is in the document, the changes you make in this dialog box will change the default settings for the entire document. You can use different page layout settings for parts of your document, however, by selecting a paragraph style or by inserting a new page layout, as explained later in the section, "Inserting a New Page Layout."

At first glance, Ami Pro's variety of settings and options may appear overwhelming. Remember, however, that the dialog box is self-explanatory. As you use each option, the change appears immediately in the example document, making the whole process fast and simple.

Setting Margins

▶ See "Design Strategies," p. 611

▶ See "Design Elements," p. 623

▶ See "Understanding Typography," p. 632

Margins are the white space between the text and the edges of the page. The page has margins along the top, bottom, left, and right sides. Default margins are set by the style sheet you use when you open the document. You can change these margins whenever you choose.

The changes you make to margin settings affect the appearance and amount of text you can fit on a page. The larger the margins, the less text-space remains. You may want to increase the left margin to allow room for notes or binding, or you may want to decrease all margins to fit more text in a page.

To change margins, follow these steps:

1. Select **M**argins & Columns in the Modify section of the Modify Page Layout dialog box. The margins and columns options appear in the dialog box.

2. Position the cursor in the **L**eft text box, and type the desired number (the size of the margin in inches) for the left margin. You can also use the arrow buttons next to the text box to select the number.

   To change the left margin with the ruler, drag the solid right-pointing arrow ( ) on the bottom left half of the page layout ruler to the desired margin setting.

3. To change the right, top, and bottom margins, position the cursor in the **R**ight, **T**op, and **B**ottom text boxes, and type the desired setting for

the margins. You also can use the arrow buttons next to the text boxes to select the setting.

To change the right margin with the ruler, drag the solid left-pointing arrow ( ) in the bottom right half of the page layout ruler (at the right margin) to the desired position. (To get to the right margin arrow, you may need to use the large advance ruler arrow ( ) at the right of the ruler.)

You also can click-and-drag on the bottom of the ruler to change the margins but maintain the same line length. (This works for 1-column layout only.)

If you want to change the unit of measurement displayed in the ruler, click the unit of measurement button next to the **S**et Tab button. You can use inches, centimeters, picas (1/6 inch), or points (1/72 inch).

Tip

The section, "Working with Rulers," later in this chapter provides a more complete description of how Ami Pro uses rulers.

Note

You also can specify margins with the keyboard and the page layout ruler. Press Tab to move the cursor to the ruler. Press the left- or right-arrow key to position the solid black line at the desired margin position. Then press the space bar to set the margin.

Setting Tabs

The ruler comes with default tab settings that you often may need to change. If you have columns of numbers, dates, lists, and so on, for example, you may want to set a tab for each individual item. You can change tab settings with the **M**argins & Columns options in the Modify Page Layout dialog box.

Note

Use the Modify Page Layout ruler to set the tabs you use most often in your document. You can use the current ruler (explained in the section "Working with Rulers" later in this chapter) to set tabs that appear only once or twice in the document.

The tab buttons appear below the page layout ruler; reading left to right, the buttons create left tabs, right tabs, decimal (numeric) tabs, and center tabs. The following table lists the types of tabs and their actions. Examples of each are shown in figure 5.3.

Tab Type	Action
Left tab	Left-aligns text
Right tab	Right-aligns text
Center tab	Evenly centers text on both sides of the tab location
Decimal tab	Aligns the decimal point in numbers on the tab

Tip
A line leader is perfect for fill-in lines on forms, signatures, and so on.

You can add a *leader* to the tabs in your document. A leader is a series of characters that precedes the tab and its following text. For leader characters, you can use periods, dashes, or underlines. For a right tab, for example, you may want a series of periods (a *dot leader*). You use a dot leader when you want to lead the reader's eye from the text on the left to the text on the right. Figure 5.3 demonstrates the different types of tabs.

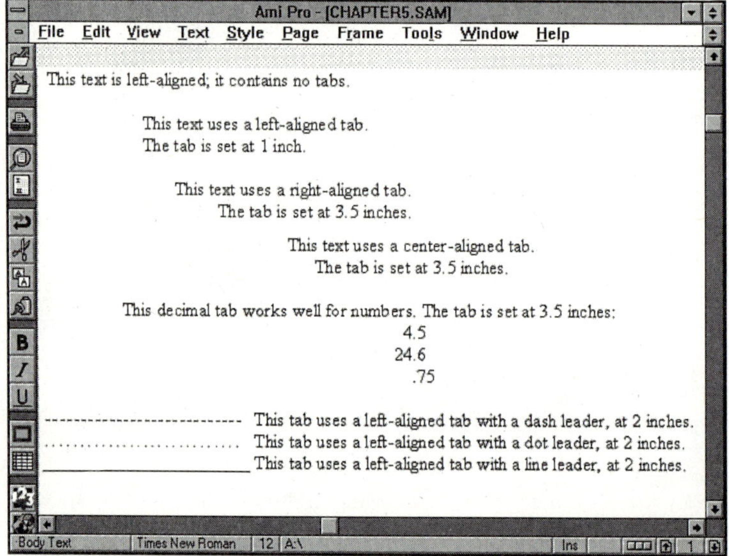

Fig. 5.3
Different tab and leader types.

To select a tab type, follow these steps:

1. Select **M**argins & Columns in the Modify section of the Modify Page Layout dialog box. The margins and columns options appear in the dialog box.

2. In the tab bar, click the button for the tab type you want. With the keyboard, press Tab until the cursor moves to the first tab button, and then use the right- and left-arrow keys to move between the tab buttons.

3. If you want to use a leader character, click the leader character button next to the tab buttons until you see the character you want showing on the top of the buttons. Figure 5.4 shows the tab buttons displaying dot leaders; the mouse cursor in the figure points to the leader character button.

4. After you have selected the type of tab (and leader) you want, position the mouse pointer in the ruler where you want to place the tab (pointing toward the upper part of the ruler) and click. (With the keyboard, press Shift+Tab until the cursor is in the ruler and then use the arrow keys to move the cursor to the position you want. Press the space bar to add the tab.)

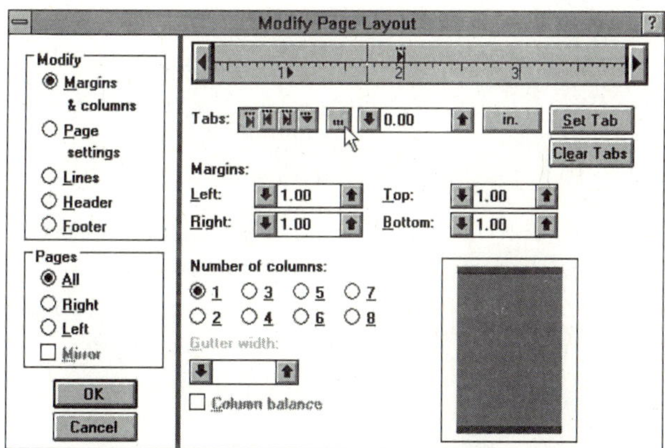

Fig. 5.4
The tab buttons showing dot leader characters.

If you want to place the tab at a specific location, type the desired position in the Tabs text box (for example, type **2.0**) and choose **S**et Tab.

You also can use the increment and decrement arrows next to the text box to specify a particular tab location.

If you want to change the unit of measurement displayed in the ruler, click the unit of measurement button next to the **S**et Tab button. You can use inches, centimeters, picas (1/6 inch), or points (1/72 inch.)

You can place up to 22 tabs in the page layout ruler.

Tip
Because you cannot insert a new tab where a tab already exists, remove unwanted tabs from the ruler first. To remove a tab, click-and-drag it off the ruler.

Tip
All rulers, whether in the Modify Style dialog box or an inserted ruler, work the same as the Modify Page Layout ruler.

To move an existing tab, click-and-drag its indicator with the mouse. With the keyboard, use the arrow keys to move the cursor to the tab, and then press and hold the space bar while pressing the appropriate arrow key to move the tab to the new position.

To delete all tabs on the ruler, select the Cl**e**ar Tabs button.

Setting Columns

Columns have many uses in word processing. Text in two or three columns often is easier to read and more pleasing to the eye than text that spans the entire width of the page. Newsletters, brochures, price lists, flyers, forms, and even books can use multiple-column formats. Ami Pro offers newspaper-style columns; the text flows from the bottom of column one to the top of column two automatically. Alternatively, you can use frames and tables to produce columns. (For more information, see Chapter 19, "Desktop Publishing with Ami Pro," Chapter 16, "Using Frames," and Chapter 13, "Working with Tables.")

▶ See "Types of Documents," p. 615

▶ See "Creating a Purchase Order Form," p. 652

Working with multiple columns of text is impossible if you try to use tabs to create the columns. Use tabs to set up columns of numbers or lists; use Ami Pro's column feature for text. As you type, Ami Pro enters the text into formatted columns. As with the other page layouts, the default number of columns is determined by the style sheet you use when you open the document.

Suppose that you want to place columns in a sample document, such as the document shown in figure 5.5. To specify columnar text, select **M**argins & Columns in the Modify section of the Modify Page Layout dialog box. The **M**argins & Columns options appear in the dialog box. Then specify the number of columns you want in the Number of Columns section of the dialog box. You can choose from one to eight columns.

Figure 5.6 shows the sample text after choosing 2 for the Number of Columns option. Figure 5.7 shows the same text after choosing 3.

In figure 5.8, you see that the example box in the Modify Page Layout dialog box shows the page layout you select. When you choose 3 columns, for example, the sample box shows a page divided into 3 columns.

You can specify additional options as you work with columns. The space between columns is known as the *gutter*. You can modify the spacing between columns by using the Gutter Width text box.

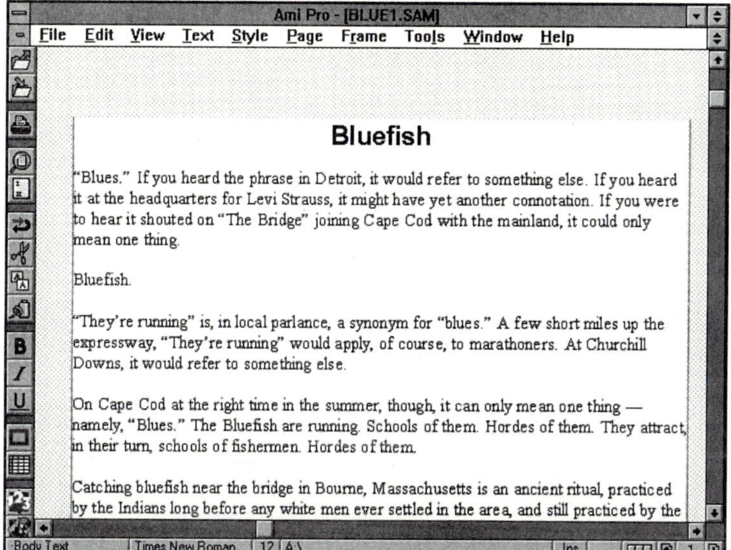

Fig. 5.5
The sample text in one column.

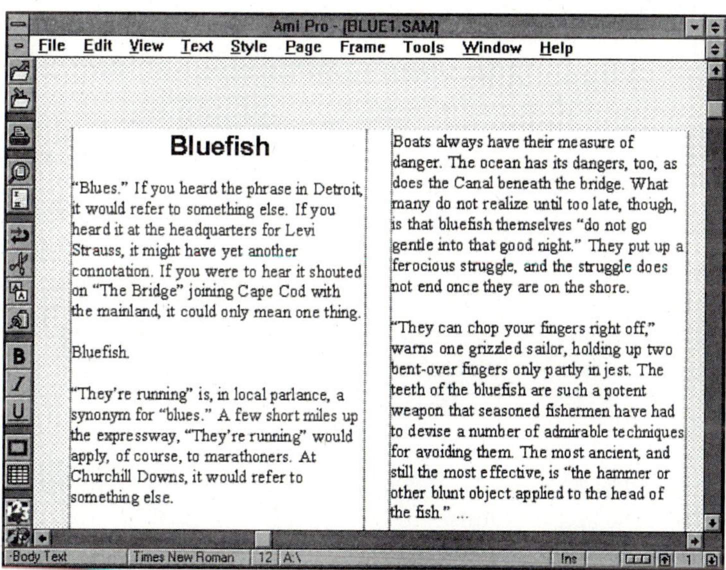

Fig. 5.6
The sample text in two columns.

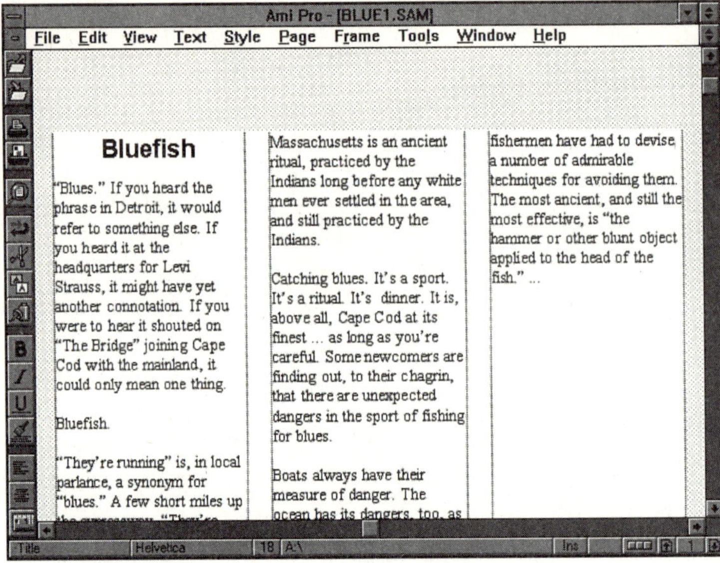

Fig. 5.7
The sample text in three columns.

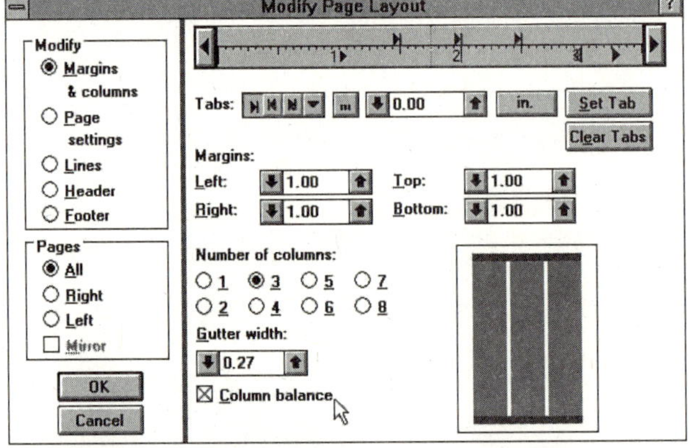

Fig. 5.8
Selecting the number of columns and gutter width.

The default gutter width is .17 inches, but in most documents this gutter width makes the text in columns too close for comfortable reading. To ensure that the text in your documents is easy to read, make the gutter at least .25 inches, and even more if possible (up to .5 inches).

You can modify column and gutter widths using the Ruler Bar in one of three ways:

- If you position the mouse between the right margin indicator for one column and the left margin indicator for the adjacent column, and drag the mouse, you can adjust the width of the columns while maintaining the gutter width.

- If you want to modify the width of a gutter and a column, position the mouse over a column margin indicator, and drag it to the desired position.

- If you want to modify the gutter width while maintaining the column width, position the mouse between the left and right column margin indicators for one column, then drag the mouse until the gutter is the desired width.

If you select the **C**olumn Balance option, Ami Pro balances the columns vertically so that you end up with the same amount of text in each column. Ami Pro automatically balances columns on all but the last page without using this option. Figure 5.9 shows the sample text with balanced columns.

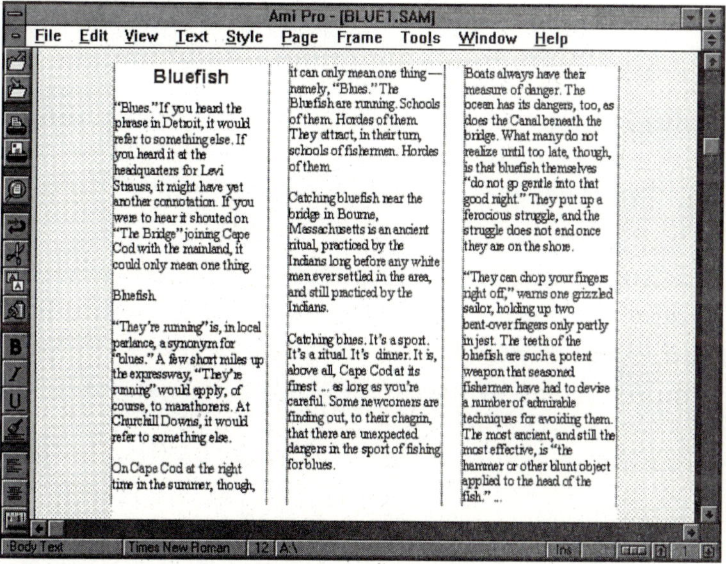

Fig. 5.9
The sample text after selecting **C**olumn Balance.

► See "Using the Table Menu," p. 400

► See "Creating a Frame," p. 498

► See "Using Columns and Tabs in Frames," p. 525

► See "Balancing Design Elements," p. 624

► See "Creating a Newsletter," p. 658

Most of the time you don't need to use the **C**olumn Balance option. Ami Pro balances the columns on full pages. For a partial page (the last page in a document, for example) you may want to use **C**olumn Balance. As a practice, wait until you have completely entered your text before you turn on **C**olumn Balance. Otherwise, the columns balance as you type, making text jump between the columns.

Setting Size and Orientation

When you choose **P**age Settings in the Modify section of the Modify Page Layout dialog box, Ami Pro displays the options for page size and orientation in the right side of the dialog box, as shown in figure 5.10.

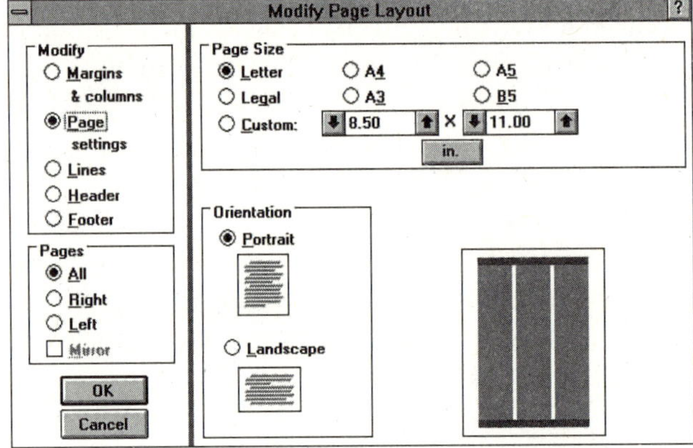

Fig. 5.10
The **P**age Settings options in the Modify Page Layout dialog box.

Tip
Use the unit of measurement button to change the units in the text boxes from inches to centimeters, picas, or points.

For standard page sizes, you can choose **L**etter (8 1/2-by-11 inches) or Le**g**al (8 1/2-by-14 inches). If the paper is a custom size, choose **C**ustom and specify the dimensions of the paper in the text boxes next to the **C**ustom option.

Ami Pro also offers four European paper size settings you can choose—A**3**, A**4**, A**5**, and **B**5. The following table shows the dimensions for these sizes, using inches as the unit of measurement. (The dimensions appear in the text boxes next to the **C**ustom option.)

Size	Length (in.)	Width (in.)
A3	11.69	16.53
A4	8.27	11.69
A5	5.83	8.27
B5	6.93	9.84

Caution

Not all printers support all sizes of paper, and some may require manual feed of custom sizes. Check your printer manual to determine your printer's capabilities.

The term *page orientation* refers to the direction of the longest measurement of the page. The orientation you choose usually depends on the kind of document you are creating. For letters, reports, and most business documents that emphasize text rather than tables or graphics, *portrait orientation* (upright, with the short side of the paper at the top) is preferable. If you are printing trifold brochures, some forms, flyers, books, or charts with multiple columns, you may want to print in *landscape orientation* (sideways, with the long side of the paper at the top).

In figure 5.10, the Orientation section displays both options. To select either option, click the button next to your choice. With the keyboard, press Tab to reach the Orientation section and press **P** or **L**. Then press the space bar to select the orientation you have designated.

In most cases, you must have a laser printer to print in landscape orientation. If you try to print in landscape orientation with a printer that doesn't support this option, Ami Pro displays a warning message; you must reconfigure the printer or change printers before continuing. See Chapter 7, "Proofreading and Printing a Document," for more information about printing.

► See "Printing Documents," p. 207

► See "Types of Documents," p. 615

Note

Because some printers require special fonts for landscape orientation, you may not have the same font choices as you do in portrait orientation. To print in landscape, you must change the setup in both Ami Pro and Windows. See your Windows documentation for details on changing the page orientation setup.

Adding Lines

With the Modify Page Layout dialog box, you can draw lines around an entire page. A box around the page, or lines bordering the top and bottom margins of a page, make your document more attractive and noticeable. See Chapter 19, "Desktop Publishing with Ami Pro," for ideas on using page boxes and lines.

You can specify whether you want lines on all sides or only certain sides of the page. You also can indicate the desired line position, and choose the style (width) of the lines.

To place lines on a page, choose **L**ines in the Modify section of the Modify Page Layout dialog box. Ami Pro displays the lines options, as shown in figure 5.11.

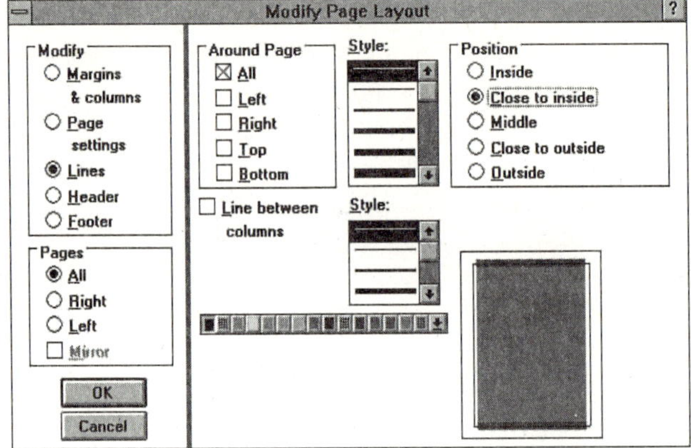

Fig. 5.11
The **Lines** option in the Modify Page Layout dialog box.

In the Around Page section of the dialog box, you specify where you want to place lines on the page. Choose **A**ll if you want to place lines on all four sides (creating a box around the page). Choose **L**eft to place a line on the left side of the page, **R**ight to place a line on the right side of the page, and so on. You can also place lines on only the top and bottom of the page, top and left, left and right, and so on.

Tip
If you choose any Position option other than **I**nside, allow at least an extra .25 inch on all sides when setting your margins to make it easier to read.

In the Position section of the dialog box, you indicate how close to the text you want Ami Pro to place the lines. Ami Pro provides a range of positions from which you can choose—from **I**nside, which places the line next to the text, to **O**utside, which creates a border at the edge of the margin. The example box in figure 5.11 shows a line around the document using the **C**lose to Inside option.

The following list explains the options in the Position box:

- ***Inside.*** Ami Pro places the line on the inside text margin (directly adjacent to the text).
- ***C****lose to Inside.* Ami Pro places the line just outside the text.
- ***M****iddle.* The line appears midway in the margin, between the text and the edge of the paper.
- ***C****lose to Outside.* Ami Pro places the line just inside the edge of the paper.
- ***O****utside.* Ami Pro positions the line on the edge of the paper.

You can use the color bar to specify the color for the lines. Click the color you want to use for the line. Select from the colors displayed in the color bar, or click the arrow button at the end of the color bar to display a full range of colors and patterns from which you can choose (see fig. 5.12). All lines you add with the Modify Page Layout dialog box are the same color.

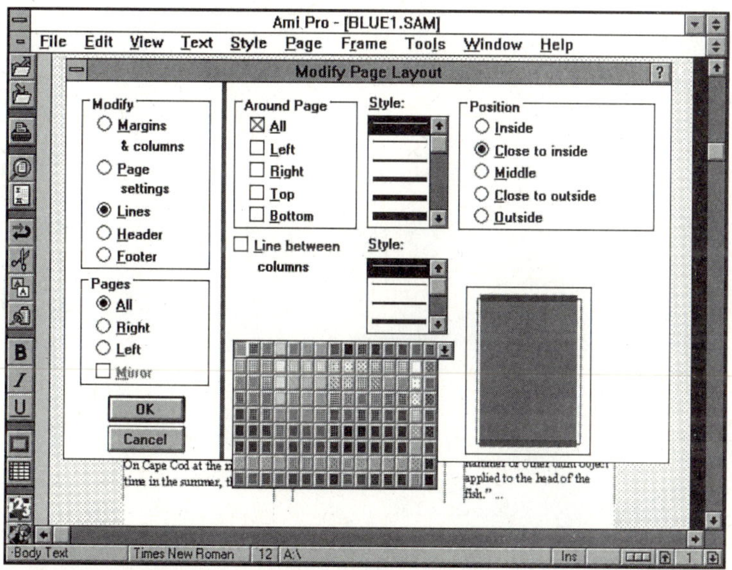

Fig. 5.12
Selecting a color for the line.

Tip
Lines set to **O**utside or **C**lose to Outside may not print on your printer if the lines fall in a "no print" zone which, on most laser printers, is between 1/4 inch and 5/8 inch from the edge of the paper.

You can create custom colors with the color palette. See Chapter 8, "Changing Your Setup," for details on adjusting the colors.

In the **S**tyle boxes, you can choose from 12 styles of lines. You use the upper **S**tyle box to select the style for the line around the text. With the lower **S**tyle box, you select the style for the lines between columns. You can scroll through the boxes to select the line style you need.

Figure 5.13 shows the three-column sample text with lines added between the columns and on all sides. The position selected for this figure is **C**lose to Inside.

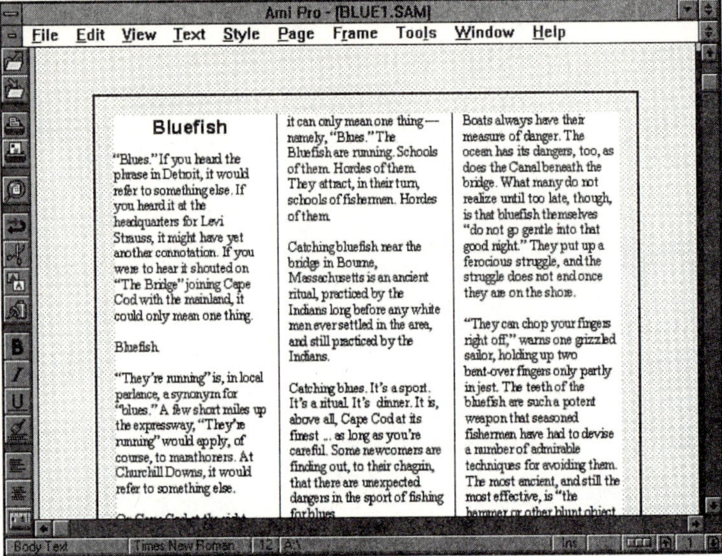

Fig. 5.13
Sample text with lines between columns and on all sides.

Working with Headers and Footers

A *header* is information (text or a picture) that appears in the top margin of a document page. For example, a header may contain the date, volume and issue numbers, and company name. A *footer* is information that appears in the bottom margin of a document page, such as a chapter name or a page number. You can use headers or footers to convey information about the document or your company.

A sample header might be the following:

```
07-15-92   The ABC Company Page 1
```

Ami Pro uses three types of headers and footers: fixed, alternating, and floating.

A *fixed* header or footer displays the same information on each page where it appears. You have some flexibility in using fixed headers and footers; the header or footer can appear on all pages, all pages except the first page, or on right or left pages only (alternating).

Alternating headers and footers display different information on the left (even-numbered) and right (odd-numbered) pages. (The first page of a document is a right page.) This book uses alternating headers and footers. In the headers, left-hand pages show the chapter number and name, and right-hand pages show the current topic discussion. The page number appears at top left on left-hand pages and at top right on right-hand pages.

You can use *floating* headers and footers if you want different header or footer information displayed for different sections of your document. Floating headers and footers also can alternate.

When you create a header or footer, Ami Pro uses the Header and Footer settings specified in the current style sheet for your document. (If you have changed the style sheet, the most recent settings apply.) The style sheet settings for your main document text, therefore, also apply to your headers and footers.

You can use all of Ami Pro's text formatting and editing features on headers and footers (paragraph styles, indenting, spell checking, text enhancements, and so forth). You also can set special margins, tabs, and columns for headers and footers by using the Modify Page Layout dialog box. You learn in the next section how to format headers and footers.

Tip

When working with headers and footers, display the margins with faint color dots. See Chapter 8, "Changing Your Setup," for instructions on displaying margins in color.

Using Fixed Headers and Footers

To create a fixed header or footer, display the document in layout mode with the top or bottom margin visible (top margin to create a header, bottom margin for a footer). You can either type the header or footer first, and then format it in the Modify Page Layout dialog box; or you can format the header or footer, then type it into your document. This section describes how to format the header or footer, then gives instructions for entering the header or footer in your document.

► See "Setting Up SmartIcons," p. 216

► See "Types of Documents," p. 615

► See "Design Elements," p. 623

The formats for headers and footers operate independently of the format for the body of the document. As figure 5.14 shows, however, the **H**eader and **F**ooter options in the Modify Page Layout dialog box are almost identical to those you use when working with page margins, tabs, and columns. (A major addition to the options with Ami Pro 3 is the **B**egin on Second Page option, discussed later in this section.) The options are the same whether you choose **H**eader or **F**ooter.

In general, the settings you change in this version of the dialog box affect only the header or footer, not the main text. Note, however, that the **T**op and the **B**ottom margin settings take into account the settings for the whole page. Ami Pro remembers the size of the page when you choose a top or bottom margin and prevents you from setting a margin that cannot fit on the page.

For headers, the top margin moves the text of the header down from the top edge of the page, and the bottom margin separates the header text from the document text. The margins work similarly (but in reverse order) for footers. If header or footer text doesn't print, it probably is in the nonprint zone, or you haven't provided a large enough area to accommodate the font and paragraph spacing.

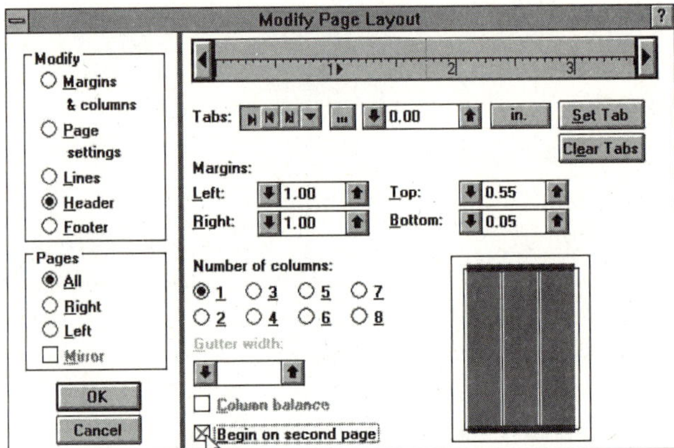

Fig. 5.14
The **H**eader options in the Modify Page Layout dialog box.

For instructions on setting the margins, tabs, and column format for the header or footer, refer to the earlier section "Setting Margins, Tabs, and Columns."

The first page of a document often shows the company logo, letterhead, newsletter nameplate, and so on, at the top of the page. Headers containing information to identify subsequent pages (such as the name of the person receiving the letter) usually begin on the second page, to avoid printing over the logo or letterhead. If you want the header (or footer) to begin on the second page, select the **B**egin on Second Page option.

Note

If you select **B**egin on Second Page and later try to create a fixed header or footer on the first page of your document, a message appears to remind you that the **B**egin on Second Page option is selected. Ami Pro also prevents you from placing the insertion point in the top or bottom margin of the first page when the **B**egin on Second Page option is selected. If this happens, return to the Modify Page Layout dialog box and deselect the **B**egin on Second Page.

After you set up the page layout for the header or footer, you type the header or footer the same way you type any other text. You then can format the text by creating a style and modifying it, or you can apply text attributes.

In layout mode, place the insertion point in the top margin and type the header or footer text. You can click the mouse cursor directly into the upper or lower margin at any time to enter the text. You also can select **P**age, **H**eader/Footer. In the Headers & Footers dialog box, choose **E**dit, then select **H**eader or **F**ooter. Select OK or press Enter. The cursor appears in the upper or lower margin.

Figure 5.15 shows a header in a document. The header is typed directly into the margin, using the tabs specified with the **H**eader options in the Modify Page Layout dialog box. The paragraph style, HEADER, is 10-point Helvetica, with a line below the text to divide it from the body text (see Chapter 10, "Working with Style Sheets," for more information on creating styles).

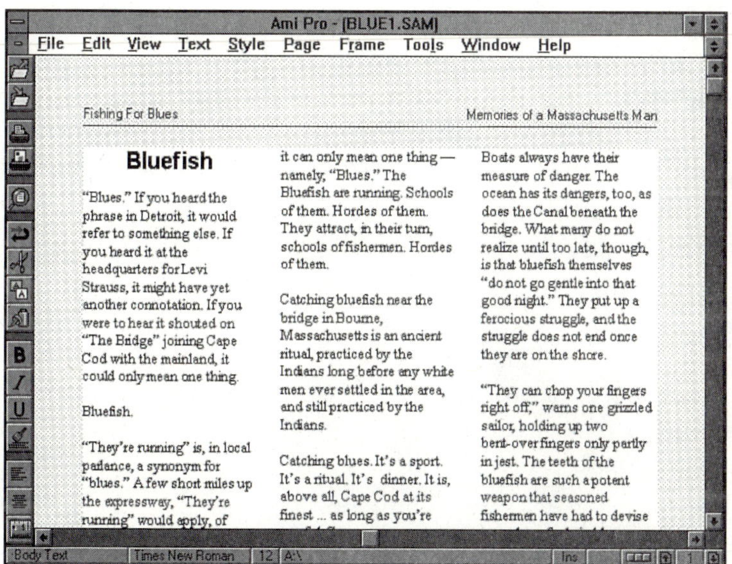

Fig. 5.15
A document with a formatted header.

The insertion point doesn't need to be in the first page of the document to create a fixed header or footer. You can create fixed headers and footers while working on any page (provided that you haven't already added a floating header or footer). If you want the header or footer to begin on the second page, however, select the **B**egin on Second Page option, as discussed earlier.

Although you can create fixed headers or footers at any point in the document, you must exercise care when you create floating headers and footers; otherwise, these headers and footers may not be in the appropriate place in your document, as the next section explains.

Note

If you use a frame for your header or footer and want to repeat the frame on every page, select **R**epeat All Pages in the Modify Frame Layout dialog box. Repeating frames also can alternate, so you can have alternating headers and footers in a frame. See Chapter 16, "Using Frames," for information on creating a frame. See Chapter 19, "Desktop Publishing with Ami Pro," for information on adding a graphic to a header in a frame.

Tip

In the Modify Page Layout dialog box, the Pages section contains an option called **M**irror, which can affect the margins in headers and footers.

After you finish typing the text for the header or footer, click anywhere in the main document text or press Esc to leave the margin and return to the main document.

To create alternating fixed headers and footers, follow the same procedure to set up the header or footer, but select **R**ight in the Pages section of the dialog box before selecting **H**eader or **F**ooter in the Modify section. After specifying the format in the dialog box, place the insertion point in the appropriate margin (top for headers, bottom for footers) of any odd-numbered page and type the desired text or create the desired frame.

Having specified a right page header or footer, Ami Pro understands that you have a corresponding left page header. Go to any even-numbered page and type the header or footer in the appropriate margin. Return to the Modify Page Layout dialog box only if you want different tabs, columns, or margins for the headers or footers on alternate pages. (Alternatively, you can begin by choosing a left page, entering the header on the page, and then entering the right page header on any appropriate right page.)

Using Floating Headers and Footers

You may want to use different headers and footers in different parts of your document. If your document has three sections, for example, you may want to have different headers and footers for each section. When writing a book, you may want to enter chapter names in the header for each chapter.

With floating headers and footers, you can change the text in a header or a footer on any page. Ami Pro then repeats the text until the program encounters another floating header or footer in the document.

Note

A frame in a header or footer (containing a logo or other graphic image) is associated with a particular location on the page rather than with the header or footer. Inserting a floating header or footer doesn't prevent the contents of such a frame from appearing throughout the document. See Chapter 16, "Using Frames," for more information.

After you create a floating header or footer, Ami Pro inserts a hidden mark that shows the location of each header or footer. As you continue to enter text, Ami Pro displays the current floating header or footer in the appropriate margin. If you change the header or footer, the changed header or footer appears on subsequent pages. A floating header or footer floats throughout the document when you edit text. If the floating header mark is located in the first sentence on the page, for example, the floating header appears on that page. When you edit (for instance, when you add text to the preceding page), you may force the sentence with the header mark to move down the page. The floating header, therefore, moves to the next page. For this reason, the best practice is to enter floating headers or footers only after you complete all editing and formatting of a document.

To create a floating header or footer, follow these steps:

1. Place the insertion point at the location in the text where you want the floating header or footer to start. To keep the floating header or footer with specific text, place the insertion point on the beginning line of the desired text. If during editing you force the text to move to another page, the floating header or footer moves along with it.
2. Choose **P**age **H**eader/Footer. The Headers & Footers dialog box appears.
3. Choose **F**loating Header/Footer. Select **OK** or press Enter. Figure 5.16 shows the Floating Header/Footer dialog box that appears.

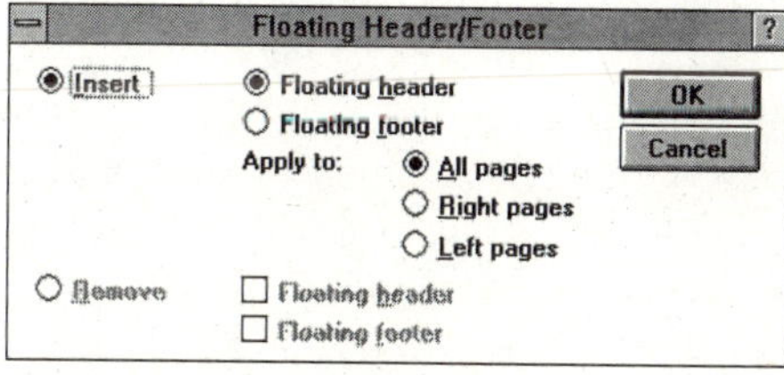

Fig. 5.16
The Floating Header/Footer dialog box.

4. Select **I**nsert, then choose Floating **H**eader or Floating **F**ooter.

5. Choose the appropriate Apply To option. Choose **A**ll Pages to place the header or footer on every page, **R**ight Pages for odd-numbered pages, or **L**eft Pages for even-numbered pages.

   The header or footer appears on pages following the page with the header or footer mark, unless the mark is on the first line of the page. In that case, the header or footer also appears on the same page as the mark.

6. Choose OK or press Enter. The Floating Header/Footer dialog box disappears.

   If you chose Floating **H**eader, the insertion point moves to the top margin of the page. If you chose Floating **F**ooter, the insertion point moves to the bottom margin of the page. If you place the insertion point on the first line of the page when you begin creating the floating header or footer, the insertion point moves to the top or bottom margin of the current page. If you place the insertion point on any other line, the insertion point moves to the top or bottom margin of the next page.

7. Type the desired text for the floating header or footer.

8. Click anywhere in the main document or press Esc to leave the margin.

Just as you can create alternating fixed headers and footers, you can use alternating floating headers and footers to display different information in the floating headers and footers for even- and odd-numbered pages. Many books, for example, use alternating floating headers with the book title on the right side and the current chapter title on the left.

Note

If, on the last page of the document, you place the cursor beyond the first line of the page, and place a floating header or footer mark for a right page when you are on a right page (or a left page when you are on a left page), Ami Pro displays the message `Cannot display the header/footer requested.` The new header or footer is to be placed two pages after the current page; Ami Pro knows about only one blank page beyond the current page.

To create alternating floating headers and footers, follow the same general procedure as that for creating floating headers and footers. Choose **R**ight pages or **L**eft pages in the Apply To section of the Floating Header/Footer

dialog box. If you choose **L**eft pages, when you exit the dialog box the insertion point moves to the margin of the next even-numbered page. If you choose **R**ight pages, the insertion point moves to the margin of the next odd-numbered page.

Finding Floating Header and Footer Marks

To display the Ami Pro mark that indicates the location of a floating header or footer, choose **V**iew View **P**references. In the View Preferences dialog box, select **M**arks. After you exit the dialog box, Ami Pro displays all marks for floating headers and footers. Figure 5.17 shows a document in which the floating header and footer marks appear.

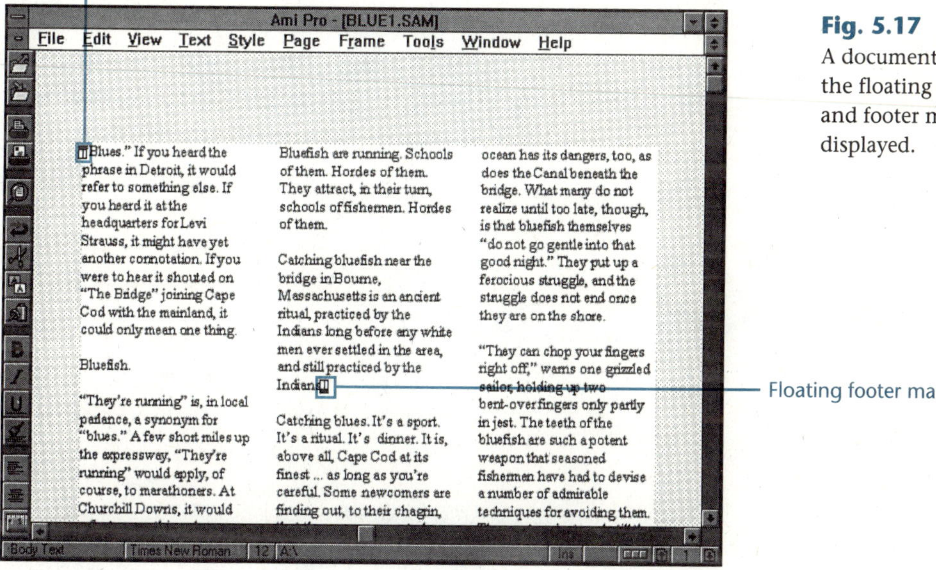

Fig. 5.17
A document with the floating header and footer marks displayed.

To move to a floating header or footer mark with the keyboard, choose **E**dit **G**o To. In the Go To dialog box, select Floating Header/Footer Mark in the **N**ext Item list box; then choose `Go To ^H` or press Enter. The insertion point moves to the next floating header or footer mark in your document.

Editing Text with Floating Headers or Footers

When you edit text containing a floating header or footer mark, keep the following facts in mind:

- If you copy or paste text containing a floating header or footer mark, Ami Pro copies or pastes the floating header or footer.
- If you try to cut text containing a floating header or footer mark, a warning box appears to remind you that you are deleting a floating header or footer. You can cancel the action or choose OK to cut the text and the associated floating header or footer.
- To help with copying, cutting, and pasting floating header and footer marks, display the marks as described in the preceding section.

Removing Headers and Footers

Tip
To remove fixed headers or footers with a line below or above, delete the text in the margin first. Then change the paragraph style of the header or footer to body text.

You can delete a floating header or footer at any time. Place the insertion point on the mark for the floating header or footer that you want to remove. Choose **P**age **H**eader/Footer. In the Headers & Footers dialog box, select **F**loating Header/Footer. The Floating Header/Footer dialog box appears. Select **R**emove. Then choose Floating **H**eader or Floating **F**ooter and choose OK or press Enter. Ami Pro deletes the floating header or footer and its mark.

To delete a fixed header or footer, position the cursor in the header or footer and delete the text in the margin.

Specifying Page Setup

In the Pages section of the Modify Page Layout dialog box (shown in fig. 5.18), you can specify which pages of your document use the modified layout—**A**ll, **R**ight, **L**eft, or **M**irror.

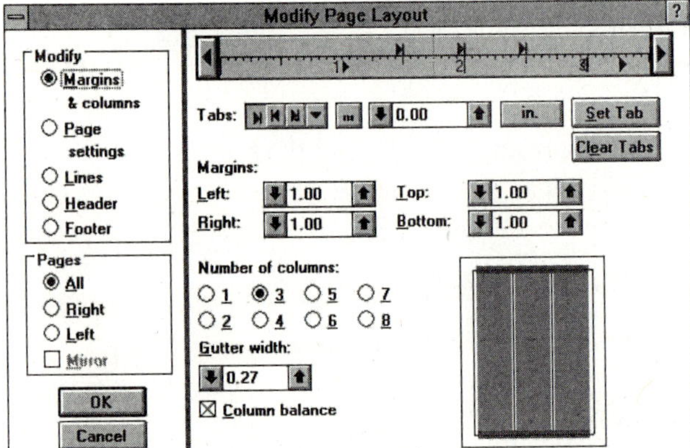

Fig. 5.18
The Pages options (at bottom left in the dialog box).

To choose the kind of page you want to use, select the appropriate option with the keyboard or mouse. Ami Pro applies the original layout that you set up, until you change the individual Pages options. The following table lists the effects of each choice.

Option	Purpose
All	Uses the specified layout for all pages
Right	Uses the specified layout only on right (odd) pages
Left	Uses the specified layout only on left (even) pages
Mirror	Uses a mirror image of the left page on the right page (using the same layout on left and right pages, but reversing the image)

Tip
The **M**irror option is grayed (the default setting) because you can mirror settings only if you apply them to a left or right page—as in facing pages.

Also known as *facing pages*, the **M**irror feature is available only if you select **L**eft or **R**ight (otherwise, **M**irror is dimmed). After you choose **M**irror, you must choose the settings for left or right page only; Ami Pro reverses the settings for the opposing page.

Inserting a New Page Layout

Sometimes you want to change the layout for only a page or a series of pages in a document. You may need to insert two pages without columns in a newsletter using a column format, for example, or perhaps you are preparing a scientific paper that contains several pages with a set of numeric tabs. To create documents such as these, you must be able to change the layout for particular pages.

You can insert a new page layout anywhere in the document. To insert a page layout, begin by choosing **P**age **I**nsert Page Layout. A cascading menu appears, as shown in figure 5.19.

When you choose **I**nsert, the Modify Page Layout dialog box opens. The available options in this version of the Modify Page Layout dialog box are identical to the options available when specifying the general page layout for the document (see the earlier section "Modifying the Standard Page Layout" for details on using the dialog box). These selections affect only the pages with the inserted layout, however, instead of all pages in the document.

The settings displayed in the dialog box are those in effect in the document at the location of the insertion point when you choose **P**age **I**nsert Page Layout.

Make any necessary changes in the settings and then choose OK or press Enter to implement those changes.

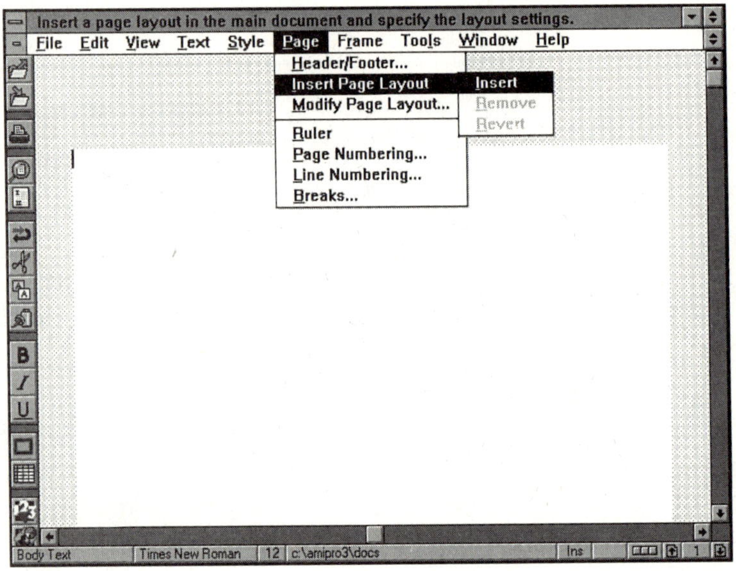

Fig. 5.19
The **I**nsert Page Layout menu.

Tip
To move the insertion point to an inserted page layout, choose **E**dit **G**o To. Select Layout Change in the **N**ext Item list box; then choose `Go To ^H` or press Enter.

By default, Ami Pro places a page break before the inserted page layout, unless you begin on a new page (the first line of a page with a hard page break preceding the first line).

To remove an inserted page layout, place the insertion point on the page with the inserted layout and choose **P**age **I**nsert Page Layout **R**emove. Ami Pro removes the page break, combines the text with the preceding page, and repaginates the document. All pages following the removed inserted page layout acquire the settings of the preceding inserted page. If no preceding inserted page exists, the pages revert to the standard page layout.

Tip
The **R**evert and **R**emove options use the same accelerator key. To choose **R**emove, press **R** once; to choose **R**evert, press **R** twice.

You also can revert to standard page layout by placing the insertion point in the inserted page and then choosing **P**age **I**nsert Page Layout **R**evert. The **R**evert option doesn't change the entire document back to the standard layout, but the option does change the current page and all subsequent pages, up to the next inserted page layout.

Working with Rulers

Rulers govern the columns, indents, and tabs you use in your document. A ruler shows the position of margins, tabs, indents, and columns. Figure 5.20 shows an activated ruler at the top of the screen.

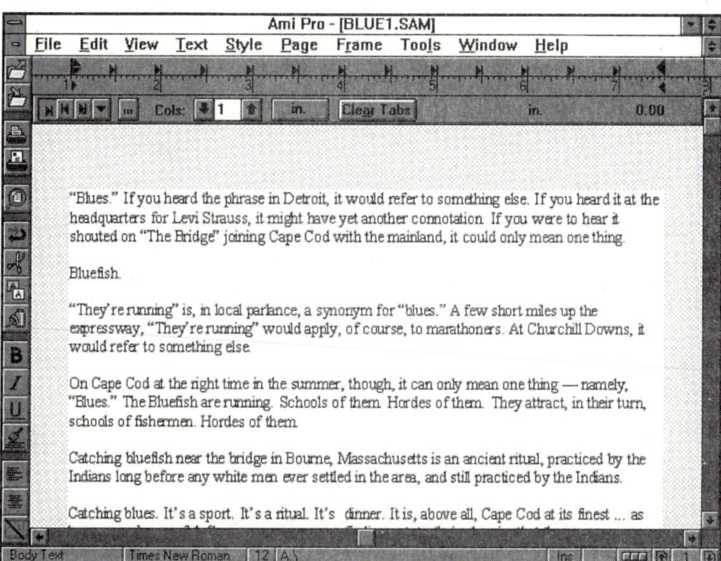

Fig. 5.20
A screen displaying an activated ruler.

You can use any of three different methods to specify the ruler:

- You use the ruler shown in the Modify Page Layout dialog box for all pages of the document.
- You can supersede the page ruler with a ruler for a specific paragraph style. You invoke the style ruler, which you can modify in the Modify Style dialog box (discussed in Chapter 10, "Working with Style Sheets") when you use a specific paragraph style in a style sheet.
- You can insert a ruler into a paragraph. The inserted ruler affects the tab settings and indents only for the paragraph in which the ruler is inserted.

When Ami Pro is in layout mode, you can show or hide the ruler by choosing **V**iew Show **R**uler or **V**iew Hide **R**uler. When you choose **V**iew Show **R**uler the current ruler appears at the top of the Ami Pro screen. The command in the **V**iew menu changes to Hide **R**uler. The section of this chapter entitled "Using an Inserted Ruler" explains how to change the current ruler.

Ami Pro also provides a SmartIcon for showing and hiding the ruler that you can add to your SmartIcons palette (see Chapter 8, "Changing Your Setup," for instructions on how to customize the SmartIcons palette).

Using the Page Layout Ruler

▶ See "Creating and Modifying Styles," p. 273

The page layout ruler in the Modify Page Layout dialog box is the document's default ruler. The default values for the page layout settings and ruler are brought into the document by whatever style sheet you are using when you open the document. If you change the page layout settings or ruler to create a customized page layout that you want to use again in other documents, you can save the modified page layout as a style sheet.

You can change the tab settings with the **P**age **M**odify Page Layout option previously discussed in the chapter. The tabs and ruler that you see in the Modify Page Layout dialog box are the settings used throughout the document (unless you insert rulers or modify paragraph styles).

Using the Current Ruler

The *current ruler* is the ruler in effect in the paragraph where the insertion point rests. When you use a special paragraph style, the ruler for that paragraph can be modified by using the Modify Style dialog box (discussed in Chapter 10, "Working with Style Sheets"). If you insert a ruler, the ruler governs tabs, columns, and indents for the entire paragraph in which the ruler is inserted. At the end of the paragraph, Ami Pro automatically reverts back to the ruler in the page layout. If you press Enter, however, Ami Pro inserts a new ruler with the same settings.

You must display a ruler in order to change its settings. First, make sure that you are using layout mode by choosing **V**iew **L**ayout Mode. Then choose **V**iew Show **R**uler. After you display the ruler, you can insert, move, and delete tabs; change margins; and change indents. When you finish using the ruler, you can hide it by choosing **V**iew Hide **R**uler. Hiding the ruler gives you more space to view the document.

Not only can you use and modify rulers in documents, you also can use rulers in tables and frames. For a discussion of using rulers in frames, see Chapter 16, "Using Frames." To understand the use of rulers in tables, see Chapter 13, "Working with Tables."

Using an Inserted Ruler

You may want to create different tab or indent settings for certain pages or paragraphs in a document. Perhaps you are quoting one document within another and want larger margins for the quoted document. You may want to create a block quotation within a document and use special tab settings for this purpose. The inserted ruler affects all text from the location where you insert the ruler until you insert another ruler or revert to a paragraph style ruler or page ruler.

Figure 5.21 shows a document that uses four different rulers for four paragraphs and then reverts to the first style. Figures 5.22 through 5.25 show the rulers for each paragraph of the document. You can display the rulers by placing the insertion point anywhere within the paragraph where the ruler is in effect (provided you choose **V**iew Show **R**uler first, in layout mode).

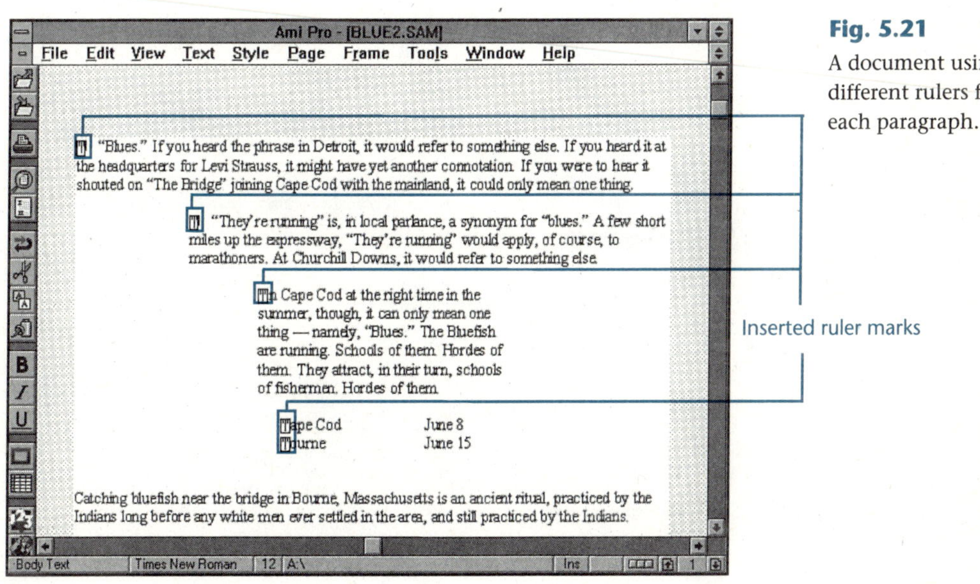

Fig. 5.21
A document using different rulers for each paragraph.

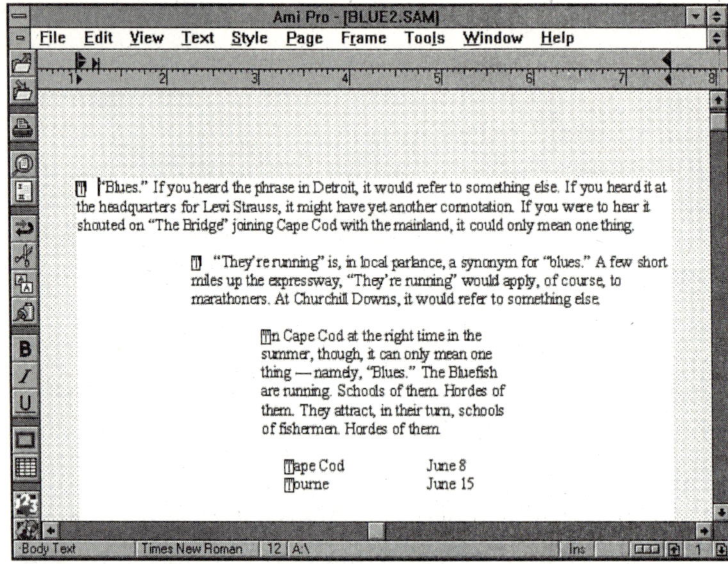

Fig. 5.22
The ruler used for the first paragraph.

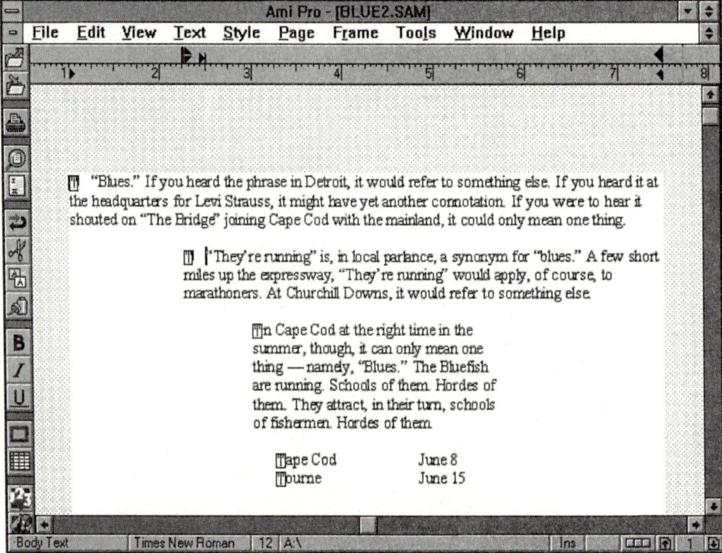

Fig. 5.23
The ruler used for the second paragraph.

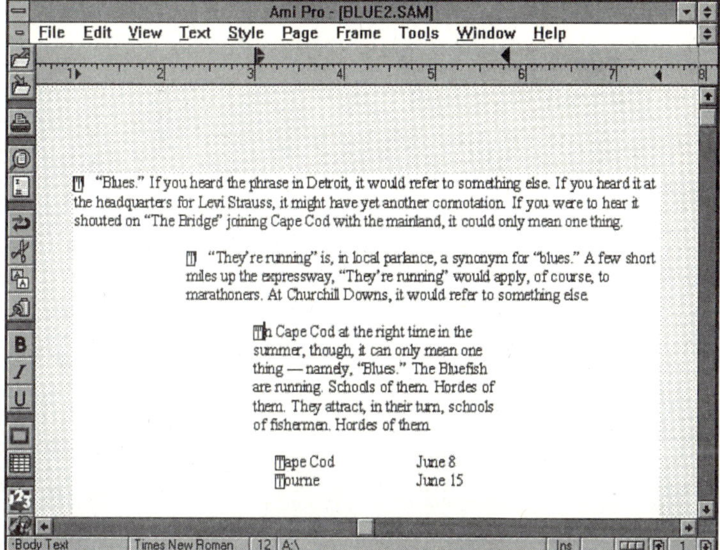

Fig. 5.24 The ruler used for the third paragraph.

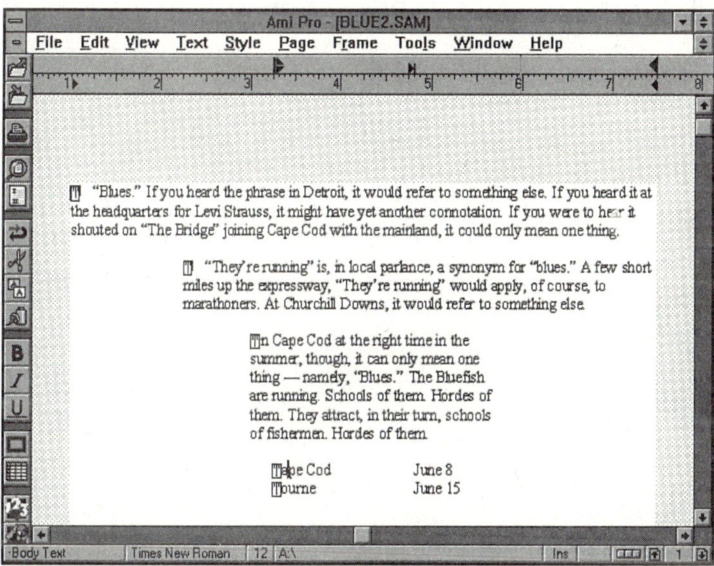

Fig. 5.25 The ruler used for the fourth paragraph.

To see the symbol for the inserted ruler in the text, choose **V**iew View **P**references. In the View Preferences dialog box, choose **M**arks.

To insert a ruler, follow these steps:

1. If a ruler isn't displayed, choose **V**iew Show **R**uler (you must be in the layout mode).

2. Place the insertion point in the document where you want to begin the new tab settings, or change the indent or columns. You also can select text—from one paragraph to several pages—to which you want to apply the inserted ruler.

3. Choose **P**age **R**uler. The Ruler menu cascades from the **P**age menu, as shown in figure 5.26.

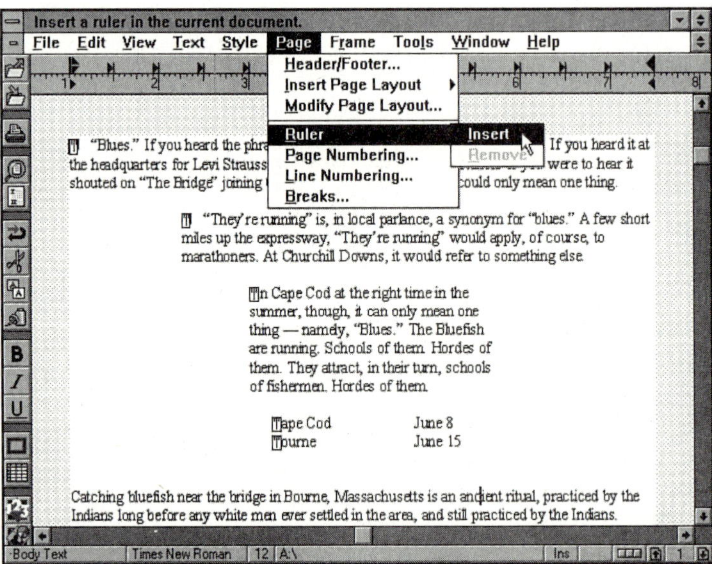

Fig. 5.26
The **R**uler menu.

4. Choose **I**nsert. Ami Pro inserts the ruler.

The inserted ruler is, in effect, a copy of the previous ruler. Inserting a new ruler places a mark in the paragraph (as in figure 5.21), but the format of the text doesn't change until you actually modify the ruler. When you modify the ruler, Ami Pro reformats the text of the affected paragraph.

Note

A shortcut to inserting a ruler is to click the ruler displayed at the top of the screen. Ami Pro then inserts a ruler at the beginning of the paragraph where the insertion point is located and uses the modified ruler for the paragraph. This technique produces the same effect as the preceding steps with less effort.

To copy an inserted ruler to another place in the document, place the insertion point in the text that uses the ruler. Activate the ruler at the top of the screen by clicking anywhere on it and then choose **E**dit **C**opy; then move the insertion point to the location where you want to insert the ruler, and choose **E**dit **P**aste.

Modifying a Ruler

In a ruler you can insert, move, and delete tabs. Inserting tabs simplifies organizing your text into lists or columns. Moving and deleting tabs makes editing easy. You also can change indents, margins, and columns. Using the ruler to modify tabs, indents, and so on saves time in formatting a document. You can apply the current ruler settings to one paragraph or to many paragraphs without formatting paragraph styles.

◀ See "Paragraph Formatting," p. 105

▶ See "Creating and Modifying Styles," p. 273

Modifying Ruler Tabs

To insert a tab, follow these steps:

1. Display the ruler. From layout mode, choose **V**iew Show **R**uler.

2. Activate the displayed ruler by clicking it with the mouse. (From the keyboard, choose **E**dit **G**o To. In the **N**ext Item list, select **R**uler and then choose Go to ^H.) When you click the displayed ruler, Ami Pro displays the tab bar beneath the ruler (see fig. 5.27).

3. To create a tab, select a type of tab (left tab, right tab, decimal tab, or center tab) from the tab buttons in the tab bar. From the keyboard, press Tab until you reach the tab buttons, and then use the right- and left-arrow keys to move between the tab buttons. (See the section "Setting Tabs" earlier in this chapter for a complete discussion of the types of tabs and an example of each tab in use.)

You can set, change, customize, and remove tabs from the ruler, using the techniques covered in the earlier section of this chapter, "Setting Margins, Tabs, and Columns." To exit the ruler, click in the main document or press Esc.

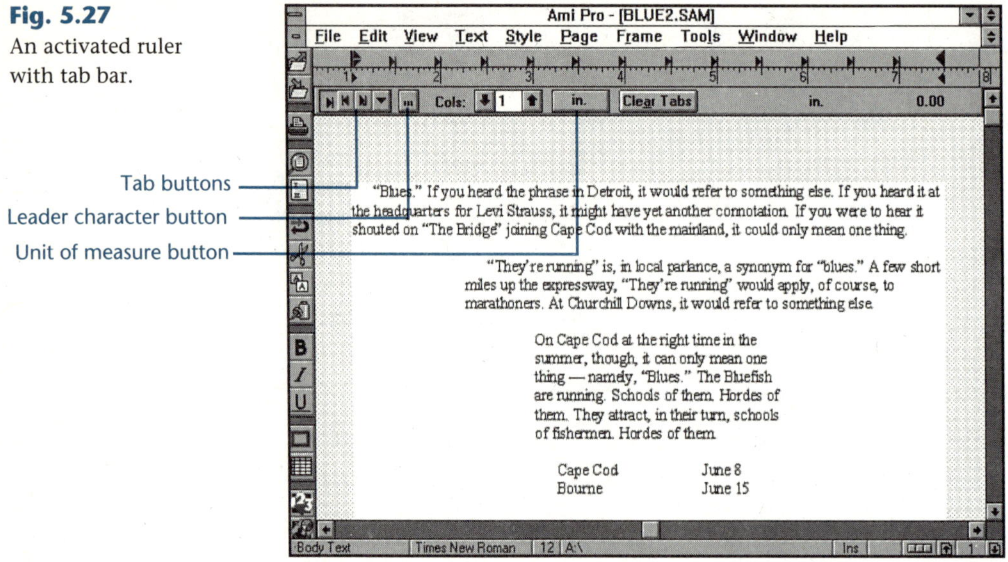

Fig. 5.27
An activated ruler with tab bar.

Tab buttons

Leader character button

Unit of measure button

As you modify the ruler, Ami Pro immediately applies the changes in the ruler to the text governed by the ruler (the paragraph that contains the insertion point or selected text).

Modifying the Indentions in the Ruler

The indentions are beginning and ending points on the line for the paragraph. Figure 5.28 shows a document with paragraphs using four different indentions.

You can change the indentions for the paragraph by using the indention arrows in the upper half of the ruler bar (see fig. 5.29). When you move the indention arrows, a guideline appears on the page. With Ami Pro, you can indent the first line of the paragraph differently from the other lines.

You can modify the indention in various ways—or all the lines in a paragraph, for example, or for the first line only. The following list explains the different ways you can modify indention for your Ami Pro document.

- To modify the indention for all lines in the paragraph, click the indention arrows and drag them to the desired location in the ruler (as in figure 5.29). Alternatively, press the arrow keys to move the dotted insertion line in the ruler; then press **0** to set the indention. Use this type of indent to set off a paragraph from the remainder of the body text.

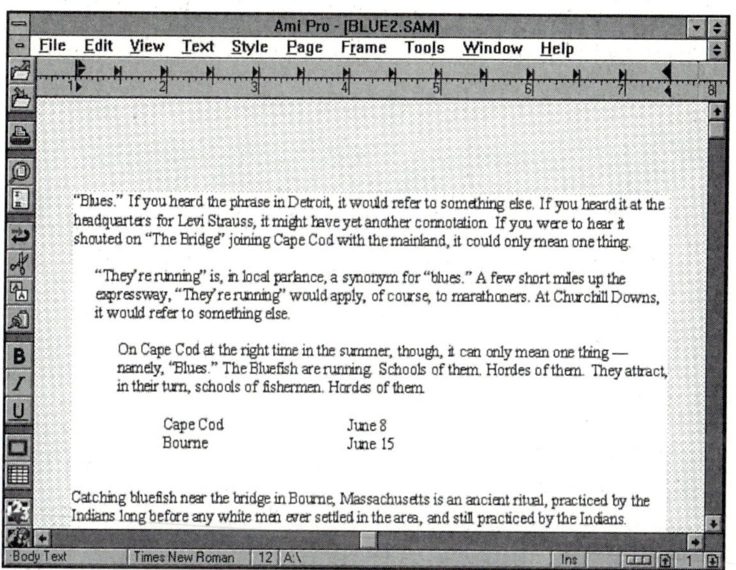

Fig. 5.28 A document with paragraphs using different indentions.

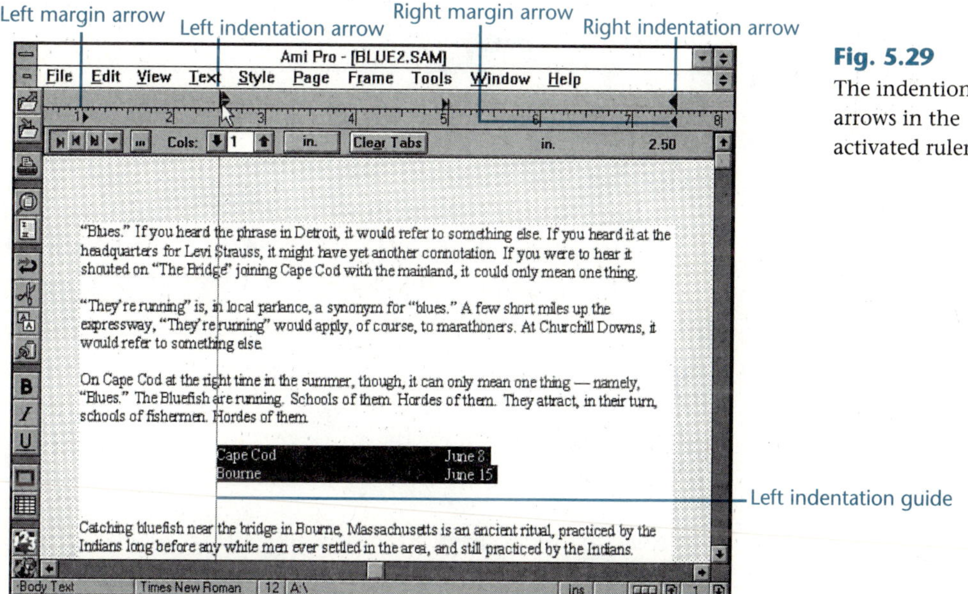

Fig. 5.29 The indention arrows in the activated ruler.

- To modify the indention for the other lines of a paragraph when you have a special indention for the first line, click the bottom half of the indention arrow and drag it to the desired location. Alternatively, press the arrow keys to move the dotted insertion line in the ruler; then press **2** to set the indention for the other lines of the paragraph.

Figure 5.30 shows a ruler set for different indentions for the first line and remaining lines of a paragraph. In this example, a hanging indent at "Blues" introduces the indented paragraph.

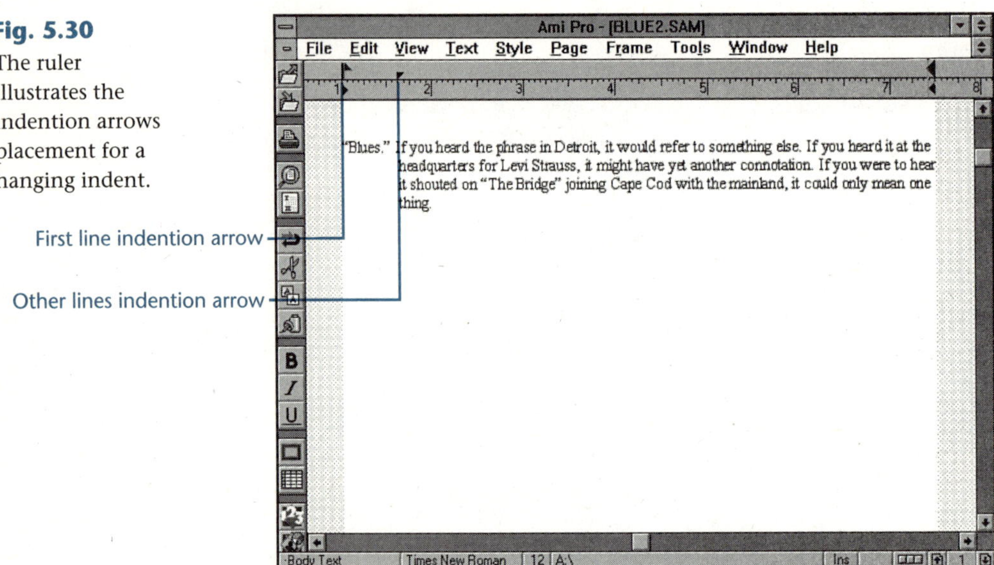

Fig. 5.30
The ruler illustrates the indention arrows placement for a hanging indent.

- To modify the indention for the first line only in the paragraph, click the upper half of the indention arrow and drag it to the desired location (see fig. 5.31). Alternatively, press the arrow keys to move the dotted insertion line in the ruler; then press **1** to set the indention for the first line of the paragraph. Use this indention style for normal body text paragraphs that you want to indent.

- To modify the indention on the right side of a paragraph, click the indention arrow on the right side of the ruler and drag it to the desired position. Alternatively, press the arrow keys to move the dotted insertion line in the ruler; then press **3** to set the right indention.

To exit the ruler, place the cursor in the document text and click, or press Esc. Ami Pro implements the new ruler in the paragraph where the insertion point or selected text is located as you modify the ruler.

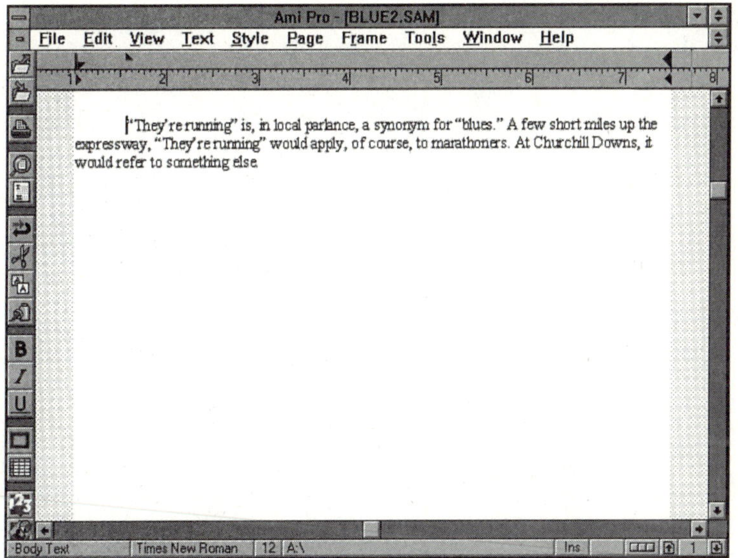

Fig. 5.31
A first line indent. Note how the positions of the indention arrows in the ruler differ from those in figure 5.30.

Modifying Margins and Columns in a Ruler

The margins and columns are indicated in the bottom half of the activated ruler (see fig. 5.32).

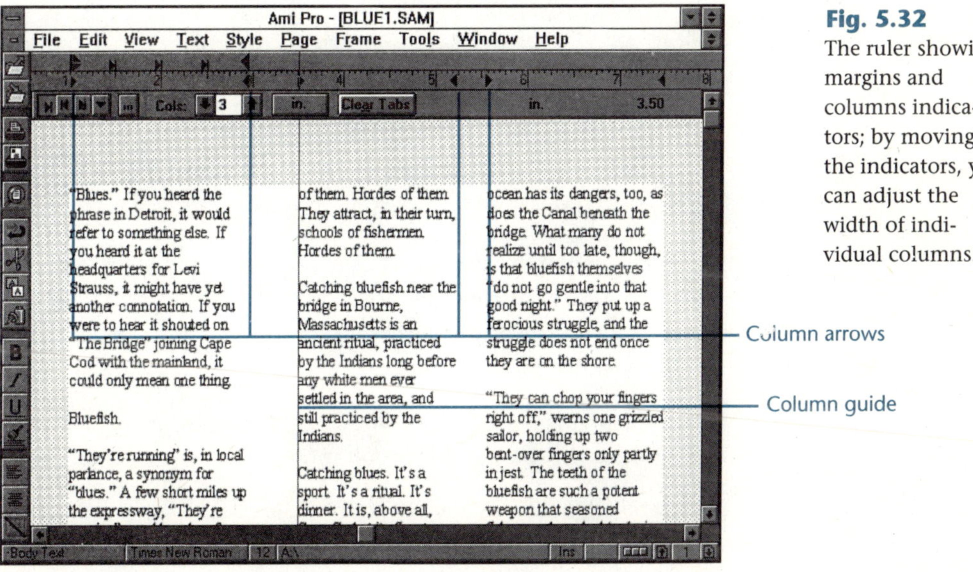

Fig. 5.32
The ruler showing margins and columns indicators; by moving the indicators, you can adjust the width of individual columns.

Note

Changes to margins and columns in the ruler affect the entire document. If your document requires pages with and without columns, insert a new page layout at the beginning of the section containing the changed layout (see "Inserting a New Page Layout" earlier in this chapter). With this technique, changes to margins or columns in the ruler affect only the section governed by the page layout ruler.

Tip
You can return the indentions to their previous settings by selecting the text and choosing **T**ext In**d**ention Revert to **S**tyle, by changing the rulers, or by removing the rulers.

To modify margins, choose **V**iew Show **R**uler in layout mode; then follow these steps:

1. Click in the displayed ruler. Alternatively, choose **E**dit **G**o To. In the **N**ext Item list, choose **R**uler; then choose Go to ^H or press Enter.
2. To modify the left margin, click the far left arrow in the bottom half of the ruler bar and drag the arrow to the new location. Alternatively, use the arrow keys to move the dotted insertion line in the ruler; then press **[** (left bracket) to set the left margin.
3. To modify the right margin, click the far-right arrow in the bottom half of the ruler bar and drag the arrow to the new location. Alternatively, use the arrow keys to move the dotted insertion line in the ruler; then press **]** (right bracket) to set the right margin.
4. To change the location of the margins but keep the same length of text on a line, click the bottom half of the ruler between the two margin arrows and drag the entire section to the left or right.

To modify columns, use the same steps you used to modify margins. The following list explains the different ways you can modify columns.

- *Modify the number of columns.* Click the columns indicator in the tab bar below the ruler and select the number of columns. Alternatively, press Tab to select the measurement text box and type the desired measurement.
- *Modify the width of a single column.* Change the position of the arrow indicator for the margin of the column you want to change.
- *Move a column without changing its width.* Click the lower half of the arrow bar between the left and right indicators for the column and drag the column to its new position.

- *Change the width of two adjacent columns.* Click the lower half of the ruler in the space between the columns (the gutter), and drag the mouse in the desired direction.

As you change the columns in the ruler, Ami Pro changes the text in the document to match the new settings.

Removing an Inserted Ruler

Follow these steps to remove an inserted ruler:

1. Within the text of the document, place the insertion point on the inserted ruler (or at any point in the text affected by the ruler).

2. Choose **P**age **R**uler **R**emove. Ami Pro removes the ruler, and the symbol disappears from the text.

Tip
When you remove an inserted ruler, the text reverts to the format of the original page layout ruler.

If you want to remove multiple rulers, select the text containing the rulers and choose **P**age **R**uler **R**emove.

Just as you can specify custom settings for tabs, margins, and columns, you can use custom settings for page and column breaks, as the next section explains.

Customizing Page and Column Breaks

Tip
To keep the page above the break from appearing unbalanced, select **V**ertically Center Text Above Page Break in the dialog box.

Ami Pro automatically places page breaks according to the directions you specify for the page layout, paragraph styles, user setups, frame layout, and **T**ext menu. In the Modify Page Layout dialog box, for example, you select margins. Based on the margins you set, Ami Pro places appropriate page breaks.

In the Modify Style dialog box for paragraphs, you can specify page (or column) breaks before or after paragraphs for a particular paragraph style.

In your user setup, you can select widow/orphan control to prevent single lines on a new page. You can anchor a frame to certain text so that the text and frame stay on the same page. In the **T**ext menu, you choose spacing for the document.

◄ See "Character Formatting," p. 95

► See "Setting Defaults," p. 228

In addition to all the page breaks Ami Pro uses based on the directions you specify, you also can place a manual page break or column break wherever you need it in the text. You may want a manual page break when you begin a new section of text, for example.

To insert a manual page or column break, place the insertion point where you want to begin the new page or column and choose **P**age **B**reaks. Ami Pro displays the Breaks dialog box, shown in figure 5.33.

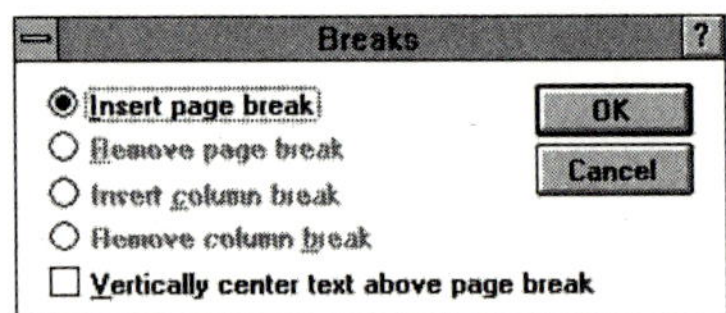

Fig. 5.33
The Breaks dialog box.

Select the page break or column break in the dialog box; then choose OK or press Enter. Ami Pro inserts the page break at the location of the insertion point.

A column break is useful if you want to place certain text in particular columns. If you use a manual column break, you can control the division of text in columns. This option is only available in the Breaks dialog box if your document contains more than one column.

You also can use the Breaks dialog box to remove page and column breaks. In layout mode, place the insertion point anywhere in the paragraph containing the page break or column break you want to remove. In draft mode, place the insertion point before the column or page break symbol.

Note

To move the insertion point to a page break or column break mark, choose **E**dit **G**o To. In the Go To dialog box, select Hard Pg Break or Column Break in the **N**ext Item list box; then choose Go To ^H or press Enter. Next, press Del to remove the break; Ami Pro gives you a warning message to confirm that you want the break removed.

Figure 5.34 shows a document with a page mark displayed.

In addition to changing the appearance of the printed page, you can change how the document appears on-screen as you work, as explained in the next section.

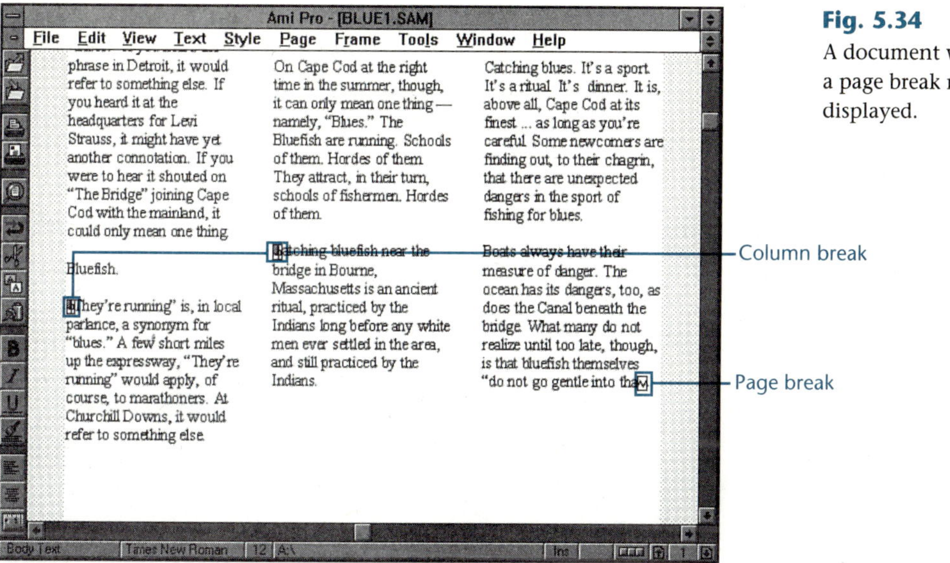

Fig. 5.34
A document with a page break mark displayed.

Using Views

Typically, you work in a single view in Ami Pro (the document appears on-screen in one particular fashion, with your favorite options available). You probably work most often in Custom view. For special purposes, however, you can use the **V**iew menu to select additional views of the document (see fig. 5.35): **F**ull Page, **C**ustom, **S**tandard, **E**nlarged, or F**a**cing Pages.

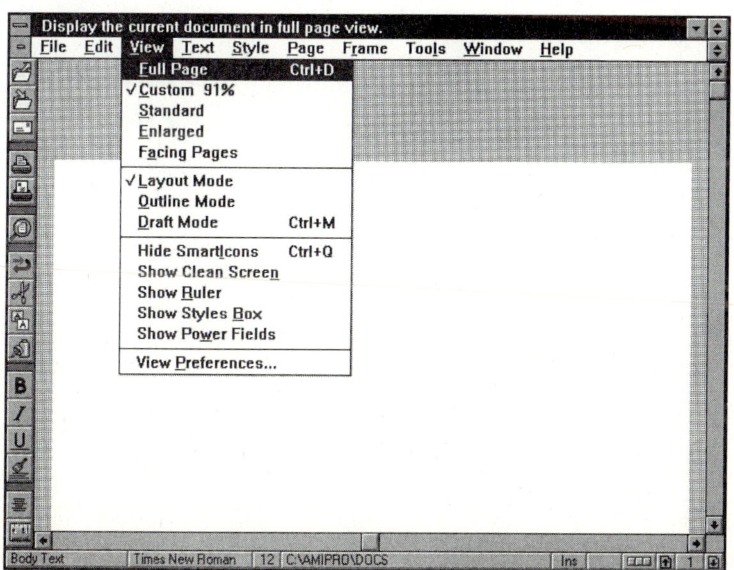

Fig. 5.35
The **V**iew menu.

Two of the page views—**F**ull Page and F**a**cing Pages—work only when the document is in layout mode. In the following sections, you explore Ami Pro's display modes. For now, choose **V**iew **L**ayout Mode to place a sample document in layout mode. **S**tandard view shows the page in the same size as other Microsoft Windows applications.

Full Page View

To see an entire page of the document, choose **V**iew **F**ull Page or press Ctrl+D. (Ami Pro must be in layout mode to choose **F**ull Page view.) You see the entire page in a reduced size, as shown in figure 5.36.

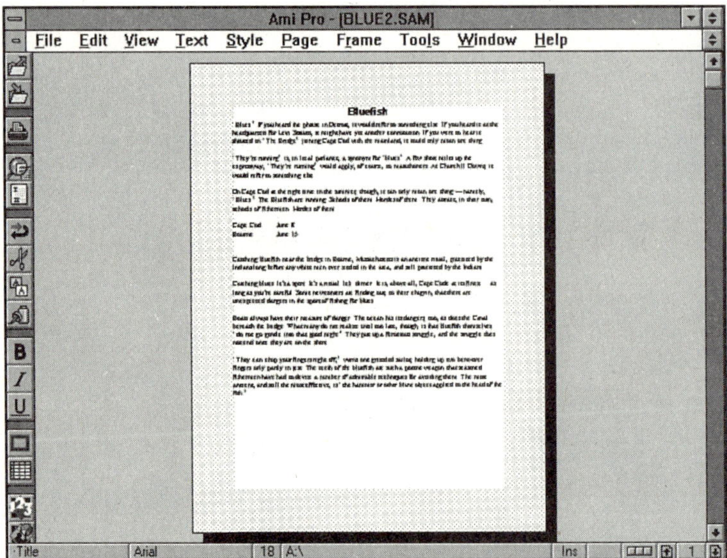

Fig. 5.36
The Full Page view of a document.

Tip
The text may be hard to read and work with in full Page view if you use small fonts or fonts that Ami Pro cannot display in that view.

The **F**ull Page option shows how text and graphics look on the page. The most significant difference between full page view and the preview mode used in DOS based word processing packages is that you can edit the text in full page view.

Standard View

To see the *standard view* of a document, choose **V**iew **S**tandard. A standard view displays the page in the same size as the pages of other Windows documents and files (see fig. 5.37). You can edit a document in Standard view.

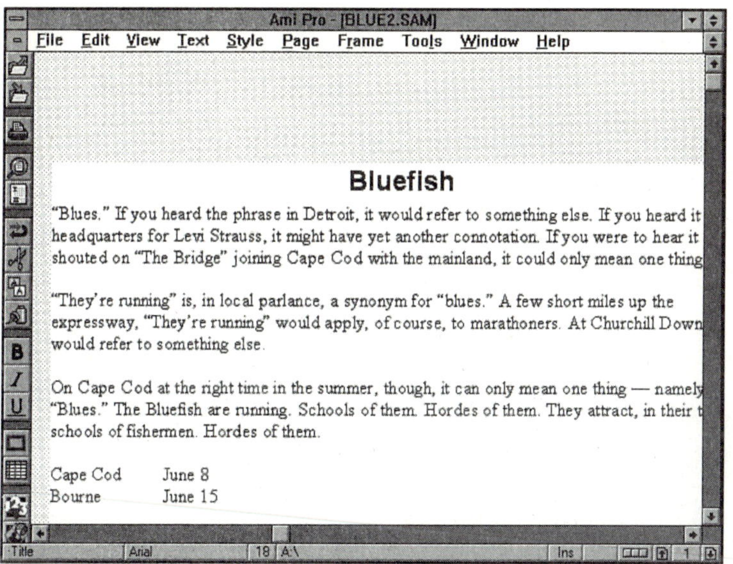

Fig. 5.37
The Standard view of a document.

In standard view, you may not be able to see the beginnings and ends of lines. If you encounter this problem, use the horizontal scroll bar to move the text so that you can see the remainder of the line. (To avoid the problem, switch to Custom view.)

Custom View

To see the *custom view* of a document, choose **V**iew **C**ustom (which is followed by a percentage on the menu). The document's text appears on-screen in readable characters. Custom view is valuable because you can set the degree or percentage of magnification to change the size of the characters on-screen. If you cannot see the entire line of your text due to video resolution, size of page, or width of margins, you can adjust the current **V**iew **C**ustom option percentage to alleviate the problem. Because editing is easiest in this view, you typically create and edit documents in Custom view.

Note

The FIT2SCRN.SMM macro adds another option, **F**it to Screen, to the **V**iew menu for the current work session. When you exit Ami Pro,the option disappears. The **F**it to Screen option adjusts the view so the full line of text shows (from left margin to right margin). Ami Pro assigns a SmartIcon to the **F**it to Screen macro.

Figure 5.38 shows the custom view of a document, with the **V**iew View **P**references dialog box. You can make the characters in the custom view larger or smaller by setting the custom view as a percentage of the standard view.

In the bottom right corner of the View Preferences dialog box, you select the percentage of the **V**iew **C**ustom option.

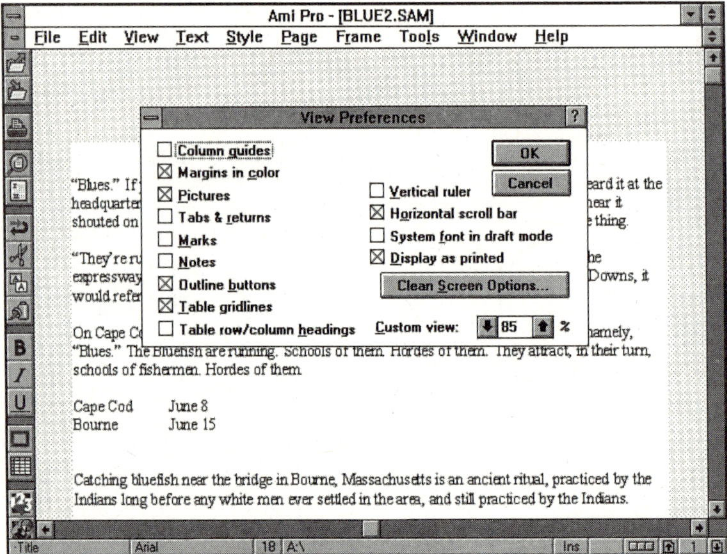

Fig. 5.38
The Custom view of a sample document and the View Preferences dialog box.

To use the Custom view method to change the on-screen size of the characters, choose **V**iew View **P**references. (Note that Ami Pro must be in layout mode before you can see the Custom view as a percentage of the Standard view.) Specify a percentage between 10 percent and 400 percent. A 50 percent setting, for example, makes the text half as large as Standard view; 100 percent makes the text the same size as Standard view; and 400 percent makes the text four times larger than Standard view text.

See Chapter 8, "Changing Your Setup," for more information on using the View Preferences dialog box and setting the Custom view as a percentage of the Standard view.

You can use Custom view in either layout or draft mode. In layout mode, the custom view is figured as a percentage of the standard mode. Layout and draft modes are explained in the section "Using Display Modes." Layout mode shows the document on-screen in a page-by-page format. Draft mode enables you to work on a document without the inconvenience of page breaks and columns.

Enlarged View

To enlarge a portion of a page so that you can see fine details of the page layout, choose **V**iew **E**nlarged. Enlarged view—200 percent of standard view—is particularly helpful for positioning frames precisely on a page, for viewing text set in a small typeface, for creating equations, or for making fine edits in a drawing.

Enlarged view shows a portion of the current page, like the sample in figure 5.39. The portion of the page displayed depends on the location of the insertion point when you choose **V**iew **E**nlarged.

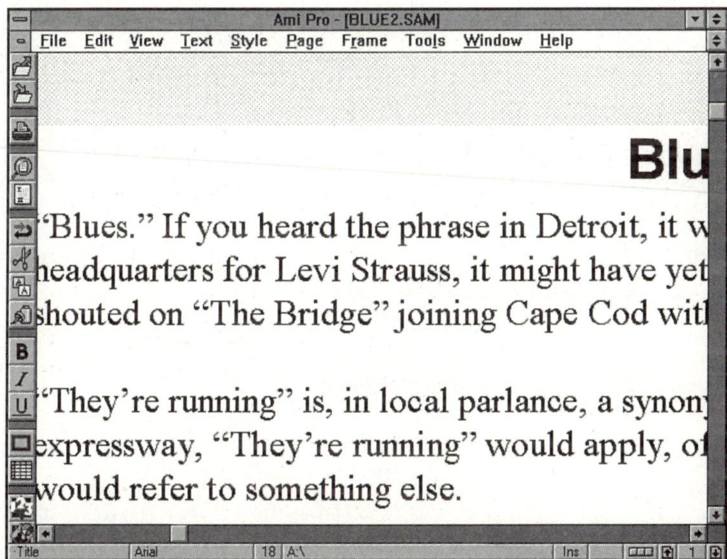

Fig. 5.39
The Enlarged view of a document.

You can edit a document using an enlarged view. Use the horizontal and vertical scroll bars to move to other parts of the page or document.

▶ See "Setting Up SmartIcons," p. 216

Facing Pages

To display two *facing pages* side-by-side, choose **V**iew F**a**cing Pages. Facing pages view is helpful if you want to review the effects of layout and formatting changes on two consecutive pages; for example, to balance the amount of text on each page. You also may want to see how page numbers, footnotes, frames, or other elements affect the appearance of the facing pages.

The current page and the facing page appear together, as shown in figure 5.40.

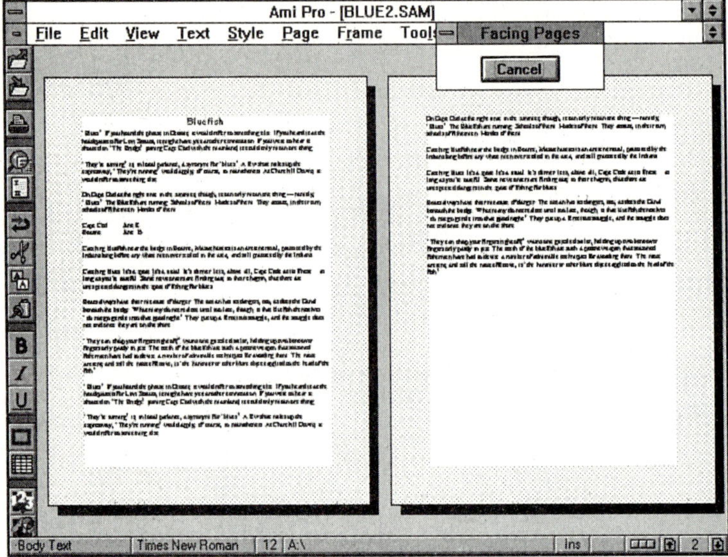

Fig. 5.40 Viewing two facing pages.

You cannot edit a document in a facing pages view. After you finish viewing facing pages, choose Cancel or press Esc to return to the previous page view.

Using Display Modes

Views, as explained in the preceding sections, affect the appearance of the document while editing. *Display modes* affect not only how the document appears on-screen, but also provide you with different options for working with the document.

▶ See "Setting Defaults," p. 228

▶ See "Understanding Outline Mode," p. 298

Ami Pro provides three display modes for presenting documents on-screen. In *layout mode*, you see how the document looks when printed. In *outline mode*, you work with the document in collapsible outline form. In *draft mode*, you cannot see how the document appears on the page; instead, you see a less formatted, working version of the document.

Views determine the degree of magnification, whereas modes determine what items are displayed and how they are displayed. For example, layout mode displays line and page breaks. Layout mode,therefore, must calculate printer font widths and line and page lengths, and takes a little more time to redraw than draft mode. If you want to see text placement exactly as it will appear on the printed page, use layout mode. Draft mode, on the other hand, shows the text without obeying page breaks or column guides. For ease of entering text, use draft mode.

You can move from one display mode to another at any time while working with a document. Choose the mode you want from the **V**iew menu.

Layout Mode

To see a WYSIWYG (what you see is what you get) view of a document, choose **V**iew **L**ayout Mode. Ami Pro shows how the document will appear when printed (see fig. 5.41). Notice that you see the columns in layout mode. (Contrast this view with figure 5.42, which shows the same document in draft mode.)

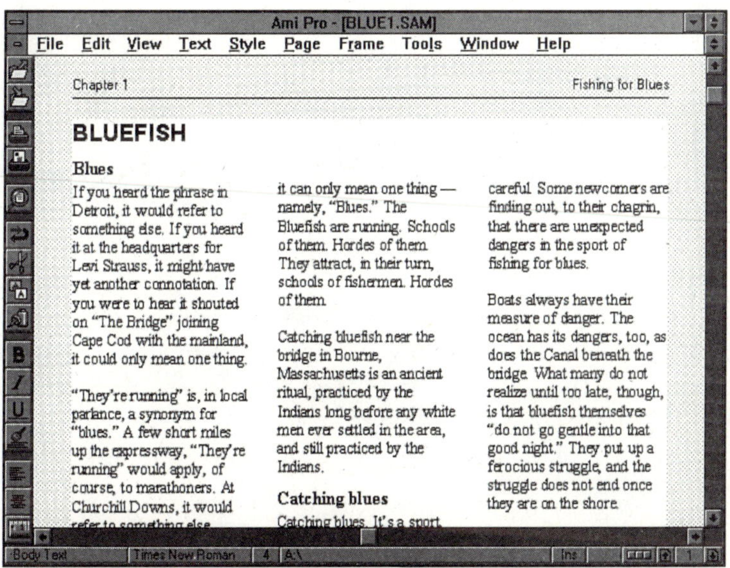

Fig. 5.41
The sample document displayed in layout mode.

The text is displayed with specified typefaces and font sizes, as well as all specified attributes, alignment, indentation, columns, and spacing. Tables, pictures, headers, footers, and footnotes also appear.

Tip
The Clean Screen options enable you to show or hide parts of the Ami Pro screen. See Chapter 8, "Changing Your Setup," for details.

Draft Mode

For quick maneuvering and text editing within a document, choose **V**iew **D**raft Mode. You see a less formatted view of the document, as shown in figure 5.42. The program displays text enhancements and attributes, but no page breaks, columns, headers, footers, footnotes, unanchored frames, drawings, or charts.

Text and pictures in anchored frames appear in the correct locations, but other kinds of frames don't appear at all. You can edit the contents of a frame in draft mode, but you cannot create, cut, copy, or move a frame.

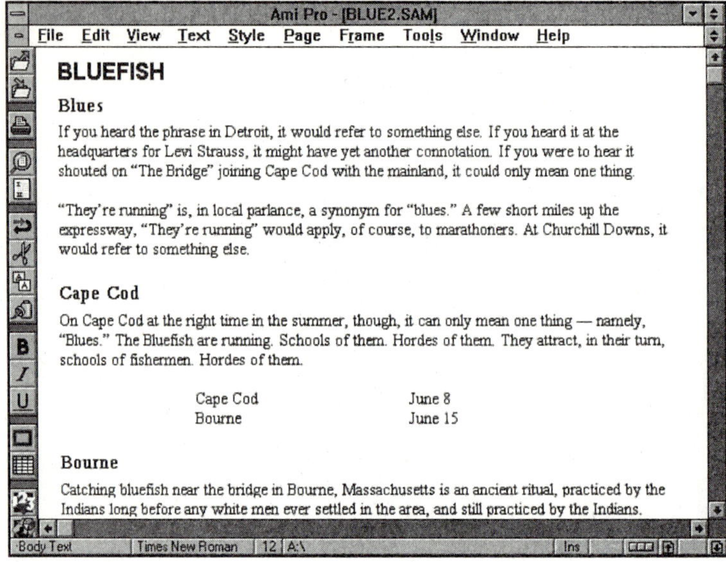

Fig. 5.42
The sample document in draft mode.

Outline Mode

To see how a document is organized and to limit the screen to showing specific paragraph styles (headings only, headings and subheadings only, and so on), choose **V**iew **O**utline Mode. Ami Pro also can display all text in the document. Each paragraph is marked according to paragraph type. An **O**utline menu appears in the Menu Bar. Figure 5.43 shows a document in outline mode.

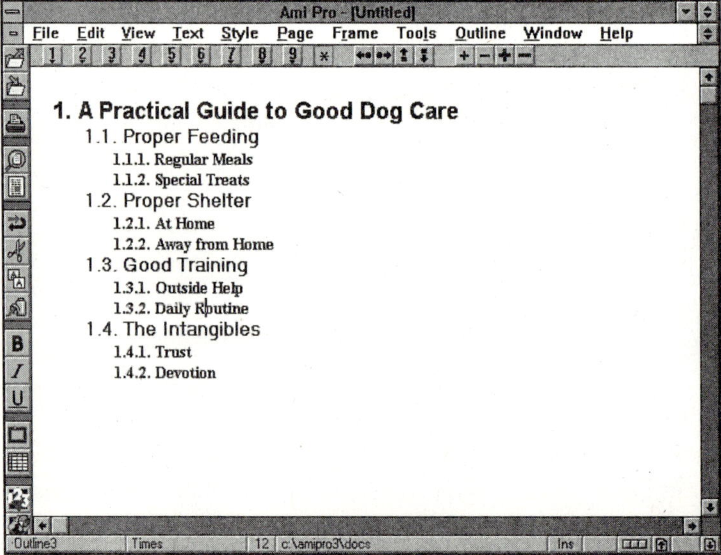

Fig. 5.43
A document in outline mode.

In outline mode, you can show all the text in a file, limit the text displayed to specified paragraph styles, rearrange sections of text, and create a new outline order for the document. Chapter 11, "Outlining a Document," provides instructions on using outline mode and the **O**utline menu.

Numbering Pages

Ami Pro offers several ways to handle page numbering. You can assign page numbers for your entire document, or you can start page numbering on any specified page. You can specify the starting page number (for example, page 2 or 3 instead of page 1). You also can use leading text (such as *Page 1*) with page numbers. You can locate page numbers in the top or bottom margin, at the left, right, or in the center. The page number can be placed in the header or footer. See the section "Working with Headers and Footers" for details on adding page numbers to a header or footer.

Using Automatic Page Numbering

To assign page numbers, begin with the document in layout mode. You can number the document manually by editing the header or footer on the initial left or right page and inserting the correct page number.

To use automatic page numbering, follow these steps:

1. Place the insertion point in the top or bottom margin of any page in your document.

2. Choose **P**age Numbering. The Page Numbering dialog box appears (see fig. 5.44).

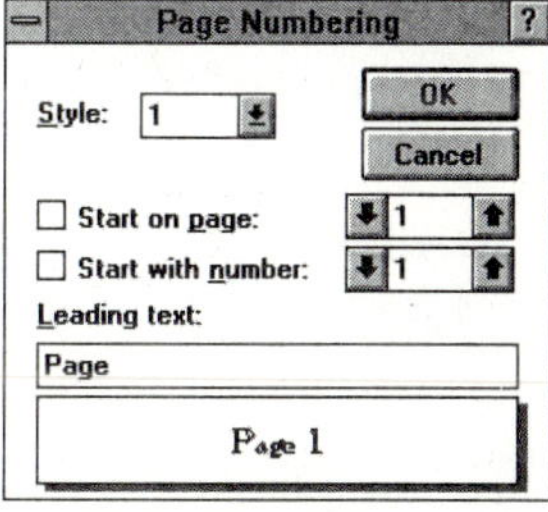

Fig. 5.44
The Page Numbering dialog box.

3. In the **S**tyle list box, specify the numbering style that you want to use for the page numbers. To see a list of available page numbering styles, click the down-arrow button by the **S**tyle list box.

4. If you want to start numbering pages after page 1, select Start on **P**age and specify, from the list of numbers, the page on which you want numbering to begin.

5. If you want to start numbering with a number other than 1, select Start with **N**umber and specify the starting page number.

6. If you want text to precede the page numbers, place the insertion point in the Leading Text text box and type the desired text. (You can type up to 30 characters and spaces.)

7. After you finish specifying numbering features, choose OK or press Enter. The Page Numbering dialog box disappears. Ami Pro numbers the document pages according to your page numbering specifications.

Tip

If you type leading text that includes a following space, as in the example *Page 1*, you must type the space, too.

When you add leading text, the example box at the bottom of the Page Numbering dialog box displays the number as it appears with leading characters or text.

If you want to add following text or spaces after Ami Pro inserts the page numbers, go to the margin where the page number appears and type the desired text. You also can enhance the page numbers and accompanying text with italics, boldfacing, display fonts, paragraph styles, and so on.

Ami Pro can number assign section-page numbers within the document; for example, Section 1-Page 1, Section 1-Page 2, and so on, followed by Section 2-Page 1, Section 2-Page 2, and so on. To use this type of numbering style, create a floating header or footer on the first line of each page where you want the section-page numbering to begin. (See the earlier section "Using Floating Headers and Footers" for details on this process.) Then access the Page Numbering dialog box and use the Start on **P**age, Start with **N**umber, and **L**eading Text options to create the desired section-page numbers for each section.

Changing Page Numbers

Ami Pro usually compensates automatically for deleted text; therefore, you very rarely need to renumber the pages of a document. If you used page numbering in a floating footer and removed the mark, however, you must renumber the pages. After you finish the changes to your document, choose **P**age Numbering. When the Page Numbering dialog box appears, specify the desired options for starting page, starting number, or leading text. Then choose OK or press Enter. The Page Numbering dialog box disappears, and Ami Pro renumbers the pages of the document.

Summary

In this chapter, you explored the opportunities of working with page layout. You now know how to use the Modify Page Layout dialog box to customize your documents—setting up margins, tabs, columns, page size, orientation, and lines. You learned how to use headers and footers, and how to number the pages of a document. You also learned how to use the ruler, how to use page and column breaks, how to change the display of text on-screen and the uses of the draft, layout and outline modes.

In the next chapter, you learn how to use the Find & **R**eplace, **G**o To, and **B**ookmark features in Ami Pro.

Chapter 6

Tools for Marking and Searching Text

Ami Pro provides several ways to move through a document quickly to find information, instead of searching line-by-line or page-by-page. In this chapter, you learn how to search through documents by using methods that include bookmarks, the Find & **R**eplace feature, and the **E**dit **G**o To command.

This chapter shows you how to use bookmarks to tag specific locations and items in your document for quick reference. You learn how to move directly to any specified page from any location in the document, and how to move to each occurrence of a particular item (header, footer, frame, note, and so on) in the document.

This chapter also discusses how to find specific words, phrases, and symbols in a document, and how to replace those items with new items (for example, how to find the word *full* and replace it with *fullness*).

Finally, you learn how to find and replace a specific style from the style sheet.

Using a Bookmark

Just as you insert a piece of paper between the pages of a book so that you can find your place again, you can use *bookmarks* in Ami Pro documents. With a document bookmark, you can return quickly to the specified location to insert text, make revisions, and so on.

Using the default style sheet, type the following sample text (type the first line in the top margin, as a header):

The History of the Buffalo in Montana

A history of Montana would not be complete without a discussion of the buffalo. Some of the state's most fascinating moments surround the discovery, hunting, and domestication of the buffalo.

Montana pioneers quickly discovered that the buffalo herds were a prime source of food, fuel, and hides. The relationship proved to be a balanced one, with pioneers taking only what they needed from the great herds and leaving the balance of nature basically unchanged. But then the white buffalo hunters arrived, and they began eliminating entire herds in a single hunt.

B. A. Skinner, noted sharpshooter and buffalo hunter, defended the activities of the hunters in an 1869 interview with a Missoula newspaper reporter: "The cattlemen needed them wide-open spaces for their steers, and the buffalo herds was competin' for the same grass. We put a lot more meat on a lot of American tables by makin' sure the prairie grass was reserved for the big cattle herds."

After you finish typing the sample text, you can add a bookmark, as explained in the next section.

Adding a Bookmark

To add a bookmark, you begin by moving the insertion point to the document location where you want to place the bookmark. In this example, you mark B.A. Skinner's quotation in the sample text so that you can find it quickly later.

To add a bookmark, follow these steps:

1. Move the insertion point to the location in the text where you want to place the bookmark. For this example, place the insertion point after B. A. Skinner's name in the sample text.

2. Choose **E**dit **B**ookmarks. The Bookmarks dialog box appears, as shown in figure 6.1.

3. Type a name for the bookmark in the **B**ookmark text box. (A bookmark name can be up to 17 characters long but cannot have spaces or consist only of numbers.) For this example, type **Skinnerquote**.

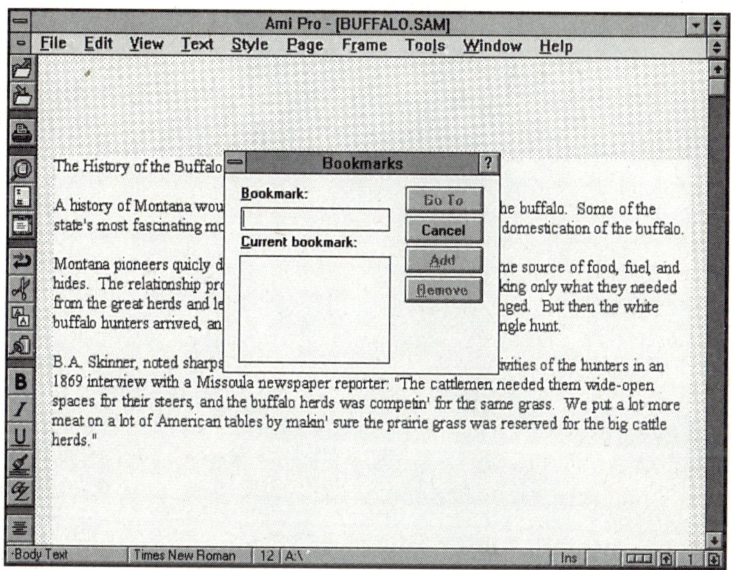

Fig. 6.1
The Bookmarks dialog box.

4. After assigning the bookmark name, choose **A**dd or press Enter. Ami Pro creates a bookmark at the insertion point and assigns the specified name to the bookmark. In this example, the bookmark named **Skinnerquote** appears after Skinner's name.

The dialog box disappears, and Ami Pro returns to the document.

Repeat these steps to place a bookmark named **Missoula** at the beginning of the word *Missoula* in the next sentence of the sample text.

Another way to access the Bookmarks dialog box is by using the Bookmark SmartIcon. This icon looks like a book with a bookmark (red bookmark on a color monitor). To access the Bookmarks dialog box, click the Bookmark SmartIcon.

Tip
If your SmartIcon set doesn't include the Bookmark SmartIcon, you can customize the set. See Chapter 8, "Changing Your Setup."

Finding a Bookmark

After you establish a bookmark in your document, you can return to that spot quickly.

To return to the B.A. Skinner quote in the sample document, follow these steps:

1. Choose **E**dit **B**ookmarks. The Bookmarks dialog box appears. The **C**urrent Bookmark list box lists all the bookmarks in your document, as shown in figure 6.2.

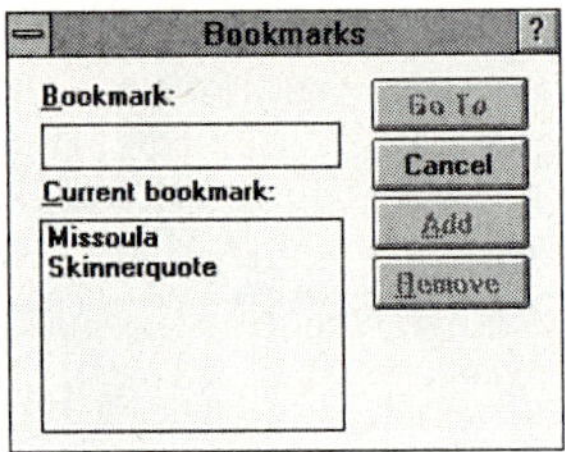

Fig. 6.2
The Bookmarks dialog box, with bookmarks listed in the **C**urrent Bookmark list box.

2. In the **C**urrent Bookmark list box, highlight the name of the bookmark you want to find. For this example, select `Skinnerquote`.

3. Choose the `Go To ^H` button. The dialog box disappears, and the insertion point moves to the specified bookmark. In this example, the insertion point moves to the end of B. A. Skinner's name, which is the location of the **Skinnerquote** bookmark.

You also can use **E**dit **G**o To to find bookmarks, footnotes, page breaks, notes, and so on, as explained later in this chapter.

Removing a Bookmark

If a bookmark no longer is useful, you can remove it from your document. In this example, you remove the Missoula bookmark from the sample text.

To remove a bookmark, follow these steps:

1. Choose **E**dit **B**ookmarks. The Bookmarks dialog box appears.

2. In the **C**urrent Bookmark list box, select the name of the bookmark you want to remove. For this example, select Missoula.

3. Choose **R**emove. The dialog box disappears. Ami Pro removes the specified bookmark and returns to the document. (If you choose **E**dit **B**ookmarks again, you can see that the **Missoula** bookmark no longer is listed.)

Using Go To

Ami Pro's **G**o To feature enables you to move around quickly in your document—to a bookmark, a particular page, a specific item (header, footer, note) within the document, and so on. You can use **G**o To in layout mode or draft mode, with one limitation: In draft mode you cannot use **G**o To to find page numbers because there are no page numbers in draft mode.

Move the insertion point to the beginning of the sample document. For this example, work in layout mode. To check the current mode, choose **V**iew; if there is no check mark before the **L**ayout Mode option, choose that option and return to your document.

In this example, you use **G**o To to find the next bookmark in the sample document. Follow these steps:

1. Perform one of the following actions: Choose **E**dit **G**o To, click the page number on the Status Bar, press Ctrl+G, or click the Go To SmartIcon. The Go To SmartIcon looks like three arrows pointing to the right (blue and black on a color monitor). If your SmartIcon set doesn't include the Go To SmartIcon, you can customize the set. See Chapter 8, "Changing Your Setup," for details on customizing the SmartIcon set.

   The Go To dialog box appears, as shown in figure 6.3.

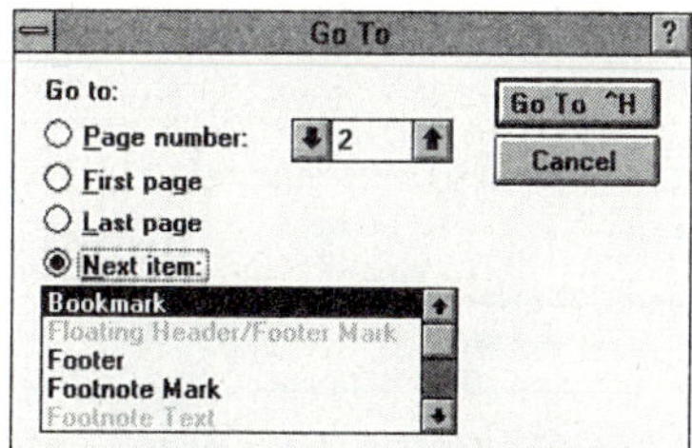

Fig. 6.3
The Go To dialog box.

2. Select the page option or item you want to locate.

   To go to a particular page number, the first page of the document or the last page of the document, choose **P**age Number, **F**irst Page, or **L**ast Page. If you choose **P**age Number, indicate the desired page in the list box.

   To go to a particular item in the document, choose **N**ext Item and select the desired item in the list box. The list box displays only five items at once. If the item you want isn't in the box, scroll through the items by clicking the up-arrow or down-arrow button at the side of the box, or pressing Tab to move to the list box and then pressing the arrow keys on your keyboard.

   For this example, choose **N**ext Item and highlight `Bookmark` in the list box.

3. Click the `Go To ^H` button or press Ctrl+H. Ami Pro moves the insertion point to the specified location or item. The insertion point moves to

Tip

If you use **G**o To to find an item (bookmark, header, footer, and so on), you can go to the next occurrence of that item by pressing Ctrl+H.

the next bookmark in the document—in this example, the bookmark after B. A. Skinner's name.

Note that using this method to go to a bookmark doesn't allow you to specify which bookmark to move to. Ami Pro moves to the next bookmark it finds in the document.

The options in the Go To dialog box move the insertion point as indicated in the following table.

Option	Action
Page Number	Moves to the top line of the specified page
First Page	Moves to the top line of the first page
Last Page	Moves to the top line of the last page
Next Item	Moves to the next occurrence of the specified item

The following table describes how Ami Pro moves the insertion point to the specified items in the **N**ext Item list box.

Item	Action
Bookmark	Moves to the next bookmark in the document
Floating Header/ Footer Mark	Moves to the next floating header or footer mark
Footer	Places the insertion point in the footer on the current page
Footnote Mark	Moves to the next footnote reference number
Footnote Text	Moves from the footnote mark to the first character of the footnote text (you must go to the footnote mark before you can go to the text of the footnote)
Frame	Moves to the first frame on the current page (use Ctrl+H to move from the first to the second, and so on)
Hard Pg Break	Moves to the next inserted page break mark
Header	Places the insertion point in the header on the current page
Layout Change	Moves to the next inserted page layout mark
Next Field	Moves to the next special field (merge field, power field, index entry field, document description field, and so on)

Item	Action
Note	Displays the next note; close the note to return to the document
Ruler	If the tab ruler is displayed, moves to the tab ruler
Ruler Mark	Moves to the next inserted ruler mark

Tip
If you have footnotes in your document, each footnote is marked with its own reference number.

If Ami Pro cannot find the specified item in your document, you see the message `Go To could not find a match for that item` (see fig. 6.4). The message indicates that the item doesn't exist, or that you started the Go To process at a location in the document past the item you are trying to find.

To clear the message, choose OK or press Enter. Ami Pro returns to the document.

For more information on the items displayed in the **N**ext Item list box, consult the chapters of this book, as shown in the following table.

Item	Chapter
Bookmarks	"Using a Bookmark" section of this chapter
Headers/footers	Chapter 5
Footnotes	Chapter 12
Frames	Chapter 16
Page layout	Chapter 5
Notes	Chapter 21
Ruler	Chapter 5

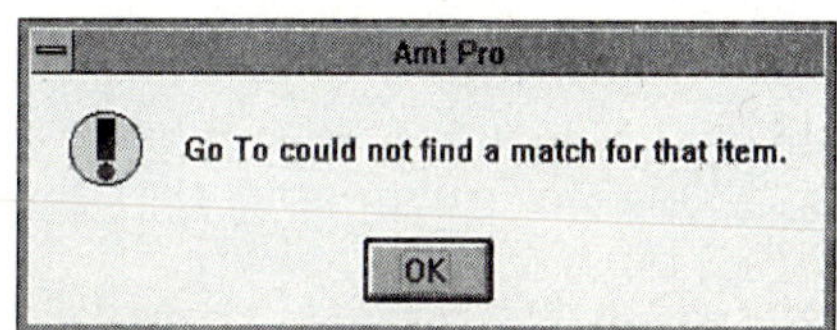

Fig. 6.4
The warning message that appears when Ami Pro cannot find the specified **N**ext Item.

As you have seen, Ami Pro's **G**o To feature enables you to move the insertion point to specific locations in the document. The next section describes another valuable Ami Pro feature, Find & **R**eplace, which enables you to find a specific section of text and replace it with different text.

Using Find & Replace

Ami Pro's Find & **R**eplace feature can find a particular word, symbol, or paragraph style in your document and replace the found item with something different. You can find and replace words (replacing *alive* with *lively*), symbols (replacing *$* with *%*), or paragraph styles (finding each paragraph with an Indent 1 style and replacing that style with Body Text).

You access the Find & Replace dialog box by choosing **E**dit Find & **R**eplace, by pressing Ctrl+F, or by clicking the Find & Replace SmartIcon (it looks like a flashlight). If your SmartIcon set doesn't include the Find & Replace SmartIcon, you can click the SmartIcons button on the Status Bar and select the Editing SmartIcon set. See Chapter 8, "Changing Your Setup," for details on SmartIcon sets.

Figure 6.5 shows the Find & Replace dialog box. In the dialog box, you specify the search text or paragraph style in the **F**ind text box and the replacement text or paragraph style in the Replace **W**ith text box.

The text you specify in the **F**ind text box can be a few letters, a word, a phrase, or a short sentence containing up to 40 letters, characters, spaces, and wild-card characters.

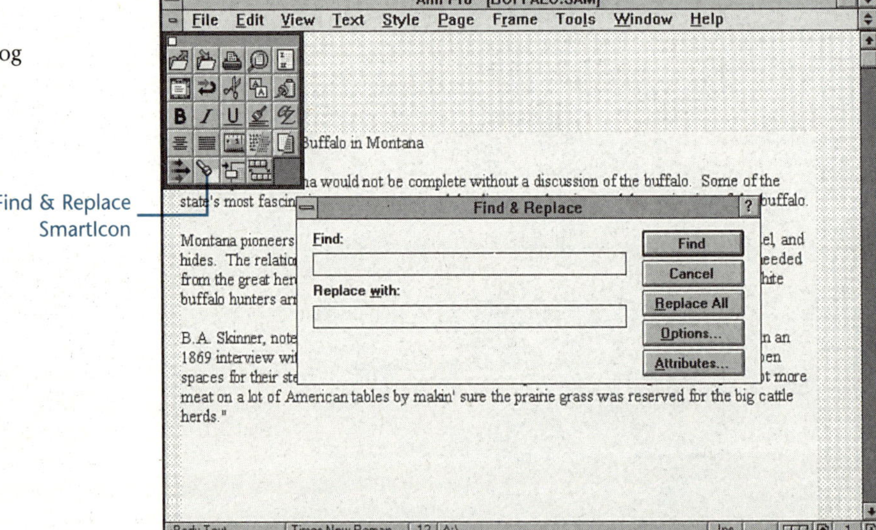

Fig. 6.5
The Find & Replace dialog box.

You use *wild-card characters* (* and ?) to search for different words that share similar characteristics. The question mark wild-card character replaces a single character in the word, and the asterisk wildcard character represents any number of characters.

To search for words beginning with *part* (such as particle and participate), for example, you type **part***. To search for words with one letter between the letters *c* and *t*, you type **c?t**. To search for words with two letters between the letters *n* and *t*, you type **n??t**. To search for words with one letter between *th* and *n* and any number of letters following (such as thinning or thence), you type **th?n***.

Tip
To cancel a Find & **R**eplace operation, choose Cancel.

To search for tabs, place the insertion point in the **F**ind text box, and press Ctrl+Tab to find tabs. The tab symbol (>) appears in the **F**ind text box. To search for carriage returns, place the insertion point in the **F**ind text box and press Ctrl+Enter. The carriage return symbol (¶) appears in the **F**ind text box. To search for a question mark or an asterisk in the text, type the character surrounded by angle brackets: **<?>** or **<*>**.

For information regarding using Find & **R**eplace with paragraph styles, see the later section of this chapter, "Finding and Replacing a Paragraph Style."

Searching Text Streams

Ami Pro treats different parts of a document as separate *text streams*. The main document text is considered one text stream, text in fixed frames is another text stream, and so on. Text streams in Ami Pro have the following priority:

1. Main document text
2. Text in fixed frames (frames set to **W**here Placed in the Modify Frame Layout dialog box)
3. Footnote text
4. Text in floating frames (frames set to With **P**ara Above or **F**low With Text in the Modify Frame Layout dialog box) and text in tables
5. Text in floating headers and footers
6. Text in fixed headers and footers, and text in repeating frames (frames set to **R**epeat All Pages or Repeat Right/**L**eft in the Modify Frame Layout dialog box)

The order of priority is important only if you want to include lower-priority text streams in a Find & **R**eplace operation.

If the insertion point is in the main document text and you want a Find & **R**eplace operation to include headers and footers, choose **O**ptions in the Find & Replace dialog box and then choose **I**nclude Other Text Streams in the Find & Replace Options dialog box. When you use this option with the insertion point in the main document text, Ami Pro includes all text streams in the search.

Tip
You cannot search for text in notes or drawings.

If the insertion point is in a text stream other than main document text, Ami Pro automatically searches that text stream and all lower-priority text streams. Note that Ami Pro starts the search at the beginning of the document, regardless of the location of the insertion point.

Note

To search a specific area of the document, select the text before choosing **E**dit Find and **R**eplace. Ami Pro searches the selected text only. If you do not preselect text and begin a Find & **R**eplace operation, Ami Pro searches from the location of the insertion point to the end of the document, only.

Replacing Text

When you type replacement text in the Find & Replace dialog box, you indicate whether you want Ami Pro to find and replace *all* occurrences of the specified text or only *selected* occurrences (those you specify). To find and replace specified occurrences, choose the `Find` button in the Find and Replace dialog box. To find and replace *all* occurrences, choose the **R**eplace All button. If you tell Ami Pro to find each occurrence of the search text, a second Find & Replace dialog box appears, as shown in figure 6.6.

The second Find & Replace dialog box shows the search text, the specified replacement text, and the text stream Ami Pro is searching. You can use the options in this dialog box as described in the following table.

Option	Action
Replace & **F**ind Next	Replaces the highlighted text with the replacement text and searches for the next occurrence of the search text
Find **N**ext	Continues searching for the next location of the search text without replacing the current instance
Replace Remaining	Finds and replaces all remaining occurrences of the search text
Cancel	Stops the search and returns to the document

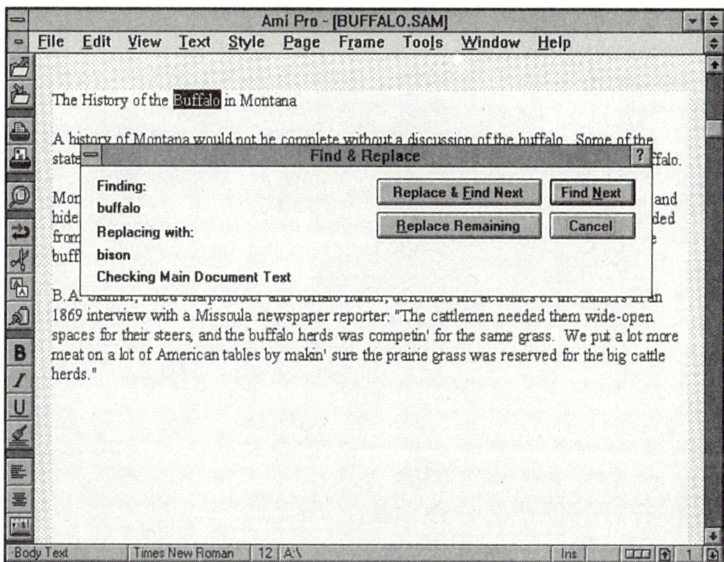

Fig. 6.6
The second Find & Replace dialog box.

After completing the Find & **R**eplace operation, Ami Pro displays a brief message in the Status Bar at the bottom of the screen. This message indicates the number of times Ami Pro found the search text and the number of replacements made. The Find & Replace dialog box disappears, and Ami Pro returns to the text stream where you began the search. The insertion point is at the last occurrence of the search text.

Note

If you use Find & **R**eplace in draft mode, the insertion point may end up in a different text stream than you anticipated. In draft mode, only one text stream can appear on the screen at a time. You can return to layout mode to determine where the insertion point is and to move it to the desired location in the text.

Specifying Find & Replace Options

You can make the search parameters of the Find & **R**eplace procedure more exact by choosing **O**ptions in the Find & Replace dialog box. The Find & Replace Options dialog box appears, as shown in figure 6.7.

In the Find & Replace Options dialog box, you can select from the options described in the following table.

Tip
The **B**eginning of Document and **I**nclude Other Text Streams options aren't available if the insertion point is in any text stream other than main document text.

Option	Description
Whole Word Only	Searches for whole words (text with a space before and after it), not parts of words (if searching for *buffalo*, Ami Pro skips occurrences of *buffaloes*).
Exact Case	Searches for or replaces text with the upper- and lowercase letter combination specified in the **F**ind or Replace **W**ith text boxes. If **E**xact Case is not selected, Ami Pro finds all occurrences, regardless of capitalization.
Exact **A**ttributes	Searches for or replaces text with the attributes (boldface, underline, italics, and so on) specified in the Find & Replace Attributes dialog box.
Beginning of Document	Searches entire document, regardless of current insertion point location (if deselected, begins search at current insertion point position).
Include Other Text Streams	Searches the text stream the insertion point is in, and all lower-priority streams; when deselected, searches only the text stream the insertion point is in.
Find Backwards	Searches main document text, backward from insertion point to document beginning; if insertion point is in text stream other than main document, Ami Pro searches only that text stream.
Text	Indicates that you want to find and replace text.
Style	Indicates that you want to find and replace a paragraph style.

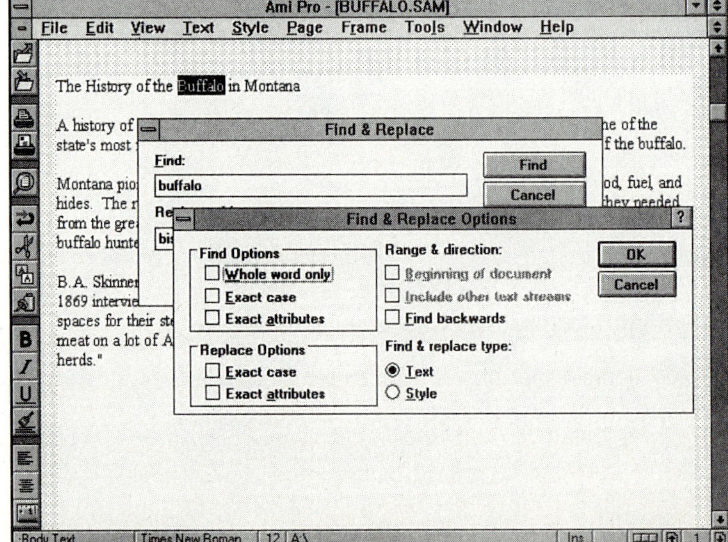

Fig. 6.7
The Find & Replace Options dialog box.

Specifying Find & Replace Attributes

Ami Pro's Find & Replace **A**ttributes option enables you to find enhanced text (boldface, italics, underline) or to enhance replacement text. When you choose **E**dit Find & **R**eplace **A**ttributes, The Find & Replace Attributes dialog box appears, as shown in figure 6.8.

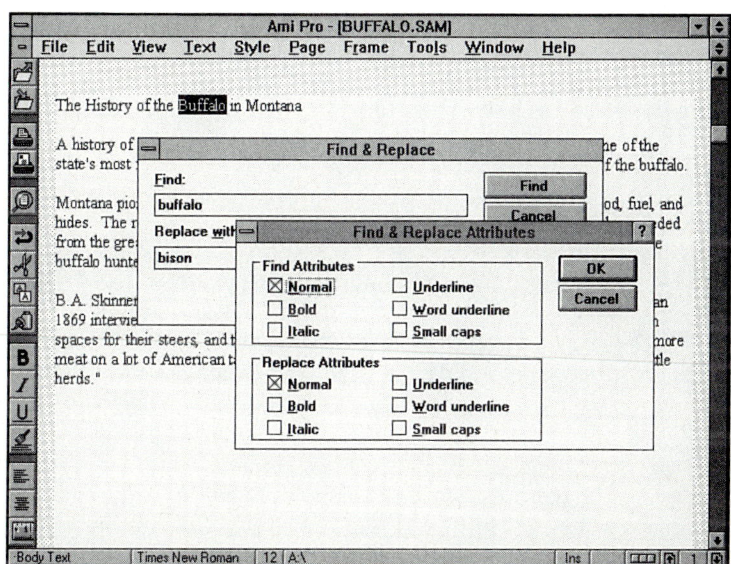

Fig. 6.8
The Find & Replace Attributes dialog box.

By default, the **N**ormal options are selected for both the Find Attributes and Replace Attributes sections.

You can limit the search to enhanced text by indicating the enhancements you want Ami Pro to find (**B**old, **I**talic, **U**nderline, **W**ord Underline, or **S**mall Caps) in the Find Attributes box. You can choose combinations of attributes to search for, such as in a boldfaced and underlined word.

To enhance the replacement text (for example, if you want the replacement text to be in italics), you indicate the desired enhancements in the Replace Attributes section.

When you have finished selecting attributes, choose OK or press Enter to close the Find & Replace Attributes dialog box. Ami Pro returns to the Find & Replace dialog box.

Performing a Simple Find & Replace Operation

In this example, you use Find & **R**eplace to find and replace the word *buffalo* in the text of the sample document with the word *bison*. Your sample document includes the following header:

```
The History of the Buffalo in Montana
```

To search through the entire document, including the header, and limit the search to the whole word *buffalo*, follow these steps:

1. Place the insertion point at the beginning of the document.

2. Choose **E**dit Find & **R**eplace, click the Find & Replace SmartIcon, or press Ctrl+F. The Find & Replace dialog box appears (refer to fig. 6.5).

3. Place the insertion point in the **F**ind text box and type the text you want to find; for this example, type **buffalo**.

4. Choose **F**ind. Ami Pro moves to the first occurrence of the word *buffalo*, highlights the word, and displays the Find & Replace dialog box. To end the search operation, choose Cancel or press Esc, and skip the following steps.

5. To replace the word *buffalo* with the word *bison*, place the insertion point in the Replace **W**ith text box and type **bison**. (For this example, you accept the default **N**ormal setting for both Find Attributes and Replace Attributes.)

6. Choose **O**ptions. The Find & Replace Options dialog box appears (refer to fig. 6.7).

7. Specify the desired Find & Replace options in the dialog box. For this example, select **W**hole Word Only, **T**ext, **B**eginning of Document, and **I**nclude Other Text Stream. When you finish specifying options, choose OK or press Enter. The Find & Replace dialog box reappears.

8. For this example, choose Find, so you can find each occurrence of the search text separately and decide at that point whether to replace it.

   Ami Pro finds the first occurrence of the search text *buffalo* in the first line of the document, and highlights the word. The second Find & Replace dialog box appears (refer to fig. 6.6).

9. Choose Replace & **F**ind Next. Continue to choose Replace & **F**ind Next until Ami Pro finds the word *buffalo* in the phrase *white buffalo hunters*. The word *buffalo* is better suited to this phrase than is the word *bison*.

10. Leave this occurrence of the search text unchanged by choosing Find **N**ext. The insertion point moves to *buffalo* in the next paragraph, in the description of B. A. Skinner as a buffalo hunter. Again, choose Find **N**ext to leave this text unchanged. Repeat this procedure for the use of buffalo in the Skinner quotation.

11. Assume that you now have saved all appropriate uses of the word *buffalo*. Choose **R**eplace Remaining. Ami Pro finds and replaces all remaining occurrences of *buffalo* in the sample document.

When the operation is complete, Ami Pro displays a message in the Status Bar that indicates the number of occurrences of the search text and the number of replacements made, and then returns to the document.

Tip
You can move the second Find and Replace dialog box to get a better view of the highlighted text.

If you use Find & **R**eplace while your document is in draft mode, and you choose the **I**nclude Other Text Streams option, the insertion point returns to the last occurrence of the search text. Returning to the last occurrence may place the insertion point in a fixed frame, footnote, or header instead of the main text of your document.

If you plan to use the **I**nclude Other Text Streams option, and you want to see the exact location of the insertion point in the document after the Find & **R**eplace operation is completed, switch to layout mode before selecting **E**dit Find & **R**eplace.

Finding and Replacing a Paragraph Style

The steps required to find and replace a paragraph style are nearly identical to the steps for finding and replacing text.

When you want to find and replace a paragraph style, you enter the **F**ind text box and type the name of the paragraph style you want to find, or press the appropriate function key for that paragraph style. Similarly, in the Replace **W**ith text box, type the name (or press the function key) of the paragraph style you want to use as a replacement.

If you press the appropriate function key (F2, F3, and so on) for the paragraph style you want to find, Ami Pro inserts that paragraph style's name in the Find text box.

Note

You may find it useful to activate the Styles box (**V**iew Show Styles **B**ox) before using Find & **R**eplace with styles. This box shows the appropriate function key next to the paragraph style name and can be used as a quick reference for which function keys correspond to which paragraph styles.

If you type the paragraph style name, be sure to type it exactly as shown in the style sheet for your document (capitals, spelling, and so on).

When using Find & **R**eplace with **S**tyles, if you choose Find rather than **R**eplace All, Ami Pro finds the first occurrence of the specified paragraph style, highlights the paragraph, and displays the second Find & Replace dialog box. As when you use Find & **R**eplace with **T**ext, you then can choose Replace & **F**ind Next, Find **N**ext, **R**eplace Remaining, or Cancel.

The example in this section uses the sample document shown earlier. Modify the document by making the Skinner quotation a separate paragraph.

To use Find & **R**eplace to find the Skinner quotation and replace that paragraph's Body Text paragraph style with the Bullet paragraph style, follow these steps:

1. Place the insertion point at the beginning of the document in order to perform the search throughout the entire document, or select the text on which you want to perform the search.
2. Choose **E**dit Find & **R**eplace, or click on the Find & Replace SmartIcon, or press Ctrl+F. The Find & Replace dialog box appears.
3. For this example, type **Body Text** in the **F**ind text box (see fig. 6.9).

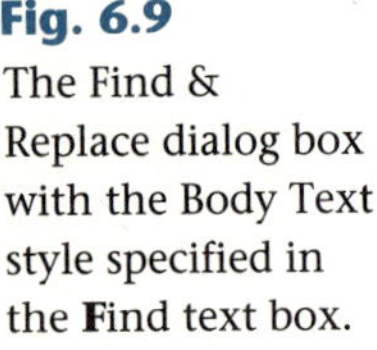

Fig. 6.9
The Find & Replace dialog box with the Body Text style specified in the **F**ind text box.

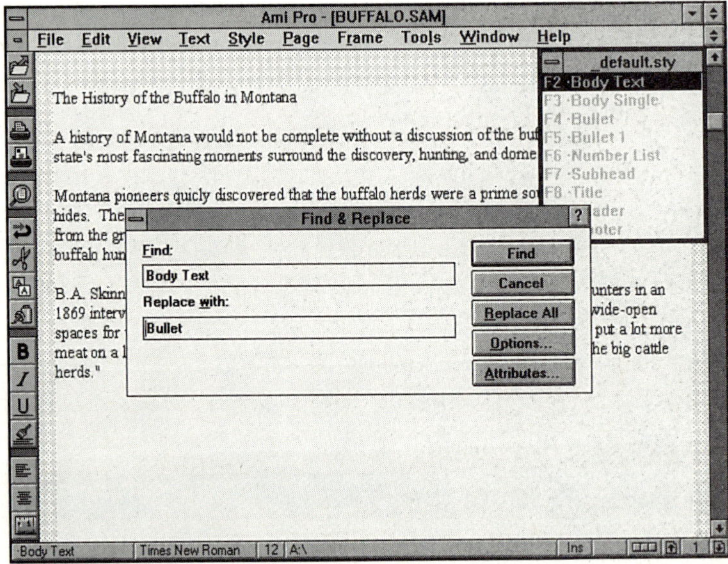

4. In the Replace **W**ith text box, press F4 for the Bullet style.

5. Choose **O**ptions. The Find & Replace Options dialog box appears.

6. Indicate the desired options. For this example, select **S**tyle as the Find & Replace Type; the options shown in the Find Options and Replace Options sections are dimmed (see fig. 6.10). You cannot use these options when you find and replace a style. To see a list of styles with function keys, select the **S**tyle **S**elect a Style command. The _DEFAULT.STY dialog box appears.

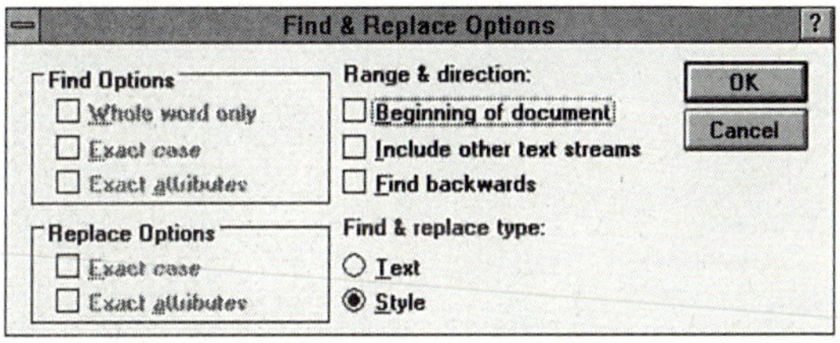

Fig. 6.10
The Find & Replace Options dialog box, showing the **S**tyle option selected and the Find Options and Replace Options dimmed.

7. For the search range in this example, select **B**eginning of Document; then choose OK or press Enter. The Find & Replace dialog box reappears.

8. Choose Find. In this example, the first paragraph with the selected style isn't the paragraph you want to change. Choose Find **N**ext to leave Body Text as the style for the selected paragraph and find the next occurrence of the Body Text style.

9. Continue choosing Find **N**ext until Ami Pro highlights the Skinner quotation, as shown in figure 6.11. Choose Replace & **F**ind Next. Ami Pro replaces the Body Text style in the Skinner quotation with the Bullet style.

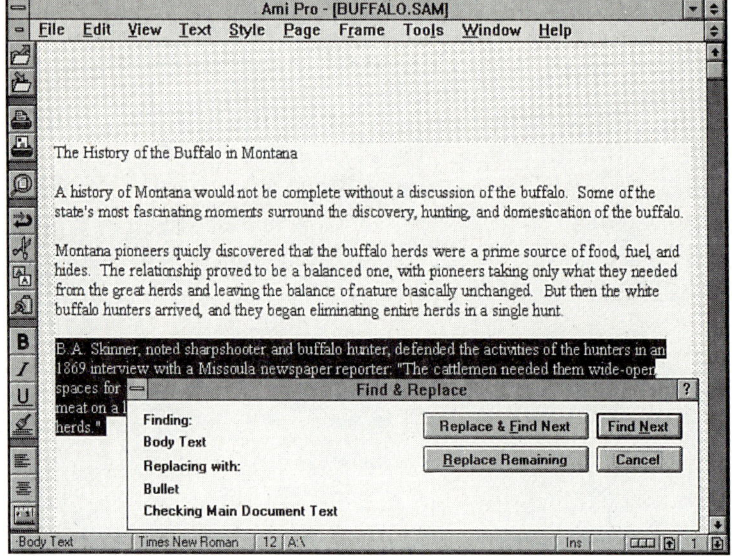

Fig. 6.11
The last paragraph with Body Text paragraph style, and the second Find & Replace dialog box.

Summary

In this chapter, you learned how to use bookmarks to find locations or items in your document, and how to add bookmarks, find bookmarks, and remove them. You learned how to use the **G**o To function to locate footnote text, footnote marks, page numbers, page breaks, rulers, and even page layout changes. You also experimented with the Find & **R**eplace function, and learned how to find and replace text and styles, and how to use the Find & **R**eplace options to search for text attributes or particular text streams.

In the next chapter, you prepare your documents for printing. You first learn how to use Ami Pro to check the spelling and grammar in your text, and then how to print the finished document.

Chapter 7

Proofreading and Printing a Document

Before you print a document, you need to check it for errors. This action saves you time (in reprinting the document later) and embarrassment (in releasing a document that contains errors). One of the most important proofreading tools in word processing is a spelling checker; this feature rapidly finds and highlights the misspellings in a document for correction.

The Spell Check feature, like other Ami Pro tools, is powerful and flexible. You can check a single word or an entire document. Unless you specify otherwise, the program checks the spelling in the main body of the document and in frames, margins, and other special locations. A customizable user dictionary enables you to copy custom words into the dictionary. With this feature, you can avoid frequent stops to spell check custom words, such as proper names ("AT&T"). Ami Pro 3 enables you to add an expanded dictionary that contains medical and scientific terms. By purchasing this dictionary, you can cut down the number of times the program stops to spell check the special words you use in your business.

Ami Pro's new Grammar Check feature is another important proofreading tool that enables you to check a document for correct grammar and use of language. You can specify grammar rule and writing style options to customize the grammar checker to meet your specific needs.

In this chapter, you learn how to proof a document before you print it to make sure that all words are spelled correctly. You also learn how to choose options for the Spell Check feature and how to use the various choices available as you check the document. You examine the Grammar Check feature, learn how to choose grammar rule and writing style options, and use the various options available as you search the document for grammar errors. Then the chapter turns to using Ami Pro's electronic Thesaurus, a writer's tool for finding synonyms.

After you proof the document, you are ready to print. You learn how to set up the printer, choose the options you want to use for printing the document, and then print the document.

Using Spell Check

Ami Pro checks the spelling of each word in a document against a 115,000-word dictionary that comes with the program. This dictionary includes legal, business, finance, and insurance terms. Spell Check can find misspelled words, suggest correctly spelled replacements, and find words that appear twice, such as *the the*. If the document contains words not included in Ami Pro's main dictionary, you can add those words to a separate dictionary that Ami Pro uses with the main dictionary in future spell check operations.

With Ami Pro, you can check an entire document or any portion, beginning at any point in the document. You decide whether you want to check the text in frames, headers, and footers.

You specify the Spell Check options and begin the spell check operation with the Spell Check dialog box. To access the dialog box, choose Too**l**s **S**pell Check; the Spell Check dialog box appears (see fig. 7.1).

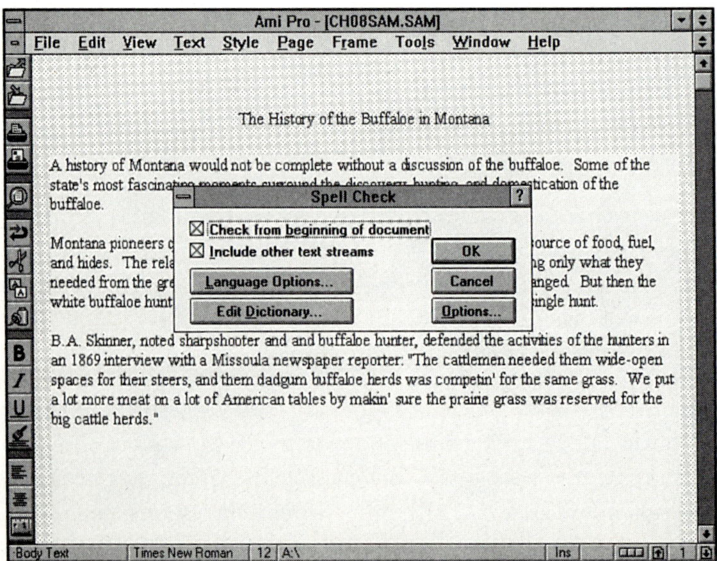

Ami Pro - [CH08SAM.SAM]
File Edit View Text Style Page Frame Tools Window Help
The History of the Buffaloe in Montana
A history of Montana would not be complete without a discussion of the buffaloe. Some of the
Spell Check
Check from beginning of document
Include other text streams
OK
Language Options...
Cancel
Edit Dictionary...
Options...
B.A. Skinner, noted sharpshooter and and buffaloe hunter, defended the activities of the hunters in an 1869 interview with a Missoula newspaper reporter: "The cattlemen needed them wide-open spaces for their steers, and them dadgum buffaloe herds was competin' for the same grass. We put a lot more meat on a lot of American tables by makin' sure the prairie grass was reserved for the big cattle herds."
Body Text
Times New Roman
12
A:\
Ins

Fig. 7.1
The Spell Check dialog box.

If you want Ami Pro to search through the entire main document text stream, regardless of the location of the insertion point, choose Check from **B**eginning of Document. Deselect this option if you want the search to begin from the current position of the insertion point.

Different parts of a document are treated as separate text streams; the main document text is considered one text stream, text in fixed frames is another, and so on. To check all parts of a document, choose **I**nclude Other Text Streams.

You can select both the **B**eginning of Document and **I**nclude Other Text Streams options. If you start the spell check in a text stream other than the main document text, however, these options are dimmed (unavailable). In this case, Ami Pro selects **I**nclude Other Text Streams automatically and begins the spell check at the beginning of the document. Only the current text stream (the text stream in which the insertion point appears) and any lower priority text stream(s) are checked.

Text streams in Ami Pro have the following priority:

Main document text

Text in fixed frames

Footnote text

Text in floating frames

Text in tables

Text in floating headers and footers

Text in fixed headers and footers, and text in repeating frames

This order of priority is important only if you want to include the lower-priority text streams in a spell check (or if you are using information tools such as Find & Replace—see Chapter 6, "Tools for Marking and Searching Text," for details). If the insertion point is in the main document text and you want the spell check to include headers and footers, for example, choose **I**nclude Other Text Streams. When you use this option, Ami Pro includes the main document text and all other lower-priority text streams in the spell check.

After you finish a spell check, the insertion point remains at the last checked word. If you spell check while the document is in draft mode and choose **I**nclude Other Text Streams, the insertion point may stop in a fixed frame, footnote, or header, rather than the main text of the document.

Note

If you want to see exactly where the insertion point is in the document after the spell check is complete, switch to layout mode. (See Chapter 5, "Working with Page Layout," for an explanation of the different modes to use when displaying and working with documents.)

Use the following sample document to help you learn how to use Spell Check and print your work. Type the document exactly as you see it here; the intentional errors in the document show up when you use Spell Check. Type the first (single) line in the top margin, as a header.

The History of the Buffaloe in Montana

A history of Montana would not be complete without a discussion of the buffaloe. Some of the state's most fascinating moments surround the discovery, hunting, and domestication of the buffaloe.

Montana pioneers quickly discovered that the buffaloe herds were a prime source of food, fuel, and hides. The relationship proved to be a balanced one, with pioneers taking only what they needed from the great herds and leaving the balance of nature basically unchanged. But then the white buffaloe hunters arrived, and they began eliminating entire herds in a single hunt.

B.A. Skinner, noted sharpshooter and and buffaloe hunter, defended the activities of the hunters in an 1869 interview with a Missoula newspaper reporter: "The cattlemen needed them wide-open spaces for their steers, and them dadgum buffaloe herds was competin' for the same grass. We put a lot more meat on a lot of American tables by makin' sure the prairie grass was reserved for the big cattle herds."

To check the spelling of a single word or paragraph, you select the word or paragraph and choose Too**l**s **S**pell Check. Ami Pro checks the selected text immediately, without using the Spell Check dialog box. (You also can check the entire document by selecting it and choosing Too**l**s **S**pell Check.) During the spell check operation, if Ami Pro finds an error, the Spell Check dialog box appears with the misspelled text highlighted. If no misspellings exist, Ami Pro returns to the document.

To spell check a document, follow these steps:

1. Make the document you want to check the active document and position the insertion point in the location where you want to begin the spell check. For this example, position the insertion point anywhere in the main document text area of the sample document. Because this example is designed to check the entire document, the insertion point must be in the main text area.

2. Choose Too**l**s **S**pell Check or click the Spell Check SmartIcon (it looks like a book with *abc* on the cover). The Spell Check dialog box appears (refer to fig. 7.1).

3. If desired, choose the **B**eginning of Document option and the **I**nclude Other Text Streams option. For this example, choose both options.

4. Choose **O**ptions if you want to review and choose additional spell check options. The Spell Check Options dialog box appears (see fig. 7.2).

   For this example, choose the Check for **R**epeated Words option and the Check Words with **I**nitial Caps option. (These options are discussed following these steps.)

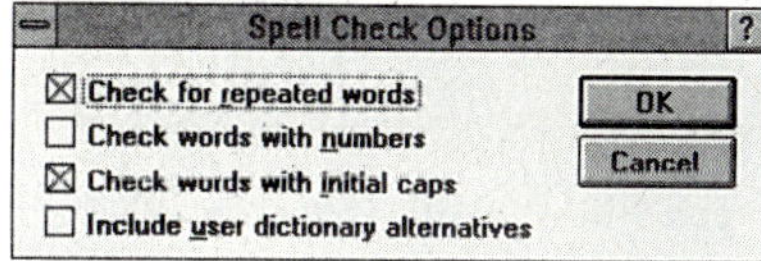

Fig. 7.2
The Spell Check Options dialog box.

5. Choose OK or press Enter to close the Spell Check Options dialog box.

6. To start the spell check, choose OK or press Enter in the Spell Check dialog box.

The following options are available in the Spell Check Options dialog box:

- *Check for **R**epeated Words*. Use this option to check the document for duplicate words (words that appear twice in a row). When you find double words, you can delete the unnecessary word or make no changes.

- *Check Words with **N**umbers*. Use this option to check words that contain numbers, such as *beta12*. If you don't use this option, Spell Check skips these types of words.

- *Check Words with **I**nitial Caps*. Use this option to check words that begin with a capital letter. If you use titles and subtitles with initial capitals, for example, and you want to include those words in the spell check, you must select this option. Otherwise, Spell Check skips text with an initial capital letter.

- *Include **U**ser Dictionary Alternatives*. Use this option to add words to a user dictionary separate from the main dictionary. (For instructions, see the next section, "Making Corrections.") If you use an unusual word (such as *whizbang*) in the document and Spell Check finds it, you can add this word to the user dictionary.

  This option displays the user dictionary words in the A**l**ternatives list box during a spell check. This option also enables you to use the words in the user dictionary along with the main dictionary during a spell check.

If you start a spell check and see a message indicating that Ami Pro cannot find a dictionary to use, choose **L**anguage Options in the Spell Check dialog box. When the Spell Check Language Options dialog box appears, type **\AMIPRO** (or whatever path you used when you installed Ami Pro) in the Language **P**ath box. This procedure instructs Ami Pro to use the standard dictionary included with the program.

Making Corrections

When Spell Check finds a misspelled word, the program highlights the word in the document and displays the word in a different version of the Spell Check dialog box. At this point, you can decide whether to correct the word, add it to the dictionary, or ignore it. Figure 7.3 shows this new version of the Spell Check dialog box and displays the first misspelled word in the main text of the sample document. Notice that the Replace **W**ith text box highlights and displays the word.

After Ami Pro locates a word that may be misspelled, you can choose any of the following actions:

- ***S**kip All and S**k**ip*. If the word is correct, choose **S**kip All. Ami Pro then ignores all occurrences of the word during this spell check. If the word is spelled appropriately in this instance but you want to look for the same word in the rest of the document, choose S**k**ip. Ami Pro leaves this particular word as is but finds any other occurrences of the word and enables you to change the spelling.

- *Replace and **R**eplace All.* If the word is incorrect, scan the list of alternative spellings provided in the A**l**ternatives list box. (Use the arrow buttons to scroll the list if all the alternatives don't fit in the box.) If you find the correct spelling of the word in the A**l**ternatives list box, select the correct spelling. Ami Pro inserts the selected word in the Replace **W**ith text box.

- If you don't find the correct spelling in the A**l**ternatives list box, edit the word (delete undesired characters or type the correct spelling) in the Replace **W**ith text box.

- If you want to replace only this occurrence of the highlighted word with the word you specified in the Replace **W**ith box, choose R**e**place. Ami Pro replaces the incorrect word with the word you specified, and moves on. The spell check stops at the next occurrence of the word you just replaced.

- If you want to replace all occurrences of the highlighted word in the rest of the document, choose **R**eplace All. Ami Pro replaces all occurrences of the incorrect word with the word you specified in the Replace **W**ith text box.

- ***A**dd To Dictionary.* If you want to add the highlighted word to the user dictionary, choose **A**dd To Dictionary. Ami Pro considers this word spelled correctly in any future spell check. The program also lists this word in the A**l**ternatives list box as an alternative spelling in future spell check operations.

Caution

Spell Check doesn't prompt you to verify additional replacements when you choose **R**eplace All. Make certain that you want to replace all instances. If you mistakenly choose **R**eplace All, you can restore the original words by choosing **E**dit **U**ndo immediately.

In the sample spell check, the suggested spellings *buffaloed* and *buffaloes* are offered in the A**l**ternatives list box. To correct the spelling, type **buffalo** in the Replace **W**ith text box. Choose R**e**place to replace *buffaloe* with *buffalo.*

After you choose R**e**place, the spell check finds the next occurrence of *buffaloe.* Again, type **buffalo** in the Replace **W**ith text box, and then choose R**e**place.

At this point, you realize that *buffalo* is misspelled throughout the document and you want the word corrected in all cases. To make this change, choose **R**eplace All. Ami Pro replaces *buffaloe* with *buffalo* throughout the document.

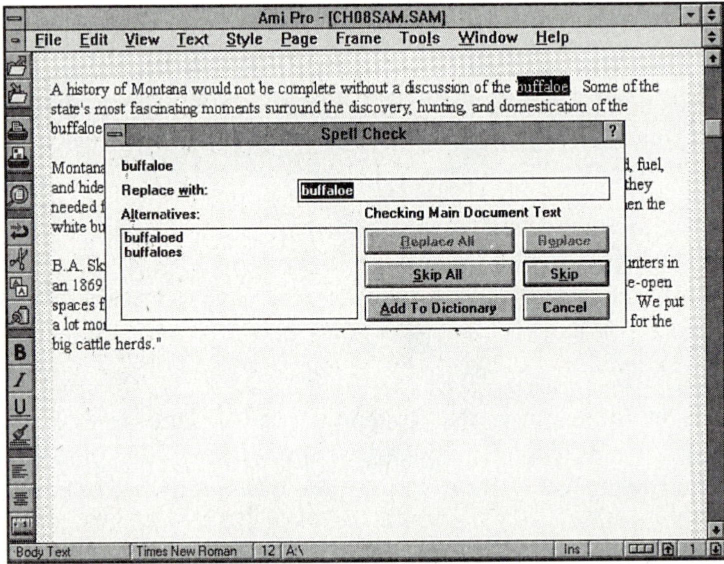

Fig. 7.3
The Replace **W**ith text box, highlighting the misspelled word *buffaloe.*

Tip
Ami Pro doesn't verify whether capitalization is correct. If you choose the Check Words with **I**nitial Caps option in the Spell Check Options dialog box, Ami Pro checks the spelling of such words.

Ami Pro doesn't recognize the abbreviation *B.A.* and stops. Choose S**k**ip to ignore this word.

As the operation continues, Spell Check stops at *and and*, highlighting the second occurrence of *and*. (Spell Check caught this error because you selected the Check for **R**epeated Words option before you started the spell check.)

A message box appears, indicating that the word preceding the highlighted word is spelled in the same way (see fig. 7.4).

Choose OK or press Enter to return to the Spell Check dialog box. The word *and* is highlighted in the **R**eplace With text box (see fig. 7.5).

To delete the second occurrence of *and*, press Del and then choose R**e**place. The second *and* disappears.

Ami Pro doesn't recognize the proper noun *Missoula* and stops. Choose S**k**ip to ignore this word.

Next, Spell Check stops and highlights the word *dadgum*. You want to use this word in the quotation and add the word to the user dictionary. To add the highlighted word to the user dictionary, choose **A**dd To Dictionary.

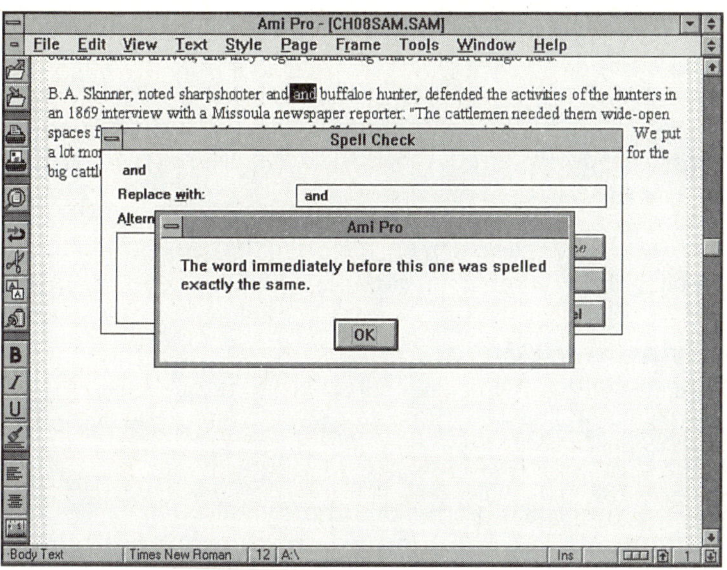

Fig. 7.4
The identical word message box.

Tip
As with many other Ami Pro defaults, the settings for the Spell Check options from the last Spell Check session remain in effect each time you begin a Spell Check operation.

Ami Pro adds *dadgum* to the user dictionary. (If you want to use the word during a future spell check, select Include **U**ser Dictionary Alternatives at that time, before you continue the spell check.)

Ami Pro doesn't recognize the contractions *competin'* and *makin'* in the quotation and stops at each. Choose S**k**ip to ignore these words.

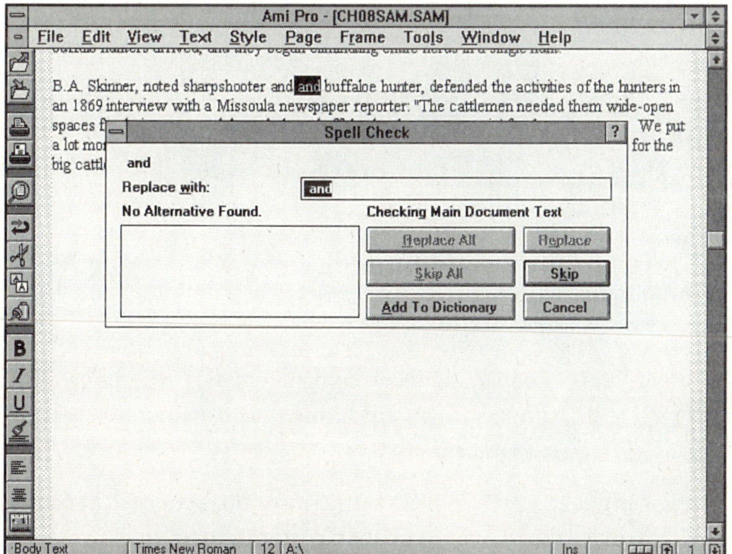

Fig. 7.5
The Spell Check dialog box.

The spell check now stops at the misspelled word *Buffaloe* in the header. Note that Ami Pro differentiates between words that begin with an initial capital letter and words that begin with a lowercase character. Thus, *Buffalo* and *buffalo* are stored as two distinctly different entries in the dictionary and are checked independently of each other. Select *Buffalo* from the alternatives list and choose R**e**place.

The spell check is complete. Ami Pro returns to the text of the sample document, leaving the insertion point at the last word checked (*Buffalo*).

Specifying a Dictionary

Tip
You can purchase dictionaries for other languages from Lotus Development Corporation, 1000 Abernathy Road, Atlanta, GA 30328 (1-800-831-9679).

Ami Pro comes with a main dictionary printed in the language of the country in which the program is sold, and a second (user) dictionary you can customize to meet your needs.

Ami Pro loads the main dictionary during the installation process. If you must specify the path for your dictionary (for example, if Ami Pro cannot find the dictionary when you start a spell check), or if you want to specify another dictionary, follow these steps:

1. Choose Too**l**s **S**pell Check. The Spell Check dialog box appears.

2. Choose **L**anguage Options. The Spell Check Language Options dialog box appears (see fig. 7.6).

Fig. 7.6
The Spell Check Language Options dialog box.

3. The cursor moves to the Language **P**ath text box. Type the path name (directory and any subdirectories) where the dictionary you want is stored; for example, type **C:\AMIPRO**.

4. In the Default Language for **N**ew Documents list box, choose the language of the dictionary you want to use for future documents. For this example, choose `American`.

5. In the Language for **C**urrent Document list box, choose the language of the dictionary you want to use for the current document. Again, for this example, choose `American`.

6. Choose OK or press Enter. The Spell Check Language Options box closes.

7. Choose OK or press Enter to close the Spell Check dialog box.

Editing the User Dictionary

As you learned earlier in this chapter, you can add words to a separate user dictionary as you perform a spell check, making those words available for future spell checks. You also can edit the user dictionary, adding new words or deleting unwanted words as necessary.

To edit the user dictionary, follow these steps:

1. Choose Too**l**s **S**pell Check.

2. Choose Edit **D**ictionary. Ami Pro displays the contents of the user dictionary in a separate window (see fig. 7.7). This window displays all numbers, symbols, capitalized words, and lowercase words you added to the user dictionary.

   If you spell checked the sample document earlier and added the word *dadgum* to the user dictionary, that word is listed, along with any other words you added during spell checks.

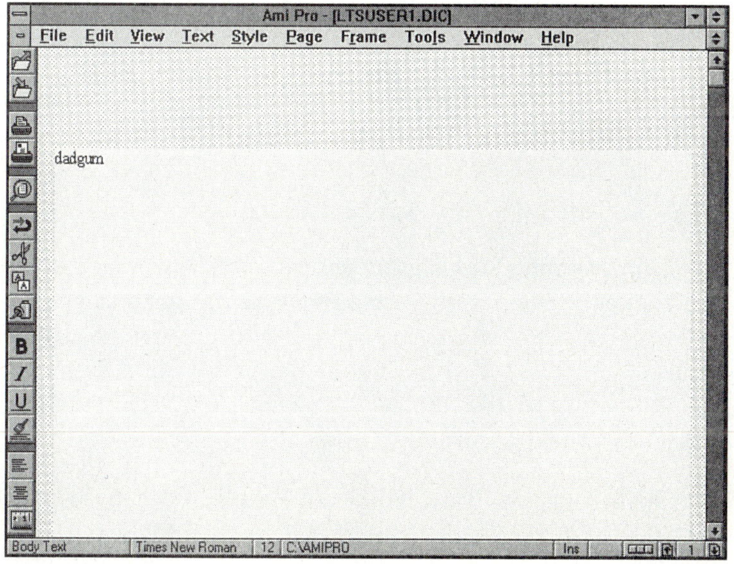

Fig. 7.7
The user dictionary.

3. To add new words to the list, move the insertion point to the beginning of the first available (blank) line. Type the word you want to add and press Enter. The insertion point moves to the next line. Repeat this step for each new word you want to add to the user dictionary, entering only one word per line.

4. To delete an unwanted word from the user dictionary, select the word and press Del to remove the word from the list. Repeat this step for any other unwanted words.

5. Save the updated user dictionary by making the user dictionary the active window and choosing **F**ile **S**ave. Ami Pro saves the updated dictionary and re-sorts all entries to reflect the changes you made.

6. To leave the user dictionary window, choose **F**ile **C**lose. Ami Pro closes the window.

In most cases, you don't need to edit the dictionary beyond adding words during a spell check.

Using an Expanded Dictionary

Ami Pro enables you to supplement the main dictionary with an expanded dictionary that contains medical and scientific terms. You can purchase the expanded dictionary from Lotus Development Corporation, 1000 Abernathy Road, Atlanta, GA 30328 (1-800-831-9679). You install the expanded dictionary with the Ami Pro Install program. Then you can spell check your document, using the Too**l**s **S**pell Check command as you normally would.

Using Grammar Check

Tip
Grammar checking doesn't eliminate the need for proofreading, but reduces the amount of proofreading you need to do.

In Ami Pro, you can proofread a document for correct grammar and use of language. The program examines each sentence in the document and determines whether the text conforms to various grammar, style, usage, and punctuation rules. If a sentence appears to break one or more of these rules, the Grammar Checker dialog box displays the sentence that contains the error and suggestions for its revision.

You can customize the grammar check by specifying grammar rule and style options to meet your specific needs. For example, you can disable rules that don't apply to your writing style, or specify options for finding errors such as split infinitives.

Checking the Document

After you spell check the document and correct any misspelled words, you can use the grammar check to check the grammar, usage, style, and punctuation of sentences in your document.

To check grammar in a document, follow these steps:

1. Make the document you want to check the active document and move the insertion point to the location where you want to begin the grammar check. For this example, position the insertion point anywhere in the main document text of the sample document. (Remember that the last spell check exercise left the insertion point in the header of the sample document.)

2. Choose Too**l**s **G**rammar Check or click the Grammar Check SmartIcon (it looks like a book with *G* on the cover). The Grammar Check dialog box appears (see fig. 7.8).

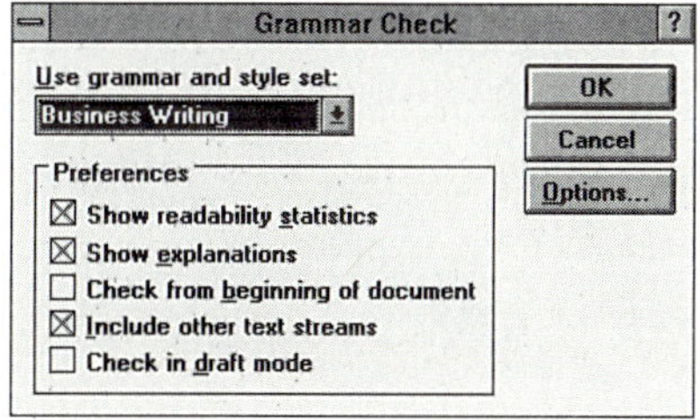

Fig. 7.8
The Grammar Check dialog box.

3. If you want, choose a writing style option from the **U**se Grammar and Style Set list box. For this example, choose `Business Writing`.

4. If you want, choose other options. For this example, choose Show Readability **S**tatistics, Show **E**xplanations, and **I**nclude Other Text Streams. (These options are discussed following these steps.)

5. Choose **O**ptions to review and choose additional grammar check options. The Grammar and Style Options dialog box appears (see fig. 7.9).

   For this example, leave the default settings for the Gra**m**mar Rules, St**y**le Rules, and **W**ord Order Rules options. (These options are discussed following these steps.)

6. Choose OK or press Enter to close the Grammar and Style Options dialog box.

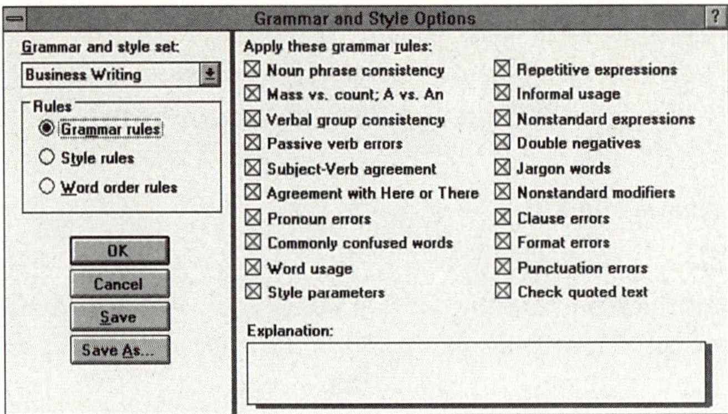

Fig. 7.9
The Grammar and Style Options dialog box.

7. To start the grammar check, choose OK or press Enter in the Grammar Check dialog box.

The following options are available in the Grammar Check dialog box:

- *Show Readability **S**tatistics*. Use this option to display the Readability Statistics box. The Readability Statistics box shows the number of characters, words, sentences, and paragraphs in the text, as well as several standard measurements of the readability of the document.

- *Show **E**xplanations*. Use this option to display an explanation of any highlighted rule.

- *Check From **B**eginning of Document*. Use this option to search through the entire main document text stream, regardless of the location of the insertion point in the main document text. Deselect this option if you want the search to start from the current position of the insertion point.

- ***I**nclude Other Text Streams*. Use this option to search the main document text and all other lower-priority streams in the grammar check. If the insertion point is located in a text stream other than the main document text, this option is selected automatically.

- *Check in **D**raft Mode*. Use this option to allow sentences that span columns or pages to appear in their entirety during the grammar check.

The following options are available in the Grammar and Style Options dialog box:

- *Gra**m**mar Rules*. Use this option to specify the basic grammar rules, usage, and punctuation the grammar check should use to check the grammar in the document.

- *Style Rules*. Use this option to specify a particular writing style to check the effectiveness of sentences and word choice. Ami Pro offers eight levels of grammar checking: Business Writing, All Rules, Legal Writing, Technical Writing, Fiction Writing, Academic Writing, Format Writing, and Casual Writing.

- ***W**ord Order Rules*. Use this option to check sentences that contain split infinitives, consecutive nouns, and prepositional phrases.

After making your choices, you are ready to make corrections to the errors in grammar or style in your document.

Making Corrections

When Grammar Check locates a grammar or style error in a sentence, the program highlights the sentence in the document and displays it in the Sentence box of the Grammar Checker dialog box. An explanation of the grammar rule appears in the **S**uggestions list box. Ami Pro displays the error in the sentence in red on a color monitor and in boldface on a monochrome monitor. At this point, you can decide whether to correct the sentence or ignore it. Figure 7.10 shows this new version of the Grammar Checker dialog box, displaying the first grammar error in the sample document. Notice that the Sentence box highlights and displays the sentence.

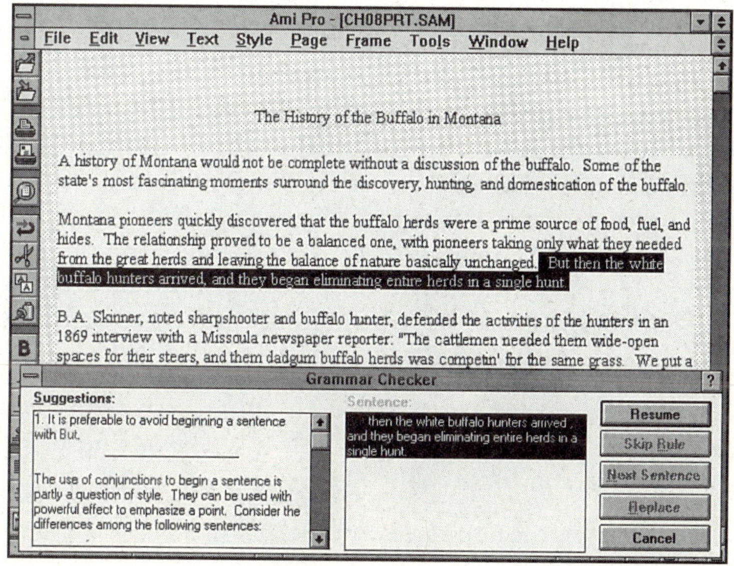

Fig. 7.10
The Grammar Checker dialog box displays the highlighted sentence in the Sentence text box.

After Ami Pro locates a sentence that may contain a grammar or style error, you can choose any of the following actions:

- If you don't want to change the text, choose Resume.
- *Skip **R**ule.* If several correct sentences fall under the same rule, choose Skip **R**ule. Ami Pro ignores the rule that appears in the **S**uggestions list box (and similar rules within a group of grammar or style rules) for the rest of the document.
- ***N**ext Sentence.* If you want to skip the rest of the errors in this sentence, choose **N**ext Sentence. Ami Pro skips the current suggestion in the **S**uggestions list box and checks the following sentence.
- ***R**eplace.* If the sentence is incorrect, choose **R**eplace to replace the incorrect sentence with the suggested sentence. Ami Pro executes the suggestion that appears in the **S**uggestions list box and changes the sentence. If the **R**eplace button is unavailable, press Alt+F6 or click the document to activate the document; make the changes to the sentence in the document, and then choose Resume to continue checking grammar.

In the sample grammar check, Ami Pro finds a sentence that begins with the conjunction *But* and displays the sentence in the Sentence box. To correct the sentence, press Alt+F6 or click the document to move to the document. To delete the word *But* in the highlighted sentence, double-click the word and press Del, and then change the *t* in *then* to a capital *T*. Finally, choose Resume to continue the grammar check.

After you choose Resume, the grammar check locates the next sentence that contains a potential punctuation error. The opening quotation mark appears at the beginning of the highlighted sentence and the closing quotation mark appears at the end of the next sentence. Because the grammar check looks at only one sentence at a time, the program didn't find the closing quotation mark at the end of the next sentence. Choose Skip **R**ule to ignore the rule for matching quotation marks for this sentence and the rest of the document.

After you finish responding to the grammar checks, the Readability Statistics dialog box appears and displays the number of characters, words, sentences, and paragraphs in the text, as well as several standard measurements of the readability of the document (see fig. 7.11).

Choose Close to close the Readability Statistics dialog box and return to the document.

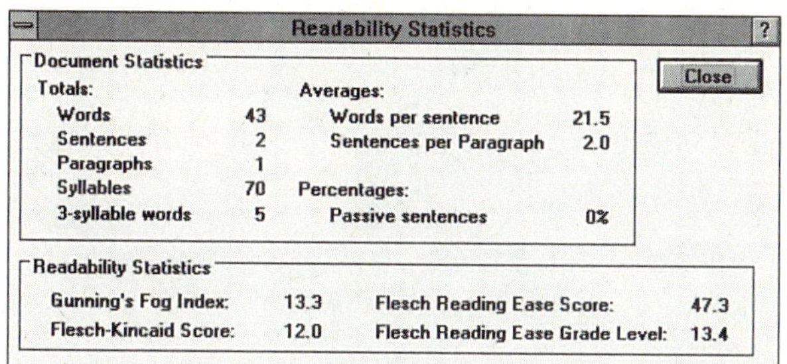

Fig. 7.11
The Readability Statistics dialog box.

The grammar check is complete. Ami Pro returns to the text of the sample document, leaving the insertion point at the last sentence checked.

If the Grammar Check feature finds inappropriate word usages, you may need to substitute synonyms that improve the readability of the text. In these situations, Ami Pro's thesaurus is a handy feature, as described in the next section.

Tip
As with many other Ami Pro defaults, the settings for the Grammar Check options from the last Grammar Check session remain in effect each time you begin a Grammar Check operation.

Using the Thesaurus

You may be accustomed to using a printed thesaurus to help you find synonyms for words. An electronic thesaurus is faster than a printed thesaurus. Besides providing synonyms, the Ami Pro thesaurus provides definitions and enables you to place a selected synonym directly into a document. The Ami Pro thesaurus contains 1,400,000 definitions, variations, and synonyms for 40,000 root words.

To look up a word in Ami Pro's electronic thesaurus, follow these steps:

1. Select the word you want to find (or place the insertion point on the word). *Select only one word.* If you select more than one, the thesaurus looks up only the first word. Figure 7.12 shows the word `parlance` selected in a sample document named BLUE.SAM.

2. Choose Too**l**s **T**hesaurus or click the Thesaurus SmartIcon (it looks like a blue block with the letter *T*). The Thesaurus dialog box appears, as shown in figure 7.12.

The following information is displayed in the dialog box:

- The Word Looked Up section shows the word you selected in the document.

- The Meaning **V**ariations list box lists various shades of meaning of the word in the Word Looked Up section.
- The **M**eaning text box displays the definition of the term selected in the Meaning **V**ariations box.
- The **S**ynonyms list box lists alternate words you can use for the selected term in the Meaning **V**ariations list box.
- The Replace **W**ith text box shows the synonym you select from the **S**ynonyms or Meaning **V**ariations list box. You also can choose Replace **W**ith and type your own term in the text box (for example, if you think of a useful term and want to use **L**ookup and other capabilities in the dialog box to analyze the word).

To find a substitute for the selected word, move the highlight over the terms in the Meaning **V**ariations and **S**ynonyms list boxes. If you see a synonym you want to use, highlight that synonym in the **S**ynonyms or the Meaning **V**ariations list box. (The word you highlight also appears in the Replace **W**ith text box.) Figure 7.12 shows the word *phraseology* selected.

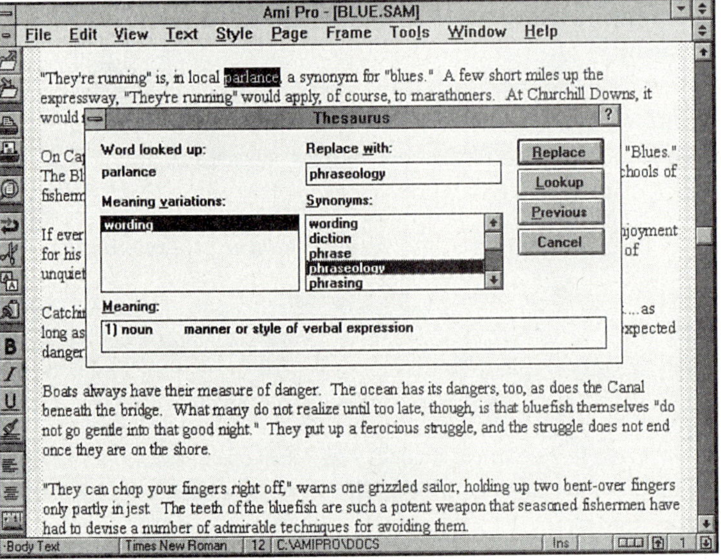

Fig. 7.12
The Thesaurus dialog box.

Choose the **L**ookup button if you want to see definitions in the **M**eaning text box for the terms in the Meaning **V**ariations list box.

If you don't see a synonym you want to use when scrolling through the **S**ynonyms and Meaning **V**ariations list boxes, choose Cancel or press Esc to return to the document.

Another way to look up a term—even if that term isn't shown in the **S**ynonyms list box—is to type the term in the Replace **W**ith text box and choose **L**ookup. Ami Pro displays the definition in the **M**eaning text box.

If you want to go back to the word last shown, choose **P**revious. The previous word appears in the Replace **W**ith, Meaning **V**ariations, and **S**ynonyms boxes. The definition appears in the **M**eaning box.

When the synonym you want to use is displayed in the Replace **W**ith text box, choose OK or press Enter. Ami Pro replaces the selected word in the text with the selected word from the Thesaurus dialog box.

Printing Documents

In most cases, your work with a document is not complete until you print the document. In Ami Pro (as in other word processing software), you install a printer when you install the program. If you don't change the printer, and you are satisfied with the results you get when you print, you can simply print a document without worrying about setup.

Often, though, you may need to change printers or change requirements for the current printer. Perhaps you want draft-quality printing sometimes and letter-quality printing at other times. You may want to print *landscape style* (the wide part of the page at the top) rather than the usual *portrait style* (the narrow part at the top).

In the following section, you learn how to set up the printer and its options.

Changing the Printer Setup

Microsoft Windows controls the printer; you specify how you want Windows to handle the necessary setup options such as paper size, printer cartridges, and optional soft fonts. For this purpose, you use several dialog boxes.

To select the printer you want to use, choose **F**ile Prin**t**er Setup. The Select Printer dialog box appears (see fig. 7.13).

The **P**rinter for This Document list box displays the different types of printers available. (If the printer you need doesn't appear on the list, you may not have installed the correct printer during installation of Windows, or the correct printer driver may not be available. For information on printer drivers, consult your Windows documentation.)

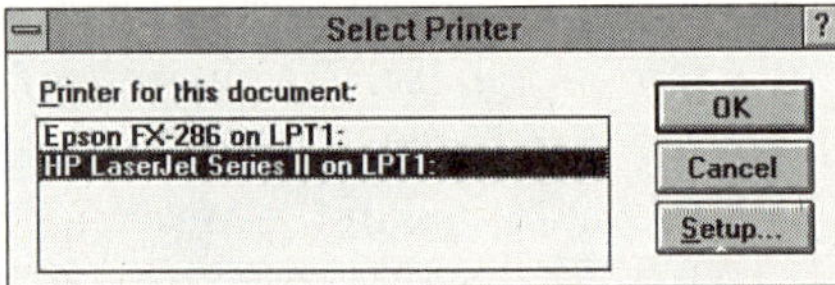

Fig. 7.13
The Select Printer dialog box.

To specify the setup options for the selected printer, choose **S**etup. The dialog box that appears specifies the setup options for the selected printer, and the Title Bar of the dialog box displays the name of the selected printer (see fig. 7.14).

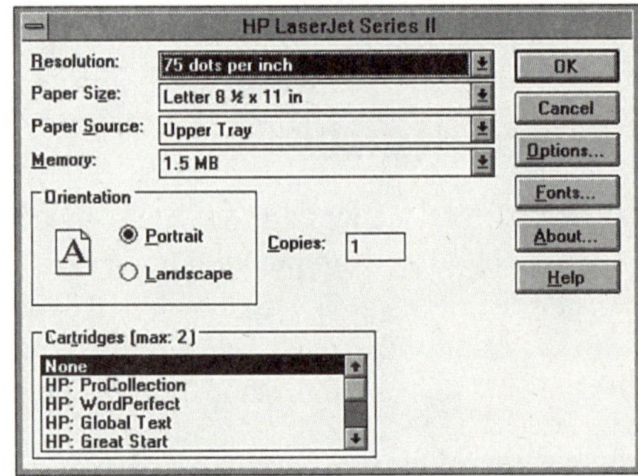

Fig. 7.14
The printer setup dialog box for a laser printer.

The printer setup dialog box varies for different types of printers. For a dot-matrix printer, for example, the dialog box displays dot-matrix printer setup options. If you use a laser printer, the setup options for a laser printer appear. The example in fig. 7.14 displays laser printer options.

Help usually is available in this dialog box. Choose **H**elp; the type of printer you selected is listed at the top of the resulting Help window (see fig. 7.15).

The Help dialog box provides help for every selection in the printer setup dialog box. Using the index, browsing, and moving from one topic to the next work the same as these features in any other Windows Help dialog box. (See Chapter 1, "Getting Acquainted with Ami Pro," for complete instructions on using a Help dialog box.) To exit the Help dialog box and return to the printer setup dialog box, press Esc or choose **C**lose from the Control Menu of the Help window.

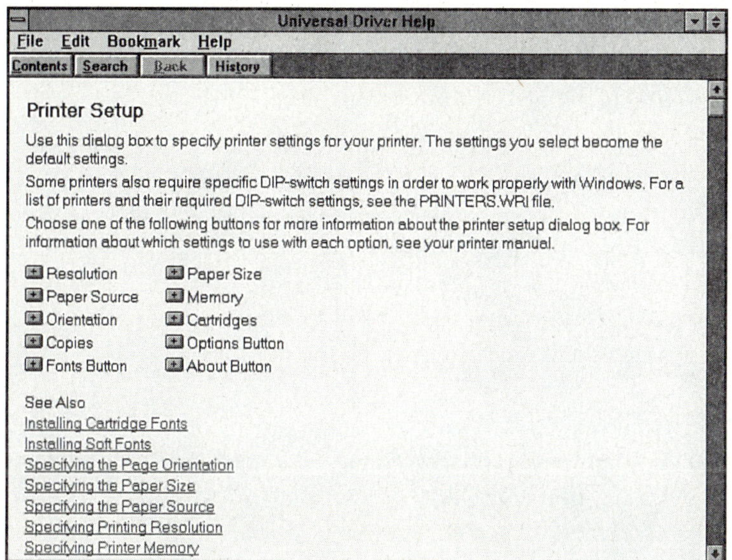

Fig. 7.15
The Help dialog box for a printer driver.

As necessary, modify the options for paper source, paper size, and so on in the printer setup dialog box. (Choosing some of the buttons in the dialog box accesses additional dialog boxes where you can specify more setup options.) Keep in mind the following items as you specify the printer setup:

- When you change printer setup options, you affect the current document and all documents subsequently printed on that printer. You also affect other Windows programs using that printer.

- To use landscape orientation, you must change the Windows printer setup *and* change Ami Pro's page layout (to landscape orientation) and paragraph style (to a landscape font) for *all* documents with landscape pages. If a document uses both portrait and landscape orientation, you must insert a page layout and change the orientation to accommodate landscape or portrait orientation. See Chapter 5, "Working with Page Layout," for instructions on inserting page layouts and changing the orientation.

- If you change the graphics resolution setting, keep in mind that the more dots per inch (dpi) you choose, the better the printout.

- If you specify Cartridges, you can select only cartridges you installed in the printer. Choosing a cartridge that isn't installed doesn't give you the fonts you want, but probably prints Courier.

- To use Ami Pro's Adobe Type Manager soft fonts, you must specify the fonts, using the **T**ext **F**ont command. See Chapter 4, "Formatting a Document," for instructions on specifying fonts.

- If you want to install new soft fonts, consult your soft font vendor's instructions or technical support department. (*Soft fonts* are special software fonts—not cartridges—that you can download to a printer, usually a laser printer.)

After you specify your printer setup, you can choose printer options for the current document and print the document.

Printing the Document

After you select and set up the printer, you can specify print options such as number of copies, page range to be printed, and items to include in the printing, such as pictures and notes. Then you can print the document.

To choose print options and print a document, follow these steps:

1. Choose **F**ile **P**rint, click the Print Document SmartIcon, or press Ctrl+P. The Print dialog box appears (see fig. 7.16).

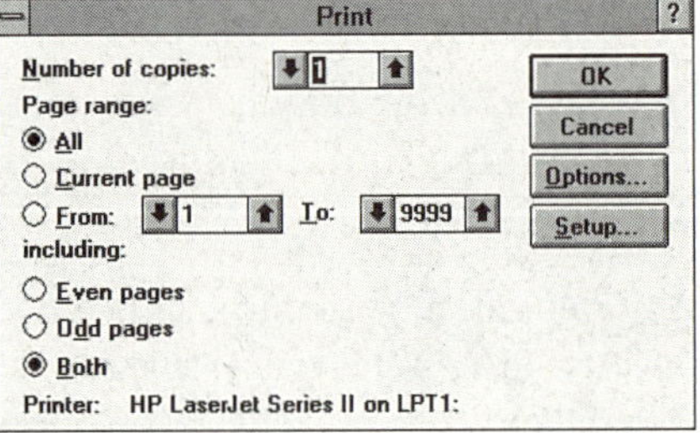

Fig. 7.16
The Print dialog box.

   Ami Pro displays the name of the selected printer and port in the lower left corner of the Print dialog box. You selected this printer when you last used the printer setup. To change the printer, exit the dialog box, choose **F**ile Prin**t**er Setup, select a different printer, and change the setup options as necessary. To change the printer options for the current printer, select the **S**etup button in the Print dialog box and change the setup options as necessary.

2. Specify the **N**umber of Copies you want. Type the number in the box provided or use the arrow buttons to select the desired number. For the sample document, specify two copies.

3. Specify the page range you want to print. To print the entire document, choose **A**ll. To print only a range of pages (for example, pages 1 to 3 or 5 to 8), choose **F**rom to specify the beginning page number in the text box and **T**o to specify the ending page number. For the sample document, choose **A**ll.

4. Specify the type of pages (left, right, or both) you want to print. Choose **B**oth to print even-numbered (left-hand) and odd-numbered (right-hand) pages. Choose **E**ven Pages to print only even-numbered (left-hand) pages. Choose O**d**d Pages to print only odd-numbered (right-hand) pages. For the sample document, choose **B**oth.

5. To review and choose print options and printer bin options, choose **O**ptions. The Print Options dialog box appears, as shown in figure 7.17. (A description of the options in the dialog box follows these steps.)

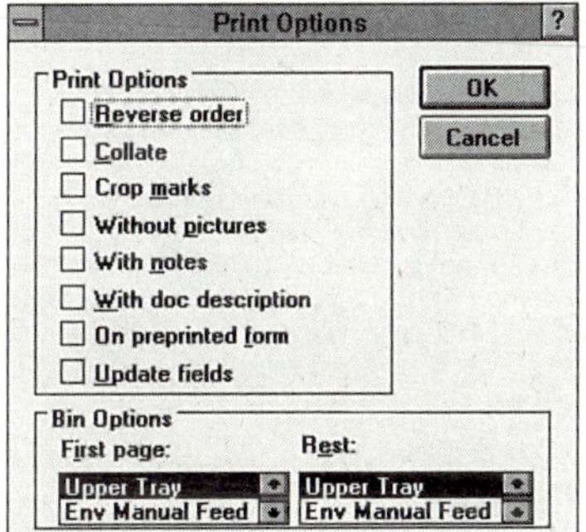

Fig. 7.17
The Print Options dialog box.

6. After you finish selecting print options, choose OK or press Enter to return to the Print dialog box.

7. To print the document, choose OK or press Enter.

   Ami Pro displays a message that indicates the document is printing. This message remains on-screen until the entire document is sent to the printer. Figure 7.18 shows the printed document.

The following options are available in the Print Options dialog box for times when your printing needs require special document handling:

- ***R**everse Order.* Prints the document in reverse order (last page prints first).

- *Collate*. Prints the entire document before printing another copy. If you request more than one copy in the Print dialog box and don't choose this option, Ami Pro prints the requested number of copies for page 1, for page 2, and so on. This option collates each copy of the document for you. Note that printing collated is slower than printing uncollated.
- *Crop Marks*. Prints *crop marks* (marks you can use for trimming the page) 1/2 inch outside the document margins.
- *Without Pictures*. Prints only document text; if any frames in the document contain pictures, the frames print as empty frames. The document prints faster if you use this option.

Fig. 7.18 The printed document.

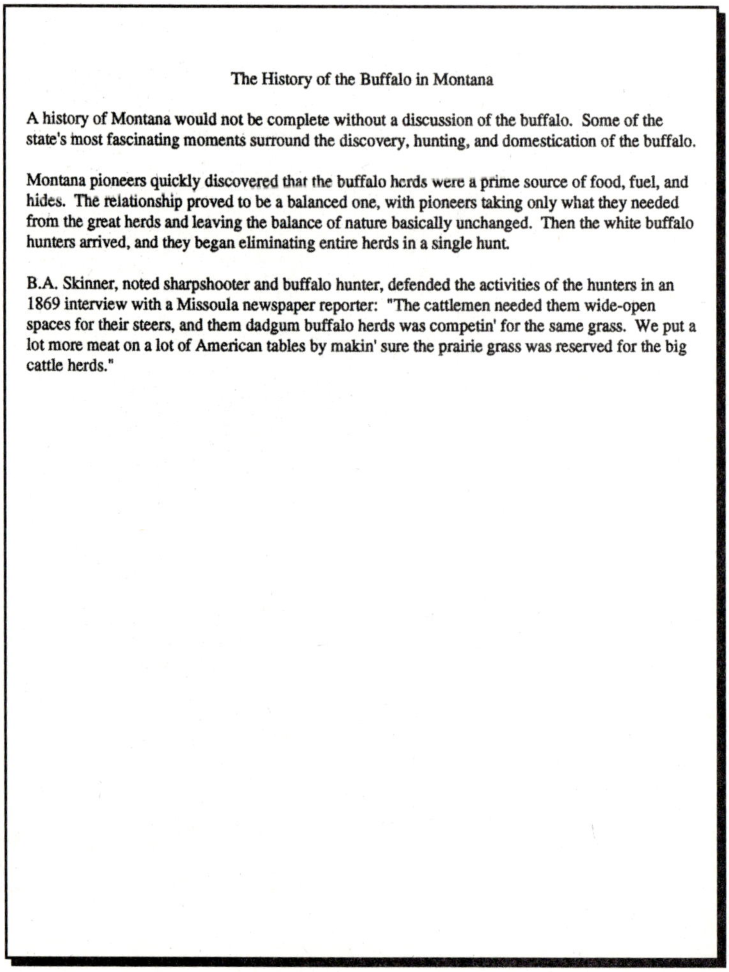

The History of the Buffalo in Montana

A history of Montana would not be complete without a discussion of the buffalo. Some of the state's most fascinating moments surround the discovery, hunting, and domestication of the buffalo.

Montana pioneers quickly discovered that the buffalo herds were a prime source of food, fuel, and hides. The relationship proved to be a balanced one, with pioneers taking only what they needed from the great herds and leaving the balance of nature basically unchanged. Then the white buffalo hunters arrived, and they began eliminating entire herds in a single hunt.

B.A. Skinner, noted sharpshooter and buffalo hunter, defended the activities of the hunters in an 1869 interview with a Missoula newspaper reporter: "The cattlemen needed them wide-open spaces for their steers, and them dadgum buffalo herds was competin' for the same grass. We put a lot more meat on a lot of American tables by makin' sure the prairie grass was reserved for the big cattle herds."

- *With **N**otes*. If the document contains notes, this option prints the initials at the location of each note within the main text. The text of all the notes prints at the end of the document.
- ***W**ith Doc Description*. Prints the document description as the cover page for the document if you used the document description feature to identify the document.
- *On Preprinted **F**orm*. Prints the document on a preprinted form. Ami Pro doesn't print protected text or lines and shading for frames and tables.
- ***U**pdate Fields*. If the document contains any power fields, Ami Pro prints the information referenced by those fields. (See Chapter 24, "Creating Smart Documents with Power Fields," for an explanation of power fields.)
- *Bin Options*. In this section of the dialog box, you indicate which printer bin you want to use for the F**i**rst Page of the document (such as letterhead) and for the R**e**st of the document.

To cut down the amount of time the print message remains on-screen while a document is printing, choose the Print in **B**ackground option in the User Setup dialog box (choose Too**l**s **U**ser Setup to access the dialog box). See Chapter 8, "Changing Your Setup," for more information.

Note

You can easily print an envelope by selecting **F**ile Print Envelope. Ami Pro will select the text that looks like the format of an address and prompt you through the dialog boxes for additional information like Return Address. Print Envelope Options include choices such as determining if there is an envelope feeder installed on the printer or choosing the orientation of the envelope or the feed position of the envelope. If the default layout doesn't work, you can choose the adjust button in the Options dialog box. Then adjust either the return address or the recipient's address.

Summary

In this chapter, you learned how to use Spell Check and Grammar Check to proofread the document. You explored the possibilities for enhancing the word usage of a document with the Thesaurus. You also learned how to set up the printer to accommodate your special printing considerations, choose print options such as the number of copies, and print an Ami Pro document.

◄ See "Modifying Fonts," p. 96

◄ See "Setting Size and Orientation," p. 130

The next chapter explains how to change your Ami Pro setup for everything from the default directory for storing your documents to setting up a macro to run when you load or exit the program.

Chapter 8

Changing Your Setup

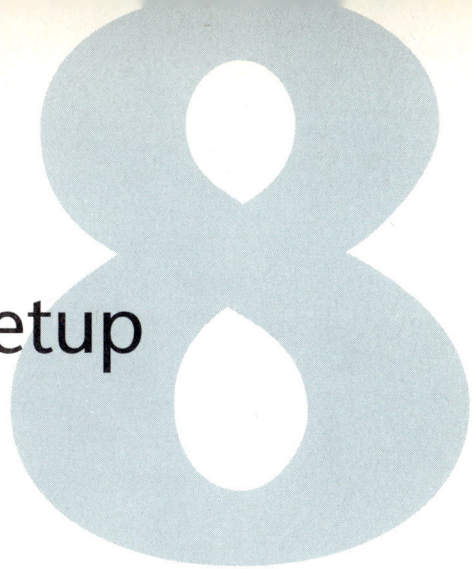

When working with a new software program, you may be tempted to get started quickly and not spend much time setting up. Developing a sense of what you need before you spend much time on setup probably is a good idea, but setting up the software in such a way that it perfectly suits your purposes can save time. Changing the location of the SmartIcons palette, for example, may not sound like a timesaver, but moving the palette near the area where you work on-screen (instead of moving across the screen repeatedly to reach the palette) can be important if you repeat the operation 50, 100, or 500 times daily.

Ami Pro makes changing your defaults easy; nowhere is the software's versatility more apparent than in the number of defaults Ami Pro enables you to set. Your working environment can be precisely what you want. Setting the defaults to suit your purposes can save time and make your work more efficient.

In this chapter, you learn about Ami Pro's many default settings. You begin by learning how to set up SmartIcons and position them on-screen. You can customize the SmartIcons so that the SmartIcons you use most often appear as you work. You can even create your own SmartIcons and attach macros to them. This chapter also explains how to activate program defaults when you work in Ami Pro, and the effect those defaults have; for example, whether you have automatic backups and how many previous actions you are able to undo.

Certain default settings apply to documents—such as how Ami Pro handles hyphenation, and whether *widows* and *orphans* (single lines at the top and bottom of the page, respectively) are acceptable when you print. This chapter explains how to set all such document defaults.

Other default settings apply to paths. Ami Pro uses default paths as you work—paths for the document, for example, and for macros. You can save time by setting defaults that correspond with the paths you use most. This chapter details how to set default paths.

You also learn how to make the default settings take effect when you load a document; for example, defaults such as the view Ami Pro uses initially and whether the Styles box is visible. Finally, you learn how to set view preferences. These settings control such features as whether margins appear in color in layout mode and whether pictures are visible on-screen.

Setting Up SmartIcons

Ami Pro gives you a choice: you can display or not display the SmartIcons. If the SmartIcons are on-screen, you can place them on the left side of the screen, the right, the top, or the bottom, or "floating" so that you can move them around as you want.

Displaying SmartIcons

Tip
You can toggle quickly between showing and hiding the SmartIcons by pressing Ctrl+Q.

You can display or hide a SmartIcon set in several ways. Using the Ami Pro menus, choose **V**iew Hide (Show) Smart**I**cons. When the SmartIcons are displayed, the menu choice is Hide Smart**I**cons. When the SmartIcons are hidden, the menu choice is Show Smart**I**cons.

The main reason to hide the SmartIcons is to create more room on-screen as you work. If you develop the habit of pressing Ctrl+Q to toggle between showing and hiding the SmartIcons, you have the advantage of using *floating* SmartIcons (with as many SmartIcons displayed as you want) that can be hidden to prevent blocking the text on-screen. On the other hand, the major advantage of SmartIcons is that you can save time by using the SmartIcons with one click of the mouse; hiding the SmartIcons defeats that purpose.

For more information on displaying SmartIcons, see the section "SmartIcon Sets," later in this chapter.

Positioning the Palette

Most of the time when you are working on text, you probably want Ami Pro to display SmartIcons on the left side of the screen. In this position, the SmartIcons don't compete with the menus (top), scroll bars (right and bottom), or Status Bar (bottom). Placing the SmartIcons is largely a matter of personal preference. If you are working with graphics, equations, or in one part of the screen, you may prefer to set up the SmartIcons near the area where you are working. If you are used to working with other Windows-based software products (such as Word for Windows) where the icons are automatically placed at the top of the screen just below the menu, you may want to place your SmartIcons at the top of the Ami Pro screen. With this placement, you don't need to think about the location of the SmartIcons when you want to use them; you move the mouse to the top of the screen as a habit.

To specify the position of the SmartIcons, choose Too**l**s Smart**I**cons. The SmartIcons dialog box appears (see fig. 8.1). In the **P**osition list box, you specify the desired position for the SmartIcons. The **P**osition options are Floating, Left, Right, Top, and Bottom.

If you choose Left, Right, Top, or Bottom, the SmartIcons appear along the specified side of the screen in a vertical or horizontal line. Figures 8.2 through 8.5 show the results of choosing each of these four options. Notice that the horizontal versions of the SmartIcon palette include six more SmartIcons than will fit in the vertical palettes.

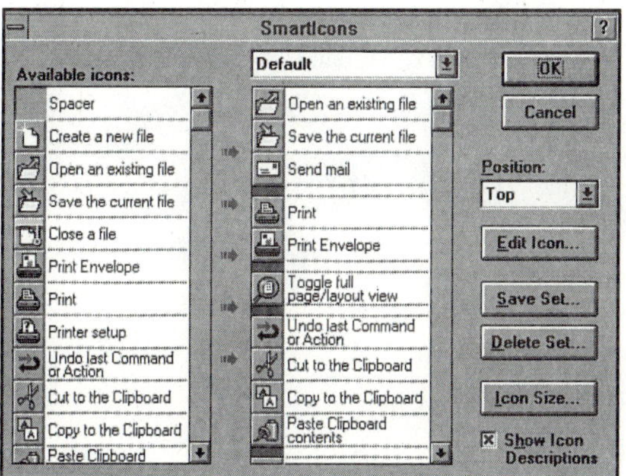

Fig. 8.1
The SmartIcons dialog box.

If you choose the Floating position, Ami Pro displays the SmartIcons as a rectangular palette, which first appears in the top left corner of the window. At the left side of the floating SmartIcons palette is a solid bar with a white square at the top. Clicking the white box with the mouse hides the floating palette. Selecting any other portion of the solid bar enables you to drag the palette anywhere on-screen. You also can resize and reshape the floating SmartIcon palette. If you point to the edge of the palette (the mouse pointer becomes a two-headed arrow), you can increase or decrease the palette size. The palette shows as many SmartIcons as will fit in the palette size you specify this way. Figure 8.6 shows a palette of floating SmartIcons, and figure 8.7 shows the palette expanded to a larger size.

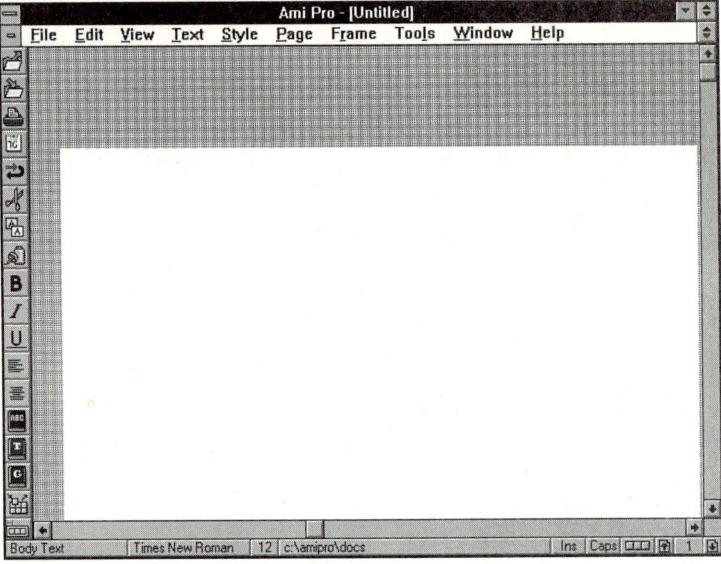

Fig. 8.2
SmartIcons displayed along the left side of the screen.

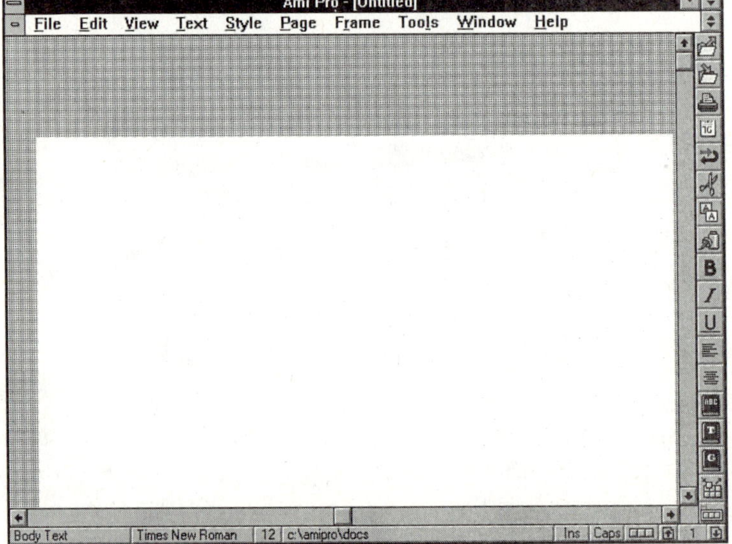

Fig. 8.3
SmartIcons displayed along the right side of the screen.

When you display the SmartIcons in any way other than floating, you see a limited number of SmartIcons (18 on a VGA display). When you switch to floating SmartIcons, you see all the SmartIcons that are in the current palette (as explained in the following section).

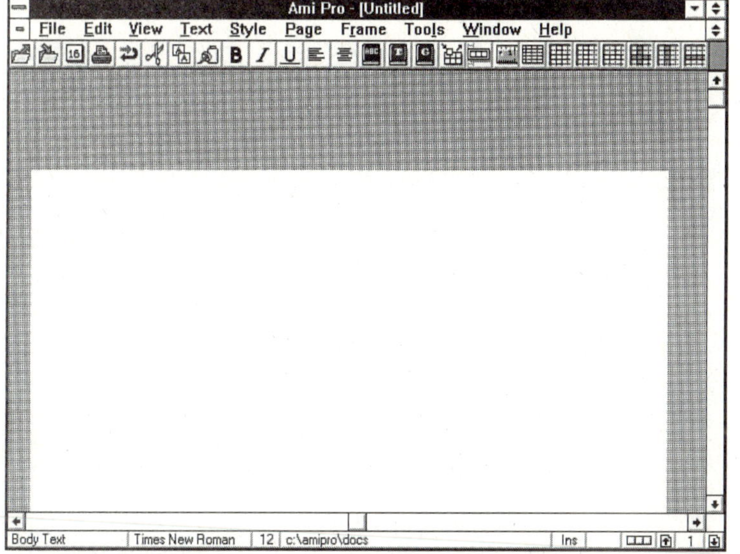

Fig. 8.4
SmartIcons displayed along the top of the screen.

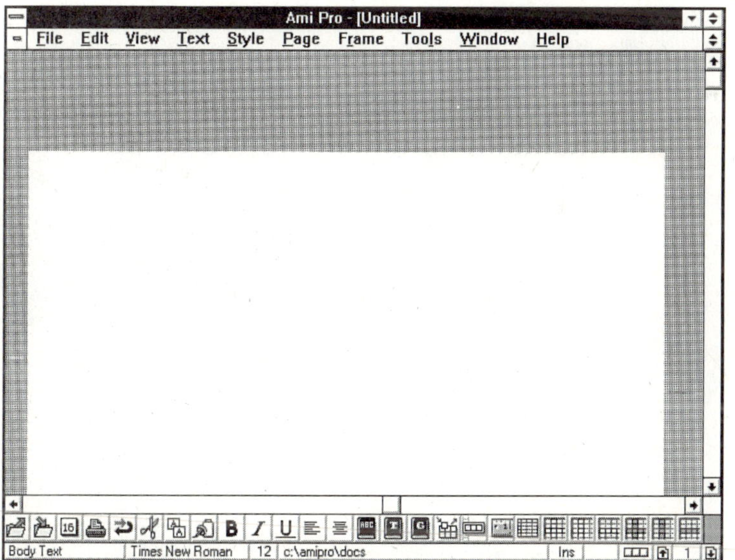

Fig. 8.5
SmartIcons displayed along the bottom of the screen.

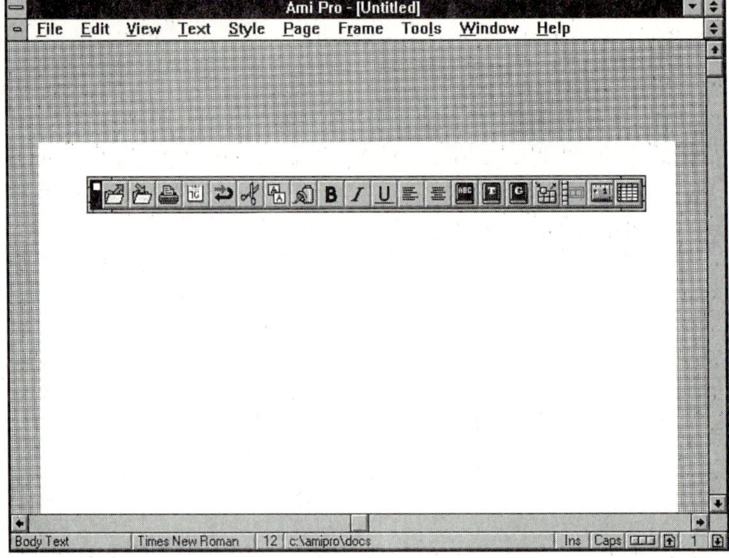

Fig. 8.6
An example of floating SmartIcons.

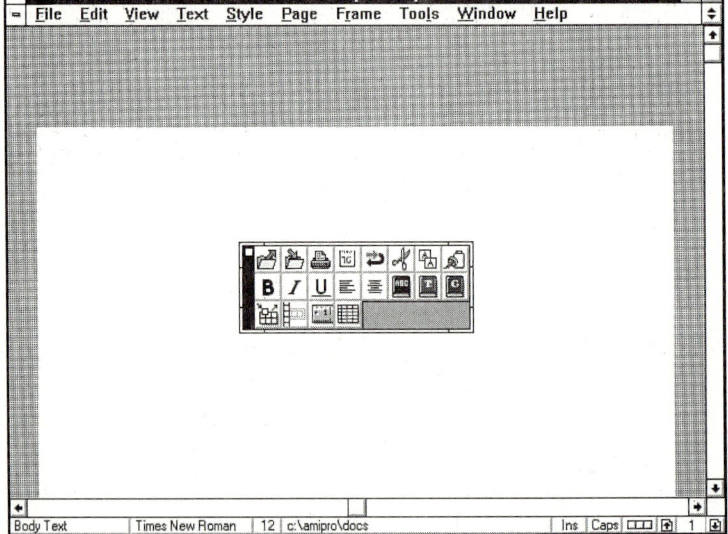

Fig. 8.7
The floating palette in a different shape.

Customizing the Palette

In addition to deciding when and where to display SmartIcons, you can specify the size of the SmartIcons, which SmartIcons you want to see, and the order in which you want to display them. When you begin using Ami Pro, you may not be certain which SmartIcons you need most. You may want to tinker with the palette until it meets your needs. Perhaps you create frames often and want to use the SmartIcon that adds a frame; or perhaps you want SmartIcons for find-and-replace operations, drawing, changing text to superscript, or toggling between outline and layout modes. You may even want to create sets of SmartIcons to be displayed when working on a particular type of document.

To customize the palette, access the SmartIcons dialog box (choose Too**l**s Smart**I**cons). The SmartIcons dialog box appears (refer to fig. 8.1).

Note

Just as you need a mouse to operate a SmartIcon, you need a mouse to drag a SmartIcon from one position to another in the SmartIcons dialog box. You can use the keyboard in the dialog box to select the buttons (OK, Cancel, **E**dit Icon, and so forth), and the **P**osition list, but you must use the mouse to move the SmartIcons.

In the SmartIcons dialog box, you choose the SmartIcons you want to display based on the activities you perform most. (Ami Pro's initial set of SmartIcons may suit your purposes well.) In the following sections, you learn how to use the SmartIcons dialog box to customize the palette by changing the order of SmartIcons, adding and removing SmartIcons, and creating custom SmartIcons and SmartIcon sets.

The SmartIcons dialog box has two list boxes containing SmartIcons and their descriptions. The list box on the left contains all available SmartIcons—those currently in use and any stored in BMP files in the \AMIPRO\ICONS directory. The list box on the right shows the SmartIcons that make up the active set. Initially, the current SmartIcons set is displayed. You can display any SmartIcon set by choosing its name from the drop-down list box at the top of the dialog box.

Changing the Order of SmartIcons

You can change the order of the SmartIcons without changing which ones appear. In the active palette section of the SmartIcons dialog box (the list box on the right), point to the SmartIcon whose position you want to change. Drag the SmartIcon so that it covers the icon that will follow it in the active palette section. The other SmartIcons adjust to make room for the repositioned SmartIcon.

Adding and Removing SmartIcons

To add SmartIcons to the palette, point to the SmartIcon you want in the Available Icons section of the SmartIcons dialog box. Drag the SmartIcon to the desired position in the active palette section. The other SmartIcons in the active palette section move to make room for the new SmartIcon, keeping the same columnar order.

Note

You can add as many SmartIcons to the current palette as will fit, even using all the available SmartIcons if you want.

When you add a SmartIcon to the active palette, Ami Pro copies the SmartIcon from the Available Icons section of the dialog box. The Available Icons palette never changes; you can create multiple SmartIcon sets containing many of the same SmartIcons.

To remove a SmartIcon from the active palette, point to the SmartIcon you want to remove in the active palette section and drag the SmartIcon to the Available Icons section, or just drag it out of the active palette section.

Adding and Removing Spacers

Ami Pro provides solid rectangles called *spacers* for use in grouping SmartIcons on the SmartIcons palette. (Figure 8.1 shows the spacer icon at the top of the Available Icons list.) Spacers are added to and removed from the palette in the same way as other SmartIcons. You may need to add multiple spacers to achieve a desired visual effect.

Tip
To use the custom SmartIcon procedure described in this section, you must be familiar with Ami Pro macros (see Chapter 23, "Using Macros").

Creating Custom SmartIcons

You can create a custom SmartIcon of your own and assign a macro to it—in fact, you can create as many custom SmartIcons as you want. You can create a SmartIcon that places your logo at the top of a document, for example, or one that deletes all instances in the document where you have two carriage returns in a row.

Many useful macros come with Ami Pro. If you use a macro often, create a SmartIcon for it and add that SmartIcon to your current palette. If you create your own macro, give it the same name as the SmartIcon drawing for easy identification. Macros have the extension SMM, and drawings have the extension SDW.

Ami Pro includes many bitmap icons that you can use to create new SmartIcon designs. Using an existing SmartIcon is probably the easiest way to create a custom SmartIcon. To use this technique, follow these steps:

1. Record and save (in the \AMIPRO\MACROS directory) the macro that will be associated with the SmartIcon.

2. From the SmartIcons dialog box, choose **E**dit Icon. The Edit SmartIcon dialog box appears (see fig. 8.8).

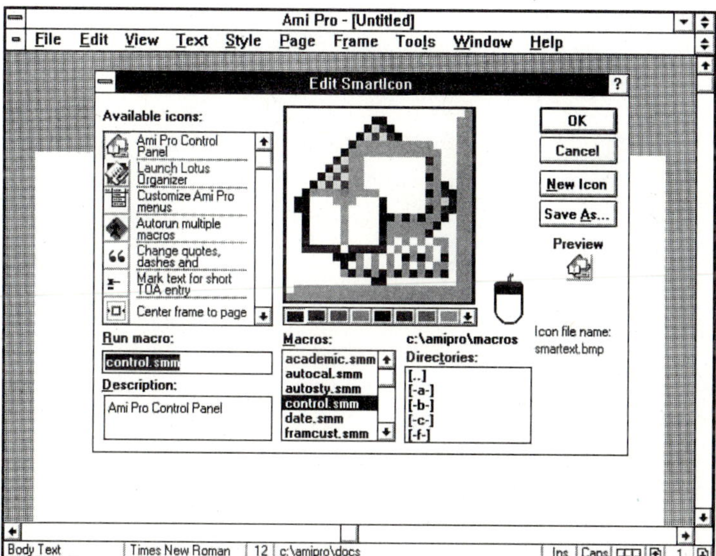

Fig. 8.8
The Edit SmartIcon dialog box.

3. Scroll through the Available Icons list until you find a SmartIcon similar to the one you want to create, and click that SmartIcon. If it isn't one of the standard Ami Pro SmartIcons, it appears in the bitmap edit box (to the right of the Available Icons list); otherwise, the program prompts you to save the image in a new file before you can alter it.

4. Make the desired changes by selecting colors from the color bar and using the mouse to click different squares in the bitmap edit box.

5. From the **M**acros list box, choose the macro to be associated with the SmartIcon. The macro file name appears in the **R**un Macro text box.

6. In the **D**escription text box, enter a description of the SmartIcon's function.

7. Select Save **A**s or **N**ew Icon. In either case, the Save As a New SmartIcon dialog box appears.

8. Type a file name and choose OK or press Enter. The new SmartIcon is added to the Available Icons list along with its description.

> **Note**
>
> You can create a bitmap from scratch by using AmiDraw or Windows Paintbrush to create a picture. If you are using a VGA display adapter, the ideal drawing size is 21 by 21 pixels; if you use another size, Ami Pro scales the picture for you. (See Chapter 17, "Using the Draw Feature," for more information on drawing.)

You can now add this SmartIcon to any existing SmartIcon set, or build a new SmartIcon set around it.

Using SmartIcon Sets

Rather than having a comprehensive SmartIcon palette, you may prefer to create palettes that are task- or document-oriented. Ami Pro provides seven preconfigured SmartIcon sets for you to use. All contain common word processing functions (such as **F**ile **O**pen, **F**ile **S**ave, Cu**t**, and **P**aste) and add other functions based on type of document or Ami Pro task (graphics, tables, and so on).

To see the SmartIcons available in each predefined SmartIcon set, activate the SmartIcons dialog box (choose Too**l**s Smart**I**cons) and select the name of the desired SmartIcon set from the name list box (see fig. 8.9). The SmartIcons in the selected set appear in the active palette list box. Use the scroll bar to view each SmartIcon and its description.

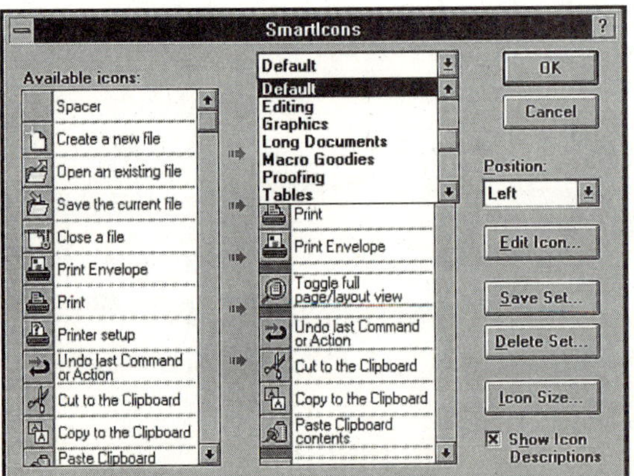

Fig. 8.9
The drop-down list of available SmartIcon sets.

To create a SmartIcon set, follow these steps:

1. Select Too**l**s Smart**I**cons. The SmartIcons dialog box appears.
2. Select a SmartIcon set to use as a base for the new set.
3. Remove the SmartIcons you don't need, and (if necessary) replace them with new ones from the Available Icons list.
4. Select Save **S**et. The Save Set of SmartIcons dialog box appears (see fig. 8.10).

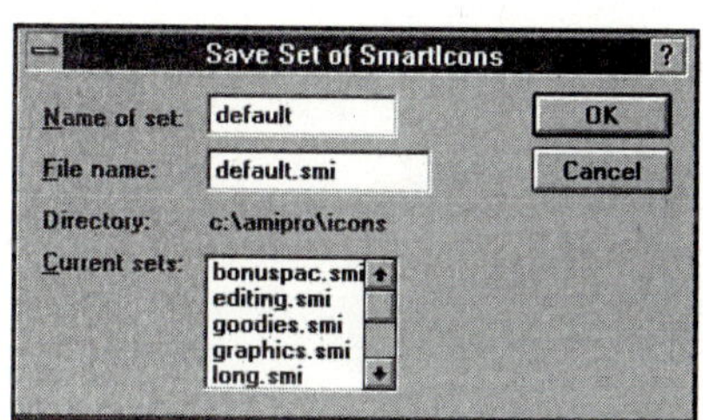

Fig. 8.10
The Save Set of SmartIcons dialog box.

5. Replace the active set name in the **N**ame of SmartIcon Set text box with a new set name.

   Note that if you base a new SmartIcon set on the default SmartIcon set, when you select **S**ave Set in the SmartIcons dialog box, no name appears in the **N**ame of SmartIcon Set text box. You must type a name for the SmartIcon set.

6. In the **F**ile Name text box, type a new file name (this step is optional). Ami Pro assigns a file name based on the name of the SmartIcon set (specified in step 5) and automatically attaches the SML extension.
7. Choose OK or press Enter. This new set becomes the active set.
8. After you finish creating SmartIcon sets, choose OK or press Enter in the SmartIcons dialog box to return to the document.

To display a different SmartIcon set, click the SmartIcon button on the right side of the Status Bar. As figure 8.11 shows, a menu of available SmartIcon sets pops up. Choosing a new set name displays that set in place of the current SmartIcon set.

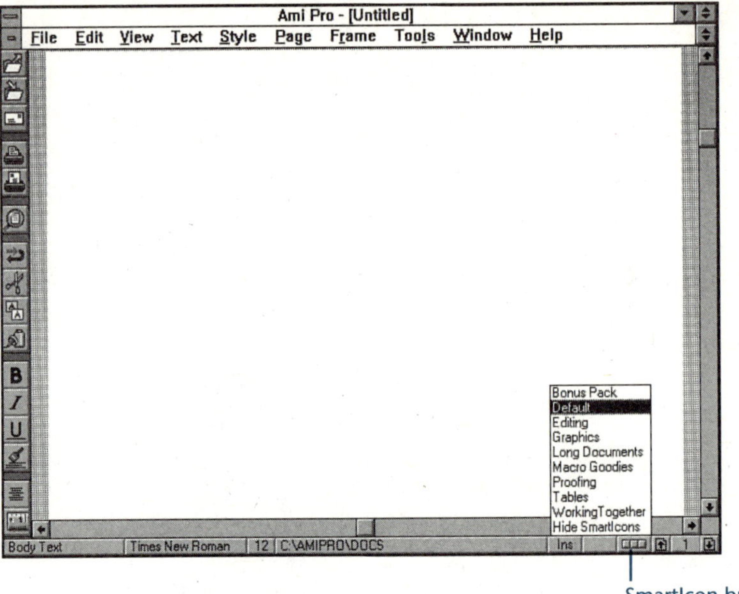

Fig. 8.11 The SmartIcon sets.

Specifying SmartIcon Size

In addition to positioning the SmartIcons in any part of your screen, you can display the SmartIcons in one of three sizes: small, medium, or large. To change the SmartIcon size, choose **I**con Size in the SmartIcons dialog box. The Icon Size dialog box appears (see fig. 8.12).

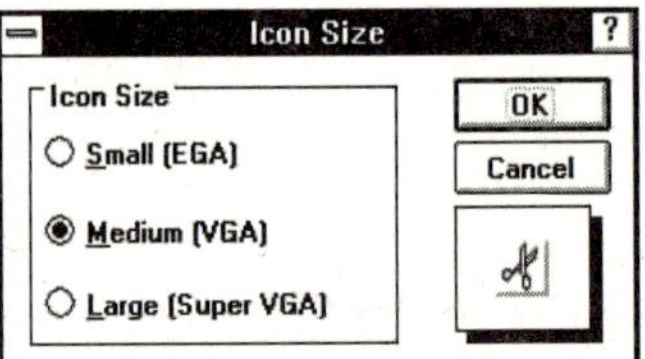

Fig. 8.12 The Icon Size dialog box.

Ami Pro sets the initial icon size based on your monitor type, but you aren't restricted to small if you have an EGA monitor, or to large if you have a super VGA monitor. Specify the size you want to use; then choose OK or press Enter. When Ami Pro returns to the document, the SmartIcons reappear in the selected size. Figure 8.13 shows the large size SmartIcons.

Note

If you're using a limited SmartIcon set, display the SmartIcons in **M**edium or **L**arge. This method makes the SmartIcon image clearer and easier to view (especially if the SmartIcon contains descriptive text). If you are using an extensive SmartIcon set displayed down the left or right side, choose the **S**mall size to display more SmartIcons.

Caution

The SmartIcon size affects the way the SmartIcons are displayed in the palette and the SmartIcons dialog box. This fact is important when you are creating or altering SmartIcons because the descriptive text may be cropped at the top and bottom, making it difficult to read.

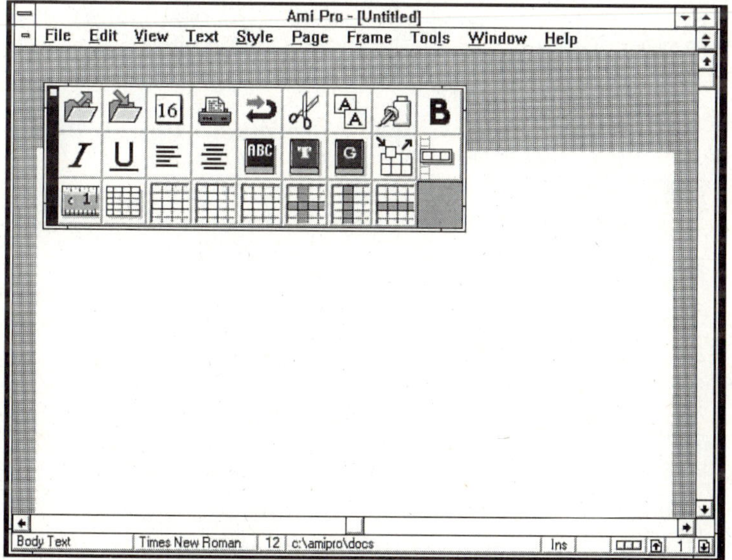

Fig. 8.13
The SmartIcons shown in large size.

SmartIcons are powerful tools for speeding the creation of many types of documents. After the SmartIcon is created, you need never worry about forgetting how to perform a function or accidently pressing the wrong key. All you need to do is click the SmartIcon! In the next section, you learn how to specify which SmartIcon palette is loaded at the beginning of each Ami Pro work session, and you explore other default settings that can simplify and speed your use of Ami Pro.

Setting Defaults

You can customize the way Ami Pro works by setting the many defaults the program offers. You can indicate whether you want automatic backups, set the number of actions Ami Pro can undo, disable warning messages, choose colors for document notes, use automatic macros, specify default paths, and set document defaults (such as the number of spaces at the end of the line before Ami Pro hyphenates text).

As you use the program and establish a special style of working, you can set up Ami Pro to suit that style. If you have multiple authors adding notes to documents, for example, setting the defaults for notes may be important to you.

To set defaults, you use the User Setup dialog box (see fig. 8.14). To access the User Setup dialog box, choose Too**l**s **U**ser Setup.

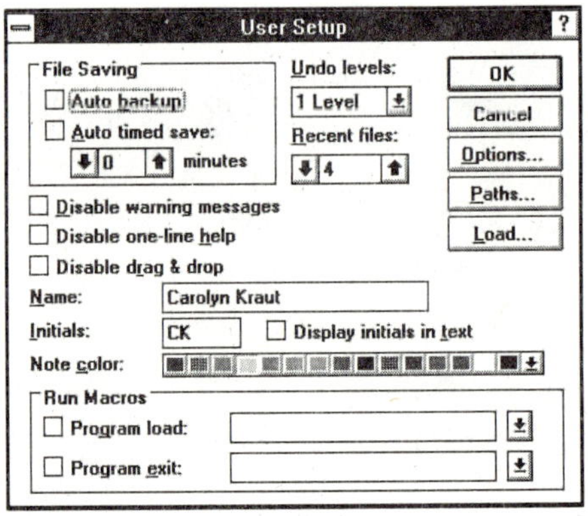

Fig. 8.14
The User Setup dialog box.

Setting Program Defaults

The options available in the User Setup dialog box are described in the following sections. After you finish setting defaults in the User Setup dialog box, choose OK or press Enter to exit the dialog box. These defaults are implemented each time you start Ami Pro.

Auto Backup

▶ See "Changing the Document Directory," p. 863

When the Auto **B**ackup option is selected, each time you save the current document Ami Pro creates on disk a duplicate copy of that document. Because the backup copy has the same name as the original file, give the backup a different name than the one where you save your working documents. If your working directory is C:\AMIPRO\DOCS and your backup directory is C:\AMIPRO\BACKUP, for example, your files are saved to

C:\AMIPRO\DOCS, and a duplicate of each file is placed in C:\AMIPRO\BACKUP. For information on naming your backup directory, see "Setting Default Paths," later in this chapter.

Auto Timed Save

Choose the **A**uto Timed Save option if you want Ami Pro to save your document at periodic intervals. Specify how often you want the program to save the document (in minutes, from 1 to 99). When you are using a document and Ami Pro is saving automatically, the mouse pointer becomes an hourglass symbol and the message `Saving Document` appears in the Status Bar to indicate that your file is being saved.

> **Caution**
>
> **A**uto Timed Save isn't active when you work with the drawing, charting, image processing, or equations features of Ami Pro. The document is saved only when you return to word processing mode.

Undo Levels

The **U**ndo Levels option specifies how many successive actions you can undo with the **E**dit **U**ndo command. You can undo the last one to four actions executed. Each successive time you use **E**dit **U**ndo, Ami Pro returns to the preceding action, up to the number you specify with the **U**ndo Levels option in the User Setup dialog box.

> **Note**
>
> The highest allowable undo level is 4, but you probably should specify a smaller number. For each additional undo level, Ami Pro stores deleted or changed material. Storing this material takes time and disk space.

> **Tip**
>
> The list of recent files really saves time in searching for files. If you use many documents during a given time period, choose a high number for the Recent Files option.

Recent Files

When you access the **F**ile menu, Ami Pro lists at the bottom of the menu the recent files on which you have worked. (You can open one of the files by clicking the name in the list.) With the **R**ecent Files option, you can specify the number of files (from zero to five) that Ami Pro lists at the bottom of the **F**ile menu.

Disable Warning Messages

Choose the **D**isable Warning Messages option when you want to prevent Ami Pro from displaying warning messages. Warning messages normally appear when you delete text containing notes, page breaks, footnotes, tables, floating headers or footers, inserted page layouts, anchored frames, DDE links, or power fields. (Ami Pro continues to display help and error messages even if you select the **D**isable Warning Messages option.)

> **Caution**
>
> Only experienced users should disable warning messages; these messages can help prevent irreversible mistakes that result in data loss.

Disable One-Line Help

If you don't want command descriptions to appear in the Title Bar, you can choose Disable One-Line **H**elp. (You may find that you don't use the messages or that they are distracting.) You may find these messages useful, however, even after you know the program well.

Disable Drag & Drop

Ami Pro 3 enables you to disable the program's drag-and-drop capability by choosing Disable D**r**ag & Drop. If drag-and-drop is disabled, you cannot highlight text and copy or move it to a new location by using the mouse.

Locking Options (Name)

If you plan to lock documents, type your name in the **N**ame text box. This option enables all users to add notes but prevents them from revising the document. (You also must choose **L**ock for Annotations in the Doc Info dialog box, as explained in Chapter 21, "Managing Files and Documents.")

Note Options (Initials, Display Initials in Text, and Note Color)

If you type your initials in the **I**nitials text box and choose the Display Initials in **T**ext option, your initials appear in the text in brackets when you add a note, to distinguish your notes from those of other users.

On the Note **C**olor bar, you can click the color you want to use for your notes. (The notes appear in the selected color.) To display additional colors, click the arrow button at the right end of the color bar. The bar expands to display additional colors from which you can choose (see fig. 8.15).

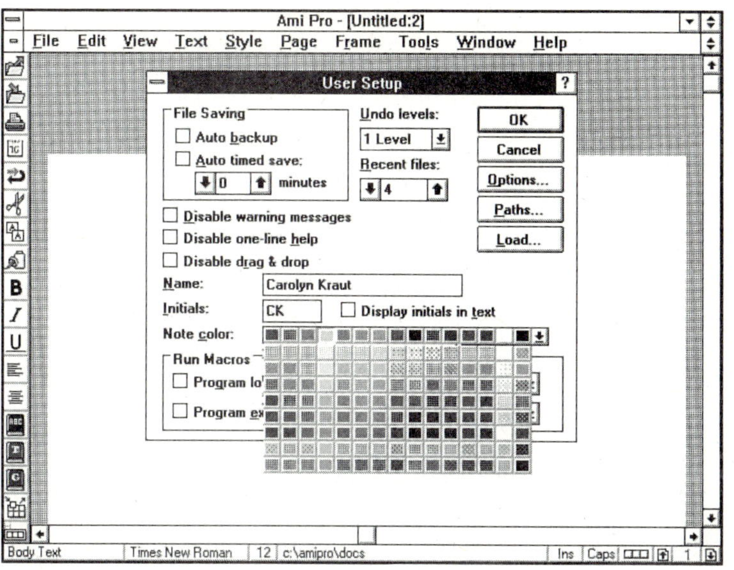

Fig. 8.15
Additional colors in the Note **C**olor bar.

You can create custom note colors. In the Note **C**olor bar, double-click the color you want to change. The Custom Colors dialog box appears, as shown in figure 8.16. The large multicolored box displays all the possible color choices; the medium-size box to the right displays the current color selection. The small color box displays the spectrum for the current color. Use the mouse to select a new color in the big color box. When you choose a new color, it appears in the medium and small color boxes. To select a different shade of the same color, adjust the color by dragging the arrow that points to the small color bar (drag left or right) until you see the color you want. Dragging the mouse adjusts the hue, saturation, and luminosity of the color and its red, green, and blue qualities.

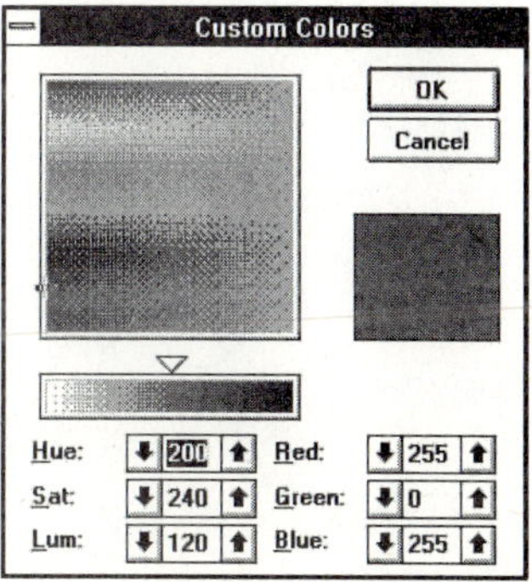

Fig. 8.16
The Custom Colors dialog box.

Tip
You can reset the note color palette to the Ami Pro defaults by returning to the User Setup dialog box, holding down the Ctrl key, and clicking anywhere on the Note **C**olor bar.

You also can make custom color adjustments with the **H**ue, **S**at (saturation), **L**um (luminosity), **R**ed, **G**reen, and **B**lue text boxes. A higher number in the **R**ed, **G**reen, or **B**lue text boxes increases the percentage of red, green, or blue (respectively) in the custom color. A higher **H**ue number decreases the amount of red. A higher **S**at number increases the amount of green and decreases the amount of red and blue. A higher **L**um number increases the amount of red, green, and blue.

When the custom color is correct, choose OK or press Enter to return to the User Setup dialog box.

Macro Options (Program Load and Program Exit)

In the Run Macros section of the User Setup dialog box, you can tell Ami Pro to execute a macro automatically when you load the program (Pro**g**ram Load) or when you exit the program (Program **E**xit). If you always use Ami Pro with 1-2-3 for Windows, for example, you can execute the macro 123W.SMM each time you start Ami Pro. If you plan to work with a group of documents, you may want to run WORKGRUP.SMM at the outset.

To use automatic macros, follow these steps:

1. Choose Pro**g**ram Load to run a macro when you load Ami Pro; choose Program **E**xit to execute a macro when you exit Ami Pro.

2. Click the arrow button at the right end of the option's text box to display a list of existing macros.

3. Select the macro you want to run. The macro name appears in the text box. (If you prefer, you can type the name of the macro in the text box.)

The following section describes other options and features available from the User Setup dialog box.

Setting Document Defaults

Several document defaults are related to typography and speed; these defaults determine how Ami Pro works with documents. You access these options from the User Setup Options dialog box shown in figure 8.17. To access the User Setup Options dialog box, choose the **O**ptions button in the User Setup dialog box.

The following sections describe the two main areas in the User Setup Options dialog box: Typographic Options and Speed Options.

Setting Typographic Options

With the **H**yphenation Hot-Zone option, you can specify the number of spaces (from two to nine) that must be available between the end of the last word on a line and the right margin before Ami Pro hyphenates a word. In other words, you specify how many characters (including the hyphen) you want to allow in a hyphenated word at the end of a line. If fewer spaces than needed are available (if you specified five spaces, for example, and the word is six characters long), the whole word wraps to the next line.

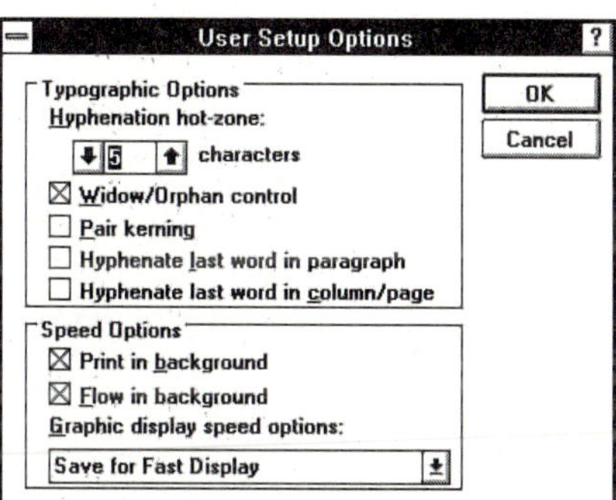

Fig. 8.17
The User Setup Options dialog box.

If you choose the **W**idow/Orphan Control option, Ami Pro eliminates widows and orphans from your documents. *Widows* and *orphans* are single lines of a paragraph appearing at the top and bottom of a page, respectively. Ami Pro moves the single line to the next page (orphans) or the preceding page (widows).

Tip
You use the Modify Style dialog box to determine whether Ami Pro uses hyphenation at all. See Chapter 4, "Formatting a Document," for more information.

Pair Kerning reduces the amount of space between certain letters and characters; this option applies only to printers that support kerning (PostScript printers, for example). When you choose **P**air Kerning, Ami Pro kerns the text automatically. The result is a more professional appearance, but kerning reduces Ami Pro's speed.

Two additional hyphenation options are Hyphenate **L**ast Word In Paragraph and Hyphenate Last Word In **C**olumn/Page. When you select the Hyphenate **L**ast Word in Paragraph option, if the last word in a paragraph doesn't fit on the line Ami Pro may hyphenate the word. If this option is deselected, that last word is placed on the next line. The **C**olumn/Page option works similarly. When this option is deselected, the last word isn't hyphenated; the entire word is moved to the next column and/or page (whichever applies).

Setting Speed Options

Ami Pro's current speed may be adequate for you. If you don't use many graphics or don't print often, the default speed settings may not affect your work noticeably. If you must increase your processing speed, however, the speed options in the User Setup Options dialog box can be very useful.

Select the Print in **B**ackground option to continue working on documents while printing.

If you choose the **F**low in Background option, you can continue working on a document while Ami Pro is reformatting a page in that document.

The **G**raphic Display Speed Options list box accesses three speed options pertaining to working with graphics: Conserve Disk Space, Save for Fast Display, and Save While Open. To choose one of these options, click the arrow button and choose the desired option from the drop-down list. When you are satisfied with the options you have selected, choose OK or press Enter.

When you use graphics, Ami Pro creates a screen snapshot file for any graphic you display. Unless you specify otherwise, the program saves the file as an ~ISD*.TMP file on the hard disk while you have the document open, and as part of the document when you use the **F**ile **S**ave command. The snapshot file enables Ami Pro to display the picture quickly. Your choices for the **G**raphic Display Speed Options affect disk space or speed in the following ways:

- Use the Conserve Disk Space option if you use many graphics and don't have much disk space on your computer. When you choose this option, Ami Pro doesn't save screen snapshot files on your disk but stores them in RAM. Storing the files in RAM saves disk space, but slows the speed at which Ami Pro can display pictures.

- If you choose Save for Fast Display, Ami Pro creates screen snapshot files, stores them as temporary files on the hard disk as you work, and includes them in the document when you save it. This option increases the speed at which pictures can be displayed, but also increases the size of the document. Use the Save for Fast Display option if you have plenty of disk space and value the increased speed as you work.

  Snapshots can be quite large; if you use the Save for Fast Display option, monitor your free disk space often.

- If you choose Save While Open, Ami Pro creates screen snapshot files, stores them as temporary files while you work on the document, and deletes them when you close the document. Use the Save While Open option if you want greater working speed but don't want to use up disk space to store snapshot files permanently.

After specifying the desired options in the User Setup Options dialog box, choose OK or press Enter to return to the User Setup dialog box.

Setting Default Paths

A *path* is like an address for a file; it consists of a drive (such as drive C) and a directory or directories (such as \AMIPRO\MACROS). You can specify the default paths for documents, style sheets, backup files, and macros. Ami Pro uses these paths to find and store files. To set the default paths, choose the **P**aths button in the User Setup dialog box. The Default Paths dialog box appears (see fig. 8.18).

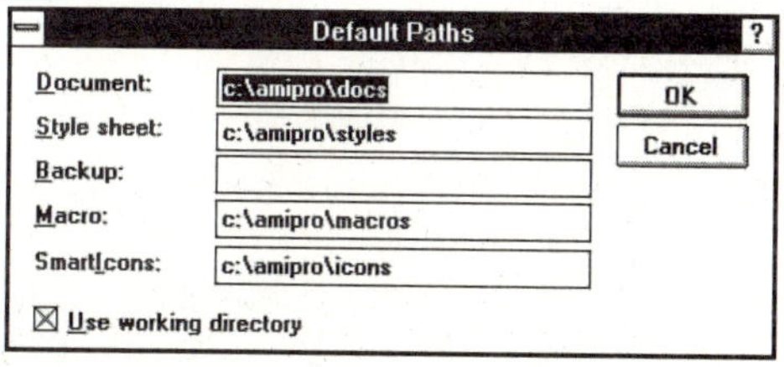

Default Paths

Document: c:\amipro\docs
Style sheet: c:\amipro\styles
Backup:
Macro: c:\amipro\macros
SmartIcons: c:\amipro\icons
☒ Use working directory
OK
Cancel

Fig. 8.18
The Default Paths dialog box.

Tip
When you install Ami Pro, the setup program requests path information and suggests defaults for documents, styles, and macros; these paths are indicated in the dialog box.

To set up default paths, choose the appropriate option from the following list and specify the desired path. Choose OK or press Enter to return to the User Setup dialog box.

- The **D**ocument path (usually C:\AMIPRO\DOCS) indicates where Ami Pro stores and retrieves documents. If you use DOS directories as a way of organizing your files on disk, you may want to change the default directory occasionally so that the default document directory is the one where you work most often at a given time.

- The **S**tyle Sheet path (usually C:\AMIPRO\STYLES) specifies where Ami Pro stores and retrieves style sheets. Unless you work with many style sheets other than those that come with the program, you probably don't need to change the default. If you create custom style sheets of your own, you may want to keep them separate from the Ami Pro style sheets. You can keep your custom style sheets in a different directory and set up a default path to that directory.

- The **B**ackup option indicates the path you want Ami Pro to use for documents you save with the automatic backup feature. (To use automatic backups, see the section "Auto Backup," earlier in this chapter.) The backup file has the same name as the original, with no special extension (such as BAK). Use the backup if you accidentally delete some or all of the working file.

- The **M**acro path (usually C:\AMIPRO\MACROS) indicates the directory for storing and retrieving macro files. Ami Pro creates the directory during installation. To use a different directory, you must create it yourself.

- Ami Pro also enables you to set the default path for Smart**I**cons. When you install Ami Pro, the program places its predefined SmartIcon sets and SmartIcons in \AMIPRO\ICONS. To use these SmartIcon sets, specify this directory as the default.

- Another feature in the Defaults Path dialog box is the capability to use the working directory. When you choose the **F**ile **S**ave or **F**ile **O**pen commands, Ami Pro displays a list of *.SAM files located in the previously defined default directory. If you choose the **U**se Working Directory option, each time you open or save a file Ami Pro looks at the current (working) directory of the last file opened. Suppose that your default document directory is specified as C:\AMIPRO\DOCS and you create a new document called API.SAM. Instead of saving the new document in C:\AMIPRO\DOCS, you want to save it in C:\API\DOCS, so you use the **F**ile Save **A**s command. The next time you open a file during the current session, Ami Pro automatically displays the documents in C:\API\DOCS instead of C:\AMIPRO\DOCS.

Setting Load Defaults

Tip
The load default options don't take effect immediately. You must exit and restart Ami Pro to see the results of your selections.

Ami Pro uses the load defaults options when you invoke the Ami Pro program. These defaults specify how to set up the screen, and they save you from having to make initial changes. The load defaults include the mode, view, and style sheet you want to use when you start Ami Pro. Other load options control whether the Styles box is displayed, whether the Ami Pro window is maximized, and whether the Ami Pro logo is displayed.

To set up load defaults, choose the **L**oad button in the User Setup dialog box. The Load Defaults dialog box appears (see fig. 8.19).

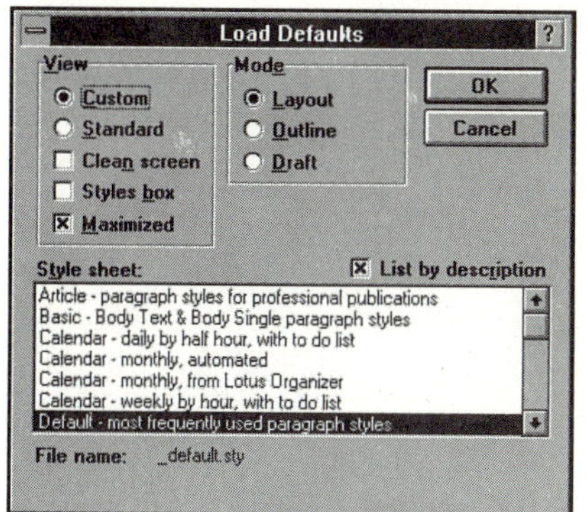

Fig. 8.19
The Load Defaults dialog box.

The following sections describe the options in the Load Defaults dialog box. After specifying the desired options, choose OK or press Enter to return to the User Setup dialog box.

View Options. You use the **C**ustom and **S**tandard view options to specify which view you use each time you load Ami Pro. Notice that these options use radio buttons; you must choose one or the other. (See Chapter 5, "Working with Page Layout," and the section "Setting View Preferences," later in this chapter, for more information on views.)

If you choose the Styles **B**ox option, the Styles box appears when you load Ami Pro. If you choose **M**aximized, the Ami Pro window is maximized (expanded to take up the whole screen) when you start Ami Pro. These options are toggles; each is selected or deselected, as indicated by the X in the check box.

Mode Options. The Mode options specify which mode Ami Pro uses when you load the program. Choose **L**ayout, **O**utline, or **D**raft. (See Chapter 5, "Working with Page Layout," for a discussion of modes.)

Style Sheet Options. In the S**t**yle Sheet list box, you can choose a default style sheet. Each new document you open then has the default style sheet highlighted in the **S**tyle Sheet for New Document text box (in the New dialog box). Ami Pro's initial default style sheet is ~DEFAULT.STY.

You can browse the style sheet list by file name or style description. If you want to list the styles by description, choose List by Desc**r**iption. The highlighted style's file name appears below the Style Sheet list box.

After you finish specifying load defaults, choose OK or press Enter to return to the User Setup dialog box.

Default settings are a great tool for customizing your Ami Pro work environment. Taking the time to set defaults means a reduction in the time necessary for Ami Pro to perform certain functions, as well as a reduction in the number of keystrokes or mouse clicks necessary to file operations or set up a view. The next section describes how to set up the default view.

Setting View Preferences

The options in the View Preferences dialog box (see fig. 8.20) determine how the Ami Pro screen appears. Ami Pro sets initial defaults, but you can set your own view preferences and change them as necessary. To specify view preferences, choose **V**iew View **P**references. The View Preferences dialog box opens.

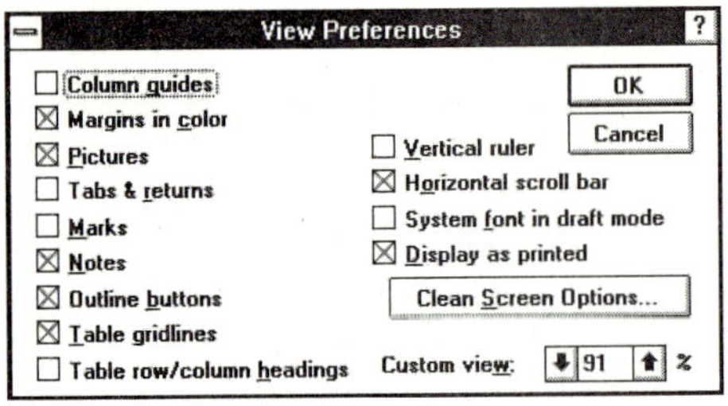

Fig. 8.20
The View Preferences dialog box.

In the View Preferences dialog box, you choose from the options described in the following sections. After you finish selecting options, choose OK or press Enter to return to the document.

Column Guides

Select Column **G**uides to display a light dotted line for each column margin in layout mode. The advantage of this option is that you can see the page layout before you type text in the columns. The disadvantage is that the lines are one more item on a screen that already displays menus, scroll bars, SmartIcons, text, and possibly rulers.

Tip
Change the margin color in the Windows Control Panel with the Colors option. Ami Pro uses a dithered (dotted) shade of the color you specify with this option.

Margins in Color

The Margins in **C**olor option displays margins in color (or dotted on a monochrome screen) in layout mode. If you don't choose this option, seeing the margins can be difficult. At times, if you cannot see the margins, you may think that you are using draft mode when you actually are using layout mode—the margins are the most visible difference between the two modes.

Pictures

Select **P**ictures to display graphics. If this option is deselected, Ami Pro displays an X in any graphic frames you create; you lose the advantage of seeing the pictures in the frames. As you work with pictures, you probably want to see them, but Ami Pro works more quickly without pictures. You can turn off this option when you need the speed and don't need to see the pictures.

Tip
After you see the graphics in a document, turn off the **P**ictures option to improve the speed at which Ami Pro runs.

Tabs & Returns

Use the Tabs & **R**eturns option to display symbols where tabs and returns are located in the document. As you work with document styles, you may not be able to tell where you have placed carriage returns or inserted extra spaces. This option can be useful, for example, for eliminating unnecessary returns between paragraphs.

Marks

The **M**arks option displays symbols for column breaks, page breaks, inserted rulers, inserted page layouts, floating headers, and floating footers. You may want to use this option occasionally to make certain that you haven't inadvertently entered marks you don't want, or to see that the marks appear where you want them.

Notes

To display notes as small colored rectangles, choose **N**otes. (See the "Setting Program Defaults" section of this chapter for instructions on changing the color of the rectangles.) For more details on Ami Pro notes, see Chapter 21, "Managing Files and Documents."

Outline Buttons

Select the Outline **B**uttons option to display only in the outline view the outline buttons that indicate whether a section of text contains additional headings under it. (See Chapter 11, "Outlining a Document," for a full discussion of outlining.)

Table Options (Table Gridlines and Table Row/Column Headings)

Use **T**able Gridlines to display light dotted lines between columns and rows in a table. Some users prefer to work without gridlines, but gridlines help you identify in which table cell you are working at any time.

The Table Row/Column **H**eadings option displays the headings of rows and columns in a table when you place the insertion point in the table. Numbers at the left identify rows; letters across the top identify columns. If you are using multiple rows and columns or need to identify cell addresses, this option is helpful. Otherwise, deselect this option to avoid having unnecessary information on your screen.

For more information on using Ami Pro's table feature, see Chapter 13, "Working with Tables."

Vertical Ruler

If you choose **V**ertical Ruler, Ami Pro displays a vertical ruler on the left side of the screen in layout mode. You can use the ruler to set top and bottom page margins. The ruler also is useful when you want to see the precise vertical location of the insertion point, such as when using the Draw program. For more information on using the ruler, see Chapter 5, "Working with Page Layout."

Horizontal Scroll Bar

Select H**o**rizontal Scroll Bar to display the horizontal scroll bar at the bottom of the screen. This scroll bar is useful if you are working in a document wider than the screen display.

System Font in Draft Mode

Choose System **F**ont in Draft Mode if you want Ami Pro to use (in draft mode) the Windows system font rather than the font you specify in paragraph style or the font you apply with the **T**ext menu or the Status Bar. Ami Pro runs faster in draft mode with this option selected, but you lose the advantage of seeing on-screen the font that appears when you print.

Display as Printed

The **D**isplay as Printed option causes Ami Pro to show a document on-screen as it will print. The advantage of using this option is that you can see how the font, line endings, and pagination appear with true WYSIWYG (What You See Is What You Get) capability. Keep in mind, however, that the **D**isplay as Printed option causes Ami Pro to work more slowly. With this option deselected, Ami Pro speeds up and gives you an approximate display of the font, line endings, and pagination.

> **Caution**
>
> Be sure to choose the **D**isplay as Printed option before printing, creating an index, or creating a table of contents. Otherwise, the pagination you see as you work may not be the same as that of the printed document.

When you choose **D**isplay as Printed, Ami Pro calculates the line endings and fonts by storing the font size information from the printer driver in memory, and using the driver as if you were printing the document. You may find that certain words appear distorted, especially with large or italic fonts. To eliminate this effect, you can use standard view or adjust the view level (with the Custom Vie**w** option on the **V**iew menu) until you correct the distortion. For more information on views, see Chapter 5, "Working with Page Layout."

Clean Screen Options

The Clean Screen feature of Ami Pro enables you to use more of the screen when displaying a document. To accomplish this, you hide various parts of the window. The parts of the window that can be hidden are the **T**itle Bar, **m**enu, Smart**I**cons, **S**tatus Bar, **v**ertical scroll bar, and **h**orizontal scroll bar. The clean screen options also enable you to indicate whether you want Ami Pro to display an icon that returns the document to the default view. If you choose not to display this icon, you can access the main menu with the menu accelerator keys; Alt+H displays the Help menu, Alt+V displays the **V**iew menu, and so on.

Tip
Selecting the **T**itle Bar option automatically selects and grays the **M**enu option.

To choose the elements that are displayed when a clean screen is active, choose Clean **S**creen Options in the View Preferences dialog box. The Clean Screen Options dialog box appears (see fig. 8.21). Select the desired options, then choose OK or press Enter.

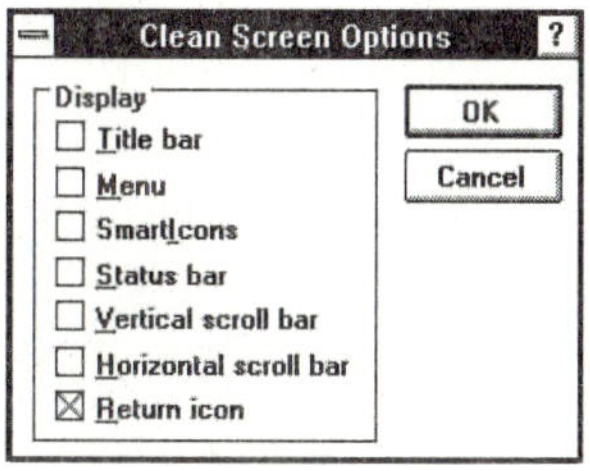

Clean Screen Options

Display
- ☐ Title bar
- ☐ Menu
- ☐ SmartIcons
- ☐ Status bar
- ☐ Vertical scroll bar
- ☐ Horizontal scroll bar
- ☒ Return icon

OK
Cancel

Fig. 8.21
The Clean Screen Options dialog box.

Summary

In this chapter, you learned how to set up your display preferences, particularly with respect to the SmartIcons. You learned how to set up a number of defaults—defaults affecting how quickly Ami Pro works with a document, default paths for files, and defaults that determine the mode and the style sheet you use when you start Ami Pro. Finally, you learned how to set view preferences to specify such options as whether margins appear in color when you are using layout mode.

Tip
To view your document in clean screen format, you must choose **V**iew Show Clean Scree**n** from the Ami Pro menu.

The next chapter begins a new phase in learning Ami Pro—how to use the special features of the program to improve your word processing. You start by learning how to use a fundamental feature of Ami Pro—the style sheet.

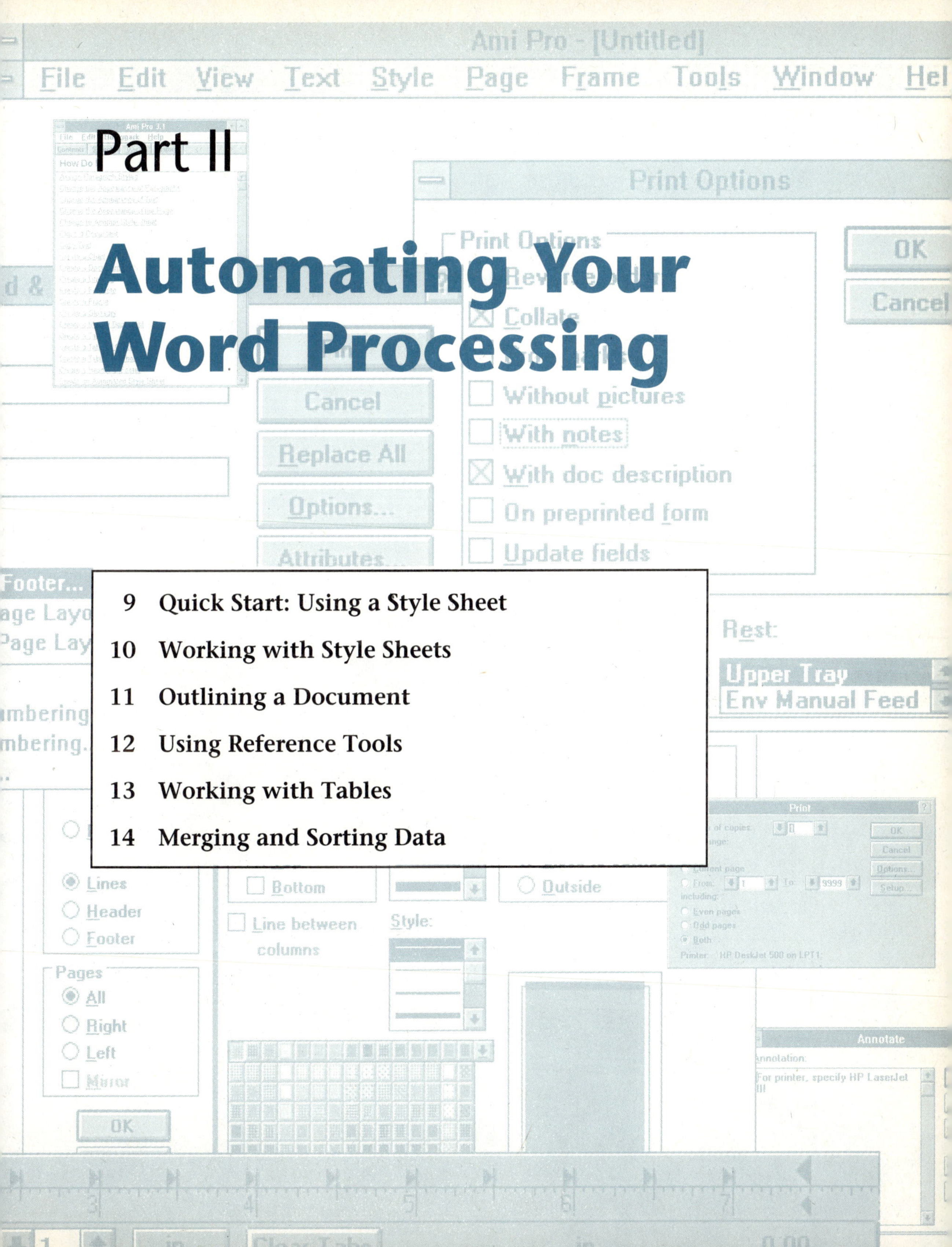

Part II

Automating Your Word Processing

Ami Pro - [Untitled]
File Edit View Text Style Page Frame Tools Window
Print Options
Print Options
Reverse order
Collate
Crop marks
Without pictures
With notes
With doc description
On preprinted form
Update fields
Bin Options
First page:
Rest:
Upper Tray
Env Manual Feed
Find
Cancel
Replace All
Options...
Attributes...
Modify Page
Around Page
All
Left
Right
Top
Bottom
Style:
Line between columns
Position
Inside
Close to inside
Middle
Close to outside
Outside
Page settings
Lines
Header
Footer
Pages
All
Right
Left
Mirror
OK
Print
Number of copies:
Page range:
Current page
From:
To:
including:
Even pages
Odd pages
Both
Printer: HP DeskJet 500 on LPT1:
Options...
Setup...
Annotate
Annotation:
For printer, specify HP LaserJet III
Clear Tabs
in.
0.00

Chapter 9

Quick Start: Using a Style Sheet

A *style sheet* is a collection of paragraph styles and page layout information that formats the current document. A paragraph style contains formatting information for an entire paragraph, including typeface and font size of the text; indention; spacing between characters, lines, and paragraphs; and special effects such as bullets, lines, and numbering. Page layout includes margins, tab settings, columns, and header and footer formatting. Some style sheets even include text and graphics that you can use to construct boilerplate media, such as newsletters and fax cover sheets.

Ami Pro provides over 50 style sheets for use in creating or editing a document. The different style sheets contain specific styles or paragraph formatting that you can use to format the paragraphs of the document.

Ami Pro styles are easy to use. Formatting a paragraph with a bullet and special indention can be as quick and easy as clicking the mouse button or pressing a function key. An even greater advantage lies in the ease with which you can make changes to paragraphs you already have formatted.

Suppose that you type a report and format 20 separate headings, each centered with a 24-point Helvetica bold font. Later, you decide to change the headings to 18-point Times Roman, flush with the left margin. If you formatted those 20 headings without using a style, you must go back and reformat each heading individually to make the desired changes. If you used a style to format the headings, however, you just edit the style and all the headings change automatically. For changes in format and appearance, you may prefer to make changes by using styles. Chapter 19, "Desktop Publishing with Ami Pro," offers suggestions for creating your own style sheets.

In this quick start lesson, you learn how to choose a style sheet, how to assign a paragraph style, how to create a new style or modify the styles in the style sheet you are using, and how to create a new style sheet so that the new or modified styles can be used in other documents.

Choosing a Style Sheet

In this section, you create a brochure. You can enter your own information, copy text from another Ami Pro document, or type the text used in the following example. The finished document need not look exactly like the sample text for you to learn how to use styles and style sheets. For ease of comparison, however, choose text with one- or two-line paragraphs or break the text into one-sentence paragraphs similar to those in the example.

When you begin a new document, you can choose a style sheet for use with the document. (If you don't choose a style sheet, Ami Pro assigns the style sheet for the document, using the default style sheet you specify by choosing Too**l**s **U**ser Setup.) For this lesson, you create a brochure by using the _PRESS1.STY style sheet.

To begin a new document, follow these steps:

1. Choose **F**ile. The **F**ile menu appears, as shown in figure 9.1.

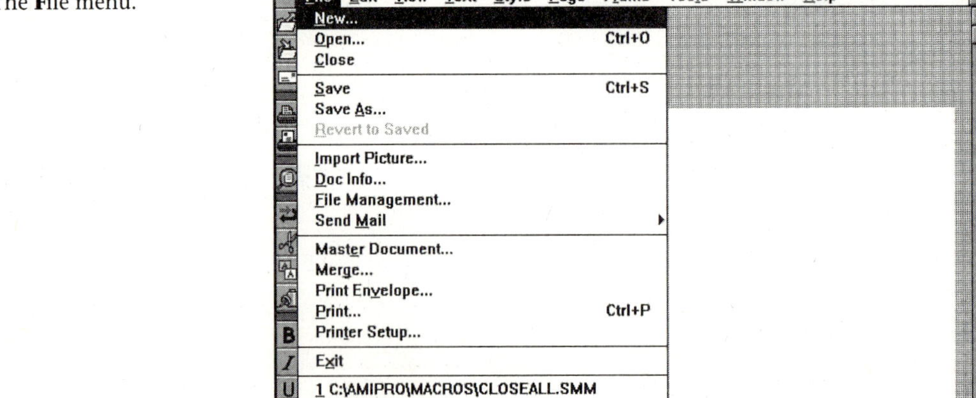

Fig. 9.1
The **F**ile menu.

2. Choose **N**ew. The New dialog box appears, as shown in figure 9.2. Choose List by **D**escription.

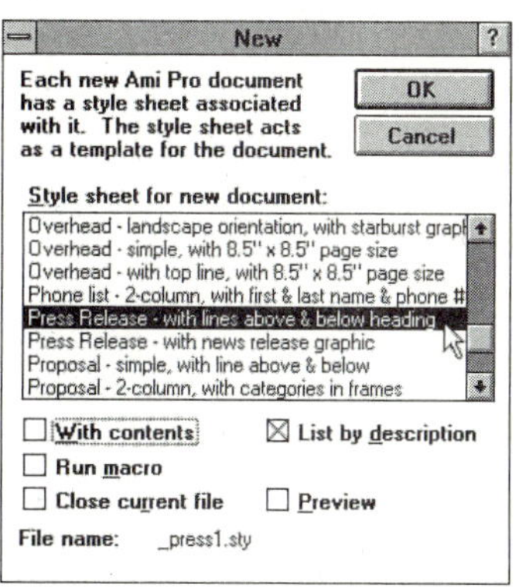

Fig. 9.2
The New dialog box.

3. Choose **S**tyle Sheet for New Document. This list box contains the names and descriptions of style sheets. If you don't choose a different style sheet by using Too**l**s **U**ser Setup, the default style sheet appears in reverse video. (Ami Pro automatically assigns the default style sheet if you don't choose another style sheet.)

   For this example, choose the first press release style sheet described as having lines above and below the heading. The name Press Release and the description appear in reverse video to indicate that it is selected. Note that the file name for this style (located at the bottom of the dialog box) is `_press1.sty`.

4. Turn off **W**ith Contents and Run **M**acro by selecting each of these options. The X in the box beside each option disappears when you choose it, signifying that the option is off.

5. Choose OK or press Enter. The dialog box disappears and a new document screen appears (see fig. 9.3).

6. The cursor appears in the upper left corner of the page; the paragraph style is Body Text. Type your own text, or type the following text, pressing Enter as indicated:

   Discover Iowa's State Parks<Enter>

   Did you know that there are 84 state parks and recreational areas comprising 53,000 acres in Iowa?<Enter>

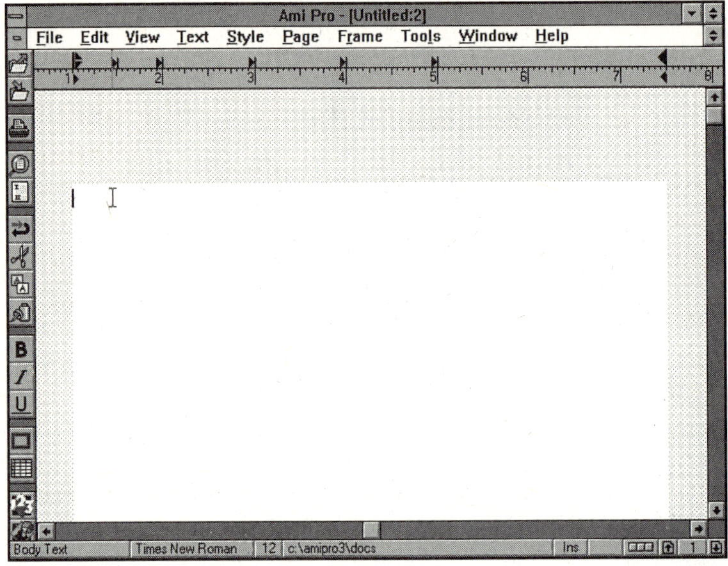

Fig. 9.3
A blank document using the _PRESS1.STY style sheet.

And that these areas contain approximately 45,000 acres of lakes and reservoirs?<Enter>

This doesn't even include another 1,100 county parks. That's a lot of woods and water.<Enter>

Iowa ranks 11th in the nation in the number of state parks and recreational areas.<Enter>

For a land known for its farms, Iowa also has green forests, hills, valleys, prairies, and caves. Within the parks are often found scenic lakes, rivers, and streams.<Enter>

State parks are a great place to spend a day or weekend.<Enter>

You can swim in a cool lake on a hot Iowa summer day.<Enter>

Picnic in the spring when the woods awaken with new color or in the fall and enjoy the red, gold, and orange shades of autumn.<Enter>

You can canoe or wind surf on the lakes.<Enter>

If you're interested in the natural landscape of Iowa, you can hike on self-guided nature trails that educate you about the land.<Enter>

7. Choose **S**tyle **S**elect A Style. The Styles box appears in the upper right corner of your screen. The name `_press1.sty` appears at the top of the Styles box to indicate that _PRESS1.STY is the style sheet being used with this document.

   The Styles box contains preassigned paragraph styles for body text, bullets, headings, titles, and so on. To see the entire list, position the cursor along the bottom edge of the box. Click and drag the cursor down to enlarge the box (the cursor shape turns into a double arrow, as shown in fig. 9.4). Alternatively, you can use the scroll bar in the box to view the styles.

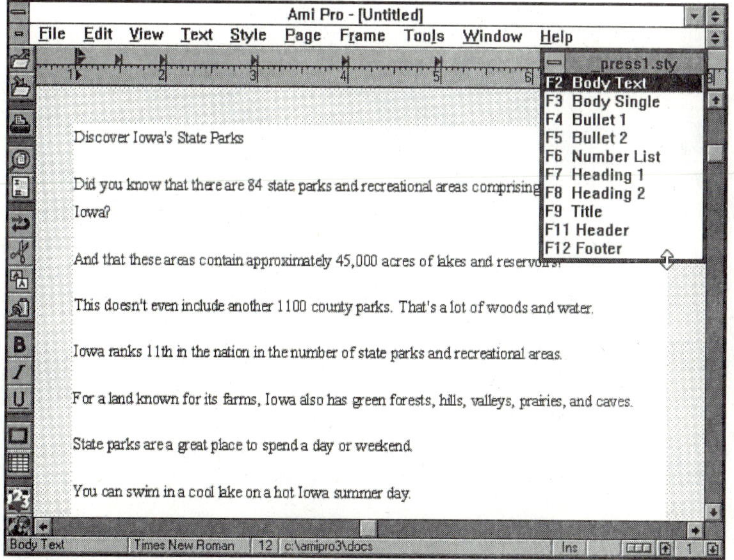

Fig. 9.4
The Styles box, lengthened to view the entire styles list.

Assigning a Paragraph Style

As you typed the text for the sample document, it may have looked different from text you have typed in other documents. The text looks different because Ami Pro assigned the Body Text paragraph style, and the Body Text style in the press release style sheet is different from the Body Text style in many of the other style sheets. If you don't choose another paragraph style, Ami Pro assigns the Body Text style to paragraphs as you type.

To use a style from _PRESS1.STY to format the title of the document, follow these steps:

1. Place the insertion point in the first line of text.

2. Using the mouse, choose the word Title from the list of paragraph styles in the Styles box.

   If the entire Styles box is not showing, point to the down-arrow button in the Styles box and hold the left mouse button down to scroll until you see the word Title.

3. Click `Title`. The Title style name appears in reverse video in the Styles box, and the paragraph where the insertion point is located immediately changes. The text becomes larger, and thick gray lines appear above and below the text (see fig. 9.5). The font size and gray lines are formatting contained in the Title style.

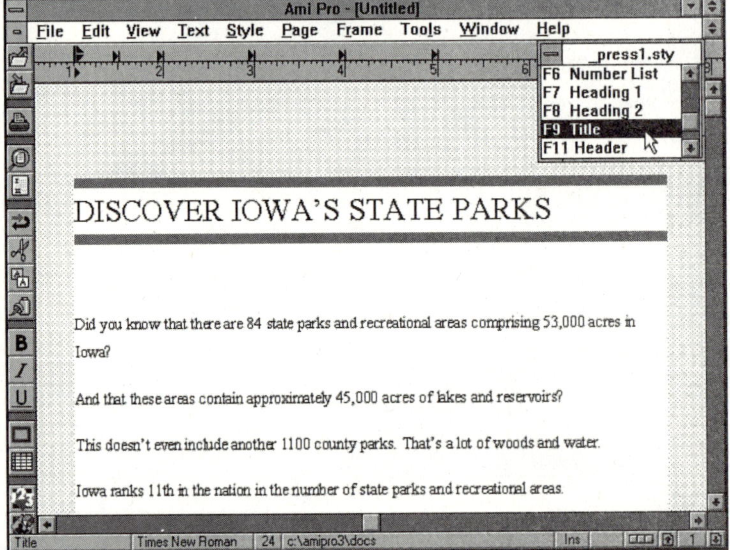

Fig. 9.5
The title of the sample document after applying the Title style.

Note

You can apply a style by pressing a function key instead of scrolling and clicking in the Styles box. Notice that the function key a style uses appears to the left of the style name in the Styles box. If you use a style frequently, you soon learn which function key invokes that style. In this example, instead of scrolling and clicking Title, you can place the insertion point in the paragraph you want to format and press F9 to apply the Title style.

Creating a Style

Applying a style from an existing style sheet is easy; you place the insertion point in the paragraph you want to format and click the style in the Styles box. But what if the available styles don't provide the formatting you want? You can apply a style and then override certain characteristics with formatting changes. If you have many paragraphs that need changes, however, the formatting process can be time-consuming. You need to create your own styles so that you can use them to format your documents.

When you create a style, you gain the ease and speed of using styles to format paragraphs, and you can specify the formatting you want. In this section, you create a new style and apply it to a paragraph in the sample document.

Suppose that you want to create subheadings that are 14-point Times Roman, boldface, and all uppercase. Follow these steps:

1. Position the insertion point in the second line of text.
2. Choose **S**tyle **C**reate Style. The Create Style dialog box appears (see fig. 9.6). Ami Pro places the cursor in the **N**ew Style text box so that you can type a name for the new style.
3. Type **Subhead** for the new style's name.
4. In the Based On section of the dialog box, specify whether the new style is based on an existing **S**tyle or Selected **T**ext. For this example, choose **S**tyle.

   By default, Ami Pro uses the existing style, which is highlighted.

   If the insertion point is in body text, this style has the characteristics of the body text in the press release style sheet (Times New Roman, 12-point, left-aligned, and so on).

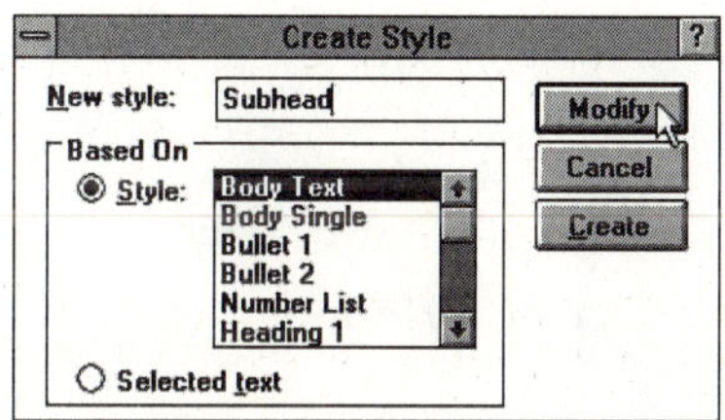

Fig. 9.6
The Create Style dialog box.

II

Automating

5. For this example, highlight Body Text—the style you want to use as the basis for the new style.

   At this point, the new style is the same as the Body Text style. You need to modify the attributes of the style to include the attributes you want for the subheadings.

6. Choose Modify. The Modify Style dialog box appears, as shown in figure 9.7.

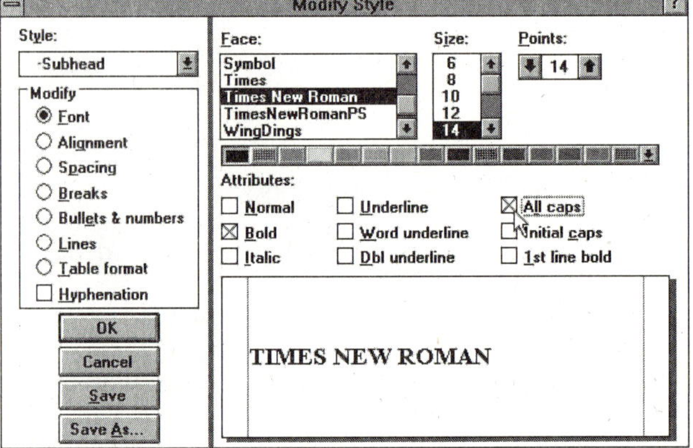

Fig. 9.7 The Modify Style dialog box, with the correct choices for the Subhead style.

As figure 9.7 shows, the name of the new style, Subhead, appears in the Style list box. In the Modify section of the dialog box, the **F**ont option is selected. The **F**ace list box lists various typefaces; for this example you want to use Times New Roman.

7. Choose **F**ace; then scroll the list in the list box until Times New Roman is highlighted (if TrueType isn't installed, use Times). Notice that the example box in the lower right corner of the dialog box indicates that you chose the Times New Roman font.

   As you complete the following steps, notice that each change is reflected in the example box.

8. Choose S**i**ze. This list box lists the different type sizes. For this example, highlight 14 to use 14-point type.

9. The Attributes section lists the different attributes you can give to the text. Because you want to use boldface for this example, choose **B**old. An X appears in the **B**old check box to indicate that the option is selected.

10. Select A**l**l Caps. An X appears in the A**l**l Caps check box.

11. Choose OK or press Enter. Ami Pro returns to the document.

    You have created a new style called Subhead. The text of the document isn't affected yet because you haven't applied the new style to any text. You can see the new style name, however, by scrolling to the bottom of the Styles box, as shown in figure 9.8.

    In the Styles box, scroll by clicking the scroll arrows. If you click any of the styles, you change the style of the current paragraph.

12. Now use the new style on a line of text in the document. Place the insertion point in the line `State parks are a great place. . ..`

13. Scroll the Styles box until Subhead is visible.

14. Click `Subhead`; the line of text should resemble that shown in figure 9.8.

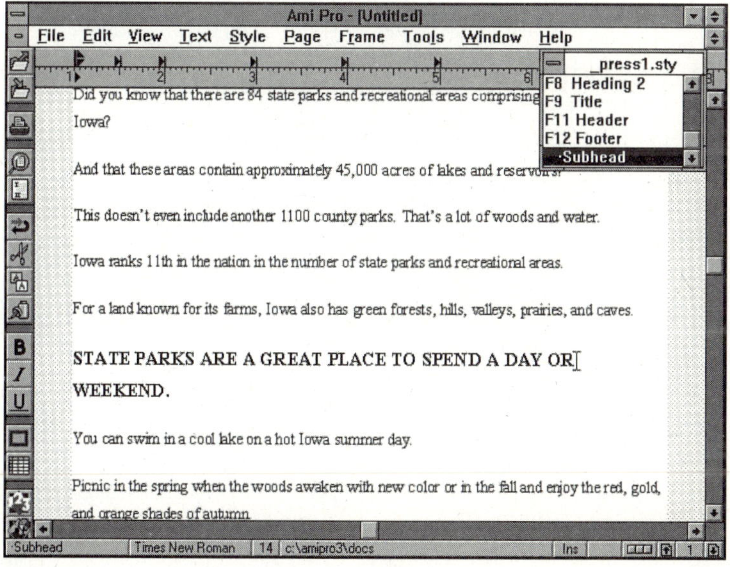

Fig. 9.8
The Subhead style in the Styles box and assigned to the sample text.

Modifying a Style

The real advantage of using styles becomes apparent when you need to change text in a document that has been formatted. Suppose that your document has subheadings formatted with the Subhead style and you want the subheadings to use italics instead of capitals. To make this change, edit or modify the Subhead style by performing the following steps:

1. Choose **S**tyle **M**odify Style. The Modify Style dialog box appears.

   If you haven't moved the insertion point since the last example, the style name `Subhead` appears in the St**y**le list box. If a different style name appears, scroll the box until Subhead is highlighted to ensure that you modify Subhead and not some other style.

2. Choose A**l**l Caps to deselect this option. Notice that the X in the A**l**l Caps check box disappears and the text in the example box changes to initial caps.

3. Select **I**talic. An X appears in the **I**talic check box and the text in the diagram appears in italics. Figure 9.9 illustrates the Modify Style dialog box with the changes.

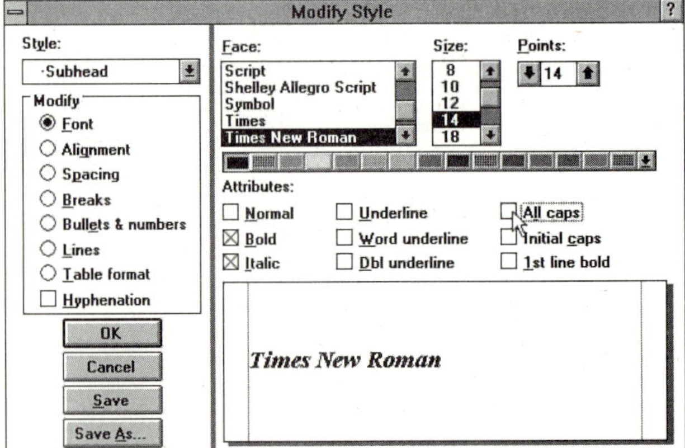

Fig. 9.9
The Modify Style dialog box with the changes to the Subhead style.

4. Choose OK or press Enter. Ami Pro returns to the document screen. Notice that all the text you formatted with the Subhead style has changed. The text, now italicized instead of in capitals, should look like that shown in figure 9.10.

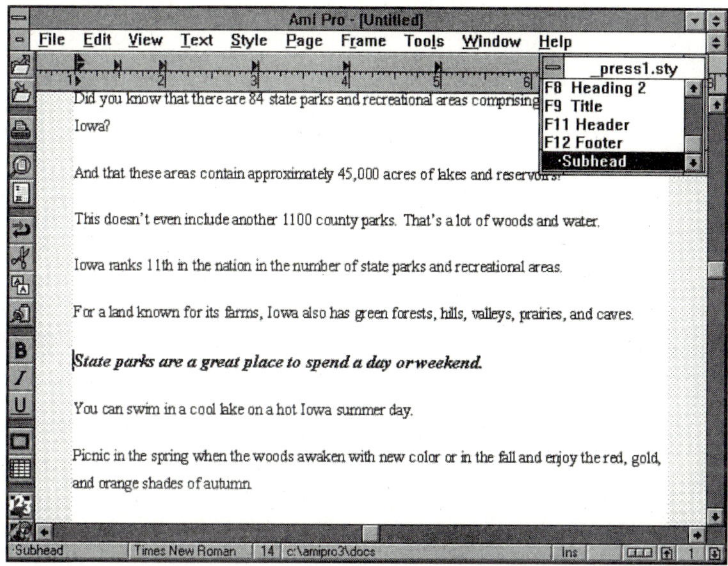

Fig. 9.10
The line of text after modifying the Subhead style.

To complete the document formatting, do the following:

1. Select the text from Did you know... to Iowa also has green forests.... Select the text by clicking and dragging the mouse cursor from the beginning sentence to the ending sentence. The text appears in reverse video when selected. Alternatively, position the cursor at the beginning of the sentence `Did you know. . .`. Hold the Shift key while pressing the down arrow until the text is selected.

2. In the Styles box, choose `Bullet 2` to apply to the selected text.

3. Repeat the formatting with the text from `You can swim. . .` to the end of the document. Figure 9.11 illustrates the sample text after formatting.

You can modify existing Ami Pro styles, but you must be careful. If you save the modifications to the style sheet, you can affect text in other documents formatted with the same styles—even documents you have already created, if you haven't saved the format with the document. If you want, you can save the modified and created styles to a new style sheet. This technique keeps the styles from affecting other documents. The next section describes how to save a new style sheet.

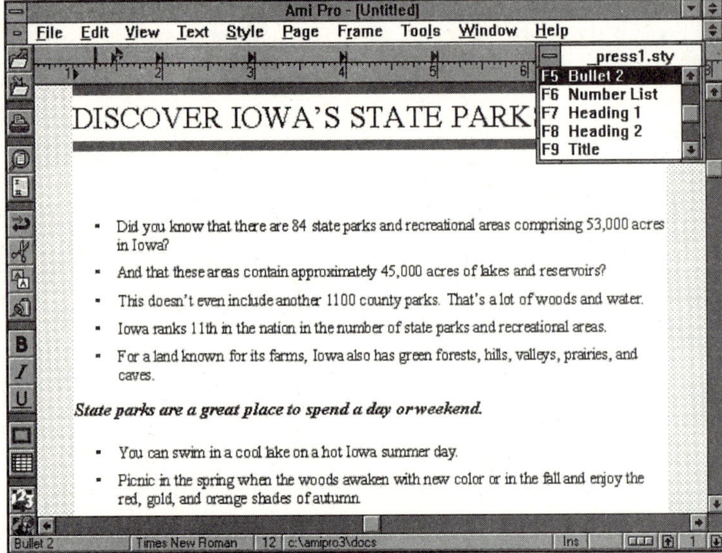

Fig. 9.11
The sample text with the Bullet 2 style applied.

Creating a Style Sheet

When you create or modify a style, the style is attached to the current document. The new style doesn't apply to other documents, even those using the same style sheet, unless you save the new style to the current style sheet or a new style sheet.

At this point in the chapter, you have created a style, used it to format some text, and modified the style to change the text formatting. This style is available only when you are working on this document. To use this style in other documents, you must do one of the following:

- Create a new style sheet.
- Permanently modify the existing style sheet you are using (_PRESS1.STY).

To avoid making permanent changes to Ami Pro styles in this quick start, you created a new style. You have the option to permanently modify existing style sheets, but you should use this option only when you are sure that you want the changes to be permanent. If you aren't careful, you may be unpleasantly surprised by the changes in other documents in which you used the same style sheet.

Caution

If you modify the _PRESS1.STY style sheet, you change it permanently. In this case, the change isn't a problem because you merely added a new style. If you modify one of the styles provided with Ami Pro (such as Body Text or Title), and then modify the style sheet, that style is changed for future documents and for any documents created with the _PRESS1.STY style sheet.

In this section, you create a new style sheet: BROCHURE.STY. This step enables you to use the new style in other documents. To create BROCHURE.STY, follow these steps:

1. Choose **S**tyle. The Style menu appears.
2. Choose Sa**v**e as a Style Sheet. The Save as a Style Sheet dialog box appears. Notice that the name _press1.sty is listed in the **F**ile Name text box. If you don't type a new name, the _PRESS1.STY style sheet is modified.
3. Choose **F**ile Name and type **BROCHURE.STY** in the text box.
4. Notice that if you accepted the default paths during installation, the Sty**l**e sheet path is C:\AMIPRO\STYLES. This is the subdirectory in which Ami Pro stores all style sheets.

   Notice, too, that the **D**escription of the style sheet is the same as the _PRESS1.STY sheet. To change the description, click the cursor in the **D**escription text box. Alternatively, choose **D**escription.

   Type your own description for the style sheet, or use the one shown in figure 9.12.
5. Deselect **W**ith Contents and **R**un Macro. Choose OK or press Enter. The dialog box disappears, and the style sheet name in the Styles box changes to BROCHURE.STY.

When you want to use the Subhead style in a document, you now can choose the BROCHURE.STY style sheet.

Note

You can save your document at any point by selecting **F**ile Save **A**s. In the resulting dialog box, type the document name in the File **N**ame text box. You can name the document anything you want (STATE, BROCHURE, or FIGURE1, for example), as long as the name contains no more than eight characters and follows standard DOS file-naming conventions. Ami Pro attaches the SAM extension automatically.

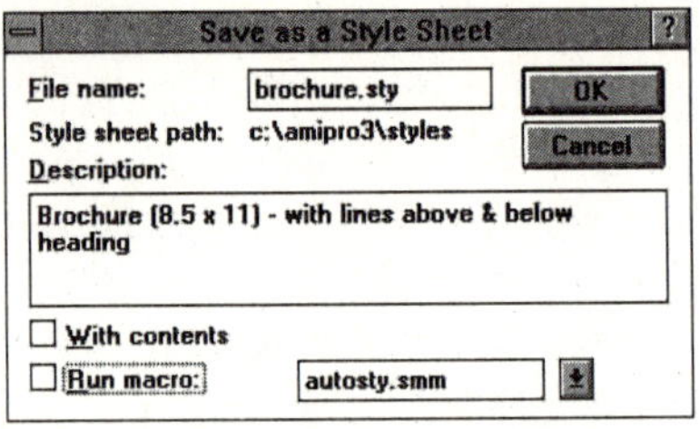

Fig. 9.12
The Save as a Style Sheet dialog box, with changes made to save BROCHURE.STY.

Modifying the Page Layout

In addition to its collection of paragraph styles, a style sheet contains page layout information, including formatting for margins, columns, and tab settings. (For detailed information on changing page layout in a document, see Chapter 5, "Working with Page Layout.") In this lesson, you change one attribute of the page layout and save that change to the style sheet so that you can use the new page layout when you use the style sheet.

The brochure you currently are creating is set with 1-inch margins all around. To change the margins of the page, follow these steps:

1. Choose **P**age. The **P**age menu appears.

2. Choose **M**odify Page Layout. The Modify Page Layout dialog box appears.

3. Change the **L**eft margin to 1.50. Use the scroll arrows to choose the measurement, or type in the text box. Change the **R**ight and **B**ottom margins to 1.50. Change the **T**op margin to 2.00.

   Notice that the sample page in the lower right corner of the Modify Page Layout dialog box changes as you change the margin measurements. Figure 9.13 illustrates the Modify Page Layout dialog box with changes.

4. Choose OK or press Enter. Ami Pro returns to the document screen, which shows the page with the wide margins. Figure 9.14 shows a full-page view of the modified page.

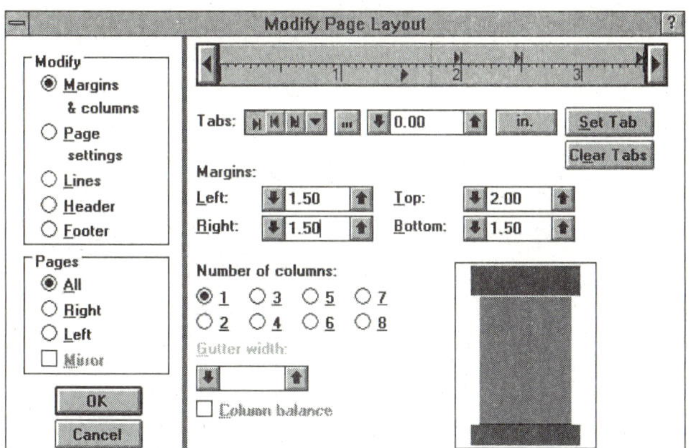

Fig. 9.13
The Modify Page Layout dialog box after you change the margin measurements.

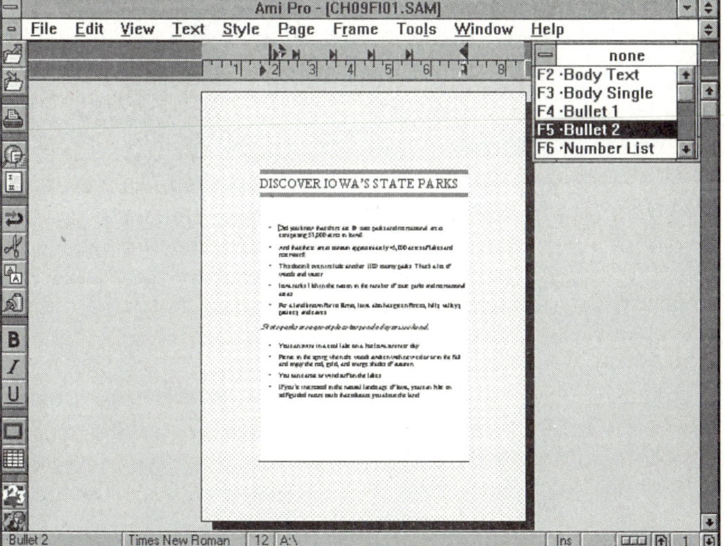

Fig. 9.14
The sample document after you modify the margins, in full-page view.

Modifying a Style Sheet

At this point, if you save the document with the modified margins, the change isn't saved to the style sheet, and the format doesn't apply to other documents even when you use BROCHURE.STY as the style sheet. To be able to use the new page layout with another document, you must perform one of the following actions:

- Create a new style sheet.
- Modify an existing style sheet.

Because you just created a new style sheet (BROCHURE.STY) and you will use this page layout for other brochures, the most efficient method is to modify the BROCHURE.STY style sheet rather than create a new style sheet. To modify the style sheet, follow these steps:

1. Choose **S**tyle. The Style menu appears.
2. Choose Sa**v**e as a Style Sheet. The Save as a Style Sheet dialog box appears with the name `brochure.sty` in the **F**ile Name text box. (If you type a new name here, you create another new style sheet.)
3. Choose OK. Ami Pro displays the message box shown in figure 9.15. The program is warning you that BROCHURE.STY already exists and that, if you proceed, you will replace it.

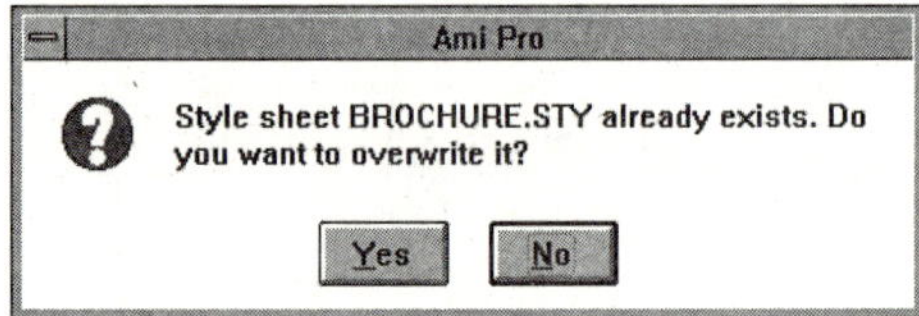

Fig. 9.15
A message box indicating that the named style sheet exists.

4. If you want to replace the style sheet, choose **Y**es. (Notice that the default is **N**o.) For this example, choose **Y**es. Ami Pro returns to the document screen.

The next time you use BROCHURE.STY, the wide margins are included in the style sheet.

Chapter 10

Working with Style Sheets

In Ami Pro, a *style sheet* is a file containing paragraph style instructions and page formatting instructions. Each style sheet has multiple paragraph styles (such as styles for body text, indented paragraphs, bulleted text, and so on) and one page layout (settings for margins, tabs, columns, and special settings such as lines around the page).

The availability and quality of style sheets (sometimes referred to as *templates*) vary among word processing programs. Some programs, like WordPerfect, offer only rudimentary style sheets. If you want predefined styles in those programs, you must create the styles yourself. Some recent programs (like Word for Windows) offer a library of useful style sheets. Ami Pro has taken style sheets to heights unimagined by other word processing packages.

Style sheets define most of the page layout and paragraph styles you need in a document. Ami Pro 3 has more than 50 predefined style sheets, including styles for indexes, tables of contents, calendars, outlines, letters, memos, newsletters, and more.

One advantage of Ami Pro's predefined style sheets is that they provide expertly designed formats for most of the documents you will want to create. You can create calendars, newsletters, and fax cover sheets of your own, but the process for designing each can be time-consuming; Ami Pro's creators have done the work for you. See Chapter 9, "Quick Start: Using a Style Sheet," and Chapter 19, "Desktop Publishing with Ami Pro," for more information on style sheets.

Ami Pro also offers automated style sheets. Many of the predesigned style sheets included with Ami Pro contain macros to speed up your work.

Macros are shortcuts that enable you to combine and record multiple keystrokes or commands, then perform them as one operation. You used one such macro, SMARTYPE.SMM, in Chapter 9, "Quick Start: Using a Style Sheet," to convert quotes, apostrophes, and dashes to typographical characters. The macros included in some of Ami Pro's style sheets work the same way.

Some of the style sheets run a macro only the first time it is open. When you begin a new document with one of these style sheets, a dialog box appears. The dialog box supplies a section in which you enter information such as your name, address, and phone number. Ami Pro then stores this information in the style sheet for later use. The Calendars, Letters, and Memos style sheets are just a few of the style sheets using this type of macro.

Some Ami Pro style sheets use a macro that totals columns and rows of numbers in a table. This macro works each time you use the style sheet. Two style sheets that contain this macro are the Expense Report and the Invoice style sheets. For more descriptions of Ami Pro's style sheets (both with and without macros), see the Appendix, "A Guide to Style Sheets." For more information on macros, see Chapter 23, "Using Macros."

This chapter details the techniques for using the Ami Pro style sheets and teaches you how to create your own style sheets (a process that offers you complete control and creativity). In addition to creating new styles, you learn to edit existing styles and save styles so that you can use them with other style sheets and other documents. After you select and use a style sheet, you may decide that another style is more suitable for your document. As you learn in this chapter, changing a document's style sheet is easy with Ami Pro.

You may want to expand your collection of style sheets. This chapter explains the basic features to create, manage, and save style sheets. Chapter 19, "Desktop Publishing with Ami Pro," explains the design and typographical elements that help you produce quality style sheets and professional-looking documents.

Using Style Sheets and Paragraph Styles

Style sheets make styling tasks easy. If you want to place bullets in front of a paragraph, indent all lines of a paragraph from the left margin or set decimal tabs for a column of numbers. The style sheet enables you to handle the task with a click of the mouse or the touch of a function key.

In this section, you learn how to assign a style sheet to the current document and how to assign individual paragraph styles to paragraphs within that document. You also learn how to reassign a style sheet to a document if your needs change.

Assigning Style Sheets

When you create a new document, Ami Pro prompts you to assign a style sheet to the document. If you don't specify another style sheet, Ami Pro assigns the general purpose style sheet _DEFAULT.STY to your new document.

> **Note**
>
> You can select any style sheet as the default. The default style sheet appears highlighted in the **S**tyle Sheet for New Document section of the New dialog box. To change the default style sheet, choose Too**l**s **U**ser Setup and then choose **L**oad. In the S**t**yle Sheet dialog box, choose the style sheet you want. Select OK or press Enter twice.

Table 10.1 lists Ami Pro's predefined style sheets. Included in the New dialog box (choose **F**ile **N**ew) is an option, List by **D**escription, that briefly describes each Ami Pro style sheet. (See the Appendix for specific details on using the predefined style sheets.)

Table 10.1 Ami Pro Predefined Style Sheets

Purpose	Style Sheet	Description
All-purpose	_DEFAULT.STY	The most frequently used paragraph styles
	_BASIC.STY	Body text and body single paragraph styles
Memos	_MEMO1.STY	Informal, with a line down the left margin
	_MEMO2.STY	Informal, with memo text in a gray frame
	_MEMO3.STY	Informal, with a line above the memorandum text
	_MEMO4.STY	Informal, with a sawtooth graphic across the to
	_MEMO5.STY	Informal, with memo text and a gray bar across the top

(continues)

II

Automating

Table 10.1 Continued

Purpose	Style Sheet	Description
	_MEMO6.STY	Informal, with a diamond graphic across the top
Letters	_LETTER1.STY	Business-oriented, with a globe graphic
	_LETTER2.STY	Business-oriented, with a border around the page
	_LETTER3.STY	Business-oriented, informal, with a company name
	_LETTER4.STY	Business-oriented, with a company name
Reports	_REPORT1.STY	Simple, with a line under the title
	_REPORT2.STY	2-column, with sections
	_REPORT3.STY	2-column, with a title in a frame spanning the columns
	_REPORT4.STY	1-column, with categories in frames
Proposals	_PROPOS1.STY	Simple, with a line above and below
	_PROPOS2.STY	2-column, with categories in frames
Dissertations	_DISSERT.STY	Paragraph styles for theses and dissertations
Term papers	_TERMPPR.STY	Paragraph styles for research papers
Newsletters	_NEWSLT1.STY	2-column, with frames for graphics
	_NEWSLT2.STY	1-column, with a title in a frame that includes a fill pattern
	_NEWSLT3.STY	3-column, with frames for graphics
	_NEWSLT4.STY	3-column, with a frame for a graphic
	_NEWSLT5.STY	2-column, with a fountain pen graphic
Articles	_ARTICLE.STY	Paragraph styles for professional publications

Purpose	Style Sheet	Description
Outlines	_OUTLIN1.STY	The most frequently used outline paragraph styles
	_OUTLIN2.STY	Includes a large left margin and a line across the top of the page
	_OUTLIN3.STY	Includes a large left margin for notes
	_OUTLINE.STY	Used in Outline mode
Press releases	_PRESS1.STY	Includes lines above and below the heading
	_PRESS2.STY	Includes a news release graphic
Overheads	_OVERHD1.STY	Portrait orientation, with a number graphic
	_OVERHD2.STY	Landscape orientation, with an arrow graphic
	_OVERHD3.STY	Landscape orientation, with a starburst graphic
	_OVERHD4.STY	Simple, with a page size of 8 1/2 by 8 1/2 inches
	_OVERHD5.STY	Includes a top line, with a page size of 8 1/2 by 8 1/2 inches
	_HANDOUT.STY	Portrait orientation based on Freelance for Windows
Titles	_TITLE1.STY	Formal, with a title page and a frame that includes a shadow border
	_TITLE2.STY	Formal, includes a frame with a double-line border
	_TITLE3.STY	Informal, includes a frame with a gray background
Faxes	_FAX1.STY	Plain, without borders
	_FAX2.STY	Includes a large top border in black
	_FAX3.STY	Includes a fill pattern in the top border
Business forms	_EXPENSE.STY	Expense report with self-totaling columns and rows
	_LOANPAY.STY	Create a loan payment table based on loan assumptions such as interest rate, length of loan, minimum and maximum amounts

(continues)

Table 10.1 Continued

Purpose	Style Sheet	Description
	_MORTGAG.STY	Mortgage real estate calculation sheet which is automated and includes loan amount, origination fees, closing costs in a professional looking format
	_INVOICE.STY	Includes self-totaling columns
Phone list	_PHONLST.STY	2-column, with first and last name and phone number
Merge	_MERGDAT.STY	Includes merge field names and delimiters
	_MERGLET.STY	_LETTER1.STY with merge fields
Calendars	_CALDAY.STY	Daily by half hour, with To Do list
	_CALWK.STY	Weekly by hour, with To Do list
	_CALMON.STY	Monthly, automated
Labels and envelopes	_LABEL.STY	Compatible with Avery laser labels
	_ENVELOP.STY	Includes return address area
	_~AMIENV.STY	Used for automatic envelope printing
Macro	_MACRO.STY	Used when writing macros
Table of contents	_TOC.STY	Used when creating a TOC
Index	_INDEX.STY	Used when creating an index

Note

Notice that the name for each original Ami Pro style sheet begins with an underline (_). Ami Pro lists keyboard characters (underline, tilde, ampersand, and so on) first in the File **N**ame list box; alphabetic listings follow. You can begin your style sheets with a different keyboard character so that your style sheets are in front of Ami Pro's. The number sign (#), for example, is listed before the percent sign (%), the ampersand (&), and so on. Ami Pro doesn't allow certain symbols, such as the plus sign (+) and the asterisk (*), in style sheet names.

Each style sheet is designed to help you create a particular type of document. _FAX2.STY, for example, helps you type fax cover sheets quickly, and _CALDAY.STY provides a form for your schedule. (See the Appendix for a description of each style sheet's features.) As you become acquainted with these style sheets, you can select the one that best meets your needs for a particular type of document.

To assign a style sheet as you create a new document, follow these steps:

1. Choose **F**ile **N**ew. The New dialog box appears, as shown in figure 10.1.

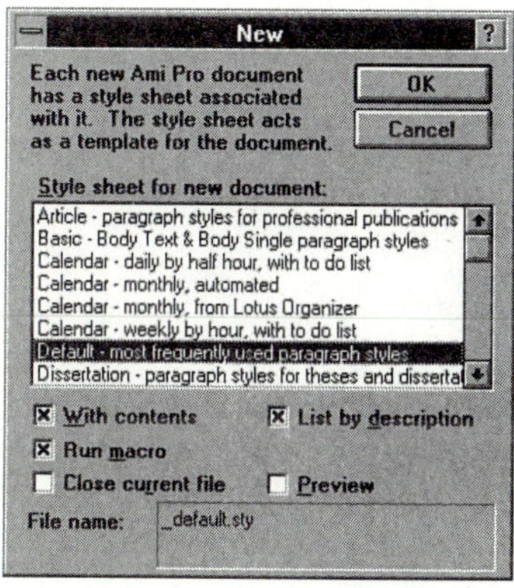

Fig. 10.1
The New dialog box.

2. The **S**tyle Sheet for New Document list box contains a list of available style sheets with their descriptions. Scroll through the list of style sheets and select the one you want.

3. Select the **W**ith Contents option if you want the contents of the style sheet file (graphic lines or perhaps some text) to appear in the new document. An X appears in the check box when you select this option.

4. Choose OK or press Enter.

Note

Using the **W**ith Contents option when you create a new document can save time. For the _FAX2.STY style sheet, for example, Ami Pro copies the FAX title, TO: and FROM: lines, and other information from the style sheet to the blank document. You just fill in the blanks.

Another option in the New dialog box is Run **M**acro. Some style sheets contain macros that help you complete information in the new document, such as company name, address, phone, and so on. The Appendix identifies the style sheets that use macros. Figure 10.2 shows one such style sheet opened on-screen.

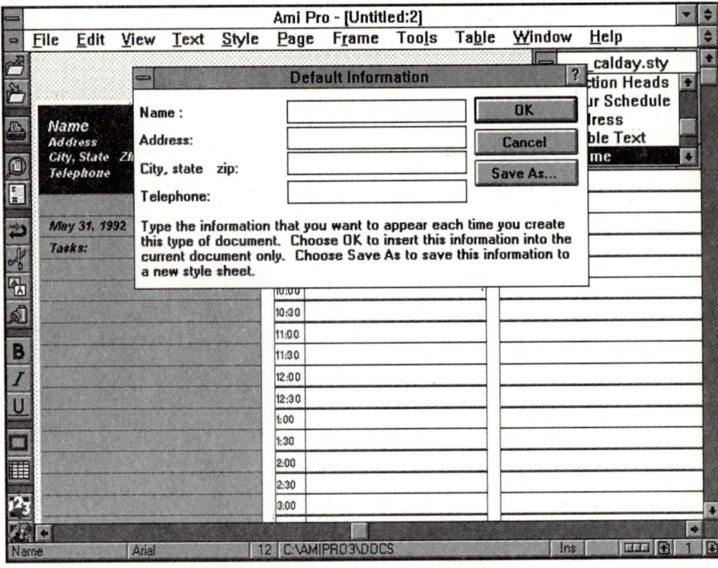

Fig. 10.2
The CALDAY.STY style sheet.

Tip
You also can access styles by clicking the far left button in the Status Bar (the Style button). In the pop-up list (the Styles list), click the style you want.

The CALDAY.STY style sheet provides a daily calendar, lines, and dates. This style sheet also begins a new document by asking you to enter your name, address, and phone number.

For a discussion of the other options in the New dialog box (Close Cu**r**rent File, **P**review, and List by **D**escription), see Chapter 3, "Editing Techniques."

When you close the New dialog box, a new document window appears. Notice that the Styles box in the screen's upper right corner shows the name of the style sheet you select. (If the Styles box isn't visible, choose **S**tyle **S**elect a Style or press Ctrl+Y.) The Styles box also shows the paragraph styles available from the current style sheet and the function keys you use to access those styles. You can access the styles by clicking them with the mouse cursor or by using the function keys displayed next to the style names.

Note that the Styles box functions much like other windows, such as document or application windows. You can move or enlarge the Styles box to suit your purposes. You can move the Styles box to another area of the screen for easy editing; enlarge the Styles box to view all style options at one time. (To move the Styles box, click its Title Bar and drag the box to a new location.) If you want to use only a small number of styles, you can shrink the Styles box to show only the desired styles.

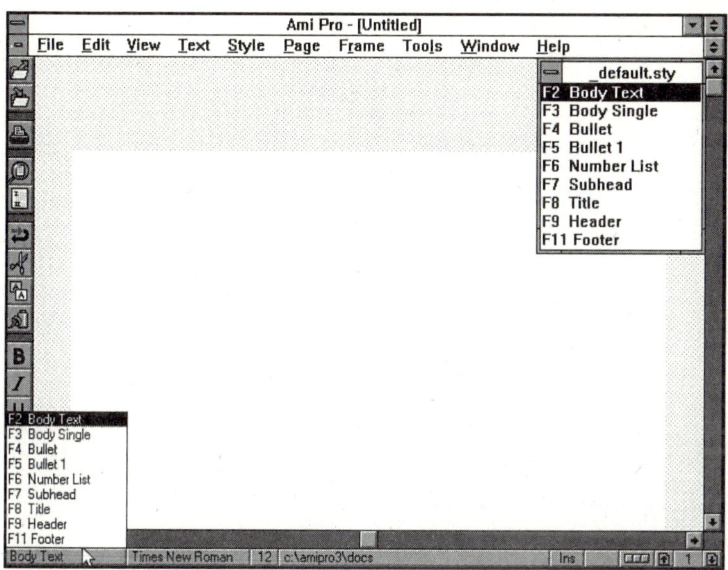

Fig. 10.3
Two ways to assign a paragraph style.

When you create a new document, the Styles box retains the same location or dimensions as in the preceding document. If you don't want the Styles box to appear when you load a document, deselect the Styles Box option in the Load Defaults dialog box. (Choose Too**l**s **U**ser Setup Load to access the Load Defaults dialog box. In **V**iew, choose Styles **B**ox, select OK, or press Enter twice.)

After you become familiar with the styles in a style sheet, you can choose the style sheet by name when you create a document. With this method, the styles for that style sheet are available when you create the document. If you don't know the styles in a style sheet, refer to the Appendix or choose **P**review in the New box to view the style sheet. You can use the **W**ith Contents option to see how the document looks on-screen. **P**review gives you a mini-preview of the style sheet without actually opening a document. If you don't like the sample you see, choose another style.

After you specify the style sheet, you can use it to assign paragraph styles in your document, as explained in the next section.

Assigning Paragraph Styles

Assigning paragraph styles is a simple procedure. To assign a style to a paragraph, place the insertion point in that paragraph and click the style you want in the Styles box.

Tip
Applying a different paragraph style is a quick way to indent several paragraphs, set multiple tabs, use bullets, and so on.

Suppose that you want to assign styles from the style sheet _DEFAULT.STY. Begin by creating a document with the _DEFAULT.STY style sheet. After the document is in place, you can assign individual paragraph styles. To select a new style for a paragraph, follow these steps:

1. Place the insertion point in the paragraph you want to format (or select the text if you are formatting more than one contiguous paragraph).

   If you are typing new text, select the style first (as explained in steps 2 and 3) and then type the text.

2. Using the mouse, click one of the styles in the Styles box and then click the up- or down-arrow button to scroll the styles in the Styles box.

3. Click the style you want to apply. Figure 10.4, for example, shows the Title style selected and the cursor positioned in `Bluefish`. The format of the paragraph or selected text changes to reflect the new style.

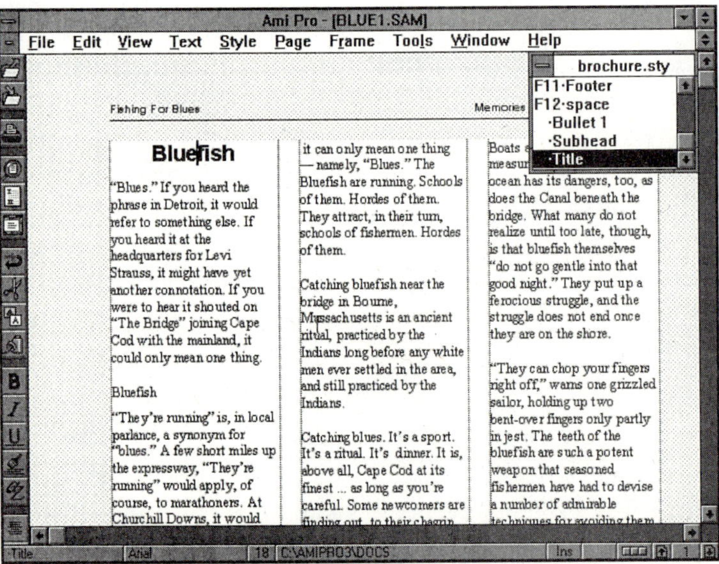

Fig. 10.4
Selecting a new paragraph style.

Tip
Ami Pro enables you to assign new function keys to any style. For details, see the section "Managing Styles," later in this chapter.

Instead of clicking the paragraph style name in the Styles box, you can assign a paragraph style by pressing the function key (listed next to the style) corresponding to that style. Instead of clicking Title, for example, you can press F8. After you learn the function key shortcut for a particular style, you may find using the function key faster than using the mouse.

If you find the on-screen Styles box distracting (if it blocks your view of the Minimize icon, for example), you can use the Style button on the Status Bar instead. Choose **V**iew Hide Styles **B**ox to close the Styles box. When you want to choose a style, click the Style button (extreme left on the Status Bar) and choose a style from the pop-up list (as shown in fig. 10.3).

Note

Assigning a paragraph style with the Styles box changes the entire paragraph. To affect only a portion of the paragraph, select that portion and use the Text menu or the SmartIcons to change the formatting instead of assigning a new style to the entire paragraph. To boldface a few words in a paragraph, for example, select the text and click the appropriate SmartIcon.

The Fast Format feature speeds up formatting. Use this feature, for instance, if you need several words, letters, or paragraphs changed but don't want to create a style for that format. First, format the text in the style you want repeated (for example, 18-point, bold, Helvetica, centered). This formatted style is called the *base format*. Select the text and access Fast Format by selecting **T**ext Fas**t** Format or by pressing Ctrl+T.

If you select an entire paragraph, a dialog box opens asking if you want the format to be text attributes (**T**ext menu) or paragraph styles (**S**tyle menu). (If you select only a portion of a paragraph's text, no dialog box opens and Ami Pro automatically selects text attribute formatting.) The mouse pointer changes to an I-beam and paint brush (see fig. 10.5). Select any text you want to change to the base format. After you choose and press Enter, you can fast format as many words, paragraphs, and so on as you want. The cursor remains in Fast Format until you select **T**ext Fas**t** Format again or press Ctrl+T.

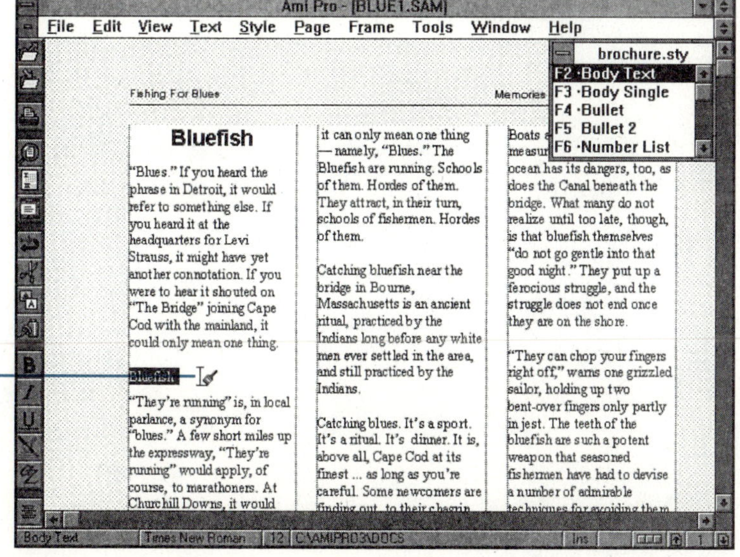

Fig. 10.5
The base format (the original style) in which the Fast Format cursor appears next to the selected text.

Reassigning Style Sheets

You can reassign style sheets if you decide that a different style sheet is more suitable for an existing document. To select a style sheet for an existing document or to replace the current style sheet with a different style sheet, follow these steps:

1. Choose **S**tyle **U**se Another Style Sheet. The Use Another Style Sheet dialog box opens, as shown in figure 10.6.

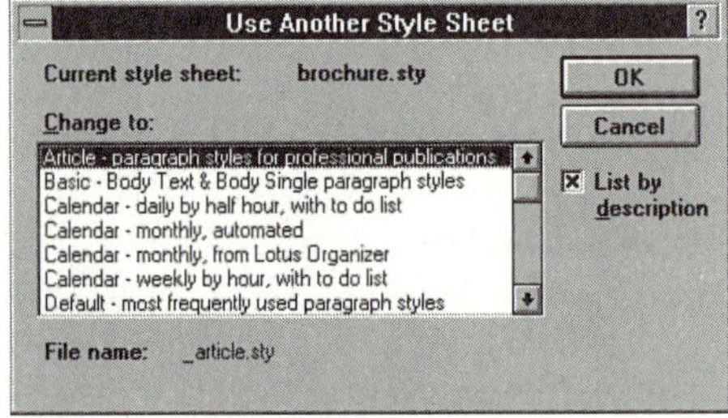

Fig. 10.6
The Use Another Style Sheet dialog box.

2. In the **C**hange To box, which lists the available style sheets, scroll through the choices and select the style sheet you want to apply.

3. Choose OK or press Enter. The dialog box disappears, and the name of the new style sheet appears in the Styles box.

Because the specified style sheet is now available, you can choose from the styles in that style sheet for any additional text you create (see fig. 10.7).

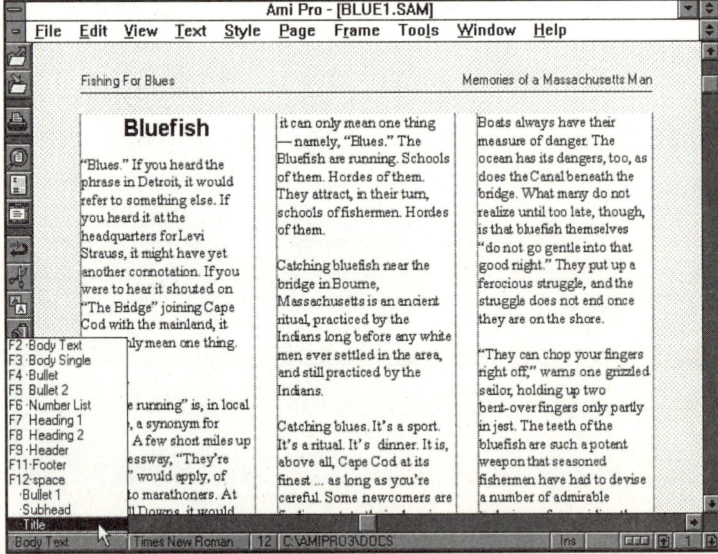

Fig. 10.7
The styles added from the _ARTICLE.STY style sheet.

Note

Ami Pro doesn't automatically apply the styles from the new style sheet to the document. If the document stored formatting information (you selected the **K**eep Format With Document option in the Save **A**s dialog box when you saved the document), the document retains that information until you assign new styles.

In addition to controlling which style sheet is applied to a document, you can revise the styles included in a particular style sheet. The next section explains how to customize styles.

Creating and Modifying Styles

Ami Pro provides many style sheets with formatted styles, but you may have special uses for which you want to create your own styles and style sheets. In this section, you learn how to create new styles and edit existing styles.

Creating New Styles

You can use two methods to create a new style. In the first method, you select text in your document that is formatted with the enhancements you want to include in the style or choose characteristics from a series of dialog boxes and apply this new style to text. If you have formatted a heading, for example, and have several more headings in the document to format, you can create a style based on the formatted heading. Follow these steps to format a heading and to create a style based on the heading:

1. Select the text (as shown in fig. 10.8). Next, use the **T**ext menu to format the heading as Times Roman, 14-point, bold, italic. (The body text is 12-point Times Roman.)

2. Choose **S**tyle **C**reate. The Create Style dialog box appears (as shown in fig. 10.9).

3. In the **N**ew Style text box, type a name for the style. In figure 10.9, the style name is `Title 2`. (The name can be up to 13 characters.)

4. In the Based On section of the dialog box, choose the Selected **T**ext option.

5. Choose **C**reate. The dialog box disappears, and Ami Pro returns to the document.

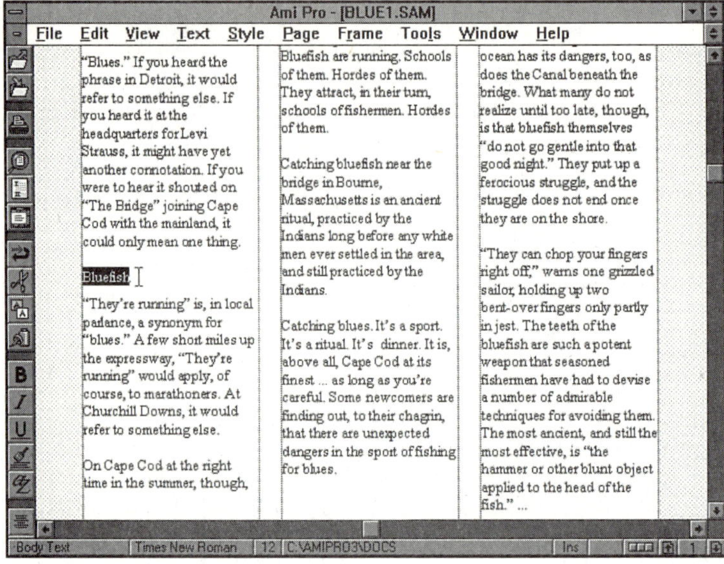

Fig. 10.8
Select the text to create a new style, and then format with the **T**ext menu or SmartIcons.

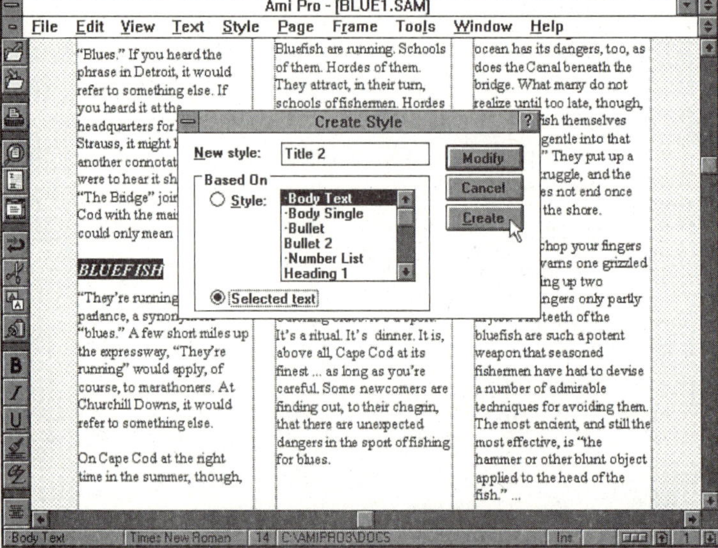

Fig. 10.9
The Create Style dialog box and the formatted text.

Note

Ami Pro assigns the new style to the first available function key in the Styles box. If no function keys are available, the software places the new style at the end of the list with a bullet next to the style (the bullet indicates that no function key was available for the new style).

The new paragraph style is available for use within the current document only. If you want to use the new style in other documents, you must save the style to the style sheet (as explained later in this chapter, in the section "Saving Styles to a Style Sheet").

Note

When naming styles, you don't need to follow DOS naming conventions (you even can use spaces in the name), but you may want to follow Ami Pro style-naming conventions. Title, Bullet, Heading, and Body Text are style names Ami Pro frequently uses. To create a variation of the Ami Pro name, add a number, such as Title 2 (specify a number that currently isn't used in the document). With this method, if you move the new style into an existing style sheet, the new style name is consistent with the existing style names and is easy for you to recognize.

The second method of creating a new style is to base it on an existing style and add modifications. In this method, you have no formatted text on which to base the new style. Suppose that you type the text for your Titles with the Body Text style that Ami Pro assigns by default. Then you decide to add another Title format (Helvetica, 28-point, bold, italic). To change the formatting, you start with the Create Style dialog box and assign the attributes you want.

To create a new style without an existing format, follow these steps:

1. Choose **S**tyle **C**reate. The Create Style dialog box appears (see fig. 10.10).

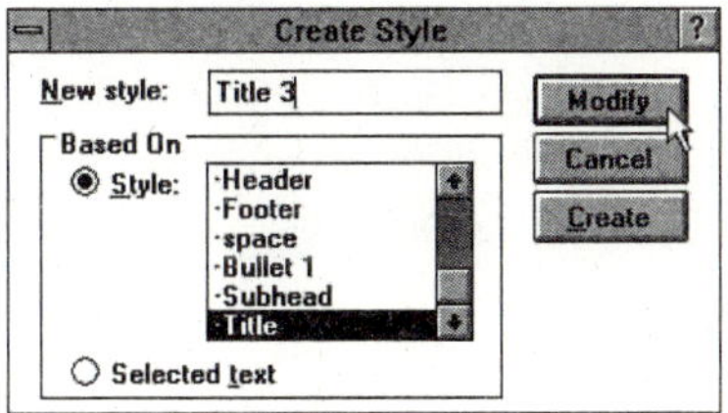

Fig. 10.10
The Create Style dialog box.

2. In the **N**ew Style text box, type a name for the new style. For this example, type **Title 3**. (Note that the Modify and **C**reate buttons dim until you type a name for the new style.)

3. Select **S**tyle and specify the style you want to modify (use the style most like the one you want to create). For this example, select Title. The selected style appears in reverse video.

4. Choose Modify. The Modify Style dialog box appears (as shown in fig. 10.11).

5. Choose **F**ont. The font options appear in the right side of the dialog box. Note that the example box (at the bottom of the dialog box) shows an example of the font for the selected style.

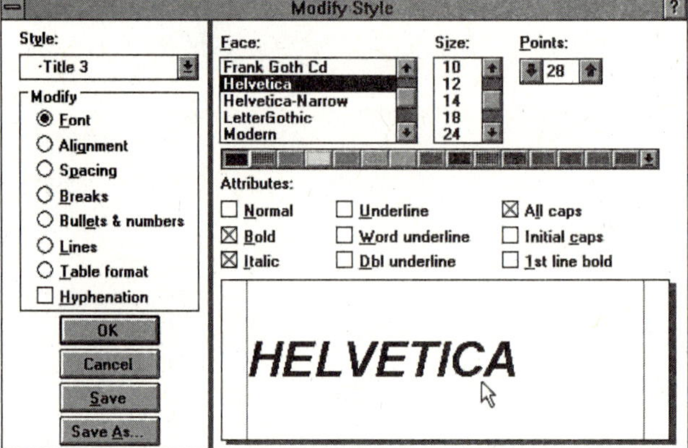

Fig. 10.11
The completed Modify Style dialog box.

6. In the **F**ace section, scroll through the list of typefaces and select the typeface you want to use for the new style. For this example, choose Helvetica. The example box shows the new typeface.

7. In the **P**oints section, scroll to the size you want or type the size. In this example, use 28.

Note

Use the **P**oints option when you want a type size not listed in the S**i**ze section. If the **P**oints option is dimmed, you cannot use a custom point size. In this case, select the point size you want by scrolling to it in the S**i**ze section. Note that you cannot change the unit of measurement. The sizes in the S**i**ze section depend on the typeface in the **F**ace section and on your printer's capabilities.

8. In the Attributes section, select the attributes you want to use for the new style. For this example, choose **B**old, **I**talic, and A**l**l Caps. (If your printer doesn't have a bold italic font, these options aren't available.)

9. After you finish selecting attributes for the new style, choose OK or press Enter. Figure 10.11 shows the completed Modify Style dialog box.

If you choose **S**ave or Save **A**s instead of OK, Ami Pro saves your changes but keeps the dialog box open for you to make additional changes (Ali**g**nment, S**p**acing, **B**reaks, and so on).

After you choose OK, the dialog box disappears, and Ami Pro returns to the document.

The text's appearance doesn't change with the new style until you apply the new style to the paragraphs you want to reformat. (Refer to the earlier section, "Assigning Paragraph Styles," for more information.)

In some situations, you may not need to create a new style to achieve the format you need. The next section of this chapter explains how to modify an existing style.

Modifying Existing Styles

You can modify any existing style in your document, regardless of whether you create the style or it's present in the current style sheet. In this section, you learn the options available for modifying existing styles.

Caution

When you modify an existing style, you automatically modify all paragraphs assigned that style in the current document. If you make the style changes permanent (by selecting St**y**le **S**ave), you also modify paragraphs in other documents using that style sheet and style. If you want to change certain sections of text—but not all text using a particular style—select the text and change the attributes with the **T**ext menu.

To begin modifying an existing style, choose **S**tyle **M**odify. (Your insertion point can be anywhere in the document.) The Modify Style dialog box appears. Select the style you want to modify in the St**y**le section (see fig. 10.12).

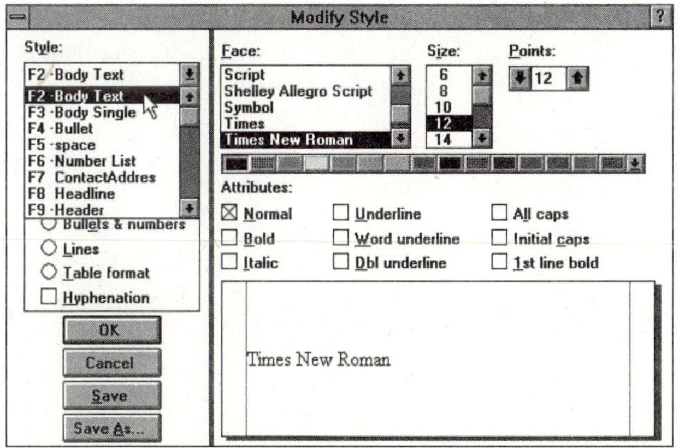

Fig. 10.12
Selecting a style to modify in the Modify Style dialog box.

Note

Rather than using the **S**tyle menu, you can move directly to the Modify Style dialog box by clicking the Modify a Paragraph Style SmartIcon, pressing Ctrl+A, or double-clicking the desired style in the Styles box. An added feature in Ami Pro 3 is the use of the right mouse button. Position the cursor in text that uses the style you want to modify, then click the right mouse button. The Modify Style dialog box appears with that style already selected.

The following sections describe the steps necessary to display and use each group of Modify options in the dialog box. Note that you don't have to use all the Modify options. Select only the options you want to modify for the style you are editing.

After you finish making selections in the Modify Style dialog box, choose OK or press Enter. Ami Pro returns to the document. Paragraphs formatted with the modified style change to reflect your selections.

Changing Fonts

The first options that appear in the Modify Style dialog box apply to the font used in the style (refer to fig. 10.12). You can select the typeface, size, color, and other attributes. The preceding section describes most of these options.

Tip
Double-clicking a color button brings up the Custom Colors dialog box. The newly created color is assigned to the color button you click.

To modify color for the style, click the down-arrow button next to the color bar in the **F**ont options. Then click the new color for the style. (Monitor the color changes in the example box.)

Changing Alignment

To modify paragraph alignment for the style, choose Ali**g**nment in the Modify section of the dialog box. The alignment options appear in the dialog box, as shown in figure 10.13. The following paragraphs describe the alignment options.

In Chapter 5, "Working with Page Layout," you learn how to use the ruler for setting tabs and margins. In the Modify Style dialog box, you can use the ruler in the same way to set the characteristics of a particular style rather than the characteristics of a page or section of text.

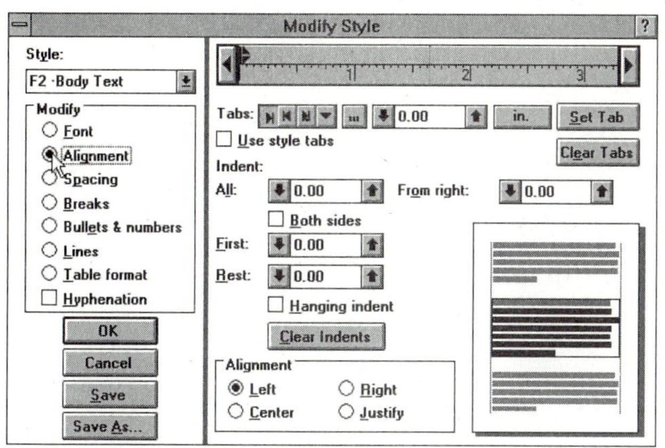

Fig. 10.13
The Modify Style dialog box.

Tabs

To select a tab type, click the button for the tab type you want (if you are using the keyboard, press Tab until the cursor moves to the first tab button and then use the right- and left-arrow keys to move between the tab buttons). The tab buttons (from left to right) create left tabs, right tabs, decimal (numeric) tabs, and center tabs.

You also can specify a leader character by choosing the leader character button located to the right of the tab type buttons. The character you choose appears between the tabs in place of spaces. For a right tab, for example, you may want a series of periods (a *dot leader*) to appear before the tab and its following text. Click the Leader Character button until the character you want appears above the tabs on the tab buttons. Figure 10.14 shows the tab buttons displaying dot leaders.

After you select the type of tab you want to use, move the mouse pointer to the position in the ruler where you want to place the tab and click. With the keyboard, press Shift+Tab to place the cursor in the ruler and use the arrow keys to move the cursor to the position you want. Press the space bar to add the tab. To place the tab at a specific location, type the measured location in the tab bar text box and choose Set **T**ab.

If you want to change the unit of measurement displayed in the ruler, click the unit of measurement button next to the **S**et Tab button. You can use inches, centimeters, picas (1/6 inch), or points (1/72 inch).

To move an existing tab, click and drag the tab indicator. With the keyboard, use the arrow keys to move the cursor to the tab. Press the space bar together with the appropriate arrow key to move the tab to the new position.

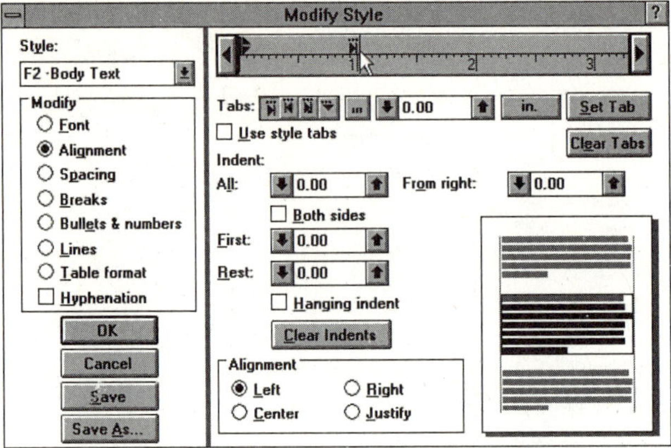

Fig. 10.14
The tab buttons showing the dot leader characters.

To delete a tab, click-and-drag it off the ruler. With the keyboard, move the cursor to the tab and then press Del. To delete all tabs on the ruler, select Cl**e**ar Tabs.

When you set tabs for a style, note that Ami Pro doesn't automatically apply the new tabs for documents using that style sheet. You must select the **U**se Style Tabs option to use the tabs for the style instead of the tabs set in the page-layout process.

Indention and Justification

You also can set paragraph indention in the alignment section of the dialog box. You can indent all lines from one or both sides of each paragraph defined by this style (A**l**l), only the first line (**F**irst), or all lines except the first line (**R**est). To indent from the right, specify an indention amount in the From Right text box. The Fr**o**m Right option indents all lines from the right margin by the amount you specify in the text box.

The middle paragraph of the example box shows the effect of the indention settings. The first line (magenta on a color monitor) shows the setting for the **F**irst option. The middle lines (blue on a color monitor) show the setting for **R**est. Together they show the setting for A**l**l.

To indent from both sides by the amount you specify, select the **B**oth Sides option. When **B**oth Sides is selected, you increment both the A**l**l and Fr**o**m right options when you increment either of them. The **B**oth Sides option is useful for setting off quotations and other material in your documents.

To adjust the indention, click the up- or down-arrow buttons next to the A**l**l, **F**irst, and **R**est text boxes or type the amount of indention you want in the text box for each option. When you click the arrow buttons, Ami Pro increments the amount in the text box by .05 inches in the direction you indicate. (You can change the unit of measurement by clicking the unit of measurement button next to the **S**et Tab button.) Setting A**l**l to .40, **F**irst to .00, **R**est to .70, Fr**o**m Right to .40, and selecting **B**oth Sides, for example, creates the indent shown in the example box in figure 10.15. (The example box is in the lower right corner of the dialog box.)

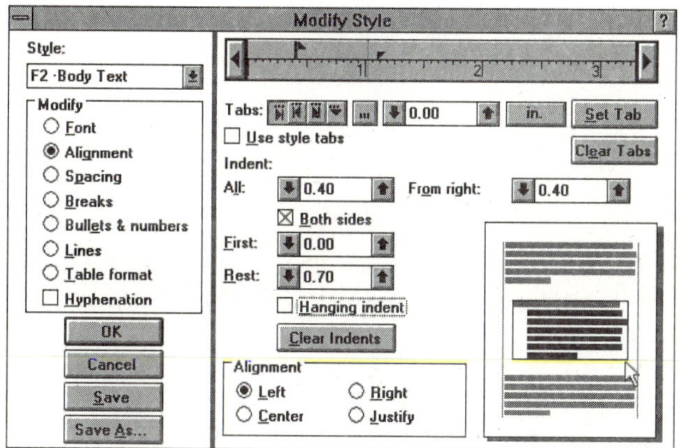

Fig. 10.15 The Modify Style dialog box with Ali**g**nment options.

To set a hanging indent, select the **H**anging Indent option. In a hanging indent, the first line is flush left, and all other lines are indented by the amount you specify. The difference between using a hanging indent and simply indenting all lines after the first line is that in the hanging indent, even text in the first line is indented if it follows a tab. A hanging indent is useful for setting up a term-and-description section where the term you are defining comes before the indent in the first line and is followed by the description.

To specify the paragraph justification, choose **L**eft, **C**enter, **R**ight, or **J**ustify in the Ali**g**nment section.

Changing Spacing

To set spacing options for the style, choose Spacing in the Modify section of the Modify Style dialog box. The spacing options appear in the dialog box, as shown in figure 10.16. In this dialog box, you can set line spacing or leading (the distance each line occupies, including the typeface and the space below each line), paragraph spacing (the distance between paragraphs), and text tightness (the width of characters on the line). Text tightness controls kerning. Kerning is the reduction of space between individual letters so that the characters look aesthetically pleasing.

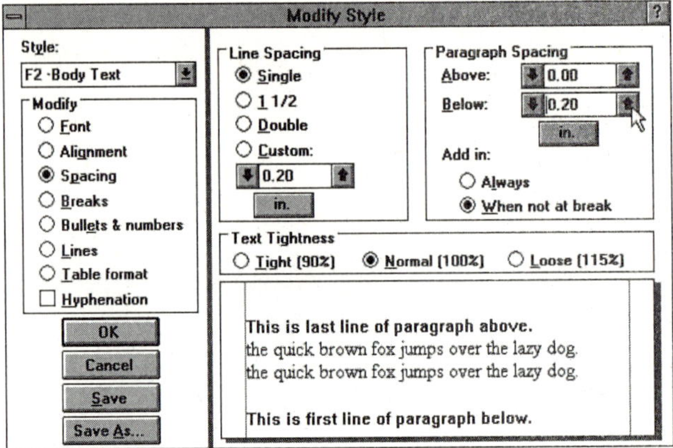

Fig. 10.16
The Modify Style dialog box with Spacing options.

For the Line Spacing options, choose **S**ingle, **1** 1/2, **D**ouble, or **C**ustom. If you choose **C**ustom, type the desired line spacing (in inches) in the text box. You also can use the arrow buttons to set custom spacing. Each time you click the arrow button, the distance increments by .05 inches. To change the unit of measurement, use the unit of measurement button as described in the preceding section.

In the Paragraph Spacing section, use the **A**bove and **B**elow options to specify the amount of space you want to insert before and after the paragraph, respectively. The **A**bove option specifies the amount of space before the first line of the paragraph. The **B**elow option specifies the amount of space after the last line of the paragraph in that style. (Again, you can change the unit of measurement as desired.) Figure 10.16 illustrates Paragraph Spacing **B**elow of .20; notice the spacing in the example box.

Note

Be consistent in how you use paragraph spacing in a style sheet. If you specify spacing **A**bove for certain styles in the sheet, use the same option for all other styles. If you have space above some paragraphs and below others, you may end up with what appears to be too much space between some paragraphs and too little between others.

Note

When deciding how much space to use, think about how much text you want on each page. Extra space between paragraphs can make text easier to read, but too much space places too little text on each page and forces the reader to turn pages frequently.

The Add In option tells Ami Pro when to apply the indicated paragraph spacing—**A**lways or **W**hen Not at Break. If you select **Al**ways, less text and extra space appear on the page. With this option selected, Ami Pro applies paragraph spacing even if a paragraph is first or last on a page. To increase the amount of text on each page and make the pages appear uniform, select **W**hen Not at Break.

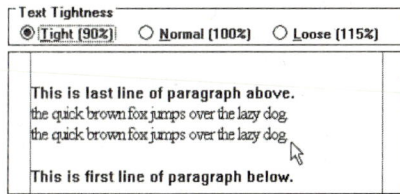

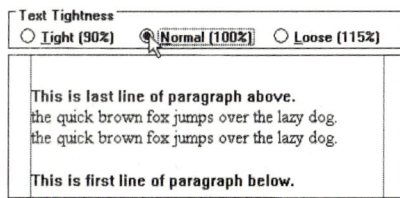

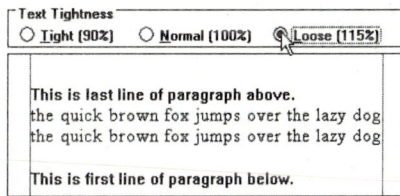

Tip

For ease of reading, choose **N**ormal Text Tightness for body text, or any text 14-point and smaller. You can use the **T**ight or **L**oose options, however, for larger type sizes.

For the Text Tightness options (kerning), choose **T**ight if you want the text characters to occupy only 90 percent of their usual space. Choose **N**ormal if you want the characters to occupy their usual amount of space (100 percent). Choose **L**oose to increase character space to 115 percent of its usual space. The example boxes in figures 10.17, 10.18, and 10.19 show the effects of selecting **T**ight, **N**ormal, and **L**oose, respectively.

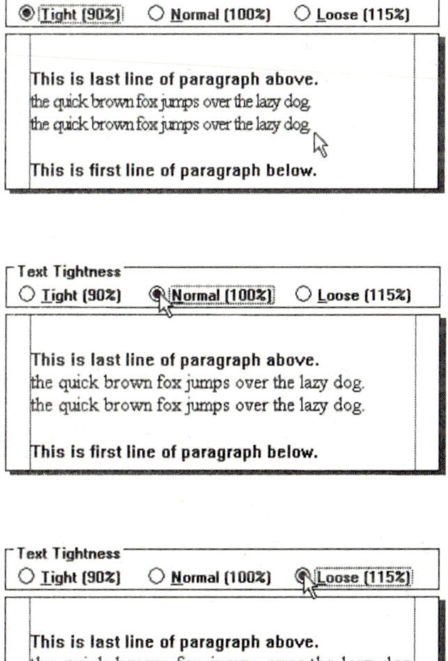

Tight (90%)
Normal (100%)
Loose (115%)
This is last line of paragraph above.
the quick brown fox jumps over the lazy dog
the quick brown fox jumps over the lazy dog
This is first line of paragraph below.

Tight (90%)
Normal (100%)
Loose (115%)
This is last line of paragraph above.
the quick brown fox jumps over the lazy dog
the quick brown fox jumps over the lazy dog
This is first line of paragraph below.

Fig. 10.17 Text shown with the **T**ight option selected.

Fig. 10.18 Text shown with the **N**ormal option selected.

Fig. 10.19 Text shown with the **L**oose option selected.

Changing Page Breaks

Tight (90%)
Normal (100%)
Loose (115%)
This is last line of paragraph above.
the quick brown fox jumps over the lazy dog.
the quick brown fox jumps over the lazy dog.
This is first line of paragraph below.

To specify page breaks for your style, choose **B**reaks in the Modify section of the Modify Style dialog box. The Breaks options appear in the dialog box, as shown in figure 10.20.

The following paragraphs describe the effects you achieve with the Breaks options.

- *Page Break* ***B****efore Paragraph.* Ami Pro places a page break before each paragraph using this style. This option isn't appropriate for most styles but is useful for a style that must appear at the top of a page, such as a chapter heading.
- *Page Break* ***A****fter Paragraph.* Ami Pro places a page break after every paragraph in this style. This option can be appropriate for some title pages.

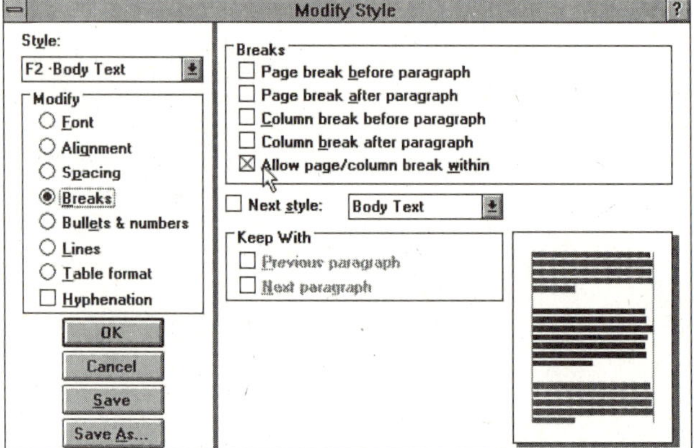

Fig. 10.20
The Modify Style dialog box with options for creating breaks.

- ***C****olumn Break Before Paragraph.* Ami Pro places a column break before each paragraph containing this style. This option is useful for material that must appear at the top of a column, such as titles for columns of data or lists.
- *Column* ***B****reak After Paragraph.* Ami Pro inserts a column break immediately after a paragraph in the selected style. This option can be useful, for example, if you use a particular style for summing up the contents of a column.
- *Allow Page/Column Break* ***W****ithin.* Using this option avoids unnecessary blank space on pages and in columns. Text using this paragraph style can continue from one column to another or from one page to another. If this option is deselected, Ami Pro moves any paragraph that cannot be completed within a column or page to the succeeding column or page. This is a default Body Text setting in most Ami Pro style sheets.

Below the Breaks section of the dialog box is another option you may find useful for special cases—Next **S**tyle. A list box showing the styles in the

The Add In option tells Ami Pro when to apply the indicated paragraph spacing—**A**lways or **W**hen Not at Break. If you select **A**lways, less text and extra space appear on the page. With this option selected, Ami Pro applies paragraph spacing even if a paragraph is first or last on a page. To increase the amount of text on each page and make the pages appear uniform, select **W**hen Not at Break.

For the Text Tightness options (kerning), choose **T**ight if you want the text characters to occupy only 90 percent of their usual space. Choose **N**ormal if you want the characters to occupy their usual amount of space (100 percent). Choose **L**oose to increase character space to 115 percent of its usual space. The example boxes in figures 10.17, 10.18, and 10.19 show the effects of selecting **T**ight, **N**ormal, and **L**oose, respectively.

Tip

For ease of reading, choose **N**ormal Text Tightness for body text, or any text 14-point and smaller. You can use the **T**ight or **L**oose options, however, for larger type sizes.

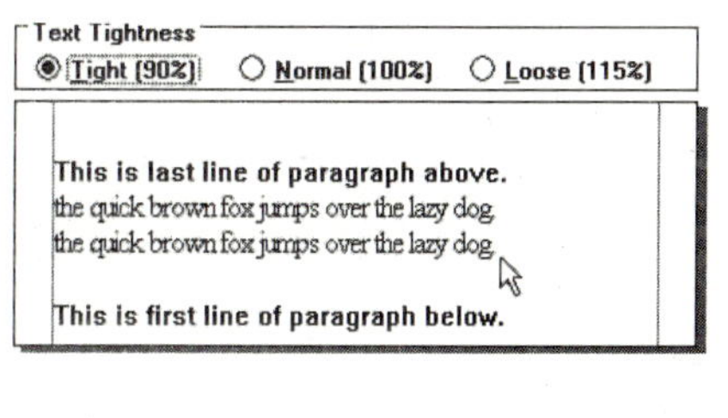
Text Tightness
Tight (90%)
Normal (100%)
Loose (115%)
This is last line of paragraph above.
the quick brown fox jumps over the lazy dog
the quick brown fox jumps over the lazy dog
This is first line of paragraph below.

Fig. 10.17
Text shown with the **T**ight option selected.

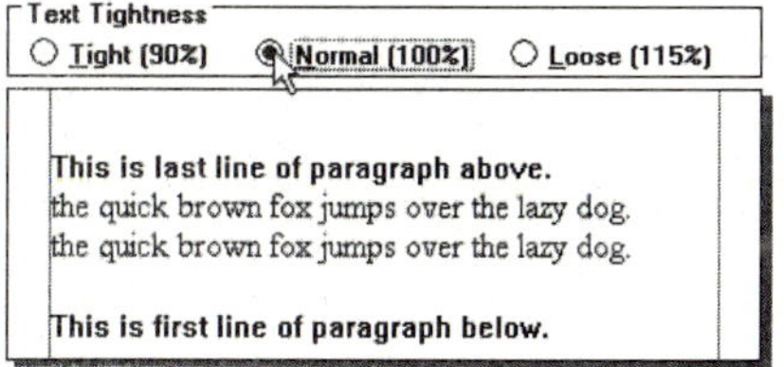
Text Tightness
Tight (90%)
Normal (100%)
Loose (115%)
This is last line of paragraph above.
the quick brown fox jumps over the lazy dog.
the quick brown fox jumps over the lazy dog.
This is first line of paragraph below.

Fig. 10.18
Text shown with the **N**ormal option selected.

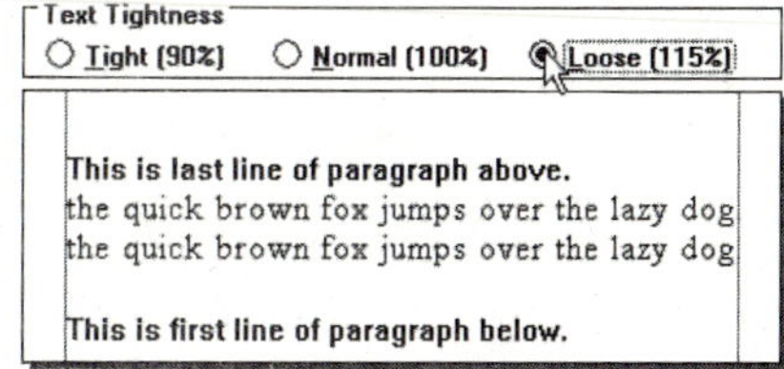
Text Tightness
Tight (90%)
Normal (100%)
Loose (115%)
This is last line of paragraph above.
the quick brown fox jumps over the lazy dog
the quick brown fox jumps over the lazy dog
This is first line of paragraph below.

Fig. 10.19
Text shown with the **L**oose option selected.

Changing Page Breaks

To specify page breaks for your style, choose **B**reaks in the Modify section of the Modify Style dialog box. The Breaks options appear in the dialog box, as shown in figure 10.20.

The following paragraphs describe the effects you achieve with the Breaks options.

- *Page Break **B**efore Paragraph.* Ami Pro places a page break before each paragraph using this style. This option isn't appropriate for most styles but is useful for a style that must appear at the top of a page, such as a chapter heading.

- *Page Break **A**fter Paragraph.* Ami Pro places a page break after every paragraph in this style. This option can be appropriate for some title pages.

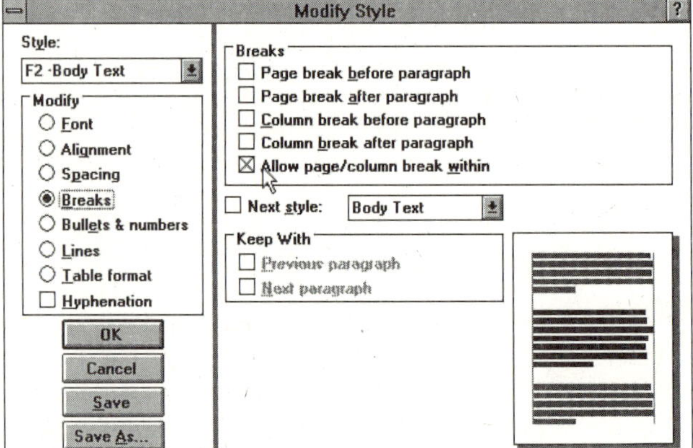

Fig. 10.20
The Modify Style dialog box with options for creating breaks.

- ***C**olumn Break Before Paragraph.* Ami Pro places a column break before each paragraph containing this style. This option is useful for material that must appear at the top of a column, such as titles for columns of data or lists.

- *Column **B**reak After Paragraph.* Ami Pro inserts a column break immediately after a paragraph in the selected style. This option can be useful, for example, if you use a particular style for summing up the contents of a column.

- *Allow Page/Column Break **W**ithin.* Using this option avoids unnecessary blank space on pages and in columns. Text using this paragraph style can continue from one column to another or from one page to another. If this option is deselected, Ami Pro moves any paragraph that cannot be completed within a column or page to the succeeding column or page. This is a default Body Text setting in most Ami Pro style sheets.

Below the Breaks section of the dialog box is another option you may find useful for special cases—Next **S**tyle. A list box showing the styles in the document accompanies this option. Perhaps you want every paragraph in a certain style to be followed by a paragraph in another style; for example, you may want every main title to be followed immediately by a subtitle.

The Next **S**tyle option takes effect when you press Enter at the end of a paragraph. If you press Enter in the middle of an existing paragraph, however, the new paragraph keeps the style of the preceding paragraph.

The Breaks section of the dialog box also displays two Keep With options. If you select **P**revious Paragraph, Ami Pro prevents a page break between a paragraph using this option and the paragraph that precedes it. This option is useful for certain list formats. If you select **N**ext Paragraph, Ami Pro prevents a page break from occurring between a paragraph using this option and the paragraph that follows it.

Changing Bullets and Numbers

Special design effects include bullets, numbers, and text that Ami Pro displays before paragraphs formatted in a certain style. To modify bullets and numbers, choose Bull**e**ts & Numbers in the Modify section of the Modify Style dialog box. The Bull**e**ts & Numbers options appear in the dialog box, as shown in figure 10.21.

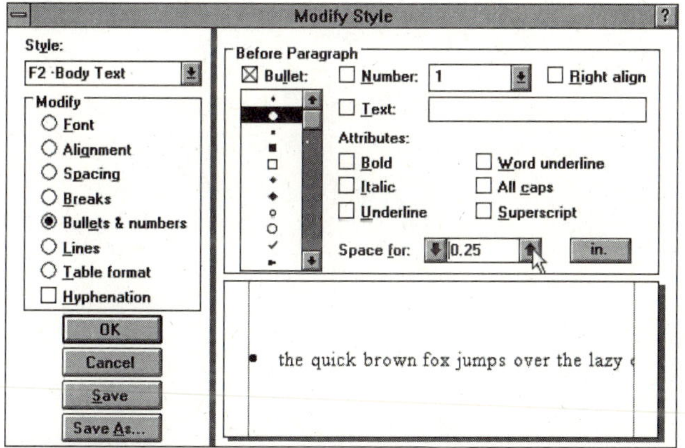

Fig. 10.21
The Modify Style dialog box with Bull**e**ts & Numbers options.

The Before Paragraph section enables you to set up a bullet, a number, or text to appear before paragraphs formatted in the specified style. Normally, you use only one of the three possibilities (bullet, number, or text) although Ami Pro accepts all three in any combination. If you combine all three options, the generally accepted sequence is the bullet first, followed by the number, and then the text.

To include a bullet, select Bu**l**let and specify the bullet style you want in the list box. Again, refer to figure 10.21. The sample text shows the selected bullet. Notice, too, that the Space For option allows for .25 inches of space between the bullet and the text.

To insert a number, select **N**umber and indicate the desired numbering style in the list box (choose from upper- or lowercase Roman numerals, Arabic numerals, or upper- or lowercase letters). Ami Pro uses the number style you select and automatically numbers series of paragraphs. If another number style interrupts the series, Ami Pro restarts the numbering.

In addition, Ami Pro enables you to right-align the numbers in your paragraph styles. This option should be used any time you combine one-, two-, and three-digit numbers in your list (as in 9, 10, and 100). To effect this change, choose **R**ight Align to the right of the **N**umber option in the Before Paragraph section.

To include text before the paragraph, select **T**ext and type the desired text in the text box. You can use such words as Item or Resolved (see fig. 10.22). You can specify up to 30 keyboard characters, including letters, numbers, spaces, and symbols.

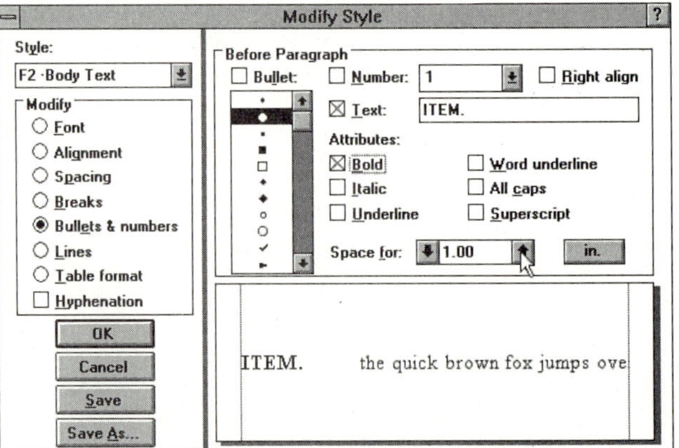

Fig. 10.22
The Modify Style dialog box with Bu**l**lets & Numbers options.

You can specify attributes for the special effects bullet, number, or text. Select or deselect **B**old, **I**talic, **U**nderline, **W**ord Underline, All **C**aps, or **S**uperscript, as desired. As you make changes, you see the effects in the example box. The special effect can be a bullet, a number, some text, or any combination of the three options. Remember, however, that you cannot modify the attributes of just one option; the attributes you assign apply to all selected options.

In the Space **F**or text box, you can specify the amount of space between the bullet and text, the number and text, or the text and following text. Click the arrow buttons next to the box to increment by .05 inches or type the amount of space you want. (As usual, you can change the unit of measurement with the button to the right of this option.)

Changing Lines

By choosing **L**ines in the Modify section of the Modify Style dialog box, you can access options to control the style, length, and color of lines above and below each paragraph formatted in that style (see fig. 10.23).

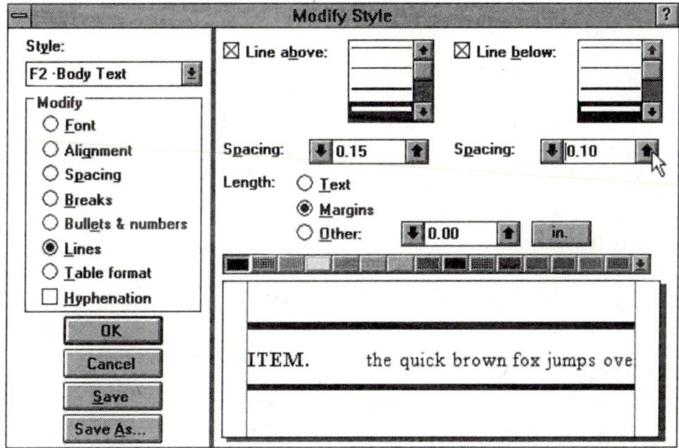

Fig. 10.23
The Modify Style dialog box with **L**ines options.

You indicate where you want Ami Pro to place the line or lines by selecting Line A**b**ove or Line **B**elow. With the mouse, click the option. With the keyboard, press **B** twice. (Pressing **B** once selects **B**reaks in the Modify section; pressing **B** again moves to the Line A**b**ove option. If you press **B** a third time, you can move to the Line **B**elow option.) Press the space bar to select the option. (You can specify one option, or both options as in figure 10.23.) When you specify the style for each line (thick, thin, single, double, and so on), keep in mind that you can use a different line style for each location. Specify how far you want Ami Pro to space the line from the paragraph text by choosing S**p**acing and typing or selecting the desired distance between the line and the text.

The Length options refer to whether the line extends to match the text (**T**ext), stretches from margin to margin (**M**argins), as in figure 10.23, or extends a specified length (**O**ther). If you select **O**ther, the line begins at the left margin, or at the start of the line of text; you specify the desired line length in the text box or scroll the box to choose the desired length. (Change the unit of measurement if desired.)

You can specify the color of the line by selecting a color from the color bar. To display more color options, select the arrow button to the right of the color bar. Then choose the desired color.

Note

If you specify a color but don't have a color printer, the color still appears on your (color) monitor. When you print, Ami Pro translates the color into an appropriate gray shade. Ami Pro also contains gray shades in the color bar. If you are not printing to a color printer, use a gray shade so you have more control over your output.

Changing Table Format

You can change the format of tables in the style by choosing **T**able Format in the Modify section of the Modify Style dialog box. The table format options appear, as shown in figure 10.24.

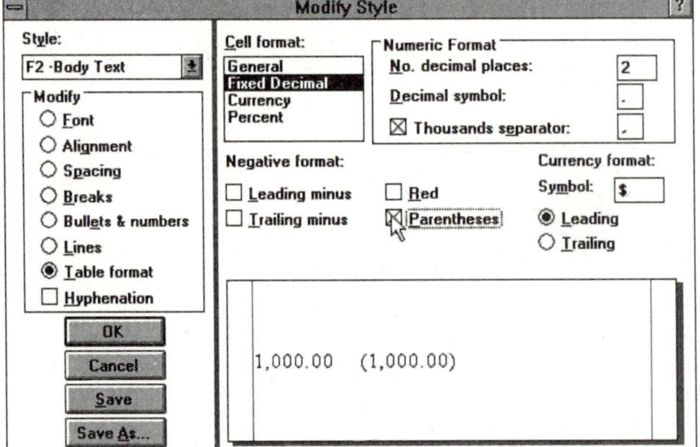

Fig. 10.24
The Modify Style dialog box with **T**able Format options.

Use the table options if you are using numeric data in tables in the paragraphs formatted with this style. Choices in this version of the dialog box fall into four categories: **C**ell Format, Numeric Format, Negative Format, and Currency Format. The following paragraphs describe the categories and options.

Cell format refers to the way Ami Pro displays numbers in the table. The **C**ell Format section of the dialog box offers four types of cell format display, described in the following list:

- *General*. Numbers are displayed with no decimal places.

- *Fixed decimal.* Numbers are displayed with the decimal places you specify.
- *Currency.* Numbers are displayed with the currency symbol you specify.
- *Percent.* Numbers are displayed with a percent symbol.

In the Numeric Format section, you can specify the following options:

- ***N**o. Decimal Places.* This option specifies the number of decimal places for cells formatted as Fixed Decimal.
- ***D**ecimal Symbol.* Use this option to specify the symbol used for the decimal point in Fixed Decimal format (the symbol can be a period or some other character).
- *Thousands S**e**parator.* This option specifies the character Ami Pro uses to separate thousands from the rest of the number (usually a comma or no separator character).

In the Negative format section of the dialog box, you decide how Ami Pro displays negative numbers in a table. Following are descriptions of the four choices:

- ***L**eading Minus.* With this format (the most common, therefore the default), a minus sign appears in front of negative numbers.
- ***T**railing Minus.* Use this option to display a minus sign at the end of negative numbers.
- ***R**ed.* Selecting this option displays in red any negative numbers and the symbols (such as the minus sign) associated with them. **R**ed prints red if you have a color printer. If your printer only prints black, those negative numbers specified as **R**ed just print as a dark screen. With small numbers (10- or 12-point), the numbers resemble those printed on a dot-matrix printer.
- ***P**arentheses.* This option displays parentheses around negative numbers.

The Currency format options are useful if you are working with international currencies. You have the following choices:

- *Sy**m**bol.* When you select this option, currency is displayed with the symbol you specify in the text box. You can use any ANSI or ASCII symbol.

- *Leading.* Using this option displays the currency symbol at the beginning of the number.

- *Trailing.* Select this option to display the currency symbol at the end of the number.

In figure 10.24, the example box shows the result of specifying a fixed decimal format with two decimal places, using a period for the decimal symbol and a comma for the thousands separator. The fixed decimal format in this case uses parentheses for negative numbers.

Changing Hyphenation

You can specify whether hyphenation is on or off for paragraphs formatted with this style by selecting **H**yphenation in the Modify section of the Modify Style dialog box. Unlike the other choices in the Modify Style dialog box, the **H**yphenation option doesn't display a set of additional options. This option acts as a toggle—it is selected or deselected.

In Ami Pro, you control hyphenation with paragraph styles, but you choose the size of the hyphenation hot-zone in the User Setup Options dialog box (choose Too**l**s **U**ser Setup **O**ptions to access the dialog box and then choose **H**yphenation Hot-zone to specify the hot-zone setup). Chapter 7, "Proofreading and Printing a Document," contains more details on hyphenation.

Tip
Always select **H**yphenation when the body text is justified. Otherwise, the resulting "rivers" of white space are distracting and make the text hard to read.

Hyphenation affects the appearance of the document. If you use hyphenation, Ami Pro can fit more characters on each line. If your text is left-aligned, the right side of the page looks less ragged if you use hyphenation. If you use full justification, selecting hyphenation usually means less white space between the words on the page.

You can override hyphenation for a particular word. Select the word you don't want to hyphenate (for example, a long proper noun). Choose **E**dit **M**ark Text and then choose **N**o Hyphenation to deselect hyphenation for that word.

You also can specify where Ami Pro hyphenates a word. Position the insertion point at the location in the word where you want the discretionary hyphen. Press Ctrl+- (hyphen) to set up a marker. If Ami Pro needs to hyphenate the word, the software hyphenates at the point you place the marker.

To control hyphenation for the style, select or deselect the hyphenation option in the Modify Style dialog box. Ami Pro applies the following principles in hyphenating.

- If the entire word cannot fit on a line, Ami Pro hyphenates the word instead of wrapping to the next line.
- Within a paragraph, no more than two consecutive lines are hyphenated.
- Words separated by a nonbreaking space (words between which you press Ctrl+space bar) aren't hyphenated.
- Words containing numerals aren't hyphenated.

Managing Styles

When you create or modify a style while working in a document, Ami Pro saves that style with the document. If you create new styles or modify existing styles while working with a document, you may want to make those styles a permanent part of the style sheet. This action makes the styles available to other documents using that style sheet.

This section explains how to manipulate your styles so you can use newly created or modified styles with other style sheets. You also can use selected styles from multiple style sheets in the same document.

The Style Management dialog box shown in figure 10.25 shows the options you use for moving, removing, and undoing changes in styles. You can access the dialog box by choosing **S**tyle Style Ma**n**agement.

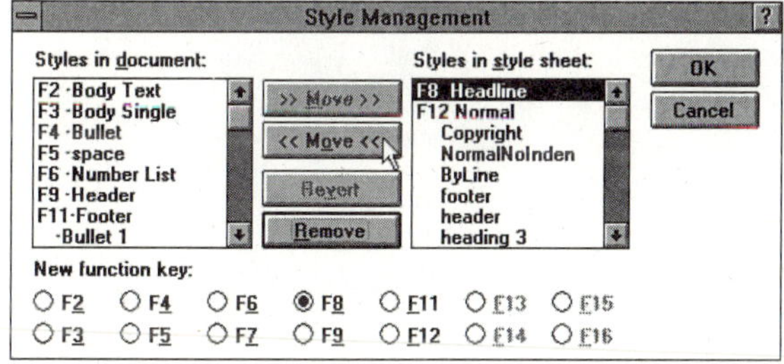

Fig. 10.25
The Style Management dialog box.

The following sections describe the options in the Style Management dialog box.

Moving Styles to a Style Sheet

Adding a style to a style sheet by using the Style Management dialog box enables you to permanently assign to that style sheet a particular style that you created for a document. After the style is assigned to the style sheet, you can use the style with other documents as well. You also can use the Style Management dialog box to remove unwanted styles from the document or the style sheet. When you remove a style, any text formatted in that style reverts to the body text format.

The unmodified styles that Ami Pro provides with the style sheet for the current document appear in the Styles in **S**tyle Sheet list box in the Style Management dialog box. Styles that you create or modify while editing the current document appear in the Styles in **D**ocument list box.

If you leave the current document and later access the style sheet again, only the styles you store with the style sheet are available. Use the Style Management dialog box if you want styles you created in the document to become a permanent part of the style sheet.

If you want to move your modified style to the style sheet, highlight the name of the style in the Styles in **D**ocument list box. Notice that the top **M**ove button (with arrows pointing right) changes from gray to black to indicate the direction in which you move the style. Choose **M**ove to add the style to the style sheet. The style name moves from the Styles in **D**ocument list box to the Styles in **S**tyle Sheet list box, and the style becomes part of the style sheet. That style sheet then has the new style available for future use.

Caution

If you move a style name from the Styles in **D**ocument list box to the Styles in **S**tyle Sheet list box, that style replaces any style with the same name. If you modify a style and then move it to the Styles in **S**tyle Sheet list box, you lose the old style with the same name in the style sheet. This change affects all documents retaining the link to this style sheet and all documents using this style.

You also can move a style from the style sheet to the document. This action ensures that you maintain the original style from the style sheet for the current document (even if you later change the style in the style sheet).

Reversing Changes to the Style Sheet

You easily can undo changes made to existing styles by using the Re**v**ert option in the Style Management dialog box (refer to fig. 10.25). Re**v**ert returns a style to the characteristics of the original style.

> **Caution**
>
> If you select the **K**eep Format With Document option in the Save **A**s dialog box when you save the document, you cannot use the Re**v**ert option. To revert to another style, choose Style **U**se Another Style Sheet (even if the style sheet you use is the one you used originally, before saving the format with the document).

To undo modifications made to a style not yet saved, highlight the style (for example, the Byline style) in the Styles in **D**ocument list box and choose Re**v**ert. The style name (in this case, Byline) moves to the Styles in **S**tyle Sheet list box. Choose OK or press Enter. Ami Pro returns to the document; paragraphs formatted with the Byline style revert to the characteristics of the original style.

Removing Styles

Perhaps you don't like the look of a style or you realize that a new style is redundant with the others you have available. When this situation occurs, you can remove a style from the document or from the style sheet.

To remove a style, highlight the style name in the Styles in **D**ocument or Styles in **S**tyle Sheet list box and choose **R**emove (refer to fig. 10.25).

> **Caution**
>
> If you try to remove a style listed in the Styles in **S**tyle Sheet list box, Ami Pro warns you that removing the style affects other documents in which you have used that style. If you want to cancel the procedure, choose **N**o in the warning box. If you want to proceed, choose **Y**es.

If you remove any style from the Styles in **S**tyle Sheet list box, Ami Pro changes paragraphs formatted with that style to the Body Text style. If you remove a modified style from the Styles in **D**ocument list box, paragraphs formatted in that style revert to the style with the same name in the Styles in **S**tyle Sheet list box. If no style with that name exists, the paragraphs revert to Body Text style.

Tip
You cannot delete the Body Text style from the Styles in **S**tyle Sheet list box. You also cannot delete the Footnote or Table Text style if a footnote or table still exists in the document.

Assigning Function Keys

Ami Pro enables you to assign styles to function keys. Using function keys to format may be faster than pointing and clicking with the Styles box or the Status Bar. Ami Pro assigns styles in style sheets to function keys. After you create a new style, Ami Pro assigns it to the first available function key.

To change the arrangement of function key assignments, begin by highlighting the desired style in the Styles in **D**ocument or Styles in **S**tyle Sheet list box. If the highlighted style has a current function key assignment, that function key is selected in the New function key section of the dialog box (refer to fig. 10.25). To assign a function key to the highlighted style, press the desired function key or select the appropriate function key button in the dialog box.

Ami Pro assigns the new function key and, if necessary, repositions the style in the Styles in **S**tyle Sheet list box. If another style is assigned to the function key you choose, that style loses its current function key assignment. You have the option of assigning another function key to that style.

Creating a New Style Sheet

When you create a new style or modify an existing style, Ami Pro saves that style with the document in which it is created. To make your new or modified styles available in other documents, you can save the styles to an existing style sheet (as discussed earlier) or create a new style sheet.

You can benefit from creating your own style sheets. The style sheets that come with Ami Pro are a "best guess" by the manufacturer of what your needs are likely to be. You can create style sheets, however, that fit your needs exactly. You can create a letter style sheet to use with your letterhead or a memo format that follows your company's conventions. If you prepare papers or chapters according to a certain style, you can set up a style sheet to reflect those requirements. Chapter 19, "Desktop Publishing with Ami Pro," contains detailed information about creating your own style sheets.

To create a new style sheet, choose **S**tyle Sa**v**e as a Style Sheet from within an open document. The Save as a Style Sheet dialog box appears, as shown in figure 10.26. The existing style sheet name appears in the **F**ile Name text box. Type a new name for the style sheet in the text box. Follow the DOS naming conventions; type from one to eight characters, a period, and **STY** to identify the file as an Ami Pro style sheet. Then choose OK or press Enter. Ami Pro returns to the document, and the new style sheet's name appears in the Styles box.

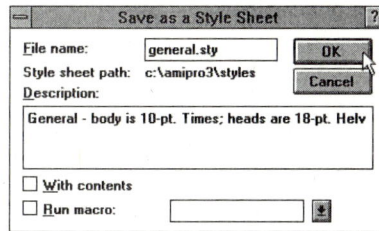

Fig. 10.26
The Save as a Style Sheet dialog box, with a new style sheet name in the **F**ile name text box.

Caution

You can use the name of an existing style sheet in the Sa**v**e as a Style Sheet text box. If you overwrite one of the style sheets that comes with Ami Pro, you must reinstall the program to restore the original styles in that style sheet. If you aren't sure that you want to replace an existing style sheet, save your style under a different name.

Note

If you have text that you want to appear in every document using a particular style sheet, select **W**ith Contents when you use the Save as a Style Sheet dialog box to save the style sheet. This option is useful, for example, if you want the company letterhead to appear at the top of the first page of the document.

You can make the purpose of a style sheet obvious by providing sample contents. You even can include sample text that you later can delete so that you can see how the styles in the style sheet look. For a letter style sheet, for example, you can type prompts for the date, the address, and so on. You can assign macros to automate these prompts (use **R**un Macro in the Save as a Style Sheet dialog box). In addition, Ami Pro offers some style sheets with macros that prompt you for this information. See the Appendix, "A Guide to Style Sheets," for more information on Ami Pro's style sheets. Chapter 23, "Using Macros," contains more information about writing and assigning macros.

In addition to styles, style sheets contain page-layout specifications such as margins, columns, and tab settings. If you change the page layout in your document, Ami Pro saves those changes with the document but doesn't change the style sheet. If you want to use the new page layout as part of a style sheet (so that you can use the layout in other documents), be sure to save the style sheet under a new name, using the procedures described in this section.

Summary

In this chapter, you learned how to use style sheets to create good-looking documents without having to design your own layouts and typefaces. You learned how to select and change a style sheet, how to create new styles, how to modify existing styles, and how to manage styles so that you can use them with more than one document.

In the next chapter, "Outlining a Document," you learn how to take your document's organization one step further, by using Ami Pro's outlining feature to plan and organize your writing.

Chapter 11

Outlining a Document

Writing an outline is sometimes tedious and time-consuming, but outlining is the best method for organizing a writing project. An outline displays a document in an easy-to-read and quick-to-analyze layout. Ami Pro's outlining features are powerful and make creating an outline a simple task.

Ami Pro offers two approaches to creating an outline. You can create an outline in *layout mode* or *draft mode* using an outline style sheet, or you can create an outline in *outline mode*. As you have already learned, with the default style sheet assigned, layout mode and draft mode are unstructured, open work areas. This type of work area is highly flexible and enables you to create whatever type of document you require.

Outline mode, on the other hand, is a highly structured work area. Outline mode enables you to break up your document into headings, subheadings, and paragraphs quickly. Each heading, subheading, and paragraph is indented to a specific level. The benefit of working in outline mode is that you can manipulate a document in ways unavailable in draft or layout mode. In outline mode, you can *collapse* a document so that you see only the main headings. Collapsing a heading subordinates all subheadings and paragraphs; therefore, if you move or delete the collapsed heading, you move or delete all its subordinate subheadings and paragraphs, which enables you to change your document quickly. By moving the collapsed headings, you can rearrange an entire document with only a few keystrokes.

Ami Pro offers three outline style sheets that structure the layout mode or draft mode like a traditional outline. As you learned in Chapter 10, all files in Ami Pro have an assigned style sheet—a fax style sheet, a memo style sheet, an outline style sheet, or the default style sheet. Ami Pro has 60 different predefined style sheets! The style sheet sets the structure and the style of the document. When you execute a **F**ile **N**ew command to open a new document, you must assign a style sheet before the new document appears on-screen. The default style sheet in layout mode and draft mode is a blank work area. To set a specific structure in layout mode or draft mode (for a fax or an outline, for example), you assign a fax or an outline style sheet to the document.

You don't need to use an outline style sheet if you are going to work in outline mode. Because you don't need a set structure in outline mode (the mode itself is structured) and the default style sheet assigns different styles to the levels of the outline (and you can change the styles at any time as you work with the outline), you should use the default style sheet if you are going to work in outline mode.

In this chapter, you learn how to create an outline using outline style sheets in layout mode and draft mode, and how to create an outline using outline mode. You learn how to access outline mode and how to use the capabilities of outline mode to expand and contract an outline and to promote, demote, and move levels. You discover how to edit a document quickly, using the standard icons available only in outline mode.

You also learn the process of printing specific levels of the document—a useful printing option also available in outline mode only.

This chapter also discusses how to assign an outline style sheet in layout mode and draft mode and how to use the style sheet to create an outline in those modes. You also learn how to change the format of the style sheets (default and outline) to fit your needs best. You can change the style sheet, for example, so that the Title style is bordered Times Roman bold 25, left-aligned, rather than unbordered Courier italic 30, center-aligned.

Finally, you learn how to create your own outline numbering system to display in any mode—outline, draft, or layout.

Understanding Outline Mode

Outline mode is a powerful utility for organizing a document. When you use outline mode, you work with a multilevel structure. Each level has a heading and can contain subordinate headings and paragraphs. As explained in the "Editing an Outline" section of this chapter, you can choose to view only the main headings of your document (known as the first level); the first and second level headings; the first, second, and third level headings; and so on. You can change the level of a section, a heading, or a paragraph any time (a heading and its subordinate headings and paragraphs is known as a *section*). You can change a third-level section to a second-level section, for example.

Besides the outline structure, the outline style is another important facet of working in outline mode. The outline style refers to the typeface (Courier, Arial, and so on), point size (12, 18, and so on), and attribute (bold, italic, and so on) for the level. Each level is assigned a different outline style.

Outline mode has a few restrictions not found in other modes. In outline mode, Ami Pro cannot display text or pictures in unanchored frames, but can display tables, text, and pictures in anchored frames. You can edit the contents of an anchored frame, but you cannot create, cut, copy, or move a frame. See Chapter 16, "Using Frames," for more information on frames.

◄ See "Using Display Modes," p. 164

Using the Outline Menu, Icons, and Buttons

Outline mode offers methods for manipulating your document in ways that you may find indispensable when you become familiar with this mode. You can contract a document to display main headings only and then expand all or part of those headings. You can reposition a section swiftly by clicking and dragging it to a new position. You learn about such capabilities in "Editing an Outline," later in this chapter.

Figure 11.1 shows a document typed in outline mode. The *outline level icons* and *command icons* appear along the top of the document window (below the SmartIcons if you have the SmartIcons displayed at the top of the document window). *Outline buttons* appear to the left of each heading and paragraph, and the **O**utline menu appears in the Menu Bar. All the outline headings and paragraphs are at the same level and therefore have the same outline button. The outline is structured when you type the document into outline mode.

Note

If the outline buttons don't appear, choose **V**iew View **P**references or the View Preferences SmartIcon to access the View Preferences dialog box. Choose the Outline **B**uttons option; choose OK or press Enter to exit the dialog box. (See Chapter 8, "Changing Your Setup," for more information.)

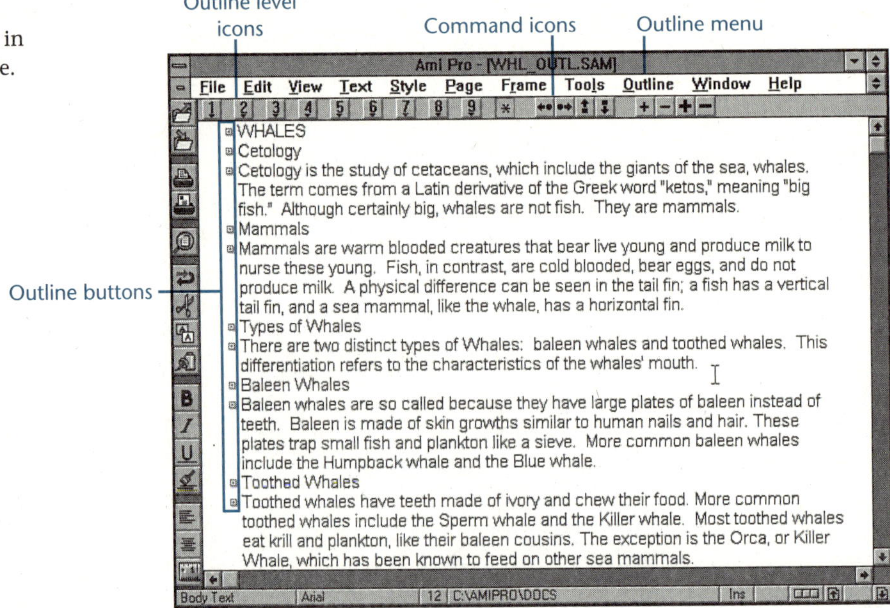
Outline level icons
Command icons
Outline menu
Outline buttons
Ami Pro - [WHL_OUTL.SAM]
File Edit View Text Style Page Frame Tools Outline Window Help
WHALES
Cetology
Cetology is the study of cetaceans, which include the giants of the sea, whales. The term comes from a Latin derivative of the Greek word "ketos," meaning "big fish." Although certainly big, whales are not fish. They are mammals.
Mammals
Mammals are warm blooded creatures that bear live young and produce milk to nurse these young. Fish, in contrast, are cold blooded, bear eggs, and do not produce milk. A physical difference can be seen in the tail fin; a fish has a vertical tail fin, and a sea mammal, like the whale, has a horizontal fin.
Types of Whales
There are two distinct types of Whales: baleen whales and toothed whales. This differentiation refers to the characteristics of the whales' mouth.
Baleen Whales
Baleen whales are so called because they have large plates of baleen instead of teeth. Baleen is made of skin growths similar to human nails and hair. These plates trap small fish and plankton like a sieve. More common baleen whales include the Humpback whale and the Blue whale.
Toothed Whales
Toothed whales have teeth made of ivory and chew their food. More common toothed whales include the Sperm whale and the Killer whale. Most toothed whales eat krill and plankton, like their baleen cousins. The exception is the Orca, or Killer Whale, which has been known to feed on other sea mammals.
Body Text
Arial
12 C:\AMIPRO\DOCS
Ins

Fig. 11.1
A document in outline mode.

> **Note**
>
> To change your Ami Pro setup to use outline mode as the default mode, choose Too**l**s **U**ser Setup to access the User Setup dialog box. Choose **L**oad to access the Load Defaults dialog box; choose **O**utline in the Mode section of the dialog box. Choose OK or press Enter twice to exit the two dialog boxes and return to the document.

Use the mouse to manipulate these icons and buttons. Figure 11.2 points out the individual command icons you use to promote, demote, and move text—the processes that structure your outline.

Many mouse operations, including demoting and promoting text, have keyboard equivalents on the **O**utline menu. Figure 11.3 shows the **O**utline menu.

Figure 11.4 shows the document after the headings and paragraphs have been promoted and demoted to shape the outline. Each heading is considered to be at a specific level after you promote and demote the text.

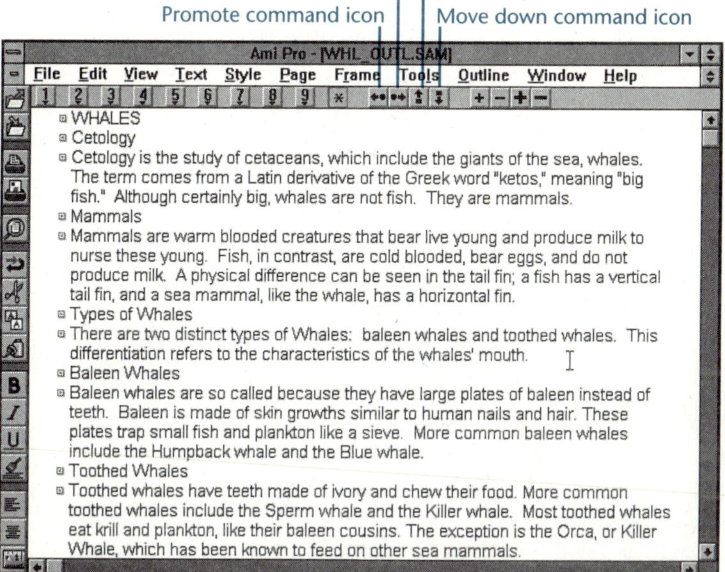
Demote command icon
Promote command icon
Move up command icon
Move down command icon
Ami Pro - [WHL_OUTL.SAM]
File Edit View Text Style Page Frame Tools Outline Window Help
WHALES
Cetology
Cetology is the study of cetaceans, which include the giants of the sea, whales. The term comes from a Latin derivative of the Greek word "ketos," meaning "big fish." Although certainly big, whales are not fish. They are mammals.
Mammals
Mammals are warm blooded creatures that bear live young and produce milk to nurse these young. Fish, in contrast, are cold blooded, bear eggs, and do not produce milk. A physical difference can be seen in the tail fin; a fish has a vertical tail fin, and a sea mammal, like the whale, has a horizontal fin.
Types of Whales
There are two distinct types of Whales: baleen whales and toothed whales. This differentiation refers to the characteristics of the whales' mouth.
Baleen Whales
Baleen whales are so called because they have large plates of baleen instead of teeth. Baleen is made of skin growths similar to human nails and hair. These plates trap small fish and plankton like a sieve. More common baleen whales include the Humpback whale and the Blue whale.
Toothed Whales
Toothed whales have teeth made of ivory and chew their food. More common toothed whales include the Sperm whale and the Killer whale. Most toothed whales eat krill and plankton, like their baleen cousins. The exception is the Orca, or Killer Whale, which has been known to feed on other sea mammals.
Body Text
Arial
12 C:\AMIPRO\DOCS
Ins

Fig. 11.2
The command icons.

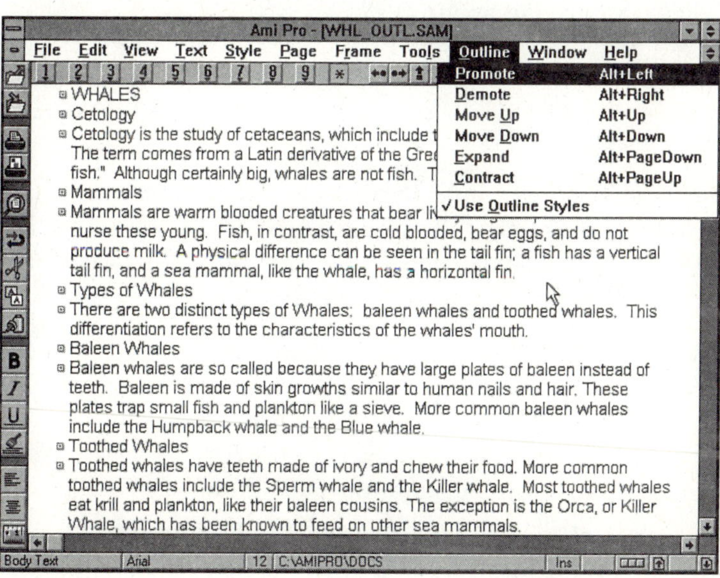
Ami Pro - [WHL_OUTL.SAM]
File Edit View Text Style Page Frame Tools Outline Window Help
Promote Alt+Left
Demote Alt+Right
Move Up Alt+Up
Move Down Alt+Down
Expand Alt+PageDown
Contract Alt+PageUp
✓Use Outline Styles
Body Text
Arial
12 C:\AMIPRO\DOCS
Ins

Fig. 11.3
The **Outline** menu, with keyboard shortcuts at right.

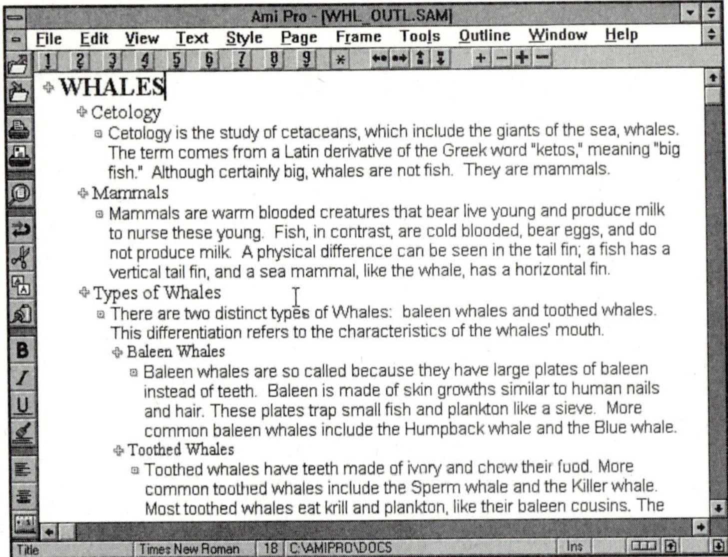
Ami Pro - [WHL_OUTL.SAM]
File Edit View Text Style Page Frame Tools Outline Window Help
WHALES
Cetology
Cetology is the study of cetaceans, which include the giants of the sea, whales. The term comes from a Latin derivative of the Greek word "ketos," meaning "big fish." Although certainly big, whales are not fish. They are mammals.
Mammals
Mammals are warm blooded creatures that bear live young and produce milk to nurse these young. Fish, in contrast, are cold blooded, bear eggs, and do not produce milk. A physical difference can be seen in the tail fin; a fish has a vertical tail fin, and a sea mammal, like the whale, has a horizontal fin.
Types of Whales
There are two distinct types of Whales: baleen whales and toothed whales. This differentiation refers to the characteristics of the whales' mouth.
Baleen Whales
Baleen whales are so called because they have large plates of baleen instead of teeth. Baleen is made of skin growths similar to human nails and hair. These plates trap small fish and plankton like a sieve. More common baleen whales include the Humpback whale and the Blue whale.
Toothed Whales
Toothed whales have teeth made of ivory and chew their food. More common toothed whales include the Sperm whale and the Killer whale. Most toothed whales eat krill and plankton, like their baleen cousins. The
Title
Times New Roman
18
C:\AMIPRO\DOCS
Ins

Fig. 11.4
The sample document with headings and paragraphs at different outline levels.

Outline Hierarchy

Outline mode has 10 different outline levels (1 to 9, and none). All paragraphs are at level none. All headings are assigned a level from 1 to 9. The 10 different outline levels are arranged in a hierarchical structure. Level 1 is highest in the hierarchy, then level 2, and so on. Within this hierarchy, the following rule applies:

> Any heading or paragraph at a particular outline level is subordinate to any other heading above it that has a lower level number. If heading B or paragraph B is subordinate to heading A, whatever action you perform on heading A directly affects heading B or paragraph B.

Figure 11.4 is an example of an outline with several levels. The top heading in this figure, Whales, is assigned level 1. Because Whales is at level 1, all the headings and paragraphs below this level are subordinate to it. The headings Cetology, Mammals, and Types of Whales are at level 2. The headings are independent of each other, but are all subordinate to the level 1 heading. The headings Baleen Whales and Toothed Whales are level 3 headings and are subordinate to the level 2 heading, Types of Whales. Each heading has a subordinate paragraph, except the level 1 heading, Whales. This example shows no level 4 to level 9 headings.

The idea of a heading or paragraph being subordinate to another heading is the basis of the power of the outline view. If you delete a heading, any subordinate headings and paragraphs also are deleted. If you reposition a heading, any subordinate headings and paragraphs can be simultaneously repositioned.

Outline Buttons

After you structure the outline, the outline buttons that appear to the left of each heading indicate whether the heading has subordinate headings and/or paragraphs. You can double-click the buttons to display and hide the subordinate headings and paragraphs. This process is called *expanding* and *contracting*. Double-clicking a plus button contracts a heading with subordinate headings and paragraphs, which hides the subordinate headings and paragraphs. Double-clicking a filled plus button expands a heading to show the hidden headings and paragraphs. (Double-clicking a minus or box button has no effect.) Table 11.1 explains the use of the outline buttons.

Table 11.1 Outline Buttons

Button	Use
Plus	Appears next to a heading set to level 1 to 9; indicates that the heading has subordinate text.
Filled Plus	Appears next to a heading set to level 1 to 9; indicates that the heading has hidden subordinate text.
Minus	Appears next to a heading set to level 1 to 9; indicates that the heading has no subordinate text.
Box	Appears next to text with an outline level of None. Paragraphs appear with a box.

The outline buttons also are powerful tools for repositioning text in your document. You learn how to use the outline buttons for repositioning in the "Editing an Outline" section, later in this chapter.

Command Icons

The *command icons* provide functions similar to the outline buttons. You can use the command icons, as you can the outline buttons, to hide, display, or reposition text. To use the command icons, click the insertion point at the heading or paragraph you want to change, and then click a command icon. Command icons enable you to move a heading without its subordinate headings and paragraphs, something you cannot do using the outline buttons. To move a heading with its subordinate headings and paragraphs using the command buttons, you must select the heading and all its subordinate headings and paragraphs, and then click a command icon. As you learn in the "Editing an Outline" section of this chapter, clicking and dragging the outline buttons to reposition a heading and all its subordinate text is easy.

Table 11.2 summarizes the uses of the command icons.

Table 11.2 Command Icons

Command Icon	Keyboard Equivalent	Use
Asterisk	Alt+0	Displays all headings and paragraphs.
Promote	Alt+left arrow	Changes the indicated heading to the next higher level (moving from level 3 to level 2, for example).
Demote	Alt+right arrow	Changes the indicated heading to the next lower level (moving from level 3 to level 4, for example).
Move Up	Alt+up arrow	Each click moves the indicated heading or paragraph above the preceding heading or paragraph. This command does not change the level of the heading or paragraph but moves it up through the document at the same level. To move a paragraph above the two that directly precede it, for example, click the insertion point at that paragraph and click the Move Up icon twice.
Move Down	Alt+down arrow	Each click moves the indicated heading or paragraph below the following heading or paragraph. This command does not change the level of the heading or paragraph but moves it down through the document at the same level.
Small Plus		Displays hidden subordinate text for the indicated heading, one level at a time, starting with the next highest level.

Command Icon	Keyboard Equivalent	Use
Small Minus		Hides displayed subordinate text for the indicated paragraph, one level at a time, starting with the lowest level.
Large Plus	Alt+PgUp	Displays all hidden text for the indicated heading.
Large Minus	Alt+PgDn	Hides all displayed text for the indicated heading.

Outline Level Icons

When you click an outline level icon, Ami Pro displays all text at or above that level. If you click the icon for outline level 3, for example, you see all headings at levels 1, 2, and 3. The other headings and any paragraphs are hidden (*collapsed*).

Tip

You cannot display individual levels below level 1—if you display levels 2 and 3, for example, you also display level 1.

You can use the keyboard, if you prefer, to display specific levels. Press Alt+1 to display the level 1 headings, press Alt+2 to display the level 2 headings, and so on. To display all the text in the document (all headings and all paragraphs), press Alt+0.

Figure 11.5 shows the sample document contracted to level 2.

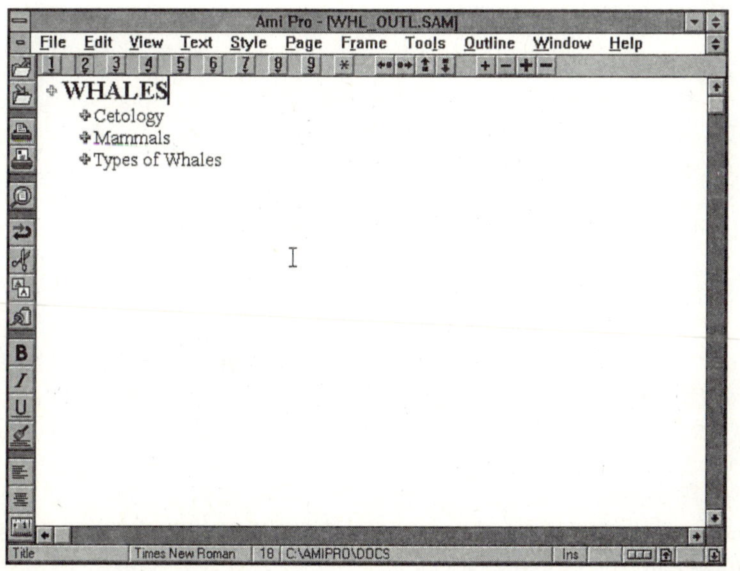

Fig. 11.5
The sample document after clicking the number 2 outline level icon.

Outline Menu

◄ See "Using the Mouse," p. 16

◄ See "Making Choices," p. 27

◄ See "Setting Defaults," p. 228

◄ See "Setting View Preferences," p. 238

As illustrated in other places in Ami Pro, using the keyboard occasionally offers some advantages over using the mouse. In outline mode, for example, you can use the mouse or the **O**utline menu to perform many of the operations described earlier. Using the menu enables you to read the name of a command before you implement it, which is useful as you learn how to use outline mode. After you become familiar with the keyboard equivalents, you can decide whether using the mouse or the keyboard to perform operations suits you best.

Besides the commands for manipulating the outline (**P**romote, **D**emote, Move **U**p, Move **D**own, **E**xpand, and **C**ontract), the **O**utline menu offers the Use **O**utline Style option, which is explained in the section "Changing Styles," later in this chapter.

Outline Structure

You promote and demote the text of the document to structure your outline. When you promote and demote text, you are setting the text at a specific outline level. Once you promote and demote text to set the structure of the outline, you can expand and contract specific headings of the outline, specific sections of the outline, or even the entire outline.

Promoting and Demoting Text

As noted earlier, headings in Ami Pro can have an outline level of 1 through 9, and paragraphs have an outline level of None. (Each level has a corresponding style, as explained in the section "Changing Styles," later in this chapter.) In the sample document, the headings are promoted and demoted to structure the outline. The title WHALES is at level 1. The headings Cetology, Mammals, and Types of Whales are at level 2. Baleen Whales and Toothed Whales are subheadings under Types of Whales, and are at level 3. Each heading and subheading has a paragraph. Paragraphs are assigned a level of None and are subordinate to the heading directly above.

When you promote or demote a heading, you change the level of the heading. Each level has a different indentation. If you promote a heading from level 3 to level 2, for example, the indentation of the level changes to the level 2 indentation. Also, because each level is assigned a different font style, when you promote or demote a heading, you change the font style of the text. If you promote a heading from level 3 to level 2, for example, the font style of the heading changes because the font style assigned to level 2 (TimesNewRoman 14) is different from the font style assigned to level 3 (TimesNewRoman 12).

To promote a heading, follow these steps:

1. Place the insertion point in the heading you want to promote.
2. Click the Promote command icon to promote the heading one level, or press Alt+left arrow or choose Outline Promote.

To demote text, follow these steps:

1. Place the insertion point in the heading you want to demote.
2. Click the Demote command icon to demote the text one level, or press Alt+right arrow or choose Outline Demote.

Repeat these operations as many times as needed to move the heading to the desired level. Paragraphs, which have an outline level of None, aren't promoted or demoted; they move with the heading directly above the paragraph as that heading is promoted or demoted. All headings in a document are assigned a level of None until you promote and demote the headings (as shown in figure 11.3).

After the outline is structured so that subheadings are subordinated to main headings, you can promote or demote sections.

To promote a section (a main heading and its subheadings and/or paragraphs), follow these steps:

1. Select the section by clicking the outline button for the main heading.
2. Click the Promote command icon to promote the section one level, or press Alt+left arrow or choose **O**utline **P**romote.

To demote a section, follow these steps:

1. Select the section by clicking the outline button for the main heading.
2. Click the Demote command icon to demote the section one level, or press Alt+right arrow or choose **O**utline **D**emote.

Contracting and Expanding the Outline

When you contract an outline, you select an outline level to appear, and all subordinate levels are hidden. When you expand an outline, the hidden levels reappear.

You can choose to expand or contract the entire outline, a section, or a heading. To expand and contract the entire outline, use the outline level icons.

Click the outline level icon for the level you want to display; for example, click the level 2 icon to display only the headings at level 2, or press Alt+2 on the keyboard. Figure 11.5 shows the sample document contracted to show only level 2 headings.

To expand a section (main heading with subheadings and paragraphs), place the insertion point in the main heading you want to expand. Then click the large plus command icon, double-click the paragraph's filled plus button, press Alt+PgDn, or choose **O**utline **E**xpand. Any of these methods expands the outline to show all hidden text under the selected heading. Figure 11.6 shows the sample document after expanding the Types of Whales section.

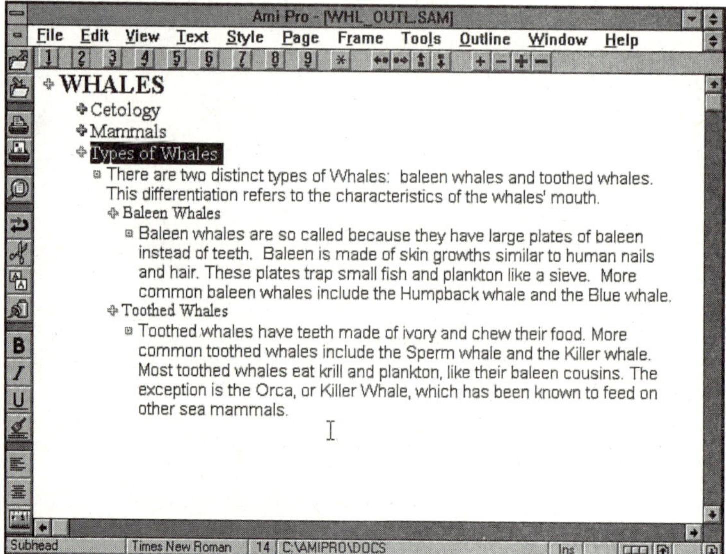

Fig. 11.6
The sample document with only the Types of Whales section expanded.

You can expand the entire outline quickly by clicking the asterisk (*) command icon, or by pressing Alt+0 on the keyboard. Figure 11.7 shows the sample document after clicking the asterisk command icon.

To contract text on a local level, place the insertion point in the heading of the section you want to contract. Then contract with one of four methods: click the large minus command icon, double-click the paragraph's plus button, press Alt+PgUp, or choose **O**utline **C**ontract. This operation contracts the outline to hide all text under the selected heading. Figure 11.8 shows the sample document after contracting the Types of Whales section.

Expanding or contracting a heading involves hiding or displaying the paragraph of that heading, and you use the same section methods described above to expand or contract.

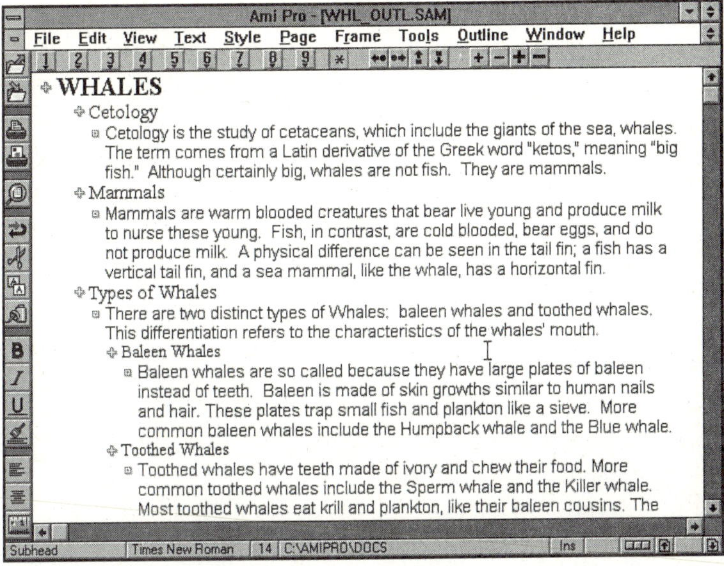
Ami Pro - [WHL_OUTL.SAM]
File Edit View Text Style Page Frame Tools Outline Window Help
1 2 3 4 5 6 7 8 9 *
WHALES
Cetology
Cetology is the study of cetaceans, which include the giants of the sea, whales. The term comes from a Latin derivative of the Greek word "ketos," meaning "big fish." Although certainly big, whales are not fish. They are mammals.
Mammals
Mammals are warm blooded creatures that bear live young and produce milk to nurse these young. Fish, in contrast, are cold blooded, bear eggs, and do not produce milk. A physical difference can be seen in the tail fin; a fish has a vertical tail fin, and a sea mammal, like the whale, has a horizontal fin.
Types of Whales
There are two distinct types of Whales: baleen whales and toothed whales. This differentiation refers to the characteristics of the whales' mouth.
Baleen Whales
Baleen whales are so called because they have large plates of baleen instead of teeth. Baleen is made of skin growths similar to human nails and hair. These plates trap small fish and plankton like a sieve. More common baleen whales include the Humpback whale and the Blue whale.
Toothed Whales
Toothed whales have teeth made of ivory and chew their food. More common toothed whales include the Sperm whale and the Killer whale. Most toothed whales eat krill and plankton, like their baleen cousins. The
Subhead
Times New Roman
14
C:\AMIPRO\DOCS
Ins

Fig. 11.7
The sample document fully expanded.

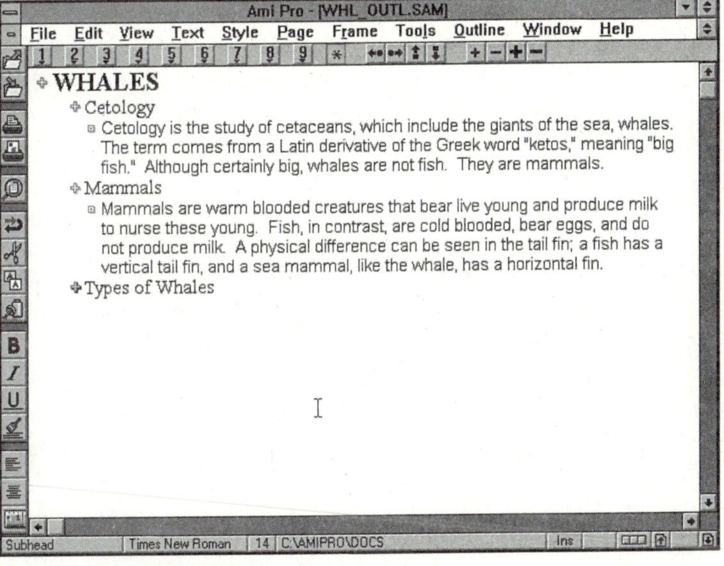
Ami Pro - [WHL_OUTL.SAM]
File Edit View Text Style Page Frame Tools Outline Window Help
1 2 3 4 5 6 7 8 9 *
WHALES
Cetology
Cetology is the study of cetaceans, which include the giants of the sea, whales. The term comes from a Latin derivative of the Greek word "ketos," meaning "big fish." Although certainly big, whales are not fish. They are mammals.
Mammals
Mammals are warm blooded creatures that bear live young and produce milk to nurse these young. Fish, in contrast, are cold blooded, bear eggs, and do not produce milk. A physical difference can be seen in the tail fin; a fish has a vertical tail fin, and a sea mammal, like the whale, has a horizontal fin.
Types of Whales
Subhead
Times New Roman
14
C:\AMIPRO\DOCS
Ins

Fig. 11.8
The sample document with the Types of Whales section contracted.

Caution

Be careful when you check spelling or try to find text while you are in outline mode. The Spell Checker checks only the displayed text, and the search searches only the displayed text. Any collapsed text is ignored. Be sure to display all the text in a document before performing a spell check or a find and replace.

◀ See "Using Find & Replace," p. 178

◀ See "Using Spell Check," p. 190

Editing an Outline

In outline mode, you can perform all the editing tasks that you can perform in the other modes. You can select text and change its attributes, select text and delete it, and copy text and paste it. Outline mode also provides features unavailable in the other modes. In outline mode, for example, you can move levels and quickly manipulate large sections of the document at one time. As mentioned already, however, you cannot work with unanchored frames or create new frames.

Moving Text

In outline mode, you can move a section, a heading, or a paragraph. You can move a heading or a paragraph up or down the outline, or move a section or a heading to a different outline level.

To move a section (main heading with its subordinate headings and paragraphs) up or down the outline, click the appropriate outline button and drag the button up or down to position the section in a new location. You also can move a section by clicking the outline button and using the Move Up or Move Down command icon (as described earlier). Contracting all headings and paragraphs under the main heading and moving the main heading is another way to move a section. All contracted headings and paragraphs move with the main heading. You can move a heading with only subordinate paragraphs using the same methods.

To move a heading without its subordinate headings and paragraphs, place the insertion point in the heading you want to move. Make certain that the heading is expanded—moving a contracted heading moves subordinate headings and paragraphs with the main heading—and click the Move Up or Move Down command icon. Each click moves the heading one position up or down in the outline. Clicking doesn't change the level of the heading, only its position. You also can move a heading without its subordinate material by pressing Alt+up arrow, by choosing **O**utline Move **U**p, by pressing Alt+down arrow, or by choosing **O**utline Move **D**own. To move a paragraph up or down the outline, place the insertion point in the paragraph you want to move and click the Move Up or Move Down command icon. If you are moving several paragraphs, select the paragraphs and click the Move Up or Move Down command icon.

To promote or demote a single heading, place the insertion point in the heading and click the Promote or Demote command icon. When you move a heading to a different level, the style of that level immediately is assigned to the heading. All heading paragraphs move with the heading.

Note

Moving a heading without its subordinate headings and paragraphs doesn't change the outline level of the heading, only the placement of the heading. If you aren't careful, moving headings can result in lower-level headings appearing before higher-level headings. Contracting the document to the specific level you are moving within before executing the move is highly recommended. In the example, if you are moving the Types of Whales section up in the document, contract the document to level 2 (by clicking the 2 outline level icon) before executing the move. This procedure ensures that this level 2 section is not moved beneath a level 3 section accidentally.

Note

The simplest way to reposition text—section, heading, or paragraph—is to click-and-drag the outline button. When you click an outline button and drag it up or down through the outline, you move that text to a new location. When you drag an outline button left or right, you promote or demote that text to a new outline level at the same location. The simple click-and-drag repositioning of text makes the outline mode a simple-to-use (yet potent) outlining environment.

A horizontal line appears across the outline, indicating the position of the moved text as you drag text up or down. A vertical line appears through the outline, indicating the level of the moved text as you drag text left or right.

If the move isn't successful, you can undo the change by choosing **E**dit **U**ndo, clicking the Undo SmartIcon, or pressing Ctrl+Z.

Caution

Make sure that undo isn't set to Off before executing an outline move. The Undo Levels under Tools User Setup must be set to at least Level 1 for undo to be on.

Tip

Saving the file before altering the structure is highly recommended. If you perform several move commands and then decide you prefer the original structure, you can just retrieve the file rather than reconstruct the original structure.

Deleting Text

To delete text in outline mode, select the text and press Del. You can use outline mode procedures to delete a section, a heading, or a paragraph. Follow these steps to delete a section in outline mode:

1. Place the insertion point in the main heading of the section you want to delete.

2. Contract the section by clicking the large minus command icon or by using the equivalent keyboard or menu commands.

   You also can contract the section by double-clicking the outline button at the main heading.

3. Press Del.

◄ See "Basic Editing," p. 73

◄ See "Undoing Actions," p. 84

To delete a heading and its subordinate paragraphs, click the outline button for the heading and press Del. To delete a paragraph, click the outline button for the paragraph and press Del. To delete several paragraphs, select the paragraphs and press Del.

Manipulating a Document in Outline Mode

Ami Pro, like many Windows programs, offers multiple ways to accomplish a task. The following is a summary of the best methods for manipulating a document in outline mode:

- *Expand the entire outline.* Click the asterisk (*) command icon.
- *Contract the entire outline to a specific level.* Click the outline level icon.
- *Expand or contract a heading and all its subordinate text.* Double-click the outline button for that heading.
- *Expand a heading one level at a time.* Click the insertion point anywhere in the heading and click the Expand One Level control button (the small plus sign). Each click of the control button displays the next level of subordinate text.
- *Contract a heading one level at a time.* Click the insertion point anywhere in the heading and click the Contract One Level control button (the small minus sign). Each click of the control button hides the next level of subordinate text.
- *Reposition a heading and its subordinate text.* Click the outline level button corresponding to the level of the heading being repositioned. This step ensures that all subordinate text is hidden and thereby moves with the heading. Click-and-drag the outline button for the heading up or down to where you want to reposition the heading.

- *Reposition a heading without its subordinate text.* Click the insertion point anywhere in the heading and click the Move Up or Move Down control button as many times as needed. Each click moves the heading up or down by one paragraph. The level of the heading does not change. All subordinate text must be displayed.
- *Reposition multiple paragraphs.* Select the paragraphs and click the Move Up or Move Down control button as many times as needed. All the selected paragraphs move together in the direction chosen.
- *Change the level of a heading and all its subordinate text.* Click the outline button for the heading and drag it to the left or right until the heading is positioned correctly.
- *Change the level of a heading without its subordinate headings.* Click the insertion point anywhere in the heading and click the Promote or Demote command icon. Paragraphs are always repositioned with the heading when the heading level changes.
- *Delete a section.* Click the outline button for the main heading, and press Del.
- *Delete a heading and its subordinate paragraphs, or delete a paragraph.* Click the outline button for the heading or the paragraph, and press Del.

Printing in Outline Mode

If you print a document from outline mode, Ami Pro prints only the displayed text and doesn't print hidden subordinate text.

To print a document in outline mode, follow these steps:

1. Collapse or expand the document so that the text you want to print is displayed and the text you don't want to print is hidden.
2. Choose **F**ile **P**rint. The Print dialog box appears. Choose printer settings as necessary.
3. Choose OK or press Enter.

Because printing in outline mode prints only the displayed text, you can print only the subheadings of a document by collapsing the outline to display only the subheadings and then printing. Being able to print selected text is a major advantage of using outline mode.

◄ See "Printing Documents," p. 207

Changing Styles

The outline style controls the display of the outline. The default style sheet is good for outlining and, like all style sheets, enables you to change the style for any level to fit your needs. Figure 11.9 displays the sample document, contracted to level 3, in outline mode using the default style sheet. You can see that the level 1 heading (the title) is clearly a different style from the level 2 headings and that the level 2 headings are different from the level 3 headings.

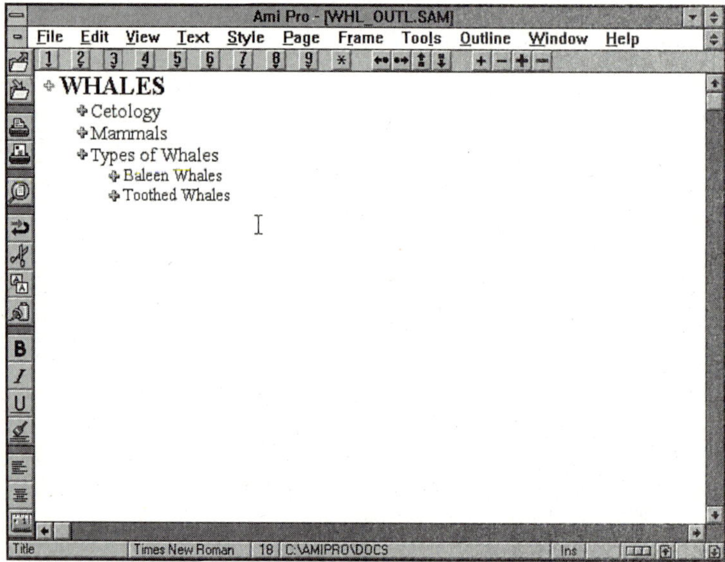

Fig. 11.9
The sample document in outline mode using the default style sheet.

The default style sheet doesn't assign distinct styles for levels 4 to 9. If you are creating an outline with levels beyond 1, 2, and 3, you should change the styles for the higher levels to make the document outline easier to use.

Displaying Text in Outline Mode

Each level of a structured outline has a different style. In the sample document, for example, WHALES appears at level 1 and is therefore assigned the Title style according to the default style sheet. You display the Styles box, which shows the possible styles for the style sheet being used, by pressing Ctrl+Y or by selecting **S**elect a Style from the **S**tyle menu. Figure 11.10 shows the document with the Title style highlighted in the Styles box. The Title style is highlighted in the Styles box because the insertion point is in the level 1 heading, WHALES. You can see the name of the Styles box is _DEFAULT.STY, indicating that this is the default style sheet. If you change

WHALES from level 1 to level 3 by clicking the demote icon two times, the corresponding style changes from Title to Outline 3, because Outline 3 is the style in the default style sheet for level 3. As you see in figure 11.11, Outline 3 is now the highlighted style.

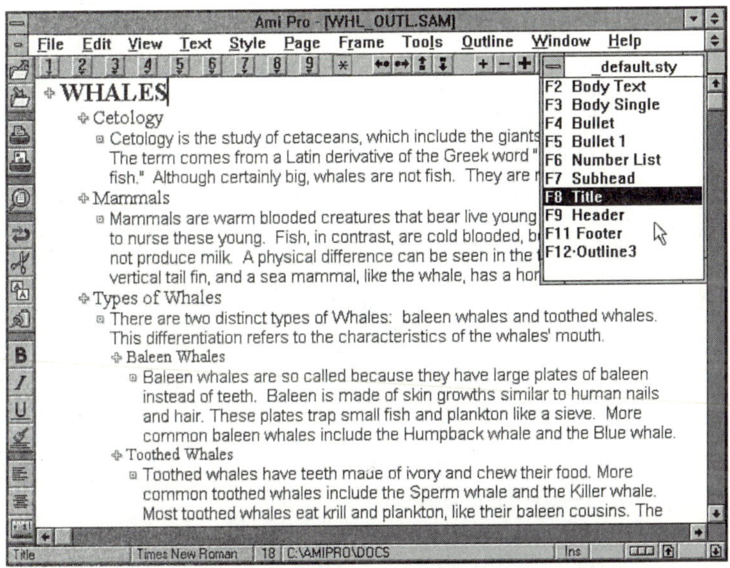

Ami Pro - [WHL_OUTL.SAM]
File Edit View Text Style Page Frame Tools Outline Window Help
_default.sty
F2 Body Text
F3 Body Single
F4 Bullet
F5 Bullet 1
F6 Number List
F7 Subhead
F8 Title
F9 Header
F11 Footer
F12·Outline3
WHALES
Cetology
Cetology is the study of cetaceans, which include the giants
The term comes from a Latin derivative of the Greek word "
fish." Although certainly big, whales are not fish. They are
Mammals
Mammals are warm blooded creatures that bear live young
to nurse these young. Fish, in contrast, are cold blooded, b
not produce milk. A physical difference can be seen in the
vertical tail fin, and a sea mammal, like the whale, has a hor
Types of Whales
There are two distinct types of Whales: baleen whales and toothed whales.
This differentiation refers to the characteristics of the whales' mouth.
Baleen Whales
Baleen whales are so called because they have large plates of baleen
instead of teeth. Baleen is made of skin growths similar to human nails
and hair. These plates trap small fish and plankton like a sieve. More
common baleen whales include the Humpback whale and the Blue whale.
Toothed Whales
Toothed whales have teeth made of ivory and chew their food. More
common toothed whales include the Sperm whale and the Killer whale.
Most toothed whales eat krill and plankton, like their baleen cousins. The
Title | Times New Roman | 18 | C:\AMIPRO\DOCS | Ins

Fig. 11.10
The level 1 heading with the Title style.

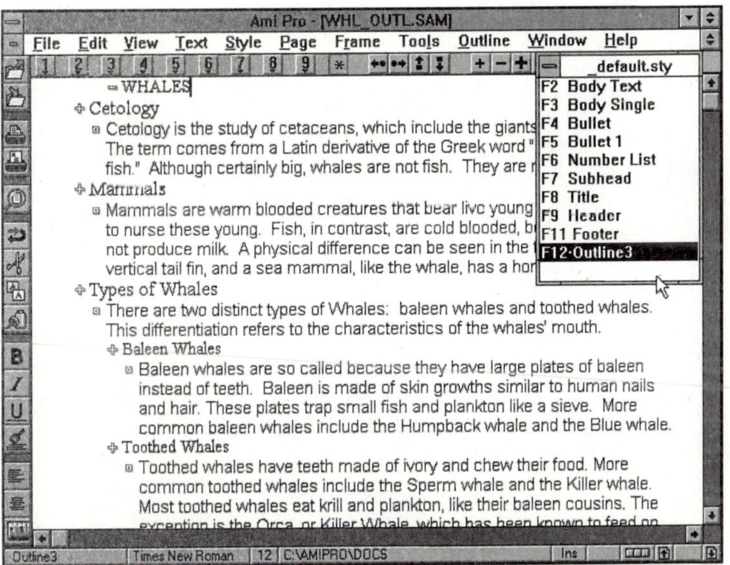

Fig. 11.11
The demoted heading (now level 3) with the Outline 3 style.

Because each level is assigned a distinct style, you can change a level by clicking that heading and selecting a different style from the Style box. You could click the cursor in WHALES and select Outline 3 from the Styles box to make WHALES a level 3 heading. Note that each style has a function key associated with that style; you can change the style (and the level) of a heading or paragraph by placing the insertion point at that location and pressing the function key.

You change a style sheet by pressing Ctrl+A or by selecting **M**odify Style from the **S**tyle menu. You can change any style assigned to a level by changing the style sheet used by the outline. In outline mode, to see any changes made to a level style, you must click off the Use Outline Styles choice on the **O**utline menu.

Figure 11.12 shows the Modify Style dialog box. The current style sheet, in this case the default style sheet (_DEFAULT.STY), is the style sheet being used.

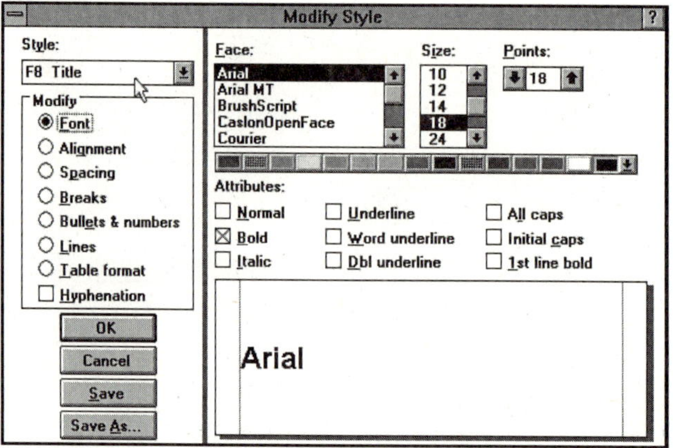

Fig. 11.12
The Modify Style dialog box.

Tip
When working in outline mode, you must click off the Use **O**utline Styles choice on the **O**utline Menu to see any changes made to a level style.

The style being modified, Titles, appears in the Style box in the upper left corner of the dialog box. To change a different style, you click the St**y**le list box and make a selection. Several categories of a style can be changed, such as the font, the alignment, or the spacing. When the Modify Style dialog box is selected, the **F**ont button is chosen by default in the Modify box. You can see that the Titles style is bold, typeface is Arial, and size is 18 points. You change these settings to create a different Titles font style. Figure 11.13 shows Titles font style settings changed to bold, typeface BushScript, and size 36 points. Figure 11.14 shows the Title in outline mode after the font style change.

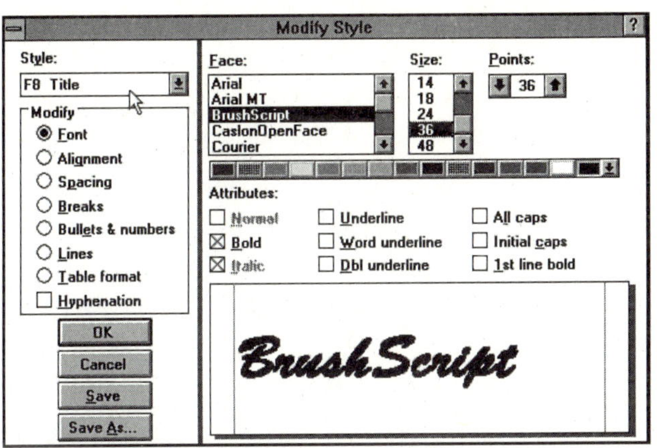

Fig. 11.13
The Font style changes for the Titles style.

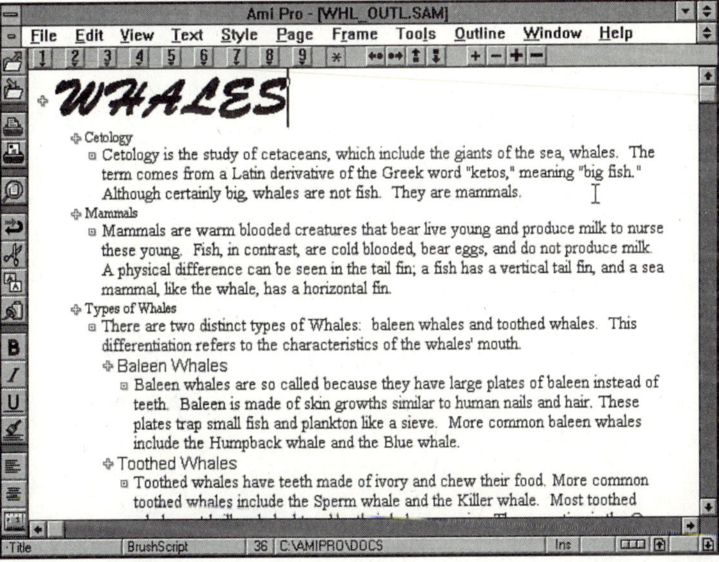

Ami Pro - [WHL_OUTL.SAM]
File Edit View Text Style Page Frame Tools Outline Window Help
WHALES
Cetology
Cetology is the study of cetaceans, which include the giants of the sea, whales. The term comes from a Latin derivative of the Greek word "ketos," meaning "big fish." Although certainly big, whales are not fish. They are mammals.
Mammals
Mammals are warm blooded creatures that bear live young and produce milk to nurse these young. Fish, in contrast, are cold blooded, bear eggs, and do not produce milk. A physical difference can be seen in the tail fin; a fish has a vertical tail fin, and a sea mammal, like the whale, has a horizontal fin.
Types of Whales
There are two distinct types of Whales: baleen whales and toothed whales. This differentiation refers to the characteristics of the whales' mouth.
Baleen Whales
Baleen whales are so called because they have large plates of baleen instead of teeth. Baleen is made of skin growths similar to human nails and hair. These plates trap small fish and plankton like a sieve. More common baleen whales include the Humpback whale and the Blue whale.
Toothed Whales
Toothed whales have teeth made of ivory and chew their food. More common toothed whales include the Sperm whale and the Killer whale. Most toothed
Title
BrushScript
36
C:\AMIPRO\DOCS
Ins

Fig. 11.14
The changed style for Titles in outline mode.

Note

You cannot change a style sheet by making style changes with the Typeface or Size buttons on the Status Bar, the **T**ext menu, or the SmartIcons. If you select the title of the outline and then change the typeface and size by using the Typeface and Size buttons, for example, you change only the look of that text. Other text at level 1 (the Title level) doesn't take on that style change. You shouldn't use these methods for changing the look of text in an outline unless you want to make a change to the selected text only.

Figure 11.15 shows the Modify Style dialog box again. This time, the change is being made to the Subhead style, which is the level 2 style. The style being modified, Subhead, appears in the Style box in the upper left corner of the dialog box. The change this time is to the type style bold, typeface Roman, and a size of 18 points.

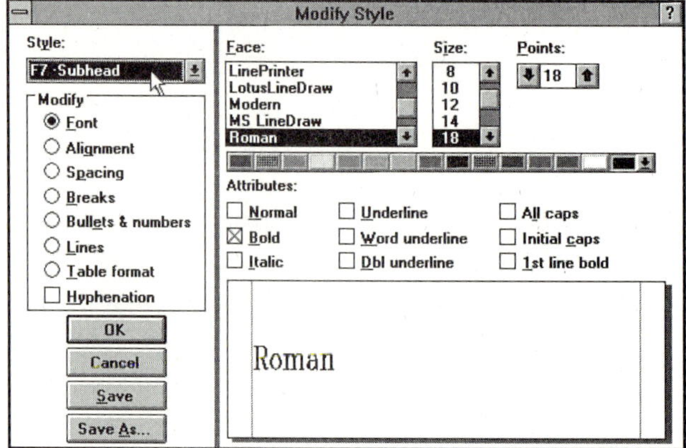

Fig. 11.15
The settings to change the Subhead style to Roman 18 Bold.

Finally, you change the level 3 style, called outline 3, to typeface LetterGothic, size 12, Bold, Double underline. The changes to level 2 and level 3 are displayed in outline mode in figure 11.16.

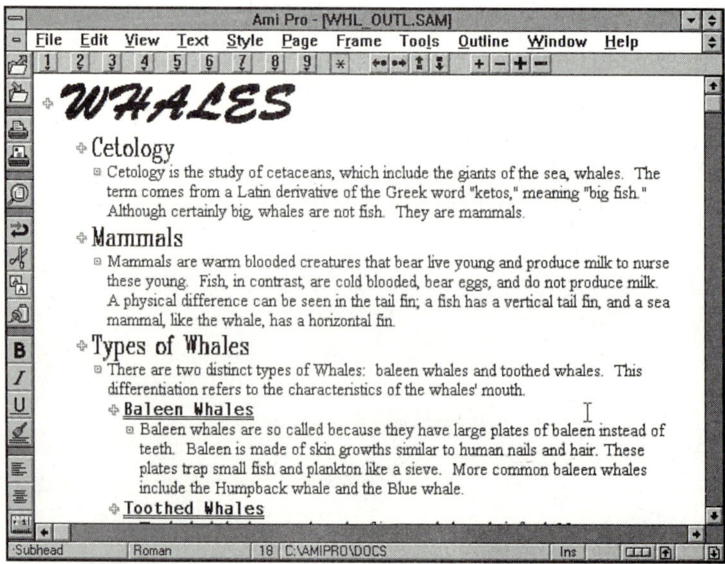

Fig. 11.16
The Subhead style font changed to Roman 18 Bold and the Outline 3 style font changed to LetterGothic 12 Bold Double underline.

If you make changes to the default style sheet and want to save the modifications, saving the changes as a new style sheet is highly recommended. You save the changes to a new style sheet by choosing **S**tyle Sa**v**e as a Style Sheet. The dialog box shown in figure 11.17 appears. For this example, type the new style name **WHL_STYL** to save the changed default style sheet as a new style sheet named WHL_STYL. Also, change the **D**escription to correspond to the style sheet changes. This process creates a custom style sheet you can use like any other style sheet.

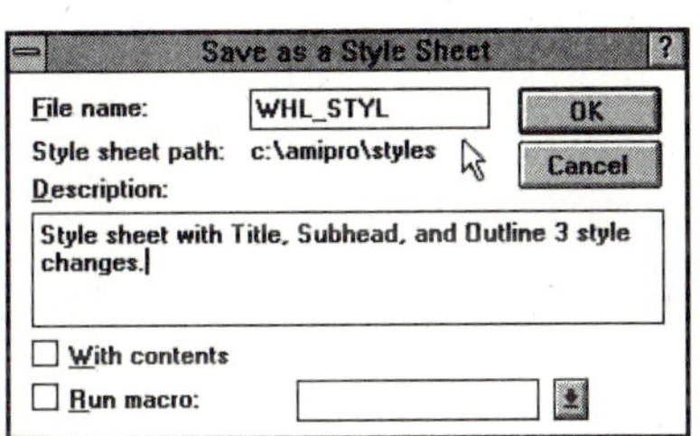

Fig. 11.17
The Save as a Style Sheet dialog box.

As you have seen, you can adjust any level style in a style sheet and make your outline appear exactly as you need.

Displaying Text in Layout Mode

When you change from outline mode to layout mode or draft mode, the level style font changes carry over with the document. However, the outline mode indentations don't carry over to layout mode or draft mode. In the Modify a Style dialog box, you can change the font of a style, the indentation, and all the other elements of a regular paragraph style. Figure 11.18 shows the sample document in layout mode.

You switch to layout mode by choosing the toggle layout/outline mode SmartIcon, by pressing Ctrl+M, or by choosing **V**iew **L**ayout Mode.

As you can see, the level style font changes are carried over with the document, but the indentations don't carry over. At times, you may want to add indentation to an outline level or change the alignment of an outline level after you switch to layout mode. In these cases, you can change the style sheet in layout mode like you can when you are in outline mode. Note that by default the title is center aligned when you switch to layout mode. For this example, you want to indent the level 2 headings, add a line border above and below the level 2 headings, and right-align the level 3 headings. Figure 11.19 shows the Modify Style dialog box with the Alignment options; the settings for a 1/2-inch indentation for all level 2 (Subhead) headings have been implemented. Figure 11.20 shows the **L**ines button selected under

Modify, the Line A**b**ove and Line **B**elow boxes checked with the third line style selected, and the **O**ther Length set to 1.75. Figure 11.21 shows the change for right alignment for level 3 (outline 3). Figure 11.22 shows the document in layout mode after the changes to the level 2 and level 3 styles.

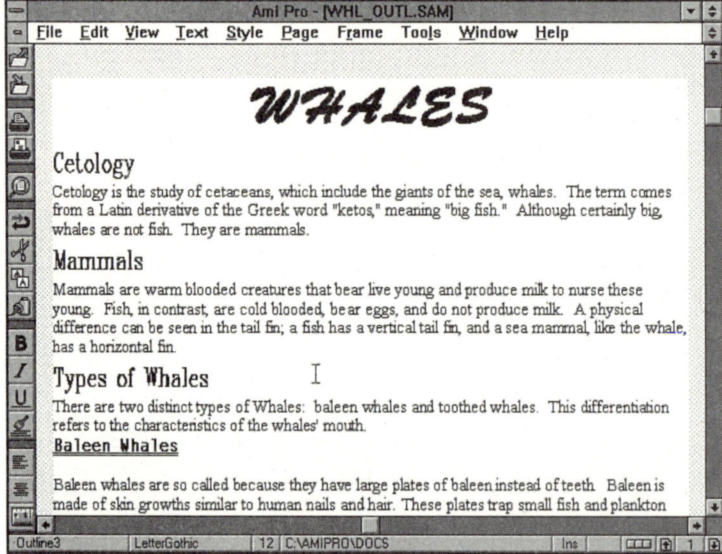
Ami Pro - [WHL_OUTL.SAM]
File Edit View Text Style Page Frame Tools Window Help
WHALES
Cetology
Cetology is the study of cetaceans, which include the giants of the sea, whales. The term comes from a Latin derivative of the Greek word "ketos," meaning "big fish." Although certainly big, whales are not fish. They are mammals.
Mammals
Mammals are warm blooded creatures that bear live young and produce milk to nurse these young. Fish, in contrast, are cold blooded, bear eggs, and do not produce milk. A physical difference can be seen in the tail fin; a fish has a vertical tail fin, and a sea mammal, like the whale, has a horizontal fin.
Types of Whales
There are two distinct types of Whales: baleen whales and toothed whales. This differentiation refers to the characteristics of the whales' mouth.
Baleen Whales
Baleen whales are so called because they have large plates of baleen instead of teeth. Baleen is made of skin growths similar to human nails and hair. These plates trap small fish and plankton
Outline3
LetterGothic
12
C:\AMIPRO\DOCS
Ins

Fig. 11.18
The sample document in layout mode.

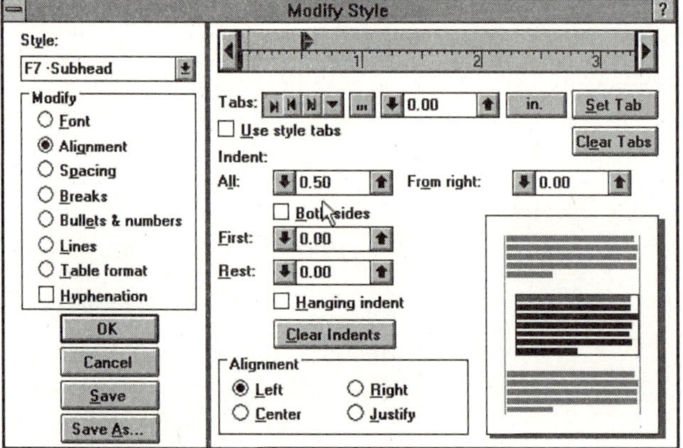
Modify Style
Style:
F7 ·Subhead
Modify
Font
Alignment
Spacing
Breaks
Bullets & numbers
Lines
Table format
Hyphenation
OK
Cancel
Save
Save As...
Tabs:
0.00
in.
Set Tab
Use style tabs
Clear Tabs
Indent:
All:
0.50
From right:
0.00
Both sides
First:
0.00
Rest:
0.00
Hanging indent
Clear Indents
Alignment
Left
Right
Center
Justify

Fig. 11.19
Level 2 indentation set to 0.50 inches.

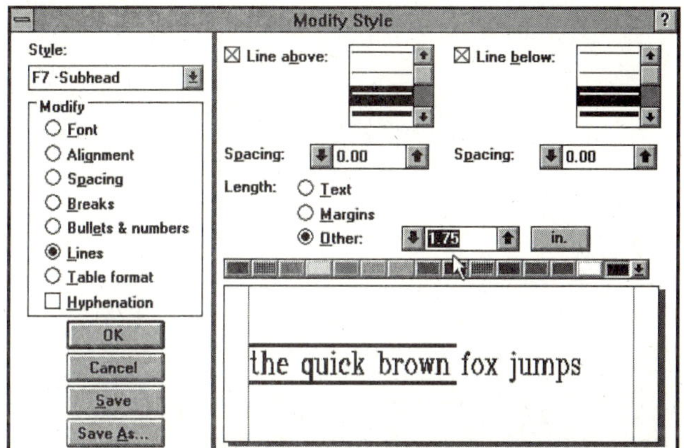

Fig. 11.20 Line settings for a Line Above and Line Below level 2 headings.

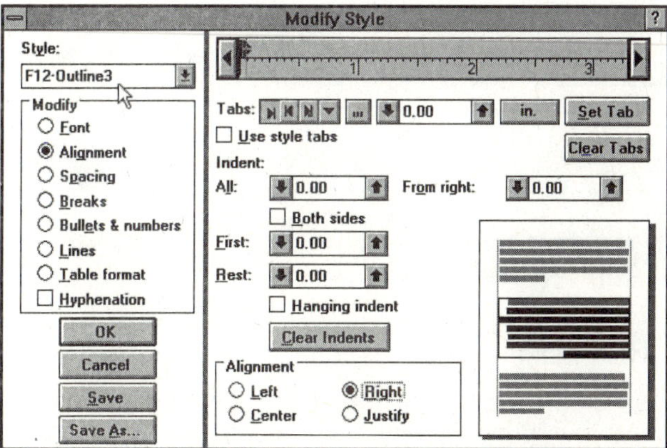

Fig. 11.21 Level 3 headings changed for right alignment.

Because outline mode is a structured environment, any changes you make to the indentation or alignment while in layout mode aren't displayed if you switch back to outline mode. The Lines don't display in outline mode either. The flexibility of layout mode offers greater opportunity for you to create an exact look for your outline before printing it.

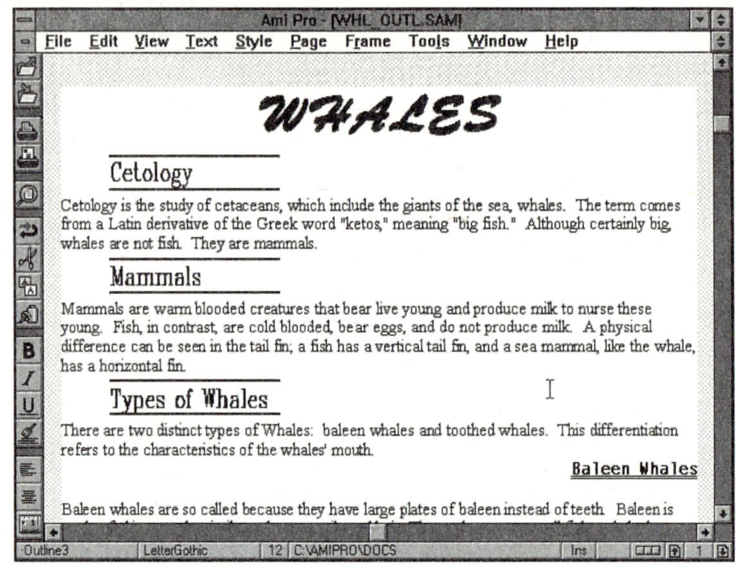
Ami Pro - [WHL_OUTL.SAM]
File Edit View Text Style Page Frame Tools Window Help
WHALES
Cetology
Cetology is the study of cetaceans, which include the giants of the sea, whales. The term comes from a Latin derivative of the Greek word "ketos," meaning "big fish." Although certainly big, whales are not fish. They are mammals.
Mammals
Mammals are warm blooded creatures that bear live young and produce milk to nurse these young. Fish, in contrast, are cold blooded, bear eggs, and do not produce milk. A physical difference can be seen in the tail fin; a fish has a vertical tail fin, and a sea mammal, like the whale, has a horizontal fin.
Types of Whales
There are two distinct types of Whales: baleen whales and toothed whales. This differentiation refers to the characteristics of the whales' mouth.
Baleen Whales
Baleen whales are so called because they have large plates of baleen instead of teeth. Baleen is
Outline3
LetterGothic
12 C:\AMIPRO\DOCS
Ins

Fig. 11.22
The document in layout mode after level 2 and level 3 style changes.

◄ See "Layout Mode," p. 165

◄ See "Creating and Modifying Styles," p. 273

◄ See "Creating a New Style Sheet," p. 294

Creating an Outline in Layout Mode

You can use an outline style sheet in layout mode or draft mode to create an outline. An outline style sheet structures layout mode or draft mode like a traditional outline; if you are going to create an outline in layout mode or draft mode, you certainly want to use one of the outline style sheets to make the outline readable and workable. These style sheets also simplify paragraph numbering, if that is all you require for your document.

Using the _OUTLIN1.STY Style Sheet

Tip
The **W**ith Contents box must be checked when you open the new file with a style sheet.

When you execute a **F**ile **N**ew command, you must assign a style sheet before the document appears on-screen. Ami Pro has four outline style sheets. Three outline style sheets (_OUTLIN1.STY, _OUTLIN2.STY, and _OUTLIN3.STY) are outline templates that structure the layout mode in a traditional outline manner (indentation, different styles for each level, numbers, letters, Roman numeral headings, and so on). The fourth style sheet (_OUTLINE.STY) is not an outline template. This style sheet provides no indentation, but it does have different styles for each level of the outline.

Figure 11.23 shows a document in layout mode with the _OUTLIN1.STY style sheet assigned. As you can see, this style sheet structures the outline like a traditional outline.

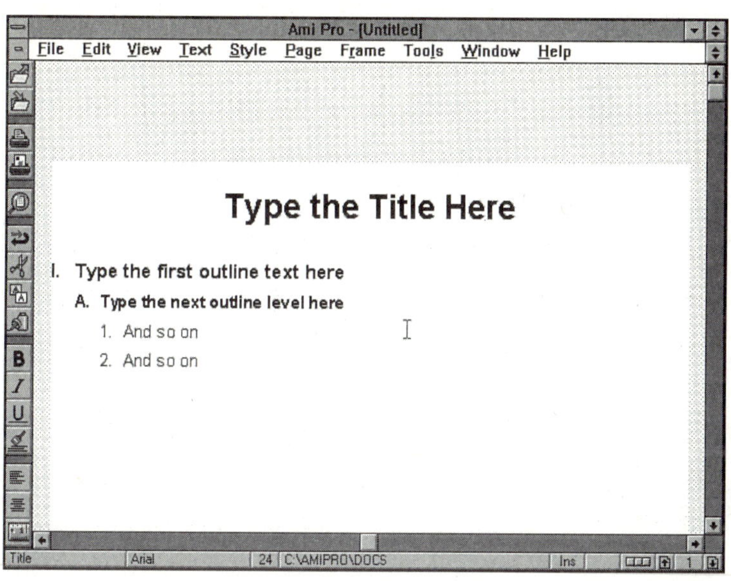

Fig. 11.23 The _OUTLIN1.STY style sheet assigned to a document.

You begin to enter the text of your document with the help of the template prompts; for example, you type the title of the document where the style sheet prompts `Type the Title Here`. You use the style sheet to structure the document as you enter the text. Display the Styles box on-screen so that you can easily structure the outline as you create it. You access the Styles box by pressing Ctrl+Y or by choosing **S**tyle **S**elect a Style. Figure 11.24 shows a document after the title and the first outline level heading are entered. When you press Enter after typing **Cetology**, the outline, which thinks you are going to enter the second heading of that level, displays the Roman numeral II. The heading *Cetology* has a paragraph; however, the next level needs to be Body Text (all paragraphs have a level of Body Text (None)). Make sure that the cursor is at the Roman numeral II and choose Body Text from the Style box. Figure 11.25 shows the document after you choose Body Text and enter the paragraph text.

You continue to type in the document, adjusting the level of the text using the styles in the Styles box. Figures 11.26 and 11.27 show the text of the entire document.

Figure 11.28 shows the document switched into outline mode. You switch to outline mode by choosing the toggle layout/outline mode SmartIcon or by choosing **V**iew **O**utline Mode. The levels are set automatically when you switch to outline mode. Note also that the font and numbering are carried over to outline mode. You can use all the conventions described in the section "Using the Outline Menu, Icons, and Buttons," earlier in this chapter, to rearrange your document.

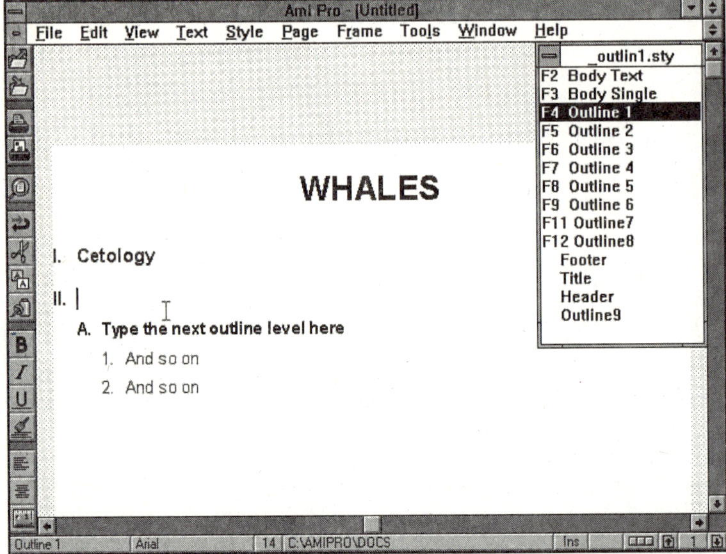

Fig. 11.24
The title and first heading entered in the document assigned the _OUTLIN1.STY style sheet.

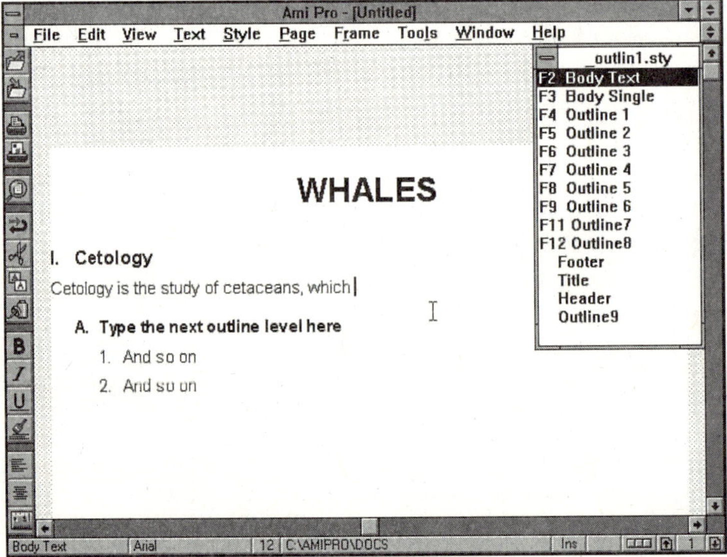

Fig. 11.25
The Body Text level assigned and the beginning of the paragraph.

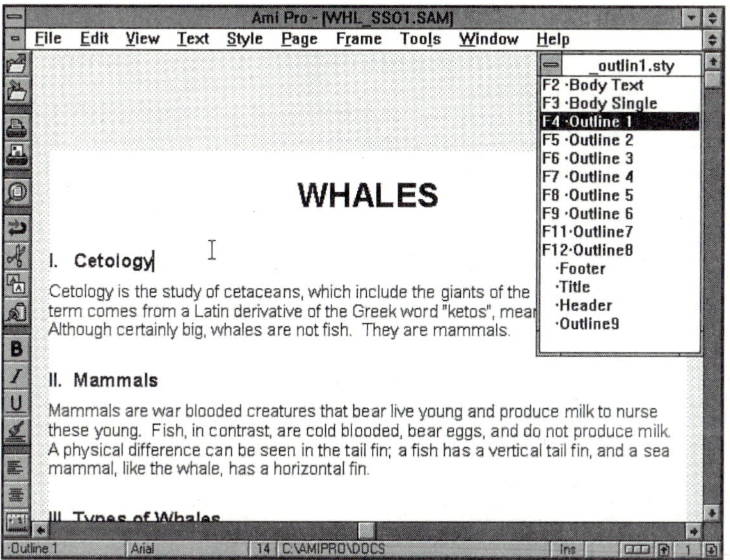

Fig. 11.26
The title and first section of the sample document.

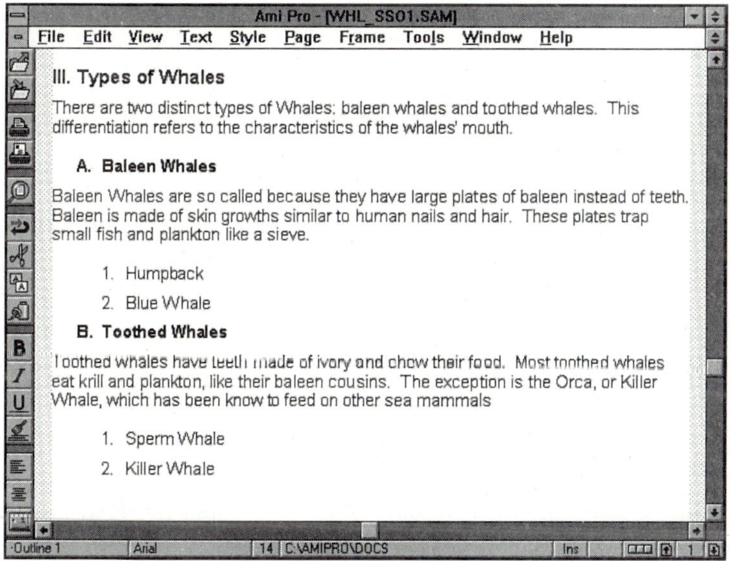

Fig. 11.27
The second section of the sample document.

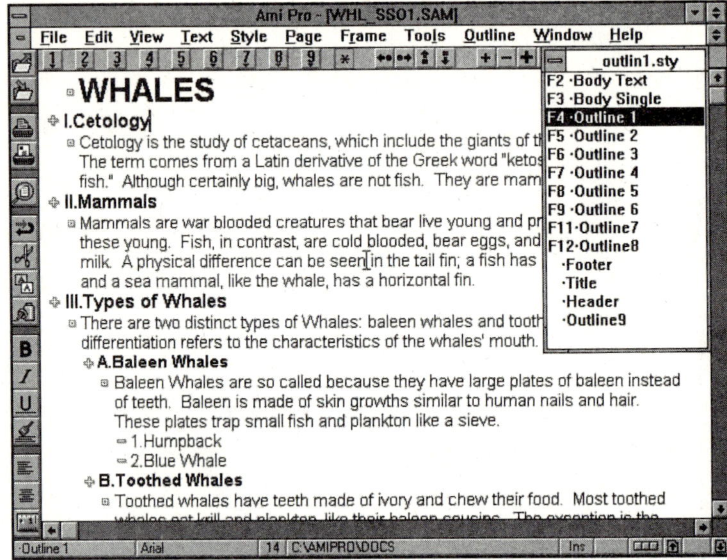

Fig. 11.28 The sample document displayed in outline mode.

The _OUTLIN2.STY and _OUTLIN3.STY style sheets are similar to the _OUTLIN1.STY style sheet in that they structure the layout mode or draft mode. These style sheets offer different level styles than _OUTLIN1.STY offers.

The _OUTLINE.STY style sheet does not provide an outline template. This style sheet provides no level indentation but provides different styles for levels 1 through 3. The _OUTLINE.STY style sheet is a helpful style sheet to apply a numbering scheme to so that you can differentiate the levels more easily.

Using the _OUTLIN2.STY Style Sheet

The _OUTLIN2.STY style sheet gives you the following elements:

- The structure for your outline
- A line (in the margin at the top of the page) spanning the width of the page from the left to the right margins
- A frame in the margin at the top left of the page with the sample text Heading Here
- A large left margin

Figure 11.29 displays the _OUTLIN2.STY style sheet with the style box open, as it appears when assigned to a new file. You can see the Heading Here frame at the top left of the page. To create a heading in this frame, double-click the heading to activate the frame. Select the Heading Here text and type the heading for your outline. The heading you type is typed over the Heading Here text. Add the correct headings and text for your outline in the structured outline work area.

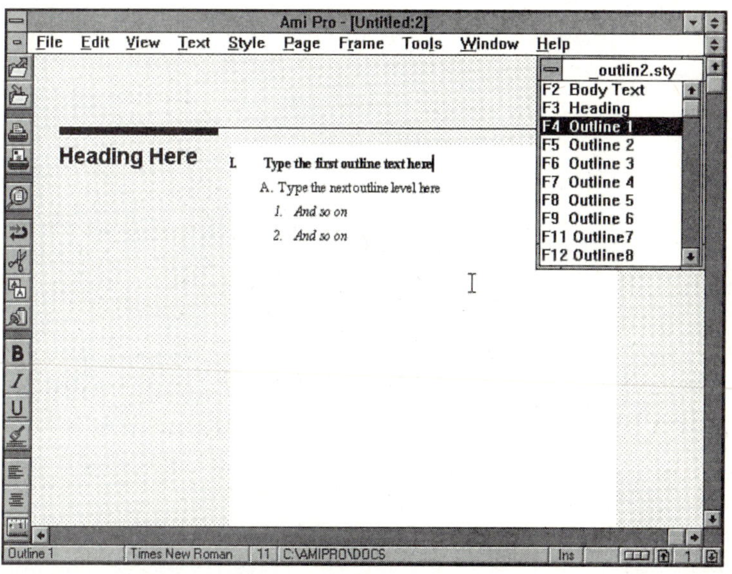

Fig. 11.29
The _OUTLIN2.STY style sheet.

Figure 11.30 shows the document after a heading, the first outline level heading, and a paragraph are added.

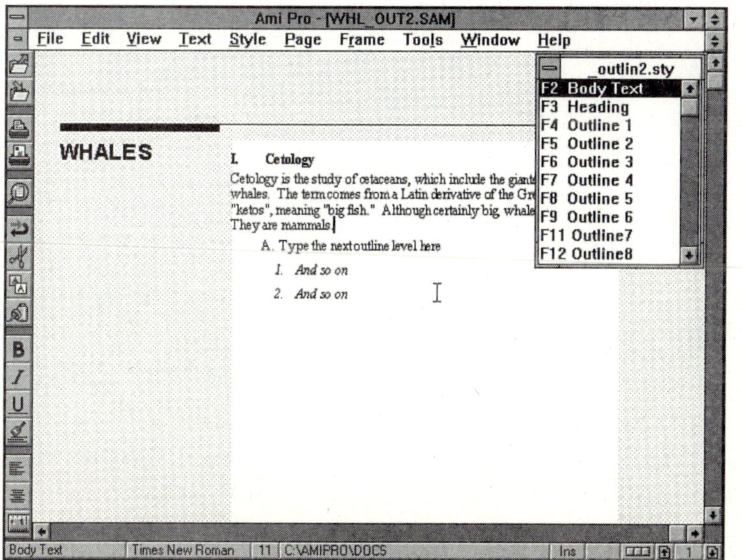

Fig. 11.30
The beginning of a document outlined with the _OUTLIN2.STY style sheet.

Using the _OUTLIN3.STY Style Sheet

The _OUTLIN3.STY style sheet gives you the following elements:

- The structure for your outline
- A border around the page
- A frame in the margin at the top left of the page with the sample text notes
- A frame along the left side of the page from the top to the bottom margins containing sample text for outline notes
- A large left margin

Figure 11.31 displays the _OUTLIN3.STY style sheet with the style box open, as it appears when assigned to a new file. You can see the Notes frame at the top left of the page. To create a heading in this frame, double-click the heading to activate the frame. Select the Notes text and type in the heading for your outline. Add the correct headings and text for your outline in the structured outline work area. Add notes in the left margin of the outline as you see the need for them.

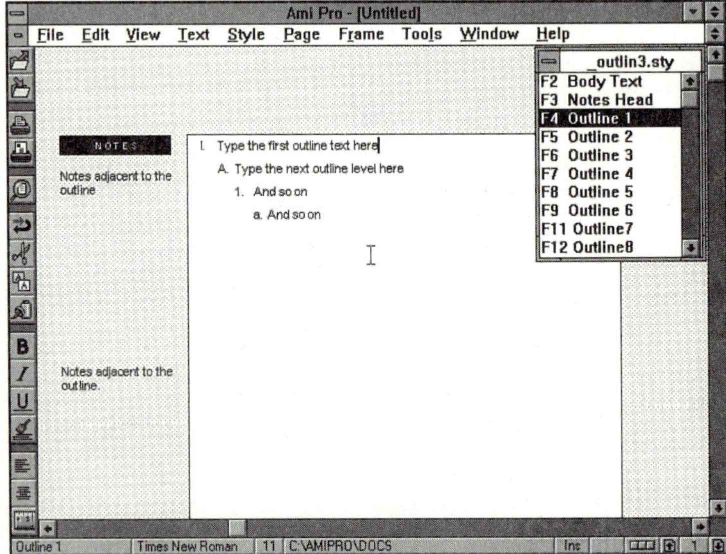

Fig. 11.31
The _OUTLIN3.STY style sheet.

◄ See "Using Style Sheets and Paragraph Styles," p. 262

◄ See "Assigning Style Sheets," p. 263

Figure 11.32 shows the document after a heading, the first outline level heading, a paragraph, and a note have been added to the outline.

These two style sheets offer basic additions to the structured outline offered by the _OUTLIN1.STY style sheet; all three can be used comfortably to create an outline in layout mode or draft mode.

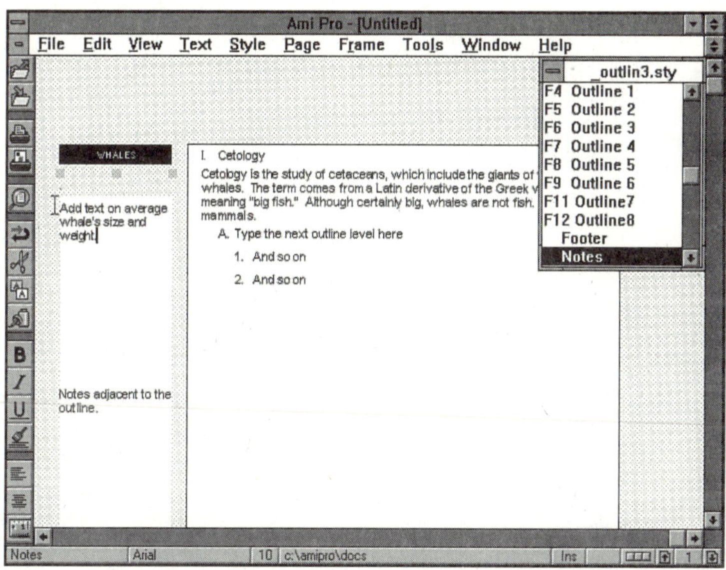

Fig. 11.32
The beginning of a document outlined using the _OUTLIN3.STY style sheet.

Creating a Numbering Scheme

You can create a numbering scheme quickly and easily in outline mode or in layout mode. A numbering scheme makes breaking down the document into its individual sections easier.

Creating a Numbering Scheme in Outline Mode

In outline mode, after you have the outline structured, select **S**tyle **O**utline Styles to display the Outline Styles dialog box (see fig. 11.33). The sample document has three levels; three levels are set in the dialog box, corresponding to each of the three levels in the document. You can set individual level numbering or use one of the two Quick Numbering choices. Figure 11.34 shows the dialog box after clicking the first Quick Numbering button. Figure 11.35 shows the change to the document. (Note that the Use **O**utline Styles option on the **O**utline menu must not be checked if you want to see the numbering in outline mode.)

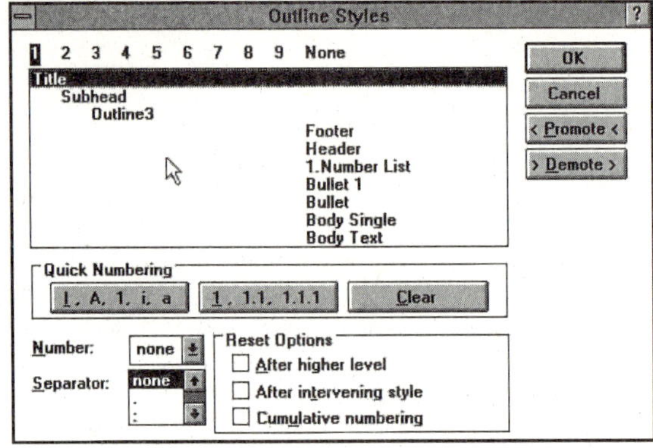

Fig. 11.33 The Outline Styles dialog box.

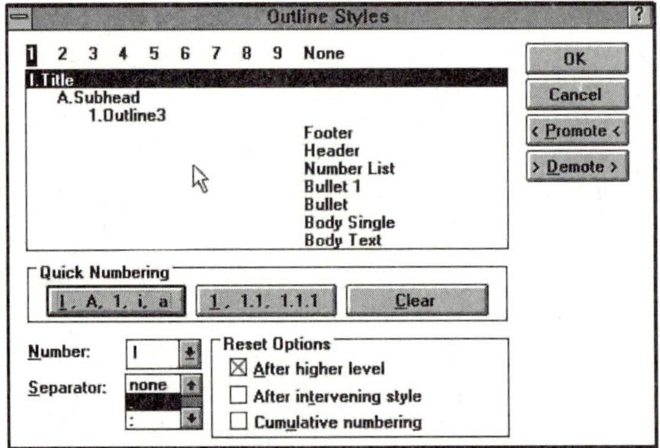

Fig. 11.34 The dialog box after clicking the first Quick Numbering button.

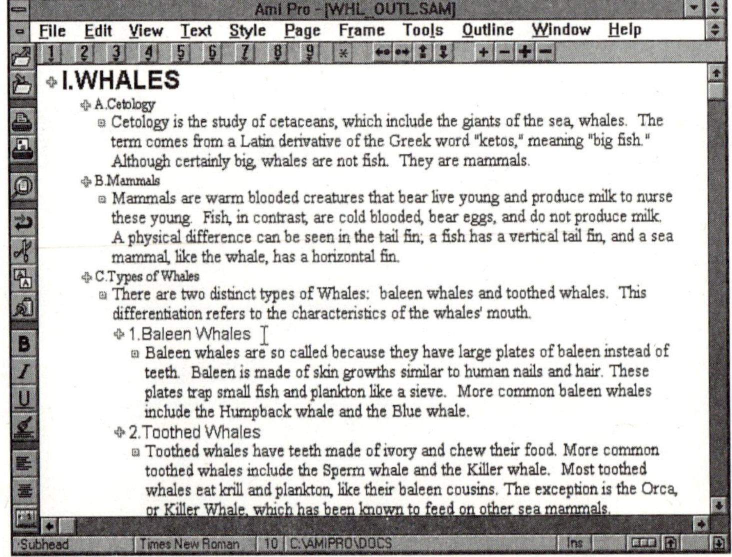

Fig. 11.35 The sample document displayed in outline mode after adding numbering.

The second Quick Numbering button sets legal outline numbering, as shown in figure 11.36. Choose **S**tyle **O**utline Styles to access the Outline Styles dialog box; then click the second Quick Numbering button to change the numbering to a legal numbering system.

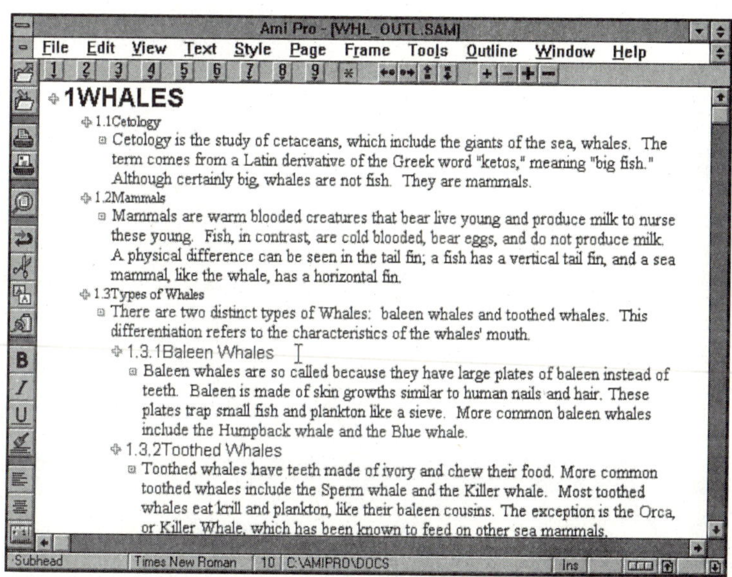
Ami Pro - [WHL_OUTL.SAM]
File Edit View Text Style Page Frame Tools Outline Window Help
1WHALES
1.1Cetology
Cetology is the study of cetaceans, which include the giants of the sea, whales. The term comes from a Latin derivative of the Greek word "ketos," meaning "big fish." Although certainly big, whales are not fish. They are mammals.
1.2Mammals
Mammals are warm blooded creatures that bear live young and produce milk to nurse these young. Fish, in contrast, are cold blooded, bear eggs, and do not produce milk. A physical difference can be seen in the tail fin; a fish has a vertical tail fin, and a sea mammal, like the whale, has a horizontal fin.
1.3Types of Whales
There are two distinct types of Whales: baleen whales and toothed whales. This differentiation refers to the characteristics of the whales' mouth.
1.3.1Baleen Whales
Baleen whales are so called because they have large plates of baleen instead of teeth. Baleen is made of skin growths similar to human nails and hair. These plates trap small fish and plankton like a sieve. More common baleen whales include the Humpback whale and the Blue whale.
1.3.2Toothed Whales
Toothed whales have teeth made of ivory and chew their food. More common toothed whales include the Sperm whale and the Killer whale. Most toothed whales eat krill and plankton, like their baleen cousins. The exception is the Orca, or Killer Whale, which has been known to feed on other sea mammals.
Subhead
Times New Roman
10
C:\AMIPRO\DOCS
Ins

Fig. 11.36
The sample document displayed in outline mode with legal numbering.

If you don't want to see the document with only the numbering, remove the outline buttons by choosing **V**iew View **P**references or the View Preferences SmartIcon to access the View Preferences dialog box. Click off the Outline **B**uttons option; choose OK or press Enter to exit the dialog box.

Creating a Numbering Scheme in Layout Mode

Ami Pro offers two predefined numbering schemes, but you may have specialized numbering requirements. You can create your own numbering scheme using the Outline Styles dialog box. Creating the numbering scheme is a four-step process. Choosing a style, a number, and a separator is a simple process, but when assigning the number scheme to each paragraph level, you must be careful to maintain consistency among the levels.

> **Caution**
>
> Ami Pro increments outline numbering based on the outline level. If two paragraph styles use the same outline level, Ami Pro increments the numbering when it encounters either style. To avoid possible confusion later, assign only one paragraph style to each level when you are creating your own numbering scheme.

In this section, you create your own numbering scheme for the sample document shown in figure 11.37 (using the style sheet _OUTLINE.STY).

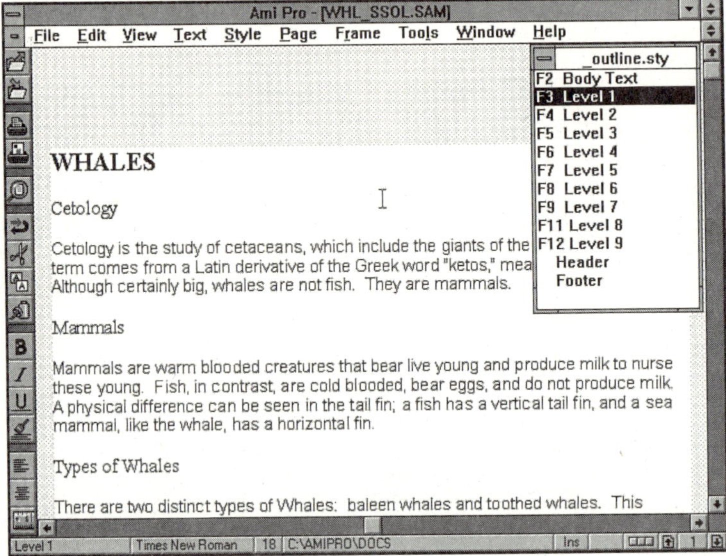

Ami Pro - [WHL_SSOL.SAM]
File Edit View Text Style Page Frame Tools Window Help
_outline.sty
F2 Body Text
F3 Level 1
F4 Level 2
F5 Level 3
F6 Level 4
F7 Level 5
F8 Level 6
F9 Level 7
F11 Level 8
F12 Level 9
Header
Footer
WHALES
Cetology
Cetology is the study of cetaceans, which include the giants of the
term comes from a Latin derivative of the Greek word "ketos," mea
Although certainly big, whales are not fish. They are mammals.
Mammals
Mammals are warm blooded creatures that bear live young and produce milk to nurse these young. Fish, in contrast, are cold blooded, bear eggs, and do not produce milk. A physical difference can be seen in the tail fin; a fish has a vertical tail fin, and a sea mammal, like the whale, has a horizontal fin.
Types of Whales
There are two distinct types of Whales: baleen whales and toothed whales. This
Level 1
Times New Roman
18
C:\AMIPRO\DOCS
Ins

Fig. 11.37 The sample document before assigning a numbering scheme.

Follow these steps to create a numbering scheme:

1. Choose **S**tyle **O**utline Styles. The Outline Styles dialog box opens (see fig. 11.38).

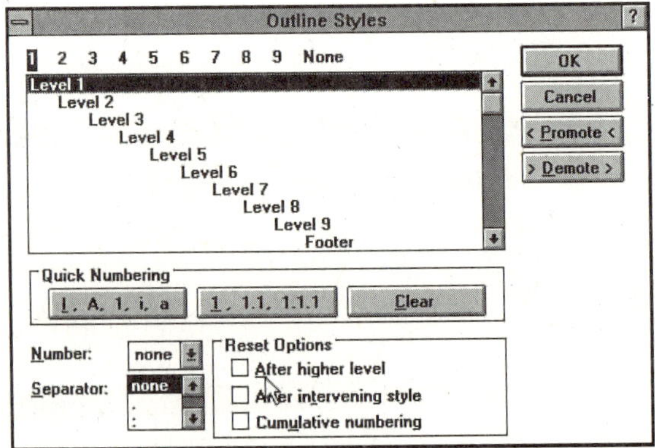

Outline Styles
1 2 3 4 5 6 7 8 9 None
Level 1
Level 2
Level 3
Level 4
Level 5
Level 6
Level 7
Level 8
Level 9
Footer
OK
Cancel
< Promote <
> Demote >
Quick Numbering
I. A. 1. i. a
1. 1.1. 1.1.1
Clear
Number:
none
Separator:
none
Reset Options
After higher level
After intervening style
Cumulative numbering

Fig. 11.38 The Outline Styles dialog box before assigning a numbering scheme.

2. Select the style set to level 1—the Level 1 style, in this example.

3. Choose **N**umber and select from the drop-down list the number you want to use for the paragraph style—none, 1, I, i, A, or a.

4. In the **S**eparator list box, select the separator you want to use to separate the number from the text. You can select no separator (none), a period (.), a colon (:), a closing parenthesis ( )), a closing bracket (]), a set of brackets ([ ]), a period and closing parenthesis (.)), or a set of parentheses (( )).

5. Repeat steps 3 through 5 to assign numbering styles to each level.

Figure 11.39 shows the Outline Styles dialog box with the numbering scheme assigned for each outline level.

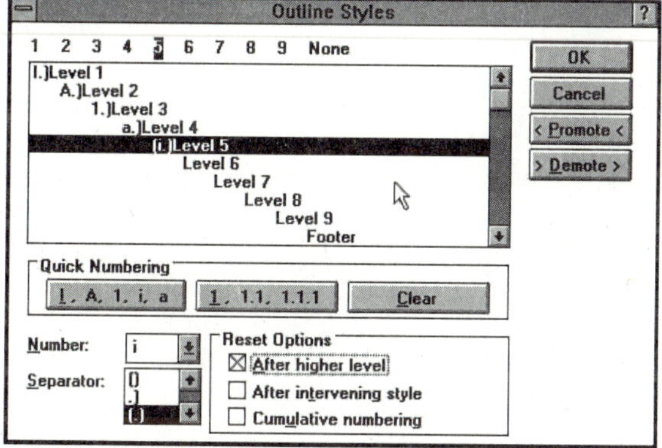

Fig. 11.39 The Outline Styles dialog box with the numbering scheme in place for each outline level.

If you use _OUTLINE.STY, which does not indent levels, the document is much easier to read and work with if you have assigned a number scheme to each level. Figure 11.40 shows the document in layout mode after the number scheme has been implemented.

The Outline Styles dialog box also contains a Reset Options section. You use the reset options to tell Ami Pro where in the document you want to reset the numbering to the first number and begin incrementing from there. This feature can be valuable; if you don't use a reset option, Ami Pro numbers every paragraph in the document, using the paragraph style with the assigned numbering scheme. The next section explains the reset options.

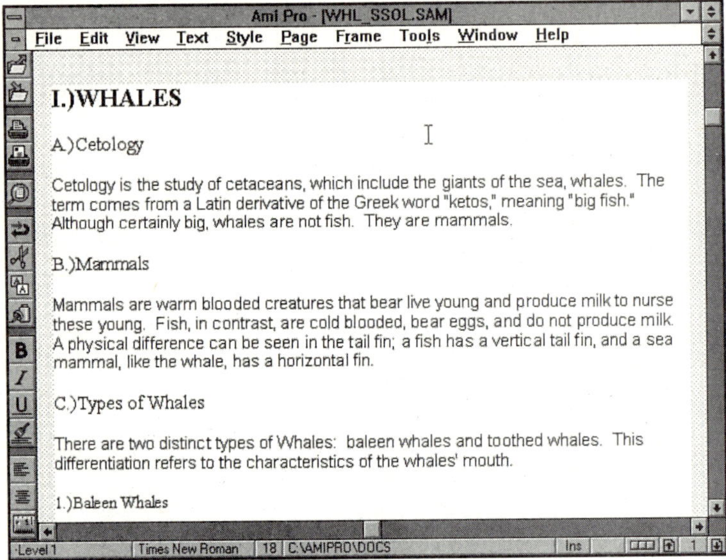

Ami Pro - [WHL_SSOL.SAM]
File Edit View Text Style Page Frame Tools Window Help
I.)WHALES
A)Cetology
Cetology is the study of cetaceans, which include the giants of the sea, whales. The term comes from a Latin derivative of the Greek word "ketos," meaning "big fish." Although certainly big, whales are not fish. They are mammals.
B.)Mammals
Mammals are warm blooded creatures that bear live young and produce milk to nurse these young. Fish, in contrast, are cold blooded, bear eggs, and do not produce milk. A physical difference can be seen in the tail fin; a fish has a vertical tail fin, and a sea mammal, like the whale, has a horizontal fin.
C.)Types of Whales
There are two distinct types of Whales: baleen whales and toothed whales. This differentiation refers to the characteristics of the whales' mouth.
1.)Baleen Whales
Level 1
Times New Roman
18
C:\AMIPRO\DOCS
Ins
1

Fig. 11.40
The document custom numbering displayed in layout mode.

Using Reset Options

Reset options can be confusing initially, but the examples in this section should make clear the value of using the reset options. The following paragraphs explain the reset options.

Tip
Reset options must be set separately for individual outline levels.

If you choose the **A**fter Higher Level option, Ami Pro restarts the numbering for a heading set to a lower number (with any outline style), if the heading follows text with a style set to a higher level. Such restarting is normal for most outlines. If a heading has the number *I*, for example, the heading following (at a lower level) begins with *A*. Following the number *II*, the numbering begins again with *A*.

If you select the After **I**ntervening Style reset option, Ami Pro restarts the numbering for a heading (in any outline style), if the heading follows text set to another outline level or to None. If a style has the level 6, for example, numbering restarts when a heading with that style follows a heading with the level 1 through 5 or 7 through 9.

This feature is most useful if you are creating a document with several different sections and want the numbering to begin again within each section. If you use the Cum**u**lative Numbering reset option, Ami Pro uses the numbering scheme 1, 1.1, 1.1.1, 2, 2.1, 2.1.1, and so on.

> **Caution**
>
> If you use the cumulative numbering system, you may need to modify the style so that the entire number appears and prints.

If you create your own numbering scheme, you probably need to use the reset options to avoid incorrect numbering sequences in your documents.

◄ See "Creating and Modifying Styles," p. 273

Summary

In this chapter, you learned about Ami Pro's outlining capability, which is invaluable for organizing a document. You learned the distinction between outline mode and outline styles, explored the outline icons, menu, and buttons, and learned how to edit and print in outline mode. You learned the relationship between outline styles and the document display in outline mode and the document display in layout mode. Finally, you learned how to number an outline with the quick-numbering feature or by creating your own numbering schemes.

In the next chapter, you learn about other useful Ami Pro capabilities—creating references such as an index, footnotes, or a table of contents.

Chapter 12

Using Reference Tools

In many word processing programs, creating the table of contents, the table of authorities, and the index can be surprisingly time-consuming. Creating an *accurate* table of contents or index in which all entries match in wording, capitalization, spacing, and spelling can be particularly challenging.

Ami Pro automates the tasks of creating a table of contents, a table of authorities, footnotes, and an index. Even these automated tasks demand careful attention, however. First, you must set up the document appropriately. When creating an index, for example, you need to go through the document and mark the text that you want to include in the index. Nevertheless, automated reference tools like those in Ami Pro can save you much time and improve your accuracy.

In this chapter, you learn how to work with footnotes. You find out how to create them, how to go to them quickly, and how to edit them. Next, you learn how to use a glossary; not an alphabetical listing of terms at the end of a document, but a document in which you store frequently used text.

In the last three sections of the chapter, you learn step-by-step how to use three powerful reference tools: the table of contents, the table of authorities, and the index. You learn how to set up a document so that you can create a table of contents and how to generate the table of contents itself. Next, you learn first how to set up a document so that you can create a table of authorities and how to generate the table of authorities itself. Finally, you find out how to mark the text in a document so that you can create an index, how to generate the index, and how to use the powerful Ami Pro tools for editing an index.

Using Footnotes

Creating *footnotes* without using a word processing program, such as Ami Pro, can be a headache. Fitting the footnotes onto the page can be tricky. Maintaining a consistent appearance for the footnotes from page to page can be difficult. If you have a line between the bottom of the text and the footnotes, for example, you must be certain that the line is identical on each page. If you eliminate one footnote, you must renumber all other footnotes correctly.

You also can choose to use *endnotes* with your document. Endnotes are placed at the end of the document (an approach often used in books) rather than at the bottom of each page to accompany the footnote numbers on that page.

Ami Pro automates the process of creating footnotes and endnotes and builds in much of the consistency that is so difficult to maintain manually. This section discusses how to create and edit footnotes.

Creating Footnotes

Often, if you are writing footnotes as you go along, you may not be sure how much space you will need for them. You may have a difficult time planning for the footnotes and splitting them over additional pages as necessary. Revising footnotes (and changing their length) can be a nightmare if you are working manually. But Ami Pro takes care of all such problems for you. Almost all you have to do is indicate in the text where the footnote numbers should appear and type the footnotes.

Although typing a footnote may be a simple matter of typing text at the bottom of the page or at the end of a document, you have many options and choices to make. You must decide whether endnotes (notes at the end of a chapter) or footnotes (notes at the bottom of the page) are better for your document. You also must choose a starting number for the note; the starting number doesn't have to be 1. You also must specify the length of the line on which the note appears.

When you insert a footnote into an Ami Pro document or a table cell, Ami Pro inserts the reference number for the footnote in two places: at the location of the insertion point in the document and at the bottom of the page or table (the area that the program creates for the footnote text). The footnote can be any length and can have multiple paragraphs. After you have a footnote in place, you can use additional Ami Pro techniques to go to, edit, and remove the footnote.

Follow these steps to create a footnote:

1. Place the insertion point where you want the reference number for the footnote. Figure 12.1 shows a sample document with the insertion point positioned for a footnote.

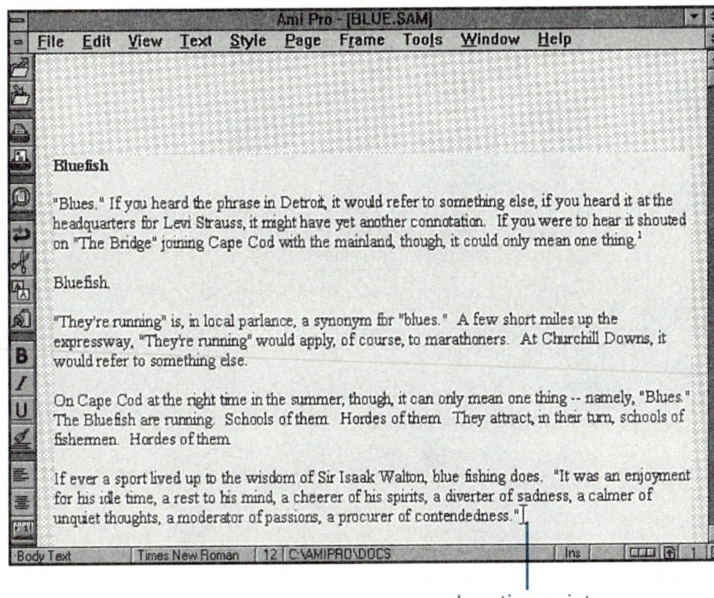

Fig. 12.1 Placing the insertion point in a document to add the footnote.

2. Choose Too**l**s **F**ootnotes or click the Insert Footnote SmartIcon (in the Long Documents SmartIcon set; the Insert Footnote SmartIcon looks like a sheet of paper with a 1 in the bottom left corner).

   The Footnotes dialog box appears, as shown in figure 12.2.

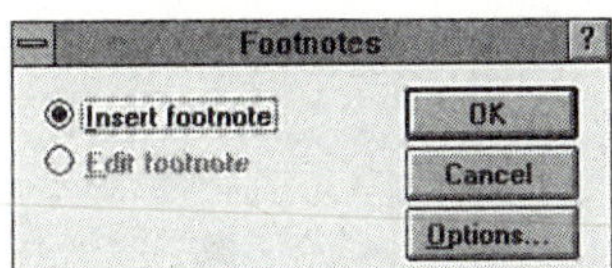

Fig. 12.2 The Footnotes dialog box.

3. If you want to specify footnote options, choose the **O**ptions button. The Footnote Options dialog box appears, as shown in figure 12.3.

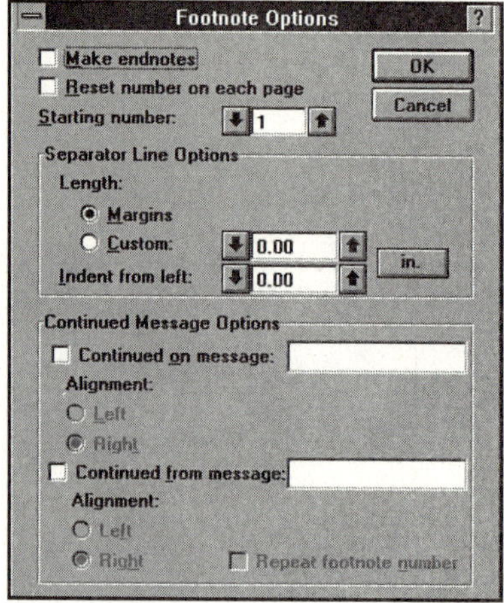

Fig.12.3 The Footnote Options dialog box.

4. Make your choices in the Footnote Options dialog box. (The options are explained in table 12.1, following these steps.)
5. Choose OK or press Enter to return to the Footnotes dialog box.
6. In the Footnotes dialog box, choose **I**nsert Footnote.
7. Choose OK or press Enter.

   The insertion point moves to the footnote area, where you type the text of the footnote (see fig 12.4).

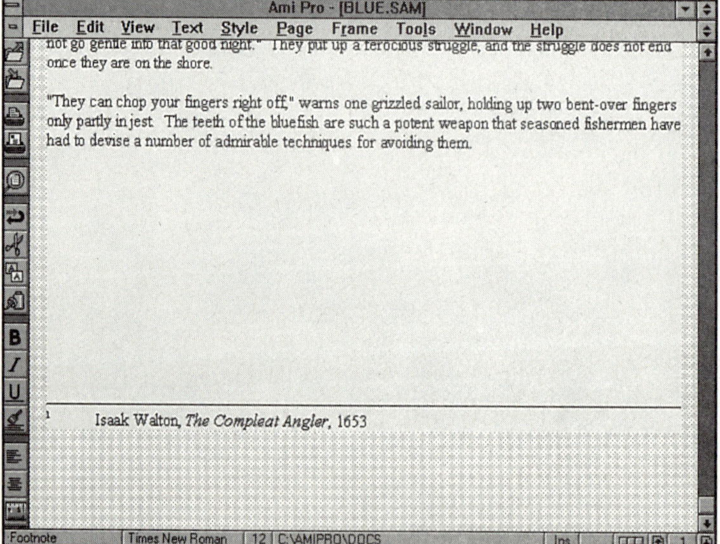

Fig. 12.4 Footnote area containing sample text at the bottom of the page.

8. Type the text for the footnote. Ami Pro places a reference number at the insertion point position in the document (see fig. 12.5).

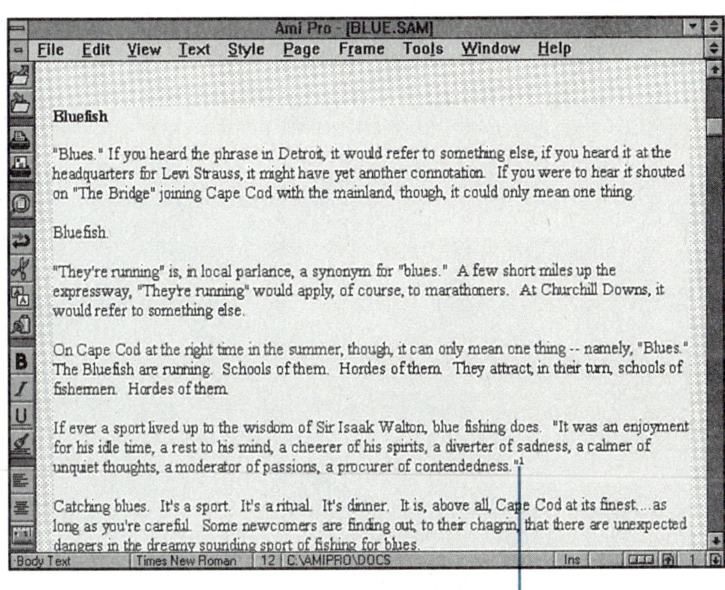

Fig. 12.5
The footnote reference number inserted into text.

9. Press Esc or click anywhere in the document. Ami Pro returns to the main document, and your footnote is complete.

Table 12.1 Footnote Options

Option	Action
Make Endnotes	Makes notes into endnotes (placed at the end of the document) rather than footnotes (placed at the bottom of the page)
Reset Number on Each Page	Resets the numbering of footnotes on each page instead of numbering consecutively throughout the document
Starting Number	Specifies a particular number for the first footnote; 1 is the default
Margins	Extends the separator line from left to right margin
Custom	Specifies the length of the separator line, starting at the left margin; you can select **C**ustom in conjunction with **I**ndent from Left

(continues)

Table 12.1 Continued

Option	Action
Indent from Left	Separator line begins at a specified distance from the left margin
Continued **o**n message	Available if you are unable to fit the entire footnote on one page. Prints up to 64 characters on the line below footnote text and aligns either left or right
Continued **f**rom message	Prints 64 character message on the first line above the continued footnote and aligns either left or right
Unit of measure button	Specifies the units used for a custom line length or indention; choose among inches, picas, points, and centimeters

If you insert multiple footnotes, Ami Pro fits them on the bottom of the page. Footnotes fill up from the bottom margin of the page as you create them. Sufficient space must be available for the note below the lowest frame on the page. If insufficient space is available below the lowest frame, Ami Pro splits the footnote over additional pages.

Figure 12.6 shows a sample document with four footnotes at the bottom of the page. Because Ami Pro automatically makes room for the footnotes, you don't need to adjust the length of the footnotes or the length of the text on the document page to make the footnotes fit (see fig. 12.7).

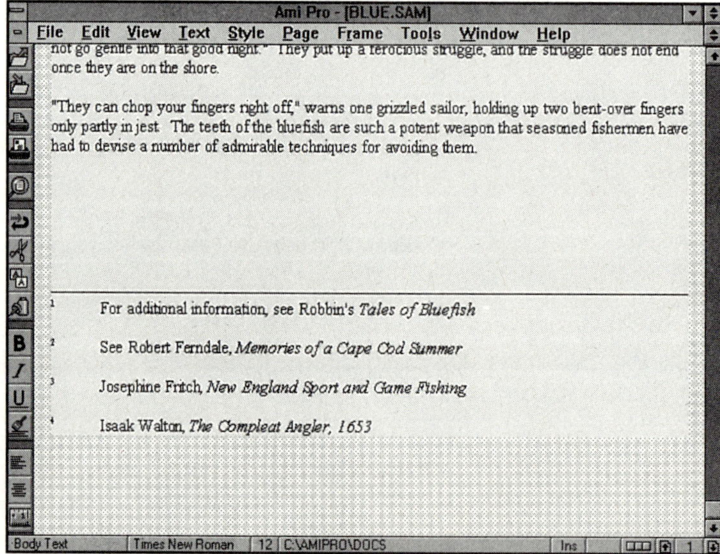

Fig. 12.6
A sample document with four footnotes at the bottom of the page.

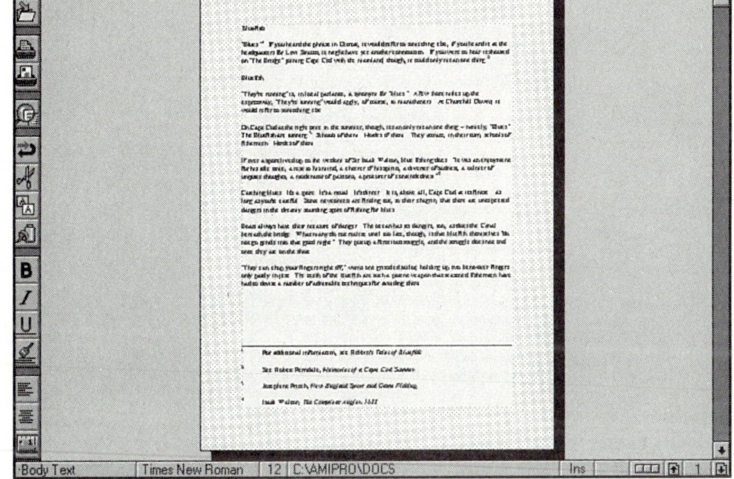

Fig. 12.7
The full-page view of a sample document, enabling you to see the page with the footnotes at the bottom.

Going to Footnotes

As you create a document, you may enter footnotes as you go along. Later, as you are preparing the final version of the document, you may want to proof the footnotes by moving to each one in succession.

You can move easily from one footnote mark in the text to the next and from footnote text to footnote text. Follow these steps to move from mark to mark:

1. Place the insertion point anywhere in the main document.

2. Choose **E**dit **G**o To or press Ctrl+G. You also can click the Page button on the Status Bar or click the Go To SmartIcon (in the Editing SmartIcon set; the Go To SmartIcon shows three arrows pointing right). The Go To dialog box appears.

3. In the **N**ext Item list box, choose Footnote Mark (see fig. 12.8).

4. Choose the Go To ^H button or press Ctrl+H.

The insertion point moves to the next footnote reference number in the document. The next section explains how to move from the footnote mark to the footnote text.

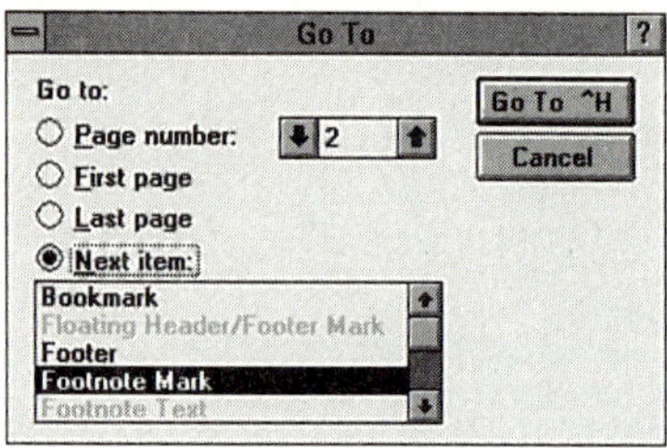

Fig. 12.8
The Go To dialog box.

If no footnote numbers exist after the location of the insertion point, when you choose Go To ^H Ami Pro responds `Go To could not find a match for that item`. Choose OK or press Enter to return to the document.

Editing Footnote Text

You can edit footnote text just as you edit main text. The trick is to get the insertion point where you want it before you begin editing. Follow these steps:

1. Move to the footnote text. With the mouse, click the footnote text in layout mode. With the keyboard, choose **E**dit **G**o To Footnote Text.

2. Edit the footnote text as you edit any other text. See Chapter 3, "Editing Techniques," for more information on text editing.

3. After you finish editing the footnote text and are ready to return to the main document, press Esc or click anywhere in the main text.

In layout mode, you can move from footnote text to footnote text by pressing the down-arrow key. You can select text, however, within a single footnote only.

Changing Paragraph Style in Footnotes

When you add a footnote to a document, Ami Pro automatically adds a Footnote style to the Styles box (if the style isn't there already). To change the footnote style, you follow the same steps you use to change paragraph style in a document, as explained in Chapter 4, "Formatting a Document." You may want to change the style of the footnote numbers (to letters, for example), the attributes of the footnote numbers (such as whether the numbers are superscripted), or the amount of space you use for footnote numbers.

Suppose that you want to change a sample footnote style so that the footnote number doesn't appear as a superscript. Follow these steps:

1. With the insertion point in the footnote, choose **S**tyle **M**odify Style, press Ctrl+A, click the right mouse button anywhere in the text, or click the Modify Paragraph Style SmartIcon (in the Editing SmartIcon set; the Modify Paragraph Style SmartIcon looks like a sheet of paper with large dots on the left and small dots on the right). The Modify Style dialog box for the selected footnote style appears (see fig. 12.9).

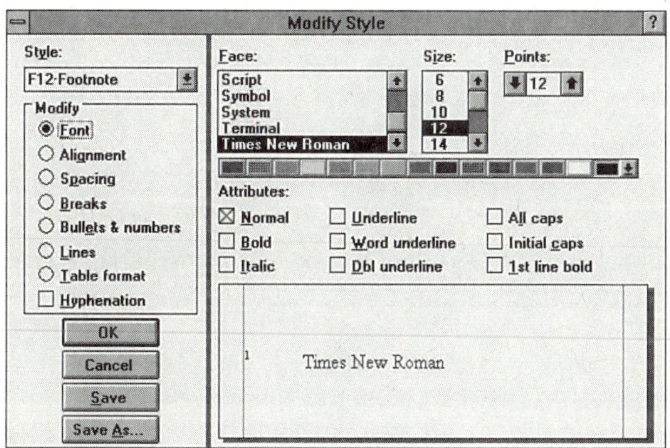

Fig. 12.9
The Modify Style dialog box for the Footnote style.

2. Choose Bull**e**ts & numbers from the group of Modify options on the left side of the dialog box. The Modify Style dialog box changes to show bullets and numbers options, as shown in figure 12.10.

3. Deselect **S**uperscript, which is selected by default.

   Notice that the example box in the lower right corner of the dialog box changes so that the footnote number no longer appears as a superscript (see fig. 12.11).

4. Choose OK or press Enter.

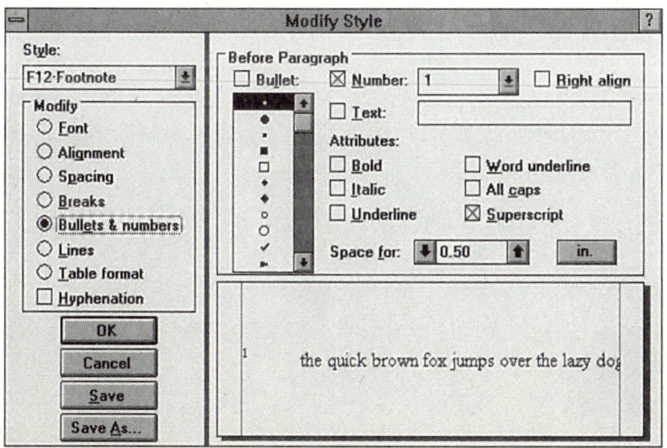

Fig. 12.10
The Modify Style dialog box for editing footnote bullets and numbers.

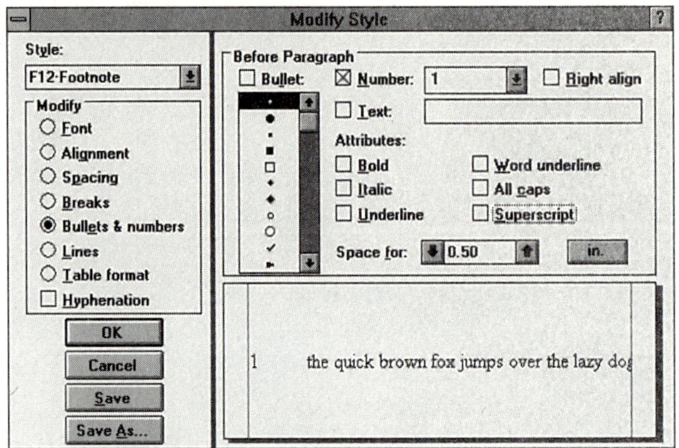

Fig. 12.11
The dialog box after the **S**uperscript option is turned off. Note the different position and size of the footnote number in the example box.

To use a bullet rather than a number, choose Bu**l**let. You also can combine bullets and numbers by choosing both the Bul**l**et check box and the **N**umber check box.

In the list box, highlight the appropriate style of bullet. In this dialog box, you can change these styles just as you would change any other styles. See Chapter 10, "Working with Style Sheets," for information on setting styles.

You may want to make several other changes. To change the **N**umber style, for example, choose the style you want in the text box for **N**umber. You can use the styles 1, A, or i or you can choose the new cumulative symbols, such as the asterisk (*) and the dagger (á). These symbols increase by one for each footnote reference mark; for example, the first footnote mark contains one asterisk (*); the second contains two asterisks (**), and so on.

Another footnote reference feature you may want to use is to right-align the reference number character. Choose the **R**ight Align option to use this feature.

To have a period appear after a footnote number, select **T**ext and type a period in the **T**ext text box.

You may want to change the text attributes of the footnote numbers—for example, to have them appear in boldface. Choose **F**ont in the Modify section of the dialog box; then choose the appropriate attributes in the Attributes section of the dialog box.

Removing Footnotes

Removing a footnote is a simple matter of deleting the reference number. Follow these steps to delete a footnote:

1. Move the insertion point to the reference number of the footnote you want to delete.

2. Select the reference number.

3. Press Del. Unless you have disabled warning messages during setup, as explained in Chapter 8, "Changing Your Setup," Ami Pro displays a message asking whether you want to continue (see fig. 12.12). Choose **Y**es or press Enter.

Tip
You also can use drag-and-drop to move the footnote reference number. If necessary, Ami Pro repositions the footnote text automatically.

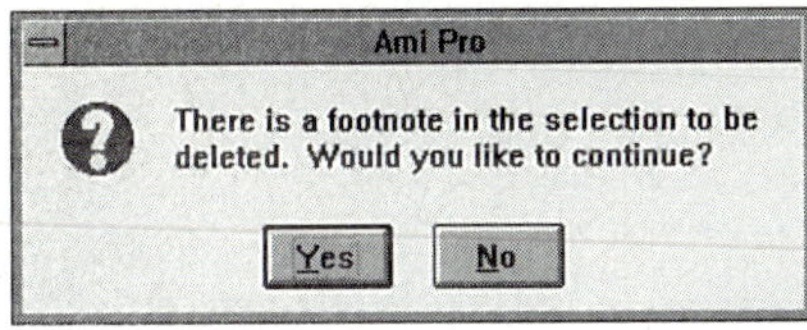

Fig. 12.12
The warning message that appears when you try to delete text containing a footnote.

Ami Pro deletes the footnote number and text, and then renumbers all the other footnotes accordingly.

Using a Glossary

A *glossary* is a document containing frequently used text. Your glossary can have any number of entries. The text may be boilerplate text, such as standard language for legal documents, a standard heading that you use at the top of a document, or any text that (for whatever reason) you use repeatedly. Instead of typing the text each time you need it, you can insert the text from the glossary into another document.

The next three sections explain how to create a glossary data file, how to place data into the file, and how to insert the data into other documents.

Creating Glossary Data Files

You can create any number of glossary data files, each containing standard text that you want to reuse. You might create one glossary file for standard sales information, one for legal text, and one for business letters, for example. If you don't use glossaries often, you may want to work with just one glossary file so that you don't have to search through several glossaries for an entry you want to insert.

The Glossary function is similar to the Merge function, which is explained in Chapter 14, "Merging and Sorting Data." To create a glossary data file, you must enter two *delimiters*. One delimiter marks the end of a *field* (the ID name); the other marks the end of a *record* (the actual data). When you look at the following example, you can see the difference between an ID name and a record.

The delimiters can be any characters that don't appear anywhere in the glossary data. You can use any ANSI or ASCII characters, but remember that many of these characters, such as the letters of the alphabet, are likely to appear in the text you are saving in the glossary; therefore, you may want to use symbols for your delimiters (such as $, #, !, ~, or |).

The first delimiter identifies the field. (*Field* refers to the name that describes the data to be inserted.) The second delimiter identifies the end of the *record*, which is the standard text you plan to enter.

If the delimiters are the characters ~ (tilde) and | (pipe), for example, an entry in the glossary data file may look like this:

```
Walton~The Compleat Angler, by Izaak Walton¦
```

Tip
If you use numbers for the record ID, the numbers should contain the same number of digits; for example, 001, 010, and 100 rather than 1, 10, and 100.

The first word, Walton, is the field name for the glossary entry. The tilde (~) is the field delimiter. The rest of the text (`The Compleat Angler, by Izaak Walton`) is the actual data in the glossary record. The pipe (|) is the record delimiter, indicating the end of the data in the glossary entry.

Follow these steps to create a glossary data file:

1. Create a standard Ami Pro document—using the default style sheet—to contain the glossary records. To create an example for practice, create a standard document called BOOKS.

2. On the first line of the document (the glossary data file), type the two delimiters you plan to use for the document, with no spaces or punctuation between them. For this example, type ~|. Remember that the first delimiter is for fields, and the second for records.

3. At the end of the line containing the delimiters, press Enter.

4. On the second line of the document, type the field name for the first delimiter. This name is the title for all the ID names in the document—a generic name that describes all the field names. For this example, type **Book**. The file name should match the intended use or subject of the glossary.

5. Without pressing Enter, type the field delimiter (~ in this example).

6. Type the field name you want to use for the actual records in the glossary data file. For this example, type **Full Title**.

7. Type the record delimiter (| in this example).

8. Press Enter.

The first two lines of the sample document now look like this:

```
~¦
Book~Full Title¦
```

Although you can have multiple entries, each entry can consist of only two parts: the field (followed by the field delimiter) and the record (followed by the record delimiter).

Typing Glossary Entries

After you have set up the document for accepting glossary items, you are ready to make entries into the glossary. Follow these steps:

1. On the next line of the example file, type the record name, which identifies an individual glossary entry. For this example, type **Walton**.

   You use this record name later—in the main document—to identify the record you want to insert into the document. (The field name, which you type into the document, is short. The record, which is inserted from the glossary, is long.) A record name must be unique.

2. Immediately after the record name, type the field delimiter (~ for this example).

3. Following the field delimiter, type the record (the text of the entry) followed by the record delimiter. For this example, type **The Compleat Angler, by Izaak Walton**|.

   The record can be as long as you like, even several paragraphs long if necessary.

4. Press Enter.

5. For each entry you want to place in the glossary, repeat steps 1 through 4.

Figure 12.13 shows a sample glossary containing several entries for literary references.

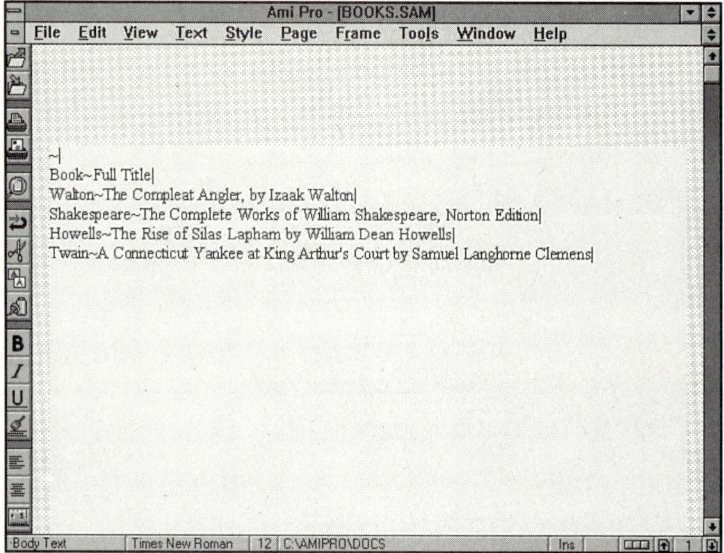

Fig. 12.13
A sample glossary containing several entries.

Ami Pro offers you another way to add entries to the glossary data file, as explained in the next section.

Creating Glossary Entries from Selected Text

You don't need to type the data for the glossary entries from scratch. You can use selected text in a document to make an entry. Follow these steps:

1. Move the insertion point to the text you want to add to the existing glossary.
2. Select the text to add to the glossary.
3. Choose **E**dit **M**ark Text **G**lossary. The Mark Glossary Record dialog box appears, as shown in figure 12.14. The first line of the selected text is in the Record Text box.

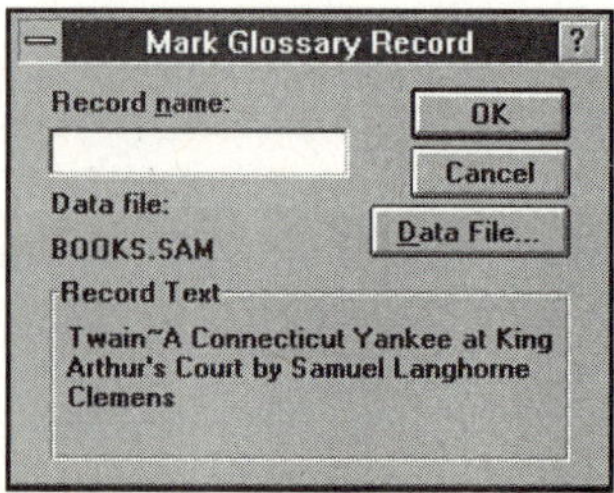

Fig. 12.14
The Mark Glossary Record dialog box.

4. In the Record **N**ame text box, type a name for the selected text. For the example, type **Twain**.

   The name corresponds to the ID name (the first of the two fields) for the data file you have established.

5. To specify a data file, choose **D**ata File. Enter the data file name in the **D**ata File text box or select a file name from the **F**iles list box. Then choose OK or press Enter. The data file name appears in the Data File section of the Mark Glossary Record dialog box.

6. Choose OK or press Enter. Ami Pro adds the record to the current glossary data file.

While you are in the Mark Glossary Record dialog box, you can have Ami Pro add the selected text as the record in a data file other than the current one. Before choosing OK or pressing Enter in the Mark Glossary Record dialog box, follow these steps:

1. Choose the **D**ata File button. The Data File dialog box appears, as shown in figure 12.15.

Fig. 12.15
The Data File dialog box.

2. From the **F**iles list box, select the data file to which you want to add the glossary record. If you prefer, you can type the file name in the **D**ata File text box.

3. Choose OK or press Enter. Ami Pro returns to the Mark Glossary Record dialog box, and displays the data file name in the Data File section of the dialog box.

4. Choose OK or press Enter to add the record to the glossary and return to the document.

After you create the glossary data file and add the entries to it, you can save much typing in the future. Instead of typing the entries contained in the glossary each time you want to use them, you can insert the entries from the glossary, as explained in the next section.

Inserting Glossary Entries

Suppose that you are creating a document and want to use the glossary data file just created (BOOKS.SAM) to save time as you insert text. To insert a glossary entry, follow these steps:

1. Open the document in which you want to insert the records from the glossary.

2. Place the insertion point at the location where you want to insert the text contained in the record in the glossary.

3. Choose **E**dit **I**nsert or click the Insert Glossary Record SmartIcon (on the Long Documents SmartIcon set; this SmartIcon shows three white bars and a piece of paper). Ami Pro cascades the **I**nsert menu from the **E**dit menu (see fig. 12.16).

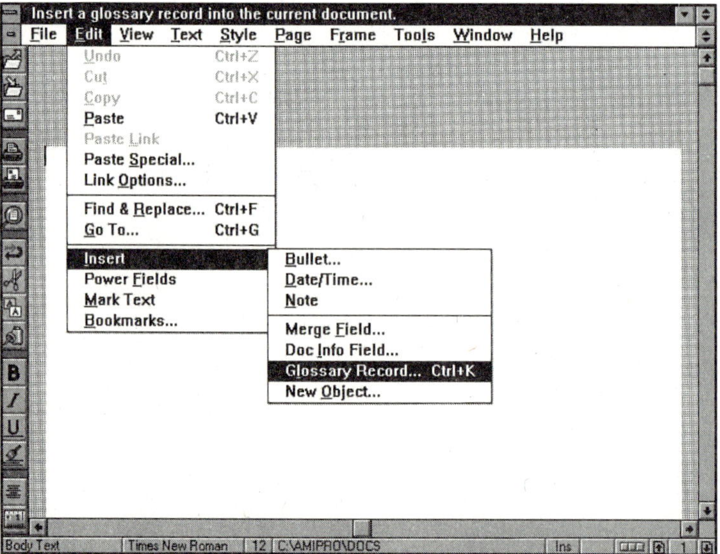

Fig. 12.16
The **I**nsert menu.

4. From the **I**nsert menu, choose G**l**ossary Record. The Insert Glossary Record dialog box opens, as shown in figure 12.17.

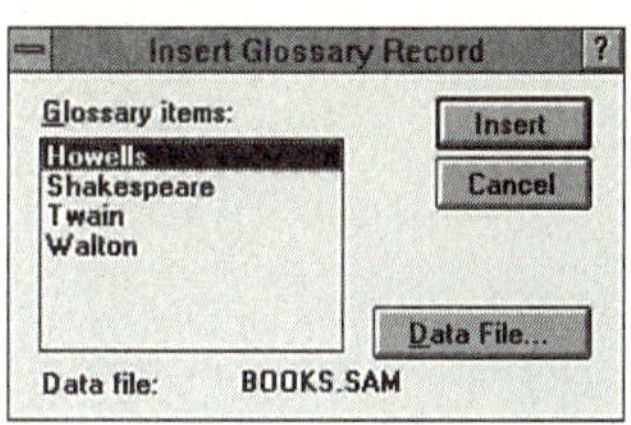

Fig. 12.17
The Insert Glossary Record dialog box.

5. If the correct data file isn't listed, choose **D**ata File. The Data File dialog box appears.

6. In the Data File dialog box, type the name of the data file (or highlight the name in the **F**iles list box). Figure 12.18 shows the name of the data file in the Data File dialog box.

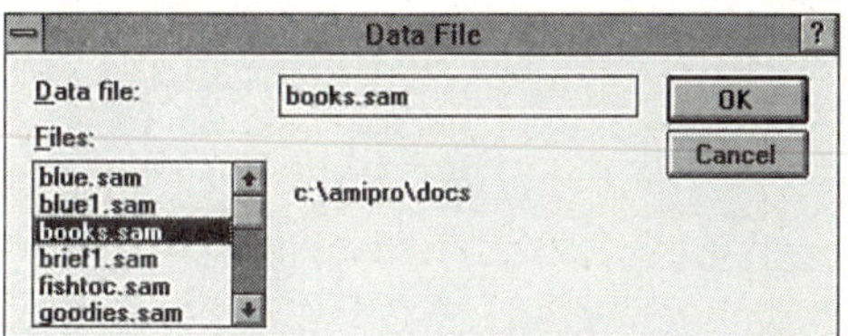

Fig. 12.18
The Data File dialog box, showing the name of the data file.

7. Choose OK or press Enter. Ami Pro returns to the Insert Glossary Record dialog box, which contains the name of the glossary and a list of the items contained in the glossary.

8. In the **G**lossary Items list box, select the record ID name of the glossary record you want to insert.

9. Choose Insert. Ami Pro inserts the glossary record into the document and returns to the document.

Tip
If you want to store and recall Ami Pro commands to perform specific tasks as well as boilerplate text, create a macro rather than a glossary.

After you have specified the glossary data file, you can use a keyboard shortcut to insert the record into the document. Move the insertion point to the place where you want to insert the record. Type the name of the record and press Ctrl+K. The glossary record replaces the record name you have typed with the record data.

Glossaries require you to spend some time in setup, but can save a good deal of time if you have reason to insert significant amounts of boilerplate text into a document.

▶ See "Recording and Playing Macros," p. 799

Another reference tool that is essential for many documents is the table of contents. The next section introduces you to Ami Pro's table of contents feature.

Creating a Table of Contents

Creating the table of contents (TOC) is a two-part process. First you assign the paragraph styles to the text you want to include in the table of contents. Then you generate the table of contents. When you generate a table of contents, you must make several decisions:

- Decide whether the page number should appear with the table of contents. A table of contents for a lengthy document isn't very useful without page numbers.
- Decide whether to right-align the page number.
- Select a separator (period, hyphen, or underscore) to use between the table of contents entry and the page number. If you have many headings in the table of contents, visible separators help the viewer line up page numbers with appropriate headings in the table of contents.
- Choose a location for the table of contents. You can place the table of contents at the top of the current document or in a separate document. If you specify an output file, Ami Pro generates the table of contents in that file. If you don't specify a file, the program places the table of contents at the top of the current document.

Tip
If you think that a document may require many revisions, and may therefore need frequent table of contents revisions, put the document in a separate file and use the master document feature to link the files together.

Assigning Table of Contents Styles

You can use existing table of contents styles, or you can create your own unique styles based on existing styles in the document. (See Chapter 10, "Working with Style Sheets," for information on creating styles.) Follow these steps to assign styles for the table of contents:

1. Place the insertion point anywhere in the document for which you want to generate a table of contents.
2. Be certain that the subheadings in the document appear the way you want them to look in the table of contents.
3. Choose **S**tyle **U**se Another Style Sheet. In the resulting dialog box, choose Table of Contents in the **C**hange To list box; then choose OK or press Enter.

4. Choose **S**tyle **S**elect a Style. The Styles box appears in the upper right corner of the screen.

   Notice in the Styles box that the sample document has three unique styles at the bottom—in this case, using the ~TOC.STY style sheet, the Styles box shows the styles Title1, Subhead1, and Subhead2 (see fig. 12.19).

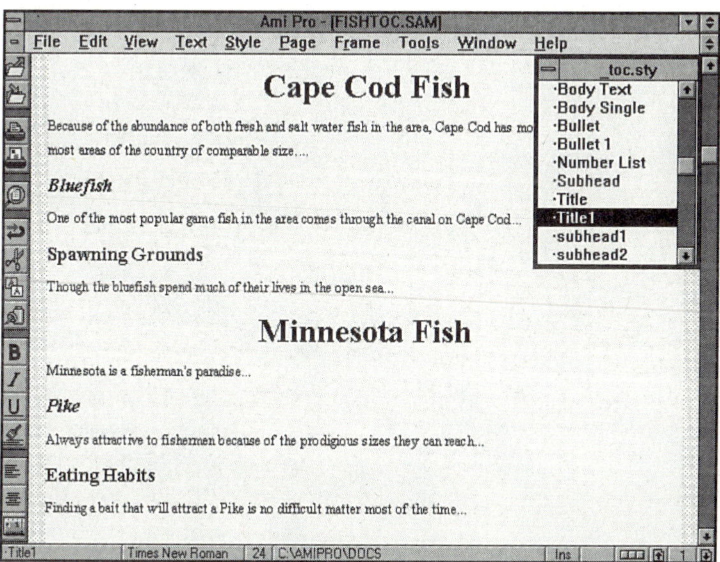

Fig. 12.19
A sample document for creating a table of contents, showing the Styles box.

5. Assign table of contents styles to the text that will appear in the table of contents. Assign one style to headings you want to appear as level 1 headings, another style to those you want to appear as level 2 headings, and so on, up to 9 levels. For this example, assign the text *Cape Cod Fish* and *Minnesota Fish* the Title1 style.

> **Caution**
>
> Don't assign styles to blank lines in the document unless you want the blank lines to appear in the table of contents.

Generating the Table of Contents

After you have assigned the appropriate styles to the text you want to include in the table of contents, only a few steps are necessary to create the table of contents in the document. To generate the table of contents, follow these steps:

1. Choose Tools TOC, Index or click the Generate TOC, Index SmartIcon (from the Long Documents SmartIcon set; this SmartIcon shows a table of contents on a page). The TOC, Index dialog box opens, as shown in figure 12.20.

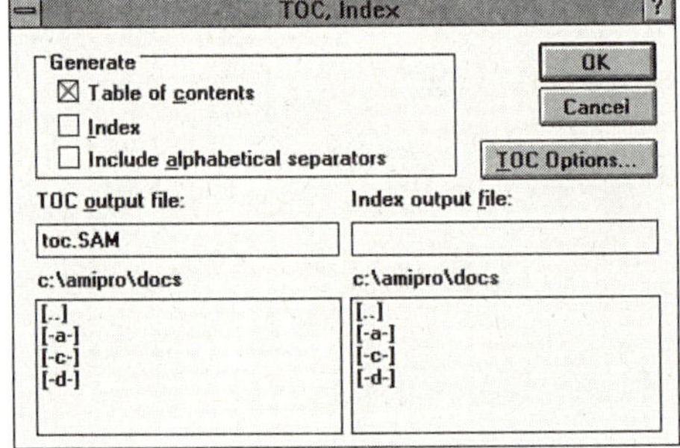

Fig. 12.20 The TOC, Index dialog box.

2. Choose the **T**OC Options button. The TOC Options dialog box appears (see fig. 12.21). In this dialog box, you specify the paragraph style that Ami Pro should recognize as the style for that level, whether the page number should appear, whether to right-align the page number, and the leader character to separate the entry from the page number in the table of contents.

3. In the dialog box, select from the list of styles the style you want to use for each level. Nine level numbers appear at the top of the TOC Options dialog box. The default styles appear in a list on the left side of the styles box and the available styles appear in a list on the right side of the box (under None).

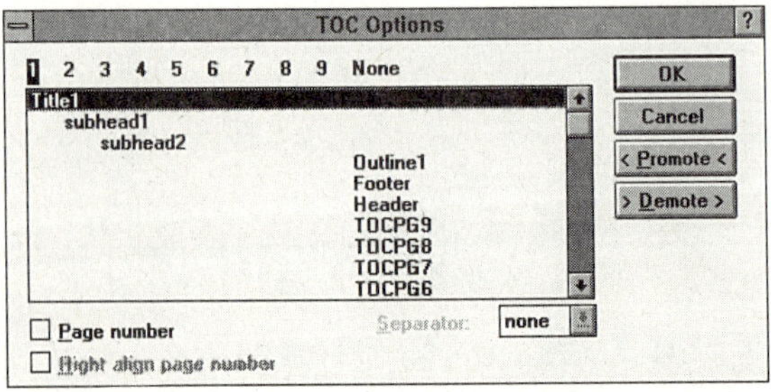

Fig. 12.21 The TOC Options dialog box.

To specify a style and level in the styles box, select the style and choose **P**romote to move the style to a higher level or **D**emote to move the style to a lower level. You also can drag the styles below the desired level number. Styles you don't want to use should be at the None level. In figure 12.21, for example, Title1 is the style for level 1, Subhead1 for level 2, and Subhead2 for level 3.

4. For each level, select **P**age Number if you want to include page numbers in that table of contents level.

5. If you selected **P**age Number and you want the page numbers aligned at the right margin, choose **R**ight Align Page Number. If you don't select **R**ight Align Page Number, Ami Pro places a single separator character (the comma) after the entry, before the page number.

6. In the **S**eparator list box for each level, select a separator character. You can use a period, a hyphen, an underscore, or no separator character.

   If you didn't select **P**age Number, **R**ight Align Page Number and **S**eparator are grayed. If you chose **P**age Number but not **R**ight Align Page Number, the only choices in the **L**eader box are none or the comma.

   Figure 12.22 shows the **P**age Number and **R**ight Align Page Number options selected in the dialog box. For this example, a dot leader is specified as the separator character.

7. Choose OK or press Enter to return to the TOC, Index dialog box. The Table of **C**ontents option is selected in the Generate section of the dialog box.

8. If you want Ami Pro to place the table of contents in a separate file, type that file name in the TOC Output **F**ile text box. If you don't specify a file, Ami Pro places the table of contents at the beginning of the current document.

9. Choose OK or press Enter to generate the table of contents.

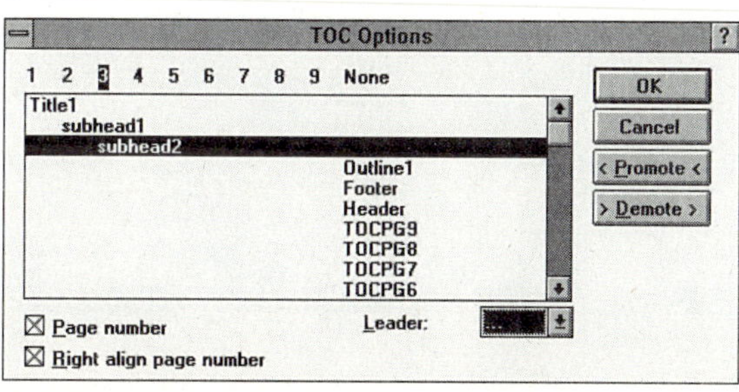

Fig. 12.22
Selected options for the table of contents.

II

Automating

Ami Pro generates the table of contents with a dot leader separator, and places it at the beginning of the current document or the file you specified (see fig. 12.23). Figure 12.24 shows the same table of contents with a hyphen separator. Figure 12.25 shows the same table of contents with the **P**age Number option deselected in the TOC Options dialog box.

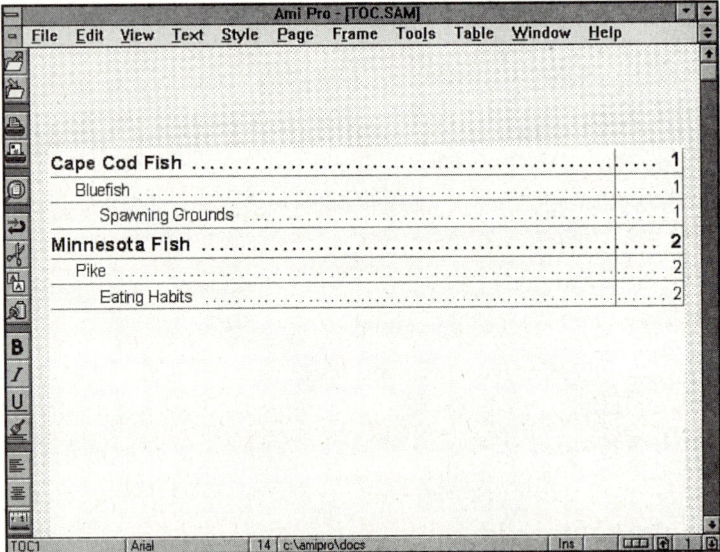

Fig. 12.23
A sample table of contents with a dot leader separator.

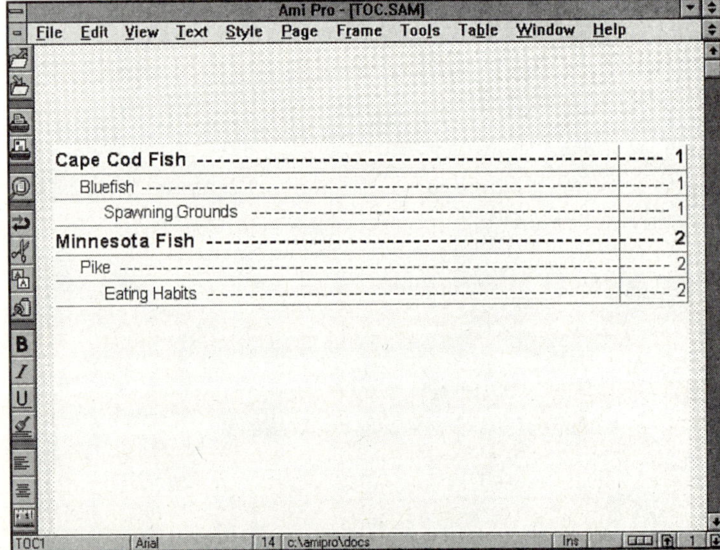

Fig. 12.24
The table of contents with a hyphen separator.

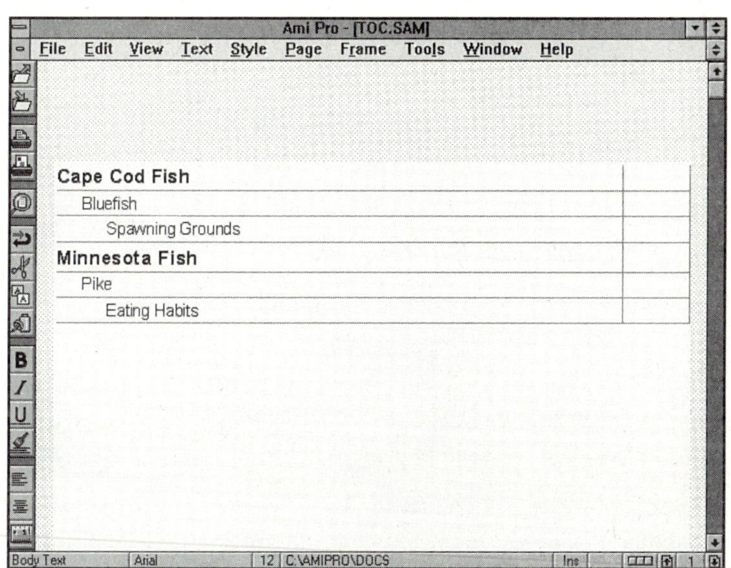

Fig. 12.25 The table of contents with no page numbers or separator character.

Tip
If you later change the document and want to update the table of contents, generate the table of contents again by repeating steps 8 and 9.

Note that Ami Pro automatically creates paragraph styles for the table of contents named TOC1 through TOC9 and TOCpg1 through TOCpg9. The program sets the alignment indentions for each paragraph style so that each level appears indented appropriately.

The fonts are based on the next lower level; that is, TOC1 uses level 2 paragraph style font, TOC2 uses level 3 paragraph style, and so on. TOC9 uses Body Text style. You can change these settings as desired.

Tip
If you place the table of contents in a separate file, Ami Pro uses the _TOC.STY style sheet for the document. You can modify _TOC.STY just as you modify any other style sheet.

Creating a Table of Contents Entry from Selected Text

You can specify text you want to include in the table of contents in addition to—or instead of—assigning table of contents levels to heading paragraph styles. You can use this method if you assign only one paragraph style, such as Body Text, to text in a short document. You also can use this method to shorten a table of contents entry if the text in a heading paragraph contains several lines.

To create a table of contents entry from selected text, begin with the document for which you want to generate the table of contents in the active window. Then follow these steps:

1. Select the text you want to include in the table of contents, or place the insertion point where you want to create a table of contents entry. You can select up to 240 characters.

2. Choose **E**dit **M**ark Text.

3. Choose **T**OC Entry.

4. In the resulting dialog box, specify the table of contents level for the text.

5. Type or edit the text for the table of contents entry.

6. Choose OK to return to the document.

7. Repeat steps 1 through 6 for any additional text you want to include in the table of contents.

When you generate the table of contents, Ami Pro includes only the selected text instead of the entire paragraph, even if you assigned a table of contents level to the paragraph style used by the text.

Tip
After you create a table of contents, if you modify or remove table of contents entries created from selected text, you should regenerate the table to reflect the changes.

The table of contents entries you create from selected text are power fields. You can modify or remove the power fields before or after generating the table of contents. If you display power fields, you can use the Find & Replace feature to find a table of contents entry and replace it with another entry.

The table of contents is an Ami Pro table—you can edit the table of contents the same way you edit any other Ami Pro table. See Chapter 13, "Working with Tables," for more information.

Just as you can create a table of contents with Ami Pro, you can create a table of authorities for legal briefs, as explained in the next section.

Creating a Table of Authorities

◄ See "Creating and Modifying Styles," p. 273

► See "Displaying Power Field Instructions," p. 875

Creating the table of authorities is a three-step process. First, you add the table of authorities options to Ami Pro's menu. (Ami Pro can execute this step automatically; see the next section.) Next, you mark the authorities and assign the categories to appear in the table of authorities. Finally, you generate the table of authorities and choose the style and leader options, similar to when you generate a table of contents. Ami Pro places the table of authorities at the end of the document.

To create a well-organized table of authorities that is easy to read, you need some specific information:

- Before you begin marking the text, determine what categories you want to include in the table of authorities. The table of authorities groups citation references under six categories: constitutional provisions, cases, rules and regulations, statutes, treaties, and other authorities. You also can create your own categories.

- When marking the text, determine whether the citations are short or long entries. A short entry contains only the case name. A long entry contains the case name and where the case can be referenced.

- Decide what separator (period, hyphen, underscore, or none) to use between the TOA entry and the page number. If you have many headings in the table of authorities, visible separators help the viewer line up page numbers with appropriate headings in the table of authorities.

Adding the TOA Options to the Menu

The table of authorities (TOA) macro adds to the **E**dit and Too**l**s menus the TOA commands used to create a table of authorities—otherwise, the TOA commands don't appear on the menus.

Note

You can tell Ami Pro to execute the TOA macro automatically when you load the program. With this strategy, each time you start Ami Pro the TOA macro plays back immediately and the TOA commands appear on the menus. For details, see Chapter 8, "Changing Your Setup," and Chapter 23, "Using Macros."

To run the TOA macro, follow these steps:

1. Choose Too**l**s **M**acros **P**layback or click the Play Back SmartIcon (in the Macro Goodies SmartIcon set; this SmartIcon shows a cassette tape with an arrow pointing right).

2. In the resulting dialog box, specify the name of the macro you want to run. For this example, select TOA.SMM in the **M**acros list box or type **TOA** in the Macro **F**ile text box.

3. Choose OK or press Enter to run the macro.

   Ami Pro adds three commands to the **E**dit **M**ark Text menu: TOA **L**ong Entry, TOA **S**hort Entry, and Remove TOA **M**ark. On the Too**l**s menu, Ami Pro adds one command: **G**enerate TOA.

Marking the Entries

When the table of authorities options are on the Ami Pro menu, you are ready to mark the entries for the table of authorities. Follow these steps:

1. Select the text for the first citation you want to include in the table of authorities. Figure 12.26 shows an example of a citation selected to be marked as an authority reference.

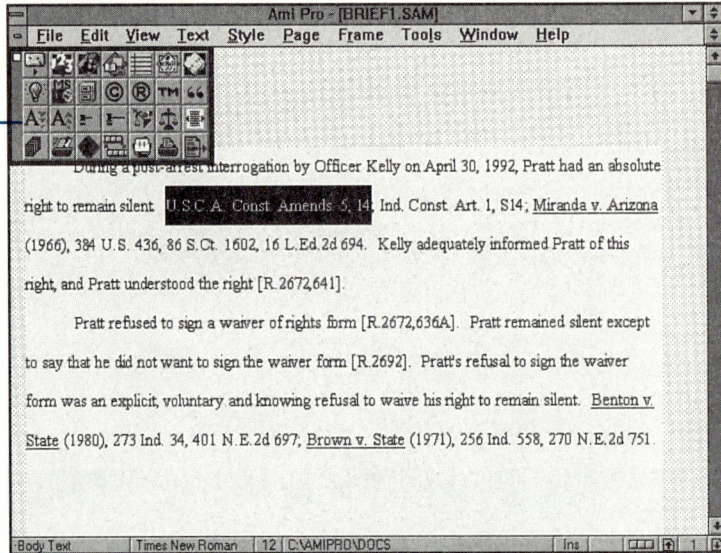

Fig. 12.26
A sample document for creating a table of authorities, with an authority reference selected.

Macro goodies SmartIcon set

2. Choose **E**dit **M**ark Text. The cascading **M**ark Text menu shows the new table of authorities entries (see fig. 12.27).

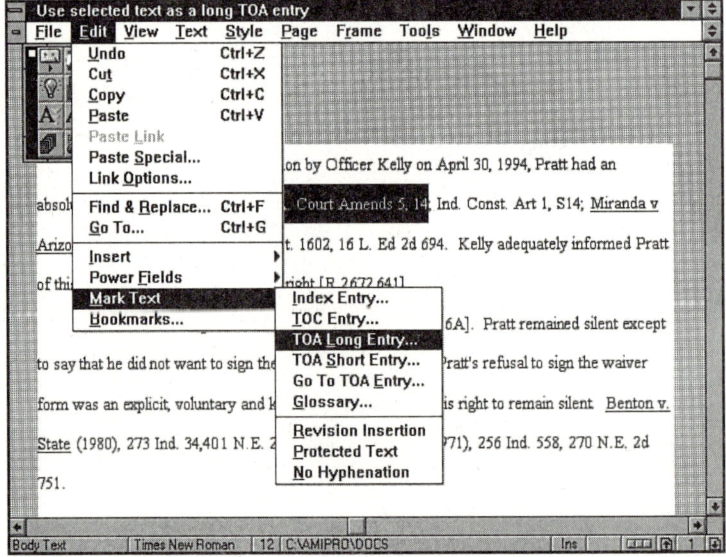

Fig. 12.27
The **E**dit **M**ark Text menu with options added by the macro TOA.SMM.

3. From the **M**ark Text menu, choose TOA **L**ong Entry or TOA **S**hort Entry. If you select TOA **L**ong Entry, the Mark TOA Long Entry dialog box opens (see fig. 12.28). If you select TOA **S**hort Entry, the Mark TOA Short Entry dialog box appears (see fig. 12.29). You can select the short entry only when an existing long entry already has been marked for the same citation.

   Alternatively, you can access the dialog boxes with the TOA Long Entry SmartIcon (shows a large gavel) or the TOA Short Entry SmartIcon (shows a small gavel). Both SmartIcons are in the Macro Goodies SmartIcons set.

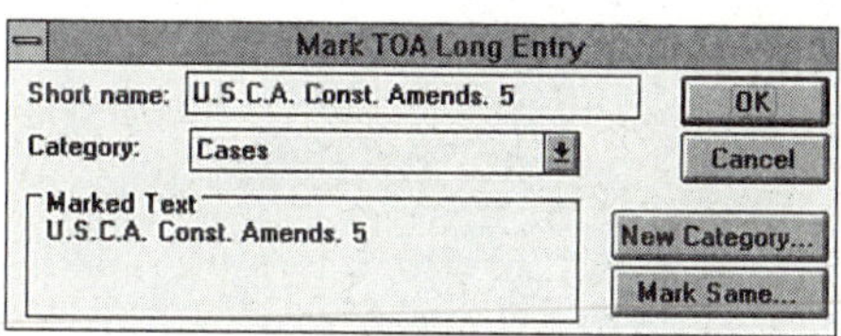

Fig. 12.28
The Mark TOA Long Entry dialog box.

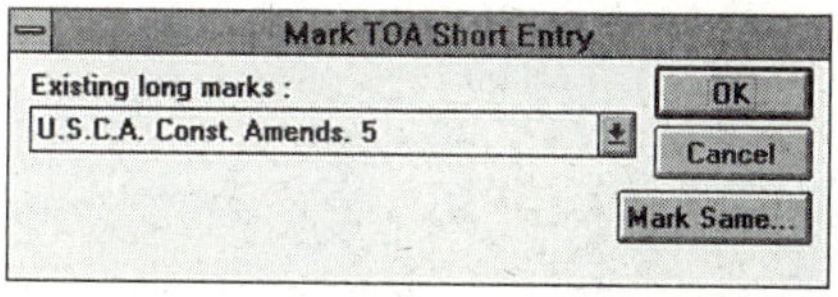

Fig. 12.29
The Mark TOA Short Entry dialog box.

4. If you selected the long entry, choose from the Category list box the category you want to assign to the authority. For the sample document, assign the first citation to the Constitutional Provisions category and the second citation to the Cases category.

   If you want to create your own category, choose New Category. The Add Category dialog box appears (see fig. 12.30). In the **N**ew Category Name text box, type a name for the new category.

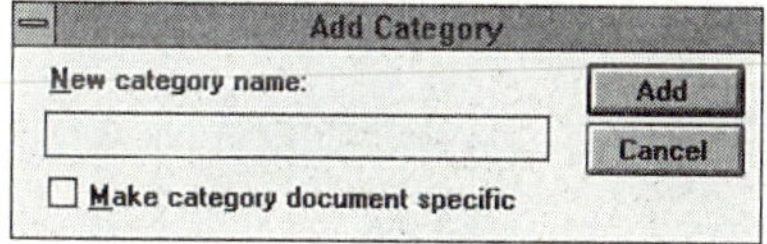

Fig. 12.30
The Add Category dialog box.

   If you want to use the new category only in this document, choose **M**ake Category Document Specific. If you don't select this option, the categories list is permanently modified for all documents.

After you finish specifying the new category and its options, choose Add to add the category name to the category list.

5. If you have more than one occurrence of a citation throughout the brief, you can mark some or all of these citations. Specify the category for the first occurrence of the citation and then choose Mark Same in the Mark TOA Long Entry or Mark TOA Short Entry dialog box. The Specify TOA Search dialog box opens (see fig. 12.31).

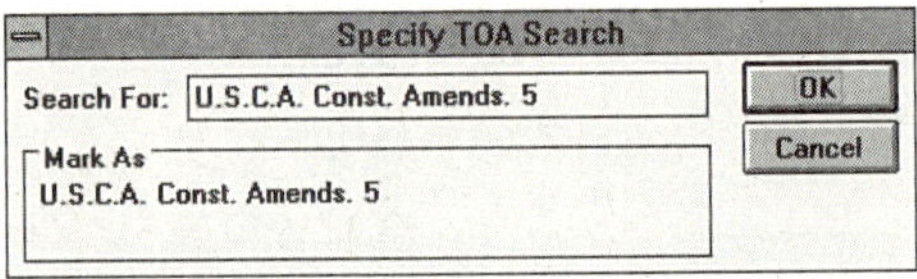

Fig. 12.31
The Specify TOA Search dialog box.

Choose OK or press Enter to search for the second occurrence of the citation. Ami Pro finds the second occurrence, highlights the citation in the document, and opens the Locate Short TOA Marks dialog box (see fig. 12.32).

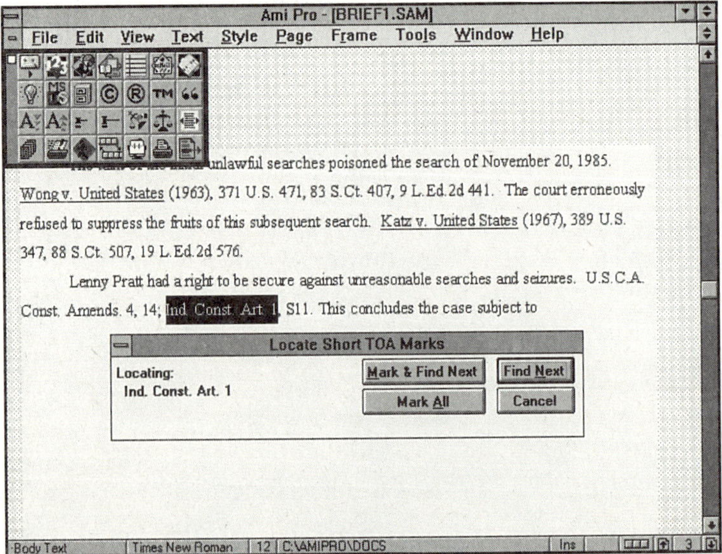

Fig. 12.32
The Locate Short TOA Marks dialog box.

To mark the text and find the next occurrence, choose **M**ark & Find Next. To skip marking the text and find the next occurrence, choose Find **N**ext. To mark all occurrences of the text, choose Mark **A**ll.

6. For each authority you want to include in the table, repeat steps 1 through 5.

Tip
You can select Go To to find a specific entry without removing it.

To remove a TOA entry, select the text with the entry, choose **E**dit **M**ark Text, and then choose Remove TOA **M**ark. (Alternatively, you can click the Remove TOA Mark SmartIcon, which shows a scale with a hand tilting the scale.) The Remove TOA Entry dialog box appears, with the entry highlighted in the Existing Entries list box. (You also can choose other entries from the list box.) If it is a long entry, Long Citation on Page (x) is selected. You also can choose Short Citation on Page (x), and select the page from the list box. Selecting Remove deletes the TOA entry.

Tip
TOA entries are power fields. For details on using power fields, see Chapter 24, "Creating Smart Documents with Power Fields."

Generating the Table of Authorities

After you mark the authorities, you generate the table of authorities. Follow these steps:

1. Choose Too**l**s **G**enerate TOA or click the Generate a Table of Authorities SmartIcon (it shows a scale). The Generate Table of Authorities dialog box opens (see fig. 12.33). In this dialog box, you specify the paragraph styles that Ami Pro should use for the categories and references, and the leader character to separate the entry from the page number in the table of authorities.

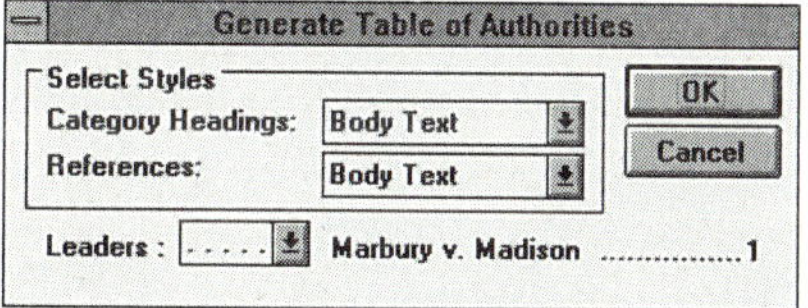

Fig. 12.33
The Generate Table of Authorities dialog box.

2. In the Category Headings list box, select from the list of styles the style that you want to use for the category headings. By default, the style is Body Text.

3. In the References list box, select from the list of styles the style that you want to use for the references headings. By default, the style is Body Text.

4. In the Leaders list box, select a separator character. You can use a period, hyphen, underscore, or no leader character.

5. Choose OK or press Enter to generate the table of authorities.

Tip
If you later change the document and want to update the table of authorities, generate the table of authorities again by repeating steps 1 through 5.

Ami Pro generates the table of authorities and places it at the end of the document (see fig. 12.34).

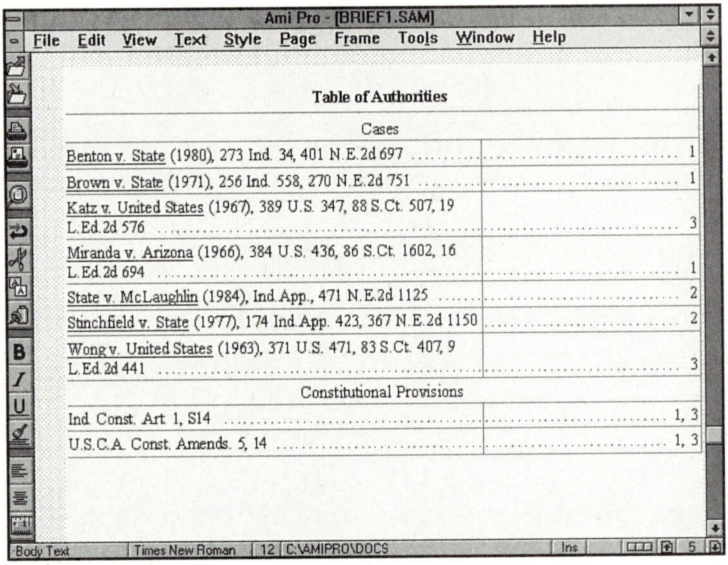

Fig. 12.34
A sample table of authorities with a dot leader separator.

Ami Pro - [BRIEF1.SAM]

File Edit View Text Style Page Frame Tools Window Help

Table of Authorities

Cases	
Benton v. State (1980), 273 Ind. 34, 401 N.E.2d 697	1
Brown v. State (1971), 256 Ind. 558, 270 N.E.2d 751	1
Katz v. United States (1967), 389 U.S. 347, 88 S.Ct. 507, 19 L.Ed.2d 576	3
Miranda v. Arizona (1966), 384 U.S. 436, 86 S.Ct. 1602, 16 L.Ed.2d 694	1
State v. McLaughlin (1984), Ind.App., 471 N.E.2d 1125	2
Stinchfield v. State (1977), 174 Ind.App. 423, 367 N.E.2d 1150	2
Wong v. United States (1963), 371 U.S. 471, 83 S.Ct. 407, 9 L.Ed.2d 441	3
Constitutional Provisions	
Ind. Const. Art. 1, S14	1, 3
U.S.C.A. Const. Amends. 5, 14	1, 3

Body Text | Times New Roman | 12 | C:\AMIPRO\DOCS | Ins | 5

Tip
The table of authorities is an Ami Pro table; you can edit the table of authorities as you'd edit any other Ami Pro table. See Chapter 13, "Working with Tables," for more information.

You also can create an index with Ami Pro, as discussed in the next section.

Creating an Index

For many documents, particularly technical documents, an index is invaluable. The index gives you an alphabetic listing of key topics and corresponding pages.

Ami Pro offers two ways to create an index. You can work within a document and mark index entries. You also can create the index entries in a separate file. In the following paragraphs, you learn how to use both of these methods to create an index.

To build an index, you must mark each word or phrase to appear in the index. You mark an entry by choosing **E**dit **M**ark Text. You can use a macro to speed the process of marking additional occurrences after you mark an entry the first time. (This macro is explained later.)

Each time you mark an index entry, you create a power field. Chapter 24, "Creating Smart Documents with Power Fields," explains power fields in depth. The point here is that you set the conditions so that when you generate the index, Ami Pro can include in the index each word or phrase you marked, according to instructions you provide.

You can designate an item as a primary entry (an entry with a separate alphabetic listing in the index) or a secondary entry (an entry beneath a primary entry). You decide whether a page number should appear with the entry, and you also can choose to add additional text, such as *See* or *See also*, after the entry.

Marking Index Entries

One way to create an index for a document is to go through the document and mark the text that should appear in the index. Then you can generate the index.

If you don't have established guidelines regarding what to mark as an index entry, deciding what to mark requires common sense and a basic knowledge of the subject matter. You must know what is important enough to mark. If you are preparing an index about Chrysler Corporation, for example, you may mark *Chrysler*, *General Motors*, and *Iacocca*. You probably wouldn't mark *car* because you would have a multitude of references to the entry. If you mark *Iacocca* as an entry, you might decide to make secondary entries for *childhood*, *publications*, and *management style*.

Ami Pro refers to the text you mark for the index as an *index reference*. A *primary reference* is a main reference. A *secondary reference* is subordinate to a primary reference.

You can mark and include in your index any number of single words or complete phrases; however, keep in mind that the limitation isn't the software but the appearance of the index. One- to three-word entries work best in an index.

> **Caution**
>
> When marking entries, be consistent in capitalization and spacing. Ami Pro's indexing treats *Bluefish*, for example, as a separate entry from *bluefish* or *blue fish*.

Follow these steps to create index entries:

1. Begin with the document you want to index in the active window.

2. Select the first portion of text you want to include in the index. Figure 12.35 shows an example of a word selected to be marked as an index reference.

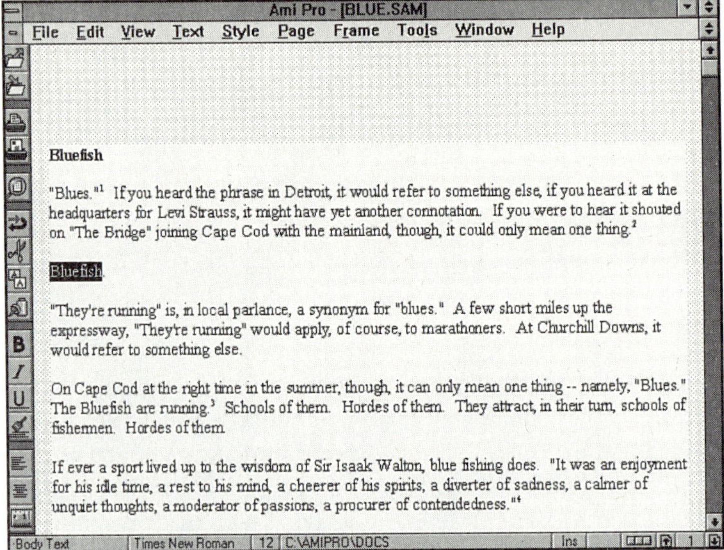

Fig. 12.35
A sample document for indexing, with an index reference selected.

3. Choose **E**dit **M**ark Text and then choose **I**ndex Entry. The Mark Index Entry dialog box opens.

4. The index reference for the selected text appears automatically in the Pr**i**mary text box. If you want to make the reference a Se**c**ondary reference, you can cut-and-paste the text from one text box to the other (press Shift+Del to cut and Shift+Ins to paste) or just type the text in the other text box.

   To ensure consistency, you can click the down arrow in the Pr**i**mary or Se**c**ondary text box to see a list of previous entries; then select the entry from the list. If you select *Bluefish* in the text and then see that the list includes only bluefish, you can select bluefish in the list to index the selected *Bluefish* under `bluefish`.

5. In the Reference section of the dialog box, choose P**a**ge Number if you want to display the entry with a page number (a useful option in an index).

6. Choose **O**ther if you want to place additional text and punctuation next to the entry in the index. You can use the **O**ther text box to add *See* or *See also*, for example, or to add a comma or space between the index entry and the text.

   The example box at the bottom of the dialog box shows the effect of your choices. In figure 12.36, the entry Bluefish is a primary entry followed by a page number. In the example box, you see `Bluefish, ##`. If you add a secondary entry or some other text, such as *See Also*, you can see the changes in the example box.

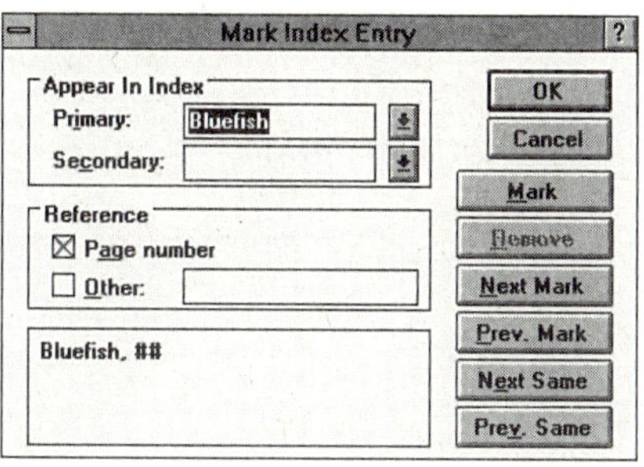

Fig. 12.36
Bluefish as a primary entry.

Because a final index can contain hundreds of entries, you should review entries as you create them. After you mark an entry and leave the dialog box, you don't see how the entry looks until you generate the index.

7. Choose **M**ark. Ami Pro marks the text as an index entry and the selected entry disappears from the Appear in Index text box. The Mark Index Entry dialog box remains open.

   You cannot specify a secondary entry without specifying a primary entry. If you choose **M**ark before you indicate a primary entry, Ami Pro displays a warning message (see fig. 12.37). Choose OK; then specify a primary entry.

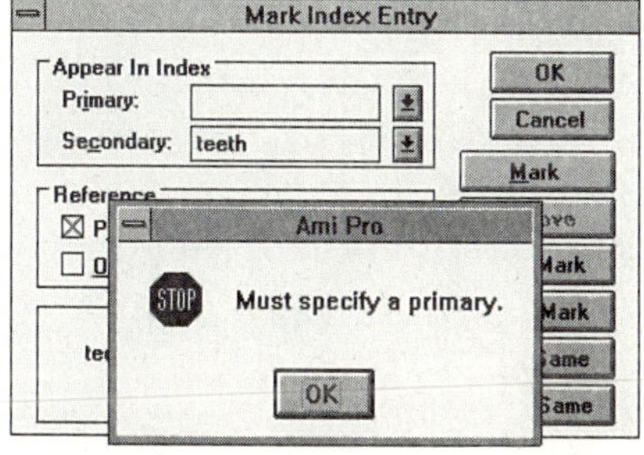

Fig. 12.37
The message that appears if you haven't specified a primary field.

8. After you specify all the index entries you want for the selected text, choose Cancel or OK. Even if you choose Cancel, Ami Pro marks the text for which you have chosen **M**ark.

II

Automating

You can place the same text as a secondary reference under additional primary entries. An entry for *Bluefish*, for example, may appear as a secondary entry under *Cape Cod Fishing* and under *Migration Patterns in Fish*. You also can list similar primary entries; for example, you can mark both *Bluefish* and *Blue Fish* as primary entries. Figure 12.38 shows a sample document with multiple power fields following the entry *Bluefish*. Each of the primary fields appears in the index, followed by the page number.

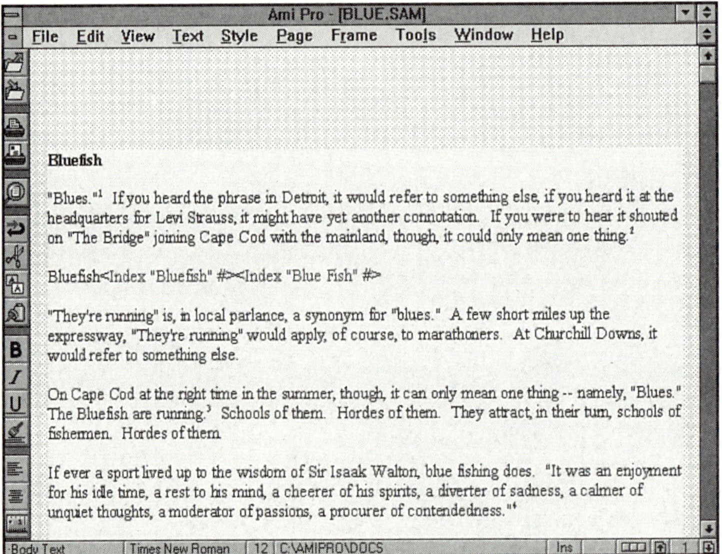

Fig. 12.38
A sample document with power fields following the entry Bluefish.

Marking Multiple Entries with a Macro

You often may mark multiple entries of the same text (such as the term *Bluefish*) within a document. Although you can mark each entry individually, Ami Pro provides a macro that marks additional instances of an entry. (See Chapter 23, "Using Macros," for details on Ami Pro macros.) Follow these steps to run the macro:

1. Choose Too**l**s **M**acros **P**layback. The Play Macro dialog box appears.
2. In the Macros list box, highlight the macro named INDEXALL.SMM.
3. Choose OK or press Enter. The macro adds the item Mark Index **A**ll to the **E**dit **M**ark Text menu (see fig. 12.39).

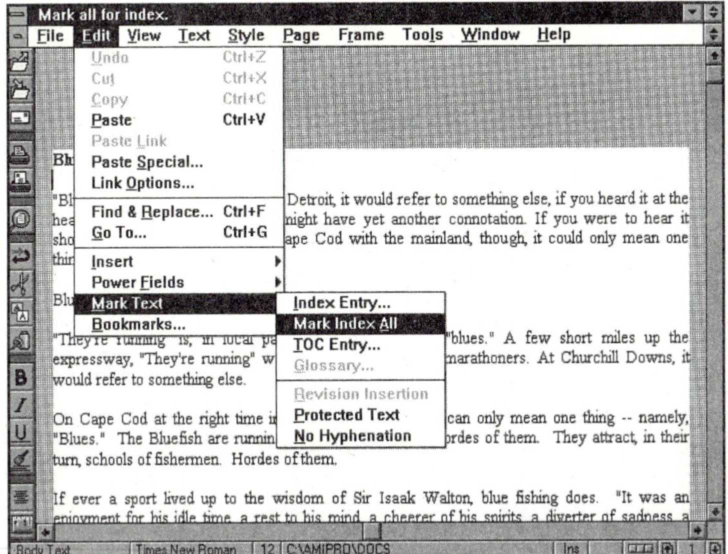

Fig. 12.39

The **E**dit **M**ark Text menu with the Mark Index **A**ll item added.

4. Select one occurrence of the term to be marked throughout the document.

5. Choose **E**dit **M**ark Text and then choose Mark Index **A**ll. Ami Pro marks every occurrence of the term as a primary index entry.

Creating Index Entries in a Separate File

Often you may want to create an index for multiple files. If you have many documents containing chapters for a book, for example, you probably don't want to combine them all into a single document to create the index. If you know a list of specific terms that you want to index, you can create the index entries in a separate file.

Setting Up the Entries

To index multiple files in a single index, you begin by specifying the entries in a special document. Follow these steps:

1. Create a new document (using the default style sheet) to contain the list of index entries.

2. On the first line of the document, type an index entry.

3. Press Enter.

4. For each index entry you want to include, type the entry on a separate line.

5. Move the insertion point to the top of the document.

6. Select the first entry.

7. Choose **E**dit **M**ark Text and then choose **I**ndex Entry. The Mark Index Entry dialog box appears.

8. To make the selected text a primary index entry, choose OK or press Enter.

9. To make the selected text a secondary index entry, specify the primary index entry in the Pr**i**mary text box, paste the selected text into the Se**c**ondary text box, and choose OK or press Enter.

10. For each index entry you want to create, select the appropriate text and follow steps 7 through 9.

11. Save and close the document.

Inserting the Index Entry File into the Main Document

After you set up the index entries in a separate file, you can mark the text in the document you are indexing. First, however, you must insert the index entry file at the end of the document you want to index. Follow these steps:

1. Make the document you are indexing the active document.

2. Move the insertion point to the end of the document.

3. Choose **F**ile **O**pen. The Open dialog box appears.

4. In the Open dialog box, specify the name of the file containing the list of index entries.

5. Choose **I**nsert.

Ami Pro inserts the document containing the list of index entries at the end of the current document.

Marking the Index References in the Main Document

The next task is to mark the index references in the text of the document. Follow these steps:

1. Move the insertion point to the beginning of the document you are indexing.

2. Select the text you want to reference in the index (as explained earlier, in the section "Marking Index Entries").

3. Choose **E**dit **M**ark Text and then choose **I**ndex Entry. The Mark Index Entry dialog box appears.

4. If you want the text to be a primary entry, click the down arrow next to the Pr**i**mary text box to display all primary index entries in the list file, and then select one of the primary index entries.

   If you want the text to be a secondary index entry, click the down arrow next to the Se**c**ondary text box to display the secondary index entries, and then select one of the secondary index entries.

5. Choose the P**a**ge Number option if you want to display a page number with the index entry.

6. If you want to include other punctuation and text with the index entry, choose **O**ther and type the punctuation and text in the text box.

7. Choose **M**ark.

8. Mark all additional entries in the same way. Select the text and follow steps 3 through 7.

9. Choose Cancel or press Esc to return to the document.

Removing the List File

After you have used the list file to create the index entries, you no longer need the list file. Follow these steps to remove it:

1. In the document containing the index entries, place the insertion point at the beginning of the inserted text.

2. Select all the inserted text. With the keyboard, you can press Shift+Ctrl+End to select all the text from the insertion point to the end of the document.

3. Choose **E**dit Cu**t**. This process removes the inserted document but doesn't remove the index references you created in the current document.

4. Save the document.

5. Repeat this process for any other document that you are indexing.

After you create the index entries, you are ready to generate the index, as described in the next section.

Generating the Index

After you mark the text for the index, regardless of the method you use, you must follow a few steps to tell Ami Pro to generate the index:

1. With the document you want to index in the active window, choose Too**l**s TOC, I**n**dex. The TOC, Index dialog box appears (see fig. 12.40).

2. In the Generate section of the dialog box, choose **I**ndex.

Fig. 12.40
The TOC, Index dialog box.

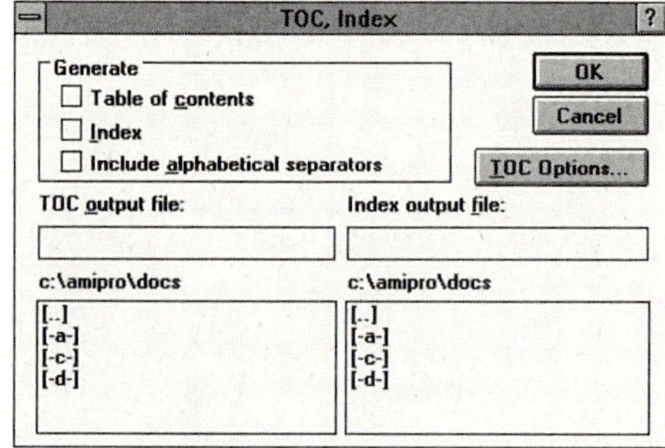

3. Choose Include **A**lphabetical Separators if you want Ami Pro to place a letter of the alphabet in the index before index entries beginning with that letter.

4. In the Index Output **F**ile text box, you must specify the name of the file in which you want to put the index. Ami Pro doesn't put the index in the current document.

5. Specify the drive and directory for the file.

6. Choose OK or press Enter.

Ami Pro creates the index, assigns paragraph styles to the index entries, inserts any specified text, inserts commas between the index entries and page numbers and between multiple page numbers for the same entry, and places the insertion point at the top of the first page of the index. Figure 12.41 shows a brief sample index.

When creating the index, Ami Pro uses a style sheet called _INDEX.STY. To primary index entries, the program assigns the Pr**i**mary paragraph style, and to secondary entries, the Se**c**ondary paragraph style. Notice that in figure 12.41 the items in the secondary paragraph style appear indented more than the entries in the primary paragraph style. Alphabetic separators appear in the Separator paragraph style.

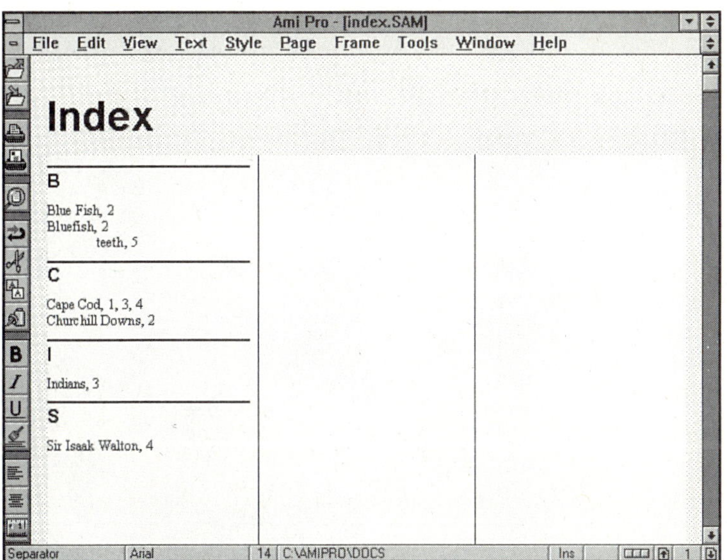

Fig. 12.41
A sample index.

Tip
To use a different style for the document, choose **S**tyle **U**se Another Style Sheet, as explained in Chapter 10, "Working with Style Sheets." You also can modify the styles in _INDEX.STY.

Changing an Index

After you generate an index, you are almost certain to want to make changes. Perhaps you inadvertently put in entries for *Bluefish* and *bluefish* and don't want both to appear as separate entries in the index. Perhaps you want to add entries or remove entries. This section describes how to edit an index.

Tip
Ami Pro's index entries are power fields. See Chapter 24, "Creating Smart Documents with Power Fields," for more information on power fields.

Note

Before you open the Mark Index Entry dialog box in the following steps, click the Document Path button in the Status Bar until the line, column, and position information appears. Even when the cursor is within a dialog box, Ami Pro indicates in the Status Bar the position of any index entry highlighted in the Mark Index Entry dialog box.

Follow these steps to modify an index:

1. With the insertion point anywhere in the document whose index you want to change, choose **E**dit **M**ark Text and then choose **I**ndex Entry.

   The Mark Index Entry dialog box appears (see fig. 12.42). Because you haven't selected any text in the document, no text appears in the Pr**i**mary text box.

2. Several buttons along the right side of the dialog box enable you to move to index entries in the document.

3. Choose **N**ext Mark if you want to move the insertion point to the next index entry in the document. You can use this option to move one-by-one through the entries in the index. Entries appear in the Pr**i**mary and (if appropriate) Se**c**ondary text boxes. The insertion point remains at the initial entry in the document as you display the subsequent index entries.

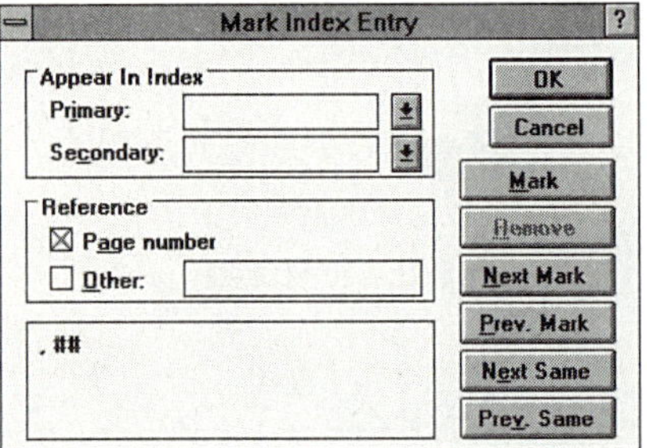

Fig. 12.42
The Mark Index Entry dialog box, as it appears if no text is selected.

Choose **P**rev. Mark if you want to move the insertion point from the present index entry to the preceding index entry in the document.

Choose N**e**xt Same if you want to move the insertion point to the next instance of the index entry displayed in the Pr**i**mary and Se**c**ondary text boxes.

Choose Pre**v**. Same if you want to move the insertion point to the preceding instance of the index entry displayed in the Pr**i**mary and Se**c**ondary text boxes.

4. To remove an entry, choose **R**emove when the entry is displayed in the Pr**i**mary or Se**c**ondary text box. You cannot remove the entry from the Pr**i**mary or Se**c**ondary list boxes if other text in the document is referenced under the entry. Ami Pro removes the mark at the position of the present entry, however.

5. When an index entry you want to change appears in the Pr**i**mary or Se**c**ondary text box (the insertion point has moved to that entry in the document), you can just type over the entry in the text box, or you can click the down arrow, scroll through the choices, and select a replacement.

6. To change the reference for an entry listed in the Pr**i**mary or Se**c**ondary text box, type the new reference in the text box. (Alternatively, you can select the Pr**i**mary or Se**c**ondary index entry you want to use in place of the listed entry.)

Ami Pro indexes the entry at the specified position in the document under the new primary or secondary reference you indicated.

7. Choose **M**ark. Your edit doesn't show up in the list boxes until you exit the dialog box and then return to the dialog box.

8. Choose Cancel or OK to return to the document.

The insertion point is at the last index entry displayed in the Mark Index Entry dialog box. To have the index reflect your changes, you generate the index again (as explained earlier, in the section "Generating the Index").

Without index-editing capabilities, reworking an existing index can be cumbersome. These tools enable you to perform operations as simple as moving one-by-one through the index entries or as advanced as changing the entire index.

Summary

In this chapter, you have become familiar with Ami Pro's powerful reference tools. You learned how to create and edit footnotes and how to create and use a glossary. You also have discovered how to create a table of contents, a table of authorities, and an index—three enormously helpful and powerful reference features.

In the next chapter, you learn about Ami Pro's table function.

Chapter 13

Working with Tables

Ami Pro tables give you great flexibility in working with words, numbers, and pictures. Using the Tables function, you can create tables to hold text, numbers, pictures, charts, equations, or drawings. You can use tables with the Mer**g**e, S**o**rt, and **C**harting functions. You can create formulas to calculate the contents of cells. You even can use tables to create standard forms, such as expense reports, that you use repeatedly.

In this chapter, you first learn the difference between a page table and a frame table. Then you learn how to create a table, how to move around the table with the keyboard and the mouse, and how to enter and edit data in the table.

After you create a table, you can change the initial settings. This chapter explains how to add and subtract rows and columns, how to change the size of rows and columns, and how to combine rows into a single row.

Because of the flexibility in its tables, Ami Pro is an excellent program for creating forms. This chapter shows you how to create forms and how to use Ami Pro tables for basic spreadsheet activities. You learn how to use a table as a standard document or a data document for performing a merge. Finally, you learn how to use a table for charting and how to sort the data in a table.

Creating Tables

To create an effective table, you must know the parts of a table. A table is organized by *columns* and *rows*. Rows run horizontally across the screen, and columns run vertically. If you choose **V**iew View **P**references and then choose **T**able Gridlines in the View Preferences dialog box, Ami Pro displays gridlines, which outline columns and rows. If you choose Table Row/Column Headings from the **V**iew View **P**references dialog box, Ami Pro displays column headings (letters) across the top of the table and row headings (numbers) along the left side of the table.

Headings are the letters above the columns and the numbers to the left of the rows. *Gutters* are spaces between columns and rows.

A *cell* is an entry box in a table. Cell names—a column letter followed by a row number—follow spreadsheet conventions. In figure 13.1, for example, the cell containing the name Tim Pyron is cell A5.

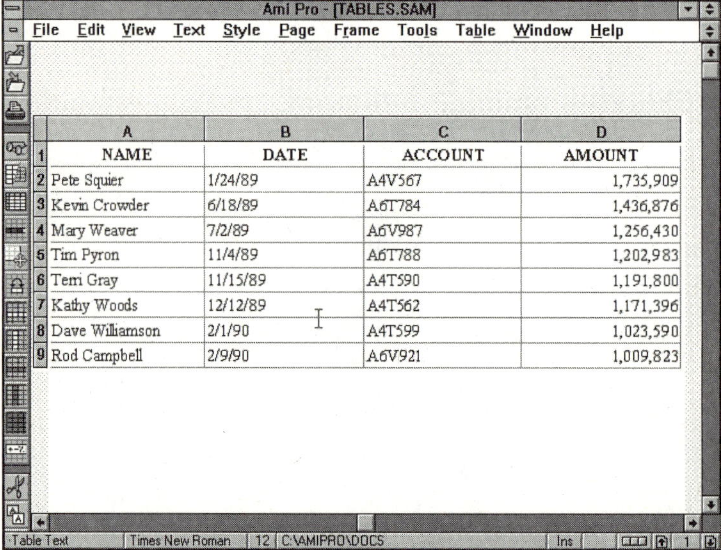

	A	B	C	D
1	NAME	DATE	ACCOUNT	AMOUNT
2	Pete Squier	1/24/89	A4V567	1,735,909
3	Kevin Crowder	6/18/89	A6T784	1,436,876
4	Mary Weaver	7/2/89	A6V987	1,256,430
5	Tim Pyron	11/4/89	A6T788	1,202,983
6	Terri Gray	11/15/89	A4T590	1,191,800
7	Kathy Woods	12/12/89	A4T562	1,171,396
8	Dave Williamson	2/1/90	A4T599	1,023,590
9	Rod Campbell	2/9/90	A6V921	1,009,823

Fig. 13.1
A table, four columns by nine rows.

Ami Pro creates two types of tables: a page table and a frame table. You determine which type of table to use by considering the requirements or limitations of the table.

A *page table*, which is inserted at the current insertion-point location (position of the cursor), appears without a frame. All the text at or below the insertion point is pushed below the inserted table. A frame is a box you create in the text. A frame can be used for a graphic or table. Text can flow around a frame, and in this way a frame is simply an object placed in the text. See Chapter 16, "Using Frames," for a detailed discussion on frames. By default, Ami Pro positions page tables at the left margin. You must use a page table if the data fills more than one page. Figure 13.2 shows a page table in a memo.

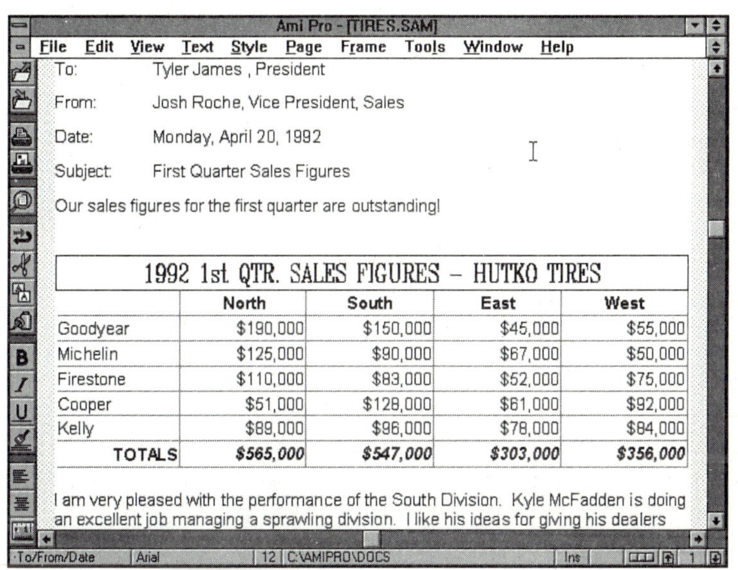

To: Tyler James , President

From: Josh Roche, Vice President, Sales

Date: Monday, April 20, 1992

Subject: First Quarter Sales Figures

Our sales figures for the first quarter are outstanding!

1992 1st QTR. SALES FIGURES – HUTKO TIRES				
	North	South	East	West
Goodyear	$190,000	$150,000	$45,000	$55,000
Michelin	$125,000	$90,000	$67,000	$50,000
Firestone	$110,000	$83,000	$52,000	$75,000
Cooper	$51,000	$128,000	$61,000	$92,000
Kelly	$89,000	$96,000	$78,000	$84,000
TOTALS	*$565,000*	*$547,000*	*$303,000*	*$356,000*

I am very pleased with the performance of the South Division. Kyle McFadden is doing an excellent job managing a sprawling division. I like his ideas for giving his dealers

Fig. 13.2
A page table in a memo.

A *frame table* is a table that you create inside a frame. The table appears wherever you position the frame, which you can position almost anywhere on the page. A frame table, however, cannot contain page breaks after rows; this means that a frame must be one page. You use a frame table, for example, if you must flow text around a table.

You can manipulate a frame-table frame in the same way you manipulate any other type of frame. You can reposition the frame, cut and paste it, and even reduce it so that some table data is hidden. (If you reduce a frame to hide table data, however, you can work only with the visible data.) Figure 13.3 shows a frame table in a memo.

Tip
When you create a table inside a frame, you cannot use that frame for any other purpose. You cannot add text, import graphics, or create drawings inside the frame.

You can create a table almost anywhere in a document, except in a header, footer, or footnote. If you intend to combine a table and text, you can enter text on the page before you create a table, and then create the table and continue with the text. Because Ami Pro can wrap text around existing tables, you also can create the table first and add text later. You cannot import a table into existing text, however.

To create a table, follow these steps:

1. To create a page table, place the insertion point in the document where you want the table to begin.

Fig. 13.3
A frame table in a memo.

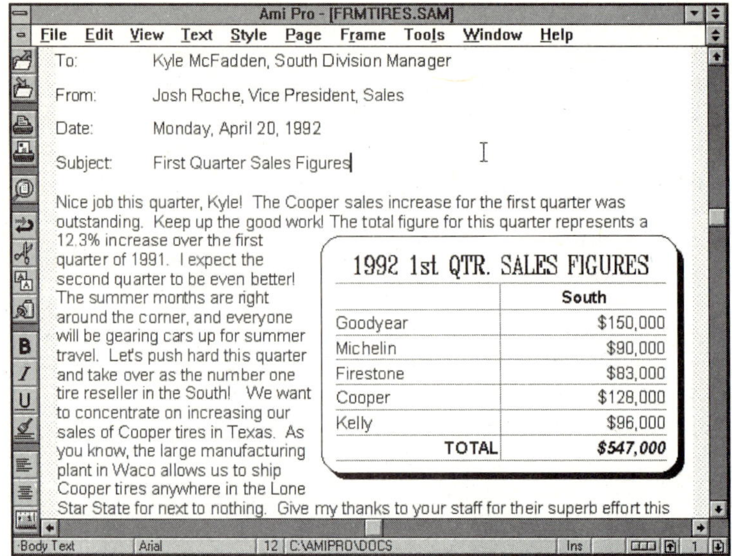

To create a frame table, begin by creating a frame in the document, making sure that the insertion point is inside the frame. See Chapter 16, "Using Frames," for complete details on creating and using frames.

2. Choose Too**l**s Ta**b**les or select the Create a Table SmartIcon. The Create Table dialog box appears, as shown in figure 13.4.

Fig. 13.4
The Create Table dialog box.

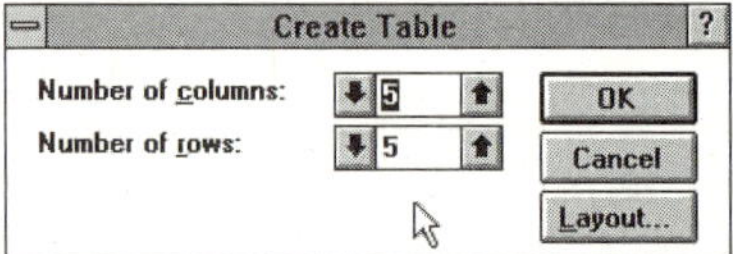

The column and row boxes contain the number of rows and columns you used in the last table you created. If you have not created a table during the current session, Ami Pro uses the default value 5 for both rows and columns.

The Tables SmartIcon palette (refer to fig. 13.1) contains 12 table-related SmartIcons. You may want to activate that palette when you work with tables.

3. Specify the Number of columns and Number of rows that you want. You can type in the number of rows and number of columns, or you can click the up arrow or down arrow next to the Number of columns and Number of rows boxes to make changes to the current settings.

If you want a table with four columns and seven rows, for example (28 cells in all), specify **4** for columns and **7** for rows. The limit is 250 columns and 4,000 rows.

4. Choose **L**ayout to set up the layout of your table. The Modify Table Layout dialog box appears, as shown in figure 13.5.

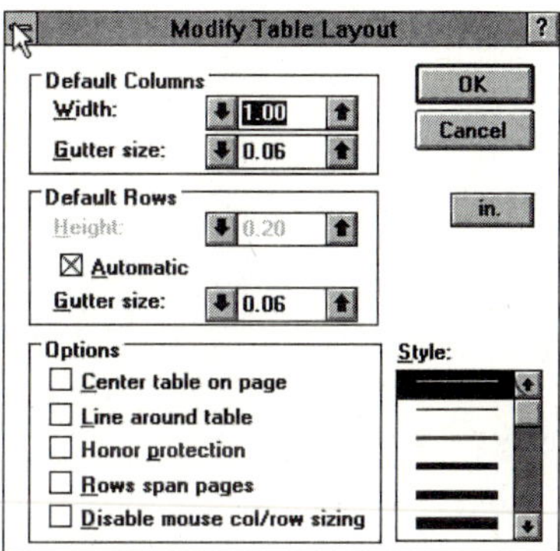

Fig. 13.5
The Modify Table Layout dialog box.

5. Use the unit of measure button (in fig. 13.5, the "in." button) to specify the unit of measurement you want to use for the table. You change to a different unit of measurement by clicking the unit of measure button. Each time you click the button, a different type of unit of measurement appears in the button. The three other units of measurement are cm (centimeters), picas, and pt. (points). For this example, use the default unit, inches.

6. In the Default Columns section of the dialog box, specify **W**idth and **G**utter Size for the columns in your table by using the arrow buttons or by typing the sizes in the entry boxes. The default **W**idth and **G**utter Size values are 1.00 inch and 0.06 inch, respectively. You can adjust the size of individual rows or columns, as explained later in this chapter.

   For this example, type **1.25** in the **W**idth entry box and **.25** in the **G**utter Size entry box.

7. In the Default Rows section of the dialog box, specify a **G**utter Size for rows. For this example, type **.10** in the **G**utter Size entry box.

   You can use the Alt+G key to access the **G**utter Size options for both columns and rows. Press Alt+G once to issue the Default Columns **G**utter Size command; press Alt+G again to issue the Default Rows **G**utter Size command.

8. If you want Ami Pro to wrap text from one line to another and adjust row height to accommodate the text, select the **A**utomatic option in the Default Rows section of the dialog box. (The **A**utomatic setting is useful if your table contains a great deal of text.) For this example, select **A**utomatic.

   If you don't want automatic row-height adjustment and text wrapping, deselect the **A**utomatic option. Deselection activates the **H**eight entry box, where you specify the default **H**eight for the rows. If you are creating a form, such as an expense report, deselect **A**utomatic; you want the form to be identical every time you use it.

9. In the Options section of the dialog box, choose the **C**enter Table on Page and **L**ine around Table options. The following table explains the table options.

Option	Function
Center Table on Page	Spaces the table evenly between the margins; available only for page tables.
Line around Table	Outlines the table; available only for page tables.
Honor **P**rotection	Activates protection function so that you cannot edit protected cells.
Rows Span Pages	Tells Ami Pro to continue table data on the next page without moving the entire row; available only for page tables and only when **A**utomatic is selected.
Disable mouse col/row sizing	Prevents the use of the mouse to manually size columns and rows.

10. Because you chose the **L**ine around Table option, choose in the **S**tyle box the type of line you want for the outline. For this example, choose the thickest line.

11. Choose OK or press Enter to save your changes and close the Modify Table Layout dialog box. (You can reopen this dialog box at any time by choosing Ta**b**le Modify Table **L**ayout or by clicking the Modify Table Layout SmartIcon.)

12. Choose OK or press Enter again to close the Create Table dialog box. Ami Pro creates a blank table according to your specifications, as shown in figure 13.6.

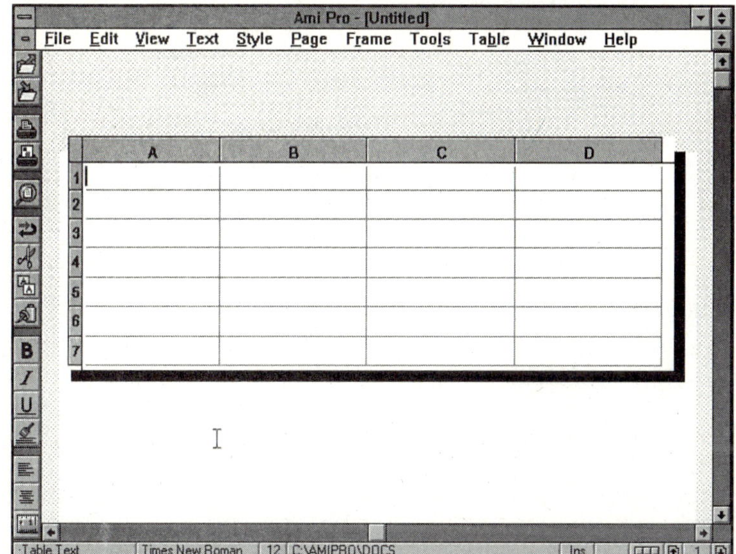

Fig. 13.6
A blank table with layout settings.

Note

The table in figure 13.6 shows column letter headings (A, B, C, and so on) and row number headings (1, 2, 3, and so on). You can choose to display or not display these headings.

Each cell in a table has a name, or *reference address*, that consists of the column letter followed by the row number. The reference address of the top left cell in a table, for example, always is A1.

You can specify whether the table shows gridlines and row or column headings by choosing **V**iew View **P**references or by clicking the View Preferences SmartIcon. Ami Pro displays the View Preferences dialog box, as shown in figure 13.7.

Select **T**able Gridlines to display light dotted lines between columns and rows. Gridlines appear only on-screen; they don't print. Select Table Row/Column **H**eadings if you want to display row and column headings in tables. Like gridlines, headings don't print; headings appear on-screen only when you put the insertion point in the table. Most people prefer to display gridlines and headings, which make cells in the table easy to identify. (The table shown in figure 13.1 contains both gridlines and headings.)

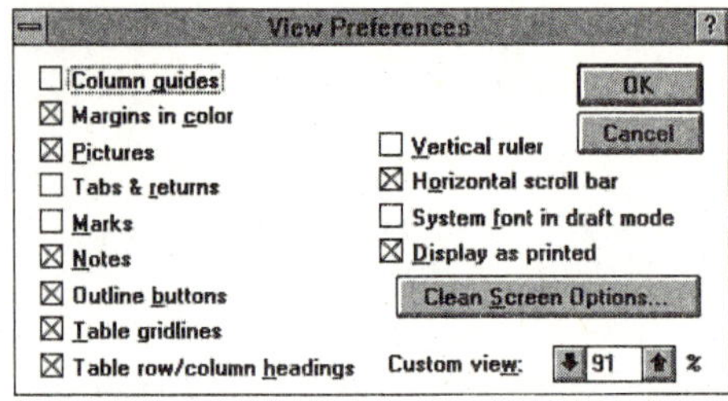

Fig. 13.7
The View Preferences dialog box.

To remove gridlines and headings, deselect the **T**able Gridlines and Table Row/Column **H**eadings options. (For more information on headings, see the "Creating Headings" section later in this chapter.)

When you create a table, Ami Pro adds a Ta**b**le menu to the menu bar (see fig. 13.8).

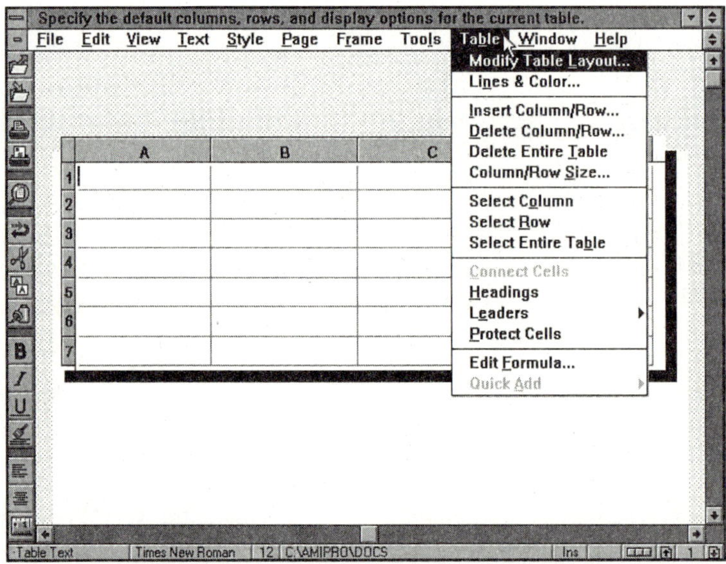

Fig. 13.8
The Ta**b**le menu.

The Ta**b**le menu appears in the menu bar only when the insertion point is in the table. (For more information on this menu, see the "Using the Table Menu" section later in this chapter.)

After you create the table, you can move around in it and select cells for various activities, as the next section explains.

Working with Cells

A table is a group of cells. Each rectangle in the table is a cell. The number of cells depends on the size of the table. To work effectively with a table, you must know how to work with a cell. You must know how to move from cell to cell, how to select cells, how to enter data into cells, and all the other aspects of working with cells. The following section explains the functionality of using cells.

Moving from Cell to Cell

When you work with a table, using the mouse is the easiest, fastest way to move from cell to cell; click a cell, and the insertion point appears in that cell.

You also can use the keyboard to move around in a table. The following list describes the table-navigation keys.

Key	Function
Right arrow	Moves one character to the right or to the next column if no more characters exist
Left arrow	Moves one character to the left or to the preceding column
Up arrow	Moves up one line
Down arrow	Moves down one line
Tab	Moves to the next cell and then to the far left column of the next row
Shift+Tab	Moves to the preceding cell and then to the far right column of the preceding row
Ctrl+arrow	Moves to the next cell up, down, right, or left (in the direction of the arrow on the key)
Home	Moves to the beginning of the current line in a cell
End	Moves to the end of the current line in a cell
Home+Home	Moves to the first cell in the current row
End+End	Moves to the last cell in the current row

Selecting Cells

Before you can manipulate cells—format, add lines, copy, and so on—you must select the cells. You can use either the mouse or the keyboard to select cells.

You can use the following mouse techniques to select cells:

- Click and drag the mouse pointer across the cells.
- Click one corner of a range (a group) of cells, drag the mouse pointer to the corner diagonally opposite, and then press Shift while you click the left mouse button.
- To select a row, move the mouse pointer to the left border of the row (or to the row number, if the headings are displayed) and click when the mouse pointer changes into a small, thick, black arrow.
- To select multiple rows, click and drag up or down the colored arrow through the rows.
- To select a column, move the mouse pointer to the top border of the column (or to the column letter, if the headings are displayed) and click when the mouse pointer changes into a small, thick, black arrow.
- To select multiple columns, click and drag the colored arrow right or left across the columns.

To select cells from the keyboard, press Shift+Ctrl+arrow key to move from cell to cell, selecting cells as you go.

Another way to select cells from the keyboard is to select and move an entire table. To select and move a table, follow these steps:

1. Place the insertion point in the table.
2. Press Esc to move the insertion point out of the table. The insertion point becomes a large, flashing vertical bar on either the right or the left side of the table.
3. If the flashing vertical bar is on the right side of the table, press Shift+left arrow. Ami Pro selects the entire table, even if the table spans several pages. If the flashing vertical bar is on the left side of the table, press Shift+right arrow. Ami Pro selects the entire table, even if the table spans several pages.

You also can use the commands Ta**b**le Select C**o**lumn, Ta**b**le Select **R**ow, and Ta**b**le Select Entire Ta**b**le to select, respectively, all the cells in a column, all the cells in a row, or all the cells in the table.

To use Ta**b**le Select C**o**lumn or Ta**b**le Select **R**ow, first click in the column or row and then make the menu choice. To use Ta**b**le Select Entire Ta**b**le, you can place the insertion point in any cell.

To deselect cells, click outside the selected cells, either inside or outside the table.

Entering Data

The obvious way to enter data into a table is to type the data. You also can import data, pictures, and text from other applications. This section discusses these data-entry methods.

Typing Text

To type text into a table, place the insertion point in the appropriate cell and begin typing. If you selected the **A**utomatic row-height option in the Modify Table Layout dialog box, Ami Pro wraps the text as you type. You can move to the next line at any time by pressing Enter.

If you don't select **A**utomatic and you type more text than fits in the cell, Ami Pro hides the characters that don't fit. If you expand the column, the hidden characters appear.

To begin typing in another cell, move the insertion point to the desired cell and then type the text.

The default paragraph style for tables is Table Text, which is a Body Text style without tabs, special effects, indentation, or spacing above and below paragraphs. (For information on changing the default settings, see the "Formatting Text and Number Cells" section later in this chapter.)

Typing Numbers

Ami Pro distinguishes between text and number cells, considering any cell that contains text characters, a space, or a comma to be a *text cell.* Ami Pro also considers any cell in which you press Enter to be a text cell. If you type both text characters and numbers in a cell, the cell still is a text cell. A *number cell*, on the other hand, can contain only numbers, plus (+) signs or minus (–) signs, and decimal points.

In number cells, Ami Pro displays numbers right-justified and without leading zeros. If you type **009.3**, for example, Ami Pro aligns the entry to the right boundary of the cell and displays 9.3. In text cells, Ami Pro displays text left-justified (aligned to the left boundary of the cell). You can, however, change the way Ami Pro displays numbers or text in cells. For more information, see the "Formatting Text and Number Cells" section later in this chapter.

Note

To preserve leading zeros in a number, type a space after the number. Ami Pro treats the cell as a text cell and doesn't remove the leading zeros. Remember, a text cell has a numerical value of 0; if you input a number as a text cell, it has a value of 0 for all calculations.

To type numbers into a table, place the insertion point in a cell, type a number, move to the next cell, and continue typing. After you leave a cell, Ami Pro right-justifies the numbers in the cell and applies any formatting instruction you specified. (Table formatting controls the appearance of numbers in the table. For information on changing the table format, see the "Formatting Text and Number Cells" section later in this chapter.)

Pasting Document Text

You can add text from an existing document to a table. First, locate and select the text, and then cut or copy it. You can add tabbed text, text from other tables, or untabbed text.

If you paste tabbed document text into a table, Ami Pro places the text following each tab in the original document in separate columns. If the table doesn't have enough columns to accommodate the tabs in the document, Ami Pro doesn't paste the additional tabs and text. In such a case, you can add extra columns to your table and paste the tabbed text again. You add extra columns using the Ta**b**le **I**nsert Column/Row command.

Carriage returns in the original document become new rows in the table. If you paste data from one table to another, the number of columns in the target table determines how much data you can paste. If the document contains returns but no tabs, Ami Pro asks whether you want to paste all data into the current cell. If you respond **N**o, Ami Pro inserts each paragraph into a separate row in the table.

If you paste data into a single cell, Ami Pro appends the data to the cell's contents at the insertion point. Pasting data into multiple cells, however, *overwrites* the existing contents of those cells.

If you select the **A**utomatic option in the Modify Table Layout dialog box, Ami Pro expands cell size as necessary to accommodate incoming data. If you don't select **A**utomatic, Ami Pro hides the data that doesn't fit in the cell. You can display hidden data by selecting **A**utomatic or by manually resizing the cells. (For information on manual resizing, see the "Changing Table Layout" section later in this chapter.)

Suppose that you want to copy information from a parts list into a table. In the parts list, the part number appears on the first line, the description on the second line, the location on the third line, and the price on the fourth line, as in the following example:

5239

Widget

bin 423

45.95

To paste this document text into a table, select the text, choose **E**dit **C**opy or **E**dit Cu**t**, place the insertion point in the cell where you want to begin inserting the text, and choose **E**dit **P**aste. For this example, place the insertion point in the first cell. When you choose Edit Paste, Ami Pro displays a dialog box, asking `Paste all data in current cell?` For this example, answer **N**o. The software pastes the data in the first column of the table, as shown in figure 13.9.

This text is created by using the Enter key to move the cursor to the next cell; therefore, this text is *Enter* (Return) *key delimited*. The delimiter is what ends one piece of data. If you press the Tab key after typing a piece of data, that data is considered Tab key delimited.

If the price list was created with tabs instead of returns, an entry may look like the following example:

5239 Widget bin 423 45.95

To paste this text into the table, follow the same procedure: select the text, choose **E**dit **C**opy or **E**dit Cu**t**, place the insertion point in the cell where you want to insert the text, and choose **E**dit **P**aste. For this example, place the insertion point in the first cell. When you choose **E**dit **P**aste, Ami Pro pastes the data directly into the row without asking `Paste all data in current cell?` The resulting table resembles figure 13.10.

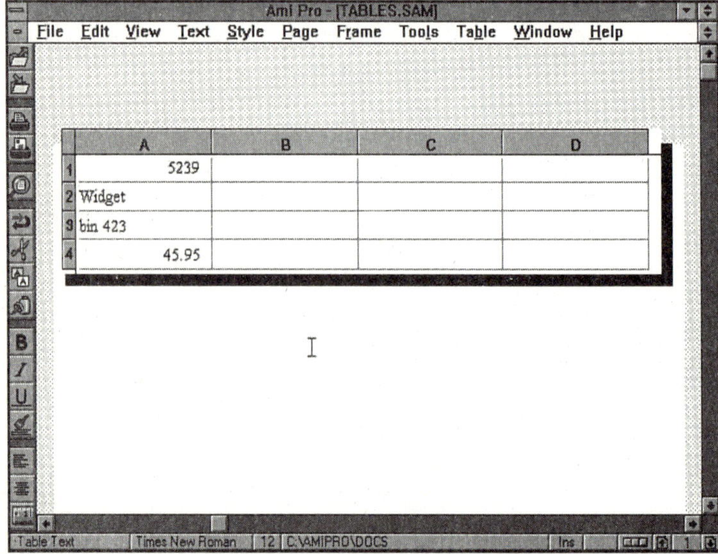

Fig. 13.9 Data pasted into a table.

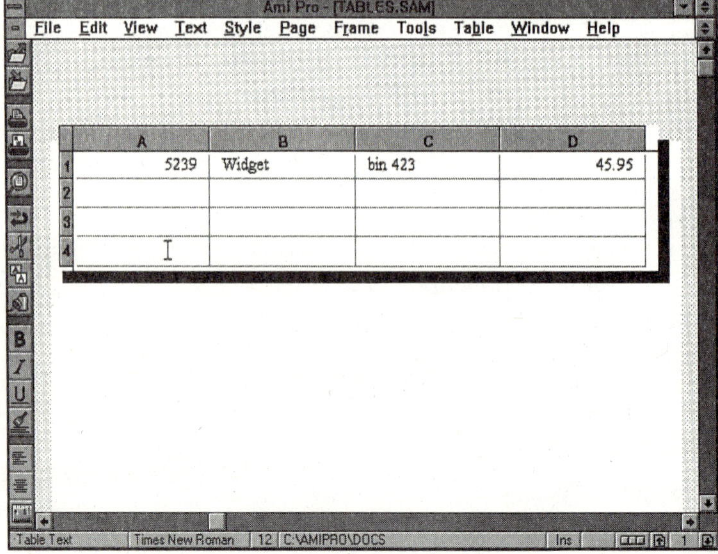

Fig. 13.10 Data with Tab key delimiters pasted into a table.

Importing Data and Pictures

You can import data from spreadsheets and databases directly into an Ami Pro table. If you're copying data from a spreadsheet, the spreadsheet cells transfer automatically. To copy data from a non-Windows file (for example, a Lotus 1-2-3 spreadsheet) into an Ami Pro table, use the File Open Insert command.

An Ami Pro table also accepts data, pictures, and charts from other word processing and graphics applications.

Chapter 20, "Importing, Exporting, and Linking Files," provides complete instructions for importing data from different applications. If you import data from applications that feature Dynamic Data Exchange (DDE) or Object Linking and Embedding (OLE), you must use the **E**dit Paste **L**ink or **E**dit Paste **S**pecial command.

When you import data, keep the following rules in mind:

- The number of columns in the table must be equal to or greater than the number of fields or columns in the spreadsheet or database.
- The number of rows in the table must be equal to or greater than the number of records or rows in the text you're importing.
- Place the insertion point in the table cell where you want to insert the data.

Similarly, you can import a picture, a drawing, or clip art from another application to a table cell.

When you import pictures, keep the following rules in mind:

- Place the insertion point in the cell where you want to insert the picture before you choose **F**ile **I**mport Picture.
- The cell must be empty before you can import a picture. An imported picture overwrites any existing data in the cell.

Creating Drawings and Charts

You can use Ami Pro's drawing or charting capabilities to create a chart or a drawing inside a table cell. Chapter 17, "Using the Draw Feature," explains how to create a drawing. Chapter 18, "Creating Charts," explains how to create a chart.

When you create a drawing or chart in a table, place the insertion point in the cell where you want to begin the drawing or picture. You also must make the cell the proper size (see the "Changing Table Cell Sizes" section later in this chapter).

To create a drawing, choose the Too**l**s **D**rawing command; to create a chart, choose the Too**l**s **C**harting command. Neither Drawing nor Charting are available when data already exists in the cell.

Typing Footnotes

Adding footnotes to a table is a simple process. You can add as many footnotes as you want, with the text of each footnote appearing in a separate row below the table. Ami Pro puts footnote numbers in the appropriate cells and numbers the footnotes sequentially, starting with 1. You can footnote either a text or a number cell.

Suppose that you want to add a footnote to the table shown in figure 13.2. Your footnote involves sales of Cooper tires in the South Division.

To add the footnote, follow these steps:

1. Place the insertion point after the entry in cell C6, where you want the footnote number to appear. Cell C6 is the intersection of Cooper and South.
2. Choose Too**l**s **F**ootnotes. The Tools Footnotes dialog box appears.
3. Click **I**nsert Footnote.
4. Choose OK or press Enter. Ami Pro inserts a superscript 1 in the cell (indicating that you are creating the first footnote for this table). A footnote cell, also numbered 1, appears at the bottom of the table.
5. Type the footnote text in this cell.
6. After you type the footnote text, press Esc. The insertion point returns to cell A6, after the footnote number.

Your footnoted table will look similar to figure 13.11.

Figure 13.11 appears with column/row headings under **V**iew View **P**references.

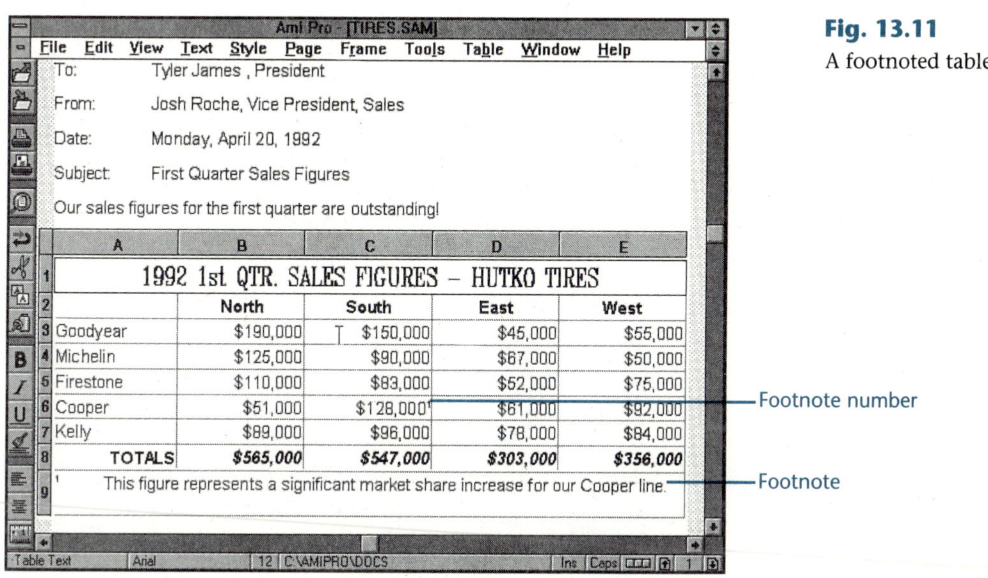

Fig. 13.11
A footnoted table.

Editing Tables

You can use all Ami Pro editing and formatting commands in table cells. This section describes familiar editing features—undoing, cutting, copying, moving, and deleting—as they apply to tables. Editing commands specific to tables, such as inserting or deleting a column or row and adding headers to a column, appear in the Ta**b**le menu and are described in the "Using the Table Menu" section later in this chapter.

◄ See "Basic Editing," p. 73

► See "Creating a Frame," p. 498

In the following sections, you learn about editing tables.

Undoing an Action

You can undo changes you make in the text of a table cell as long as the insertion point remains in that cell. You cannot undo actions you perform in multiple cells. If you select multiple cells and then delete them, for example, you cannot undo that action. Ami Pro considers connected cells to be one cell; therefore, you can undo any action you take in that "cell."

You can undo the deletion of an entire table, but you cannot undo deletions of columns, rows, or pictures. Before you make a deletion that you cannot undo, Ami Pro displays an alert box, warning you that you cannot undo the deletion and giving you the opportunity to continue or cancel.

Cutting, Pasting, and Copying Selected Data

You can cut and copy table data the way you cut and copy other data. Select the text (one cell or a range of cells) and choose **E**dit Cu**t** or **E**dit **C**opy.

When you cut data, pictures, formulas, or numbers from a table, Ami Pro stores the cut data in the Clipboard. You can paste this data from the Clipboard into another table or into another document.

When you paste table data into a text document, Ami Pro separates the data with tabs and adds a carriage return at the end of each row except the last; the insertion point appears at the end of the last row. For instructions on pasting data into a table, see the "Pasting Document Text" section later in this chapter.

Moving a Column or Row

You can quickly reposition a column or row within a table by using Ami Pro. Select the column or row to reposition by moving the mouse pointer to the column or row header (or to the column letter or row number, if the headings are displayed) and click when the mouse pointer changes to a small, thick, black arrow. Then move the mouse pointer into the column or row, and click and drag the column or row to its new position. If you select multiple columns or rows, all the columns or rows are moved to the new location. To select multiple columns or rows, click and drag the colored arrow across the columns or up or down through the rows.

Copying and Moving a Page Table

To copy or move a page table, you must select the table. First, place the insertion point in the table and press Esc. Pressing Esc moves the insertion point out of the table; the insertion point becomes a large, flashing vertical bar on the right or left side of the table.

If the vertical bar is at the right side of the table, press Shift+left arrow to select the table. If the vertical bar is at the left side of the table, press Shift+right arrow to select the table. Then choose **E**dit Cu**t** or **E**dit **C**opy.

If you want to select the text and a table, click the insertion point before the first word of the text, and then hold down the Shift key and click after the last word. The text and table are highlighted.

If you choose **E**dit Cu**t** when both text and a table are selected, Ami Pro displays the following message in a dialog box:

```
There is a table in the selection to be deleted. Would you like to
continue?
```

If you then choose **Y**es in the dialog box, Ami Pro copies the text and table (or text only) to the Clipboard and deletes your selection from the document.

If you choose **E**dit **C**opy, Ami Pro leaves the text and table (or text only) in the original location and stores an additional copy of the text and table (or text only) in the Clipboard. You then can paste the Clipboard copy elsewhere.

Next, place the insertion point where you want to move the table and choose **E**dit **P**aste. The text and table (or text only) appear in the new location. The text, which is separated by columns in the table, is separated by tabs at the new location. Ami Pro doesn't overwrite the text in the new location; the software pushes that text below the table.

Copying and Moving a Frame Table

You can easily move a frame table on a page by clicking and dragging the table. If any document text wraps around the frame, Ami Pro automatically wraps text around the frame at the table's new position.

Figure 13.12 shows a repositioning of the frame table in figure 13.3.

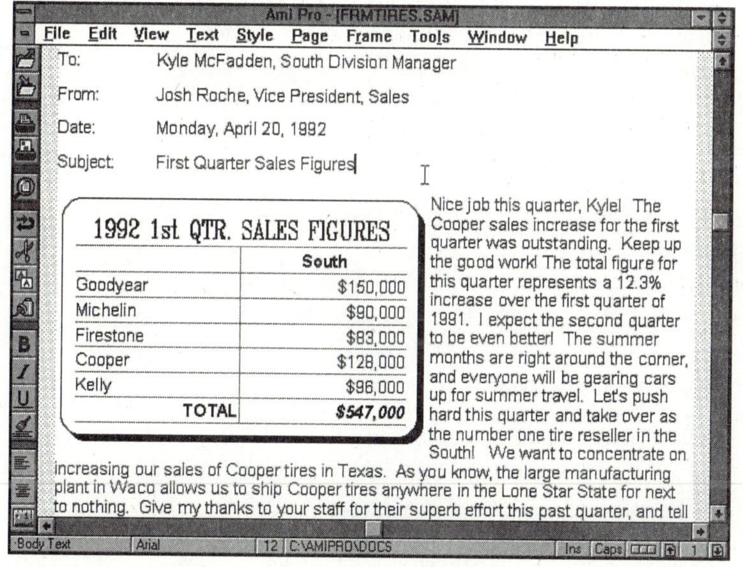

Fig. 13.12
A repositioned frame table.

To copy or move a frame table to a different page, follow these steps:

1. Select the table frame.

2. Choose **E**dit Cu**t** or **E**dit **C**opy.

3. Place the insertion point anywhere on the page to which you want to move the table.

4. Choose **E**dit **P**aste. Ami Pro pastes the frame table on the new page in the *same position* the table occupied on the original page.

5. Move the frame as needed.

Copying and pasting a frame table on the same page is tricky. First, select the frame and copy it. Then paste the frame elsewhere on the same page. The copy is placed on top of the first frame, slightly down and to the right. No matter where the insertion point is located, the copied frame is pasted on top of the original frame. Finally, you move the second frame, the copy, into position.

You cannot simultaneously move a frame table and the document text that surround the table. First, you must move the text; then you can move the frame table.

Ami Pro gives you much greater flexibility in moving a frame table than in moving a page table. Because a frame table is in a frame, you can move the table to any position quickly and easily by clicking in the frame and dragging it to a new position. If you must reposition a page table frequently or precisely, you can make your task easier by copying the page table and then pasting it into a frame; the page table becomes a frame table. To copy a page table into a frame, you must create a frame table and then paste the table data into the frame table.

Deleting Tables

You can delete a page table by itself or as part of a selection. To delete only the page table, place the insertion point in the table and then select Ta**b**le Delete Entire **T**able or click the Delete Table SmartIcon. You can undo the deletion of an entire table.

You also can delete a page table as part of a selection. To delete a page table as part of a selection, select the text and table, and then press Del. Ami Pro displays the following message in a dialog box:

```
There is a table in the selection to be deleted.
Would you like to continue?
```

If you choose Yes, Ami Pro deletes the text and table from the document. Deleting a selection that has both text and a table can be undone.

To delete a frame table, delete its frame. To delete the frame, select it and press Del. You can undo the deletion of a frame table.

For information on deleting columns and rows, see the "Using the Table Menu" section later in this chapter.

Tip

If you use Table Select Entire Table to select all the cells in a table and then press Del, you delete the contents of those cells but not the cells themselves.

Deleting Text in a Table

You delete table data the way you delete any data. To delete data in a table, select the data and press Del.

You can delete all the data in a cell or any part of the data in a cell. To delete data in several adjacent cells simultaneously, select the cells by clicking and dragging, and then press Del. You also can delete text in a table by deleting the row or rows containing the text. Similarly, you can delete text in a table by deleting the column or columns containing the text. You select a row or a column by placing the cursor on the column heading or row number and clicking (the mouse becomes a small, black arrow). You select multiple rows or columns by dragging the black arrow across the column headings or up and down the row numbers.

Deleting Pictures and Extra Spaces

Extra returns can add extra lines in cells and make your table look unbalanced. Figure 13.13 shows a table in which extra returns make the cells in row 3 too large.

	A	B	C	D
1	NAME	DATE	ACCOUNT	AMOUNT
2	Pete Squier	1/24/89	A4V567	1,735,909
3	Kevin Crowder¶ ¶	6/18/89	A6T784	1,436,876
4	Mary Weaver	7/2/89	A6V987	1,256,430
5	Tim Pyron	11/4/89	A6T788	1,202,983
6	Terri Gray	11/15/89	A4T590	1,191,800
7	Kathy Woods	12/12/89	A4T562	1,171,396
8	Dave Williamson	2/1/90	A4T599	1,023,590
9	Rod Campbell	2/9/90	A6V921	1,009,823

Fig. 13.13
A table with extra returns.

To delete extra lines or spaces in a table, follow these steps:

1. Choose **V**iew View **P**references or click the View Preferences SmartIcon. The View Preferences dialog box appears.

2. Choose the Tabs & **R**eturns option to display paragraph markers where the returns occur. Returns are marked by paragraph markers.

3. In your table, delete the paragraph markers for the extra lines by selecting them and pressing Del. For this example, select from the paragraph marker after `Kevin Crowder` down through the second paragraph marker. Press Del, and the extra lines are removed.

4. Press Del. Ami Pro deletes the extra return.

You can delete a single paragraph marker by placing the insertion point at the marker and pressing Del.

◀ See "Deleting Text," p. 83

To delete a picture, drawing, or chart from a table, select the cell that contains the material you want to delete and then press Del.

▶ See "Manipulating Frames," p. 504

Using the Table Menu

The Ta**b**le menu appears in the menu bar when you place the insertion point in a table. Some of the options in this menu enable you to insert and delete columns and rows, change table size, add borders to a table, and turn cell protection on or off (refer to fig. 13.8).

Table 13.1 briefly explains the options in the Ta**b**le menu.

Table 13.1 Table Menu Options

Option	Function
Modify Table **L**ayout	Opens the Modify Table Layout dialog box, where you can specify column size, row size, and other aspects of the table layout.
Li**n**es & Color	Opens the Lines & Color dialog box where you can specify lines in or around the table and the style of the lines. You also can specify a fill color for the selected cells.
Insert Column/Row	Opens the Insert Column/Row dialog box.
Delete Column/Row	Opens the Delete Column/Row dialog box.
Delete Entire **T**able	Deletes the table. All text below the table moves up.
Column/Row **S**ize	Enables you to specify the sizes of individual rows or columns.
Select C**o**lumn	Selects the column in which the cursor is located. If you select cells in multiple columns first, this option selects all the columns with a selected cell.

Option	Function
Select **R**ow	Selects the row in which the cursor is located. If you select cells in multiple rows first, this option selects all the rows with a selected cell.
Select Entire Ta**b**le	Selects the whole table.
Connect Cells	Turns selected adjacent cells into a single cell.
Headings	Creates a heading that displays as the first row on each page of the table.
L**e**aders	Selects leading characters.
Protect Cells	A toggle switch that enables you to turn cell protection on or off; protection is on when Honor Protection in the Modify Table Layout dialog box is on.
Edit **F**ormula	Opens the Edit Formula dialog box where you enter or edit formulas in cells.
Quick **A**dd	Adds the values in a selected row or column.

The following sections describe how to use the Ta**b**le menu.

Changing Table Layout

One of the most important features that you can access from the Ta**b**le menu is the Modify Table Layout dialog box. (Earlier in the chapter, you worked briefly with this dialog box, shown in figure 13.5.) To open the dialog box, choose Ta**b**le Modify Table **L**ayout.

The Modify Table Layout dialog box enables you to change column, row, and gutter sizes; to change the line style of a table; to customize the table's appearance; and to protect table cells from unwanted changes.

Protecting Cells

Cell protection prevents anyone from editing the contents of the cell. You may want to protect a cell that contains header information in a table that other people use.

Cell protection is a two-step process. To turn on cell protection, follow these steps:

1. Click the cell and choose Ta**b**le **P**rotect Cells. (A check mark appears next to **P**rotect if you click in a cell that already is protected and then choose Ta**b**le.)

2. Choose Ta**b**le Modify Table **L**ayout. Select the Honor **P**rotection option in the Modify Table Layout dialog box. Then choose OK.

After you turn on the Honor **P**rotection option, Ami Works protects the cell you selected. When a cell is protected, you cannot place the insertion point in the cell, so you cannot edit it or change its appearance. You can, however, select the cell again after you turn off Honor **P**rotection.

The **P**rotect Cells option functions as a toggle; if you select a protected cell and then select Ta**b**le **P**rotect Cells, you turn off the protection for that cell. Honor Protection must be turned off before you can place the cursor in a protected cell. To turn protection off for the entire table, turn off the Honor **P**rotection option in the Ta**b**le Modify Table **L**ayout dialog box.

Keeping Multiple-Line Row Data on One Page

At times, a row in a table consists of multiple lines, some of which fall after the page break. Ami Pro forces rows with multiple lines to a new page. If you want to split the multiple line rows between pages, choose **R**ows Span Pages in the Table Modify Table Layout dialog box.

If you choose **R**ows Span Pages in the Modify Table Layout dialog box, Ami Pro splits multiple line rows.

Changing Cell Sizes

When you create a table, Ami Pro makes all rows and columns the same size. You may want to have a large column for names and a small column for numbers. You also may want to adjust the size of rows and columns.

To change the default size of all the cells in your table, follow these steps:

1. Choose Ta**b**le Modify Table **L**ayout or click the Modify Table Layout SmartIcon. The Modify Table Layout dialog box appears.

2. Change the column, gutter, and row sizes as desired.

3. Choose OK to close the dialog box.

Figure 13.14 shows the column **W**idth option changed to 2.

If you make this change, Ami Pro resizes the table's columns to 2 inches, as shown in figure 13.15.

You can center the table on the page by choosing the **C**enter Table on Page option. To add a printable border around the table, choose **L**ine around Table and then choose a line **S**tyle.

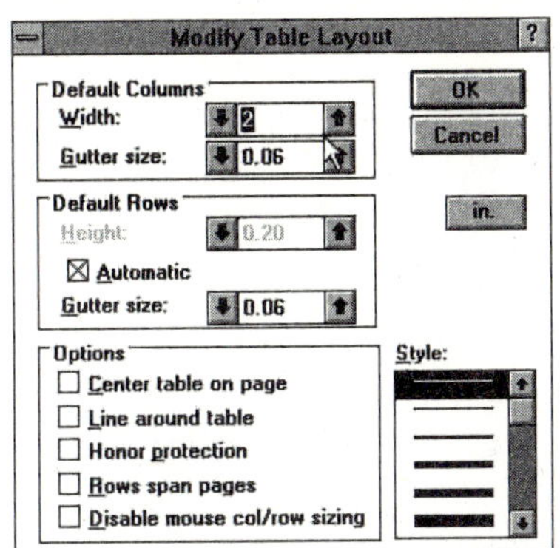

Fig. 13.14 Table layout column **Width** changed to 2.

	A	B
1	1992 1st QTR. SALES FIGURES	
2		South
3	Goodyear	$150,000
4	Michelin	$90,000
5	Firestone	$83,000
6	Cooper	$128,000
7	Kelly	$96,000
8	TOTAL	*$547,000*

Fig. 13.15 Resized columns.

If you individually resize any rows or columns in a table, these modified rows or columns aren't affected when you change the default sizes in the Modify Table Layout dialog box.

If you make the cells too small to display all the text you entered, only the text that fits in the cell appears. The other text remains hidden until you increase the cell size. If you make a column too narrow to display numbers, Ami Pro handles the problem in one of the following ways:

- If the **A**utomatic row-height option is selected, the numbers wrap to the next line in the cell.
- If the **A**utomatic row-height option is deselected, asterisks appear in the cell when you leave the cell.

You can change row and column size with the mouse instead of the keyboard if you prefer to resize cells by appearance instead of by dimension. You don't need to select cells before you use the mouse to resize a table. Even if several columns or rows are selected, you can use the mouse to resize one row or column at a time.

To size rows and columns with the mouse, follow these steps:

1. If you want to change row height, choose Ta**b**le Modify Table **L**ayout and deselect the **A**utomatic row-height option. If you don't have gridlines on your table, turn on Table Gridlines and choose OK after choosing **V**iew View **P**references.

2. Place the mouse pointer on a gridline to the right of the column or below the row that you want to size. A four-headed arrow appears. (You cannot resize a row or column by moving the mouse pointer to the row or column headings, if you are displaying headings.)

3. Click and drag to resize the cell. (Drag to the right or down to increase the size of a column or row, respectively; drag to the left or up to decrease the size of a column or row.) A vertical line follows the pointer, showing you the new dimension of the column or row.

   Remember, when you create the table, its width fills the page from margin to margin. Therefore, you must decrease the width of a column to increase the width of another column. This guideline isn't true if the table doesn't extend from the left to the right margin.

4. Release the mouse button. Ami Pro resizes the cells.

Figure 13.16 shows the four-headed arrow and the vertical line.

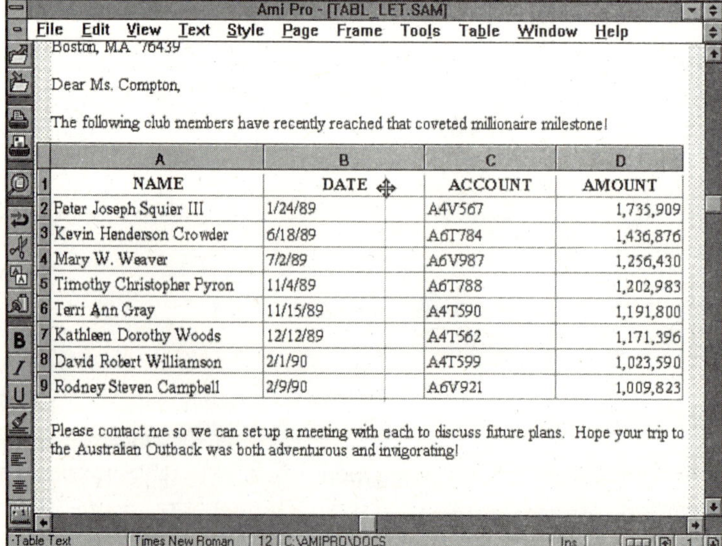

Fig. 13.16
Changing the width of column B with the mouse.

Figure 13.17 shows a resized table.

Ami Pro - [TABL_LET.SAM]

File Edit View Text Style Page Frame Tools Table Window Help

Boston, MA 76439

Dear Ms. Compton,

The following club members have recently reached that coveted millionaire milestone!

	A	B	C	D
1	NAME	DATE	ACCOUNT	AMOUNT
2	Peter Joseph Squier III	1/24/89	A4V567	1,735,909
3	Kevin Henderson Crowder	6/18/89	A6T784	1,436,876
4	Mary W. Weaver	7/2/89	A6V987	1,256,430
5	Timothy Christopher Pyron	11/4/89	A6T788	1,202,983
6	Terri Ann Gray	11/15/89	A4T590	1,191,800
7	Kathleen Dorothy Woods	12/12/89	A4T562	1,171,396
8	David Robert Williamson	2/1/90	A4T599	1,023,590
9	Rodney Steven Campbell	2/9/90	A6V921	1,009,823

Please contact me so we can set up a meeting with each to discuss future plans. Hope your trip to the Australian Outback was both adventurous and invigorating!

Table Text | Times New Roman | 12 | C:\AMIPRO\DOCS | Ins | 1

Fig. 13.17
A table with different column sizes.

You also can change the size of individual columns or rows without turning on the gridlines by choosing Ta**b**le Column/Row **S**ize or clicking the Size Columns and Rows in a Table SmartIcon. This method gives you more precise control of column and row sizes and enables you to adjust the gutters.

Tip
You cannot make a column so wide that the table doesn't fit within the margins of the page. You cannot change the size of rows if the **A**uto-matic row-height option is selected.

II Automating

Figure 13.18 shows the Column/Row Size dialog box.

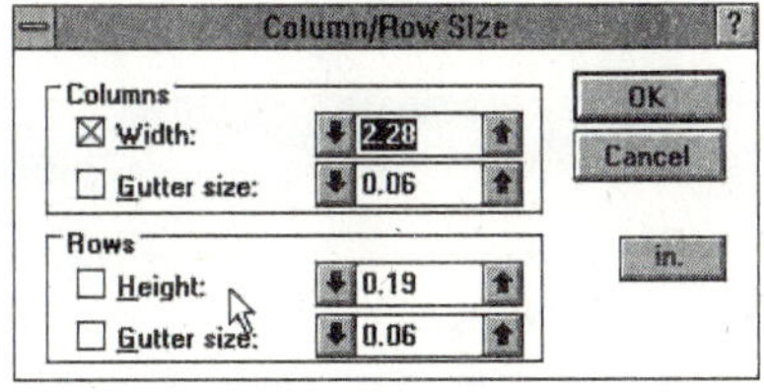

Fig. 13.18
The Column/Row Size dialog box.

Figure 13.19 shows a table in which the height and gutter settings for row 1 change from the defaults.

For row 1 of the table shown in figure 13.19, the row height was changed from the default (.20 inches) to .40 inches, and the gutter was changed from the default (.06 inches) to .20 inches.

Fig. 13.19
A table with nondefault height and gutter settings.

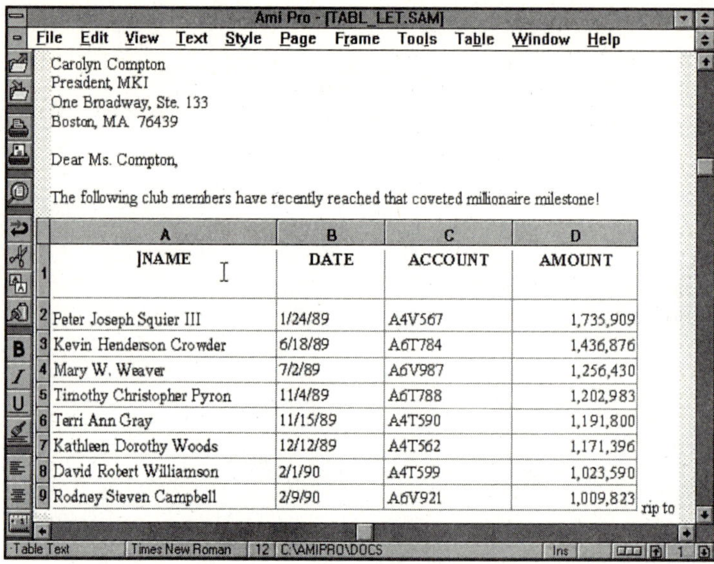

Carolyn Compton
President, MKI
One Broadway, Ste. 133
Boston, MA 76439

Dear Ms. Compton,

The following club members have recently reached that coveted millionaire milestone!

	A	B	C	D
1	]NAME	DATE	ACCOUNT	AMOUNT
2	Peter Joseph Squier III	1/24/89	A4V567	1,735,909
3	Kevin Henderson Crowder	6/18/89	A6T784	1,436,876
4	Mary W. Weaver	7/2/89	A6V987	1,256,430
5	Timothy Christopher Pyron	11/4/89	A6T788	1,202,983
6	Terri Ann Gray	11/15/89	A4T590	1,191,800
7	Kathleen Dorothy Woods	12/12/89	A4T562	1,171,396
8	David Robert Williamson	2/1/90	A4T599	1,023,590
9	Rodney Steven Campbell	2/9/90	A6V921	1,009,823

Before you change the row height, you must deselect the **A**utomatic row-height option in the Modify Table Layout dialog box.

> **Note**
>
> Changing the row height may cause problems if the row consists of multiple lines. When **A**utomatic is the row-height setting, the row height changes if the font size of the text changes or if text is added. If you set row height manually, however, the row height doesn't change as the cell contents change.

> **Note**
>
> Column or row changes you make in the Modify Table Layout dialog box while the **A**utomatic option is deselected don't affect rows or columns that you already changed by other methods. If you later select **A**utomatic, however, you lose any previous changes.

Changing Lines and Colors

Ami Pro enables you to outline or color table cells, rows and columns, or the entire table. You also can underline a cell or a row and add other printable lines to your table. You can use color to highlight totals or distinguish header cells.

Note

To print in color, you must have a color printer. You can, however, shade cells in gray tones; the grays print out on any printer.

To outline or color table cells, follow these steps:

1. Select the cells.

2. Choose Ta**b**le Li**n**es & Color or click the Modify Lines & Shades in a Table SmartIcon. The Lines & Color dialog box appears, as shown in figure 13.20.

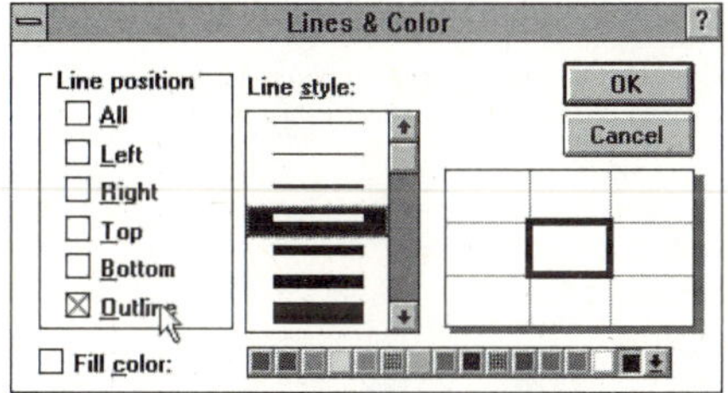

Fig. 13.20
The Lines & Color dialog box with **O**utline and a thick line selected.

3. In the Line Position section of the dialog box, indicate where you want lines to appear in the selection by clicking the check boxes of the appropriate options, as follows:

   - **A**ll places lines on every side of each selected cell.
   - **L**eft, **R**ight, **T**op, and **B**ottom place lines on the left, right, top, or bottom of each selected cell, respectively.
   - **O**utline places a line around selected cells as a block.

4. In the Line **S**tyle section, select a line style.

5. In the Fill **C**olor section, choose a color. (If the selected cells already contain color, the Fill **C**olor option is selected.) Click the box that represents the color you want; that color appears in the example box near the lower right corner of the dialog box.

   Notice the arrow button at the right end of the color bar. This button activates a drop-down color bar that contains more color options. The 135 color choices include shades of gray and various colored patterns.

6. Choose OK or press Enter.

   The cells are lined according to the choice you make and, if you choose a color, the cells are filled with that color. The text in the cells isn't eradicated by the color; the color component is a background color. Figure 13.21 shows a table with an outline around the first row.

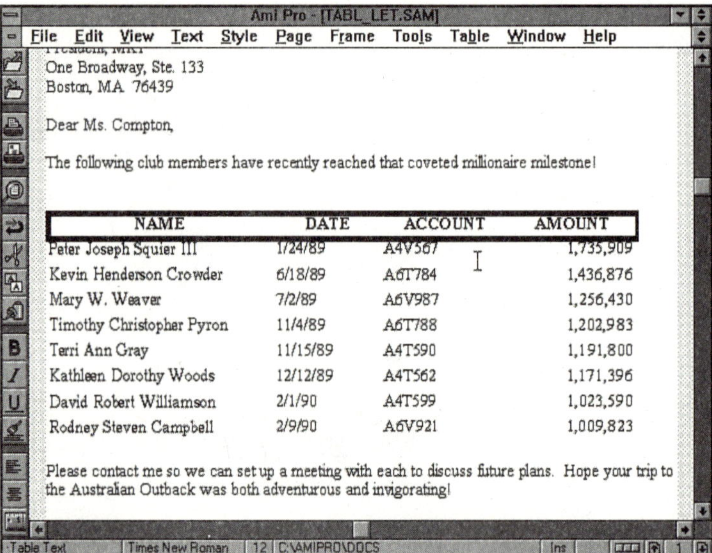

Fig. 13.21
An outline around selected table cells.

Figure 13.22 shows the same table after an outline is added for the entire table and a gray shade is added to cells D2 through D9.

You can select any of 135 colors or create a custom color. To create a custom color, follow these steps:

1. In the Fill **C**olor section of the Lines & Color dialog box, double-click the box containing the color that is closest to the color you want. The Custom Color dialog box appears, as shown in figure 13.23.

2. As you drag the arrow along the color bar, new colors appear in the example box.

3. When the color you want appears in the example box, choose OK.

You also can create a custom color by specifying each color element in the appropriate text box.

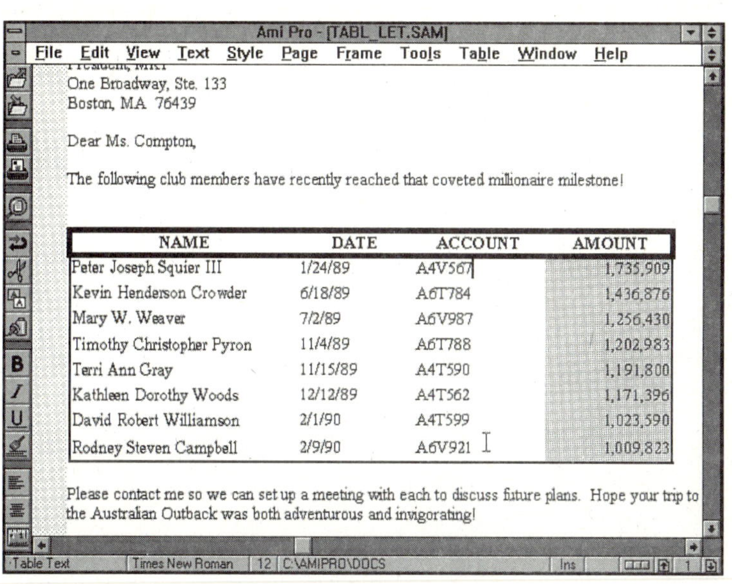

Fig. 13.22
A table with an outline and gray shade added.

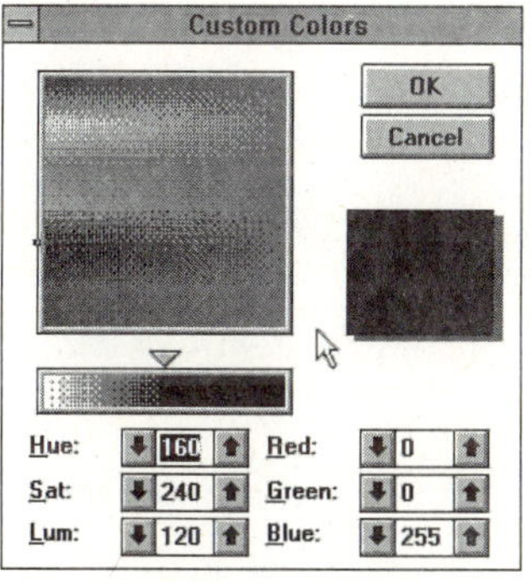

Fig. 13.23
The Custom Colors dialog box.

Inserting Columns and Rows

After you finish a table, you often must expand the table to add more rows, more columns, or both. You use the Ta**b**le menu to expand a table.

You must have enough room between margins to insert a column; if you don't have enough room, the **I**nsert Column option is dimmed. To use this option for a page table (which Ami Pro displays from the left margin to the right margin by default), you must change the default column size, which changes the sizes of all columns that you haven't sized individually.

To insert a column or row, follow these steps:

1. Place the insertion point in the table where you want to insert the new column or row.

2. Choose Ta**b**le **I**nsert Column/Row. The Insert Column/Row dialog box appears, as shown in figure 13.24.

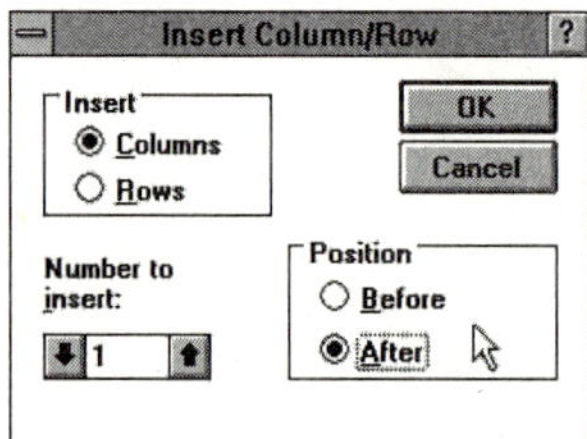

Fig. 13.24
The Insert Column/Row dialog box.

3. Click the **C**olumns or the **R**ows radio button. (If you don't have enough room in the table to insert a column or row, the appropriate option is dimmed.)

4. In the Number to **I**nsert entry box, specify the number of rows or columns to insert. (Remember that a table can have no more than 250 columns and 4,000 rows.)

5. In the Position section of the dialog box, specify whether you want to insert the new row or column **B**efore or **A**fter the cell that contains the insertion point.

   For rows, **B**efore places the new row above the row that contains the insertion point. For columns, **B**efore places the new column to the left of the column that contains the insertion point. **A**fter inserts the new row below the row that contains the insertion point and the new column to the right of the column containing the insertion point.

6. Choose OK or press Enter. Ami Pro inserts the specified rows or columns.

Figure 13.25 shows a table with a new column added.

You also can use SmartIcons to insert one row or column at a time. To use this method, follow these steps:

1. Place the insertion point in the table where you want to insert the new column or row.

2. Click the Insert Row in Table SmartIcon or the Insert Column in Table SmartIcon.

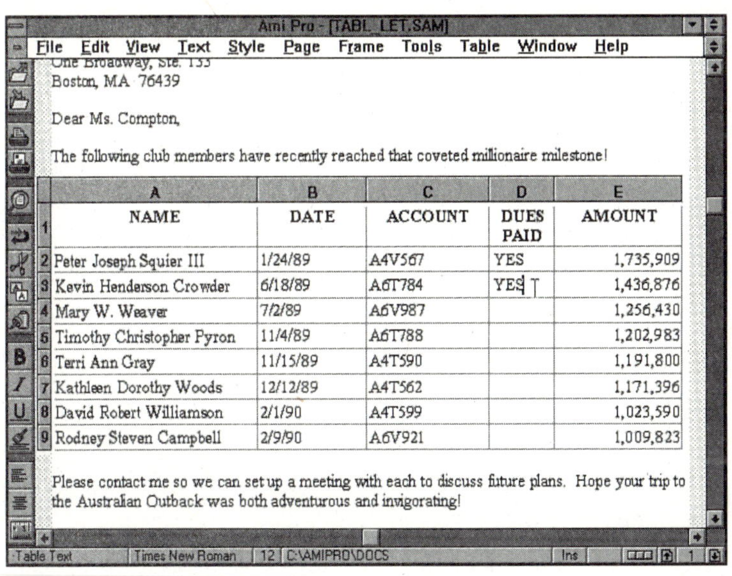
One Broadway, Ste. 135
Boston, MA 76439

Dear Ms. Compton,

The following club members have recently reached that coveted millionaire milestone!

NAME	DATE	ACCOUNT	DUES PAID	AMOUNT
Peter Joseph Squier III	1/24/89	A4V567	YES	1,735,909
Kevin Henderson Crowder	6/18/89	A6T784	YES	1,436,876
Mary W. Weaver	7/2/89	A6V987		1,256,430
Timothy Christopher Pyron	11/4/89	A6T788		1,202,983
Terri Ann Gray	11/15/89	A4T590		1,191,800
Kathleen Dorothy Woods	12/12/89	A4T562		1,171,396
David Robert Williamson	2/1/90	A4T599		1,023,590
Rodney Steven Campbell	2/9/90	A6V921		1,009,823

Please contact me so we can set up a meeting with each to discuss future plans. Hope your trip to the Australian Outback was both adventurous and invigorating!

Fig. 13.25
A new column added to a table.

Insert Row in Table inserts a single row below the current row. Insert Column in Table inserts a single column to the right of the current column.

If you select multiple rows or columns before you click a SmartIcon, Ami Pro doesn't insert any rows or columns.

Note

You cannot insert columns and rows at the same time. Instead, you must open the dialog box twice—once to insert rows and again to insert columns.

As an alternate method, you can use the keyboard to insert rows or columns. To insert a single row, place the insertion point where you want to insert the new row and press Ctrl++ (on the numeric keypad). Ami Pro inserts one row.

To insert several rows, select a number of rows equal to the number of rows you want to add and then press Ctrl++ (on the numeric keypad). Ami Pro inserts the number of rows you indicated after the row that contains the insertion point.

To insert columns, select (in a single row) a number of columns equal to the number of columns you want to insert and then press Ctrl++ (on the numeric keypad). You must select more than one cell to insert columns. If you have

Tip
If you insert a row or column into an area of a table that contains lines or color, the inserted row or column cells take on the same line or color characteristics.

only one cell selected, Ctrl++ inserts a row. Ami Pro inserts the new columns to the right of the column that contains the insertion point if you have enough room in the table to accommodate the columns. Otherwise, nothing happens.

Deleting Columns and Rows

Just as you sometimes need to add columns or rows, you sometimes overestimate the number of rows or columns you need. You can delete extra rows and columns in much the same way that you add columns and rows.

To delete a column or a row, follow these steps:

1. Select one cell in each row or column that you want to delete. (To delete a single row or column, place the insertion point in that row or column.) For the example, cells A4, A5, and A6 are selected, indicating that you want to delete rows 4, 5, and 6.

2. Choose Ta**b**le **D**elete Column/Row. The Delete Column/Row dialog box appears, as shown in figure 13.26.

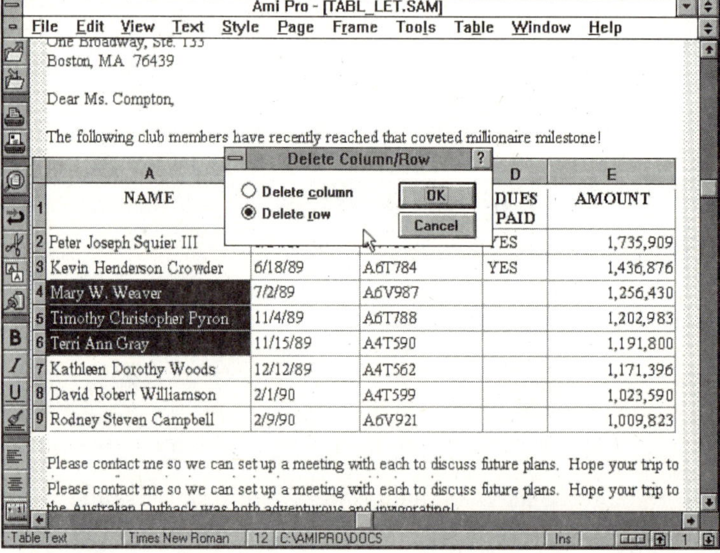

Fig. 13.26
The Delete Column/Row dialog box.

3. Choose either Delete **C**olumn or Delete **R**ow. (For this example, choose Delete **R**ow.)

4. Choose OK or press Enter. Ami Pro warns you that you cannot undo the deletion and asks whether you want to continue.

5. Choose **Y**es or press Enter to continue deleting. Ami Pro deletes the selected row or column. If you choose **N**o, Ami Pro returns to the unaltered table.

Figure 13.27 shows the preceding table after the deletion.

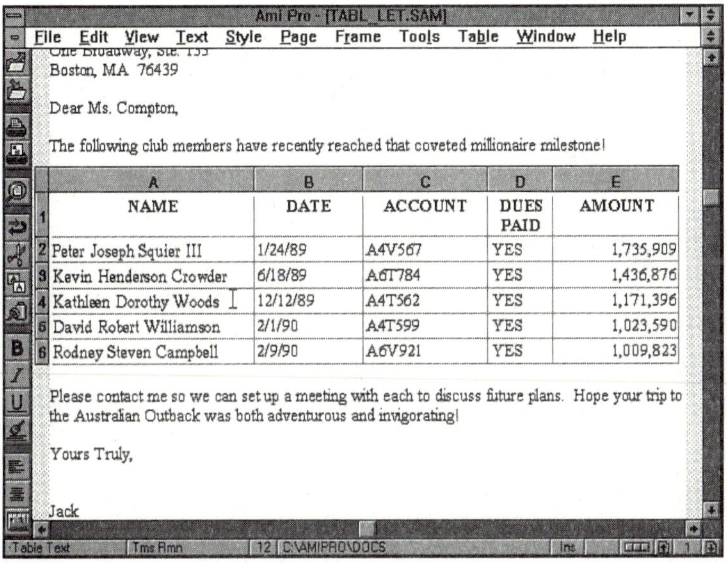

Ami Pro - [TABL_LET.SAM]

File Edit View Text Style Page Frame Tools Table Window Help

One Broadway, Ste. 155
Boston, MA 76439

Dear Ms. Compton,

The following club members have recently reached that coveted millionaire milestone!

	A	B	C	D	E
1	NAME	DATE	ACCOUNT	DUES PAID	AMOUNT
2	Peter Joseph Squier III	1/24/89	A4V567	YES	1,735,909
3	Kevin Henderson Crowder	6/18/89	A6T784	YES	1,436,876
4	Kathleen Dorothy Woods	12/12/89	A4T562	YES	1,171,396
5	David Robert Williamson	2/1/90	A4T599	YES	1,023,590
6	Rodney Steven Campbell	2/9/90	A6V921	YES	1,009,823

Please contact me so we can set up a meeting with each to discuss future plans. Hope your trip to the Australian Outback was both adventurous and invigorating!

Yours Truly,

Jack

Table Text | Tms Rmn | 12 | C:\AMIPRO\DOCS | Ins | 1

Fig. 13.27
The table after the selected rows were deleted.

You also can use SmartIcons to delete rows and columns. To use this method, follow these steps:

1. Place the insertion point in the row or column you want to delete.

2. Click the Delete Selected Row in Table SmartIcon or the Delete Selected Column in Table SmartIcon. (If you select multiple rows or columns before you click the SmartIcon, Ami Pro deletes the selected rows or columns.) Ami Pro inserts the row or column.

You also can use the following keyboard method to delete a single row:

1. Place the insertion point in the row you want to delete.

2. Press Ctrl+- (on the numeric keypad). Ami Pro warns that you cannot undo the deletion and asks whether you want to continue.

3. Choose **Y**es or press Enter to continue. Ami Pro deletes the selected row. If you choose **N**o, Ami Pro returns to the unaltered table.

To delete multiple rows, select multiple column cells in a single row and then press Ctrl+ – (on the numeric keypad). Ami Pro warns you that you cannot undo the deletion and asks whether you want to continue. Choose **Y**es or press Enter to continue. The software deletes the selected rows.

To delete columns from the keyboard, follow these steps:

1. In a single row, select the number of columns you want to delete. (Press Shift+Ctrl+arrow key to proceed in the direction you want.)

2. Press Ctrl+ – (on the numeric keypad). Ami Pro warns that you cannot undo the deletion and asks whether you want to continue.

3. Choose **Y**es or press Enter to continue. Ami Pro deletes the selected columns. Choose **N**o to return to the unaltered table.

Adding Page Breaks to a Table

You may want to use page breaks in long tables to ensure that the contents of a cell appear on one page. To insert a page break, follow these steps:

1. Place the insertion point in the row that you want to move to the next page.

2. Choose **P**age **B**reaks. The Breaks dialog box appears, as shown in figure 13.28.

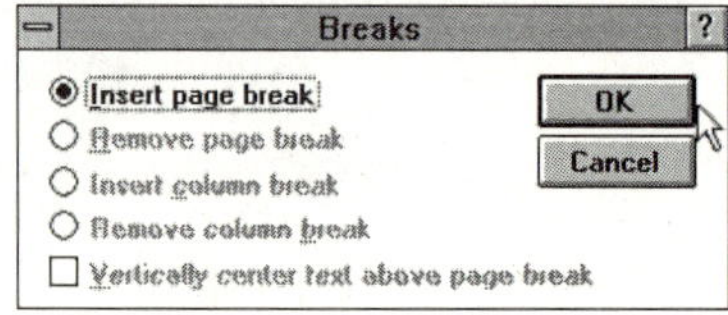

Fig. 13.28
The Breaks dialog box.

3. Select Insert Page Break.

4. Choose OK or press Enter. Ami Pro moves the row to the next page.

To remove a page break in a table, follow these steps:

1. Place the insertion point in the row immediately after the page break.

2. Choose **P**age **B**reaks. The Breaks dialog box appears.

3. Choose Remove Page Break.

4. Choose OK or press Enter. Ami Pro removes the page break.

Connecting Cells

Besides adjusting the sizes of rows and columns, you can change the size of cells by connecting them with adjacent vertical or horizontal cells to form one large cell. Connecting cells is a handy way to create a title for your table.

To connect cells, select the cells you want to connect and choose Ta**b**le **C**onnect Cells or click the Connect Selected Cells in a Table SmartIcon. Ami Pro removes the cell boundaries, making one cell.

You normally connect cells before you enter data into those cells. If you have already entered data into the cells, only the data in the extreme left cell remains visible.

To return the cells to their separate status, repeat this procedure; the **C**onnect Cells option is a toggle. If hidden data disappears when you connect the cells, that data reappears when you disconnect the cells.

Figure 13.29 shows a table with five blank cells in the last row. Figure 13.30 shows the same table with four cells connected and data added.

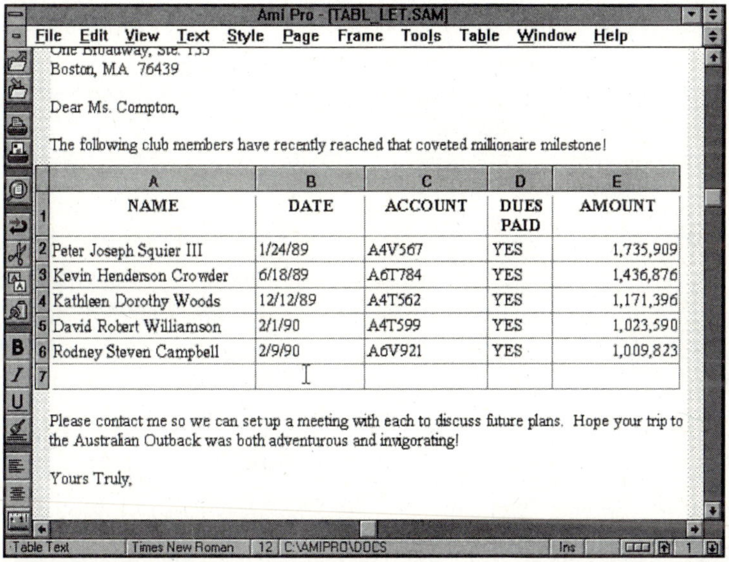

Ami Pro - [TABL_LET.SAM]

File Edit View Text Style Page Frame Tools Table Window Help

Boston, MA 76439

Dear Ms. Compton,

The following club members have recently reached that coveted millionaire milestone!

	A	B	C	D	E
1	NAME	DATE	ACCOUNT	DUES PAID	AMOUNT
2	Peter Joseph Squier III	1/24/89	A4V567	YES	1,735,909
3	Kevin Henderson Crowder	6/18/89	A6T784	YES	1,436,876
4	Kathleen Dorothy Woods	12/12/89	A4T562	YES	1,171,396
5	David Robert Williamson	2/1/90	A4T599	YES	1,023,590
6	Rodney Steven Campbell	2/9/90	A6V921	YES	1,009,823
7					

Please contact me so we can set up a meeting with each to discuss future plans. Hope your trip to the Australian Outback was both adventurous and invigorating!

Yours Truly,

Table Text | Times New Roman | 12 | C:\AMIPRO\DOCS | Ins | 1

Fig. 13.29
A table with blank cells in the last row.

Note

You cannot connect cells that appear on different pages.

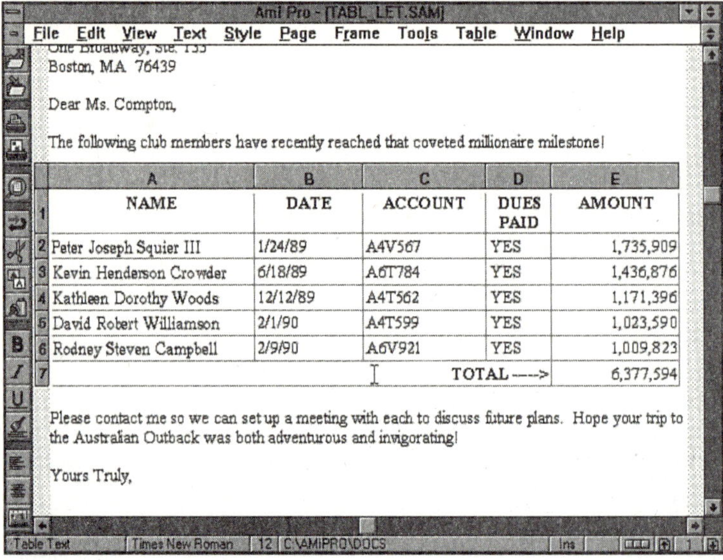

Boston, MA 76439

Dear Ms. Compton,

The following club members have recently reached that coveted millionaire milestone!

	A	B	C	D	E
1	NAME	DATE	ACCOUNT	DUES PAID	AMOUNT
2	Peter Joseph Squier III	1/24/89	A4V567	YES	1,735,909
3	Kevin Henderson Crowder	6/18/89	A6T784	YES	1,436,876
4	Kathleen Dorothy Woods	12/12/89	A4T562	YES	1,171,396
5	David Robert Williamson	2/1/90	A4T599	YES	1,023,590
6	Rodney Steven Campbell	2/9/90	A6V921	YES	1,009,823
7	TOTAL ---->				6,377,594

Please contact me so we can set up a meeting with each to discuss future plans. Hope your trip to the Australian Outback was both adventurous and invigorating!

Yours Truly,

Fig. 13.30
The table with the first four cells in the last row connected.

> **Note**
>
> You cannot undo the **C**onnect Cells command. You can disconnect the cells by putting the insertion point into one of the connected cells, however, and then choosing Table Disconnect Cells.

Creating Headings

Headings are the names of columns or rows. If a table fits on one page, you can type headings anywhere you want (although column headings usually appear in the top row and row headings usually appear to the left of the first column). You can create headings before you fill in the rest of the table, or you can add a row at the top of a completed table and fill in headings later.

If the table takes up more than one page, you can avoid the task of reentering headings on each page by using Ami Pro's Ta**b**le **H**eadings function. Figure 13.31 shows a table with the row of headings selected and the Ta**b**le **H**eadings option.

To add headings to a table that spans several pages, follow these steps:

1. Type the heading text in the top row of your table. (You can leave the cells separate or connect them first.)

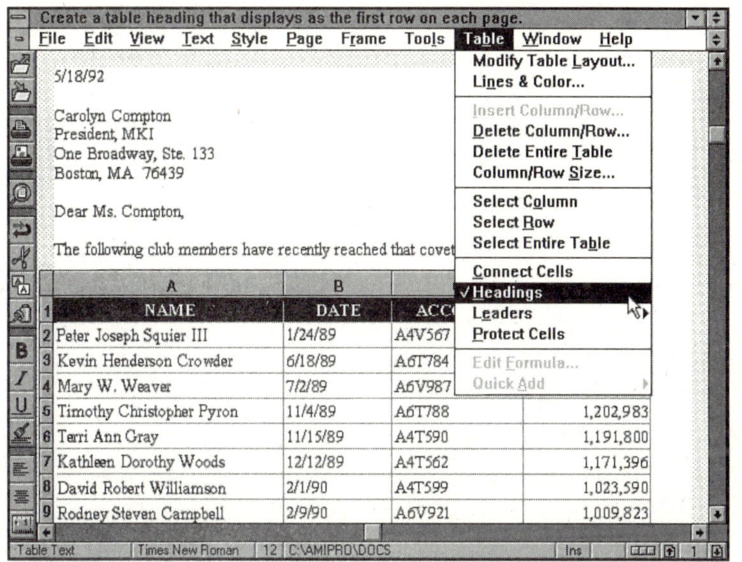

Fig. 13.31
The **H**eadings choice from the Table menu.

If data already appears in the top row of your table, first insert an empty row above the data row. (See the "Inserting Columns and Rows" section earlier in this chapter.)

2. Select the row that contains the headings. For this example, select the top row.

3. Choose Ta**b**le **H**eadings. Ami Pro inserts the selected row at the top of each page that follows. A check mark appears next to Headings in the Table menu, as shown in figure 13.31.

If you want to use different headings on subsequent pages, repeat these steps separately on each of those pages.

A check mark appears next to **H**eadings in the Table menu, as shown in figure 13.31.

You can edit headings unless you protected the cells that contain the headings. If you want to use one font for the table data and a different font for the headings, for example, use the **T**ext menu to change the heading font or choose a different paragraph style. (For detailed information, see the "Formatting Text and Number Cells" section later in this chapter.)

Creating Leaders

Leaders are characters such as dots, dashes, and underlines that appear before the first character or after the last character in a cell. If the text in a cell is left-aligned, leader characters appear after the text and fill to the cell boundary. If the data is right-aligned, leaders appear between the first character and the left cell boundary. If the data is centered, no leaders appear.

Figure 13.32 shows a table without leaders.

Fig. 13.32
A table with no leaders.

1992 1st QTR. SALES FIGURES	
	SOUTH
Goodyear	$150,000
Michelin	$90,000
Firestone	$83,000
Cooper	$128,000
Kelly	$96,000
TOTAL	***$547,000***

To create leaders in a table, follow these steps:

1. Select the cells in which you want to insert leaders.
2. Choose Ta**b**le L**e**aders. Ami Pro displays the leader styles in a cascading menu.
3. Choose the desired leader style: dots, dashes, underlines, or **N**one.

Figure 13.33 shows with dot leaders added the table shown in figure 13.32.

To remove a leader, repeat the preceding steps and choose **N**one for the desired leader.

Fig. 13.33
A table with dot leaders.

1992 1st QTR. SALES FIGURES	
	SOUTH
Goodyear	$150,000
Michelin	$90,000
Firestone	$83,000
Cooper	$128,000
Kelly	$96,000
TOTAL	***$547,000***

Formatting Text and Number Cells

You can change the appearance of text and data in a table the same way you change the appearance of document text: by using the **T**ext or **S**tyle menu options.

The **T**ext menu options enable you to change the font, alignment, spacing, and indention of selected text cells. (See Chapter 4, "Formatting a Document," for details on using the **T**ext menu.)

You may not have to use the **T**ext menu in all cases, however. If the text in a text cell is indented too far from the border of the cell, for example, choose Ta**b**le Modify Table **L**ayout and change the gutter-width option in the Modify Table Layout dialog box.

You can change the attributes of text cells by assigning a different paragraph style to the cells. (See Chapter 10, "Working with Style Sheets," for details on using the **S**tyle menu.)

You also can change the indentation of text cells by inserting a ruler into the table and then making a change to the tab settings or the indentation markers.

If you want to change the way numbers print in your tables, follow these steps:

1. To bring up the Modify Style dialog box, choose **S**tyle **M**odify Style, click the Modify Style SmartIcon or, with the cursor in the table, click the right mouse button.

2. Choose **T**able Format in the Modify section of the Modify Style dialog box. The table-formatting options appear, as shown in figure 13.34.

3. In the **C**ell Format list box, select a format for all the number cells in your table. You can choose only one cell-formatting option. (The **C**ell Format options are described later in this section.)

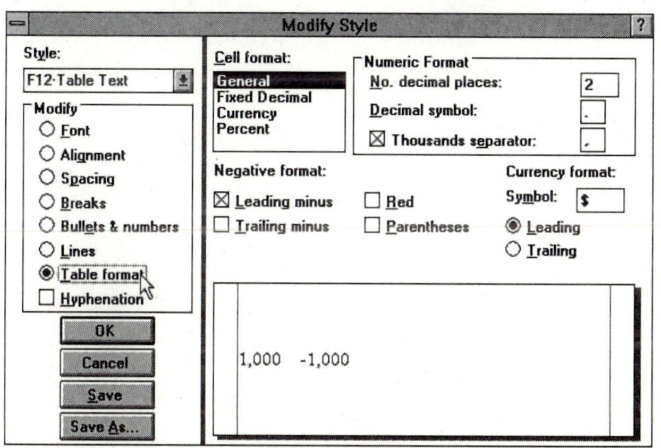

Fig. 13.34
The Modify Style dialog box with table-formatting options.

4. In the Numeric Format section of the dialog box, select a number format. (The Numeric Format options are described later in this section.)

5. In the Symbol entry box (located in the Currency Format section), type the currency symbol you want to use, and then click either **L**eading or **T**railing to indicate how you want Ami Pro to display the currency symbol in relationship to the number. The example box shows a positive and a negative number formatted according to the options you choose.

6. Choose OK or press Enter. Ami Pro reformats the table's number cells.

The following table describes the Cell Format options.

Format	Description
General	Shows numbers with no specific decimal position
Fixed Decimal	Shows numbers with a specified number of decimal places
Currency	Shows numbers with a specified currency symbol
Percent	Shows numbers with a percentage sign

Note

When you choose the Currency option in the Modify Style dialog box, Ami Pro uses the Currency format for every number in the cells you select.

The following table describes the Numeric Format options. You can change all these options, but the default settings of two decimal places, a comma as the thousands separator, and a period as the decimal symbol are the most common options.

Format	Description
No. Decimal Places	Sets the number of decimal places to be used with the Fixed Decimal format
Decimal Symbol	Specifies the character to be used for the decimal symbol (the usual choice is a period)
Thousands S**e**parator	Specifies the character to be used for a thousands separator (the usual choice is a comma or a period)

Note

Numeric Format works only in cells that contain only numbers, decimal points, and/or negative symbols. Ami Pro considers cells that contain currency symbols and commas to be text cells.

The following table describes the Negative Format options. You can select either **L**eading Minus or **T**railing Minus. After you select one of these options, you can select one, both, or neither of **R**ed or **P**arentheses.

Format	Description
Leading Minus	Places a minus sign (–) in front of negative numbers.
Trailing Minus	Places a minus sign (–) after negative numbers.
Red	Displays negative numbers in red. On a monochrome monitor, the numbers appear bold.
Parentheses	Displays negative numbers in parentheses.

When you move the insertion point to a number cell, only the numbers and any decimal points appear, so you can easily modify the data. When you leave the cell, Ami Pro redisplays the formatting characters (dollar signs, separators, and so on).

Figure 13.35 shows a table in which number cells are formatted as currency, with two decimal places.

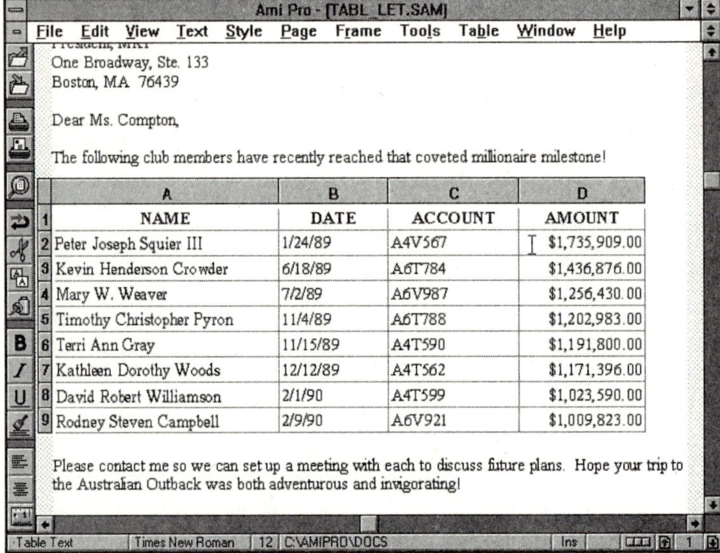

One Broadway, Ste. 133
Boston, MA 76439

Dear Ms. Compton,

The following club members have recently reached that coveted millionaire milestone!

	A	B	C	D
1	NAME	DATE	ACCOUNT	AMOUNT
2	Peter Joseph Squier III	1/24/89	A4V567	$1,735,909.00
3	Kevin Henderson Crowder	6/18/89	A6T784	$1,436,876.00
4	Mary W. Weaver	7/2/89	A6V987	$1,256,430.00
5	Timothy Christopher Pyron	11/4/89	A6T788	$1,202,983.00
6	Terri Ann Gray	11/15/89	A4T590	$1,191,800.00
7	Kathleen Dorothy Woods	12/12/89	A4T562	$1,171,396.00
8	David Robert Williamson	2/1/90	A4T599	$1,023,590.00
9	Rodney Steven Campbell	2/9/90	A6V921	$1,009,823.00

Please contact me so we can set up a meeting with each to discuss future plans. Hope your trip to the Australian Outback was both adventurous and invigorating!

Fig. 13.35
A table with formatted number cells.

You can use different formats for different numbers in a table. For each different format, create a different paragraph style; then, for each style, select formatting options. You then can apply that style to any cells you want.

Using Formulas in Tables

A *formula* is an expression that performs mathematical operations on the data in cells. You can use formulas that add, subtract, multiply, and divide in the cells of an Ami Pro table.

Formulas in Ami Pro table cells function much like formulas in spreadsheets and are useful for calculating table data.

The following table shows the operators you can use in an Ami Pro table formula:

Operator	Purpose
+	addition
–	subtraction
*	multiplication

Operator	Purpose
/	division
%	percentage

You also can use parentheses in formulas to specify the order of operations, and you can use the word *sum* to create a total of numbers in the table.

Note

You can use Lotus 1-2-3 syntax in table formulas.

Caution

If you type a comma or dollar sign in a number cell, Ami Pro considers that cell to be a text cell and doesn't format it numerically or access it correctly in formulas.

You can start a formula with an at sign (@) or an equal sign (=), or just use the operation. You specify a range of cells in the formula by typing the cell addresses (in uppercase or lowercase) with two periods (..) or a colon (:) between them. When you specify a range of cells, the formula uses the two specified cells and all the cells between them.

The following table lists some example formulas:

Formula	Action
`sum(B2..B5)`	Adds the data in cells B2, B3, B4, and B5
`sum(B2:B5)`	Adds the data in cells B2, B3, B4, and B5
`@sum(B2...B5)`	Adds the data in cells B2, B3, B4, and B5
`=B2+B3+B4+B5`	Adds the data in cells B2, B3, B4, and B5
`B2+B3+B4+B5`	Adds the data in cells B2, B3, B4, and B5
`sum(A3:A6)-C12`	Adds the data in cells A3, A4, A5, and A6, and then subtracts the data in cell C12
`(15*C3)/(A4:A10)`	Multiplies the data in cell C3 by 15 and then divides the result by the sum of the data in cells A4 through A10
`=D4*40%`	Multiplies the data cell in D4 by 40 percent

Formulas work only in cells that Ami Pro considers to be number cells. (For information on the difference between number and text cells, see the "Entering Data" section earlier in this chapter.)

Creating Formulas

To create a formula in a cell, follow these steps:

1. Place the insertion point in the cell in which you want to create a formula.

2. Choose Ta**b**le Edit **F**ormula or click the Edit Formula in Table Cell SmartIcon. The Edit Formula dialog box appears, as shown in figure 13.36.

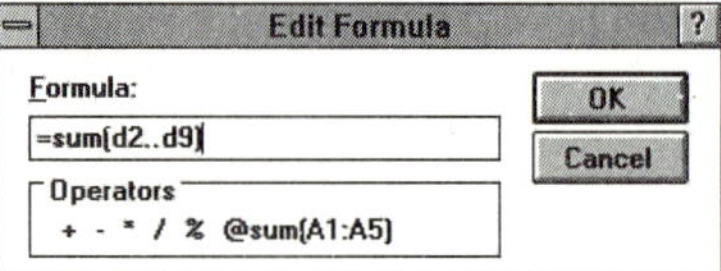

Fig. 13.36 The Edit Formula dialog box with the formula `=sum(d2..d9)`.

3. In the **F**ormula text box, type the formula you want to use. In this example, the formula totals the data in the Amounts column (cells D2 through D9).

4. Choose OK or press Enter. Ami Pro makes the specified calculation and displays the result in the cell that contains the insertion point. In this example, the result appears in cell D10, as shown in figure 13.37.

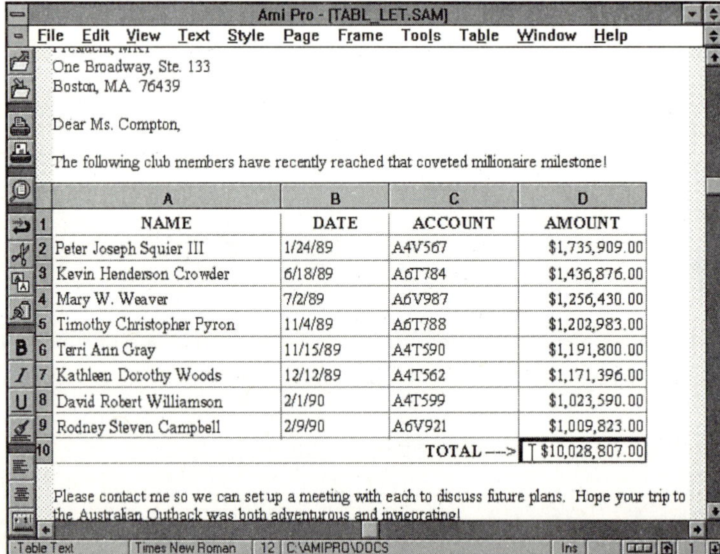

	A	B	C	D
1	NAME	DATE	ACCOUNT	AMOUNT
2	Peter Joseph Squier III	1/24/89	A4V567	$1,735,909.00
3	Kevin Henderson Crowder	6/18/89	A6T784	$1,436,876.00
4	Mary W. Weaver	7/2/89	A6V987	$1,256,430.00
5	Timothy Christopher Pyron	11/4/89	A6T788	$1,202,983.00
6	Terri Ann Gray	11/15/89	A4T590	$1,191,800.00
7	Kathleen Dorothy Woods	12/12/89	A4T562	$1,171,396.00
8	David Robert Williamson	2/1/90	A4T599	$1,023,590.00
9	Rodney Steven Campbell	2/9/90	A6V921	$1,009,823.00
10			TOTAL --->	$10,028,807.00

Fig. 13.37 The result of a formula.

If you change the data in one of the cells that the formula references, Ami Pro updates the data in the formula cell when you exit the changed cell. If you reference a text cell in your formula, Ami Pro displays Ref in the cell that contains the formula.

Editing and Deleting Formulas

To edit a formula that you enter in a table cell, follow these steps:

1. Double-click the cell containing the formula. The Edit Formula dialog box appears.

2. Edit the formula in the Formula text box.

3. Choose OK or press Enter.

As an alternative method, follow these steps:

1. Place the insertion point in the cell that contains the formula.

2. Choose Ta**b**le Edit **F**ormula or click the Edit Formula in Table Cell SmartIcon. The Edit Formula dialog box appears.

3. Edit the formula in the **F**ormula text box.

4. Choose OK or press Enter.

When you place the insertion point in a cell that contains a formula, Ami Pro places a box around the cell and prevents you from typing in that cell. You can redisplay the Edit Formula dialog box and change the formula, but you cannot type anything in the cell.

Tip
If you click a cell and the insertion point disappears, either the cell contains a formula or the cell is protected and Honor **P**rotection is in effect.

To delete a formula, select the cell that contains the formula and press Del. Deleting a formula cannot be undone.

Moving Formulas

You can move a formula to another cell in a table. When you move the formula, Ami Pro automatically changes the cells to which the formula refers.

You can use the options in the **E**dit menu to cut and paste a formula. Ami Pro changes the referenced cells when you move the formula. If you cut the formula A1+B1 in cell C1 and paste that formula into cell C2, for example, Ami Pro changes the formula to A2+B2.

Suppose that you create a complicated formula in one row of a table to calculate the withholding tax for a person listed in that row. Your formula may look like the following example:

```
((B3)*.28)+(D3/12)+((B3-C3)/52)
```

You want to use the same formula for the next person who appears in the table. When you move the formula, Ami Pro automatically changes the references to cells in the same relative position to the formula cell.

Note

To prevent Ami Pro from changing cell references when you move a formula, type a dollar sign (**$**) before the cell's address in the formula—for example, type the formula **A1+B1** as **A1+B1**. This process changes a *relative address* to an *absolute address* and prevents Ami Pro from changing the cell references when you move the formula.

Using Quick Add

If you want to add the data in a row or a column without bothering with a formula, you can use the Quick **A**dd feature.

To add the data in a column, click the cell in which you want the total to appear and choose Ta**b**le Quick **A**dd **C**olumn. To add the data in a row, click the cell in which you want the total to appear and choose Ta**b**le Quick **A**dd **R**ow.

To total in one cell the data from multiple rows or columns, select a cell in those rows or columns that you want to total and then choose Ta**b**le Quick **A**dd **C**olumn or Ta**b**le Quick **A**dd **R**ow. Ami Pro totals all the numbers in the rows or columns and places the calculation in the first cell of the selection. Multiple column or row selection doesn't total all selected cells. Only the first cell shows a total.

Caution

You can use Quick **A**dd only in a row or column that contains only number cells. If a cell to which a formula refers contains non-numeric data, Ami Pro displays REF in the cell that contains the formula, indicating an incorrect reference. To remove this message, you must change the cell reference in the formula or change the data in the referenced cell.

Using Tables in Document Applications

Tables are particularly useful in document applications such as business forms, charts, and document merges, because the rows-and-columns format of tables corresponds nicely to the lines-and-columns format of most forms and charts. You can structure a table to match the format of the document.

Keep the following ideas in mind when you use tables for general document applications:

- When you create the table and open the Modify Table Layout dialog box, choose row and column sizes that fit most of the rows and columns in your document. You can resize individual rows and columns later by choosing Ta**b**le Column/Row **S**ize. (For more information, see the "Creating Tables" and "Changing Cell Sizes" sections earlier in this chapter.)
- To ensure that the form fits your design, specify exact column and row sizes in the Modify Table Layout dialog box instead of sizing columns or rows with the mouse.
- For most forms, disable the **A**utomatic row-height option so that every copy of the form prints identically.
- Protect cells or groups of cells that contain headings, but don't turn on Honor **P**rotection in the Modify Table Layout dialog box until you finish editing the form. (For more information, see the "Protecting Cells" section earlier in this chapter.)
- Use different line styles and colors to distinguish different types of cells. (For more information, see the "Changing Lines and Colors" section earlier in this chapter.)
- Modify the appearance of text or number cells to match the design of your document. (For more information, see the "Formatting Text and Number Cells" section earlier in this chapter.)
- Use formulas to add rows or columns automatically. (For more information, see the "Using Formulas in Tables" section earlier in this chapter.)

Creating Charts

You can use the data contained in a table to create a chart. You also can cut or copy data from the table for use in a chart.

To use table data in a chart, select the cells that contain the data and then choose **E**dit **C**opy. Ami Pro copies the data to the Clipboard for use in charting.

For instructions on working with Ami Pro charts, see Chapter 18, "Creating Charts."

Creating Forms

Forms that you create from table data can include text for use in preprinted forms or text and formats for use on blank paper. You can use the table as a template. You can type text into the form and leave the original form (the template) unaltered for future use.

The expense style sheet Ami Pro provides (_EXPENSE.STY) is an excellent example of a form created from a table. The expense style sheet appears in figure 13.38.

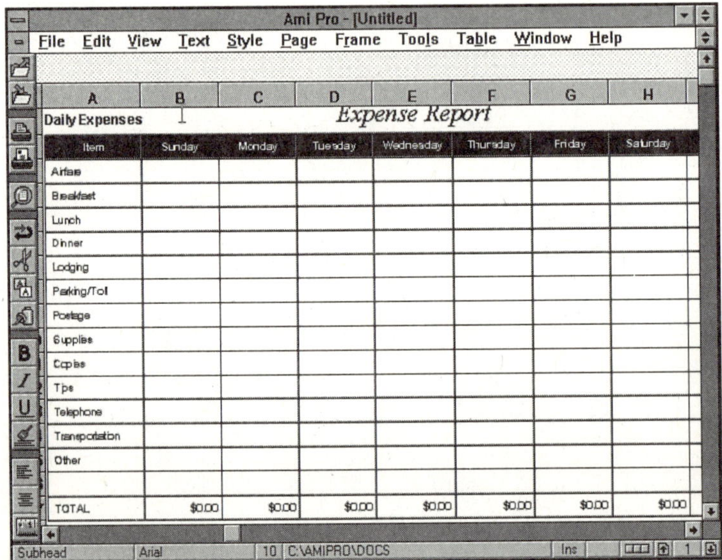

Fig. 13.38
The Ami Pro expense style sheet.

The column headings in this form are shaded so that you can distinguish the headings from the body of the table. All headings are in protected cells so that the headings cannot be edited. The cells in the Total row contain formulas that add daily expenses as these expenses are entered.

To create a form from a table, you first must design the form and its layout. Count the number of columns and rows you need and carefully measure their dimensions, and then create the table according to the directions in the "Creating Tables" section earlier in this chapter.

Following are some useful tips to keep in mind as you create a table to use as a form:

- If you intend to use the form repeatedly in different documents, save the form as a document or as a style sheet. (For more information, see the "Saving a Form" section later in this chapter.)

- If you intend to use a table for on-screen entry of data in a preprinted document, re-create the document's headings or labels in the table and then protect the cells that contain these headings or labels. When you print the document, you can tell Ami Pro not to print the protected cells, as the following section explains.

Printing a Form

If you are printing a form on blank paper, you don't need to follow any special procedures. If you want to print on a preprinted form, however, you don't want to print any heading or label cells that already appear in the preprinted form.

When you created the form, you protected those cells against editing. Now you can prevent the same cells from printing. (You also may not want to print lines or colors you added to the on-screen version of the table to make data entry easier.)

To print only text, without protected cells, lines, or colors, follow these steps:

1. Choose Ta**b**le Modify Table **L**ayout. The Modify Table Layout dialog box appears.

2. In the dialog box, deselect the Honor **P**rotection option.

3. Choose OK or press Enter.

4. In the table, select the protected cells you don't want to print.

5. Choose **E**dit **M**ark Text and specify **P**rotected Text. You see no change on-screen, but Ami Pro now knows not to print the protected cells.

6. Repeat steps 4 and 5 to mark all protected cells.

7. Choose **F**ile **P**rint. The Print dialog box appears, as shown in figure 13.39.

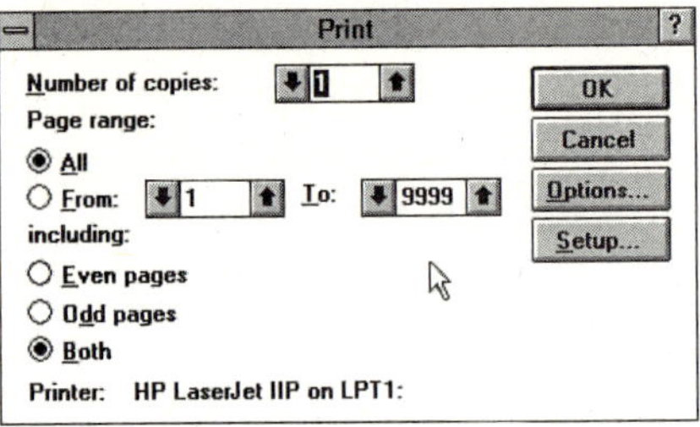

Fig. 13.39
The Print dialog box.

8. In the dialog box, choose **O**ptions. The Print Options dialog box appears, as shown in figure 13.40.

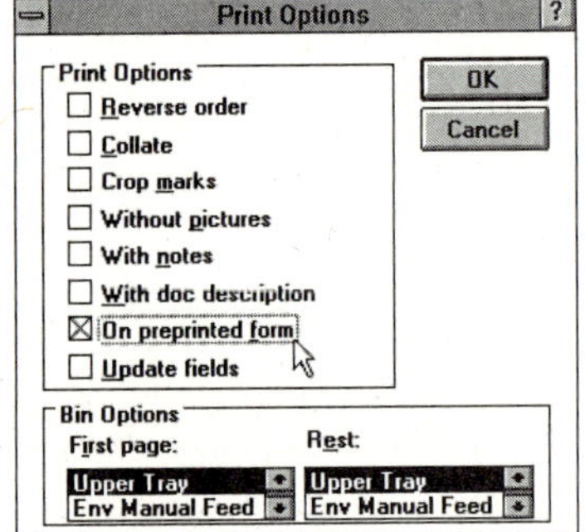

Fig. 13.40
The Print Options dialog box.

9. In the dialog box, choose On Preprinted **F**orm.
10. Choose OK or press Enter to close the Print Options dialog box. The Print dialog box remains on-screen.
11. Choose OK or press Enter to start printing.

Saving a Form

You can save a form as an ordinary Ami Pro document (by choosing **F**ile Save **A**s) or as a style sheet (by choosing **S**tyle Sa**v**e As a Style Sheet). When the Save As a Style Sheet dialog box appears, type the style sheet's name, select the **W**ith Contents option, and then choose OK or press Enter. Ami Pro saves the form as a style sheet.

The advantage of saving a form as a style sheet is that you can access and use the style sheet for other tables without re-creating the table or deleting old data from a copy of the table. Saving a form as a style sheet is particularly helpful for forms you use repeatedly.

To use a form you have saved as a style sheet, choose **F**ile **N**ew. When the New dialog box appears, select a style sheet in the **S**tyle Sheet for New Document list box, choose the **W**ith Contents option, and then choose OK or press Enter.

Using the Merge Feature with a Table

You can use the Merge feature (described in Chapter 14, "Merging and Sorting Data") with a table in either of two ways:

- The document that contains the table can serve as the data document, and you can place data in the table cells.
- The document that contains the table can serve as the standard document, and you can place the data document's merge-field names in the table cells.

Using a table makes setting up and entering fields easy. To use a table as a merge data file, follow these steps:

1. Open a new document.
2. Place the insertion point on the first page of the document and choose Too**l**s Ta**b**les. The Create Table dialog box appears.
3. In the Number of **C**olumns entry box, type a number that equals the number of fields in the data document.
4. In the Number of **R**ows entry box, type a number that equals the number of records you anticipate using in the merge data file. (You can add or delete rows later, if necessary.)
5. Choose OK or press Enter. Ami Pro uses the column and row specifications as the field and record delimiters.
6. In the first row of the table, type the field names from the data document, using a separate cell for each field name. (If the first row already contains data, insert a new row.)
7. Place the insertion point in the first column of the second row.
8. Type or import the data. (For more information on importing, see the "Importing Data and Pictures" section earlier in this chapter.)

If you want to use a table as a standard document and to insert field names into the table cells, follow these steps:

1. Create the table.

2. Place the insertion point in a cell into which you want to import a merge field.

3. Choose **E**dit **I**nsert Merge **F**ield. The Insert Merge Field dialog box appears, as shown in figure 13.41.

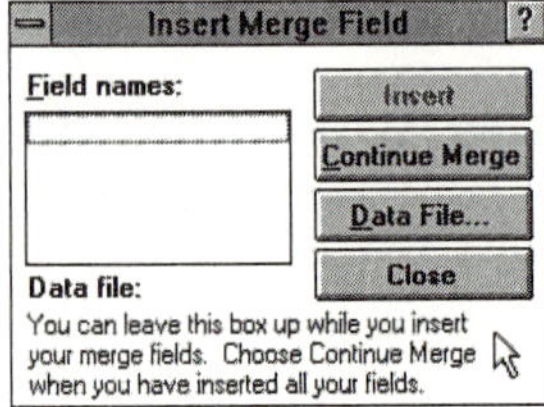

Fig. 13.41
The Insert Merge Field dialog box.

4. Choose **D**ata File. The Select Merge Data File dialog box appears, as shown in figure 13.42.

5. In the **D**ata File text box, type the name of the file that contains the merge fields you want to use.

6. Choose OK or press Enter to close the Data File dialog box. The Insert Merge Field dialog box remains on-screen.

7. In the **F**ield Names list box, type the first merge field's name.

8. Choose Insert or press Enter to import the field name into the table.

9. Move the insertion point to the cell into which you want to place the next merge field and repeat steps 7 and 8. Continue moving the insertion point and repeating steps 7 and 8 for each field name you want to insert.

Fig. 13.42
The Select Merge Data File dialog box.

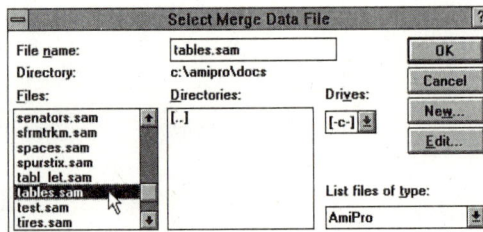

Sorting Table Data

You can use all the Ami Pro Sort options (discussed in Chapter 14, "Merging and Sorting Data") to sort data in tables. If you have a table that contains the names, addresses, and phone numbers of potential customers, for example, you may want to sort the data in this table for easy access.

Keep the following facts in mind when you sort table data:

- Ami Pro treats table columns as fields.
- Ami Pro usually treats table rows as records (but you can specify the number of rows to be used per record).
- You cannot sort the part of a table that contains a formula.
- You can specify which parts of a table Ami Pro sorts.

Summary

In this chapter, you learned how to create and move around in tables. You learned how to add and edit table data, how to change the size and shape of a table, and how to use formulas to perform basic math operations on table data. You also learned how to use Ami Pro's charting, merging, and sort capabilities with tables.

In the next chapter, you learn how to use Ami Pro's Merge function to merge data into documents.

Chapter 14

Merging and Sorting Data

In this chapter, you learn about Ami Pro's data management features: merging and sorting.

Before automation, if you wanted to send a personalized form letter to a list of people, every letter had to be typed individually. Most of the information in each letter was the same, but each person's name and address—and perhaps other information—needed to be changed for each letter.

Merges eliminate much of the unnecessary labor of this process. In an Ami Pro merge, you create a *merge document* with the information that is the same in each letter. Where the variable information (*data*) belongs, you tell Ami Pro to insert a special code. Later, when you tell Ami Pro to perform the merge, the program uses these special codes to insert the data—customizing each individual letter.

Merges are appropriate for more than just letters. Any time you want to create a standard document with data that varies, you should consider using a merge. You can merge to create mailing labels, contracts, proposals, and many other kinds of documents, as well as letters.

You maintain your data in a specially formatted Ami Pro document called a *data file*. You also can use data from a database management program (such as dBASE or Paradox) or from a spreadsheet (such as Excel or Lotus 1-2-3).

Ami Pro always has had the capacity to merge data. Before version 3, however, an Ami Pro merge required you to set up the merge document and data file manually. Ami Pro 3 has added an easy-to-use, automated procedure for creating these documents. Ami Pro's new merge procedure also provides the capacity to sort your data file—another operation that required manual effort in previous versions.

The new automated merge creation procedure is implemented as a series of macros; therefore, this feature operates somewhat more slowly than most Ami Pro operations. For all but the simplest merges, however, the time saved by automating the manual merge work more than compensates for the merge's comparatively pokey behavior.

In this chapter, you learn how to use Ami Pro 3's automated merge procedure to create standard documents and data files, and then how to combine standard documents and data files to create finished documents. You also learn how to sort data—data in Ami Pro data file format, data in tables, or data delimited by tabs or typographic characters.

Understanding Merges

A *merge* is a method of combining changing information with unchanging information, and combining a document with variable text and a document with fixed text and formatting, to produce a set of finished documents. Figure 14.1 illustrates the basic process.

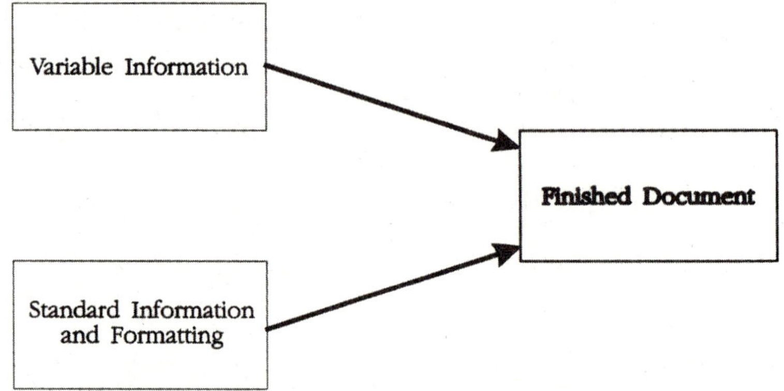

Fig. 14.1
A merge combines variable text, fixed text, and formatting to produce finished documents.

You start a merge by creating two documents. One document contains data. *Data*, as the term is used in Ami Pro merge operations, is information that varies in each finished document—such as the names and addresses of people to whom a form letter will be sent. Ami Pro calls the document containing this data the *data file*. If you use a database or spreadsheet as your source of data, however, you don't need an Ami Pro data file. The database or spreadsheet file serves as the data file.

Each data file is organized into fields. Each *field* contains one type of information. In a list of customers, for example, you may have a last name field, a first name field, a street address field, and so on.

The second document contains fixed information—information that is the same in every finished document. Fixed information usually includes standard text (such as the text of a form letter) and the formatting codes that define how the standard text and the variable data will appear. The document with the fixed information is the *merge document.* The merge document includes not only the standard text and formatting codes, but also special codes called *merge fields*. The merge fields tell Ami Pro where in the finished document the data will appear.

After you create these two documents, you tell Ami Pro to merge the documents. Ami Pro responds by creating a set of finished documents. Each finished document contains the following:

- The standard text from the merge document
- The formatting codes from the merge document
- The data pertaining to one item from the list (if the list represents customers, for example, each finished document includes the name and address of one customer)

Producing Simple Merges

In some word processing programs, you can create the standard document or the data document first. In Ami Pro, you must create the data document first, because you use the data document in the process of creating the standard document. Producing a simple merge requires three simple steps:

1. Create the data document or choose an existing data document.
2. Create the merge document.
3. Instruct Ami Pro to merge the two documents.

To begin the merge process, you choose **F**ile Mer**g**e. Ami Pro displays the Welcome to Merge dialog box (see fig. 14.2). Notice that the three choices in this dialog box correspond to the three steps to create a merge. Ami Pro keeps track of where you are in the merge process, and the default selection in the Welcome to Merge dialog box reflects the next step.

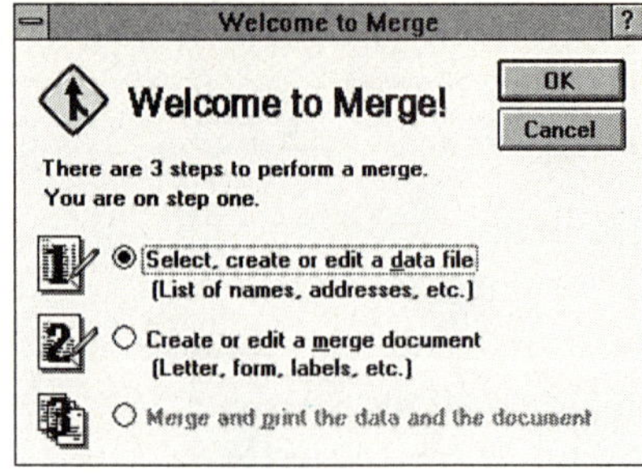

Fig. 14.2
The Welcome to Merge dialog box with the first item selected.

Ami Pro leads you through each of the steps in the merge process and the Welcome to Merge dialog box, as described in the following sections.

Creating the Data File

The first step in performing a merge operation is to create the data file—the file into which you insert the variable information. This process takes two major steps: defining the names of the fields and entering the data.

You begin the process by accessing the Welcome to Merge dialog box (choose **F**ile Mer**g**e). Because you want to create a data file, accept the default selection in the dialog box (Select, Create or **E**dit a Data File) by pressing Enter or choosing OK. Ami Pro displays the Select Merge Data File dialog box (see fig. 14.3).

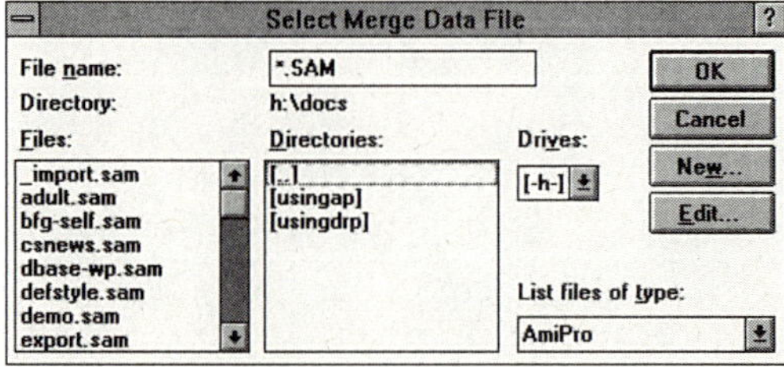

Fig. 14.3
The Select Merge Data File dialog box.

If you want to use an existing data file, you can choose one of the files in the **F**iles list box. At this point, however, because you want to create a new data file, choose Ne**w**. Ami Pro displays the Create Data File dialog box. You use this dialog box to define the field names, as described in the next section.

Defining Field Names

Because you haven't defined field names for this data file, the Create Data File dialog box is blank. The cursor is in the Field **N**ame text box; Ami Pro is waiting for you to type a field name.

Note

You can enter field names in any order in the data file, but the *first* field name should describe the item of data you will use to refer to the record. If the data file is an address list, for example, you probably refer to records by the last name. For a list of companies, you probably want to select the company name.

To enter field names, follow these steps:

1. Type the name of the first field in the Field **N**ame text box. You can use letters, numbers, and spaces, but the first character must be a letter or an underscore character. (Capitalization doesn't matter.)

   For this example, type **Last Name** in the Field **N**ame text box (see fig. 14.4).

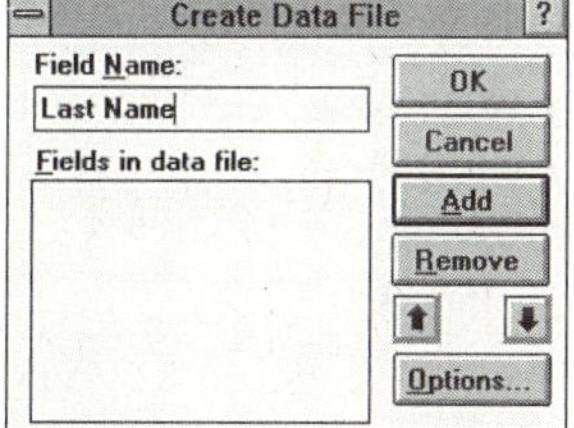

Fig. 14.4 The Create Data File dialog box with the first field name typed in the Field **N**ame text box.

2. After you type the field name, press Enter or choose **A**dd. Ami Pro moves the name you typed to the **F**ields in Data File list box and clears the Field **N**ame list box to prepare it for the next field name.

3. Repeat steps 1 and 2 for the rest of the fields.

After you finish entering the fields, the dialog box may resemble figure 14.5. Because the example contains more fields than can fit in the **F**ields in Data File list box, Ami Pro scrolls the list and adds scroll bars.

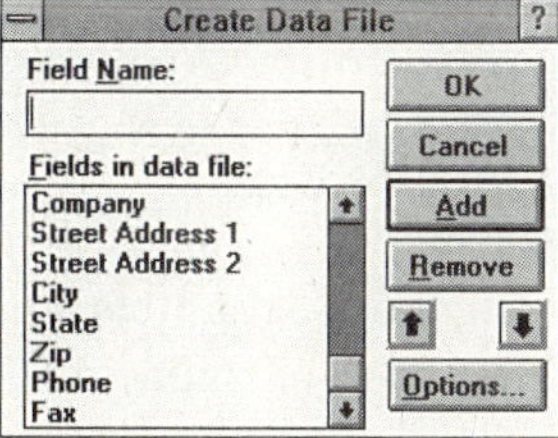

Fig. 14.5 The Create Data File dialog box with all the fields entered.

Note

Include a field for every possible item of data. If some addresses fit on one line and others require two lines, for example, define two fields—Address 1 and Address 2. Make field names long enough to be descriptive, but short enough to fit within the **F**ields in Data File list box. For a last name, "LN" is probably too cryptic, and "Last name of the client" too long. "Last Name" and "Last" are good compromises.

Changing the Field Names

If you enter a field and then decide you want to remove it, select the field in the **F**ields in Data File list box and choose **R**emove. The field disappears from the list. To edit a field name, delete the field and then retype the field name as you want it to appear.

Changing the Order of the Field Names

As mentioned earlier, the order of fields in the data file doesn't really matter (except for the first field). You can use the data in any order in the merge document, independently of the order of the data in the data file. You may want to keep fields in a certain order, however, to make data entry more convenient. If you use a phone list as a data source, for example, you may have a phone number and a fax number for each person. If the numbers are next to each other in the source document, you want to enter them together as you type records into the data file. You can accomplish this objective by placing the fields together in the file.

You can change the order of the fields as you are entering field names. To move a field up in the sequence, highlight the field name in the **F**ields in Data File list box; then click the large up-arrow button in the dialog box (between the **R**emove and **O**ptions buttons). Each time you click the arrow button, the field name moves up one position in the list box. To move a field down, follow the same procedure using the down-arrow button.

Changing the Delimiters

By default, Ami Pro uses the tilde (~) and the vertical bar (|) as *delimiters* in data files. Delimiters tell Ami Pro where one field ends and the next field begins, and where one record ends and the next record begins.

You don't need to know much about delimiters unless you plan to edit the data file directly (a practice that isn't recommended); however, make sure that Ami Pro's delimiter characters don't appear in your data. In other words, if any chance exists that a tilde (~) or vertical bar (|) is in the data, you must use some other characters as delimiters. If neither of these characters exists in the data, you can skip ahead to the next section.

Note

The field delimiter and record delimiter characters cannot be the same.

To change the delimiter characters, follow these steps:

1. In the Create Data File dialog box (refer to fig. 14.5), choose **O**ptions. The Data File Options dialog box appears (see fig. 14.6).

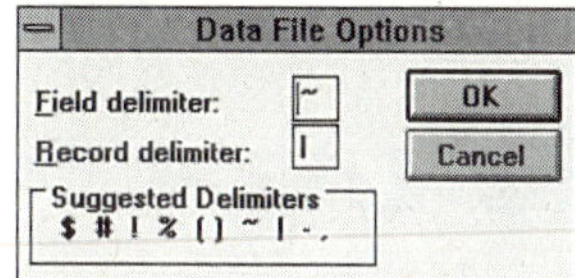

Fig. 14.6
The Data File Options dialog box.

2. To change the field delimiter, type the character you want to use in the **F**ield Delimiter text box. You can use any character on the keyboard as long as no chance exists that the character appears in the data. (One of the characters in the Suggested Delimiters list box may be appropriate.)

3. To change the record delimiter, type the character you want to use in the **R**ecord Delimiter text box. Make sure that the field and record delimiters are different characters.

4. After you define the delimiters, choose OK or press Enter.

When the field names are the way you want them, choose OK or press Enter in the Create Data File dialog box. The dialog box closes and Ami Pro pastes into the new document the chosen delimiters (or the defaults) and field names. The program then performs a series of operations on the data file. At times, Ami Pro may appear to be finished. Be patient, however; eventually, Ami Pro displays the Data File dialog box (see fig. 14.7), and you are ready to begin entering data.

In this figure, part of the data file containing the delimiters and field names is visible behind the dialog box.

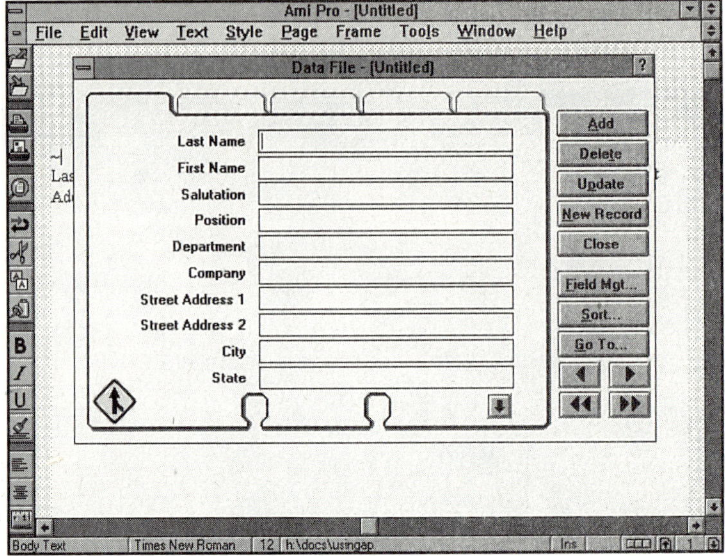

Fig. 14.7
The Data File dialog box, as it appears with no data file.

Entering Data

Notice that the Data File dialog box looks like a series of tabbed Rolodex cards. On the top card, you can see some of the field names created earlier. All you can see of the cards behind the first card is a set of blank tabs. Each tab represents one record in a data file; because you haven't entered any data, all the tabs are blank.

While you waited for Ami Pro to display this dialog box, the program was reading the field names from the data file and preparing to use them as the field names on the cards. If all the fields fit on a single card, all of them appear. If more fields exist than space on the card (as in fig. 14.7), the field names continue on subsequent pages of the card.

Each Ami Pro data file card can be longer than one page. Each card tab that appears on-screen represents one card (or one record), not one page. If you have multiple-page cards, each tab represents all the pages of a card.

To enter data in the fields on the first page of a card, type the value for the first field in the first text box. In this example, type the first person's name in the Last Name text box (see fig. 14.8).

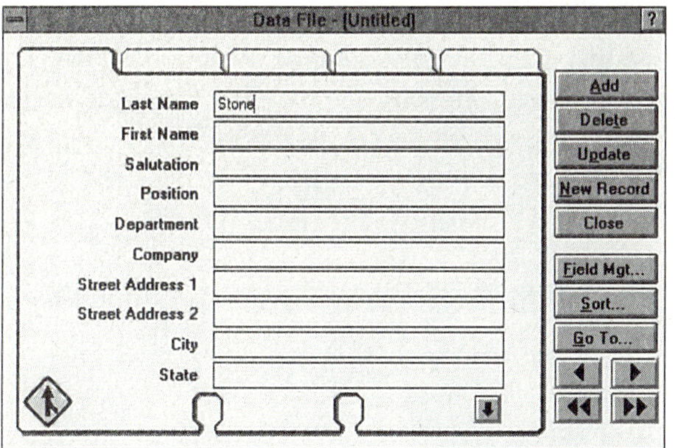

Fig. 14.8
The data file with the first field entered in the first record.

To move to the next field, press Enter, Tab, or the down-arrow key. To move back to a previous field, press Shift+Tab or the up-arrow key. You also can use the mouse to position the cursor in a field.

Continue moving from field to field and entering data. Figure 14.9 shows the completed example card.

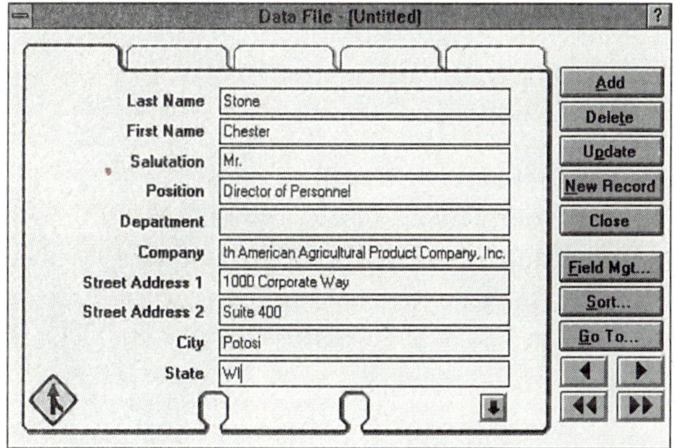

Fig. 14.9
The data file with all the data entered into the first page of the first record.

Notice that the Department field in figure 14.9 is empty. In this example, because the person doesn't work in a particular department, the field is left blank. Notice also that the entry in the Company field ("North American Agricultural Product Company, Inc.") is too long for the text box. (Ami Pro scrolls the information in the text box horizontally.) The entire company name appears in the data file, although you cannot view the entire name at one time on the card. To see the first part of the company name, position the cursor in the text box and then scroll with the left-arrow key or press Home.

If your card contains more than one page, you can move to the second page of the card by pressing Enter or the down-arrow key after you complete the last field on the first page. (Pressing Tab highlights the **A**dd button rather than moving to the next page.) You also can move to the next page by pressing PgDn or by clicking the large down-arrow button in the bottom right corner of the card. Ami Pro displays the next page (see fig. 14.10).

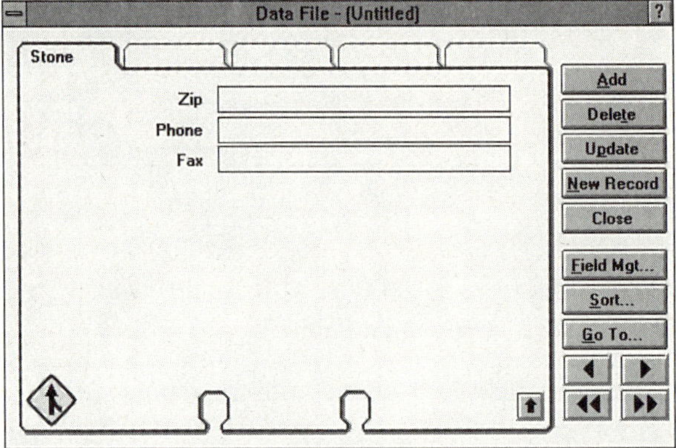

Fig. 14.10
The second page of the data file card.

Enter the data in the fields on the second page in the same way that you enter data on the first page. If you need to go back to the first page, click the up-arrow button at the bottom of the card or press PgUp.

After you enter data in the last field on the last page of the card, press Enter or choose **A**dd. Ami Pro inserts the record into the data file, "files" the card, and displays a new, blank record (see fig. 14.11). Notice that the first record (Stone) is filed behind the second (blank) record. The last name appears on the tab because the Last Name field was the first field you defined for the data file.

You enter subsequent records in the same way that you entered the first record.

By default, Ami Pro places new records on the top of the stack of cards (at the beginning of the data file). You can overcome this default and insert cards anywhere in the stack. This process is explained later in this chapter.

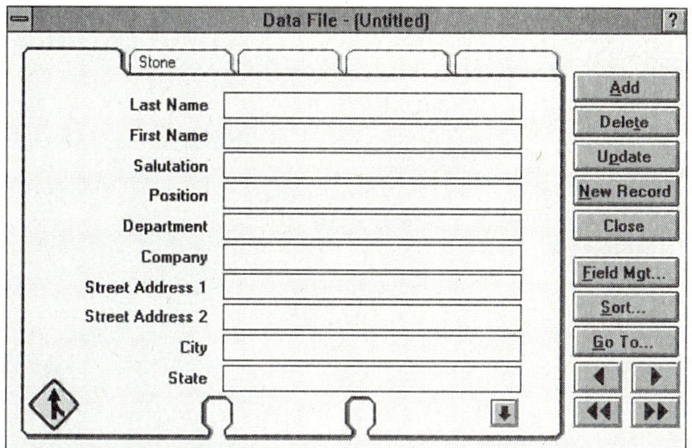

Fig. 14.11
The first page of the second record, with the first record "filed" behind it.

Moving around in the Data File

After you enter a few records in the data file, you may want to move around in the data file to insert records, edit existing records, or delete records. You can move around in a data file in the following ways:

- You can page through the data file, one record at a time, in either direction.
- You can go quickly to the first or last record in the data file.
- You can go directly to a specific record.

To page through the data file, use the large left and right triangles (◀ and ▶), located below the **G**o To button. Pressing ◀ moves toward the top of the stack of cards (forward in the file), one record at a time. Pressing ▶ moves toward the bottom of the stack, one card at a time. To go to the top of the file, click the ◀◀ symbol. To go to the bottom of the file, click the ▶▶ symbol. (If you don't have a mouse, tab to the symbol and press Enter.)

You can go directly to a specific record in two ways. If the tab for the record appears on-screen, you can display the record by clicking the tab. To go directly to a record that isn't shown on-screen, search for the record by choosing **G**o To. Ami Pro displays the Go To Record dialog box (see fig. 14.12).

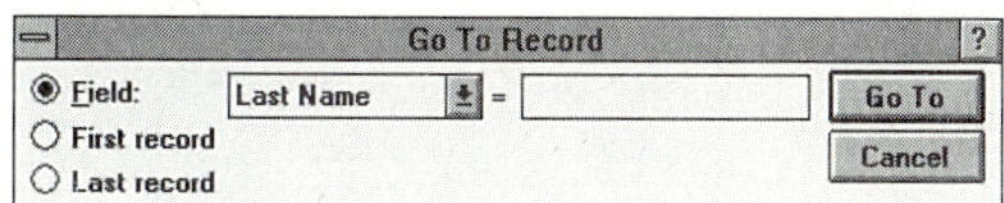

Fig. 14.12
The Go To Record dialog box.

This dialog box contains three options: **F**ield, First Record, and Last Record. First Record and Last Record go to the top and bottom of the stack of cards, respectively—they duplicate the actions of the ◀◀ and ▶▶ symbols in the Data File dialog box. The **F**ield option searches for a record, based on the value in any field.

To search for a record identified by the default field (the first field in the record—the field that appears on the tabs of the cards), type the value of the record in the text box on the right, and then choose **G**o To. If you are looking for a record with the last name Meyerson, for example, type **Meyerson** in the text box (capitalization doesn't matter), and choose **G**o To. If a matching record exists, Ami Pro displays its card; otherwise, Ami Pro displays a dialog box indicating that no match exists.

Keep in mind the following points:

- By default, Ami Pro matches only complete words. (The word doesn't need to be the first word in the field; however, it must be a complete word.) Ami Pro doesn't find Meyerson if you type **Meyer**. To search for a complete word, using only part of the word in the search, type the part of the word for which you want to search, and then add an asterisk. The asterisk (*) matches any group of letters; **Meyer*** matches Meyer, Meyerson, and Meyersen.

- Ami Pro always searches from the top of the stack and therefore always finds the first record that matches the search. If you have two Smith records, Ami Pro always finds the first one. The only way to find the second Smith is to search on some unique field, such as a Social Security number.

To search for a field other than the default (first) field, you first choose the field in the left text box by clicking the down-arrow button. A drop-down list box displays the fields defined in the data file. Select the field you want to use for the search. Alternatively, you can position the cursor in the **F**ield text box and press the down-arrow key on the keyboard until the desired field appears.

Next, type the text for which you are looking in the value box of the designated field (the text box to the right of the equal sign), and choose **G**o To.

Inserting Records

By default, Ami Pro places at the beginning of the data file any records you enter. You can override the default sequence as you enter records, however, by displaying the card you want the new record to follow, and then choosing **N**ew Record. Ami Pro displays a blank record. Complete the record and tell Ami Pro to file it by pressing Enter in the last field or by choosing **A**dd.

Editing Records

To change an existing record, display the record, make the changes, and choose **U**pdate. Ami Pro replaces the existing record in the data file with the revised record.

If you have a series of similar records to enter (for example, a group of people from the same company with the same address), you can save time by copying an existing record and then modifying the copy. Display the record you want to copy and then choose **A**dd. Ami Pro inserts another copy of the record into the data file and displays a blank record. Click the ◀ symbol to display the copy, and then make the changes you want. After you finish editing, choose **U**pdate to save the modified record.

To delete a record from the data file, display the record and then choose Dele**t**e to remove the current record from the data file.

Sorting the Data File

You can sort the records in a data file. You can sort on any field, in ascending order (A to Z and 1 to 9) or descending order (Z to A and 9 to 1). If the data includes numbers, you also can sort alphanumerically or numerically.

Suppose that the following numbers are in the data file: 10, 22, 3, 20, 1, 12, 11, 21, and 2. *Numeric sorts* look at each set of digits as a numeric quantity. With a numeric sort, Ami Pro sorts the numbers in numeric sequence: 1, 2, 3, 10, 11, 12, 20, 21. *Alphanumeric sorts* look at each digit as an individual character. With an alphanumeric sort, Ami Pro produces the sequence 1, 10, 11, 12, 2, 20, 21, 22, 3. Usually, you sort numeric data (such as ZIP codes) numerically.

To sort the data file, follow these steps:

1. Choose **S**ort in the Data File dialog box. The Sort Records dialog box appears (see fig. 14.13).

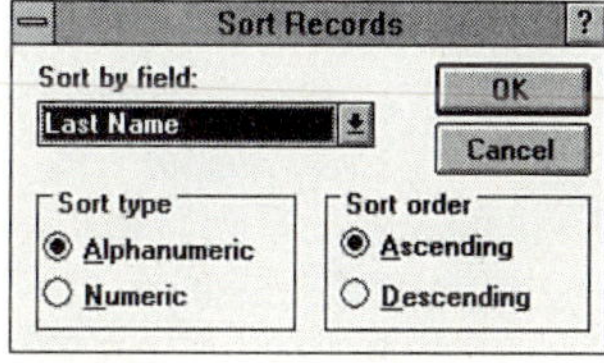

Fig. 14.13
The Sort Records dialog box.

2. To select the field you want to sort, click the down-arrow button at the right of the Sort by Field list box to display a drop-down list of fields. (If you aren't using a mouse, tab to the box and press the down-arrow key on the keyboard.) Then select the field you want.

3. The default sort type is **A**lphanumeric. To sort numerically, choose the **N**umeric option.

4. The default sort order is **A**scending. To sort in descending order, choose **D**escending.

5. When the options are set correctly, choose OK or press Enter. Ami Pro sorts the data file.

When you sort the data file, Ami Pro displays on the tabs of the cards the first few characters of the field on which you sorted. If you sort by ZIP code, for example, the cards appear as shown in figure 14.14. To redisplay the first field in the tabs, sort the data file by the first field.

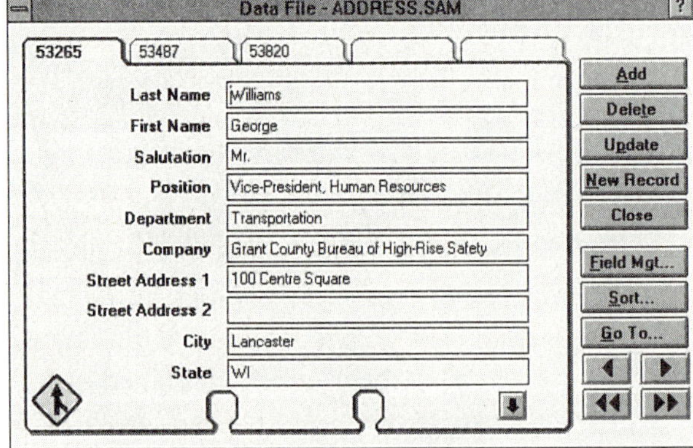

Fig. 14.14
The Data File dialog box after the data file is sorted by ZIP code.

This automated procedure enables you to perform simple sorts, such as sorts on a single field. You can perform more sophisticated sorts on the data file by using the S**o**rt option on the Too**l**s menu (described later in this chapter).

Note

If you need to perform a multilevel sort and want to use the automated procedure, sort the least important field first. Then sort the next most significant field. Continue until you have sorted all the relevant fields. If you want to sort clients by company, company by last name, and last name by first name, for example, sort by the least important field—first name. Then sort by the next most important field—last name. Finally, sort by the most important field—company.

Adding Fields during Data Entry

When entering data, you may realize that you forgot to define a field that you need. You can add fields by using the Data File dialog box. To add a field, follow these steps:

1. Choose **F**ield Mgt from the Data File dialog box. The Field Management dialog box appears.

2. In the Fields in Data File list box, select the field to appear immediately before or after the field you are about to insert. Then type the name of the new field in the Field Name text box. If you want to insert a field for the country of the addressee between the Zip field and the Phone field, for example, select Zip in the Fields in Data File list box, and then type **Country** in the Field Name text box (see fig. 14.15).

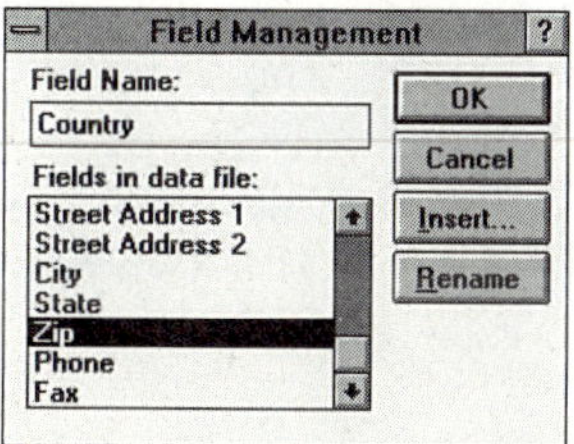

Fig. 14.15 The Field Management dialog box, ready to insert the Country field.

3. Choose OK or press Enter. The Insert Field dialog box appears (see fig. 14.16).

4. Depending on whether you want the new field to appear before or after the Zip field, choose **B**efore Selected Text or **A**fter Selected Text. For this example, because you want Country to appear after Zip, choose **A**fter Selected Text.

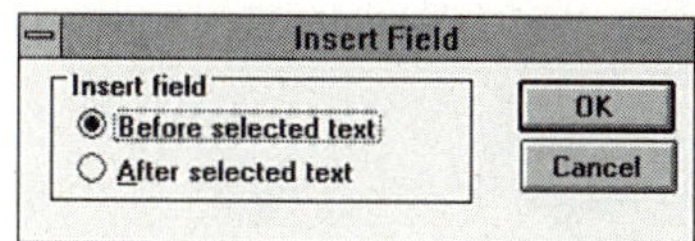

Fig. 14.16 The Insert Field dialog box.

5. Choose OK or press Enter. Ami Pro redisplays the Field Management dialog box with the field inserted in the Fields in Data File list box.

6. Choose OK or press Enter. Ami Pro displays the current record containing the new field. In figure 14.17, the Country field appears in the current record.

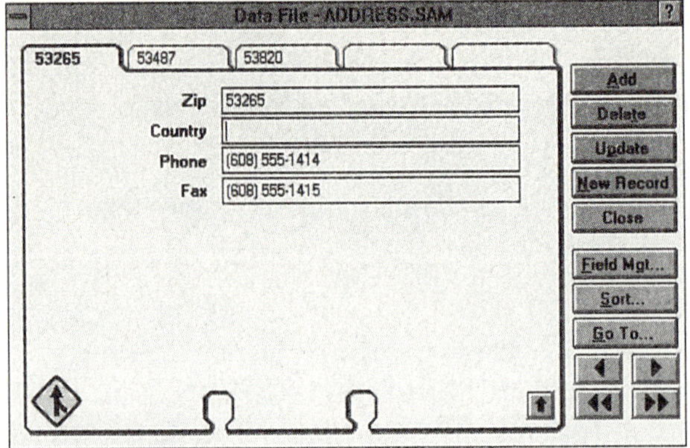

Fig. 14.17 The new field (Country) appears between the Zip and Phone fields.

Note

After you close the Field Management dialog box, Ami Pro goes through the entire data file and inserts a blank field in every existing record. If you have many records, this process may take a long time (if you also have a slow computer, a *very* long time). To avoid this wait, determine the fields you need before you enter data.

Renaming Fields during Data Entry

You can rename fields during data entry. To rename a field while entering data, follow these steps:

1. Choose **F**ield Mgt from the Data File dialog box. The Field Management dialog box appears (refer to fig. 14.15).
2. In the Fields in Data File list box, select the field you want to rename. In the Field Name text box, type the new field name.
3. Choose **R**ename. Ami Pro displays the new field name in the Fields in Data File list box.
4. Choose OK or press Enter. Ami Pro renames the field in the data file and displays the current record card, including the new field name.

Closing the Data File

When you finish entering data, choose the Close option in the Data File dialog box. Ami Pro displays the Save As dialog box. Save the file as you do any other Ami Pro file. Ami Pro redisplays the Welcome to Merge dialog box with the second item, Create or Edit a **M**erge Document, as the default (see fig. 14.18).

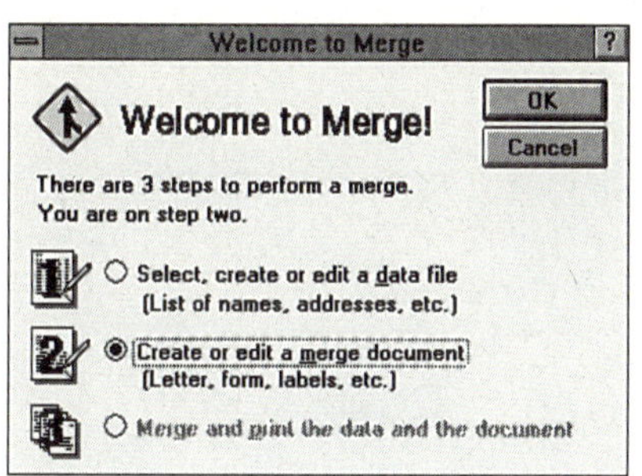

Fig. 14.18
The Welcome to Merge dialog box, ready to begin creation of the merge document.

Even if you go on to the next step in merging (creating the merge document), you always can come back to the data file and add, delete, or change records.

Using a Table as a Data File

You can use an Ami Pro table as your data file. When you use a table, each *row* of the table represents one record and each *column* represents one field. You don't supply delimiters if you use a table—Ami Pro uses the table formatting to organize the document into records and fields. You must supply field names, however, by entering the field names in the top row in the table. The first record appears in the second row of the table.

> **Note**
>
> When you use an Ami Pro table as a data file, the table must begin on the first page of the document and must be the only thing in the document.

To use a table as a merge data file, create the table, enter the field names, and enter the data. Keep in mind the following conditions:

- You can use a page table or a frame table. Page tables enable you to enter as many records as you want. Frame tables restrict you to the number of records on a single page.
- The number of columns should equal the number of fields for the merge.
- The number of rows should at least equal the number of records you plan to enter. (If the table contains blank rows, Ami Pro ignores them.)
- You can increase or decrease the columns or the rows later.
- When Ami Pro reads the data in the table during the merge, any formatting specified in the table is ignored.

- In the first row of the table, type the field names, one field name per column. The field names can wrap to more than one line if necessary.
- Type the data beginning in the second row. Put each record on a separate row, with the record fields in the appropriate columns. Data can wrap to more than one line if necessary.

Using an External File as a Data File

Keeping data in an Ami Pro data file document and using that data in merges is a satisfactory solution if your data management needs are relatively simple. Dedicated database and spreadsheet programs have much richer capabilities for managing data. But these applications cannot compare with Ami Pro when combining data with standard text and presenting the combined information in a nicely formatted style.

Fortunately, Ami Pro enables you to use the following types of files (created by many of the most popular database and spreadsheet programs) as data files:

1-2-3 (through Release 3)

Comma-delimited or fixed-length ASCII

dBASE II, III, and IV

Data Interchange Format (DIF)

Microsoft Excel (through version 4.0)

Paradox

SuperCalc

You don't have to convert the files or import them into Ami Pro. You simply tell Ami Pro what kind of file you're using, and then set up the merge as usual.

Note

If you have data in an application not listed here, you may be able to import the data into an Ami Pro table and then use the table as your data file. See Chapter 20, "Importing, Exporting, and Linking Files," for information on importing data into Ami Pro.

To use an external data file, Ami Pro must have field names for the data in that file. For some formats, you may need to supply a *description file* that tells Ami Pro what kind of file is being used and the names of the fields in that file.

In many cases, Ami Pro can determine the field names. If the external file is a database file from dBASE or Paradox, Ami Pro uses the field names stored in that file; you don't need a description file. If the external file is a spreadsheet file or an ASCII file, and the first record in the file contains the field names, you can tell Ami Pro to use the first record as the field names, and you don't need a description file. You only need to supply a description file if you are using a spreadsheet or ASCII file and the first record in the file doesn't contain the field names.

Creating a merge with an external data file is very much like creating a merge with an Ami Pro data file. You choose **F**ile Mer**g**e and select the first option in the Welcome to Merge dialog box. Ami Pro displays the Select Merge Data File dialog box (refer to fig. 14.3).

In the **F**iles list box, select the file type you want to use, then choose OK or press Enter. Unless the selected file type is dBASE or Paradox, Ami Pro displays the Merge Data File Fields dialog box.

If the first record in the data file contains the names of the fields, accept the default option (Field Names in First **R**ecord of Data File). Otherwise, create or specify the description file. After you finish this process, close the Merge Data File Fields dialog box by choosing OK or pressing Enter, and proceed with the rest of the merge operation as you do with an Ami Pro data file.

Creating the Merge Document

After you finish creating the data file, you are ready for the second major step in merge operations: creating the merge document (the file that contains the standard information and formatting). To begin creating the merge document, follow these steps:

1. Choose Create or Edit a **M**erge Document in the Welcome to Merge dialog box. Ami Pro displays the Merge Document dialog box (see fig. 14.19).

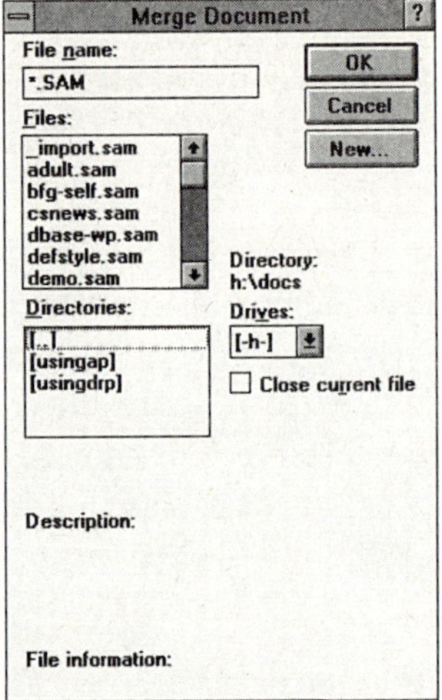

Fig. 14.19 The Merge Document dialog box.

2. Choose New to instruct Ami Pro to create a new merge document. Unless you have changed the defaults, Ami Pro displays the New dialog box with the default style _DEFAULT.STY highlighted.

3. Select the style you want to use and then choose OK or press Enter. (See Chapter 10, "Working with Style Sheets," for information on selecting style sheets. For the example in this chapter, use _DEFAULT.STY.)

4. Ami Pro displays a new document. In the upper right corner of the screen, Ami Pro displays the Insert Merge Field dialog box (see fig. 14.20).

> **Note**
>
> If you have a merge document format you use often, enter the standard information, formatting, and merge fields; then save the document as a style sheet with contents. Chapter 10, "Working with Style Sheets," offers information on saving new style sheets.

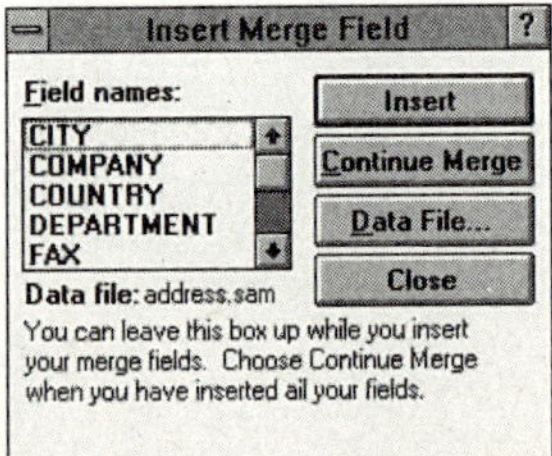

Fig. 14.20 The Insert Merge Field dialog box.

Note

The Insert Merge Field dialog box isn't like most Ami Pro dialog boxes. Most Ami Pro dialog boxes are *modal*; you must complete the entries in the dialog box and then close the dialog box (usually by choosing OK or Cancel) before Ami Pro allows you to do any more work in the document. The Insert Merge Field dialog box is a *nonmodal* dialog box; you can move back and forth freely between the dialog box and the document, and you don't need to close the dialog box. The nonmodal nature of the Insert Merge Field dialog box makes it a useful tool when creating a merge document.

The Insert Merge Field dialog box in figure 14.20 contains the list of the fields defined in the data file created earlier. The fields are listed alphabetically and in uppercase (regardless of how you typed them in the data file). Any spaces used in the field names have been replaced in the Insert Merge Field dialog box by underscores.

Tip

If you inadvertently close the Insert Merge Field dialog box, you can redisplay it by choosing **E**dit **I**nsert and then choosing Merge **F**ield.

Building the Basic Document

To create a letter by using the fields in the Insert Merge Field dialog box, follow these steps:

1. Type the date of the letter in the document.

2. Position the insertion point where you want the name of the addressee to appear (in the format "Mr. Chester Stone").

3. Select the SALUTATION field from the Insert Merge Field dialog box (see fig. 14.21). Note that *salutation* in this example refers to the honorifics Mr., Ms., and so on.

4. Choose Insert or double-click the field name to place the field name at the insertion point in the standard document. The merge field name appears between angle brackets (see fig. 14.22).

   The text and angle brackets aren't the merge field—they are an indicator that a merge field has been inserted. The merge field is an invisible code; therefore, you cannot insert merge fields just by typing angle brackets and field names. Ami Pro recognizes only the field names you insert by choosing from the Insert Merge Field dialog box.

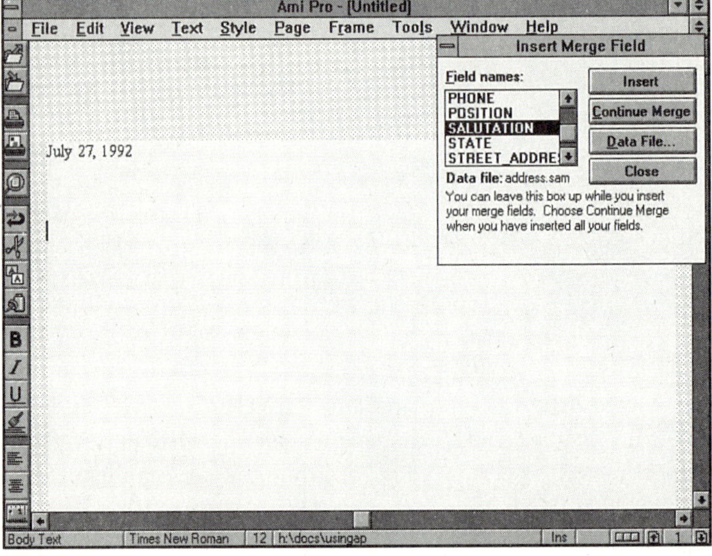

Fig. 14.21
The Insert Merge Field dialog box with the SALUTATION field selected.

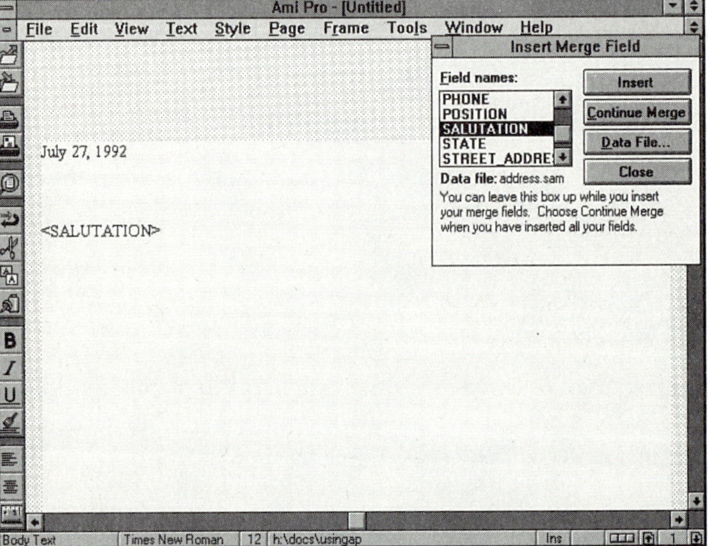

Fig. 14.22
The field is inserted in the document.

5. Type a space after the closing angle bracket in the <SALUTATION> field, and leave the insertion point at that position. Then repeat steps 3 and 4, selecting the FIRST_NAME field.

6. Continue entering the rest of the fields in the address block. Position the insertion point in the document where you want the field to appear. Use spaces, commas, and hard returns as needed to format the text properly. Include the following fields:

    LAST_NAME (after FIRST_NAME)

    POSITION (line 2 of the address block)

    DEPARTMENT (line 3)

    COMPANY (line 4)

    STREET_ADDRESS_1 (line 5)

    STREET_ADDRESS_2 (line 6)

    CITY (line 7)

    STATE (following CITY, a comma, and a space)

    ZIP (following STATE and a space)

   Don't worry if some of the fields in the records are blank. If a field is blank and the only object on a line, Ami Pro skips the line. If STREET_ADDRESS_2 is blank, for example, the line with CITY, STATE, and ZIP immediately follows the line with STREET_ADDRESS_1.

7. At the point where you want the salutation to appear, type **Dear** followed by a space.

8. Select SALUTATION from the Insert Merge Field dialog box, and then type a space. This step repeats the honorific Mr., Ms., and so on.

9. Select LAST_NAME from the Insert Merge Field dialog box, and then type a colon (:). Figure 14.23 shows the document at this point.

10. Type the rest of the text for the document (see fig. 14.24).

Editing Merge Fields

You can delete, cut, copy, and paste merge fields in much the same way that you perform those operations on text. Copying and pasting are relatively straightforward, as long as you include the text and both angle brackets in your selection. Cutting and deleting, however, can be tricky.

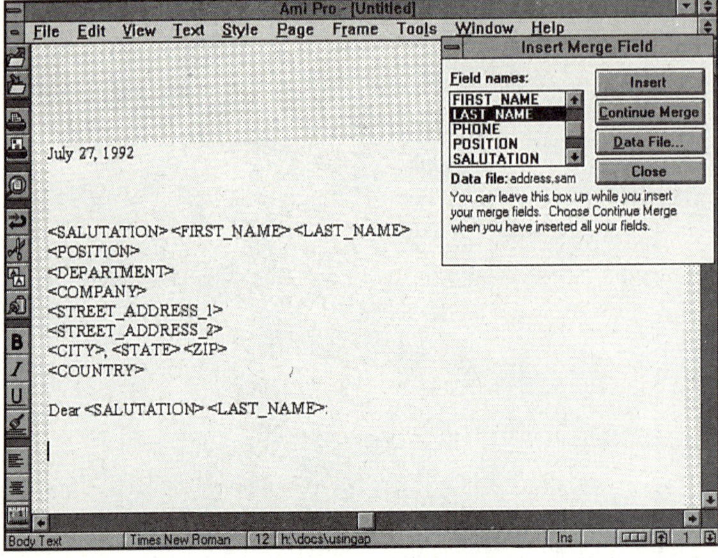

Fig. 14.23 The document with the address block and salutation inserted.

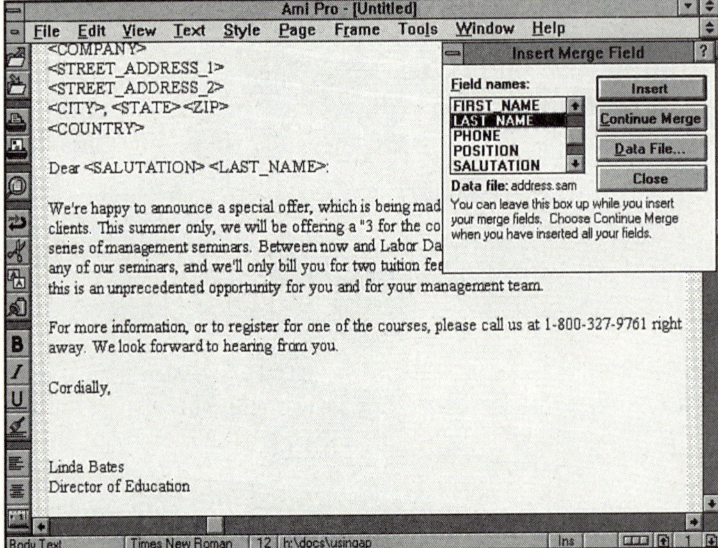

Fig. 14.24 The completed merge document.

The best way to delete a merge field is to select the entire field, including both angle brackets, and then press Del (or choose the Delete SmartIcon). If you use the Del key or Backspace key to delete a merge field character-by-character, you may delete only the text that marks the merge field and not the merge field itself. To make sure that you delete the merge field, choose the entire field and then press Del.

If you try to delete or cut a merge field or a larger selection containing a merge field, Ami Pro displays a dialog box to warn you that you are deleting a field. If this dialog box doesn't appear, you haven't included the merge field code in your selection. To delete the field, choose **Y**es. To cancel, choose **N**o.

Tip

Merge fields are a type of *power field*. To choose a power field, place the insertion point in the document prior to the field, choose **E**dit Power **F**ields, and then choose **N**ext Field.

Caution

You cannot undo a merge field cut or delete operation. Ami Pro restores only the text and angle brackets, not the merge field.

Enhancing Text in Merge Fields

You can enhance the appearance of the text that appears in the merge fields in the finished document (by boldfacing or underlining, for example) by applying the enhancements from the **T**ext menu to the merge fields in the merge document. When Ami Pro merges data into the standard document, the text appears with the enhancements you applied to the merge fields.

To enhance a merge field, select the field, including the text and the angle brackets. Select the desired enhancement from the **T**ext menu. See Chapter 4, "Formatting a Document," for more information on text enhancements.

Performing the Merge

When the merge document is ready, choose **C**ontinue Merge from the Insert Merge Field dialog box. The dialog box disappears and the Welcome to Merge dialog box appears, with the third option selected (see fig. 14.25).

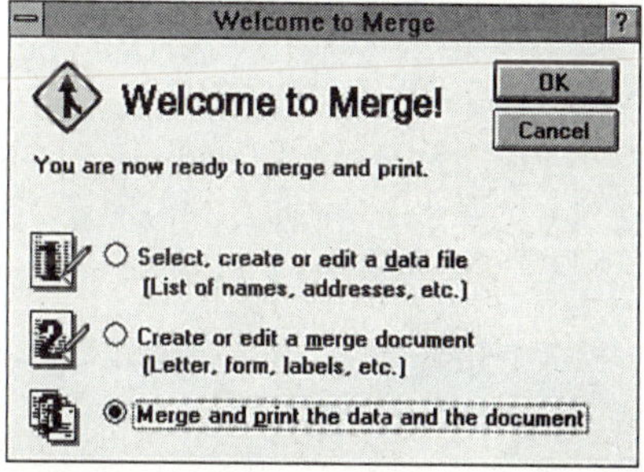

Fig. 14.25
The Welcome to Merge dialog box with the third option selected.

Note

If you choose Close rather than **C**ontinue Merge in the Insert Merge Field dialog box, the dialog box disappears, but the Welcome to Merge dialog box doesn't appear. To continue the merge, you must choose **F**ile Mer**g**e, choose the third option in the Welcome to Merge dialog box, and reselect the data file and merge document.

After you finish the data file and the merge document, most of the work is done. The actual merge operation is a simple procedure that can generate a large volume of personalized documents quickly. When you perform the merge operation, the result is a new letter or some other form for each record in the data file.

To merge the two files, choose the third option (Merge and **P**rint the Data and the Document) from the Welcome to Merge dialog box. The Merge dialog box appears (see fig. 14.26).

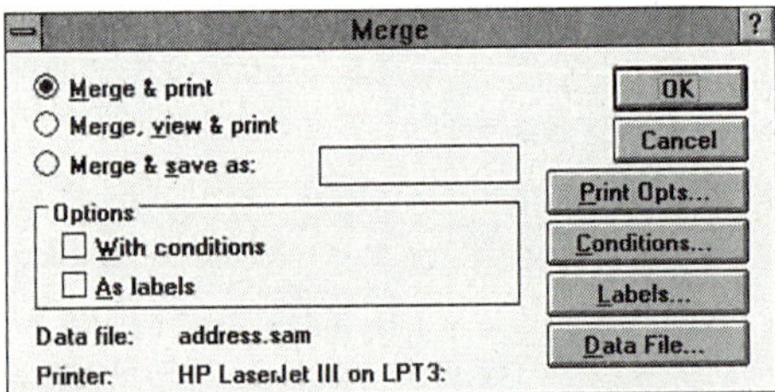

Fig. 14.26
The Merge dialog box.

Note

If you need to change printer options before merging, choose **P**rint Opts from the Merge dialog box to access the Print dialog box. (If you choose **F**ile **P**rint to access the Print dialog box, Ami Pro sends the file to the printer instead of returning to the Merge dialog box.) See Chapter 8, "Proofreading and Printing a Document," for details on using the Print dialog box.

The Merge dialog box presents three options for merging and printing: **M**erge & Print; Merge, **V**iew & Print; and Merge & **S**ave As. You choose an option depending on the conditions of the merge document and the data file, and on whether you want to check the finished documents before printing them. The following sections describe these options. For the example merge, use the Merge, **V**iew & Print option (described in the third section).

Note

Even when you plan to use one of the other options, begin by selecting Merge, **V**iew & Print. By viewing the completed first record, you can determine whether the merge document is okay. Then you can cancel the operation and make corrections or start merging and printing with the option you want to use.

Caution

Don't choose Merge & **P**rint or Merge & **S**ave As unless you are sure the merged document will contain no errors. If you have a field in the merge document that doesn't match a field in the data file, for example, Ami Pro displays two error messages for each record during the merge. The only option available when Ami Pro displays one of these messages is OK, which just removes the dialog box and continues with the merge. If this problem occurs during a Merge & **P**rint or Merge & **S**ave As operation, you cannot stop the merge and correct the situation, short of rebooting the computer. You must choose OK two times per record until the merge is finished. If you have hundreds of records in your data file, this process takes a very long time.

Merge & Print

Choose **M**erge & Print to send the merged documents directly to the printer (without displaying them) as Ami Pro creates them. If you choose this option, you don't see the documents on-screen before they print, and the documents aren't saved in a file. If you find a mistake, you must correct and reprint the documents affected by the mistake. If you are sure that the merged documents will be correct, this option is the fastest and least labor-intensive way to print them.

Merge & Save As

Use the Merge & **S**ave As option to perform the merge and save the merged document as a separate file that you can view or print later. This is the only option that enables you to print the documents later without rerunning the merge. (Merged document files created from large data files usually are huge; therefore, you must have plenty of disk space to use this option.) With this method, Ami Pro asks you to provide a file name before beginning the merge.

Merge, View, & Print

Choose Merge, **V**iew & Print if you want to view each document before printing it. This option enables you to skip printing a document or to make minor editorial corrections before sending a document to the printer. After looking at some of the documents, if you find a major mistake that needs to be corrected, you can cancel the merge, correct the problem, and then restart the merge.

When you choose Merge, **V**iew & Print, the Merge dialog box disappears and Ami Pro displays the first merged document. This document has the standard text and formatting from the merge document and the data from the fields in the first record of the data file. The field data is in the locations you specified when you created the merge document. A second, smaller Merge dialog box appears (see fig. 14.27).

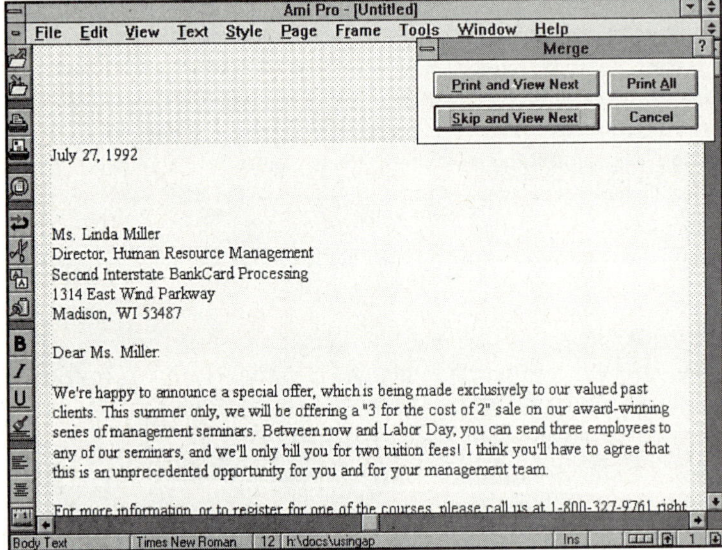

Fig. 14.27
The Merge dialog box that appears for the Merge, **V**iew & Print option.

Choose one of the following options from the smaller Merge dialog box:

- Choose **P**rint and View Next to print the document and review the next document on-screen. Selecting this option repeatedly enables you to review and print the letters individually.
- Choose **S**kip and View Next if you don't want to print the displayed document. Ami Pro shows the next document.
- Choose Print **A**ll if the first merged letter appears to be correct and you want to print the rest of the letters without reviewing them.
- Choose Cancel if you notice a general problem (for example, a field in the wrong place) or if you don't want to print the merged documents.

After the merge is complete, Ami Pro redisplays the merge document. If at some later point you want to rerun the merge with the existing files, choose **F**ile Mer**g**e and repeat the merge procedure.

Reusing Merge Files

You can reuse data files and merge documents for later merges, using these files "as is," or modifying them. Ami Pro's automated merge feature guides you through this process.

To begin, choose **F**ile Mer**g**e. Ami Pro displays the Welcome to Merge dialog box. Choose Select, Create or Edit a **D**ata File. The Select Merge Data File dialog box appears. Earlier in this chapter, you chose Ne**w** in this dialog box to create a new data file (refer to fig. 14.3). Now you want to reuse an existing data file. You have the following choices:

- Select the file in the **F**iles list box and choose OK or press Enter (or just double-click the file name) to designate an existing data file to be used without changes.

- Select the file and choose **E**dit to edit the data file—add records, delete records, or modify records. Ami Pro displays the Data File dialog box (refer to fig. 14.7). You can use the techniques you learned earlier in the chapter to edit the file. When you finish editing the file, choose Close in the Data File dialog box.

Note that no matter which option you choose, you can choose only data files. If you try to choose any other type of file, Ami Pro displays an error message indicating that the file you chose isn't in valid data file format.

After you select and (if necessary) edit the data file, Ami Pro redisplays the Welcome to Merge dialog box. Choose the second option, Create or Edit a **M**erge Document. Ami Pro asks whether you want to use the current document as the merge document. If you choose **Y**es, Ami Pro skips the next step (selecting a merge document). Otherwise, Ami Pro displays the Merge Document dialog box (refer to fig. 14.19). Select a file and choose OK or press Enter (or just double-click the file name).

Ami Pro "remembers" when you use a data file with a merge document. When you choose an existing merge document, Ami Pro responds by displaying the document along with the Insert Merge Field dialog box (refer to fig. 14.20). The field names in the Insert Merge Field dialog box are those from the data file you last used with the selected merge document.

To use the merge document with a different data file, choose **D**ata File in the Insert Merge Field dialog box. The Select Merge Data File dialog box appears (refer to fig. 14.3). Then select a new data file.

Note

If you want to use the data file from the last merge, and if the data file doesn't need editing, choose **F**ile Mer**g**e and then choose Create or Edit a **M**erge Document in the Welcome to Merge dialog box. By default, Ami Pro assumes that you want to use the most recent data file for the merge document you select.

Tip
If you selected the wrong data file, choose **D**ata File from the Insert Merge Field dialog box. Ami Pro displays a dialog box from which you can choose the correct data file.

You also can edit the merge document, using the techniques described earlier in this chapter. When you're ready to go on, choose **C**ontinue Merge from the Insert Merge Field dialog box. Ami Pro displays the Welcome to Merge dialog box with the third option (Merge and **P**rint the Data and the Document) selected. The procedure from this point duplicates that which was described earlier in this chapter.

Using Merge Conditions

The standard merges described earlier in this chapter create one finished document for each record in the data file. Sometimes you may want to merge selectively, skipping some records in the data file, depending on what those records contain.

Suppose that you have a standard mailing list containing the addresses of customers from many different states. You are located in New Jersey. You want to send a notice to your out-of-state customers (those whose address isn't New Jersey) regarding sales tax. Or perhaps you want to send an executive-level briefing only to customers with the title of President; or only to customers with ZIP codes between 53000 and 53999; or only to customers with addresses in Madison or Milwaukee.

You can merge records selectively by using the merge conditions feature of Ami Pro. You give Ami Pro one or more conditions, and Ami Pro merges only those records that meet the conditions.

To set up a merge condition, you specify a field name, a value, and an operator. The field name must be defined in the active data file. In the first example cited (sending a letter to customers whose address isn't New Jersey), the field name is STATE.

The *value* is the contents of the field that Ami Pro uses to decide whether to merge the record. In this example, the value Ami Pro checks is *NJ* (the abbreviation for New Jersey).

The *operator* tells Ami Pro what relationship to find between each record and value. The operator in this example is *not equal to*—you want Ami Pro to merge records where the STATE field is not equal to the value New Jersey. The symbol for not equal to is !=. The condition is as follows:

```
STATE != NJ
```

Following are "translations" of the other examples.

To merge only records where the position is President, you tell Ami Pro to merge when POSITION is equal to the value President:

```
POSITION = President
```

To merge only records where the ZIP code is between 53000 and 53999, you need two conditions. You want all records where ZIP is greater than or equal to the value 53000 and where ZIP is less than or equal to the value 53999:

```
ZIP >= 53000 AND ZIP <= 53999
```

Notice that in this example you need field names, operators, values, and a *connector* to tie the conditions together. In this example, the connector is the word *AND*.

You also need two conditions to choose all customers with addresses in Milwaukee or Madison:

```
CITY = Madison OR CITY = Milwaukee
```

The connector that ties these conditions together is *OR*.

You access the merge conditions feature by choosing the **C**onditions button in the Merge dialog box (refer to fig. 14.26). Ami Pro responds by displaying the Merge Conditions dialog box (see fig. 14.28).

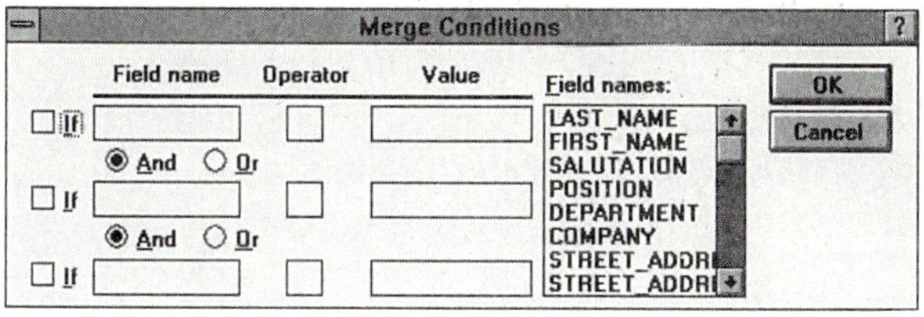

Fig. 14.28
The Merge Conditions dialog box.

To specify merge conditions, follow these steps:

1. Place the cursor in the first Field Name text box.

2. Select the desired field name from the **F**ield Names list box, or type the field name in the Field Name text box. To restrict the merge to people who live in a particular city, for example, choose the CITY field. Ami Pro checks the check box to the left of the Field Name text box.

3. Place the cursor in the first Operator text box. Ami Pro displays a list of operators in the **O**perators list box (see fig. 14.29). If the operators don't appear, position the mouse pointer on the Operator text box and click. (Table 14.1, following these steps, describes the purpose of each operator.)

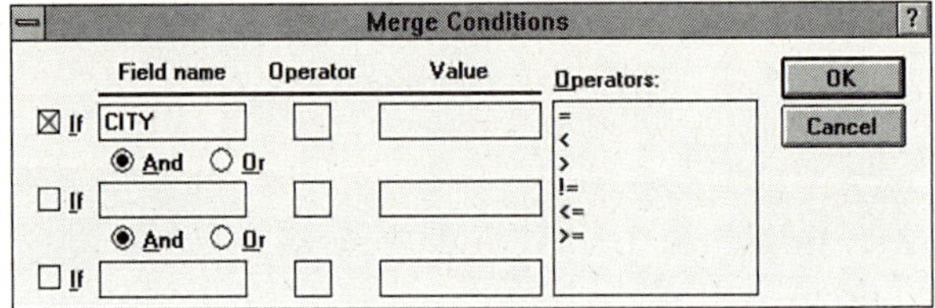

Fig. 14.29
The Merge Conditions dialog box, showing the available operators.

4. Select one of the operators from the list box, or type the operator in the text box.

5. Place the cursor in the Value text box and type the value of the expression.

   A text value must be typed *exactly* as it appears in the data file. Capitalization must be correct. If you type **milwaukee**, for example, Ami Pro doesn't select a record where the city is Milwaukee.

6. If you need only one merge condition, skip to step 7. Otherwise, enter the second merge condition in the second set of boxes. If necessary, enter a third merge condition in the third set of boxes. Make sure that the correct connecting word, **A**nd or **O**r, is selected to connect each pair of conditions.

7. After you finish specifying merge conditions, choose OK or press Enter to return to the Merge dialog box. When the Merge dialog box reappears, **W**ith Conditions is checked. If you decide not to use the conditions just defined, deselect **W**ith Conditions.

8. Proceed with the merge.

Table 14.1 Operators in the Merge Conditions Dialog Box

Operator	Purpose
= (equal to)	Merges records where the designated field in the record is equal to the value typed in the Value text box
!= (not equal to)	Merges records where the designated field in the record *isn't* equal to the value typed in the Value text box
< (less than)	Merges records where the designated field in the record is less than the value typed in the Value text box

Operator	Purpose
<= (less than or equal to)	Merges records where the designated field in the record is less than or equal to the value typed in the Value text box
> (greater than)	Merges records where the designated field in the record is greater than the value typed in the Value text box
>= (greater than or equal to)	Merges records where the designated field in the record is greater than or equal to the value typed in the Value text box

Creating Labels

Creating mailing labels requires special consideration because most labels are printed with multiple copies on a single sheet of paper. Ami Pro's labels feature makes printing labels in conjunction with a merge operation very easy.

Two basic techniques are available to create labels in Ami Pro. You can use the LABEL macro (supplied with Ami Pro), or you can create labels manually. Both techniques are described in the sections that follow.

Using the Label Macro

The LABEL macro runs automatically when you tell Ami Pro to create a new document with the _LABEL.STY style sheet. The LABEL macro has two big advantages: it automates much of the labor involved with creating labels, and it provides a huge variety of predefined label formats. The documents you can create with the LABEL macro include standard address labels, shipping labels, disk labels, tab labels for tabbed dividers or file folders, audio and video cassette labels, Rolodex cards, name badges, and postcards.

The predefined labels are referenced to part numbers of label forms manufactured by Avery. You can cross-reference most labels from other manufacturers to an Avery product that is reasonably close. You also can modify any of the label definitions provided by the label macro.

To create a label document, choose **F**ile **N**ew. When the New dialog box appears, choose the _LABEL.STY style sheet. Make sure that the **W**ith Contents and **R**un Macro options are selected, and then choose OK or press Enter.

Ami Pro displays a new document, which appears as a small label in the center of the screen (see fig. 14.30). Ami Pro begins running the LABEL macro.

Tip
If you have an untitled document open, you can run the LABEL macro independently of the _LABEL.STY style sheet. Choose Too**l**s **M**acros **P**layback and specify LABEL.SMM.

Watch the Status Bar at the bottom of the screen to see the progress of the macro.

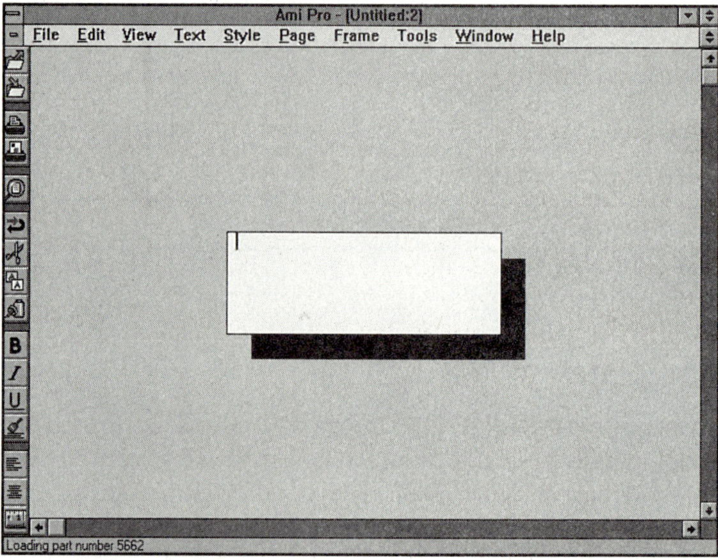

Fig. 14.30 A new label document.

Eventually, Ami Pro displays the Labels dialog box (see fig. 14.31). The list box shows a large selection of labels, each with the Avery part number.

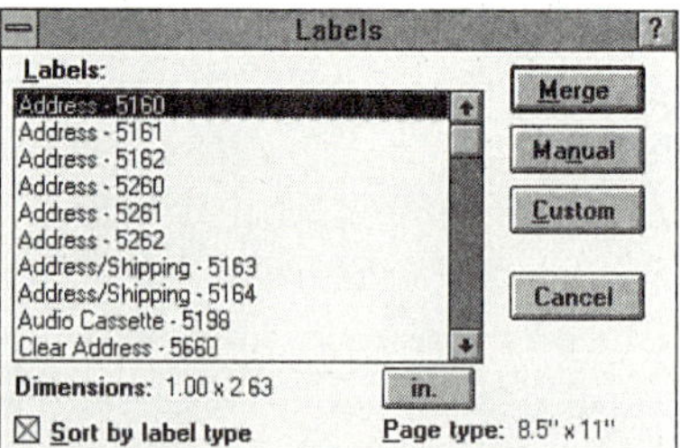

Fig. 14.31 The Labels dialog box.

Using Predefined Labels

To use a predefined label definition, choose the definition in the Labels dialog box and then choose **M**erge. Ami Pro displays the Select Merge Data File dialog box (refer to fig. 14.3). Select or create the data file. When you complete this task, Ami Pro displays the label and the Insert Merge Field dialog box. Insert the fields in the label.

Note

If merge field names are too long, they wrap to the next line of the label. This action may cause some label fields to wrap to the next page (the next label). As long as the label is wide enough to hold the longest line produced by the data in the data file, however, this isn't a problem. After you run the merge, if you find that some labels don't contain all the data you expect, try using a smaller font size (or a larger label).

When the label is formatted correctly, choose **C**ontinue Merge in the Insert Merge Field dialog box. Ami Pro displays the Welcome to Merge dialog box with the third option selected. When you instruct Ami Pro to execute the third option, the Merge dialog box appears. To merge the data file and the merge document, choose **M**erge & Print or Merge & **S**ave As (Merge, **V**iew & Print isn't available when you merge to labels).

Defining a Custom Label

To define a custom label, choose the closest predefined label to your custom size in the Labels dialog box. Then choose **C**ustom. Ami Pro displays the Modify Page Layout dialog box. Make the changes you want to the page layout and then choose OK or press Enter to close the Modify Page Layout dialog box. Ami Pro displays the Select Merge Data File dialog box. From this point, proceed as you do for a predefined label. For details on changing page layout, see Chapter 5, "Working with Page Layout."

Tip
After the page layout is correct, save the empty document as a style sheet. See Chapter 10, "Working with Style Sheets," for more information on saving style sheets.

Creating Manual Labels with the LABEL Macro

You can use the LABEL macro to create manual labels—labels that aren't associated with a data file. When you specify manual labels, Ami Pro creates a table. Each cell in the table is the size of one label. Type the data and then print the document as you do any other document.

To create the manual labels, choose the predefined label that corresponds to the desired label size from the Labels dialog box. Then choose Ma**n**ual. Ami Pro creates the table and places the insertion point in the first cell.

Tip
Use manual labels only for data you plan to use once, or for data that will never change. If you need to insert and remove labels, use the merge file techniques discussed in this chapter.

Creating Labels Manually

You also can create labels manually during the merge process. You perform the same steps you normally carry out when you're creating a merge, with three additions:

- When you create the merge document, define a page size for the document equal to the size of one label (not a sheet of labels).

- Use the Merge Labels dialog box to define how the individual labels will be laid out on the paper.
- In the Merge dialog box, tell Ami Pro to perform the merge as labels.

After the individual labels have been defined, create a merge document using that definition. Select the appropriate data file, insert the merge fields, and format the labels as appropriate. After your individual labels are defined and your merge document has been created, you are ready to lay out the sheet of labels. To define a sheet of labels, follow these steps:

1. In the Merge dialog box (refer to fig. 14.26), choose **L**abels. The Merge Labels dialog box appears (see fig. 14.32).

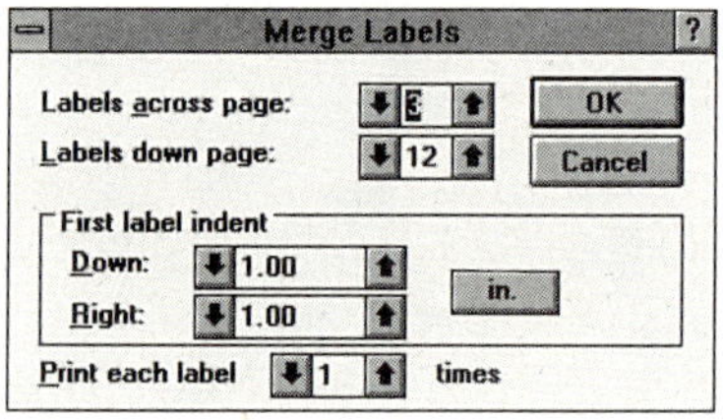

Fig. 14.32
The Merge Labels dialog box.

Merge Labels

Labels across page:	3	OK
Labels down page:	12	Cancel

First label indent

Down:	1.00	in.
Right:	1.00	

Print each label 1 times

2. In the Labels **A**cross Page text box, indicate how many labels you want to appear horizontally on the page (across the sheet).

3. In the **L**abels Down Page text box, specify the number of labels you want to appear vertically on the page (down the sheet).

4. In the First Label Indent section of the dialog box, specify the position for the upper left corner of the top left label (the first label on the sheet). In the **D**own text box, indicate how far down from the top edge of the sheet Ami Pro should place the top edge of the first label. In the **R**ight text box, specify how far from the left edge of the page Ami Pro should place the left edge of the first label.

   To use measurements other than inches, use the unit of measure button to the right of the **D**own and **R**ight text boxes. You can choose inches, centimeters, picas, and points.

5. In the **P**rint Each Label *x* Times text box, specify how many times Ami Pro should print each label.

6. Choose OK or press Enter. Ami Pro returns to the Merge dialog box. The **A**s Labels option is checked and the only print option available is Merge & **P**rint.

Using the Sort Tool

Earlier in this chapter, you learned how to do simple, single-field sorts by using the **S**ort option in the Data File dialog box. With Ami Pro's Sort feature, you also can sort data in lists or tables. Each field in a record is a *level*; the first field is the first level, the second field is the second level, and so on. You specify whether to sort in ascending or descending order, how many levels to sort (up to three), which word to sort on, and whether the sort is alphanumeric or numeric.

Tip
You can sort multiple paragraphs, portions of a document or table, or entire documents or tables. You don't need to set up your data in a particular way to sort it.

Ami Pro sorts data in a table by rows. If you enter one record per row, you can keep the records intact when you sort the data.

A simple sort uses only one sort field and doesn't include multiple paragraphs in each record. Suppose that you want to sort an address list that contains the names Karen Miller, John Smight, Rudy Jones, and Ann Wilson.

Tip
Before sorting, copy your document. Making a copy ensures that you can recover the original list or table if you don't like the results of the sort.

When sorting a list, you indicate how Ami Pro can find the individual fields in each record. *Tab delimited files* separate the fields in each record with tabs. *Field delimited files* use a special character to distinguish the fields.

The procedures for sorting a list and for sorting a table are similar. Follow these steps:

1. If you want to sort only part of the document, select the part you want to sort. Don't select items that you don't want to sort, such as column heads or titles.

2. Choose Too**l**s S**o**rt. The Sort dialog box appears, as shown in figure 14.33. (If you haven't selected anything in the document, Ami Pro displays a warning message. Choose OK to continue and sort the entire text stream. If you want to select a portion of the text to sort, choose Cancel, select the text, and choose Too**l**s S**o**rt again.)

   You can sort on up to three levels. In this example, you want to sort on just one level—the name.

3. In the **L**evel 1 Field text box, specify the number of the field to use for primary sorting.

   The example list contains four records, each with the field's name, street address, and phone number, separated by commas. For this example, because you want to sort by last name, which is the first field, specify **1** as the **L**evel 1 designation. (If you want to sort by street address, use **2**; for phone number, use **3**.)

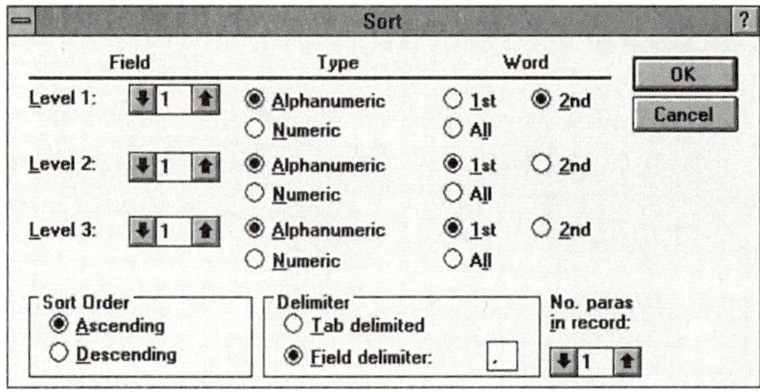

Fig. 14.33
The Sort dialog box.

4. If you want to sort by additional fields, specify those fields in the **L**evel 2 and **L**evel 3 text boxes.

5. For each of the levels, specify the type of sort you want: **A**lphanumeric or **N**umeric. For this example, choose **A**lphanumeric.

6. Specify which word in each field you want to sort on: the first (**1**st), second (**2**nd), or all words (A**l**l).

   In the example, because last name is the second word in the first field, choose **2**nd.

7. Choose **A**scending or **D**escending for the sort order. For the example, choose **A**scending.

8. Specify how the fields are separated in the data file by selecting **T**ab Delimited or **F**ield Delimiter. If you indicate that the data uses a field delimiter, specify the character in the text box.

   In the example, the fields are separated by commas; select **F**ield Delimiter and type a comma as the delimiter. If you are sorting a table, the Delimiter box is grayed. In a table sort, each column serves as a delimiter.

9. For the No. Paras **I**n Record option, indicate the number of paragraphs in each record. (Remember that a carriage return at the end of a record and a blank line between records count as two paragraphs in a record.) For the example, type or choose **1**.

   For this option, specify a number other than 1 only if each record has the *same* number of paragraphs. Otherwise, the sort may scramble your data.

10. Choose OK or press Enter. Ami Pro sorts the data according to your specifications. Figure 14.34 shows the sorted example list.

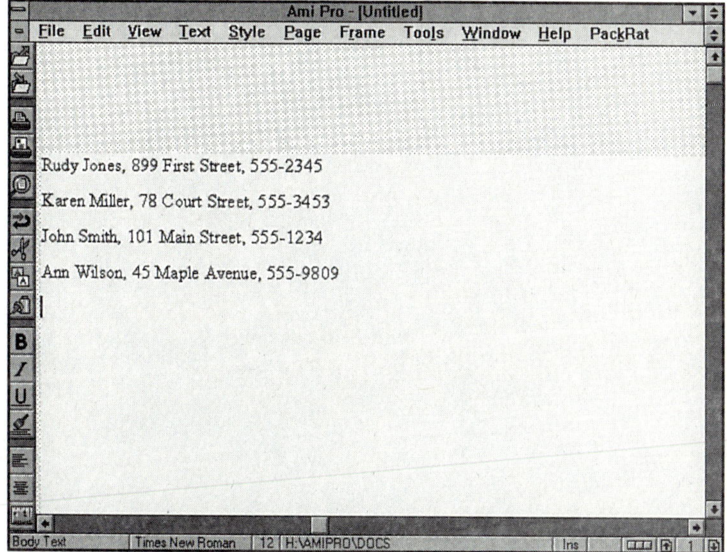

Fig. 14.34
The sorted list of names and addresses.

Summary

In this chapter, you learned about the data management features of Ami Pro: merging and sorting. You use merges to create documents that combine standard information from a merge file with variable information from a data file. The data file can be a specially formatted Ami Pro file, an Ami Pro table, or an external file from a program such as Excel or Paradox. You can use Ami Pro's sorting ability on regular text, or to sequence the records you plan to use in merges.

In the next section, you learn how to produce professional output with Ami Pro.

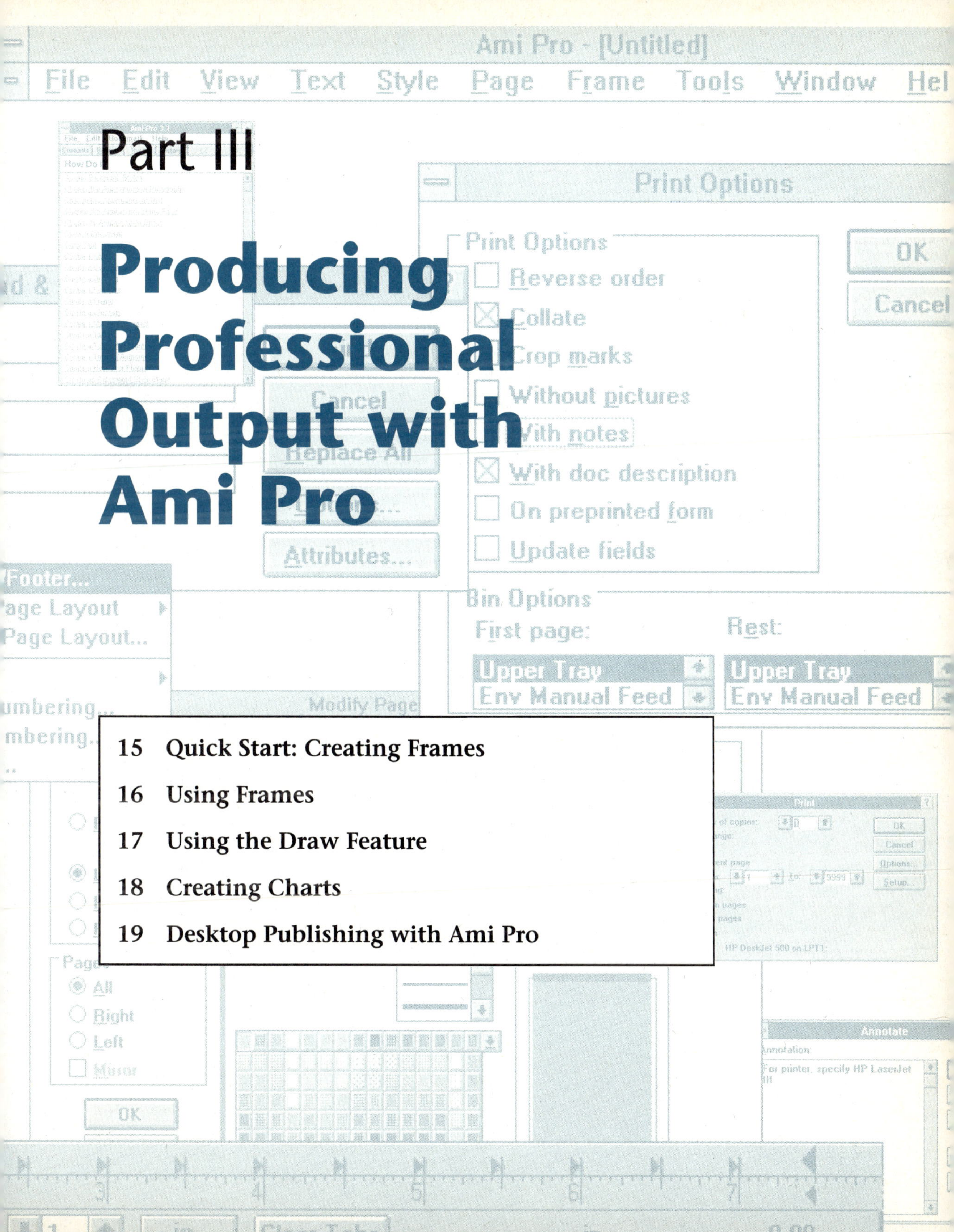

Part III

Producing Professional Output with Ami Pro

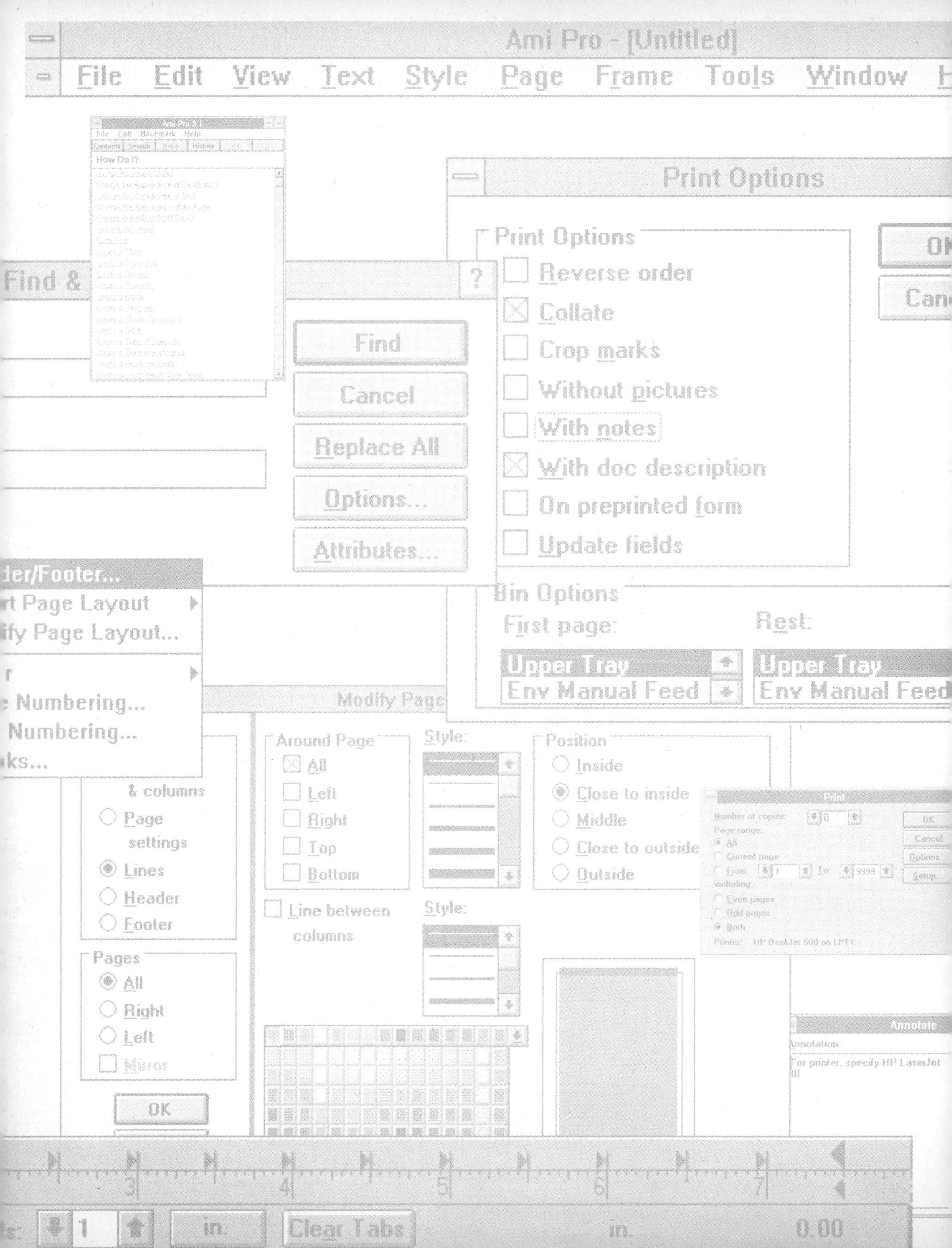
Ami Pro - [Untitled]
File Edit View Text Style Page Frame Tools Window
Print Options
Print Options
Reverse order
Collate
Crop marks
Without pictures
With notes
With doc description
On preprinted form
Update fields
Bin Options
First page:
Rest:
Upper Tray
Env Manual Feed
Find
Cancel
Replace All
Options...
Attributes...
Modify Page
Around Page
All
Left
Right
Top
Bottom
Style:
Position
Inside
Close to inside
Middle
Close to outside
Outside
Line between columns
Pages
All
Right
Left
Mirror
OK
Lines
Header
Footer
Page settings
Clear Tabs
Annotate
Annotation:
For printer, specify HP LaserJet III
Print
Number of copies:
Page range:
Printer: HP DeskJet 500 on LPT1:

Chapter 15

Quick Start: Creating Frames

Ami Pro frames are an excellent way to add text, graphics, drawings, charts, and so on to your document. Ami Pro frames are easy to create, place, and modify, providing you with additional control over document design.

If you haven't used non-Windows word processing (or Windows software that doesn't use frames), you probably don't recognize what a breakthrough frames represent. In character-based word processing, for example, you often must work on a blank screen to create special text or graphics; then you place a code in the document to represent the item. To see how the item looks in the document, you use some form of document preview. Moving or resizing the item is a complex operation, and wrapping text around the item is impossible or extremely difficult.

With Ami Pro, creating a frame, adding text or graphics to the frame, and moving or resizing the frame are easy operations.

In this quick start, you learn two methods of creating a frame: drawing a frame with the mouse, and having Ami Pro draw the frame from specified measurements. You also learn how to modify a frame by adding lines, a background screen, text, tabs, and a picture. Because frames contribute to the overall design of an Ami Pro document, this quick start lesson also illustrates using a frame for a three-column heading, a callout, a repeated frame with a graphic, and a table of contents. Chapter 19, "Desktop Publishing with Ami Pro," offers a more detailed look at frames and design in documents.

Before you begin creating frames, you can type some sample text or retrieve an existing document and save it with a new name; if you prefer, use a blank document. The example figures in this quick start use the sample text introduced in Chapter 5, "Working with Page Layout." Your results don't need to look like these examples for you to learn the basics of creating and using frames.

Creating a Basic Frame

In this section, you learn how to create a basic frame by "drawing" it with the mouse or keyboard. You also learn how to create an automatic frame by specifying dimensions and letting Ami Pro draw the frame. In later sections, you learn how to add text to the frame, modify the frame layout, and modify text in a frame.

The sample document used in this section is a three-column newsletter; the frame you create contains a heading that spans three columns. Figure 15.1 illustrates the sample document in layout mode and custom view.

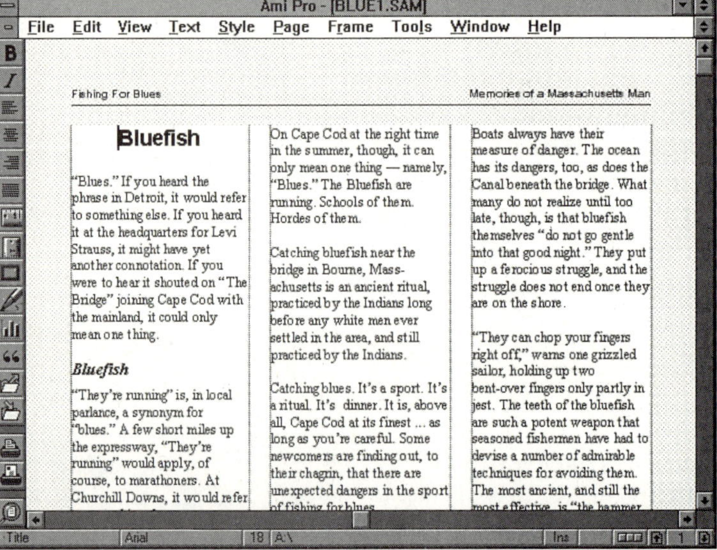

Fig. 15.1 A sample document shown in custom view (85 percent of full size).

> **Note**
>
> Before you create the frame, make sure that Ami Pro is in layout mode and in the custom view by choosing **V**iew. When the **V**iew menu appears, look for check marks to the left of the **C**ustom and **L**ayout Mode options. If you need to select both options, you must start at the main menu a second time to select the second option.

Drawing the Frame Manually

Working with Ami Pro's frame feature is simple if you use a mouse; using the keyboard is a little more complicated. The following steps describe both methods of drawing a frame:

1. Choose F**r**ame **C**reate Frame. The Create Frame dialog box appears, as shown in figure 15.2.

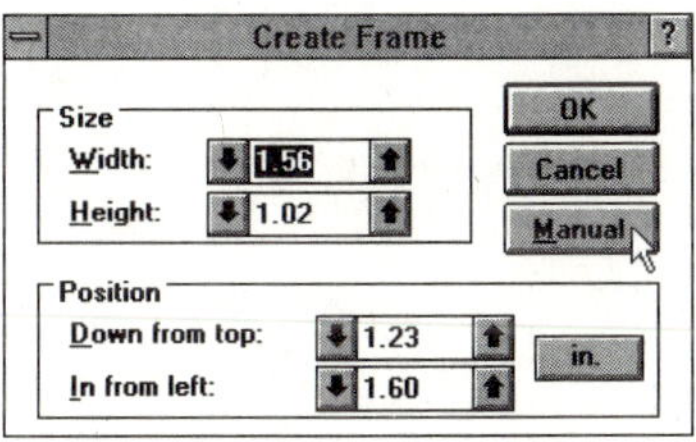

Fig. 15.2
The Create Frame dialog box.

2. Choose **M**anual. The dialog box disappears and Ami Pro displays the document. The mouse cursor appears as a small box with thick borders—the *frame icon*..(An alternative mouse method for accessing the frame icon is to click the Add a Frame SmartIcon. See Chapter 16, "Using Frames," for details.)

   At this point, the mouse and keyboard methods diverge. In the following step, the mouse method is described first, and then the keyboard method.

3. To specify the frame with the mouse, position the frame icon at the left margin of the page, hold down the left mouse button and drag the cursor diagonally to the right margin of the page.

   A dashed box appears, showing the boundaries of the frame as you draw (see fig. 15.3). The frame should be about one inch tall.

   To specify the frame with the keyboard, press and hold the space bar while pressing the right-arrow key. The frame extends to the right side of the page. Continue holding the space bar, and press the down-arrow key until the frame is about one inch tall.

4. When the box is the right size (seven inches by one inch in this example), release the mouse button or the space bar. The frame forces the text in each column down the page. Ami Pro rewraps the text in the columns, and some text may move to the top of the next page.

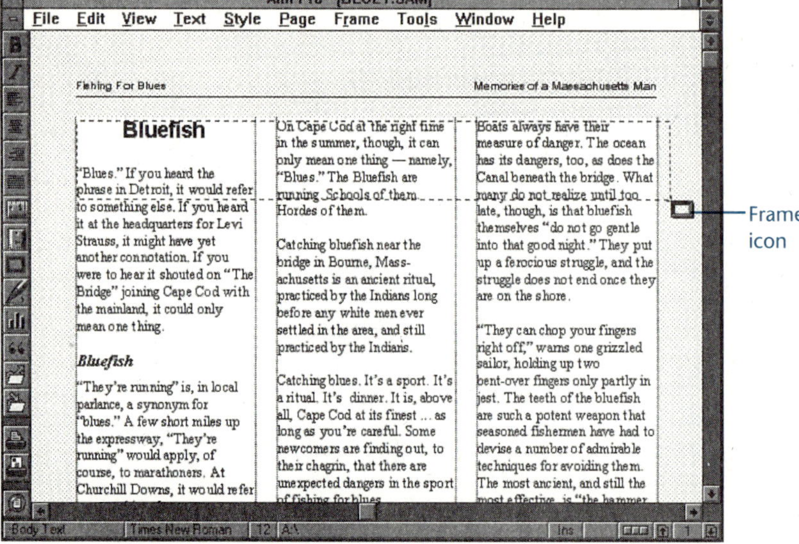

Fig. 15.3 The dashed outline illustrates the frame being created.

Tip
If the frame doesn't look right, press Del to delete the selected frame, and then start again.

The frame appears as a rectangle with eight small black boxes around its boundaries—one box at each corner and one at the midpoint of each side of the frame (see fig. 15.4). These boxes are called *handles*; the handles indicate that the frame is *selected*.

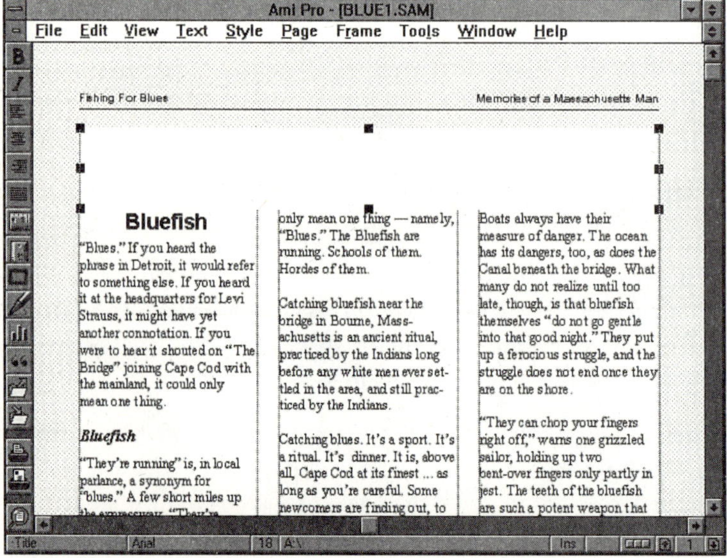

Fig. 15.4 A selected frame with handles.

Note

Ami Pro uses default settings for frame characteristics; if these defaults have been changed in the Modify Frame Layout dialog box, your frame may not resemble the one in figure 15.4. For now, use the frame you created. In the following section, you change the default frame.

Creating an Automatic Frame

When you created the frame in the preceding section, you drew the frame on-screen with the mouse or keyboard. That method is a quick and easy way to create frames, but Ami Pro provides another approach. If you know the precise measurements for the height and width of the frame, you can create a frame in your document by specifying the dimensions and placement of the frame. In this section, you create a sample frame two inches wide by two inches tall in the sample document.

Using this method, you can create the frame with the mouse or the keyboard. To create an automatic frame, follow these steps:

1. Choose F**r**ame **C**reate Frame. The Create Frame dialog box appears.

2. Choose **W**idth and specify the desired width for the frame in the **W**idth text box. If you used the Tab key to move to the **W**idth text box, the default width is highlighted; just type the new width (this action deletes the old width). If you prefer, click the arrow buttons next to the text box to move the dimensions up or down by .05 with each click. For this example, type **2**. You don't need to type the decimal point or zeros.

3. The default measurement is in inches; to use points, picas, or centimeters, click the unit of measure button until it displays the measurement standard you want to use. With the keyboard, press Tab to select the unit of measure button; then press the space bar to change the measurement. For this example, if the unit of measure button shows in., you can skip this step.

4. Choose **H**eight and specify the desired height for the frame in the **H**eight text box. For this example, type **2**.

5. Choose **D**own from Top to change the position of the frame from the top of the page; specify the measurement you want Ami Pro to use. For this example, type **1.90** in the **D**own from Top text box.

6. Choose **In** from Left to change the position of the frame respective to the left edge of the page; specify the measurement you want Ami Pro to use. For this example, type **3.22** in the **In** from Left text box.

   At this point, the Create Frame dialog box should resemble figure 15.5.

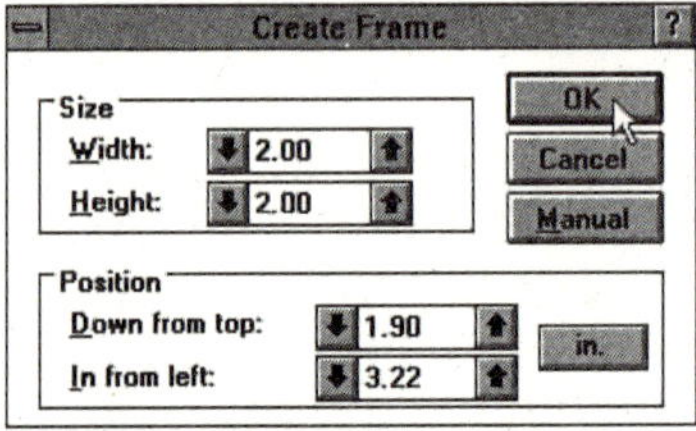

Fig. 15.5
The Create Frame dialog box with the measurements for the sample frame.

7. Choose OK or press Enter. Ami Pro returns to the document and displays the frame (see fig. 15.6).

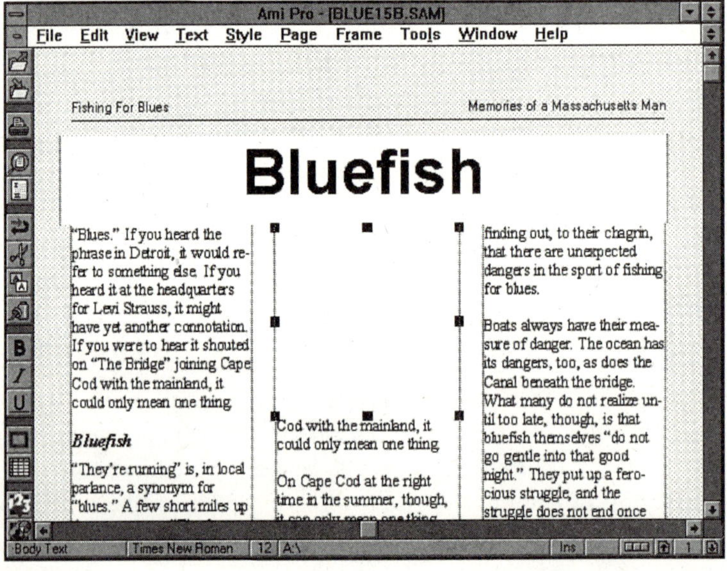

Fig. 15.6
The automatic frame.

The frame you create with this procedure appears only on the current page, in the center column, and stays at this position on the page even if you edit the text around the frame. Ami Pro's default positioning of the frame is **W**here Placed. You can change this setting in the Placement section of the default Modify Frame Layout dialog box. You also have other choices such as **F**low With Text, Keep **W**ith Paragraph Above, and so on (see Chapter 16, "Using Frames," for details).

Tip
Although the Go To method of selecting a frame is time-consuming, mouse users may find this method beneficial if a frame is hard to click because other objects are too close to it.

The default frame has no lines or shadows (as shown in the figure), but you can identify the frame from the black handles on each corner and side of the frame. Your frame may look different if you have changed the defaults.

The next section describes some ways that you can modify a frame—by changing the way that text wraps around the frame and by modifying the line style.

Wrapping Text around the Frame

Ami Pro offers many options for changing an existing frame: you can specify the margins, placement, size, and so on. Each of these options is described in detail in Chapter 16, "Using Frames." For this quick start, you modify only how the text of a document wraps around a frame.

The frame you created in the last section still is selected (handles appear on the corners and sides). If the frame you want to modify isn't currently selected, click the frame to select it. Alternatively, choose **E**dit **G**o To. When the Go To dialog box appears; choose **N**ext Item and specify Frame in the list box. Then choose Go To ^H. Ami Pro returns to the document; the frame is selected.

To modify the frame layout, follow these steps:

1. Choose Fr**a**me **M**odify Frame Layout. The Modify Frame Layout dialog box appears (see fig. 15.7).

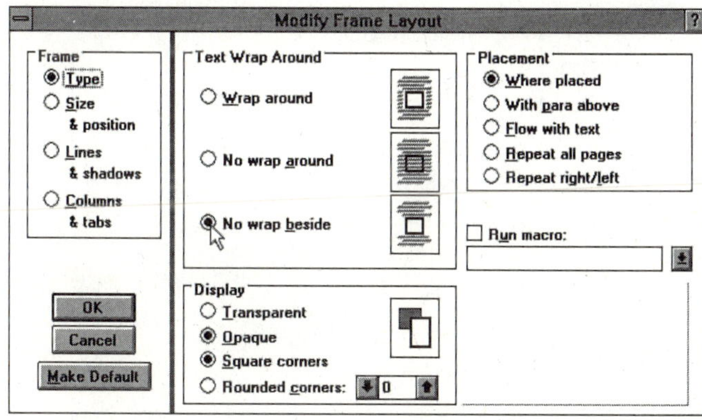

Fig. 15.7
The Modify Frame Layout dialog box.

Mouse users can position the mouse pointer over the frame and press the right mouse button to access the Modify Frame Layout dialog box.

At the left side of the Modify Frame Layout dialog box is a Frame section, offering categories of options for the selected frame. When you choose a Frame option, additional options appear to the right in the dialog box. In figure 15.7, the **T**ype options are shown in the dialog box. (**T**ype is the default Frame setting.) Notice the example box in the lower right corner of the dialog box; it shows an example frame with the options you specify. (Chapter 16, "Using Frames," discusses each option in the Modify Frame Layout dialog box.)

2. In the Text Wrap Around section of the dialog box, a sample page beside each option graphically displays the use of that option. Choose the wrapping option you prefer. For this example, choose No Wrap **B**eside.

3. In the Display section, indicate the display options you want to apply to the frame. For this example, choose **S**quare Corners and **O**paque.

4. In the Frame box, choose **L**ines & Shadows. The **L**ines and Shadows options appear in the dialog box, as shown in figure 15.8.

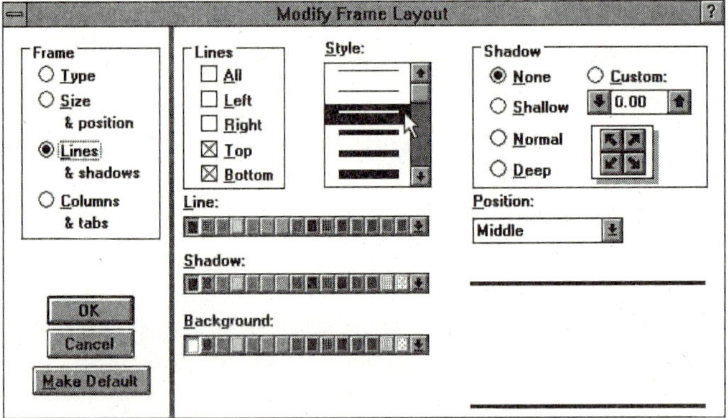

Fig. 15.8
The Modify Frame Layout dialog box with **L**ines & Shadows options.

5. In the Lines box, indicate where you want frame lines to show. For this example, choose **T**op and **B**ottom.

6. In the **S**tyle list box, specify the line style you want to use. For this example, choose the third line pattern from the top.

7. In the Shadow section, choose the appropriate options to create a drop shadow for the frame. For this example, select **N**one.

8. If you want to use the same settings each time you create a frame, choose **M**ake Default. These default settings remain in effect until you specify new settings and choose **M**ake Default again. For this example, don't choose **M**ake Default.

9. Choose OK or press Enter. The dialog box disappears, and Ami Pro returns to the document (see fig. 15.9).

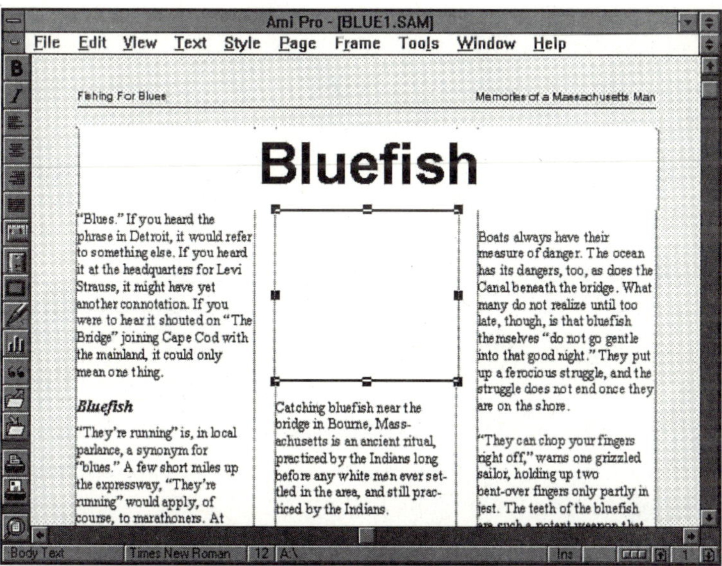

Fig. 15.9
The document with the formatted frame.

Note

Use the **M**ake Default option when you draw the first frame of any new document that will contain many frames. A four-page newsletter like the sample document may use eight or ten frames (for callouts, graphics, advertising, and so on). Most frames within the same document should be consistent in line type, placement, and width. By creating and modifying a frame, and then saving it as a default, you guarantee that subsequent frames created in the newsletter will be consistent.

You can draw the frame past the margins of the page to prevent text from wrapping around a frame; however, choosing the No Wrap **B**eside option is faster, easier, and guarantees that no text will appear along the sides of your frame.

The frame you created in this section can hold a graphic or text. The next section describes two ways to add text to a frame.

Working with Text in Frames

Entering and setting up text in a frame is similar to entering and setting up text on the page. You can structure margins, columns, tabs, and so on in the frame in much the same way as in the document. In this section, you use the example frames in the newsletter to add a heading, create a pull-out quote, and create a table of contents. You set margins, add a background screen, and work with frame tabs.

For more Ami Pro frame design possibilities, see Chapter 16, "Using Frames," and Chapter 19, "Desktop Publishing with Ami Pro."

Copying Text into a Frame

To add a heading to the manual frame created earlier in this chapter (refer to fig. 15.4), follow these steps:

1. Select the word *Bluefish* from the top of the first column of text in the newsletter; cut the text to the Windows Clipboard by choosing **E**dit Cu**t**. (See Chapter 3, "Editing Techniques," for more information on selecting, cutting, and pasting text.)

2. Position the cursor in the frame by double-clicking anywhere in the frame.

   With the keyboard, select the frame by choosing **E**dit **G**o To **N**ext Item, specifying Frame, and choosing Go To ^H. Ami Pro returns to the document, with the frame selected. Press Enter to activate the cursor within the frame.

3. Choose **E**dit **P**aste to copy the text from the Clipboard into the frame at the cursor position. The cursor normally appears in the upper left corner of the frame. Because the text in this case (*Bluefish*) was formatted as a title, however, the formatting was copied with the text—therefore, when pasted, the word *Bluefish* appears in the top center of the frame (see fig. 15.10).

To format the text in the heading frame, select the text (*Bluefish*) and change the typeface to 48-point Helvetica. Then boldface and center the text. (See Chapter 4, "Formatting a Document," for complete details on character formatting.) Figure 15.11 shows the finished heading.

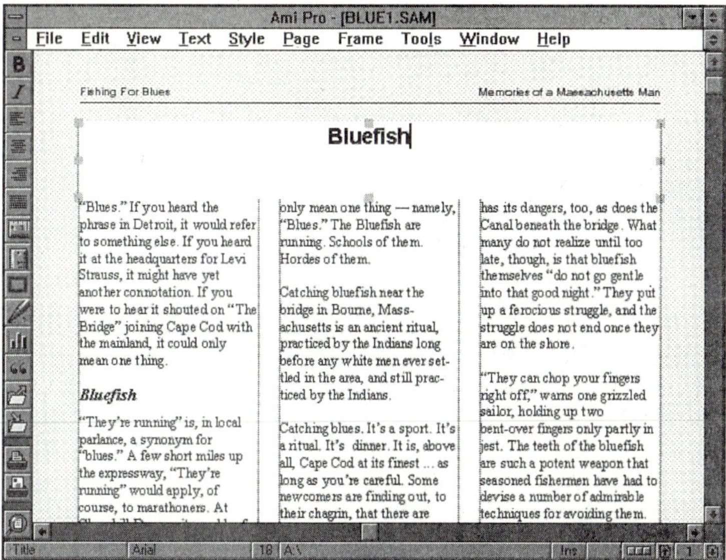

Fig. 15.10
The pasted text carries the previous formatting when cut or copied.

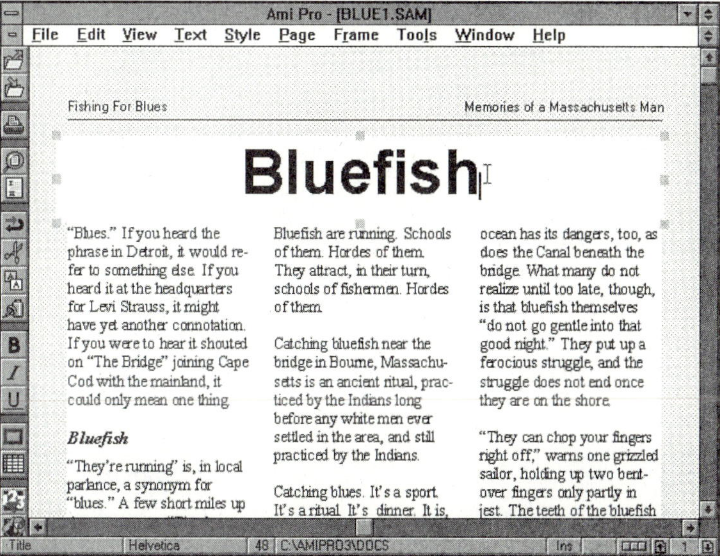

Fig. 15.11
The finished heading text in the frame.

Typing Text in a Frame

In this section, you create a simple pull-out quote by adding text to the 2-inch-square automatic frame you created and modified earlier (refer to fig. 15.6).

A *pull-out quote* attracts attention to an article or story by using an interesting phrase or sentence from the article or story. The pull-out quote usually is enclosed in a frame (see fig. 15.12); the frame can be boxed, bordered, or screened. The typeface used for the quote should be larger than the body text and boldfaced or italicized; the text can be centered or left-aligned. (Only use right-aligned pull-out quotes if everything in your page and text design supports that formatting. See Chapter 19, "Desktop Publishing with Ami Pro," for information about good design.)

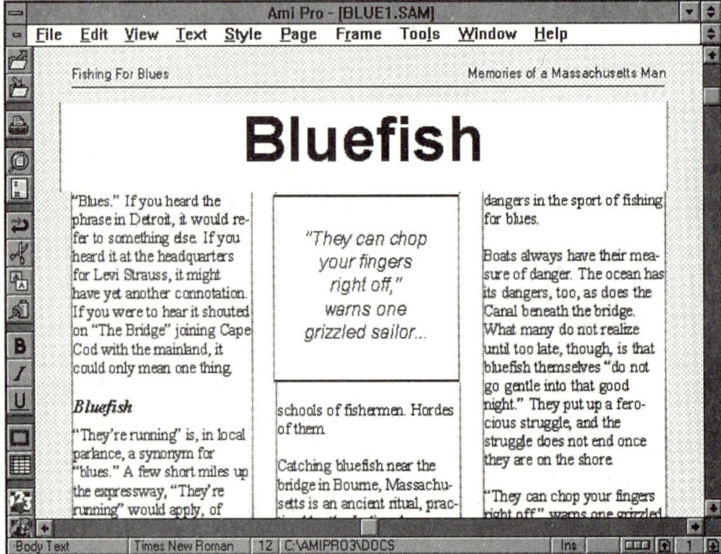

Fig. 15.12
The newsletter with a pull-out quote in the center column.

To add the pull-out quote to the frame, follow these steps:

1. Position the cursor in the frame (see the preceding section for details).
2. Press Enter.
3. Type the desired text, or copy and paste the text from the article or story. For this example, type the text shown in figure 15.12: **"They can chop your fingers right off," warns one grizzled sailor...**
4. To exit the frame, click outside the frame or press Esc.

To format the pull-out quote as shown in figure 15.12, select the text; then change the formatting to 14-point Helvetica, italicized and center-aligned. See Chapter 4, "Formatting a Document," for more information on character formatting.

Improving the Appearance of the Frame

In this section, you create a table of contents for the newsletter. Figure 15.13 shows the finished version of the screened frame with the text for the table of contents. With this example, you learn how to use columns, tabs, margins, and shading to improve the appearance of a frame and its text.

The lines bordering the top and bottom of the table of contents frame are consistent with other frames used in the sample newsletter. The screened background adds emphasis to the frame.

Tip

Notice that the background screen in the example is a light screen. Don't use heavy (dark) screens with text in a frame; the text may not be visible against the screen.

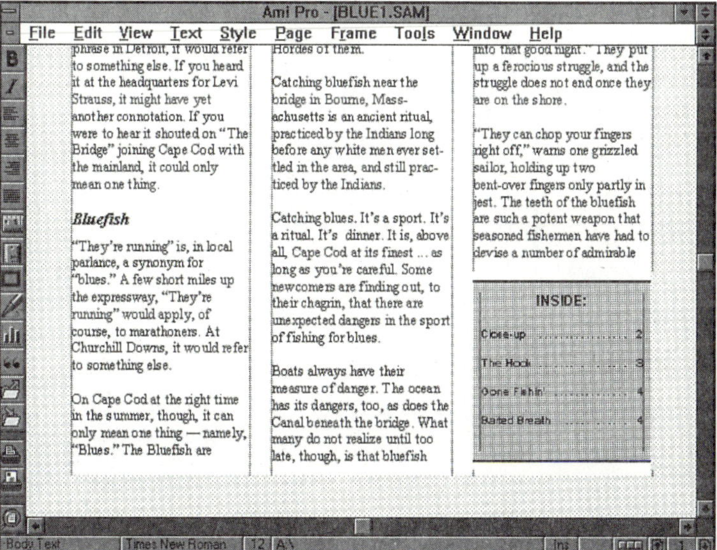

Fig. 15.13
The table of contents for the newsletter.

Formatting the Frame

To begin creating the table of contents, create a frame in the lower right corner of the page. You can draw the frame manually or automatically, using the techniques discussed earlier in this chapter. Then size, position, and screen the frame with the following steps:

1. Select the frame.

2. Choose F**r**ame **M**odify Frame Layout or press the right mouse button. The Modify Frame Layout dialog box appears.

3. In the Frame section, choose **T**ype (the default). The **T**ype options appear in the dialog box (refer to fig. 15.7).

4. In the Text Wrap Around section, choose the appropriate settings for text wrapping around the frame. For this example, choose No Wrap **B**eside. In the Display section, indicate how you want the frame to be displayed. For this example, choose **S**quare Corners and **O**paque.

   If you changed the default frame settings earlier in the chapter, you may not need to change these settings.

5. In the Frame section, choose **S**ize & Position. Figure 15.14 shows the Size & Position version of the Modify Frame Layout dialog box with changes made for the sample frame.

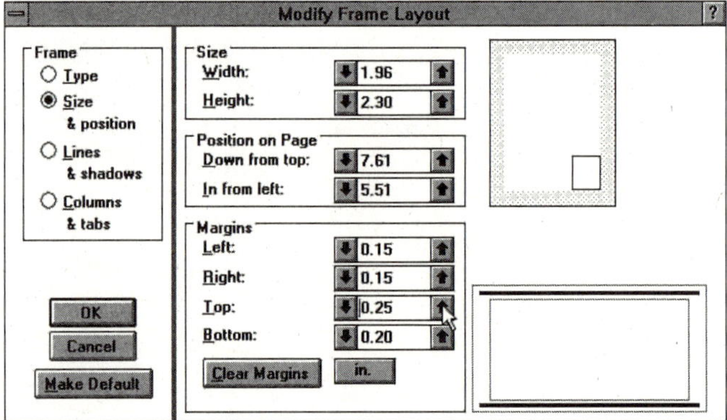

Fig. 15.14
The Modify Frame Layout dialog box with the **S**ize & Position options.

6. Change the Size and Position on Page options to show the desired amounts. If you don't know the exact position where you want the frame to appear, you can make some initial guesses and adjust the position later. For this example, use the amounts shown in figure 15.14 (**W**idth **1.96**, **H**eight **2.30**, **D**own from Top **7.61**, and **I**n from Left **5.51**).

   The example frame in the upper right corner of the dialog box shows the frame's placement on the page. The example frame in the lower right corner of the dialog box shows the frame formatting (the top and bottom border lines and the margins).

7. In the Margins section, specify the margin settings you want to use for the frame. If you place text in a frame with border lines, use at least a .15-inch margin to keep the text from butting up against the border lines.

For this example, set the **L**eft and **R**ight margins to **.15**; set the **T**op margin to **.25** and the **B**ottom to **.20**. The measurement is in inches; you can type the amount in the text boxes or use the arrow buttons to change the number in .05-inch increments.

8. In the Frame section, choose **L**ines & Shadows; the **L**ines & Shadows options appear in the dialog box.

9. In the Lines section, indicate where you want lines to appear in the frame. For this example, choose **T**op and **B**ottom.

10. In the **S**tyle list, specify the style for the lines. For the sample document, choose the third line pattern from the top.

11. In the Shadow section, specify the kind of drop shadow you want to use for the frame. Because the table of contents frame doesn't use a drop shadow, choose **N**one in this case.

12. In the **B**ackground color bar, click the down-arrow button to display a drop-down box of color and pattern options (see fig. 15.15). Some **L**ine, **S**hadow, and **B**ackground colors may not be suitable for a non-color printer, but each color bar includes gray scale choices appropriate for printing in black and white. (You may need to experiment with your printer to see which screen works best.)

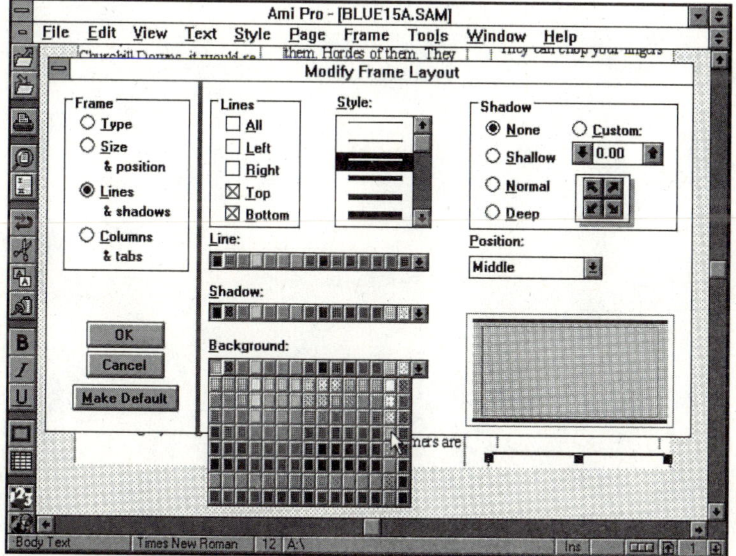

Fig. 15.15
The drop-down color box; the mouse pointer shows the background screen for the table of contents frame.

Select the desired color or pattern; for this example, choose the option in the second column from the right, fifth pattern from the top.

13. Choose OK or press Enter. Ami Pro returns to the document; the frame is complete.

Structuring the Text

To enter the text in the table of contents frame, begin by positioning the cursor in the frame (the cursor automatically appears in the upper left corner of the frame). Then type the text. Don't space between the title of each article and its page number; instead, type the text and press the keys enclosed in angle brackets (<>) as indicated in the following list:

INSIDE:<Enter>

Close-up<Tab><space bar>**2**<Enter>

The Hook<Tab><space bar>**3**<Enter>

Gone Fishin'<Tab><space bar>**4**<Enter>

Baited Breath<Tab><space bar>**4**<Enter>

Format the heading for the table of contents (the word *INSIDE*) as 12-point Helvetica, boldfaced, and center-aligned. Figure 15.16 shows the frame at this point.

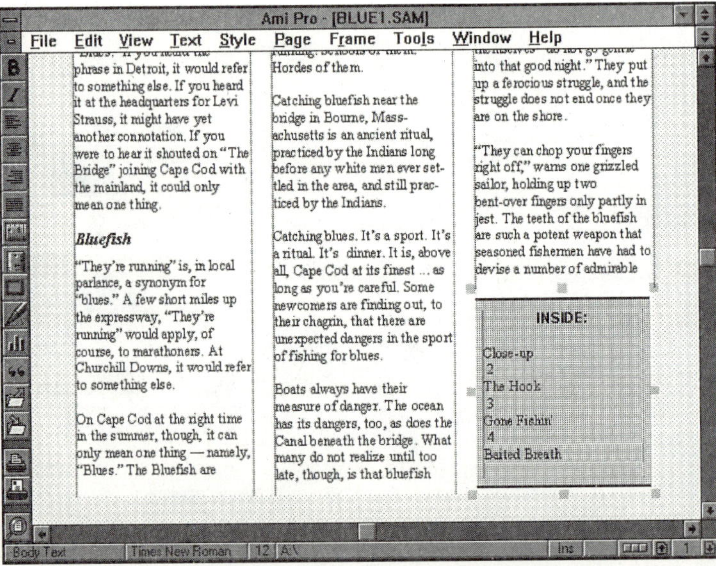

Fig. 15.16 The table of contents frame with the text entered.

Notice that the page numbers appear on the lines *following* the article names (except for the last number, which will reappear later). When you restructure the text with columns later in this section, the page numbers will be restored to the correct lines, and the last page number will be visible.

Format the remaining text in the frame as 10-point Helvetica. For information on character formatting, see Chapter 4, "Formatting a Document."

In this example, the table of contents uses a *dot leader* (a line of periods running from one column to the next) between the article name and its page number. When you typed the preceding text, you pressed the space bar to add a space between the dot leader (this setting is added shortly) and the page number. Without this space, the dot leader runs into the page number, causing a crowded and unprofessional look.

To format the tabs, including the dot leader tab, you use the Modify Frame Layout dialog box. To access the dialog box, choose F**r**ame **M**odify Frame Layout. Then choose **C**olumns & Tabs in the Frame section of the dialog box. The column and tab options appear in the right side of the dialog box (see fig. 15.17). Notice the tab ruler in the top section of the dialog box. Below the tab ruler is a series of buttons displaying symbols that represent the types of tabs you can select for the frame.

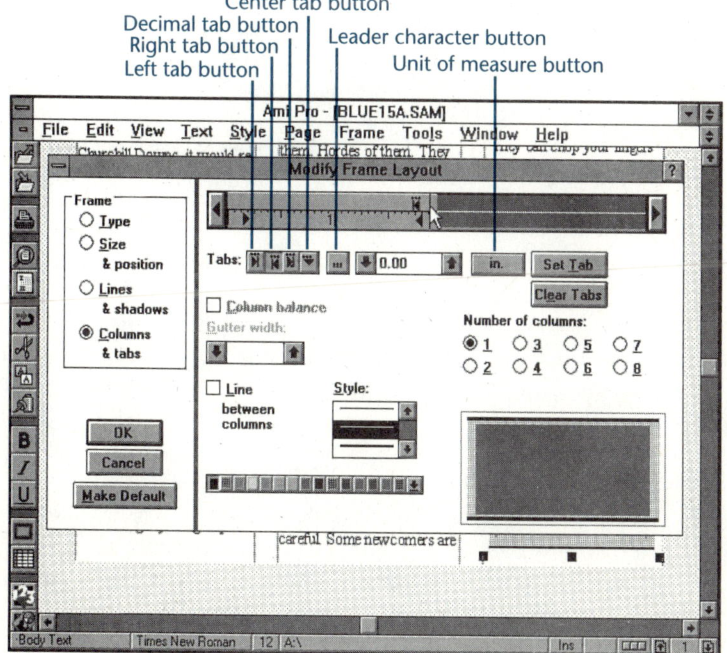

Fig. 15.17
The Modify Frame Layout dialog box with the **C**olumns & Tabs options selected.

Note

The tab ruler in the Modify Frame Layout dialog box is similar to the tab ruler in the Modify Page Layout dialog box; however, the frame ruler applies only to the text in the frame.

Before you position a tab, you must specify the type of tab you want to insert. For a table of contents, the page numbers should be right-aligned; for this example, you use a right tab with a dot leader. (For a detailed discussion of tabs, see Chapter 5, "Working with Page Layout.")

The tab buttons below the tab ruler specify the types of tabs you can use. The buttons represent (reading left to right) a left tab, a right tab, a decimal tab, and a center tab. The fifth button is the Leader Character button. You click the Leader Character button to see the leader characters (none, dots, dashes, or underlines) that you can combine with the tab. (With the keyboard, press Tab until the cursor is on the Leader Character button, and then press the left- or right-arrow key to change the leader characters.)

To set up tabs in the frame, follow these steps:

1. Select the frame.

2. Choose F**r**ame **M**odify Frame Layout to display the Modify Frame Layout dialog box.

3. In the Frame section, choose **C**olumns & Tabs. The column and tab options appear.

4. Click the Leader Character button until the leader character you want appears on the tab buttons. In this case, use the dot leader (...).

5. Choose the type of tab you want. For this example, click the right tab button.

6. To specify where you want Ami Pro to insert the tab, move the mouse pointer to the desired location (placing the pointer on the upper half of the tab ruler) and click.

   To set tabs with the keyboard, press Tab to move the cursor to the ruler. Use the arrow keys to move the black line to the desired position; then press the space bar to set the tab in the ruler. Alternatively, you can specify a precise tab location after choosing the tab style by typing the position for the tab in the tab bar text box (next to the Leader Character button) and then choosing **S**et Tab.

For this example, place a tab at about two inches from the left margin. A symbol appears at the specified location on the tab ruler, representing the type of tab you chose.

7. Repeat step 6 for each tab you want to set. You can set up to 22 tabs in the ruler, in any combination you want.

8. If you don't want to measure in inches, click the unit of measure button (the button reads `in.` in fig. 15.17). You can choose from picas, points, centimeters, and inches (the default).

9. When the tabs are correct, choose OK or press Enter.

To complete the setup, select the last page number in the frame (4) and format it to match the other text. Then position the cursor after each page number and press Enter to add extra space between the lines of type. The tab is set for the last number (4); however, if you changed the typeface or type size of the other text in the frame, you must apply that formatting to the last number as well.

Your table of contents frame now should resemble the one in figure 15.18. The vertical lines you see within the box are the nonprinting margin guides. Notice that they keep the text from running to the edge of the frame.

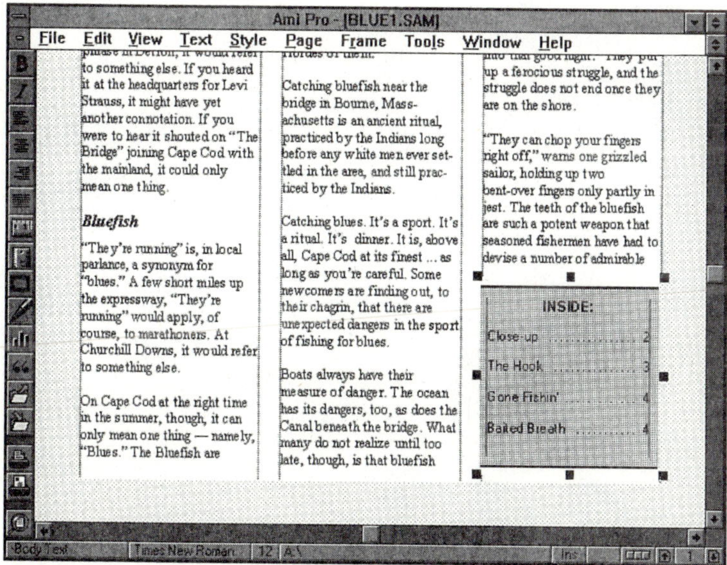

Fig. 15.18
The formatted text in the frame.

Chapter 16

Using Frames

Frames often are an "ah ha" experience—a breakthrough discovery for people who use character-based word processing programs. Frames provide a logical way to insert special text or graphics into a document and help to organize text on the page. Frames also contribute to the appearance of your document; the design possibilities with frames are almost endless. Frames have a number of uses, including holding headers, footers, mastheads, tables of contents, forms, stories, and articles. Frames can display clip art, scanned halftones, images from drawing programs, tables, and spreadsheets. The list of potential uses for Ami Pro frames goes on and on.

In character-based word processing, you insert graphics or special text by placing a code in the document and then create the graphics or text on a separate screen. Only when you print or preview the document can you see how the insert looks.

When you create an Ami Pro frame, you see how the insert looks as you create it. The frame's flexibility is a big bonus; text wraps around the frame, and Ami Pro adjusts the text if you move the frame. You even can create frames within frames. Ami Pro's frame feature is integral to successful page layout and design.

In this chapter, you learn how to create frames. (Creating the frame can be as simple as clicking-and-dragging with the mouse.) You learn how to manipulate a frame by selecting it, sizing it, moving it, or deleting it. You also learn how to enter text or graphic images into the frame, modify the layout of the frame on the page, and use columns and tabs in the frame.

This chapter also discusses special frame capabilities such as grouping frames, using layered frames, and using repeating frames. As you discover in this chapter, Ami Pro's creators have made these advanced capabilities accessible through simple selections from a dialog box and with the use of SmartIcons.

Creating a Frame

When creating or editing a frame, you must use layout mode rather than draft or outline mode. To determine which mode you are using, choose **V**iew. A check mark appears next to the current mode. To switch to layout mode, choose **L**ayout Mode.

You can create a frame in one of two ways: by using the mouse or keyboard to manually draw the frame, or by specifying the dimensions and position in the Create Frame dialog box and letting Ami Pro draw the frame automatically. In this chapter, you learn both methods.

Creating an Automatic Frame

Creating an automatic frame in Ami Pro is useful in two particular circumstances: when the frame must be an exact size (such as when creating a border for a sized photograph), and when the frame must be placed in a specific location on the page (as when adding a postal permit or address to a business reply card). To create an automatic frame, you use the F**r**ame menu's **C**reate Frame command, shown in figure 16.1.

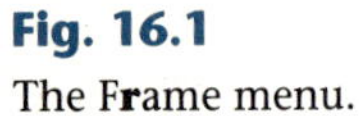

Fig. 16.1
The F**r**ame menu.

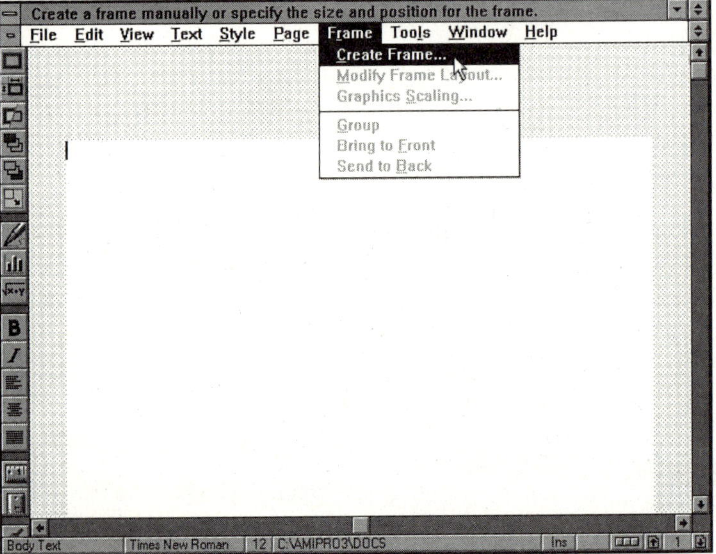

After you choose the **C**reate Frame command, the Create Frame dialog box appears, as shown in figure 16.2. The Size and Position sections of the dialog box show the options for specifying the dimensions of your frame and for placing the frame on the page.

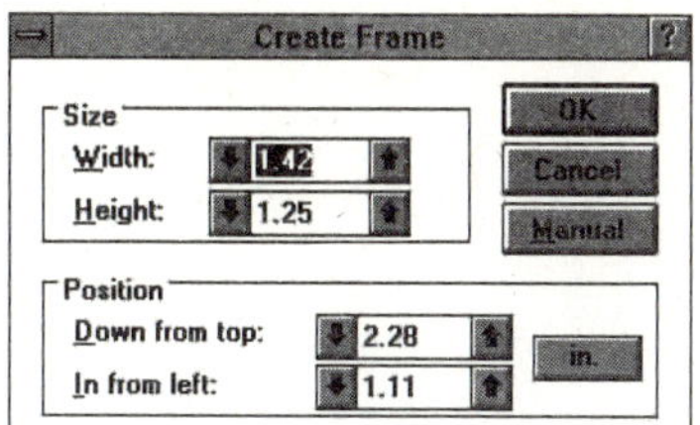

Fig. 16.2
The Create Frame dialog box.

> **Note**
>
> The initial sizes you see in the Create Frame dialog box are the sizes you used for the last frame created.

If you know the exact dimensions for the frame, and you know where you want to place the frame on the page, specify those settings. You specify dimensions, for example, if you are following established requirements for a newsletter or other document.

In the Size section, you specify the width and height of the frame. You can type the desired measurements in the **W**idth and **H**eight text boxes, or you can click the up- and down-arrow buttons to increase or decrease the width and height dimensions shown in the text boxes. When you use inches, the amount changes by .05 inches each time you click the button.

In the Position section, you specify the frame's position on the page. The measurements indicate the placement of the upper left corner of the frame. Ami Pro measures down from the top of the page and in from the left edge of the page to place the upper left corner of the frame. You can type the desired measurements in the **D**own From Top and **I**n From Left text boxes, or you can click the arrow buttons to specify the dimensions in the text boxes.

> **Note**
>
> In the next section, "Creating a Frame with the Mouse or Keyboard," you learn the freedom and ease a mouse brings to the process of creating frames. Note, however, that you sometimes can create frames with greater precision by using the automatic method.

If you don't want to measure the frame in inches (the default unit of measure), click the unit of measure button in the lower right corner of the dialog box (labeled `in.` in the figure). The button label changes to `cm.` (centimeters) and the numbers for the Size and Position options change to reflect measurements in centimeters.

If you click the unit of measure button again, you change the unit to `picas`. With additional clicks, you can change the unit to points `(pt.)` and then back to inches.

To change the units with the keyboard, press the Tab key to select the unit of measure button. Then press the space bar to change the units.

Note

You must use the same measurement (inches, centimeters, and so on) for width, height, and placement. You cannot use points to measure width and height, for example, and use inches to measure the position of the frame.

To create an automatic frame with specified dimensions and placement, follow these steps:

1. Choose F**r**ame **C**reate Frame. The Create Frame dialog box appears (refer to fig. 16.2).
2. Choose **W**idth and specify the desired width for the frame. For this example, specify **4.35** inches.
3. Choose **H**eight and specify the desired height for the frame. For this example, specify **1.95** inches.
4. Specify the desired placement for the frame in the **D**own From Top and **I**n From Left text boxes. For this example, specify **1.64** inches down from the top and **1.97** inches in from the left.
5. Choose OK or press Enter. Ami Pro displays the frame in the document.

Figure 16.3 shows a sample frame specified with exact dimensions.

You can use the mouse or keyboard for a faster (if somewhat less exact) method of sizing and placing the frame, as described in the following section.

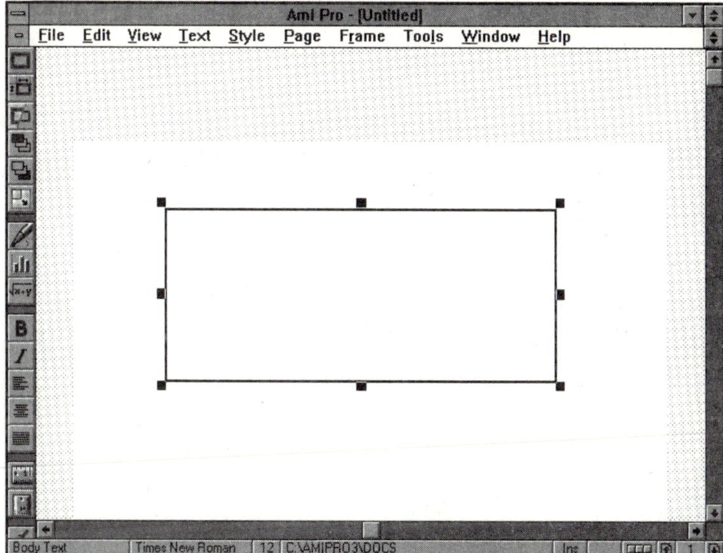

Fig. 16.3
A sample frame using specified dimensions.

Creating a Frame with the Mouse or Keyboard

As a general practice, you should create frames with the mouse. The mouse makes working with frames quick and easy; you just click-and-drag to create a frame of the appropriate size and in the correct location. You create a "manual" frame with the mouse by using one of two methods: using the Frame menu, and using SmartIcons. A third method uses the keyboard instead of the mouse. This section describes all three techniques.

Using the Frame Menu To Create a Frame

To create a frame with the mouse and the Frame menu, follow these steps:

1. Choose Frame Create Frame to display the Create Frame dialog box.
2. Choose Manual.
3. Click OK. Ami Pro returns to the document; the mouse pointer changes to the frame icon—a small picture frame.
4. Position the frame icon where you want the upper-left corner of the finished frame to appear.
5. Hold down the left mouse button and drag the frame icon to the location where you want the opposite corner of the frame to appear. A box bordered by a dashed line appears on-screen, showing the borders of the frame as you draw (see fig. 16.4).

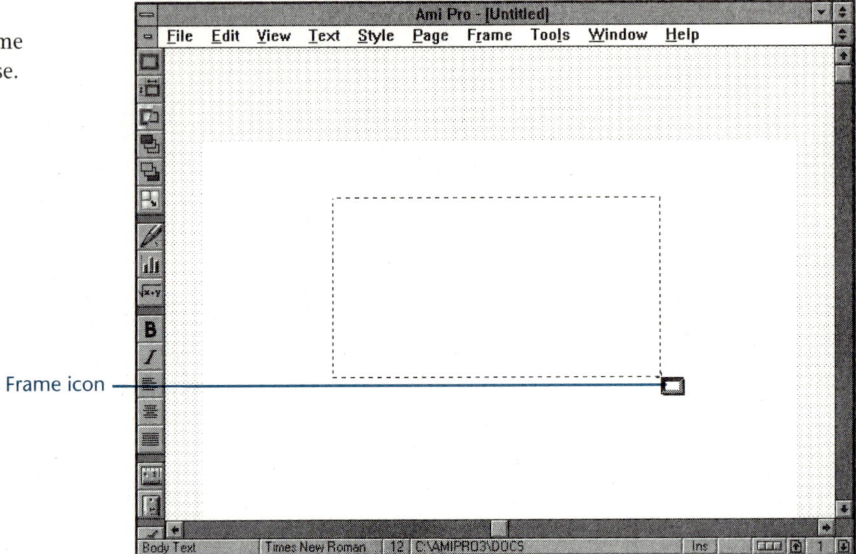

Fig. 16.4
Creating a frame with the mouse.

6. Release the mouse button. A box appears with eight small black boxes (*handles*) along its edges (see fig. 16.5). The handles indicate that the frame is *selected.*

You also can use the keyboard to create a frame manually. Follow these steps:

1. Choose F**r**ame **C**reate Frame.

2. Press the Tab key to select **M**anual (or press Alt+M). The pointer appears as a frame icon.

3. Press and hold the space bar while pressing the right-arrow key. The frame extends further toward the right side of the page with each press of the key. When the frame is as wide as you want it, release the right-arrow key, but continue to hold the space bar. Then press the down-arrow key with the space bar until the frame is as tall as you want it (with each keypress, the frame grows one line taller). For this example, make the frame about one inch tall. Release the keys; the frame displays the selection handles.

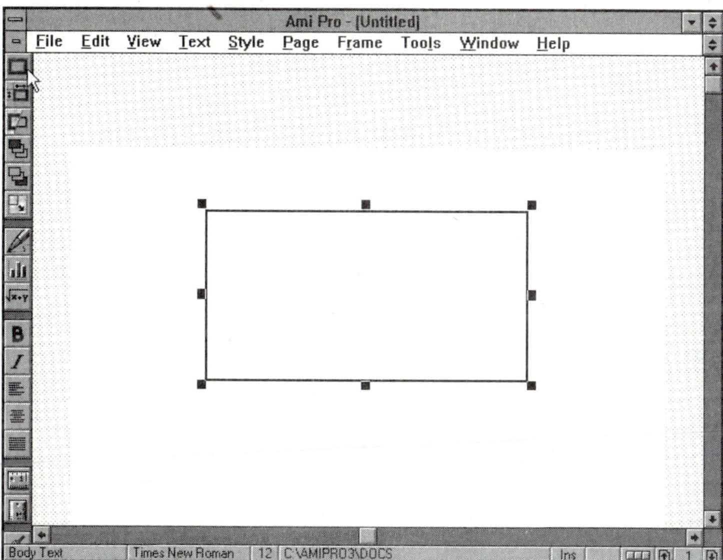

Fig. 16.5
The completed frame.

Note

To deselect a frame, click the mouse outside the frame or press Esc. The insertion point returns to the document text, and the handles disappear from the frame.

Using SmartIcons To Create a Frame

Another fast method of creating a frame in Ami Pro is with the Add a Frame SmartIcon (for mouse users only). Figure 16.6 shows the frame-related SmartIcons. By clicking the mouse on the Add a Frame SmartIcon, you bypass steps 1 through 3 in the preceding set of steps. The mouse cursor immediately changes to the frame icon, and you can draw your frame. (For information about customizing SmartIcons, see Chapter 8, "Changing Your Setup.")

Another SmartIcon displayed in figure 16.6 adds a frame by using previous settings. Use this SmartIcon to revert to the settings you used last in the Create Frame dialog box. If you need several frames of the same size, for example, you can simply click this SmartIcon for each frame; identical frames appear automatically. (You can copy the frame, but using the SmartIcon is faster.) This SmartIcon also is useful when you need a frame of the same size and in the same location on several different pages; just go to the next page and click the SmartIcon. You learn uses for the other frame SmartIcons later in this chapter.

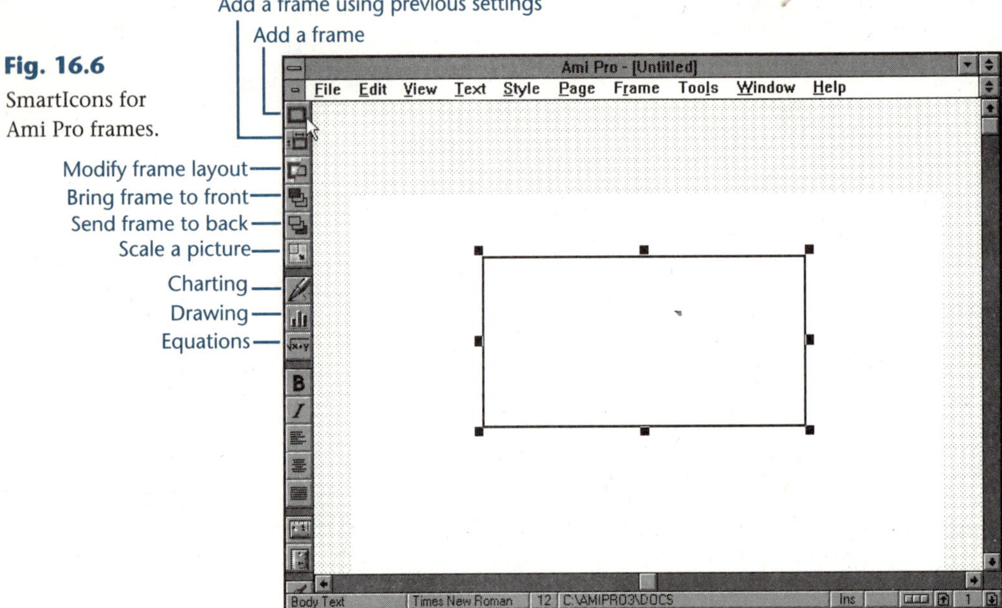

Fig. 16.6
SmartIcons for Ami Pro frames.

Note

The icons for scaling pictures, drawing, charting, and equations access functions that Ami Pro performs in conjunction with the frame feature. You can customize your SmartIcon palette to include all of these SmartIcons—or any combination of SmartIcons that you regularly use—in sets of SmartIcons for specific features. See Chapter 8, "Changing Your Setup," for details on customizing SmartIcons.

You can move, resize, delete, or manipulate the frame in various ways, as described in the next section.

Manipulating Frames

After placing the frame in your document, you may want to change the frame's size and location. You don't have to learn special editing commands to work with frames. In this section, you learn the basics of manipulating a frame.

Selecting and Deselecting the Frame

You must select a frame before you can move, resize, copy, or delete it. To select the frame, move the mouse pointer within the borders of the frame. (The mouse pointer changes to an arrow.) Click the mouse; handles appear around the frame. To deselect the frame, move the mouse pointer outside the frame and click. The handles disappear, indicating that the frame no longer is selected.

With the keyboard, you can select a frame by using the Go To feature. Begin on the page containing the frame you intend to select; then follow these steps:

1. Choose **E**dit **G**o To or press Ctrl+G. The Go To dialog box appears, as shown in figure 16.7.

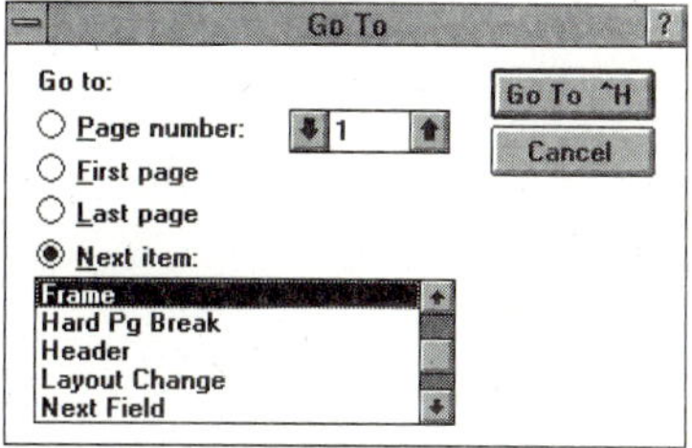

Fig. 16.7
Selecting a frame with the Go To dialog box.

2. Choose **N**ext Item.

3. Select `Frame`.

4. Choose Go to ^H. Ami Pro selects the next frame on the current page.

Tip
Ctrl+H (abbreviated ^H) is the shortcut for Go To Next Item. Holding Ctrl and pressing H takes you to the next occurrence of the item you went to last. Because ^H cycles through all the frames on a page, using ^H is especially helpful when you stack frames.

Sizing the Frame

You can change the size of a frame by increasing or decreasing its width or height. To change a frame's size, follow these steps:

1. Select the frame.

2. Move the mouse pointer over one of the handles. (With the keyboard, use the arrow keys to move the pointer to a handle; then press and hold the space bar to select the handle. The pointer changes to an arrow.)

   Use a corner handle to change both the width and height of the frame. Use a handle in the middle of one side of the frame to change just the height or width.

3. Hold down the mouse button or space bar and drag the handle out to increase the size, or in to decrease the size (with the keyboard, use the arrow keys). Notice that the handles disappear, and the dashed box appears to show the borders of the resized frame as you draw (see fig. 16.8).

4. Release the mouse button or space bar. The borders of the frame and the handles reappear.

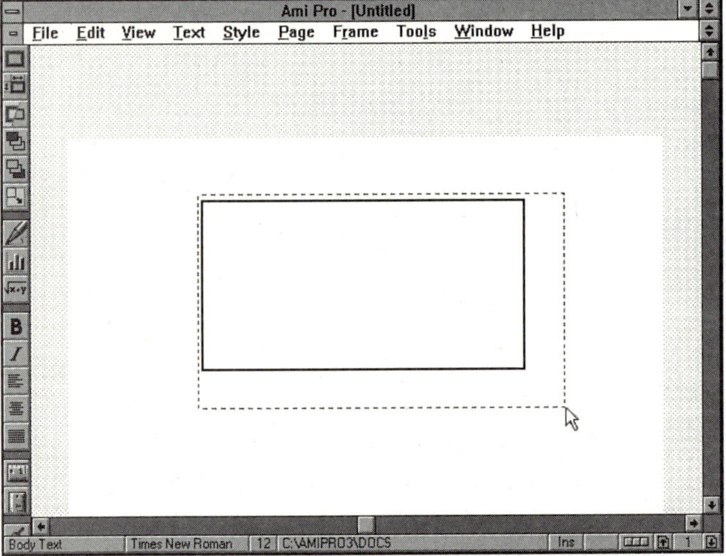

Fig. 16.8
The dashed box shows the borders of the frame as you resize.

You also can resize the frame by using the Modify Frame Layout dialog box. For details, see the "Modifying the Appearance of Frames" section of this chapter.

Note

If a frame is set in text (for example, to hold a picture in a newsletter), resizing the frame may affect the flow of the text. If you enlarge a frame on a specified page, for example, Ami Pro may wrap some of the text to the next page. See the section "Wrapping Text Around a Frame" later in this chapter for details on how to make text and frames flow together.

Copying the Frame

You may want to insert a copy of an existing frame, either on the same page as the original or on another page. You copy a frame in much the same manner as you copy text in any Windows word processing program. Follow these steps to copy a frame:

1. Select the frame.
2. Choose **E**dit **C**opy.
3. Choose **E**dit **P**aste.

Tip
The keyboard shortcut for **E**dit **C**opy is Ctrl+C; the keyboard shortcut for **E**dit **P**aste is Ctrl+V.

If you paste the copy on the same page as the original frame, the copy appears slightly offset from the position of the original (see fig. 16.9). The copy remains selected. You can use the mouse to move the frame to another position, as described in the next section.

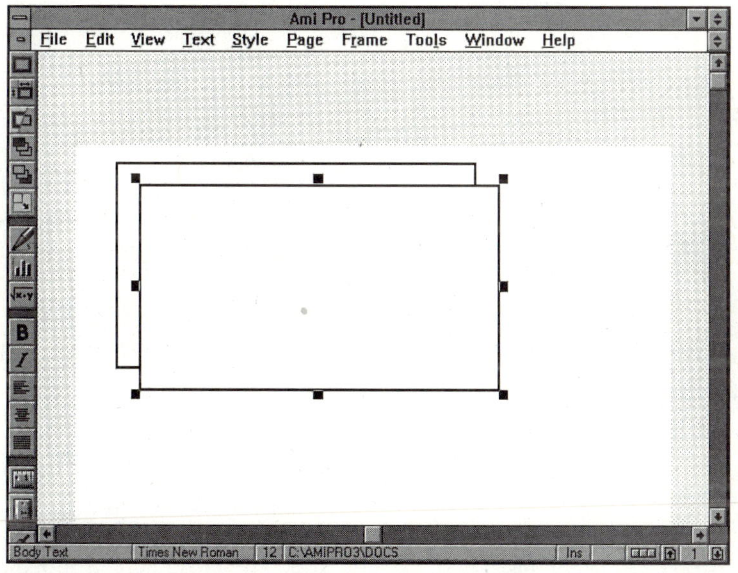

Fig. 16.9
The original and copied frames; the handles appear on the copied frame.

Moving the Frame

Moving a frame is a simple operation with the mouse or the keyboard. To move a frame with the mouse, follow these steps:

1. Select the frame.
2. Move the mouse or I-beam pointer near the center of the frame (not on the handles).

3. Holding down the mouse button or pressing the space bar and arrow keys, drag the frame to the appropriate position on the page. As you drag, a dashed representation of the outline of the frame indicates the new position (see fig. 16.10).

4. Release the mouse button or space bar. The frame moves to the new position and remains selected.

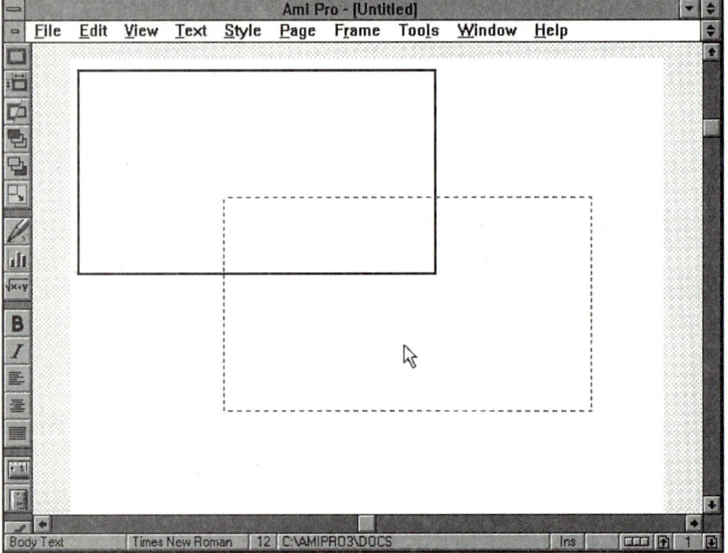

Fig. 16.10
The outline illustrates the new position of the moving frame.

Tip
You can use **E**dit Cu**t** and **E**dit **P**aste to move the frame to another page or to another document. When you use Cu**t** and **P**aste, the copied frame appears in the same position on the new page as on the original page.

You can control the exact placement of a frame you have created by using the Modify Frame Layout dialog box. For details, see the "Modifying the Appearance of Frames" section of this chapter.

Grouping Frames

You may have occasion to work with multiple frames in Ami Pro. Grouping the frames makes these tasks much easier. You can manipulate grouped frames together, maintaining their position and proportion in relationship to one another. You can move grouped frames simultaneously, for example, or cut and paste them to another page or another document.

Suppose that you have two frames on the page and want to copy them. Follow these steps to select a group of frames so that you can manipulate them together:

1. Select one of the frames. The frame's handles appear.

2. Hold down the Shift key and move the mouse until an arrow appears over the second frame, or press Ctrl and the arrow keys to move the pointer to the second frame.

3. Click the mouse on the second frame, or press Ctrl+Shift+space bar to select the second frame. The handles appear around the second frame (see fig. 16.11).

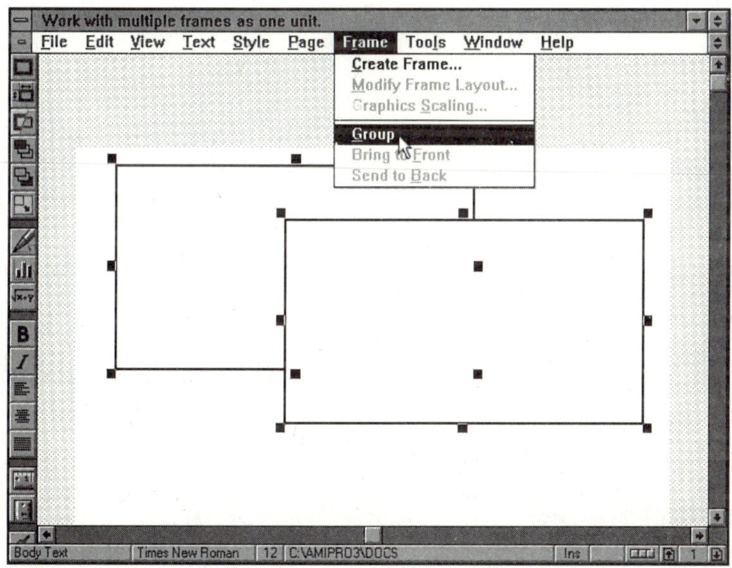

Fig. 16.11
Select multiple frames by holding the Shift key and clicking with the mouse.

4. To select additional frames, repeat steps 2 and 3 until you have selected all frames that you want to group.

5. Choose F**r**ame **G**roup.

6. To copy the frames, select **E**dit **C**opy and then **E**dit **P**aste. The frames appear offset slightly from the original frames (see fig. 16.12).

To move the group of frames, follow these steps:

1. Place the mouse pointer over one of the frames or, with frames selected, press the arrow keys to move the pointer inside one frame.

2. Hold down the mouse button or press the space bar plus the arrow keys, and drag the frames to the target location. Dashed boxes appear, representing the outlines of the frames.

3. After you have positioned the frames, release the mouse button or space bar.

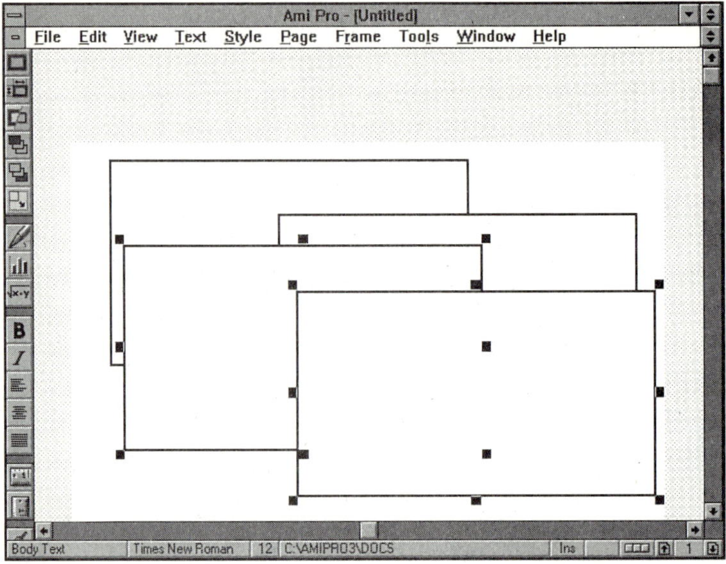

Fig. 16.12
Two frames are copied at the same time.

If you used the keyboard, the frames remain selected. To free the group of frames from each other, choose F**r**ame **G**roup again to remove the check mark next to the **G**roup option on the F**r**ame menu.

Layering Frames

In Ami Pro, you can use text or a graphic image in a frame. You cannot use both, however, in the same frame. You can overcome this limitation by *layering* one or more frames over another frame in the document. Layering frames is useful for creating a graphic logo using several boxes, for example, or for combining text and a drawing. Figures 16.13 and 16.14 show two layered frames used to create a newsletter nameplate; the newsletter name is contained in one frame (fig. 16.13) and the map graphic is in a different frame (fig. 16.14). You can combine text with an Ami Pro drawing, but not with a graphic image imported from another program.

In this example, both frames are opaque. If you want text or graphics in the first (bottom layer) frame to show through the second (top layer) frame, the second frame must be transparent.

Layering frames essentially involves moving one frame over another, and isn't a difficult procedure. You follow the same basic steps used to move a selected single frame; click the frame and drag it into position, or hold down the space bar while pressing the arrow keys.

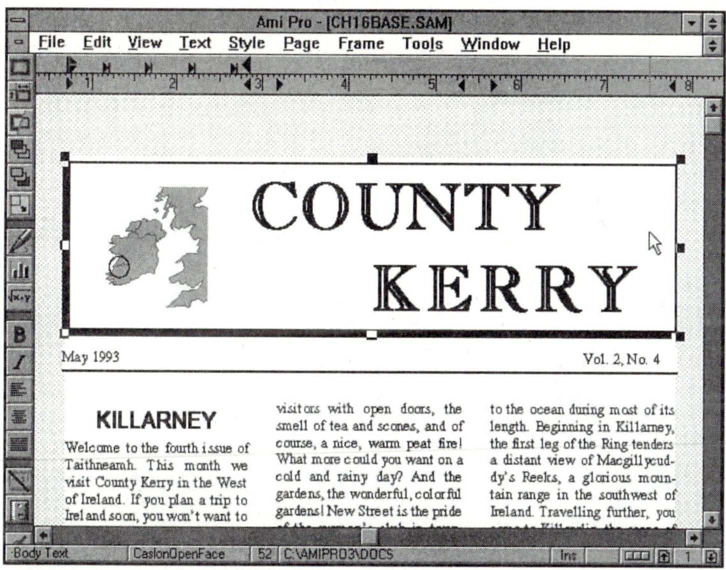

Fig. 16.13
A frame containing the newsletter name.

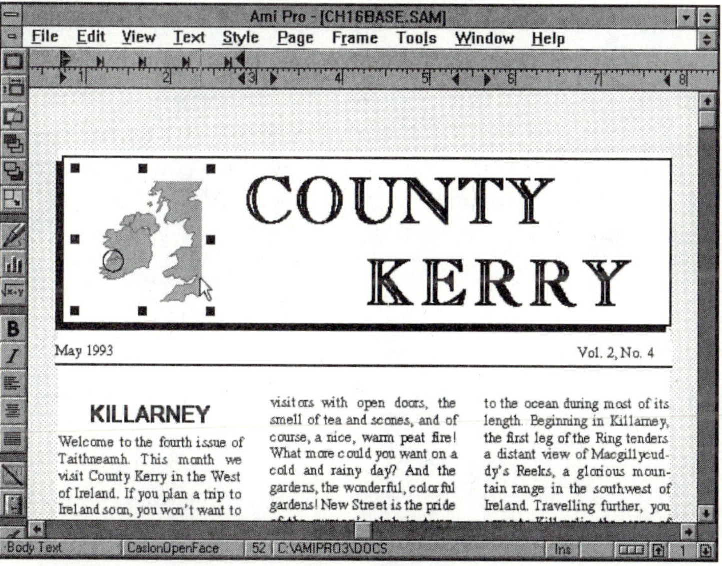

Fig. 16.14
A second frame contains the map graphic.

Note

If you have trouble selecting a layered frame (one that is completely covered by another), hold the Ctrl key while clicking the frame. Each time you click the mouse, the handles of a different frame in the layer appear. Continue clicking until the frame you want is selected.

You may want to rearrange the order of layered frames, or use a different frame in the foreground. To change the order of layered frames, follow these steps:

1. Select the frame you want to move.
2. Choose F**r**ame.
3. Choose Bring to **F**ront or Send to **B**ack to change the position of the selected frame. The menu disappears and Ami Pro changes the frame position in the layered arrangement. The frame remains selected.

Deleting the Frame

Tip
If you use a mouse, you can move the frame quickly between back and front by clicking the Bring Frame to Front SmartIcon or the Send Frame to Back SmartIcon (refer to fig. 16.6).

Deleting a frame is just like deleting text in a document. To delete a frame, select it and press Del. The frame disappears. If you change your mind immediately, you can undo the deletion by choosing **E**dit **U**ndo. The frame reappears in the same position on the page that it occupied when you deleted it. If you have deleted something else in the meantime, however, you cannot use **U**ndo to restore the frame.

Note

If you think you may want to undo a deletion, choose **E**dit Cu**t** , which copies the frame to the Windows Clipboard. Deletions (performed with the Del key) aren't copied to the Clipboard but to a special Undo buffer. For Undo to work, you must have the Undo option enabled in the User Setup dialog box (choose Too**l**s **U**ser Setup). You can set the Undo option for up to four levels; for more information on this procedure, see Chapter 8, "Changing Your Setup."

Entering Text and Graphics in Frames

A primary benefit of Ami Pro's frame feature is that frames can hold text and graphics. You can enter text in a frame, and format the frame text as you would page text (columns, indents, tabs, and so on).

Ami Pro frames not only are easy to use, they also are flexible. In the newsletter example (shown earlier in the "Layering Frames" section), layered frames combine text and graphics, creating a nameplate. By placing text in a frame that spans three columns, you can create the dateline for the newsletter, as shown in figure 16.15. Figure 16.16 shows a preview of the first page of the newsletter; the sidebar accompanying the article (left column) is another frame. A frame also can enclose a pull-out quote (see fig. 16.17).

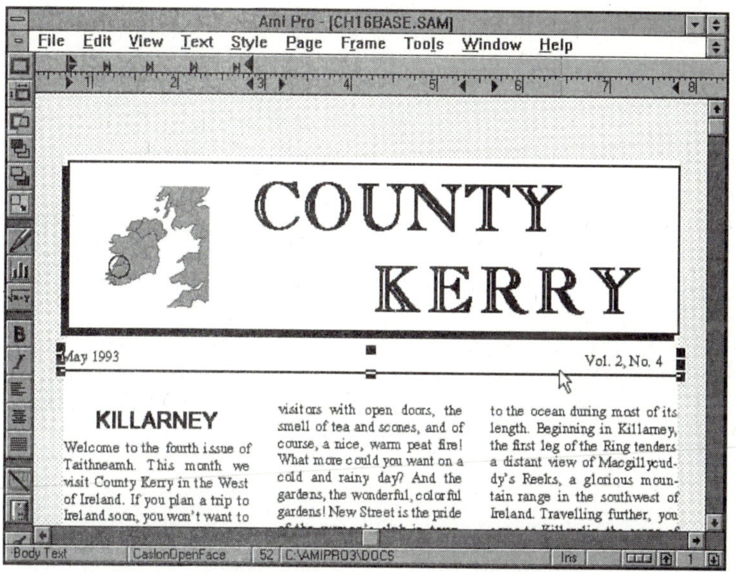

Fig. 16.15
A frame that encloses a dateline, spanning three columns of type.

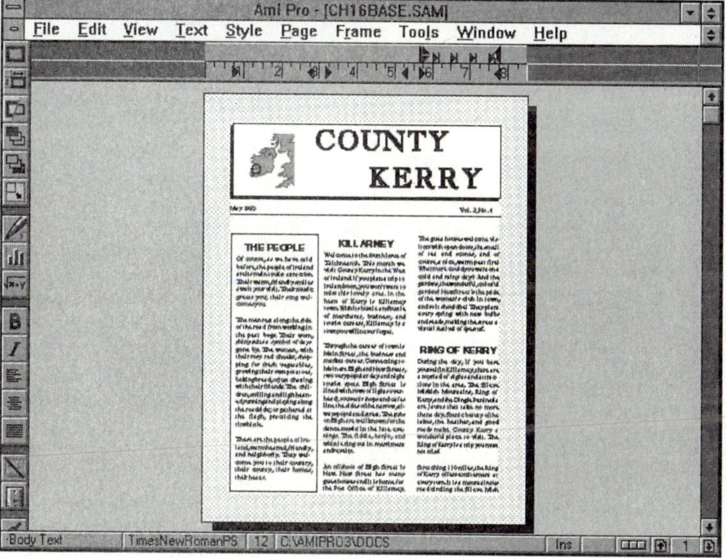

Fig. 16.16
A sidebar created with a frame.

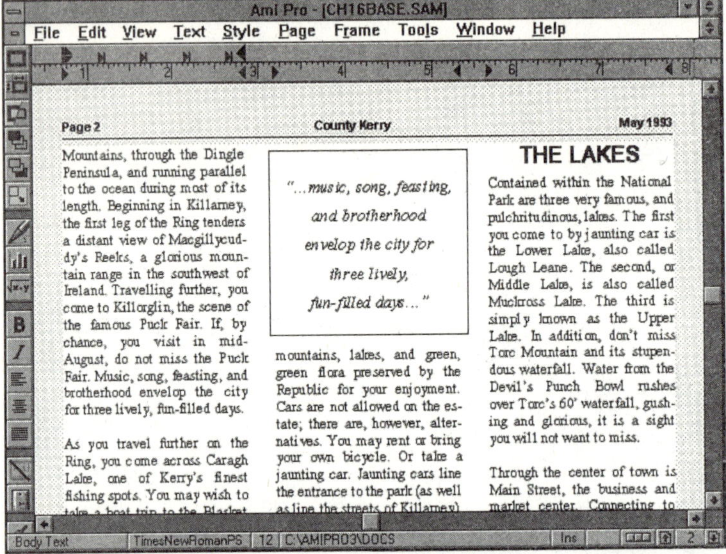

Fig. 16.17
A pull-out quote bordered by a frame.

Note

Other chapters in this book provide detailed information for using frames in specific applications. See Chapter 17, "Using the Draw Feature," for more information about using frames with the drawing feature and scanned images. See Chapter 18, "Creating Charts," for more information about using frames with charts and graphs. Chapter 19, "Desktop Publishing with Ami Pro," also offers material on using frames.

To type text in a frame, follow these steps:

1. Move the mouse pointer within the frame where you want to type text, or select the frame with the keyboard.
2. Double-click the mouse or press Enter. The selection handles turn gray and a cursor appears inside the frame.
3. Type the desired text.
4. After you finish typing text in the frame, click the mouse outside the frame or press Esc to return to the main portion of your document.

Note

You can format the frame text as you would any text in your document. Specify the font and point size with the **T**ext menu, the status bar, the SmartIcons, or—best of all—with the Styles box. Because you use the same techniques to format document text and frame text, see Chapter 4, "Formatting a Document," for more information.

You can specify the alignment of frame text: centered, right-aligned, left-aligned, or justified in the frame. (See Chapter 10, "Working with Style Sheets," for details on text alignment.) Ami Pro aligns the text in relation to the borders of the frame. Later in this chapter, you learn how to set tabs and columns for the text in a frame.

Tip
For ideas and information about designing with frames and typefaces, see Chapter 19, "Desktop Publishing with Ami Pro."

Modifying the Appearance of Frames

You can modify the layout and appearance of a frame by anchoring the frame, changing its margins, setting document text to wrap around the frame, and selecting the frame's line and background style. You make all of these changes with the Modify Frame Layout dialog box. (To access the dialog box, choose F**r**ame **M**odify Frame Layout.) The sections of the dialog box change to reflect the current options you are using for your frame, as described in the following sections.

Note

The mouse gives you quick access to the Modify Frame Layout dialog box. Select the frame you want to modify, and click the right mouse button. The Modify Frame Layout dialog box appears. You also can click the Modify Frame Layout SmartIcon to access the dialog box (refer to fig. 16.6).

When you select one of the options in the Frame section of the dialog box, the options in the right section of the dialog box change. Figure 16.18 shows the Modify Frame Layout dialog box with the **T**ype options. Later sections of this chapter describe other Frame options that appear in the dialog box.

Note

The example box in the lower-right corner of the Modify Frame Layout dialog box displays the frame margins, lines, shadows, and so on. This feature of Ami Pro enables you to preview the options you are considering without actually changing the frame in your document.

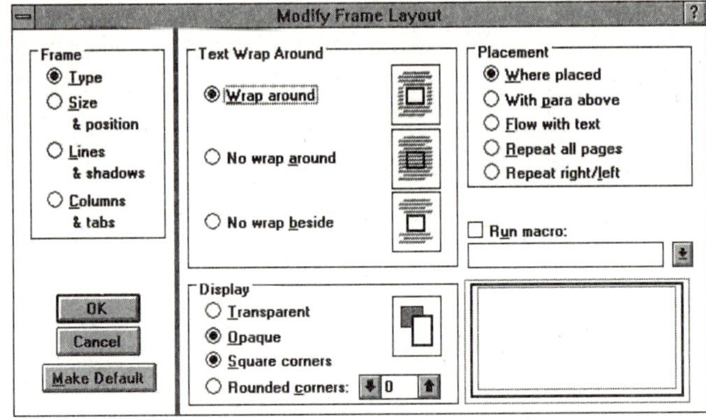

Fig. 16.18
The **Type** version of the Modify Frame Layout dialog box.

Setting Display Characteristics

The options in the Display section of the Modify Frame Layout dialog box enable you to manipulate the frame's appearance. You can select from the following options:

- ***T**ransparent.* This option enables you to see any text or pictures behind the frame.
- ***O**paque.* This option obscures any text or pictures behind the frame.
- ***S**quare Corners.* This option applies square corners to any lines you specify with the **L**ines & Shadows options.
- *Rounded **C**orners.* This option rounds the corners of any lines you specify with the **L**ines & Shadows options. You can set the degree of rounding between 0 and 100.

Tip
You can exit the dialog box at any time by choosing Cancel. Be aware, however, that this technique doesn't save changes you made to the options in the dialog box.

Tip
To display a frame as a circle, begin with a frame of equal width and height. Choose Rounded **C**orners and specify **100** as the degree of rounding.

Wrapping Text Around the Frame

Ami Pro enables you to control the way text wraps around a frame with the following options in the Text Wrap Around section of the dialog box:

- ***W**rap Around.* Use this option to wrap text around the frame. In a two-column format, for example, text flows down the page at the left side of the frame (column 1) and then moves to the right side of the frame (column 2). This option fills even small spaces with text (see fig. 16.19).
- *No Wrap **A**round.* This option flows text through the frame, as if no frame exists. Unless you make the frame opaque, text shows within the boundaries of the frame and on both sides (see fig. 16.20). Select No Wrap **A**round, for example, if you want to place text over a "ghosted" graphic.

Mountains, through the Dingle Peninsula, and running parallel to the ocean during most of its length. Beginning in Killarney, the first leg of the Ring tenders a distant view of Macgillycuddy's Reeks, a glorious mountain range in the southwest of Ireland. Travelling further, you come to Killorglin, the scene of the famous Puck Fair. If, by chance, you visit in mid-August, do not miss the Puck Fair. Music, song, feasting, and brotherhood envelop the city for three lively, fun-filled days.

As you travel further on the Ring, you come across Caragh Lake, one of Kerry's finest fishing spots. You may wish to take a boat trip to the Blasket Islands, or Skellig Rock. Skellig Michael is a massive rock, jutting 700 feet high out of the Atlantic; what a sight to behold! Or perhaps you will take a side trip to Puffin Island, Kerry's own bird sanctuary where over 10,000 puffins gather each year to breed.

Whether you travel south or west on the ring, to the Islands or the Burrin, you will never forget the beauty and solitude of the landscape, and the love of life from the people. It is a memory to cherish your whole life through.

MUCKROSS ESTATE

Also located near Killarney, County Kerry, is a tremendous National Park called Muckross Estate. Over 10,000 acres of mountains, lakes, and green, green flora preserved by the Republic for your enjoyment. Cars are not allowed on the estate; there are, however, alternatives. You may rent or bring your own bicycle. Or take a jaunting car. Jaunting cars line the entrance to the park (as well as line the streets of Killarney), ready to transport you to this scene of serenity and beauty. The horse-drawn carriages are driven by gents who spin tales and weave stories of old Ireland, Killarney, Muckross, and the fairies.

Your first stop on the Estate is Muckross Abbey. A Francisian Abbey built in the 15th century, it is one of the best kept and restored abbeys in all of Kerry. Your next stop is Muckross House. A monumental 19th century home donated, along with the land, to the people of Ireland by its former owners. The house is filled with intricately hand-carved furniture, home-made crafts, tapestries, and original art works. The basement contains a stable, and fully stocked print shop, pub, blacksmith shop, kitchen, and all the conveniences of home.

THE LAKES

Contained within the National Park are three very famous, and pulchritudinous, lakes. The first you come to by jaunting car is the Lower Lake, also called Lough Leane. The second, or Middle Lake, is also called Muckross Lake. The third is simply known as the Upper Lake. In addition, don't miss Torc Mountain and its stupendous waterfall. Water from the Devil's Punch Bowl rushes over Torc's 60' waterfall, gushing and glorious, it is a sight you will not want to miss.

Fig. 16.19 A transparent frame (no lines or shadows) with the **W**rap Around option activated.

- *No Wrap **B**eside.* Choose this option to prevent text from appearing on the right or left side of the frame. Text skips from a line above the frame to a line below the frame, leaving blank the space on the left and right sides next to the frame (see fig 16.21).

Fig. 16.20
A transparent frame (with lines to show placement) with the No Wrap **A**round option activated.

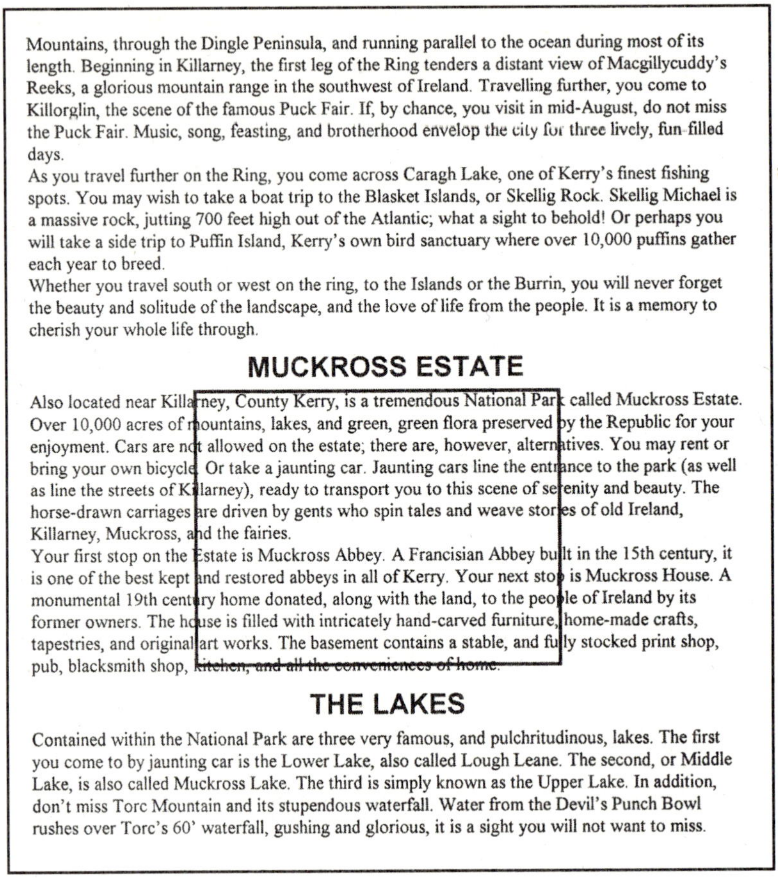

Mountains, through the Dingle Peninsula, and running parallel to the ocean during most of its length. Beginning in Killarney, the first leg of the Ring tenders a distant view of Macgillycuddy's Reeks, a glorious mountain range in the southwest of Ireland. Travelling further, you come to Killorglin, the scene of the famous Puck Fair. If, by chance, you visit in mid-August, do not miss the Puck Fair. Music, song, feasting, and brotherhood envelop the city for three lively, fun-filled days.
As you travel further on the Ring, you come across Caragh Lake, one of Kerry's finest fishing spots. You may wish to take a boat trip to the Blasket Islands, or Skellig Rock. Skellig Michael is a massive rock, jutting 700 feet high out of the Atlantic; what a sight to behold! Or perhaps you will take a side trip to Puffin Island, Kerry's own bird sanctuary where over 10,000 puffins gather each year to breed.
Whether you travel south or west on the ring, to the Islands or the Burrin, you will never forget the beauty and solitude of the landscape, and the love of life from the people. It is a memory to cherish your whole life through.

MUCKROSS ESTATE

Also located near Killarney, County Kerry, is a tremendous National Park called Muckross Estate. Over 10,000 acres of mountains, lakes, and green, green flora preserved by the Republic for your enjoyment. Cars are not allowed on the estate; there are, however, alternatives. You may rent or bring your own bicycle. Or take a jaunting car. Jaunting cars line the entrance to the park (as well as line the streets of Killarney), ready to transport you to this scene of serenity and beauty. The horse-drawn carriages are driven by gents who spin tales and weave stories of old Ireland, Killarney, Muckross, and the fairies.
Your first stop on the Estate is Muckross Abbey. A Francisian Abbey built in the 15th century, it is one of the best kept and restored abbeys in all of Kerry. Your next stop is Muckross House. A monumental 19th century home donated, along with the land, to the people of Ireland by its former owners. The house is filled with intricately hand-carved furniture, home-made crafts, tapestries, and original art works. The basement contains a stable, and fully stocked print shop, pub, blacksmith shop, kitchen, and all the conveniences of home.

THE LAKES

Contained within the National Park are three very famous, and pulchritudinous, lakes. The first you come to by jaunting car is the Lower Lake, also called Lough Leane. The second, or Middle Lake, is also called Muckross Lake. The third is simply known as the Upper Lake. In addition, don't miss Torc Mountain and its stupendous waterfall. Water from the Devil's Punch Bowl rushes over Torc's 60' waterfall, gushing and glorious, it is a sight you will not want to miss.

To select a text wrap style, make sure that the frame is selected; then follow these steps:

1. Open the Modify Frame Layout dialog box.
2. Choose **T**ype (the default) in the Frame section of the dialog box.
3. Choose one of the options in the Text Wrap Around section of the dialog box.
4. Choose OK or press Enter. Ami Pro uses the specified wrapping style for the frame.

Mountains, through the Dingle Peninsula, and running parallel to the ocean during most of its length. Beginning in Killarney, the first leg of the Ring tenders a distant view of Macgillycuddy's Reeks, a glorious mountain range in the southwest of Ireland. Travelling further, you come to Killorglin, the scene of the famous Puck Fair. If, by chance, you visit in mid-August, do not miss the Puck Fair. Music, song, feasting, and brotherhood envelop the city for three lively, fun-filled days.

As you travel further on the Ring, you come across Caragh Lake, one of Kerry's finest fishing spots. You may wish to take a boat trip to the Blasket Islands, or Skellig Rock. Skellig Michael is a massive rock, jutting 700 feet high out of the Atlantic; what a sight to behold! Or perhaps you will take a side trip to Puffin Island, Kerry's own bird sanctuary where over 10,000 puffins gather each year to breed.

Whether you travel south or west on the ring, to the Islands or the Burrin, you will never forget the beauty and solitude of the landscape, and the love of life from the people. It is a memory to cherish your whole life through.

MUCKROSS ESTATE

Also located near Killarney, County Kerry, is a tremendous National Park called Muckross Estate. Over 10,000 acres of mountains, lakes, and green, green flora preserved by the Republic for your enjoyment. Cars are not allowed on the estate; there are, however, alternatives. You may rent or bring your own bicycle. Or take a jaunting car. Jaunting cars line the entrance to the park (as well

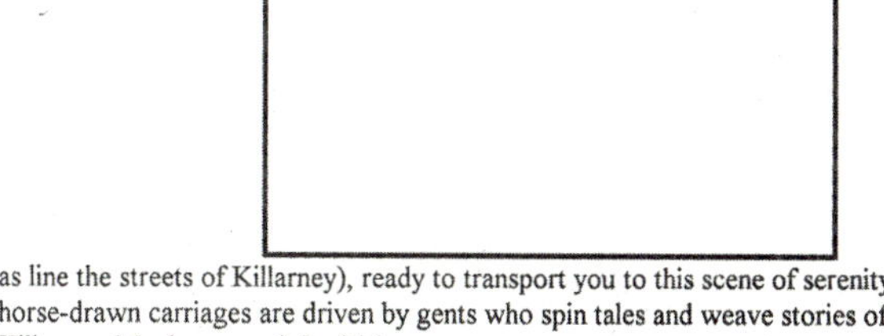

as line the streets of Killarney), ready to transport you to this scene of serenity and beauty. The horse-drawn carriages are driven by gents who spin tales and weave stories of old Ireland, Killarney, Muckross, and the fairies.

Your first stop on the Estate is Muckross Abbey. A Francisian Abbey built in the 15th century, it is one of the best kept and restored abbeys in all of Kerry. Your next stop is Muckross House. A monumental 19th century home donated, along with the land, to the people of Ireland by its former owners. The house is filled with intricately hand-carved furniture, home-made crafts, tapestries, and original art works. The basement contains a stable, and fully stocked print shop, pub, blacksmith shop, kitchen, and all the conveniences of home.

Fig. 16.21
Text doesn't wrap beside a frame with the No Wrap **B**eside option activated.

Caution

When Ami Pro wraps text around a frame, the software splits words—even after a single letter—but doesn't hyphenate. When you place the frame in text, be sure to check for unwanted text beside the frame, and choose the proper Text Wrap Around option to correct any problems. Alternatively, you can position the insertion point before the split word and press Shift+Enter to force the word to the next line.

Note

Choose No Wrap **B**eside or lap the frames into the margin slightly to prevent Ami Pro from wrapping text between the margin and a frame. You get strange layouts when the program places text down an area wide enough for only one character.

Determining how the text flows around the frame is just one of the ways you can control the relationship between text and frame. The next section describes how you can make sure that a frame remains close to a particular paragraph of text, no matter what editing changes affect the page.

Anchoring the Frame

Ami Pro usually anchors the frame on the page and then flows text around the frame. Even if editing changes move the text to another page or to another position on the same page, the frame and its contents stay in place.

This type of anchoring is appropriate for many frames, such as those in figure 16.16, but may not be appropriate for others. For example, if you are inserting a pull-out quote (a box containing part of the text, such as a quotation from an interview) to emphasize the text and catch the reader's eye, you need to anchor the frame containing the pull-out quote to the section of the article containing the entire quotation. This anchoring ensures that if the text moves, the pull-out quote goes with it.

To anchor a frame in place, you choose **T**ype in the Modify Frame Layout dialog box. In the Placement section, choose **W**here Placed (the default).

The following paragraphs describe the anchoring options:

- ***W****here Placed.* Select this option (the default) to anchor the frame in the current location on the page, no matter what happens to the text around the frame.
- *With* ***P****ara Above.* This option anchors the frame to the paragraph of text immediately preceding the frame.
- ***F****low with Text.* Choose this option if you want to attach the frame to the text surrounding the frame.
- The ***R****epeat All Pages* and *Repeat Right/****L****eft* options deal with repeating frames. You can assign a frame to appear in the same spot on every page, on every right page, or on every left page. See the section "Using Repeating Frames," later in this chapter, for more information on these options.

To specify anchoring options, select the frame, open the Modify Frame Layout dialog box, and choose one of the options from the Placement section. Finally, choose OK or press Enter.

Setting Frame Margins

In Ami Pro, the word *margin* refers to the blank space surrounding a frame's border—the gap between the contents of the frame and the contents of the document. The margin setting controls how text wraps both inside and outside the frame. If you set the frame margins to 1/4 inch, for example, text wraps outside the margin boundaries to within 1/4 inch of the border, and the text fills the inside of the frame to within 1/4 inch of the border.

Tip
The example box in the upper-right corner of the dialog box displays the selected frame's position on the page.

To set the margins for a frame, you use the **S**ize & Position options in the Modify Frame Layout dialog box (see fig. 16.22).

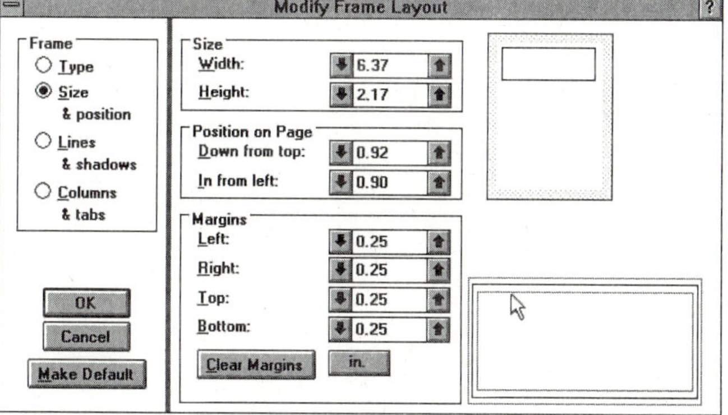

Fig. 16.22
The Modify Frame Layout dialog box with size and position options.

Follow these steps to change the margins of a frame:

1. After selecting the frame, open the Modify Frame Layout dialog box and select **S**ize & Position. The dialog box changes to show the size and position options.

2. For each margin setting—**L**eft, **R**ight, **T**op, and **B**ottom—type the desired measurement in the text box or click the arrow buttons to increase or decrease the measurement. You can modify a single margin or any combination of margins.

   To clear all current margin settings or to change all the settings to 0, choose **C**lear Margins. (With 0 settings, note that text extends to the borders of the frame.)

3. After you finish setting margins for the frame, choose OK or press Enter. The dialog box disappears, and Ami Pro returns to the document.

Figure 16.23 shows the dialog box with the left margin set to 1.5 inches, the top margin to .75 inches, and the right and bottom margins set to .25 inches. Notice how the example frame in the bottom right corner of the dialog box changes to show the new margin settings. The solid line in the example frame is the document frame. The dotted lines on the outside and inside of the solid line represent the outer and inner margins.

Note

You can use inches, centimeters, picas, or points as the unit of measure for the margins. Click the button labeled in. to change increments. (See "Creating an Automatic Frame," earlier in this chapter, for more information on specifying the frame size and its position on the page.)

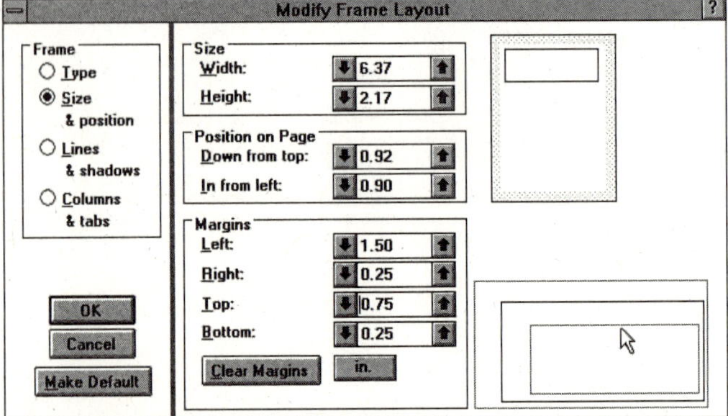

Fig. 16.23
Size and position options; notice the uneven margins in the example frame.

Selecting Line, Drop Shadow, and Background Styles

Ami Pro provides many variations in color and pattern for the line borders, drop shadows, and background of frames. The default background for a frame is white and opaque, for example, but you can choose from a variety of colors and patterns. You even can specify your own default settings for a frame.

Figure 16.24 shows four combinations of lines, drop shadows, and backgrounds. Each frame uses a different line style. The top left frame shows a custom drop shadow of .22 inches. The top right frame uses no shadow, with a top and left line position only. The bottom left frame has corners rounded at 70 degrees and a black background. Finally, the bottom right frame has rounded corners (19 degrees) and gray-screened frame lines.

> **Caution**
>
> Using a pattern or screen for the background of a frame makes any text you place in the frame difficult to read.

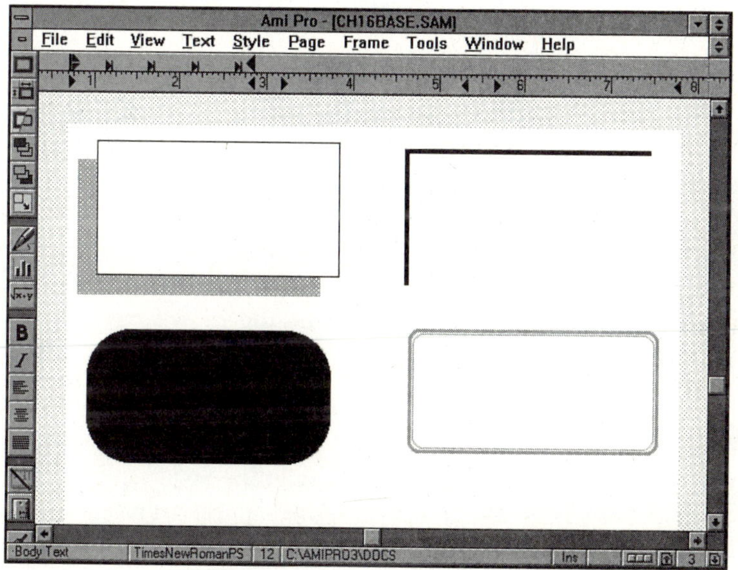

Fig. 16.24
Combinations of lines and shadows.

To begin modifications, you select the frame, open the Modify Frame Layout dialog box and choose **L**ines & Shadows (see fig. 16.25).

The following sections describe the options available in the **L**ines & Shadows version of the Modify Frame Layout dialog box for modifying the lines, background, and shadow of a frame in Ami Pro.

After the line styles, shadows, and patterns meet with your approval, you choose OK or press Enter in the Modify Frame Layout dialog box. Ami Pro returns to the document. The new frame options are reflected on-screen, and the frame still is selected.

> **Tip**
> To make more frames with the same styles, shadows, and patterns, choose **M**ake Default. The default remains in effect for all future sessions until you change the defaults again.

Line Styles

To begin modifying the frame's line borders, choose the desired option in the Lines section of the dialog box. To border all sides, choose **A**ll. To border one to three sides, choose **L**eft, **R**ight, **T**op, or **B**ottom as appropriate. For a text box, for example, you may want borders only on the top and bottom.

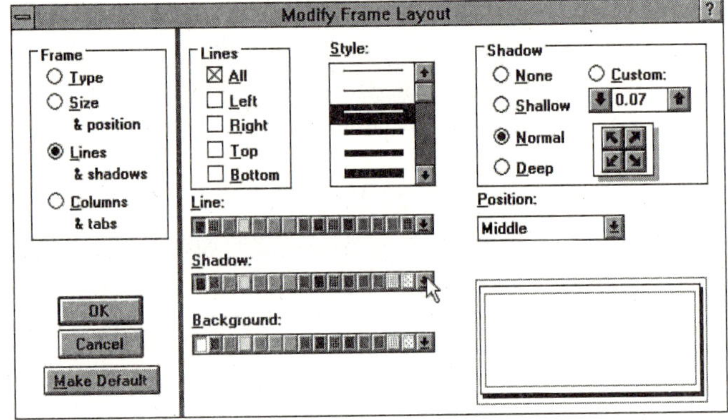

Fig. 16.25 The Modify Frame Layout dialog box with line, shadow, and background options.

The **S**tyle option shows several line styles. The current style appears in reverse video. Click the arrow buttons to scroll through the other line styles. (With the keyboard, tab to the **S**tyle section and press the arrow keys to highlight your choice.) The choices range from thin to thick lines and from single- to triple-line designs.

To choose a line style, click the representation of the line style you want to use. With the keyboard, press the Tab key to exit the **S**tyle section after you choose the line style. The chosen line style then appears in reverse video.

Shadow Styles

You use the options in the Shadow section of the dialog box to add a drop shadow to the frame. Choose **N**one if you don't want a shadow. Choose **S**hallow for a .04-inch shadow, **N**ormal (the default) for a .07-inch shadow, or **D**eep for a .12-inch shadow. You also can choose **C**ustom and specify in the text box (in inches) the size of the shadow you want. The custom-sized shadow can be from .01 inches to .23 inches wide.

To specify the location of the shadow, use the quartet of boxes containing arrows in the lower-right corner of the **S**hadow section. Choose the arrow that indicates in which direction you want the shadow to lie. Choosing the upper-left arrow, for example, places a shadow at the top and left sides of your frame; choosing the lower-right arrow makes the shadow appear around the bottom and right sides of the frame. Ami Pro shows the placement of the chosen shadow in the example frame (refer to fig. 16.25).

Coloring and Shading

Use the **L**ine, **S**hadow, and **B**ackground options in the middle of the dialog box to specify the color and shading patterns for those elements of your frame. Each option name is followed by a palette of boxes containing different colors as well as shades of gray (on a monochrome monitor, the colors appear as different patterns of white, gray, and black). The default background color is white and the default line and shadow color is black.

To change one of these patterns, click the appropriate box. (You also can tab to a color bar and use the arrow keys to select your choice.) Selected colors appear "pressed in." Use a gray scale for the shadow, for example, or a background of patterned gray. The example frame in the lower right corner of the dialog box illustrates the changes you make.

Tip
Use lighter background screens for black type and darker screens for white (reversed) type. (See Chapter 19, "Desktop Publishing with Ami Pro," for more information about background screens and reversed type.)

Using Columns and Tabs in Frames

You can specify columns and tab settings that apply only to a frame. For a Table of Contents box, for example, you may want to set a right tab with dot leaders to make the text easier to read. You may have a box of text that you want to divide into columns and stretch across the page. These and other options are available to you with Ami Pro frames, as described in the following sections.

To use columns and tabs in your frames, choose the **C**olumns & Tabs option in the Modify Frame Layout dialog box (see fig. 16.26). The following sections explain the options in the dialog box. After you finish specifying column and tab settings, choose OK or press Enter to close the dialog box and return to the document.

Tip
To create more frames with the same column and tab settings, choose **M**ake Default before leaving the dialog box.

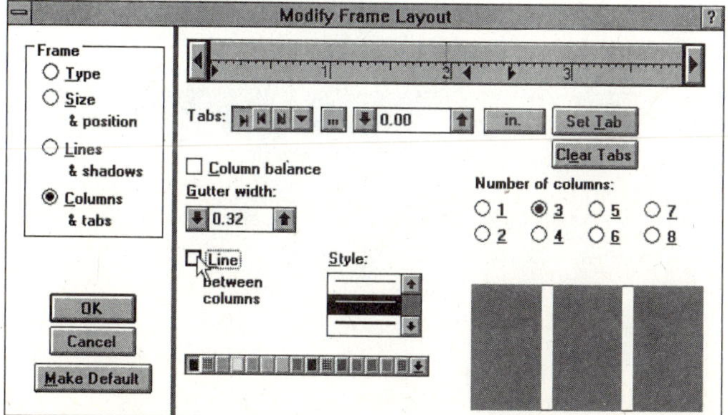

Fig. 16.26
The columns and tabs options in the Modify Frame Layout dialog box.

Specifying Columns

To set columns, choose the desired number of columns from the Number of Columns section (**1** through **8**). The example frame in the lower right corner of the dialog box shows the number of columns and the *gutter width* (white space between columns). The example frame in figure 16.26, for example, shows three columns.

By default, Ami Pro sets the gutter width to .17 inches. To change the gutter width, choose **G**utter Width and increase the increment. The gutter width changes appear in the example box.

Note

If you edit the width by typing a new value, Ami Pro doesn't update the example box until you move the cursor to another item in the dialog box or use the arrow buttons to increment or decrement the value.

If you want to place a line between columns, choose the **L**ine between Columns option.

To change the style of the line between the columns, choose **S**tyle and specify the desired line style. The styles range from thin to thick lines and from single to triple lines. The changes appear in the example box.

Note

In figure 16.26, the gutter width is set at .32 inches. Ami Pro's default gutter width of .17 inches isn't enough space between columns of text. Always set the gutter width to at least .25 inches for more readable text. Add even more to the gutter width if your text is justified; wide gutters help the reader's eye to keep from jumping between columns while reading the text.

Tip

If your columns contain text, use only the first or second line style from the **S**tyle list. The other line styles make the page look cluttered and dense.

Note

If you choose the **L**ine between Columns option, and you are placing text in the frame columns, be sure to add extra gutter space so the page doesn't look too gray. A gray appearance results from the contrast between text (and graphics) and the white space—margins, gutters, and so on—of the page.

The color bar at the bottom of the dialog box specifies the color or shading pattern of the lines between columns. You may want a gray line, for example, rather than black. Click the box that shows the color pattern you want to use for the lines. (You also can choose a color or pattern with the arrow keys.)

Figure 16.27 shows a completed sample frame with three columns of justified text and lines between columns. Note the gutter width of .32 inches, allowing "breathing room" between the columns.

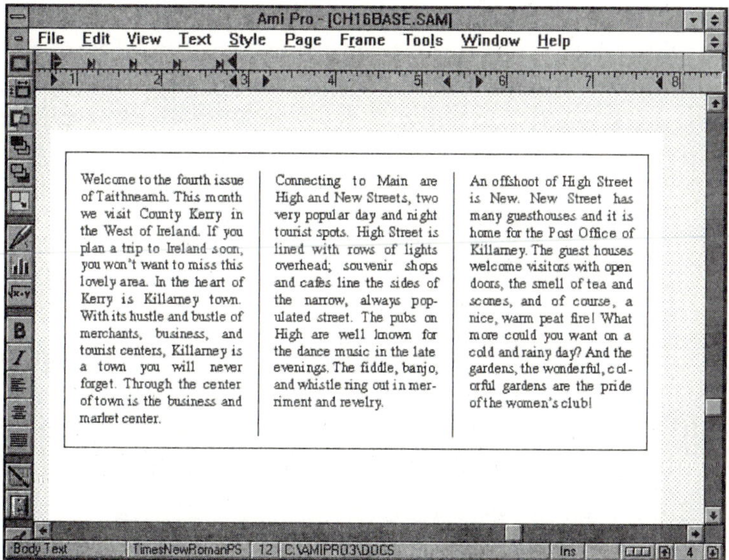

Fig. 16.27
A sample frame with text set in columns.

Selecting Tabs

Notice the tab ruler at the top of the Columns & Tabs version of the Modify Frame Layout dialog box. This ruler represents the width of the frame; if you are using columns in the frame, the columns are marked in the ruler. In this example, the ruler illustrates the width of the frame and a line leader tab set on the ruler (refer to fig. 16.26).

Tab Styles

If you want a leader tab rather than a basic tab, click the leader character button (to the right of the four tab buttons below the tab ruler—see fig. 16.28) until the leader character you want appears on the tab buttons. You can choose dots, dashes, underlines, or no leader character.

The tab buttons represent (reading left to right) the four basic types of tabs: left, right, decimal, and center. Click the appropriate button to select the type of tab you want to use. (For more information on setting tabs, see Chapter 5, "Working with Page Layout.")

Tab Settings

Move the mouse pointer to the ruler and click the location where you want to place the tab setting. The symbol representing the tab type you chose appears at that spot on the tab ruler.

If you prefer to use the keyboard to set the tab, move to the desired tab button and press the space bar to select it. Then type the exact location of the tab setting in the tab bar text box and choose Set **T**ab. Alternatively, you can press Shift+Tab to move to the ruler, position the tab, and press the space bar to set the tab.

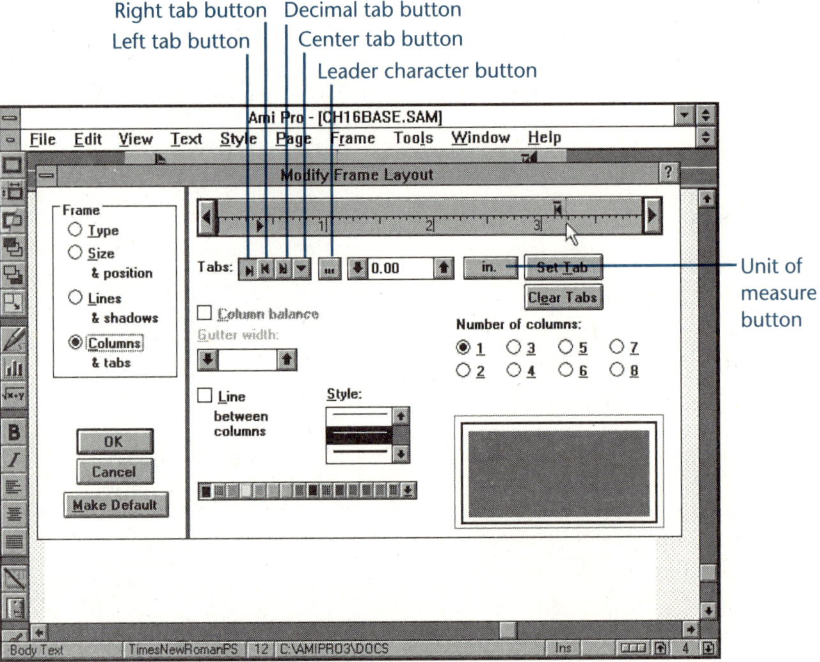

Fig. 16.28
Tab settings in the Modify Frame Layout dialog box.

To move the tab setting, use the mouse to click-and-drag the symbol to another area of the tab ruler. To remove any tab setting, drag the symbol off the tab ruler. The symbol disappears. To remove all tab settings, select the Cl**e**ar Tabs button. With the keyboard, press Shift+Tab to move to the ruler; then press the arrow keys plus the space bar to move the solid black line to the desired position. To delete a tab, move to the tab on the ruler and press Del.

Click the unit of measure button (labeled `in.`) if you want the tabs to be measured in a unit other than inches (the default setting). Each click cycles to a different measurement unit. You can select centimeters, picas, or points as an alternative to inches.

Tip
You can use the current ruler to adjust tabs in a frame. For more information about the current ruler, see Chapter 5, "Working with Page Layout."

Figure 16.29 illustrates an example of a frame containing text with right-aligned, line leader tabs. Line leader tabs are perfect for forms, signature lines, and so on. After choosing the tab position and the line leader, you just press the Tab key in your text to create a line. (See Chapter 19, "Desktop Publishing with Ami Pro," for more information about using line leaders.)

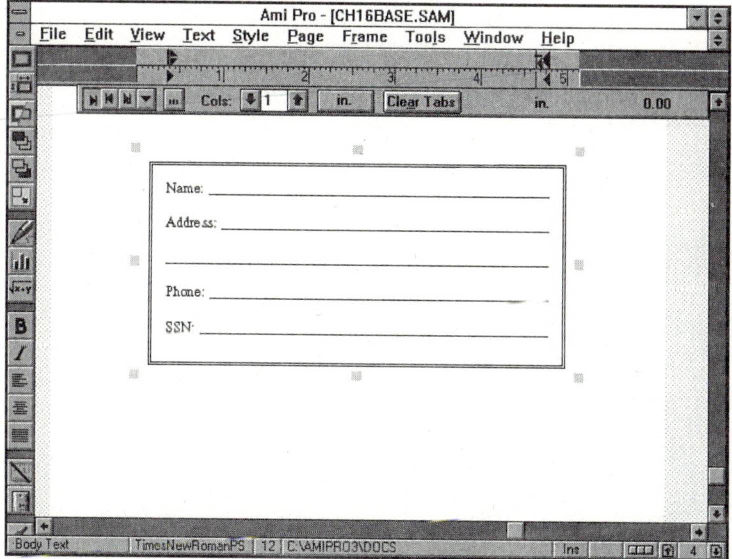

Fig. 16.29
A frame using right-aligned, line leader tabs to create a form.

Using Repeating Frames

In a report, newsletter, or other document, you may want to repeat a particular frame—a page number or running title, for example—on every page. You also may need a frame to appear on alternating pages, if your document will be printed on both sides of the paper and bound so that it opens to two pages at once. Or you may want to create a graphic header or footer for a two-page spread.

Suppose that you want the Ireland graphic from figure 16.14 to repeat on the left pages of your newsletter. To repeat an existing frame, select the frame, choose F**r**ame **M**odify Frame Layout **T**ype (see fig. 16.30), and then choose one of the following options in the Placement section of the dialog box:

- To repeat the frame on every page, select **R**epeat All Pages.
- To repeat the frame on alternating pages, select Repeat Right/**L**eft. Ami Pro repeats the frame on all left pages if the selected frame is currently on a left page or on all right pages if the selected frame is located on a right page. (If your document begins with page 1, right pages are odd-numbered; left pages are even-numbered.)

Tip
To check the frame placement of left and right pages, select **V**iew F**a**cing Pages.

After you finish specifying the placement of the frame, choose OK or press Enter. The dialog box disappears, and Ami Pro returns to the document.

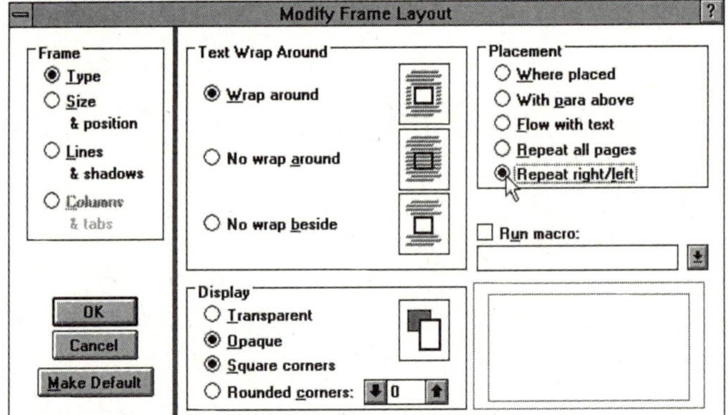

Fig. 16.30
The Modify Frame Layout dialog box with the **Type** options selected.

Figure 16.31 illustrates the Ireland graphic in a repeating frame, on page two of the newsletter. Note that a border was added to the frame (the border wasn't in the original nameplate) to separate it from the text and make it stand out on the page.

To add interest to the newsletter, you also could add the Ireland graphic to right pages, paralleling the graphic on the left pages.

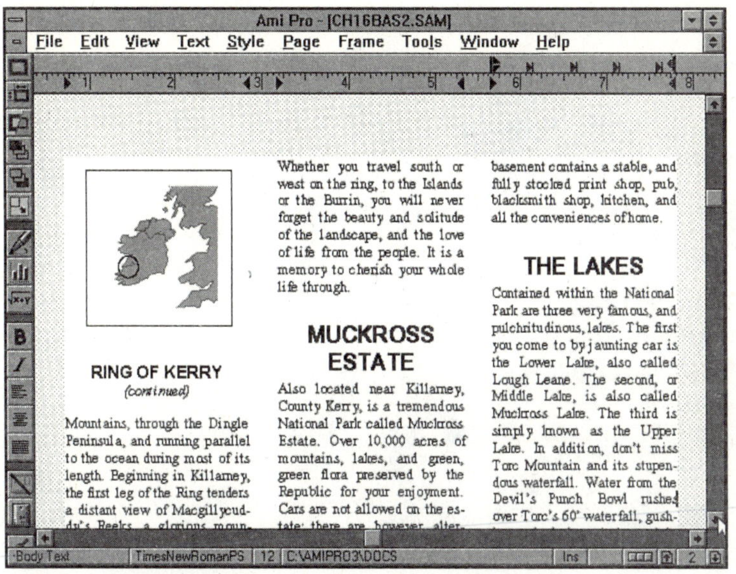

Fig. 16.31
The Ireland graphic as a repeating frame on left pages.

Using an Imported Picture in a Frame

An Ami Pro frame can hold graphic images from many different programs. *Graphic images* (pictures, line art, halftones, tables, and so on) add interest and comprehension to the written word. Ami Pro 3 includes over 90 clip art files for you to use with documents. In this section, you import one of these clip art files into an Ami Pro frame.

> **Note**
>
> If you didn't install the clip art files with Ami Pro, or if you want to import a different graphic file, see Chapter 20, "Importing, Exporting, and Linking Files," for information on additional file types you can use.

You can use the Bluefish document (from earlier chapters) for this section, or choose another Ami Pro document. Be sure that Ami Pro is in layout mode and custom view.

Scroll to the bottom of the page and create a frame. Then import the drawing by following these steps:

1. Select the frame.

2. Choose **F**ile **I**mport Picture. The Import Picture dialog box appears.

3. In the File **T**ype list box, choose `AmiDraw`.

4. In the **F**iles list box, choose `USA.SDW`, or another clip art file (extension SDW).

5. Select the **C**opy Image option (below the File **T**ype list box).

6. Choose OK or press Enter. Ami Pro returns to the document and displays the imported drawing in the frame (see fig. 16.32). The image fills the frame proportionately. If you enlarge the frame, Ami Pro enlarges the image to match.

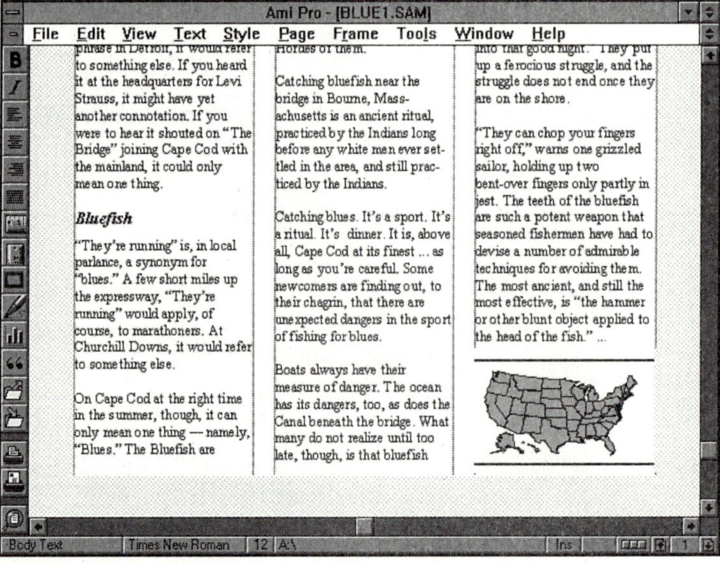

Fig. 16.32
Clip art imported into a frame.

Tip
You can size, crop, and modify the drawing. For more information, see Chapter 17, "Using the Draw Feature."

Summary

In this chapter, you learned how to create and manipulate frames—how to enter text in a frame, modify the layout and appearance of a frame, and use columns and tabs in a frame. You also learned how to work with multiple frames by grouping and layering. Finally, you learned how to use repeating frames and how to import a picture into a frame.

In the next chapter, you learn about another powerful graphics tool—Ami Pro's Draw feature.

Chapter 17

Using the Draw Feature

Ami Pro comes with a fully equipped Draw feature—the type of feature you may expect to find only in a dedicated drawing package. By working in a frame in your Ami Pro document, you can create nearly any shape or drawing and then add text to the drawing. After your drawing is in place, you can select, copy, and move the objects drawn. When you combine the power of frames with the power of drawing, you have a capability unmatched by any other word processing software currently on the market.

Note

You must have a mouse to use the Draw feature. You cannot create a drawing in a frame that contains text or a non-drawing graphic.

In this chapter, you learn how to start the Draw feature. You examine the uses for the *Drawing icons* (selection arrow, lines, ellipse, rectangle, polygon, and so on) and learn how to use these basic tools to create a drawing.

In addition to Drawing icons, the Ami Pro Draw feature includes a series of *Command icons* (Group, Bring to Front, Rotate, and so on) on the top-right of the Draw screen. Many of these icons provide shortcuts for menu commands. This chapter details how to use commands to group, rotate, and flip objects. This chapter also explains how to create rotated text in the Draw feature, how to import clip art, and how to use Ami Pro's Image Processing feature.

You also learn how to select a single object, multiple objects, or all objects in a drawing and then how to copy, move, enlarge, reduce, and delete objects. You also learn how to change the line style and color, and the object fill, color, and pattern of a drawing.

Starting the Draw Feature

Tip
To specify a size and location for the frame, choose Frame Create Frame, set the specifications, and then choose Tools Drawing.

To produce a drawing, you must use a frame. If you don't create your own frame, Ami Pro creates a frame for you when you start the Draw feature. (Note that you cannot create a drawing in a frame that contains text or a nondrawing graphic.) If Ami Pro creates the frame, the feature uses the current settings in the Create Frame dialog box. (See Chapter 16, "Using Frames," for information on creating frames.)

To start the Draw feature, choose Too**l**s **D**rawing. If you select a frame, Ami Pro uses that frame; otherwise, the Draw screen appears with an empty frame in which you can draw. Figure 17.1 shows the Too**l**s menu.

After you choose **D**rawing from the Too**l**s menu, Ami Pro returns you to the screen. Your frame now contains grayed handles and a new icon bar—the Drawing icon bar—appears at the top of the screen. Figure 17.2 illustrates the Drawing screen. Notice that the Menu Bar now offers a **D**raw menu, which you use to implement Draw commands. Table 17.1 describes the Drawing icons in the icon bar at the top of the screen.

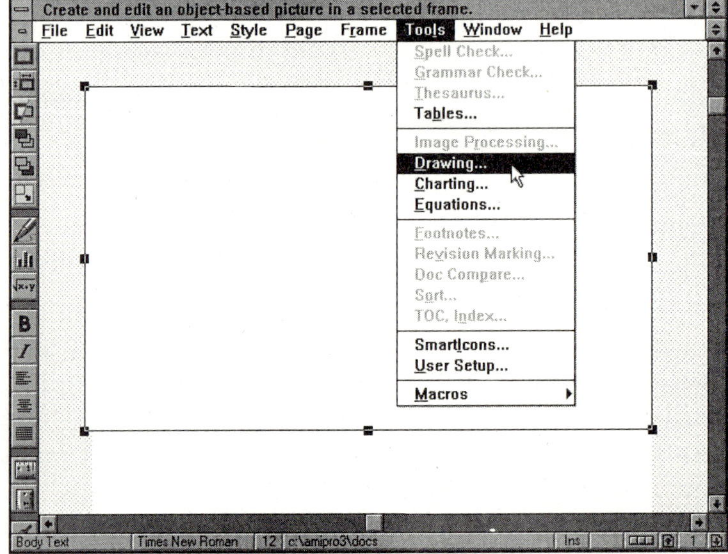

Fig. 17.1
The Too**l**s menu with **D**rawing selected.

Tip
If you use the Draw feature frequently, add the drawing SmartIcon (the Pencil icon in fig. 17.1) to the SmartIcons palette.

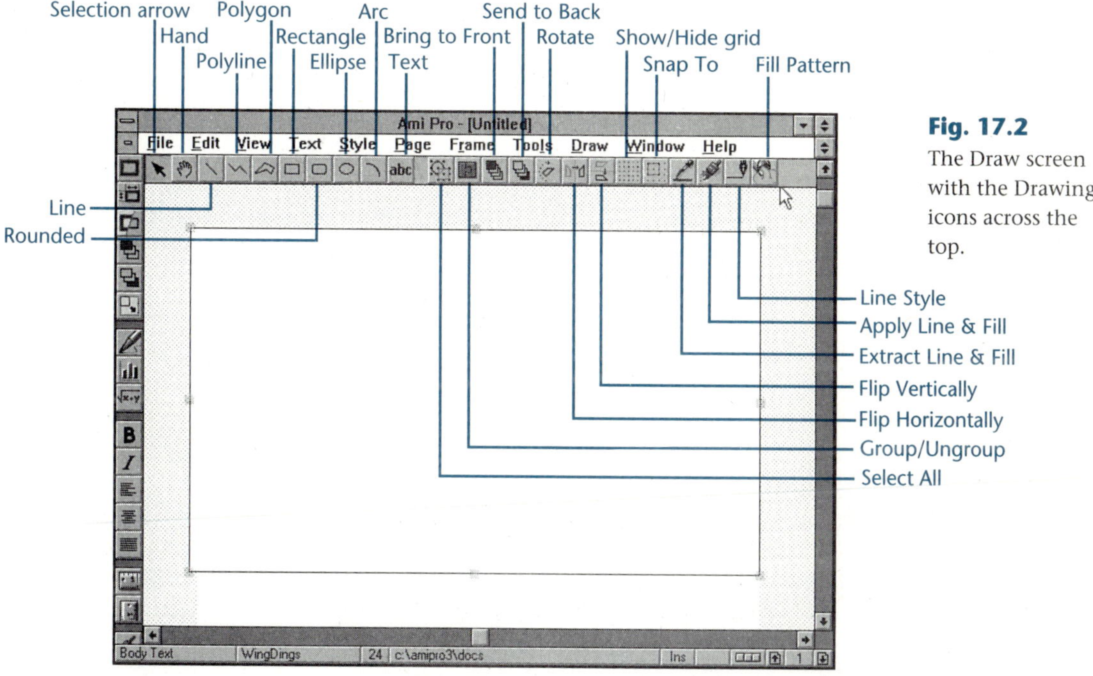

Fig. 17.2 The Draw screen with the Drawing icons across the top.

Table 17.1 The Ami Pro Drawing Icons

Drawing Icon	Function
Selection Arrow	Selects or sizes an object or group of objects.
Hand	Selects the contents of the frame; positions the drawing within the frame; used for moving objects.
Line	Draws a straight line when you drag the mouse pointer; draws the line at a 45-degree angle from the previous setting if you press and hold down Shift and drag the mouse pointer; displays the prospective line in increments of 45 degrees until you release the mouse button to accept the line.
Polyline	Draws a line that connects two points; draws multiple connected lines if you click the Polyline tool and click multiple lines inside the Drawing frame; draws free-form lines if you press and hold the Shift key while you draw.
Polygon	Draws a polygon when you click at each point where you want a corner of the polygon and then double-click the last corner.
Rectangle	Draws a rectangle; draws a square if you press and hold down Shift as you click and drag.

(continues)

Table 17.1 Continued

Drawing Icon	Function
Rounded Rectangle	Draws a rectangle with rounded corners; draws a rounded square if you press and hold down Shift as you click and drag.
Ellipse	Draws an ellipse; draws a circle if you press and hold down Shift as you click and drag.
Arc	Draws a parabolic arc.
Text	Enables you to type text in the frame as part of the drawing.

As a shortcut to many of the features, you can use the Command icons, which appear across the top right of the Draw screen. Figure 17.2 shows the Command icons, and table 17.2 summarizes their functions.

Note

The appearance of the Line & Fill Command icons changes with the contents of the drawing. If you are using a heavy line style for your objects, for example, the line that appears below the pencil on the Line Style Command icon reflects the heavy line style you are using.

Table 17.2 The Drawing Command Icons

Command Icon	Function
Select All	Selects or deselects all objects in a frame.
Group/Ungroup	Groups or ungroups all selected objects in a frame.
Bring to Front	Brings the selected object in front of all other objects at that location.
Send to Back	Places the selected object behind all other objects at that location.
Rotate	Rotates the selected object clockwise or counterclockwise by the specified amount.
Flip Horizontally	Flips the selected object or objects by swapping left and right sides.

Command Icon	Function
Flip Vertically	Flips the selected object or objects by swapping top and bottom.
Show/Hide Grid	Displays or hides a grid, which helps in drawing and placing objects.
Snap To	Enables you to align objects on the grid you specify for the frame.
Extract Line & Fill	Changes the current line style and fill pattern to those of the selected object.
Apply Line & Fill	Applies the current line and fill pattern to the selected object.
Line Style	Displays the options for setting line style, color, and endings.
Fill Patterns	Displays options for color and fill patterns.

Note

After you leave Draw mode (or if you leave it accidentally by clicking outside the frame), you can return to Draw mode by double-clicking inside the frame. Ami Pro returns to a frame you drew previously, and the Drawing icons appear across the top of the screen.

Creating a Drawing

On the Draw screen, Ami Pro displays Drawing icons below the Menu Bar (refer to fig. 17.2 again). You use the Drawing icons to produce basic shapes which Ami Pro refers to as objects. A drawing can be one object or a combination of objects. To use the Drawing icons, you first click an icon that represents the object you want to draw. Then you move the mouse pointer in the frame to draw the object.

To create a rectangle, follow these steps:

1. Click the icon for the object you want to draw. For this example, click the Rectangle icon.

2. Position the mouse pointer in the frame at the location you want to place one end of the object. For this example, position the mouse pointer near the middle left side of the frame to mark the top of the rectangle.

3. Drag the mouse pointer to the location you want the other end of the object to appear. For this example, drag the mouse down and slightly to the right. Figure 17.3 illustrates the finished rectangle. Notice the mouse pointer in the figure (at the lower right corner of the rectangle) appears as a cross.

   As you drag, you can see the object on-screen. Until you release the mouse button, you can continue to drag the object into various shapes until you have a shape that suits you.

Fig. 17.3
You can use the Rectangle tool to create a rectangle.

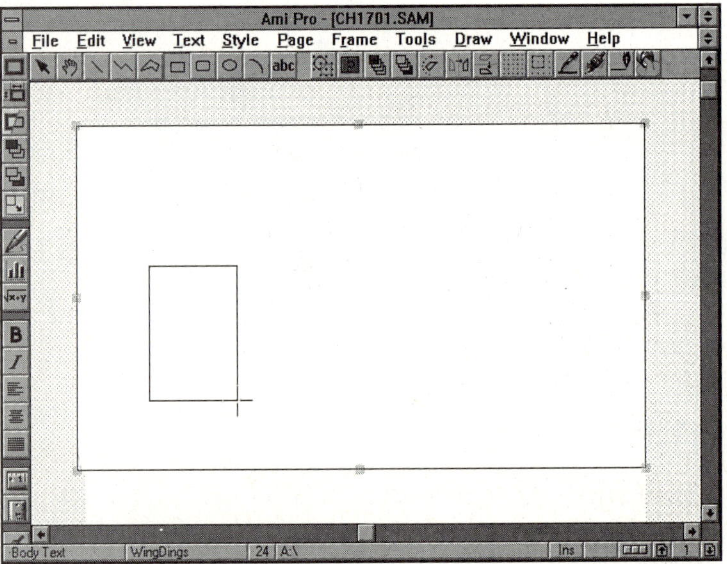

4. Release the mouse and the rectangle is complete.

Suppose that you want to transform this rectangle into a house. The next step is to add a roof. To do this, select the Line icon and draw two diagonal lines to form a roof on top of the rectangle. The Line icon works similarly to the Rectangle icon. Figure 17.4 illustrates a line drawn to form a roof on the house.

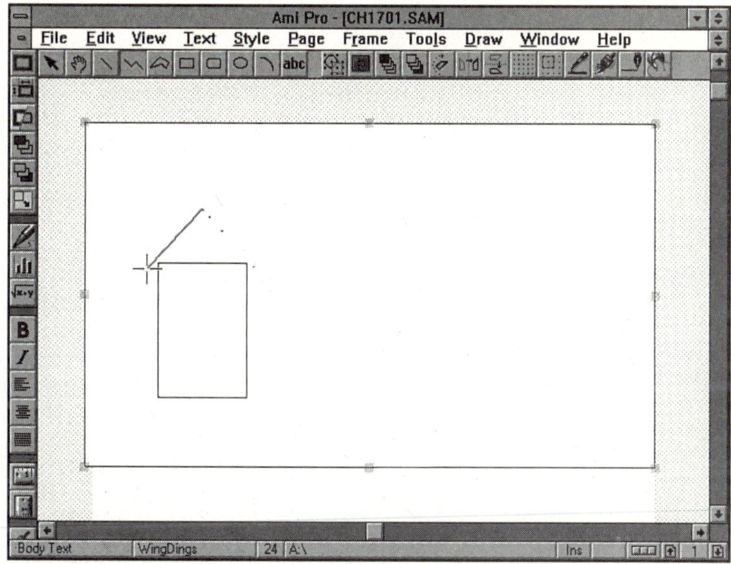

Fig. 17.4
You can draw a line by using the Line icon.

As you add to the house in the drawing, you need to perform certain editing functions, such as copying, moving, and deleting. The next section explains these procedures.

◀ See "Creating a Frame," p. 498

◀ See "Manipulating Frames," p. 504

◀ See "Modifying the Appearance of Frames," p. 515

Note

When editing and drawing, you may need to change views of the screen. For some drawings, the enlarged view works best; for other drawings, you may need to change the custom view. To change the custom view, select **V**iew View **P**references. In **C**ustom view, select the percentage you want. The figures in this chapter were drawn at various percentages in **C**ustom view.

Editing Objects

Editing in the Draw feature isn't much different from editing in Ami Pro. You select the objects you want to edit; then you edit the objects using the menus or the SmartIcons.

Selecting and Deselecting Objects

If you have used the mouse, you should have no trouble selecting objects in Ami Pro Draw because Ami Pro follows the same mouse procedures used in Windows. Selecting small or thin items (such as a line) is sometimes difficult with the selection arrow. The selection arrow doesn't select from the tip but from somewhere near the center of the arrow. Practice helps you master selecting small objects more easily.

Note

If you have objects that overlap or are very close to each other, sometimes it may be difficult to select the one you want. If you have trouble selecting an object, press and hold Ctrl while you select the object in question; this helps you zero in on the object you want more easily.

To select a single object, click the Selection Arrow icon and then click the object you want to select. Handles appear around the object (or at the end of lines) to indicate it's selected. The frame in which you are drawing contains dimmed selection handles (refer to fig. 17.4 again).

Tip
When selecting an object without pressing and holding Shift, you deselect all other objects.

To select multiple objects, follow the same steps you use to select a single object, but press and hold down Shift as you point to the objects you want to select. To select the multiple objects, for example, click the Selection Arrow icon, click the first object, press and hold down the Shift key, and then click each additional object you want to select.

Figure 17.5 illustrates the house drawing in progress. Notice that the two selected lines in the drawing have handles on either end. Copying these two lines rather than drawing more lines speeds up the drawing process in this case. To copy and paste two or more objects, you must first group them, as explained in the next section.

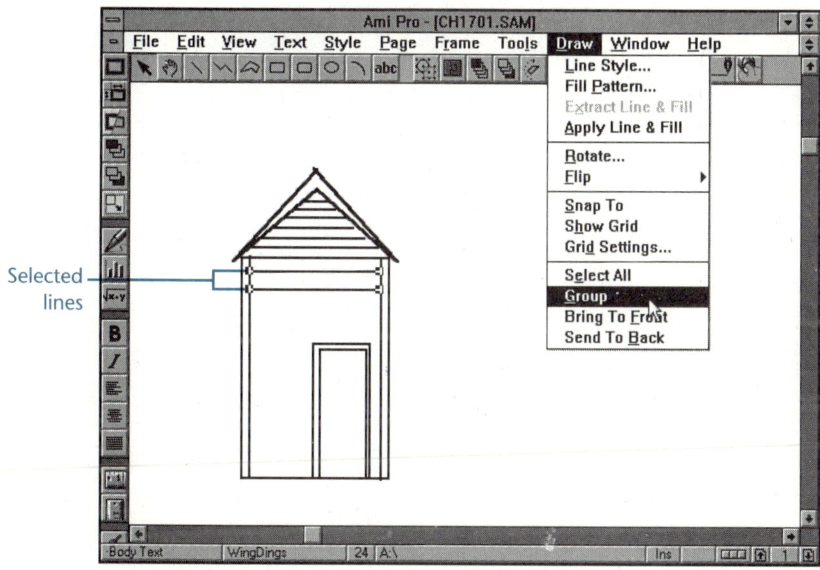

Fig. 17.5
Two lines selected in the drawing.

Grouping Objects

As described in the preceding section, you can select some or all the objects in a drawing and perform some operations on them simultaneously, such as copying and pasting. Forming the objects into a group you can treat as a single object enables you to perform more operations, such as moving and resizing. As shown in figure 17.5, you can select two objects (lines in this case), group them, and then copy and paste them. To group two or more objects, follow these steps:

Tip
After you group the lines, you can copy and paste them together.

1. Select the first object by clicking the selection arrow on the object.

2. Press and hold the Shift key and select a second object. Each selected object contains its own handles. Continue to hold the Shift key and select any additional objects.

3. Select **D**raw **G**roup (refer to fig. 17.5 again). The menu disappears, and the objects are grouped. The group of objects now contains one set of handles to identify it as a group.

Tip
You can use the Command icons for Group/Ungroup, and you also can perform other editing functions on grouped objects, such as moving, deleting, enlarging, and reducing.

Tip
In Ami Pro, you first move the insertion point and then select **E**dit **P**aste. In the Draw feature, you choose **E**dit **P**aste and then select the location by dragging the object to the location you want.

Note

Group, in the **D**raw menu, now has a check mark beside it to indicate that the objects are grouped. You cannot select, cut, copy, move, or otherwise modify one part of this group until you select **D**raw **G**roup again and deselect the **G**roup option.

You are now ready to copy and paste the grouped objects, as explained in the next section.

Copying Objects

To copy an object, select the object or group of objects you want to copy. For this example, select the two lines you grouped in the last section. Choose **E**dit **C**opy. Ami Pro copies the object to the Windows Clipboard. Choose **E**dit **P**aste. Ami Pro pastes the object from the Clipboard over the original object; point to the copy with the mouse pointer and drag the copy to the desired location in the frame (see fig. 17.6).

Note

By using the mouse, you can bypass the menus when you copy an object or group in the Draw feature. With the mouse pointer on or inside the object, press and hold the Shift key, click and drag the object to a new position, and release the mouse button. Ami Pro copies the object.

Note

You can add to your SmartIcons palette a SmartIcon for copying. To copy using the SmartIcon, select the object, and then click the SmartIcon. Ami Pro copies the selected object to the Clipboard. The same is true for the SmartIcon you use to paste objects. See Chapter 8, "Changing Your Setup," for information on customizing the SmartIcon palette.

Note

You can copy and paste individually selected objects, but to move the pasted objects, you must select and move each object separately. The easiest method is to group objects, and then copy, paste, and move them as one object. You can always ungroup them later.

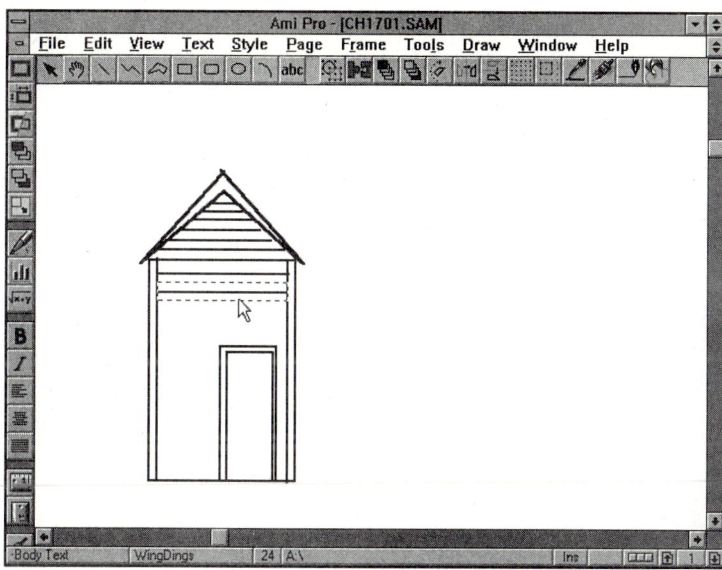

Fig. 17.6
The sample drawing after copying and pasting the lines; the selection arrow is moving the copied lines to a new location.

Selecting Multiple Objects without Grouping

Ami Pro offers another multiple-object selection method that is faster than clicking each object; however, to use this method, the objects must be adjacent (located next to each other). To select adjacent objects, click the Selection Arrow icon; then drag the mouse pointer across the objects you want to select (as if to draw a box around the adjacent objects). As you move the mouse pointer, a dotted rectangle appears (see fig. 17.7).

Tip
The object doesn't need to be completely enclosed by the selection rectangle. The Draw feature selects any objects that are partially enclosed by the rectangle.

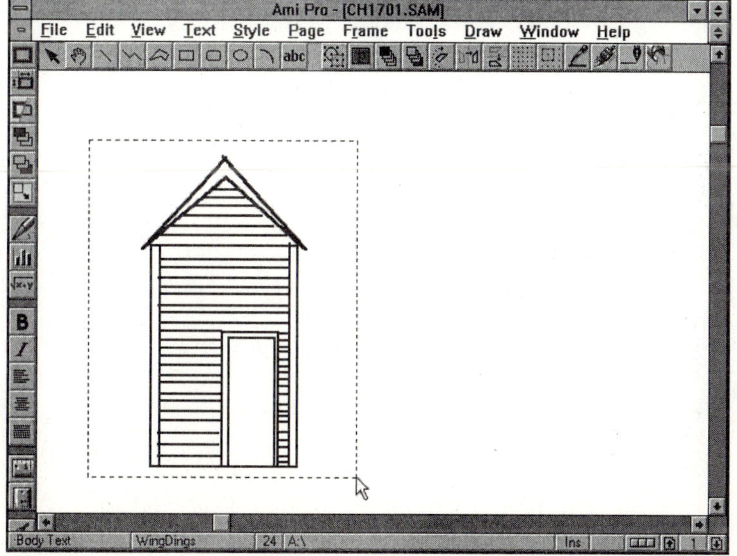

Fig. 17.7
The dotted rectangle appears when you select adjacent objects.

Release the mouse when the rectangle surrounds the objects you want to select. Handles appear around each selected object (see fig. 17.8).

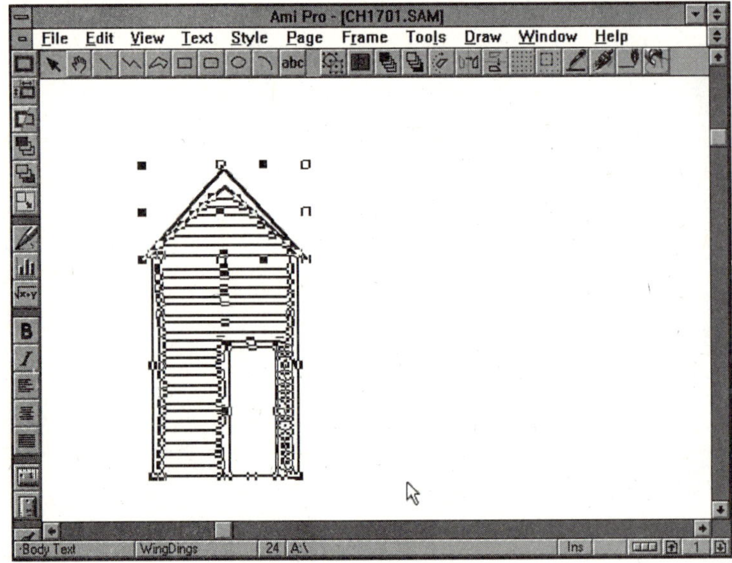

Fig. 17.8
The handles indicate selected multiple objects.

To deselect one or more objects, click outside the selected object (but still inside the frame). The handles disappear.

Selecting multiple objects enables you to perform editing functions such as deleting, copying, and pasting.

Changing the Order of Layered Objects

When drawing, you can place objects on top of other objects. Sometimes an object may hide another object entirely. Unless you change the order, the most recently drawn object appears on top.

After drawing several layered objects, you may decide that you want to change the order of the objects. To bring an object to the front, select that object and click the Bring to Front Command icon (or choose **D**raw Bring to **F**ront). The selected object moves in front of all the other objects.

To select an object hidden behind another object or objects, press and hold down Ctrl and click inside the top object until the object you want is selected. Selection handles indicate the selected object (refer to fig. 17.8).

The Send to Back Command icon (or **D**raw Send to **B**ack) works in the same way but with the opposite effect. When you select an object and click the Send to Back icon, the object moves to the back of the group of layered objects.

You also can change line and fill styles to objects as explained in the next section.

Changing the Current Line Style

When you first start the Draw feature, the current line style—the style of line Ami Pro uses when you draw a Line, or the style the feature applies when you choose **D**raw **L**ine Style—is a solid black line (shown in the Line Style Command icon).

You can change the current line style. In figure 17.8, the line style used to draw the house (the default line style), is too thick. You can change it by using the **D**raw menu or the Command icon. To set a line style, follow these steps:

1. Select the line and choose **D**raw **L**ine Style or click the **L**ine Style Command icon. The Line Styles dialog box appears (see fig. 17.9).

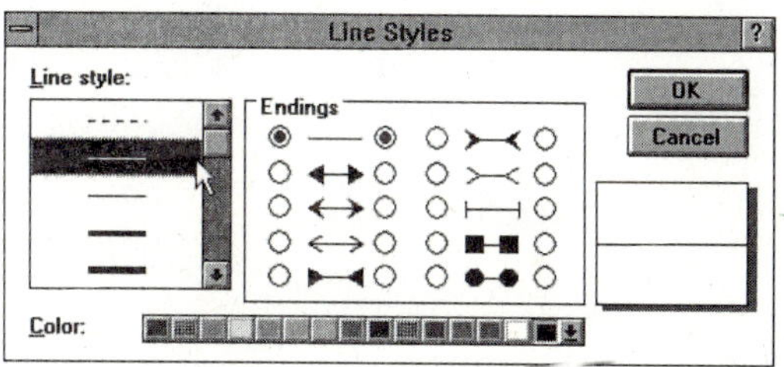

Fig. 17.9 The Line Styles dialog box.

2. In the **L**ine Style section, choose a line style. You can choose various thicknesses or a broken line. For this example, choose the second line from the top of the list.

   The example box in the lower right corner of the dialog box displays an example of your changes.

3. In the Endings box, select a line ending by clicking the selection button. You can have an ending at either end of the line, both ends of the line, or neither end of the line. You also can have different endings on each end, such as a circle on one end and an arrow on the other. For this example, choose no ending—the top option—for both ends of the line.

4. Use the **C**olor bar to specify a line color. You can click the arrow button to see additional choices. For this example, use black.

5. Click OK or press Enter. The current line style changes to the one you selected. The line style remains in effect—even into your next session—until you set it again.

Tip
You also can choose the line style and color before you begin drawing a line.

In addition to changing line styles, you can change the fill pattern of closed objects, such as ellipses, rectangles, polygons, and so on. The next section explains how to change the fill pattern of an object.

Changing the Fill Pattern

Changing the fill pattern is similar to changing the line style. When you choose **D**raw **F**ill Pattern or click the Fill Pattern Command icon, the Fill Pattern dialog box opens (see fig. 17.10). In the Color section of the dialog box, select the color you want to fill the selected object and then select a pattern from the Pattern bar. The example box displays your choices. When you are satisfied with your selections, click OK or press Enter. The pattern you selected becomes the default fill pattern.

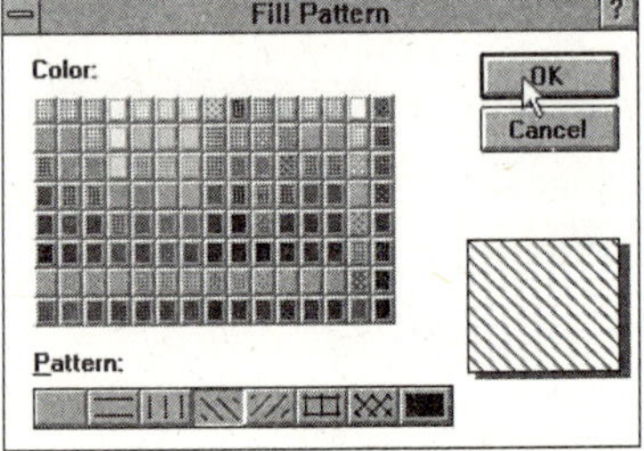

Fig. 17.10
The Fill Pattern dialog box with the fourth pattern selected.

In the sample drawing of a house, add a fill pattern to the door of the house. To do this, first draw a rectangle for the door (to use the fill pattern, you must use a closed object) and select it. Select the **D**raw menu and then choose Fill **P**attern. Select a pattern and then select OK or press Enter. Figure 17.11 illustrates the door of the house with a fill pattern.

The fill pattern in the door uses black lines for the pattern. You also can use any color or shade of gray in conjunction with a fill pattern, as shown in fig. 17.12. **P**attern is the sixth icon from the left (when selected, the button looks "pressed"). The Color in the example is the second column from the right, fourth pattern from the top (the selection arrow is pointing to the gray shade box).

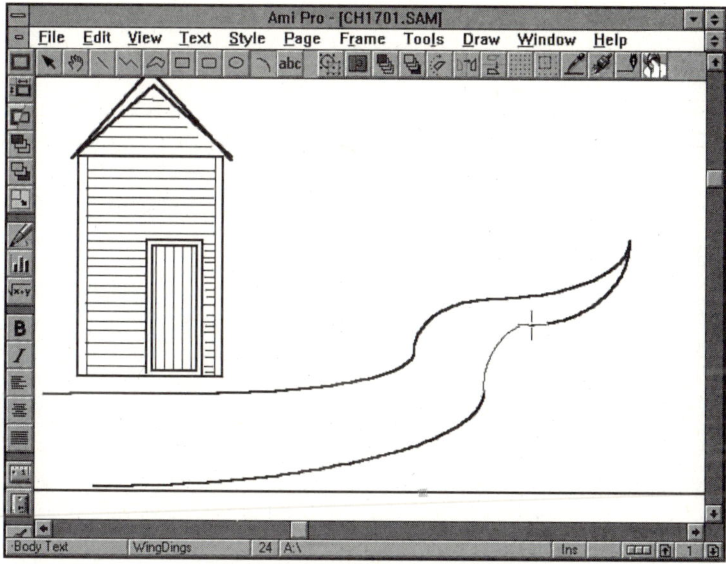

Fig. 17.11
The door to the house is filled with a pattern, and the road is drawn using the arc.

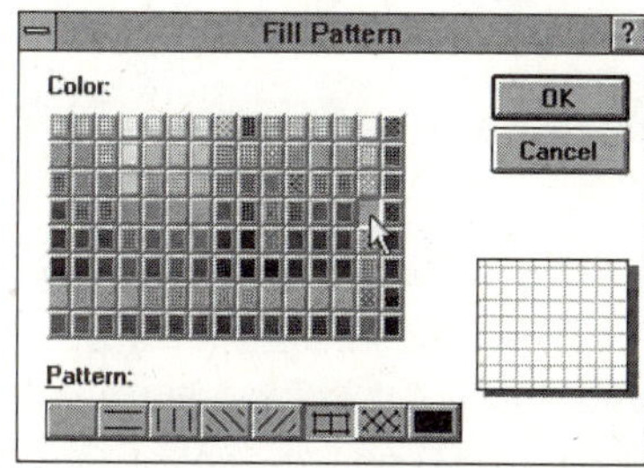

Fig. 17.12
A fill pattern that appears in a shade of gray.

Note

The first button in the row of **P**attern boxes is a blank and contains no pattern. You can use this button with a color or gray shade for a solid fill pattern.

Note

By using different shades of gray in your objects, you can create perspective (depth) in your drawings. Darker objects appear near the front of a picture, are larger, and are lower on the page. Lighter objects appear toward the back and are smaller and higher on the page (see fig. 17.13).

Figure 17.13 illustrates the beginning of another house created using the gray shaded pattern. The left side and beginning of a roof for the new house are drawn using the Polygon tool.

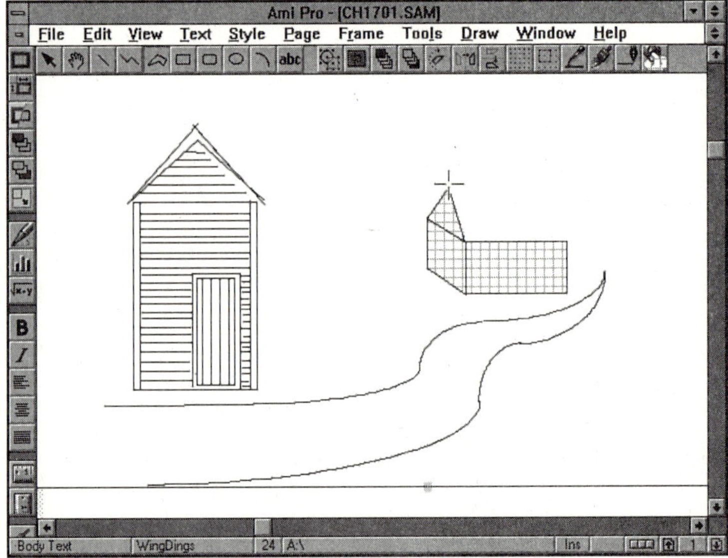

Fig. 17.13 The sample drawing with a second house; this house is smaller, lighter gray, and higher on the page to create depth in the drawing.

Modifying Multisided Objects

So far in this chapter, you have worked with lines and rectangles as examples. But Ami Pro also gives you the power to work with multisided objects. You may want to experiment with the Polygon tool in the Drawing icons. As is shown in figure 17.13, a polygon shape is perfect for drawing parts of a house in perspective. After drawing a polygon, you can add sides and angles to its shape by following these steps:

1. Click the Selection Arrow tool and then select the polygon.
2. Double-click inside the polygon. The object displays handles.
3. Double-click inside the polygon again; rotation arrows and the center of the rotation circle appear on the polygon.
4. Position the mouse pointer on the line in the polygon on which you want to create a new point.

Tip
Using a polygon in this manner, you easily can add several more houses to the sample drawing.

5. Click and drag the mouse in the direction in which you want to create the new point (see fig. 17.14).

6. When the line is the way you want it, release the mouse. Ami Pro stretches the original line and changes it to two lines at the point to which you dragged the mouse pointer.

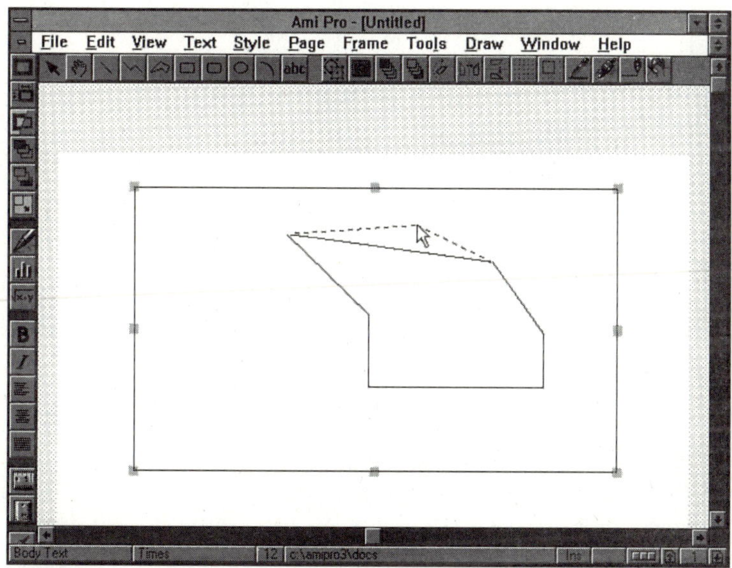

Fig. 17.14
You can drag a point in a polygon to create a new line.

Tip
Creating and using new points along the line of an object works only when using the Polygon tool in the Drawing Icons. You can alter other shapes by clicking and dragging one of their handles.

To delete a line from a polygon, follow these steps:

1. Select the object.

2. Double-click inside the object to display the handles and rotation arrows.

3. Position the mouse pointer on a handle.

4. Click the right mouse button once or double-click the left mouse button. Ami Pro deletes the point and redraws the object without it.

Fig. 17.15 The second house, created with polygons and a gray shaded pattern.

Tip

Notice in figure 17.15 the addition of the tree and bushes by the roadside. To draw the organic lines, choose the Polyline tool. Press and hold the Shift key while drawing with the tool to create natural lines.

Extracting a Line Style and Fill Pattern

When using the Line Style and Fill Pattern commands, if you create a line style and fill pattern that you particularly like, or if you see patterns you like in one of Ami Pro's predrawn symbols from the \AMIPRO\DRAW and \AMIPRO\DRAWSYM subdirectories, you can make that style and pattern the current line style and fill pattern. You even can extract line style, line color, line endings, fill pattern, and color from a drawing to use for the current line style and fill pattern. (See Chapter 19, "Importing, Exporting, and Linking Files," for details on importing drawings.)

Suppose that you want to use the line and fill pattern of an object as the current fill pattern and style for other objects in a drawing. To extract the fill pattern, select the object and then click the Extract Line & Fill Command icon (or choose **D**raw E**x**tract Line & Fill). The Command icons for line style and fill pattern change to reflect the line style and fill pattern of the selected object.

Applying the Current Line Style and Fill Pattern

You may want to apply the current line style and fill pattern to selected objects. Perhaps you have created an object, using the previous line and fill pattern, and now decide you want the object to have the current line style and fill pattern. You can change to the current line style and fill pattern for that object by selecting the object (or group of objects) and clicking the Apply Line & Fill Command icon (or choosing **D**raw **A**pply Line & Fill). The selected objects change to the current line style and fill pattern.

Figure 17.16 displays a set of fence posts. The first fence post is created, and then the line style and fill pattern are extracted. The other fence posts are created, and then the line style and fill pattern from the original fence post are applied to the other fence posts.

Moving Objects

To move an object, you click the selected object or group of objects and drag the object to a new location in the frame. Begin by selecting the object. Position the mouse pointer on the object, in the center—not on one of the selection handles. Using the mouse, click-and-drag the object to the position you want. A dotted rectangle shows the position of the selected object as you drag (see fig. 17.17). When you release the mouse button, the object appears in the new position.

Tip
If you click and hold a selection handle, you resize the object rather than move it.

Fig. 17.16
The fence posts are repeated using the E**x**tract Line & Fill and **A**pply Line & Fill features.

Fig. 17.17
You can move an object by using the mouse.

Moving objects and drawing objects may be easier if you use the Grid feature of Ami Pro. The next section describes how to use the grid.

Working with the Grid

A grid is invaluable for placing items in exact positions in a drawing. By using a grid, you can line up objects to ensure that all the objects contain the same baseline, for example, or you can be exact in the spacing between objects by placing columns of the grid between objects. To display a grid, click the Grid Command icon or choose **D**raw S**h**ow Grid. You also can choose **D**raw Gri**d** Settings. To hide the grid, click the Grid Command icon again or choose **D**raw **H**ide Grid.

In the Grid Settings dialog box, you can choose a style of spacing: **F**ine, **M**edium, or **C**oarse. In the text box, you can specify the distance between gridlines or dots for each type of spacing. For the unit of measurement, use inches, centimeters, picas, or points. In the Grid Line section, you can choose the style of line: **D**ots at Intersect or Dotted **L**ine. To display the settings every time you use a grid, choose M**a**ke Default.

Positioning objects manually on the grid isn't necessary. If you use **D**raw **S**nap To, Ami Pro makes the objects snap to the grid so that they align neatly on the grid. To align objects on the grid as you draw them, click the Snap To Command icon or choose **D**raw **S**nap To. To turn off **S**nap To, click the Command icon again or choose **D**raw **S**nap To again.

Caution

If you have the **S**nap To feature in effect, objects align whether or not the grid is visible. If you're dealing with objects that mysteriously resist moving to the location you want, check to make sure that **S**nap To is turned off.

Resizing Objects

To change the size of an object, select the object and then point to one of the handles with the mouse pointer. If you use a side handle, you change the width of the object. If you use a top or bottom handle, you change the height of the object. If you use a corner handle, you change the width and the height at the same time. Drag the mouse in the appropriate direction to change the size.

Tip
To decrease the size of the object, drag the handle toward the middle of the object.

Figure 17.18 shows the drawing with the flower resized by dragging the top corner handle out.

Fig. 17.18
You can resize the flower by moving the top corner handle.

Rotating Objects with the Rotation Arrows

As discussed earlier, to select an object, click the Selection Arrow icon, and then click the object. If you double-click a selected object, however, you select it in a special way. The selected object shows rotation arrows and a black circle with a plus sign (+) in it rather than handles. The plus sign marks the center of rotation for the object (see fig. 17.19).

To rotate an object, follow these steps:

1. Select the object.
2. Move the mouse pointer anywhere within the object and double-click. The selected object displays rotation arrows and the center-of-rotation circle.
3. Move the mouse pointer to one of the rotation arrows.

Fig. 17.19
The flower with rotation arrows and the center-of-rotation mark.

4. Click and drag the arrow in the direction in which you want to rotate the object. For this example, drag the top left corner arrow down (see fig. 17.20).
5. When you're satisfied with the drawing, release the mouse button.

If you move the center-of-rotation mark, the object rotates based on that placement. To move the center-of-rotation mark, click the selection arrow on the mark and drag it to the new position (see fig. 17.21). Then continue to rotate by clicking and dragging the arrows.

Figure 17.22 shows the flower rotated the same number of degrees as in fig. 17.20; however, in figure 17.22 the center of rotation has changed.

Fig. 17.20
You can rotate the flower.

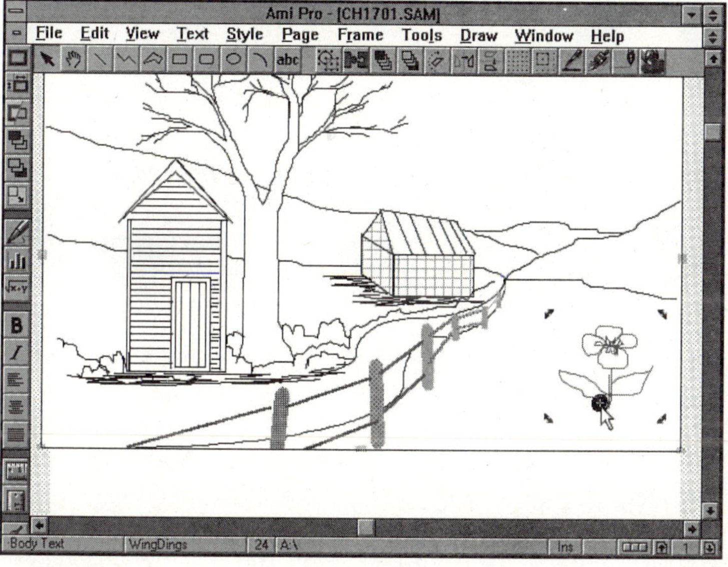

Fig. 17.21
The center-of-rotation mark in the flower is lowered to change the rotation of the object.

Deleting Objects and Drawings

Deleting an object is just like deleting text in word processing. You select the object and press Del, and Ami Pro deletes the object. To delete a complete drawing—all the objects located within a frame—select all the objects in the frame and press Del. You can select objects by pressing and holding down Shift and using the Selection tool or by choosing **D**raw S**e**lect All.

> **Caution**
>
> After you delete a drawing from a frame, you can use the frame only for another drawing, not for text. If you want to use an identical frame in the same location for text or a picture other than a drawing (such as an imported picture), you must delete the frame and the drawing and redraw the frame. To delete the frame and the drawing, select the frame and press Del. See Chapter 16, "Using Frames," for information on deleting frames.

Fig. 17.22
The flower object rotated with a different center of rotation.

Creating and Modifying Text Objects

Ami Pro enables you to add text to your drawings with two methods. The first method is using drawing mode; the second method is using a transparent frame that holds text only. If you want to add a great deal of text (more than a sentence or two), the best method is to create another transparent frame to place on top of the frame containing the drawing. Chapter 16, "Using Frames," explains this procedure in detail.

Adding text to the drawing frame is a second possibility; however, reserve this technique for small amounts of text. You cannot easily control line spacing, alignment, kerning, and so on with text in the drawing feature. In addition, each line of text is a separate object in the drawing feature, making it difficult to work with large bodies of text.

Adding text to the drawing frame, however, is useful in several situations. You can add numbers, letters, titles, phrases, captions, labels, and so on, to your drawings, while ensuring the text remains with the drawing. Another interesting use for text in the drawing mode is rotated text.

You can rotate text 45, 90, or 180 degrees in Ami Pro's drawing feature; you even can rotate text to an odd amount, such as 16, 23, or 142 degrees. You can rotate the text manually or by using the menu (as described in the section "Flipping and Rotating Objects," later in this chapter).

Tip
You also can rotate a drawn object, clip art, or some imported pictures in the drawing feature of Ami Pro.

An invaluable use of rotated text is to add a mailing panel to a brochure. Normally, a three-panel brochure, set in landscape mode, needs a mailing panel with rotated text. (See Chapter 19, "Desktop Publishing with Ami Pro," for complete instructions for producing a brochure of this type.) The option of rotating text in the drawing mode adds to the ease of creating this type of brochure. The following section explains how to create text in the drawing feature, how to format the text, and how to rotate the text.

Creating Text in the Drawing Feature

Each line of text (a line of text is created when you press Enter) is a separate object in the Draw feature. This line of text *can* be moved, cut, copied, rotated, and edited separately from any other text or graphic object in the drawing. This line of text *must* be formatted, aligned, and spaced separately from other objects in the drawing.

To create a text object in a drawing, click the Text Drawing icon (abc). Position the cursor at the point you want the text to begin. Type the text as you do normally. To align the text (center, left, or right), choose the selection arrow and click the text block. Small handles appear (as with a drawing object). You now can move the text block to align it.

Formatting the text block is slightly different than formatting text. The next section explains two methods of formatting the text.

Formatting the Text

When using the Draw feature in Ami Pro, you cannot select text by dragging the cursor across it, as with normal text. In drawing, selecting the text means using the selection arrow to select the block of text or object. When selecting the text object in this manner, the text object can only be treated as a draw object (moved, copied, deleted, and so on). To apply formatting, such as typeface, size, and style, you must use the cursor. You can format text in two ways.

One way to format the text is to enter the text and then format it by using the Status Bar or the **T**ext menu. To enter and format a line of text, follow these steps:

1. Draw a frame for the text.

2. Select Too**l**s **D**rawing.

Tip
DomCasual is an ATM (Adobe Type Manager) font that comes packaged with Windows 3.1 (see fig. 17.24). For information about using the ATM fonts in documents, see Chapter 19, "Desktop Publishing with Ami Pro."

3. Click the Text icon (abc) at the top of your screen.

4. Position and click the cursor in the location you want the word to begin and type. For this example, type the name of your company.

Note

You cannot align text in the drawing feature by choosing alignment choices from the SmartIcons or the **T**ext menu. The location in which you position the cursor is the point to which the text is left aligned. To align the text, you must select it with the selection arrow and move it as a text object.

5. Position the cursor at the beginning of the line of text and click.

6. Select **T**ext **F**ont; the Font dialog box appears (see fig. 17.23).

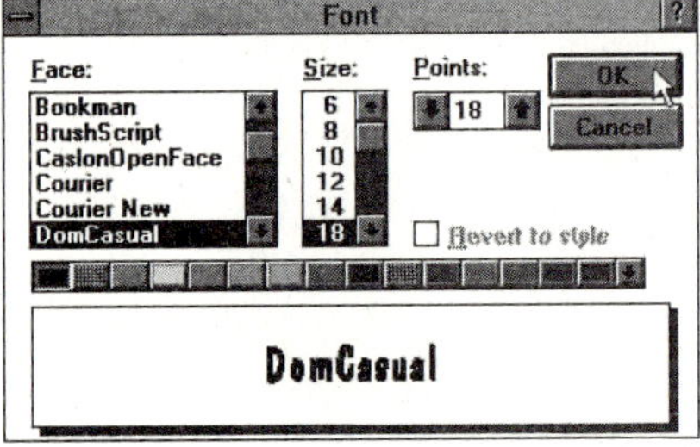

Fig. 17.23
The Font dialog box contains the choices you make for the sample text.

7. Select the **F**ace, **S**ize, and color for the text. In this example, the text is 18-point DomCasual.

8. Select OK or press Enter. Ami Pro returns you to the frame that contains the formatted text.

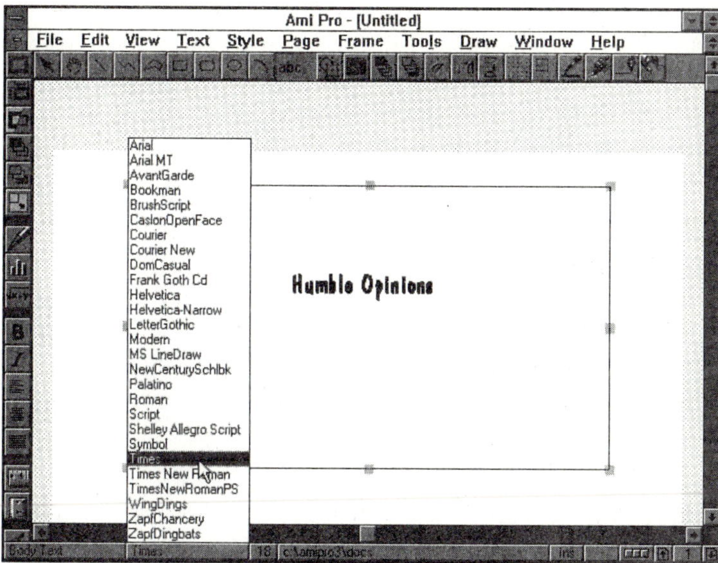

Fig. 17.24
You can choose the typeface of the text object before you enter the text.

Tip
You also can boldface or italicize type in the text object by using the SmartIcon or the text shortcuts (press Ctrl+B for bold or Ctrl+I for italic).

The other method you can use to format text in the Draw feature is to choose the typeface, size, and color before you enter the text. You can accomplish this task by using the **T**ext menu or the Status Bar. To format and enter a second line of text, follow these steps:

1. Click the Text icon (abc).

2. Select the typeface and type size of the second line of type. In this example, the second line of type is 12-point Times.

   Figure 17.24 illustrates the first line of text entered for the example is DomCasual. Figure 17.24 also shows the use of the Status Bar to choose the typeface for the second line of type before the text is entered.

3. Position the cursor below the first line of type (the company name) and type the street address of your company.

4. Press Enter at the end of the second line, and then type the name of the city and the state on the third line.

> **Note**
>
> Although you pressed Enter to begin the third line of text, it isn't connected in any way to the second line. Each line is a separate text object.

Note

The third line (and fourth, fifth, and so on) remains formatted in the last chosen typeface and size until you change it by using the Status Bar or the **T**ext menu.

Grouping the Text Objects

You can rotate the three lines of type separately; however, aligning and placing them is difficult. An easier method is first to group the three lines and then rotate them. To group the three lines of text, follow these steps:

1. Choose the selection arrow from the Drawing icons. Click the first line of type to select it.

2. Press and hold the Shift key and select the second line of type and then select the third line of type.

3. Choose **D**raw **G**roup. Figure 17.25 shows the **D**raw menu and the three selected lines of text.

   Note

   Group is a toggle command; a check mark appears beside the word *Group* in the menu to indicate that it's activated. Choosing the command again deactivates the group option, and the check mark disappears.

4. Ami Pro returns you to the screen. The three text objects are now one object that contain one set of handles.

The next section describes how to rotate the text group.

Rotating Text

You can rotate the text group by using the **D**raw menu or the rotation arrows. To rotate the text group by using the rotation arrows, follow these steps:

1. Choose the selection arrow from the Drawing icons.

2. Select the text group. The handles appear.

3. Double-click the selected group, and the double arrows appear.

4. Choose a corner arrow and swing the text until it's rotated the way you want. Figure 17.26 shows the rotated text group.

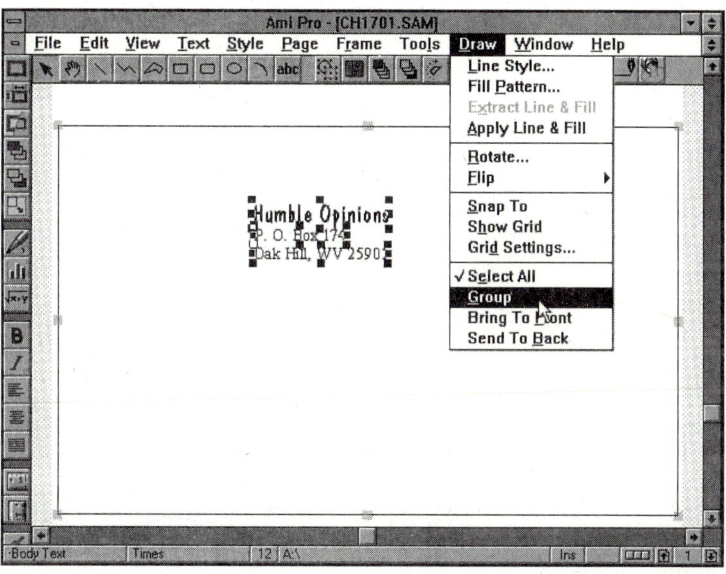

Fig. 17.25 The **D**raw menu and selected sample text.

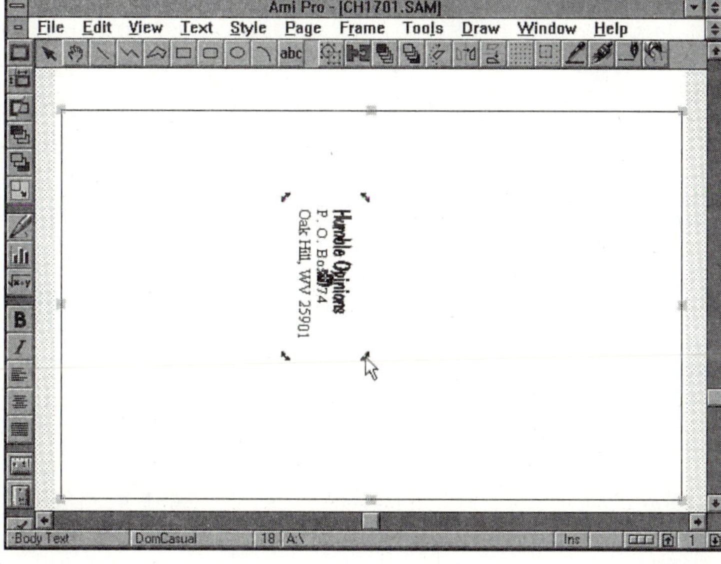

Fig. 17.26 The text group rotated with the rotation arrows.

◀ See "Character Formatting," p. 95

◀ See "Paragraph Formatting," p. 105

Modifying Imported Objects

Tip
These methods don't work with scanned half-tones. See the next section, "Modifying a Scanned Image," for information.

Modifying imported objects includes moving and cropping (hiding part of the object from view) within the frame, and enlarging and reducing, flipping, and rotating the object. Imported objects include those from clip art programs, other draw or paint programs, and so on. (See Chapter 20, "Importing, Exporting, and Linking Files," for information about compatible file formats.) For the following example, you can use a file from Ami Pro's clip art collection (AmiDraw) or one of your own files.

To import an AmiDraw file, create a frame. Select the frame, and then choose **F**ile **I**mport Picture. From File **t**ype, choose AmiDraw. From the list of **F**iles, choose any piece of AmiDraw clip art. Select OK or press Enter. The following steps use the RTARROW.SDW file. Ami Pro returns you to the document with the clip art imported to your frame.

Note

If you use a frame in the drawing mode to import an AmiDraw file, the command in the **F**ile menu changes to **I**mport Drawing.

Tip
After selecting an imported object, you can cut, copy, or paste it as with any other object in the Draw feature. You even can add text to clip art as described in the previous section.

To modify the imported object, select the frame and go to Too**l**s, **D**rawing. You must select the object within the frame. Use the selection arrow to click the object. The selection handles appear around the object.

Moving and sizing an imported object is different from moving and sizing other draw objects, as the following section explains in detail.

Moving the Object

To move or crop the object within the frame, you must use the Hand tool from the Drawing icons. The selection arrow, when used with imported pictures, enlarges and reduces the object. To move an object, select it, and then use the Hand tool to manipulate it in the frame. To move the object (in this case the right arrow), follow these steps:

1. Select the Hand tool from the Drawing icons.
2. Position the hand over the object, and then click and drag the object around in the frame. A dashed box appears as you drag the object (see fig. 17.27).

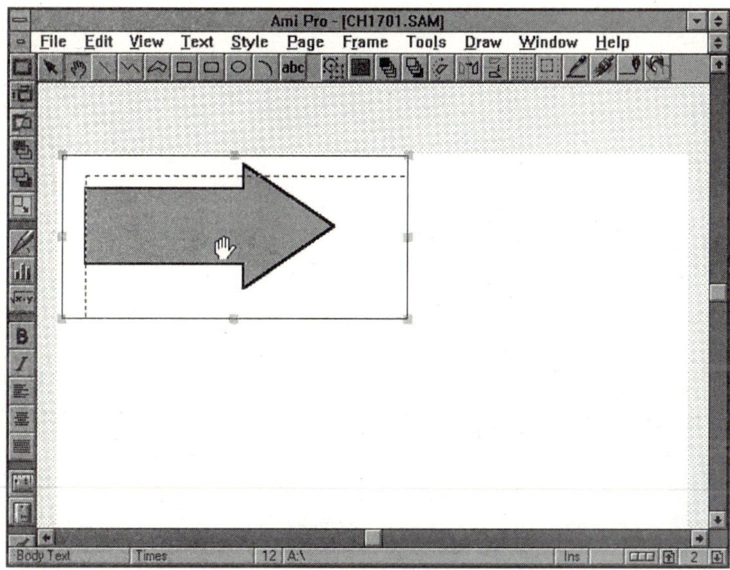

Fig. 17.27
You can use the Hand tool to move the imported object within the frame.

3. When you release the mouse button, the object is in place, and the dashed box disappears.

Tip
The Hand tool remains active until you choose another tool.

To crop the clip art file, use the Hand tool to move the object off any edge of the frame. You can hide a quarter, half, or all of an object by pushing it out of the frame using the Hand tool. To bring the object back in view, use the Hand tool to drag the dashed box in the opposite direction.

Tip
If you have trouble finding the object after you push it completely out of the frame, enlarge the frame to locate it.

Enlarging and Reducing the Imported Object

You enlarge and reduce Draw objects by using the selection arrow. You also enlarge and reduce imported objects by using the selection arrow, but not by selecting a handle. Moving the imported objects with the selection arrow enlarges or reduces an imported object. To reduce an imported object, follow these steps:

1. Choose the selection arrow from the Drawing icons.
2. Click and drag the imported object diagonally to the lower right corner. Figure 17.28 illustrates the motion with the dashed rectangle.
3. To move the object back to the center of the frame, use the Hand tool as described in the previous section.

Caution

Don't use the selection arrow to reposition the object; moving the object back to the center by using the selection arrow enlarges it again.

To enlarge an imported object, drag the object in the opposite direction (towards the upper left corner of the frame). Figure 17.29 illustrates the reduced arrow from the preceding steps. The dashed box that appears in the figure pushes the arrow to the upper-left corner to enlarge it.

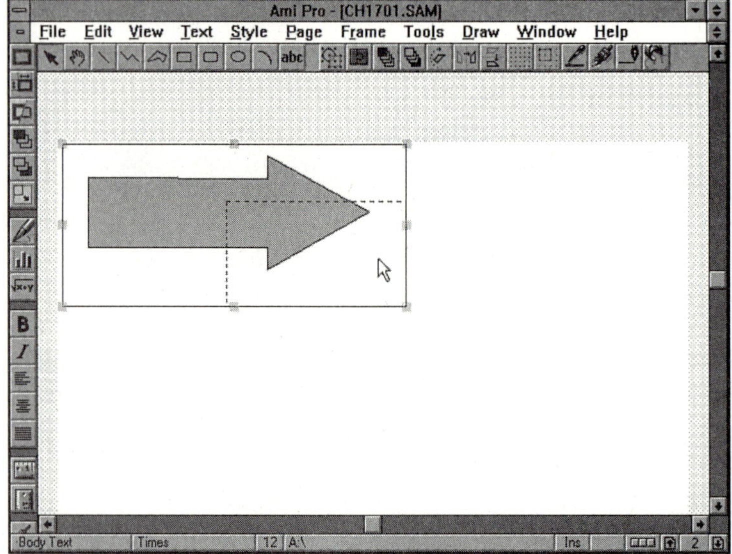

Fig. 17.28 You can reduce the imported object by dragging it to the lower right corner of the frame.

You must reposition the enlarged object by using the Hand tool to bring it back into the middle of the frame. You can flip imported and drawing objects, as described in the next section.

Flipping and Rotating Objects

Imported objects don't move, crop, enlarge, or reduce the same as drawn objects, but they do flip and rotate the same way. Figure 17.30 illustrates the procedure for flipping the right arrow to change it to a left arrow.

Tip
You cannot flip text objects.

To flip the drawn or imported object, select it by using the selection arrow. Choose **D**raw **F**lip. Select Horizontal from the cascading menu.

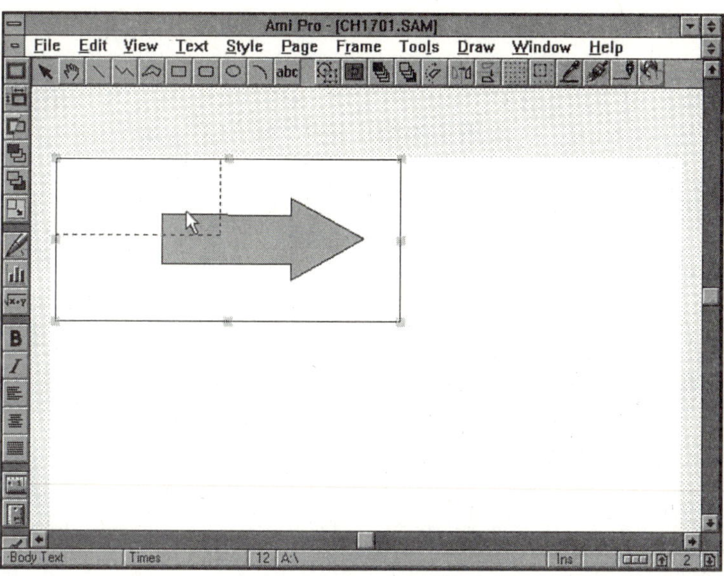

Fig. 17.29
The reduced arrow is repositioned, and the dashed box illustrates the procedure you use to enlarge the clip art.

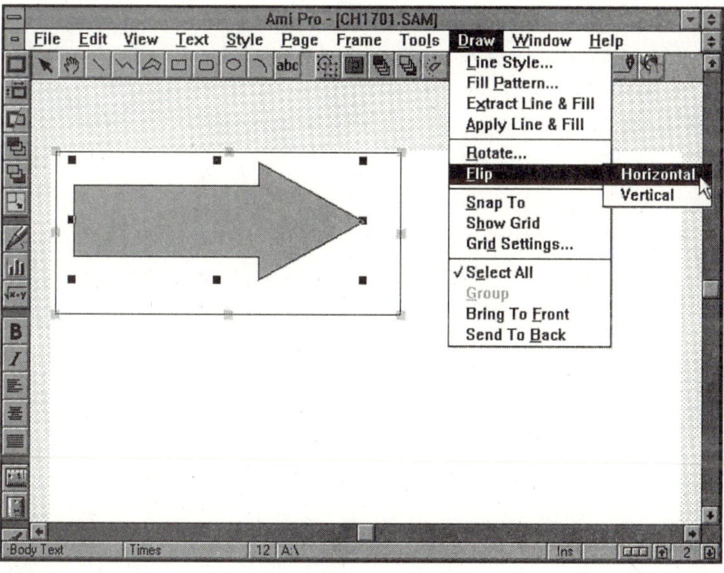

Fig. 17.30
You can change the right arrow to a left arrow by flipping it.

You also can flip an object vertically. In this example, the arrow looks no different when flipped vertically.

You also can rotate a drawn, imported, or text object, as explained in the next section.

Tip
You can use the Command icons rather than the **D**raw menu to flip objects and access the Rotate dialog box (see fig. 17.31).

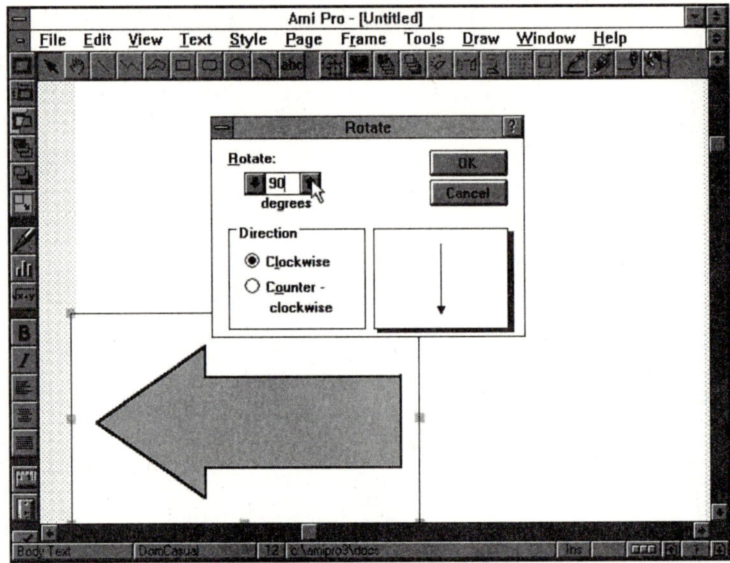

Fig. 17.31
The flipped arrow and the Rotate dialog box.

Rotating Objects with the Menu

You can rotate text and drawn or imported objects by using the rotation handles (as described in previous sections) or the **D**raw menu. To rotate an object by using the **D**raw menu, follow these steps:

1. Select the object.
2. Choose **D**raw **R**otate.
3. In the **R**otate box, type the number of degrees you want to rotate the object (you can choose in increments of one from 0 to 359 degrees).
4. Select the Direction in which you want to rotate the object: C**l**ockwise or C**o**unter-clockwise (again, refer to figure 17.31). It displays the Rotate dialog box. Notice that the example box in the right corner shows the results of your choices.
5. Select OK or press Enter when you are satisfied with your choices. Ami Pro returns you to the document with rotation changes in effect. Figure 17.32 illustrates the sample arrow rotated 90 degrees clockwise.

◄ See "Entering Text and Graphics in Frames," p. 512

► See "Importing Graphics," p. 691

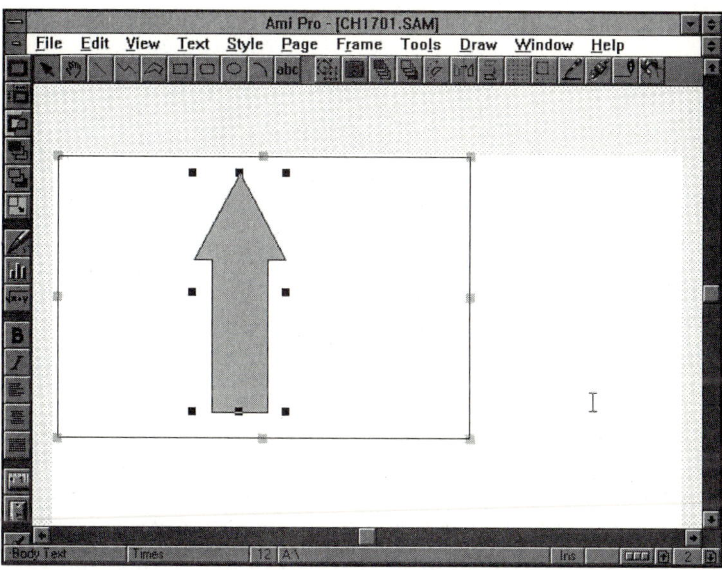

Fig. 17.32
The arrow is rotated 90 degrees.

Modifying a Scanned Image

Although image processing isn't really a part of the drawing feature, it is, nevertheless, an important part of working with images in Ami Pro if you use a scanner. This section briefly explains Image Processing using a scanned image (halftone). For more information about Image Processing, first refer to the Ami Pro reference manual and then experiment with your scanned images.

Tip
You can scan an image in a line art or halftone format. Line art is black-and-white and contains no gray tones. You work with a line art in the same way you work with a drawn object in the Draw feature.

A scanned image, or halftone, is an image that uses a series of dots to form a picture. These dots, both large and small, create the image. The more (and larger) dots within the image, the darker (or blacker) is that part of the image; the fewer (and smaller) dots, the lighter (or grayer) is the image.

True black-and-white photographs use black and various shades of gray dots to form an image, producing true gray tones. A printer cannot produce those gray tones. Instead, a printer uses a halftone with black dots in different sizes and density to imitate the look of gray tones.

Note

When scanning a halftone, you can adjust the brightness and contrast of the halftone in the scanning program; doing this is best. It gives you more control over the image processing in the scanning program, and the halftone prints from Ami Pro more quickly if you use no image processing in Ami Pro.

Tip
Image Processing is not a part of the Draw feature in Ami Pro; therefore, you can adjust the image by using the keyboard or the mouse.

You may need to adjust the brightness or contrast to your halftones in Ami Pro. In these instances, you can accomplish the adjustments by using Image Processing. First, you need a halftone with which to work. If you don't have a scanned image of your own (TIFF or PCX format), you can use the halftone that Ami Pro supplies. (See Chapter 20, "Importing, Exporting, and Linking Files," for information about importing a scanned image.)

To import the halftone from Ami Pro, follow these steps:

1. Draw a new frame and then select it.

2. Choose **F**ile **I**mport Picture.

3. In File **N**ame text box, type ***.TIF**.

   Typing ***.TIF** is a wild-card method that enables you to locate all files that end in the extension TIF. The * (asterisk) is a wild-card character that means *all*; therefore, typing an asterisk followed by a period (*.) in a file name box instructs Ami Pro to display all files that end with a particular extension (TIF in this case).

4. Change directories to the \AMIPRO\DOCS directory. If your hard drive isn't C, change to the correct drive. (For information about changing directories, see Chapter 3, "Editing Techniques.")

5. From the File **T**ype list, choose TIFF. The PUPS.TIF file name appears in the list of **F**iles.

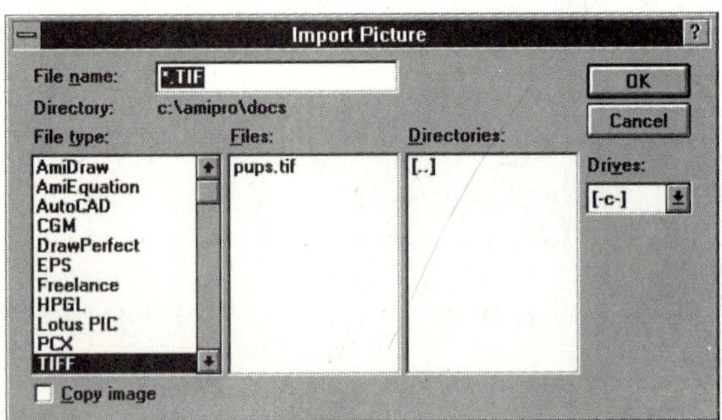

Fig. 17.33
The Import Picture dialog box, with the selection arrow pointing to the directory in which the PUPS.TIF file is located.

6. Choose PUPS.TIF from the list of **F**iles and then choose OK or press Enter. Ami Pro returns you to the document; the image appears in your frame (see fig. 17.34).

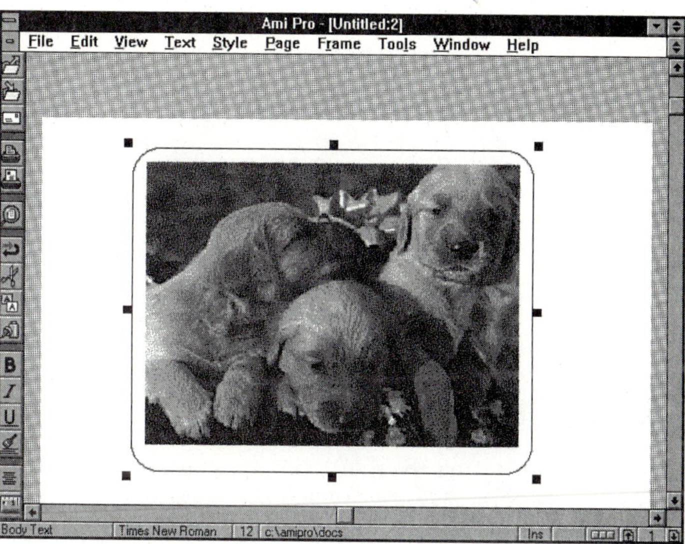

Fig. 17.34
The PUPS.TIF image as it appears when imported.

Note

Because the halftone image isn't in draw mode, you cannot use any of the Draw features or tools. If you position the cursor over the image, however, the cursor changes to a hand. The hand works similarly to the hand in the Draw feature and enables you to move and crop the image.

Notice that the **I**mage menu has been added to the Menu bar. Figure 17.35 shows the **I**mage menu.

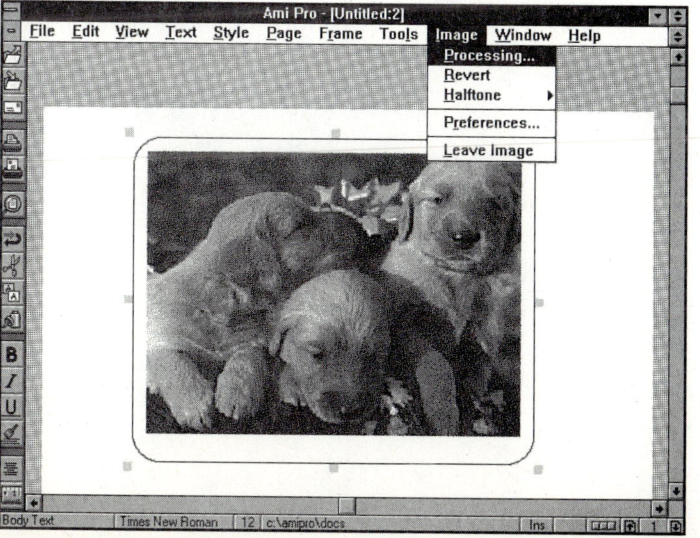

Fig. 17.35
The **I**mage menu is added to the Menu Bar when you select **I**mage **P**rocessing from the Tools menu.

Following is a brief explanation of the **I**mage menu and command choices:

- ***P****rocessing*—When you choose Processing, the Image Processing dialog box appears. The following options used to change the image are included within the dialog box:

    - *Brightness*—Controls the mix of black-and-white dots in the image. Increase the brightness and more white appears; decrease the brightness and more black appears. The brightness applies uniformly to the image.

    - *Edge Enhancement*—Controls the contrast between edges of the picture and the background and between the edges within the picture; brings out more details.

    - *Contrast*—Controls the sharpness of the image by increasing the difference between black and white and by reducing the amount of grays in the image.

    - *Smoothing*—Blends harsh or jagged edges and removes stray dots. Smoothing gives a softer look to the image.

    - *Invert Image*—When checked, changes an image from black to white, creating a reverse of the original image.

- ***R****evert*—Restores the image to the original version.

- ***H****alftone*—Presents a cascading menu that contains commands that enable you to control printing speed and quality. Following is a list and brief explanation of the Halftone commands:

    - ***F****astest Printing*—Prints the image quickly; however, the quality of the image is sacrificed. This print option is good for proofing pages.

    - ***B****est Picture Quality*—Produces a fine print quality, however, prints more slowly.

    - ***A****utomatically Selected*—Produces a higher quality print of a scaled image without taking as long to print.

    - ***P****osterize*—Provides halftones with a special poster effect and changes all grays to black or white.

    - ***L****eave Image*—Hides the **I**mage menu.

To adjust the image processing for a halftone, follow these steps:

1. Select the frame that contains the image and double-click it to activate the **I**mage menu.

   When you first import an image, the **I**mage menu appears. If you select **L**eave Image, the **I**mage menu disappears. To show the Image menu again, double-click the image.

2. Choose **I**mage **P**rocessing. The Image Processing dialog box appears (see fig. 17.36).

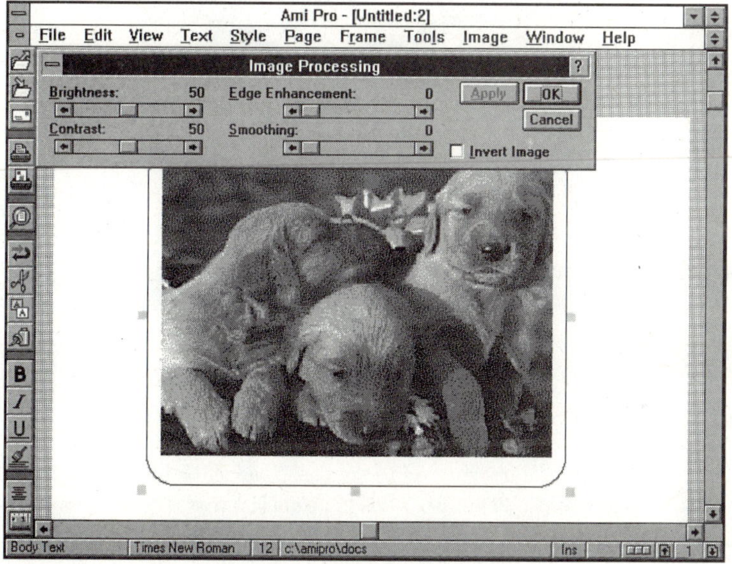

Fig. 17.36
The Image Processing dialog box.

Tip
By clicking Apply rather than OK, the dialog box remains on-screen, and your changes are made to the image.

3. Using the arrows on the Brightness bar and Contrast bar, adjust the Brightness and Contrast (in this example, the Brightness is 70 and the Contrast is 80), and then click Apply.

4. Make other adjustments to the image as you want. When you're satisfied with the image, select OK or press Enter.

Figure 17.37 illustrates the processed image after you apply the changes from the Image Processing dialog box.

Fig. 17.37 The image after you add more Brightness, Contrast, and Smoothing.

> **Note**
>
> If possible, complete all sizing of an image before you import it into Ami Pro. Resizing a halftone in Ami Pro causes two results. First, a resized halftone takes longer to print. Second, a resized image doesn't look as good as the original because of those same dots used to create the halftone. The dots stretch, distort, and space differently when you resize the halftone in Ami Pro, and this results in an inferior product. The best solution to this problem is to resize the image before you scan it. Most scanning programs offer this option. See the reference manual of the scanning program you use for more information on sizing a picture before you scan it.

Summary

Ami Pro's Draw feature is a full-fledged drawing feature with plenty of flexibility. With the powerful Draw and Command icons and the **D**raw menu, you can create a number of fixed shapes and free-form shapes, and you can import and modify draw objects.

In this chapter, you learned how to draw, select, move, copy, resize, and change objects. You also learned how to apply more extensive modifications to selected objects—grouping, changing the order of layered objects, rotating, flipping horizontally and vertically, and customizing line patterns and fill patterns. You also learned how to work with AmiDraw files and how to process scanned images. With this knowledge, you can use Ami Pro's Draw feature to accomplish your drawing objectives.

In the next chapter, you learn how to use Ami Pro's Charting feature to create and edit graphs for use in reports and presentations.

Chapter 18

Creating Charts

Using charts to represent numeric information in graphic form for business presentations has been a standard practice for some time. Charts help to interpret large or small volumes of data in a style that is easy for an audience or readers to understand. Presenters routinely use bar charts, pie charts, or line-and-picture charts to represent data. Many people who may not use drawing features or add other enhancements to their data are willing to use charting capabilities.

Because Microsoft Windows makes working with simultaneous multiple programs so easy, you may use a full-fledged graphics program such as Lotus Freelance for Windows or Microsoft PowerPoint to create your charts. Ami Pro's charting program is powerful enough, however, that you can use it for many of your charting needs.

In this chapter, you first learn how to set up the data to use in your charts. You cannot build an Ami Pro chart without specifying the data for the chart or charts you plan to create. (If you don't provide data, Ami Pro presents a dialog box in which you can specify the data.)

After learning the basics of creating a chart, you examine the available Ami Pro chart types, learn when each type is appropriate, and explore how to use each type. (A pie chart, for example, is best when you want to show the relationship of parts to the whole.) You also learn how to apply useful chart options, such as displaying a legend or using a grid.

Because an Ami Pro chart is a drawing program file, you can edit the chart as you do other drawings. In this chapter, you learn how to delete a chart, how to use drawing to add elements such as clip art and explanatory text, and how to change the chart type (for example, from a columnar chart to a pie chart).

Finally, you learn how to change chart defaults—the default pictures that appear in picture charts and the default colors and patterns that appear in all charts.

Supplying Chart Data

Before you can create a chart in Ami Pro, you must provide the data for the chart to display. You can use one of two methods. You can cut or copy data from another Ami Pro document, from a table, or from another application (see Chapter 20, "Importing, Exporting, and Linking Files," for information on using other applications). You also can type the data in a dialog box. In this section, you learn how to use both methods.

The data must follow these guidelines for Ami Pro to use the data in a chart:

- If you aren't using a table, you must use numeric data arranged in columns and separated by tabs or spaces. The data can include negative or exponential numbers and decimals. Ami Pro ignores currency symbols or commas and doesn't use them in the chart.

- To include a legend or labels along the axes (not applicable to pie charts), type the desired text in the first row before the numeric data. The labels appear along the x-axis (the bottom axis) for all charts except the stacked bar, where Ami Pro places the labels on the y-axis (the side axis).

- A pie chart lacks axes but can include a legend or labels. Type the legend or labels above the numeric data. If you have enhanced the text for the labels or data (in an Ami Pro document, as opposed to the Charting Data dialog box), Ami Pro uses the text as labels or data but ignores the enhancements.

- You can use only as many columns and rows as the chart can accommodate. The maximum is 5,000 columns and rows (but you must have enough available memory to support that amount).

Tip
You can enhance the text in charts with the drawing feature, as explained later in this chapter.

Using Existing Data

If you use existing data in your chart, the data can be in an Ami Pro document or table or even in another application. Suppose that you have a document containing a table of sales information (see fig. 18.1). You can copy this table into a chart.

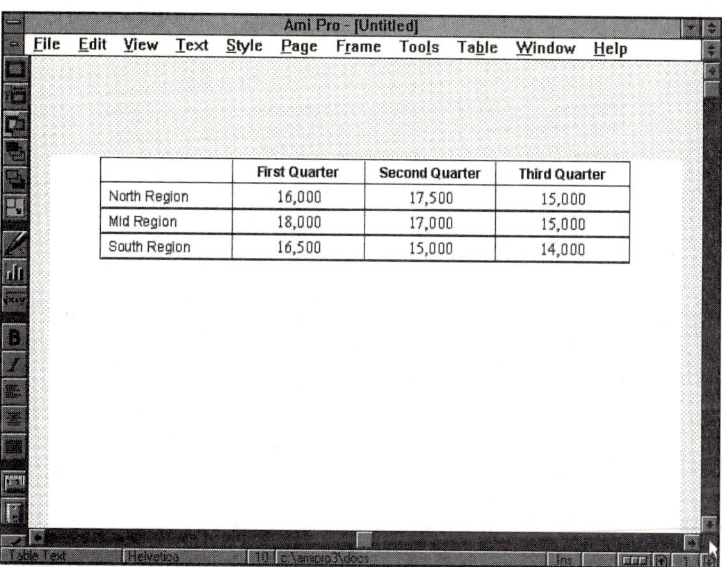

	First Quarter	Second Quarter	Third Quarter
North Region	16,000	17,500	15,000
Mid Region	18,000	17,000	15,000
South Region	16,500	15,000	14,000

Fig. 18.1
A sample table.

For the following steps, assume that you want to copy all the data from the sample table in figure 18.1. Follow these steps to copy data from an Ami Pro document to a chart:

1. In the document containing the data, select the portion of the data you want to use in the chart. For this example, select the whole table.

2. Choose **E**dit **C**opy (to retain the data). Ami Pro copies the data to the Windows Clipboard. (You can use **E**dit **C**ut if you don't want to keep the original data in the table.)

3. Make the document in which you want to place the chart the active window; or use the same document that holds the table.

4. Create a frame in which you want the chart to appear. (Note that the frame doesn't need to be visible. See Chapter 16, "Using Frames," for information.)

   Alternatively, you can choose Too**l**s **C**harting without first drawing a frame, and Ami Pro draws the frame automatically (using the dimensions listed in the Create Frame dialog box).

5. Select the empty frame.

6. Choose Too**l**s **C**harting.

Tip
To create a label that includes a number (such as 1993), type an underscore before the number (for this example, type _**1993**).

Tip
For multiple-word labels, such as Regional Sales, use an underscore between words. Ami Pro replaces the underscore with a space when creating the chart.

If the frame you created isn't large enough, Ami Pro displays the following message:

```
The frame is too small to create a chart. You must enlarge
the frame before continuing.
```

If you haven't copied or cut data to the Clipboard, Ami Pro displays a message indicating that the Clipboard is empty and prompts you to enter data.

If the frame is large enough to hold the chart and the Clipboard contains data, the Charting dialog box appears, as shown in figure 18.2. The dialog box shows the data from the Clipboard in a chart format in the example box.

7. Specify the desired options in the Charting dialog box (the options are explained later in this section). For this example, use the default settings.

8. Choose OK or press Enter. Ami Pro creates the chart.

The following paragraphs briefly explain the options in the Charting dialog box. The section "Using Charting Options," later in this chapter, discusses the charting options in the dialog box in more detail.

At the left side of the dialog box is the Chart Type section, in which you select the chart type you want to use. (The default is a column chart.) Click a chart type to select it; Ami Pro displays a sample chart in the example box in the center of the dialog box. The example box shows the indicated chart type, reflecting the selected data for the chart you are creating.

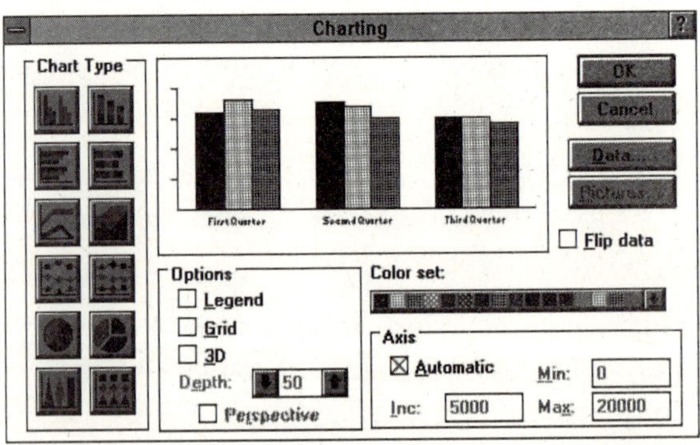

Fig. 18.2
The Charting dialog box (with default settings).

In the Options section, you can elect to use a legend instead of labels, display a grid, have the chart appear in three dimensions, and specify the depth and perspective for the three-dimensional chart. (You can preview the effects of your choices for depth and perspective in the example box.)

With the Color Set color bar, you can choose the set of colors you want to use for the chart. You can even create new custom colors. (For details on specifying colors, see Chapter 8, "Changing Your Setup.")

If you choose **D**ata, you can edit the data in your table by adding, deleting, or changing the data. (See "Editing Chart Data," later in this chapter, for more information.)

The **P**ictures option is dimmed unless you select one of the four kinds of picture charts in the Chart Type section of the dialog box. Choosing this button produces more picture options.

With the **F**lip Data option, the program uses the data from the first column (instead of the first row) as labels or legends and creates the rest of the chart accordingly.

In the Axis section, select **A**utomatic if you want Ami Pro to set the axes automatically. With this option, the program uses a scale with a minimum of 0 and a maximum appropriate for the data represented (the scale must allow the largest number to fit on the chart) and reasonable increments between the tick marks on the axis. If you prefer, you can deselect **A**utomatic and set the **M**in (minimum), Ma**x** (maximum), and **I**nc (increments) for the axes.

In figure 18.3, the names of the regions (in the first column of the table) don't appear, and the chart has no title. The first row from the table, showing the quarter headings, appears here as labels. Notice that Ami Pro has used an appropriate scale for the y-axis, ranging from 0 to 20,000 (abbreviated here as 20K). You can make many improvements in the chart, as explained later in this chapter. From this example, however, you can see that you can create a quick chart by entering the data and using the default chart settings. This figure shows a vertical bar chart based on the sample data in figure 18.1. Later in the chapter, you learn how to create other chart types.

Typing Chart Data

Creating a chart from data in an existing document is convenient, but you may not have such data available. For standard applications you use repeatedly, on the other hand, you may want to experiment and project possible results using sample data. For these situations, you can type data by following these steps:

1. Create or select an empty frame of the size you want. (See Chapter 16, "Using Frames," for details on using frames.)

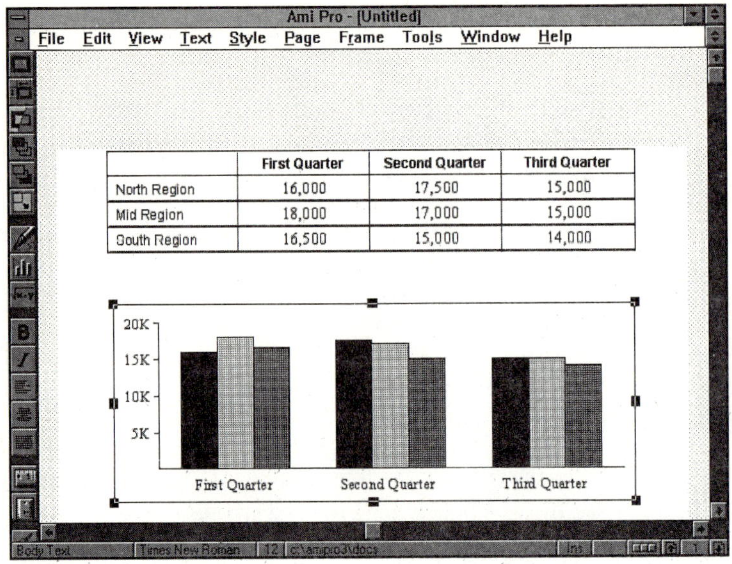

Fig. 18.3
A bar chart based on the sample data in figure 18.1.

If you prefer, you can let Ami Pro create the frame for you; however, creating your own frame is faster. If you draw the frame, you don't need to resize the one Ami Pro creates.

2. Choose Too**l**s **C**harting. Ami Pro checks the Clipboard to see whether you have data there. If the program doesn't find any data, you see the message shown in figure 18.4.

Fig. 18.4
The message that appears when no data is in the Clipboard for use in charting.

3. Choose OK or press Enter. Ami Pro displays the Charting Data dialog box with a blank text box so you can enter the chart data.

4. Type the desired data in the text box by following the rules described after these steps.

5. Choose OK or press Enter to close the Charting Data dialog box.

6. Choose OK or press Enter to close the Charting dialog box. Ami Pro creates the chart.

When typing data for the chart in the dialog box, note the following rules:

- You cannot use the Tab key; use the arrow keys or click with the mouse to move between characters and rows.
- You cannot press Enter at the end of a line (this is the same as choosing OK).
- Press Ctrl+Enter to move to the next line.
- Use spaces to separate the columns. You may want to use more than one space to distinguish the columns.

Figure 18.5 shows a sample set of typed data in the Charting Data dialog box, and figure 18.6 shows a pie chart based on that data.

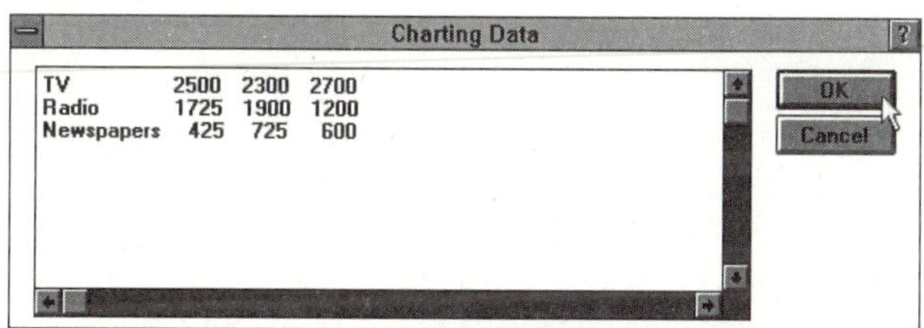

Fig. 18.5
Sample data in the Charting Data dialog box.

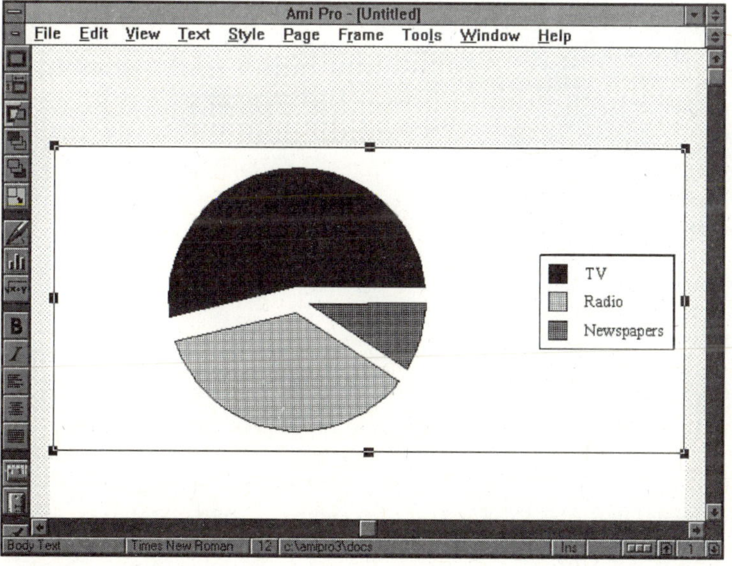

Fig. 18.6
A sample pie chart, with legend, based on the sample data in figure 18.5.

Editing Chart Data

You can edit the chart data in the Charting dialog box but not in the same way you edit text with the **E**dit menu. You cannot cut, copy, paste, or add attributes. You can delete characters or words with the Del or Backspace keys, and insert new text by typing new characters. You can edit data typed in the dialog box or data imported from the Clipboard.

Note

If the amount of data is limited, edit the data in the Charting Data dialog box. If you have many changes to make, however, return to the original document to edit the text. In the original document, you have full Ami Pro editing capabilities. You then can copy the edited data and create a new chart.

Note

Changes you make in the Charting Data dialog box don't affect the original data in a table or another file. The two files aren't *hot-linked*.

Note

You can double-click an existing chart to display the Charting dialog box. If you use the Draw program to edit the chart, you may see the draw mode when you double-click. You see the mode you used last: charting or drawing. To switch modes, click outside the frame to exit draw mode. Then select the frame and choose Too**l**s **C**harting.

Tip
In figure 18.7, the Charting Data dialog box allows room for additional columns and rows. You can use the scroll bars to view the data.

Follow these steps to edit the chart data in the Charting dialog box:

1. Select the frame containing the chart.
2. Choose Too**l**s **C**harting.
3. In the Charting dialog box, choose **D**ata. Ami Pro opens the Charting Data dialog box, which displays the current data.

   Figure 18.7 shows the data from the chart in the sample document (created earlier in this chapter) in the Charting Data dialog box.
4. Edit the chart text as necessary (inserting and deleting characters). Use the space bar to separate columns.

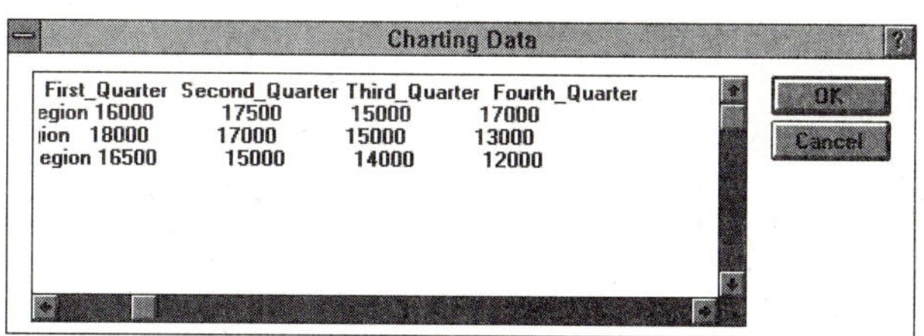

Fig. 18.7
The Charting Data dialog box with edited data.

5. Choose OK or press Enter when you are satisfied with your changes. Ami Pro returns to the Charting dialog box and displays an example chart in the dialog box based on the chart data.

Figure 18.8 illustrates the edited sample chart (in the example box).

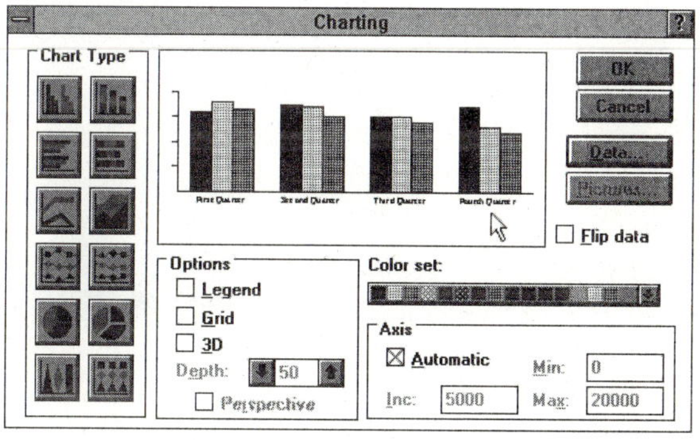

Fig. 18.8
The sample chart with new information added (in the example box).

The next section explains how to create a chart by using the options in the Charting dialog box.

◄ See "Creating Tables," p. 379

◄ See "Creating a Frame," p. 498

► See "Importing and Exporting Text," p. 676

Creating the Chart

With your data in place, finishing the chart is a matter of selecting the chart type you want, choosing the options you want (such as **3**D or **L**egend), and choosing OK. Thanks to the WYSIWYG (what you see is what you get) format, you can see your choices in the example chart in the dialog box before you implement those choices.

The chart types and chart options available are described in detail in the sections that follow. The basic procedure for completing a chart after your data is prepared and entered in the Charting dialog box involves the following steps:

1. In the Charting dialog box, click one of the Chart Type icons (see fig. 18.9). Press Tab to select a chart type. The example chart at the top of the dialog box changes to reflect the chosen chart type.

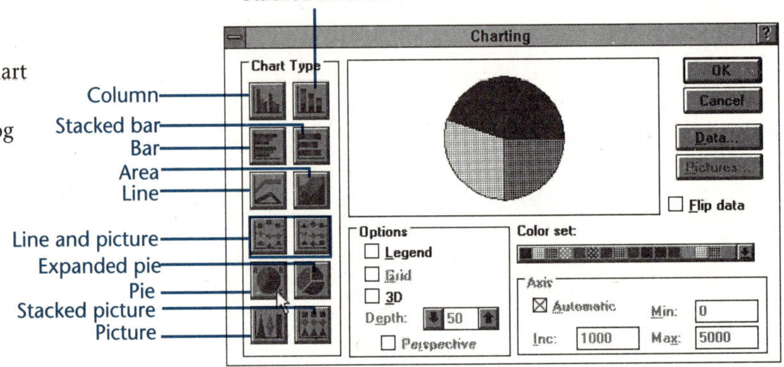

Fig. 18.9
Choosing a chart type in the Charting dialog box.

2. Select any desired options.

3. Choose OK or press Enter.

After you finish creating the chart, save it. To save the chart, save the document containing the chart by choosing **F**ile Save **A**s or **F**ile **S**ave (if the document already has been saved).

Choosing Chart Type Variations

You choose a chart type by clicking the appropriate icon in the Charting dialog box. If you click a selected chart type icon again, however, Ami Pro displays the variations for that chart type, such as varying the color for column and bar charts or having the label text displayed inside or outside a pie chart. Each chart type can have up to four variations.

Tip
The Pie icon shows the next choice, not the current choice.

The basic pie chart appears after you click the pie chart icon once (see the example box in fig. 18.9). Figure 18.10 shows the same pie chart data after clicking the pie chart icon again—notice that the icon changes with the example in the example box. Figure 18.11 shows the same pie chart data after clicking a third time. (With the keyboard, press the space bar instead of clicking.) The first figure shows the pie chart without labels. In the second figure, the labels appear outside the pie; in the third figure, the labels are on the pie slices.

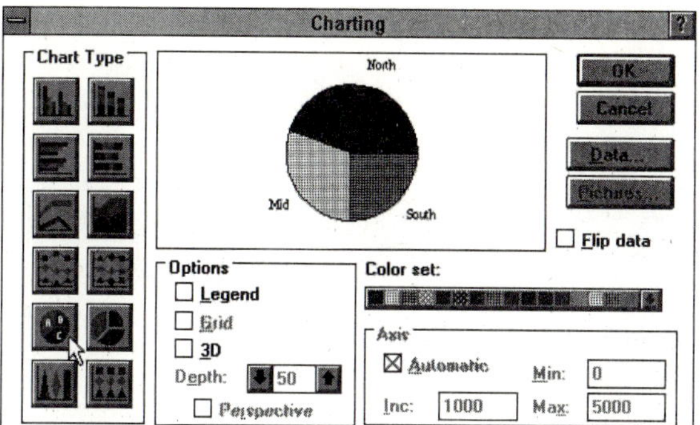

Fig. 18.10
The dialog box after clicking the Pie Chart icon a second time (labels outside the pie).

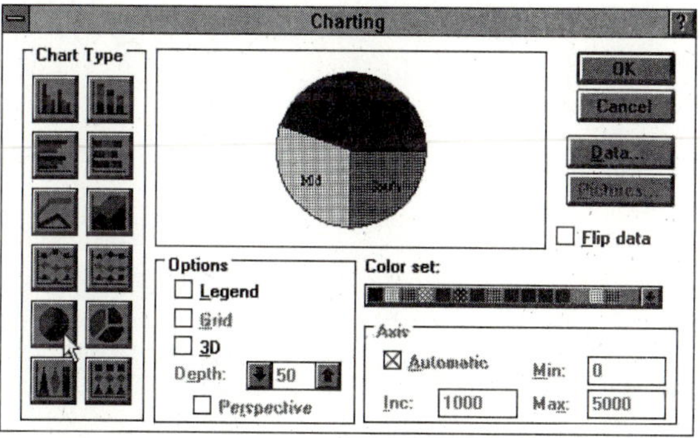

Fig. 18.11
The dialog box after clicking the Pie Chart icon a third time (labels inside the pie slices).

Selecting a Chart Type

To choose the right chart type, you must be familiar with the types of charts represented by the chart type icons on the left side of the Charting dialog box. These icons represent the following chart types: column, stacked-column, bar, stacked-bar, line, area, line-and-picture, pie, expanded-pie, picture, and stacked-picture. The following sections discuss each chart type in detail and provide examples to help familiarize you with Ami Pro's many chart types.

Column Chart

A *column chart*, also known as a *vertical bar chart*, shows the data in columns. The column chart in figure 18.12 is based on the data in the sample document used earlier (refer to fig. 18.1). In this case, the sample column chart has several options in effect. A *legend* (the key or caption to explain the chart) appears in the box to the right of the chart. The chart uses a *grid*—the broken parallel lines appearing behind the columns—and the three-dimensional option. The chart also uses a black-and-white color set to help distinguish the individual bars. (You can choose colors or shades for the chart from the Color Set bar in the Charting dialog box.)

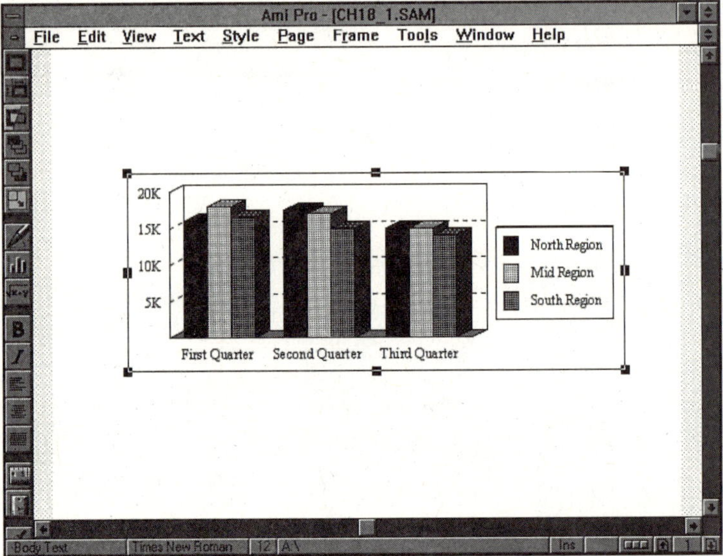

Fig. 18.12 A sample column chart with enhancements.

In this example, the first set of three columns (reading from the left) represents the first quarter figures from the table in figure 18.1. The first quarter figure for the North Region appears in the far left column of the chart, followed by the first quarter for the Mid Region (center), and the first quarter for the South Region (right). The second set of three columns shows the results of the second quarter, and the third set shows the results of the third quarter.

Column charts are particularly useful for showing data over time, with earlier periods appearing on the left and later ones to the right. A column chart can show a decline in yearly sales over a five-year period, for example, with each column representing sales for a particular year.

Stacked-Column Chart

The *stacked-column chart* in figure 18.13 is similar to a column chart. Instead of showing related data (the data from a single column) in a group of vertical bars, however, a stacked column chart shows related data in a single vertical bar. In the figure, the sample data for the first quarter appears in the left stacked column, the second quarter in the second stack, and so on. As the legend shows, the North Region data is at the bottom of each stack, topped by the Mid Region and then the South Region. This example includes the grid, legend, and 3D enhancements.

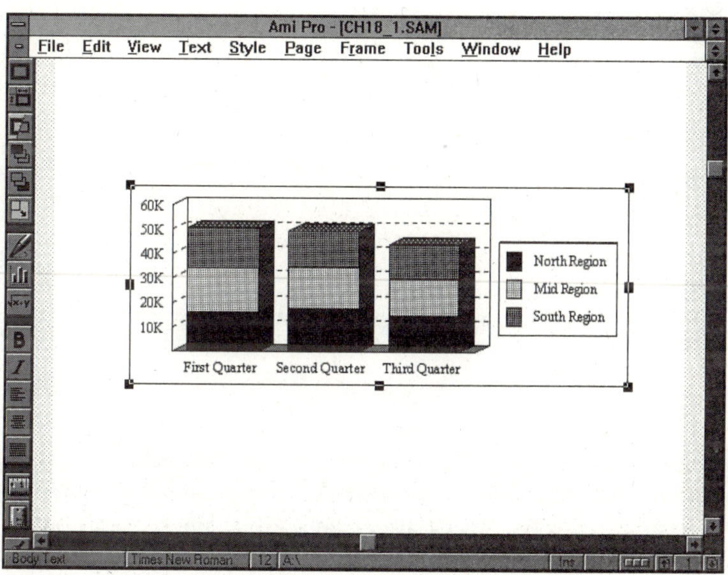

Fig. 18.13
A sample stacked-column chart.

With a stacked-column chart, you can compare more easily the total values for each column with one another—for example, the totals for the first quarter with those of the second and third quarters in the sample data.

Bar Chart

In Ami Pro, a *bar chart* (also known as a *horizontal bar chart*) shows bars projected horizontally from the y-axis. Instead of comparing data over time, a bar chart is useful for comparing data at a single point. If you use the sample data in a bar chart, as shown in figure 18.14, the emphasis shifts from changes in sales over time to the sales figures in each bar irrespective of time. In the sample chart, the emphasis changes from the threat of a decline in sales from the first quarter to the third quarter to the individual performance of each quarter. This chart includes the legend enhancement only.

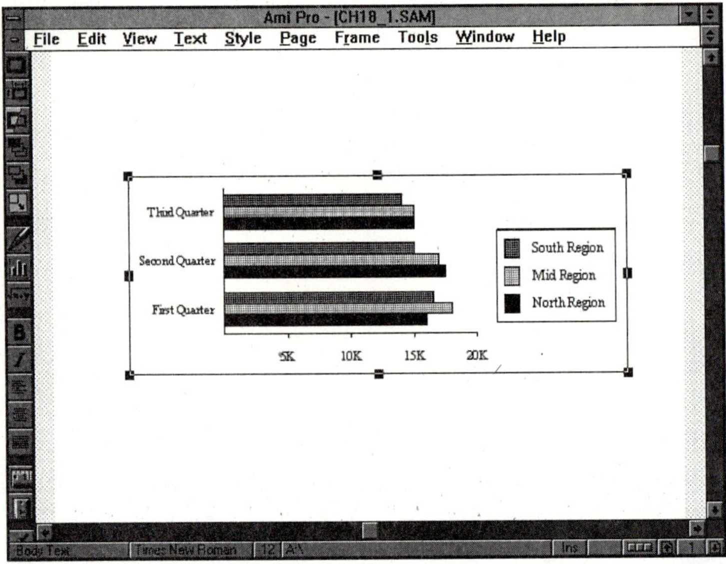

Fig. 18.14
A sample bar chart.

Stacked-Bar Chart

Like a stacked-column chart, a *stacked-bar chart* enables you to compare more easily the total values for each bar rather than the individual values emphasized in a bar chart. Figure 18.15 shows the sample data projected as a stacked-bar chart with a legend. In this example, you easily can see the total performance for each quarter, without paying attention to the trends in regional performance.

Line Chart

A *line chart*, like a column chart, emphasizes changes in data values over time. Whereas column charts emphasize the values for each period (such as the first quarter, second quarter, and third quarter in the example), line charts emphasize the overall trend. Line charts are particularly useful when you have many data points to chart. Figure 18.16 shows a line chart version of the sample data with a legend.

If you view the lines in color and add a legend (as shown in this figure), you can see that sales in the Mid and South regions declined steadily while sales in the North Region rose in the second quarter before declining in the third.

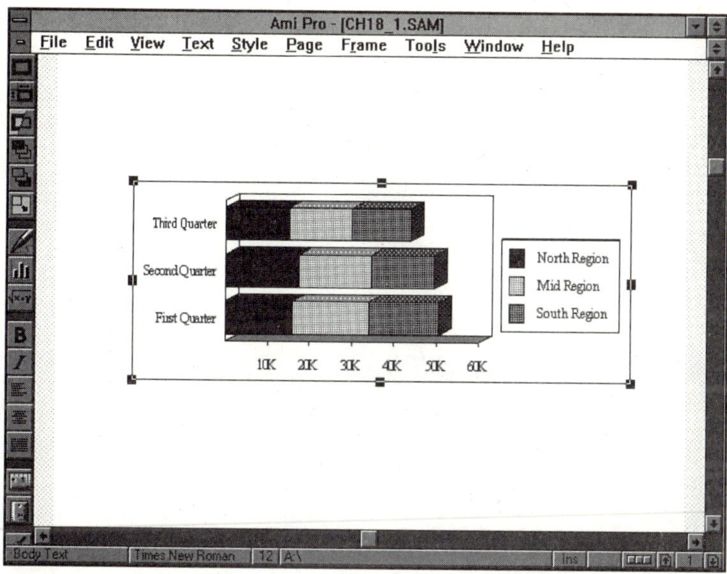

Fig. 18.15
A sample stacked-bar chart.

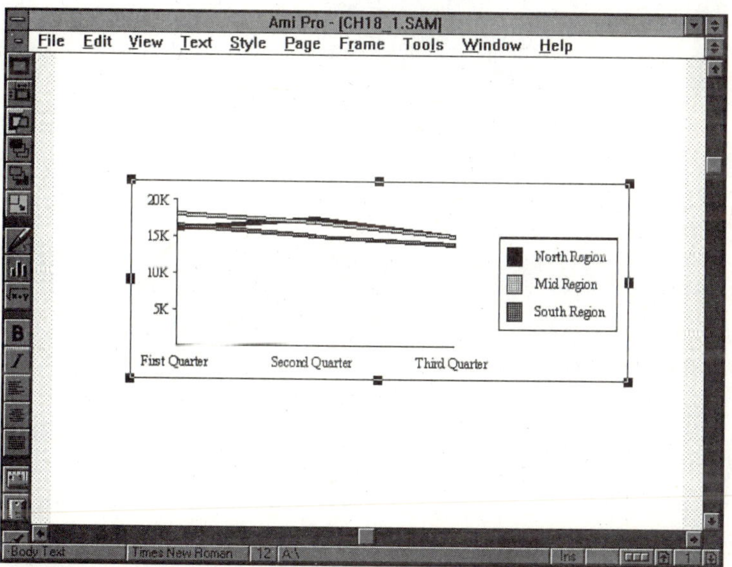

Fig. 18.16
A sample line chart.

III

Professional Output

Area Chart

Like a stacked-column chart, an *area chart* compares values for a number of different data sets (in the example, sales for different regions). In the stacked-column chart, the emphasis is on comparing sales in individual periods—the sales for the first, second, and third quarters. In the area chart, on the other hand, the emphasis is on comparing overall trends in sales over time—in this case, the gradual decline from the first to the second quarter, and the steeper decline from the second to the third quarter. Figure 18.17 shows the sample area chart with a legend.

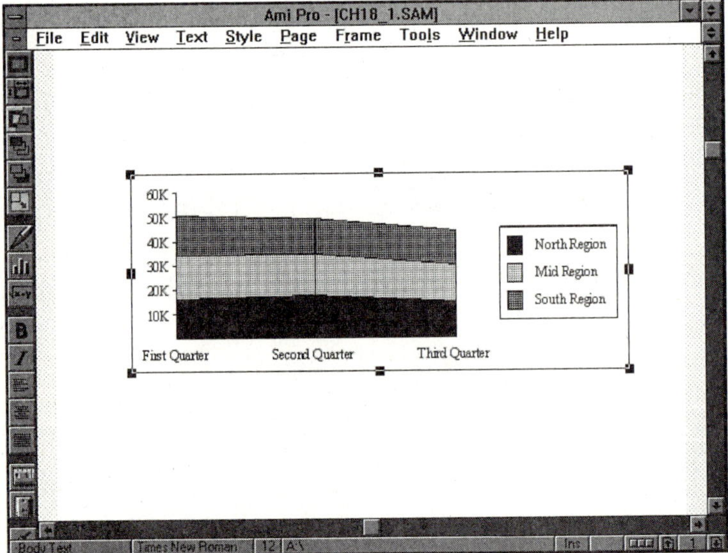

Fig. 18.17
A sample area chart.

Line-and-Picture Chart

A *line-and-picture chart*, as its name implies, is an enhanced line chart. Like a line chart, a line-and-picture chart shows trends over time. The "pictures" (symbols representing data points) also help you see the distinct data points and compare the points with one another. Figure 18.18 shows a line-and-picture chart using the sample data; the legend shows what each picture represents.

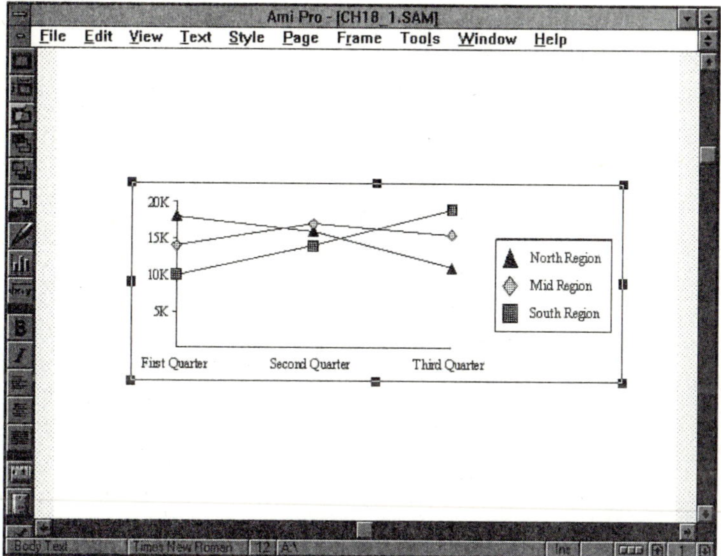

Fig. 18.18

A sample line-and-picture chart.

Pie Chart

A *pie chart* is useful for comparing parts with the whole rather than primarily comparing parts with one another (as in a column chart, for example). The sample pie chart in figure 18.19 shows sales from each region as a part of overall sales. This figure shows that each region carries its own weight, with about a third of the overall sales. If one region is markedly larger in sales than the others, management may want to know why. The sample pie chart includes a legend and the 3D effect.

Expanded-Pie Chart

Ami Pro offers a choice between two kinds of pie charts. The standard pie chart is a simple pie with slices connected (see fig. 18.19). The *expanded-pie chart*, on the other hand, shows the pieces of the pie expanded from the whole, thereby helping you see and compare individual slices. Figure 18.20 shows an example of an expanded-pie chart, with a legend and in 3D.

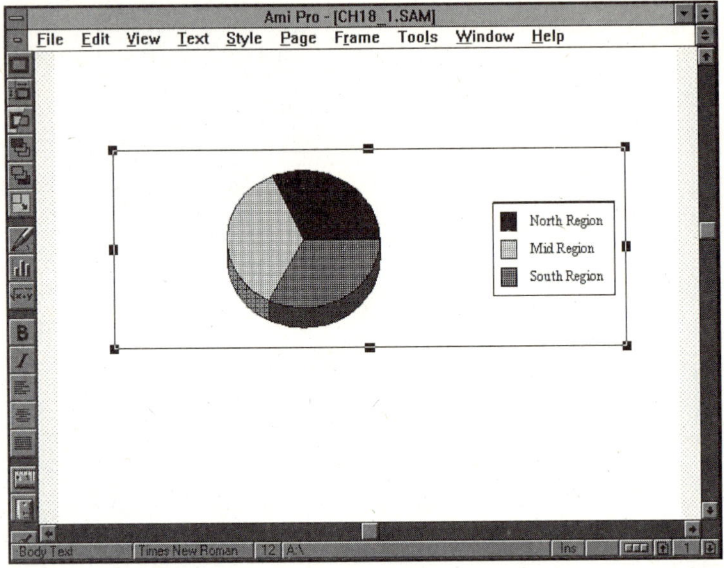

Fig. 18.19 A sample pie chart.

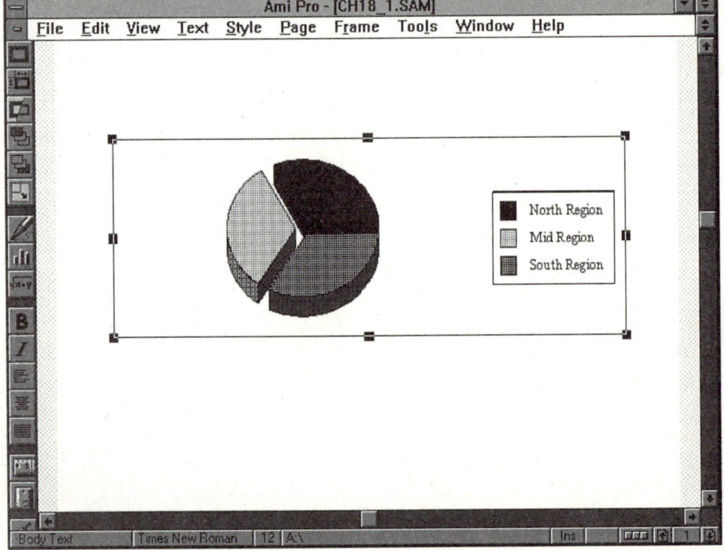

Fig. 18.20 A sample expanded-pie chart.

Picture Chart

A *picture chart* is a column chart with one difference. Each column is an individual picture, so you can see each column distinctly. In the chart in figure 18.21, the group of pictures that makes up a column represents sales for a quarter. Each picture within the group represents a sales region, as shown in the legend.

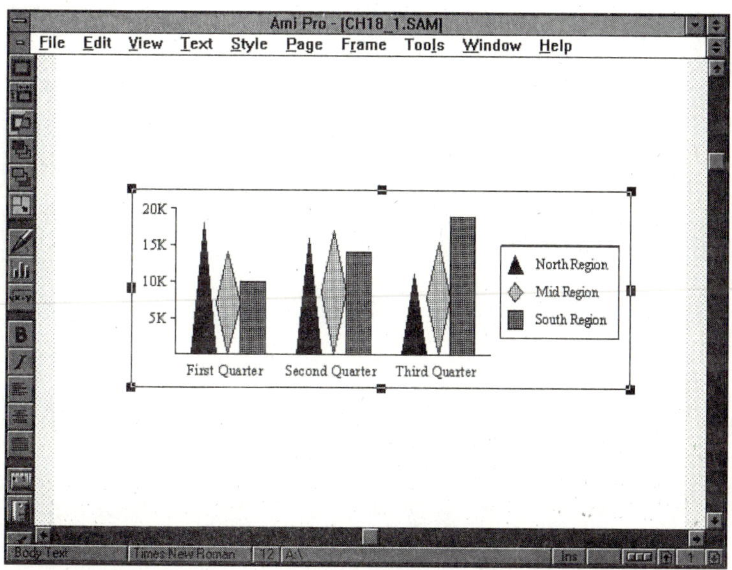

Fig. 18.21
A sample picture chart.

Stacked-Picture Chart

A *stacked-picture chart*, like a stacked-column chart, emphasizes the total values for each data set. The pictures, as in a regular picture chart, enable you to see individual values distinctly. Figure 18.22 shows a sample of a stacked-picture chart that calls attention to the sales of each individual region (as shown in the legend).

Using Charting Options

As noted earlier in the chapter, Ami Pro's charting feature offers a number of options, such as using a legend or grid, changing the color set, and changing the baseline (**M**in) for a chart. You specify the options in the Charting dialog box (see fig. 18.23).

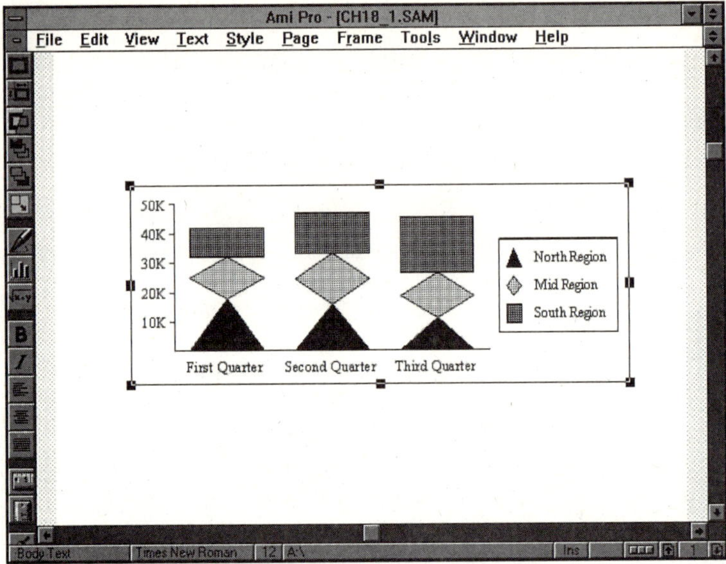

Fig. 18.22
A sample stacked-picture chart.

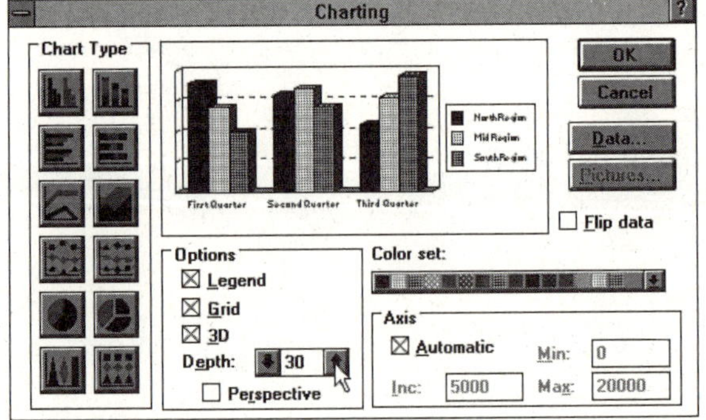

Fig. 18.23
The Charting dialog box, showing a column chart in the example box.

Keep in mind that not all options are available for all chart types. The **G**rid option isn't available for a pie chart, for example, because a grid helps compare elements horizontally and vertically and doesn't make sense for elements presented as parts of a circular whole. The **3**D option isn't available for a line chart because a line cannot appear in three dimensions. The **L**egend option, however, is available for all chart types.

The following sections explain how to use the Charting dialog box options for your charts.

Adding a Legend

Understanding a chart can be difficult if the chart doesn't have a *legend* (an explanation of the symbols, patterns, or colors). All of the sample charts shown in the previous figures have included a legend to help clarify the data.

After you select the **L**egend option in the Charting dialog box, Ami Pro displays the text from your first column of data as a legend. If you don't have the text for the legend in the first column of data, edit the data to add the legend text.

Adding a Grid

After you select **G**rid in the Charting dialog box, Ami Pro displays a grid of dashed lines behind the chart. The lines align with the values on the axis of your chart (horizontal or vertical—the direction that makes sense for the chart—Ami Pro determines which way the gridlines run). Gridlines give you the advantage of being able to see exact values more easily.

Displaying a Chart in Three Dimensions

You can display many of your charts in three dimensions—all but the various forms of line charts and picture charts. In the Charting dialog box, select the **3**D option; then specify a depth from 1 to 100 in the D**e**pth text box.

Note

When you use three dimensions, the area of a bar or column or pie no longer is an exact representation of the data. The non-three-dimensional face of the chart represents the data precisely, but the three-dimensional portion is for effect only and doesn't represent the data. If you don't need the area object to represent the data exactly (often you may not), three-dimensional bars, columns, and pies often look more finished and impressive than flat objects.

The default setting for **3**D is 30. If you change the setting, the new setting becomes the default (the initial setting) for the next chart you create. The setting isn't based on a unit of measure but is a relative measure of depth (a percentage of the total depth Ami Pro accepts). Using **3**D is an aesthetic decision above all, as is deciding what percentage of 3D to use. Consider what looks good for your purposes; if you want to give the impression of depth and solidity, you may opt for a higher depth setting.

Figure 18.24 illustrates a column chart with the **3**D option selected. The D**e**pth setting of 60 is also in use; however, the Pe**r**spective option is not selected. The **L**egend and **G**rid options are also selected for this example.

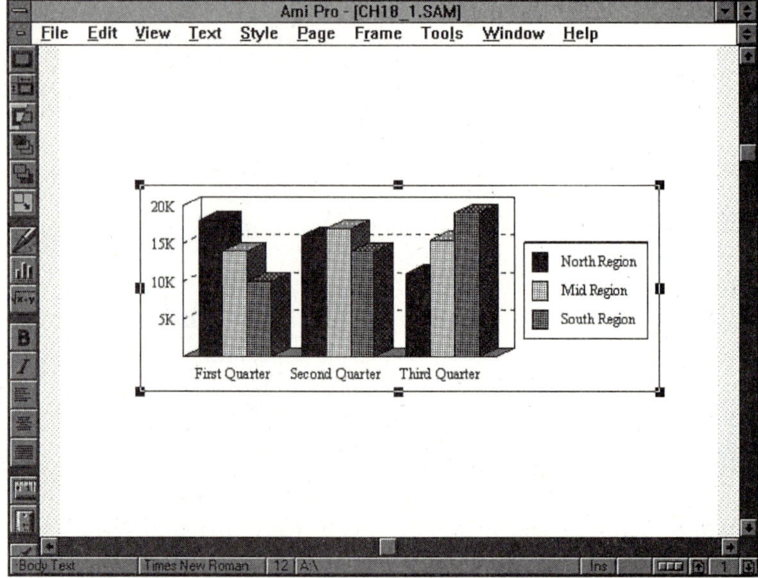

Fig. 18.24
A column chart with the **3**D option selected and a D**e**pth setting of 60.

The Pe**r**spective option in the Charting dialog box is available only after you select **3**D. If you select Pe**r**spective, Ami Pro enhances the three-dimensional effect in the chart by increasing the effect. Figure 18.25, for example, shows the chart in figure 18.24 after the Pe**r**spective option has been selected. The D**e**pth is still 60, and the **L**egend and **G**rid are selected, as well.

Tip
Colors look nice on-screen, but you need a color printer. Choose different patterns or shading from the Color Set color bar for black-and-white printers.

Changing Colors

If you prefer, you can change the colors displayed in the current chart by using the Color Set color bar in the Charting dialog box. (To change the colors displayed in all your charts, you must change the default color set or the default position of the colors.)

The first color on the left in the Color Set color bar is the color for the first row or column of data, the second color is for the second row or column, and so on. To change the colors for the current chart, click the down-arrow button on the Color Set color bar to display the full palette of colors. Figure 18.26 shows the wide range of possible colors from which you can choose.

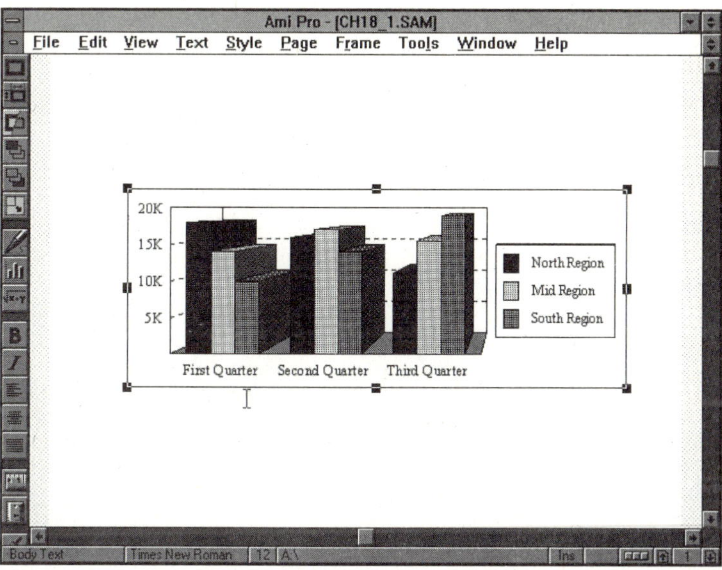

Fig. 18.25
The sample chart with the Perspective option selected.

Click the palette (the row of colors) you want to use as the current color set. That row moves to the top position as the current color set. To move a color within the current color set, click the color you want to move and drag it to the column where you want it to appear. The new color replaces the former color. The other colors shift to make room for the new color.

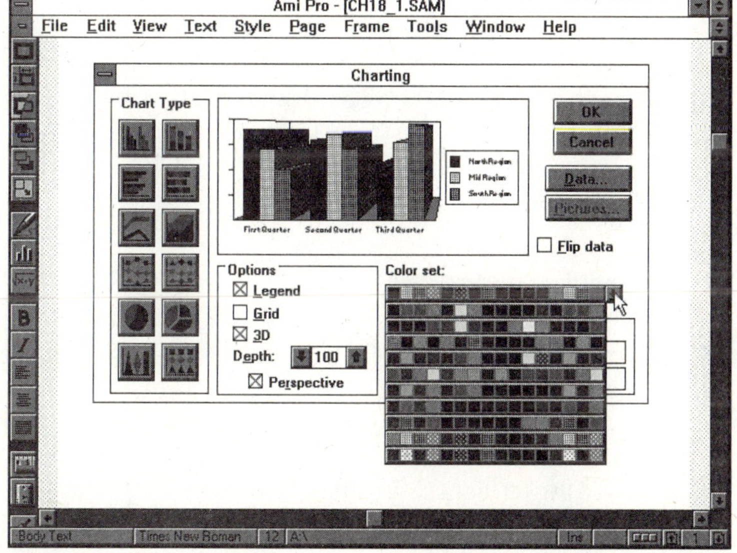

Fig. 18.26
The Color Set color bar after clicking the down-arrow button to display all the colors.

Tip
The color set retains all its colors after you change the order. You cannot move a color from one color set (row) to another.

You can replace a color in the color set by following these steps:

1. Double-click a color to access the Fill Patterns dialog box (shown in fig. 18.27).

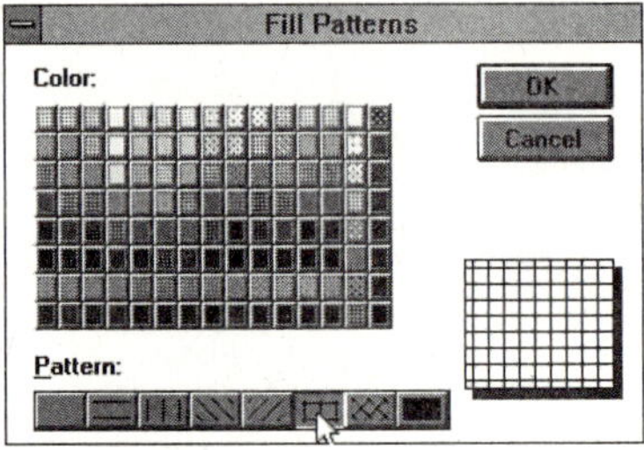

Fig. 18.27
The Fill Patterns dialog box.

2. Click a new Color or **P**attern in the Fill Patterns dialog box. If you have no more changes to make, skip to step 6.

3. If you want to create a custom color, double-click the color you want to use as the basis for your new color. The Custom Colors dialog box appears, as shown in figure 18.28.

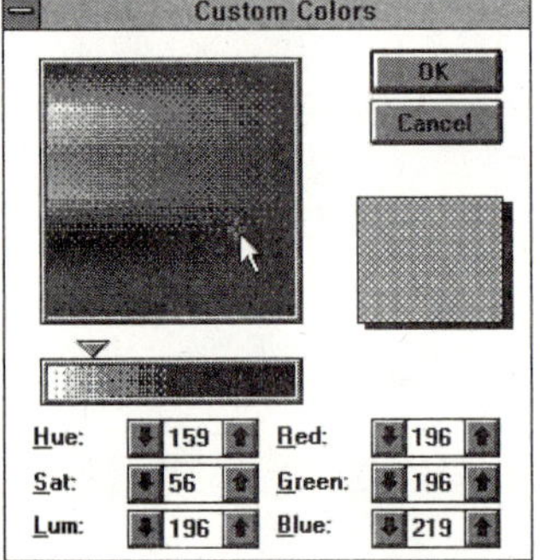

Fig. 18.28
The Custom Colors dialog box.

4. Drag the mouse in the color bar to create a new color. You also can adjust hue, saturation, and so on (for specific details on using the Custom Colors dialog box, see Chapter 8, "Changing Your Setup").

5. Choose OK or press Enter to close the Custom Colors dialog box and return to the Fill Patterns dialog box.

6. Choose OK or press Enter to close the Fill Patterns dialog box and return to the Charting dialog box.

Figure 18.29 illustrates the sample column chart with changes made in the patterns used for each column.

Modifying Picture Defaults

Earlier in this chapter (in the section "Selecting a Chart Type") you reviewed examples of Ami Pro chart types, including a line-and-picture chart, a picture chart, and a stacked-picture chart. Sixteen pictures (or symbols) are available for use in these picture chart variations—one for each data set you can use in an Ami Pro chart. These pictures are adequate for most purposes. If you prefer, however, you can choose another picture, perhaps one that corresponds to a theme of your presentation. You may be creating a presentation on transportation, for example, and want to use a picture of a truck in your charts.

You can substitute Ami Pro Draw files for the 16 default pictures by using clip art files from AMIPRO\DRAWSYM files you saved as Ami Pro Draw files, or files you import from other programs. The pictures appear in the current chart and any future charts (until you change the pictures again).

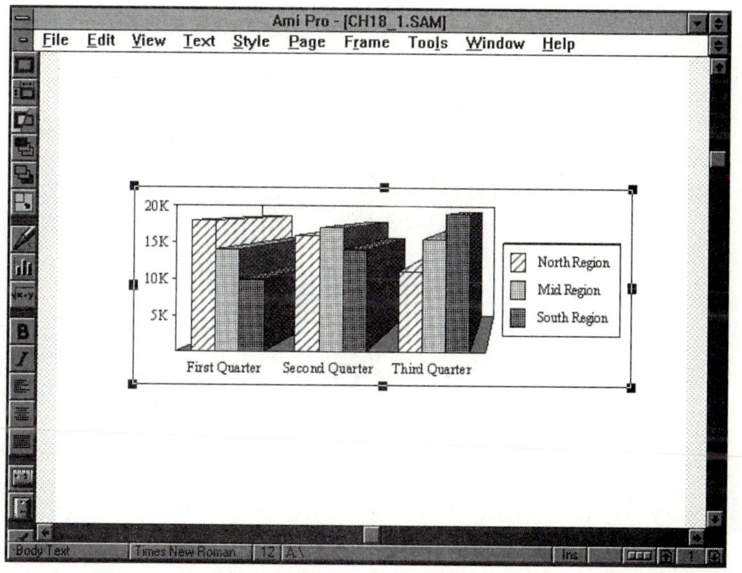

Fig. 18.29
New patterns added with the Fill Patterns dialog box.

You can set up separate defaults for each chart type that uses pictures (line-and-picture charts, picture charts, and stacked-picture charts).

Follow these steps to change one or more of the picture defaults:

1. Choose Too**l**s **C**harting.

2. In the Charting dialog box, select one of the chart types that uses pictures: line-and-picture, picture, or stacked-picture. Notice that the **P**ictures button on the right side of the dialog box darkens, indicating that the option is available.

3. Choose **P**ictures. The Charting Pictures dialog box opens, as shown in figure 18.30.

4. From the numbered list of pictures, select the picture you want to change.

   The numbers in the numbered list coincide with the picture for a data set. Pictures are available for up to 16 data sets in a chart. If you have more than 16 data sets, Ami Pro repeats the pictures.

   To use another type of picture (clip art, drawing, and so on), follow steps 1 through 3, skip step 4, then continue with step 5.

Tip
If you change your mind and want to return to the original picture for any number, select the picture and then click the Default button in the Charting Pictures dialog box.

5. Click the **D**rawing button. The Drawing dialog box appears.

6. In the Directories list box, specify the directory containing the file you want to use for the picture. For this example, the directory is C:\AMIPRO3\DRAWSYM.

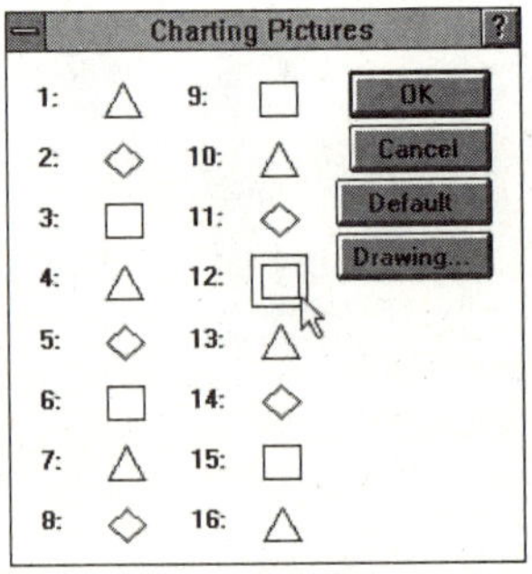

Fig. 18.30
The Charting Pictures dialog box.

7. In the **F**iles list box, select the desired file with the extension SDW. (If you prefer, you can specify the file name or the path and file name in the File **N**ame text box.)

The specified picture appears in the example box in the lower right corner of the Drawing dialog box. Figure 18.31 shows the picture that appears if you select the file BIGTRUCK.SDW.

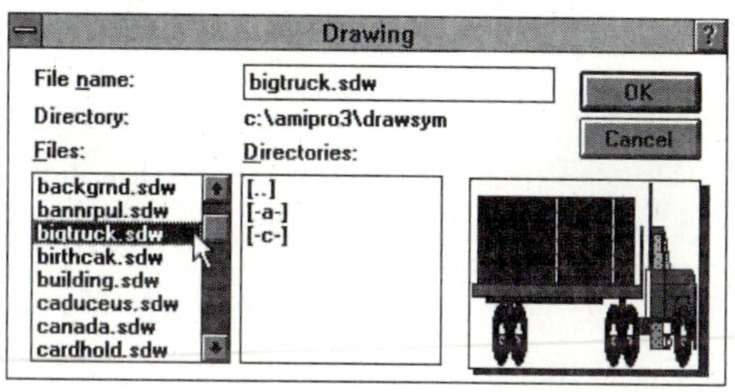

Fig. 18.31 The Drawing dialog box with the selected picture in the example box.

8. Choose OK or press Enter. Ami Pro returns to the Charting Pictures dialog box. The new picture is next to the number you selected.
9. Repeat steps 4 through 8 for each picture you want to substitute.
10. Choose OK or press Enter to close the Charting Pictures dialog box and return to the Charting dialog box.

Figure 18.32 illustrates a stacked-picture chart using the BIGTRUCK.SDW picture.

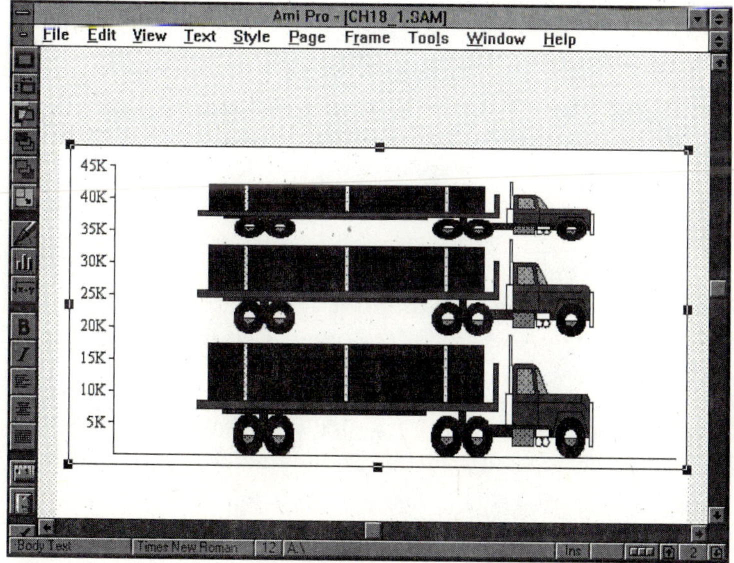

Fig. 18.32 A stacked-picture chart using an AmiDraw clip art file.

Modifying Axis Options

Ami Pro provides default axis options that work well for most situations. If you use the default, the minimum number on each axis is 0—the number most people expect as the baseline when viewing a chart. The default maximum depends on your chart data. You can change the axis options for most chart types. (Pie and expanded-pie charts don't use axes.)

The following paragraphs explain the axis options (located in the Axis section in the lower right corner of the Charting dialog box).

By default, the **A**utomatic option is selected, and Ami Pro sets the numbers on the x-axis or y-axis based on the numbers in the Charting Data dialog box. If you select **A**utomatic in the Axis section, the **I**nc (increment), **M**in (minimum), and Ma**x** (maximum) options appear dimmed—you cannot adjust them. Deselect **A**utomatic if you want to adjust these settings.

You can increase or decrease the number of values displayed on the axis by changing the values Ami Pro uses for placing numbers on the chart. In the **I**nc text box, you type the number for the increment you want to use.

The y-axis doesn't need to begin at 0; you can use any range you want for the **M**in and Ma**x** options. If all your data begins at 30,000, for example, you can use 20,000 or even 30,000 as the minimum. To change the minimum number, type in the **M**in text box the number you want to use.

> **Caution**
>
> Be careful—small changes in your data can appear quite large if you move the baseline up too far. Furthermore, data that's close to the baseline number (or below it) may not show at all.

Figure 18.33 shows the column chart with the minimum set to 0. Figure 18.34 shows the same chart with the minimum set to 13,000. Notice that the differences between the bars appear accentuated. In addition, the 10,000 columns do not show.

Just as the axis doesn't need to begin at 0, it doesn't need to end at the number Ami Pro has set. To change the maximum number, type in the Ma**x** text box the number you want to use.

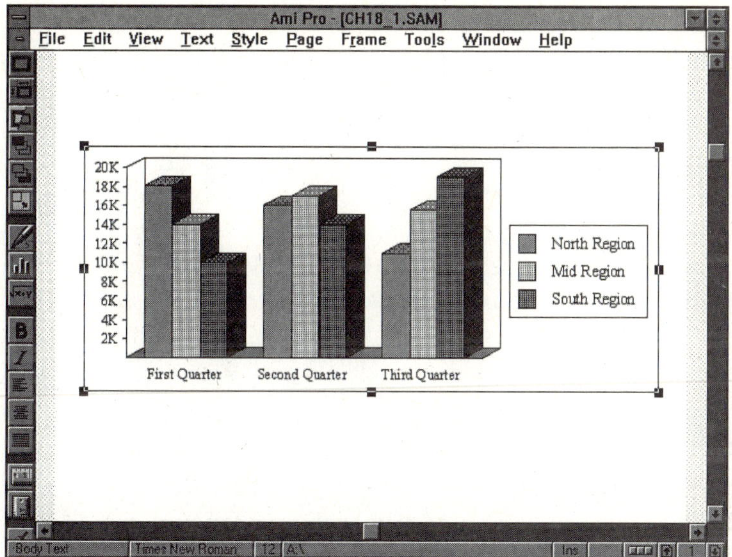

Fig. 18.33
A sample column chart with minimum set to zero.

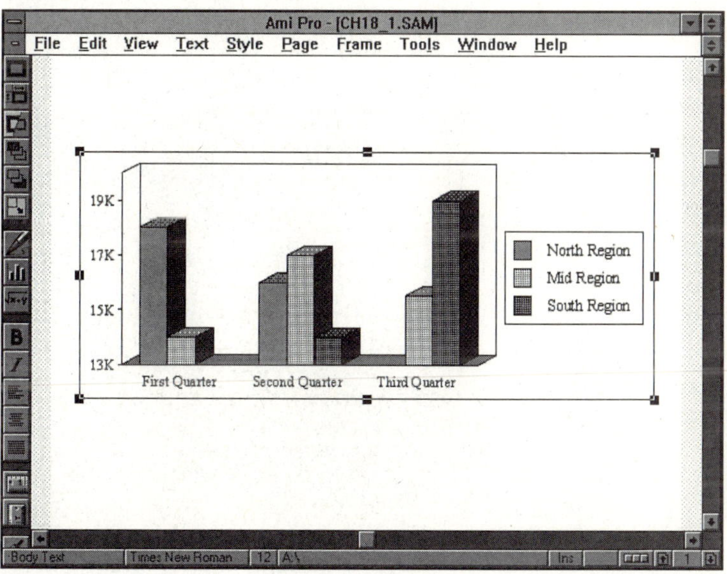

Fig. 18.34
The sample column chart with minimum set to 13,000.

Tip
If you specify values that cause the maximum or minimum number to disappear from the chart, the chart can disappear.

Flipping the Data

After preparing the chart data, you may change your mind and decide that you want to use the first column rather than the first row for the chart's labels. For the sample data from figure 18.1, for example, you may want to show each quarter rather than each region as a pie piece in the chart. In the Charting dialog box, you select the **F**lip Data option to tell Ami Pro to transpose the data in the table when creating the chart. The rows become columns, and the columns become rows. Figure 18.35 shows the chart from the sample data. Figure 18.36 shows the pie chart with the data flipped. The advantages of **F**lip Data show up particularly well with a pie chart.

Editing the Chart

You learned earlier how to edit the data you are using in a chart (see "Editing Chart Data," earlier in this chapter). You also can edit the chart itself in certain ways. Chapter 16, "Using Frames," explains how you can resize a chart within a frame, and Chapter 20, "Importing, Exporting, and Linking Files," tells you how to scale a graphic.

This section introduces you to the basic editing tasks you can perform with a chart. You can delete the chart and use the Draw program to change the chart's appearance by moving, deleting, or modifying the segments of the chart, such as the slices in a pie chart or the columns in a column chart.

Deleting a Chart

Tip
You can bypass the preceding steps by selecting the frame containing the chart and then deleting the frame and its contents.

To delete a chart, you use Ami Pro's Draw program and the same procedure you use to delete any other drawing. Select the frame containing the chart you want to delete. Choose Too**l**s **D**rawing. The drawing icons appear at the top of the Draw screen, and the **D**raw option appears in the Menu Bar, as shown in figure 18.37.

Click the Select All command icon or choose **D**raw **S**elect All; then press Del. Ami Pro deletes the chart.

After you delete a chart from a frame, you cannot treat the frame as a new frame. You cannot enter text (except Draw text) or another type of picture (other than a chart or an Ami Pro drawing) into the frame. To eliminate such restrictions, select and delete the entire frame and create a new one.

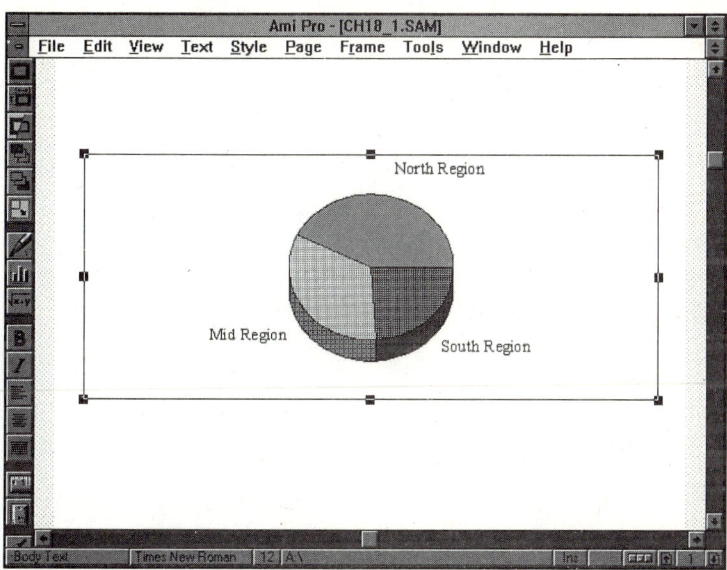

Fig. 18.35 A pie chart showing the regions.

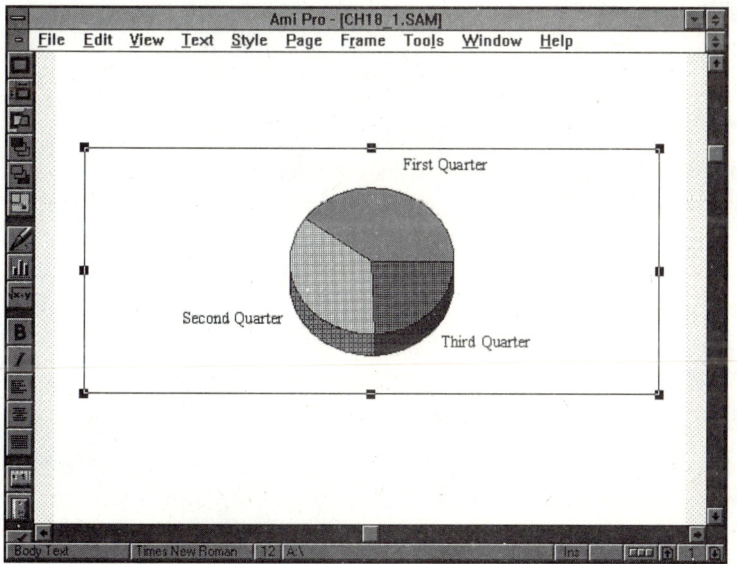

Fig. 18.36 The same data, with the Flip Data option selected; the pie chart now shows quarters.

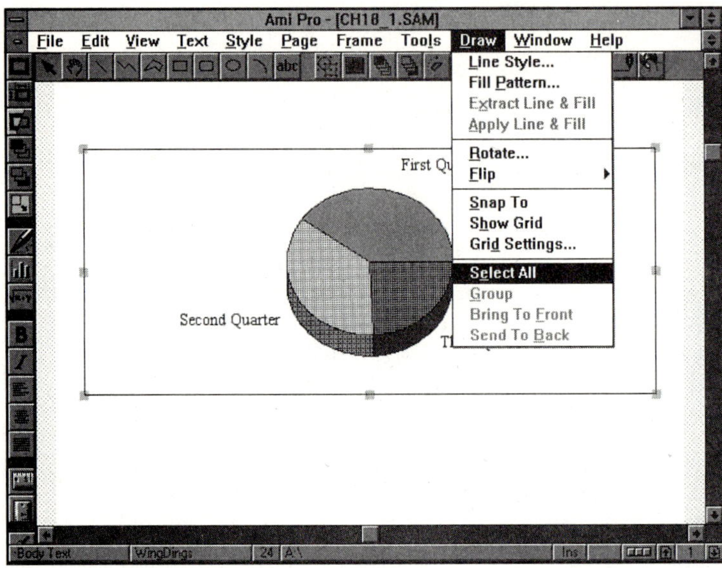

Fig. 18.37
A chart in draw mode, with the **D**raw menu.

Modifying a Chart with the Draw Program

You often can make your charts communicate more effectively by enhancing them with drawing. You can invoke Ami Pro Draw while you are in a frame containing an Ami Pro chart.

Tip
You also can change the fill pattern of the truck in the drawing mode (see Chapter 17, "Using the Draw Feature"). If you make the truck screens lighter, you can use black type.

To call attention to part of a chart, you can add text, such as a label, heading, or comment. You also can format the text by changing the typeface, size, style, and so on. You may want to add clip art to the chart to make it appear more attractive. You even can use drawing to substitute pictures (a truck or an airplane, for example) for the bars in a chart, thereby creating a pictorial bar chart. Figure 18.38 illustrates a stacked-picture chart with text added in the draw program. Since the pictures (trucks) are dark screens, white is selected in **T**ext **F**ont as the color of the type.

You can use the Draw program with a chart in all the same ways you can use the program with a drawing. (See Chapter 17, "Using the Draw Feature," for explanations of how to use all the drawing tools.)

Figure 18.39 illustrates another chart, a pie chart, that is enhanced with the drawing program. The clip art stars are added, the type is reformatted, and the pie pieces are moved around.

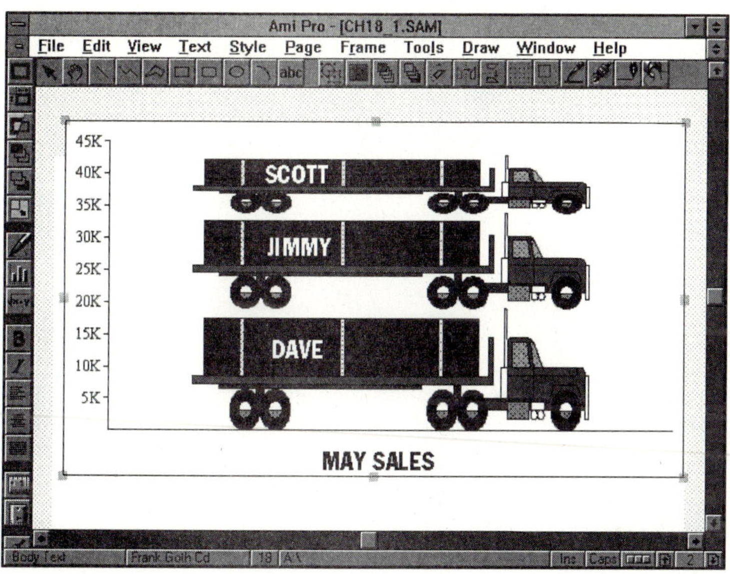

Fig. 18.38
A stacked-picture chart enhanced with the drawing feature.

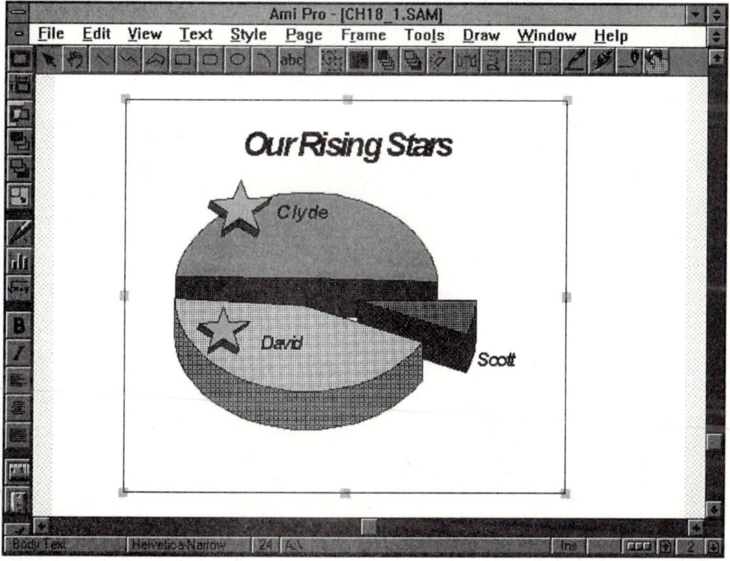

Fig. 18.39
A pie chart enhanced with the drawing program.

> **Caution**
>
> Select the chart type you want before changing the chart with the Draw program. If you change the chart type or the data and then re-create your original chart, Ami Pro deletes the previous chart—along with any enhancements you have made to the chart with the Draw program.

◀ See "Modifying the Appearance of Frames," p. 515

◀ See "Creating a Drawing," p. 537

◀ See "Editing Objects," p. 539

▶ See "Editing Imported Graphics," p. 701

Summary

Ami Pro's charting features are powerful enough to handle many of your presentation needs. You can create column, bar, line, pie, and picture charts, and other variations. In this chapter, you learned how to supply the data for your charts, how to create and edit charts (for example, by using drawing tools), and how to use the charting options.

In the next chapter, you learn how to bring text and graphics together to create finished, professional-looking documents.

Chapter 19

Desktop Publishing with Ami Pro

In this chapter, you learn how to use Ami Pro's features to produce successful and professional-looking documents. You learn how to maintain consistency in a design, yet add emphasis for interest. You discover the roles that page layout, design elements, and typography play in creating an attractive document. You explore the components of design, such as white space, balance, and graphic elements (rules, screens, borders). You learn the basics of typography (the art of setting type or the style of the typeset page), such as which typeface to use in your documents, proper type size, line and paragraph spacing, and so on. You find out how to add graphic images such as line art, halftones, spreadsheets, and charts so your document attracts attention and looks professional. In addition, you learn to apply many Ami Pro features to a good design. You learn how to use the frame feature to produce design variation on a page. You learn to use tables to help organize information on the page. You learn to use the drawing and charting features to add to your documents, and you learn to create a style sheet for repeat use in documents.

Near the end of this chapter, you discover several document designs that you can reproduce in Ami Pro, including a letterhead, order form, brochure, newsletter, and business report. Each section about specific documents contains instructions for Ami Pro settings, tips for producing the document, and samples of output. After you complete this chapter, you're on your way to producing attractive, professional-looking designs.

Introduction to Desktop Publishing

Personal computers are now capable of performing page layout and design tasks that once were only attempted in print shops by conventional typesetters. The capability to write a document and design it completely in one's own home or business saves the desktop publisher time, money, and effort. The benefits of doing your own page layout become apparent as you learn more about Ami Pro and its special features. This section discusses some of those features and how you can benefit from desktop publishing with Ami Pro.

What Is Desktop Publishing?

◄ See "Using Style Sheets and Paragraph Styles," p. 262

◄ See "Creating and Modifying Styles," p. 273

◄ See "Entering Text and Graphics in Frames," p. 512

◄ See "Using Columns and Tabs in Frames," p. 525

In *desktop publishing*, you use the personal computer to create a formatted document, usually for widespread distribution. The personal computer, in this case, includes the software program used for formatting the page. Ami Pro is a powerful tool for page formatting. In addition, other programs, such as spreadsheet, drawing, scanning, and so on, combine with Ami Pro for a comprehensive and effective end result.

Desktop Publishing Benefits

The obvious benefit of desktop publishing is the professional-looking document you produce. In addition, desktop publishing with Ami Pro affords you many other benefits, such as saving you time and money, allowing you more control over your documents, and letting you integrate other software programs to produce more comprehensive documents.

You save time and money by formatting your own documents. You don't need to travel back and forth to a print shop or professional typesetter; you don't waste time correcting someone else's mistakes or explaining what you want. You don't need to wait for the print shop to call you with your proof or work around typesetting schedules. By producing your own page layout, you don't have to pay for professional typesetting.

Formatting your own documents gives you control over your document. You can experiment with various type and graphic elements to see which way looks best. You can edit or add text at the last minute, update a spreadsheet or chart, or change dates and times in a program. You don't need to wait for the print shop to complete your changes or pay for alterations to the original document.

Another advantage of doing your own page layout is using other software programs to enhance your documents. You can add a spreadsheet or scanned art to your document, then modify the document to suit your purpose. For more information about integrating other software programs with Ami Pro, see Chapter 20, "Importing, Exporting, and Linking Files."

Ami Pro Features for Desktop Publishing

Ami Pro is a word processing package with features that expedite day-to-day chores, such as typing and editing documents, spell and grammar checking, performing mail merge, and so on. Ami Pro is also a powerful tool to use for page layout and design. You can easily produce professional-looking designs by using Ami Pro features, such as frame capabilities.

With *frames*, mini-documents within the main document that can hold text or graphic images, you can add special text, graphic images, tables, or spreadsheets. You can add a drawing, chart, or equation in a frame. Frames make page layout easy and attractive with added options such as borders, lines, and screens. The document sections at the end of this chapter give you several ideas for using frames in various documents. For detailed information on using Ami Pro's frame feature, see Chapter 16, "Using Frames."

Another feature well-suited to desktop publishing are Ami Pro's style sheets. Style sheets enable you to save page and paragraph formatting for use in other documents. Suppose, for example, that you create a company newsletter that must go out each month. By saving the original paragraph and page settings in a style sheet, you have a base with which to begin each month's newsletter. The documents are formatted similarly, guaranteeing consistency. Style sheets save time. Later sections explain more about using Ami Pro's style sheets. In addition, see Chapter 10, "Working with Style Sheets," for detailed information about producing and saving style sheets in Ami Pro.

Ami Pro possesses many more features, covered in this chapter, that make the software perfect for desktop publishing: drawing, charting, Adobe Type Manager fonts, graphics control, column control, and so on. Ami Pro may be the most valuable tool you use in formatting and designing your business documents.

Design Strategies

Creating a successful design involves many steps. Because each step builds on the last, the first step is the most important: planning and preparing your design for a specific purpose. The main purpose of all printed material is to convey a message to the reader. Likewise, the main purpose of design is to convey its own message—a message that attracts the reader's attention and persuades the reader to pick up and read the printed material. This section helps you define the purpose of your document, gives you hints to plan your piece, and includes ways to create consistency within a document and add emphasis for interest.

Determining the Purpose of the Document

◀ See "Character Formatting," p. 95

◀ See "Paragraph Formatting," p. 105

◀ See "Using Style Sheets and Paragraph Styles," p. 262

When you begin planning a document for publication, you need to know the specific *purpose* of that document. What do you want to achieve? Who is your audience? What do you want to communicate? Answers to these questions help you define the purpose of your document.

What do you want to achieve with your document? Are you selling a new product? Are you having a sale? Are you informing employees of new benefits? Are you explaining new employee services? What do you want to communicate? Deciding the desired results helps you determine purpose.

Who is your intended audience? Who are you trying to reach with your document: customers or prospective customers; fellow employees; your boss? Are you trying to reach a group of professionals or the general public? Are your readers men or women, young or old, rich or poor? You cannot successfully communicate with readers unless you know who they are. Each audience has its own communication needs. The more you know about your readers, the easier it is to plan and prepare the appropriate design for your document. Answer these questions, and your document will have a successful purpose.

Planning the Document

Planning your document includes writing and organizing the copy, selecting the format, and determining the document's size. Each decision you make depends on the purpose of your document. If you're announcing a sale, for example, you want to include the word *Sale* in the document, adding prices, discounts, and so on. You also want to announce the sale on a sheet of paper large enough to be seen and in a suitable format, such as a flier. How you distribute the flier depends on your audience. The decisions you make when planning your document determine its success or failure.

When writing and organizing your copy, keep the copy's purpose in mind. Organize your main topics and subtopics first, then form them into well-written, interesting copy. The main topics, or heads, of the document should pique the reader's interest and persuade the reader to read the copy. Any added graphic images, such as charts, drawings, photographs, and so on, should contribute to gaining the reader's interest. Remember that everything—heads, body copy, images, design—must support the message and interest the reader.

The format of your document—flier, brochure, letter, newsletter, and so on—depends on the purpose of the document, the document's size, and the method of distribution. If the method of distribution is the mail, for example, the document must conform to postal regulations for size, shape, and weight of mailable pieces. A list of common document formats and their purposes is at the end of this section.

The size of a particular document depends on the amount of copy, the format, the quantity printed, and the method of distribution. Most document formats conform to common sizes used in the printing industry. A newsletter, for example, may be 8 1/2 inches by 11 inches, 11 inches by 17 inches, or 17 inches by 22 inches, then folded to the finished size. Naturally, if you produce a document on your printer, you also must conform to the printer's size limits. Common sizes for many document formats are listed at the end of this section.

Maintaining Consistency

First impressions are critical in a printed document. If the document doesn't impress a reader at first glance, the reader ignores the document. *Consistency* can help you create a positive first impression. A consistent page is clear, organized, and simple. Consistency in design and typography is vital to the success of any document. Design elements, such as balance, margins, columns, rules, and screens promote consistency. *Balancing*, or distributing, the type and design elements on the page creates a pleasing typeset piece. Keeping individual pages balanced throughout the document, for example, by using the same number of columns and the same margin widths enhances consistency. The section "Using Design Elements" later in this chapter explains these design elements and how to keep them consistent.

You also can achieve consistency by repeating design and type elements. To create consistency, for example, you can use 2-point lines above all heads or end each section with the company logo, or you can use the same size and style of heads throughout the document. Figure 19.1 illustrates consistency within an advertisement. Notice the typeface, type size, margins, and graphics. Figure 19.2 shows the same ad with much less consistency.

Fig. 19.1
Consistency in a newspaper advertisement.

GRAND OPENING
humble opinions
OFFERING INSTRUCTION
• Desktop Publishing
• Word Processing
June 3
9:00 a.m. - 5:00 p.m.
117 E. Main Street • (304) 555-2323

Fig. 19.2
Inconsistency in the same advertisement.

Grand
Opening
humble opinions
OFFERING INSTRUCTION
• Desktop Publishing
* Word Processing
June 3
9:00 A.M. - 5:00 P.M.
117 E. MAIN STREET
(304) 555-2323

Adding Emphasis

As mentioned earlier, first impressions influence a reader. You can generate a favorable first impression by using design elements consistently. Another tool you can use to create a good first impression is *emphasis*.

You can emphasize a subject in a variety of ways. You can use a graphic element to frame a photograph, for example, or white space to offset a story, or a pie chart to track profits, or lines to lead the reader's eye to an important item.

It is just as important to know when *not* to use emphasis as it is to know when to use it. Too much emphasis in a document creates disorder and clutter. The reader may not understand the important information because everything stands out. Figure 19.3, for example, shows a flier with the proper amount of emphasis added. Figure 19.4 demonstrates the abuse of emphasis in the same flier. Remember to add emphasis to only one idea or topic per page.

Tip

Typography is another way to add emphasis. For instance, you can use 72-point type to emphasize the word *Sale* and 24-point type to make the names of products stand out. You also can use bullets, pull-out quotes, boldface, italics, and so on.

Types of Documents

You can create numerous documents, such as brochures, newsletters, books, forms, magazines, and programs—the variety is endless. The following list describes some of the most common kinds of documents and sizes. Some sample layouts are included.

Fliers

A *flier* is a quick-sell advertisement designed to announce, introduce, or remind. A flier briefly describes sales, grand openings, new products, and so on.

Use a flier to attract immediate attention and to get the point across quickly. When you design the flier, use a short, hard-sell technique that includes a list of the products, items, or services, or a short list of dates, times, and places. Use no unnecessary explanations. Use descriptive adjectives and a minimum of type.

You can print a flier on one side of paper, one column or two, with large type and bullets. Common flier sizes, in portrait (vertical) or landscape (horizontal) orientation, include 5 1/2 by 8 1/2 inches, 8 1/2 by 11 inches, or 8 1/2 by 14 inches.

◀ See "Opening a New Document," p. 50

◀ See "Paragraph Formatting," p. 105

◀ See "Modifying the Standard Page Layout," p. 120

▶ See the Appendix, "A Guide to Style Sheets," p. 923

Note

The orientation and placement of text and graphics depend on the copy.

Figure 19.5 shows a sample layout of a flier.

OPENING NIGHT!

Manhattan Players Present

BEYOND ENMITY

A PLAY BY S. J. BENDER

featuring

Erin Linkous

Brandon McIntyre

Hattan Theatre

111 W. 24th Street

Fig. 19.3
Emphasis applied properly.

Tip
If you're marketing a product, make sure that the information in the brochure will interest the customer. Customers want to know what you can do for them, not what you're doing for yourself.

Brochures

A *brochure* explains, instructs, details, or informs; therefore, the customer will keep this document for future reference. A brochure may include a list and description of products, a detailed explanation of services, or a price list.

Design the cover (page 1 or front panel—whatever is appropriate for the document) for soft-sell to gently invite the reader to open and read the contents. Inside the document, describe the details of the service or product, perhaps with art, logos, or pictures. Titles, headlines, subheads, and captions accompany body text in a brochure. The back panel contains summary points in a bulleted or numbered list, return address, logo, and often a mailing panel. A logical development of ideas leads the eye through the brochure, starting with the front panel or cover, continuing through the inside, and finishing with the back panel.

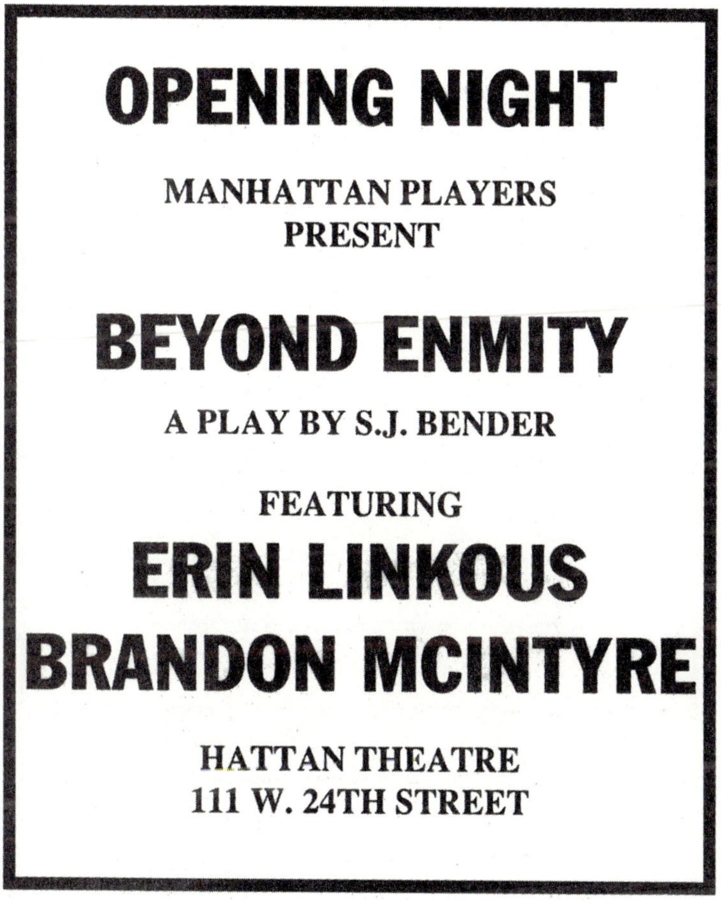

OPENING NIGHT

MANHATTAN PLAYERS
PRESENT

BEYOND ENMITY

A PLAY BY S.J. BENDER

FEATURING

ERIN LINKOUS
BRANDON MCINTYRE

HATTAN THEATRE
111 W. 24TH STREET

Fig. 19.4
Overuse of emphasis.

Figure 19.6 shows a sample layout for the outside panels of a six-panel brochure. A graphic image is used on panel 1 (the right panel) with several large headlines. The middle panel (panel 6) is for mailing, and panel 5 (to the far left) contains a summary of points and the company's address.

Tip
To rotate text, use frames and drawing text.

On the inside of the brochure (from left, panels 2, 3, and 4, respectively), figure 19.7 shows a rule above the text to tie the three columns together. In this example, one graphic image and the type are set up in a simple three-column format.

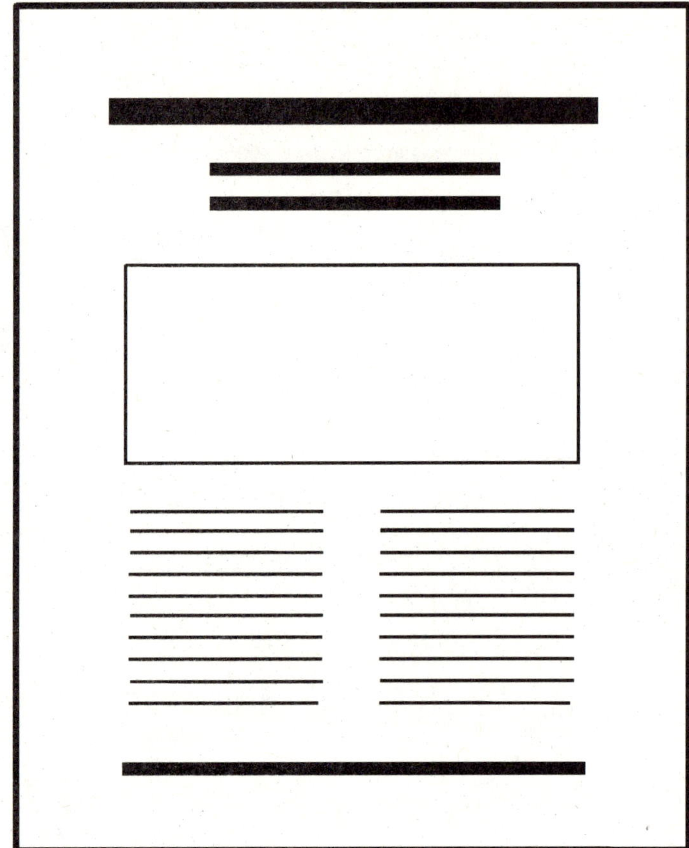

Fig. 19.5
Sample layout of a flier in portrait mode.

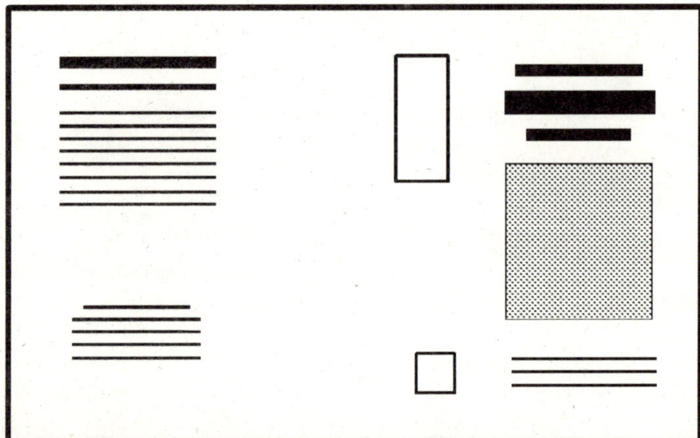

Fig. 19.6
The outside panels of a six-panel brochure.

Brochures usually are printed in landscape mode (11 inches by 8 1/2 inches for three columns or 14 inches by 8 1/2 inches for four columns). A brochure also can be in portrait mode (11 inches by 17 inches, folded to 8 1/2 inches by 11 inches; or 8 1/2 inches by 11 inches, folded to 5 1/2 inches by 8 1/2 inches; or 8 1/2-inch-by-11-inch single sheets, fastened together). See the section "Creating a Brochure," later in this chapter for information on creating an 11-inch-by-8 1/2-inch, three-panel brochure.

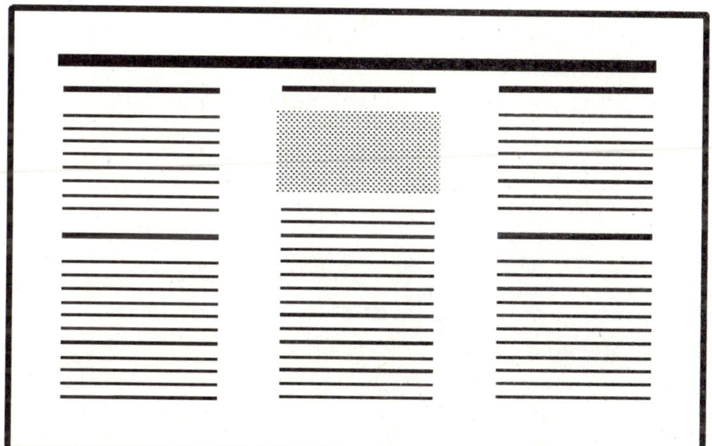

Fig. 19.7 The inside three panels of a six-panel brochure.

Newsletters

Newsletters come in many sizes, shapes, and designs. A newsletter generally has 1 to 16 pages with one to four columns per page, in either portrait or landscape mode (portrait is the most common).

Newsletters can explain, instruct, detail, inform, announce, introduce, repeat—just about anything. Some companies use newsletters to inform clients or employees; many companies use newsletters to sell products and services. Some companies even make a business of selling informational newsletters.

The first page of a newsletter contains a *nameplate*. A nameplate is an identifier for the newsletter. A nameplate consists of the name of the newsletter, or the company's name, a catchy phrase, an abbreviation, and may include a graphic image. Any type in the nameplate is usually in a different typeface from the body text and heads. You can create a nameplate in Ami Pro, in a draw or paint program, or an artist can hand draw a nameplate. The type can be display, stretched or condensed, slanted, vertical, on an arc, or changed in any way that makes it stand out.

The nameplate also can contain a logo. A *logo* is an easily recognized symbol—decorative type, catchy word, short phrase—that appears on every issue (remember that consistency is important). A dateline, or folio, also should appear under the nameplate. Sometimes centered, sometimes on the left and right margins, the dateline can include the date and perhaps the volume and document number.

Headers or footers also provide consistency. Although some printers say that these elements are unnecessary in a four-page document, a header or footer always adds a professional touch. Never place a header or footer on the first page, however. A header should include the page number and may also give the publication's name, the date, the volume, or issue number.

Although not absolutely necessary, a table of contents is a good idea if the newsletter is more than four pages long. By placing a small box on the first page that showcases four or five items of interest in the publication, you help draw the reader into the newsletter.

Always include a *masthead*, usually on page two. A masthead contains the editor's name and address, circulation, contact people, reporters, deadlines for copy, volume number, date, fees, credits, and so on.

If you send a newsletter by mail, you need to provide each copy with a return address, postage permit, and a place for the mailing label.

Note

Be sure that the postage permit is agreeable with the Post Office. The U.S. Postal Service has many regulations that govern the exact placement, wording, and even punctuation in a postage permit box. Check with your Postmaster to be safe.

The most important design point of a newsletter is consistency between issues. Individual page layouts differ from issue to issue, but the masthead, dateline, publication information, and design elements (column number and width, balance, gutter space, white space, and so on) should remain nearly the same each time. (Gutter space is the white space between columns.) Type styles, spacing, and graphic elements also need to be the same. A newsletter also should reflect the design of other publications produced by the same company to tie all the publications together and make them quickly recognizable. You can accomplish this consistency by adding the company's logo in a particular spot each time or by using the same colors of ink or paper.

Popular sizes for newsletters are 8 1/2 inches by 11 inches, printed on both sides; 11 inches by 17 inches, folded to 8 1/2 inches by 11 inches or smaller, for mailing (refer to fig. 19.7); or 22 inches by 17 inches, printed on both sides, folded to 11 inches by 17 inches and then to 8 1/2 inches by 11 inches (see fig. 19.8).

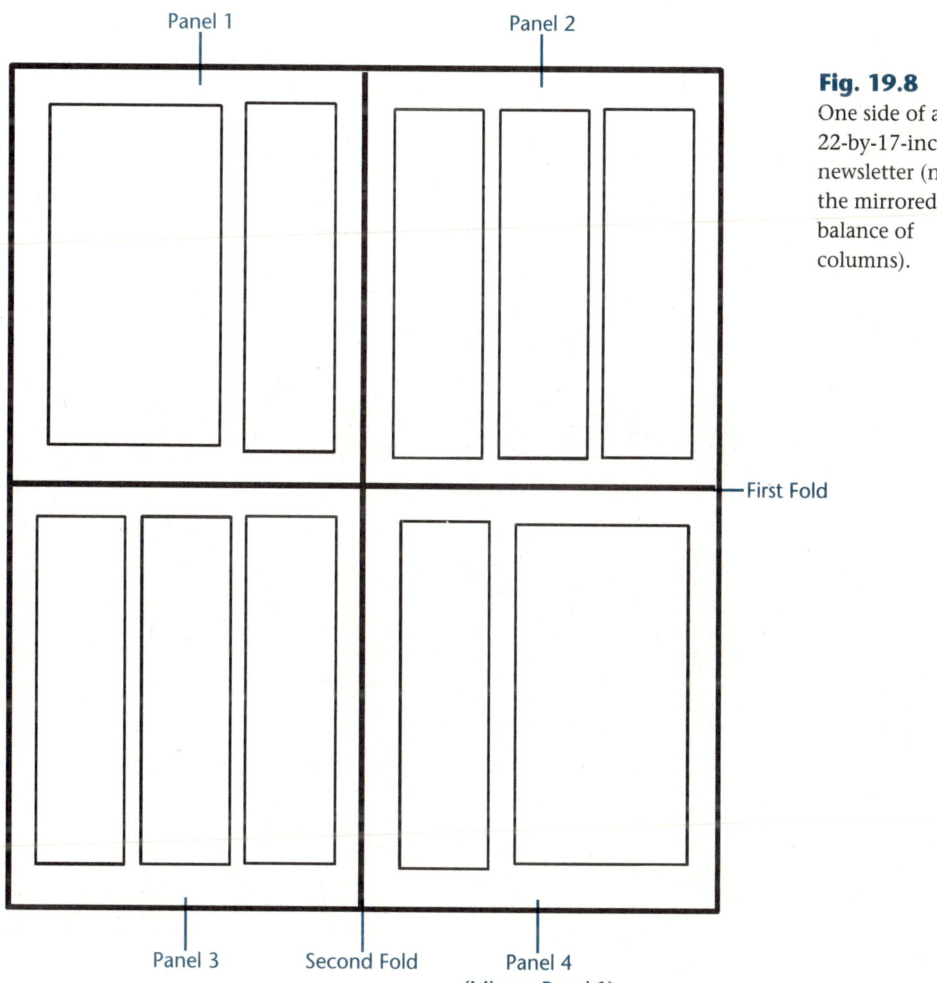

Fig. 19.8 One side of a 22-by-17-inch newsletter (notice the mirrored balance of columns).

Forms

So many different *forms* are used in business every day so identifying all of them is impossible. A form usually contains text, lines, boxes, and whatever information you want to add.

Most forms leave spaces for information such as name, address, phone number, perhaps descriptions of items, quantities, total costs, sales tax, and so on. For every form, as many kinds of fill-in formats exist.

With Ami Pro for Windows, you can produce forms easily with the Table format features (described in the section "Creating a Purchase Order Form" later in this chapter).

Books

With *books* of 8 to 12 pages or more (excluding newsletters and magazines), use headers and footers, page numbers, a table of contents, and an index.

When publishing a book with many chapters and miscellaneous elements, organizing the directories or floppy disks properly is important. Organize all information—such as text files, graphics, spreadsheets, and formatting—according to individual chapters. Save all related data in the same directory or on the same disk. (See Chapter 21, "Managing Files and Documents," for information on master documents.)

Note

The computer works faster and more efficiently if you work off the hard drive (rather than a floppy disk) and then save to a floppy disk or tape backup after you complete each chapter. With large projects, backups are especially important.

Creating or loading a style sheet from Ami Pro to apply to each chapter is a good idea. A style sheet defines page orientation, margins and columns, headlines, body text, headers, footers, page numbers, and so on. A style sheet also can help you achieve consistency throughout the book.

Traditionally, book margins are designed for easy reading. The bottom margins are usually the largest, inside margins the next largest (to accommodate a binding), and the top and outside margins are the same.

No single design solution can fit all documents. The design and typography elements you choose for your documents should depend on the specific purpose of the document, the audience, the copy, and your personal preferences. The following sections of this chapter offer guidelines to help you make these decisions, with suggestions that allow your creativity to shine through.

Design Elements

After you determine the specific purpose of a document, your next step is to choose the document design. The document design includes *design elements*: size, shape, format, and layout. These and other elements help make a document attractive, practical, and effective. The primary purpose of any document is to communicate a message to readers, so effective use of basic design elements can help you accomplish this task. In this section, you learn about using the elements of design to produce professional-looking documents. (For more information about page layout, see Chapter 5, "Working with Page Layout.")

◀ See "Modifying Character Attributes," p. 98

◀ See "Paragraph Formatting," p. 105

◀ See "Modifying the Standard Page Layout," p. 120

◀ See "Adding Lines," p. 131

◀ See "Modifying a Ruler," p. 151

◀ See "Using Style Sheets and Paragraph Styles," p. 262

Choosing Page Orientation

A basic element of design is the *page orientation* of the document: portrait (vertical) or landscape (horizontal). Each orientation has specific uses and each employs the design elements in certain ways. Which orientation you choose depends on the purpose of your document and the size of your copy.

Traditionally, the purpose of a piece dictates its shape. Documents must be easy to read, easy to use, and easy to store to attract the reader's attention. The printing trade, therefore, assigns orientations to particular documents. If, for example, a document is designed for a standard three-ring binder (a vertical format), the orientation is portrait.

Determine how much copy you have and how the information flows on the pages. Is the copy in short lists that you can include in a narrow column, or is it in long paragraphs of text that need wide columns? Is the art horizontal or vertical? Can the text fit the same orientation as the artwork? If so, mirror this orientation with the page.

Portrait Orientation

Although *portrait* orientation is vertical, or tall, it's measured by width first and then height (8 1/2 inches by 11 inches, for example). Lists of words or short sentences, graphics or photos that are taller than they are wide, shorter headlines, and many subheads fit portrait orientation. You can use large amounts of text if you use two or three columns per page.

Tip
Usually, you produce letters, newsletters, resumes, and business reports in portrait orientation. Some types of fliers and books, however, also can be portrait-oriented.

Landscape Orientation

Landscape, or wide, orientation also is measured width first, then height (11 inches by 8 1/2 inches). Long headlines, wide graphics or photos, and more pictures than text use this orientation. This mode also is well suited for spreadsheets, tables, charts, fliers, brochures, envelopes, programs, some forms, and some books.

Balancing Design Elements

Tip
You can use large amounts of text in landscape orientation by dividing the text into two, three, or four columns.

Text and graphics must *balance* on the page; one element cannot dominate the other. A balanced page of text and graphics is designed so well that the page attracts readers to the document and leads them through the document in logical steps. A balanced document also helps readers mentally organize the information after one reading, which helps the reader retain the information longer. Page layout uses three major kinds of balance: symmetrical, asymmetrical, and modular. Staying with one kind of balance throughout the document avoids confusion for the reader.

Using Symmetrical Balance

Symmetrical balance is the equal distribution of the text, graphics, and white space on a page. Size, form, and arrangement of page elements correspond on opposite sides of a point (usually the center). What you see on one side of the center guide is replicated on the opposite side. Figure 19.9 shows two examples of symmetrical balance; the center guide on both samples is the gutter space between columns.

The text and graphics, however, aren't exactly the same; you must measure the visual weight of each page by the elements. Consider text as the gray of the page (a page of nothing but type gives the impression of being gray). Graphics, art, photos, and illustrations are gray if they are light but black if very dark or heavy. Measure the white of the page in margins, gutter space, the area around headlines and graphics, and even within the text (left-aligned or right-aligned text has more white space than justified text). By balancing the grays, blacks, and whites on a page, you end up balancing the actual text, graphics, and white space.

Symmetrical balance is a formal, sophisticated, even balance that gives consistency to a document.

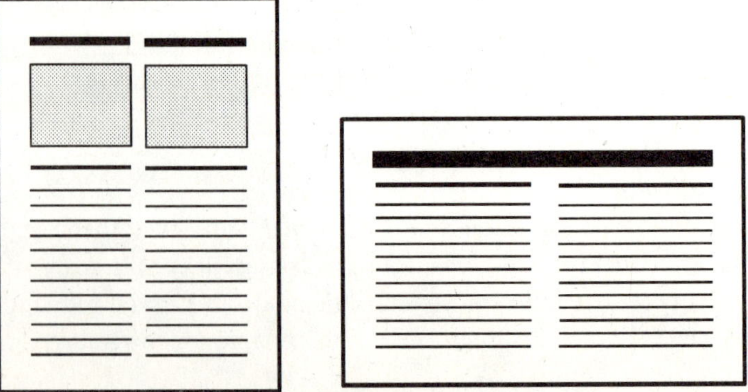

Fig. 19.9
Symmetrical balance in portrait (left) and landscape (right) orientations.

Using Asymmetrical Balance

With *asymmetrical balance*, the elements on either side of the center guide don't exactly correspond, but the overall weight of the elements remains about the same. In this mode, you balance large areas of gray with large areas of white, or small black areas with larger gray areas. Asymmetrical balance results in a more free-form, informal, and interesting document to look at than symmetrical balance. Asymmetrical balance is a harder balance to use properly and consistently (see fig. 19.10).

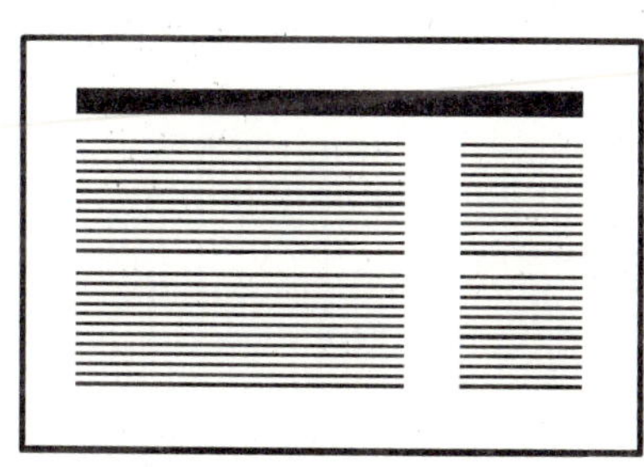

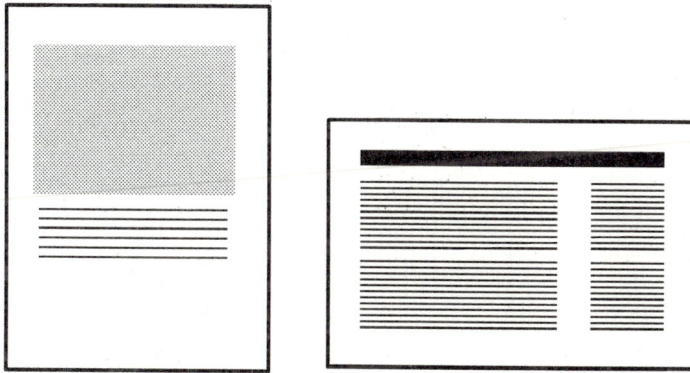

Fig. 19.10
Asymmetrical balance in portrait (left) and landscape (right) orientations.

Using Modular Balance

Modular balance uses intersecting guidelines to form boxes across the page and places text and graphics in the boxes to form an ordered, systematic layout. You can begin forming the grid, or modules, by dividing the page into two or three sections. Then divide these sections into two or three more sections (see fig. 19.11). To help you divide the page, you can draw a frame that covers the page. Make the frame transparent with no wrap-around. You can use the Drawing feature to add vertical and horizontal lines to form the grid. (See Chapter 17, "Using the Draw Feature," for more information.)

The modular layout can be symmetrical or asymmetrical. You achieve symmetrical balance by dividing the page in half, either vertically or horizontally, and then placing the text and graphics within the guidelines. You achieve asymmetrical balance with the grid by combining several boxes to construct various size areas for text or by varying placement. Figure 19.12 shows the preceding sample grid with asymmetrical balancing of text and graphics. Using figure 19.12 as an example, you can achieve asymmetrical balance by combining the first two grid blocks into one. You also can combine the last two grid blocks. Ami Pro's frame feature can help you. Draw a frame over the grid and place text or graphics in the frame.

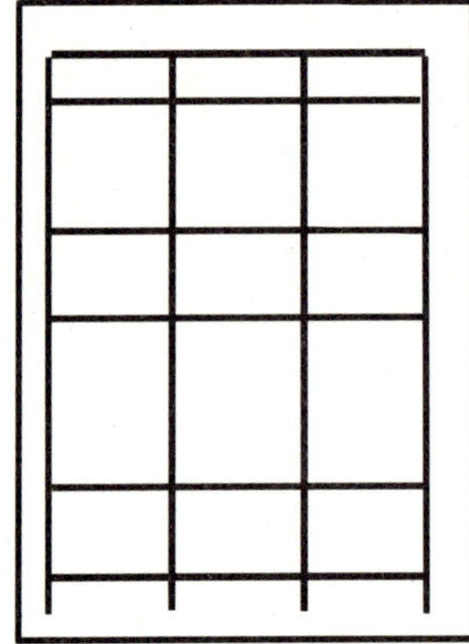
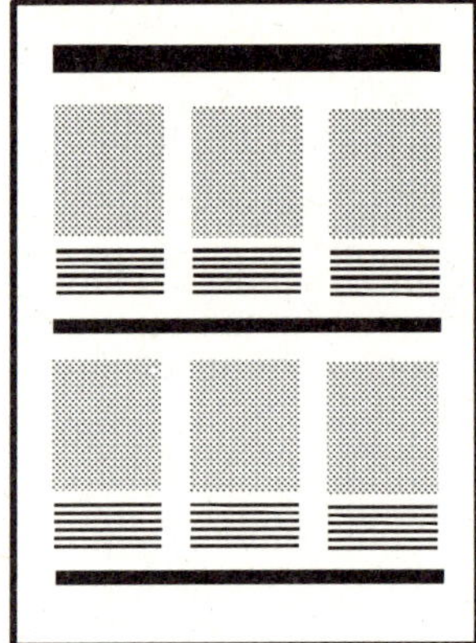

Fig. 19.11 The grid modules on the left, converted to a page using symmetrical balance.

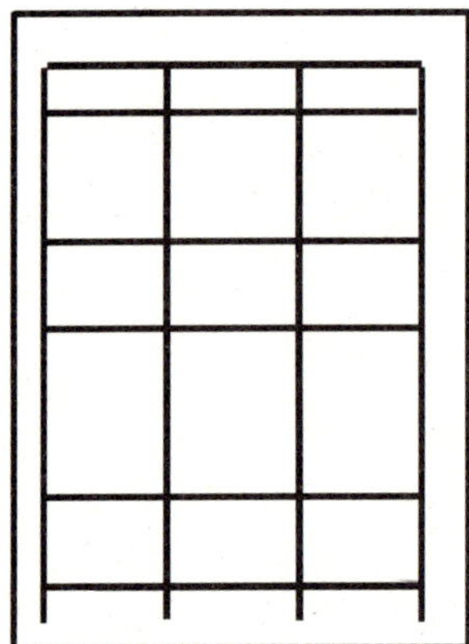

Fig. 19.12 The grid, converted to an asymmetrically balanced layout.

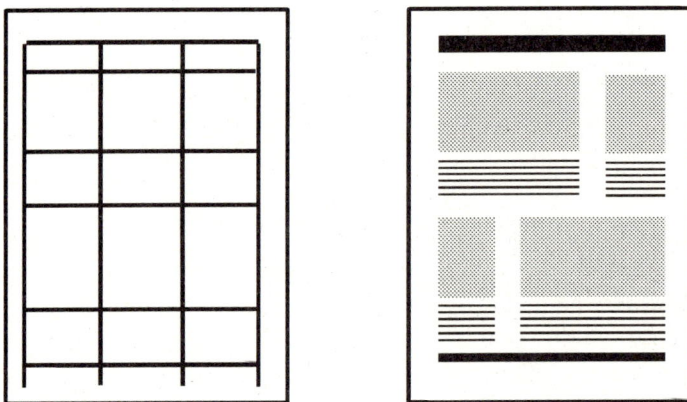

Tip
The balance you choose needs to be consistent throughout the document. Slight variations, such as adding white space within asymmetrically balanced pages, can add emphasis and interest.

Using White Space for Contrast

To provide contrast, emphasis, and a rest for the reader's eyes, use white space within a document. A headline, text, or a graphic has far more impact when surrounded by white space. As a rule, balance white space throughout the page with text and graphics (gray space) on a 50-50 ratio. This amount of white space may seem like a lot, but many ways are available to apply white space.

Margins are perhaps the most effective way of implementing white space. If you have a small amount of copy, you can make the margins one inch, two inches, or even wider. The margins don't have to be even on top, bottom, left, and right. Often, a design is more effective with a large margin on one side and smaller, equal margins on the other three sides.

When designing your page, squeeze white space to the outside of the page. Sometimes, this practice can result in odd-shaped margins, but that's better than trapping large pockets of white space inside the page. Such pockets prevent you from achieving balance, waste a lot of valuable space, and are obstacles to the eye. See figure 19.13 for an example of good use of white space.

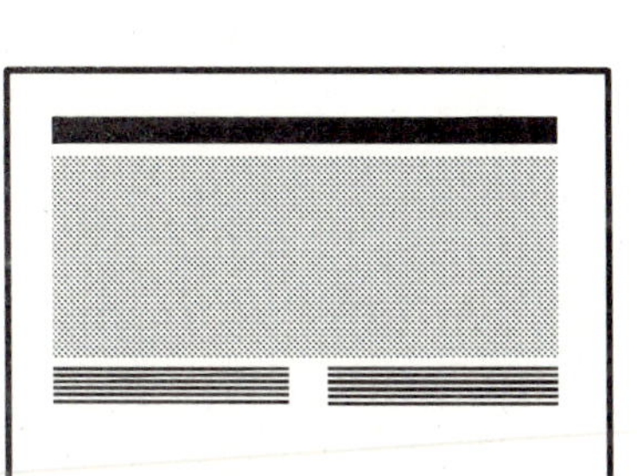

Fig. 19.13
A document showing good use of white space.

Establishing Margins

Margins are important to any document. Margins are the areas surrounding the text blocks and the graphics. This space serves as white space and as "breathing room" in contrast to the gray areas of text and graphics. Although gray space is often referred to as the "active" or "live" part of the page, don't consider the white space a dead area. White space serves an important function, especially when used as margins; white space provides ease of reading, higher impact, and emphasis on the message.

Margins also help provide consistency from page to page throughout a document. After you choose a formula for the margins of a particular document, stay with that formula throughout the document. Don't change margins just for design's sake (unless you mirror the margins for facing pages); don't change the margins to squeeze in an extra bit of text. For information on setting margins in Ami Pro, see Chapter 5, "Working with Page Layout."

Note

Most printers have an invisible margin around the edge of the paper that doesn't print. Your margin may be 3/8 inch or 1/2 inch. You can easily test the printer by creating a 1-inch-thick ruled box around the edges of an 8 1/2-inch-by-11-inch page, and then print the page. Alternatively, open and print Ami Pro's Print.SAM file (C:\AMIPRO\DOCS) to test your printer's capabilities. Measure the portion of the rule the printer doesn't print and use it as a guideline for the smallest possible margin.

If you want contrast, emphasis, and the reader's attention, use more margin. A gray page of text and crowded graphics may distract the reader.

Figure 19.14 shows common margins for a newsletter and a brochure. These layouts have three columns surrounded by margins and separated with gutters. Figure 19.15 shows a more creative use of margins and white space.

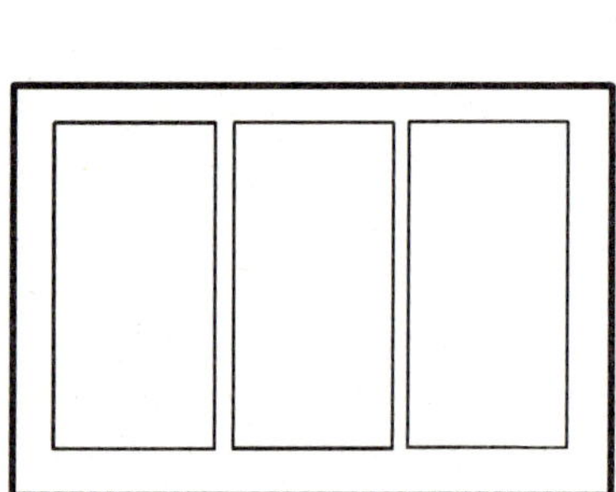

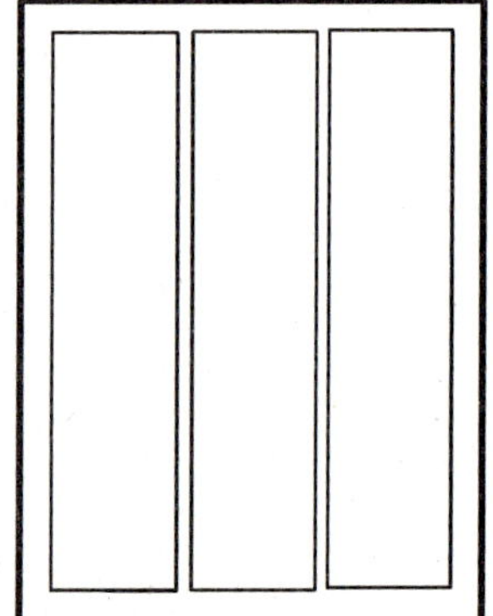

Fig. 19.14 Landscape (left) and portrait (right) orientations using common margins for a newsletter and brochure.

Planning Columns

Some documents may require a division of copy by *columns*. Columns help you organize the placement of text and graphics. Nonprinting vertical guides create boundaries by which you lay out the columns on the page. The first point to remember when designing columns is that you read from left to right. Text, therefore, should flow from the left column to the right. Because the main purpose of the document is to present information to the reader in an easy-to-understand, easy-to-follow format, don't confuse the reader by using overly creative columns. The flow of text must be logical (see fig. 19.16).

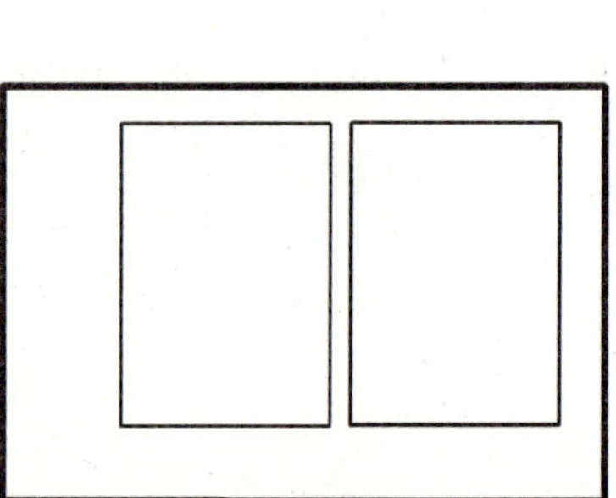

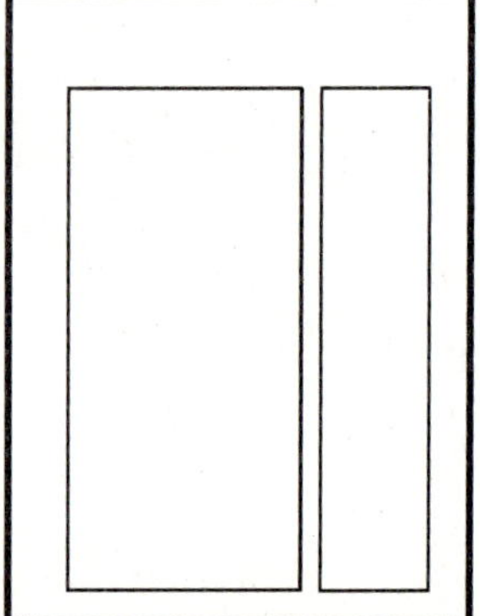

Fig. 19.15 Columns surrounded by unequal margins create a different perspective than even margins.

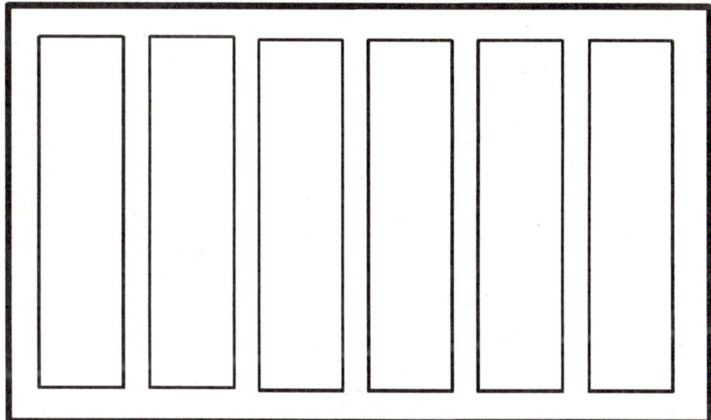

Fig. 19.16 A document divided by columns.

On portrait-oriented pages, use no more than four columns per page; on landscape-oriented pages, use no more than six columns per page. Too many columns can clutter and are hard to follow. Lines of text have to be short to fit in narrow columns, and small graphics may be ineffective.

For design purposes, columns don't need to be equal widths (see fig. 19.17). You can combine wide and narrow columns on the page to create interest. Beginning with a grid, experiment with various column widths as you plan the design. Lay out one wide column and three narrow columns or two wide and one narrow. When you're satisfied with the layout, fit your copy into the columns according to content. Include a brief, bulleted list or a tall, thin graphic in the narrow columns; or place a wide photograph or a lengthy story in the wide columns. Remember to be sure that your copy fits the column layout throughout the entire document and be consistent with the column width and placement.

When you have columns, you have gutters. A *gutter* (sometimes referred to as an alley) is the white space between two columns. Think of a gutter as a margin or "breathing room." Leaving enough space between columns is important. Narrow gutters can make the text in columns hard to read or force a reader's eye to jump to the column to the left or to the right. Very wide gutters, on the other hand, tend to separate ideas or a continued story. Limiting gutters to between 1/4 inch and 1/2 inch is a good compromise. Remember to keep the gutters consistent throughout the document. For information about setting columns and gutters in Ami Pro, see Chapter 5, "Working with Page Layout."

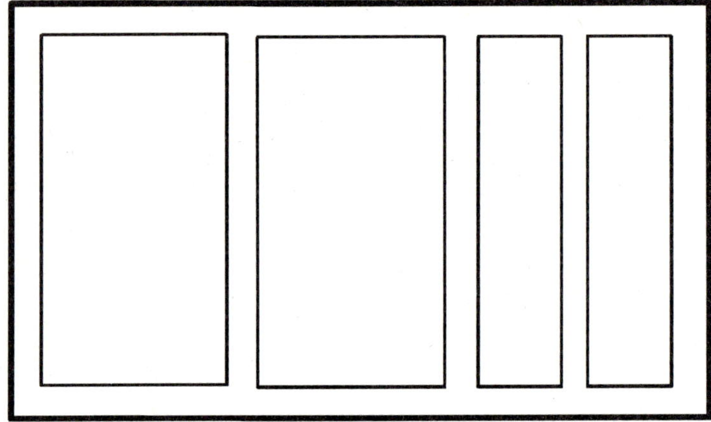

Fig. 19.17
A brochure using landscape orientation and uneven columns.

Enhancing the Page with Graphics

Besides the design elements previously mentioned, *graphics*—including horizontal lines, borders, boxes, screens, vertical lines, and images—are essential components to good design. Using graphic elements on the page adds interest and diversity. Too many elements, however, can create chaos. The purpose of using graphics is to enhance, not ornament or decorate, the text. Decorating the text can distract the reader from the message. This section covers the guidelines that govern the judicious use of graphics. (Graphic images are discussed later in this chapter in the sections "Using Graphic Images" and "Integrating Text and Graphics.")

Using Lines

A *line* can extend from margin to margin, gutter to gutter (to border a column), or add emphasis to a word, phrase, or headline by extending the width of the type. Lines are usually measured in points and can be of varying widths.

In Ami Pro, you choose lines by selecting a line pattern, or sample. Use a line to direct the eye. Use a wide line above a major head, for example, and thinner lines above the subheads. This design strategy helps tie together the main points of the document, as shown in figure 19.18.

Use lines to tie together certain elements, such as columns or pages within a document. Adding a margin-to-margin line to a header or footer establishes continuity between pages. Lines placed above or below columns also tie these elements to each other and to columns on other pages. A line also can establish a stopping point for the eye. A thick line at the bottom of the page can signal the reader to stop.

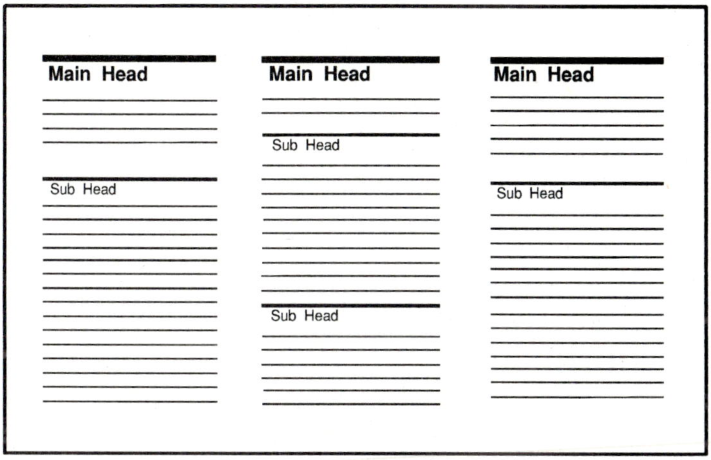

Fig. 19.18
A brochure design that incorporates lines to tie together main topics and the subheads.

Caution

Be careful where you place thick, stopping lines; use a stopping line only if you want the reader to stop, like at the end of a page or at the end of an article.

Vertical lines are useful in designing the document. Vertical lines come in the same widths as horizontal lines. Use vertical lines to separate columns of left-aligned text. A thin line between the columns keeps the reader's eye from jumping to the adjacent column.

Don't use vertical lines in place of gutter space. Add the line to the gutter space. Also, don't place a vertical line in a fold. The gutters of a brochure, for example, are for the folds. If you place a line in the gutter, you defeat the purpose of the fold (to divide the columns), and you make it difficult for the person who has to fold the brochures exactly on the line. A line in the fold doesn't look good and may cost more money.

Don't use vertical lines with justified text; the page is already gray enough. The white gutter space is more important than a line. With left-aligned text, however, the line endings create white space naturally, and a line here becomes a desirable element to add.

Using Borders

A *border*, or box, is another graphic element you can use to direct attention to specific items.

Including white space with any box you use is important. Never draw a box into the gutters; instead, draw no further than the column guides. The outside of a box shouldn't butt against other type; leave room around the box. Elements within the box, whether type or text, must also have space around them. Otherwise, the box just clutters the document. For information on how to set margins and borders in a frame, see Chapter 16, "Using Frames."

Use a box to isolate certain messages from the rest of the copy and use related information in the box. Assume that in a newsletter on design, for example, an article about margins and columns takes up two of the three columns on a page. In the third column, you can add a box with a short article about the importance of white space on the page.

A box can encompass the entire page, one column, or part of a column. A box can divide cells and rows in a table and can contain text or graphic images. Only your imagination limits the uses.

Adding Screens

Use *screens* as you use boxes. A screen, or frame background, is a shade of gray added to a box. Add a screen to an announcement or a story. You also can add a border around the screen. Screens are transparent, so type shows through; but be careful that you keep the screen light enough to read the type. Observe the same margin rules when using screens. When using a screen without a border, don't run the type to the very edge of the screen. Allow the screen to exceed the line of type by one or two characters. Your document will look better. (See Chapter 16, "Using Frames," for more information.)

Understanding Typography

◀ See "Setting Defaults," p. 228

◀ See "Using Style Sheets and Paragraph Styles," p. 262

◀ See "Creating and Modifying Styles," p. 273

One of the most important elements of design is *typography*. Typography is the style, arrangement, or appearance of typeset matter; typography also refers to the general appearance of the printed page. The subject of typography is so comprehensive that it merits an entire book by itself, and many typography books are on the market. This section presents information about typography as it applies to desktop publishing and Ami Pro.

Typefaces

A *typeface* is a specific style or design of the actual letters of type. Helvetica, for example, is a typeface, and so is Times Roman. These two typefaces are the most commonly used in desktop publishing programs and word processors.

If you don't have Helvetica and Times, you probably have some comparable typefaces.

Times and Helvetica are examples of *serif* and *sans serif* typefaces, respectively. Serifs (Times) are the fine cross strokes across the ends of the main strokes of the characters. Serif type has a varied stroke (the thickness of the lines that form the letter) and adds a horizontal flow to the type, making the letters easily recognizable to the reader.

Sans serif (Helvetica) has no serif but has a uniform stroke. Many sans serif typefaces are hard to read in large quantities—such as body text—but can be used successfully in captions, headlines, forms, and so on.

In many documents, you can use a serif typeface for body text and a sans serif for the heads, subheads, and captions. Using the two typefaces in this way creates variety and interest in the document.

In addition, Ami Pro comes packaged with *ATM* (Adobe Type Manager) fonts. These fonts (typefaces) give you a variety of choices for your documents. If you don't install ATM with your program, consider doing so before you produce any documents. See later sections in this chapter on producing specific documents for samples of ATM fonts.

Tip
Don't use more than two typefaces in any one document. Too many typefaces distract the reader and look unprofessional.

Type Sizes

The main portion of any document is the body text. The common sizes for body text are 9-, 10-, 11-, and 12-point. Type smaller than 9-point is too small to read comfortably, although a great deal of advertising text today is written in sizes smaller than 9-point. Body text larger than 12-point type is difficult to read, unless the text is geared to visually impaired readers.

For major headings (*heads*), 18-, 24-, 36-, or 48-point type serves best. Heads can be boldface, boldface italic, or, if short (two to four words), all uppercase. An 18-point head, for example, fits 10-point body type well and is comfortable to read.

Tip
If you need more space in a document to fit copy, you can reduce the type sizes of body text (no less than 9-point) and heads (no less than 14-point).

Use a *subhead* to categorize main topics. The subhead is more significant than the body text, yet less important than the heads. Usually boldface, italic, or all uppercase (if short), a subhead can be 12- or 14-point type, depending on the size of the document. The larger the page, the larger the point size.

Display type is large, sometimes ornamental type, used sparingly in documents to grab attention. The size of display type depends on the size of the document, the length of the word or words, and the space the rest of the copy occupies. Display type sizes can be 48-, 60-, 72-point, or even larger.

Using Attributes To Improve Your Document

You use *attributes* to emphasize a word or group of words. Examples of attributes are boldface, italic, boldface italic, all capital letters, and condensed or expanded type. Applying an attribute to a small amount of text is more emphatic than applying an attribute to large blocks of text. Don't use too many different attributes in a document. A little boldface and italic is fine, but using boldface, italic, all uppercase, and condensed type in one document is too much.

Note

It's easy to misuse attributes. For example, don't underline anything except a column of numbers. Underlining makes reading the document more difficult and looks unprofessional. Use italics instead of underlining. Double underlining should be reserved for under the total of a column of numbers.

Using Spacing

You need to include white space in your document. This space is important to your document for the sake of design and for readability. Crowded text—words too close together—and too much "gray" on the page fatigues a reader's eyes. To include white space in a document, you can use wider margins. You also can increase the white space by controlling the spacing within the text.

When reading, the eye doesn't look closely at each word. Instead, the reader uses the shape of words—the shape of the ascenders (*b, d, f, h, k, l, t*) and descenders (*g, j, p, q, y*) in relation to the body of the word—to recognize what the word is. (This condition is one reason all uppercase is so hard to read.) You can use the spacing of letters, words, lines, and paragraphs to help your reader get through your material quickly and easily.

Four main categories of spacing are used in typesetting documents: letter spacing, word spacing, line spacing, and paragraph spacing. When applying any kind of spacing, be consistent. Consistency in spacing keeps the reader on track, offering no diversions to interrupt the train of thought.

Spacing between Letters

The spacing between the letters of a word can make it easier or harder to read. Certain letters fit together to form instantly recognizable pairs: *th*, *er*, *sp*, and *ly* are just a few of many familiar pairs of letters. When you have too much space between letters, recognizing letters as pairs is more difficult. This problem is the main reason typesetters rarely use monospaced fonts, such as Courier, for documents. In a monospaced font such as Courier, each letter takes up exactly the same amount of space, no matter if the letter is an *i* or an *m*. Figure 19.19 shows both Courier and Helvetica type. Notice the difference in the letter spacing. Helvetica is easier to read. *Kerning* is the reduction of space between certain pairs of letters—such as capital *V*, *W*, and *A*—so that the characters print in an aesthetically pleasing manner. Ami Pro automatically kerns letter pairs (Tools User Setup Options Pair Kerning). Most kerning takes place in heads that are 18-point or larger because the uneven letter spacing is more noticeable in the larger type sizes.

Courier is a monospaced font. Each letter and punctuation mark occupies exactly the same amount of space. For this reason, Courier is difficult to read.

Helvetica is a proportionally spaced font. Each letter is only as wide as it needs to be. Helvetica is much easier to read than Courier.

Fig. 19.19
Different letter spacing in Courier and Helvetica typefaces.

Spacing between Words

The correct spacing between words is critical to ease of reading. Words too close together create a dense gray page, uninviting to a reader. On the other hand, words spaced too far apart create "holes" on the page. Large areas of white space between words are apparent in the overall gray of the page. Too much or too little spacing makes the reader work hard to get through the message (see fig. 19.20).

Tip
Fully justified text—aligned flush left and flush right—can cause problems with spacing and create large gaps between words or letters.When fully justifying text, be sure to turn on hyphenation.

Note

One final note about *word spacing*: never use two spaces after a period. This method is a leftover from the typewriter days and monospaced fonts. When you are typesetting, two spaces at the end of a sentence creates holes in the text. If you can't remember not to press the space bar twice, you can type the way you usually do and then perform a search and replace to get rid of the double spaces. See Chapter 3, "Editing Techniques."

Fig. 19.20
Words too close together (top) and too far apart (bottom) make documents difficult to read.

Wordscanbespacedtooclosetogether.If word spacing is tootight, the gray of the page is too dense, causing the reader to search for each individual word. Justified text can be the root of the problem, combined with a column that is too narrow.

Word spacing is important to readability. Too much space between words can create "rivers" of white space that flow through the page. Text that is justified tends to create wide word spacing if hyphenation is turned off.

Spacing between Lines

Line spacing, interline spacing, and *leading* (LED-ing) all refer to the amount of space between two lines of text. You may be familiar with single-, one-and-a-half-, and double-line spacing from your typewriter; Ami Pro uses the same terms to describe line spacing. In Ami Pro, you also can measure line spacing in points (by selecting the measurement box in any dialog box). As a default, Ami Pro automatically spaces lines for you, increasing the space in proportion to the size of the type. Most of the time, you probably don't need to adjust the spacing.

Note

If you have extra copy you need to fit in a document, you can add extra space for the copy by reducing the leading. Remember, the smaller the type, the less line spacing required. Sans serif type, because of its vertical emphasis, needs extra leading to improve readability. Headlines may need less leading for effortless reading; body text may require more for the same purpose. You can enlarge the spacing as much as you need to meet the needs of your document; however, you can reduce the leading only to the size of the body type. For example, 10-point type on 10-point leading, 14-point type on 14-point leading, and so on.

Spacing between Paragraphs

After the letters, words, and lines of your document have the proper spacing, you may want to add extra space between *paragraphs*. Remember this simple rule: if you indent the first line of the paragraph, don't add an extra line of space between paragraphs; if you don't indent the first line, add at least one line of space between each paragraph.

Using Text Alignment

Alignment is a method of organizing text. Body text, headlines, tabs, and all text must have an alignment (left aligned, right aligned, centered, or fully justified). Keep the alignment consistent throughout the entire document. Changes in alignment from page to page can be confusing and disconcerting to the reader. Figure 19.21 illustrates each of the four alignments discussed.

Tip
One disadvantage to left-aligned text is that you cannot fit in as much copy as you can with fully justified text. If you have a lot of copy and few pages on which to set it, left-aligned text may take up too much space.

Left Alignment

Left-aligned text has a flush left margin and a ragged right margin. Using left-aligned text for body text has many advantages. The ragged right margin adds valuable white space to break up the page. Of course, if your right margin is too ragged, the white space can be distracting. To avoid a too-ragged right margin, turn on hyphenation. Never use more than two hyphens in succession. (Two hyphens is the default in Ami Pro.) If the right margin is too ragged or has many hyphens, adjust your column width.

Another advantage of left-aligned text is that equal word spacing occurs naturally and provides an even texture to the gray of the page. Left-aligned text also works well in narrow columns because the reader can find the beginning of a line easier and faster. The flush left alignment directs the eye easily. When you use left-aligned headlines and subheads, readers are able to find the next topic easily. This alignment adds additional white space (on the right). When left-aligning text, you can place a vertical rule in the gutters to help divide the columns. Remember, don't use a rule in the gutter if the piece folds on that gutter.

Tip
Never use right-aligned text for any head or subhead more than three or four lines long. Never use right alignment in a caption or pull-out quote. Never use right-alignment for body text because it's difficult to read.

Right Alignment

Right-aligned text has a flush right margin and a ragged left margin. Don't use right-alignment for body text. Usually, right alignment is reserved for a headline or subhead to attract attention. If you use right-aligned heads, be sure to use uppercase and lowercase (never all uppercase). Make sure that the heads are very short and that the overall design of the piece reflects and reinforces the use of right-aligned text.

Center Alignment

Centered text has ragged left and right margins. Center alignment most often is used for headlines, subheads, captions, datelines, and so on. Center alignment provides to the document even word spacing, visual interest, and an air of dignity.

Fig. 19.21
Examples of left-aligned, right-aligned, centered, and fully justified type.

Left-Aligned Subhead

Left-aligned heads, subheads and body text provide consistency of design. The reader always knows where the next line begins. In addition, the ragged right line endings create white space.

Right-Aligned Subhead

Text that is right-aligned should be short and very interesting.

Center-Aligned Subhead

Any centered text should be short and be well-arranged. Also make sure that the line length is pleasing to the eye.

Justified Text

Never justify a subhead or head. Because the type is larger, it will space unequally to fit. It would not look good. Therefore, this justified text has a left-aligned head. Again, justified text allows you to fit more copy on the page.

Tip
Center-aligned heads work well with fully justified body text.

Although rarely used for body text, you can center-align certain items: lists of names or dates, invitations or announcements, and very short lines of text in a flier. Center-aligned body text is hard to read; the reader must search for the beginning and end of each line.

Full Justification

Fully justified text has a flush-left and flush-right margin. Fully justified text is perfect for long materials, such as books, articles, and reports. The page appears organized, quiet, and comfortable for the reader.

Fully justified alignment enables you to fit more copy on the page. Avoid any temptation to reduce gutters with justified text; because of the even gray appearance of the page, you need the white space in the gutters. Add extra space to the gutter if possible.

Tip

Never use fully justified text for headlines. A headline or subhead is larger type than the text. Large type is hard to justify without unequal and unsightly word spacing.

Watch out for uneven word spacing with fully justified text. Justification sometimes forces long words to the next line or squeezes short words to the current line. When using fully justified text, always make sure that automatic hyphenation is turned on. *Manual manipulation* of the line sometimes is necessary. Manual manipulation includes editing the text or adjusting the letter spacing of just one line of text (or both). Discretionary hyphens (Ctrl+hyphen) often are handy, too.

Using Graphic Images

A *graphic image* can originate from any number of sources: Ami Pro's drawing or charting features, other paint or draw programs, scanners, or any graphic program that can save images in TIFF (Tagged Image Format File), EPS (Encapsulated PostScript Standard), HPGL (Hewlett-Packard Graphics Language), PIC (1-2-3 Graphics), WMF (Windows Metafile), WPG (DrawPerfect), and so on. (See Chapter 20, "Importing, Exporting, and Linking Files," for a complete list of compatible files.) Ami Pro enables you to scale, crop, and add a border around images. The borders available for the frame of a picture are the same as rules and boxes (see fig. 19.22).

◀ See "Entering Text and Graphics in Frames," p. 512

◀ See "Modifying Imported Objects," p. 562

◀ See "Modifying a Scanned Image," p. 567

▶ See "Importing Graphics," p. 691

▶ See "Editing Imported Graphics," p. 701

Note

Be sure that a graphic image is surrounded by enough white space to let the image breathe. Scaling or cropping gives you control over white space within a framed graphic. The space on the outside of the graphic also is important. Place a margin on all sides of the frame between the graphic and the text.

See Chapter 16, "Using Frames," for information about borders, boxes, and lines. See Chapter 17, "Using the Draw Feature," for information about using an AmiDraw file, scanned images, and the drawing program. See Chapter 18, "Creating Charts," for information about Ami Pro's charting feature.

Fig. 19.22
A framed graphic image surrounded by plenty of white space.

GRAPHIC IMAGES

Import graphic images such as paint and draw programs, scanned images, spreadsheets, and clip art to Ami Pro for Windows. Ami Pro makes it easy with frames. Refer to Appendix B for more information.

Included with your Ami Pro package is a drawing program. You can use it to crop or alter any of your graphic images.

Graphic images must have white space. To effectively use white space, include it both inside the frame and outside.

Left-aligned text in columns, such as this example, affords plenty of white space for any graphic you might add. The graphic to the left has a border with white space inside, and outside. Allow graphic images to breathe. They have more impact on the reader if they are surrounded by sufficient space.

Producing Style Sheets

A *style sheet* refers to the formatted page and type. The style sheet is the overall design: columns, margins, tabs, and so on. The style sheet also lists paragraph styles that describe typeface, type size and style, spacing, alignment, and indents. You use a particular style sheet for a particular type of document. A newsletter style sheet, for example, is different from a form style sheet.

Note

You, of course, can individually format each paragraph of body text, each head, each tab, and so on. Formatting the item once, however, is so much easier. Save the format as a paragraph style and use it over and over again throughout the document and then later in similar documents.

A style sheet is an excellent way of ensuring consistency in a document and between documents. Suppose, for example, that in the first issue of a newsletter, all major headings are set in 18-point Helvetica, boldface, and centered; body text is 12-point Times Roman and justified. The document contains three columns per page, headers, page numbers, and a table of contents. Next month, when you produce the second issue of the newsletter, you can use the style sheet created for the first newsletter. The style sheet ensures that the two issues look alike. Using a style sheet saves you much time in setting up the paragraph styles.

Ami Pro has built-in style sheets. You also can create your own style sheets. For consistency and efficiency, use a style sheet with any document you frequently produce. See Chapter 10, "Working with Style Sheets," for information about creating and saving a style sheet in Ami Pro. See the Appendix, "A Guide to Style Sheets," for information about Ami Pro's built-in style sheets.

◀ See "Working with Headers and Footers," p. 134

◀ See "Using Style Sheets and Paragraph Styles," p. 262

◀ See "Creating and Modifying Styles," p. 273

Integrating Text and Graphics

As mentioned earlier in this chapter, the main purpose of all printed material is to convey a message to the reader; the main purpose of design is to attract the reader's attention. By successfully integrating text and graphics within your document design, you can accomplish both of these purposes (see fig. 19.23). Text includes body copy, headlines, subheads, captions, and display type. Graphics include *elements* (rules, screens, borders, and boxes) and *images* (clip art, line art, tables, charts, scanned images, and so on).

If you follow the guidelines presented in the previous sections of this chapter, you get an idea of how to design your page with text and graphics. This section presents examples of designs and brief critiques so you can see how text and graphics combine to make interesting, readable, and attractive documents. All designs are created in Ami Pro 3.

The first example, which illustrates a fax cover sheet, combines text and graphic elements, (see fig. 19.23). The shadow box frames help divide and organize the information. The design created by the frames is attractive and eye-catching. In figure 19.24, graphic elements and an image mix with text in an example of a newspaper advertisement.

In figure 19.24, lines border the top and bottom of the ad. The AmiDraw clip art represents a logo for the craft shop. Note that the text and the graphic image are right-aligned. Because the use of white space and alignment is unusual, this ad will stand out in a crowded newspaper.

Ami Pro includes over 100 clip art files to spice up your document. (SmartPics for Windows contains another 2,000 pieces of clip art.) You also can import your own files (see Chapter 20, "Importing, Exporting, and Linking Files," for more information). Figure 19.25 illustrates a letterhead that uses four clip art files as a logo for the company.

In figure 19.25, each image is bordered by a rounded-corner frame; the four images grouped together repeat the square shape. The same rounded corners and line style enclose the text in a frame. Repeating the elements creates consistency; varying the images creates emphasis in this design.

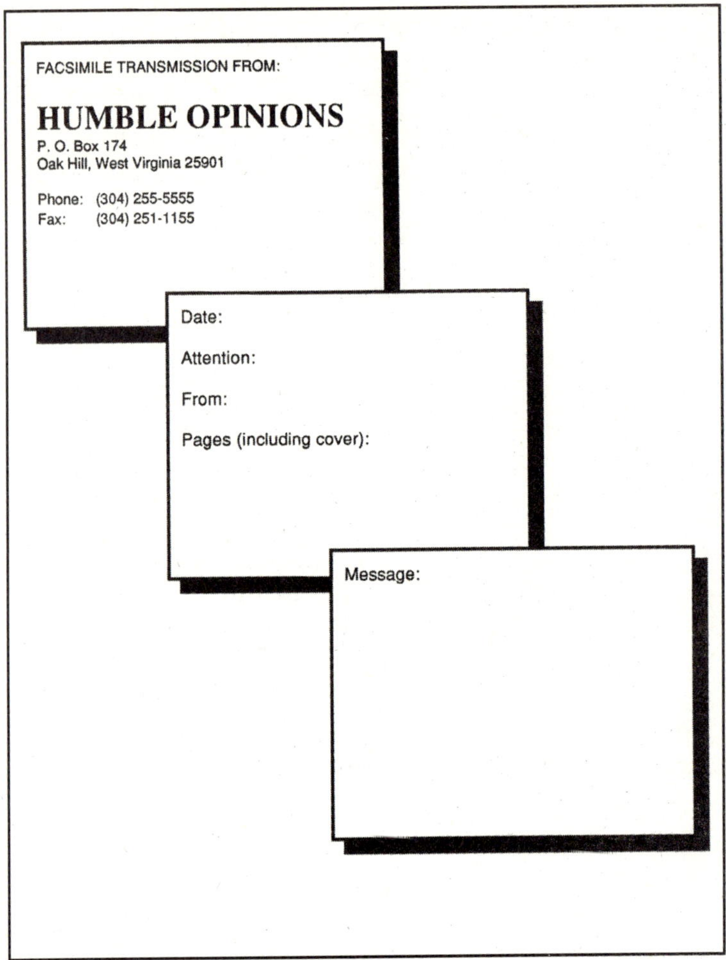

FACSIMILE TRANSMISSION FROM:
HUMBLE OPINIONS
P. O. Box 174
Oak Hill, West Virginia 25901
Phone: (304) 255-5555
Fax: (304) 251-1155
Date:
Attention:
From:
Pages (including cover):
Message:

Fig. 19.23
A fax cover sheet combining text and graphic elements.

◀ See "Adding Lines," p. 131

◀ See "Entering Text and Graphics in Frames," p. 512

Another combination of a graphic element and image appears in figure 19.26. The image, an airplane, is rotated in Ami Pro's drawing feature to create an unusual effect. The placement and formatting of the text allows the contents to breathe with plenty of white space.

Graphic elements can divide and organize information on the page. Figure 19.27 is a sample of a newsletter design that uses lines to do just that. The page borders (double lines) help define the margins and hold the page together. Another double line defines the end of the nameplate. Thin lines between each column help the reader determine the line endings of the left-aligned text. Finally, similar line styles border the pull-out quote in the center column to make it stand out.

MARIE'S
CRAFT SHOP
POTTERY
WEAVINGS
JEWELRY
CANDLES
PAINTINGS
Handmade Gifts
Open Daily 10 to 5
MARIE'S
CRAFT SHOP
3041 Elks Circle
Huntington, WV
(304) 311-5505

Fig. 19.24
Graphic elements, an image, and text create an innovative advertising design.

There is plenty of white space on this page to make reading comfortable (see fig. 19.27). The left-aligned heads and body text create white space; wide gutters also contribute. Interparagraph spacing and the addition of the pull-out quote combine to create more breathing room.

Figure 19.28 illustrates page two of the same newsletter. The page and intercolumnar lines are repeated for consistency within the newsletter. The same type of frame used for the pull-out quote on page one is repeated on page two. The top frame contains a scanned image relating to the story; white space surrounds the image, creating a light effect. The bottom frame contains an advertisement. The type and image in the ad combine to create a different look to the page, making the ad stand out. Subsequent pages (not shown here) would follow a similar layout to these two pages.

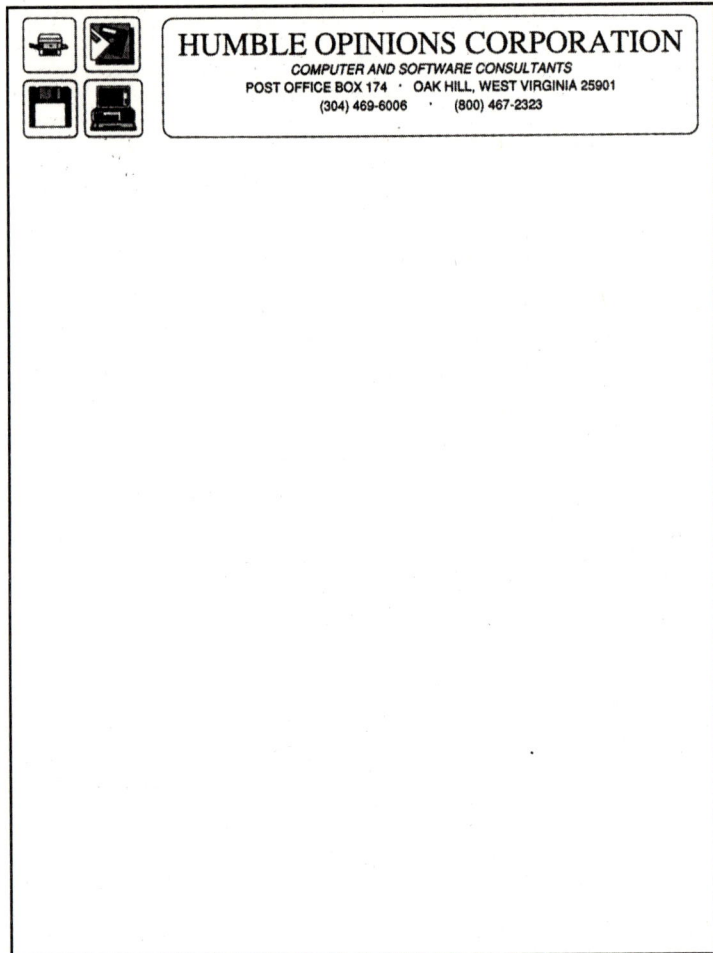

HUMBLE OPINIONS CORPORATION
COMPUTER AND SOFTWARE CONSULTANTS
POST OFFICE BOX 174 · OAK HILL, WEST VIRGINIA 25901
(304) 469-6006 · (800) 467-2323

Fig. 19.25
A letterhead design using repeated graphic elements for consistency.

Fig. 19.26
An attention-getting flier design.

Fig. 19.27
Page one of a newsletter using graphic elements to organize the information and define the page.

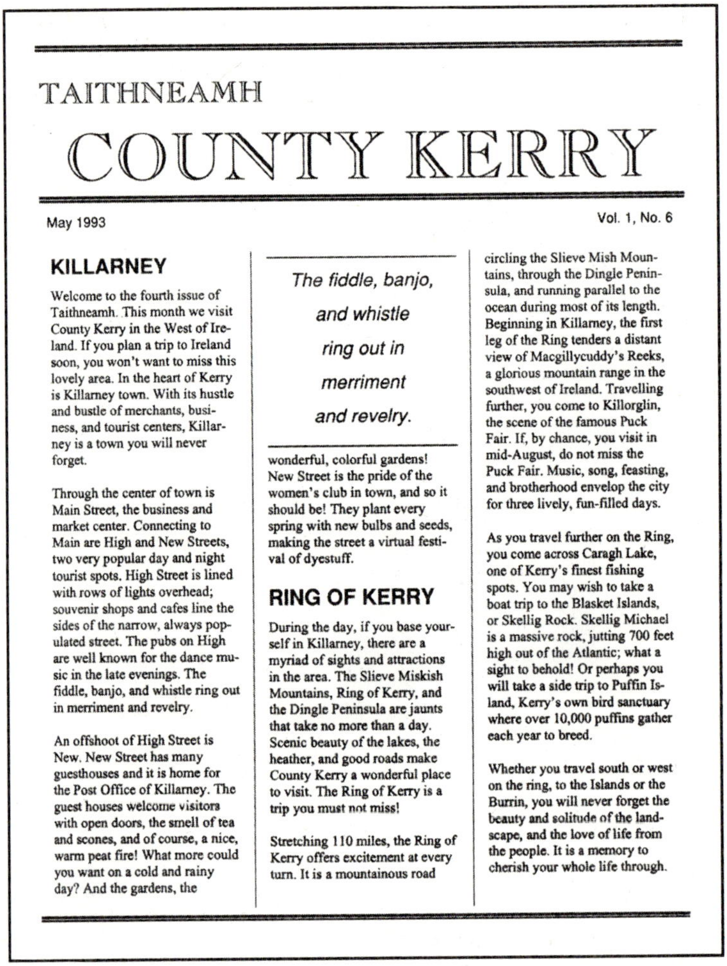

TAITHNEAMH

COUNTY KERRY

May 1993

Vol. 1, No. 6

KILLARNEY

Welcome to the fourth issue of Taithneamh. This month we visit County Kerry in the West of Ireland. If you plan a trip to Ireland soon, you won't want to miss this lovely area. In the heart of Kerry is Killarney town. With its hustle and bustle of merchants, business, and tourist centers, Killarney is a town you will never forget.

Through the center of town is Main Street, the business and market center. Connecting to Main are High and New Streets, two very popular day and night tourist spots. High Street is lined with rows of lights overhead; souvenir shops and cafes line the sides of the narrow, always populated street. The pubs on High are well known for the dance music in the late evenings. The fiddle, banjo, and whistle ring out in merriment and revelry.

An offshoot of High Street is New. New Street has many guesthouses and it is home for the Post Office of Killarney. The guest houses welcome visitors with open doors, the smell of tea and scones, and of course, a nice, warm peat fire! What more could you want on a cold and rainy day? And the gardens, the

The fiddle, banjo, and whistle ring out in merriment and revelry.

wonderful, colorful gardens! New Street is the pride of the women's club in town, and so it should be! They plant every spring with new bulbs and seeds, making the street a virtual festival of dyestuff.

RING OF KERRY

During the day, if you base yourself in Killarney, there are a myriad of sights and attractions in the area. The Slieve Miskish Mountains, Ring of Kerry, and the Dingle Peninsula are jaunts that take no more than a day. Scenic beauty of the lakes, the heather, and good roads make County Kerry a wonderful place to visit. The Ring of Kerry is a trip you must not miss!

Stretching 110 miles, the Ring of Kerry offers excitement at every turn. It is a mountainous road circling the Slieve Mish Mountains, through the Dingle Peninsula, and running parallel to the ocean during most of its length. Beginning in Killarney, the first leg of the Ring tenders a distant view of Macgillycuddy's Reeks, a glorious mountain range in the southwest of Ireland. Travelling further, you come to Killorglin, the scene of the famous Puck Fair. If, by chance, you visit in mid-August, do not miss the Puck Fair. Music, song, feasting, and brotherhood envelop the city for three lively, fun-filled days.

As you travel further on the Ring, you come across Caragh Lake, one of Kerry's finest fishing spots. You may wish to take a boat trip to the Blasket Islands, or Skellig Rock. Skellig Michael is a massive rock, jutting 700 feet high out of the Atlantic; what a sight to behold! Or perhaps you will take a side trip to Puffin Island, Kerry's own bird sanctuary where over 10,000 puffins gather each year to breed.

Whether you travel south or west on the ring, to the Islands or the Burrin, you will never forget the beauty and solitude of the landscape, and the love of life from the people. It is a memory to cherish your whole life through.

beauty and solitude of the landscape, and the love of life from the people. It is a memory to cherish your whole life through.

MUCKROSS ESTATE

Also located near Killarney, County Kerry, is a tremendous National Park called Muckross Estate. Over 10,000 acres of mountains, lakes, and green, green flora preserved by the Republic for your enjoyment. Cars are not allowed on the estate; there are, however, alternatives. You may rent or bring your own bicycle. Or take a jaunting car. Jaunting cars line the entrance to the park (as well as line the streets of Killarney), ready to transport you to this scene of serenity and beauty. The horse-drawn carriages are driven by gents who spin tales and weave stories of old Ireland, Killarney, Muckross, and the fairies.

Your first stop on the Estate is Muckross Abbey. A Franciscan Abbey built in the 15th century, it is one of the best kept and restored abbeys in all of Kerry. Your next stop is Muckross House. A monumental 19th century home donated, along with the land, to the people of Ireland by its former owners. The house is filled with intricately hand-carved furniture, home-made crafts, tapestries, and original art works. The basement contains a stable, and fully stocked print shop, pub, blacksmith shop, kitchen, and weavers shop; all have presenters working as you tour, answering any and all questions.

THE LAKES

Contained within the National Park are three very famous, and pulchritudinous, lakes. The first you come to by jaunting car is the Lower Lake, also called Lough Leane. The second, or Middle Lake, is also called Muckross Lake. The third is simply known as the Upper Lake. In addition, don't miss Torc Mountain and its stupendous waterfall. Water from the Devil's Punch Bowl rushes over Torc's 60' waterfall, gushing and glorious, it is a sight you will not want to miss.

THE PEOPLE

Of course, as we have said before, the people of Ireland are its main tourist attraction. Their warm, friendly smiles await your visit. Their music greets you; their song welcomes you. Men resting along the side of the road from working in the peat bogs. Their worn, shiny suits a symbol of days gone by. The women, with their rosy red cheeks, shopping for fresh bread and potatoes; chatting with their

TRAVEL AIRLINES

presenting our

Spring Specials

Round Trip to Shannon	$695
Round Trip to Dublin	$795

Restrictions and limits apply
Call for information and prices

CALL TOLL FREE
1-800-009-9900

Fig. 19.28 Page two of the newsletter, integrating text, graphic elements, and graphic images.

Creating a Letterhead

An attractive letterhead is one of the most important tools of a successful business. When a customer receives an appealing document from your business, the customer is more likely to read the document. An impressive letterhead sells a business and its products and services. The company's name, address, and phone number serve as a reminder of that business each time a customer receives a letter.

Tip
Be careful not to clutter the letterhead with too much information; leave space for the actual letter.

In addition to the company's name, address, and phone number, you can add the president's name, a list of board members, office and home phone numbers, addresses of subsidiaries, graphic elements, a logo, and so on.

This section illustrates two letterheads created in Ami Pro. The first design is a basic type and graphic design; the second design incorporates a logo. A matching envelope design appears with each letterhead.

◀ See "Adding Lines," p. 131

◀ See "Creating and Modifying Styles," p. 273

Note

When you create a letterhead design you like, save it as a style sheet *with contents*. By saving with contents, meaning the company name, address, phone number, logo, lines, and so on, each time you open the style sheet, the letterhead appears. All you do is type the letter. For information about saving style sheets with contents, see Chapter 10, "Working with Style Sheets."

To use the table, select the menu listed under Element in the table. In the resulting dialog box, choose the Option listed in the table, then apply the Settings.

Producing a Basic Letterhead

This section presents a formal letterhead and envelope design and the page and style settings to produce them. Figure 19.29 illustrates the completed letterhead.

Lines separate the company name and address from other text. Below the second line are the names and phone numbers of the president and vice-president of the company. This design uses two typefaces: Helvetica and Times. This design also uses a right-aligned tab for the vice-president's name and phone number.

Ami Pro makes it easy to produce your own envelopes. You can create your own style sheet or use one of Ami Pro's envelope styles (see the Appendix, "A Guide to Style Sheets"). Figure 19.30 illustrates a matching envelope to the letterhead in figure 19.29.

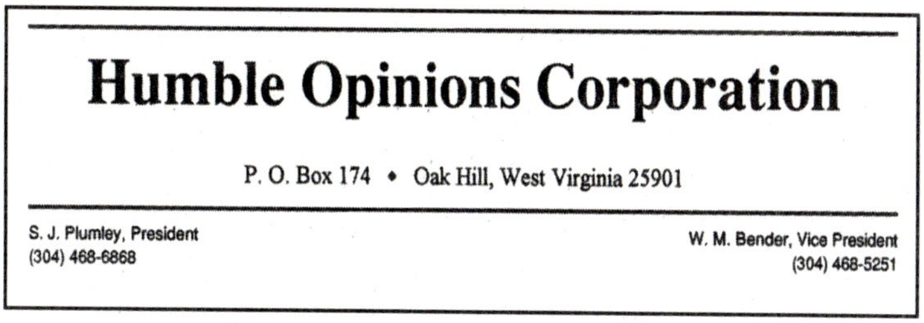

Humble Opinions Corporation

P. O. Box 174 • Oak Hill, West Virginia 25901

S. J. Plumley, President
(304) 468-6868

W. M. Bender, Vice President
(304) 468-5251

Fig. 19.29
A formal letterhead.

Caution

Ami Pro's envelope style sheet, AMIENV.STY, may need to be customized to work with your printer. Refer to Chapter 10, "Working with Style Sheets," for more information.

Notice that the overall size of the envelope design is smaller; the lines are shorter and the type is proportionally smaller. The typeface, the placement, and the style, however, remain the same as in the letterhead.

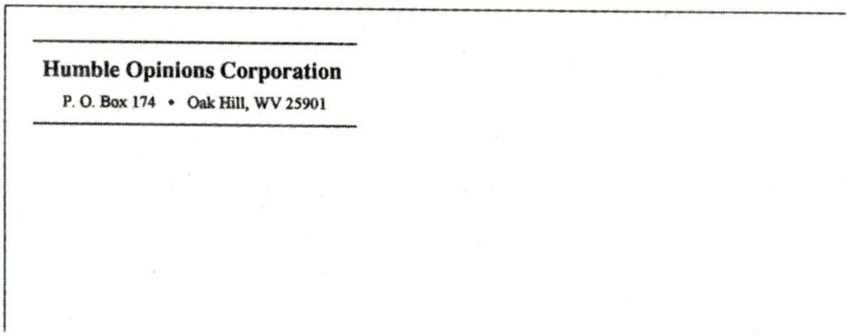

Humble Opinions Corporation

P. O. Box 174 • Oak Hill, WV 25901

Fig. 19.30
An envelope design to match the letterhead.

The following table shows the specifications for the letterhead.

Element	Option	Settings
Style Sheet	Default	
Page, Modify, Layout	Margins	All to .45 inches
Style, Create Style Head (Create)	Font Alignment Spacing	Times, 36-point, Bold Center Paragraph Spacing: Above: 0, Below: .10 inches

(continues)

Tip
Within the address line is a bullet. From the list of bullets (in Edit, Insert), choose the first diamond style; the type size of the bullet is 14-point.

Element	Option	Settings
Lines		Line above, 3rd style Spacing: .10 Length: Margins
Address (Create)	Font Alignment Lines	Times, 14-point Center Line below, 3rd style Spacing: .15
Names/Phone (Create)	Font Alignment	Helvetica, 10- point Right tab at 8 inches

The following table shows the specifications for the matching envelope.

Tip
The bullet used in the address line of the envelope is the same as the one used in the letterhead; however, select just the bullet and change the type size to 8-point so the bullet is proportional to the type of envelope design.

Element	Option	Settings
Style Sheet		Choose to fit your printer
Styles, Create Style Head	Font Alignment Spacing Lines	Times, 14-point, Bold Center tab at 1.62 inches Paragraph Spacing: Below: .05 Line above, 2nd style Spacing: .10, Length: Other at 2.75 inches
Address	Font Alignment Lines	Times, 10-point Center tab at 1.62 inches Line below, 2nd style Spacing: .10, Length: Other at 2.75 inches

Creating a Logo

Ami Pro offers you many features to help you create a logo: frames, drawing, ATM fonts, AmiDraw clip art, and so on. Following are four sample logo designs that may give you an idea for your company logo. Figure 19.31 illustrates the four designs. All are created by using the frame feature (see Chapter 16, "Using Frames").

The first design (in the top left corner) is created by using two frames. The first frame contains the *h* and uses an outline around the frame. The second frame contains the *O* with no lines or shadows. Both frames are transparent, and both use the *no wrap around option* in the Modify Frame Layout dialog box. The *h* in the first frame is Shelley Allegro Script (an ATM font) and is centered. The *O* is Times and centered. One frame overlaps the other.

The second logo (in top right corner) is simple but striking. The typeface is DomCasual (an ATM font) in all lowercase. The type is boldface and white. The frame contains no outlines, but it does have the background option turned to black (in Frame, Modify Frame Layout, Lines & Shadows). (See Chapter 4, "Formatting a Document" for information about modifying fonts.)

The third logo design (lower left corner) is created with the drawing feature. The typeface is CaslonOpenFace (an ATM font), but the type sizes are 36-point for the initial letters and 18-point for the rest. Creating four text blocks enables you to move the initial letters to any position you like. (See Chapter 17, "Using the Draw Feature," for information about text in the drawing feature.)

The final logo (lower right corner) incorporates AmiDraw clip art within one frame and type in another transparent frame. The company name is 18-point Shelley Allegro Script, lowercase, and white.

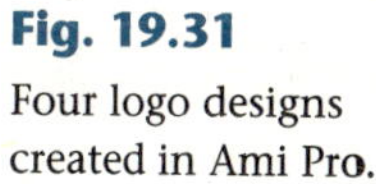

Fig. 19.31
Four logo designs created in Ami Pro.

Figure 19.32 illustrates the use of one of these logos in a letterhead. Another frame, one with a border, is added to contain the address and phone numbers. The two frames contrast to provide interest. Because the logo type is sans serif (DomCasual), the type in the address is serif (Times) to create even more interest. The envelope design is similar to the letterhead; however, the logo is shortened to include only the initials of the company name.

Creating a Purchase Order Form

A form organizes the information so it can be filled in quickly and effortlessly. A form also helps you understand and summarize the completed information. To successfully accomplish these tasks, you can customize most forms to fit specific purposes. Ami Pro provides many features that help you create the forms you need in your business.

◀ See "Creating and Modifying Styles," p. 273

◀ See "Creating Tables," p. 379

◀ See "Using the Table Menu," p. 400

◀ See "Using Tables in Document Applications," p. 427

Some useful Ami Pro features that you can use for forms are frames, tables, write protection, screens, lines, and tabs. These features enable you to customize any form to suit your purpose. In this section, the examples use the table feature to create two purchase order forms. For more information about the table feature, see Chapter 13, "Working With Tables"; for more information about frames, see Chapter 16, "Using Frames."

The first form includes screened areas for filling in purchasing, billing, and shipping information and for adding the subtotal, tax, and total of the purchase order. The specifications are listed so you can reproduce this form. Figure 19.33 illustrates the first purchase order form.

Fig. 19.32
A letterhead and envelope design with a logo.

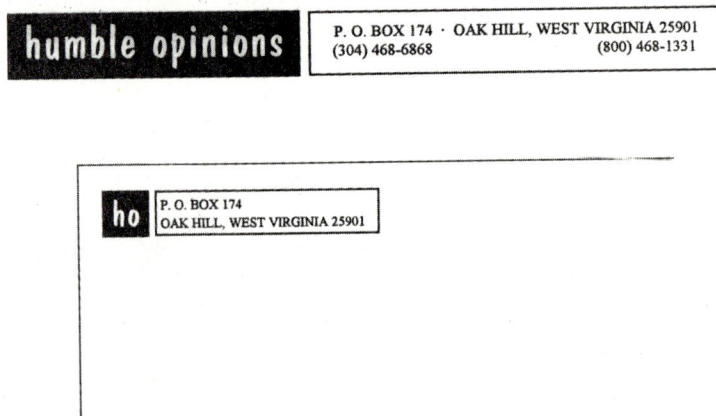

> **Note**
>
> Ami Pro's versatility lets you add screens to an entire table, one row or column, or even one cell (Frame Modify Frame Layout Lines & Shadows Background). Be sure that any screen you add is light enough for the type to show through.

HUMBLE OPINIONS CORPORATION

P. O. BOX 174 ▪ OAK HILL, WV 25901 ▪ (304) 255-1000

PURCHASE ORDER

DATE:	PO NUMBER:
PURCHASED FROM:	
SHIP ATTENTION TO:	
BILL ATTENTION TO:	
CONFIRMING ORDER REQUESTED BY:	SHIP BY:
TERMS:	

QTY	ITEM NUMBER	DESCRIPTION	UNIT PRICE	TOTAL PRICE
			SUBTOTAL	
			STATE TAX	
			TOTAL	

Fig. 19.33 A purchase order form produced with two tables in Ami Pro.

The following table shows the type and table specifications for the form.

Element	Option	Settings
Style Sheet	Default	
Page, Modify Styles, Create Style	Margins	All to .40 inches
Head	Font Alignment	Times, 24-point, bold Center
Address	Font Alignment	Times, 12-point Center

(continues)

Tip
To add a tab within a table (in first table in fig. 19.33: PO NUMBER and SHIP BY), press Ctrl+Shift+Tab. Pressing only the Tab key moves you to the next cell.

Tip
The text in the second table remains in the Table Text style; however, select the text and change it to boldface and centered through the Text Menu.

Element	Option	Settings
Purchase Order (PO)	Font	Helvetica, 14-point, bold
Styles, Modify	Alignment	Center
Table Text	Font Alignment Spacing	Helvetica, 10-point Left, Indent: All to .10 inches Paragraph Spacing: Above: .05 inches, Add in: Always
FIRST TABLE		
Tools, Tables	Number of columns Number of rows	1 9
Layout	Default Columns Default Rows Options	Width: 7.50 inches Height: .25 inches Center table on page
Table	Lines & Color	Line position: All, 2nd style Fill color: choose a light screen
SECOND TABLE		
Tools, Tables	Number of columns Number of rows	5 18
Modify Layout	Default Columns Default Rows Options Column/Row Size	Width: 1.15 inches Height: .25 inches Center table on page First column: .75 inches Second column: 1.15 inches Third column: 3.10 inches Fourth and fifth columns: 1.15 inches
Table	Lines & Color	Line position: All, 2nd style
FIRST ROW, SECOND TABLE		
Table	Lines & Color	Fill color: choose a light screen

Figure 19.34 illustrates another purchase order form, but this example is in landscape orientation. In a table, Ami Pro allows you to print only selected lines. This table shows the results of selected vertical and horizontal rules. See Chapter 5, "Working with Page Layout," for information about page orientation and Chapter 13, "Working with Tables," for information about selecting and hiding table rules.

HUMBLE OPINIONS

P. O. BOX 174 OAK HILL, WEST VIRGINIA 25901 (304) 255-5555

PURCHASE ORDER

PO NUMBER:

DATE:

QTY.	ITEM #	DESCRIPTION	ITEM PRICE	TOTAL PRICE

SHIP ATTENTION TO:

BILL ATTENTION TO:

APPROVED BY:

Fig. 19.34
A landscape-oriented purchase order form.

Creating a Brochure

A brochure is one of the most effective forms of advertising. A brochure explains and details information about a company's products or services. A brochure is soft-sell, meaning it invites the customers to read at their leisure and refer back to it often. When designing a brochure, include information that is stable. Facts such as sale dates, price lists, and other temporary material seldom go into a brochure; these facts are not stable. Instead, describe unchanging information such as descriptions of the product or service, maps, addresses, and phone numbers; describe what you can do for the customer. Organize this information in a way that logically guides the customer through the brochure.

◀ See "Modifying the Standard Page Layout," p. 120

◀ See "Adding Lines," p. 131

◀ See "Working with Rulers," p. 145

◀ See "Creating and Modifying Styles," p. 273

◀ See "Creating and Modifying Text Objects," p. 556

▶ See "Importing a Picture," p. 694

Lead the eye in a methodical way. Tell the customer who you are and what you offer. Explain, in detail, how this information is beneficial. Finally, tell where to purchase the product or service and if you have room, briefly describe the main benefits again. Strengthen the effect of your organized copy with the brochure's design.

The cover design invites the reader to open the brochure by attracting attention. The next panel (or page) may list general services, a summary of benefits to the customer, special attractions, and so on—they persuade the customer to read further. The following panels (or pages) depend on the copy, the design, and graphic images to maintain interest—they explain the details. You also may add mailing information or repeat valuable information, such as the company name, phone number, benefits, and so on.

Figure 19.35 illustrates the outside panels of an 11-inch-by-8 1/2-inch brochure. This brochure is divided into three columns and includes two parallel folds.

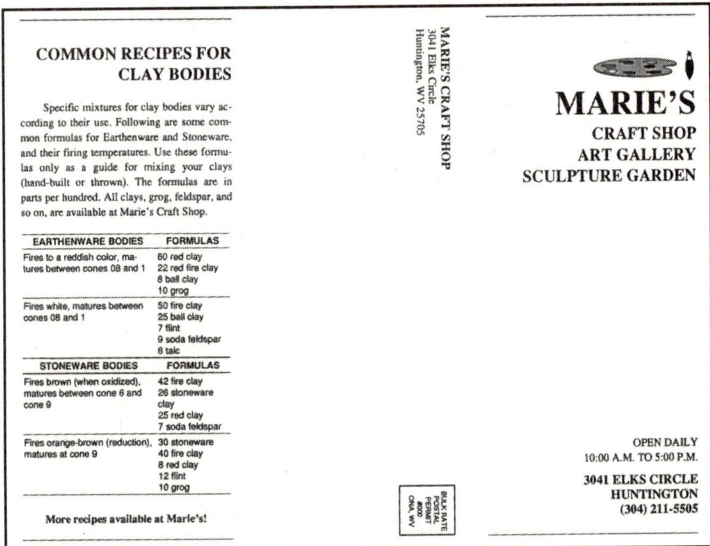

COMMON RECIPES FOR CLAY BODIES

Specific mixtures for clay bodies vary according to their use. Following are some common formulas for Earthenware and Stoneware, and their firing temperatures. Use these formulas only as a guide for mixing your clays (hand-built or thrown). The formulas are in parts per hundred. All clays, grog, feldspar, and so on, are available at Marie's Craft Shop.

EARTHENWARE BODIES	FORMULAS
Fires to a reddish color, matures between cones 08 and 1	60 red clay 22 red fire clay 8 ball clay 10 grog
Fires white, matures between cones 08 and 1	50 fire clay 25 ball clay 7 flint 9 soda feldspar 8 talc
STONEWARE BODIES	**FORMULAS**
Fires brown (when oxidized), matures between cone 6 and cone 9	42 fire clay 26 stoneware clay 25 red clay 7 soda feldspar
Fires orange-brown (reduction), matures at cone 9	30 stoneware 40 fire clay 8 red clay 12 flint 10 grog

More recipes available at Marie's!

MARIE'S CRAFT SHOP
3041 Elks Circle
Huntington, WV 25705

BULK RATE
POSTAL
PERMIT
#000
ONA, WV

MARIE'S
CRAFT SHOP
ART GALLERY
SCULPTURE GARDEN

OPEN DAILY
10:00 A.M. TO 5:00 P.M.

3041 ELKS CIRCLE
HUNTINGTON
(304) 211-5505

Fig. 19.35
The outside panels of a landscape oriented brochure.

In figure 19.35, notice that the front panel (the right column) attracts attention. The right-aligned text, logo, and line art are the first things a customer sees. Panel five (the left column) is likely to be the next panel the customer sees when opening the brochure. A table of information on this panel makes the brochure valuable to potters because it contains recipes for various clay bodies. Finally, the middle column is a mailing panel. Both the postal permit and the return address are created, grouped and rotated 90 degrees clockwise in Ami Pro's drawing feature. For more information about the drawing feature and rotating text, see Chapter 17, "Using the Draw Feature."

The inside of the brochure describes the shops and some of the available crafts. Figure 19.36 illustrates the inside panels.

The typeface, type sizes, and styles on the inside are the same as the outside of the brochure. Times, 18-point, right-aligned heads attract attention and provide interesting white space. The body text is also Times, with slightly more interline spacing for easier reading.

MARIE'S CRAFT SHOP

Marie's Craft Shop stocks the area's largest selection of arts and crafts. With more than 2,500 square feet of property, there is not only a craft shop, but also an art gallery and sculpture garden.

The Craft Shop separates into two specialized areas. One is completely stocked with the materials you need to create hundreds of crafts. Materials such as wax and wick, clay and glazes, gold, pewter and silver, looms and fibers; any and all of your craft needs. The other area of the store is filled with completed, original, hand-made crafts. Pottery, hand-blown glass, weavings, quilts, candles, jewelry, and much, much more, gathered locally!

Marie's Craft Shop also includes two rooms set apart as an art gallery. Paintings and photographs from the area are displayed for your enjoyment. All art works are for sale.

Finally, Marie's Craft Shop has an outside sculpture garden. Beautiful trees, flowers, and sculpted bushes encompass the area's finest bronze, wooden, and steel sculptures. Some works are as tall as 50 feet, other smaller ones hide and peek from the flora.

Visit Marie's Craft Shop, Art Gallery and Sculpture Garden. Open daily from 10:00 a.m. to 5:00 p.m. Special tours are available.

POTTERY

Beautiful earthenware, stoneware, and porcelain pottery are stocked at Marie's Craft Shop. Many pieces are functional, many are art works. No lead glazes are used in any of the pottery we sell. All are completely save for eating and drinking. Over 50 potters represented.

JEWELRY

Pewter, silver, gold and polished stones adorn the lovely selections at Marie's Craft shop. Earrings, necklaces, bracelets, pins, and more created by local artists. Recently acquired inlaid onyx earrings fill out our selection of fine jewelry.

LEATHERWORK

Belts, wallets, and purses hand-made of buckskin, calfskin, and suede are available. Exquisite tanned hides, sewn and laced with narrow strips of leather, create a fine craft only available at Marie's Craft Shop.

DECOUPAGE

Wood, glass, and ceramic pieces ornately hand-painted and lacquered with the most attractive prints and photographs. Many include gold leaf.

CANDLES

Handsome molded, dipped, and layered candles in a variety of shapes and colors. All prepared with the finest mixture of paraffin, tallow, and beeswax for a slow, even burning candle.

BASKETS

Baskets of all kinds including coiled, plaited, twined, and wicker for sale at Marie's Craft Shop. Made from materials such as white ash, fiber rush, sea grass, raffia, and even corn husks. Our baskets make lovely gifts for you and a friend.

WEAVING

Brilliant colors and textures liven any room in these extraordinary wall hangings. Created from all natural fibers including wool, silk, and cotton. From checks to plaids to inlays and leno, our weavings are breathtaking!

BATIK

Imported Indian designs in both batik and tie-dye made from silk, cotton, and linen in dazzling colors. Many of our batiks were created with all natural dyes, such as onion skins, turmeric, and logwood.

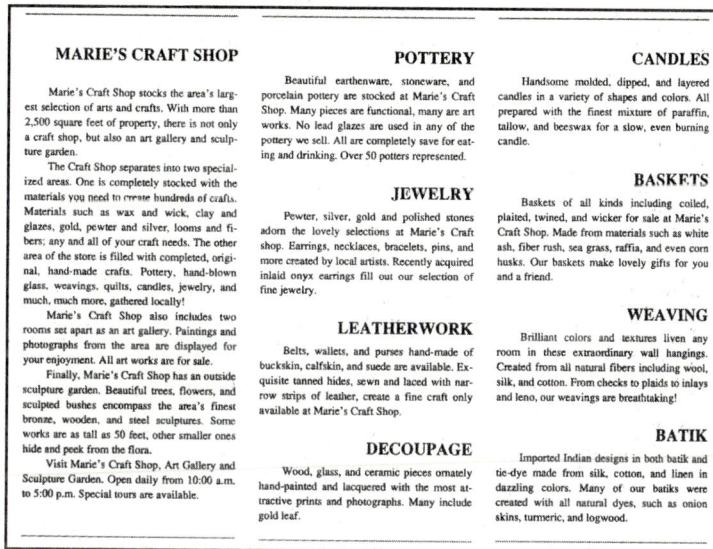

Fig. 19.36 Inside panels of the brochure.

The following table shows the specifications for the brochure.

Element	Option	Settings
Style Sheet	Default	
Page, Modify Layout	Margins	All to .35 inches Number of columns: 3 Gutter Width: .35 inches
	Page Settings	Landscape
Styles, Modify Body Text	Font	Times, 12-point
	Alignment	Justify Indent: First .35 inches
	Spacing	Line spacing: Custom .22 inches
	Hyphenation	On
Styles, Create Head	Font	Times, 18-point, bold
	Alignment	Right
Line Above	Font	10-point
	Alignment	Justify
	Spacing	Line spacing: Custom .24 inches
	Lines	Line above, 1st style Spacing: .10 Length: Margins

(continues)

Tip
Create the styles Line above and Line below for the sole purpose of adding lines to each panel of the brochure. You can use a column break after the Line below style for ease of handling.

Tip
Because you have chosen the Automatic option (Default Rows) when creating the table, Ami Pro enables you to press Enter while in a cell. Pressing Enter adds a line of text to the cell.

Element	Option	Settings
Line Below	Font Alignment Lines	10-point Justify Line below, 1st style Spacing: .10 Length: Margins
Styles, Modify Table Text	Font Alignment	Helvetica, 10-point Left
MAILING PANEL		
Name	Text	Times, 14-point, bold
Address	Text	Times, 12-point
Permit	Text	Helvetica, 8-point
TABLE		
Tools, Table	Number of columns Number of rows	2 6
Layout	Default Columns Default Rows Column/Row Size Lines & Color	Width: 1 inch Automatic Col. 1: 2 inches, Col. 2: 1 inch Select horizontal lines only

Note

The text on the front panel is modified using the Text menu, Font, and Alignment as follows: Marie's (36-point), the address and phone (14-point, right-aligned), Open Daily and the times (12-point, right-aligned). (Refer to fig. 19.35.)

Creating a Newsletter

A newsletter informs, announces, reminds, advises, instructs, advertises, and communicates. Newsletters address employees, customers, prospective customers, executives, and the general public. Because newsletters are flexible, you can design them to fit any purpose.

A significant factor in all newsletter design is consistency. Your design must be consistent. Consistency within the issue makes reading comfortable and easy to read. Consistency in a newsletter familiarizes the reader with the style and makes the reader comfortable and willing to continue reading.

The most certain method of guaranteeing consistency in your newsletter is to use a style sheet (for information on creating and saving a style sheet, see Chapter 10, "Working with Style Sheets"). You also want to include points of emphasis in your newsletter for interest. Callouts, art work, graphic rules, boxes, and screens are all prospects (see the section, "Explaining Design Strategies" in this chapter for more information).

◄ See "Modifying the Standard Page Layout," p. 120

◄ See "Setting Margins, Tabs, and Columns," p. 122

◄ See "Working with Headers and Footers," p. 134

◄ See "Using Style Sheets and Paragraph Styles," p. 262

◄ See "Entering Text and Graphics in Frames," p. 512

This section concentrates on a four-page newsletter design. Using a box to define the page and graphic rules to separate elements on the page give the newsletter an attractive and professional look. Figure 19.37 shows page one of the newsletter.

Earlier in the chapter, the section "Types of Documents" describes many useful items to use in a newsletter, one of which is a nameplate. In this example, the nameplate uses an unusual typeface, CaslonOpenFace, for the identifier of the newsletter. The size of the initial caps is 60-point; the size of the remainder of the caps is 36-point. The type sizes combined with the unusual typeface creates an unforgettable nameplate. In addition, the folio in this example doesn't contain a date, volume number, and so on; instead, the folio contains a brief description of the newsletter set in 12-point Helvetica.

This design divides the page into three columns of type. A point of emphasis to the page is the first column, which contains a pull-out quote. The type in the pull-out quote is larger (14-point) than the body text and is italic so it attracts the reader's attention.

Figure 19.38 illustrates page two of the newsletter. Note that this example uses the same layout: a pull-out quote in column one and a continuation of the article in columns two and three.

Notice, too, that page two contains the page number in the bottom margin. Ami Pro's automatic page numbering makes it easy to add any format of numbering you prefer. See Chapter 5, "Working with Page Layout," for information on automatic page numbering.

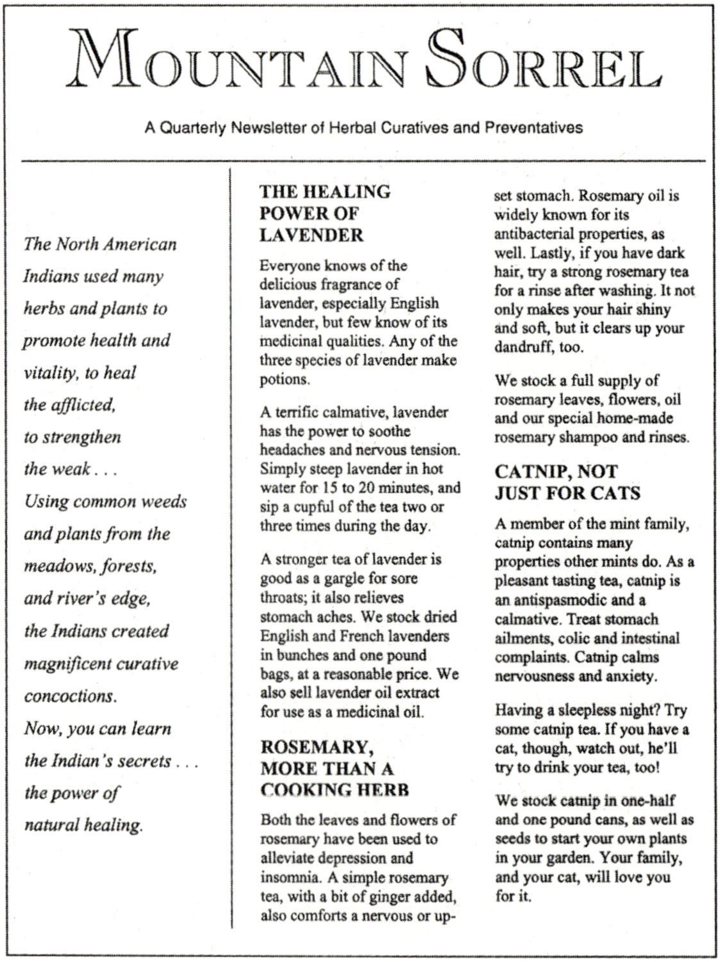

Fig. 19.37
Page one of a newsletter.

MOUNTAIN SORREL

A Quarterly Newsletter of Herbal Curatives and Preventatives

The North American Indians used many herbs and plants to promote health and vitality, to heal the afflicted, to strengthen the weak . . . Using common weeds and plants from the meadows, forests, and river's edge, the Indians created magnificent curative concoctions. Now, you can learn the Indian's secrets . . . the power of natural healing.

THE HEALING POWER OF LAVENDER

Everyone knows of the delicious fragrance of lavender, especially English lavender, but few know of its medicinal qualities. Any of the three species of lavender make potions.

A terrific calmative, lavender has the power to soothe headaches and nervous tension. Simply steep lavender in hot water for 15 to 20 minutes, and sip a cupful of the tea two or three times during the day.

A stronger tea of lavender is good as a gargle for sore throats; it also relieves stomach aches. We stock dried English and French lavenders in bunches and one pound bags, at a reasonable price. We also sell lavender oil extract for use as a medicinal oil.

ROSEMARY, MORE THAN A COOKING HERB

Both the leaves and flowers of rosemary have been used to alleviate depression and insomnia. A simple rosemary tea, with a bit of ginger added, also comforts a nervous or upset stomach. Rosemary oil is widely known for its antibacterial properties, as well. Lastly, if you have dark hair, try a strong rosemary tea for a rinse after washing. It not only makes your hair shiny and soft, but it clears up your dandruff, too.

We stock a full supply of rosemary leaves, flowers, oil and our special home-made rosemary shampoo and rinses.

CATNIP, NOT JUST FOR CATS

A member of the mint family, catnip contains many properties other mints do. As a pleasant tasting tea, catnip is an antispasmodic and a calmative. Treat stomach ailments, colic and intestinal complaints. Catnip calms nervousness and anxiety.

Having a sleepless night? Try some catnip tea. If you have a cat, though, watch out, he'll try to drink your tea, too!

We stock catnip in one-half and one pound cans, as well as seeds to start your own plants in your garden. Your family, and your cat, will love you for it.

Tip
When you set a page to three columns of text, you must use a frame to create a name-plate, or any other type that spans two or three columns of the text.

Page three of the newsletter maintains consistency by following the same page layout, type styles, and use of graphics as the two previous pages (see fig. 19.39). This newsletter creates white space in several ways: left-aligned type, interparagraph spacing, wide gutters, and interline spacing within the pull-out quote. The pull-out quote's different typeface and type style create emphasis, as does the vertical rule separating columns one and two.

The last page of any newsletter is usually different from the others. Consistency must be maintained, but requirements of the final page of a newsletter sometimes make it difficult to follow the precise style of the previous pages. Figure 19.40 illustrates the last page of this newsletter.

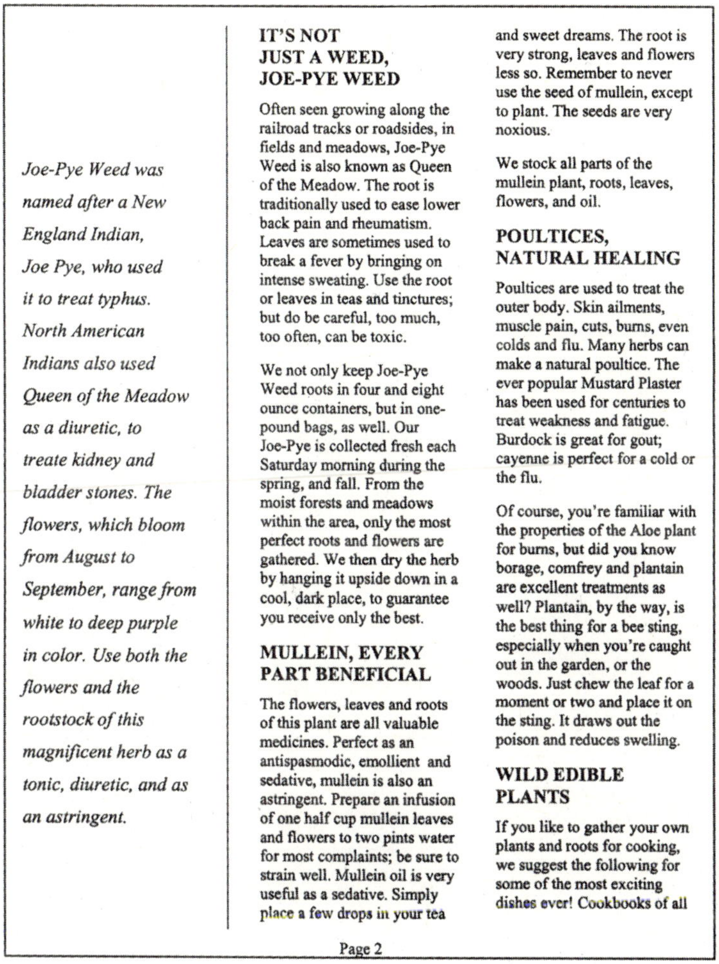

Joe-Pye Weed was named after a New England Indian, Joe Pye, who used it to treat typhus. North American Indians also used Queen of the Meadow as a diuretic, to treate kidney and bladder stones. The flowers, which bloom from August to September, range from white to deep purple in color. Use both the flowers and the rootstock of this magnificent herb as a tonic, diuretic, and as an astringent.

IT'S NOT JUST A WEED, JOE-PYE WEED

Often seen growing along the railroad tracks or roadsides, in fields and meadows, Joe-Pye Weed is also known as Queen of the Meadow. The root is traditionally used to ease lower back pain and rheumatism. Leaves are sometimes used to break a fever by bringing on intense sweating. Use the root or leaves in teas and tinctures; but do be careful, too much, too often, can be toxic.

We not only keep Joe-Pye Weed roots in four and eight ounce containers, but in one-pound bags, as well. Our Joe-Pye is collected fresh each Saturday morning during the spring, and fall. From the moist forests and meadows within the area, only the most perfect roots and flowers are gathered. We then dry the herb by hanging it upside down in a cool, dark place, to guarantee you receive only the best.

MULLEIN, EVERY PART BENEFICIAL

The flowers, leaves and roots of this plant are all valuable medicines. Perfect as an antispasmodic, emollient and sedative, mullein is also an astringent. Prepare an infusion of one half cup mullein leaves and flowers to two pints water for most complaints; be sure to strain well. Mullein oil is very useful as a sedative. Simply place a few drops in your tea and sweet dreams. The root is very strong, leaves and flowers less so. Remember to never use the seed of mullein, except to plant. The seeds are very noxious.

We stock all parts of the mullein plant, roots, leaves, flowers, and oil.

POULTICES, NATURAL HEALING

Poultices are used to treat the outer body. Skin ailments, muscle pain, cuts, burns, even colds and flu. Many herbs can make a natural poultice. The ever popular Mustard Plaster has been used for centuries to treat weakness and fatigue. Burdock is great for gout; cayenne is perfect for a cold or the flu.

Of course, you're familiar with the properties of the Aloe plant for burns, but did you know borage, comfrey and plantain are excellent treatments as well? Plantain, by the way, is the best thing for a bee sting, especially when you're caught out in the garden, or the woods. Just chew the leaf for a moment or two and place it on the sting. It draws out the poison and reduces swelling.

WILD EDIBLE PLANTS

If you like to gather your own plants and roots for cooking, we suggest the following for some of the most exciting dishes ever! Cookbooks of all

Page 2

Fig. 19.38 Page two of the newsletter, consistent with page one.

In this case, the last page of the newsletter contains a masthead and a mailing panel, so it's hard to design this page like the others. The masthead (boxed in the upper left corner) informs the reader of material such as publication information, editor's name, prices, disclaimers, and so on. To make the masthead stand out, the text is a different typeface and smaller than the other pages (Helvetica, 9-point). The mailing panel and "Our Spring Specials" also make the page layout appear different.

The differences in page four are usual and acceptable when designing a newsletter. The page is still consistent to the other pages in use of margins, columns, page border, typeface, type size, and style.

Fig. 19.39
Page three of the newsletter.

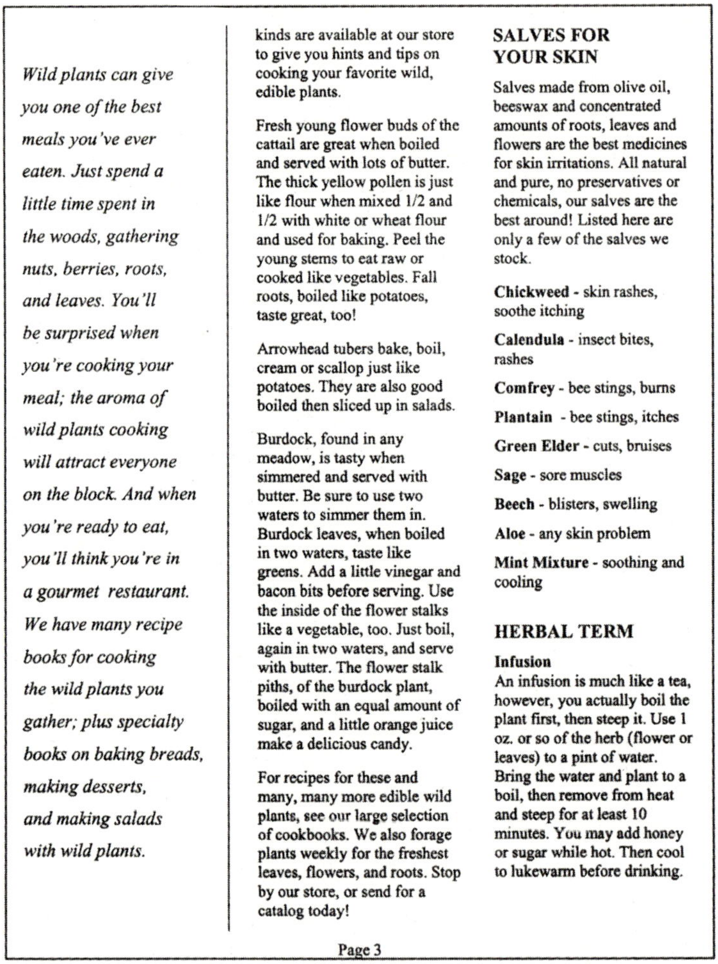

Wild plants can give you one of the best meals you've ever eaten. Just spend a little time spent in the woods, gathering nuts, berries, roots, and leaves. You'll be surprised when you're cooking your meal; the aroma of wild plants cooking will attract everyone on the block. And when you're ready to eat, you'll think you're in a gourmet restaurant. We have many recipe books for cooking the wild plants you gather; plus specialty books on baking breads, making desserts, and making salads with wild plants.

kinds are available at our store to give you hints and tips on cooking your favorite wild, edible plants.

Fresh young flower buds of the cattail are great when boiled and served with lots of butter. The thick yellow pollen is just like flour when mixed 1/2 and 1/2 with white or wheat flour and used for baking. Peel the young stems to eat raw or cooked like vegetables. Fall roots, boiled like potatoes, taste great, too!

Arrowhead tubers bake, boil, cream or scallop just like potatoes. They are also good boiled then sliced up in salads.

Burdock, found in any meadow, is tasty when simmered and served with butter. Be sure to use two waters to simmer them in. Burdock leaves, when boiled in two waters, taste like greens. Add a little vinegar and bacon bits before serving. Use the inside of the flower stalks like a vegetable, too. Just boil, again in two waters, and serve with butter. The flower stalk piths, of the burdock plant, boiled with an equal amount of sugar, and a little orange juice make a delicious candy.

For recipes for these and many, many more edible wild plants, see our large selection of cookbooks. We also forage plants weekly for the freshest leaves, flowers, and roots. Stop by our store, or send for a catalog today!

SALVES FOR YOUR SKIN

Salves made from olive oil, beeswax and concentrated amounts of roots, leaves and flowers are the best medicines for skin irritations. All natural and pure, no preservatives or chemicals, our salves are the best around! Listed here are only a few of the salves we stock.

Chickweed - skin rashes, soothe itching

Calendula - insect bites, rashes

Comfrey - bee stings, burns

Plantain - bee stings, itches

Green Elder - cuts, bruises

Sage - sore muscles

Beech - blisters, swelling

Aloe - any skin problem

Mint Mixture - soothing and cooling

HERBAL TERM

Infusion
An infusion is much like a tea, however, you actually boil the plant first, then steep it. Use 1 oz. or so of the herb (flower or leaves) to a pint of water. Bring the water and plant to a boil, then remove from heat and steep for at least 10 minutes. You may add honey or sugar while hot. Then cool to lukewarm before drinking.

Page 3

Tip
Never add a page number to the first or last pages of a newsletter.

When creating the design for the newsletter, you must add one frame on page one for the nameplate and two frames on page four (one for the masthead and one for the "Spring Specials" and mailing panel). The vertical rule that divides column one from column two, on every page, is created with a frame. You cannot display only one column rule on a three-column page. Instructions for creating the frame are included in the specifications list in the following table. See Chapter 16, "Using Frames," for more information on manipulating frames.

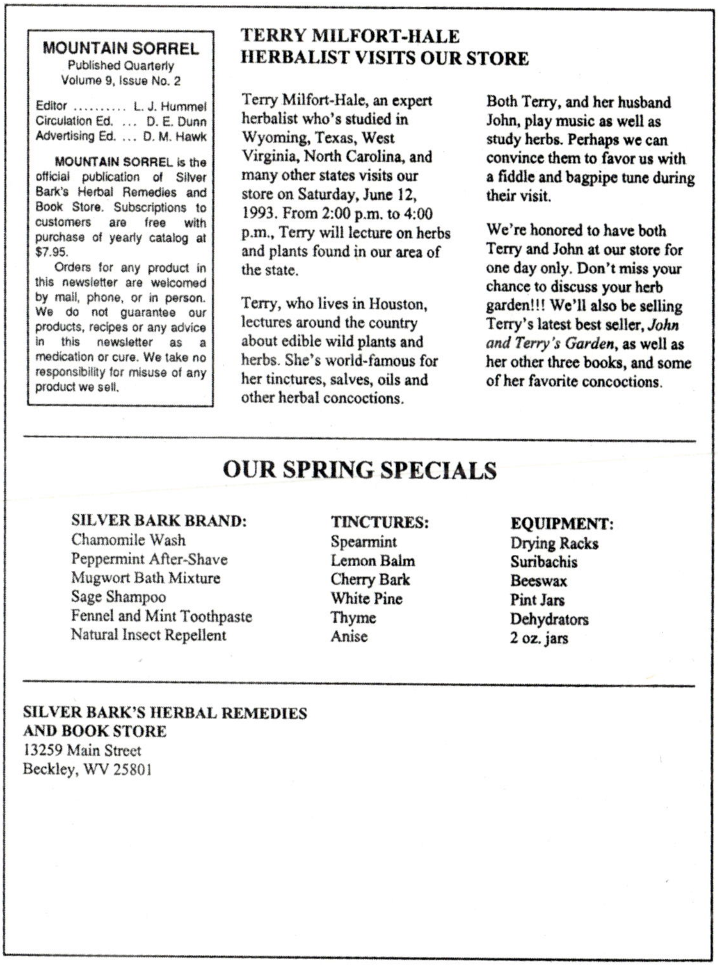

MOUNTAIN SORREL
Published Quarterly
Volume 9, Issue No. 2

Editor .... L. J. Hummel
Circulation Ed. ... D. E. Dunn
Advertising Ed. ... D. M. Hawk

MOUNTAIN SORREL is the official publication of Silver Bark's Herbal Remedies and Book Store. Subscriptions to customers are free with purchase of yearly catalog at $7.95.

Orders for any product in this newsletter are welcomed by mail, phone, or in person. We do not guarantee our products, recipes or any advice in this newsletter as a medication or cure. We take no responsibility for misuse of any product we sell.

TERRY MILFORT-HALE HERBALIST VISITS OUR STORE

Terry Milfort-Hale, an expert herbalist who's studied in Wyoming, Texas, West Virginia, North Carolina, and many other states visits our store on Saturday, June 12, 1993. From 2:00 p.m. to 4:00 p.m., Terry will lecture on herbs and plants found in our area of the state.

Terry, who lives in Houston, lectures around the country about edible wild plants and herbs. She's world-famous for her tinctures, salves, oils and other herbal concoctions.

Both Terry, and her husband John, play music as well as study herbs. Perhaps we can convince them to favor us with a fiddle and bagpipe tune during their visit.

We're honored to have both Terry and John at our store for one day only. Don't miss your chance to discuss your herb garden!!! We'll also be selling Terry's latest best seller, *John and Terry's Garden*, as well as her other three books, and some of her favorite concoctions.

OUR SPRING SPECIALS

SILVER BARK BRAND:	TINCTURES:	EQUIPMENT:
Chamomile Wash	Spearmint	Drying Racks
Peppermint After-Shave	Lemon Balm	Suribachis
Mugwort Bath Mixture	Cherry Bark	Beeswax
Sage Shampoo	White Pine	Pint Jars
Fennel and Mint Toothpaste	Thyme	Dehydrators
Natural Insect Repellent	Anise	2 oz. jars

SILVER BARK'S HERBAL REMEDIES AND BOOK STORE
13259 Main Street
Beckley, WV 25801

Fig. 19.40
Page four of the newsletter.

Element	Option	Settings
Style Sheet	Default	
Page, Modify Layout	Margins	Left, Right, and Top margins to .75 inches Bottom margin to 1 inch Number of columns: 3 Gutter Width: .35 inches
	Lines	Around Page: All, 2nd line style Position: Close to inside

(continues)

Element	Option	Settings
Styles, Modify Body Text	Font Alignment Spacing Hyphenation	Times, 12-point Left Paragraph Spacing: Below .15 inches On
Styles, Create Head	Font Alignment Spacing	Times, 14-point, bold Left Paragraph Spacing: Below .10 inches
Pull-out	Font Alignment Spacing	Times, 14-point, italic Left Line Spacing: 1 1/2
Masthead	Font Alignment Hyphenation	Helvetica, 9-point Justify Indent: First line .20 inches Tabs: right dot leader at 1.75 inches On
NAMEPLATE FRAME		
Frame, Modify Layout	Size & Position Lines & Shadows	Width: 7 inches Height: 1.56 inches Down from top: .60 inches In from left: .75 inches Clear margins Position: Bottom, 2nd style Shadow: None
MASTHEAD FRAME		
Frame, Modify Layout	Type Size & Position Lines & Shadows Shadow: None	Opaque, Square corners Width: 2.08 inches Height: 3.98 inches Down from top: .75 inches In from left: .75 inches Margins: All .15 Position: All, 2nd style
SPRING SPECIALS FRAME		
Frame, Modify Layout	Size & Position Columns & Tabs Lines & Shadows	Width: 7 inches Height: 5.43 inches Down from top: 4.77 inches In from left: .75 inches Clear margins Left at .5, 3.25, and 5 inches Lines: None Shadow: None

Element	Option	Settings
FRAME WITH VERTICAL LINE		
Frame, Modify Layout	Size & Position	Width: .15 inches Height: 9.20 inches Down from top: .76 inches In from left: 2.9 inches
	Lines	Position: Left, 1st style Shadow: None
PAGE NUMBERING		
Page	Page Numbering	Style: 1 Start on page: 2 Start with number: 2 Leading text: Page (space)

Creating a Business Report

Business reports usually focus on one specific project or one aspect of a project. Progress reports, annual reports, sales reports, inventory summaries, and marketing plans are only a few subjects for a business report. Almost all reports contain specific information regarding progress, profits, and expenditures. Finally, business reports incorporate figures, charts or graphs, spreadsheets, and text to explain these elements.

Tip
Business proposals are similar to business reports; therefore, you can use a similar design and layout for a proposal.

Some reports may include photographs. You also can add art work or illustrations. Predominant, however, are spreadsheets or other figures to represent the budget, profit, or losses in easy-to-understand terms. If you use a spreadsheet program or graph maker, your figures easily import to Ami Pro. Microsoft Excel and Lotus 1-2-3 are two examples of spreadsheet program files you can import. Lotus Freelance for graphs and charts is another good program; Ami Pro even contains a charting feature that you can use to create your own charts and graphs. For specific information about saving and importing files to Ami Pro, refer to Chapter 20, “Importing, Exporting, and Linking Files.”

A traditional business report consists of a cover, text, tables, spreadsheets, charts, or any combination of graphic elements. The following design contains all these elements and is organized by using headers and footers.

Tip
Ami Pro's excellent TOC features enable you to gather a table of contents with ease. For more information about creating a table of contents in Ami Pro, see Chapter 12, "Using Reference Tools."

The example report in this section is a Marketing Summary. Four representative pages of that report appear in this section. Figure 19.41 illustrates the title page of the report.

This report is designed for a binding margin on the left to allow room for side stitching or spiral binding. As part of the design, the left margin is much larger than necessary for a binding margin but makes the line length of the body text comfortable to read.

The rules bordering the top and bottom of the title page are created in narrow frames to make this page consistent with the following pages. Clip art was added to the front; however, you can use another graphic image, or photograph, instead.

Note

Notice in figure 19.41 the small logo above Pear Associates. This symbol is from a Wingding font that comes packaged in the ATM fonts supplied with Ami Pro and as a TrueType in Windows 3.1. Wingdings consist of symbols such as bullets, pointing hands, scissors, stars, and arrows. Using a few Wingdings in your documents adds spice.

Tip
Use OLE (Object Linking and Embedding) and DDE (Dynamic Data Exchange) to easily update the data in your imported spreadsheets and charts.

A sample page of the report appears in figure 19.42. The headers and footers remain consistent with the rules on the title page.

Figure 19.43 illustrates a pie chart within the report. Data from a spreadsheet is used to create this chart in Ami Pro's charting feature. For information on how to produce charts, see Chapter 18, "Creating Charts."

The sample page of the report, shown in figure 19.44, illustrates an imported spreadsheet, with enhancements added in Ami Pro. Notice that the page design remains consistent with other pages in the report.

MARKETING
SUMMARY
FOR
HUMBLE OPINIONS

❖

BY PEAR ASSOCIATES, LTD.
JUNE 4, 1993

Fig. 19.41
The title page of a marketing report, with graphic rules and graphic image.

Fig. 19.42
A sample page of the marketing summary.

MARKETING SUMMARY FOR HUMBLE OPINIONS

JUNE 4, 1993

Humble Opinions, a corporation dedicated to quality computer software training, initiated the Marketing Plan on June 4, 1992. Involved in this plan were many strategies for client expansion and increased financial gain. This sum-mary analyzes the success of the Marketing Plan in terms of customer base increase and profit from services offered.

Current economic trends in our area greatly affect the figures of the past three months; however, earlier reports reveal that the basic premise of the Marketing Plan is working. Should future trends prove to follow the same path as the past three months, a new Marketing Plan will then be developed. We do suggest this plan be followed for an additional period of six months before any long-term decision is made.

Despite this recent decline in profits and sales, the Marketing Plan proved to be both beneficial and profitable to Humble Opinions in the first nine months of execution. The first three months, from June 1992 to August 1992, were considered the initiation period. Although contact with clients increased considerably, profits increased only slightly. During the second three months of the Marketing Plan, from September 1992 to November 1992, profits showed incredible growth. This is attributed to initial planning and advertising to build the customer base. The three-month period from December 1992 to February 1993 proved to support the objectives of the Plan through substantial client referrals and increased profits for the company.

We estimate the Marketing Plan, with minimum modifications, can and will benefit the company in countless ways over the next six months. Customer lists will continue to expand; profits will continue to rise at a reliable and constant rate.

MARKETING SUMMARY

SUMMARY OF DATA

The pie chart in figure 1 illustrates a comparison between profits from the three marketing techniques. The actual figures are represented in the following spreadsheet.

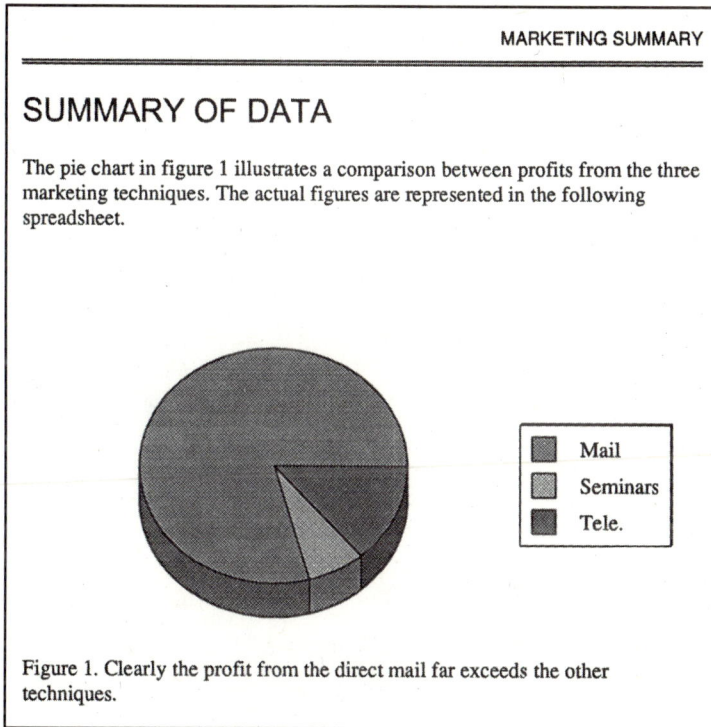

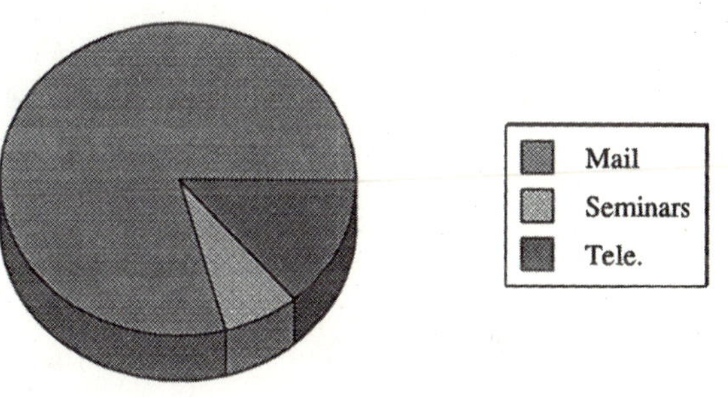

Figure 1. Clearly the profit from the direct mail far exceeds the other techniques.

Fig. 19.43 A sample page with a pie chart created in Ami Pro.

MARKETING SUMMARY

Following is a spreadsheet of the previous data so you can compare expenditures and profits as they applied to these three specific activities. Clearly, the direct mailing has demonstrated the highest return for the invested monies with 84.6% of total income from the three marketing methods. Telemarketing has an 8.8% share; the free seminars and demonstrations only 6.6%.

	DIRECT MAIL	SEMINARS	TELEMARKETING
No. of Contacts	5,000	120	2,500
No. of Sales	490	42	75
Gross Income	$71,050.00	$6,090.00	$10,875.00
Cost of Marketing	$1,645.00	$300.00	$1,250.00
Cost of Class	$49,000.00	$4,200.00	$7,500.00
Gross Profit	$20,405.00	$1,590.00	$2,125.00
Market. Cost/Contact	$0.33	$2.50	$0.50
Total Cost/Sale	$103.36	$107.14	$116.67
Marketing Cost/Sale	$3.36	$7.14	$16.67
Profit/Sale	$41.64	$37.86	$28.33

Fig. 19.44 An imported spreadsheet.

The following table lists the specifications for creating the business report.

Element	Option	Settings
Style Sheet	Default	
Page, Modify Layout	Margins	Left: 2 inches Right: 1.15 inches Top and Bottom: 1.25 inches
	Header, Margins	Left: 2 inches Right: 1.15 inches Top: .75 inches Bottom: 0 inches Begin on second page
	Footer, Margins	Left: 2 inches Right: 1.15 inches Top: .15 inches Bottom: .75 inches Begin on second page
Styles, Modify Body Text	Font Alignment Spacing Hyphenation	Times, 12-point Left Paragraph Spacing: Below .20 On
Styles, Create Heads	Font Alignment Spacing	Arial, 18-point, Normal Left Paragraph Spacing: Below .10
Subhead	Font Alignment Spacing	Times, 14-point, bold, italic Left Paragraph Spacing: Below .10
Styles, Create Page one head	Font Alignment Spacing	Times, 36-point, bold Left Line Spacing: Custom .64 inches
Header	Font Lines	Helvetica, 10-point Line below, 1st double line style, Spacing .10, Length: Margins
Footer	Font Lines	Helvetica, 10-point Line above, 1st double line style, Spacing .10, Length: Margins
FRONT PAGE FRAME		
Frame, Modify Layout Size & Position	Size	Width: 5.40 Height: .20
Lines & Shadows	Position	Top, 1st double rule

Element	Option	Settings
PAGE NUMBERING		
Page	Page Numbering	Style: 1 Start on page: 2 Start with number: 2

◄ See "Setting Size and Orientation," p. 130

◄ See "Creating a Table of Contents," p. 354

◄ See "Creating the Chart," p. 583

► See "Importing and Exporting Text," p. 676

► See "Importing Graphics," p. 691

► See "Using Master Documents," p. 744

Summary

Professional-looking documents are the key to a successful business. Whether you create forms, newspaper ads, letters, brochures, newsletters, or business reports, the documents you use in business represent your company. To make a positive impression, your documents need to be well-designed, consistent, and functional.

Proper use of the elements of design, typography, graphic images, and so on, makes your documents look professional and stand out among your competitors. In addition, Ami Pro's advanced features—such as style sheets, tables, frames, drawing, and charting—make creating those documents easy. Take time to plan the text, illustrations, and related materials of your document and plan the design by using the guidelines outlined in this chapter.

In the next chapter, "Importing, Exporting, and Linking Files," you learn graphics capabilities, such as importing graphics from other applications.

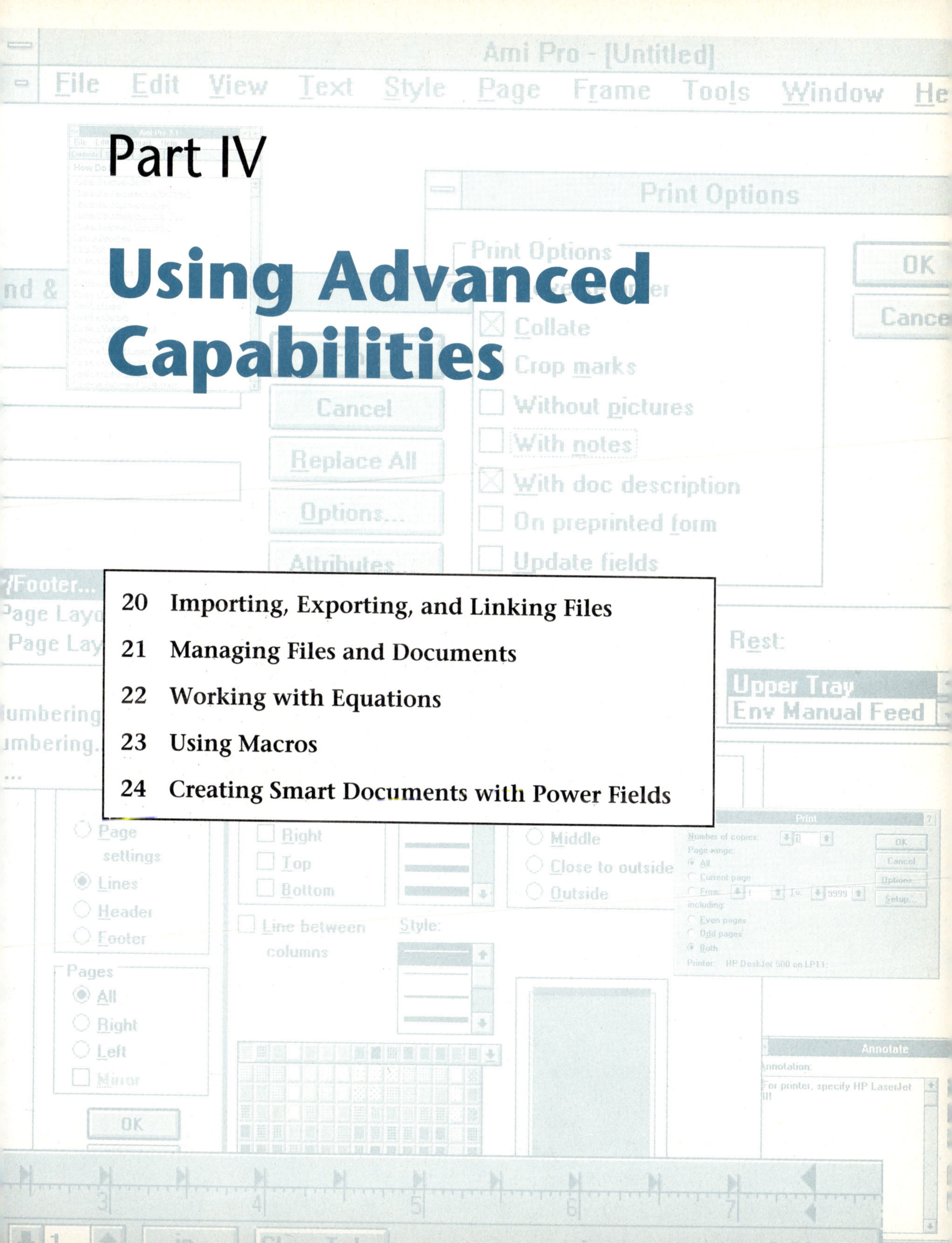

Part IV

Using Advanced Capabilities

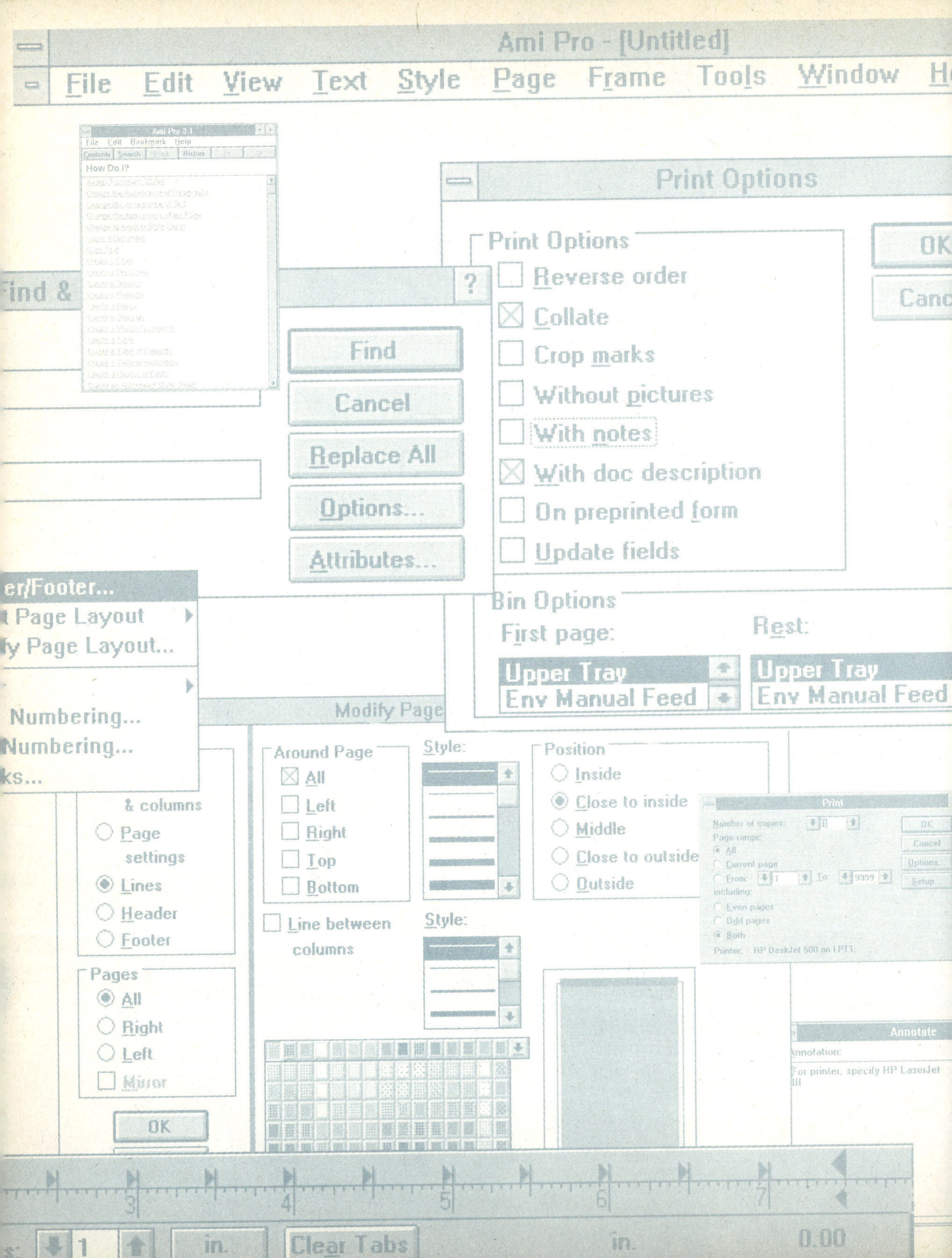
Ami Pro - [Untitled]
File
Edit
View
Text
Style
Page
Frame
Tools
Window
Ami Pro 3.1
How Do I?
Print Options
Print Options
Reverse order
Collate
Crop marks
Without pictures
With notes
With doc description
On preprinted form
Update fields
OK
Canc
Bin Options
First page:
Rest:
Upper Tray
Env Manual Feed
Upper Tray
Env Manual Feed
Find
Cancel
Replace All
Options...
Attributes...
er/Footer...
Page Layout
fy Page Layout...
Numbering...
Numbering...
ks...
Modify Page
& columns
Page
settings
Lines
Header
Footer
Pages
All
Right
Left
Mirror
OK
Around Page
All
Left
Right
Top
Bottom
Style:
Line between
columns
Style:
Position
Inside
Close to inside
Middle
Close to outside
Outside
Print
Number of copies:
Page range:
All
Current page
From:
To:
including:
Even pages
Odd pages
Both
Printer: HP DeskJet 500 on LPT1:
OK
Cancel
Options...
Setup...
Annotate
Annotation:
For printer, specify HP LaserJet III
Clear Tabs
in.
in.
0.00

Chapter 20

Importing, Exporting, and Linking Files

You can create impressive graphics with Ami Pro, using the program's drawing and charting capabilities. Often, however, importing someone else's drawing is easier than creating your own from scratch. Even if you can create certain symbols or charts yourself, you may not want to take the time to do so.

You can greatly enrich the appearance of your documents by using artwork created by other people. Ami Pro offers an excellent collection of symbols. Clip art is available from a variety of sources and in many formats; you can access libraries of existing drawings containing everything from cartoon figures to elephants to flags.

In the first part of this chapter, you learn about the three ways you can import graphics that aren't Ami Pro drawings:

- Import a graphic file with the **F**ile **I**mport Picture command
- Paste a picture by using the Windows Clipboard
- Paste-link a file from another Windows application that supports DDE (Dynamic Data Exchange) or OLE (Object Linking and Embedding)

In the second part of this chapter, you learn how to edit pictures. After your picture is inside a frame, you can touch up the drawing by scaling, cropping, or image processing. Unless a picture is an Ami Pro drawing, or you have converted it to an Ami Pro drawing (Lotus PIC files, for example), you actually cannot edit the image.

Importing and Exporting Text

Often you may want to use text created in a program other than Ami Pro. Occasionally you may want to use Ami Pro text in another word processing package, such as WordPerfect or WordStar.

Once upon a time in the ancient history of word processing (perhaps 10 years ago), you had almost no choice but to retype your text to move from one word processing program to another. Later, you could convert the text in the original file to ASCII (a standard text style, with no formatting—no paragraph styles or page styles). In the other program, you would import the ASCII text and add formatting later. More recently, you could "import" the text you wanted in your word processing package and preserve all or most of the formatting, but importing sometimes was a fairly elaborate process.

Word processing is heading toward an ideal world—where you simply open the document you want to import, or save the document to a different file format to export it to another software package. Although the world of document exchange hasn't arrived at the ideal yet (you still encounter special considerations when importing from or exporting to certain formats), Ami Pro's importing and exporting features are close to the ideal. If you are familiar with the **F**ile **O**pen and **F**ile Save **A**s commands, you already know almost everything you need to know about importing documents into Ami Pro from another word processing package (or database or spreadsheet) and exporting documents from Ami Pro to another software.

When importing or exporting files, many word processing packages (including Ami Pro) use a *filter* software program. The filter does the work of converting the text from its original file type (such as WordPerfect) into the new file type (such as Ami Pro), preserving as much of the original formatting as possible.

The Ami Pro documentation provides coverage of importing text that discusses the special considerations of importing certain file formats. A similar discussion covers exporting documents from Ami Pro to other file types. Unless you use all the file types described in the documentation, however, you don't need to know about the idiosyncrasies of all the file types.

In this chapter, you learn the basic operations of importing and exporting. The text in the following sections explains the choices you encounter in the dialog boxes as you import or export; you can learn all you need to know to conduct the process successfully. If you need detailed information about importing or exporting to a specific file type, such as WordStar or WordPerfect 5.1, however, refer to the Ami Pro documentation.

Importing Text and Data Files

Importing text means converting it from another file format into Ami Pro format. You use the Open dialog box to specify the type of file you are importing and the location and name of the file. Ami Pro's filter does the rest of the work to convert the document into an Ami Pro document; you can work with the imported document just as you work with any other Ami Pro document.

You can import the following file types:

- AdvanceWrite
- Ami Pro
- Ami Pro Macro
- ASCII
- dBASE (Versions III, III+, and IV)
- DCA/FFT
- DCA/RFT
- DIF
- DisplayWrite 4 and 5
- E-mail
- Enable (Versions 1.5 to 2.5, Lotus 1-2-3 format)
- Excel (Versions 4.0 and earlier)
- Exec MemoMaker
- Lotus 1-2-3 (Releases 1, 1A, 2, 2.01, 3, and 3.1)
- Lotus 1-2-3 for Windows
- Lotus Symphony (Versions 1.0, 1.01, and 1.1)
- Lotus Manuscript (Versions 2.0 and 2.1)
- Microsoft Word (Versions 4.0, 5.0, 5.1, and 5.5)
- MultiMate (Version 3.3)
- MultiMate Advantage II
- Navy DIF

- Office Writer
- Paradox (Versions up to 3.5)
- PeachText (Versions 2.11 or prior)
- Rich Text Format
- Samna Word
- SmartWare (Version 1)
- SuperCalc (Versions 3 and 4)
- Windows Write
- Word for Windows (Versions 2.0 and earlier)
- WordPerfect (Versions 4.2, 5.0, and 5.1)
- WordPerfect for Windows (Version 5.1)
- WordStar (Versions 3.3, 3.4, 4.1, and 5.0)
- WordStar 2000 (Versions 1 and 3)

When you import a document, Ami Pro may not keep all formatting from the original text. In addition to the normal text characters you see on your keyboard, the filters generally convert the following types of formatting:

- Text alignment (centering, justification, and so on)
- Capitalization, including small caps
- Dates
- Fonts
- Footnotes
- Text frames
- Headers and footers
- International characters, such as those used in French and Spanish
- Line spacing (single, double, or specified distances between lines)
- Page numbering
- Paragraph styles
- Character formatting, such as hard hyphens and hard spaces

- Text attributes (boldface, underline, double underline, italics, overstrike, strikethrough, superscript, subscript, and so on)
- Page format (page breaks, tab rulers, tab settings)

Note

If no default tab settings are in the imported document, Ami Pro places a tab ruler at the beginning to set tabs every 1/2 inch. You can delete or change this tab ruler. See the discussion of the tab ruler in Chapter 5, "Working with Page Layout."

You can import the document as a new document or insert it into a current document. To import a document, follow these steps:

1. Choose **F**ile **O**pen. The Open dialog box appears, as shown in figure 20.1.

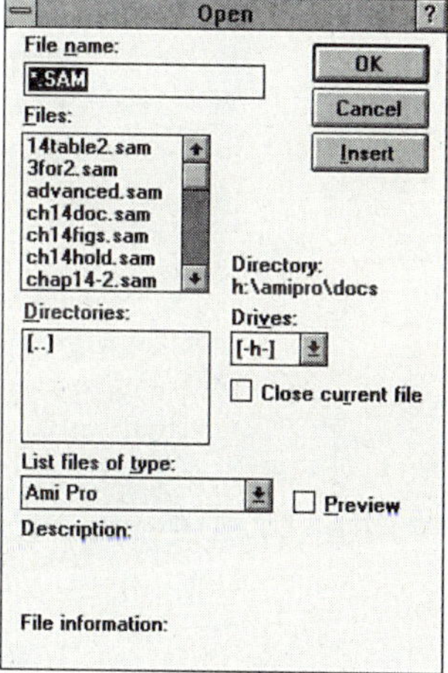

Fig. 20.1 The Open dialog box.

2. In the List Files of **T**ype list box, click the arrow button to display a list of available file types (see fig. 20.2). The list includes all of the file types mentioned at the beginning of this section.
3. In the List Files of **T**ype list box, specify the file type you want to convert. For this example, select WordPerfect 5.0 & 5.1.

   If the specified file type uses a default extension (such as DOC for MultiMate files), that extension appears in the File **N**ame list box. If necessary, type the extension you want in the list box.

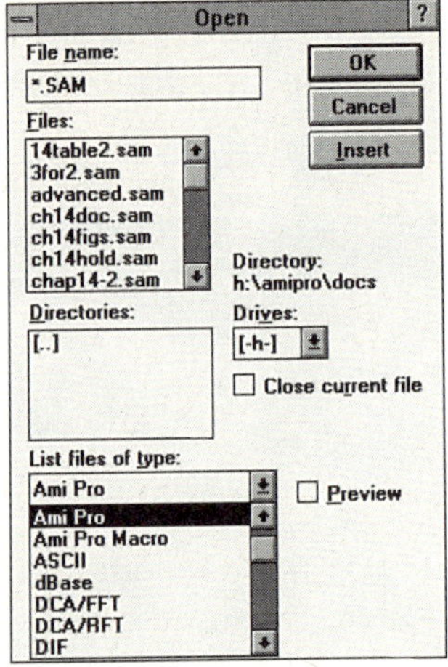

Fig. 20.2
The List Files of Type drop-down list.

4. In the Drives list box, indicate the drive location of the document you want to convert; for example, drive D.

5. Ami Pro lists the directories in the specified drive in the **D**irectories list box. If necessary, use the list box to specify the directory of the document you want to convert.

6. Ami Pro lists the files with the correct extension (from the specified drive and directory) in the **F**iles list box. Select the file you want to convert. (If you prefer, you can type the file name in the File **N**ame text box.)

7. Select the Close Current File option if you want the new document to replace the document currently open.

8. Choose OK or press Enter.

At this point, depending on the file type you are converting, Ami Pro opens a dialog box that enables you to select certain import options. Specify the options you need and choose OK. The following sections describe the options you may see.

Note

To insert an imported file into an existing document, place the insertion point where you want the new file to appear within the existing document. Then follow steps 1-7 as listed here. At step 8, choose **I**nsert instead of choosing OK or pressing Enter. Next, complete the Import Options dialog box, and choose OK or press Enter.

Word Processing Options

When you import word processing documents, you choose from a number of options related to paragraph styles, as described in the following list. Not all options appear for all formats; you see only the options that apply to the format you are importing.

- *Convert Styles.* When you are converting from word processing software that uses styles, this option creates paragraph styles in the Ami Pro version of the document; the styles match the paragraph style names and formatting information in the original document.
- *Apply Styles.* You see this option when converting from word processing programs that use styles. Select this option if you want all the attributes in the original document to be applied as text enhancements in the Ami Pro version of the document.
- *Keep Style Names.* If the current Ami Pro style sheet has paragraph style names identical to those in the document being converted, Ami Pro can assign the matching names to the imported text. The text then appears using the settings specified for the Ami Pro paragraph styles.
- *Ignore Styles.* If you choose this option, only character and paragraph attributes assigned independently of paragraph styles in the original document are applied as text enhancements in the Ami Pro version.
- *Import Style Sheet.* Select this option if you want Ami Pro to create paragraph styles in the Ami Pro document that match the paragraph style names and formatting information of the styles in the original document.
- *Convert Levels into Styles.* This option appears when importing from a word processing package that has "levels" (such as Lotus Manuscript). If you select this option, Ami Pro converts the levels into Ami Pro styles.
- *Apply Levels.* Select this option if you want attributes in the original document to appear as text enhancements (attributes) in the Ami Pro document.

Spreadsheet and Database Options

When you are importing from a spreadsheet or database program, you specify the area of the spreadsheet or database that you want to import. For spreadsheets, you indicate how much of the spreadsheet you want to import with one of the following options:

- ***Entire File.*** Imports the entire spreadsheet file you have designated.
- ***Active Worksheet.*** Imports the active worksheet. This option appears only if the spreadsheet format supports multiple worksheets.
- ***Range.*** Imports only the range specified.

For databases, you choose from the following options:

- ***Entire File.*** Imports the entire database file.
- ***Selected Fields.*** Imports only the database fields you specify.

For one database program, Paradox, Ami Pro displays a list of all the available fields and enables you to remove those you don't want to import.

Note

If you installed the WordPerfect SwitchKit when you installed Ami Pro and you told Ami Pro to add it to the **H**elp menu, you can convert WordPerfect 5.0, WordPerfect 5.1, and WordPerfect for Windows 5.1 files in batches by choosing **H**elp from the main menu. From the **H**elp menu, choose For **W**ordPerfect Users; then choose Batch **C**onvert.

Importing Linked Text or Data

When you import a text or data file, you accept it "as is"—as the originating program created it. This condition means essentially two things:

- Although some formatting survives format transfer, you usually need to do some reformatting within Ami Pro.
- If the original application changes text or data, those changes aren't reflected in what you already have imported into Ami Pro.

In many cases, these restrictions aren't serious. If the originating document and the imported material are linked, however, these restrictions may create a problem. Ami Pro has the ability to implement two important features of Microsoft Windows—*Dynamic Data Exchange* (*DDE*) and *Object Linking and Embedding* (*OLE*). DDE and OLE create *links* between the originating document and Ami Pro. DDE continually updates the text or data *in Ami Pro* when the corresponding text or data changes *in the originating application*. OLE gives to the originating application the responsibility for managing the display or printing of the imported material. In addition, OLE enables you, by double-clicking the linked data, to open the originating application to edit the data.

Note

This section deals primarily with Ami Pro as a *client application*—a receiver of linked DDE or OLE data from another application. Ami Pro also fully supports DDE and OLE *server operations*—which means that you can link your Ami Pro data into other DDE- and OLE-capable applications. To support server operations, you copy to the Windows Clipboard the Ami Pro data you want to link, using the **E**dit **C**opy command. Then, in the client (receiving) application, you perform whatever steps are necessary to create the link.

Using Dynamic Data Exchange (DDE) Links

A DDE link establishes a connection between Ami Pro and another Windows application. When the data changes in the other application, Ami Pro—in cooperation with Windows and with the other application—updates its copy of the data.

To create a link between a file in another application and an Ami Pro document, follow these steps:

1. Start the application and open the file containing the data you want to link to Ami Pro. If you want to link a range in an Excel spreadsheet to your document, for example, start Excel and load the spreadsheet from which you want to link. (The originating document must have a name—it cannot be "Untitled.")

2. Select the data you want to incorporate into your Ami Pro document. In the Excel spreadsheet example, select the range of cells you want to link to your document.

3. Copy the selected data to the Windows Clipboard. (In almost all applications, you do this by selecting the Copy function from the application's Edit menu.) Be sure to leave the application running—at least as an icon.

4. In Ami Pro, open (or create) the Ami Pro document into which you want to link the data. Place the insertion point where you want the data to appear. If you want to insert the data into a frame, select an empty frame. If you want to put the data in a table, place the insertion point in the table cell where you want the data to begin.

5. Choose **E**dit Paste **L**ink.

Ami Pro inserts the Clipboard data from the other application at the current location of the insertion point, and establishes a DDE link to the other application. If the originating application supports Rich Text Format (RTF) through DDE, Ami Pro keeps the original fonts, colors, and attributes.

If the DDE link is in main document text, Ami Pro encloses the data between blue brackets. (To see the blue brackets, choose View Preferences from the **V**iew menu and select **M**arks.)

As long as the Ami Pro document is open, if the data changes in the other application, the application sends Ami Pro a message. Ami Pro responds to the message by updating the data to reflect the change in the other application. If you make a change in your linked Excel spreadsheet, for example, and that change affects several cells in the linked range, Ami Pro makes the same changes in its copy of the data.

Each time you open an Ami Pro document containing a DDE link, Ami Pro asks whether you want to update the link. If you answer *yes*, Ami Pro checks to see whether the originating application is running. If the originating application is running, Ami Pro sends it the commands necessary to load the source file and, if the data has changed, to update the data in Ami Pro.

If the other application *isn't* running, Ami Pro asks whether you want to start it. If you answer *yes*, Ami Pro tries to start the application. If Ami Pro cannot locate the application (because its executable file isn't in the DOS path), Ami Pro displays a message telling you that the program cannot update the link. If you want to update the link, perform the following steps:

1. Start the application that owns the file.
2. In Ami Pro, choose **E**dit Link **O**ptions. The Link Options dialog box appears.
3. In the Link Options dialog box, highlight the name of the link.
4. Choose Update.

Using Object Linking and Embedding (OLE) Links

In an OLE link, the original data becomes an object linked to or embedded within your Ami Pro document. The OLE object appears as an icon, a Windows metafile, or as text. The OLE object also contains the original data in the native format of the supplying application.

Two methods are available to bring an OLE object into Ami Pro; you use one method when the object to be linked or embedded exists, and the other method when you need to create the object.

To create an OLE link when the object exists, follow these steps:

1. Start the application and open the file containing the data you want to link or embed.

2. In the originating application, select the data you want to use as the OLE object and copy it to the Windows Clipboard.

3. In the Ami Pro document, place the insertion point at the location where you want the object to appear.

4. Choose **E**dit Paste **S**pecial.

5. Ami Pro displays a list of the OLE formats supported by the originating application. If OLE Embed is available, choose that format to get the most complete OLE support. If OLE Embed isn't available, select OLE Link. (If neither format is available, the other application doesn't support OLE as a server application.)

6. Choose OK or press Enter. Ami Pro embeds the data in your document as an OLE object.

To create an OLE object when the object doesn't exist, follow these steps:

1. In Ami Pro, place the insertion point where you want the object to appear.

2. Choose **E**dit **I**nsert New **O**bject. Ami Pro displays the Insert New Object dialog box (see fig. 20.3). The list of object types varies, depending on which Windows applications you have on your system.

3. The **O**bject Type list box shows all your Windows applications that support OLE as server applications. If an application supports more than one type of OLE document (Microsoft Excel, for example, supports both charts and worksheets as OLE documents), both types are listed. Select the object type you want to create and embed into your Ami Pro document.

   Ami Pro creates a frame for the object, starts the other application (if it isn't running), creates a new document in that application, and makes that application active. The new document has a cryptic name such as `AmiProDocument÷(Untitled)÷Frame` plus a frame number. You can ignore this name.

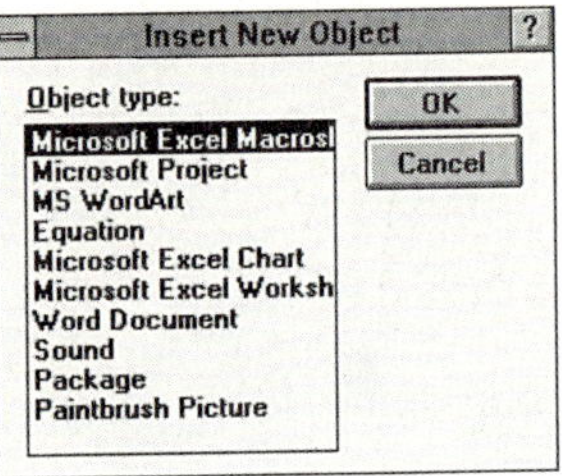

Fig. 20.3
The Insert New Object dialog box.

4. Use the facilities of the other application to create the object you want to embed in your Ami Pro document.

5. Access the **F**ile menu in the other application. In most applications, the File menu's Save option disappears and is replaced with Update. Choose Update.

   When you choose Update, the other application *doesn't* save the document as a file on disk. To save the document as a disk file, use the other application's File Save As command. (Consult the other application's documentation for details.)

6. Close the other application (or the individual document). Windows returns to Ami Pro; the object you just created is pasted into the empty frame in your Ami Pro document.

No matter which method you use to place the object in your Ami Pro document, you can double-click the object to open the other application and edit the object. (Note that double-clicking some objects may launch the object's function.) After you finish editing the object, choose the other application's File Update command and then close the application (or document).

Maintaining Links

Most of the time, working with DDE and OLE links is relatively seamless. You create the link by using the methods just described; then let Ami Pro, Windows, and your other Windows applications take care of the maintenance chores. Occasionally, however, you may need to update, unlink, deactivate, or edit a link—or perhaps just view information about a link.

To view or maintain the links in a document, choose **E**dit Link **O**ptions. Ami Pro displays the Link Options dialog box (see fig. 20.4).

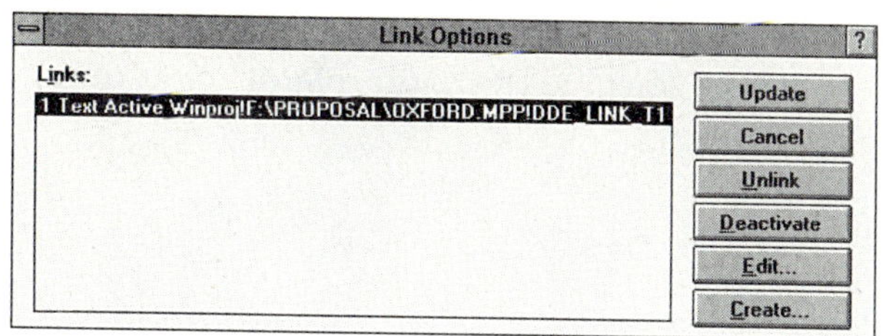

Fig. 20.4
The Link Options dialog box.

Select the link you want to modify and then make the desired modifications. The following list describes the options available:

- To update the link with the most current data from the application containing the original data, choose Update.
- To permanently remove the selected link, choose **U**nlink.
- To maintain a link but stop updating it temporarily, choose **D**eactivate. (An inactive link requires less memory.) To reactivate a deactivated link, choose Update.
- Choose **E**dit to specify a different Windows application, a different path or file, or a different range for the original data.
- Choose **C**reate to establish a new link. Ami Pro prompts you for the **A**pplication (for DDE, the application name and path; for OLE, the object type), the **T**opic (the drive, directory, and file name), and the **I**tem (the location or name of the original data, such as a range of cells or a named spreadsheet range).

After you have made your modifications, choose OK or press Enter to return to the Ami Pro document.

Exporting Documents

Exporting a document means converting it from Ami Pro file format into some other format. Ami Pro uses filters that convert the document into the new file format.

The most common reason for exporting a document to another format is as a courtesy to someone who uses the other format. You can pass along the file in the format the person uses for his or her work. Another reason may be that you do work for a client who specifies that you provide disk files in a given format.

Tip
If you need to create heavily formatted files for use with a different program, consider creating the files in that program instead of Ami Pro.

Ami Pro provides export filters for a variety of text file formats. You can save the current Ami Pro document to any of the following text file formats:

- AdvanceWrite
- Ami Pro
- Ami Pro Macro
- ASCII
- DCA/FFT
- DCA/RFT
- DisplayWrite 4
- E-mail
- Enable (Versions 1.5 through 2.5)
- Executive MemoMaker
- Lotus Manuscript 2.0 and 2.01
- Lotus Symphony
- Microsoft Word (Versions 1.X, 2.X, and 4.X)
- MultiMate (Version 3.3, 4.0, and MultiMate Advantage II)
- Navy DIF
- Office Writer
- PeachText (Version 2.11 and earlier)
- Professional Write
- Q and A Write (Versions 1.X, 3.0, and 4.0)
- Rich Text Format
- Samna Word
- SmartWare (Version 1)
- Wang (IWP)
- Windows Write
- Word for Windows through Version 6.0
- WordPerfect (Versions 4.2, 5.0, and 5.1)
- WordPerfect for Windows (Version 5.1)

- WordStar (Versions 3.3, 3.4, 4.1, and 5.0)
- WordStar 2000 (Versions 1.0 and 3.0)
- XY Write III, III Plus, IV, Windows

You can save an Ami Pro file as one of the export file types. Suppose that you want to export a sample Ami Pro file called EXPORT.SAM into Microsoft Word (DOS) format as INFOMATE.DOC. Follow these steps:

1. Choose **F**ile Save **A**s. The Save As dialog box appears, as shown in figure 20.5.

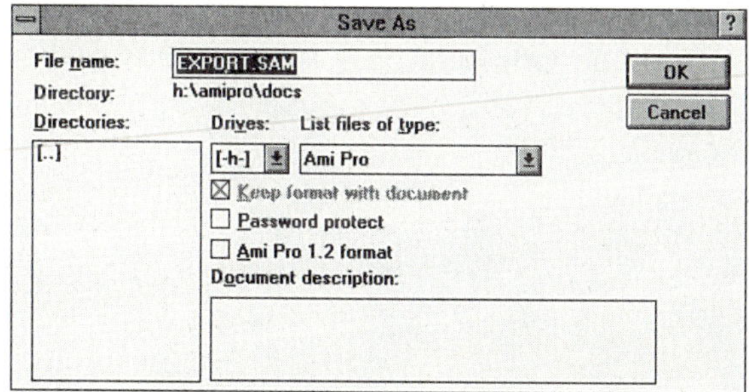

Fig. 20.5
The Save As dialog box.

2. In the List Files of **T**ype list box, select the file type for the application to which you are exporting. For this example, select Microsoft Word.

3. In the Dri**v**es list box, select the drive to which you want to export the file.

4. In the **D**irectories list box, select the directory to which you want to export the file. If you specify a path for the file, Ami Pro automatically changes to that directory the next time you open that type of file or specify that file type in the Save As dialog box.

5. In the File **N**ame text box, type the name you want for the exported document. If you are exporting to a different directory, you can use the current file name for the new document, but you may need a different extension if required by the other application. (If you prefer, you can type the full path and file name for the document in the File **N**ame text box.)

Figure 20.6 shows the completed Save As dialog box for exporting the example document.

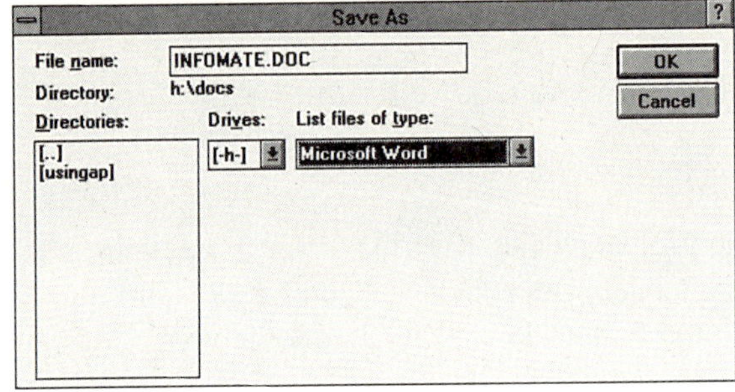

Fig. 20.6
The completed Save As dialog box for exporting the example document.

6. Choose OK or press Enter.

7. Depending on the file type specified, Ami Pro may display a dialog box providing export options (see fig. 20.7 for the Export Options dialog box for this example). Specify the appropriate option or options and choose OK or press Enter.

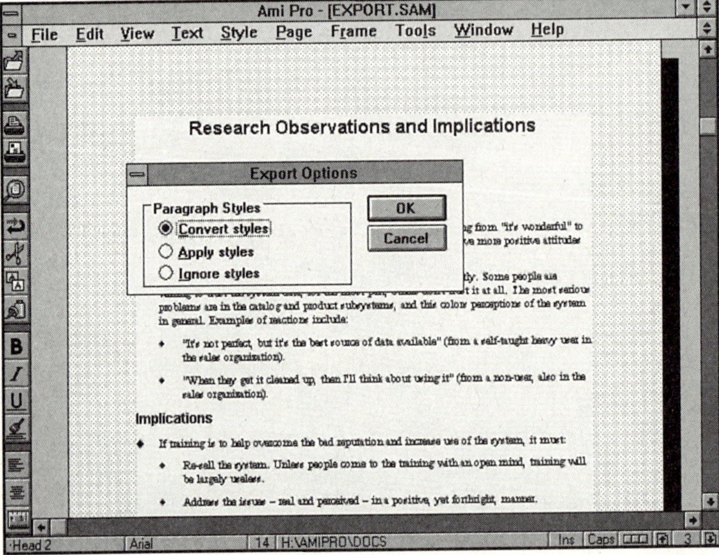

Fig. 20.7
The Export Options dialog box for the example document.

The export options are the same as the import options explained earlier in this chapter, in the section "Importing Text and Data Files." For information on options for specific programs, see your Ami Pro documentation.

In general, Ami Pro maintains the following formatting information in the exported document:

- Alignment (center, flush left, flush right, justification)
- Capitalization, including small caps
- Dates
- Fonts
- Footnotes (if footnotes aren't supported by the other program, Ami Pro converts them to regular text and places them at the end of the document)
- Headers and footers (fixed)
- International characters
- Line spacing
- Other formatting, such as hard hyphens, nonbreaking spaces, and so on
- Page formatting, including page breaks, tabs and tab rulers (tab ruler is set to a default of one tab every 1/2 inch; if the other program doesn't have center, numeric, or right tabs, all tabs become left tabs)
- Page numbering (if the other program doesn't support page numbering, page numbers are converted to regular text)
- Paragraph styles
- Text attributes (boldface, underline, double underline, italics, overstrike, superscript, subscript, and so on)
- Text frames (if anchored, frames appear at the anchoring location; if unanchored, at the end of the document)

Note

The information that Ami Pro imports and exports varies between filters. Lotus Development Corporation revises the filters with each new software release. Sometimes new filters are developed between releases. Check with Lotus (or check the LOTUSWP forum on CompuServe) for the latest release of the filter you need.

Importing Graphics

So far in this chapter, you have learned about importing and exporting text and data—but you also can import and export graphics from a variety of graphic formats. In this section, you learn four techniques for importing graphics into an Ami Pro document.

First you learn how to import pictures that you can use as Ami Pro drawings. With these methods (importing the AmiDraw, DrawPerfect/WordPerfect, Windows metafile, or Windows bit-map file types), you can use the drawing icons and tools (described in Chapter 17, "Using the Draw Feature") to resize, rotate, and otherwise edit the drawings. If you can import pictures to drawings, you have great flexibility in working with the files.

If you cannot import a picture as a drawing, however, you still may want to import the picture in some other form. Additional methods are described here for importing graphics—methods that don't convert the pictures into Ami Pro drawings (files with the extension SDW). Although nondrawing files have limitations, you can edit them; the techniques are described in this section.

Importing a Drawing in Draw Mode

You have the most flexibility in working with imported drawings if you can apply the tools of Ami Pro's draw mode to them. (In this section, note that a *drawing* is an Ami Pro Draw file, and a *picture* is any imported drawing.) In draw mode, you can import these types of charts and drawings:

- AmiDraw files
- Windows bit-map files
- Windows metafiles

Suppose that when you are using draw mode you want to import one of the symbols from the Ami Pro DRAWSYM subdirectory. Follow these steps to import a file in draw mode:

1. If you aren't already using draw mode, choose Too**l**s **D**rawing. Ami Pro creates a frame and switches to draw mode.
2. Choose **F**ile **I**mport Drawing. The Import Drawing dialog box appears, as shown in figure 20.8.
3. In the Format section of the dialog box, select the file format you want to import: **A**miDraw, Windows **M**etafile, or Windows **B**itmap.
4. In the **F**iles list box, select the file you want to import (or type the name in the File **N**ame text box). The picture appears in the example box, in the lower right corner of the dialog box. Figure 20.9 shows the example file BIGTRUCK.SDW in the dialog box.

5. Choose OK or press Enter. Ami Pro imports the drawing into the frame, as shown in figure 20.10.

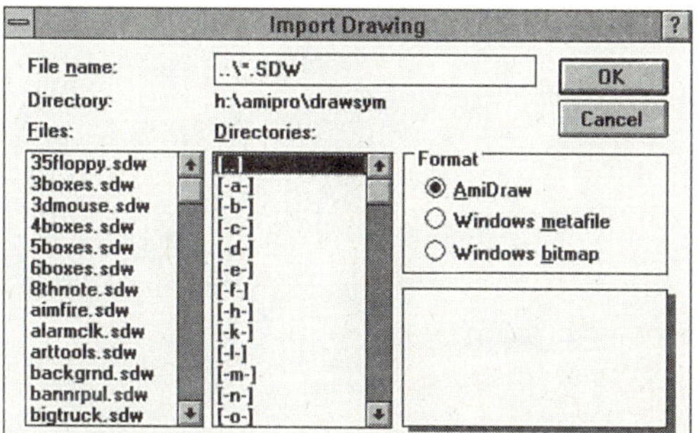

Fig. 20.8
The Import Drawing dialog box.

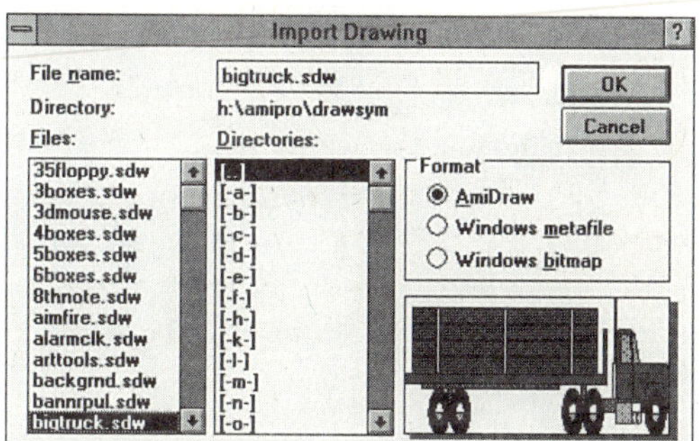

Fig. 20.9
Viewing the selected picture in the example box.

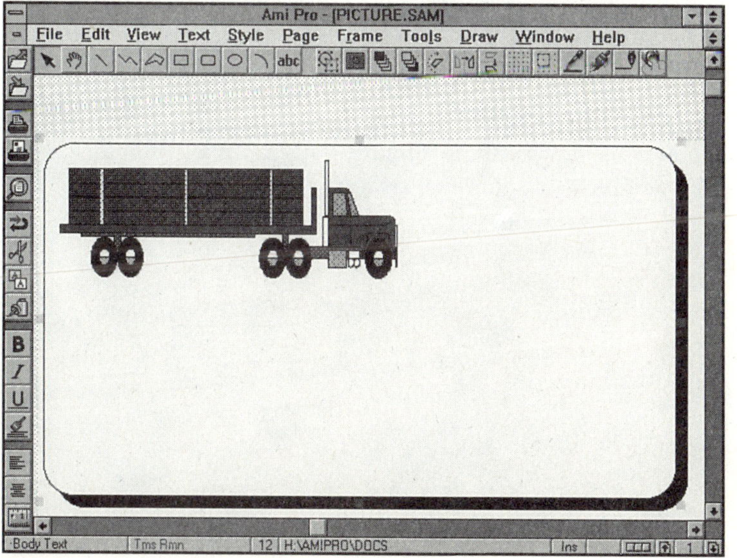

Fig. 20.10
The picture imported into an Ami Pro frame.

Note

Often you cannot judge clip art by an eight-character file name; you need to see the picture. Use the example box in the Import Drawing dialog box to review clip art samples quickly and make a selection before you take the final step of importing the art into your document.

You can use the drawing icons (shown in fig. 20.10 at the top of the document window) to edit the picture. You also can scale the drawing so that it fits in the frame. In figure 20.10, for example, you cannot see the front of the truck. See this chapter's "Editing Imported Graphics" section for more details.

Note

To edit files in HPGL (Hewlett-Packard Graphics Language) and CGM (computer graphics metafile) formats, convert the files to Windows metafiles by using the Windows Clipboard.

Begin by importing the HPGL or CGM file as a picture (as explained in the next section, "Importing a Picture"). Then double-click the frame containing the picture. The cursor changes to a hand shape. Choose **E**dit **C**opy (or press Ctrl+Ins) to place the graphic image from the frame into the Clipboard and, in the process, convert the image to Windows metafile format.

Next, create or select a frame of the size you want to use for the picture. With the frame selected, choose **E**dit **P**aste (or press Shift+Ins). Ami Pro pastes the image into the frame. You then can use the drawing tools to edit the image.

Importing a Picture

A picture must be imported into a frame. You can create the frame before you import the picture; if you don't create a frame first, Ami Pro creates one for you with the current settings in the Create Frame dialog box. (See Chapter 16, "Using Frames," for a full discussion of frames.)

Table 20.1 shows the import file formats that Ami Pro supports.

Table 20.1 Import File Types

File Type	Extension
AmiDraw	SDW
AmiEquation	TEX
AutoCAD	DXF
Computer graphics metafile (converts to Windows metafile when imported)	CGM
DrawPerfect/WordPerfect (converts to AmiDraw SDW file when imported)	WPG
Encapsulated PostScript	EPS
Freelance (converts to AmiDraw SDW file when imported)	DRW
Hewlett-Packard Graphics Language (HPGL) (converts to Windows metafile when imported)	PLT
Lotus 1-2-3 graphics (converts to AmiDraw SDW file when imported)	PIC
PC Paintbrush	PCX
Scanned images	TIF
Windows bit-map	BMP
Windows metafile	WMF

To import a picture, such as a stored symbol from the Ami Pro library of images, begin in the active window with the document into which you want to import the picture. So that you can practice importing a picture, create a sample document called PICTURE.SAM. Then follow these steps:

1. If you prefer, create or choose a frame of the size you want. (For this example, don't create a frame—let Ami Pro create it for you.)

2. Choose **F**ile **I**mport Picture. The Import Picture dialog box appears, as shown in figure 20.11.

3. Select a file type in the File **T**ype list box. For this example, accept the default file type, AmiDraw.

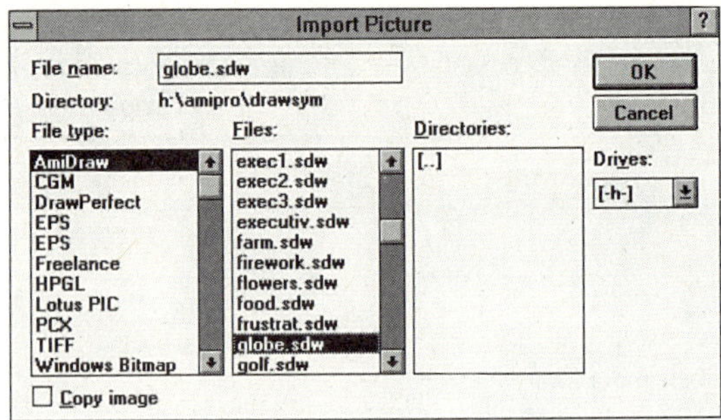

Fig. 20.11
The Import Picture dialog box.

4. In the Dri**v**es and **D**irectories list boxes, specify the path for the picture you want to import; then select the file from the **F**iles list box. For this example, accept the default drive and directory where Ami Pro installed its SDW files (C:\AMIPRO\DRAWSYM) and select the file GLOBE.SDW. (If you prefer, you can type the full path and file name in the File **N**ame text box.)

5. Select the **C**opy Image option if you want Ami Pro to copy the original picture file to a document image file. With this option, the program displays the image quickly when you print or display a page containing the image, because Ami Pro doesn't need to access the original each time. (If you change the original after creating the image, however, the image doesn't reflect the change.)

   If **C**opy Image isn't selected, and you later move the document to another directory, Ami Pro cannot find the graphics files. If you use Ami Pro's File Manager to move the document file, however, you can tell the File Manager to keep all related files together. For more information on the File Manager, see Chapter 21, "Managing Files and Documents."

   For this example, leave the **C**opy Image option deselected.

6. Choose OK or press Enter. Ami Pro fits the picture inside the frame. The *aspect ratio* (the ratio of the height to the width) remains the same, so the picture isn't distorted. Figure 20.12 shows the sample imported SDW file.

7. If you selected Computer Graphics Metafile format in step 3, the Ami Pro CGM Filter dialog box appears, as shown in figure 20.13.

8. Select the desired options in the dialog box and choose OK or press Enter. (The options are described in table 20.2.) Ami Pro imports the CGM file into the frame. Figure 20.14 shows an imported CGM file in its frame.

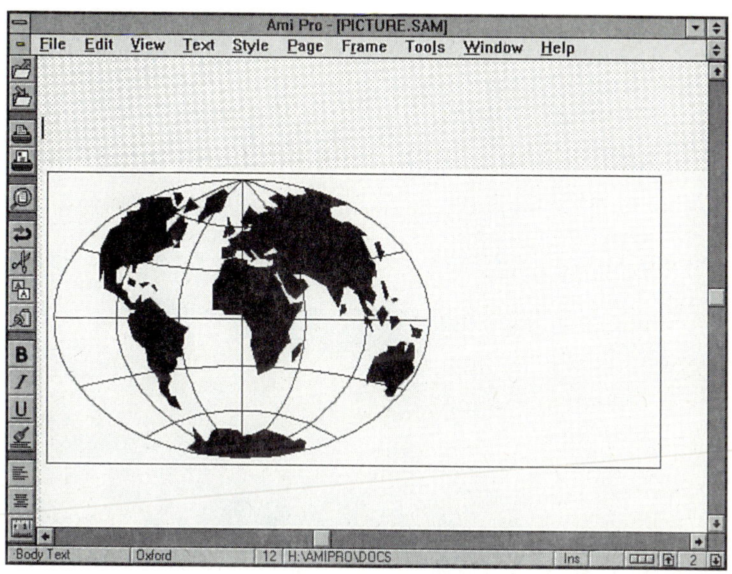

Fig. 20.12
An imported SDW file.

Ami Pro CGM Filter

☒ Ignore background
☐ Force vector fonts
☐ Dot lines
☐ Default color table

OK
Cancel
Help...

Complete :
0% 100%

© Copyright 1990,1991
Access Softek Corp. All rights reserved

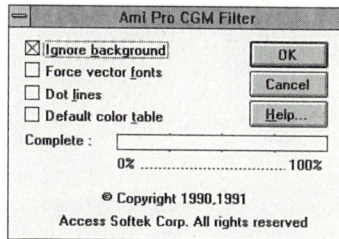

Fig. 20.13
The Ami Pro CGM Filter dialog box.

Table 20.2 describes the options for importing CGM files in the CGM Import dialog box.

Table 20.2 Options for Importing Computer Graphics Metafiles

Option	Function
Ignore **B**ackground	This option makes the picture appear transparent, without the background rectangle on which it's drawn.
Force Vector **F**onts	This option changes *raster fonts* (bit-mapped fonts) from the original into vector fonts in Ami Pro. (*Vector fonts* are generated from mathematical descriptions.) You can scale vector fonts to any size, but you can scale raster fonts only to the sizes supported by your printer.

(continues)

Table 20.2 Continued

Option	Function
Dot **L**ines	This option retains dotted lines in an imported picture. If the option is deselected, dotted lines become solid lines.
Default Color **T**able	Use this option for Harvard Graphics CGM files to assure that colors in the original file are converted correctly.

Fig. 20.14
An imported CGM file.

Pasting a Picture from Another Windows Application

Thanks to the power of Microsoft Windows, pasting a picture from another Windows application isn't much different from cutting and pasting a picture within an application. You copy the picture to the Clipboard in one application and then paste the picture into the Ami Pro document.

Note

The other application must support a Clipboard format that Ami Pro supports—usually Windows metafile or Windows bit-map format. If the other application doesn't support the format, the Windows Paste option is dimmed.

Follow these steps to paste a picture from another Windows application:

1. In the other application, make the window containing the picture the active window.
2. Select the picture in the other application.
3. Use that application's Edit Copy command to place the picture in the Windows Clipboard.
4. Activate the Ami Pro document window that will contain the picture.
5. Create (or select) a frame of the size you want, to contain the picture. If you don't create a frame, Ami Pro creates one for you.
6. Choose **E**dit **P**aste or press Shift+Ins. The picture appears in the frame.

Tip
If the imported picture isn't exactly as you want it, you can easily edit it with Ami Pro's drawing tools (such as those for selecting and moving) and with the tools described in the section "Editing Imported Graphics."

Figure 20.15 shows a drawing of the space shuttle *Atlantis* imported from the popular Windows graphics program CorelDRAW!.

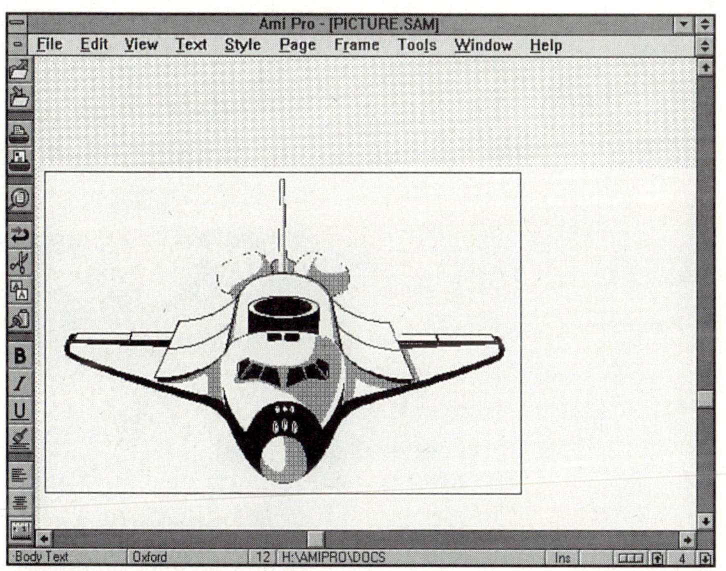

Fig. 20.15
A picture pasted into Ami Pro by way of the Windows Clipboard.

Paste-Linking a Picture

After you paste a picture into Ami Pro, the pasted picture doesn't remain linked to the original picture. If you update the original—a chart, for example—the changes in the original aren't passed to the copy in Ami Pro. If you want to maintain a link to the original picture, you can use the Paste **L**ink or Paste **S**pecial command from the **E**dit menu.

Paste **L**ink sets up a connection over *DDE* (*Dynamic Data Exchange*), a Microsoft facility for connecting applications that support DDE. Paste **S**pecial uses *OLE* (*Object Linking and Embedding*), a second Microsoft Windows utility that enables you to choose the format for the picture you paste into Ami Pro.

To see whether an application supports Paste **L**ink, first copy something from the application to the Clipboard. Then check the **E**dit menu in Ami Pro. If Paste **L**ink is available (dark rather than dimmed), the application supports Paste **L**ink.

To paste-link a picture, follow these steps:

1. Start the other application and open the file containing the picture you want to import.

2. Select the picture you want to import.

3. Choose Copy from the other application's Edit menu to copy the picture to the Windows Clipboard. *Don't close the application.* (You can minimize its window to an icon, if you want.)

4. Make the Ami Pro document in which you want to place the link the active document.

5. Create or select a frame for the graphic. If you don't create a frame, Ami Pro creates it for you.

6. Choose **E**dit Paste **L**ink for DDE applications. For OLE applications, choose **E**dit Paste **S**pecial.

The picture from the linked document appears in the Ami Pro document. As long as the link is active—that is, you don't close either application—any change to the original application appears in the Ami Pro application. If you close the Ami Pro document, the link remains in effect, and changes made in the original application appear when you reopen the Ami Pro document. If you close the other application, you end the link.

If you reopen the Ami Pro document, Ami Pro asks whether you want to reestablish the DDE link. If you choose **Y**es and if the other application still is running, Ami Pro reestablishes the link and updates the data in the Ami Pro document if necessary.

If the other application *isn't* running, Ami Pro asks whether you want to start it. If you choose **Y**es, Ami Pro tries to start the application. If Ami Pro cannot locate the application (because its executable file isn't in the DOS path), the program displays a message indicating that Ami Pro cannot update the link.

If you want to update the link, do the following:

1. Start the application that owns the file.
2. In Ami Pro, choose **E**dit Link **O**ptions. The Link Options dialog box appears.
3. In the dialog box, highlight the name of the link.
4. Choose Update. Ami Pro updates the information in the document.

Editing Imported Graphics

As you learned earlier in this chapter, pictures you import may not look exactly the way you expect. Sometimes, even if an imported picture looks exactly like the original, you still may want to change it.

In addition to modifying a picture with the drawing tools (described in Chapter 17, "Using the Draw Feature"), you can *scale* an imported graphic (change its size), *crop* it (move it within a frame without changing the graphic's size), and—for TIFF images—use *image processing* to change the *gray scale* (the mixture of black and white) in the image.

Changing the Size of a Graphic (Scaling)

Whether you're dealing with imported or drawn graphics, you frequently must change the size of a graphic so that it fits better in the frame. Suppose that you want to change the size of the truck in figure 20.10 so that the picture fills the frame. To change the size of (*scale*) a graphic, select the frame that contains the picture you want to scale. Then choose F**r**ame Graphics **S**caling. The Graphics Scaling dialog box appears, as shown in figure 20.16.

Tip
You also can resize the picture if you need it larger or smaller for purposes of proportion in the document.

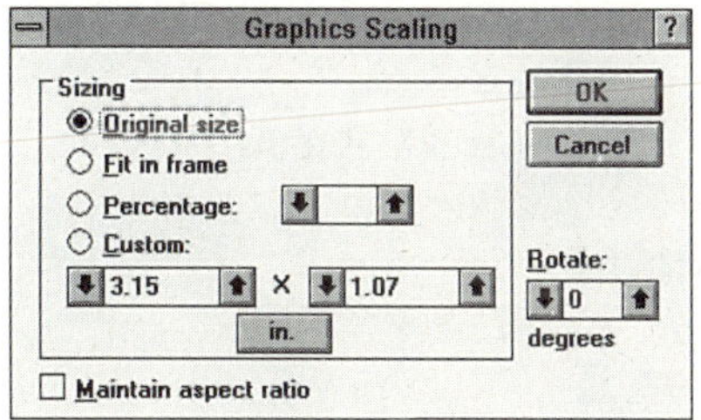

Fig. 20.16
The Graphics Scaling dialog box.

Choose the desired scaling options. You can use a custom size and specify the desired unit of measure, or let Ami Pro set the size. As you select options (except the **C**ustom option), if the option uses a list box the numbers in the list box change to show the dimensions Ami Pro assigns. The following list describes the options available:

- ***Original Size.*** This option rescales a picture to its original size (the imported size when you began the session).
- ***Fit in Frame.*** With this option, you change the size of the graphic so that it fits within the frame. This option is useful if you don't need exact dimensions for the picture.
- ***Percentage.*** This option changes the size of a picture to the percentage of the original you specify.
- ***Custom.*** This option changes the size of the picture by the amount you specify in the text boxes.
- ***Maintain Aspect Ratio.*** To keep the height proportional to the width when you scale an object, use this option. To prevent graphics from becoming distorted, choose **M**aintain Aspect Ratio before scaling. (If you select **C**ustom when you have turned on **M**aintain Aspect Ratio, just select one dimension. Ami Pro computes the other one for you.)
- ***Rotate.*** This option turns a picture clockwise within the frame by the amount you specify. For details, see the section "Rotating an Image" later in this chapter.

Figures 20.17 through 20.21 show some results of using the Graphics Scaling options on the truck from figure 20.10. Figure 20.17 shows the picture of the truck after **F**it in Frame is selected. Notice that although the truck fits in the frame, the picture appears distorted. To avoid such distortion, select **M**aintain Aspect Ratio. Figure 20.18 shows the truck after it is scaled to 160 percent of its original size.

Tip
With the mouse, you can scale the picture and the frame simultaneously. Hold down the Shift key and drag one of the corner handles of the frame.

Figure 20.19 shows the original picture after specifying the **C**ustom dimensions of 4.25 inches by 2 inches. Figure 20.20 shows how the example truck looks if you select **F**it in Frame and **M**aintain Aspect Ratio.

Rotating an Image

You can rotate an image if the image is an AmiDraw, DrawPerfect, Freelance, Lotus PIC, PCX, non-gray scale TIFF, or Windows bit-map graphic.

Figure 20.21 shows an image from the ArtRight Image Portfolio, a commercial clip art package available in a variety of formats. (This image was in DrawPerfect format when imported into Ami Pro.)

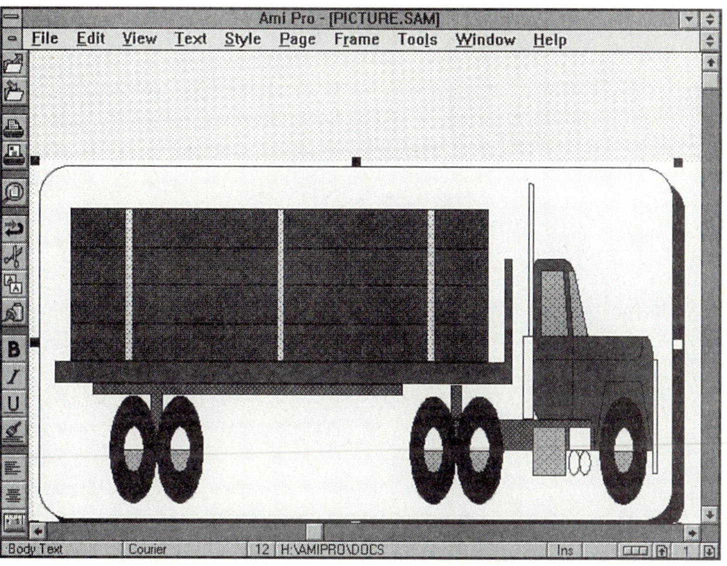

Fig. 20.17
The picture scaled with the Fit in Frame option.

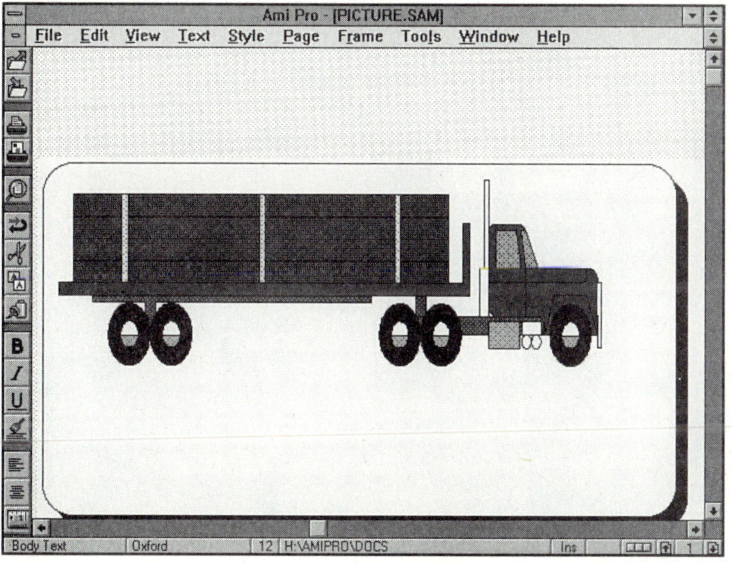

Fig. 20.18
The picture scaled to 160 percent of its original size.

To rotate the image, select the frame; then choose F**r**ame Graphics **S**caling. Ami Pro displays the Graphics Scaling dialog box (refer to fig. 20.16). In the **R**otate text box, type the number of degrees you want Ami Pro to rotate the image (between 0 and 359). Then choose OK or press Enter. Ami Pro rotates the graphic. Figure 20.22 shows the airplane graphic rotated 30 degrees.

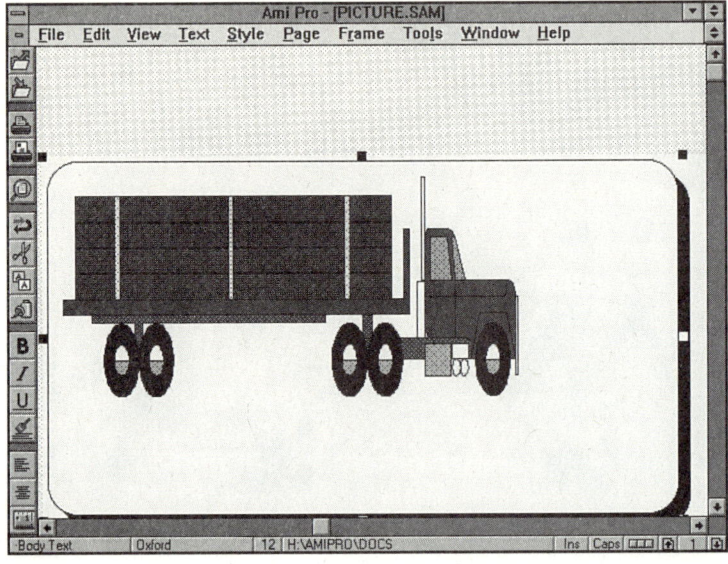

Fig. 20.19
The picture displayed in a specified custom size.

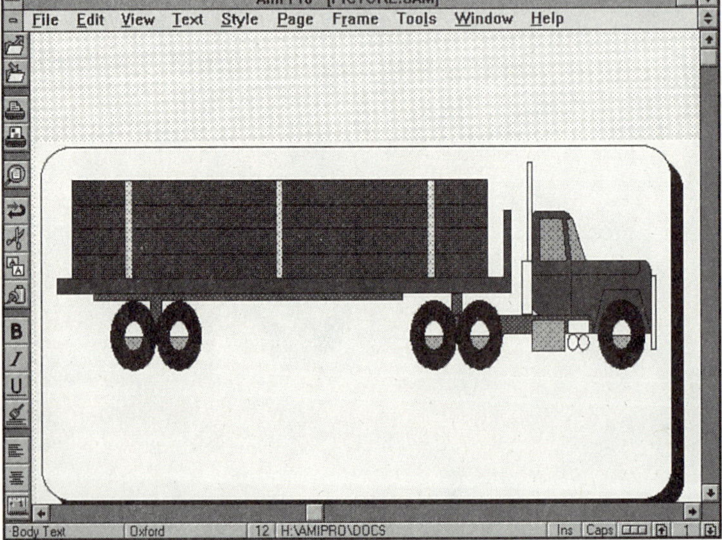

Fig. 20.20
The picture with aspect ratio maintained.

Changing the Position of a Graphic (Cropping)

A picture may not appear in the exact position you want within the frame. Ami Pro offers a cropping feature, however, that enables you to move a picture anywhere within a frame. Begin by selecting the frame containing the picture. Then double-click inside the frame (or press Enter), and drag the object to the place where you want the picture. Then release the mouse button.

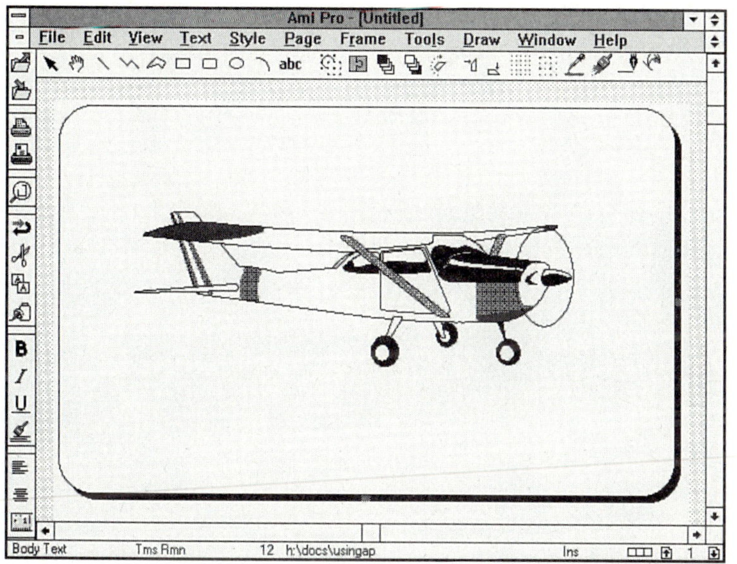

Fig. 20.21
A graphic image imported into Ami Pro.

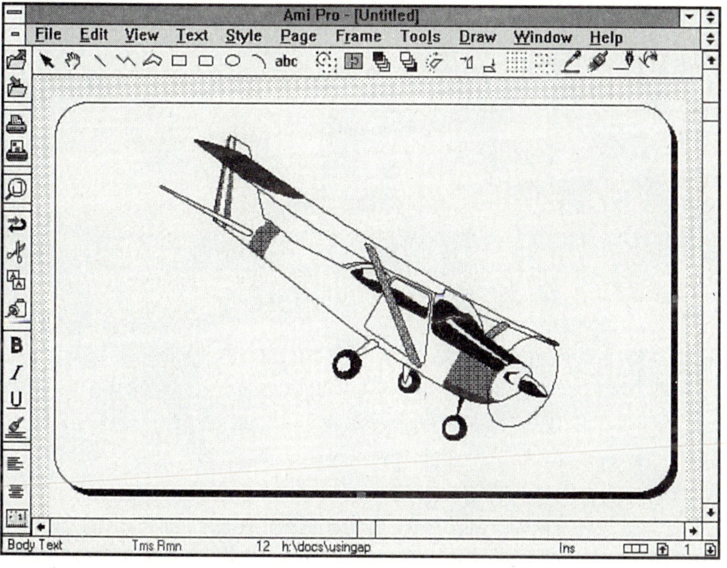

Fig. 20.22
The graphic after being rotated 30 degrees.

If you prefer, you can use the arrow keys to move the picture in small increments, or hold down Ctrl and use the arrow keys to move the picture in larger increments.

Note

If the object is a drawing, you cannot use the keyboard to crop. You must change to draw mode, click the hand icon, and drag the mouse to the drawing's new location.

Perhaps you want to show only part of a picture, such as the front of the truck in the sample picture. You can crop the picture to show only the part you want by dragging the picture over the edge of the frame (see fig. 20.23).

Fig. 20.23 Cropping the picture.

Modifying Shades of Gray (Image Processing)

Tip
Not all TIFF files can be image processed; some don't have information about shades of gray.

Unlike other images, which consist of collections of black dots and white dots, *Tagged Image File Format* (*TIFF*) images consist of gray scales—different shades of gray. With these images, you can perform image processing—changing the appearance of the gray scales in the picture, sometimes with dramatic effect. You can adjust the brightness and contrast, enhance the edges, smooth the picture, and invert the shading to change the appearance of an image and make it look attractive.

First, you must import the image into a frame. Figure 20.24 shows an imported TIFF image.

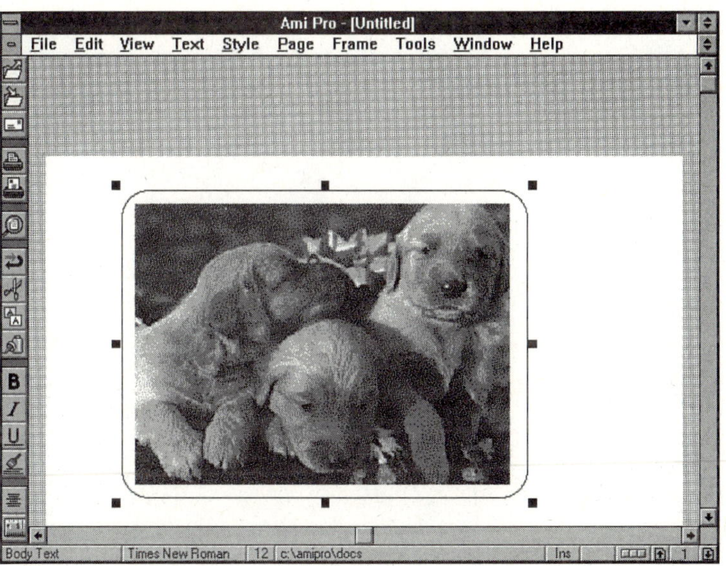

Fig. 20.24
An imported TIFF image before image processing.

Follow these steps to process the image:

1. Select the frame containing the TIFF image.
2. Choose Tools Image Processing. The Image Processing dialog box appears (see fig. 20.25).

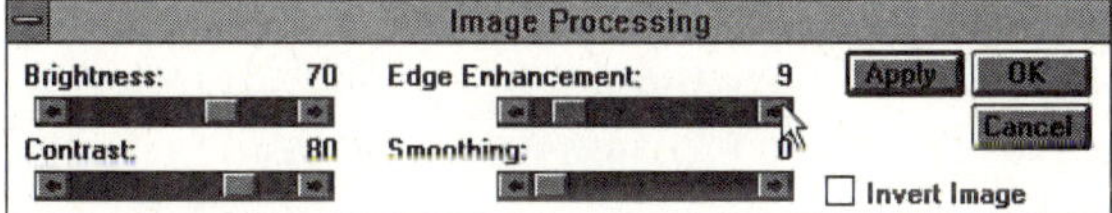

Fig. 20.25
The Image Processing dialog box.

3. Choose the options you want in the dialog box. The available options are listed in table 20.3. To use each option in the Image Processing dialog box, drag the scroll box in the scroll bar beneath each option, or click the arrows at the end of the bar as with other scroll bars. With the keyboard, press Tab to move to the scroll bar you want and press the left- or right-arrow key to move the scroll box within the bar.
4. Choose Apply. Ami Pro applies the changes to the picture in the frame but leaves the Image Processing dialog box on-screen. After you see the effect of a change, you may want to make other changes.
5. When you're satisfied with the changes, choose OK or press Enter. Ami Pro closes the Image Processing dialog box and returns to the document.

Table 20.3 Options in the Image Processing Dialog Box

Option	Purpose
Brightness	If you increase brightness in the image, you increase the number of white dots (*pixels*) in the image and decrease the number of black dots. Black turns increasingly gray, and light gray turns increasingly white. If you decrease brightness, on the other hand, gray turns increasingly black and white begins to turn gray.
Edge Enhancement	If you enhance the edges, you increase the contrast between edges in the picture and the rest of the picture. Details in the picture become more distinct.
Contrast	If you increase contrast, you decrease the amount of gray in the picture and increase the amount of white and black. If you decrease contrast, you increase the amount of gray. Blacks and whites blend together.
Smoothing	This option softens a picture by blending stray dots, jagged edges, or unwanted lines into the rest of the picture.
Invert Image	This option reverses black and white in the picture.

Summary

In this chapter, you learned how to import text and graphics, export text, paste a picture from another Windows application, and paste-link a drawing. You also learned how to change the size of a picture, how to move it around within the frame, and—for TIFF images—how to apply image processing.

In the next chapter, you learn how to use Ami Pro's file management features to manage files and documents.

Chapter 21

Managing Files and Documents

Ami Pro offers you powerful ways to work within and manage your documents. You can use Ami Pro's file management utility to manage all your Ami Pro files. With the File Manager, you can perform many activities that you also can perform with the Windows File Manager: copying files, moving files, renaming files, and changing directories.

You can use the Doc Info option to learn key information about a document, including the number of words in the document and the time and date of the document's creation and revision. With revision marking, you can compare the differences between two documents. With notes, you can make suggestions for revising a marked document.

Ami Pro provides a special way to work with multiple documents: a *master document*. You can use a master document to work with multiple files (perhaps the chapters in a book). You can combine the files in a master document and generate a table of contents, a list of figures, and an index for all the documents in the master document. This chapter familiarizes you with all these file- and document-management features.

File Management with the Ami Pro File Manager

Ami Pro's File Manager is a special facility for managing files on your computer. File Manager is a *self-running program*. The File Manager is called a self-running program because it runs independently of Ami Pro; it has its own menu independent of the main Ami Pro menu, and can actually remain open if you exit Ami Pro. You should use the File Manager only when Ami Pro is open and only to work with Ami Pro files. The File Manager duplicates some of the functions of the Windows File Manager and DOS. Ami Pro's File Manager, however, is designed to work specifically with Ami Pro documents. These documents can have associated files (such as style sheets and graphics files) that must be accessible to the main Ami Pro documents. To work with these associated files, always use Ami Pro's File Manager to handle Ami Pro files, instead of using the Windows File Manager or DOS.

In this section, you learn how to open the File Manager, change its directory, and control what files are listed. You learn how to copy, move, rename, and delete files and how to change file attributes.

Opening the File Manager

To access the File Manager, choose **F**ile **F**ile Management or click the File Management SmartIcon. The Ami Pro File Manager window appears, as shown in figure 21.1. By default, only Ami Pro documents and Ami Pro macros (which have the extensions SAM and SMM) appear in the file list. As you learn in the next section, you can have other types of files appear in the file list. The files appear in alphabetic order. The description next to each file is the document description provided when the file was saved. If no document description was entered when saving the file, there is no description for the file in the File Manager.

Changing the File Manager Directory

When you open the File Manager, it lists the files in the default directory. If you prefer to see the files in a different directory, choose the File Manager's **F**ile menu, shown in figure 21.2, and then choose C**h**ange Directory. The Change Directory dialog box appears, as shown in figure 21.3. The current path appears in the dialog box. You can type over this path to display files in a completely different location, or you can click the insertion point in the path and make only a quick change to the current path.

In the **C**hange To text box, specify the path to the directory containing the files you want to list in the File Manager. Then choose OK or press Enter.

You also can use the **C**hange To text box to show files on a floppy drive. Type **A**: in the **C**hange To text box, for example, to look at the files in drive A. An easy way to look at files on a floppy drive is to scroll the file list in the File Manager window to the end of the list. As shown in figure 21.4, the floppy drives and the hard disk drive are listed at the end of the file list. Click the drive from which you want to read files to display those files in the File Manager. [..] represents the parent directory of the current directory.

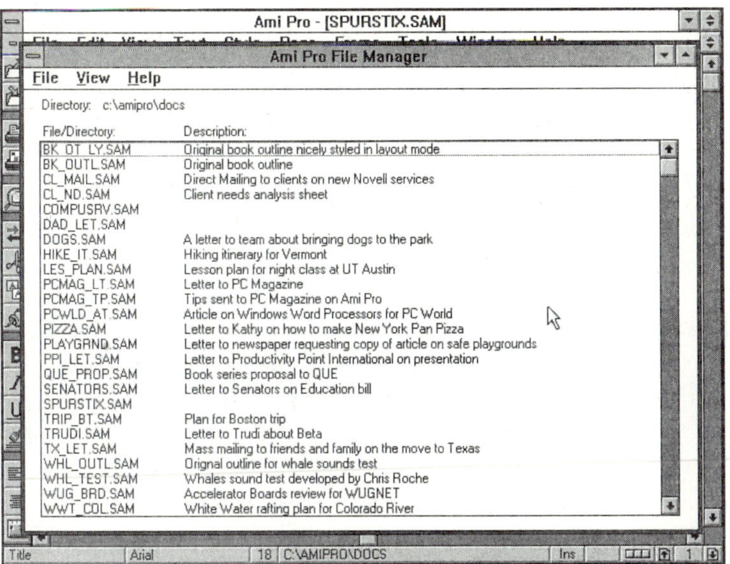

Fig. 21.1
The Ami Pro File Manager window.

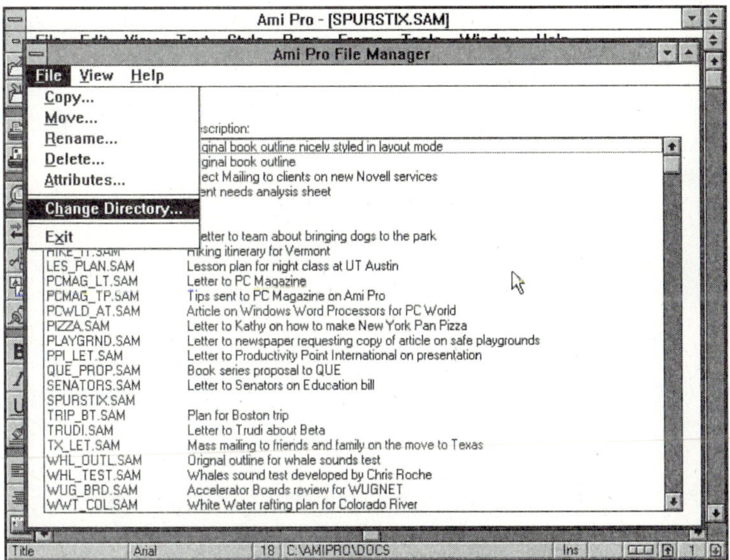

Fig. 21.2
The **F**ile menu.

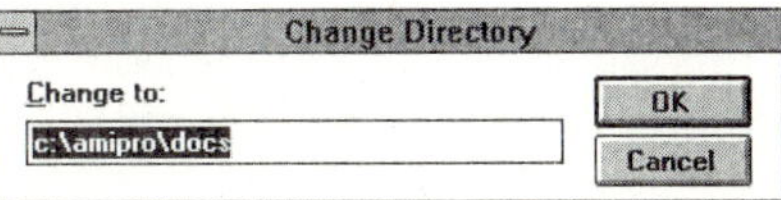

Fig. 21.3
The Change Directory dialog box.

Tip
All drives available on your system, including all network drives, appear at the end of the File Manager file list.

Note

You can double-click the directory name in the path shown in the File Manager window to change the directory. If the path shown is C:\AMIPRO\CLIENTS\PPI\PROPOSALS, for example, double-clicking the CLIENTS directory name changes the directory to C:\AMIPRO\CLIENTS and lists the files in that directory.

Limiting the File List

If the File Manager window lists too many files and you cannot find the file you want, you can use wild-card characters to specify the files you want to see. You also can use wild-card characters to limit the number of displayed files to a specific group. To restrict the file list, choose **V**iew from the File Manager menu. Figure 21.5 displays the **V**iew menu. Choose one of the displayed options (*.**S**?M Files, **A**ll, or **P**artial) to limit the list of files displayed.

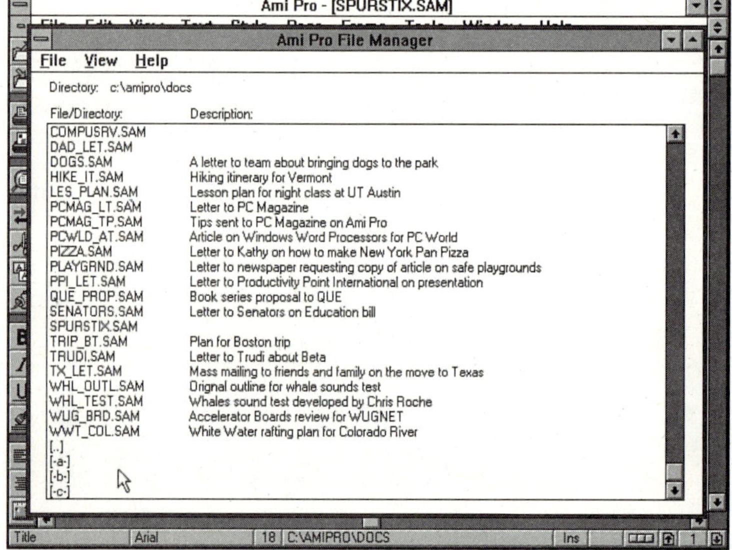

Fig. 21.4
Available drives, listed at the end of the files.

The following list describes these three options.

- **.**S**?M Files.* This option lists all files with any three-character extension beginning with *S* and ending with *M*. You get a list of all Ami Pro documents and macros.

- ***All.*** This option displays all files in the directory.
- ***Partial.*** This option accesses a dialog box that enables you to list any type of file. You can use the wild cards * and ? to specify which files you want to list. If you type ***.STY**, for example, and then choose OK or press Enter, Ami Pro lists all the style sheets, because all style sheets have the STY extension. Figure 21.6 shows the Partial dialog box set to display only the Ami Pro documents that begin with the letter *P*. (If you choose **V**iew **P**artial, you can search for files in the specified directory only.) Figure 21.7 shows the File/Directory list box limited to the Ami Pro documents beginning with *P*.

If you select All, any files that aren't Ami Pro files have the description `Not an Ami Pro File`.

You can quickly change back to looking at all your Ami Pro documents by selecting *.**S**?M Files from the **V**iew menu. You also can change to another disk drive and/or directory by using the **P**artial Option. To view all the Ami Pro documents in the directory CLIENTS on drive D, for example, type **D:\CLIENTS*.SAM** and press Enter.

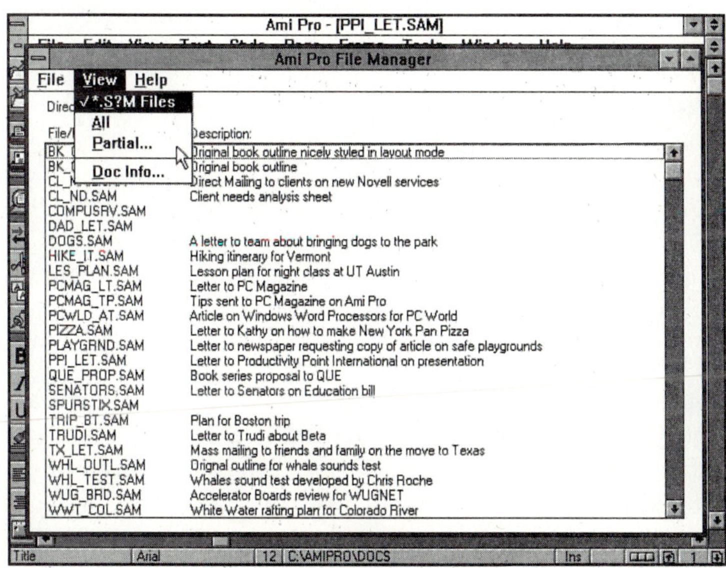

Fig. 21.5
The **V**iew menu.

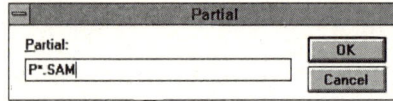

Fig. 21.6
The Partial dialog box for SAM files that begin with P.

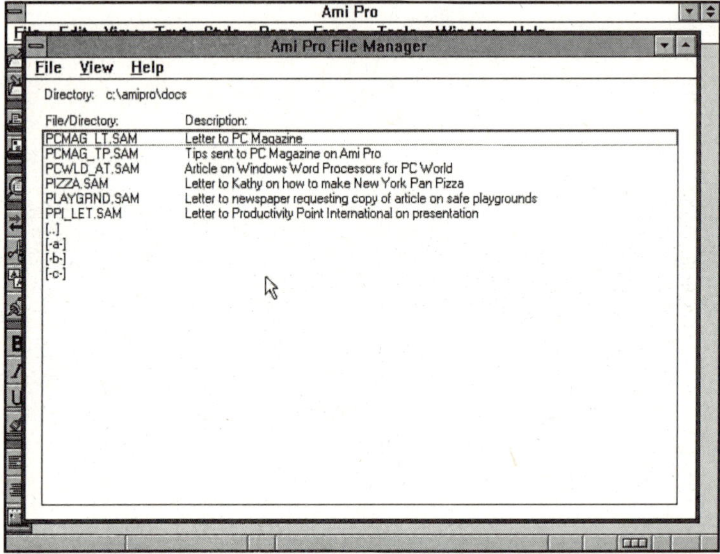

Fig. 21.7
The File Manager File/Directory list box, displaying Ami Pro documents that begin with P.

Copying Files

When you copy a file, Ami Pro duplicates the file in the location you specify and leaves the original file in its current location. You can select one file or multiple files to copy. To select a file, click the file name in the File/Directory list box. If you make a mistake, click the file name again to deselect it. If you prefer to use the keyboard, use the arrow keys to move to the appropriate file name; then press the space bar to select or deselect the file.

When all the files you want to copy are highlighted, choose **F**ile **C**opy from the File Manager menu. The Copy dialog box appears. In the **T**o text box, specify the destination for the files. Then choose OK or press Enter. Figure 21.8 displays the Copy dialog box set to copy a group of files to the directory \YEAR92\PUBLISH on drive E. You must specify the full destination path for the file's target location. The **C**opy box lists all the files to be copied, but not all of them can be seen in the box.

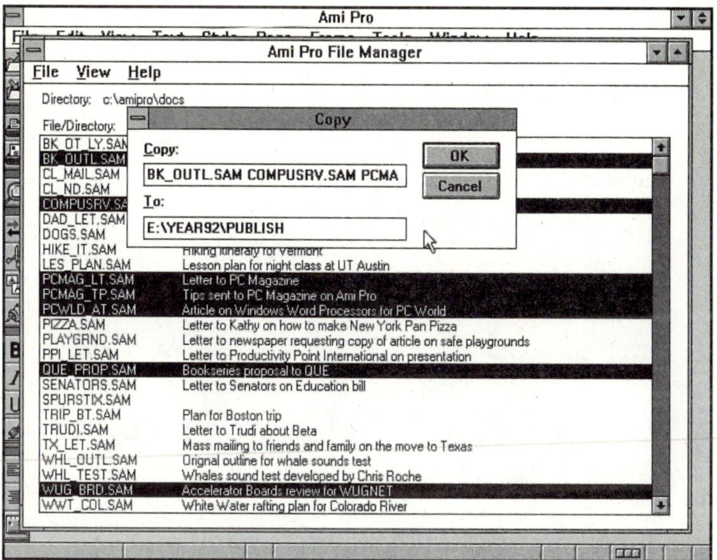

Fig. 21.8
The Copy dialog box, set to copy selected files to a different drive and directory.

You can copy a group of files to a floppy disk by entering the floppy disk drive in the **T**o box. Enter **A:** in the **T**o box, for example, to copy the selected files to a floppy disk in drive A.

> **Note**
>
> You can copy and rename a file at the same time by specifying a different file name along with the target location in the **T**o box. If BK11_OUT.SAM is a file name for the outline of Chapter 11 of a book, for example, you can copy the file to a floppy disk in drive A by entering **A:\OUTL_11.SAM**.

> **Note**
>
> You cannot copy and rename multiple files simultaneously. If you select multiple files to copy, and provide a different name for each in the **T**o box, Ami Pro displays the error message `Multiple destinations not allowed.` If you provide a single name for multiple files, Ami Pro displays the message `Cannot copy multiple files to a single destination.`

Moving Files

Moving a file is like copying a file, except that the original file is deleted from its location. To move a file, select the name of the file in the File/Directory list box. (Again, you can select any number of files.) Next, choose **F**ile **M**ove.

The Move dialog box opens, as shown in figure 21.9. In the **T**o text box, specify the full destination path; then choose OK or press Enter.

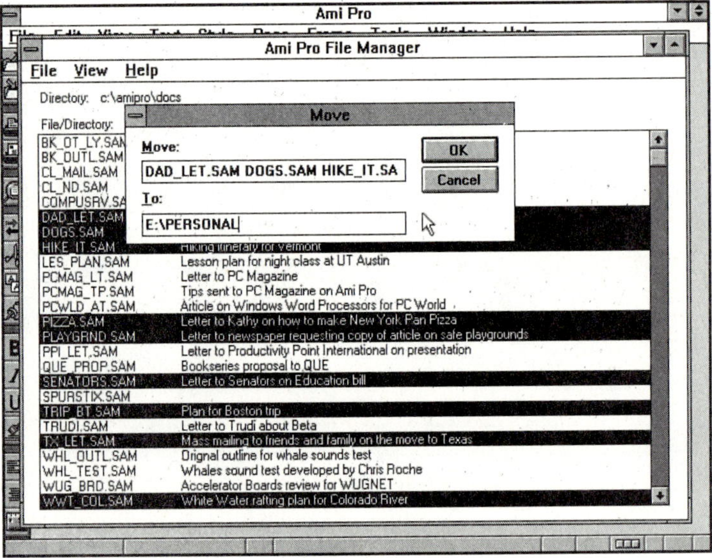

Fig. 21.9
The Move dialog box, set to move a group of files to E:\PERSONAL.

Tip
You can move and rename a file at the same time by specifying a different file name along with the target location in the **T**o box. You cannot move and rename multiple files simultaneously.

You can move a group of files to a floppy disk by entering the name of the floppy disk drive in the **T**o box.

Taking Associated Files

When you use the Ami Pro File Manager to copy or move a file, you often must take the associated graphics and style sheet files along with the file.

Graphics files are necessary only if your graphics are stored in separate files. If you draw the graphics with the Ami Pro Draw feature, paste the graphics from the Clipboard, or insert the graphics with **C**opy Image (an option in the Import Picture dialog box), they are an integral part of the document. You don't need to take any associated graphics files. If you don't choose **C**opy Image when you import a graphic, however, you may want to take graphics; otherwise, you cannot display or print the graphics.

To learn whether a document has any associated files, choose **F**ile **D**oc Info and look at the Import Files box to see whether any associated files are listed.

When you choose OK or press Enter in the Copy or Move dialog box, Ami Pro displays the File Copy Options dialog box or the File Move Options dialog box, depending on the operation. Figure 21.10 displays the File Copy Options dialog box set to copy COMPUSRV.SAM with its assigned style sheet to drive B.

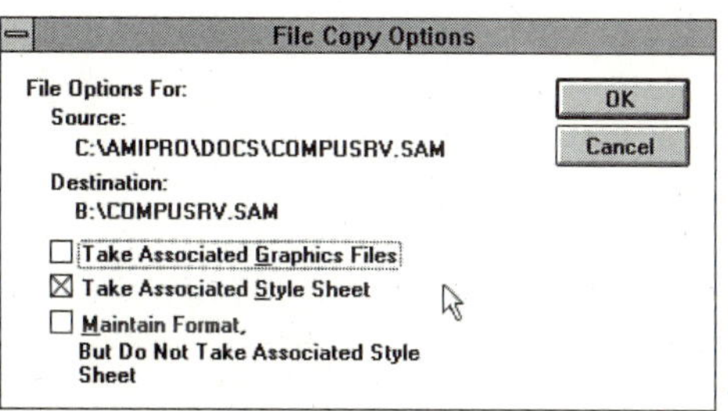

Fig. 21.10
The File Copy Options dialog box.

The File Copy Options dialog box offers the following options:

- *Take Associated **G**raphics Files.* Choose this option to copy or move original graphics files to the same location as the document.

- *Take Associated **S**tyle Sheet.* This option copies or moves the style sheet to the same location as the document. If you copy a document to a floppy disk so you can work with it on another computer, for example, you can use this option to copy the required style sheet for that document.

- ***M**aintain Format, But Do Not Take Associated Style Sheet.* This option stores paragraph styles in the document. Use this option to import your Ami Pro document into another program that cannot use Ami Pro style sheets. You also can use this option to use the document on another computer that has a style sheet with the same name but different settings.

Figure 21.11 shows the two files COMPUSRV.SAM and _ARTICLE.STY (the assigned style sheet for COMPUSRV.SAM) copied to drive B. Notice that the directory is listed as B:\.

Because every file has an assigned style sheet (whether the default or a specific style sheet) the File Copy Options dialog box or the File Move Options dialog box always appears when you copy or move a file or group of files.

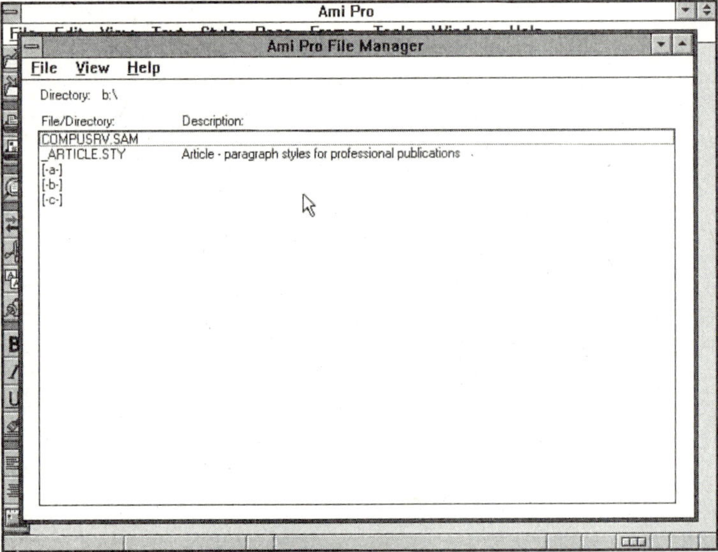

Fig. 21.11
The file and the style sheet are copied to drive B.

Renaming Files

Renaming a file with the Ami Pro File Manager is similar to renaming a file in DOS or Windows. You type a new name that replaces the previous name for the document.

In the File Manager window, select the file you want to rename and choose **F**ile **R**ename. The Rename dialog box appears. Type the new name in the **T**o text box. Choose OK or press Enter.

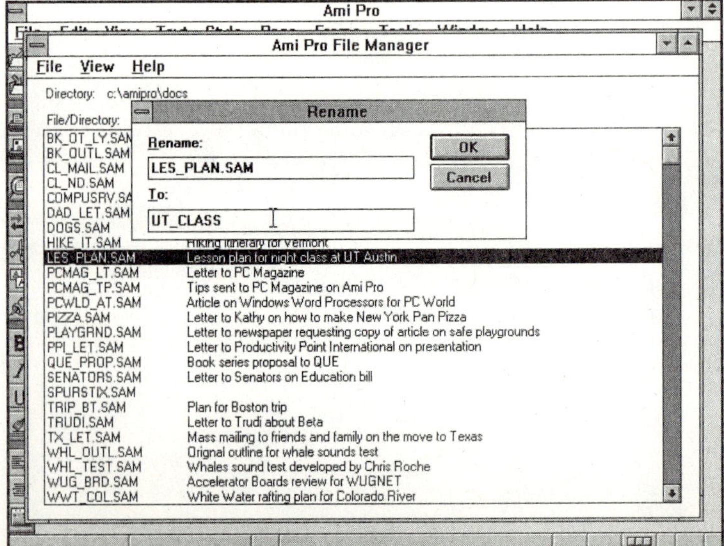

Fig. 21.12
Renaming the LES_PLAN.SAM file to UT_CLASS.SAM.

You don't have to type the extension when renaming a file; Ami Pro automatically adds the same extension. After you rename the file, the File/Directories list box organizes the files alphabetically. If you want to use a different extension for the file, type the extension when renaming the file. Remember that the default view shows only SAM files; if you rename LES_PLAN.SAM to UT_CLASS.PLN, Ami Pro doesn't list the file unless you specify the PLN extension. If you change the extension, the file description changes to `Not an Ami Pro file`.

To change the location of a file when renaming it, type the location and the new name in the **T**o text box.

> **Caution**
>
> You must provide the extension when renaming a password-protected file. All password-protected files appear with the description `Encrypted File` in the File/Directory list box.

Deleting Files

The process for deleting a file is similar to renaming or copying a file. Select the file you want to delete in the File Manager File/Directory list box and choose **F**ile **D**elete. The Delete dialog box opens, as shown in figure 21.13. If the file name is correct, choose OK or press Enter to delete the file.

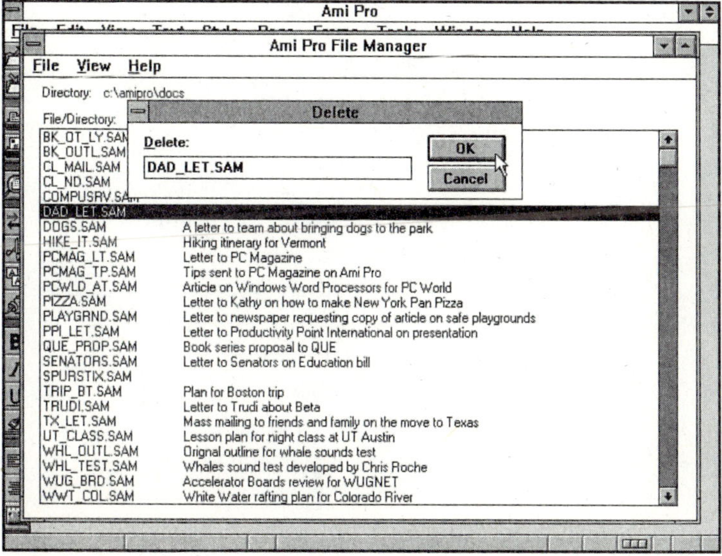

Fig. 21.13
Deleting the file DAD_LET.SAM.

You can select multiple files and then choose **F**ile **D**elete to delete them simultaneously. If a file has a Read Only attribute, you cannot delete the file. You receive the error message `Failed to Delete`. You learn about file attributes in the next section.

Tip
Instead of using the **F**ile menu, you can press Del to delete the selected file.

Caution

Use this command with extreme caution. You cannot undo or revert a delete command! Also, Ami Pro deletes password-protected files without prompting you for the password. All password-protected files appear with the description `Encrypted File` in the File/Directory list box.

Changing File Attributes

The Ami Pro File Manager can manipulate two file attributes: read-only and read-write. Most files are *read-write* files, which means that you can display (*read*) and edit (*write*) the file. If you don't want any changes to be saved to a file, or if you don't want the file to be deleted, you can give the file a *read-only* attribute.

Follow these steps to change file attributes:

1. In the File Manager File/Directory list box, select the file whose attributes you want to change.
2. Choose **F**ile **A**ttributes. The File Attributes dialog box appears, as shown in figure 21.14.
3. Choose Read **O**nly or **R**ead-Write.
4. Choose OK or press Enter.

When you make a file read-only, you are protecting it from modification in Ami Pro and by another software, including Windows and DOS. If someone opens the Windows File Manager, for example, and accidentally tries to delete CL_ND.SAM file, the read-only attribute prevents the file from being deleted. You can select multiple files and then choose **F**ile **A**ttributes to change the attributes of several files simultaneously. When you select **F**ile **O**pen and try to open a file with a read-only attribute, Ami Pro displays the message `Filename is currently protected. You cannot save any changes to it` to warn you that you cannot edit the file. Choose OK or press Enter to bring the file on-screen. The Title Bar of the document window shows `Read Only` next to the document name.

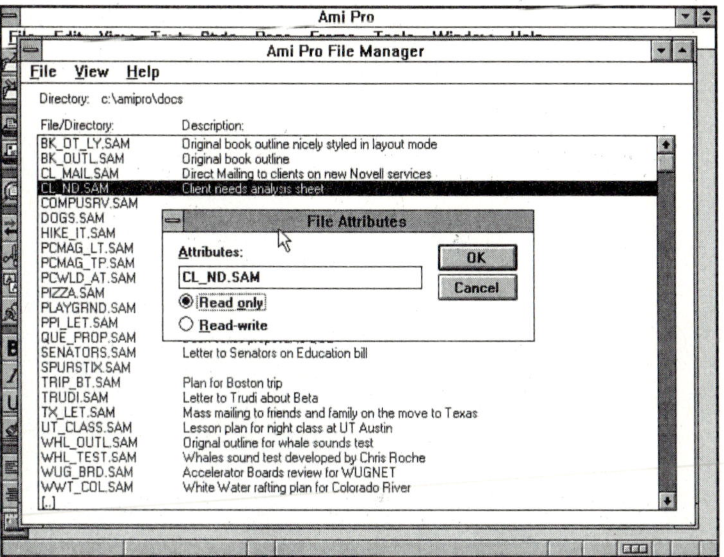

Fig. 21.14
The File Attributes dialog box, setting the file CL_ND.SAM to Read **O**nly.

The Ami Pro File Manager enables you to accomplish many of the same activities as the Windows File Manager, but the Ami Pro File Manager is designed specifically for working with Ami Pro files. The Ami Pro **F**ile menu also offers other ways of working with a document, as explained in the next section.

Viewing Document Information

You can view document information by selecting **D**oc Info from the **V**iew menu. The Doc Info dialog box appears for the selected file. This is the same dialog box that appears if you choose **F**ile **D**oc Info in the main Ami Pro program. This dialog box, however, cannot update the file statistics information. The Doc Info dialog box also cannot change the Lock for Annotations or Run Frame Macros options. The Doc Info dialog box contains a variety of information on a file: the number of pages, the date and time created, and the style sheet assigned to the document.

You cannot view the Doc Info of a password-protected file. If PROPOSAL.SAM is a password-protected file, for example, and you select PROPOSAL.SAM and then choose **V**iew **D**oc Info, Ami Pro displays the message `PROPOSAL.SAM is an encrypted file. De-encrypt and try again.`

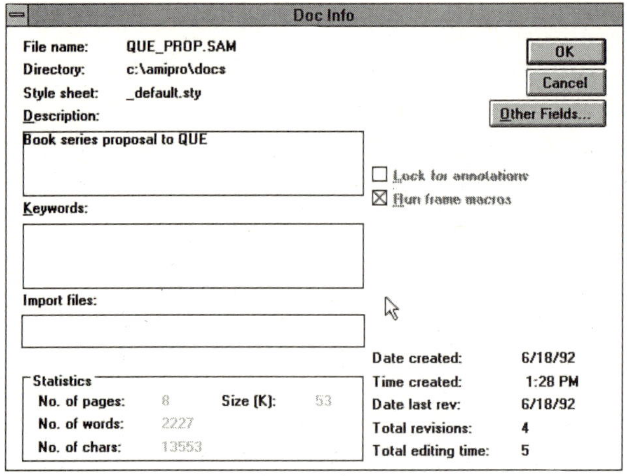

Fig. 21.15
The Doc Info dialog box for the QUE_PROP.SAM file.

Exiting the File Manager

◀ See "Saving the Active Document," p. 59

◀ See "Importing and Exporting Text," p. 676

To exit the File Manager, choose **F**ile E**x**it. Because the File Manager is a self-running program and appears in its own window, you also can close the File Manager by clicking the Control Menu in the upper left corner of the window and choosing Close. One advantage of having the File Manager appear in its own window is that the File Manager can be minimized and kept active. If you keep the File Manager active, you can switch to it, as you do in any other Windows application, by using the Windows Task List (press Ctrl+Esc). The benefit of keeping the File Manager active is that when you later switch to it, the last selection for drive and directory is still active. When you exit the File Manager and then open it again at a later time, the drive and directory revert to the default drive and directory.

Document Management with the File Menu

You can use the **F**ile menu in Ami Pro for some document-management tasks. With the **F**ile Save **A**s command, you can save an open document to a new name (or to the same name in a different directory). You also can use the **F**ile **D**oc Info command to access the Doc Info dialog box. In this dialog box, you can specify a number of options to help you track and identify documents.

Copying the Current Document

Sometimes you may want to copy and rename your Ami Pro document. Perhaps you made some tentative changes and want to retain the original document until you decide which version to use. You also may want to use a copy as a prototype for other versions.

Follow these steps to save a duplicate document:

1. Choose **F**ile Save **A**s from the Main Menu. The Save As dialog box appears (see fig. 21.16).

2. In the File **N**ame text box, type a new name for the current document. This action doesn't delete the current file and create a new one. Instead, this action keeps the current file under the old name and creates a new file with the new name.

   If necessary, use the Dri**v**es and **D**irectories options to change the path, or type the path with the file name in the File **N**ame text box.

3. If necessary, specify Ami Pro for the List Files of **T**ype option.

4. Select the **K**eep Format with Document option if you want to include formatting information in the document rather than in a separate style sheet.

5. Select the **P**assword Protect option if you want Ami Pro to request a password when the file is opened.

6. In the D**o**cument Description text box, type a description or comment up to 119 characters. (This step is optional but recommended.)

7. Choose OK or press Enter.

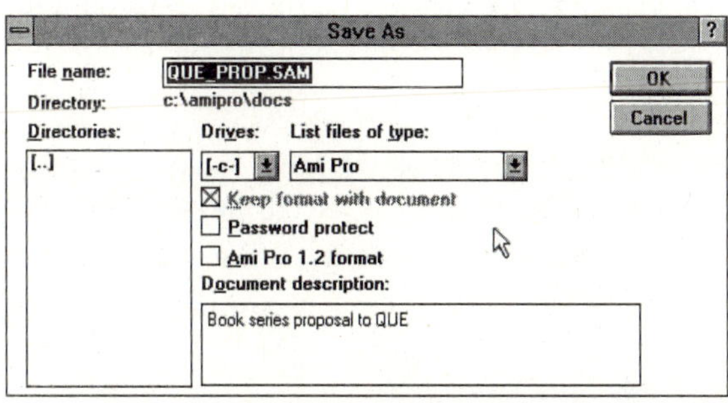

Fig. 21.16

The Save As dialog box.

Tip

If a file with the new name exists, Ami Pro displays a message that asks whether you want to overwrite the existing file. To overwrite the existing file, choose **Y**es. To return to the dialog box without overwriting the file, choose **N**o.

When you copy information to a floppy disk, you can copy the style sheet with the file by choosing **F**ile **F**ile Management and selecting the Take Associated **S**tyle Sheet option in the File Copy Options dialog box.

Caution

Before looking in the \STYLES directory for the assigned style sheet, Ami Pro looks in the directory that contains the document file. If you save a file and its assigned style sheet in the \DOCS directory, therefore, Ami Pro uses that version of the style sheet for any document using that style sheet in the \DOCS directory.

You can save selected text to a new file by using a SmartIcon. Begin by selecting the text in the current document. Then click the Save Selected Text to New File SmartIcon. In the resulting dialog box, specify a file name for the new file and choose OK or press Enter. Ami Pro creates a new file with the selected text.

Using the Doc Info Feature

The **D**oc Info option on the **F**ile menu serves several functions. You can use Doc Info in the following ways: to view information about a specific document; to add descriptions and keywords to help you identify that document later; to lock the document to control changes; to specify the running of frame macros; and to specify additional fields to insert. In this section, you learn how to take advantage of all these functions.

Viewing Document Information

The Doc Info feature provides detailed information about your document: the file name, path (including directories), style sheet, date and time created, date and time last revised, total revisions, and total editing time. To view this information, choose **F**ile **D**oc Info. The Doc Info dialog box appears, as shown in figure 21.17.

If your document has associated graphics files, Ami Pro lists these files in the Import Files list box. Choose **U**pdate to see current information on the number of pages, words, and characters, and the file size in kilobytes. This information is dimmed until you choose **U**pdate.

Adding Descriptions and Keywords

Displaying document information isn't the only purpose of the Doc Info dialog box. You also can use this dialog box to add information to help you identify the document later. This information is the same as the information used in the Save As dialog box.

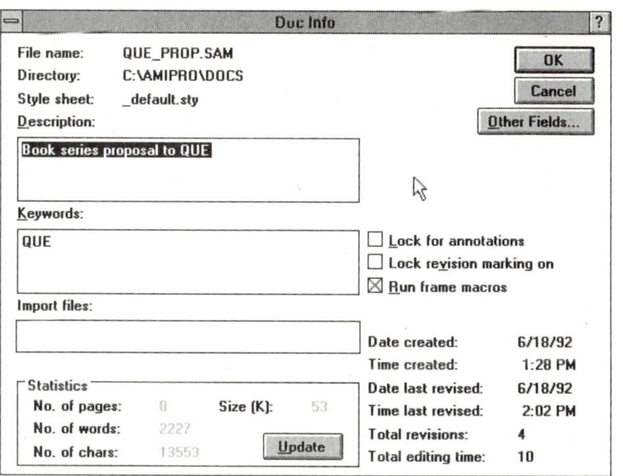

Fig. 21.17
The Doc Info dialog box.

You can type a description for your document in the **D**escription text box of the Doc Info dialog box. This description then appears in the following places:

- In the Description text box in the Open dialog box.
- Next to the file listing when you choose **F**ile **F**ile Management.
- In the Description text box when you choose **F**ile **N**ew and select the style sheet for the new document in the New dialog box. If you select List by Description, the style sheets are listed by description rather than by style sheet name in the Style Sheet for New Document list box.

You can modify the description in the Doc Info dialog box or the Save As dialog box. This modification changes the information every place where it appears.

In the **K**eywords text box, you can type any words that help you identify or work with your document. Because Ami Pro doesn't check for keywords in the document, these keywords are for your own reference and don't need to be words that appear in the document. Ami Pro also doesn't restrict the number of keywords you enter or what you use (for example, commas, periods, and spaces) to separate keywords from each other.

Keywords are important if you use the Locate Files by Doc Info SmartIcon to locate files based on the information provided in the Doc Info dialog box. This information includes keywords. Unless you know in advance what you want to type in a document, typing the keywords before you create the document is difficult. After you complete the document, however, you can identify keywords easily. If you work with many documents that you intend to keep for long periods of time, the keywords can help you identify a document and distinguish one document from other documents with similar names.

Locking Documents

The Doc Info dialog box offers two options that enable you to control whether and how changes are applied to the document: **L**ock for Annotations and Lock Re**v**ision Marking On.

To enable people to add notes to the document (see "Using Notes," later in this chapter), but otherwise prevent any changes to the document, select the **L**ock for Annotations option. Ami Pro then accepts notes but doesn't allow any changes to the document. The word Locked appears after the file name in the Title Bar when this option is selected.

Select Lock Re**v**ision Marking On if you want all changes to the document to be marked as revisions. All text entered or edited in the document appears in a different color and typeface attribute than the original text. The changes appear in blue and italics by default. Also, if you edit or delete text, the changed text remains in the document in red with a strikethrough character. You can adjust the appearance of the changes with the revision marking feature, which is explained later in this chapter. Figure 21.18 shows a document with changes made after selecting Lock Re**v**ision Marking On in the Doc Info dialog box. The words `Revision Only` appear after the file name in the Title Bar.

When you select this option, you also lock on revision marking in the Revision Marking dialog box, accessed from the Too**l**s menu (see "Using the Revision Marking Feature," later in this chapter). This option turns on `REV` in the Status Bar. To unlock this option, you must enter your name in the User Setup dialog box.

Running Frame Macros

You also can set frame macros in the Doc Info box. If you create macros that you want to run each time you select a frame, select **R**un Frame Macros in the Doc Info dialog box to execute the macros.

If you activate this option (which applies only to the document in which you activated the option), and then you assign a macro to a frame in the document, you also must select the R**u**n Macro option in the Modify Frame Layout dialog box to run the frame macro.

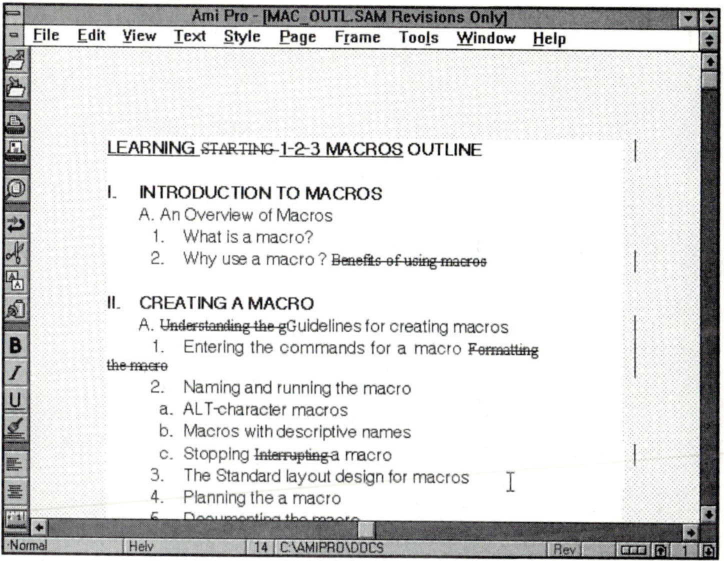

Fig. 21.18
The revised document with Lock Revision Marking On selected.

The **R**un Frame Macros option in the Doc Info dialog box is a deceptively powerful feature. If you assign a macro to a frame and have this option in effect, Ami Pro runs the macro when you choose the frame. The frame becomes a "button." With the **R**un Frame Macros option you can use any macro; for example, you can run GAME.SMM, which initiates a game that the Ami Pro designers built into the program. When you choose the frame, Ami Pro runs the macro and starts the game as a separate program.

Specifying Other Fields To Insert

Fields refers to several categories in the Doc Info dialog box: Filename, Path, Style Sheet, Document Description, and so on. You can insert the fields into your document. You use the **E**dit **I**nsert menu to insert a field. You are probably familiar with the **E**dit **I**nsert option from other chapters of this book. When you choose **E**dit **I**nsert, the **I**nsert menu appears, as shown in figure 21.19.

When you choose Doc **I**nfo Field from the **I**nsert menu, the Doc Info Field dialog box appears (see fig. 21.20). Position the insertion point where you want the information to appear in the document. Highlight the field you want to insert in the Insert Doc Info Field list box and choose Insert. The program inserts the field information into the document at the insertion point location. When you finish inserting fields, choose Cancel to return to the document. Figure 21.21 shows a document with Doc Info fields inserted to create a quick document summary as the last page of the document.

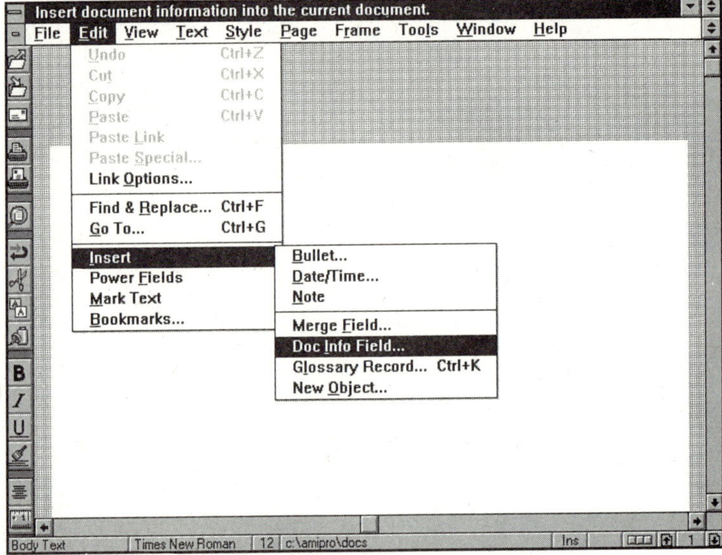

Fig. 21.19
The **E**dit **I**nsert menu.

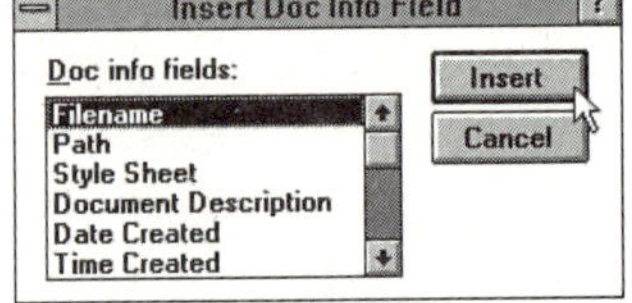

Fig. 21.20
The Insert Doc Info Field dialog box.

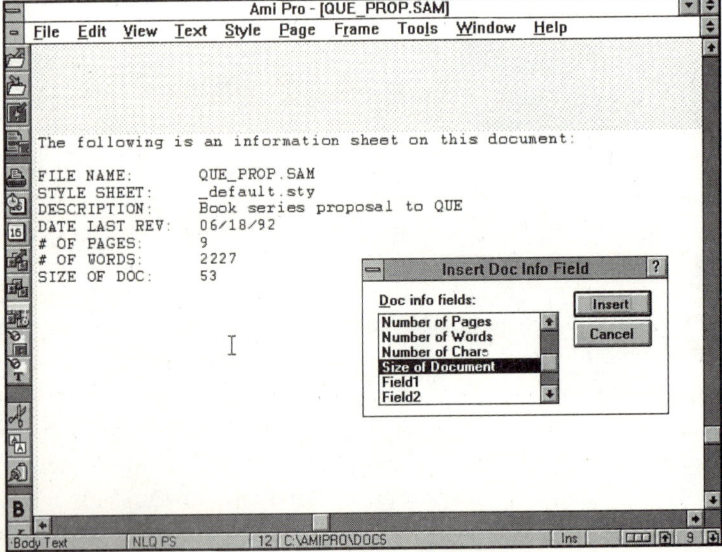

Fig. 21.21
Creating a document summary with Doc Info fields.

Note

Be sure to update the Doc Info dialog box statistical fields (Number of Words, Number of Pages, and Number of Chars) before inserting them into a document. You update these fields by opening the Doc Info dialog box and clicking **U**pdate in the Statistics section.

Another valuable feature available in the Doc Info dialog box is the capability of customizing fields for insertion into a document. Follow these steps to customize the fields that you can insert:

1. Choose **O**ther Fields. The Doc Info Fields dialog box appears, as shown in figure 21.22.
2. Choose **R**ename Fields to rename the fields to correspond to the information in the field. The Rename Doc Info Fields dialog box appears. Rename the fields as desired. Figure 21.23 shows the changes to fields 1 through 4.
3. Type the information into the fields. The information in this example is the author, company, business phone, and CompuServe ID (see fig. 21.24).
4. Choose OK or press Enter to return to the Doc Info dialog box; then choose OK or press Enter to return to the document.

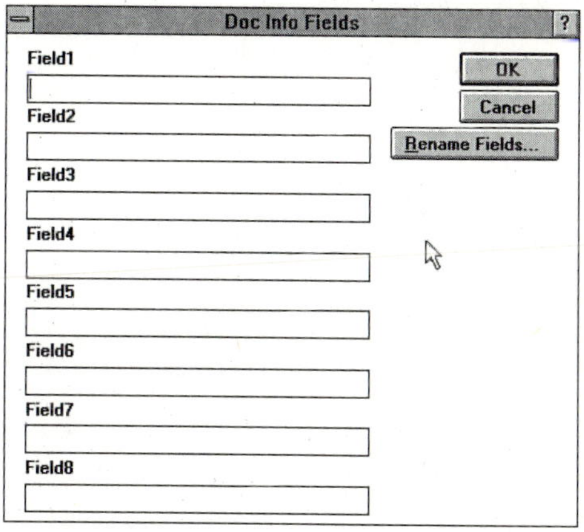

Doc Info Fields

Field1

Field2

Field3

Field4

Field5

Field6

Field7

Field8

OK

Cancel

Rename Fields...

Fig. 21.22
The Doc Info Fields dialog box.

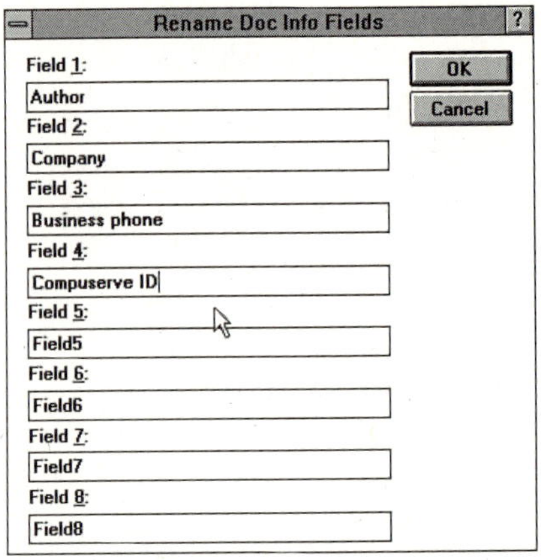

Fig. 21.23
The Rename Doc Info Fields dialog box with fields 1 through 4 renamed.

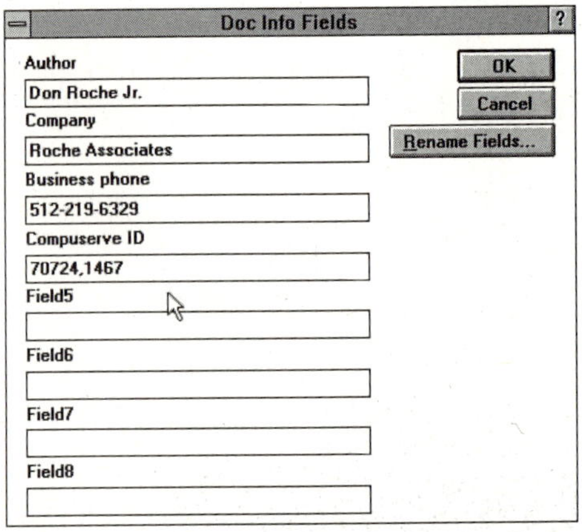

Fig. 21.24
The completed dialog box.

Figure 21.25 shows the QUE_PROP.SAM document with the information inserted from the newly created fields.

Ami Pro saves the Doc Info with the file when you execute a **F**ile **S**ave command. If you need to adjust the Doc Info frequently, you can save by clicking the Save with Doc Info SmartIcon. This SmartIcon opens the Doc Info dialog box for editing or updating before the save operation executes.

You can incorporate a few other special fields into a document. When you choose **E**dit **I**nsert **D**ate/Time, Ami Pro displays the Insert Date/Time dialog box (see fig. 21.26). You also can click the Date/Time SmartIcon to access the dialog box.

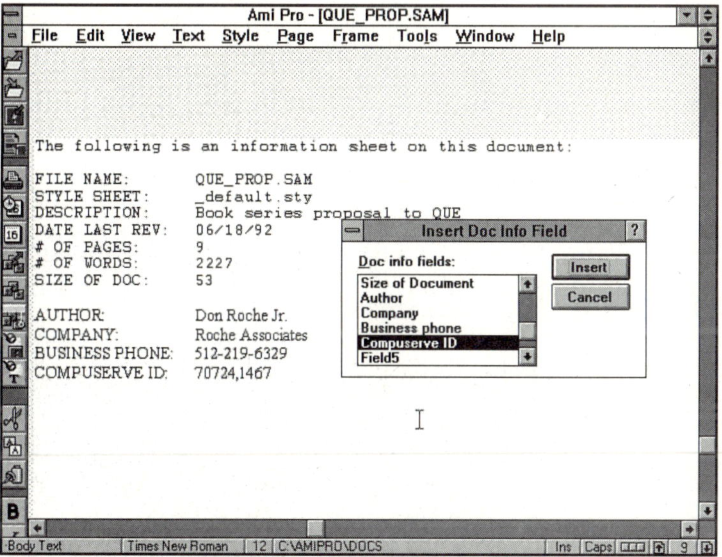

Fig. 21.25 The document summary is now complete, with the author information inserted from the Doc Info dialog box.

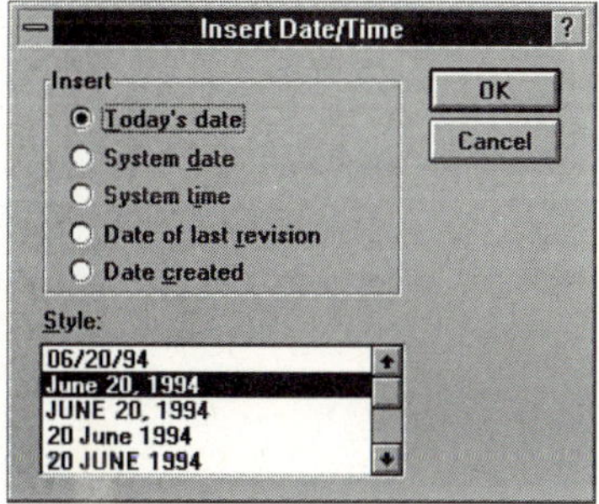

Fig. 21.26 The Insert Date/Time dialog box.

In this dialog box, you can choose from the options described in the following list:

- *Today's Date*. This option inserts the current system date; you can choose from many date formats. (The date isn't inserted as a field.) You also can insert the current date by clicking the Insert Date SmartIcon. If you insert the current system date into a document and then open the document tomorrow, the date displayed is the system date at the time the date was inserted.
- *System Date*. This option displays the current date.
- *System Time*. This option displays the current time.

◀ See "Basic Editing," p. 73

◀ See "Setting Defaults," p. 228

◀ See "Creating a Frame," p. 498

◀ See "Modifying the Appearance of Frames," p. 515

▶ See "Recording and Playing Macros," p. 799

- *Date of Last **R**evision.* This option is the same as the Date Last Revised option in the Insert Doc Info Field dialog box.
- *Date **C**reated.* This option is the same as the Date Created option in the Insert Doc Info Field dialog box.

Using the Revision Marking Feature

Besides the file management and Doc Info capabilities discussed earlier, Ami Pro provides additional tools for managing documents. Another useful way to manage a document is to track revisions.

Revision marking enables you to recognize and identify changes to a document. You can specify how you want revisions to appear so that the revisions stand out from prior versions of the text. All insertions and deletions of text, tables, frames, and graphics appear as revisions.

After you finish making revisions, you can review, accept, or cancel the revisions. Accepted revisions become part of the normal text. In the following paragraphs, you learn how to take advantage of Ami Pro's revision-marking feature. This feature can be particularly helpful if a document is created through the collaborative efforts of several people. If the revisions of one author are marked, for example, another author easily can discern revisions from original text. The other author doesn't have to be present when the revisions are made.

Marking Revisions

Before you begin marking revisions in a document, you must set the options to control how the revisions appear. Because you must be able to identify your revisions (including text added to and deleted from the original) you may want the revisions to be a particular color or to use a particular typeface attribute. You also can use the time-honored technique—in technical documentation—of indicating revised text with a mark in the margin.

Note

You can turn on revision marking quickly by clicking the Insert/Typeover button on the Status Bar. Click the button until Rev appears on the button. This action turns on revision marking, using the default settings.

Follow these steps to set the options and mark the revisions:

1. Choose Too**l**s Re**v**ision Marking. The Revision Marking dialog box appears, as shown in figure 21.27.

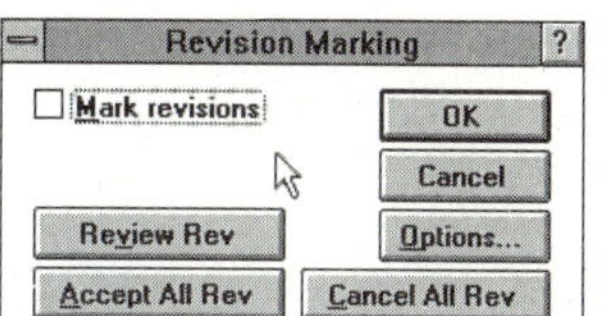

Fig. 21.27
The Revision Marking dialog box.

2. Choose **O**ptions. The Revision Marking Options dialog box opens, as shown in figure 21.28. This figure displays choices other than the default settings.

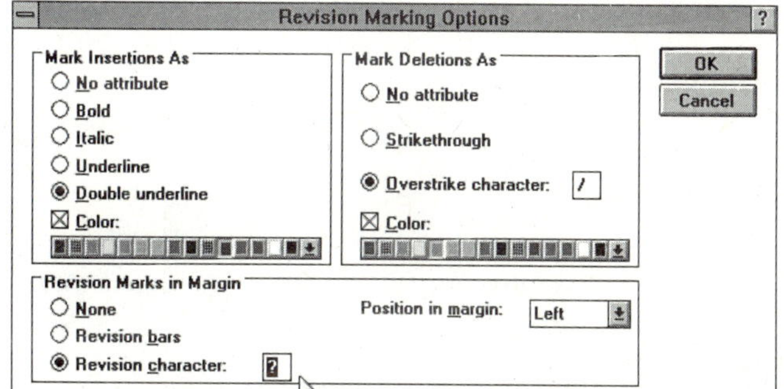

Fig. 21.28
The Revision Marking Options dialog box with setting changes.

3. In the Mark Insertions As section of the dialog box, choose a text attribute for insertions: **N**o Attribute (normal text), **B**old, **I**talic, **U**nderline, or **D**ouble Underline. The default attribute is **I**talic.

4. Select the **C**olor option and choose a color in the color bar to use for inserted text and graphics. (This step is optional but recommended.) The default color is blue.

   You can select from the colors displayed in the color bar or click the arrow button at the end of the color bar to select from a full range of colors and patterns. You can combine an attribute and a color, and you can customize the colors.

5. In the Mark Deletions As section of the dialog box, choose an attribute for deletions: **N**o Attribute, **S**trikethrough (places a line through deleted text), or **O**verstrike Character (displays a specified character over deleted text). **S**trikethrough is the default attribute for deletions.

If you choose **O**verstrike Character, type the desired overstrike character in the text box. You can type any character from the keyboard or the ANSI character set.

6. Select **C**olor and choose the desired color in the color bar for deleted text and graphics. (This step is optional but recommended.) As in step 4, you can choose from a wide palette of colors or specify a custom color.

7. In the Revision Marks in Margin section of the dialog box, indicate whether you want a character to appear in the margin to mark lines in your document containing insertions or deletions. Choose **N**one for no marker, Revision **B**ars for a vertical line, or Revision **C**haracter for a specific character. The default is Revision **B**ars for a vertical line in the margin. Left is the default choice for Position in **M**argin.

   If you choose Revision **C**haracter, type the desired character in the text box. You can use any character from the keyboard or the ANSI character set. A revision mark is especially helpful when you print because color may not be available to distinguish revised text on the printed copy.

8. From the Position in **M**argin list box, choose the location for margin revision marks: Left, Right, or Rt/Left. (Left is the default setting; use Rt/Left if your document uses facing pages.)

9. Choose OK or press Enter to return to the Revision Marking dialog box.

10. Choose **M**ark Revisions.

11. Choose OK or press Enter to return to your document.

Figure 21.29 shows a document after revisions have been made. Changes made in the document after setting up revision marking show the colors and attributes selected. The additions, deletions, and edits clearly stand out from the original text. The asterisks along the right side of the page help identify any paragraph lines with changed text. (In this black-and-white figure, of course, you cannot see that the additions are in green and the deletions are in blue.) If your document contains frames, added frames show a plus sign (+), and deleted frames show an X.

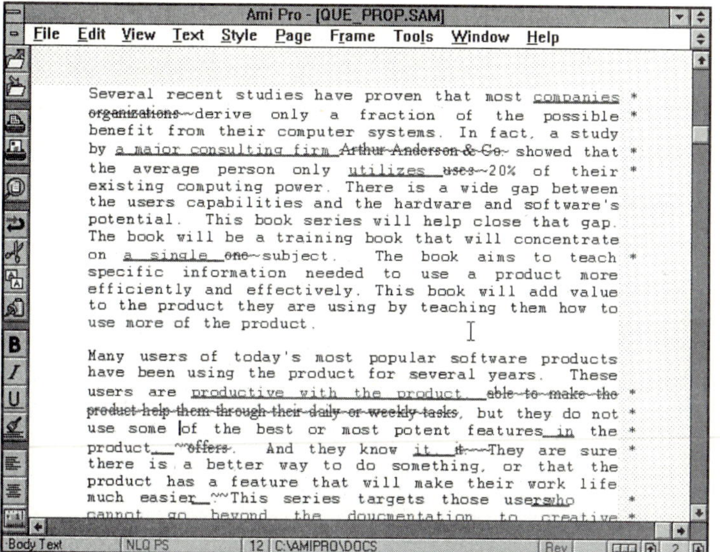

Fig. 21.29
A document after marking revisions.

> **Note**
>
> If you choose **N**o Attribute in the Mark Insertions As or Mark Deletions As sections of the Revision Marking Options dialog box, select a color with the **C**olor bar so revisions are distinct from the original version of your document.

If you modify text by using text attributes or making style changes, those changes aren't marked by Revision Marking.

When you finish making revisions and you want to return to normal editing mode, turn off revision marking by turning off the **M**ark Revisions box in the Revision Marking dialog box. You also can turn off revision marking by clicking the Insert/Typeover button (which turns to `Rev` when revision marking is on) until `Type` or `Ins` appears on the button.

Reviewing Revisions

After you make changes with revision marking, you can review the changes and choose to accept or cancel them. Begin by choosing Too**l**s Re**v**ision Marking to open the Revision Marking dialog box. Then choose one of the following options:

- Choose **A**ccept All Rev to accept and put into effect all changes made while using revision marking.

- Choose **C**ancel All Rev to revert to the original version and cancel all changes made while using revision marking.

- Choose Re**v**iew Rev to review each change individually. When you choose this option, Ami Pro highlights the first insertion in the document and displays the Review Revision Marking dialog box (see fig. 21.30). Indicate whether you want to accept, skip, or cancel the insertion. Ami Pro continues to move through the document, highlighting each revision and prompting you for a specific action, until you press Cancel or you have no more revisions to review.

If you choose **A**ccept This Insertion, Ami Pro accepts the insertion and removes the revision mark for the accepted insertion. If you choose Ca**n**cel This Insertion, Ami Pro cancels the revision by deleting the indicated insertion. If you review revisions, Ami Pro starts from the first revision of the document and indicates whether each revision is an insertion or a deletion. If you skip revisions as you are reviewing, the skipped revisions continue to appear with the attributes and colors you specified earlier for revision marking.

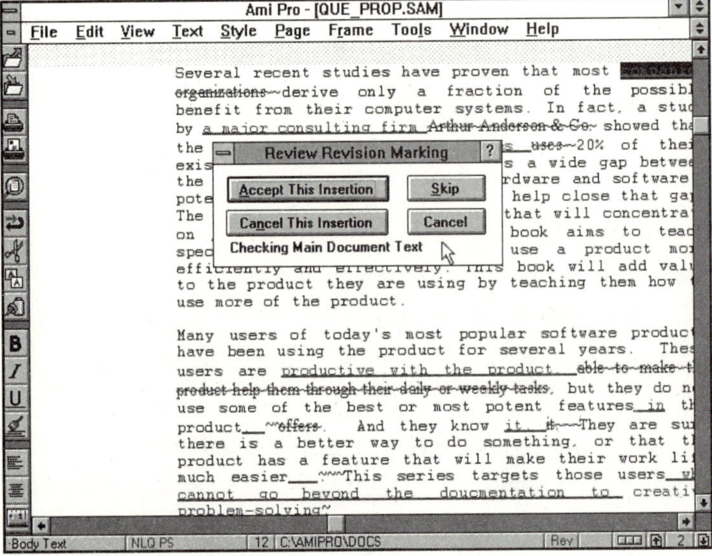

Fig. 21.30
The Review Revision Marking dialog box.

Tip
You can review a text frame by double-clicking the frame and then selecting Too**l**s Re**v**ision Marking Re**v**iew Rev.

You can review part of a document by selecting text and then selecting Too**l**s Re**v**ision Marking Re**v**iew Rev. You can check a frame or a table for revisions, however, only by checking the entire document; frames and tables are skipped if you select text and then proceed with the review.

Comparing Documents

Ami Pro's document comparison feature helps you keep track of changes made to two copies of the same document. If two or more people are editing one document on different computers, for example, ensuring that both copies of the document are updated can be difficult. In the end, you want one final, updated document.

Tip
If you close a document while still in revision marking mode and then reopen the document, Ami Pro prompts you to indicate whether you want to enter revision marking mode. Choose **Y**es or **N**o.

By comparing the two documents with Doc Compare, you can ensure that no changes are missing in the final version of the document. The differences between the two versions are marked with the same marks used in revision marking mode.

If you don't want to use the default revision markings, choose Too**l**s Re**v**ision Marking **O**ptions and specify the options you want to use for marking revisions. (See the earlier section, "Marking Revisions," for instructions on setting options.)

To compare two documents, open the document you want to compare. This *source document* is your final version. In the preceding section, for example, suppose that the QUE_PROP.SAM document was edited and then saved as QUE_REV.SAM. You can compare these two documents. Begin by opening the document QUE_REV.SAM.

◄ See "Basic Editing," p. 73

◄ See "Modifying the Standard Page Layout," p. 120

◄ See "Using the Modify Page Layout Dialog Box," p. 121

To compare the original and modified documents, follow these steps:

1. Choose Too**l**s Doc Com**p**are or click the Document Compare SmartIcon. The Doc Compare dialog box opens, as shown in figure 21.31.

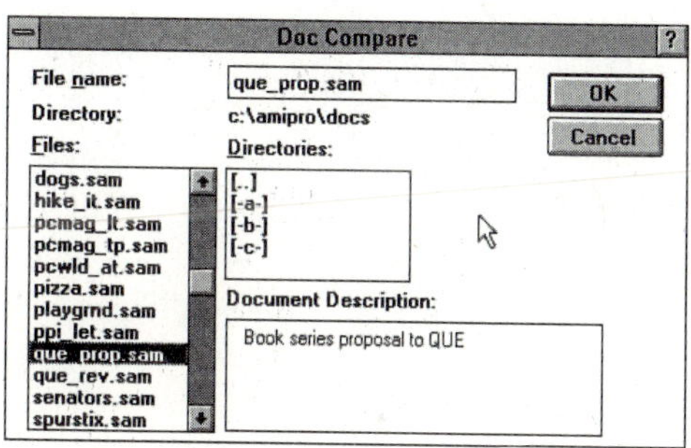

Fig. 21.31
The Doc Compare dialog box.

2. If necessary, use the **D**irectories list box to specify the drive and the directory for the second document. (If you prefer, you can type the path with the file name in the File **N**ame text box.)

3. Specify the file (the second document) that you want to compare with your current, open document. For this example, choose QUE_PROP.SAM from the **F**iles list box or type the file name in the File **N**ame text box.

4. Choose OK or press Enter.

The differences between the two documents are integrated into the source document, as shown in figure 21.32. Ami Pro displays the differences as revision insertions and deletions by using revision marking colors and attributes.

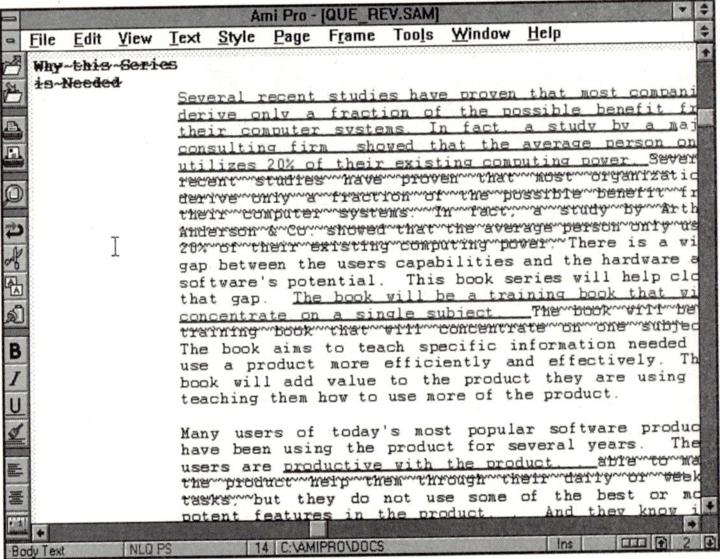

Fig. 21.32
The two documents integrated into the source document QUE_REV.SAM.

Note

Ami Pro doesn't bring pictures or tables from the second document into the current document.

As figure 21.32 shows, in cases where the text differs in the two documents, Ami Pro displays the text from the source document as revision-inserted text and the text in the second document as revision-deleted text.

After comparing the documents, you can use the Revision Marking dialog box to accept, delete, or review revisions to the original document (QUE_REV.SAM in this example). Follow these steps:

1. Choose Tools Revision Marking. The Revision Marking dialog box appears.

2. Choose Review Rev to view the differences between the two documents (as described in "Reviewing Revisions," earlier in this chapter).

3. Save the revised document.

You can use any of the following methods to save the document:

◄ See "Saving the Active Document," p. 59

- Save the changes to the source document by choosing **F**ile **S**ave.
- Don't save the changes at all; choose **F**ile **R**evert to Saved.
- Save the changes to another document by choosing **F**ile Save **A**s. In this case, the source document remains unchanged.

Using Notes

Ami Pro notes are comments that don't affect the regular text and are inserted into a document. You can insert a note anywhere within existing text—in the main body, in a header or footer, within the text in a frame, a table, or even within a footnote. Inserting notes in a document is like writing comments in the margin of a printout. Notes are especially helpful for reminding you to follow up on certain details of the text. You also can use notes to leave messages about the document to someone else working on the same document. Figure 21.33 shows a document with a note that appears as a small rectangle (next to the word `OUTLINE`). Figure 21.34 shows the note opened on-screen.

You close a note by clicking outside the note window.

Ami Pro offers several features that enable you to identify easily who has written which notes, as described later in this section.

Setting Note Defaults

In this section, you learn how to control the appearance of notes with default settings and how to insert, view, edit, remove, and print notes.

Before using notes, choose Too**l**s **U**ser Setup and specify a note color in the User Setup dialog box, shown in figure 21.35. If you want your initials to appear next to the note, specify your initials in the **I**nitials text box. Then select the Display Initials in **T**ext option.

Figure 21.36 displays the document with the note after turning on the Display Initials in **T**ext option.

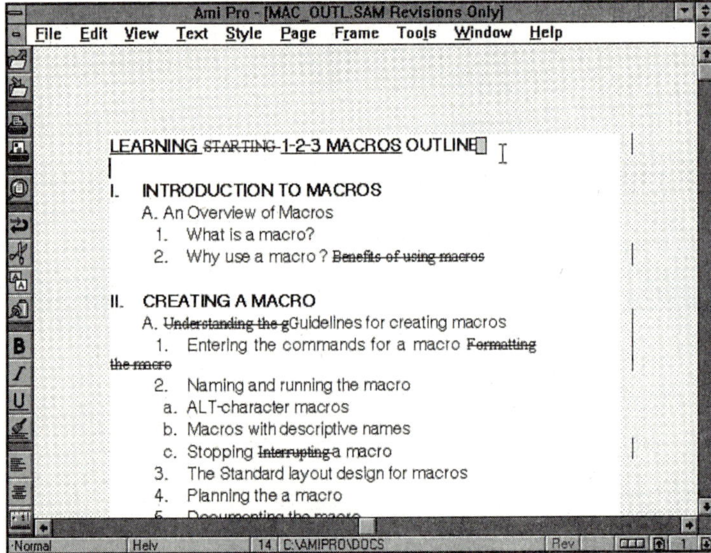

Fig. 21.33 A document containing a note.

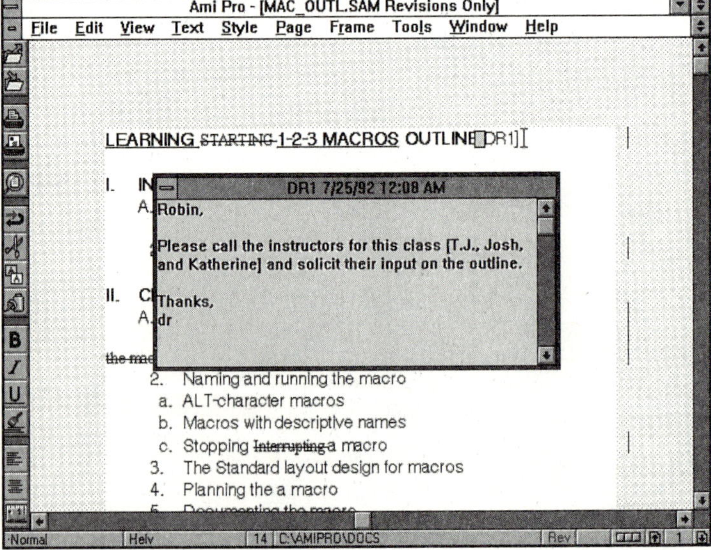

Fig. 21.34 The note opened on-screen.

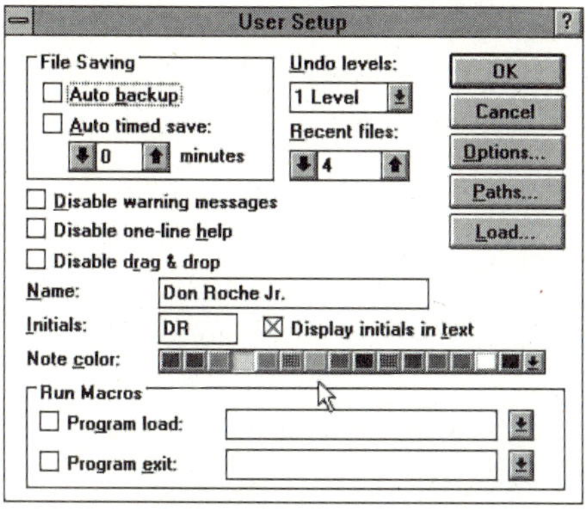

Fig. 21.35
The User Setup dialog box.

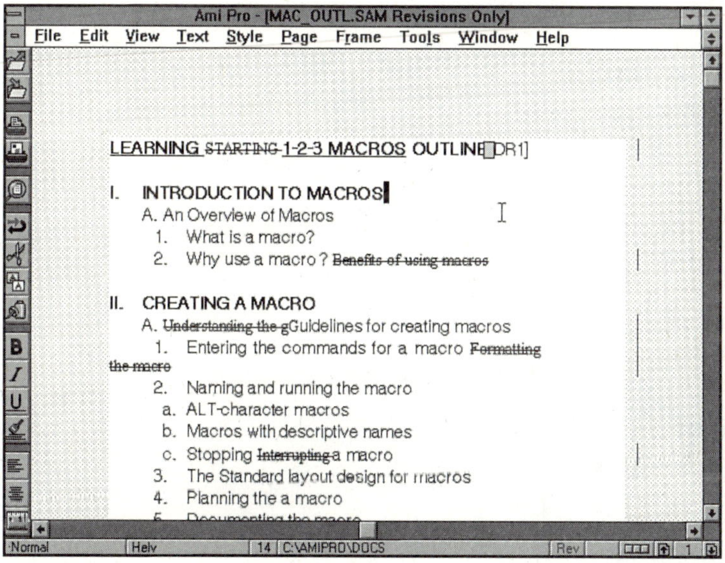

Fig. 21.36
The note with the initials of the author next to it.

To have each note appear as a small colored rectangle in the text, choose **V**iew View **P**references **N**otes. (See the Ami Pro documentation for more information.) If you don't select the option, the note doesn't appear—you can find the note with the **E**dit **G**o To command, however.

Tip
If more than one person is creating notes, specify a different color for each person to distinguish his or her notes from the notes of other users.

Inserting Notes

After choosing note defaults, you can insert notes in a document. Place the insertion point where you want the note and choose **E**dit **I**nsert **N**ote. A blank note appears on-screen with the date and time the note is created and the author's initials across the top of the window. Type the note, which can be any length, in the note window. You also can paste text copied from the main document (or any document) to create a note. To exit the note box, click the note window's Control Menu and choose Close. You also can press Esc or click outside the note window.

To reposition a note, create a note at the new position, cut the text from the current position, and paste it into the new position. Then delete the old note.

> **Note**
>
> A number for the note appears in the Title Bar and the note box after the initials. Ami Pro numbers notes sequentially (the order they appear in the text), not in the order you create them. If you create a new note before an existing note, therefore, Ami Pro renumbers all notes that follow the new one.

Viewing Notes

To view a note, you can double-click the note rectangle if the Display Notes option in the View Preferences dialog box is on. The note window opens and displays the note.

If note marks aren't visible in the document, follow these steps:

1. Choose **E**dit **G**o To, press Ctrl+G, or click the Go To SmartIcon. The Go To dialog box appears (see fig. 21.37).
2. In the **N**ext Item list box, select Note.
3. Choose `Go To ^H` or press Enter.

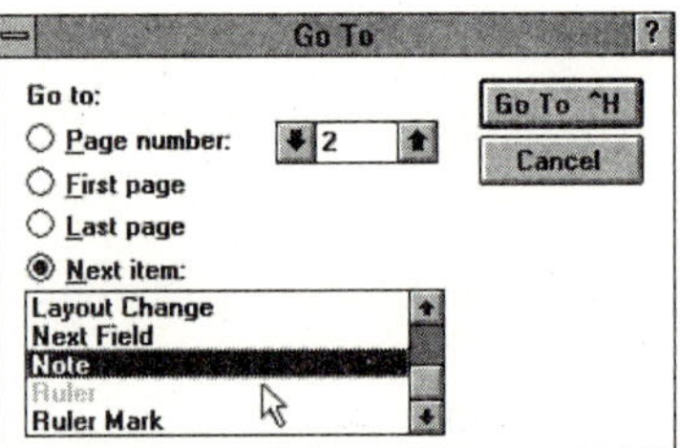

Fig. 21.37
The Go To dialog box.

◄ See "Using Go To," p. 174

When Ami Pro displays the note window, the date and time the note was created appear at the top of the window. The note writer's initials and the number of the note appear also. If this note isn't the note you want, continue to press Ctrl+H.

A Go To command ensues from the current cursor position. Position the cursor at the top of the document to make sure you find the note. (Go To doesn't scroll to the top of the document to continue searching after reaching the end of the document.)

Editing Notes

If you know how to display a note, editing a note is no different from other editing. You edit notes with the same editing keys and techniques you use to edit documents: Del, Backspace, and so on. You view the note as described in the preceding section and then edit the note just as you edit your main document. You can resize the note window to see more text if you have a long note.

Removing Notes

You can remove a note from the note window or from the text. If the note you want to delete appears in the note window, click the Control Menu in the note window (see fig. 21.38) and choose **R**emove This Note.

If the note you want to delete doesn't appear in the note window, place the insertion point on the note mark and press the Del key. Ami Pro displays a message that asks whether you want to delete the note. Choose **Y**es or press Enter to delete the note.

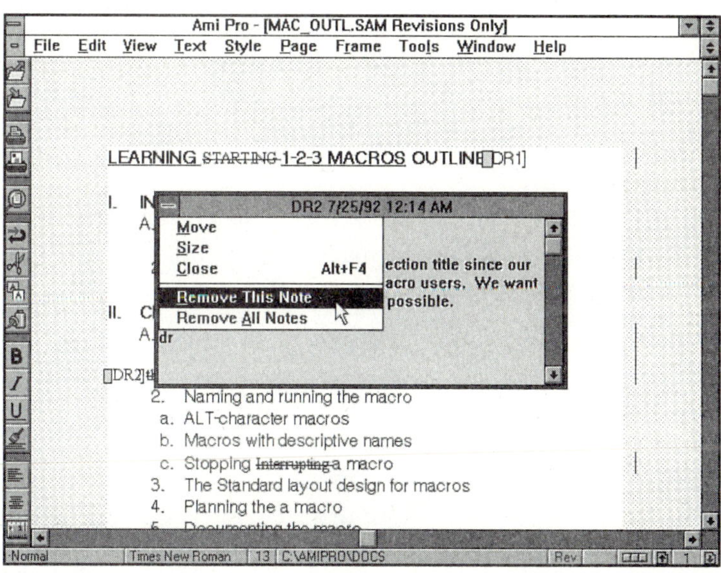

Fig. 21.38
The note window Control Menu.

After your document is in final form, you may want to remove all the notes. In this case, choose the Remove **A**ll Notes option in the Control Menu of the note window. Ami Pro removes all the notes.

Tip

If you delete text that includes a note, you also delete the note. A warning message prompts you to be certain that you want to execute the delete operation.

Printing Notes

You can print the notes with the document. Ami Pro prints the author's initials and the note number in brackets at the note's location in the text. The program also prints an index on a separate page at the end of the document, including the complete notes, author's initials, and note numbers.

Tip
If you don't specify the author's initials in the User Setup dialog box, you cannot print the initials.

Follow these steps to print notes:

1. Choose **F**ile **P**rint. The Print dialog box appears.
2. Choose **O**ptions. The Print Options dialog box opens.
3. Choose With **N**otes.
4. Choose OK or press Enter twice to return to your document.

Using Master Documents

Ami Pro's Master Document capability provides another way to manage documents. With a master document, you can manage several documents at once.

In a *master document,* multiple documents function as one document. Using master documents is valuable when you work on a long project, such as a book that contains multiple chapters. Because a computer works faster with smaller documents, making each chapter a separate document and binding the chapters with a master document is faster and more efficient than working with the chapters individually.

Ami Pro can generate a table of contents, a list of figures, an index, and consecutive page numbering for all the combined documents. With the master document, you also can print all the documents as one document.

In this section, you learn how to create a master document, add files to and remove files from a master document, specify table of contents and index options, and print a master document.

Creating a Master Document

You can use an existing file, such as the first chapter of a book, for the master document source file. Note that when you generate a table of contents or index, or print the entire master document, this document must be the current document.

If you use an existing document, and you want to include a description identifying the document as the source file (and perhaps listing the included documents), choose **F**ile **D**oc Info to add the description. (See "Adding Descriptions and Keywords," earlier in this chapter, for more information.)

To create a new file to use for the master document source file, choose **F**ile **N**ew and supply the details required in the New dialog box. To create a master document, follow these steps:

1. Choose **F**ile Mast**e**r Document. Ami Pro displays the Master Document dialog box shown in figure 21.39.

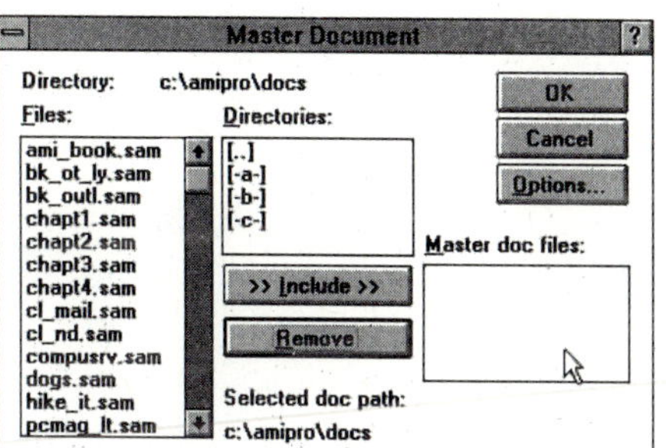

Fig. 21.39
The Master Document dialog box.

At first, files are listed in the **F**iles list box but not in the **M**aster Doc Files list box.

2. In the **D**irectories list box, specify the drive and directory of the first file you want to include in the master document.

3. In the **F**iles list box, highlight the first file you want to include in the master document. The files *must* be specified in the order you want them included in the master document because this is the order in which Ami Pro prints them and compiles the index.

4. Choose **I**nclude. The specified file appears in the **M**aster Doc Files list box, as shown in figure 21.40.

5. Repeat steps 2 through 4 for each file you want to include, specifying the files in the order in which you want them to appear in the master document.

6. Choose OK or press Enter.

After completing this procedure, you can insert files into the master document or delete files from the master document, as explained in the next two sections.

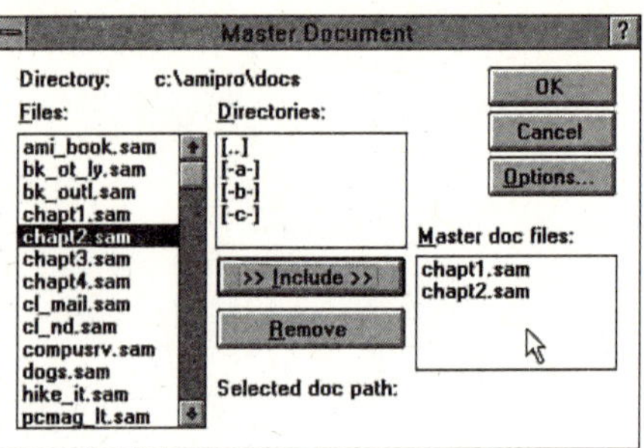

Fig. 21.40
Specifying files to include in the master document.

Inserting a File into a Master Document

You can insert a file into the master document file list rather than include the file at the end of the list. This capability is useful if you are writing a lengthy document, such as a textbook or manual, and need to insert another chapter. To insert a file into a master document, follow these steps:

1. With the master document source file open, choose **F**ile Mast**e**r Document. The Master Document dialog box appears.
2. In the **F**iles list box, select the file you want to insert.
3. In the **M**aster Doc Files list box, select the file you want the inserted file to precede.
4. Choose **I**nclude. Ami Pro lists the file in the **M**aster Doc Files list box and inserts the file into the master document.

Deleting a File from a Master Document

Deleting a file from a master document removes the files from the master document but doesn't delete the file. You may want to delete a file from a master document if the file is a chapter that you decide to remove from your book.

Follow these steps to delete a file from a master document:

1. From within the master document source file, choose **F**ile Mast**e**r Document. The program displays the Master Document dialog box.
2. In the **M**aster Doc Files list box, select the file you want to delete.
3. Choose **R**emove. Ami Pro removes the selected file from the **M**aster Doc Files list box and the master document.

You can delete a master document by deleting the master document source file. You delete only the master document collection, not the individual files.

If the master document source file is a file you must retain, however, follow the procedure just described to delete the individual files from the master document.

You can browse your master files quickly if you run the MASTRDOC macro. This macro adds the choice **M**aster Browser to the **F**ile menu. This macro also enables you to view the documents in your master document and move to the preceding or next file in the master document.

Specifying Table of Contents and Index Options

In Chapter 12, "Using Reference Tools," you learn about creating tables of contents and indexes for individual documents. You also can create a table of contents for a master document. To create an overall table of contents for the files included in the master document, the corresponding headings in each file included in the master document must be assigned the same paragraph styles.

You can specify options for master document tables of contents and indexes in the Master Document Options dialog box. From the master document source file, choose **F**ile Mast**e**r Document; then choose **O**ptions in the Master Document dialog box. The Master Document Options dialog box appears, as shown in figure 21.41.

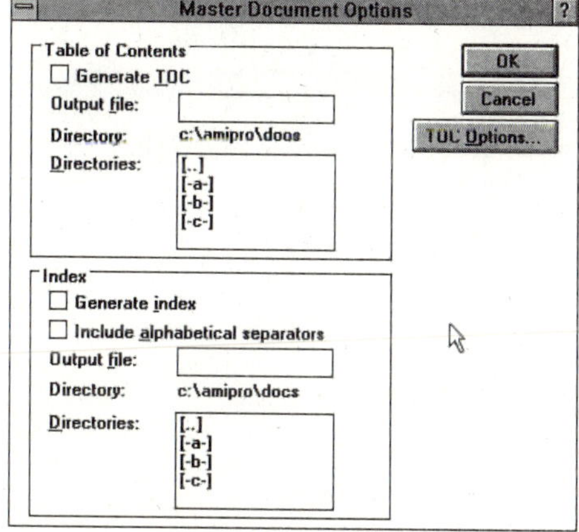

Fig. 21.41
The Master Document Options dialog box.

To set options for an index for your master document, follow these steps from the Master Document Options dialog box:

1. Select the Generate **I**ndex option.
2. Select the Include **A**lphabetical Separators option to include separators (A, B, and so on) in the index.

3. In the **D**irectories list box, specify the drive and directory for the file in which you want to store the index.

4. In the Output **F**ile text box, type the name of the file in which you want to store the index.

5. Choose OK or press Enter to generate the index and return to the master document source file. For this example, however, skip this step and continue with the table of contents options described in the next procedure.

To set options for a table of contents for the master document, follow these steps:

1. In the Master Document Options dialog box, select the Generate **T**OC option.

2. In the **D**irectories list box, specify the drive and directory for the file in which you want to store the table of contents.

3. In the Output **F**ile text box, type the name of the file in which you want to store the table of contents.

4. Choose TOC **O**ptions. The TOC Options dialog box appears, as shown in figure 21.42. In this dialog box, create different paragraph styles for the headings in the table of contents.

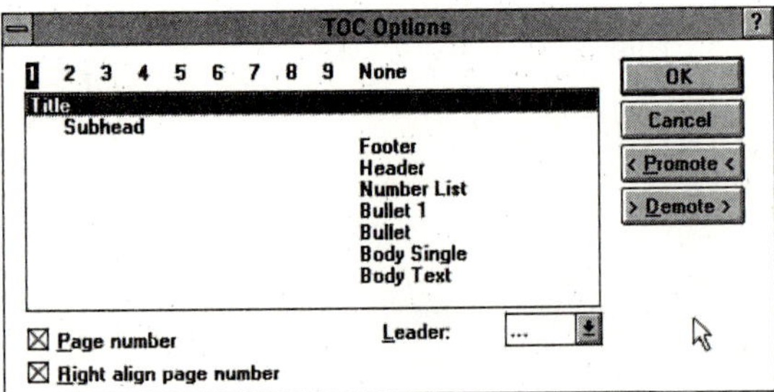

Fig. 21.42
The TOC Options dialog box.

5. Choose OK or press Enter three times to return to the master document source file. You now are ready to have Ami Pro generate the table of contents.

6. With the insertion point in the source document, choose Too**l**s TOC, I**n**dex. The TOC, Index dialog box appears. The specifications entered in the Master Document Options dialog box are retained here.

7. Choose OK or press Enter to generate the table of contents.

Generating a table of contents or an index for a master document is the same procedure you use to create a table of contents for any other document. The difference is that the process must begin from the master document source file.

Printing a Master Document

Printing a master document follows the same procedure as printing any other document, except that you must print from within the master document source file. When specifying the page range in the Print dialog box, select **A**ll. When printing a master document, if one of the included files is open you get the message `Filename.sam is already open.` You cannot save any changes to this file. Choose OK or press Enter to continue the print job. If you assign page numbers to each of the files included in the master document, Ami Pro overrides those numbers so the printout has a consecutive string of numbers. In other words, if the last page of the first file included in the master document is page 17, the first page of the second document included in the master document is page 18.

◀ See "Opening an Existing Document," p. 67

◀ See "Printing Documents," p. 207

◀ See "Creating a Table of Contents," p. 354

◀ See "Creating an Index," p. 366

▶ See "Using Predefined Macros," p. 810

Send Mail

Electronic mail and messaging have become standard office procedures. Ami Pro introduces a new feature that enables users to create mail items and send them directly to cc:Mail or Lotus Notes. Not only can you send and receive messages, but you can attach documents for review or editing purposes.

To send a mail item, follow these steps:

1. Choose **F**ile Send **M**ail.
2. Choose **C**ompose Mail Message. The Mail front end screen appears as shown in figure 21.43.
3. Fill in the subject and type the body of the message.
4. To fill in the address, put your cursor in the To: field and choose the Address button, which displays the Address dialog box. Now select the recipient(s) name from the E-mail directory or select a Public/Private Mailing List, and choose Add to insert the name(s) into the mail message. Choose OK when the list is complete. The name(s) will be added to the To: field in the Mail Memo. Use this same procedure to add addresses in the cc: and bcc: fields.
5. Choose the Send button at the top and the Send Mail Options dialog box appears, as shown in figure 21.44.

Tip
Choose the Make Default button if you want Ami Pro to automatically use the options you selected for future mail messages.

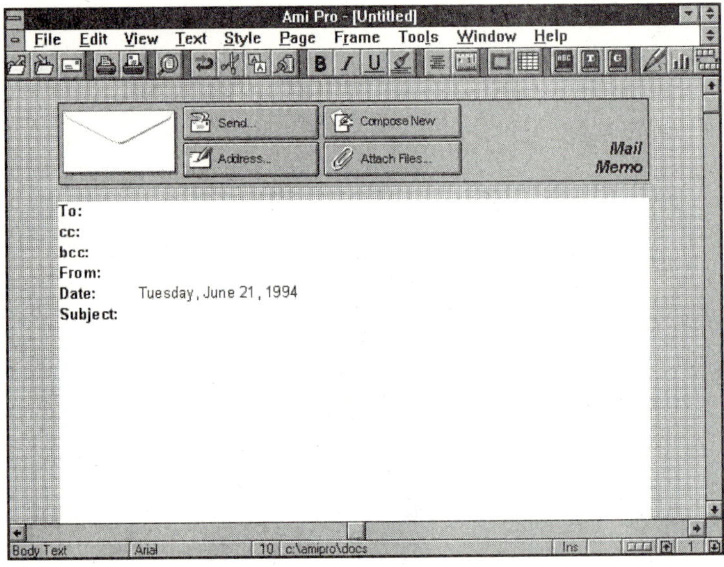

Fig. 21.43
The Mail front end screen.

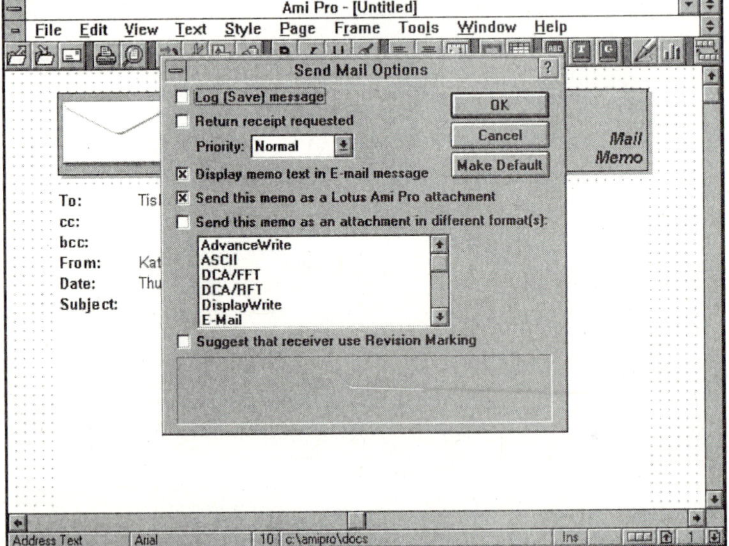

Fig. 21.44
The Mail Options dialog box.

6. Choose different Send Mail options as needed, and when you're ready to send the mail item, choose OK or press Enter.

In the Send Mail Options dialog box you have the capabilities of logging a message, being notified whether the person has received or opened the mail message, and displaying the memo text in your e-mail message. You also can attach a complete Ami Pro document or files of different formats such as ASCII.

7. When your Mail Memo has been sent, an Ami Pro Mail dialog box appears confirming that your mail item has been sent. Choose OK to close this box.

Tip
Choose Return receipt requested if you want notification that the message has been opened.

To Reply to a Mail Message

1. While in cc:Mail or Lotus Notes, open the mail notification.

2. If the sender selected Attach current Ami Pro document in the Send Mail Options dialog box, double-click the file attachment MAILMEMO.SAM which will load Ami Pro and opens the Send Mail Memo screen for your reply, as shown in figure 21.45.

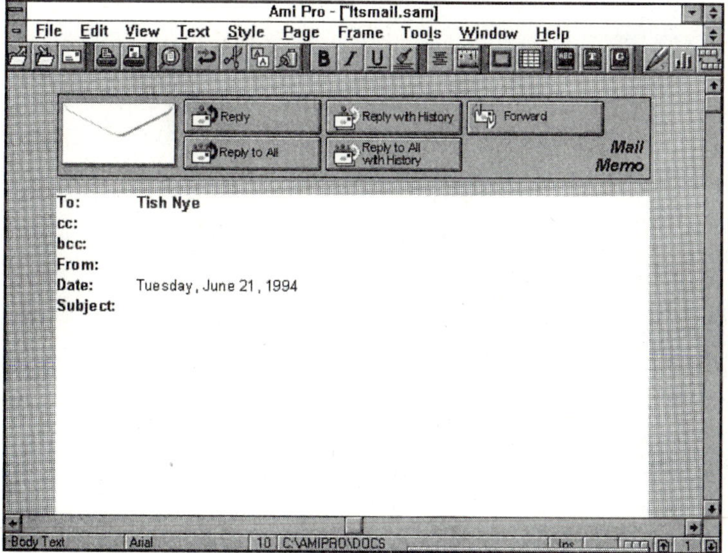

Fig. 21.45
The Ami Pro mail screen for replying to a message.

3. Select the appropriate Reply option button.

Reply	Mails a response to the sender using Send Mail Memo.
Reply to all	Mails a response to the sender as well as additional names listed in the address.
Reply with History	Mails a response to the sender with a copy of the original message.

Reply to all with History	Mails a response to the sender as well as additional names listed in the address along with a copy of the original message.
Forward	Passes the mail message to the name specified in the address.

4. After choosing the Reply option, the buttons at the top change to Send options.

5. Type your response to the mail messaage.

   Choose the Send button at the top.

6. Specify any Send Mail options from the Send Mail Options dialog box.

   Choose OK or press Enter.

Summary

In this chapter, you learned that Ami Pro offers powerful options for manipulating documents and files. You learned how to use the Ami Pro File Manager for copying, moving, and working with files and the **F**ile menu for specifying and finding information about a document. You discovered how to mark revisions, compare documents, and use notes. You also learned how to create a master document for working with multiple documents. Finally, you learned how to utilize Ami Pro to send electronic messages as well as files if you have cc:Mail or Lotus Notes installed.

In the next chapter, you explore another powerful Ami Pro feature: the capacity to create detailed equations within a document, using special equation symbols, characters, letters, and formatting.

Chapter 22

Working with Equations

Equations always have presented a problem for word processing software. They often require special characters beyond those on the standard keyboard. The equation symbols often don't occur on a single line but on multiple lines. Certain symbols—such as brackets below a line—are almost impossible to enter with conventional word processing.

Ami Pro tackles the special problems of creating equations and offers an Equation Editor. The Equation Editor provides great flexibility in entering mathematical symbols and dealing with the special effects that equations require. Ami Pro equations can include text, numerals, and mathematical function symbols of all kinds.

In this chapter, you first learn how to access the Equation Editor so you can create equations. Next, you explore the equation screen and learn how to use the equation icons to enter all the components of an equation. You learn how to navigate in equations and how to select, copy, and delete text. You learn how to edit equations and change their appearance. Finally, you learn how to import and export equations as special files called TeX files.

Note

To use the Equation Editor, you must specify Install Ami Pro with Options and select Equations when installing Ami Pro. For the equations to appear properly, you also must install a Windows Symbol font, such as the Adobe Type Manager Symbol font that comes with Ami Pro.

Entering and Exiting the Equation Editor

Before you can use equations in your document, you must access the Equation Editor by choosing Too**l**s **E**quations or by clicking the equations icon. The equations screen becomes the active window, as shown in figure 22.1.

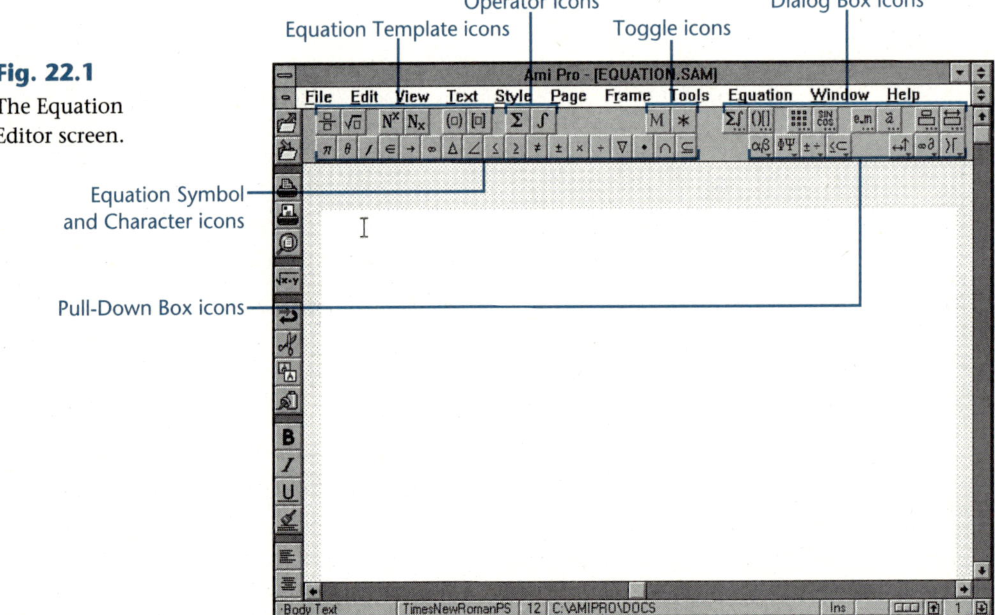

Fig. 22.1
The Equation Editor screen.

Tip
The equation icons appear under the SmartIcon Bar if the SmartIcon Bar is positioned at the top of the screen.

Equations are contained in the document in an Ami Pro frame. If you create the frame before entering the Equation Editor, the frame cannot contain any prior text. You cannot add equations to a frame containing text, but you can add text to a frame that contains equations. One frame may contain multiple equations, in addition to text describing the equations.

If you don't create a frame before entering the Equation Editor, Ami Pro creates a frame for you at the position of the insertion point when you enter the Equation Editor. When you choose Too**l**s **E**quations, Ami Pro creates a frame in your document and switches to the equations screen (refer to fig. 22.1).

You may prefer to let Ami Pro create the frame. When Ami Pro creates the frame, the program sizes and positions the frame and ensures that the frame follows standard mathematical typesetting conventions.

Note

Don't create a frame before using the Equation Editor. Ami Pro creates a frame when you click the equations icon or select Too**l**s **E**quations, and the size of this frame adjusts to the size of the equation. The size of a frame added before you bring up the Equation Editor *doesn't* adjust to the size of the equation. As the equation size changes, you must adjust the size of the frame manually.

Suppose that you need to put the quadratic equation into your document. You have entered text, so now you switch to the equation Editor by choosing Too**l**s **E**quations or by selecting the equations icon. Ami Pro creates a frame at the position of the insertion point in the document and switches to the Equation Editor. When you enter the equation, it appears on-screen, as shown in figure 22.2. The equation frame is invisible.

When you print a document containing equations, the equations appear in the printed document just as they do on-screen. You can omit printing the equation frames by selecting the Without **P**ictures option in the Print Options dialog box (choose **F**ile **P**rint **O**ptions to access the dialog box).

You can see the equation screen in standard, custom, or enlarged view. Enlarged view (choose **V**iew **E**nlarged) shows the equation much more clearly. All figures after 22.2 showing equations in this chapter show the equation in enlarged view.

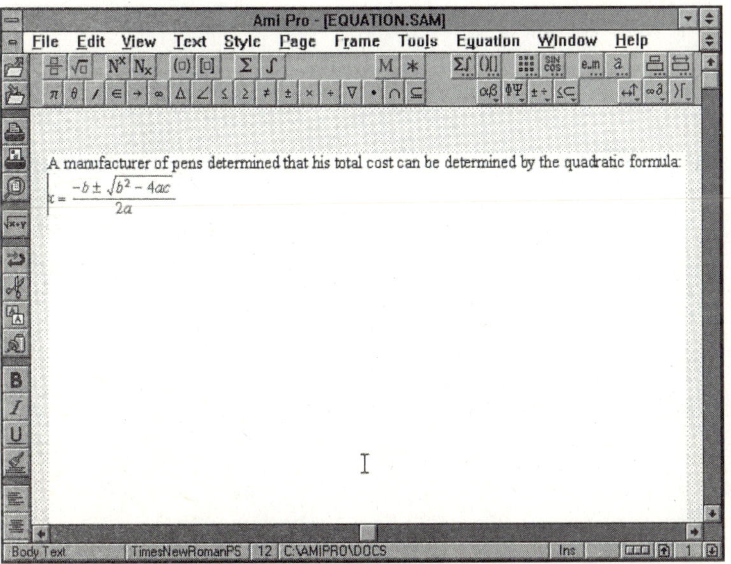

Fig. 22.2
The quadratic equation.

Tip
Create equations in enlarged view, which provides a "zoomed-in" view of your work and, therefore, a much clearer look at the equation.

To exit the Equation Editor, click the mouse outside the frame containing the equation or press Esc twice.

Because you inadvertently may leave the Equation Editor, you can reenter it from your document by double-clicking the mouse pointer inside the frame containing the equation. (With the keyboard, select the frame and press Enter.)

Using the Equation Icons

As figure 22.2 shows, two rows of icons appear at the top of the screen in the Equation Editor. To create equations, use the equation icons (as explained in the following sections). The icons act in the following ways:

◀ See "Printing Documents," p. 207

◀ See "Creating a Frame," p.498

- *Equation template icons.* Equation template icons place a *template* (or pattern) in the equation frame and enable you to add numbers or other symbols within that template. You use template icons to enter fractions, radicals, brackets, and other formats. Figure 22.3 shows an equation you can type by using the templates for brackets, parentheses, fractions, and superscripts.

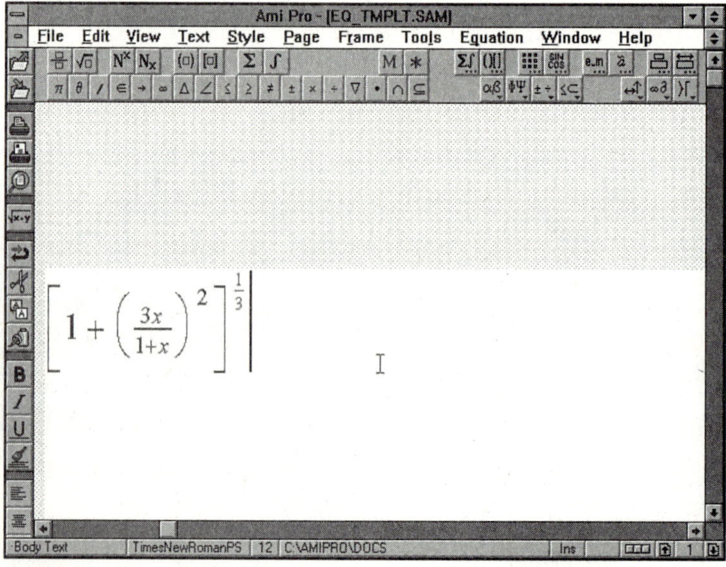

Fig. 22.3
An equation using the brackets, parentheses, fractions, and superscript templates.

- *Equation operator icons.* The equation operator icons are the symbols for sum and integral. Figure 22.4 shows an equation using the integral operator.

- *Toggle icons.* The M icon switches between mathematical characters and text within the equation frame. The * icon switches between showing and hiding input boxes and matrix lines.

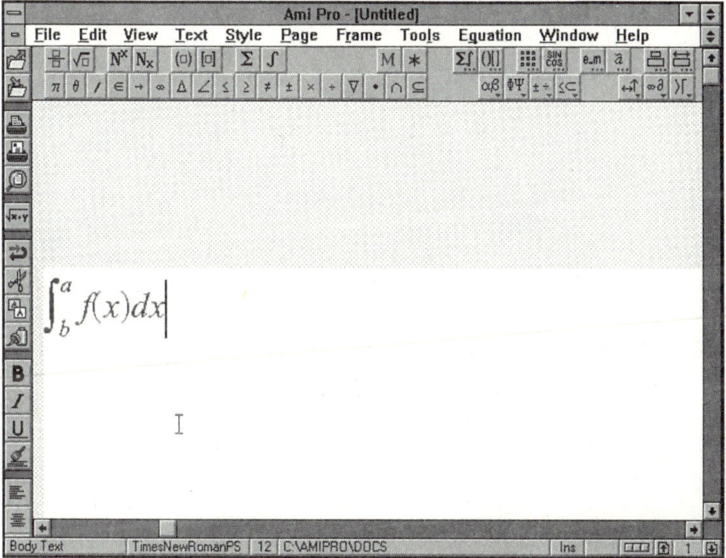

Fig. 22.4
An equation with an integral symbol.

- *Equation dialog box icons.* The equation dialog box icons access additional dialog boxes to provide even greater ranges of mathematical symbols and capabilities, such as creating a matrix, adding labels above or below the equation, or using custom brackets. Each equation dialog box has an ellipsis (...) in the lower right corner of the icon.

- *Equation symbol and character icons.* You use the equation symbol and character icons to insert into an equation 18 commonly used mathematical symbols, such as pi or the infinity symbol.

- *Equation pull-down box icons.* The equation pull-down box icons access additional symbols and operators—such as Greek letters, arrows, and delimiters—that you may need to complete your equation. Each equation pull-down box has a small downward pointing triangle in the lower right corner of the icon.

Using the Equation Template Icons

To create an expression with the equation template icons, you first select the icon for the mathematical symbol you want to use. Then you add numbers or symbols to complete the mathematical expression.

Note

On a color screen, mathematical expressions appear in red, text in black italic, and functions in gray; however, you can change the colors. (See "Setting Screen Preferences," later in this chapter.) Keep in mind that colors only appear in a printout if you have a color printer and italics appear only in a printout if your printer is capable of italic print.

Six equation template icons are located in the top left row of the equation screen: fraction, radical, superscript, subscript, parentheses, and brackets (see fig. 22.5). The sections that follow provide descriptions for using each of these icons.

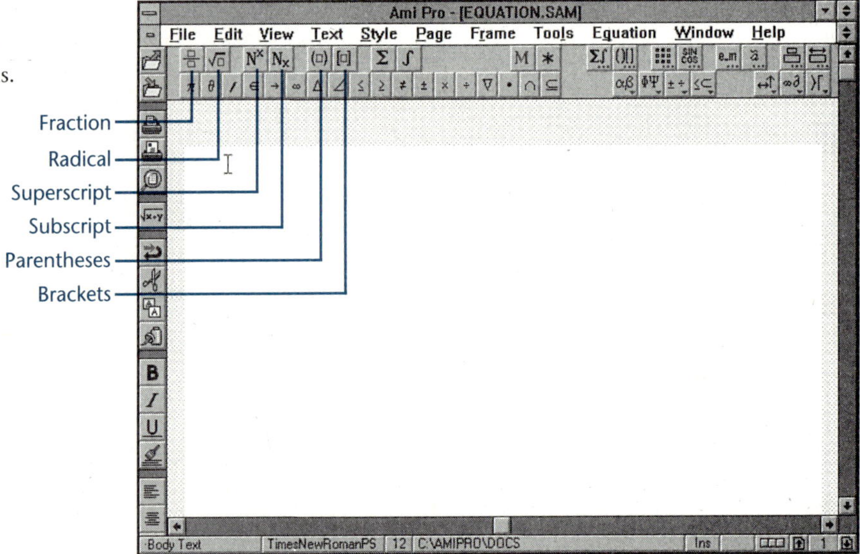

Fig. 22.5
The equation template icons.

Tip
Use the space bar in the Equation Editor to end input in any input box and to move the insertion point around in the equation.

Fractions

Suppose that you want to use a fraction in an equation, with x–2 as the numerator and y–3 as the denominator. To include the fraction in the equation, follow these steps:

1. At the point in the equation where you want to insert the fraction, click the fraction icon, press Ctrl+1, or select E**q**uation **I**nsert **F**raction. Ami Pro displays a fraction symbol with two input boxes, as shown in figure 22.6.

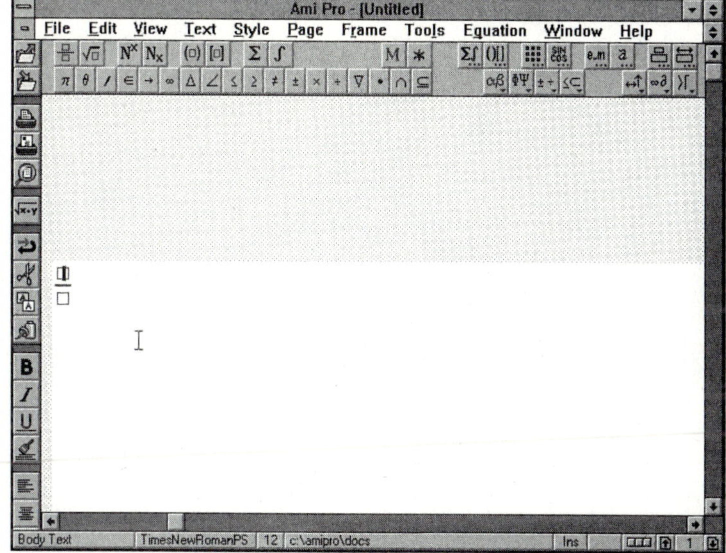

Fig. 22.6 The fraction template.

2. Type the appropriate letters or numerals to complete the mathematical expression in the first input box. (Ami Pro always positions the insertion point in the numerator input box.) For this example of a fraction, type **x–2** in the upper input box. The fraction expands as needed to hold all the characters you type.

   Ami Pro uses input boxes in all templates to show where the characters should be entered. Input boxes appear on-screen (unless you hide them, using the * toggle icon) but don't print.

3. Use Tab or click in the next text box to move to the denominator.

4. Type the mathematical expression you want to use as the denominator in the second input box. For this example, type **y–3**.

5. After you finish the fraction, click at the end of the expression or press the space bar. The insertion point moves to the right of the fraction.

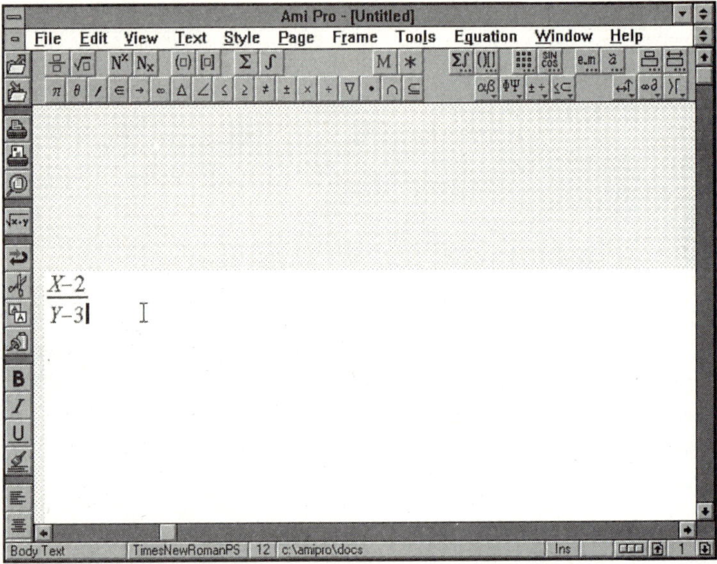

Fig. 22.7
The fraction x–2 over y–3.

Radicals

You use radicals a little differently than you use fractions. When you use the radical icon, only one input box appears, on the assumption that you are entering a square root. If you want to use a cube or some other root, however, you can press Tab to create a second input box. Then type the root.

To use the radical icon, follow these steps:

1. At the point in your equation where you want to insert the radical, click the radical icon, press Ctrl+2, or select E**q**uation **I**nsert **R**adical. Ami Pro displays a radical symbol with an input box inside, as shown in figure 22.8.

2. Type the expression that you want in the radical input box. If you want to enter the mathematical expression for the cube root of x–1, for example, type **x–1** in the input box.

3. To indicate a square root, skip to step 5; otherwise, press Tab to edit the root. When you press Tab, Ami Pro creates an input box in which you can enter the desired root (see fig. 22.9).

4. Type the root of the radical. For a cube root, for example, type **3**.

5. Click at the end of the radical or press the space bar.

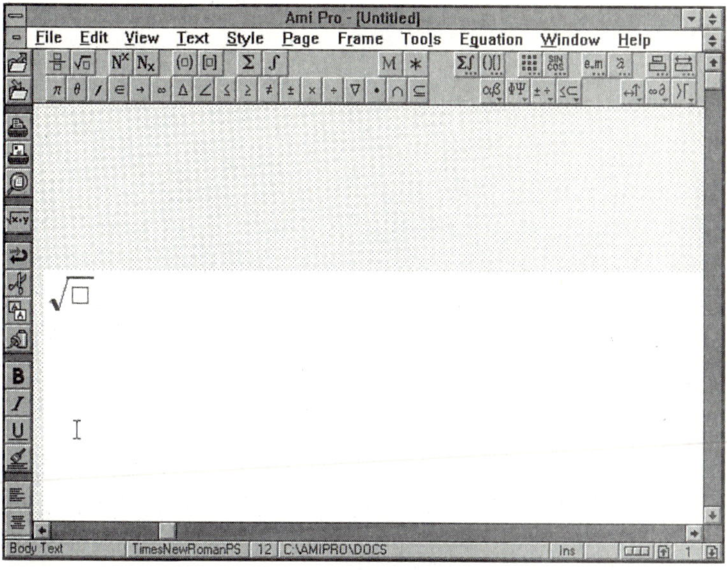

Fig. 22.8
The radical template.

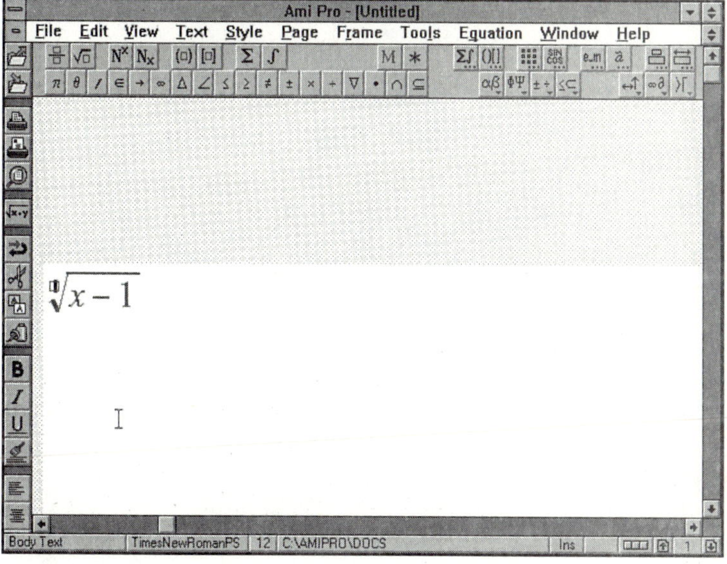

Fig. 22.9
A radical with an input box for the root.

Superscripts and Subscripts

To enter a superscript or subscript, you first enter the expression to be superscripted or subscripted. Then you click the icon and add the superscript or subscript. Follow these steps:

1. Enter the expression for which you want the superscript or subscript to operate. If you want to enter x^5 or H_2O, for example, type **x** or type **H**.

2. To superscript, click the superscript icon or press Ctrl+3, Ctrl+up arrow, or the minus (–) key on the numeric keypad. (You also can implement superscript by selecting E**q**uation **I**nsert Su**p**erscript.)

   To subscript, click the subscript icon or press Ctrl+4, Ctrl+down arrow, or the plus (+) key on the numeric keypad. (You also can implement subscript by selecting E**q**uation **I**nsert Su**b**script.)

   In either case, an input box appears (see fig. 22.10).

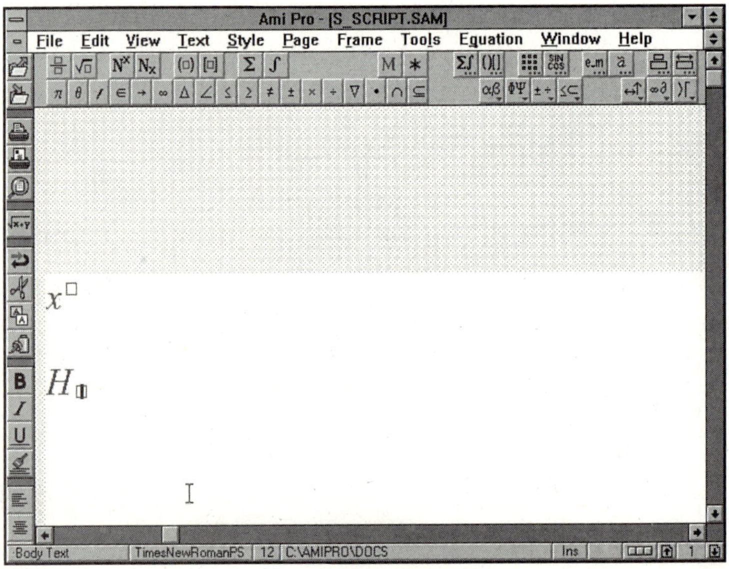

Fig. 22.10
The input box for the superscript appears slightly above and to the right of the text. The input box for the subscript (active in this figure) is slightly below and to the right of the text.

3. Type the superscript or subscript in the input box. For this example, type **5** for a superscript or type **2** for a subscript.

4. Click at the end of the superscript or subscript, or press the space bar. Then type the rest of the expression; for the subscript in this example, type **O**.

Parentheses and Brackets

You use the parentheses and brackets icons in much the same way as the other equation template icons. Follow these steps:

1. At the point in your expression where you want to insert parentheses or brackets, click the appropriate icon. You also can insert parentheses by pressing Ctrl+5, Ctrl+9, or Ctrl+0. (All of these key combinations insert parentheses.)

2. In the input box, type the expression you want inside the parentheses or brackets.

3. Click after the parentheses or brackets (or press the space bar).

Figure 22.11 shows the beginning of an equation built by clicking the brackets icon, typing **1+**, clicking the parentheses icon, then clicking the fraction icon and typing **3x** as the numerator.

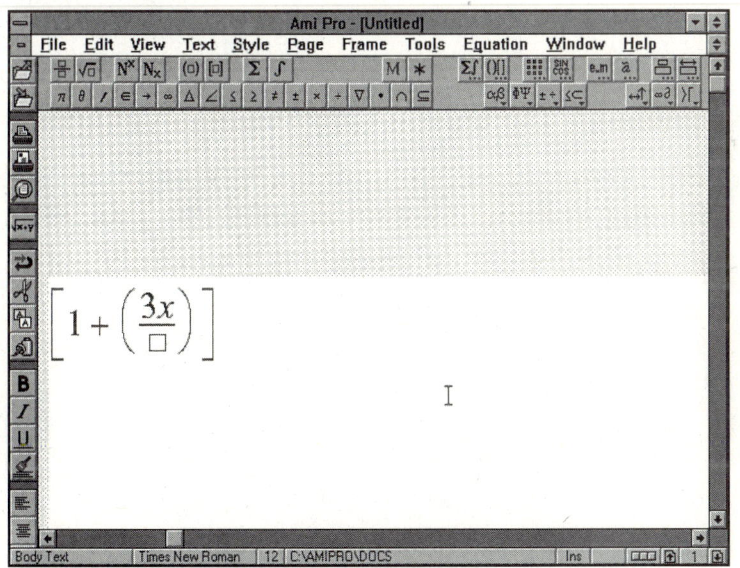

Fig. 22.11 The beginning of an equation.

Tip Templates provide input boxes to help you see where the text is to be typed. If you don't want the boxes to appear on-screen, choose E**q**uations Hide Input **B**oxes.

Using the Equation Operator Icons

The summation and integral icons in the top row of the equation screen are the equation operator icons. To place a summation or integral symbol in an equation, click the desired summation or integral icon. Ami Pro inserts the appropriate symbol. Then add superscripts and subscripts as needed.

Figure 22.12 shows a summation statement with limits for the sum above and below the summation symbol. The summation statement is a mathematical shorthand to show the same statement as the following:

```
a1 + a2 + a3 +...+ a10
```

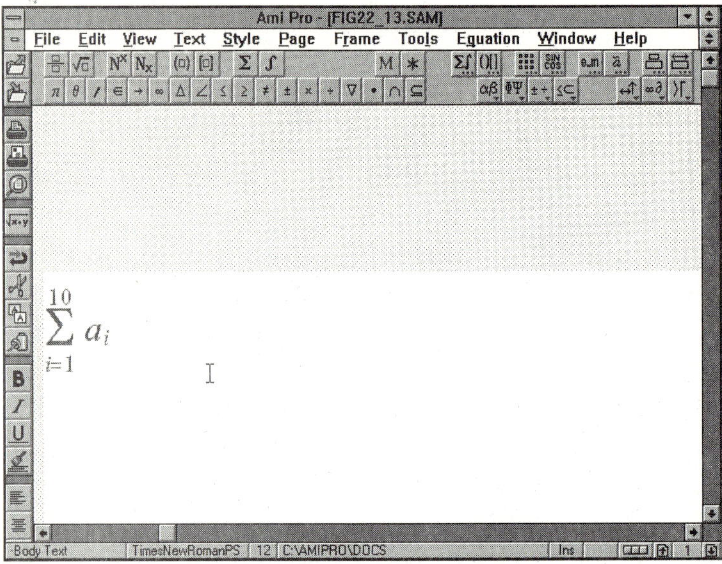

Fig. 22.12
A summation statement.

The *limits* are the little numbers (in this example, 10 and i=1) above and below the summation symbol. The limits show the end points of the values to substitute for i. The limits aren't positioned correctly as you build the formula; after you complete the formula, you must choose E**q**uation **L**imits & Size Big to correctly place the limits above and below the symbol.

To create a summation statement, follow these steps:

1. Place the insertion point where you want the summation symbol. Click the summation icon. Ami Pro places the summation symbol at the position of the insertion point.

2. Click the superscript icon, insert the upper limit in the superscript input box, and press the space bar to end the upper limit. In this example, type **10** in the input box.

   Pressing the space bar ends input in the superscript input box and repositions the insertion point to the right of the summation symbol. After you type the first limit (superscript or subscript), you also can press Tab to move the insertion point to the second limit position.

3. Click the subscript icon, insert the lower limit in the subscript input box, and press the space bar to end the lower limit. In this example, type **i=1** in the input box.

   The limits now appear as superscripts and subscripts to the summation symbol (see fig. 22.13).

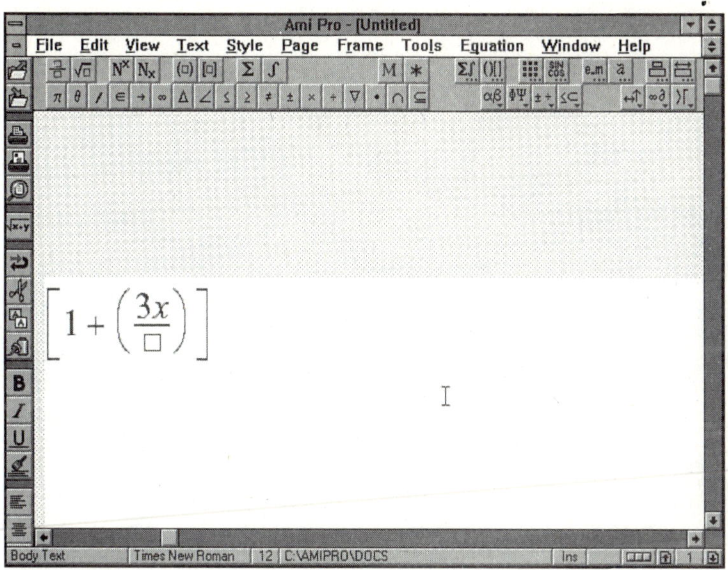

Fig. 22.13
Subscript and superscript limits.

Common mathematical convention shows summation limits above and below the summation symbol. Ami Pro places summations limits above and below the summation symbol only if you choose E**q**uation **L**imits & Size Big. When you select this option, Ami Pro correctly places the limits above and below the symbol. To complete the example equation, choose E**q**uation **L**imits & Size Big to correctly position the summation limits. Type **a** followed by a subscript **i** to complete the equation (refer to fig. 22.12).

The integral icon is beside the summation icon. An *integral* is an operation performed in calculus over a certain area. Integral symbols usually have upper and lower limits that appear as small superscripts and subscripts. The limits specify the beginning and end points for integrating. You place an integral symbol in your equation in the same way that you place a summation symbol. Integral limits are placed as superscripts and subscripts to the integral symbol and don't appear correctly positioned until you choose E**q**uation **L**imits & Size Big. (Figure 22.4 shows an integral in an equation.)

Using the Equation Dialog Box Icons

Eight equation dialog box icons appear on the right side of the top row of the equation screen: operator, brackets, matrix, function, spaces, revise character, label, and over/under. Several of the icons function like the equation template icons described earlier in this chapter, but each of the equation dialog box icons shows an ellipsis (...) at the bottom of the icon to indicate that it accesses a dialog box (see fig. 22.14).

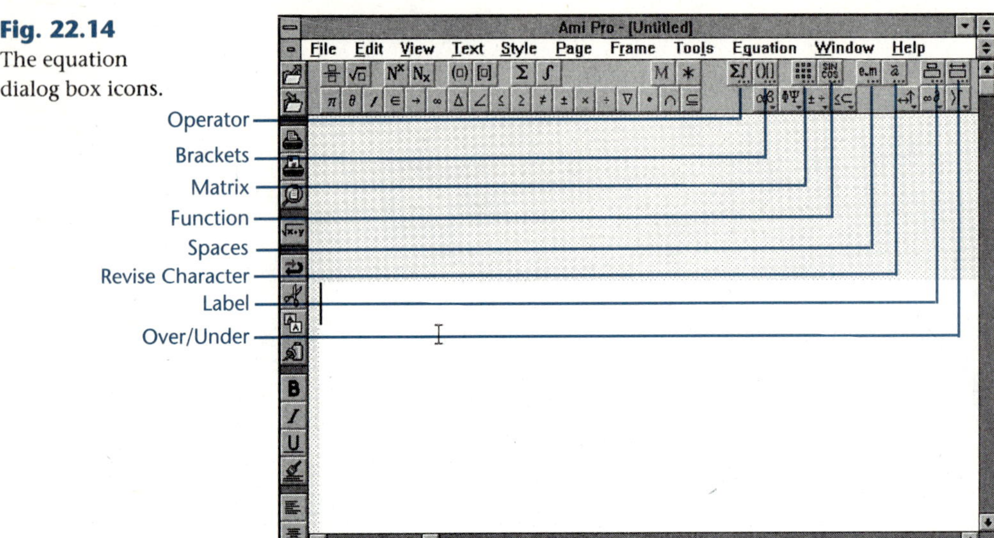

Fig. 22.14
The equation dialog box icons.

Operators

The operator dialog box icon accesses additional mathematical operators—double or triple integral signs or operators that work on sets, for example—to insert in an equation. This Ami Pro feature enables you to insert in a document almost any equation used in specialized mathematics text. In the Operator dialog box, you can specify where to place the limits for integrals or summations, and you can specify the size. Because the summation symbol and integral symbol are the most commonly used operators, they have dedicated icons next to the equation template icons.

Suppose that you want to place in your document a triple integral symbol with a superscripted *b* and a subscripted *a*. You want the integral symbol to be small and the superscript and subscript to appear directly above and below the integral symbol.

At the point in the equation where you want to insert the operator, click the operator icon or select E**q**uation **I**nsert **O**perator. The Operator dialog box appears, as shown in figure 22.15.

In the Operator dialog box, you click the appropriate operator. (For this example, click the triple integral symbol.) The operator appears in the sample box in the lower right corner of the dialog box. Then select the desired limit position. The following describe the limit positions; for this example, select Abo**v**e/Below.

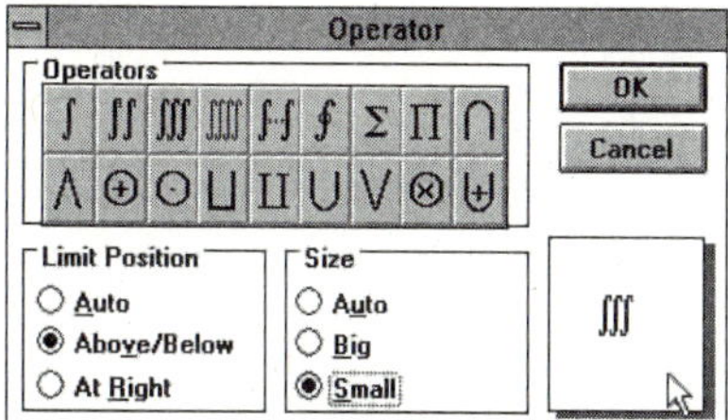

Fig. 22.15
The Operator dialog box with the triple integral operator selected.

- *Auto.* This is the default option. Select this option to place a template for a limit in the position indicated in the **L**imits and Size setting on the **E**quation menu. For more information, see "Changing Limit Position and Size" and "Using the Equation Insert Menu," later in this chapter.

- *Abo**v**e/Below.* Use this option to place the limits above or below the operator.

- *At **R**ight.* This option places the limits to the right of the operator.

In the Size section of the dialog box, you specify the desired size of the operator. The following describe the size options (for this example, select **S**mall).

- *A**u**to.* This is the default option. Use this option to follow the size specified in the **L**imits and Size setting on the E**q**uation menu.

- ***B**ig.* This option produces a large operator in mathematical conventions. Usually, when one operator precedes another, the first operator is larger. Choosing **A**uto or **B**ig makes the newly inserted operator larger than the operators that follow.

- ***S**mall.* Select **S**mall to produce a small operator, one that is the same size as the operator or expressions that follow it.

After you specify the operator, the limit position, and the size, choose OK or press Enter. Ami Pro places the specified operator in the frame, and you can continue entering the other elements of the equation. For this example, add the subscripted *b* (click the subscript icon, type **b**, and press the space bar) and the superscripted *a* (click the superscript icon and type **a**). Note that as you type the superscript and subscript entries (limits for our integral in this case) and then press the space bar, the entries are correctly positioned above and below the triple integral operator. Figure 22.16 shows the finalized triple integral operator.

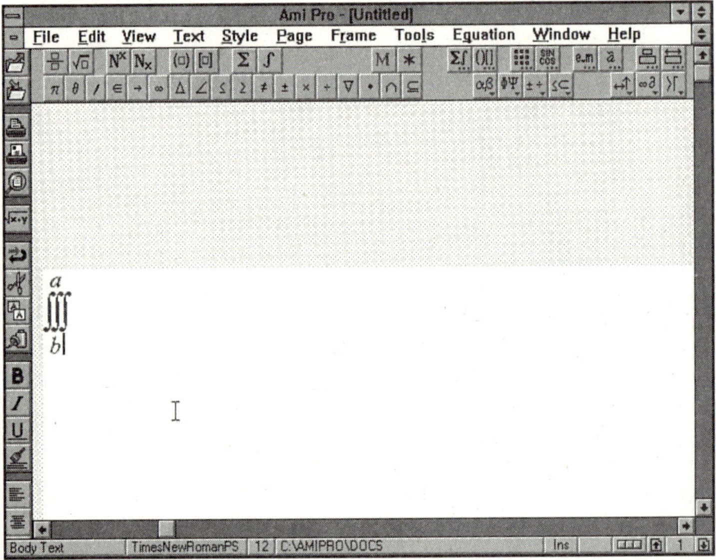

Fig. 22.16
A triple integral operator with a and b limits.

Customized Brackets

With the brackets dialog box icon, you can insert customized pairs of brackets into an equation. You can use some of these custom brackets to specify absolute value or to enclose sets. When you click the brackets dialog box icon or select E**q**uation **I**nsert Brac**k**ets, the Brackets dialog box appears (see fig. 22.17). Selecting the brackets template icon is like selecting the brackets dialog box icon except that the template icon, at the current insert point location, sets up a basic bracket ([]) with an input box. The brackets dialog box icon brings up a dialog box of brackets to choose from and is much more flexible because the icon enables you to put brackets around an existing part of an equation.

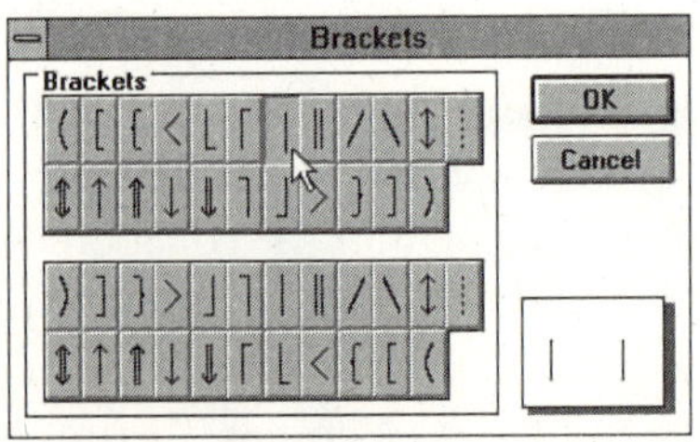

Fig. 22.17
The Brackets dialog box with the vertical lines for absolute value chosen.

Select an opening bracket from the choices in the top two rows. (The dotted lines mean no brackets at all.) If you want to enter into an equation the absolute value of *x*, for example, select the vertical line as the opening bracket.

You can select a bracket by clicking it or by moving the selector with the arrow key. Ami Pro selects the matching closing bracket, and the selected brackets appear in the example box in the lower right corner of the dialog box. For this example, two vertical lines—the symbol for absolute value—appear.

If the brackets you want aren't a matched pair, select a different closing bracket from the choices in the bottom two rows of the dialog box. You can choose a different closing bracket by clicking it or by pressing the tab key to move the selector down to the bottom two rows of bracket choices. You then can use the arrow keys to move the selector to the correct bracket.

Choose OK when the brackets are the way you want them. An input box appears between the brackets. Type the desired expression in the input box. (This input box works like the one used earlier with the equation template icon for parentheses and brackets.) For this example, type **x** (see fig. 22.18). When you finish typing the expression, click at the end of the brackets or press the space bar.

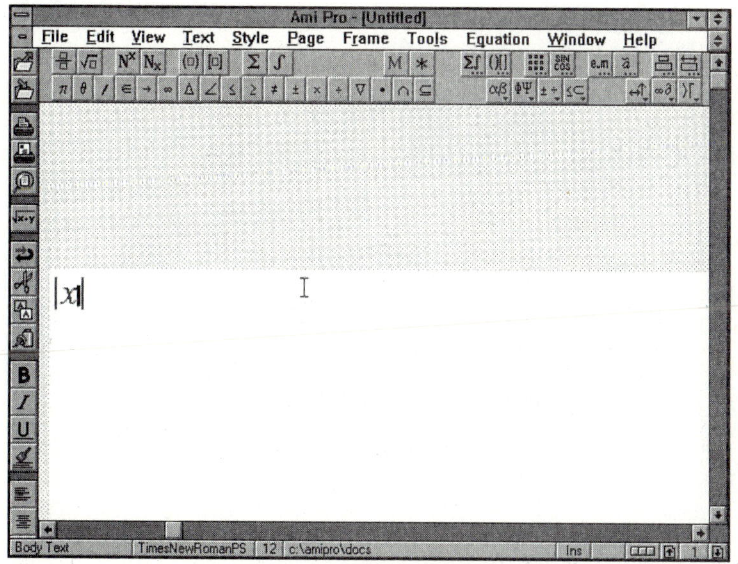

Fig. 22.18
The absolute reference of x.

Tip
To select only one bracket, click the bracket you want and then click the dotted line bracket choice for the one you don't need.

You also can use the brackets to surround an existing portion of an equation. Figure 22.19 shows an equation that is complete but needs to be bracketed to ensure that the order of operations is correct to produce the correct answer.

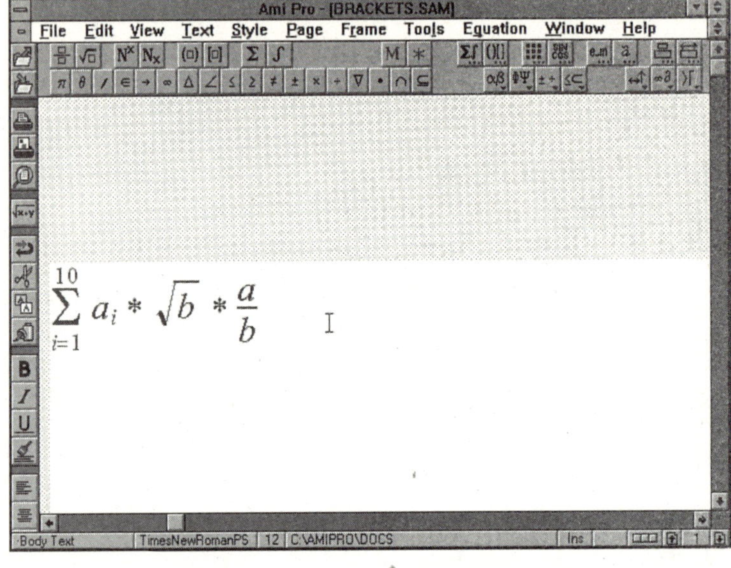

Fig. 22.19 An equation needing brackets to ensure the correct order of operations.

To surround part of an equation with brackets, you select the part of the equation to bracket and then bring up the Bracket dialog box and select the brackets. Figure 22.20 shows the selected part of the equation and a selected bracket from the Bracket dialog box (see "Editing Equations," later in this chapter, for instructions on selecting characters within equations). Figure 22.21 shows the change to the equation.

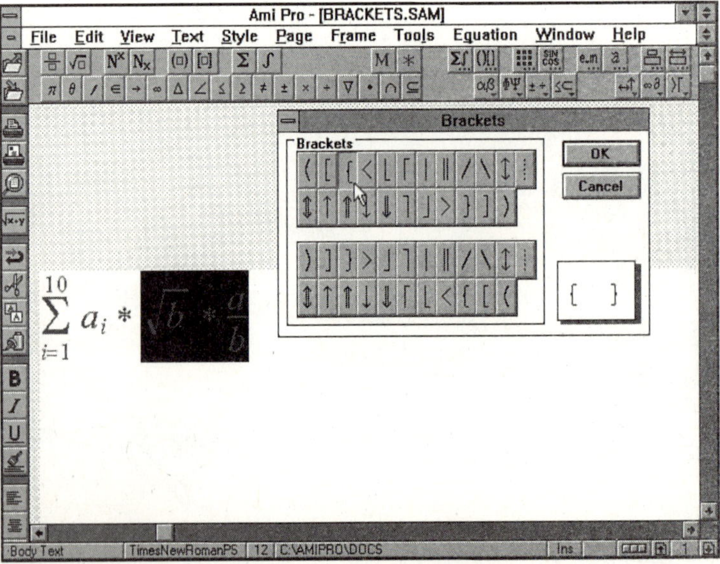

Fig. 22.20 The selected portion of the equation and a selected bracket.

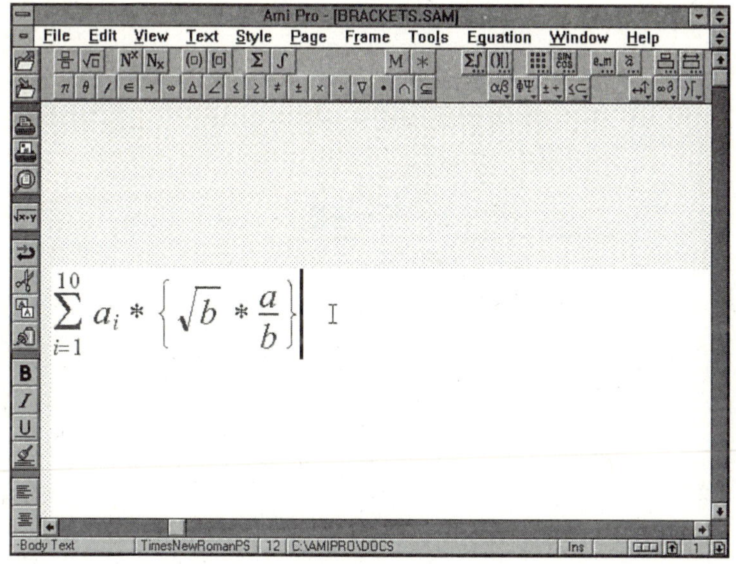

Fig. 22.21
The complete equation.

Matrices

A *matrix* is like a table with rows and columns. Ami Pro shows matrix lines for ease of input (unless you choose to hide matrix lines, using the * toggle icon or by selecting E**q**uation Hide **M**atrix Lines). Matrix lines don't print, however. A *cell* is one particular box in the matrix.

Mathematicians perform operations on matrices. These operations can affect every cell or only particular cells. This feature of equations enables you to place a matrix in a document.

The matrix icon enables you to create matrices in the size you need. You also can use this icon to create a vector, which Ami Pro treats as a matrix with only one row or only one column. Still another use is creating multiline equations where the number of rows equals the number of equations.

Suppose that you want to create a matrix with two rows and two columns and the values x, y, n, and n–1 in the cells. To create this matrix, follow these steps:

1. At the location in the equation where you want to insert the matrix, click the matrix dialog box icon or select E**q**uation **I**nsert **M**atrix. The Create Matrix dialog box appears, as shown in figure 22.22.

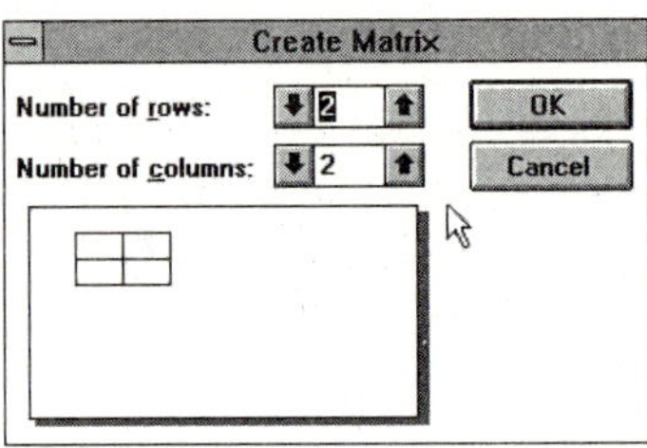

Fig. 22.22
The Create Matrix dialog box.

2. In the Number of **R**ows text box, indicate the number of rows you want in the matrix. (Type the desired number or use the arrow buttons to select the number.) The maximum number of rows accepted is 10. For this example, keep the default of **2**.

3. In the Number of **C**olumns text box, indicate the number of columns you want in the matrix. The maximum number of columns accepted is 10. For this example, keep the default of **2**.

4. Choose OK or press Enter. Ami Pro creates a template for the matrix, with an input box in each cell, and places the insertion point in the top left cell.

5. Enter the mathematical expression in the first box. (If you are creating a multiline equation, enter the first equation in this box.) For this example, type **x**.

6. Press Tab to move to the next box. You also can click the next box. (The boxes are filled from left to right before moving to the next row.) Figure 22.23 displays the matrix with the first expression entered into the first box.

7. Type an entry in the second box. For this example, type **y**.

8. Continue pressing Tab and making entries until all the boxes are filled. For this example, press Tab, type **n**, press Tab again, and type **n–1**. You also can click each box to make the entry.

   Pressing Tab moves the insertion point from box to box, left to right, top to bottom (forward). Pressing Shift-Tab moves back through the matrix. Your arrow keys move the insertion point from character to character within a box, left and right, or up and down from line to line of a multiple-line entry.

   To completely change an entry in a box after you have made an entry, double-click in the box to highlight the current entry and type in the new entry. The new entry types over the old one. To adjust an entry in a box, click in the box and use the Backspace or Del key to remove the unwanted text. Type in additional text if necessary.

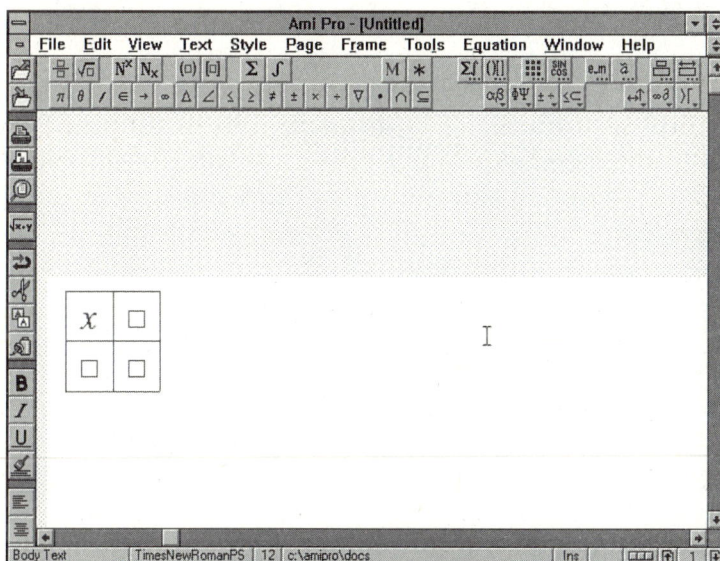

Fig. 22.23
The matrix with x entered into the first box.

9. Click to the right of the matrix, or press the space bar.

Figure 22.24 shows the completed matrix.

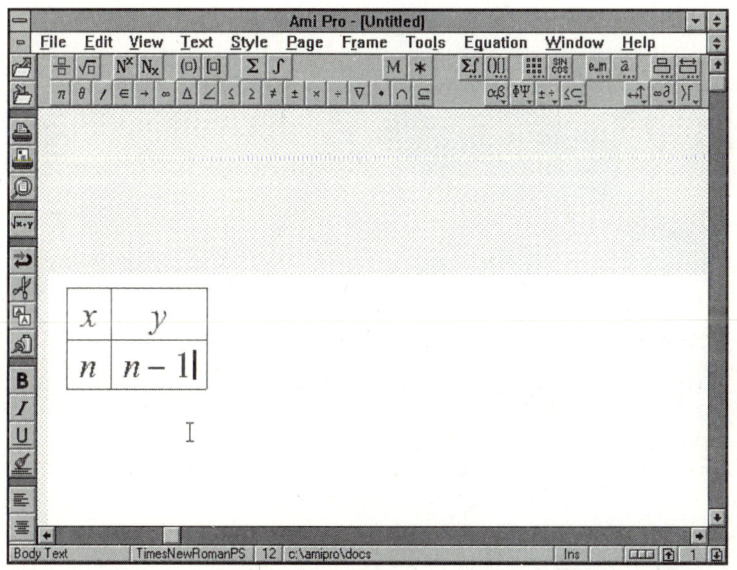

Fig. 22.24
A matrix with four entries.

Functions

The function dialog box icon enables you to enter functions (such as sine, cosine, and logarithm) and to enter customized functions. You also can specify where to place limits for certain functions. To use functions, click the function icon or select E**q**uation **I**nsert Fu**n**ction at the position in the equation where you want to insert the function. The Function dialog box appears, as shown in figure 22.25.

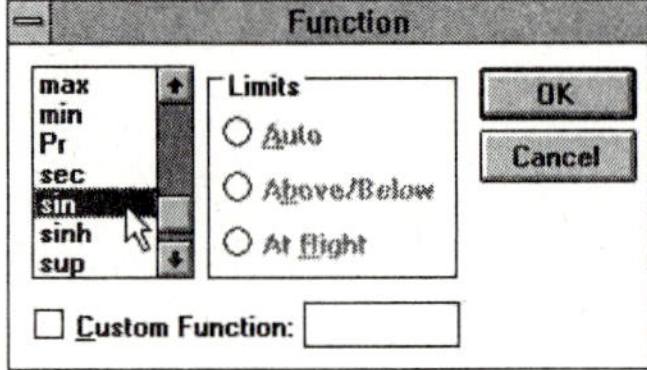

Fig. 22.25
The Function dialog box.

Select a function from the list box or select **C**ustom Function to use a custom function. The list box contains 30 functions, including trigonometric functions, logarithms, exponents, and others. If you need a function that isn't listed, select **C**ustom Function and type the function. Ami Pro places the function at the location of the insertion point. To enter sine x into an equation, for example, select sin from the list box. When you click OK, Ami Pro places *sin* at the location of the insertion point.

The Limits section of the dialog box darkens if limits apply to a highlighted function. For the DET, GCD, and INF functions, for example, you can specify a limit position. The following describe the limit positions. (Note that limits don't apply to sine.)

- ***A****uto.* Select this option to place a template for a limit in the position indicated in the **L**imits and Size setting on the E**q**uation menu, which usually is the standard position for the function. (See "Changing Limit Position and Size," later in this chapter, for more information.)

- *Abo**v**e/Below.* Use this option to place the template above or below the function.

- *At* ***R****ight.* This option places the template to the right of the function.

When you choose OK or press Enter, Ami Pro inserts the specified function, then you can finish typing the expression. For sine x, for example, type **x**.

Spaces

When you enter equations, Ami Pro inserts the correct space for mathematical typesetting conventions between characters and symbols. Ami Pro places spaces before and after +, –, and =, for example. You must use the Space dialog box to add space between characters because the space bar doesn't function normally in the Equation Editor.

Tip
You rarely need to enter spaces in equations.

To enter a space in an equation, click the space icon. The Space dialog box appears, as shown in figure 22.26.

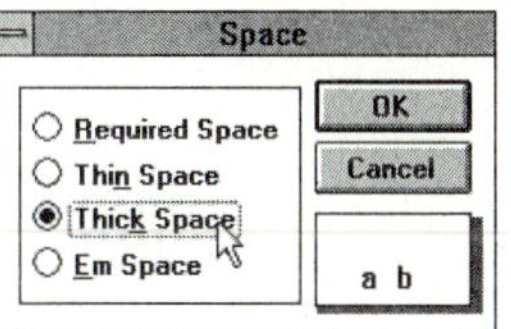

Fig. 22.26
The Space dialog box with Thic**k** Space chosen.

Select the option corresponding to the space you want to insert. The **E**m Space option produces the largest space; by comparison, the **R**equired Space option (the default) uses 1/6 of an em space. If you select Thic**k** Space, Ami Pro places 5/18 of an em space between the characters. The Thi**n** Space option uses 2/9 of an em space (see fig. 22.27). You can see the spacing differences in the example box in the Space dialog box.

Tip
To enter a required space quickly with the keyboard, press Ctrl+space bar.

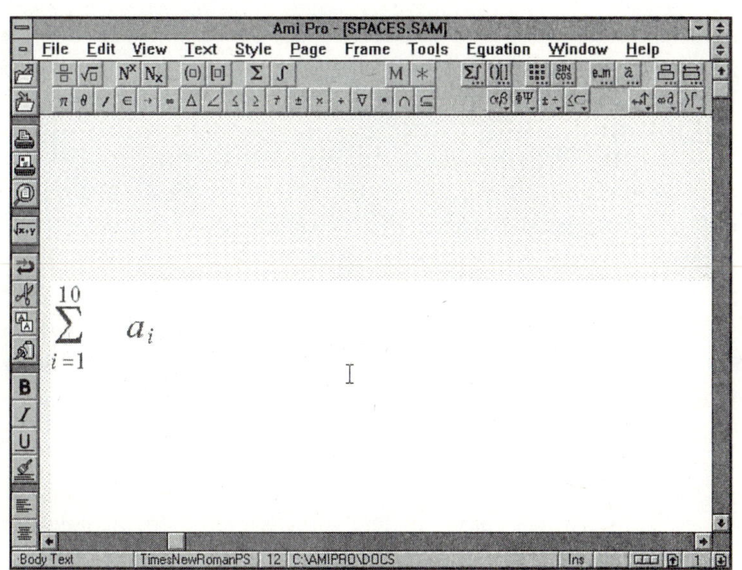

Fig. 22.27
A thick space inserted between the *i* and = in the summation lower limit, and an em space between the summation and the a_i.

Revising Characters

If the equation requires an accented or bold character or a character with a negate line through it, you use the revise character icon.

To use the revise character dialog box icon, type the character to change or, if the character has already been entered, select the character to change. If you want to boldface and add a dot over a character, *x* for example, type **x** and click the revise character icon or select E**q**uation **I**nsert Revise **C**haracter. The Revise Character dialog box appears (see fig. 22.28). The following paragraphs describe the options in the dialog box.

- *Accent on Top.* If you select this option, choose the desired accent mark from the list box to the right of the option. Click the down arrow repeatedly to scroll through the accent choices one-by-one.
- *Negate.* This option draws a slash through the character.
- *Bold.* Using this option prints the character in boldface.

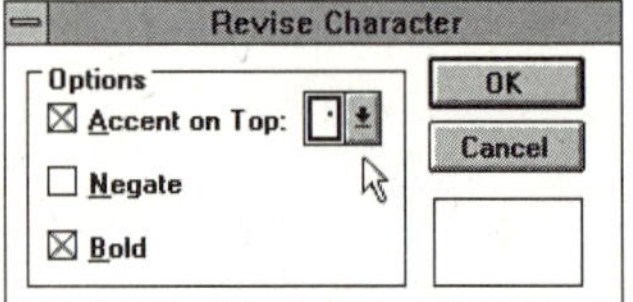

Fig. 22.28 The Revise Character dialog box.

You can specify more than one option from the dialog box. You can create a bold and accented character, for example. For this example, select **B**old and then **A**ccent on Top, and specify the dot accent.

When you choose OK or press Enter, Ami Pro modifies the character according to the options you choose. For this example, as figure 22.29 displays, a dot appears above the boldfaced *x*.

Labels

You use the label dialog box icon to enter expressions with labels attached. Clarifying an equation expression can be greatly helpful to anyone attempting to understand the equation. A label template adds two input boxes: one for the equations and one for the label. To enter a labeled expression, follow these steps:

1. At the point in the equation where you want to insert the labeled expression, click the label dialog box icon or select E**q**uation **I**nsert **L**abel. The Label dialog box opens, as shown in figure 22.30. (For this example, the input box is in the denominator.)

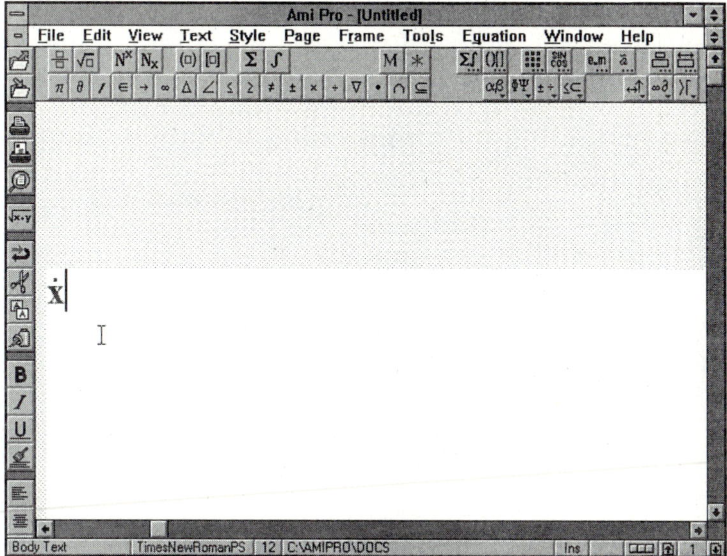

Fig. 22.29
The boldfaced x with a dot above it.

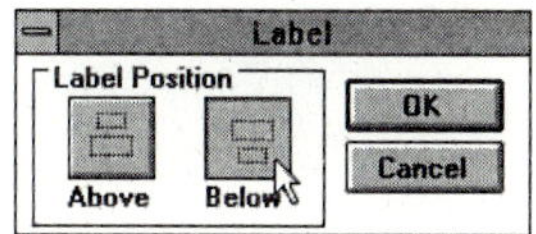

Fig. 22.30
The Label dialog box.

2. Specify where you want to place the label—Above or Below the expression. Using the mouse is easier, but you can use Tab and the arrow keys to navigate the Label dialog box.

3. Choose OK or press Enter. The program displays two input boxes: a large box for the expression and a small box for the label.

4. Enter the expression in the large input box. Figure 22.31 shows the equation with the expression, a radical, beginning to be entered. Directly below this expression is the label box.

5. Press Tab or click the insertion point in the label field.

6. Enter the label in the smaller input box.

7. Click after the expression or press the space bar. The expression appears with the label in superscript or subscript style.

To label an equation that already exists, select the equation and then access the Label dialog box. Ami Pro places the selected equation into the equation input box; then you fill in only the label input box. Figure 22.32 shows the equation selected and a Below label selected from the Label dialog box. Figure 22.33 shows the label for the equation. If you want to change the font of the label, choose **T**ext **F**ont and make a selection.

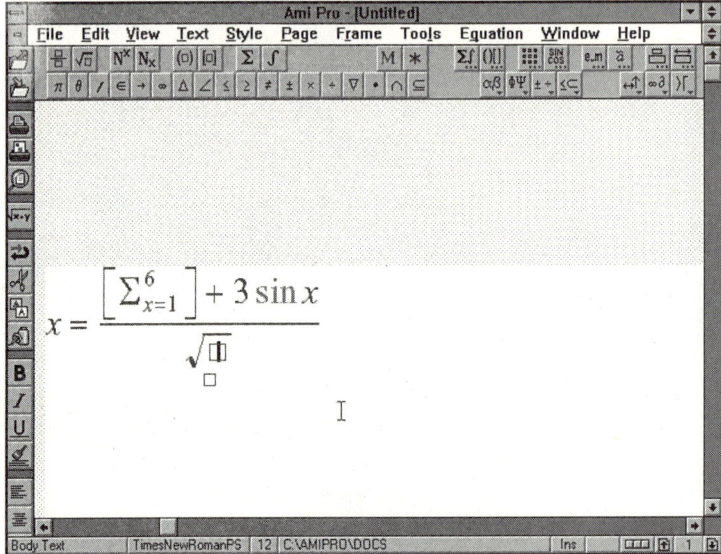

Fig. 22.31
The label box below the radical expression.

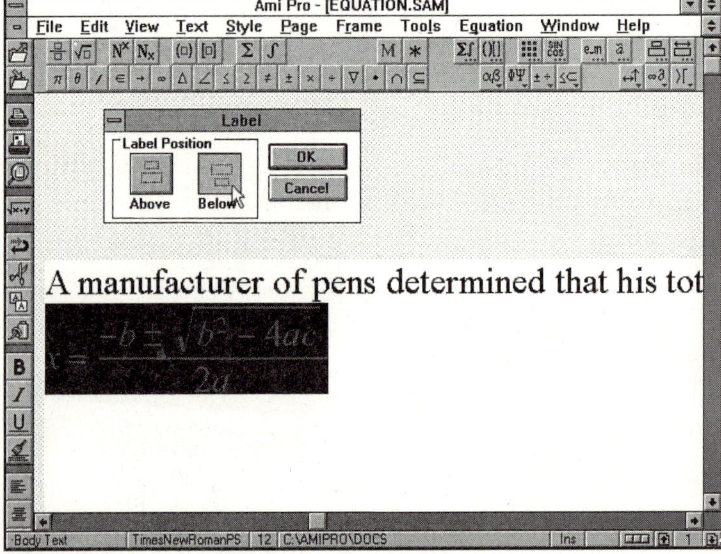

Fig. 22.32
An equation selected for a Below label.

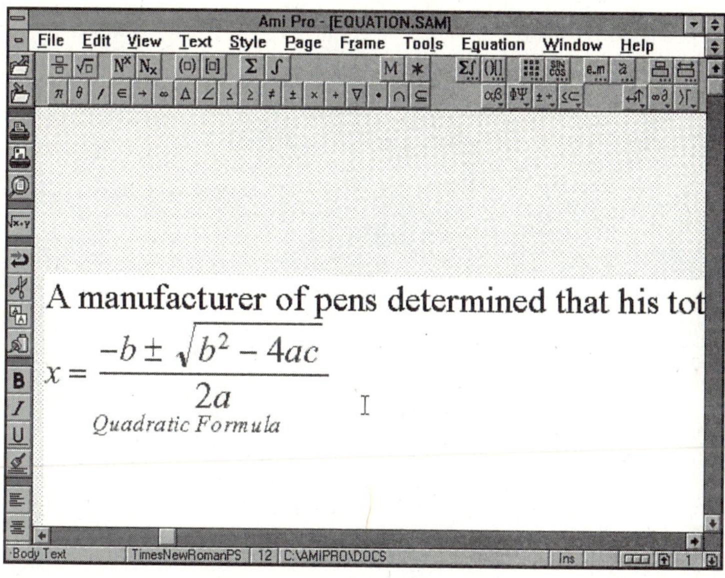

Fig. 22.33
The equation updated with a label.

Bars, Arrows, and Braces

You can add expressions with bars, arrows, or braces by clicking the over/under dialog box icon or by choosing E**q**uations **I**nsert Ov**e**r/Under. Absolute value is denoted sometimes with the bar above the expression, for example. To enter this type of expression, click the over/under icon at the point in the equation where you want to insert the expression. The Over/Under dialog box appears, as shown in figure 22.34.

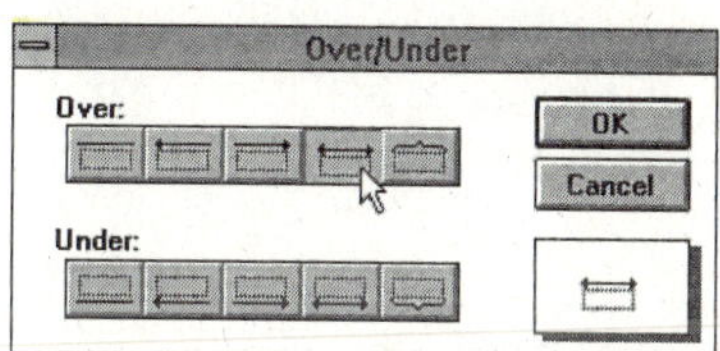

Fig. 22.34
The Over/Under dialog box.

The top row of icons (the Over row) shows the characters available to place over the expression: a bar, a left arrow, a right arrow, a two-headed arrow, and a brace. If you select one of these icons, the specified character appears above your mathematical expression. The bottom row of icons (the Under row) shows comparable characters available to place under your expression.

Click the desired character in order to select it. If you want to enter a two-headed arrow over the expression x–1, for example (see fig. 22.35), click the fourth icon in the Over row. Then choose OK or press Enter. The selected character appears with an input box over or under the selected character in the equation.

Type the desired mathematical expression in the input box. For this example, type **x–1**. Then click at the end of the expression or press the space bar.

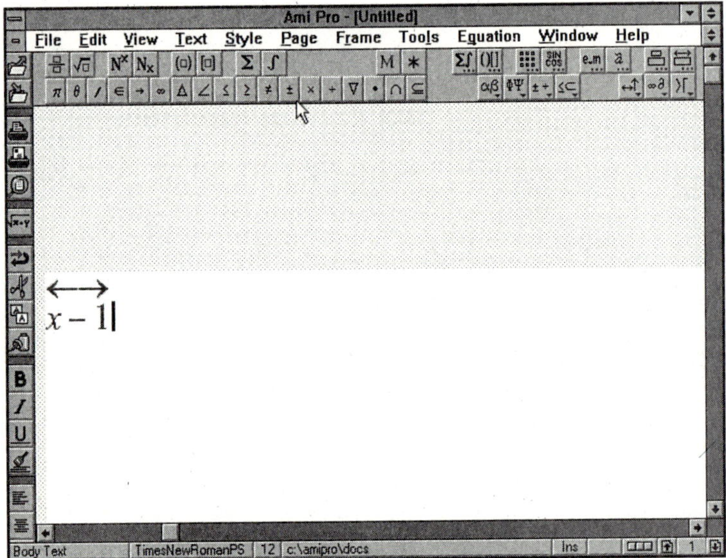

Fig. 22.35
The equation x–1 under a two-headed arrow.

Using the Toggle Icons

Ami Pro is set for mathematical characters when you first enter the Equation Editor. You cannot add an equation to a frame that contains text, but you can add text to a frame that contains equations. You can use this feature to add short explanations or transitions between equations. The M toggle icon enables you to switch from math to text characters.

The other toggle icon is the * icon. Ami Pro ordinarily shows input boxes and matrix lines in the Equation Editor. To hide the boxes and lines, you use the * icon. Because these toggle icons don't affect each other, you can use both at the same time.

To switch from entering math to entering text, click the math/text icon or press Ctrl+T. The icon displays `M` for math or `T` for text (see fig. 22.36). When you want to switch back, click the icon or press Ctrl+T again.

If you prefer, you can toggle between entering math and text by choosing E**q**uation and then choosing **M**ath Mode or **T**ext Mode, as desired.

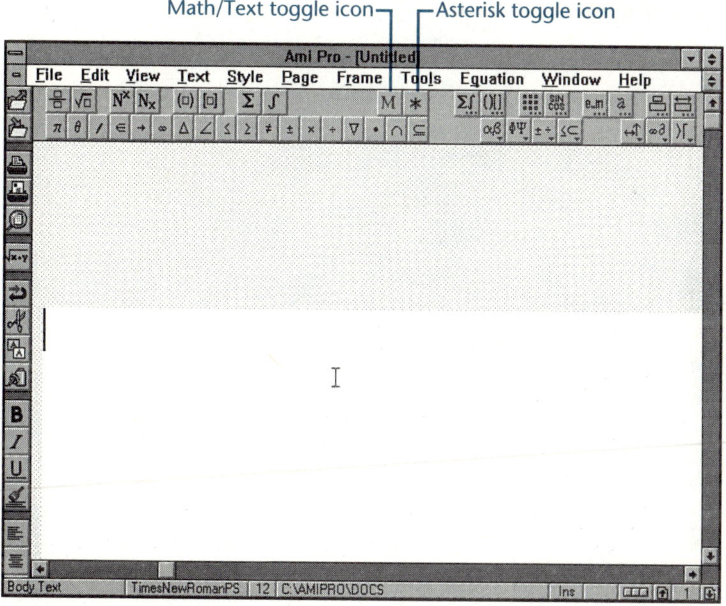

Fig. 22.36
The toggle icons.

Ami Pro displays input boxes and matrix lines although they don't print. If you want to hide the on-screen boxes so you can see what the equation will look like in print, click the * (asterisk) icon. To show the boxes, click the icon again.

If you prefer, you can show or hide both the input boxes and matrix boxes by choosing E**q**uation and then selecting Show/Hide **M**atrix Lines or Show/Hide Input **B**oxes. Like the icons, these menu options function as toggles. (If matrix lines or input boxes are hidden, clicking the icon causes both to appear.)

Using the Equation Insert Menu

As explained in this section, you can use the E**q**uation menu rather than the equation icons to insert symbols and functions. To use the menu, choose E**q**uation and then choose **I**nsert. From the **I**nsert cascading menu, select the symbol or function you want to insert.

If you want to enter a radical, for example, position the insertion point in the equation where you want the radical to appear, choose E**q**uation **I**nsert, and then choose **R**adical to insert the radical symbol. Ami Pro inserts the selected symbol or template into your equation, and you proceed as if you have selected the corresponding icon. The E**q**uation **I**nsert menu appears in figure 22.37.

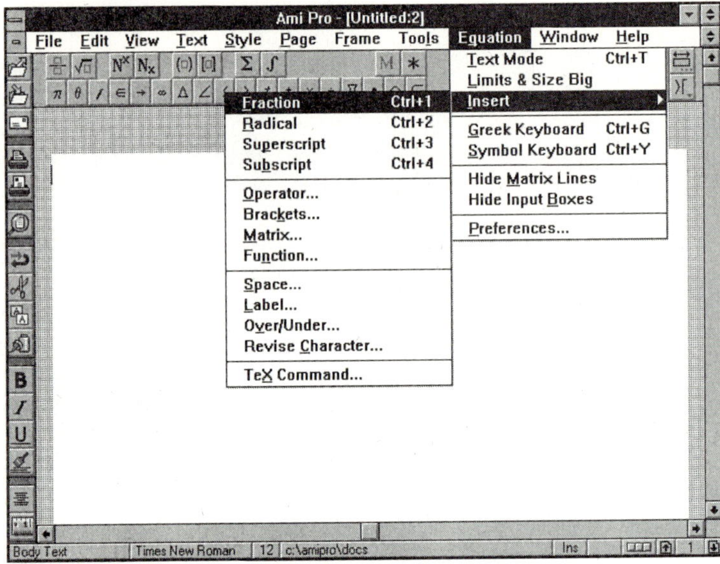

Fig. 22.37
The E**q**uations **I**nsert menu.

Now that you have learned how to use the equation template icons, equation operator icons, equation dialog box icons, and toggle icons, you are ready to learn how to enter characters into your equations.

Entering Characters into Equations

You can enter many different characters into equations. You can use any standard letters or numbers from your keyboard. (Letters appear in italics in an equation unless you choose otherwise, using the E**q**uation **P**references menu.) You also can use many specialized mathematical symbols, using the icons in the E**q**uation menus or dialog boxes. In addition, you can use Greek upper- and lowercase letters, binary operators, and almost any symbol used in mathematics or physics. If you use a specialized character frequently, you can make the icon easily available, as described later, in the section "Customizing the Equation Symbol and Character Icons." Ami Pro sizes and positions characters according to standard mathematics typesetting conventions.

Using the Equation Symbol and Character Icons

You can use in an equation any character on a standard keyboard—just type the character while in the Equation Editor. In addition to these characters, however, Ami Pro enables you to enter many more characters typically used in mathematical equations.

The icons in the second row of the equation screen enter the special characters. To enter one of the 18 characters represented by the icons beginning on the left side of the screen, you click the appropriate icon. If you want to enter an uppercase Greek delta (Δ), for example, you click the icon that displays the delta character. These icons are the equation character and symbol icons and are the most commonly used math symbols and characters.

Each of the equation pull-down box icons on the right side of the second row is marked with a red arrow pointing down—this symbol indicates that you can access a pull-down box by clicking the icon. The pull-down boxes contain additional special characters for use in equations.

The first icon (showing lowercase Greek alpha and beta) produces the pull-down box shown in figure 22.38. The second icon (showing uppercase Greek phi and psi) displays the pull-down box shown in figure 22.39.

The third icon produces the pull-down box of binary operators (see fig. 22.40). The fourth icon produces the pull-down box of binary relations symbols (see fig. 22.41).

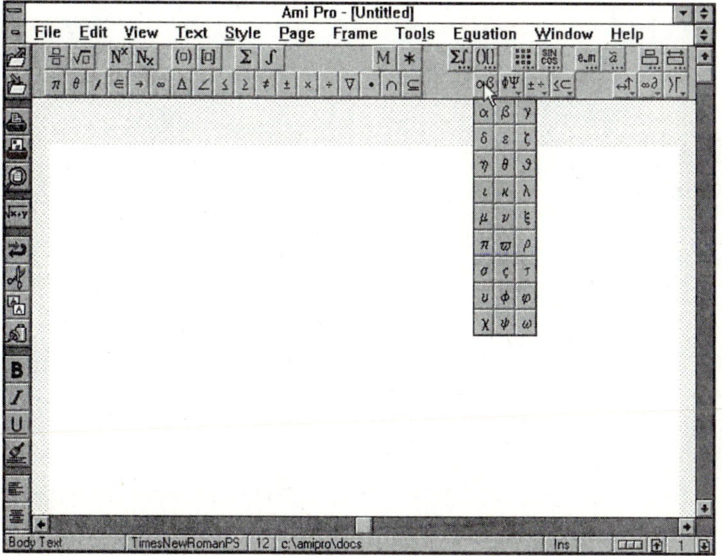

Fig. 22.38
The lowercase Greek letters pull-down box.

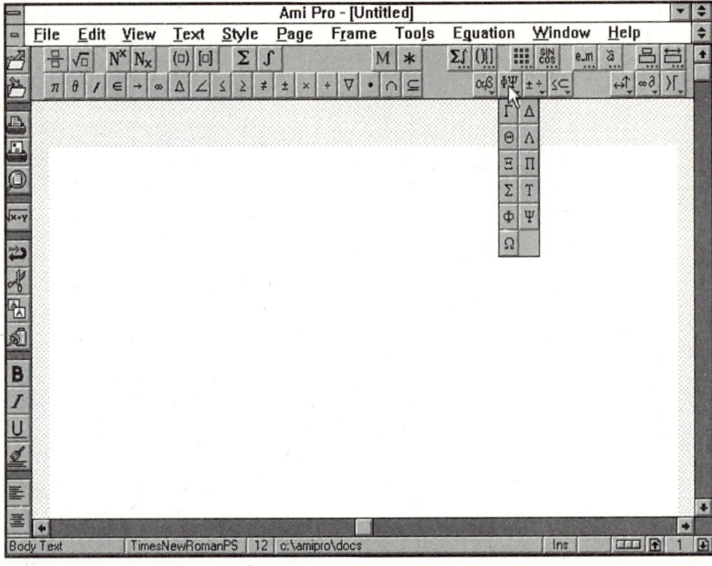

Fig. 22.39
The uppercase Greek letters pull-down box.

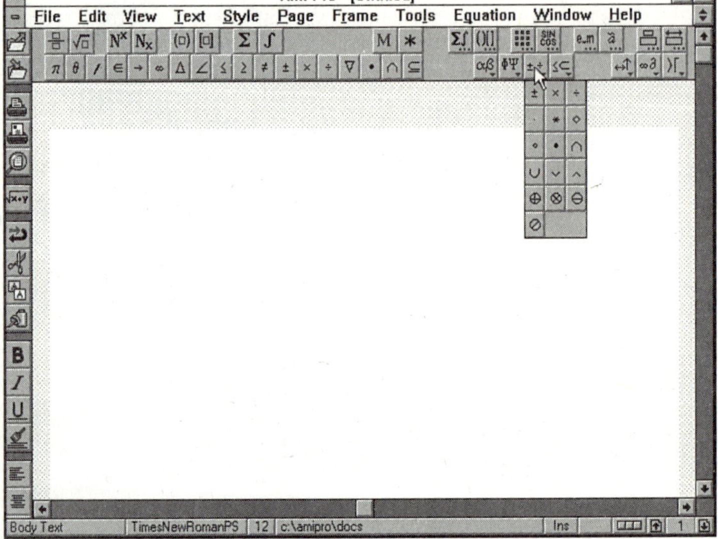

Fig. 22.40
The binary operators pull-down box.

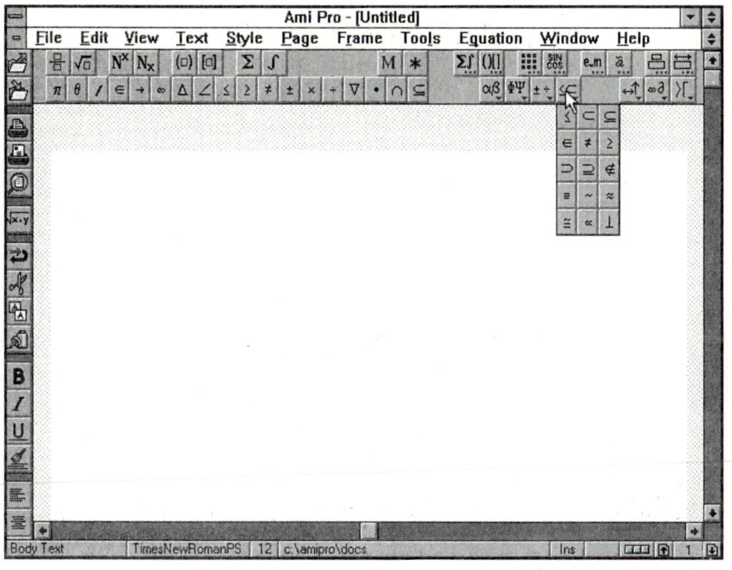

Fig. 22.41 The binary relations pull-down box.

Clicking the fifth icon displays the pull-down box of arrows, shown in figure 22.42. Clicking the sixth icon displays the pull-down box of miscellaneous characters, shown in figure 22.43. The seventh icon produces the pull-down box of delimiters, shown in figure 22.44.

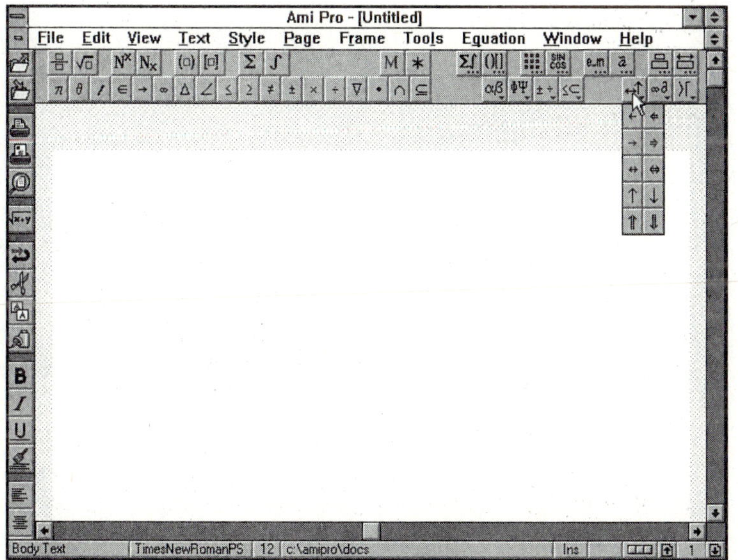

Fig. 22.42 The arrows pull-down box.

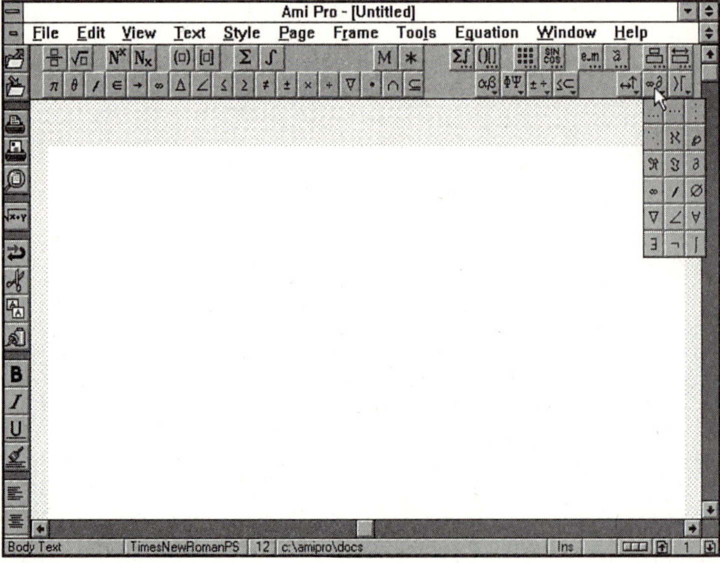

Fig. 22.43
The miscellaneous characters pull-down box.

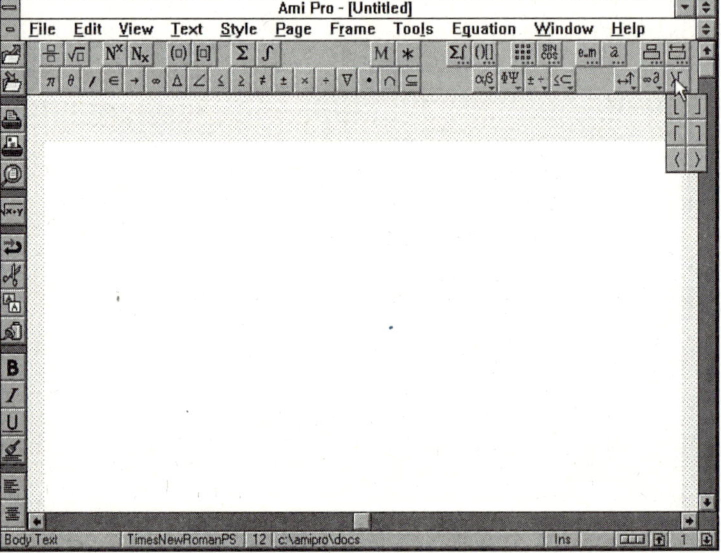

Fig. 22.44
The delimiters pull-down box.

To use a special character, click the pull-down box icon that displays the character, then click the icon for the character. The character is entered at the current insert point location.

Using Greek and Symbol Keyboards

Greek characters and mathematical symbols also can be entered into your equations by using the keyboard. The program has two alternative keyboards that make the normal keyboard keys type either Greek letters or mathematical symbols. If you tell Ami Pro to use the Greek keyboard, for example, when you type the letter **a**, the Greek letter alpha is entered rather than the letter a. Or if you tell Ami Pro to use the Symbol keyboard, when you type the letter **t**, the Tensor Product symbol is entered rather than the letter t.

To access the alternate keyboards, choose E**q**uation and then select **G**reek Keyboard or **S**ymbol Keyboard (see fig. 22.45). If you prefer, you can press Ctrl+G to access the Greek keyboard or Ctrl+Y for the symbol keyboard. With the appropriate option selected, you can enter Greek letters or mathematical symbols directly from your keyboard. (You can see the layouts for alternative keyboards in the Ami Pro *User's Guide*.)

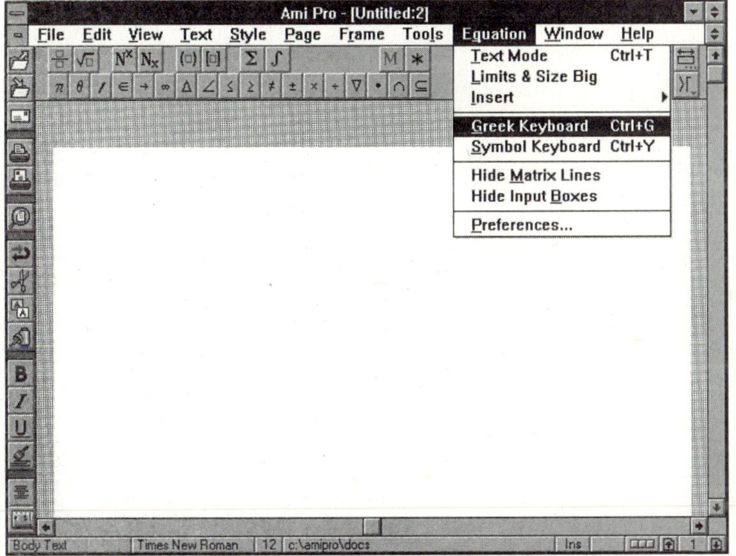

Fig. 22.45
The Greek Keyboard and Symbol Keyboard selections from the Equation menu.

All the Greek letters available from the lowercase Greek letters pull-down list and uppercase Greek letters pull-down list are available from the keyboard if you select E**q**uations **G**reek Keyboard or press Ctrl+G. All the binary operators, binary relations, arrows, miscellaneous characters and delimiters on their respective pull-down lists are available from the keyboard if you select E**q**uations **S**ymbol Keyboard or press Ctrl+Y.

When you access the Greek or Symbol keyboard, you are engaging that keyboard only for the next character you type. You aren't changing the keyboard to Greek or Symbol until you change it back to "normal." If you want to enter a series of mathematical symbols, therefore, you must press Ctrl+Y before you enter each symbol.

Customizing the Equation Symbol and Character Icons

If you use one of the special characters frequently, you can move its icon to the equation character and symbol icons list (refer to figure 22.1). This list contains the most often used character and symbol icons and appears on the left side of the second row of icons. Moving a character or symbol icon onto the equation character and symbol list allows you to access the icon quickly and easily. This rearranging process is called *customizing an equation symbol and character icon.*

Suppose that you want to replace the division sign on the equation character and symbol icons list with the Greek uppercase letter psi. To customize an equation character or symbol icon, you must first access the character you want to move. In this case, to access the Greek letter psi, you click the uppercase Greek letter icon to display the pull-down box of uppercase Greek letters.

Next, press the Shift key and click the character in the pull-down list that you want to move. For this example, Shift-click the letter psi. Then release the Shift key and click the icon on the equation character and symbol icon list you want to replace. For this example, click the division sign. Figure 22.46 shows the division sign replaced by the Greek letter psi.

Now the frequently used character has an icon of its own. The replaced division icon is still available on the binary operators pull-down box. All the character icons in the equation character and symbol icon list also are located in the pull-down boxes.

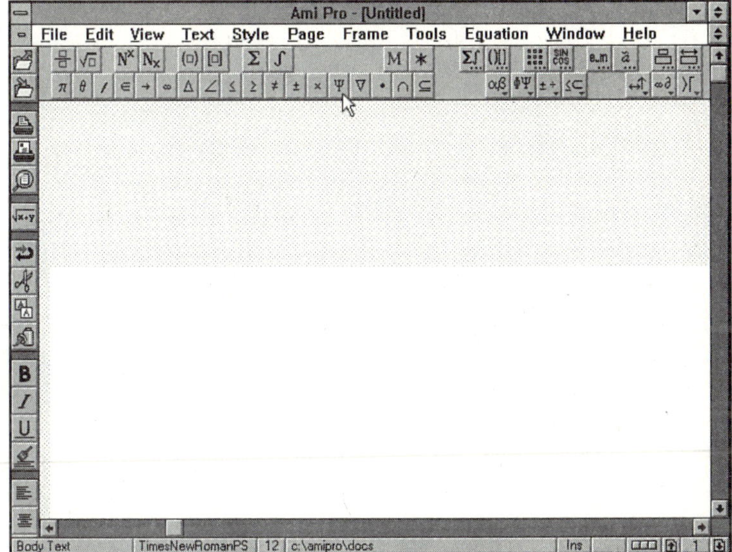

Fig. 22.46
The division sign is replaced by the Greek letter psi on the equation character and symbol icon list.

Entering TeX Commands

Ami Pro uses a mathematical typesetting language called *TeX* to create equations. When you select an icon from the equation icon bar, Ami Pro uses the TeX language to build the template, function, operator, character, or symbol. You can bypass the icon bar and use the TeX commands to build the equation directly. Most users have no reason to use TeX commands directly because creating equations with Ami Pro's Equation Editor is much easier. If you are familiar with TeX, however, Ami Pro gives you the capacity to enter TeX commands through the Equation Editor.

To enter TeX commands in your equation, follow these steps:

1. In the Equation Editor, choose E**q**uation **I**nsert Te**X** Command. The TeX Command dialog box appears, as shown in figure 22.47.

2. Select the TeX command you want to insert.

3. Choose OK or press Enter. Ami Pro enters the selected TeX command into the equation.

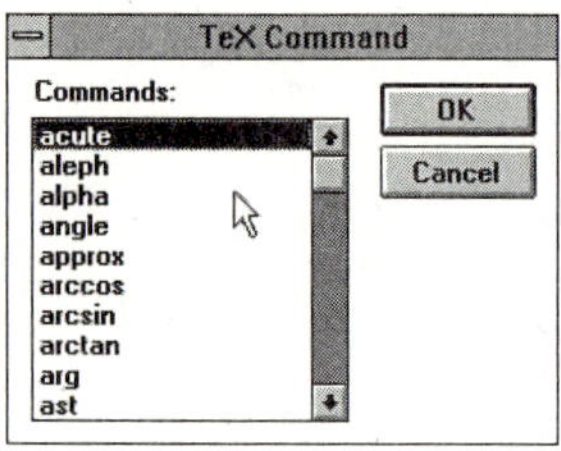

Fig. 22.47
The TeX Command dialog box.

◄ See "Saving the Active Document," p. 59

◄ See "Setting Up Smart Icons," p. 216

When you export or import an Ami Pro equation, you are creating or importing instructions in TeX. This capability enables you to share files with other applications that use the TeX language. Choose Save As Equation from the **F**ile menu to save your equation as a TeX language file (see fig. 22.48). Ami Pro adds a TEX extension to the file name you provide. You can select only part of the equation and then choose **F**ile Save As Equation to save only that part of the equation as a TeX file. To import a TeX file, select Import Equation from the **F**ile menu and select the TeX file to import.

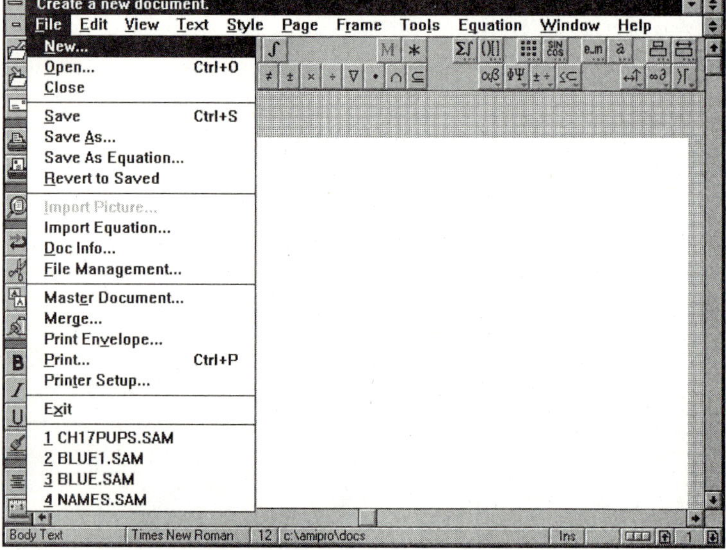

Fig. 22.48
The Save As Equation and Import Equation choices on the **F**ile menu.

Editing Equations

Navigating, selecting, and editing equations is similar to performing the same operations within other Ami Pro text. The next few sections explain how to move the insertion point within equations and how to select, deselect, copy, move, and delete equations. You also learn operations particular to equations: applying templates and editing matrices.

Selecting and Deselecting Equations

You select an equation or a part of an equation by using the same select methods for other Ami Pro text. To select an equation (or part of an equation) while in the Equation Editor, place the mouse pointer to the left of the equation. Click the left mouse button and drag the mouse pointer across the part of the equation you want to select. Then release the mouse button.

An alternate method, also using the mouse, is to move the insertion point to the left of the section you want and then place the mouse pointer to the right of the section. Hold down the Shift key and click the left mouse button to select the section.

Tip

If you prefer working right to left, you can place the insertion point to the right of the desired characters and use Shift+left arrow to select.

To select with the keyboard, place the insertion point to the left of the desired section. Press Shift+right arrow to select the next character. Continue pressing Shift+right arrow until all the desired characters are selected.

To deselect a selected equation (or part of the equation), click inside the selected frame or press an arrow key.

Copying and Moving Equations

To copy or move an equation, you use Ami Pro's standard copy-and-paste or cut-and-paste techniques. You can move or copy an equation by copying or moving the frame occupied by the equation (use the standard procedures for editing a frame).

To move an equation, select the equation (or the part of the equation that you want to move). Choose **E**dit Cu**t**. The selected material is cut from the equation and moved to the Clipboard. Place the insertion point at the desired new position for the selected material and choose **E**dit **P**aste. The selected material appears in the new location.

To copy an equation, select the equation (or the part of an equation that you want to copy). Choose **E**dit **C**opy to copy the selected material to the Clipboard. Move the insertion point to the position where you want to copy the selected material and choose **E**dit **P**aste. Ami Pro copies the selected text to the new location.

Note

If the cursor is not in a frame and if you are not in the Equation Editor, Ami Pro inserts the TeX commands that it uses to create the equation rather than the equation itself. Make sure that you have a frame selected and that you are in the Equation Editor before you paste an equation.

Deleting Equations

The procedure for deleting an equation is the same as that for deleting anything else in Ami Pro. To delete an entire equation, select the equation and press Del. To delete only part of the equation, select that section and press Del.

You also can delete parts of equations without first selecting them by using the following techniques:

- Pressing Del deletes the material following the insertion point.
- Pressing Backspace deletes material to the left of the insertion point.
- If a template for a radical, a label, an over/under symbol, parentheses, or brackets is to the right of the insertion point, pressing Del or Backspace deletes the template but leaves the contents.

Applying Templates

Suppose that you enter a mathematical expression like $x–2$ and you want to put $x–2$ inside a radical. Usually, you first select the radical icon and then place $x–2$ in the input box. This section, however, explains how to apply the radical template after you create the equation—how to put $x–2$ into the radical after you have typed $x–2$, for example.

If you want to apply a template to an existing equation or part of an existing equation, select the equation or the part of the equation to which you want to apply the template. In the case of a fraction template, the selected expression becomes the numerator of the fraction. For a matrix, the selected expression becomes the first cell of the matrix. In this example, insert $x–2$ into the radical and select $x–2$. Figure 22.49 shows $x–2$ selected. Then click the icon of the template you want to apply. In this example, click the radical icon. Figure 22.50 shows the radical applied to the selection.

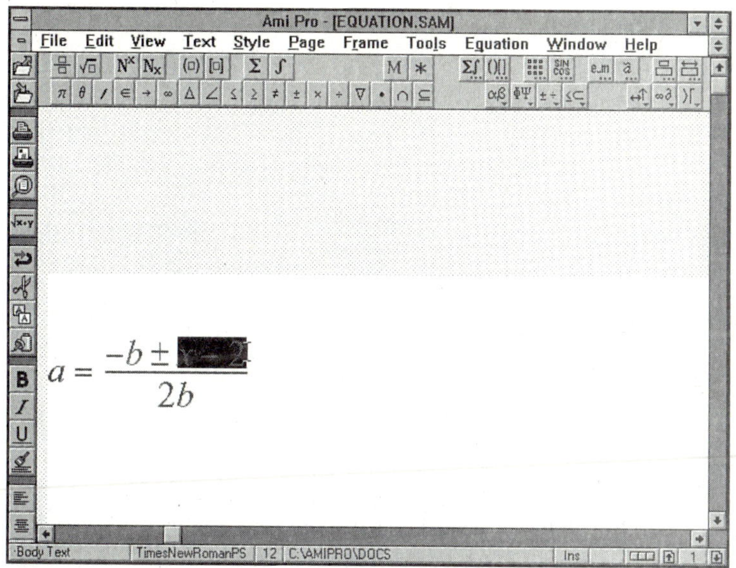

Fig. 22.49
The selected equation text.

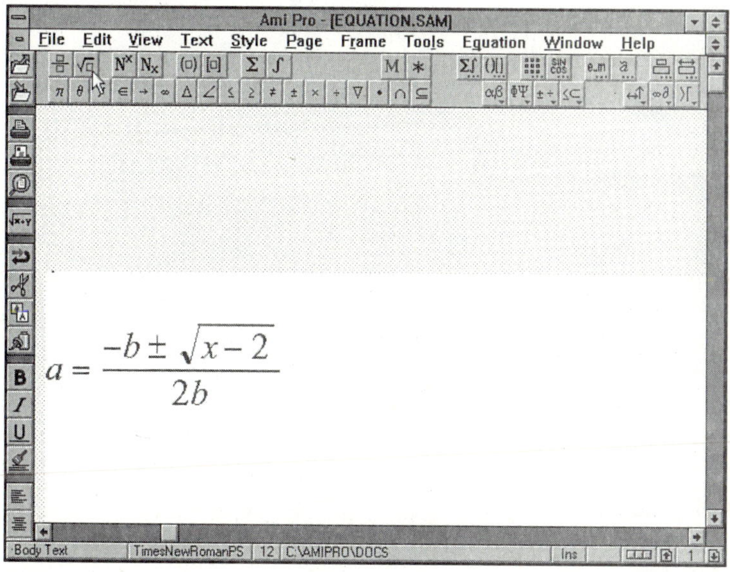

Fig. 22.50
The selected text appears inside the radical.

Editing Matrices

You can easily revise a matrix by selecting the matrix, either by clicking on the matrix dialog box icon or by selecting E**q**uation **I**nsert **M**atrix. The Revise Matrix dialog box appears. You can choose to insert rows or columns. You cannot insert both at the same time. Figure 22.51 shows the Revise Matrix dialog box set to add two columns to the end of the matrix. Note that the Number to **I**nsert text box is set to 2, and the At **P**osition box is set to 3 (which is the next column position, the end position, for this matrix). The small arrow in the sample display box shows where the columns will be inserted. Click OK to add the two columns. You have to reselect the matrix and click the matrix dialog box icon to add rows to the matrix.

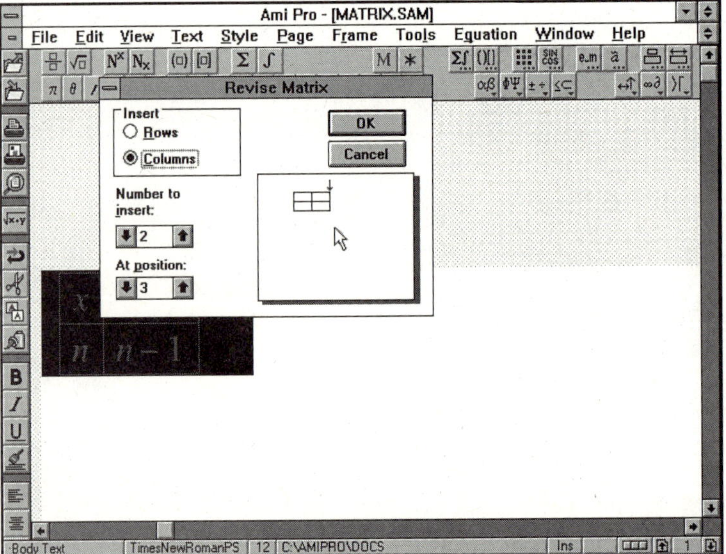

Fig. 22.51
The Revise Matrix dialog box, set to add two columns.

Figure 22.52 shows the Revise Matrix dialog box set to add one row to the bottom of the matrix. Figure 22.53 shows the changed matrix with two columns and one row added.

You can increase or decrease the number of cells in an existing matrix by splitting or combining cells. To add a cell to a matrix, move the insertion point to the position where you want to insert the cell—at the beginning, end, or middle of a mathematical expression in the cell. Press Enter. The matrix now has two cells where it originally had one cell (see fig. 22.54).

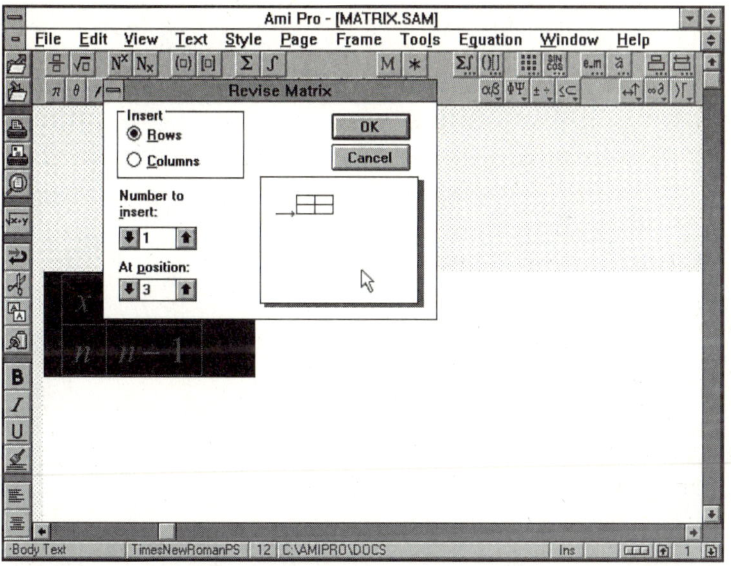

Fig. 22.52
The Revise Matrix dialog box, set to add one row.

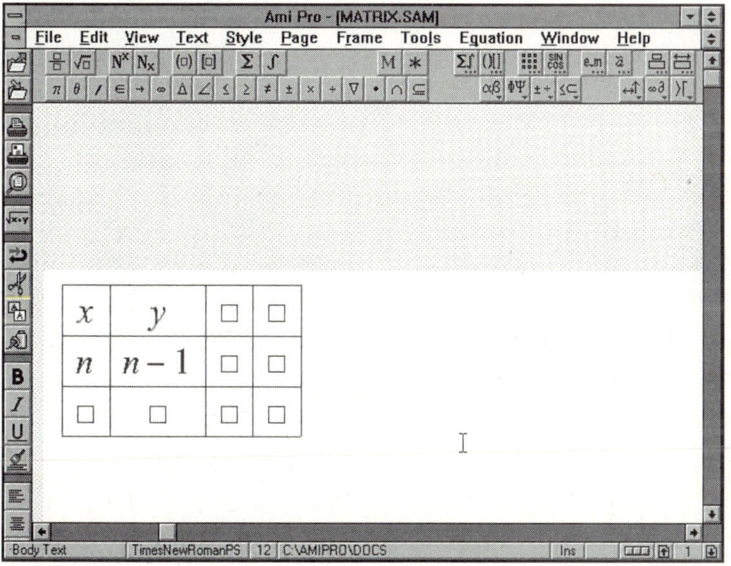

Fig. 22.53
The revised matrix.

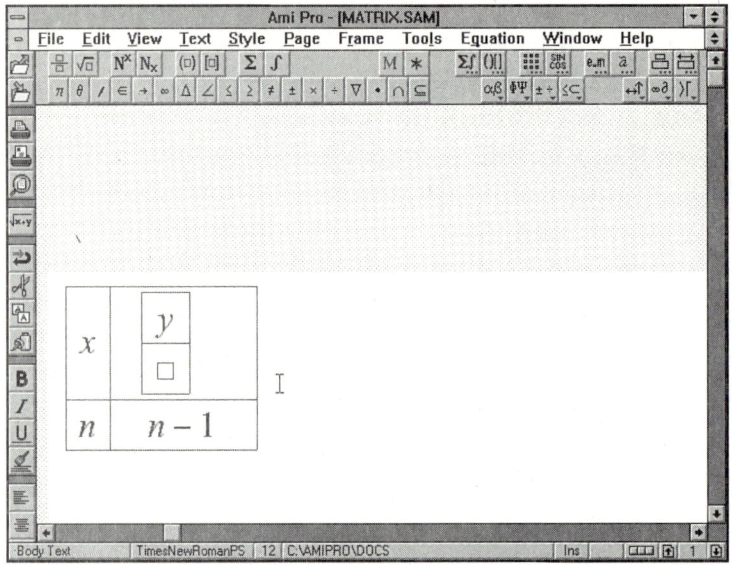

Fig. 22.54
An added cell to a matrix.

◄ See "Selecting Text," p. 76

◄ See "Moving Text," p. 79

◄ See "Copying Text," p. 81

◄ See "Deleting Text," p. 83

◄ See "Manipulating Frames," p. 504

If the matrix has only one row or column, the new cell follows the one from which it was split. Otherwise, in a matrix with several rows and columns, the new cell is inside the old cell.

To delete a cell from a matrix, place the insertion point in the cell you want to delete and press Backspace.

If you want to delete the contents of a cell but leave the cell in place, select the contents you want to delete and then press Del. If this process leaves the cell empty, an input box appears. If necessary, type a new value in the input box.

To delete a row or a column from a matrix, select the row or column you want to delete and press Del.

Changing the Appearance of Equations

You can vary the look of equations by changing the size of the symbols used, the location of the limits, and the style and color of the characters. This section explains how to alter these characteristics. Because Ami Pro automatically follows standard mathematical typesetting conventions, however, you don't need to use this option for most applications.

Changing Limit Position and Size

Limit position is the place where the limit for an operator (such as a summation or an integral) is printed. To change the default for limit position and the size of the symbols, choose E**q**uation and then choose **L**imits & Size Small or **L**imits & Size Big. (This option is a toggle switch.)

The **L**imits & Size Small option produces a smaller font and places limit templates to the right of the symbol. The **L**imits & Size Big option produces a larger font and places limit templates above or below the summation symbol.

These settings in the E**q**uation menu are only defaults. You can override the settings when you enter an operator symbol. See the "Operators" section, earlier in this chapter, for more information.

Setting Screen Preferences

You use the Preferences dialog box to change the size, type style, and screen color of the various elements of equations. To access the Preferences dialog box, shown in figure 22.55, choose E**q**uation **P**references.

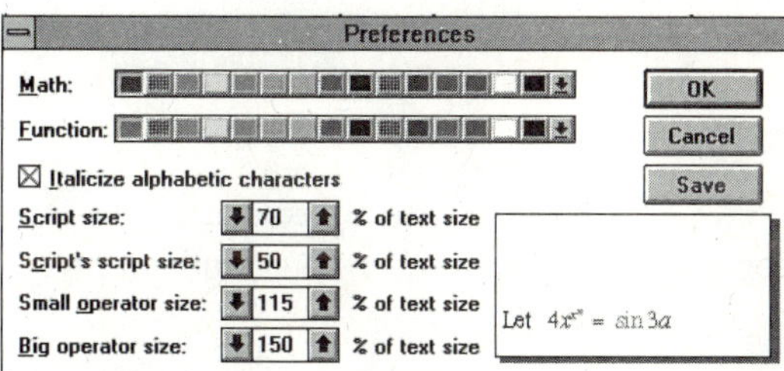

Fig. 22.55
The Preferences dialog box.

In the **M**ath color bar, specify a color for math characters. The math characters are all the characters in an equation except functions and labels. In the example box in figure 22.55, all the characters except *Let* and *sin* appear in red as math characters. In the **F**unction color bar, specify a color for function symbols. Clicking the arrow button produces more colors and patterns.

If you want letters in equations to appear in italics, select the **I**talicize Alphabetic Characters option.

For the **S**cript Size option, specify the size for subscripts and superscripts as a percentage of text size. You can use any number from 25 to 100 percent. The S**c**ript's Script Size option works in the same manner, specifying the size for script's script—subscripts and superscripts within subscripts and superscripts.

The Small **O**perator Size option specifies the size of small operators as a percentage of text size. You can use any number from 100 to 200 percent. The **B**ig Operator Size option uses the same percentage range for big operators.

After you finish specifying your preferences, choose **S**ave to save the changes. Choose OK or press Enter to leave the dialog box.

To reset your screen preferences at any time, return to the Preferences dialog box.

To change the default typeface for text in equation mode, choose **T**ext **F**ont while in equation mode. The typeface, point size, and color you choose are applied to all text in the current equation and any new equations. Existing equations that aren't selected don't change.

Summary

In this chapter, you became acquainted with Ami Pro's Equation Editor and all the equation capabilities the product offers. You learned how to enter and exit the Equation Editor. You explored the equation screen and learned how to use the equation icons. You also learned how to create, navigate, and edit equations, and how to import and save TeX files.

In the next chapter, you learn about the macro capability of Ami Pro. This feature of the program enables you to save time and keystrokes by automating repetitive or complicated tasks.

Chapter 23

Using Macros

You often may perform Ami Pro tasks requiring multiple keystrokes. If you perform the same multiple-keystroke or multiple-command task frequently, you can *record* (create) a *macro*—a shortcut that enables you to place many commands, keystrokes, and other instructions together so that you can perform them as one operation. You can create your own macros by recording the keystrokes and commands as you use them, or by writing the macros with Ami Pro's macro language. In addition, Lotus provides many prewritten macros, ready for you to use to extend the functionality of Ami Pro. You can run macros via Ami Pro menus, or assign macros to shortcut keys so that you can run the macros with quick keystrokes. You even can assign macros to SmartIcons.

In this chapter, you learn how to use menus to record and run macros. Then you learn how to use Ami Pro's macro language to modify and write macros. You discover how to make a macro play automatically—when you start or exit from Ami Pro, when you open a particular file, when you create a new file with a given style sheet, or when you select a frame. In the chapter, you also explore some macros that you may find useful to reproduce and use "as is," or use as starting points for your own efforts.

Recording and Playing Macros

Although Ami Pro provides many predefined macros, the designers may not have anticipated your specialized needs. Whether your requirements are simple or complex, you can create custom macros that meet your needs.

Suppose that you often need to change a block of text to uppercase letters. You can do this by using the **E**dit **C**aps command, of course—or you can simplify the process by creating a macro and then assigning that macro to a keystroke combination.

The number of macro possibilities literally is endless. Your custom macros can save time, increase efficiency, increase accuracy, and (in the spirit of Ami Pro) even be fun.

Recording a Macro

The simplest way to create and use macros is to tell Ami Pro to record your actions. Suppose that you often switch to outline mode and review the top level headings of your document. Follow these steps to record a macro to do the steps automatically:

1. Choose Too**l**s **M**acros. The **M**acros menu cascades from the Too**l**s menu, as shown in figure 23.1.

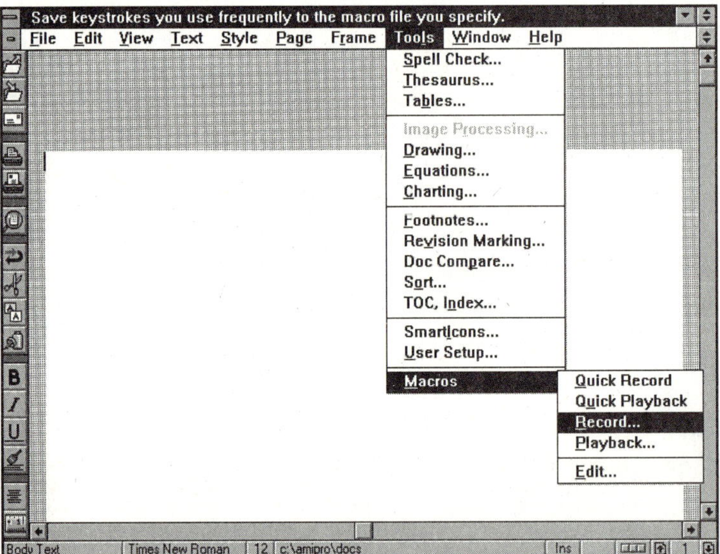

Fig. 23.1 The **M**acros cascading menu.

2. From the **M**acros menu, choose **R**ecord. The Record Macro dialog box appears, as shown in figure 23.2.

3. Type a name for the macro in the Macro **F**ile text box. (Follow the normal DOS naming conventions.) Ami Pro automatically includes an SMM file extension to identify the file as a macro.

   If you have macros in the directory you are using, Ami Pro lists those macros in the **M**acros list box. You can use one of those names for your new macro by selecting the name you want to use. (If you assign the same name, Ami Pro overwrites the original macro but warns you before taking that action.) For the sample macro, type the name `OUTLINE.SMM` in the Macro **F**ile text box.

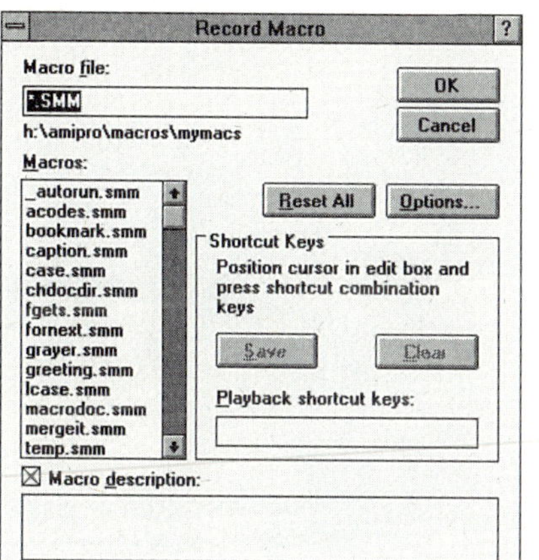

Fig. 23.2
The Record Macro dialog box.

4. Choose OK or press Enter. The menus close and Ami Pro returns to the document. In the Status Bar, where the current directory or date and time normally appear, the program displays the message `Recording Macro` to remind you that Ami Pro is recording every operation you perform as part of the macro.

5. Perform the task you want to assign to the macro. As you work, Ami Pro records your actions to create the macro.

   If you don't want to create the outlining macro described at the beginning of this section, perform the actions you want to record in your macro in place of steps 6 and 7; then skip to step 8.

6. To create the sample outlining macro described at the beginning of this section, choose **V**iew **O**utline Mode to switch to outline mode.

7. Click the `1` button to display only level 1 headings in the outline.

8. After you complete the steps you want in the macro, you are ready to end the macro. Choose Too**l**s **M**acros. The **M**acros cascading menu now offers only the End **R**ecord option, as shown in figure 23.3. (All other options are dimmed.)

9. Choose End **R**ecord to finish recording the macro. Ami Pro saves the macro and returns to the document and the Status Bar returns to normal display. Your macro is now ready for playback when needed.

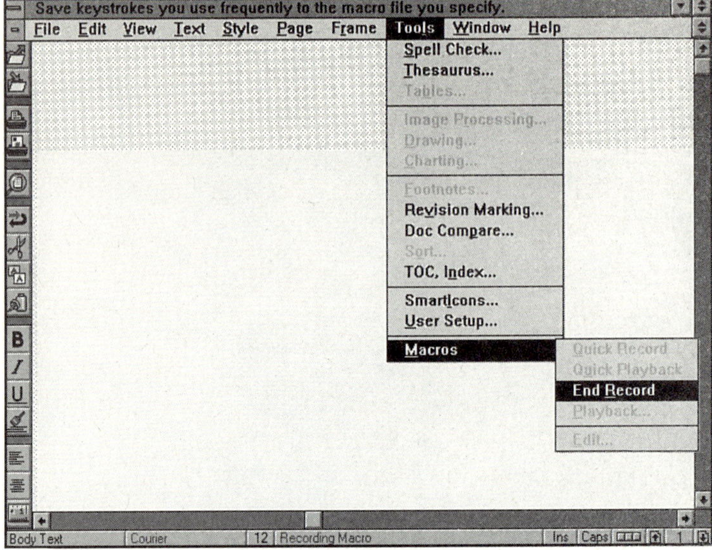

Fig. 23.3
The **M**acros cascading menu with the End **R**ecord option.

Tip
An alternate method for ending the recording is to click the area of the Status Bar that displays (in red) `Recording Macro`.

Caution

Be careful while recording a macro. If you make a mistake, that mistake becomes part of the macro.

If you make a mistake, you can edit the macro with Ami Pro. You learn how to edit macros later in this chapter.

You can record in your macro most of the operations available in Ami Pro. The few exceptions, actions that don't "take" when you record a macro, are the following operations:

- Mouse movements, such as moving the mouse pointer from one area of the screen to another (use keyboard commands to move to the desired insertion point)
- Settings in the Help, Drawing, Charting, Image Processing, Equations, File Management, Spell Check, and Thesaurus dialog boxes (Ami Pro records only the accessing of the dialog box)
- Changes made to the Status Bar to change the document path; current date and time; or the current line, column, and position
- The Find option in **E**dit Find & **R**eplace (Choosing Replace All *does* record, however)

- Menu items on the Tools Macros menu
- Text entered into a note
- System menu commands for Ami Pro document windows

Assigning Shortcut Keys

You aren't required to use a shortcut key combination for a macro. If you don't designate a shortcut key combination, you can run the macro by using the Tools Macros Playback command, or you can assign it to a SmartIcon. If you define a shortcut key combination for use with your macro, however, you can replay the macro with that key combination. This feature saves time—especially for macros that you use often.

Note

Ami Pro includes several SmartIcons that are useful for editing macros. You may want to assign these SmartIcons to your SmartIcon palette. To select and customize your SmartIcon palette, choose Tools SmartIcons and then make your changes in the SmartIcons dialog box. The predefined SmartIcons include Toggle Record Start/Stop, Play Back Macro, Toggle Quick Record Start/Stop, and Play Back a Quick Macro.

To assign a shortcut key, choose Tools Macros Edit. The Edit Macro dialog box appears (see fig. 23.4). You also can assign shortcut keys from the Play Macro dialog box—choose Tools Macros Playback and follow the procedure described in this section.

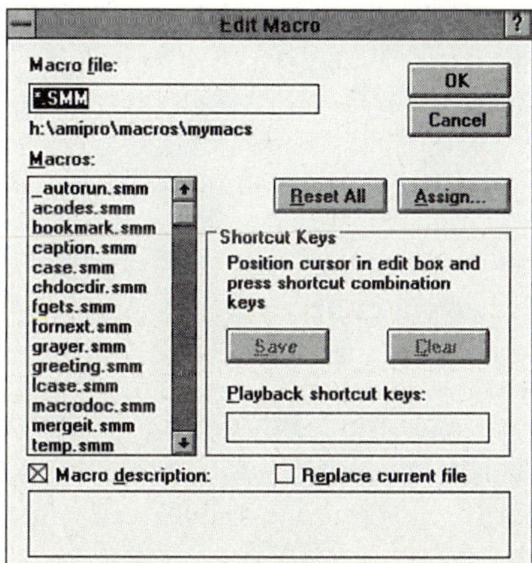

Fig. 23.4
The Edit Macro dialog box.

In the **M**acros list box, select the macro to which you want to assign shortcut keys. (If you prefer, you can type the macro name in the Macro **F**ile text box.) Next, move the cursor to the **P**layback Shortcut Keys text box and press the key combination you want to use. To designate Ctrl+F1 as the shortcut key combination for a macro, for example, hold down Ctrl and press F1. Ami Pro inserts `Ctrl+F1` in the **P**layback Shortcut Keys text box.

You can use any of the following as shortcut key combinations:

- The Ctrl key plus a function key (F1, F2, and so on); Ami Pro displays this type of combination as (for example) `CTRL+F3`. Note that you cannot use Ctrl+F10.
- The Shift key with a function key (for example, Shift+F2). You cannot use Shift+F1, however, because Ami Pro uses Shift+F1 for point-and-shoot help. You also cannot use Shift+F10; this key combination is reserved by Ami Pro and therefore is unavailable as a shortcut key sequence.
- Both Shift and Ctrl with a function key (for example, Shift+Ctrl+F2). You cannot use this combination with F10.
- Ctrl and Alt with a function key (for example, Ctrl+Alt+F7).
- Shift, Ctrl, and Alt with a function key (for example, Shift+Ctrl+Alt+F5).
- Ctrl and a letter key (for example, Ctrl+C).
- Shift, Ctrl, and a letter key (for example, Shift+Ctrl+C).

Note that all the Ctrl+*letter* key combinations are used by Ami Pro as accelerator keys for menu options. If you assign a macro to Ctrl+B (the accelerator-key combination to create boldface text), for example, you no longer can use Ctrl+B for boldfacing. If you try to assign an accelerator key as a macro, Ami Pro displays a warning message, as shown in figure 23.5.

Tip
To tell Ami Pro to revert to using the key combination as the menu accelerator key, just delete the key assignment.

After you choose OK in the message box, you still can change the shortcut key assignment; if you rarely use the accelerator key for its original purpose, though, you can go ahead and use it as a shortcut key for your macro.

Ami Pro also warns you if you are about to assign an existing macro shortcut key to a new macro. As with the accelerator key warning, you can respond by changing your shortcut key assignment or by overriding the prior assignment.

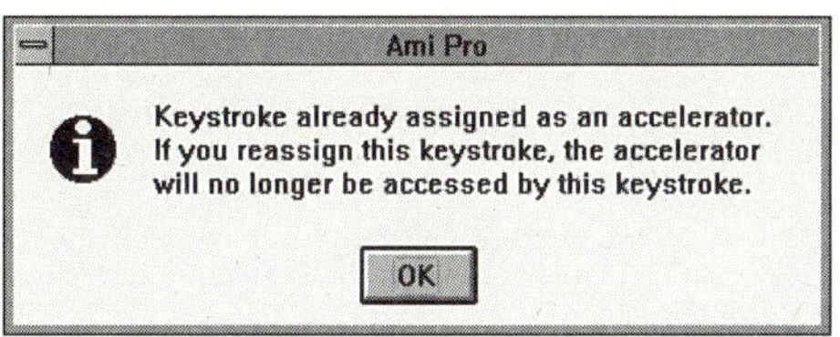

Fig. 23.5
The warning message that appears when you tell Ami Pro to assign an accelerator key to a macro.

To *reset* (clear) the shortcut keys for all macros, choose **R**eset All in the Record Macro dialog box. You also can reset all shortcut keys in the Play Macro dialog box (described later). If you attempt to reset, Ami Pro displays a warning box, as shown in figure 23.6.

This message reminds you that you are about to clear *all* custom shortcut keys. If you want to proceed, choose OK; if not, choose Cancel. Ami Pro returns to the Record Macro dialog box. If you choose OK, Ami Pro clears all your shortcut keys.

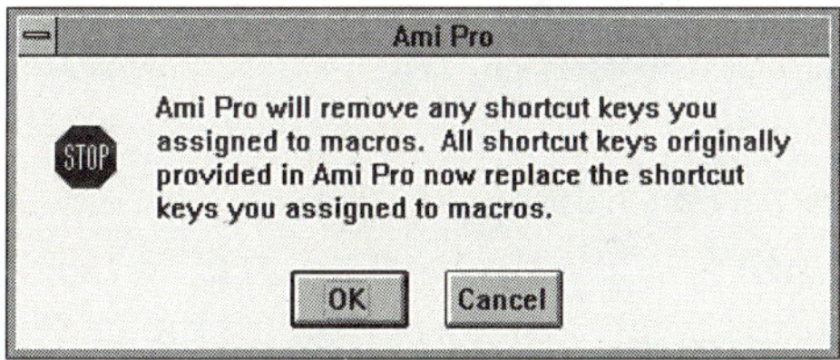

Fig. 23.6
The warning message that appears after you choose the **R**eset All option.

Playing a Macro

After you create a macro, you can play it back by choosing Too**l**s **M**acros **P**layback from the menu or by pressing the shortcut key (if you assigned a shortcut key). When you use the menu method, the Play Macro dialog box appears, as shown in figure 23.7.

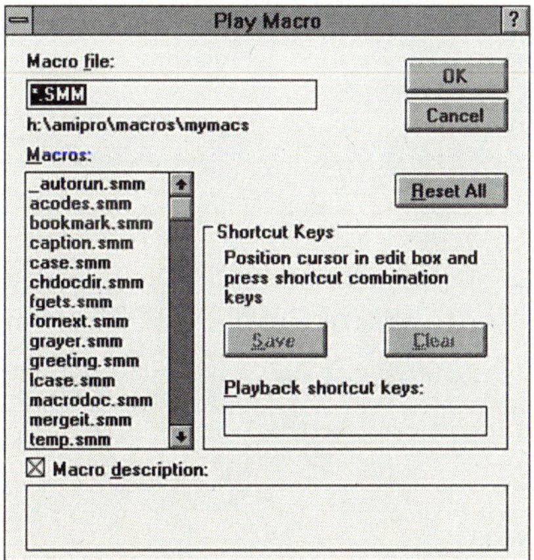

Fig. 23.7
The Play Macro dialog box.

Select the macro you want to run in the **M**acros list box or type the macro file name in the Macro **F**ile text box; then choose OK or press Enter. Ami Pro runs the macro.

> **Note**
>
> You may want to create a macro that displays a dialog box and then turns over control to the user; for example, you may want to display the Bookmarks dialog box so that the user can select a bookmark. Assigning a macro like this to a shortcut key combination can cut the time needed to access commonly used dialog boxes. If you try to record this type of macro, however, Ami Pro doesn't let you access the Too**l**s menu to end recording while the dialog box is displayed. You cannot create this kind of macro with the Record Macro feature. For most dialog boxes, you *can* use Ami Pro's macro language to write a very simple three-line macro that displays the dialog box and then lets the user decide how to use the dialog box. For details, see the section "Displaying a Dialog Box," later in this chapter.

Adding a Macro Description

A description is nearly essential for most macros. You need to be able to identify what the macro accomplishes before you play the macro and modify your document. When you record a macro, you can name it (as described earlier), but you cannot provide a description for the macro at that time.

After you have saved the macro, follow these steps to provide a description for the macro:

1. Choose **F**ile **O**pen. The Open dialog box appears.
2. In the File **T**ype list box, click the arrow button to display the available file types. Select Ami Pro Macro.

   The file name in the File **N**ame text box changes to `*.SMM` and the path name for the directory changes to the directory you set up for macros; for example, to `C:\AMIPRO\MACROS`.
3. Select the desired macro in the **F**iles list box (or type the file name in the File **N**ame text box).
4. Choose OK or press Enter. Ami Pro displays the file containing the macro (written in Ami Pro macro programming language).
5. Choose **F**ile **D**oc Info. The Doc Info dialog box appears, with the cursor in the text box for **D**escription.

6. Type the description.

7. Choose OK or press Enter.

8. Choose **F**ile **S**ave to save the description with the document.

After you add a description to a macro, Ami Pro displays the description of the macro when you highlight the macro name in any dialog box that lists macros (such as the Play Macro dialog box).

Note

As you become proficient at creating macros, you may create more than you can remember by name—or you may be unable to find your macros among the predefined macros in the list. To solve this problem, create a document that lists your macros. List each macro by file name; note the shortcut keys for the macro and a brief description of the actions the macro performs.

◄ See "Using the Keyboard," p. 16

◄ See "Setting Up SmartIcons," p. 216

◄ See "Document Management with the File Menu," p. 722

Creating and Using Quick Macros

Sometimes you may have a temporary need for a specialized macro. Suppose that you have imported an ASCII text file into Ami Pro and you need to remove hard returns at the end of some lines, converting them into spaces. You may not need a macro that performs this function in your permanent macro collection—just in your current editing session.

You can create and use a *quick macro* without saving the macro for future use. When you use the Quick Record and Quick Playback features to create and use a quick macro, that macro is available only for the rest of the current Ami Pro session. Ami Pro doesn't save the macro.

Note

You can have only one quick macro defined at any given time. When you exit from Ami Pro, you lose the quick macro. If you record a new quick macro, you overwrite any existing quick macro.

Recording and Playing Quick Macros

To create a quick macro, follow these steps:

1. Choose Too**l**s **M**acros. The **M**acros menu appears.

2. Choose **Q**uick Record. The menus close and Ami Pro returns to the document. The Status Bar displays the message `Recording Macro` to remind you that operations you perform are being recorded as part of a quick macro.

3. Perform the tasks you want to include in the quick macro.

4. Choose Too**l**s **M**acros. The **M**acros menu now displays an End **Q**uick Record option, as shown in figure 23.8.

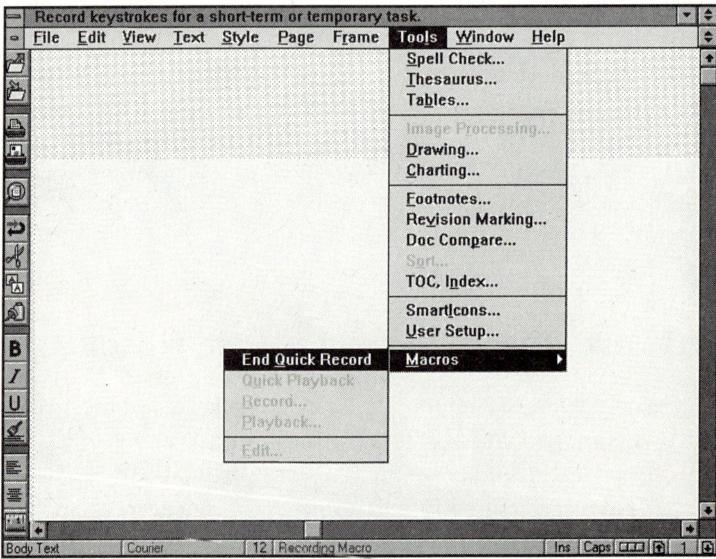

Fig. 23.8
The **M**acros menu, with the End **Q**uick Record option selected.

5. Choose End **Q**uick Record. If you prefer, you can end the macro recording by clicking the area of the Status Bar that displays (in red) `Recording Macro`. Either action ends the recording, and the Status Bar returns to its normal display.

   The menus close and Ami Pro returns to the document.

You now can use the quick macro. Just as you record a quick macro without assigning it a name, you play it back without using a name. To run a quick macro, choose Too**l**s **M**acros. When the **M**acros cascading menu appears, choose Q**u**ick Playback. Ami Pro runs the quick macro.

Note

Ami Pro saves the quick macro in the file UNTITLED.SMM. If you want to save a quick macro, choose **F**ile **O**pen and open the macro file UNTITLED.SMM. Using the **F**ile Save **A**s command, save the macro file with a name other than UNTITLED.SMM. Then you can play the macro as you do any other permanent macro.

Using Shortcut Keys with Quick Record and Quick Playback

You can make the Quick Record and Quick Playback features even faster by assigning shortcut keys to these two operations. To assign shortcut keys to the Quick Record and Quick Playback features, follow these steps:

1. Choose Too**l**s **M**acros **R**ecord to display the Record Macro dialog box (see fig. 23.9).

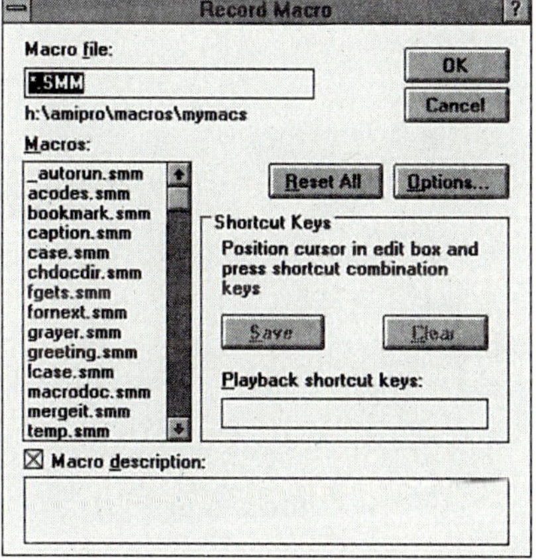

Fig. 23.9
The Record Macro dialog box.

2. Choose **O**ptions. The Quick Record Macro Options dialog box opens, as shown in figure 23.10. The cursor moves to the Start/Stop **R**ecord text box.

3. Press the key or keys you want to use as shortcut keys for the Quick Record feature. (See the section "Assigning Shortcut Keys" earlier in this chapter, for a list of keys you can use as shortcut keys.) Ami Pro inserts into the Start/Stop Record text box the names of the keys you pressed. If you hold down the Shift key and press F5, for example, `Shift+F5` appears in the text box.

Fig. 23.10
The Quick Record Macro Options dialog box.

4. Move the cursor to the Start **P**layback text box and press the key or keys you want to use as shortcut keys for Quick Playback. The names of the keys you pressed (`Shift+F6`, for example) appear in the Start **P**layback text box.

5. Choose OK or press Enter to close the Quick Record Macro Options dialog box and return to the Record Macro dialog box.

6. Choose Close in the Record Macro dialog box to return to the document.

When you want to record a quick macro, press the Quick Record shortcut keys you defined. Ami Pro begins recording a quick macro immediately. To stop recording, press the Quick Record shortcut keys again. To play back the quick macro, use the Quick Playback shortcut keys.

To see how the process works, press the sample Quick Record key combination you created in the preceding steps (Shift+F5). Notice that the `Recording Macro` message appears in the Status Bar. Perform any simple operation, such as printing a copy of your document. When you finish the operation, press Shift+F5 again. The message disappears; you have created a new quick macro.

To use your new quick macro, press the sample Quick Playback shortcut key combination, Shift+F6. The operations you recorded in the quick macro run immediately.

Using Predefined Macros

Ami Pro comes with a number of predefined macros. To try the existing macros, follow the same steps as you would to play back a macro that you created. You can assign the predefined macros to shortcut keys or to SmartIcons (some even come with their own preassigned SmartIcons). Table 23.1 describes the predefined macros.

Table 23.1 Macros Supplied with Ami Pro 3

Macro	Description
_AUTORUN.SMM	Auto-runs multiple macros
123W.SMM	Launches 1-2-3 for Windows
ACODES.SMM	Looks up regional information by area code
AMIENV.SMM	Automatic printing of envelopes in Ami Pro 3; this macro isn't intended to be run by itself
AMIMENUS.SMM	Customizes Ami Pro menus
AMIMERGE.SMM	Merge module; this macro isn't intended to be run by itself
AUTOCAL.SMM	Accessed from a power field in _CALMON.STY to automate processing monthly calendars; this macro isn't intended to be run by itself
AUTOSTY.SMM	Automates style sheets that collect information and insert that information into a new document; this macro isn't intended to be run by itself
CCMAIL.SMM	Launches Lotus cc:Mail
CHARMAP.SMM	Inserts a special character
CHGFONT.SMM	Changes the fonts in style sheets to available fonts that you can select
CLEANSCR.SMM	Displays the clean screen options
CLOSEALL.SMM	Closes all open documents
CNTRFRAM.SMM	Centers a frame horizontally on the page
COLLECT.SMM	Gathers data for the automatic style sheets
CONVERT.SMM	Automatically converts other word processing document files into Ami Pro files
COPYRITE.SMM	Inserts the copyright symbol (©)
CROSSREF.SMM	Generates cross-references between files in a master document with fewer than eight files
DATAMAN.SMM	Builds and edits a database
DOS.SMM	Shell to DOS
EDITMAC.SMM	Edits a macro

(continues)

Table 23.1 Continued

Macro	Description
FIND.SMM	Finds text in a document
FINDFILE.SMM	Finds and opens documents
FIT2SCRN.SMM	Fits view to screen
FLW.SMM	Launches Lotus Freelance for Windows
FONTDN.SMM	Makes text smaller
FONTUP.SMM	Makes text larger
FRAMCUST.SMM	Automates "click here to insert" frames in _NEWSLT?.STY; this macro isn't intended to be run by itself
FRAMGLOS.SMM	Locates and saves frames in a glossary file
FREPLACE.SMM	Finds and replaces across multiple files
FSPELL.SMM	Spell checks multiple documents
GAME.SMM	MacroMindBlaster Game
INDEXALL.SMM	Automatically marks all occurrences of a word for the index
KEYWORD.SMM	Locates files by document info
LABEL.SMM	Automates _LABEL.STY, providing the engine for Avery label-building; this macro isn't intended to be run by itself
MAKELABL.SMM	Uses the current page layout and any label settings in the Label style sheet
MARKMENU.SMM	Places document bookmarks on the main menu; selecting them allows quick access to bookmarks
MASTRDOC.SMM	Browses between files of a master document
MENULITE.SMM	Toggles between long and short menus
NEWNOW.SMM	Opens a new document, using the default style sheet
NOTES.SMM	Loads Lotus Notes
OLDKEYS.SMM	Restores the Ctrl+C and Ctrl+V keys to center and switch view levels
OPENDOCS.SMM	Selects multiple documents to open

Macro	Description
ORGANIZE.SMM	Launches Lotus Organizer
PRINTNOW.SMM	Prints all of the current document
PRNBATCH.SMM	Selects multiple files to print
PRNPAGES.SMM	Selects pages to print
PRNSHADE.SMM	Prints the selected text
QS_FIRST.SMM	Starts Ami Pro QuickStart Tutorial when Ami Pro is launched
REGMARK.SMM	Inserts the registration mark (®)
SAVEINFO.SMM	Makes the Save and Save As commands bring up Doc Info
SAVSHADE.SMM	Saves selected text to a new file
SKAUTO.SMM	Starts up Ami Pro SwitchKit for WordPerfect users
SKDATA1.SMM	Used by SwitchKit
SKDATA2.SMM	Used by SwitchKit
SKDATA3.SMM	Used by SwitchKit
SMARTEXT.SMM	Launches Lotus SmarText
SMARTFLD.SMM	Tools to build automated style sheets
SMARTPIC.SMM	Quick access to Lotus SmartPics Sampler; assign to the custom SmartIcon provided for direct access
SMARTYPE.SMM	Changes quotes, dashes, and apostrophes to typeset-style characters
SPECIALF.SMM	Installs special features for Ami Pro
SWITCH.SMM	Starts up Ami Pro SwitchKit for WordPerfect users
TILEHORZ.SMM	Tiles open documents horizontally
TM.SMM	Inserts the trademark symbol (™)
TOA.SMM	Table of Authorities application
TOAGEN.SMM	Generates a Table of Authorities
TOALONG.SMM	Marks text as a TOA long entry
TOAREMOV.SMM	Removes TOA mark

(continues)

Table 23.1 Continued

Macro	Description
TOASHORT.SMM	Marks text for a short TOA entry
TYPECHAR.SMM	Inserts special characters into the document
WINFILE.SMM	Launches Windows File Manager
WORDCNT.SMM	Displays the number of words and other information about the open document
WORKGRUP.SMM	Opens and saves groups of related Ami Pro documents

Using Automatic Macros

Ami Pro offers another handy macro feature—the automatic macro. An *automatic macro* is one that you assign to run when executing any of the following operations:

- Opening or closing a document
- Starting or exiting from Ami Pro
- Selecting a style sheet when you start Ami Pro
- Selecting a frame

The following sections describe the operation of automatic macros in each of these situations.

Running Macros When You Open or Close a File

Suppose that you want to run the OUTLINE.SMM macro (described earlier in this chapter) each time you open a document named OUTLINE.SAM. After you assign the macro to run automatically, when you open the document Ami Pro runs the macro. In this case, the program switches to outline mode and collapses the document to show only outline level 1.

To assign a macro to run automatically, follow these steps:

1. Display the file to which you want to assign a macro.
2. Choose Too**l**s **M**acros **E**dit. The Edit Macro dialog box appears (refer to fig. 23.4).

3. Choose **A**ssign. The Assign Macro To Run Automatically dialog box appears, as shown in figure 23.11.

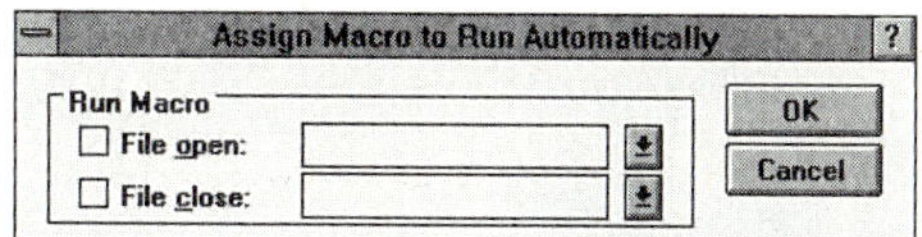

Fig. 23.11
The Assign Macro to Run Automatically dialog box.

4. To run the macro when the file is opened, select the File **O**pen option. To run the macro when the file is closed, select the File **C**lose option. For either option, click the down-arrow button in the list box to display a list of available macros.

5. Select the desired macro from the displayed list. The selected macro appears in the list box. You can select one macro to run when you open the file and one to run when you close it.

6. After you finish assigning macros, choose OK or press Enter. The dialog box closes and Ami Pro returns to the Edit Macro dialog box.

7. Choose Close to leave the Edit Macro dialog box and return to the displayed file.

8. Choose **F**ile **S**ave to resave the document with the macro run options. Depending on your specifications, the assigned macro runs when Ami Pro opens or closes the file.

Running Macros When You Start or Exit Ami Pro

You can run macros automatically when you load or exit Ami Pro. To run a single macro when you load or exit Ami Pro, specify the desired files in the Run Macros section of the User Setup dialog box (see Chapter 8, "Changing Your Setup," for details).

The limitation of the Run Macros box in the User Setup dialog box is that you can specify only one macro. What if you want to run more than one macro? To tell Ami Pro to run more than one macro automatically each time the program starts, follow these steps:

1. Choose Too**l**s **M**acros **P**layback. The Play Macro dialog appears. (Ami Pro reads the description from every macro file in the directory before it displays this dialog box, so you may need to be patient.)

2. Highlight the _AUTORUN.SMM macro, and choose OK to run the macro. _AUTORUN.SMM is one of the macros supplied with Ami Pro. The Autorun Macros dialog box appears (see fig. 23.12). The Ma**c**ros list box shows every macro in the directory. The I**n**stalled list box shows any macros that are designated to be run when Ami Pro starts.

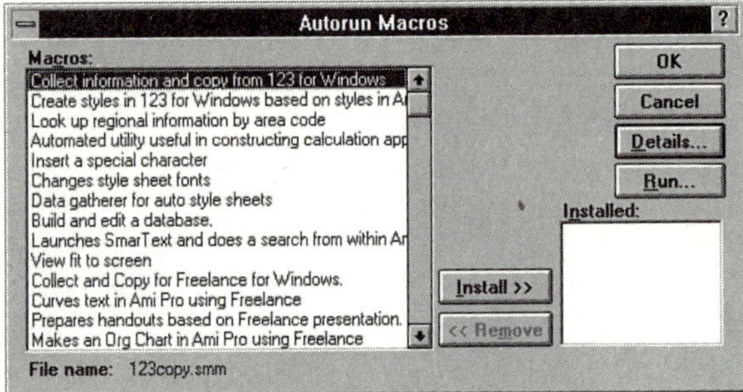

Fig. 23.12
The Autorun Macros dialog box that appears when you use _AUTORUN.SMM.

3. In the Ma**c**ros list box, highlight the first macro you want to run automatically when you start Ami Pro. Then choose **I**nstall. The macro name appears in the I**n**stalled list box. All macros in the I**n**stalled list box run automatically when you start Ami Pro. If you make a mistake, you can remove a macro from the auto-run list by highlighting its name in the I**n**stalled list box and choosing Re**m**ove.

   If you want to see more details about the functions of Ami Pro's predefined macros, choose **D**etails.

4. When all the automatic macros you want are listed in the I**n**stalled list box, choose OK or press Enter. The next time you start Ami Pro, all the selected macros run automatically.

Note

Some macros developed by Lotus Development Corporation may not appear in the Ma**c**ros list box. In the opinion of the developers, these macros shouldn't be run automatically. The developers mark these macros by putting the word `noautorun` in Field 4 of the Other Fields option in the Doc Info dialog box (see Chapter 21, "Managing Files and Documents," for more details on using Doc Info).

Note

If you run _AUTORUN.SMM, change the default macro path (with **U**ser Setup on the Too**l**s menu), and run _AUTORUN.SMM again, the macro displays the same list of files it showed you the first time—even though the path has changed. To make _AUTORUN.SMM read the files in the new macro directory, you must exit from Ami Pro and then start the program again.

Caution

After you select a set of macros to run automatically, if you change the default macro path the macros don't run automatically unless you copy them into the new macro directory.

Running a Macro When You Select a Style

To run a macro each time you create a document and select a particular style sheet, specify the macro and select the **R**un Macro option in the Save as a Style Sheet dialog box when you create the style sheet. The style sheet _ENVELOPE.STY is a good example of how macros can help automate your documents. The auto-run macro assigned to this style sheet displays a dialog box which prompts you for your default information (name, address, and so on) and then places this data on the envelope in the return address area. The macro then displays a dialog box where you can enter the addressee's data, and places this information in the appropriate area of the envelope.

Running a Macro When You Select a Frame

To run a macro each time you select a particular frame, select the R**u**n Macro option in the **T**ype version of the Modify Frame Layout dialog box when you modify the frame. You can use this feature, for example, to create "buttons" in your documents which perform a task when the reader selects them. The sample document GOODIES.SAM, which describes the macros included with Ami Pro, uses these types of frames to enable you to try the macros being described. Next to each macro description is a "button" (frame), which runs the described macro when you select it.

◀ See "Setting Defaults," p. 228

◀ See "Creating a New Style Sheet," p. 294

◀ See "Document Management with the File Menu," p. 722

Editing Macros

After you record a macro, you can modify the macro with Ami Pro's *macro language*. When modifying the macro, you can correct minor errors you may have made while recording the macro. You also can change the macro so that it performs different functions than those in the original version.

You also can use the macro language to write a macro from scratch. This feature gives you the ability to create much more sophisticated macros—macros that do more than just duplicate keystrokes and commands.

To fully use these capabilities, you need to know something about Ami Pro's macro language. A later section of this chapter, "Using Ami Pro's Macro Language," introduces you to the language. Meanwhile, in the following section you learn how to edit macros in Ami Pro and how to save new files as Ami Pro macro files.

Editing Existing Macros

To modify an existing macro, you load it into Ami Pro, edit it as you would a regular document file, and then save it. To retrieve the macro, follow these steps:

1. Choose Too**l**s **M**acros **E**dit. The Edit Macro dialog box opens, as shown in figure 23.13. A list of the macros available in the current directory appears in the **M**acros list box.

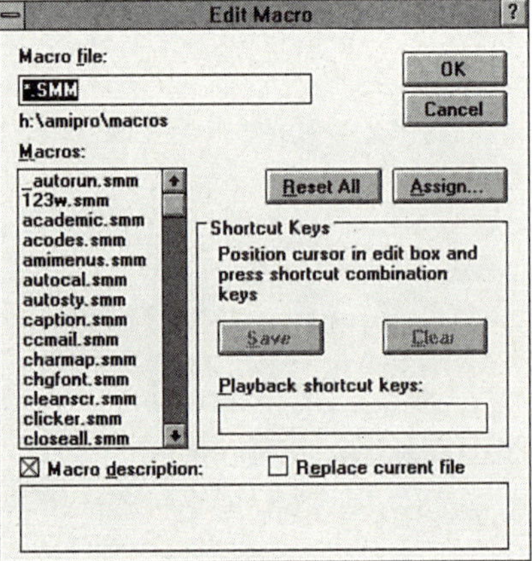

Fig. 23.13
The Edit Macro dialog box.

2. In the **M**acros list box, select the macro you want to modify. Ami Pro inserts the file name for the macro into the Macro **F**ile text box. If a description was entered for the macro (and the Macro **D**escription option is checked), the description appears in the Macro **D**escription text box. (If you prefer, you can type the file name in the Macro **F**ile text box.)

3. If you want to replace the current document with the macro file (rather than loading the macro into a new window), select the R**e**place Current File option.

4. If you want to change the shortcut keys, position the cursor in the **P**layback Shortcut Keys text box and press the key combination you want to use to invoke the macro. (Refer to "Assigning Shortcut Keys," earlier in this chapter, for a discussion of the keys you can use.)

5. Choose OK or press Enter. Ami Pro displays the macro file you have specified, with the macro's file name in the Title Bar at the top of the window. Figure 23.14 shows the macro CLOSEALL.SMM (one of the predefined macros supplied with Ami Pro) displayed in a window for editing.

Tip
You also can display a macro file for editing by using the **F**ile menu. Choose **F**ile **O**pen. Specify Ami Pro Macro in the List Files of **T**ype list box.

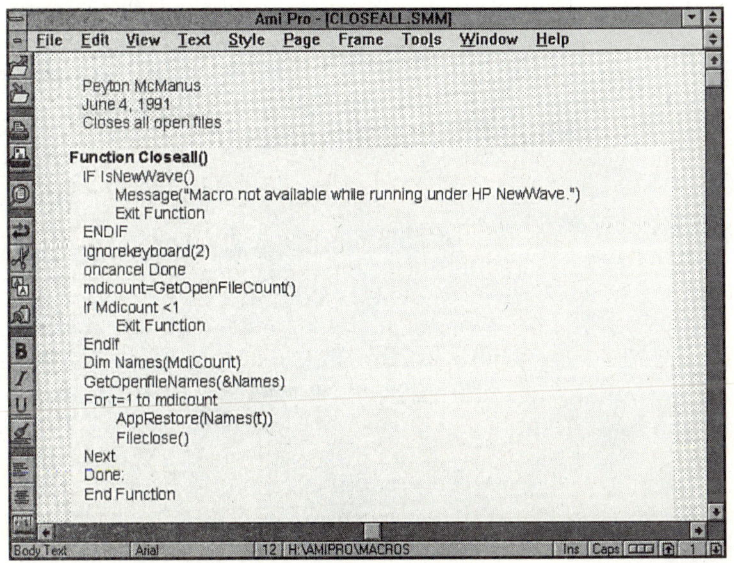
Ami Pro - [CLOSEALL.SMM]
File Edit View Text Style Page Frame Tools Window Help
Peyton McManus
June 4, 1991
Closes all open files
Function Closeall()
IF IsNewWave()
Message("Macro not available while running under HP NewWave.")
Exit Function
ENDIF
ignorekeyboard(2)
oncancel Done
mdicount=GetOpenFileCount()
If Mdicount <1
Exit Function
Endif
Dim Names(MdiCount)
GetOpenfileNames(&Names)
For t=1 to mdicount
AppRestore(Names(t))
Fileclose()
Next
Done:
End Function
Body Text
Arial
12 H:\AMIPRO\MACROS
Ins Caps

Fig. 23.14
The macro CLOSEALL.SMM (supplied with Ami Pro) displayed in a window for editing. This macro closes all open files.

The macro file contains the macro language instructions for executing the macro CLOSEALL.SMM. Notice that the file shows the macro in the Ami Pro macro language—the terms, format, and conventions that make the macro work (described later in this chapter). Edit the displayed macro file as necessary. After you finish modifying the macro file, choose **F**ile **S**ave to save the updated macro.

Tip
If you modify one of the macro files supplied with Ami Pro, save the macro under a new file name by using **F**ile Save **A**s.

When you save a macro file, Ami Pro *compiles* the macro (converts it into a special format) and checks for syntax errors. A *syntax error* is a mistake in how you wrote the macro. If Ami Pro finds any syntax errors, an error message appears and the program places the insertion point on the line of the macro where the syntax error occurred. Correct the error and save the file again. Ami Pro cannot save a macro file with a syntax error.

Note

If you want to save the file and come back later to track down the syntax error, choose **F**ile Save **A**s and change the List Files of **T**ype option to Ami Pro. Ami Pro saves the macro as a normal Ami Pro document (SAM) file. Before you can use the document as a macro, you must open it, find and correct all syntax errors, reset the file type to Ami Pro Macro, and save the file as a macro file (SMM).

Note

Syntax errors (also called *macro compilation errors*) are identified by numbers, which Ami Pro displays when the program finds an error. You can find more details on error numbers in the on-line documentation by choosing Help Macro Doc and then selecting the Macro Error Messages on the first Help screen.

Tip
Use the style sheet _MACRO.STY (supplied with Ami Pro) when writing macros. Select the style **W**ith Contents. _MACRO.STY contains some useful paragraph styles and a predefined header and footer.

Writing a New Macro

To write a new macro from scratch, simply use **F**ile **N**ew to create a new document. Enter the macro commands to perform the actions you want Ami Pro to execute. When you have entered all the commands, choose **F**ile **S**ave. Change the List Files of **T**ype option to Ami Pro Macro; then name the file and save it as you would any other file. As explained earlier, Ami Pro doesn't save a macro file if the file contains any syntax errors.

The new macro is available when you display a list of the current macros in the directory you specified for the new macro file. To assign shortcut keys to the new macro, use the Play Macro or Edit Macro dialog box.

Note

When you try again to save a macro file after Ami Pro has refused to save the file because of a syntax error, you must reselect the file type and retype the file name. If you write a long macro, you may need to repeat this cycle many times. You can simplify this process by the new macro file with just these two lines in the file:

```
FUNCTION Something()

END FUNCTION
```

Then save the file to establish the file name and type. You then can replace `Something()` with the real name of your first function and write the rest of the macro as you normally would.

Using Ami Pro's Macro Language

Ami Pro's macro language is a full-featured, rich programming language. If you aren't a programmer, don't let the words "programming language" scare you. While you need programming skills to exploit Ami Pro's programming language fully, with only a little basic understanding of the language you can edit macros you have recorded (to correct errors and change the macro operation), and write useful new macros that accomplish tasks impossible with the simple macros you can record.

In this section, you gain a basic understanding of the language you need to edit and write simple macros. If you have some programming experience, you can use this section as an introduction to the features of the language.

A full discussion of all the features of the macro programming language is beyond the scope of this book; however, Lotus provides a complete Help guide to the language in Ami Pro. Figure 23.15 shows the first Macro Documentation Help window. This window provides an overview of the comprehensive information available.

If you prefer to have the Help information in a printed form, you can order the 700-page Ami Pro for Windows *Macro Language Manual* directly from Lotus Development Corporation. Although the printed manual essentially duplicates the information already available in the Help system, it comes with some useful macro development tools. The entire package is provided for a very reasonable cost ($9.95 plus tax at the time of publication of this book). If you are serious about using Ami Pro macros, you should obtain this manual.

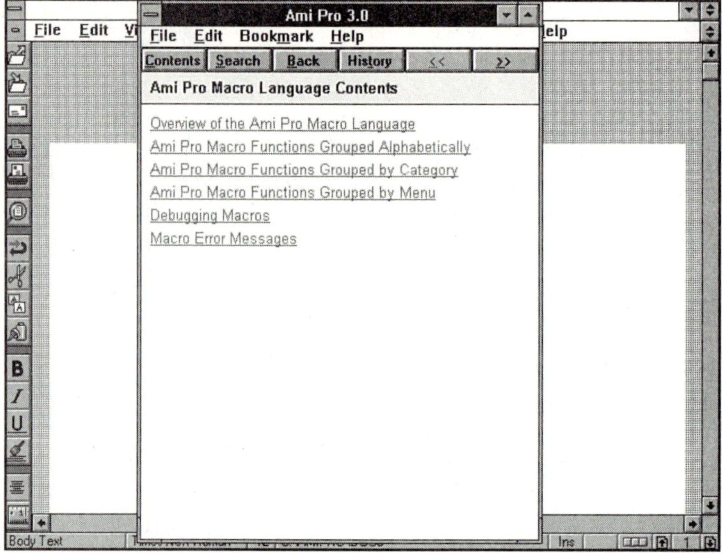

Fig. 23.15 The first Macro Documentation Help window.

This section begins with an overview of the components of the macro programming language. (Later sections show many of those features, illustrated by several useful macros that you can create with the macro language. The sample macros illustrate many of the features of the language and many of the principles of Ami Pro macro programming.)

You can format the text of a macro in any way you choose. Ami Pro ignores tabs and spaces within the text. (Macros in this chapter are formatted for readability.)

The Ami Pro macro language has three basic components: *functions*, *variables*, and *statements* (which can incorporate functions and variables). This chapter describes these components in detail. When you understand each of these components, you are well on the way to a good working knowledge of the Ami Pro macro language.

Understanding Functions

Macros you write usually contain *functions*. You can think of functions as macros; indeed, the macro documentation supplied by Lotus uses the terms *macro* and *function* interchangeably. When you record an Ami Pro macro, Ami Pro creates it as a function.

Ami Pro includes several hundred built-in functions—which are available to you to use within your macros. Suppose that you want to write a macro that includes as one of its steps closing the current document. You can do this by using the built-in function `FileClose()`. To use a built-in function, you *call* the function. You call the `FileClose()` function by writing a line of macro code with just the function name: `FileClose()` is the entire macro.

Note

All built-in functions are documented in the on-line Help macro documentation—you can access function descriptions alphabetically or by type of function. The on-line macro documentation also provides examples of the functions described. You can try the example or incorporate the example into an existing macro by copying the example to the Clipboard and then pasting it into your macro file. You may want to tile your macro document window and the macro Help window for easy access to both as you edit.

Functions, like macros, have names. A function name normally consists of alphabetic characters—and optionally, underscores and numbers—followed by a pair of closed parentheses. You can mix uppercase and lowercase letters; Ami Pro considers them equivalent. The names `MyFunction()` and `myfunction()` refer to exactly the same function.

Caution

Never give a function that you write the same name as that of a built-in Ami Pro function.

This chapter discusses many of the more commonly used macro functions and demonstrates principles that enable you to use any function. Ami Pro macro language has far too many functions for all of them to be covered in this book, however. For details on all functions, consult the Help macro documentation.

Function Return Values

Many functions *return* a value; when the function executes, it finds or calculates some value defined by the function. When the function returns—ends—it provides this value as a return value.

Consider the function `GetPageNo()`. As you may expect, this function determines the current page number. The return value of the `GetPageNo()` function is a number representing the current page number. Later in this chapter, you learn how to use this return value in macros. (To look up the meaning of the return value of any Ami Pro built-in function, refer to the Help macro documentation screen for that function.)

Function Arguments and Parameters

Tip
The `FileClose( )` example is a *fragment*—not a complete macro. To complete the function, you must assign a function name and body. See the next section for details.

Many functions need some "outside" information to work; `FileClose()` and `GetPageNo()` are exceptions to this rule. These two functions act on the current file and the current page, respectively. When you write a macro that uses one of these functions, you just write the name of the function to tell Ami Pro to use the function. To call `FileClose()`, you just write the following:

```
FileClose()
```

Now consider the `OutlineLevels()` function. The purpose of this function is to tell Ami Pro how many levels to display when in outline mode. Obviously, to use this function to display a certain number of levels, you also have to indicate how many levels you want to display. You accomplish this objective by passing an *argument* to the `OutlineLevels()` function. The argument provides additional information for the function—in this case, how many outline levels to display. When you write the macro, you place the argument inside the parentheses in the macro name. To display four outline levels, for example, you write the following:

```
OutlineLevels(4)
```

Tip
You may hear the term *parameter* used with functions. Although the two terms aren't precisely the same, for practical purposes *argument* and *parameter* can be used as synonyms.

To see the arguments that each function uses, consult the Help macro documentation for the function. Many functions require more than one argument.

Defining the Body of a Function

Earlier in this chapter, you learned that all Ami Pro macros are written as functions. Every Ami Pro function you write must be enclosed between two statements—a FUNCTION statement and an END FUNCTION statement.

The syntax of the function statement is as follows:

```
FUNCTION FunctionName()
```

You replace `FunctionName()` with the name of the function.

Suppose that you want to create a function named `MyGreeting()` to type a greeting into a document. The FUNCTION statement is as follows:

```
FUNCTION MyGreeting()
```

The syntax of the END FUNCTION statement is simpler:

```
END FUNCTION
```

The FUNCTION statement is always the first statement in a function, and the END FUNCTION statement is always the last. The FUNCTION and END FUNCTION statements define the *body* of the function. The `MyGreeting()` function, for example, can be written as follows:

```
FUNCTION MyGreeting()
     TYPE("Have a nice day![Enter]")
END FUNCTION
```

Writing Functions That Take Arguments

If a function requires *arguments*—data passed to the function when it is called from another function—you enclose the names of those arguments within the parentheses. Assume that you are going to personalize the greeting by including someone's name. Another function calls `MyGreeting()` and passes `MyGreeting()` the name of the person. In this example, the name of the person is the argument to `MyGreeting()`:

```
FUNCTION MyGreeting(greetee)
     TYPE("Have a nice day, {greetee}![Enter]")
END FUNCTION
```

The macro assigns to the variable `greetee` the value passed to the function as an argument. It then uses the variable `greetee` when it calls the `TYPE()` function.

The name you use for the argument of a function doesn't have to match the name that another function will use when it calls that function. You can write the following function, for example, to call `MyGreeting()`:

```
FUNCTION Welcomer()
     WhoIsIt = Query$("What is your name, please?")
     MyGreeting(WhoIsIt)
END FUNCTION
```

The built-in `Query$()` function displays a dialog box with a prompt string and gets a response from the user. It returns as a string whatever the user types. Suppose that the user types `Mr. Magoo` in response to the question `What is your name, please?` In this case, the function assigns the value `Mr. Magoo` to the variable `WhoIsIt`. `Welcomer()` calls `MyGreeting()`, which types into the document the text `Have a nice day, Mr. Magoo!`

Note that `Welcomer()` uses the variable name `WhoIsIt` to pass a value to `MyGreeting()`. `MyGreeting()` uses the variable name `greetee` to represent the same value.

Returning a Value from a Function

Tip

When you assign a return value to a function name, don't include the parentheses in the function name.

To write a function that returns a value, you simply assign to the function name the value you want to return. You can make this assignment anywhere within the body of the function.

Suppose that you are writing a macro to generate an invoice. The macro merges a group of items, computes the total price of all the items, and then calculates the sales tax. You decide to create a separate function, `SalesTax()`, to calculate the tax. You want to pass the sale amount to the macro, have it multiply the amount by the sales tax percentage applicable in your state, and then return the result.

If the sales tax percentage you want to use is 5 percent, you can write the function as follows:

```
FUNCTION SalesTax(SaleAmount)
     SalesTax = SaleAmount * 0.05
END FUNCTION
```

The function multiplies the value it is passed as an argument times the sales tax amount (* is the multiplication operator). Then, by assigning to the name of the function (`SalesTax`-without parentheses) the result you want to return, you cause the value to be returned to the calling function when the END FUNCTION statement is reached. A function to calculate the sales tax can use this statement:

```
InvoiceTotal = TotalGoods + SalesTax(TotalGoods)
```

This statement adds the amount of the sale (represented by the variable `TotalGoods`) to the sales tax on that amount, and assigns the total to the variable `InvoiceTotal`.

You can pass multiple arguments to a function; however, you can return only one value from a function. To pass multiple arguments, place both arguments in the parentheses following the function name. Separate the arguments with a comma.

Understanding Variables

Variables are key tools available to the macro developer for controlling the operation of a macro. Ami Pro uses variables to store information; each variable represents a specific place in the computer's memory where Ami Pro can store something. The "something" stored can be names, a file name, a keystroke—anything that can be represented as data by Ami Pro. If you tell Ami

Pro to store the current page number, for example, Ami Pro stores the page number in a variable.

Why tell Ami Pro to store data? Because you want to use the stored data later in the macro; for example, you can store a page number in a variable if later in the macro you tell Ami Pro to go to that page number or to insert that page number into the document.

Naming Variables

When you tell Ami Pro to store data in a variable, you know that the program stores the data in a location in memory; but unless you know which location the program used to store the data, you cannot find the data when you need it. You need a way to keep track of what data you put into each location.

You keep track of Ami Pro's variables by giving each one a name. For this example, you can tell Ami Pro to store the page number in the `page` variable. When you are ready to get the page number and use it, you tell Ami Pro to give you the contents of the page variable.

An Ami Pro variable name, just like a function name, can use capital letters, lowercase letters, underscore characters, and numerals. Ami Pro doesn't discriminate between uppercase and lowercase letters; `ThisVariable` and `thisvariable` refer to the same variable.

Caution

An Ami Pro variable name must have at least one letter; `this1` and `1more` are legal variable names, but 234 isn't. An Ami Pro variable name *cannot* contain a space; use an underscore instead. `Current style` isn't a legal variable name; instead, use `Current_style`.

Avoid giving an Ami Pro variable the same name as a built-in Ami Pro function.

Note

Give your variables and functions *meaningful* names. You save typing time by naming a variable x, but you may not remember what x represents after several hours of macro programming or when revising the macro a month later. If you name your variable `PageNumber`, the name provides a clue to the purpose of the variable.

Assigning Data to Variables

Assigning a value to a variable in Ami Pro is accomplished with a simple assignment statement, as in the following example:

```
page = 7
```

Each line of a macro that ends with a hard return is one *statement* (statements are discussed in more detail later in this chapter). This simple statement places the value 7 into the variable named `page`.

You can assign the value of one variable to a different variable—in effect, copying something from one memory location to a new memory location (while maintaining it in the original location). Consider these two assignment statements:

```
page = 7
CurrentPage = page
```

The first statement, `page = 7`, assigns the value `7` to the variable `page`. The second statement places the value of `page` into the variable `CurrentPage`. After both statements have executed, both variables—`page` and `CurrentPage`—have the value `7`.

Another way to get data into a variable is to assign the return value of a function to the variable. Remember that many functions return a value; `GetPageNo()`, for example, returns the current page number. To assign the return value of `GetPageNo()` to a variable, use an assignment like the following:

```
CurrentPage = GetPageNo()
```

This statement places the current page number, as returned by `GetPageNo()`, into the variable named `CurrentPage`.

Understanding Variable Types

In most programming languages, the programmer must be very careful about variable *types*—such as integers, floating point numbers, and character strings. Rather than making you worry about variable types, however, Ami Pro stores all variables as *strings* of characters. Ami Pro converts the string into integer or floating-point format when the variable is called by an arithmetic expression.

Caution

The contents of a variable aren't evaluated until needed. Even though a macro *saves* (compiles) without an error, therefore, a run-time error occurs upon running the macro if an arithmetic expression calls a variable that doesn't contain a number.

You must be aware of variable types in two situations: in assignment statements, and when you call functions that take character strings as arguments. Both situations are shown in the following paragraphs.

When you assign a character string to a variable, and that value is a character string, you must enclose the character string in double quotation marks. To assign the character string `BodyText` to the variable `CurrentStyle`, for example, type the following:

```
CurrentStyle = "BodyText"
```

The quotation marks tell Ami Pro to interpret the characters between the quotation marks as literal text to be assigned to the variable. What happens if you write the line as follows?

```
CurrentStyle = BodyText
```

In this case, Ami Pro interprets `BodyText` not as a character string variable you want to assign to `CurrentStyle`, but as a variable *name*. If you have a variable named `BodyText`, Ami Pro assigns its current value to `CurrentStyle`. If Ami Pro cannot find a variable named `BodyText`, the program displays an error message.

Now consider the other situation in which you need to worry about variable types: functions that require character strings as arguments. The `Message()` function displays a dialog box with a message to the user. Obviously, you must supply something to the function—in this case, the message you want to display. The message must be a character string; you supply the string as text enclosed with quotation marks, or as the name of a variable to which you have previously assigned a value. Following are two different legal calls to the `Message()` function:

```
Message("Have a nice day")
Greeting = "Have a nice day"
Message(Greeting)
```

Note

The assignment statement doesn't have to assign a string to the variable. The following statement is useful when you are debugging macros and want to see the value of a variable:

```
value = 7

Message(value)
```

Ami Pro knows that `Message()` needs a string argument, so the program supplies the 7 in the form of a string. (Remember that Ami Pro stores all variables as strings.)

Enclosing a Variable in a String

Sometimes you may want to include the value of a variable as part of a string. This strategy is especially useful when you use the `TYPE()` function. The `TYPE()` function performs a very simple and extremely useful job—it types the value of its argument into the current document, at the current insertion point position. The following line types `Have a nice day!` into the current document:

```
TYPE("Have a nice day!")
```

Like any other function that takes a string as an argument, `TYPE()` also can use a variable to which you have assigned a value:

```
Greeting = "Have a nice day!"
TYPE(Greeting)
```

This version performs the same function as the one-line version shown earlier.

But what if you want to *include* a variable in a string? Suppose that you want to determine the current page number with the `GetPageNo()` function, and then type into the document the text `You are on page` and the page number—on page 7, for example, to type `You are on page 7`. You can approach this problem in several ways, but the easiest way is to enclose the variable name in the string.

To enclose a variable name in a string, you place the variable name in the string and surround the variable name with braces—as in the following example:

```
num = GetPageNo()
TYPE("You are on page {num}")
```

The first line uses the built-in function `GetPageNo()`, which returns the value of the current page number. The assignment statement assigns the return value of the function to the variable `num`. The second line types into the document the text `You are on page` followed by the value of the variable. Note that the quotation marks surround both the text and the variable name.

> **Note**
>
> You can use keyboard keys in strings by enclosing the key name in brackets. To use the Backspace key, for example, type **[backspace]** (use upper- or lowercase). To use a function key, type **[F1]**, **[F12]**, and so on. The following line presses Tab, types the text and variable, and then presses Enter:
>
> ```
> TYPE("[Tab]You are on page {num}[Enter]")
> ```

> **Note**
>
> For a full list of keys, see the Help macro documentation for the TYPE() function.

Using Functions That Return Strings

As noted earlier, many functions return values. Sometimes the values are strings; sometimes numeric values; sometimes logical values (true or false). The *function return type* describes the type of value the function returns—string, numeric, or logical. The `UCASE$()` function, for example, returns a string whose value is the uppercase version of the string you pass to the function as an argument. The following lines type `HAVE A NICE DAY!` at the current insertion point position:

```
capped = UCASE$("Have a nice day!")
TYPE(capped)
```

Notice that the function name `UCASE$()` includes a dollar sign immediately before the parentheses. All built-in functions that return strings include a dollar sign in this position in the function name; this convention simplifies identifying the function return type.

Creating Statements

Statements are the basic building blocks of functions. Each line of a macro that ends with a hard return is one statement. When you run a macro, Ami Pro starts at the first statement and executes statements in sequence until the program reaches the last statement. (You can change this behavior with some of the specialized statements you learn about later in this chapter.)

You already have encountered two types of statements: the assignment statement (for example, `PageNumber = 7`) and statements that simply call functions (for example, `FileClose()`).

If you think of statements as building blocks of macros, you can think of the elements that make up statements as the raw materials. Statements are composed of five different types of raw materials. The purpose of the statement determines which of the raw materials will be present. The raw materials of statements are explained shortly; those materials include the following:

- *Variable names*
- *Literal values* (numbers or quoted strings)
- *Function names*
- *Keywords* such as `IF` and `GOTO`
- *Operators* such as + and =

By convention, statement keywords such as IF and GOTO are typed in capital letters in this book. Because Ami Pro disregards capitalization when reading a macro file, however, you can type statements, variable names, and function names in any combination of upper- and lowercase letters.

Using Operators

Operators combine other elements to form *expressions*. You can use the + operator, for example, to add two values with the following statement:

```
4 + 8
```

In this example, `4 + 8` is an expression. Expressions evaluate to values; the expression `4 + 8` evaluates to the value `12`. The *action* of the + operator upon its *operands*, `4` and `8`, is what causes the evaluation.

Ami Pro's macro language includes four types of operators—*mathematical*, *relations*, *logical*, and *bitwise*. (Bitwise operators are beyond the scope of this book. You can read about them in the Help macro documentation; you also can access them through the overview of the Ami Pro Macro Language menu selection.)

Ami Pro's *mathematical operators*, listed in table 23.2, perform mathematic operations on pairs of operands. Operands for mathematical operators must be numeric, or you get an error message while the macro is running. This condition is met by a variable that *will* have a numeric value at the time the macro is run; a function that returns a numeric value also meets this condition.

Table 23.2 Mathematical Operators

Operation	Symbol
Multiplication	*
Division	/
Addition	+
Subtraction	–

You use *relational operators* to compare values. A relational operator evaluates to TRUE or FALSE (see table 23.3). You can use numbers, strings, variables, or values—returning functions as operands with relational operators.

Table 23.3 Relational Operators

Operation	Symbol	Description
Equals	=	TRUE if the values are equal
Greater than	>	TRUE if the value on the left is greater than the value on the right
Less than	<	TRUE if the value on the left is less than the value on the right
Greater than or equal to	>=	TRUE if the value on the left is greater than or equal to the value on the right
Less than or equal to	<=	TRUE if the value on the left is less than or equal to the value on the right
Not equal to	<> or !=	TRUE if the value on the left is not equal to the value on the right

You use *logical operators* to combine several expressions into one, or to change a value from TRUE to FALSE (or vice versa). Table 23.4 shows the Ami Pro logical operators.

Table 23.4 Logical Operators

Operation	Description
AND	TRUE if both expressions are TRUE; otherwise FALSE
OR	TRUE if either expression is TRUE; otherwise FALSE
NOT	TRUE if the expression to the immediate right is FALSE, and FALSE if the expression is TRUE

Inserting Comments

One special type of statement is very useful—although it doesn't do anything! *Comments* are statements you use to document and explain macros. Liberal use of comments simplifies remembering what you did and why you did it, if you need to revise a macro months after writing it. When Ami Pro executes a macro, the program simply ignores any comments.

To insert a comment into an Ami Pro macro, type a single quotation mark. Everything after the single quotation mark is ignored—from the single quotation mark until the end of the line. In the following statement, for example, Ami Pro assigns the value `9` to the variable `MaxDocuments`. The single quotation mark indicates that the rest of the text on the line is a comment, so Ami Pro ignores it:

```
MaxDocuments = 9     ' no more than 9 documents allowed
```

If a single quotation mark is the first character on a line, Ami Pro ignores the entire line.

The only time a single quotation mark isn't interpreted as a comment is when it appears as part of a quoted string (between a pair of double quotation marks). In the following example, the single quotation mark in the contraction `I've` doesn't introduce a comment:

```
TYPE("I've had a very nice day, thank you.")
```

Caution

Make sure that you end every comment by pressing the Enter key. The hard return character inserted by the Enter key indicates the end of the comment. Comments may wrap beyond a single line.

Making Decisions with IF, ELSE, and ENDIF

If a macro does more than duplicate keystrokes, that macro may need to take different courses of action, with the choice of action based on the answer to a question. If the macro checks the value of a variable, for example, and takes action based on that value, the macro may need to execute a function and decide what to do next based on the function's return value. Or the macro may need to get some information from the user and then decide what to do next, based on the user's entry.

The IF statement and its associated statements, ELSE and ENDIF, form the basic decision-making mechanism in Ami Pro macros (and some form of these statements exists in almost every programming language).

IF and ENDIF always appear in pairs—one IF always is matched with an ENDIF. Each IF/ENDIF pair also may be matched to an ELSE statement, but ELSE statements are optional.

Using IF and ENDIF without ELSE

When Ami Pro encounters an IF statement, it evaluates the statement and decides whether it is TRUE or FALSE—in other words, whether the answer to the question implied by the IF statement is "yes" or "no." If the statement is TRUE, the commands between the IF statement and the ENDIF statement are executed (assuming no ELSE statement exists). If the answer is FALSE, the statements aren't executed, and Ami Pro jumps to the first statement following the ENDIF.

Suppose that you want to indent your text by 1/4 inch—but only if the current paragraph style is Body Text. You can write the macro this way:

```
FUNCTION Indenter()
     IF GetStyleName$() = "Body Text"
          Indent(360, 0, 0, 0)
     ENDIF
END FUNCTION
```

The built-in `GetStyleName$()` function returns a string with the name of the current paragraph style. The IF statement evaluates to TRUE if the value returned by `GetStyleName$()` is the same as the value on the other side of the equal sign: `Body Text`. (Notice that `Body Text` is enclosed in quotation marks, because you want Ami Pro to interpret it as a literal character string.)

Figure 23.16 shows the first page of the Help macro documentation for the `Indent()` statement. Notice that `Indent()` takes four arguments. In this example, you only need to specify the first argument, so you set the last three to `0`.

Also notice the reference to *twips* (Ami Pro's internal unit of measurement). Twips are specified for the arguments to all of Ami Pro's built-in functions that take measurements as arguments; Ami Pro maintains most internal measurements in twips. To indicate to `Indent()` that you want all the lines indented 0.25 inches, you multiply 1440 (one inch in twips) by 0.25.

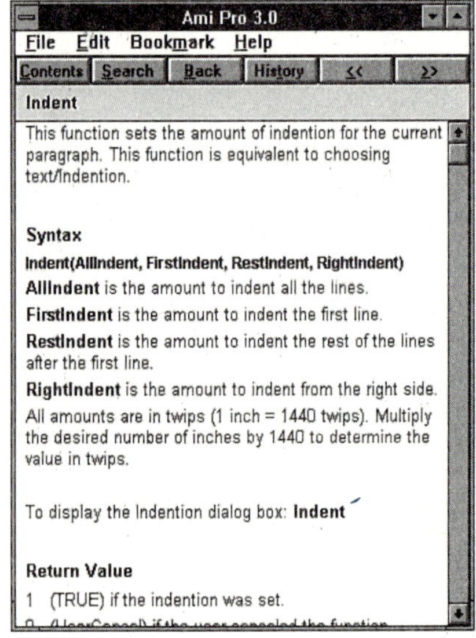

Fig. 23.16 The Help macro documentation screen for the `Indent ()` function.

Using ELSE

You use ELSE in macros when you want to supply an alternative set of commands—commands that are executed when the IF statement evaluates to FALSE. You place the ELSE statement after the condition evaluated in the IF statement and prior to the ENDIF statement.

Assume that you want to give a user the option to view the current document in draft mode. If the user chooses not to view in draft mode, you want to make sure that the view is layout mode. You can write the macro like this:

```
FUNCTION SelectView()
     answer = Decide("Do you want to use Draft Mode?")
     IF answer = 1
          DraftMode()
     ELSE
          LayoutMode()
     ENDIF
END FUNCTION
```

The `Decide()` function asks a question and presents two buttons, one labeled `Yes` and the other labeled `No`. If the user chooses the `Yes` button, the `Decide()` function returns the value `1`. If the user chooses `No`, `Decide()` returns `0`.

In this example, the macro asks a question and assigns the return value to the variable answer. If `answer` equals `1`—the user selected `Yes`—the statement between the IF statement is TRUE. The statement between the IF and ELSE statements is executed, which shifts Ami Pro to draft mode. Ami Pro then skips to the first statement after the ENDIF (in this case, simply exiting from the function).

If the IF statement is FALSE—`answer` isn't equal to `1`, because the user chose `No` and the `Decide()` function returned `0`—the statement between the ELSE and ENDIF is executed, and Ami Pro shifts to layout mode.

Note

You can eliminate a statement in this example by writing the macro as follows:

```
FUNCTION SelectView()
    IF Decide("Do you want to use Draft Mode?") = 1
    DraftMode()
    ELSE
    LayoutMode()
    ENDIF
END FUNCTION
```

Because `Decide()` returns a value, and you only need to use that value once, you can eliminate the variable by inserting the `Decide()` function directly in the IF statement.

Implementing Multiple Choice with SWITCH, CASE, DEFAULT, and ENDSWITCH

The IF keyword is useful if you want to choose between two alternatives. You can use multiple IF statements if you want to broaden the choices. In most cases when you want to choose between three or more possibilities, however, *switch blocks* are the best approach. The form of a switch block is as follows:

```
SWITCH variable
    CASE value1
        ' statements to execute if variable = value1
    CASE value2
        ' statements to execute if variable = value2
    CASE value3
        ' statements to execute if variable = value3
```

```
        CASE value4
             ' statements to execute if variable = value4
             ' ... and so on, for as many values as you need
        DEFAULT' DEFAULT statements are optional statements
             ' to execute if variable does not equal any
             ' value
   ENDSWITCH
```

SWITCH and ENDSWITCH mark the beginning and end of the block, respectively. You replace the word `variable` that follows SWITCH with the name of any variable previously defined within the function (or passed to the function as an argument). The values that follow the CASE keywords define the possible values for the variable. If the variable is equal to any of the values, Ami Pro executes the statements following that CASE statement. When Ami Pro reaches the next CASE statement (or a DEFAULT statement, or ENDSWITCH), the macro jumps to the first statement following ENDSWITCH. At most, only one set of statements—those directly following one CASE statement—is executed.

The DEFAULT keyword is optional. If you include DEFAULT, it must follow all the CASE statements. If the SWITCH variable doesn't equal any of the CASE values, Ami Pro executes the statements between DEFAULT and ENDSWITCH. If you don't include DEFAULT, and if none of the values match the variable, none of the statements execute.

Assume that you want to take an action based on the current paragraph style. If the paragraph style is Body Text or Body Single, you want to indent the entire paragraph 1/4 inch. If the paragraph style is Number List, you want to change it to Bullet. If the style is Bullet, you want to leave it alone. If the style is anything else, you want to change it to Body Text, and then indent it 1/4 inch. You can write the function this way:

```
FUNCTION FormatParagraph()
     stylename = GetStyleName$()
     SWITCH stylename
          CASE "Body Text"
               Indent(360, 0, 0, 0) 0.25" is 360 twips'
          CASE "Body Single"
               Indent(360, 0, 0, 0)
          CASE "Number List"
               SetStyle("Bullet")
          CASE "Bullet"
          DEFAULT
               SetStyle("Body Text")
               Indent(360, 0, 0, 0)
     ENDSWITCH
END FUNCTION
```

This example illustrates several features and limitations of Ami Pro's SWITCH statement.

Notice that the variable `stylename` contains a string value, because `GetStyleName$()` returns a string. As `stylename` is the SWITCH variable, and a string, all the CASE variables must be strings—they must be enclosed in quotation marks.

The actions for `CASE "Body Text"` and `CASE "Body Single"` are the same. In some programming languages, you can combine multiple CASE values that result in the same action, but you cannot do so in Ami Pro.

`CASE "Bullet"` has no statements. Because the `DEFAULT` is to change the style and indent—actions you don't want to take if the style is Bullet—you need to make sure that Bullet paragraphs aren't subjected to the `DEFAULT` actions.

Caution

The SWITCH statement must contain the name of a single variable. You cannot substitute an expression or the name of a value-returning function. The following statements cause Ami Pro to display an error message when you try to save the file:

```
SWITCH x = y              ' x = y is an expression,
                            not a single variable

SWITCH GetStyleName$()    ' you cannot use a function
                            name with SWITCH
```

Note

Ami Pro reads CASE statements in order until the program finds one with a value that matches the SWITCH variable. If that CASE statement comes early in the sequence, Ami Pro reads fewer statements, and the macro executes faster. If you have a SWITCH statement with many CASE statements, and you expect one or two CASE statements to be selected more often than the others, put those CASE statements first.

Repeating with WHILE and WEND

The WHILE and WEND keywords define a *loop*—a series of statements that can execute more than one time. WHILE marks the beginning of the loop, and WEND marks the end. The structure of a WHILE/WEND loop is as follows:

```
WHILE expression
    ' statements
WEND
```

When Ami Pro encounters a WHILE statement, it evaluates the expression following the WHILE keyword. If *expression* is TRUE, Ami Pro executes the statements within the loop (between WHILE and WEND). If *expression* is FALSE, Ami Pro skips to the first statement following the WEND, and doesn't execute the statements within the loop.

After Ami Pro has executed all the statements within the loop and reached the WEND statement, the program immediately returns to the WHILE statement and evaluates the condition again. If *expression* still is TRUE, Ami Pro executes the statements within the loop again. If *expression* is FALSE, Ami Pro exits from the loop by skipping to the first statement following WEND. This cycle continues as long as the WHILE statement is TRUE.

Caution

If none of the statements within the WHILE/WEND loop causes the WHILE expression to become FALSE, you cannot exit from the loop! Fortunately, you can break free from an endless loop by pressing any key; Ami Pro stops processing the macro and asks whether you want to continue.

For an example of a WHILE/WEND loop, see "Changing the Document Directory," later in this chapter.

Using FOR and NEXT

The Ami Pro WHILE/WEND loop described in the preceding section performs a set of operations an indeterminate number of times, until some condition within the loop causes the loop expression to evaluate to FALSE. A FOR/NEXT loop also performs a set of operations a number of times; but you normally use a FOR/NEXT loop when you want to execute the loop statements a specified number of times. (You can make a WHILE/WEND loop execute a specified number of times, but a FOR/NEXT loop is usually more convenient for this purpose.)

The syntax of a FOR/NEXT loop is as follows:

```
FOR counter = start TO finish STEP stepvar
     ' statements
NEXT
```

The syntax makes the FOR/NEXT loop look more complicated than it is. An example may make the syntax easier to understand:

```
FOR n = 1 TO 10 STEP 1
     ' statements
NEXT
```

The first time Ami Pro encounters the FOR statement, the variable *counter* is initialized to the value of *start*. In the example, the variable *n* is set equal to a value of 1.

The statements following the FOR statement then execute. When Ami Pro reaches the NEXT statement, it goes back to the FOR statement. It increments *counter* by the value of *stepvar*. In the example, the second time Ami Pro executes the FOR statement, it adds 1, the STEP value, to the current value of *n*, also 1. That action sets *n* to 2. Then Ami Pro compares the value of *n* to the *finish* value, in this case 10. If *n* is less than or equal to 10, Ami Pro executes the statements in the loop again.

When Ami Pro reaches NEXT again, the program goes back once more to the FOR statement and adds 1 (the STEP value) to *n*, which makes *n* equal 3. Because *n* still is less than or equal to 10, the loop statements execute again. This process continues for 10 complete cycles. The eleventh time Ami Pro encounters the FOR statement, *n* has a value of 10. Ami Pro adds 1 to *n*, making *n* equal 11. Because *n* no longer is less than or equal to 10, the loop statements don't execute. Instead, Ami Pro jumps to the first statement following the NEXT statement, and goes on with the macro.

Now put a real statement inside the loop:

```
FUNCTION ForNext()
     FOR n = 1 TO 10 STEP 1
          TYPE("The value of n is now {n}[Enter]")
     NEXT
END FUNCTION
```

When you execute this macro, the result is as shown in figure 23.17.

Note

If the STEP is 1, you can eliminate the STEP part of the FOR statement. The following statements are equivalent:

```
FOR n = 1 TO 10 STEP 1

FOR n = 1 TO 10
```

You also can STEP backwards:

```
FOR n = 10 TO 1 STEP -2
```

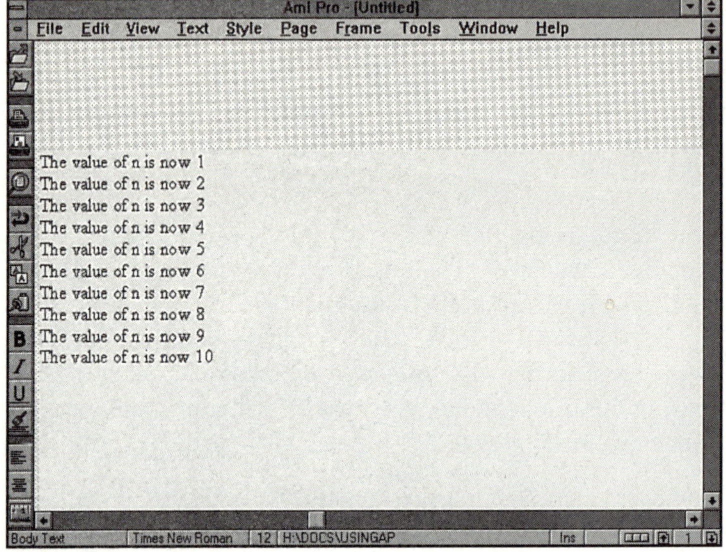

Fig. 23.17 The result of executing the FOR/NEXT example macro.

Misusing GOTO

Like most programming languages, Ami Pro's macro language has a GOTO statement. Ami Pro executes statements in a macro in the order in which they occur, except when it encounters a WEND or NEXT (which causes it to loop back to the corresponding WHILE or FOR statement) or when it selectively skips some statements because of an IF or SWITCH block. The GOTO statement tells Ami Pro to jump to a LABEL statement immediately. The LABEL statement can be anywhere within the same function as the GOTO.

The GOTO statement has the following form:

```
GOTO Label
```

The LABEL statement takes this form:

```
Label:
```

The `Label` can be any word (except a word already reserved for use as a statement keyword or function name). Note that the colon (:) must be used after the word `Label` when it appears by itself to mark the spot to which GOTO tells Ami Pro to jump, but you don't include the colon with the label name in the GOTO statement.

Following is an example of a function with a GOTO statement. The purpose of the macro is to get a list of names and type them into a document. The user is directed to type STOP when no more names are available to enter:

```
FUNCTION BadNews()
     Again:
     NameToType = Query$("Type name to insert into document
     (type STOP to quit)")
     IF NameToType <> "STOP"
          TYPE("{NameToType}[Enter]")
          GOTO Again
     ENDIF
END FUNCTION
```

The macro uses the built-in `Query$()` function to get the name from the user and assign the name to the variable `NameToType`. As long as the user types anything other than STOP, the IF expression is TRUE (`NameToType` is not equal to `STOP`), and the statements between IF and ENDIF execute. The first statement after the IF types the name into the document. The second statement, `GOTO Again`, tells Ami Pro to jump to the label `Again:` on the first line after the FUNCTION statement. Ami Pro then executes the `Query$()` function again, and continues to do so as long as the user doesn't type STOP.

The GOTO statement is frowned on by most serious programmers. In the words of Ami Pro's Help macro documentation, "Using GOTO statements to control program flow makes a macro more difficult to read, and increases the risk of causing an error if the macro is edited."

A simpler, more elegant, easier-to-read, easier-to-maintain alternative to the GOTO *always* exists. The loop just shown, for example, can use a WHILE/WEND loop:

```
FUNCTION GoodNews()
     NameToType = ""
     WHILE NameToType <> "STOP"
          NameToType = Query$("Type name to insert into
               document (type STOP to quit)")
          IF NameToType <> "STOP"
               TYPE("{NameToType}[Enter]")
          ENDIF
     WEND
END FUNCTION
```

Anyone who understands how a WHILE/WEND loop works will have no trouble discerning the intent of the macro programmer.

Occasional use of GOTO isn't very dangerous in short, simple functions like the one in this section. When functions become more complex, using GOTO makes macros more "buggy." (Unlike its partner GOTO, LABEL has a useful function, in ONERROR and ONCANCEL statements. See "Using ONCANCEL and ONERROR Statements," later in this chapter, for details.)

Using BREAK and EXIT FUNCTION

The BREAK and EXIT FUNCTION statements are for exceptions to the rules. Earlier in this chapter, you learned the following:

- A function begins with a FUNCTION statement and proceeds to an END FUNCTION statement.
- WHILE loops execute from WHILE to WEND, FOR loops execute from FOR to NEXT, and CASE blocks execute to the next CASE statement (or the DEFAULT or ENDSWITCH statement).

These rules are simplifications; you can interrupt normal flow through any function with an EXIT FUNCTION statement and through a WHILE, FOR, or SWITCH block with a BREAK statement.

Using EXIT FUNCTION

If a macro encounters an EXIT FUNCTION statement, the macro acts as if it had reached the END FUNCTION statement. The difference is that you can put an EXIT FUNCTION statement anywhere within the function, whereas the END FUNCTION statement is always (by definition) the last statement in the function. If you use EXIT FUNCTION at all, it probably is for exception processing—when something unusual happens.

When no documents are open in the Ami Pro work space, for example, most menu functions are grayed. If a macro tries to execute a grayed menu item, Ami Pro displays an error message. To avoid the error message, you can use the Ami Pro function `GetOpenFileCount()`, which returns the number of open files. If the number of open files is zero, however, you want to exit the function without performing the operation. You can write the function as follows:

```
FUNCTION MyFunction()
     IF GetOpenFileCount() = 0
          EXIT FUNCTION
     ENDIF
     LayoutMode()
     ' more statements here
END FUNCTION
```

If no files are open, the statement `IF GetOpenFileCount() = 0` is TRUE, and Ami Pro executes the EXIT FUNCTION statement; none of the other statements in the function execute. If at least one file is open, `IF GetOpenFileCount() = 0` is FALSE, and Ami Pro executes the rest of the statements, from `LayoutMode()` through `END FUNCTION`.

Note

In general, try to avoid using EXIT FUNCTION. More straightforward methods usually exist than EXIT FUNCTION. In the preceding example, you can accomplish the same result with this macro:

```
FUNCTION MyFunction()
        IF GetOpenFileCount() > 0
                LayoutMode()
                ' more statements here
        ENDIF
END FUNCTION
```

This macro probably is easier to interpret than the earlier version after several months, when you want to revise it. Another way to approach this problem is with an ONERROR and LABEL statement pair, as described later in the chapter.

Interrupting Execution with BREAK

Like EXIT FUNCTION, BREAK can interrupt the normal flow of events in a macro. In both WHILE and FOR loops, BREAK tells Ami Pro, "Ignore the normal processing logic of the loop. No matter what, go to the first statement following the WEND statement (for a WHILE loop) or NEXT statement (for a FOR loop), and continue executing there."

Suppose that you are writing a macro to create a memo with multiple addresses. You use Ami Pro's built-in `Query$()` function to get ten responses from the macro user. The macro types each response into the document; however, you want the user to be able to stop at any point by typing the word STOP. You can write the portion of the macro that gets the addressees as follows:

```
FUNCTION MemoHeader()
     TYPE("To:")
     FOR n = 1 to 10
          towhom = Query$("Type name of addressee (STOP
               to quit)")
          IF towhom = "STOP"
               BREAK
          ENDIF
          TYPE("[Tab]{towhom}[Enter]")
     NEXT
```

```
        TYPE("[Enter]From:[Tab]John Dillard")
        ' some more statements here
    END FUNCTION
```

The macro begins by typing `To:`. Then the `Query$()` function prompts the user for a name, as shown in figure 23.18. Because of the FOR loop, this process repeats ten times (so long as the user doesn't type STOP). Each time the user types a name, the name is assigned to the variable `towhom`.

If the user types anything *other* than STOP, the statement `IF towhom = "STOP"` is FALSE, and the BREAK statement doesn't execute. Ami Pro executes the rest of the FOR loop; it presses Tab, inserts the name that the user typed, and presses Enter. Assuming that this name isn't the tenth, the NEXT statement sends execution back to the FOR statement; if this name is the tenth, Ami Pro executes the statement that follows the NEXT statement.

If the user types STOP, the statement `IF towhom = "STOP"` is TRUE, and Ami Pro executes the BREAK. Execution passes immediately to the first statement after the NEXT statement; Ami Pro types the characters and text needed to start the "From" block of the memo.

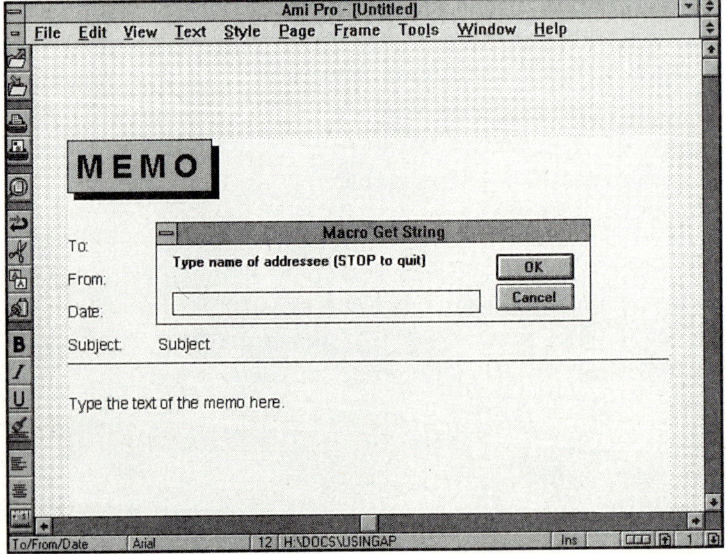

Fig. 23.18
The result of using Ami Pro's built-in `Query$()` function in the `MemoHeader()` function.

Note

A problem exists with the `MemoHeader()` macro. If the user types stop or Stop—instead of the uppercase STOP—the macro simply types the word "stop" into the memo, and prompts for the next name. You can fix this problem by converting whatever the user types into uppercase as part of the IF statement. Ami Pro's built-in `UCASE$()` function converts its argument to uppercase:

```
towhom = Query$("Type name of addressee
        (STOP to quit)")
IF UCASE$(towhom) = "STOP"
        BREAK
ENDIF
```

BREAK can be used in the same way in WHILE loops. BREAK causes Ami Pro to skip all the remaining statements in the loop, and resume processing at the first statement following the WEND.

In SWITCH blocks, BREAK works in a similar manner with some slight differences. Use BREAK within a set of CASE statements when you want to execute only some of the statements, depending on some condition.

◀ See "Using Help," p. 35

Intermediate Topics in Ami Pro Macro Programming

To this point, you have learned the basic principles of writing Ami Pro macros. You can use the techniques described thus far to write many useful macros; in this section, you learn more advanced techniques that may be helpful in special situations.

Writing Macros as Multiple Functions

When you write complex macros, you should break up the macros into multiple functions. Instead of writing one enormous function, divide the macro into functions that call each other as necessary. Each function should handle one basic task. This strategy makes macros easier to write, debug, and modify.

When you write multiple-function macros, you can put all the functions in different files, or you can put them in the same file. In general, if a group of functions go together and are intended to be used together, placing them in a single file is convenient. If you want to create some common functions and then call them from a number of unrelated macros, place the common functions in one file and call them from outside files. This procedure is discussed later in this chapter.

Putting More Than One Function in a File

Putting more than one macro function in a single file is conceptually very simple. Because every function must begin with a FUNCTION statement and end with an END FUNCTION statement, these statements serve as natural delimiters between functions.

When you tell Ami Pro to run a macro file with more than one function, Ami Pro starts executing statements with the FUNCTION statement of the first function it finds in the file. When Ami Pro reaches the END FUNCTION statement of the first function, it terminates the macro. The other functions in the file are executed only if they are called by the first function (or are called by functions that have been called previously).

Suppose that you want to put the functions `Welcomer()` and `MyGreeting()`, introduced earlier in this chapter, into one file. You can start like this:

```
FUNCTION Welcomer()
     WhoIsIt = Query$("What is your name, please?")
     MyGreeting(WhoIsIt)      ' causes an error message
END FUNCTION

FUNCTION MyGreeting(greetee)
     TYPE("Have a nice day, {greetee}![Enter]")
END FUNCTION
```

If you use this method and then try to save the file (for example, as GREETING.SMM), you get the error message shown in figure 23.19.

You get this message because when you save a macro file Ami Pro starts at the top of a file and reads down line-by-line. The program makes sure that every called function exists. A function exists if it's a built-in Ami Pro function or if Ami Pro has read the function definition (the function name following a FUNCTION keyword) some place earlier in the file.

In the example, `MyGreeting()` comes *after* `Welcomer()`. Ami Pro encounters the call to `MyGreeting()` before it knows anything *about* `MyGreeting()`. Ami Pro therefore stops and displays the error message in figure 23.19.

Two ways exist to prevent the error message. The following sections describe these two methods.

Declaring Functions. One method is to make sure that you declare a function before you use it in another function. You *declare a function* by telling Ami Pro that the function exists, the name of the function, and how many arguments it takes. You can accomplish all this in one DECLARE statement.

This example is complete, and you can save it without getting an error message:

```
FUNCTION Welcomer()
     DECLARE MyGreeting(p1)
     WhoIsIt = Query$("What is your name, please?")
     MyGreeting(WhoIsIt)
END FUNCTION
FUNCTION MyGreeting(greetee)
     TYPE("Have a nice day, {greetee}![Enter]")
END FUNCTION
```

The DECLARE statement in the `Welcomer()` function tells Ami Pro, "Somewhere in this function I will call the function `MyGreeting()`. That function takes one argument." You can use any variable name you want as the argument to the function name in the DECLARE statement. The number of variables (not the variable names) is what counts. (The convention is to use a sequence like p1, p2, p3, and so on, but this treatment is optional.)

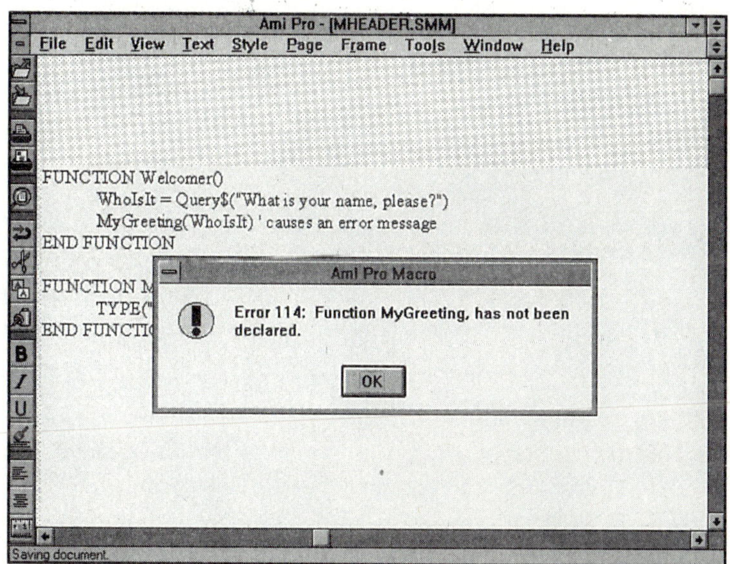

Fig. 23.19
The error message displayed when you try to save the example macro.

Using the CALL Keyword. If you don't want to bother with DECLARE, you can use CALL instead. With this strategy, you precede each call—to a macro located elsewhere in the file—with the CALL keyword. You can implement the greeting macro like this:

```
FUNCTION Welcomer()
     WhoIsIt = Query$("What is your name, please?")
     CALL MyGreeting(WhoIsIt)
END FUNCTION
FUNCTION MyGreeting(greetee)
     TYPE("Have a nice day, {greetee}![Enter]")
END FUNCTION
```

In effect, the CALL statement tells Ami Pro, "This function will be in the file when you run this macro, and it will require the number of arguments I'm passing to it with this statement." Even if the function named in the CALL statement isn't present in the macro file, Ami Pro still saves the file. When you run the macro, however, if Ami Pro cannot find the function the program displays the error message shown in figure 23.20.

The choice of which method to use is yours. Use DECLARE or CALL, whichever is most convenient.

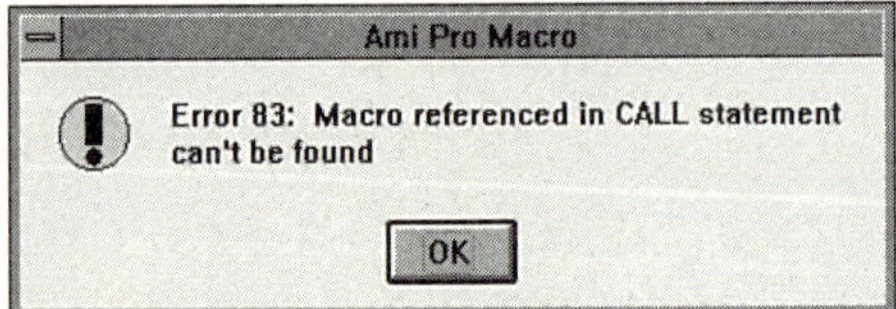

Ami Pro Macro
Error 83: Macro referenced in CALL statement can't be found
OK

Fig. 23.20
The error message displayed when Ami Pro cannot find a called macro function.

Calling Macro Functions in Other Files

When a macro function you want to call is in a different file, you use DECLARE or CALL, the same techniques you use to call a function in the same file. You also must tell Ami Pro the name of the file containing the function you want to call.

To refer to a function in another file, you use the file name (including the extension SMM), followed by an exclamation mark and the name of the function. You must include any arguments in the statement.

Assume that you save the function `MyGreeting()` in a file named NICEDAY.SMM. You can write `Welcomer()` this way:

```
FUNCTION Welcomer()
     DECLARE niceday.smm!MyGreeting(p1)
     WhoIsIt = Query$("What is your name, please?")
     niceday.smm!MyGreeting(WhoIsIt)
END FUNCTION
```

Following is a slight variation:

```
FUNCTION Welcomer()
     DECLARE niceday.smm!MyGreeting(p1) Alias Greet
     WhoIsIt = Query$("What is your name, please?")
     Greet(WhoIsIt)
END FUNCTION
```

This slightly varied example assigns an alias—`Greet`—to the function `niceday.smm!MyGreeting`. The alias saves you from having to key in the lengthy function name when you want to include it in your macro statements—simply substitute the function's alias in place of its full name.

Following is another method:

```
FUNCTION Welcomer()
     WhoIsIt = Query$("What is your name, please?")
     CALL niceday.smm!MyGreeting(WhoIsIt)
END FUNCTION
```

These forms of `Welcomer()` are the same ones you saw earlier, with the addition of `niceday.smm!` before the call `MyGreeting(WhoIsIt)`.

Using Arrays

Ami Pro macro programming language variables can be divided into two broad categories—*single element variables* and *array variables*. All the variables discussed thus far are single element variables.

Array variables enable you to assign a *set* of values to a variable with a single name. You indicate which variable in the set you want to use by following the array name with a number enclosed in parentheses. If you have a list of five files, for example, you can designate them file(1), file(2), file(3), file(4), and file(5).

The number in parentheses is called the *index*. Each separate value is called an *element*. To continue the example, you can say that the array file has five *elements*; you then know that the array uses the *indices* 1 through 5.

Arrays are useful when you need to perform the same function on a group of variables. Suppose that you want to delete five files, using the Ami Pro macro function `DOSDelFile()`. `DOSDelFile()` takes the name of the file to be deleted as its argument. You can implement the operation like this:

```
FUNCTION DeleteFiles()
     DIM file(5)      ' this statement is explained below
     file(1) = "1STFILE.TXT"
     file(2) = "2NDFILE.TXT"
     file(3) = "3RDFILE.TXT"
     file(4) = "4THFILE.TXT"
```

```
          file(5) = "5THFILE.TXT"
          FOR n = 1 TO 5
               DOSDelFile(file(n))
          NEXT
     END FUNCTION
```

Each of the statements of the form `file(1) = "1STFILE.TXT"` is a simple assignment statement. You assign a value to an array variable in exactly the same way that you assign a value to a single element variable. After executing the statement, the array variable `file(1)` has the value `1STFILE.TXT`.

The first time the FOR loop executes, the variable *n* is set equal to 1. The value of *n* becomes the subscript in the following statement:

```
DOSDelFile(file(n))
```

The macro executes the statement as the following:

```
DOSDelFile(file(1))
```

This statement is equivalent to the following statement:

```
DOSDelFile("1STFILE.TXT")
```

This statement deletes file(1), 1STFILE.TXT.

The next time the FOR loop executes, *n* is set equal to 2, so the statement executes as follows:

```
DOSDelFile(file(2))
```

This action deletes file(2), 2NDFILE.TXT.

Notice the first line in the function:

```
DIM file(5)
```

Unlike when using single element variables, before you use an array variable you must tell Ami Pro how many elements to expect to find in the array (the largest number you plan to use as a subscript). Ami Pro needs to know this number to make sure that the program allows enough memory for the variable. The DIM statement gives Ami Pro this information. The following statement tells Ami Pro to allocate enough memory for a five-element array named `file`:

```
DIM file(5)
```

Note

Unlike arrays, single element variables usually don't have to be explicitly declared. You implicitly declare a single element variable simply by assigning it a value within the macro. A few advanced built-in functions require you to make use of a variable before you declare it by assigning it a value. In these situations, you need to declare a single element variable. You can do this with the DEFSTR statement, which is described in the Help macro documentation. DEFSTR is used in the example that explains the ONERROR and ONCANCEL statements, later in this chapter.

After using the preceding statement, if you use the following statement, when you try to save the macro file Ami Pro detects a syntax error and displays an error message:

```
file(6) = "SOMEFILE.NAM"
```

Note

If you need to dynamically resize your array—that is, make it bigger, based on what happens while your macro is running—you can use the `ArrayInsert()` or `ArrayInsertByKey()` functions. If you want to sort the values in the array, you can use `ArraySort()`. These and a number of other useful array-handling functions are described in the Help macro documentation. Look in the alphabetic list of functions for those starting with the word `Array`.

Using Global Variables

By default, Ami Pro variables are *local variables*. A local variable has meaning only within the function that defines it—that is, within the FUNCTION/END FUNCTION block where it is first used. You can give the same name to variables in two different functions because, to Ami Pro, they are different variables.

If one function calls another, the local variables in the calling function aren't seen by—and cannot be affected by—the called function.

Because variables are local, when a function finishes executing—when Ami Pro executes the END FUNCTION (or EXIT FUNCTION) statement—the variables defined within that function disappear. If you later call that function again, the variables are re-initialized. They don't have the same values they had when the function finished executing the last time (unless you explicitly put those values back).

When one function passes arguments to another, Ami Pro makes a copy of each variable and passes the *copy* to the called function. Because the called function works with a copy, no changes it makes to the copy affect the value of the original variable in the calling function. When the called function returns, the copy is destroyed (along with the rest of the called function's local variables), and the original variable in the calling function is unchanged.

Local variables are fine for most purposes. The following list describes situations when using local variables is inappropriate:

- Occasionally, you may need to retain a value from a function after the function terminates.
- Many functions need access to the same variables (or set of variables), and continually passing them as arguments and handling them as return variables can be clumsy or impossible.
- A macro may need to set a value and then terminate; the next time the function executes, it may need to access the value set in the previous incarnation.
- You may want to execute a macro, have it assign a value to a variable, and then terminate, returning control to the user. Later, you may want to execute a different macro (or the same macro again) and have it refer to (and optionally change) the value originally set.

For these situations, Ami Pro provides *global variables*. Global variables last until you exit from Ami Pro or until you get rid of them. When you put a value into a global variable, the value stays there until your macro changes it.

Ami Pro includes a function to create and a function to destroy global variables.

`AllocGlobalVar()` creates a global variable (a single-element variable or an array). To create a single-element global variable named `myglobal`, you can write the following statement:

```
AllocGlobalVar("myglobal", 1)
```

The first argument to `AllocGlobalVar()` is the name of the variable. The name must be a quoted string or a number. The preceding example uses a quoted string. You can create a single-element global variable with the name `27` this way:

```
AllocGlobalVar(27, 1)
```

You can use a number to name a *global* variable. *Local* (non-global) variables must begin with a letter or an underscore character.

The second argument is the number of elements in the variable. For a single-element variable, the second argument is `1`. For a 10-element array, the second argument is `10`.

`FreeGlobalVar()` destroys the global variable named as its argument. To free the global variables created by the preceding two examples, you write the following:

```
FreeGlobalVar("myglobal")
FreeGlobalVar(27)
```

Caution

If you use many global variables—especially large global arrays—be sure to free them when you no longer need them. Global variables use memory, and memory can be a scarce commodity.

Even after you have allocated global variables, you cannot use them as you would regular local variables. If you have a global variable named `myglobal`, for example, neither of these statements is allowed:

```
TYPE(myglobal)       ' not a legal statement
myglobal = 5         ' not a legal statement
```

To put a value into a single-element global variable, you use the built-in function `SetGlobalVariable()`. This function takes two arguments: the name of the global value, and the value you are assigning to the variable. Either of these sequences puts the current page number into the global variable `PageNum`:

```
AllocGlobalVar("PageNum", 1)
SetGlobalVar("PageNum", GetPageNo())

AllocGlobalVar("PageNum", 1)
num = GetPageNo()
SetGlobalVar("PageNum", num)
```

Notice that in `SetGlobalVar()`, as in all functions that work with global variables, you must enclose the global variable name in parentheses.

To use the value of a single-element global variable, you use the function `GetGlobalVar$()`, which returns the value of the global variable. You can use `GetGlobalVar$()` where you would otherwise use the value it holds. The following macro types the number `16`:

```
FUNCTION Globler()
     AllocGlobalVar("constant", 1)       ' allocates a
          single-element global variable
     SetGlobalVar("constant", 11)        ' assigns a value
          to the global variable
     CALL Adder()
END FUNCTION

FUNCTION Adder()
     TYPE (GetGlobalVar$("constant") + 5) ' uses the
          value of the global variable
END FUNCTION
```

In some situations, you must use an assignment statement to copy the global variable into a local variable, and then use the local variable in your expression. This macro doesn't work:

```
FUNCTION Globler()
     AllocGlobalVar(name, 1)
     SetGlobalVar("name", "Stu")
     CALL MyGreeting()
END FUNCTION

FUNCTION MyGreeting()
     TYPE("Hello, {GetGlobalVar$("name")}")END FUNCTION
```

The following macro works:

```
FUNCTION Globler()
     AllocGlobalVar("name", 1)
     SetGlobalVar("name", "Stu")
     CALL MyGreeting()
END FUNCTION

FUNCTION MyGreeting()
     localvar = GetGlobalVar$("name")
     TYPE("Hello, {localvar}")      ' types Hello, Stu
END FUNCTION
```

To put values into and get values back from global arrays, you use the functions `GetGlobalArray$()` and `SetGlobalArray()` instead of `GetGlobalVar$()` and `SetGlobalVar()`. Both global array functions take an extra argument—the array index number—after the variable name. See the Help macro documentation for more information on these functions.

Using ONCANCEL and ONERROR Statements

While a macro is running, Ami Pro provides default behavior for two out-of-the ordinary types of events:

- If an error occurs (perhaps you tried to use a non-numeric argument with a function that only accepts numeric arguments) Ami Pro displays an error message in a dialog box with an OK button. When you choose the OK button, the macro terminates. The last statement Ami Pro executes from the macro is the one that caused the error. Any subsequent statements aren't executed. This process is Ami Pro's default ONERROR behavior.

- If you choose Cancel in response to a `Query$()` function dialog box, Ami Pro terminates the macro immediately. If you press a key while a macro is running, Ami Pro gives you the choice of continuing the macro or terminating it. If you choose to continue, Ami Pro resumes running the macro as though nothing had happened; but if you choose to terminate, Ami Pro terminates immediately. The last statement executed is the one that was executing when you pressed the key.

- These two situations together describe Ami Pro's default ONCANCEL behavior. If these events are what you want to happen in these circumstances, you don't do anything special. If you want to control what happens when an error occurs, however, you can do so by including ONERROR statements in your macros. If you want to control what happens when the user chooses Cancel (or presses a key during macro execution), you include ONCANCEL statements.

Caution

For most short macros, ONERROR and ONCANCEL statements are probably more trouble than they are worth. If you are writing complex macros, particularly those that use global variables or the built-in ASCII file functions, ONERROR and ONCANCEL can be crucial. Make sure that you always free global variables (unless you plan to use them later) and close any files you have opened, even when an error occurs or the user cancels.

The syntax of an ONERROR statement is as follows:

```
ONERROR Label
```

An ONERROR statement tells Ami Pro, "If an error occurs during the execution of this function, don't just display the standard error message and terminate the macro. Instead, jump to the `Label` and continue processing there." The statements following the `Label` should do whatever is necessary to "clean up" and then terminate the macro gracefully.

The syntax of the ONCANCEL statement is as follows:

```
ONCANCEL label
```

ONCANCEL works the same way as ONERROR, except that the event that "triggers" ONCANCEL is a user-initiated cancellation, either choosing Cancel in a dialog box or pressing a key during macro execution.

If you use ONERROR or ONCANCEL, put them at the beginning of the function—ideally as the first statements after FUNCTION. If an error or cancellation occurs, Ami Pro doesn't "search forward" to see if an ONERROR or ONCANCEL statement exists; so these statements only help if Ami Pro encounters them before the error or cancellation occurs.

Following is an example of ONERROR and ONCANCEL:

```
FUNCTION FileReader(filename)
     ONERROR Finish
     ONCANCEL Finish
     DEFSTR handle
     IF Assign(&handle, fopen(filename, "r")) <> 0
          text = 0
          WHILE text <> -1
               text = fgets$(handle)
               IF text <> =1
                    TYPE("{text}[Enter]")
               ENDIF
          WEND
          Finish:
          fclose(handle)
     ENDIF
END FUNCTION
```

This function is part of an advanced macro that works with ASCII text files. The `fopen()`, `fgets$()`, and `fclose()` functions are built-in functions that respectively open, read strings from, and close ASCII files. You can read descriptions of these functions in the Help macro documentation.

Notice that ONERROR and ONCANCEL are the first two statements in the function. They tell Ami Pro, "If the user cancels, or if an error occurs, jump immediately to the label `Finish` and start executing statements from there."

The IF statement in this example uses some advanced techniques; a full explanation of the function is beyond the scope of this book. A file name is passed to the macro as the argument of the IF statement. If the file exists, the IF statement opens the file and then evaluates to TRUE. (If the file doesn't exist, the IF statement evaluates to FALSE and the macro terminates normally.)

Assuming that IF is TRUE, the WHILE/WEND loop begins executing. The `fgets$()` function in the WHILE/WEND loop reads text from the file, one line at a time. As long as the text isn't equal to `-1` (which signifies that the end of the file has been reached), the TYPE statement executes and the WHILE/WEND loop repeats. When the end of the file is reached, the WHILE statement evaluates to FALSE. Ami Pro then executes the `fclose(handle)` statement, which closes the file, and the function exits.

This description assumes normal operation. But what happens if, while the macro is executing the WHILE/WEND loop and reading from the file, you press a key?

If not for the ONCANCEL statement, Ami Pro would ask if you wanted to terminate the macro immediately. If you chose Yes, Ami Pro would end the macro without executing the rest of the statements. The problem with this scenario is that the `fclose()` function would never execute. In this example, `fclose()` closes the file; if it doesn't execute, the file remains open. DOS—which provides file services to Windows—requires programs to close their files. Leaving the file open can cause DOS and/or Windows to behave unpredictably—perhaps to crash.

In this example, however, an ONCANCEL statement exists; if you press a key, Ami Pro immediately jumps to the `Finish` label and begins executing statements from there. The first statement after `Finish` is `fclose(handle)`, which closes the file. The macro still hasn't achieved its purpose—you pressed the key before all the text had been read from the file—but at least the macro didn't leave a file hanging open when terminating.

If an error had occurred during execution of the WHILE/WEND loop, the same sequence of events would have occurred, keyed by the `ONERROR Finish` statement.

Debugging Macros

Unfortunately, macros don't always run correctly the first time. (If most of your macros run correctly the first time, you are either very good or very lucky!) You need to know how to fix (*debug*) your macros. Compile-time errors—errors that Ami Pro finds when you try to save a macro—were discussed earlier in this chapter. This section discusses run-time errors—errors that occur while you are running a macro.

Run-time errors fall into two categories:

- Errors Ami Pro detects and tells you about with an error message
- Errors you discover when the macro doesn't do what it is supposed to do

The first step in debugging an error that Ami Pro detects is to look up the error—by number—in the Help macro documentation. If that source doesn't provide all the information you need, you can use two basic techniques that will help—single-stepping the macro and tracking the values of key variables.

Single-Stepping the Macro

When you include the built-in `SingleStep()` command with the argument `1` on the line after your `FUNCTION()` statement, you access *single-step mode*. To turn on single-step mode, include this statement:

```
SingleStep(1)
```

Single-step mode enables you to view each statement and then see the results of the statement. This mode displays the statements in a macro interrupt dialog box, as shown in figure 23.21.

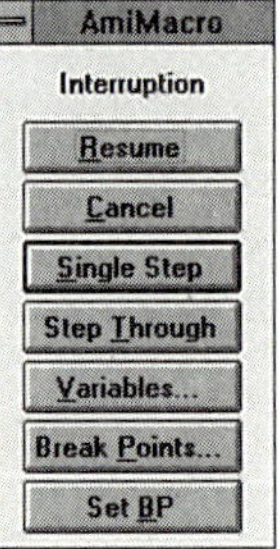

Fig. 23.21
The macro interrupt dialog box that shows each statement of a macro in single-step mode.

In response to the macro interrupt dialog box, you can choose one of the following options:

- **R**esume removes the dialog box and continues without stopping again until the end of the macro or until you reach a break point (explained later) or another `SingleStep(1)` statement.

- **C**ancel cancels the macro. If your macro has an ONCANCEL statement, Ami Pro jumps to the label designated in the ONCANCEL statement.

- **S**ingle Step continues stepping through the macro, one statement at a time.

- Unless the statement is a CALL statement, Step **T**hrough works just like **S**ingle Step. If the macro is a CALL statement, **S**ingle Step steps through every statement in the called function; but Step **T**hrough executes the called function without pausing and then pauses at the next statement in the calling function.

- **V**ariables displays a dialog box with a list of local variables, as shown in figure 23.22. In the list box, a colon and the current value of the variable follow each variable name.
- Ami Pro shows only those variables that have been declared by statements preceding the currently highlighted statement. (If no variables have been declared, nothing happens when you choose this option.) You can change the contents of any variable by highlighting the variable, typing the new value in the text box, and then choosing `Update`. (For an array variable, the number of elements in the array are shown in the dialog box and cannot be changed.)

> **Note**
>
> To see the statement highlighted in the macro file, have the macro document open when you run the macro. Each time Ami Pro pauses, it displays the macro file with the next statement to execute highlighted. When you tell Ami Pro to execute (with the **R**esume, **S**ingle Step, or Step **T**hrough button of the dialog box), Ami Pro redisplays the file from which you started the macro, before it executes the statement.

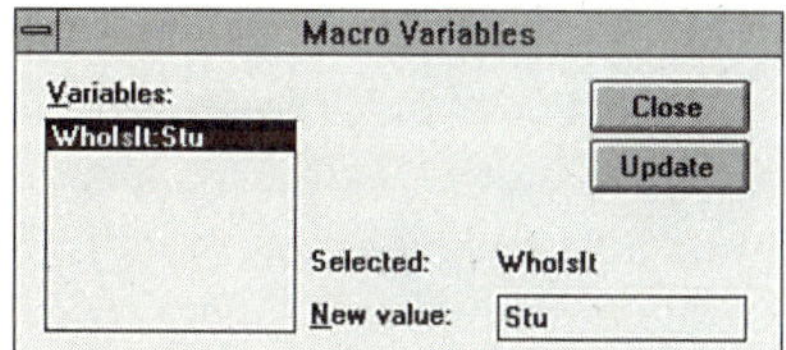

Fig. 23.22
The Macro Variables dialog box.

- Break **P**oints displays a list of the break points you have set with the Set **B**P option. Each break point is identified by the file name, the function name, and the line number within the function.
- Set **B**P sets a break point on the current line. You use break points to indicate lines where you want the macro to stop and display the interrupt macro dialog box when you choose the **R**esume option. You cannot set break points on empty or comment lines or lines with ELSE, WEND, or ENDIF. (You don't see anything happen when you choose Set **B**P. To verify that the break point has been set, choose Break **P**oints.)

Tip
If you want to single-step through only part of a function, you can turn single-step mode off with the statement `SingleStep(0)`.

After you have found the error and corrected it, remove the `SingleStep(1)` statement from your file; the next time you run your macro it executes normally.

Tracking the Value of a Single Variable

When debugging a macro, you may want to track the value of a variable as the macro changes it, without using `SingleStep()`. If you want to see the value of a variable, just include a `Message()` statement to display the variable immediately after each line that references the variable. To track the value of the variable `myvar`, for example, you can insert this statement throughout your macro:

```
Message(myvar)
```

Each time Ami Pro encounters the `Message()` statement, it displays a dialog box with the value `myvar`.

Tip

If you are tracking several variables, include the variable name in the message statement:

`Message("myvar = {myvar}")`

Some Useful Macros

This section includes several macros written with the macro language described in the preceding section. You can use these macros "as is" or use them as templates to adapt for your purposes. These macros illustrate some techniques—and the descriptions with the macros describe some built-in functions—that you haven't seen yet in this chapter.

Displaying a Dialog Box

Earlier in this chapter, you encountered the problem of trying to record a macro that simply displays a dialog box and then turns over control of the dialog box to the user. You cannot record such a macro because Ami Pro doesn't let you access the Too**l**s menu to end recording while the dialog box is displayed. But you can write a very simple macro that accomplishes this task. For most menu functions, simply use the Ami Pro macro function that implements the menu operation but, when you type the function name, omit the normal arguments and the parentheses.

If you use **H**elp **M**acro Doc to look up the function that corresponds to **F**ile **O**pen, you see this description:

```
FileOpen(Filename, Options, Appname)
```

This statement means that the `FileOpen()` function requires three arguments. But what if you just want your macro to display the Open dialog box and let the user decide how to use it? Here is a simple macro to accomplish this objective:

```
FUNCTION OpenAFile()
     FileOpen
END FUNCTION
```

Notice that the function name `FileOpen` is used without arguments and without parentheses.

Changing the Document Directory

You may follow a practice of grouping Ami Pro files into directories by projects, clients, or some other classification system appropriate for your business. By default, when you create a new file and then save the file, Ami Pro stores the file in the directory currently identified in the **D**ocument field of the Default Paths dialog box.

If you want to save a file in a different directory, you can change the directory when saving the file. If you are creating a number of similar files destined for the same directory, however, you may find changing the default document path more convenient than changing the directory for each file as you save it. With this method, you don't need to worry about saving each file in the right directory.

You can change the path by accessing the Default Paths dialog box. From the User Setup dialog box—accessed with Too**l**s **U**ser Setup—you can select **P**aths to display the Default Paths dialog box. This set of keystrokes is a fairly complex path, especially if you want to change the default path frequently.

Instead, create a macro to make changing the directory easier. You want the macro to have the same functionality as the manual method. When you access the Default Paths dialog box (shown in figure 23.23), it shows you the current document directory (along with other default directories) and enables you to enter a new directory. If you type a directory name that doesn't exist, Ami Pro displays the error message shown in figure 23.24 and redisplays the dialog box. If you select Cancel, Ami Pro abandons the operation and returns to the previous display (the User Setup dialog box).

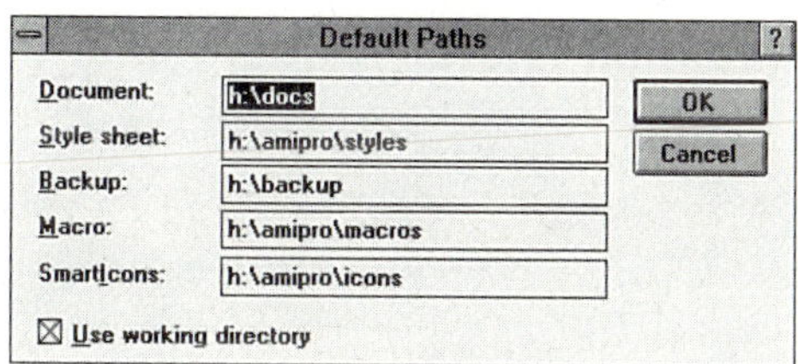

Fig. 23.23
The Default Paths dialog box, showing the current document path.

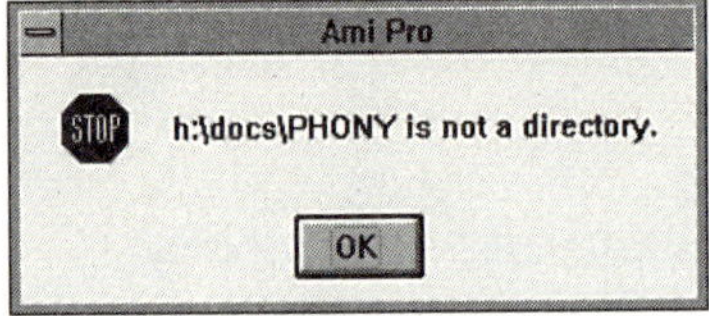

Fig. 23.24
The error message Ami Pro displays when you type an illegal path name.

The following macro implements an easily accessed operation with the same functionality as the manual method:

```
FUNCTION ChangeDocDirectory()
     currdir = GetDocPath$()
     result =-2
     while result = -2
          newdir = Query$("Document directory", currdir)
          result = SetDocPath(newdir)
          IF result = -2
               Message("{newdir} is not a directory")
          ENDIF
     wend
END FUNCTION
```

The macro begins by using the built-in `GetDocPath$()` function to assign the current document directory path to the variable `currdir`:

```
currdir = GetDocPath$()
```

Tip
When you write a loop, indent the statements inside the loop as shown in the example to simplify identifying the loop.

You will look at the next statement (`result = -2`) shortly. First, however, examine the WHILE/WEND loop, where most of the work of the macro gets done. As you have learned, a WHILE/WEND loop includes a WHILE statement, a WEND statement, and whatever statements occur between the WHILE and the WEND.

The first statement after the WHILE uses the built-in `Query$()` function to get the desired document directory from the user. As shown earlier in the chapter, `Query$()` displays a message and gets a typed response from the user. This statement asks the user to enter a path name for the document directory:

```
newdir = Query$("Document directory", currdir)
```

Earlier in the chapter, `Query$()` was used with only one argument—the *prompt string*. In this example, the prompt string `Document directory` is present, but a second argument—`currdir`—also is included (`currdir` is the variable to which you assigned the current document directory in the first statement after FUNCTION).

If you look up `Query$()` in the Help macro documentation, you see the following syntax:

```
Query$(prompt [, DefaultText])
```

This statement shows two arguments, `prompt` and `DefaultText`. But the second argument and the comma separating the arguments are enclosed in brackets. In a syntax statement, brackets represent *optional arguments* (or *optional parameters*)—that may be included when you call the function but that may be omitted if no need exists for them.

In the case of `Query$()`, the second (optional) argument, `DefaultText`, represents the default text that `Query$()` displays in the user response area of the dialog box. If the current document directory is C:\AMIPRO\DOCS, for example, the `Query$()` statement in the macro displays the dialog box shown in figure 23.25. The argument is optional because you may not have a meaningful default you want to display.

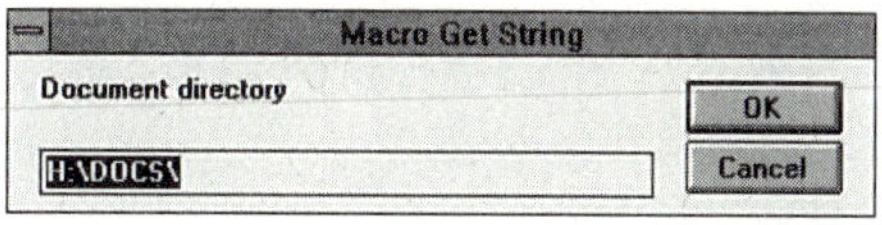

Macro Get String
Document directory
H:\DOCS\
OK
Cancel

Fig. 23.25
The dialog box with a default directory shown.

> **Caution**
>
> When you use an *optional* argument, don't type the brackets shown in the syntax statement.

When the user chooses OK, the `Query$()` function returns the text string in the box, which is assigned to the variable `newdir`. (If the user presses Cancel, the macro simply terminates.) The next statement is as follows:

```
result = SetDocPath(newdir)
```

The built-in function `SetDocPath()` sets the document directory to the path the user entered, which is passed as the argument. `SetDocPath$()` returns a value which the macro assigns to the variable result. This value is `1` if the path entered by the user exists. If the path doesn't exist, `SetDocPath$()` returns the value `-2`. (A number of Ami Pro functions return `-2` to indicate an error condition.)

The next three statements are an IF block:

```
IF result = -2
     Message("{newdir} is not a directory")
ENDIF
```

Recall the requirement for the macro stated at the beginning of this section—it must act just like the "manual" procedure. If the user enters a nonexistent directory in the Default Paths dialog box, Ami Pro displays a message box to tell the user that the directory doesn't exist. The IF block in this macro does the same thing.

If the directory doesn't exist, the preceding statement assigns the value `-2` to the variable result. The IF statement therefore evaluates to TRUE if the directory doesn't exist. (If the user enters a legal directory, however, the result equals `1` and the IF statement evaluates to FALSE.) When the IF statement evaluates to TRUE, the built-in `Message()` function displays a dialog box explaining the problem. When the user chooses OK or presses Enter, the dialog box disappears.

What happens next? The next statement in the macro is WEND, the end of the loop. Remember that when Ami Pro encounters a WEND it goes back to the previous WHILE statement and re-evaluates the expression.

This is the WHILE statement:

```
while result = -2
```

If `result` is equal to `-2` (in other words, if `SetDocPath$()` returns an error) the WHILE expression evaluates to TRUE, and the loop executes again. Ami Pro again displays the dialog box asking for a directory, attempts to set the directory to the path name typed by the user, and tests the result to see whether the attempt succeeded. If result isn't equal to `-2`, indicating that `SetDocPath$()` successfully changed the document directory, the WHILE expression evaluates to FALSE. If this condition occurs, Ami Pro immediately goes to the statement following the WEND and continues execution of the macro. In this case, as the next statement is END FUNCTION, the macro simply ends.

Tip
You can auto-run this macro when you start Ami Pro. See "Running Macros When You Start or Exit Ami Pro," earlier in this chapter.

Now you are ready to look at the statement before the WHILE:

```
result = -2
```

Whenever Ami Pro encounters a WHILE statement, the program evaluates the expression following the WHILE. In this example, because you always want the WHILE/WEND loop to execute at least once, you want the WHILE expression to be TRUE the first time Ami Pro encounters it. WHILE is TRUE if `result` equals `-2`; so you simply assign `-2` to `result` immediately in front of the WHILE statement.

Summary

In this chapter, you learned how to record a macro by performing a series of operations. You also learned how to define and use shortcut keys for a macro; how to play back a macro; how to create and use a quick macro; how to create and edit macros with Ami Pro's macro programming language; and how to assign an automatic macro to a file. While the chapter doesn't cover every aspect of the macro programming language, you now have a good basis for going as far with the language as you want to go.

In the next chapter, you explore another of Ami Pro's powerful features for automating your work—power fields.

Chapter 24

Creating Smart Documents with Power Fields

Until about a quarter century ago, the idea of a "document" had, for thousands of years, referred exclusively to collections of ink on paper. With the first magnetic-card typewriters came a new type of document, created electronically and stored magnetically—an "electronic" document.

A few years after the emergence of electronic documents, the first early, crude word processors caused a rethinking of what constituted an electronic document. Now a document could be viewed and modified on a CRT screen.

The idea of a "document" stayed at that point for about 15 years—words that could be modified interactively, stored electronically or magnetically, and reproduced on paper at will. In the mid-1980s came another advance in the idea of "electronic document," with the introduction of words and pictures integrated into the same document, first in desktop publishing programs, and then in high-end word processing packages. Documents were still passive objects, however—things that people created and manipulated.

In Ami Pro 3, you can create a new type of document: *dynamic documents.* Dynamic documents take a proactive role in their own creation; they can communicate with each other and with the document creator. The mechanism that makes this system possible is *power fields.*

In a standard word processing document, if you insert a new figure between consecutively numbered figures you must renumber all the figures that follow the new figure. Without a power field, your only choice is to renumber the figures manually. If you use power fields to number figures, however, when you insert a new figure (or delete an existing figure) Ami Pro renumbers all the figures in your document. You also can design these power fields to reference the pages on which the figures appear—and to update the references if a figure moves to a different page.

In earlier chapters of this book, you encountered several types of power fields. Bookmarks are power fields, as are index fields and merge fields. In this chapter, you learn more uses of these types of power fields and learn about other types of power fields: power fields that can insert dates or page numbers, solicit values for variables, check input for accuracy, and issue error messages. You see how power fields can automate repetitive tasks such as updating page or figure numbers. These are some of the many commonly used functions Ami Pro includes as *predefined power fields*. As this chapter explains, you also can design and save your own *custom power fields*.

In this chapter, you learn how to make documents "smarter" by combining power fields with other features of Ami Pro. Power fields work particularly well with macros—you can use most of Ami Pro's built-in macro functions in your power fields, and you even can launch your macros from a power field.

Understanding Power Field Components

Power fields have two components: the *instructions* that tell Ami Pro what to do at the power field location, and the actual *data* that the power field generates.

The contents of an instruction can range from very simple—"Insert the current page number," for example—to complex. A complex power field instruction may tell Ami Pro something like the following: "Multiply the global value *amount* by .03, and insert the result into the document at this point. When inserting the result, use two decimal places, preceded by a dollar sign. If the result is negative, enclose it in parentheses."

This example describes in plain English what the power field instruction tells Ami Pro to do. The actual instruction is more terse and cryptic:

```
FormatNum$(If amount < 0 "($" else "$" Endif,
     If amount < 0 ")" Else "" Endif, 2,amount*0.03)
```

If the value of the variable *amount* is 200, the power field inserts the data `$6.00`. If the value of *amount* is –1000, the power field inserts the data `(–$30.00)`.

The following example is moderately complex. As one of the program's predefined power fields, Ami Pro includes a field called `Seq`, which is used to display a sequence of numbers. Each time you insert a `Seq` field for the same series of numbers, it increases the number by one. If you are using `Seq` to number a series of paragraphs, which you designate as the `ParaNum` sequence, the instruction part of each `Seq` power field is `<Seq ParaNum>`. The data part of each power field is the current paragraph number.

Normally, when you view or print a document, you see only the data—which is what you *want* to see in the finished document. As explained in this chapter, however, at times you may want to display or print the power field instructions, and Ami Pro does so at your command. Using the `Seq ParaNum` example, the data appears in the document like this:

```
1.     This is the first paragraph.
2.     This is the second paragraph.
```

The numbers `1` and `2` are data; when you tell Ami Pro to show you the instructions, your document looks like this:

```
<Seq ParaNum>. This is the first paragraph.
<Seq ParaNum>. This is the second paragraph.
```

Displaying Power Field SmartIcons

If you plan to use more than a few simple power fields, consider adding the power field SmartIcons to your displayed SmartIcon set. In figure 24.1, the power field SmartIcons are shown in the displayed set (this set includes the Bookmark SmartIcon, which you use often in working with power fields).

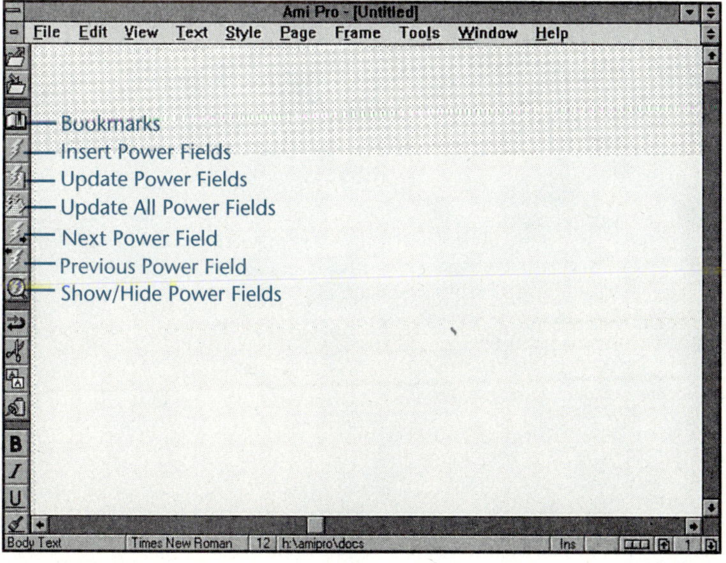

Fig. 24.1
The power fields SmartIcons added to the displayed set.

Using Predefined Power Fields

◀ See "Setting Up SmartIcons," p. 216

Ami Pro includes more than 40 *predefined power fields*. These predefined fields probably can meet most of your needs. If you need to create special power fields, however, see the section "Creating Your Own Power Fields," later in this chapter.

Inserting Simple Predefined Power Fields

Some predefined power fields are "simple"; the power field instruction consists of a single word, which you select from a list box. This section describes how to insert one of these simple power fields into a document. More complex power fields—those that require multiple-word instructions—are described in the section "Inserting More Complex Predefined Power Fields," later in this chapter.

Inserting a simple power field into a document requires only a few easy steps. Assume that you want to create a footer to display the page number in the form "Page 1 of *x*," where *x* represents the total number of pages in the document. You can easily do this with the predefined power field `NumPages`.

To create the footer with this power field, follow these steps:

1. Place the insertion point in the footer area of the document (see fig. 24.2).

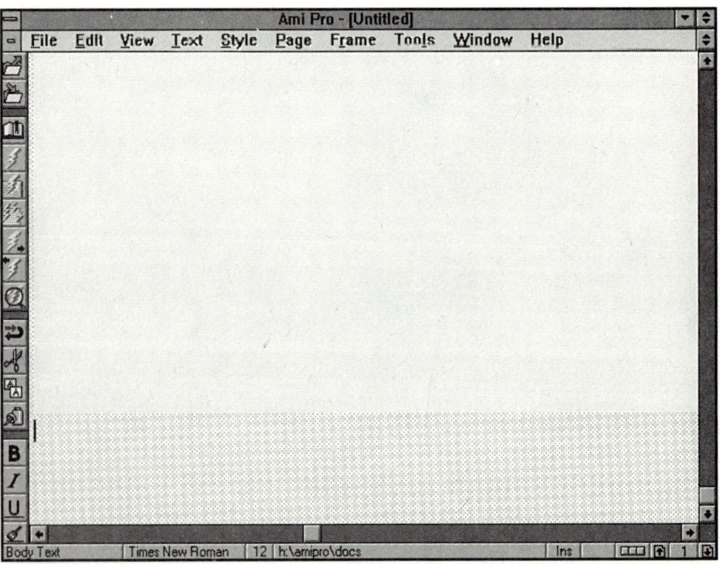

Fig. 24.2 The insertion point, shown in the footer area of the document.

2. In the document, type the word **Page** followed by a space and then choose **P**age **P**age Numbering. When the Page Numbering dialog box appears (see fig. 24.3), choose OK or press Enter to use the default settings. (For information on changing the settings, see Chapter 5, "Working with Page Layout.")

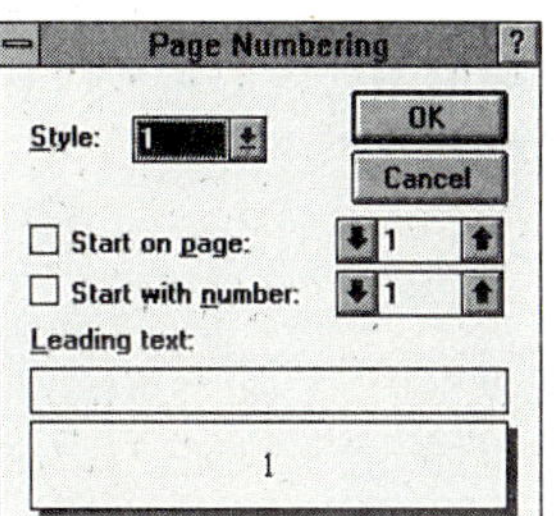

Fig. 24.3
The Page Numbering dialog box with default values.

3. Press the space bar once and then type the word **of**. Press the space bar again; then choose **E**dit Power **F**ields. The Power **F**ields cascading menu appears (see fig. 24.4).

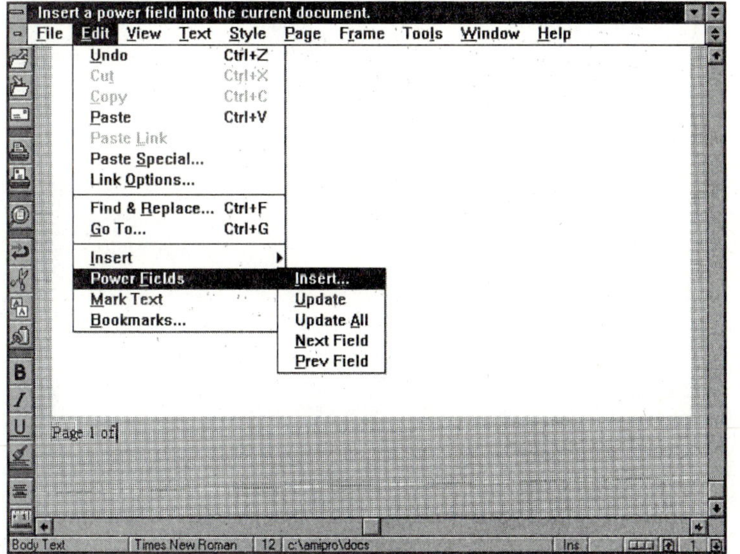

Fig. 24.4
The Power **F**ields cascading menu.

4. Choose **I**nsert. The Insert Power Fields dialog box appears (see fig. 24.5). The **F**ields list box lists the predefined power fields provided by Ami Pro.

For quick access to the Insert Power Fields dialog box, you can click the Insert Power Field SmartIcon instead of using the menu.

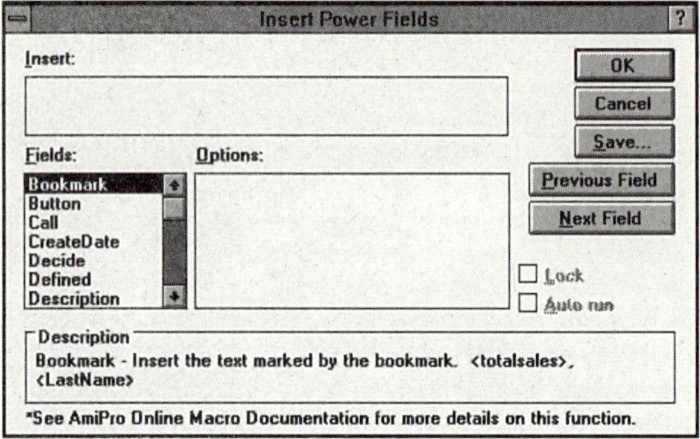

Fig. 24.5
The Insert Power Fields dialog box.

5. Scroll through the list of power fields and select the power field you want to insert. For this example, select `NumPages`. The power field is highlighted in the **F**ields list box and also appears in the **I**nsert text box. The Description text box describes the highlighted power field and the *syntax* (format) for entering the power field. When you have highlighted `NumPages`, the dialog box appears as shown in figure 24.6.

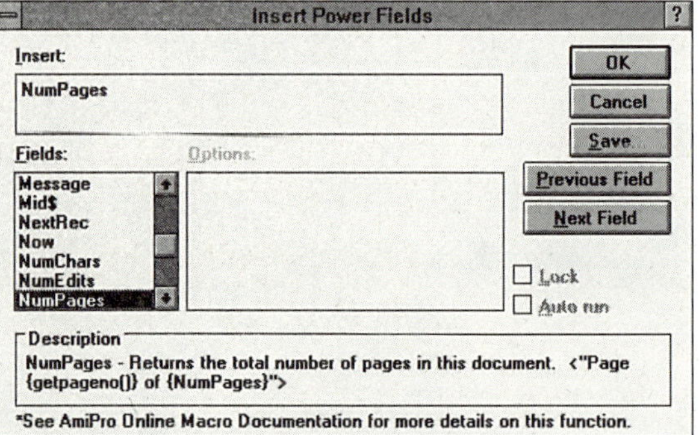

Fig. 24.6
The `NumPages` field description in the Insert Power Fields dialog box.

Caution

Although the example shown in the Description text box in figure 24.6 shows power fields surrounded by angle brackets, *never* type angle brackets in the Insert text box unless you are entering a relational operator, such as the less-than symbol (<) in an expression such as `IF x < y`.

6. With the NumPages field highlighted, choose OK or press Enter to return to the document. The footer appears as shown in figure 24.7.

Displaying Power Field Instructions

As explained earlier, a power field consists of two parts: instructions and data. Ami Pro normally shows the data, which is what you want to appear in the finished document. The NumPages power field shown in figure 24.7 is displaying data—in this case, the number of pages in the document.

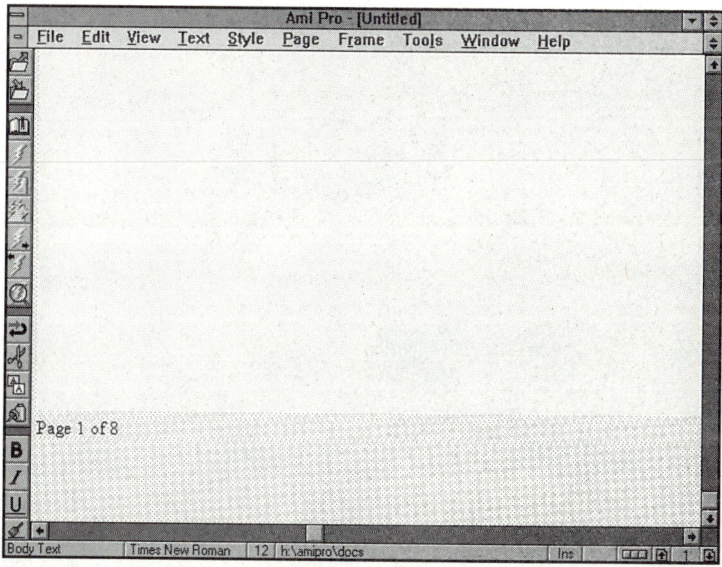

Fig. 24.7
The footer after inserting the page number and the NumPages power field.

Sometimes you may want to see the instruction part of your power fields on-screen. You may want to make sure that you place a particular power field in the right location, for example, or you may need to edit a power field. (See "Editing Power Fields," later in this chapter, for information on how to edit power fields in a document.)

To display power field instructions, choose **V**iew Show Po**w**er Fields. All power fields in the document display their instructions inside angle brackets. Everything between the angle brackets is the instruction. Figure 24.8 shows the instructions for the footer you created in the preceding example. For the NumPages power field, the data is the number of pages in the document. The instruction is the word NumPages, inside angle brackets.

Tip
Use the Show Power Fields SmartIcon to quickly toggle between displaying instructions and data.

You can continue to edit your document with power field instructions displayed, if you want, or redisplay the power fields data only when necessary. To hide all power fields in the document, choose **View**. This time, rather than Show Po**w**er Fields, the menu option reads Hide Po**w**er Fields. When you choose Hide Po**w**er Fields, the power field instructions disappear and Ami Pro again displays the power fields data.

Fig. 24.8
The footer with power field instructions displayed.

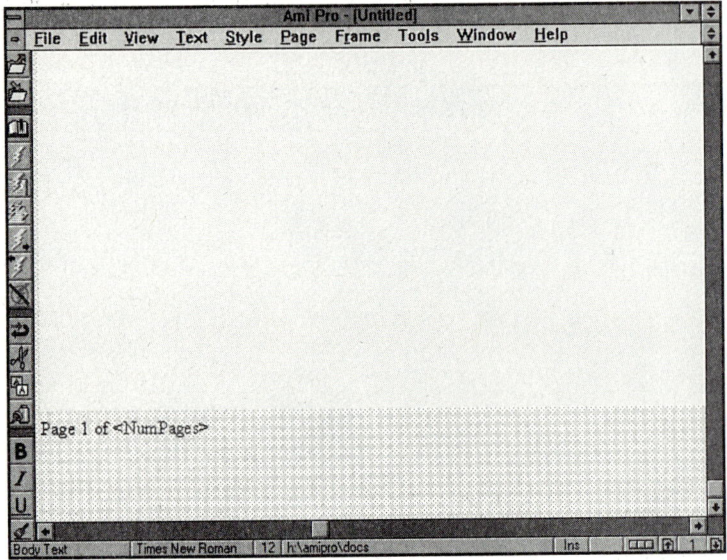

Note

"Show Power Fields" and "Hide Power Fields" are misleading terms. If a power field is the type that displays data, the power field always "shows" its instructions (when you select Show Power Fields) or its data (when you select Hide Power Fields).

Tip
To create a printed copy of your power field instructions, display instructions (choose **V**iew Show Po**w**er Fields); then print the document as you normally would.

When you save a document (or when the auto save feature saves the document automatically), Ami Pro hides the power fields (changes to the display of data) before saving the document. If your power fields suddenly and unexpectedly flip from instructions to data, Ami Pro probably is performing a timed save.

Selecting a Power Field

For many of the operations on an individual power field, you first need to select that power field. You select a power field in one of the following ways:

- Display power field instructions, as described in the preceding section, and highlight the entire power field. Make sure that the selection includes the angle bracket at the beginning of the instruction and at the end.

◄ See "Setting Program Defaults" p. 228

- Use the **N**ext Field and **P**rev Field choices from the Power **F**ields cascading menu (choose **E**dit Power **F**ields) to select the next field or preceding field in the document. You can use these options whether Ami Pro is displaying instructions or data.

Tip
Use the Next Field and Previous Field SmartIcons to move quickly between fields.

Moving, Copying, and Deleting Power Fields

To move, copy, or delete a power field, you first select the power field, using the techniques described earlier. Then you simply cut, copy, or delete the selection as you would any other selection.

Tip
You must have the *entire* field selected, or Ami Pro will not move, copy, or delete the field.

You cannot delete a power field with Backspace or Del unless you first select the power field. If instructions are displayed, Backspace and Del can delete characters within the power field instructions (anything between the angle brackets), but until you remove the angle brackets—which you can do only if you first select them—you haven't deleted the power field.

If you attempt to cut or delete a selection of text that includes a power field, Ami Pro displays the message shown in figure 24.9. To continue the operation, choose OK or press Enter; otherwise, choose Cancel.

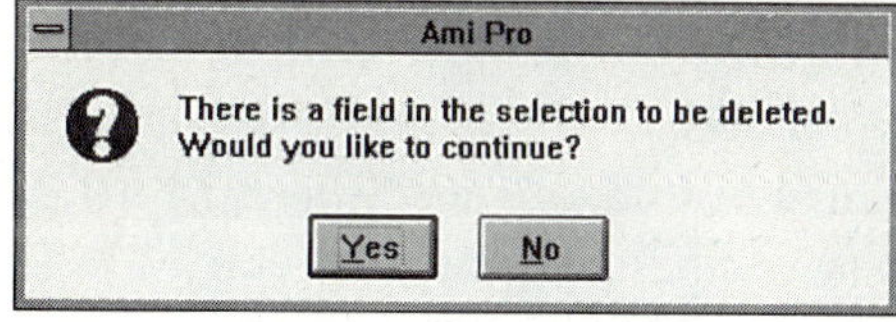

Fig. 24.9
The message Ami Pro displays when you try to move or delete a selection that includes a power field.

> **Caution**
>
> You may believe that you have selected a power field when you don't have the whole field—and you must select the *whole* field to move, copy, or delete it. This problem is likely to occur when you have several power fields in the same area, or when you have one power field nested within another. After you have moved, copied, or deleted a selection that includes power fields, display the power field instructions and verify that you have accomplished what you intended.

Updating Power Fields

When you create a new power field, Ami Pro calculates and displays the correct data for that power field *at the time you create the power field*. When you inserted `NumPages` in the earlier example, Ami Pro inserted the correct number of pages in your document.

If you make changes to your document that affect the data displayed by the power field, Ami Pro *doesn't* automatically update the power field. If you insert pages into your document or remove pages from your document, for example, the footer shown in figure 24.7 is no longer correct, because it doesn't change automatically.

You can update a power field in two ways:

- Update the power fields manually.
- Set a power field to **A**uto Run, which tells Ami Pro to update the power field each time you open the document containing the power field. (This option is covered in the section, "Updating Power Fields when Opening a Document," later in this chapter.)

Updating Power Fields Manually

Tip
If you have many power fields, Ami Pro may take a *very* long time to perform an Update **A**ll operation.

Tip
Insert a bookmark at your current location *before* you choose Update **A**ll. Then you can quickly return to that point after you update power fields.

You can tell Ami Pro to update any individual power field or all the power fields in a document.

To update all the power fields in the document, choose **E**dit Power **F**ields. From the Power **F**ields cascading menu, choose Update **A**ll.

When you choose Update **A**ll, Ami Pro updates all the power fields in your document. If power field instructions are displayed at the time you choose Update **A**ll, Ami Pro switches to data display (hiding the power fields). After power fields are updated, Ami Pro repositions the insertion point at the beginning of the document.

To update any *individual* power field, follow these steps:

1. Select the power field. If power field instructions are displayed, just place the cursor anywhere within the power field.
2. Choose **E**dit Power **F**ields. The Power **F**ields cascading menu appears.
3. Choose **U**pdate. The power field performs its assigned action and displays the updated data in your document. If you update the `NumPages` power field in the footer described earlier, for example, the footer displays the current number of pages in the document.

Updating Power Fields when Opening a Document

You can tell Ami Pro to update specific power fields within a document each time it opens that document. You do this by selecting the **A**uto Run feature in the Insert Power Fields dialog box for each power field you want to update automatically.

Tip
Use the Update Power Field SmartIcon to quickly update a selected field.

Note

You cannot turn on **A**uto Run when you first create a power field; to activate **A**uto Run, you must select this option in the Insert Power Fields dialog box *after* you create the field.

To tell Ami Pro to mark a power field for automatic update each time the program opens the document, follow these steps:

1. Select the power field. If instructions are displayed, you can simply place the cursor anywhere inside the field.
2. Choose **E**dit Power **F**ields. The Power **F**ields cascading menu appears.
3. Choose **I**nsert. The Insert Power Fields dialog box appears. (To quickly display the Insert Power Fields dialog box, you can click the Insert Power Field SmartIcon.)

   The instruction for the power field appears in the **I**nsert text box (see fig. 24.10). The **A**uto Run option (which is dimmed when you create a *new* power field) now is available.

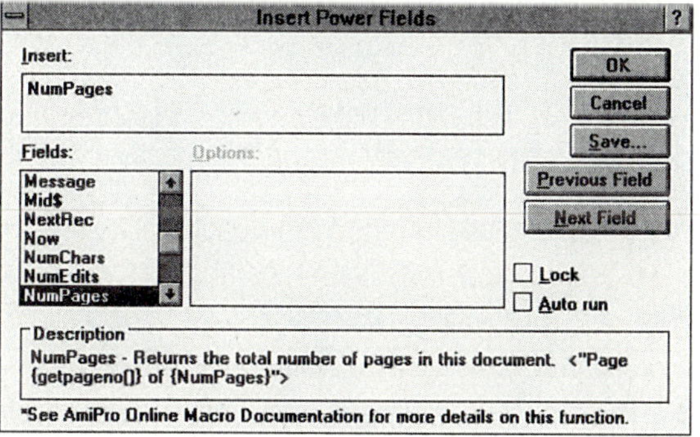

Fig. 24.10
The Insert Power Fields dialog box for an existing power field.

4. Choose **A**uto Run. An X in the check box indicates that **A**uto Run is selected.

5. Choose Cancel. The dialog box disappears. The next time you open the document, Ami Pro automatically updates the power field.

To cancel the **A**uto Run setting for the field, repeat this procedure, deselecting the **A**uto Run option.

Locking Power Fields To Prevent Updating

Tip

As with the **A**uto Run feature, when you first create a power field you cannot lock it. You must return to the Insert Power Fields dialog box to lock the field.

You may have some power fields that you don't want Ami Pro to update when you use the Update **A**ll feature. (For an example, see the section "Inserting a Complete Document," later in this chapter.) You can *lock* power fields to prevent Ami Pro from updating them.

To lock a power field, follow these steps:

1. Select the power field you want to lock.
2. Choose **E**dit Power **F**ields. The Power **F**ields cascading menu appears.
3. Choose **I**nsert. The Insert Power Fields dialog box appears. The instruction for the power field appears in the **I**nsert text box (refer to fig. 24.10). The **L**ock option (which is dimmed when you create a *new* power field) now is available.
4. Choose **L**ock. An X in the check box indicates that **L**ock is selected.
5. Choose Cancel. The dialog box disappears. Ami Pro will never update the power field again (unless you unlock the field first or select **A**uto Run and **L**ock for the same field).

Caution

Don't choose OK. Ami Pro doesn't lock the field if you choose OK.

To unlock the field, repeat this procedure, deselecting the **L**ock option.

Inserting More Complex Predefined Power Fields

So far in this chapter, you have learned how to insert simple predefined power fields; how to display instructions and data; how to select, move, copy, and delete a power field; and how to use Ami Pro's features for locking and updating power fields. All the techniques you have learned apply not only to the simple power fields used as examples thus far, but also to the more complex predefined power fields you begin exploring in this section.

The term *predefined* is something of a misnomer for these power fields; a more accurate term may be *partially defined.* When you enter a power field that requires more than a single-word instruction, you select the first word from the **F**ields list box—that's the "predefined" part. But then you must enter additional information to make the power field instruction complete. You can think of the additional information you enter as the *arguments* to the power field. (See Chapter 23, "Using Macros," for a definition and discussion of the term *argument.*)

In the Insert Power Fields dialog box, the **O**ptions list box displays the defined options for the highlighted field in the **F**ields list box. Date fields such as `CreateDate`, for example, provide a set of formatting options, as shown in the **O**ptions list box in figure 24.11.

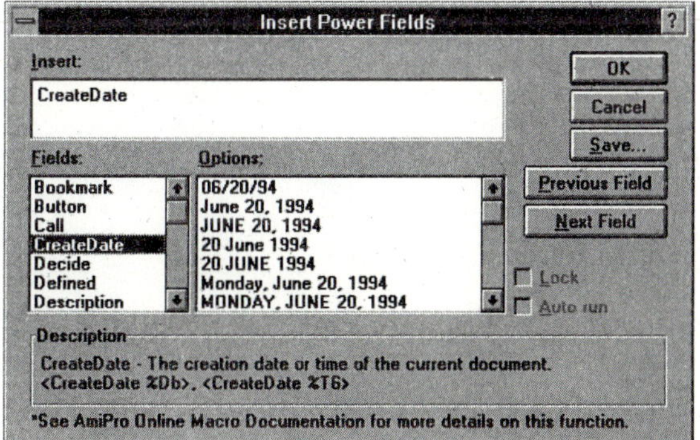

Fig. 24.11
The Insert Power Fields dialog box, showing date options.

For some power fields, you complete the instruction by selecting an item from the **O**ptions list box. In the **I**nsert text box, Ami Pro places a code representing the selected option, following the field type. For other types of fields requiring complex instructions, you enter additional information by typing text directly into the **I**nsert text box. (Some instructions may have arguments consisting of a combination of selected options and typed text.)

Using the Correct Syntax in Power Field Instructions

When typing a power field instruction, you must use the correct *syntax* (format). If you try to insert a power field with incorrect syntax, the error is indicated in the following way. First, Ami Pro displays a dialog box with an error message. Then the program inserts the field into the document; instead of the data, however, the program displays the error message from the dialog box. Finally, Ami Pro redisplays the dialog box so that you can correct the error.

◀ See "Working with Headers and Footers," p. 134

◀ See "Numbering Pages," p. 167

◀ See "Using a Bookmark," p. 171

◀ See "Using Ami Pro's Macro Language," p. 821

Each power field type has its own rules of syntax. Some rules apply to a number of different Ami Pro power field types. These rules include the following:

- Use quotation marks around *literal text*—text you want inserted in exactly the form in which you type it.
- Use quotation marks around any other text only when the Description text box for that power field type shows quotation marks.
- *Don't* use quotation marks around global variable names. Note that this rule differs from the rule about global variables in *macros*, where you *must* use quotation marks around global variable names.
- Use parentheses to enclose the arguments for any macro functions you use in your power fields. In the expression `Decide("Use Standard Form?")`, for example, the quoted text `"Use Standard Form?"` is the argument to the `Decide()` macro function.

Caution

Never use angle brackets in power field instructions, except in an expression such as `IF totalpages>5`.

Formatting Dates and Times

When you use the `CreateDate` or `EditDate` field types to insert the creation or editing date of the current document, you must include an option that specifies the format Ami Pro will use to display the date. (If you omit the option, Ami Pro displays a number that represents the date as the number of seconds since midnight, January 1, 1970, Greenwich Mean Time. Unless you plan to make calculations using the date, this number isn't particularly useful.)

You can represent the date or the time by using the option codes in Table 24.1. If you want to display date *and* time, insert two separate power fields—one with a date option, the other with a time option.

Table 24.1 Power Field Date Formats

Code	Sample of Format
%Da	06/11/92
%Db	June 11, 1992
%DB	JUNE 11, 1992

Code	Sample of Format
%Dc	11 June 1992
%DC	11 JUNE 1992
%Dd	Thursday, June 11, 1992
%DD	THURSDAY, JUNE 11, 1992
%De	June 11
%DE	JUNE 11
%Df	Thursday June 11
%DF	THURSDAY June 11
%Dg	06/11
%Dh	06/11/1992
%Di	11. June
%DI	11. JUNE
%Dj	11. June 1992
%DJ	11. JUNE 1992
%Dk	1992 June 11
%DK	1992 JUNE 11
%Dl	June, 1992
%DL	JUNE, 1992
%T1	18:11 (24-hour format)
%T2	6:11 AM
%T3	06:11 AM
%T4	6:11 A
%T5	06:11 A
%T6	6:11 am
%T7	06:11 am
%T8	6:11 a
%T9	06:11 a

Editing Power Fields

You can edit power field instructions. If you want to change the format of a `Date` power field, for example, editing the existing power field may be more convenient than deleting the power field and replacing it with another power field. Editing power fields changes only the power field instruction; for the change to be reflected in the data, you must update the power fields, as explained earlier in this chapter.

You can edit power fields directly in the document text or by using the Insert Power Fields dialog box.

To edit power fields in the document, display power field instructions by choosing **V**iew Show Po**w**er Fields or by clicking the Hide/Show Power Fields SmartIcon. Place the insertion point between the angle brackets of the power field you want to edit. Add, delete, or replace the text in the power field as desired. Be sure to obey syntax rules for the power field you are editing.

Caution

When editing a power field, be careful not to delete either angle bracket at the ends of the power field. If you remove the angle bracket, Ami Pro no longer recognizes that text as a power field. If you delete an angle bracket by mistake, delete the power field and reinsert it. You cannot just retype the angle brackets.

Tip
When you use this method, Ami Pro automatically checks the syntax of the power field and informs you if you have made a mistake.

The other way to edit power fields is to access them with the Insert Power Fields dialog box. In the document, select the power field you want to edit. Then display the Insert Power Fields dialog box. Change the text in the **I**nsert text box as necessary; then choose OK or press Enter. Ami Pro changes the power field in the document.

Using Global Variables in Power Fields

In Chapter 23, "Using Macros," you learned about *variables*. You may recall that a variable specifies a place in the computer's memory where Ami Pro can store a *value*. The value of a variable can be text (in the form of a *string*, or sequence of characters) or a numeric quantity.

You also learned in Chapter 23 that a *global variable* is a variable that stays in the Ami Pro environment until you exit from Ami Pro or until you explicitly tell Ami Pro to free (destroy) the global variable. (You can tell Ami Pro to free a global variable from within a macro.)

Global variables also are available in power fields. You can use global variables to help your document control its environment—and even to control other functions in Ami Pro and in Windows.

Assigning Values to Global Variables

You must *allocate* (assign memory to) a global variable before you can assign a value to it. In a *macro*, this process requires two separate steps. The following macro statements allocate a single-element global variable named `myvar` and assign it the value `"Have a nice day"`:

```
AllocGlobalVar("myvar", 1)
SetGlobalVar("myvar", "Have a nice day")
```

In a power field, you also can use the predefined `Set` power field to assign a value to a global variable. If the global variable doesn't exist, Ami Pro allocates the variable automatically. Unlike in macros, therefore, creating a new global variable and assigning it a value with a power field requires only one step, not two.

Caution

When you create or use a global variable in a power field (unlike in a macro), *don't* enclose the name of the variable in quotations.

The following list describes the values you assign to a global variable in a power field:

- A number, such as `Set myglobal 24`.
- A *string* in quotation marks, such as `Set myglobal "Your account is 30 days past due. Please remit payment immediately."` (See Chapter 23, "Using Macros," for more information on strings.)
- The contents of another global variable, such as `Set myglobal otherglobal`.
- The result of a mathematical expression, such as `Set myglobal 5+8` or `Set myglobal otherglobal*6`.
- Note that a bug in Ami Pro results in an error if you enter an expression that includes a subtraction; for example, the expression `8-3` doesn't

work (it evaluates to `0`). To work around this bug, use a negative number enclosed in parentheses in your expression. To perform the subtraction in this example, use `8+(-3)`.

- The contents of a merge field from a data file attached to the current document. The data file can be an Ami Pro merge data file or an external data file from a program such as dBASE, Paradox, Excel, or 1-2-3. If you have a merge field named `LASTNAME`, for example, you can enter `Set myglobal LASTNAME`.

- The return value from a built-in macro function. For example, `Set myglobal GetBookMarkCount()` sets `myglobal` to the number of bookmarks in the current document.

To assign a value to a global variable with a `Set` power field, follow these steps:

1. Place the insertion point at the position in the document where you want to locate the power field.

2. Choose **E**dit Power **F**ields. From the Power **F**ields menu, choose **I**nsert. The Insert Power Fields dialog box appears.

3. In the **F**ields list box, select `Set`. The word `Set` appears in the **I**nsert text box (see fig. 24.12).

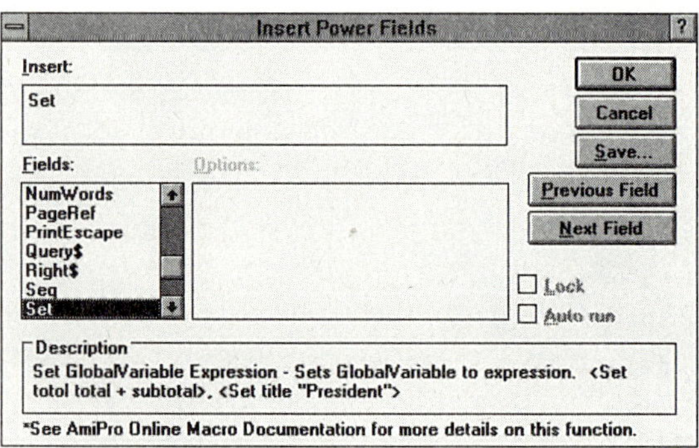

Fig. 24.12
The Insert Power Fields dialog box with the `Set` field selected.

4. Place the cursor in the **I**nsert text box, immediately following the word `Set`. Type a space and then the name of the global variable. You can use any combination of letters, numbers, and underscore characters, as long as the name contains at least one letter. The name cannot include spaces.

   For this example, name the variable `myglobal`.

5. Type a space after the variable name and then type the value you want to assign to the global variable. (The values you can assign are described following these steps.)

   If you have created a global variable named `othervariable` and assigned it a numeric value, and then you assign global variable `myglobal` the value `otherglobal*1.2`, the dialog box resembles figure 24.13.

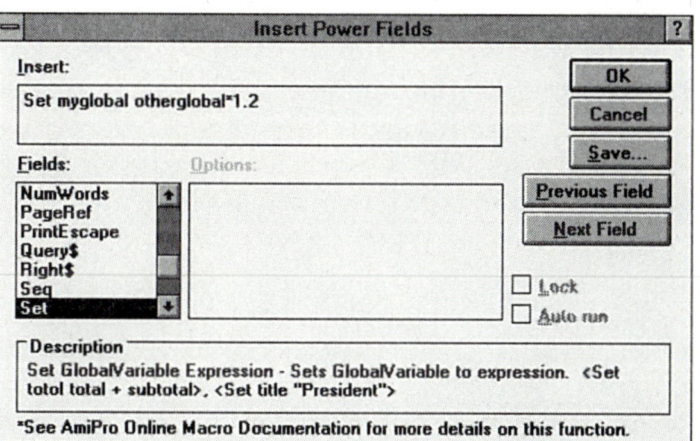

Fig. 24.13
The Insert Power Fields dialog box with the complete Set expression entered.

6. Choose OK. Ami Pro inserts the power field into the document.

   A `Set` power field displays no data. You can see the instructions you just inserted by choosing **V**iew Show Po**w**er Fields or by clicking the Show/Hide Power Fields SmartIcon (see fig. 24.14).

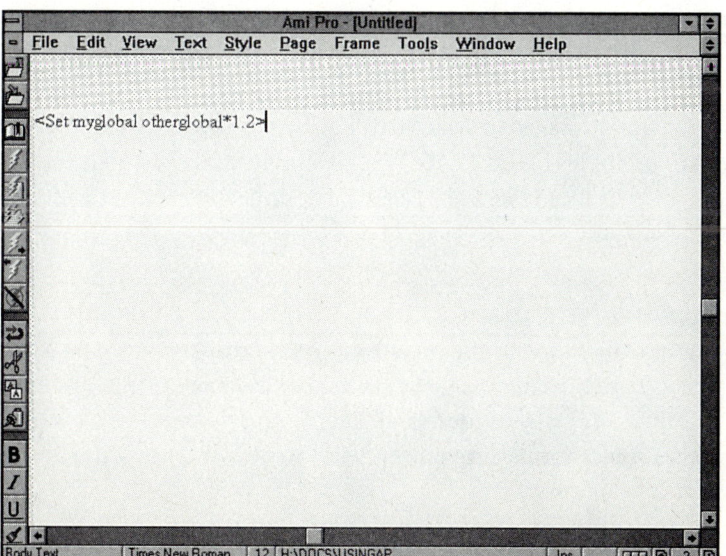

Fig. 24.14
The example `Set` power field with instructions displayed.

Displaying the Value of a Global Variable

To display the value of a global variable, you create a power field with an instruction consisting solely of the name of the global variable. To display the value of the variable `myglobal` created in the preceding section, follow these steps:

1. Place the insertion point at the position in the document where you want the value of the global variable to appear.
2. Choose **E**dit Power **F**ields. From the cascading Power **F**ields menu, choose **I**nsert. The Insert Power Fields dialog box appears.
3. In the **I**nsert text box, type the name of the global variable (see fig. 24.15).

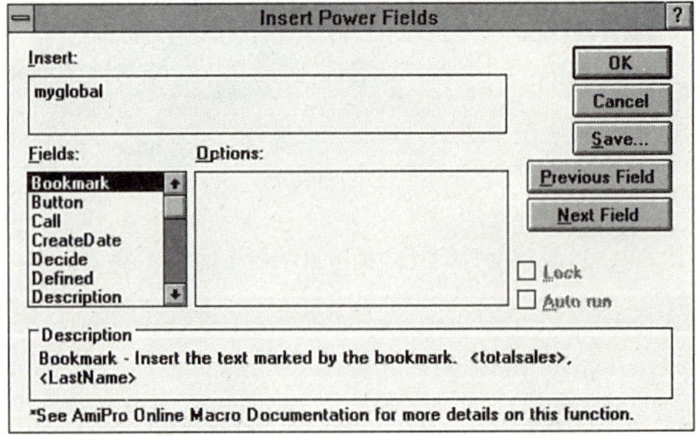

Fig. 24.15
The Insert Power Fields dialog box, ready to insert the value of the global variable `myglobal`.

4. Choose OK or press Enter. Ami Pro inserts the power field into the document.

   With data displayed (power fields hidden) in this example, the document resembles figure 24.16. With instructions displayed (power fields showing), it looks like figure 24.17. The angle brackets indicate that the variable name is the instruction of a power field.

Formatting Numbers

The technique described in the preceding section displays the data in a default format. But you can change the format of the data, using Ami Pro's number-formatting options (described later in this chapter) or by using the predefined number-formatting power field `FormatNum$`. The syntax of `FormatNum$` is as follows:

```
FormatNum$("prefix", "suffix", decimals, expression)
```

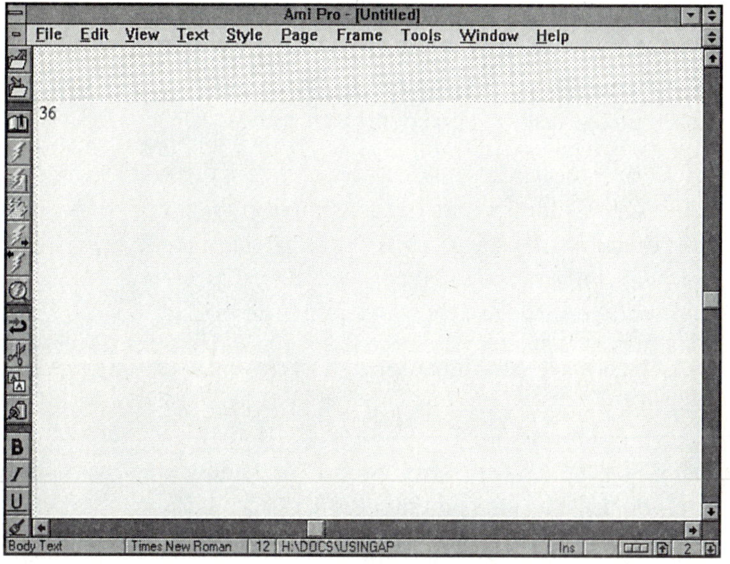

Fig. 24.16
The value of the global variable `myglobal` shown in the document.

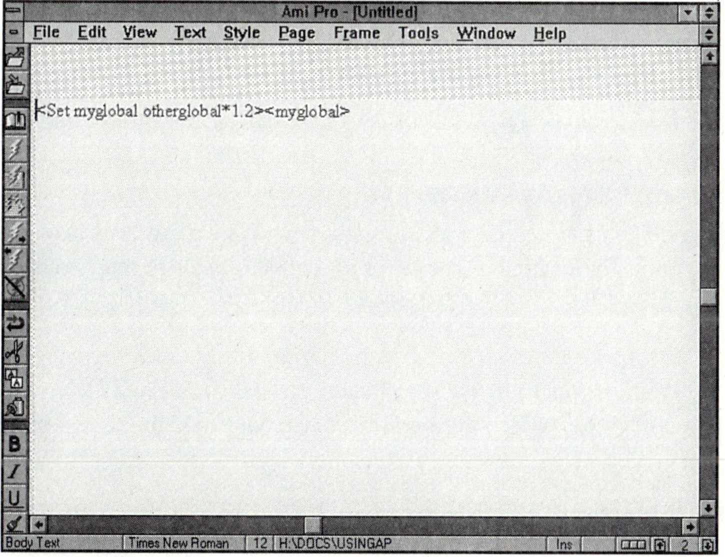

Fig. 24.17
The instructions for the power field. Note that both global variables are assigned values by these power fields.

FormatNum$ has four arguments. You must supply a value for all four. When you use a `FormatNum$` power field, you use the arguments as shown in the following list:

- For *prefix*, specify the character or characters you want to precede the number. You must enclose the characters in quotation marks. To precede the number with a dollar sign, for example, type **"$"**. (If you don't want a prefix, just type two quotation marks: "".)
- For *suffix*, indicate the character or characters you want to follow the number. You must enclose the characters in quotation marks. If you want the number to be followed by a space and the letters *CR* (an accounting convention meaning *credit*), for example, type **"CR"**. (If you don't want a suffix, just type two quotation marks: "".)
- Replace *decimals* with the number of decimal places you want. For standard currency format, for example, type **2**. To display only the whole number portion of the number, type **0**. (Note that `FormatNum$` doesn't *round*—it *truncates*. If the number is 1.9999 and you tell Ami Pro to display 0 decimals, the program displays `1`.)
- For *expression*, substitute the number, global variable, or mathematic expression that represents the value of the number. To display the result of multiplying the value of the global variable `TotalSale` times the value of the global variable `SalesTax`, using standard currency format, you create a `FormatNum$` power field with the following syntax:

```
FormatNum$("$","",2,TotalSale*SalesTax)
```

Using Global Variables

Although you can only create global variables with a `Set` power field (or with a macro), you can insert the name of a global variable into many different types of power fields.

When you choose OK after creating a power field incorporating a global variable, Ami Pro checks to see whether the global variable exists. A global variable exists if it has been defined by a `Set` power field or created by the `AllocGlobalVariable()` function in a macro you have run at least once.

If you specify a global variable that doesn't exist, Ami Pro displays the error message shown in figure 24.18. Choosing OK causes Ami Pro to display the error message in the document in place of the data that would normally appear. When you later create the variable (by defining a `Set` power field or by running a macro that allocates the variable), update the power field with the reference to the global variable. Ami Pro then replaces the displayed error message with the value of the data.

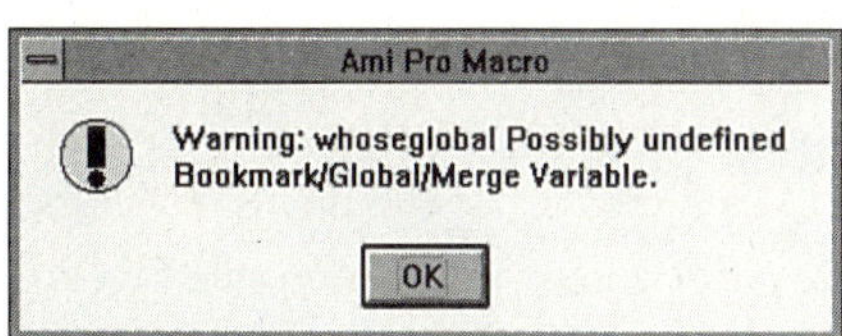
Ami Pro Macro
Warning: whoseglobal Possibly undefined Bookmark/Global/Merge Variable.
OK

Fig. 24.18
The error message displayed when you reference an undefined global variable.

Caution

When you run a macro that can change the value of a global variable referenced in one or more power fields, you must update all the power fields with references to that variable, or the values will not be correct.

When you choose OK after defining a power field, Ami Pro tries to figure out what each word in your power field instruction means. If you entered the instruction correctly, the program has no trouble. If Ami Pro finds a word it cannot interpret, however, it assumes you are referencing an undefined global variable and displays the message shown in figure 24.18. If you get this message, but didn't intend to reference a global variable, you probably made a syntax error.

Creating Extended Documents

Global variables embedded in a document can extend the reach of the document far beyond its own boundaries. After you have created a global variable with `Set` (or modified a global variable created with a macro, through the action of a `Set` power field in your document) you can use the variable in another power field in the same document. But you also can use a global variable to insert data from your document into a power field in a different document—because the variable is *global*, it is accessible by any Ami Pro document.

Because a global variable also is accessible to *macros*, you can use the global variable you created or modified in a document to control the action of the macro. The macro can open another document based on the value of the power field in your document, perform operations in that (second) document based on the value of the power field—even use the value of the variable to control any other Windows application that supports Dynamic Data Exchange (DDE).

◄ See "Producing Simple Merges," p. 437

◄ See "Intermediate Topics in Ami Pro Macro Programming," p. 847

Documents controlling other documents and documents controlling macros (rather than the other way around) is a radically new idea in word processing. As you may imagine, this chapter can only hint at the many possible applications for power fields.

Creating Smart Numbers with Power Fields

Suppose that you have a document where you need to document procedures by inserting a series of numbered steps in various places. (This book is such a document.) You want to number the steps automatically so that if you move, delete, or insert a step, all the steps retain the correct numbers. The first step in each procedure, of course, must be numbered `1`.

In the earlier section "Understanding Power Field Components," you saw an example of how you can use the `Seq` field to display a series of numbers. Because a `Seq` field can use many of the types of instructions available in power fields—as well as being very useful in its own right—this section works through an example using `Seq`.

Inserting the First Step in a Series of Steps

You begin by inserting the first step, which always must be numbered `1`. This requirement creates a complication—but one that you can handle quite easily with the tools available for use with `Seq`.

Begin by choosing **E**dit Power **F**ields **I**nsert. The Insert Power Fields dialog box appears. In the **F**ields list box, select the field `Seq` (see fig. 24.19).

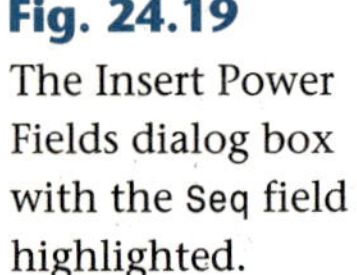

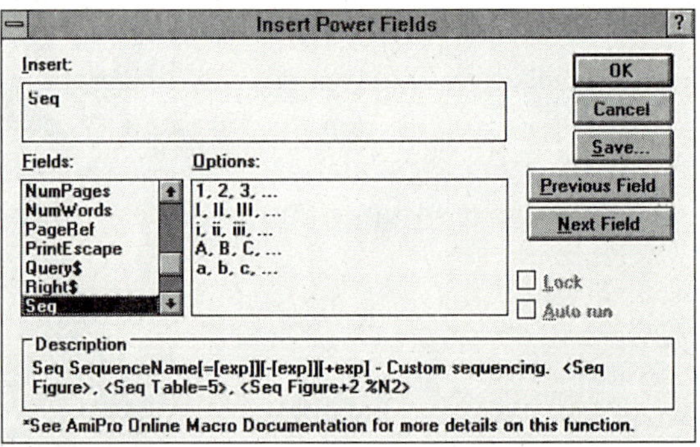

Fig. 24.19
The Insert Power Fields dialog box with the `Seq` field highlighted.

The **D**escription text box of figure 24.19 shows what is euphemistically called a "description." (It probably confuses you more than it enlightens you—but it is important.) The following paragraphs break down the description into its component parts.

The segment `Seq SequenceName[=[exp]][-[exp]][+exp]` describes the syntax of the `Seq` power field. In a syntax description, brackets (`[]`) enclose parts of the syntax that are optional. The required part of the syntax, therefore, consists of two words: `Seq SequenceName`. `Seq` is the field type, which Ami Pro has entered into the **I**nsert text box for you. `SequenceName` represents the name you will assign to the sequence.

In this example you need only one sequence at a time, but you may want to number paragraphs with one sequence, tables with another, chapter sections with a third, illustrations with a fourth, and so on. You can have as many sequences as you want running simultaneously.

You replace `SequenceName` with a descriptive name for the specific sequence. The name can be any combination of letters, numbers, and underscore characters, but cannot contain any spaces. The name should describe what you're numbering.

Note that you *must* assign a name, even if you plan to have only a single sequence in your document. If you try to insert a power field with just the word `Seq`, Ami Pro displays the error message shown in figure 24.20. This message also is displayed as the data of the power field until you correct the problem.

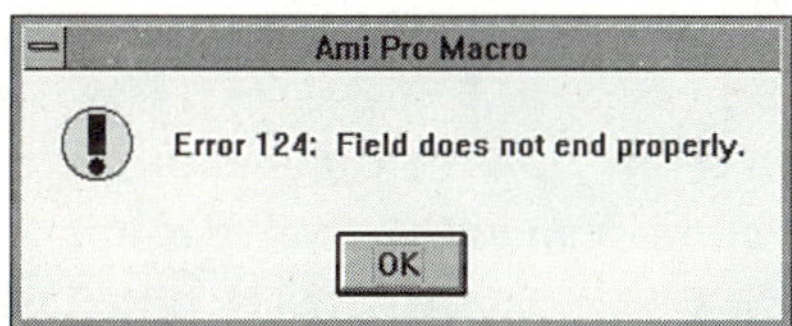

Fig. 24.20
The message Ami Pro displays when you enter an incomplete power field.

Because this example numbers steps, call the sequence `Steps`. To insert the name, move the cursor into the **I**nsert text box. Type a space after the word `Seq`, and then type **Steps** (see fig. 24.21).

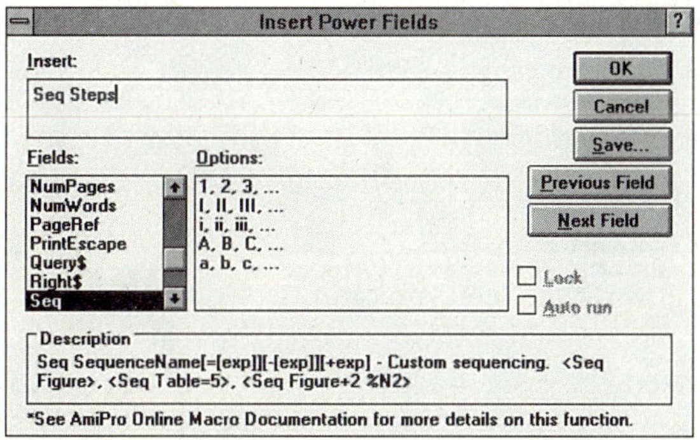

Fig. 24.21
The Insert Power Fields dialog box after you have entered the name for the sequence (`Steps`).

For the second and subsequent steps in any procedure, this instruction is sufficient—the field type Seq followed by the sequence name Steps. Because you are numbering the first step—and because this example uses the same sequence name (Steps) for each procedure—you must make sure that the sequence always starts with 1.

Note

You could solve this problem with a different approach—using a different sequence name for each procedure. As you see later in the chapter, however, one advantage of the approach chosen here is the ease with which it can be automated, using a simple, easy-to-record macro. Using different sequence names makes such a macro more complex to write and more cumbersome to use.

If you haven't used the Steps sequence before in this document, the first step will be numbered 1. If this is the second procedure for which you are using the Steps sequence, however, Ami Pro doesn't know that you want to start over with 1. Fortunately, a method exists for telling Ami Pro to restart the sequence; unfortunately, that method returns to the convoluted description.

Look at the first optional part of Seq SequenceName[=[exp]][-[exp]] [+exp]—the part that is expressed [=[exp]]. As mentioned earlier, the square brackets indicate optional material; you can assign a value to any Seq field, rather than letting Ami Pro number it automatically. The key is that when you assign such a value, Ami Pro starts Seq counting from that specified value.

Look at the second example in the **D**escription text box. (Examples are enclosed in angle brackets in the description; however, *don't* type the angle brackets in the **I**nsert text box.) The second example is <Seq Table=5>, which sets a sequence named Table to the value 5. The data inserted into the field will be 5. When the program reaches the *next* field with an instruction Seq Table, Ami Pro assigns the value 6.

To assign a value of 1 to the first step in your procedure (the step-numbering sequence), type =1 immediately following the word Steps in the **I**nsert text box (see fig. 24.22).

The power field now is complete; you can insert it into the document by choosing OK or pressing Enter. After you have inserted the field in the document, type the step to be referenced by the step number. For this example, type **Create a new document.** Figure 24.23 shows the result.

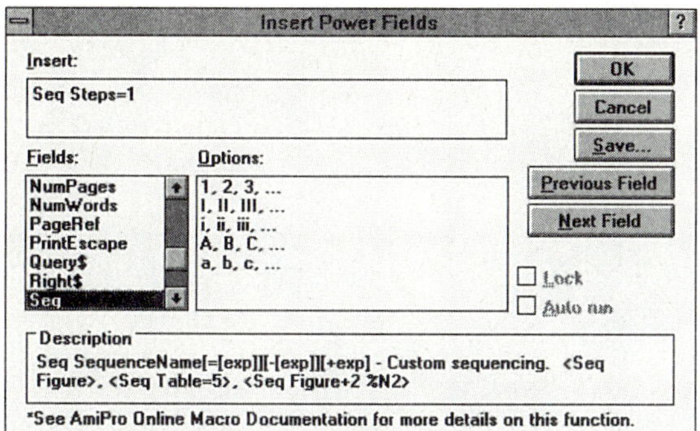

Fig. 24.22
The power field to number step 1 and start the sequence counting from 1.

If you tell Ami Pro to display power field instructions (show power fields), the document looks like figure 24.24.

Numbering Subsequent Steps in a Series

The procedure for numbering subsequent steps is exactly the same as that for numbering the first step, except that you don't need to tell Ami Pro what number to use; Ami Pro uses the next number in the sequence. In the process of creating the power field, your entry in the **I**nsert text box of the Insert Power Fields dialog box should read `Seq Steps` (refer to fig. 24.21).

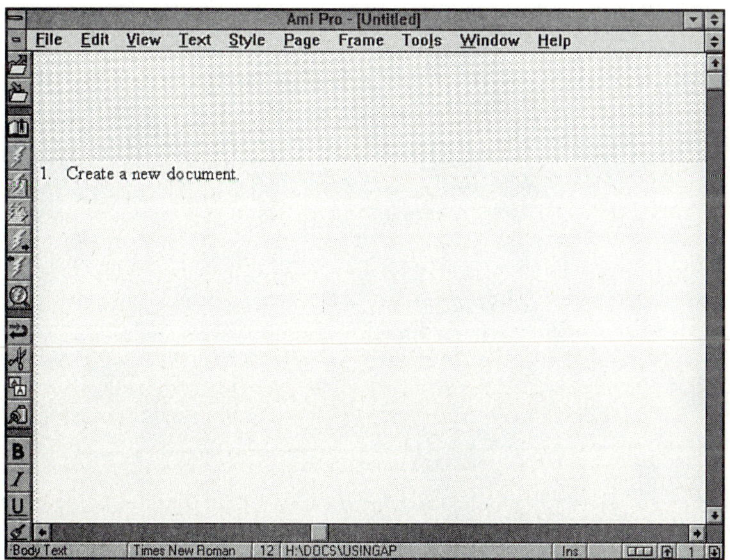

Fig. 24.23
The document showing step 1.

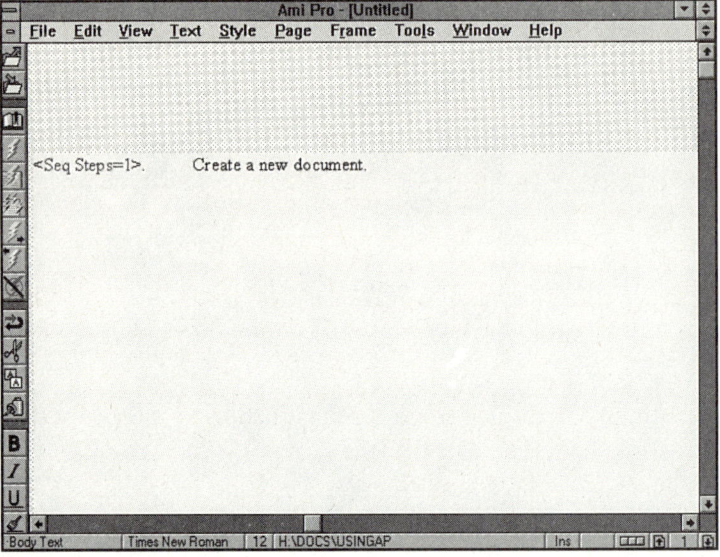

Fig. 24.24
The document showing the instruction that produces the step numbered 1.

After you have entered several `Seq Steps` power fields, your document resembles figure 24.25. If you choose to show power fields, it resembles figure 24.26.

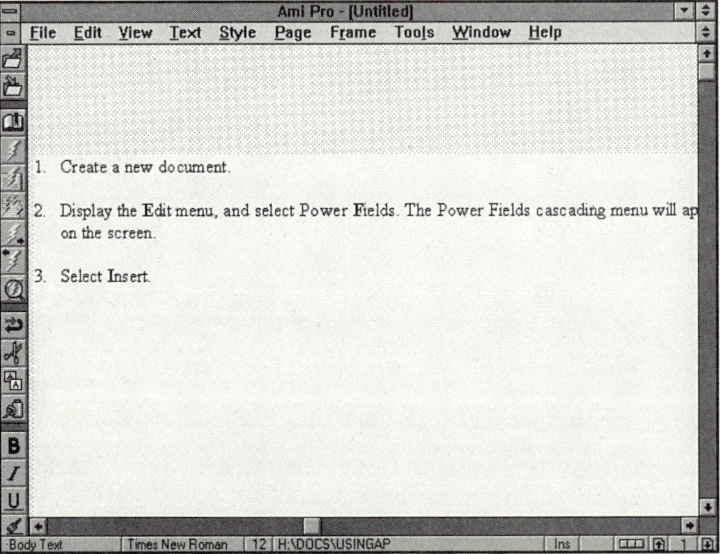

Fig. 24.25
The document with three steps entered and numbered.

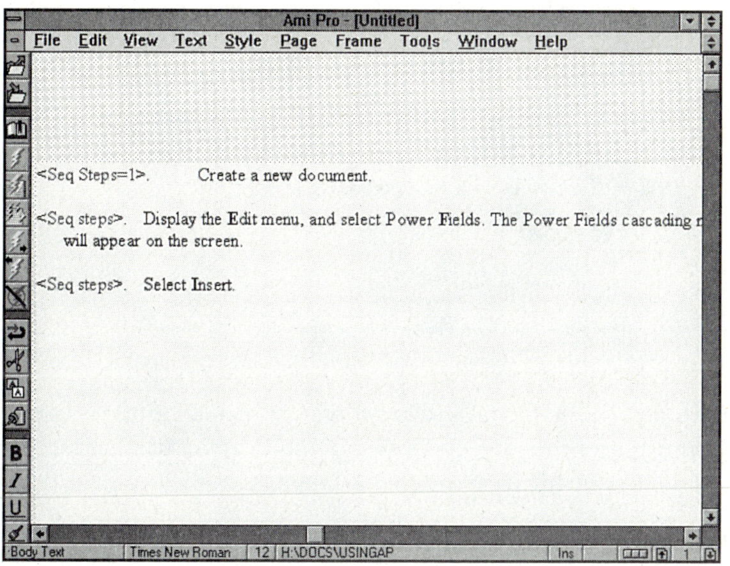

Fig. 24.26
The instructions that produce the data shown in figure 24.25.

If you move, delete, or add a step, Ami Pro renumbers some of the steps immediately. To make sure that all the steps are renumbered correctly, update your power fields.

> **Caution**
>
> If you change the order of steps so that the original step 1 no longer is step 1, be sure to move the power field `<Seq Steps=1>` to the new first step.

Changing the Format of the Smart Numbers

By default, the `Seq` power field creates a sequence of numbers in the format `1`, `2`, `3`, `4`, and so on. But what if you want to number your steps `A`, `B`, `C`, `D`, and so forth?

Notice the five choices in the **O**ptions list box in figure 24.27. Each choice represents a format for representing the numbers in a sequence. The first choice (`1`, `2`, `3`) represents the default format. If you want to use capital letters instead of numbers, select the next-to-last option (`A`, `B`, `C`). When you make this change, Ami Pro inserts a format code at the end of the instruction (see fig. 24.27).

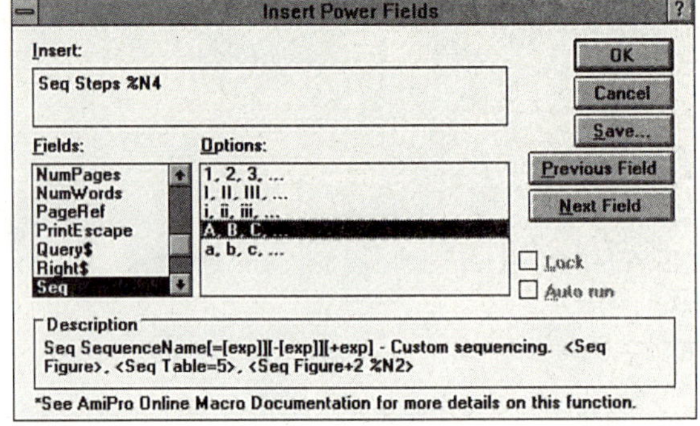

Fig. 24.27
The **Insert** text box contains a format code to use capital letters.

When you choose the capital letters option (and make the same change in the power fields for the subsequent step numbers), your document resembles figure 24.28. The instructions in the document resemble figure 24.29.

When you edit power fields directly in your document (see "Editing Power Fields," earlier in this chapter), you can change the numbering format by using the codes shown in table 24.2. These codes can also be used to format other power fields that insert numeric data into text.

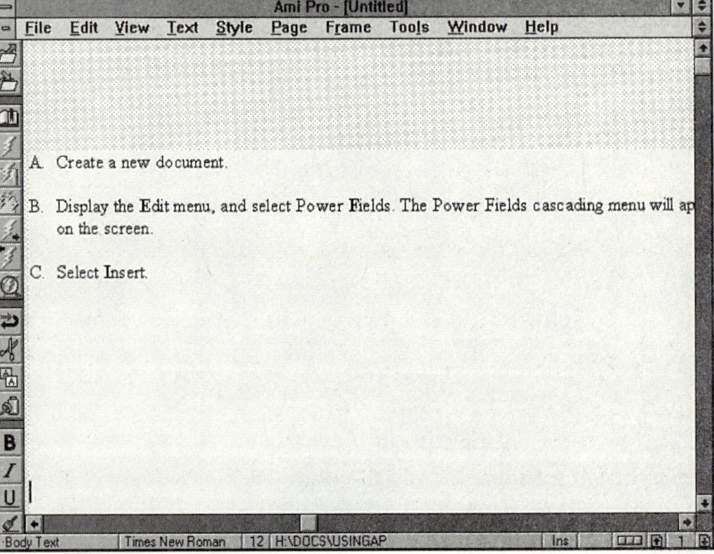

Fig. 24.28
The document with the steps "numbered" A, B, and C.

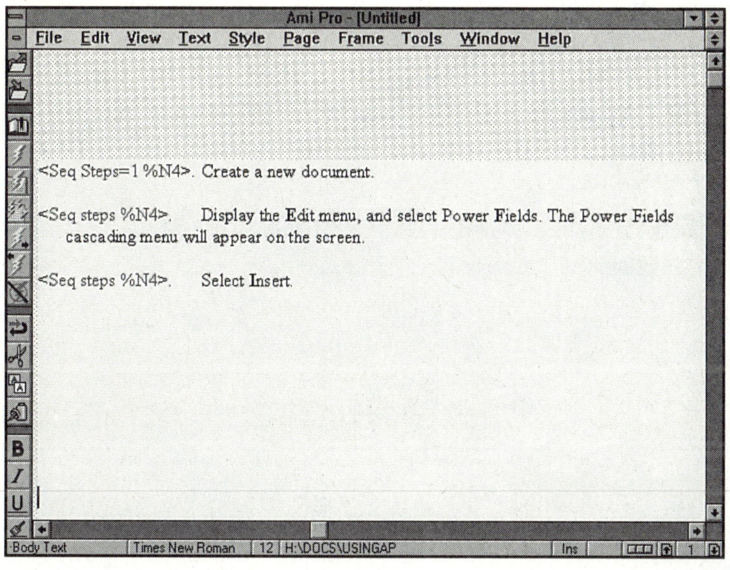

Fig. 24.29 The instructions that produce the data in figure 24.28.

Table 24.2 Number Format Codes for Power Fields

Format	Sequence
%N1	1, 2, 3 ...
%N2	I, II, III ...
%N3	i, ii, iii ...
%N4	A, B, C ...
%N5	a, b, c ...

Automating Smart Numbers with a Macro

When you plan to insert a common power field many times within a document—for example, when you create a power field that you use like `Seq Steps`—you can save time by creating a macro that inserts the power field and then assigning that macro to a shortcut key combination. To automate `Seq Steps` with a macro, follow these steps:

1. Choose Too**l**s **M**acros. From the **M**acros cascading menu (see fig. 24.30), choose **R**ecord. Ami Pro displays the Record Macro dialog box (fig. 24.31).

2. In the Macro **F**ile text box, type a file name for the macro. For the `Seq Steps` macro, type `seqsteps`.

3. In the **P**layback Shortcut Keys text box, press the key combination you want to assign to the macro. For this example, press Ctrl+F7 (see fig. 24.3).

4. Choose OK or press Enter. Ami Pro returns to the document. The Status Bar displays the message `Recording Macro`.

5. Choose **E**dit Power **F**ields **I**nsert. The Insert Power Fields dialog box appears.

6. In the **F**ields list box, select `Seq`. The word `Seq` appears in the **I**nsert text box.

7. Place the cursor in the **I**nsert text box following the word `Seq`, type a space, and then type `Steps`.

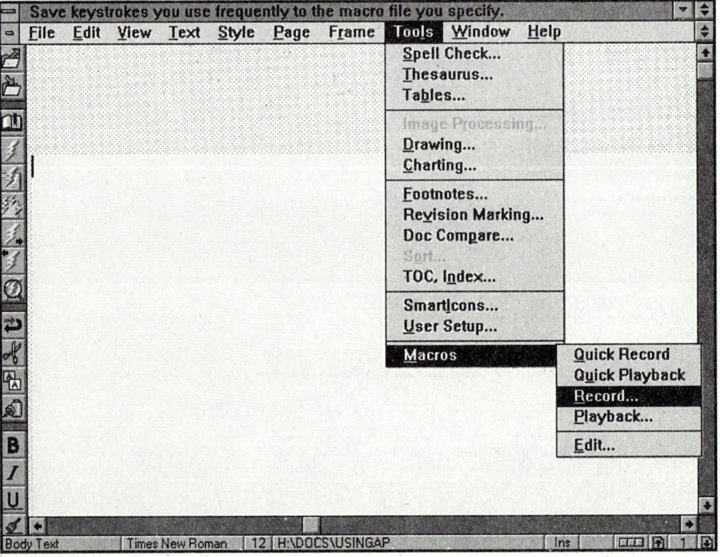

Fig. 24.30
The **M**acros cascading menu wih **R**ecord selected.

8. Choose OK or press Enter. Ami Pro inserts the power field into the document.

9. Choose Too**l**s **M**acros End **R**ecord. Ami Pro returns to the document.

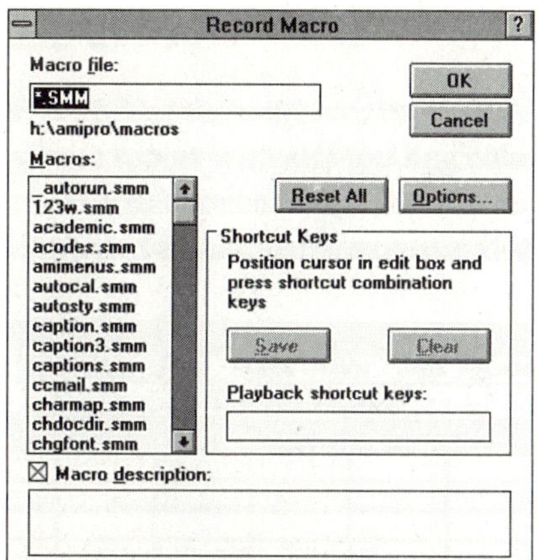

Fig. 24.31
The Record Macro dialog box.

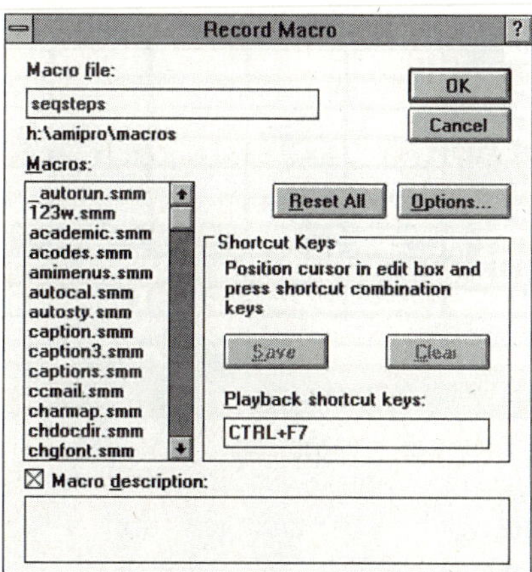

Fig. 24.32
Specifying the macro file name and playback shortcut key combination.

After you finish recording the macro, you can press the assigned shortcut key combination (Ctrl+F7, in this example) to insert a sequence number. To add the necessary =1 to the instruction for the first step in each sequence, you either can edit each first-step power field, adding the text to the end of the instruction (see "Editing Power Fields," earlier in this chapter), or record another macro (with a different file name and a different shortcut key combination) and include =1 in the instruction.

Supercharging Bookmarks

Chapter 6 discusses Ami Pro bookmarks. After you have placed a bookmark in a document, you can move quickly to the location of the bookmark. If you place a bookmark named *Recommendations* at the beginning of the recommendations section of your report, for example, you can jump directly to your recommendations by telling Ami Pro to "Go To Recommendations."

This function is unquestionably useful. In conjunction with other types of power fields, however, bookmarks can do much more than be passive targets for Go To commands. You can put things *inside* bookmarks, for example, and then use a `GetBookmark` field to insert copies of those things anywhere else in a document. The `Include` field enables you to insert the contents of a bookmark in a different document at the location of the field. You also can use a `PageRef` field to insert a field containing the page number of a bookmark anywhere in your document.

The ability to reproduce the contents of a bookmark anywhere within the document enables you to create "smart" references—references that can adjust themselves automatically to changes in the source. The bookmark (including the text and codes it encloses) is the *source*; a power field such as `GetBookmark` provides the *reference*.

Creating Smart References

You can use this capability to insert references to figures that you have numbered with a `Seq` field. If you later insert or remove figures prior to a referenced figure, the sequence number changes—and, because that number is referenced by `GetBookmark` power fields within the text, when you update power fields all references to the figure number also change.

You also can use referencing to insert the titles of chapter and section headings (such as the heading "Creating Smart References" at the beginning of this section) anywhere within a document. If you change the title, all references to it change when you update power fields.

Inserting the Source

The first step in creating an automatic reference is to insert the source; that is, what you want to reference. Suppose that you want to refer to the table number in figure 24.33. Every time you refer to the table, you want the word *Table* and the correct number to appear in the text. Figure 24.34 shows the text from figure 24.33 with power field instructions displayed. (Note the `Seq` field used to create the table number.)

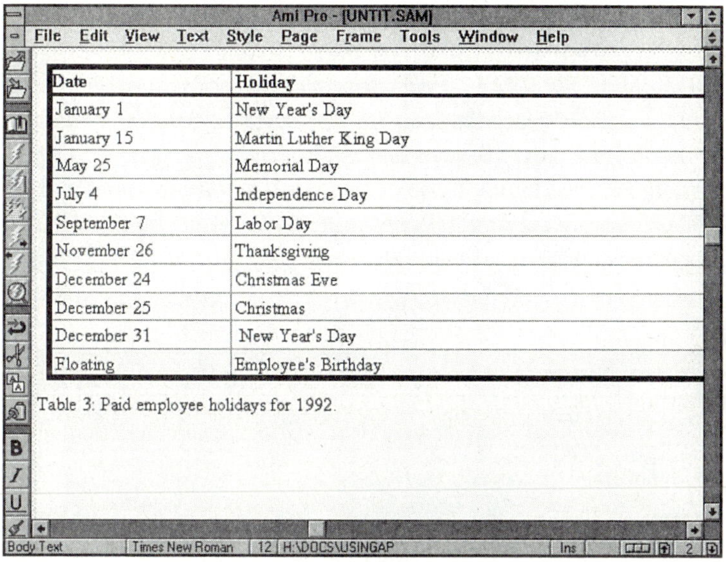

Ami Pro - [UNTIT.SAM]

File Edit View Text Style Page Frame Tools Window Help

Date	Holiday
January 1	New Year's Day
January 15	Martin Luther King Day
May 25	Memorial Day
July 4	Independence Day
September 7	Labor Day
November 26	Thanksgiving
December 24	Christmas Eve
December 25	Christmas
December 31	New Year's Day
Floating	Employee's Birthday

Table 3: Paid employee holidays for 1992.

Body Text | Times New Roman | 12 | H:\DOCS\USINGAP | Ins | 2

Fig. 24.33
A table number that you want to reference elsewhere in the text.

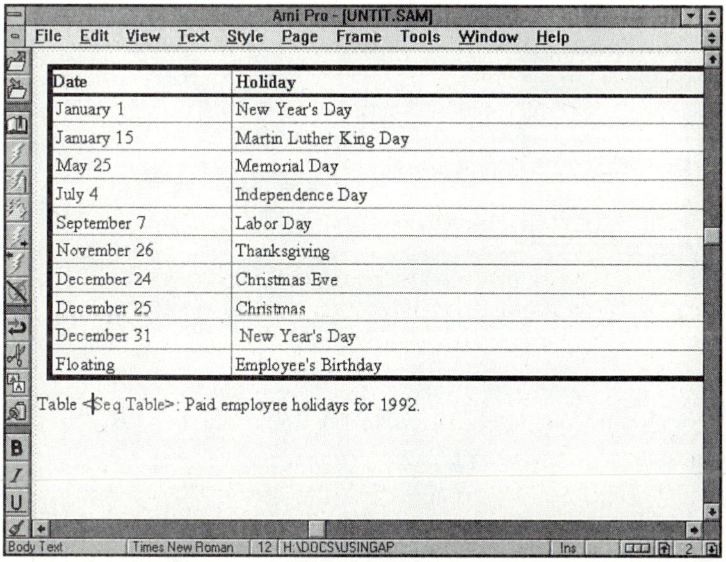

Ami Pro - [UNTIT.SAM]

File Edit View Text Style Page Frame Tools Window Help

Date	Holiday
January 1	New Year's Day
January 15	Martin Luther King Day
May 25	Memorial Day
July 4	Independence Day
September 7	Labor Day
November 26	Thanksgiving
December 24	Christmas Eve
December 25	Christmas
December 31	New Year's Day
Floating	Employee's Birthday

Table <Seq Table>: Paid employee holidays for 1992.

Body Text | Times New Roman | 12 | H:\DOCS\USINGAP | Ins | 2

Fig. 24.34
The power field used to create the table number in figure 24.33.

To create the source, follow this procedure:

1. Find the item you want to use as the source, and select that item. Figure 24.35 shows the selected source for this example.

Fig. 24.35
The selected text.

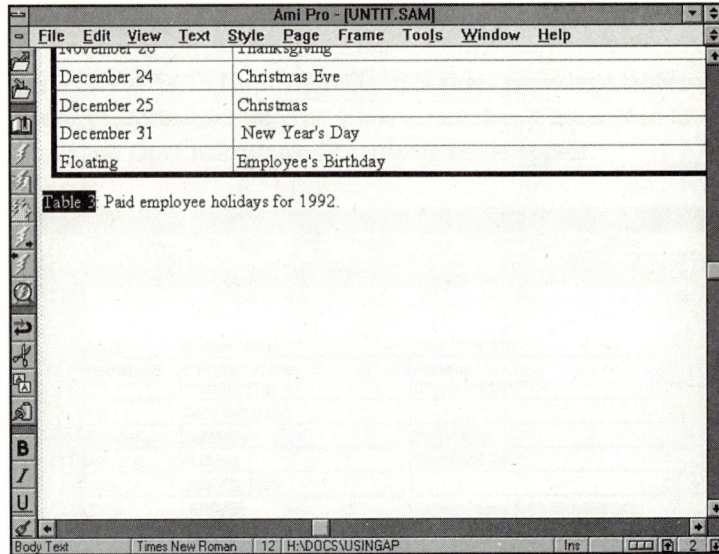

2. Choose **E**dit **B**ookmarks or click the Bookmarks SmartIcon. The Bookmarks dialog box appears, with the insertion point in the **B**ookmark text box (see fig. 24.36).

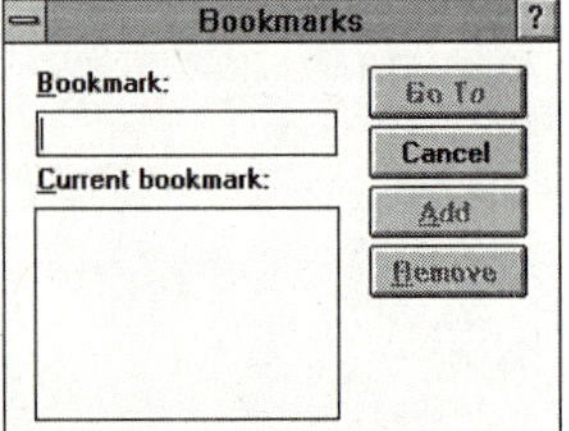

Fig. 24.36
The Bookmarks dialog box.

3. Type a name for the bookmark in the **B**ookmark text box. For this example, type **HolidayTable**.

4. Choose **A**dd.

The bookmark isn't visible unless instructions are displayed. To display instructions, choose **V**iew Show Po**w**er Fields. With instructions displayed (power fields shown), the document resembles figure 24.37.

Notice the angle brackets surrounding `<Table <Seq Table>>`. The angle brackets represent the boundaries of the bookmark `HolidayTable`. As this example illustrates, you can enclose a power field within a bookmark.

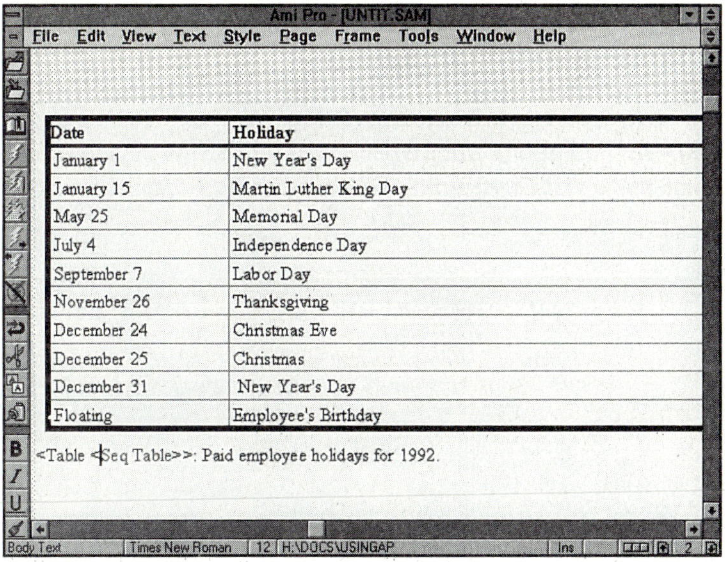
Ami Pro - [UNTIT.SAM]
File Edit View Text Style Page Frame Tools Window Help
Date
Holiday
January 1
New Year's Day
January 15
Martin Luther King Day
May 25
Memorial Day
July 4
Independence Day
September 7
Labor Day
November 26
Thanksgiving
December 24
Christmas Eve
December 25
Christmas
December 31
New Year's Day
Floating
Employee's Birthday
<Table <Seq Table>>: Paid employee holidays for 1992.
Body Text
Times New Roman
12
H:\DOCS\USINGAP
Ins

Fig. 24.37
The bookmark enclosing the referenced text `Table <Seq Table>`.

Creating the Reference

After you have named the source by enclosing it in a bookmark, you are ready to create the reference to the source. Follow these steps:

1. Move the cursor to the point in the text where you want the reference to the table to occur.
2. Choose **E**dit Power **F**ields **I**nsert. The Insert Power Fields Box appears.
3. In the **F**ields list box, select `Bookmark`. A list of currently defined bookmarks appears in the **O**ptions list box.
4. In the **O**ptions list box, select the bookmark you want to reference.
5. Choose OK or press Enter to insert the field (see fig. 24.38).

Tip
The name of the bookmark *doesn't* appear in the document.

In this example, you added a reference to a table. You use the same procedure if you want to add a reference to an illustration, a paragraph number, a chapter heading, or anything else in your document. Just enclose what you want to reference inside a bookmark.

Tip
If the bookmark you reference is empty, Ami Pro displays an error message. You can insert references only to bookmarks containing something.

Note

You cannot put anything inside a bookmark when the bookmark is inside a frame. Solve this problem by placing the bookmark outside the frame, and specify that you want the frame to flow with text, or keep the frame with the paragraph above it (see Chapter 16, "Using Frames," for details).

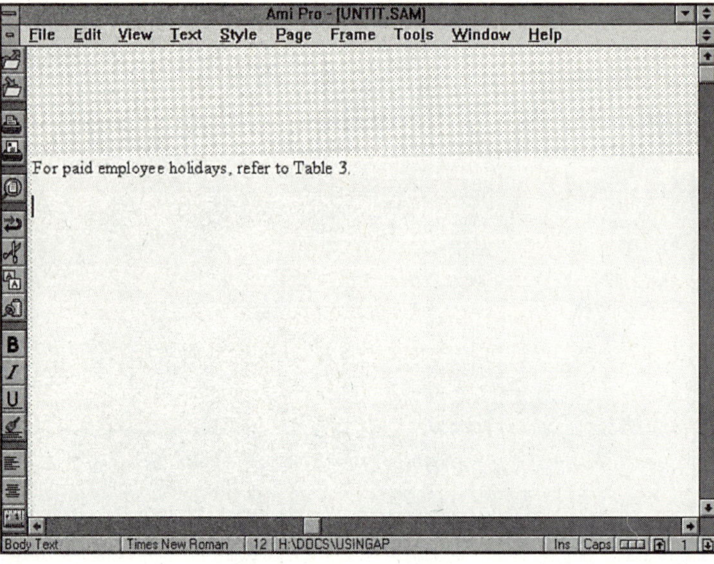

Fig. 24.38 The document with the reference to the table shown in the text.

Adding Page Number References

Tip You can create multiple references to a single source. Follow the procedures in this section and use the same bookmark as the source for each reference.

What you have done so far is very useful. If you insert a new Table 2, for example, when you update power fields all your references to Table 3 automatically change to Table 4. But you can go a step farther and insert an automatic reference to the *page number* where the reader can find your table.

Actually, you have done half the work of adding the page number, because you use the source that you used for the reference in the last section. The procedure for adding a reference to a page number is similar to that for adding the reference.

Note

You can add a page number reference without first creating a reference of the type described in the preceding section. Simply create your source bookmark then create the reference as described in this section.

To add a page number reference, follow these steps:

1. If you have not done so, create a source bookmark on the page you want to reference, following the procedures described earlier in the section, "Inserting the Source."

2. Move the insertion point to the position where you want the reference to the page number to appear. Type the text you want to precede the reference (such as **on page** followed by a space).

3. Choose **E**dit Power **F**ields **I**nsert. The Insert Power Fields Box appears.

4. In the **F**ields list box, select the field type `PageRef`. Ami Pro places the word `PageRef` in the **I**nsert text box.

5. Move the cursor to the **I**nsert text box, type a space after the word `PageRef`, and then type the name of the bookmark you are referencing *with no quotation marks*. If you are using the same example as in the preceding section, type **HolidayTable** (see fig 24.39).

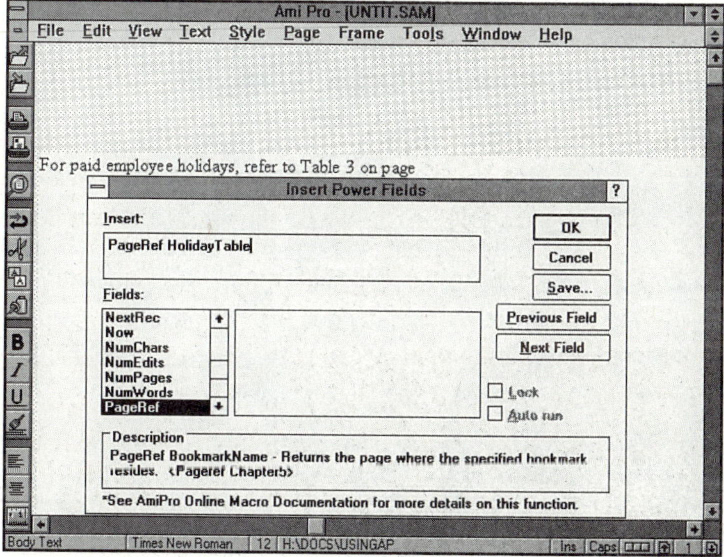

Fig. 24.39
The Insert Power Fields dialog box with the name of the bookmark whose page you want to reference.

6. Choose OK or press Enter to insert the page reference. The document resembles figure 24.40 with power fields hidden.

Caution

If you are working in draft mode or outline mode, the `PageRef` field always evaluates to page 1. To correct the page number references, switch to layout mode. Then either update the specific `PageRef` power field or update all power fields. Refer to the procedures earlier in this chapter for details on how to update power fields.

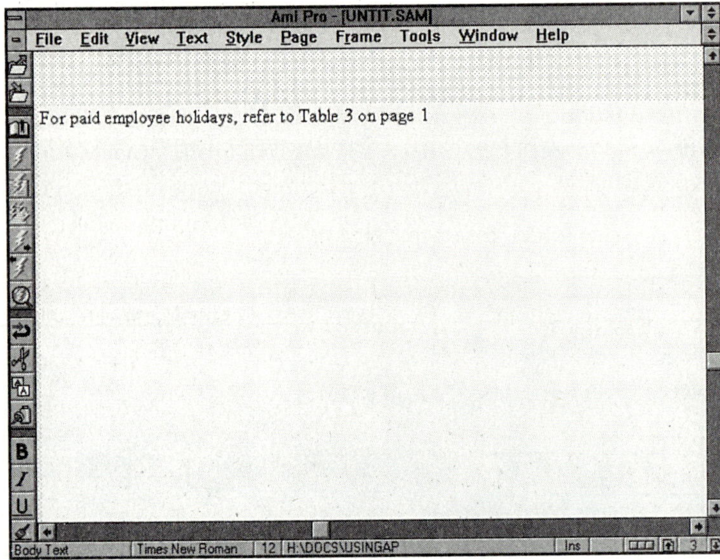

Fig. 24.40
The page reference inserted into the document.

Creating a Smart Boilerplate

If you have text that you often include in your documents—perhaps standard contract payment terms, biographies of your staff, or descriptions of product options—you can collect these pieces of boilerplate information into one or more source documents and then reference those source documents from any document that needs to include the boilerplate text.

To accomplish this feat, you use `Include` power fields. You use the first form to insert a complete document:

```
Include "docname"
```

Use the second form to insert the contents of a bookmark from another document:

```
Include "docname!bookmark"
```

Inserting a Complete Document

To use the first form, replace `docname` with the name of your document (including the path name if it isn't your default document directory). Suppose that you have standard payment terms in a document named TERMS.SAM, which you keep in the directory C:\AMIPRO\DOCS\CONTRACT. Nothing else is in the document—just the paragraph or two of standard terms. To insert the standard terms into any other document, follow these procedures:

1. Open the document where you want the terms to appear—in this example, the contract document. (Note that the source document—the document where you store the boilerplate—doesn't need to be open.)

2. In the contract document you are creating, place the insertion point where you want the standard terms to appear.

3. Choose **E**dit Power **F**ields **I**nsert. The Insert Power Fields dialog box appears.

4. From the **F**ields list box, select `Include`. Ami Pro inserts the word `Include` into the **I**nsert text box.

5. Move the cursor into the **I**nsert text box, type a space following `Include`, and then type the name (and path, if necessary) of the source document. Enclose the name in quotation marks. For this example, type the following (see fig. 24.41):

   "C:\AMIPRO\DOCS\CONTRACT\TERMS.SAM"

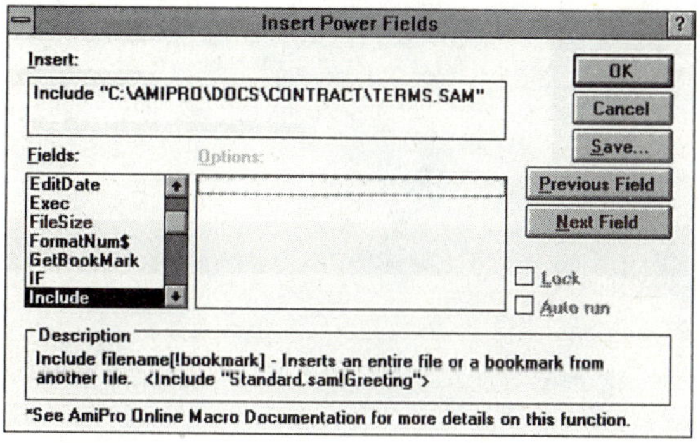

Fig. 24.41
The Insert Power Fields dialog box, ready to insert boilerplate text from the named document.

6. Choose OK or press Enter to insert the boilerplate text into the contract document (see fig. 24.42). If you choose **V**iew Show Po**w**er Fields, Ami Pro displays the instructions, as shown in figure 24.43.

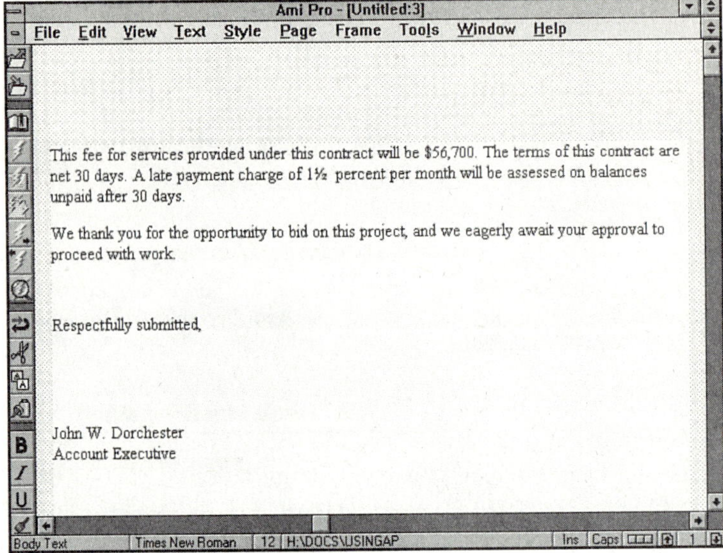

Fig. 24.42
The boilerplate contract terms in the contract.

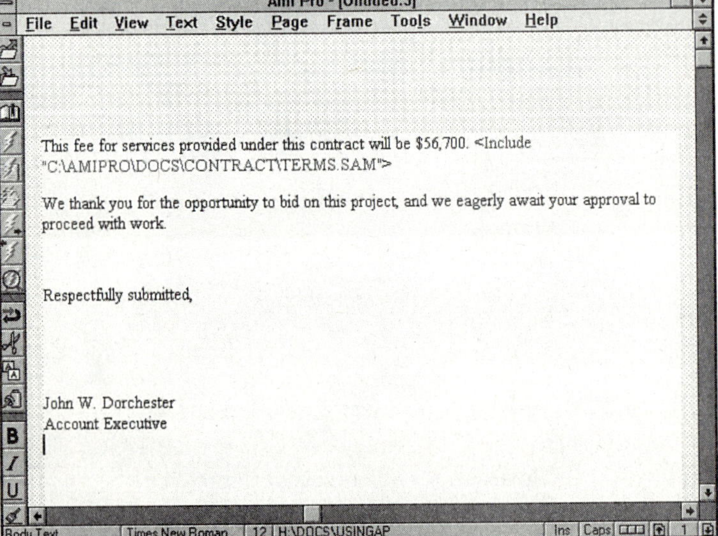

Fig. 24.43
The instruction that produces figure 24.42.

Caution

Be careful with `Include`. Suppose that you want to change your standard terms and incorporate the changes into TERMS.SAM. At some later time, you reopen a contract document that referenced the old terms (perhaps the client has requested changes

> that don't affect the terms). If you update power fields in the contract document, the new terms from TERMS.SAM replace the existing terms from the original version of TERMS.SAM.
>
> To prevent this error, *lock* the `Include` power field in each contract you create, following the procedures described earlier in this chapter in the section, "Locking Power Fields to Prevent Updating."

Inserting a Selection from a Document

Suppose that you have several dozen people in your company. You often include in your proposals the names of the people who will work on the proposed project, along with a brief biography of each person.

You could put everyone's biography in a separate file and then use the `Include` statement as described in the preceding section to insert the contents of the appropriate files into each proposal. This strategy may be cumbersome to maintain. Another option is to put the biographies into the same file and use the second form of `Include`.

If you choose to keep multiple entries in a single file, the first step is to create the source file. (In this example, assume that you name the source file BIOS.SAM, and keep it in the directory C:\AMIPRO\DOCS\PROPOSAL.) Create the source file as an ordinary Ami Pro file. Type a paragraph or two (or as much text as you want) about each individual. Then enclose each person's biography in a bookmark, following this procedure:

1. Select all the text you want to include in the first person's biography.
2. Choose **E**dit **B**ookmarks. The Bookmarks dialog box appears (see fig. 24.44).
3. In the Bookmark text box, type the person's name. (If you type a first name and a last name, don't put a space between them.) Assume that the person's name is Warren Nixon; in this case, type **WarrenNixon**.
4. Choose OK or press Enter. When you display power field instructions (choose **V**iew Show Po**w**er Fields), Ami Pro displays the selected text, enclosed in angle brackets (see fig. 24.45). The angle brackets show the boundaries of the bookmark.
5. Repeat steps 1 through 4 for each person whose biography you want to include.

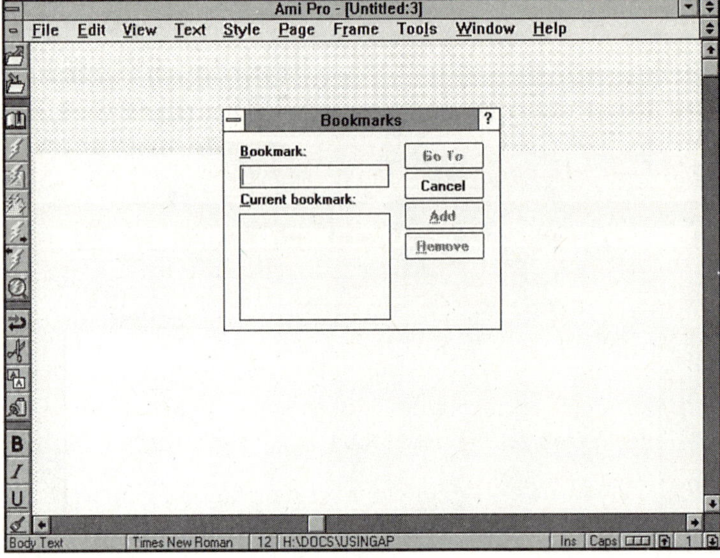

Fig. 24.44
The Bookmarks dialog box.

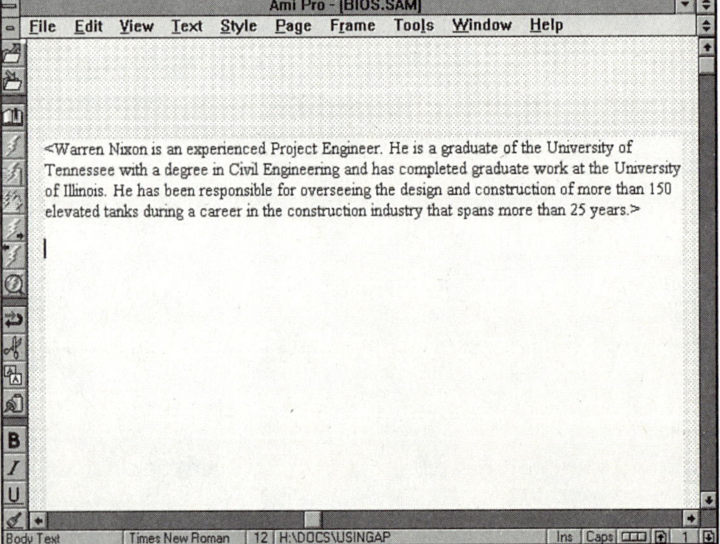

Fig. 24.45
A biography enclosed in a bookmark in the source document.

You now can insert any biography into any proposal by using an `Include` power field. Follow these steps:

1. Open the document where you want the biography to appear and position the insertion point where you want it.

2. Choose **E**dit Power **F**ields **I**nsert. In the Insert Power Fields dialog box, select `Include` in the **F**ields list box. Ami Pro inserts the word `Include` into the **I**nsert text box.

3. Move the cursor into the **I**nsert text box, type a space following `Include`, and then type the name of the reference as follows:

   C:\AMIPRO\DOCS\PROPOSAL\BIOS.SAM!WarrenNixon

   Be sure to type the bookmark name exactly as it appears in the source document, including capitalization. If the bookmark name in BIOS.SAM is *WarrenNixon*, the `Include` statement must specify *WarrenNixon*, not *warrennixon*.

4. Choose OK or press Enter to insert the biography into the contract document.

Note that you type the name of the source document and append the name of the bookmark that designates the specific text you want to insert from the source. To tell Ami Pro where the file name ends and the bookmark name begins, you use an exclamation point (!).

Understanding the Limitations of Include

You cannot use `Include` to include text from a table or a frame in another document. `Include` only brings in straight text, with formatting such as paragraph breaks and tabs, and text enhancements like boldface or italics. If you have standard documents that include tables and frames, consider incorporating them into other documents by using the Master Document feature of Ami Pro.

◄ See "Using Master Documents," p. 744

Creating Smart Forms

In the application in this section, you set up a smart document to guide a user through the process of completing the document.

Suppose that each salesperson in your office must create weekly expense reports, using an electronic form. You can use power fields to solicit the salesperson's name when he or she opens the electronic expense report form. The power fields also can supply the date on which the expense report is updated, query whether the user wants to fill in the standard format, and provide the format if she or he responds affirmatively. If you display the power field instructions, your document may resemble figure 24.46. The completed document, with the salesperson's name, the date, and the standard report format may resemble the document shown in figure 24.47.

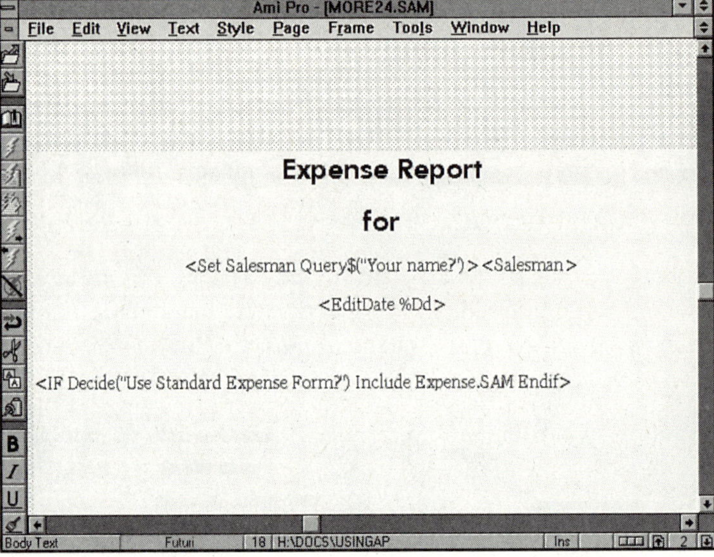

Fig. 24.46
A sample expense report with power fields displayed.

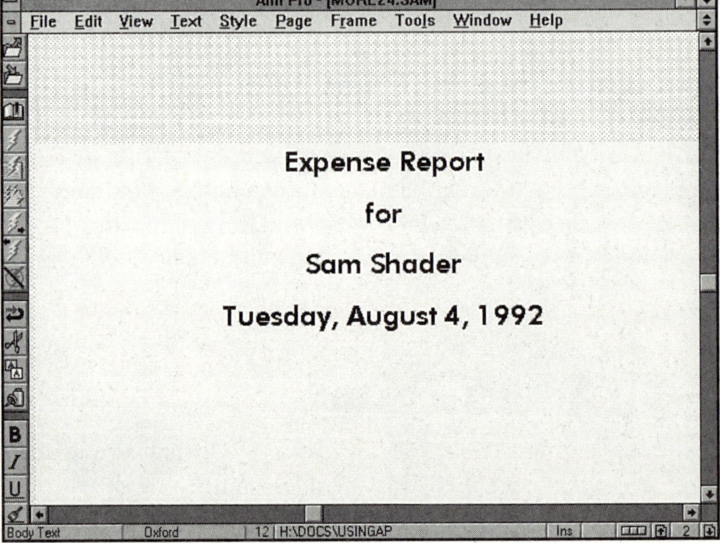

Fig. 24.47
The sample document from figure 24.46 with the data in the power fields.

The sample document uses a combination power field that combines a `Set` field and a `Query` field. This field displays a message on-screen to ask the salesperson's name, and then assigns that name to the global variable `salesman`. Another power field—the name of the variable—displays the name of the salesperson making the report with the document.

Directly below the name on the expense report, you can use the `EditDate` power field to display the date on which the report is updated.

The last power field is a combination of three power field expressions. This custom power field gives the person who completes the expense report the option to use the standard form. The syntax of the power field is as follows:

```
<IF Decide("Use Standard Expense form?") Include
    "C:\AMIPRO\EXPENSES.SAM" EndIF>
```

This example uses the `IF` power field, the `Decide` power field, and the `Include` power field. The `IF` power field tests a condition, decides what is required, and performs the action. The `Decide` power field presents a question and Yes/No buttons in a dialog box. If the user answers Yes, `Decide` evaluates to `TRUE`. In the power field expression, a Yes answer makes the `IF` condition true, so the `Include` power field is evaluated. The `Include` field specifies which file to insert into the document at the position of the power field.

Playing Macros from Power Fields

You can *play back* (execute) any macro—one you have written or one of the many macros supplied with Ami Pro—by creating a `Call` power field. Whenever you update the power field, the macro runs. To launch a macro from a power field, follow this procedure:

1. Choose **E**dit Power **F**ields **I**nsert. Ami Pro displays the Insert Power Fields dialog box.

2. From the **F**ields list box, select `Call`. Ami Pro inserts the word `Call` in the **I**nsert text box.

3. Move the cursor into the **I**nsert text box, type a space after the word `Call`, and then type the name of the macro you want to launch. Enclose the name in quotation marks. To play back the macro that launches the Lotus CC:Mail application, for example, type **CCMAIL.SMM( )** as shown in figure 24.48. If the macro is anywhere other than in the default macro directory, you must precede the macro name with the path name of the macro file. If the macro requires arguments, put them inside the paired parentheses.

4. Choose OK or press Enter. Ami Pro inserts the power field into the document. The macro executes immediately and executes again each time you update the power field.

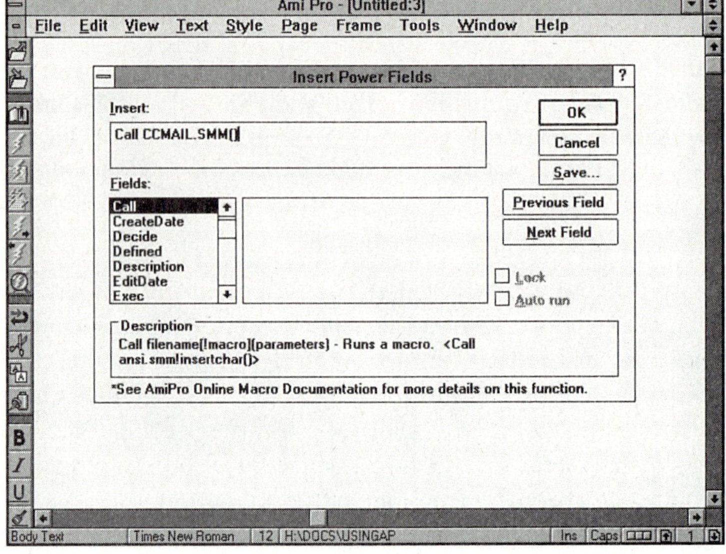

Fig. 24.48
The Insert Power Field dialog box, ready to insert a field that runs the CCMAIL macro.

Note

If you want to run a specific function within a macro file, add the name of the function after the macro file name in the **I**nsert text box of the Insert Power Fields dialog box. Separate the file name and the function name with an exclamation mark, and put the paired parentheses (with any arguments) after the function name. To execute the function `Function1()` in the file MYMACRO.SMM, for example, type **MYMACRO.SMM!Function1( )**.

Tip
To pass a value from your document to a macro, put the value into a global variable; then reference that global value in the macro. Any changes the macro makes to the value of the global value will be reflected in your document.

Creating Your Own Power Fields

Earlier in this chapter, you learned how to use a predefined power field to perform multiple actions in an expense report. If you want to use the same `IF`, `Decide`, and `Include` power fields again, you can simplify the process by creating a custom power field.

Custom power fields are useful when you plan to reuse a complex field. When you create a custom power field, Ami Pro adds the field name to the **F**ields list box in the Insert Power Fields dialog box. This action enables you to select and use the power field in the same way that you select and use Ami Pro's predefined power fields.

Creating a Custom Power Field

To create and save a custom power field, follow these steps:

1. Move the insertion point to the position where you want to insert the power field.

2. Choose **E**dit Power **F**ields **I**nsert. The Insert Power Fields dialog box appears.

3. In the **I**nsert text box, type the custom power field. If you want to create the custom power field used earlier for the `IF`, `Decide`, and `Include` functions, type the following text:

```
IF Decide("Use Standard Expense form?") Include
    "c:\amipro\expense.SAM" EndIF
```

   Figure 24.49 shows the sample power field text in the Insert Power Fields dialog box. For the example to work, you must have a file called EXPENSE.SAM in the C:\AMIPRO subdirectory. The file must contain the expense report you intend to include.

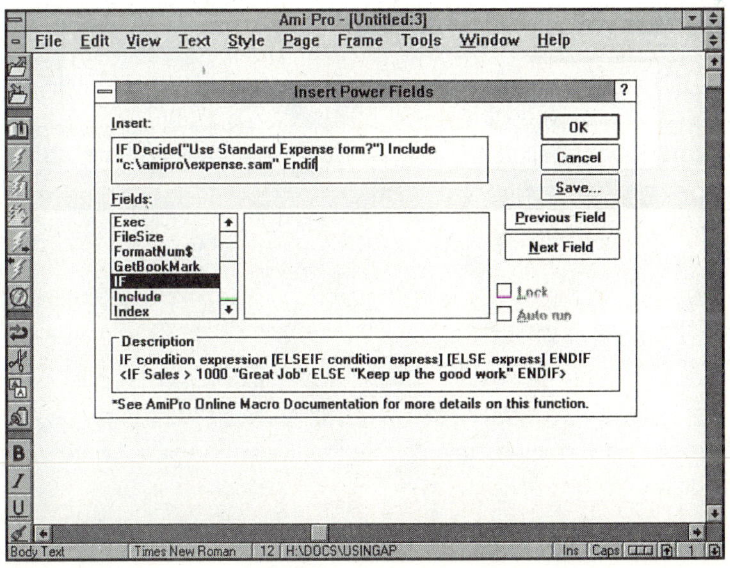

Fig. 24.49
The sample text in the Insert Power Field dialog box.

4. Choose **S**ave. Ami Pro displays the Save Power Field dialog box, as shown in figure 24.50.

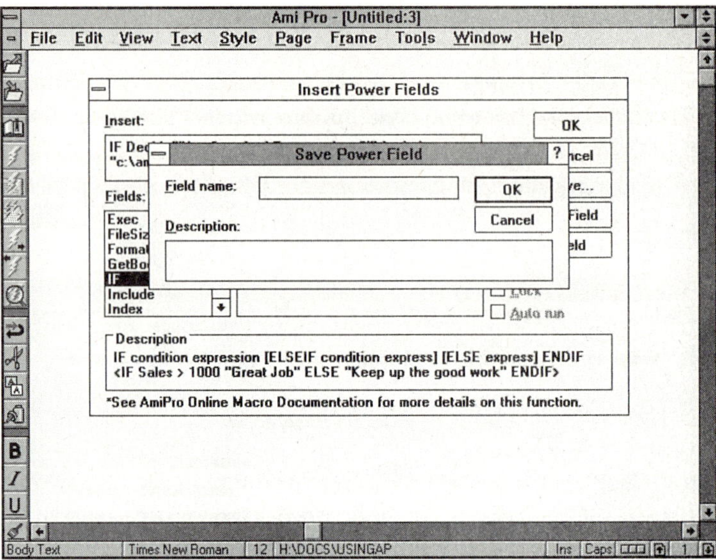

Fig. 24.50
The Save Power Field dialog box.

5. In the **F**ield Name text box, type a name for the custom power field. For this example, type **ExpenseForm**.

6. If desired, enter a description of the custom power field in the **D**escription text box. The **D**escription text box is a useful place to describe syntax or any peculiar feature of the custom power field. For this example, type the following text in the **D**escription text box:

    This power field includes a standard expense report after displaying a decision box.

7. Choose OK or press Enter to close the Save Power Field dialog box and return to the Insert Power Fields dialog box.

8. Choose OK or press Enter to close the Insert Power Fields dialog box and return to the document. Ami Pro inserts the power field into the document.

The next time you open the Insert Power Field dialog box, the custom power field you created is listed as a choice in the dialog box.

Deleting a Power Field from the List of Power Fields

The preceding section explained how to save a power field so that it appears on the power field list in the Insert Power Fields dialog box. You may decide that you don't need a field you saved. Unfortunately, no "Remove" button is provided in the Insert Power Fields dialog box, and the field appears every time Ami Pro displays the dialog box, because the fields are global—that is, not stored with individual documents, but available in any document.

You can remove fields you have created (but not *predefined* power fields) by using a text editor like Windows Notepad. Use the editor to open the file AMIPRO.INI, which is in the Windows directory. Then locate a line that says `[Fields]`. Under that line are the names and definitions of all the fields you have saved. If you have saved one field named *Captions*, for example, your file may look like this:

```
[Fields]
Captions=Seq Table %N1~
```

To eliminate the `Captions` field from the list of fields, use the text editor to delete the line describing `Captions`. The next time you display the Insert Power Fields dialog box, `Captions` is gone.

> **Caution**
>
> Don't make any other changes to AMIPRO.INI unless you know what you are doing!

Summary

In this chapter, you learned the value of Ami Pro's unique power fields feature. Power fields enable you to automate many cumbersome tasks and save time and effort when you work with Ami Pro documents. You learned how to insert a predefined power field, how to create a custom power field, and how to display, edit, and update power fields.

The next section of this book describes how to install Ami Pro on your computer and provides a complete guide to the Ami Pro style sheets.

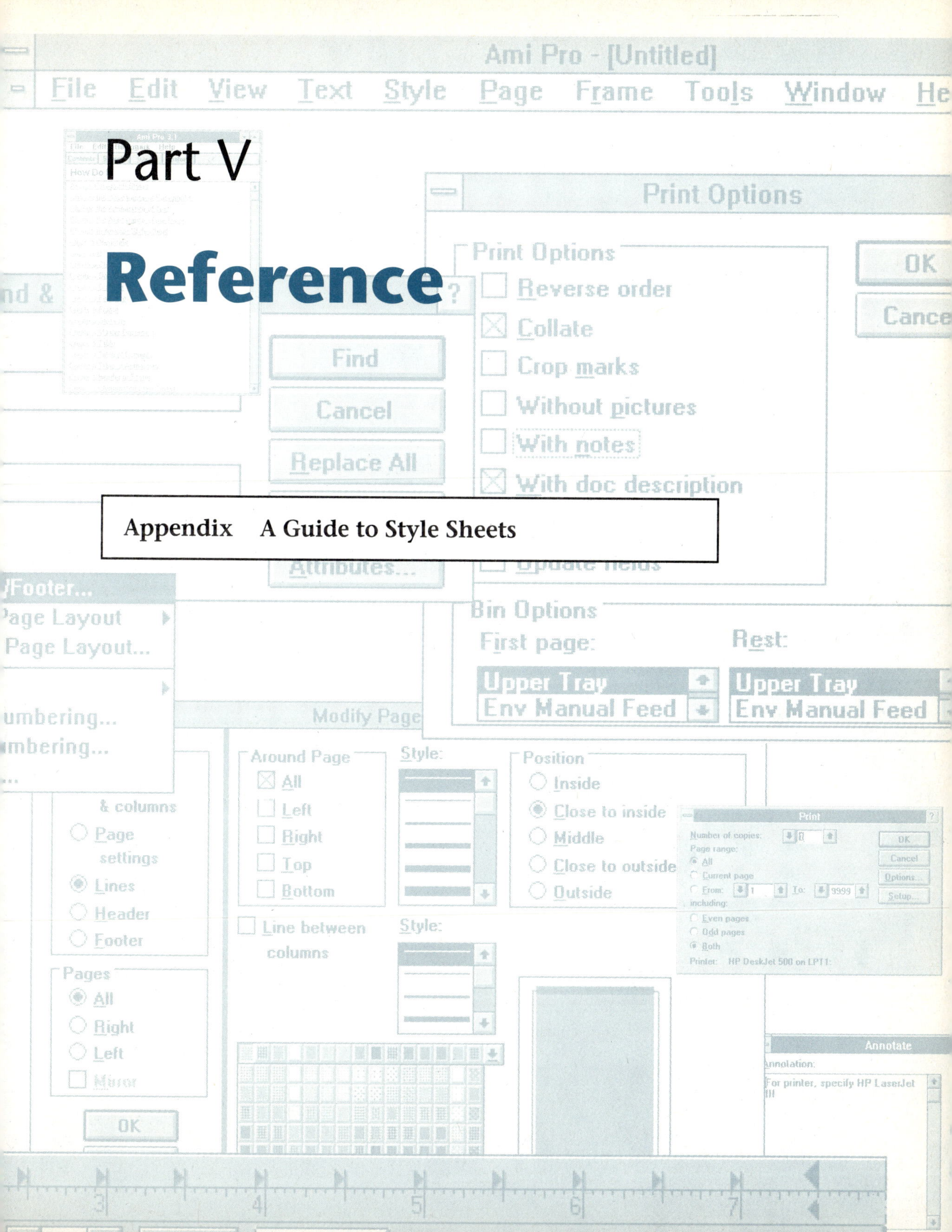

Part V
Reference

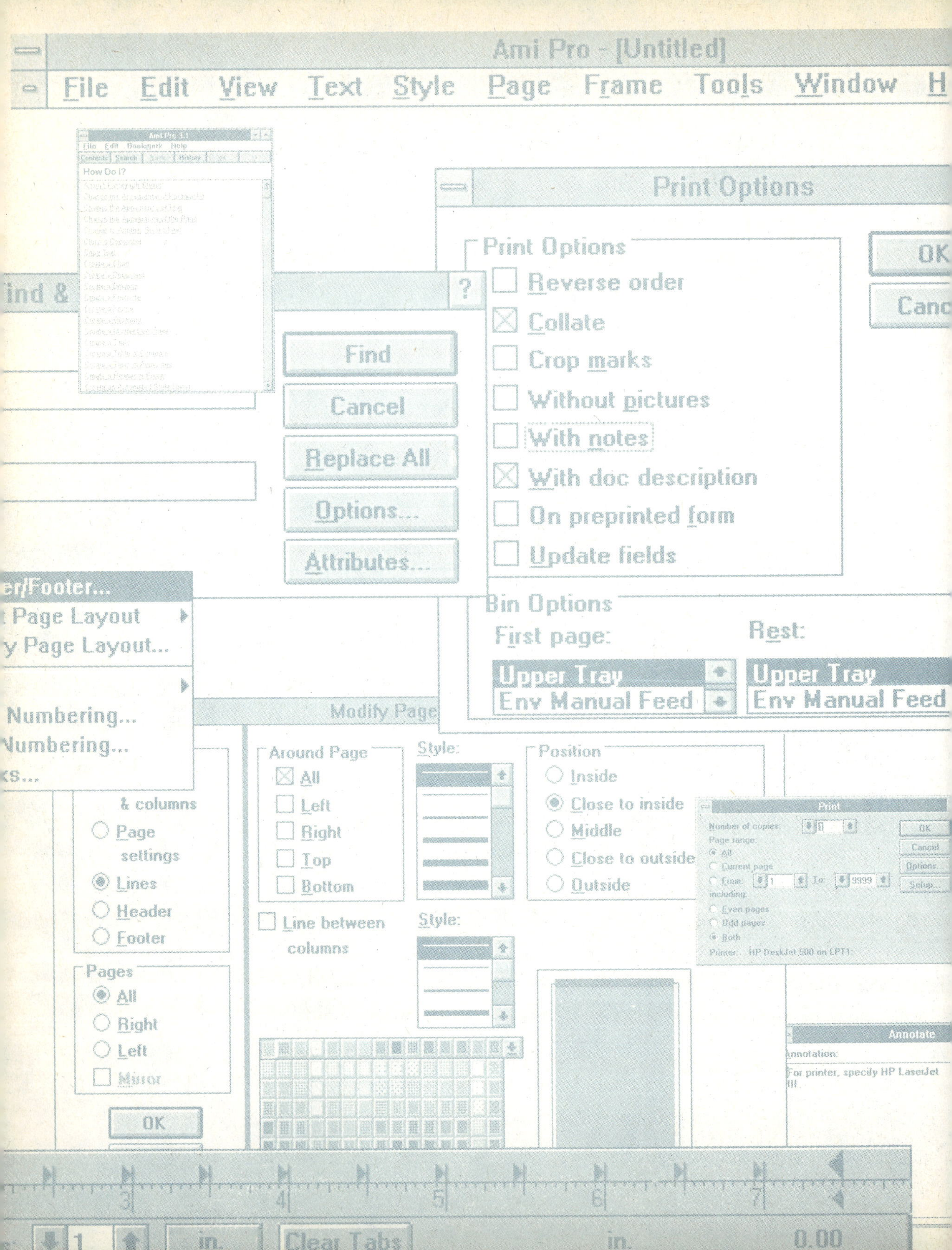

Ami Pro - [Untitled]
File
Edit
View
Text
Style
Page
Frame
Tools
Window
Ami Pro 3.1
How Do I?
Print Options
Print Options
Reverse order
Collate
Crop marks
Without pictures
With notes
With doc description
On preprinted form
Update fields
OK
Bin Options
First page:
Rest:
Upper Tray
Env Manual Feed
Upper Tray
Env Manual Feed
Find
Cancel
Replace All
Options...
Attributes...
Page Layout
Numbering...
Numbering...
Modify Page
& columns
Page
settings
Lines
Header
Footer
Pages
All
Right
Left
Mirror
OK
Around Page
All
Left
Right
Top
Bottom
Style:
Line between
columns
Style:
Position
Inside
Close to inside
Middle
Close to outside
Outside
Print
Number of copies:
Page range:
All
Current page
From:
To:
including:
Even pages
Odd pages
Both
Printer: HP DeskJet 500 on LPT1:
OK
Cancel
Options...
Setup...
Annotate
Annotation:
For printer, specify HP LaserJet III.
Clear Tabs
in.
in.
0.00

Appendix

A Guide to Style Sheets

As you have learned throughout this book, Ami Pro is rich in capabilities. When you work with paragraph styles, for example (as explained in Chapter 4, "Formatting a Document"), you can use lines above or below the paragraph and decide how you want those lines to look. You can choose typefaces from Arial to Wingdings, and set attributes for the typefaces. You can set up the spacing between paragraphs and the spacing between the appearance of bullets in bulleted lists.

When you work with page layout, you can specify the setup of margins, columns, and tabs. You decide whether to have lines around the page, how thick the lines are, how close they are to the text, and what color they are. You also can set up the page size and the orientation.

You also can create frames, add pictures, use notes, insert the system date and time, and much, much more.

You may not be able to learn all these capabilities in time to use them for a given project. You may never have the time to learn how to use all these features, yet you may need the benefits of the features.

Style sheets place Ami Pro's advanced capabilities at your disposal from the time you first use the program. You don't even need to know how to use those advanced capabilities. You only need to know how to choose a style sheet to obtain the desired results.

A *style sheet* is a file that contains paragraph and page formatting instructions for a document. Each style sheet has multiple paragraph styles (at least two) and one page layout.

If you choose the **W**ith Contents option in the New dialog box when you create a new document and choose a style sheet, you may see in your style sheet additional text, frames, tables, pictures, notes, and inserted fields.

Ami Pro includes, with many of the style sheets that follow, some fields and automatic macros. These automatic macros help you fill in information that remains in the style sheet. This capability customizes the style sheet for your use. Using macros enables you to apply the completed information to only one document.

Trained graphic artists designed these style sheets for you to use in your documents. Use these style sheets to produce professional-looking documents, and you may discover ideas to apply to your own style sheets.

Note

Feel free to revise Ami Pro's style sheets to suit your purpose. You can change the typeface or type size, rework the page layout, add gutter space between columns, or add frames, drawings, and charts. Experiment with the style sheets and save the ones that work for you.

If you open a new document with Ami Pro style sheets and choose Run **M**acro and **W**ith Contents, a dialog box appears on-screen. The automatic macro runs the dialog box. When you open the new style, the automatic macros included with many of the style sheets create one or two dialog boxes. The first dialog box is Default Information. This dialog box asks for your name, sometimes the company name, address, phone number, and so on. Depending on the style sheet, this dialog box asks for other information. The second dialog box may ask you to list tasks, fill in a customer's name and address, or enter headings in a form. You can save this information to the style sheet so it opens with the new style sheet, or you can use the entered information with the current document only. You also can cancel the dialog box if you plan to customize the style sheet. If you fill in the requested information in the first dialog box, a second dialog box appears.

The second dialog box is Optional Information. This dialog box asks for information specific to the document, such as customer's name and address, the week, day, year, and so on. This information applies only to the current document. You also can cancel this dialog box if you plan to customize the style sheet.

The following style sheet descriptions include the types of dialog boxes that the style sheet uses.

_ARTICLE.STY

This style sheet is for legal articles and contains a table for your personal information. Five paragraph styles are included for your use. Courier is the body text style. The _ARTICLE.STY style sheet has automated macros. This style sheet uses both the Default Information and Optional Information dialog boxes if you choose **W**ith Contents and Run **M**acro when beginning a new document.

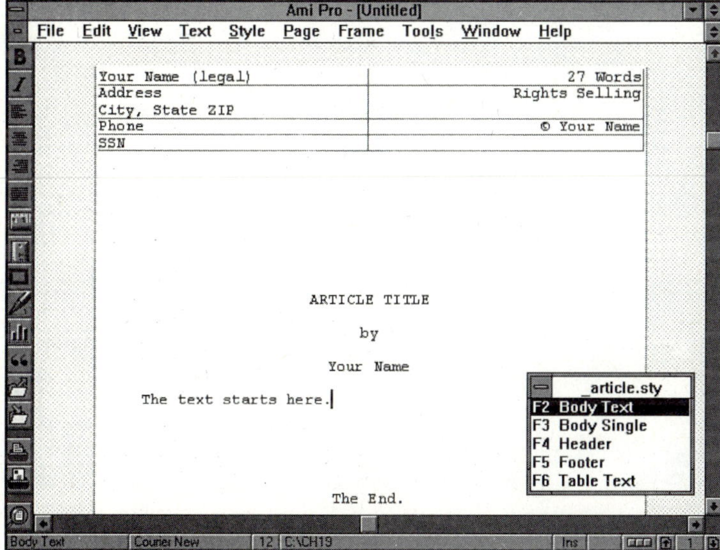

Fig. A.1
_ARTICLE.STY

_BASIC.STY

The _BASIC.STY style sheet is appropriate for building your own style sheets. Four paragraph styles in Times Roman are included (Times New Roman PS if you install ATM, or Times New Roman—a TrueType font—if you use Windows 3.1). You also can use this style if you need a very basic document.

Fig. A.2
_BASIC.STY

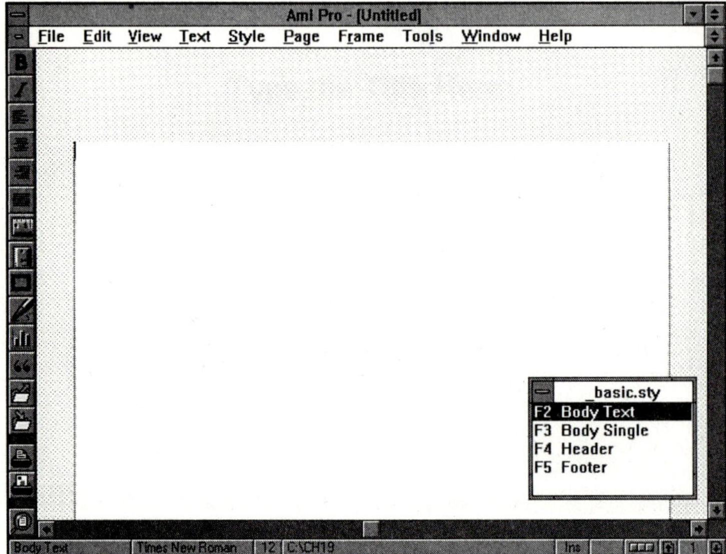

_CALDAY.STY

Ami Pro's convenient daily calendar includes half-hour time slots, a to-do list, and room for notes (if you choose **W**ith Contents). The Default Information dialog box asks your name, address, and telephone number (if you choose Run **M**acro). Today's date automatically appears, although you can change it easily. Several paragraph styles are included; you can reformat the styles if you like. Also included are sections with the headings Appointments, Notes, Contacts, and Expenses.

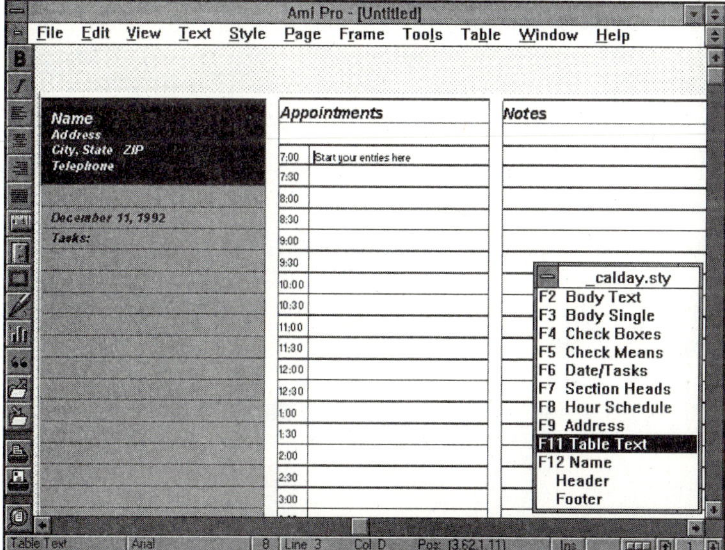

Fig. A.3
_CALDAY.STY

_CALMON.STY

Ami Pro also furnishes you with a monthly calendar. The automatic macro asks you the year and month, and Ami Pro automatically fills in the applicable current dates. Use **W**ith Contents and Run **M**acro to get the most from this style sheet.

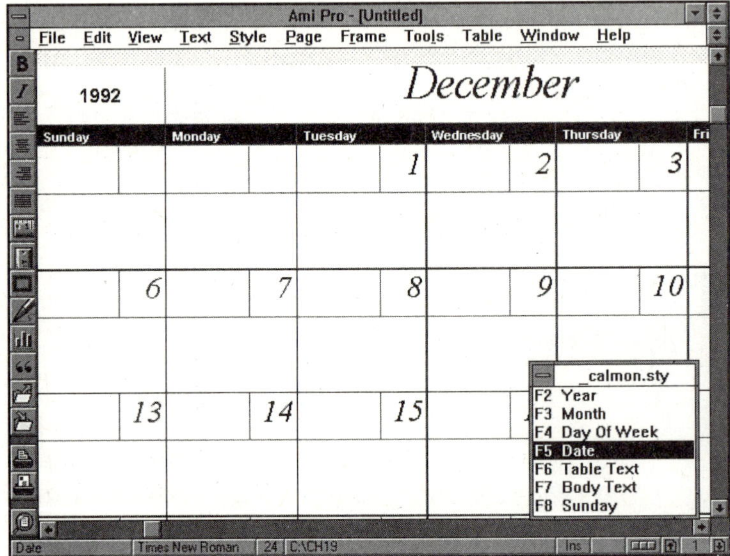

Fig. A.4
_CALMON.STY

_CALWK.STY

The last Ami Pro calendar style is _CALWK.STY. Your hourly work week and a task list are included with several paragraph styles. The automatic macro used with this style sheet is the Default Information dialog box.

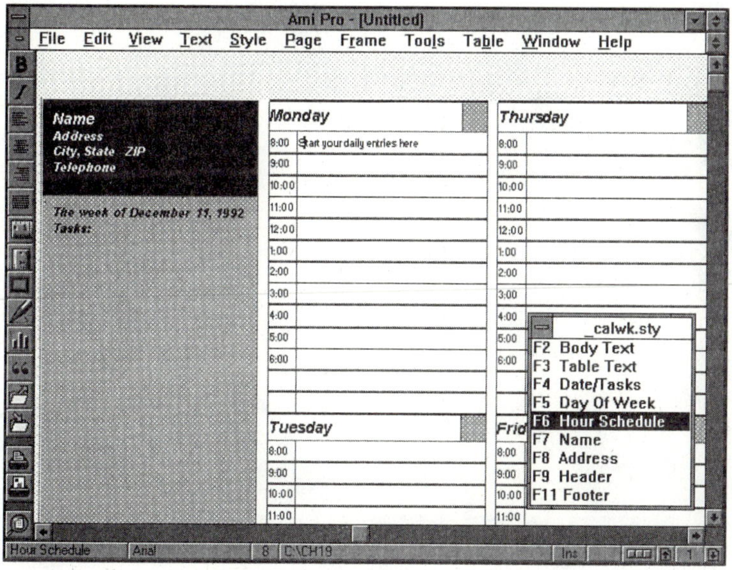

Fig. A.5
_CALWK.STY

_DEFAULT.STY

The most frequently used style sheet is _DEFAULT.STY. This style sheet has more paragraph styles than the _BASIC.STY style sheet. This style sheet is excellent to use to build your own style sheets.

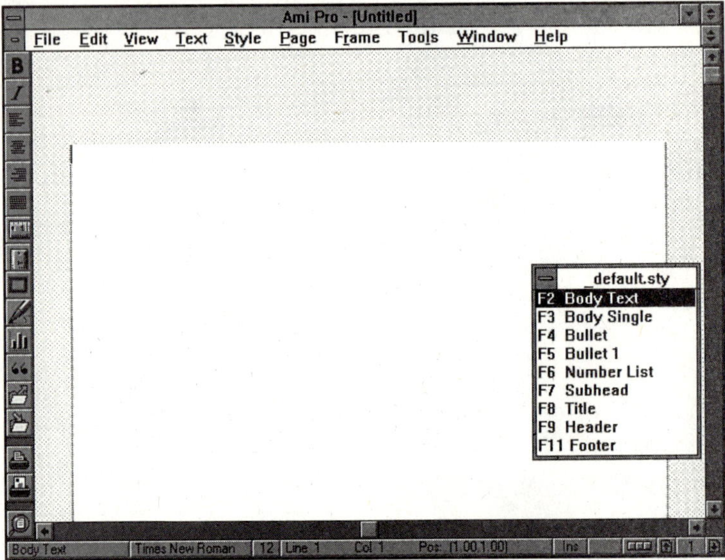

Fig. A.6
_DEFAULT.STY

_DISSERT.STY

Perfect for theses and dissertations, the _DISSERT.STY style sheet includes several paragraph styles, such as Prose and Poetry Quotes, Footnotes, and Footer styles.

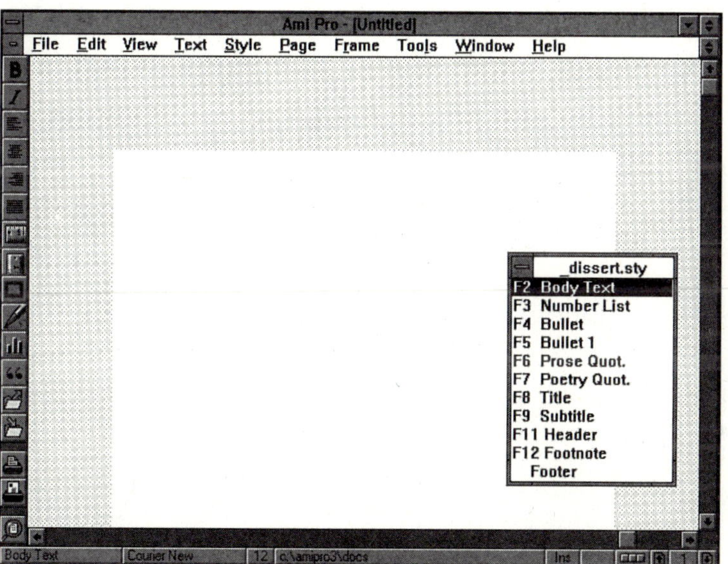

Fig. A.7
_DISSERT.STY

_ENVELOP.STY

If you choose **W**ith Contents, this envelope style sheet sets the margins for easy entry of the recipient's address and indicates the position for your return address. Enter your name and address in the Default Information dialog box (when using Run **M**acro). Then enter Optional Information for the recipient's name and address. Format the text, and then use **S**ave Sa**v**e as a Style Sheet to use ready-made return addresses when you type envelopes.

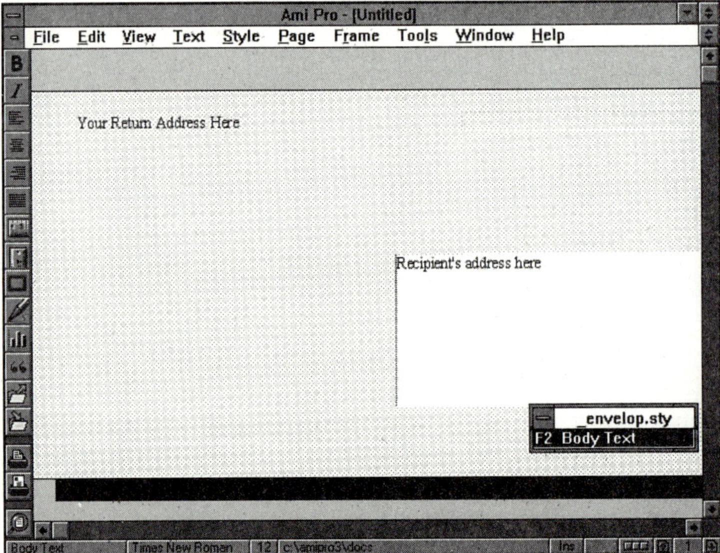

Fig. A.8
_ENVELOP.STY

_EXPENSE.STY

When you choose the **W**ith Contents option, this style sheet provides a format to generate an expense report with self-totaling columns and rows. Also contained within the style sheet are entertainment expenses, daily expenses, and other expenses; totals and adjustments; notes; and signature lines.

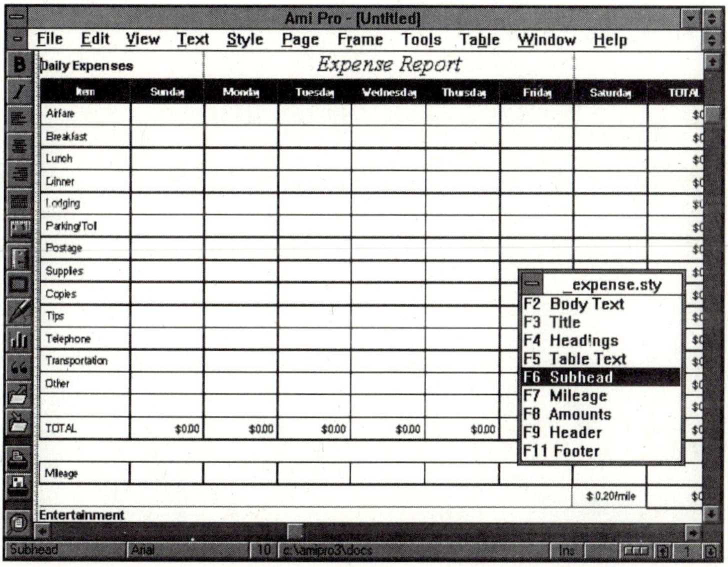

Fig. A.9
_EXPENSE.STY

_FAX1.STY

When you choose the **W**ith Contents option, this style sheet provides a format for fax transmissions, including banner lines such as To, From, Date, and so on. Choose Run **M**acro and complete the Default and Optional Information; Ami Pro places the information you type in the proper areas.

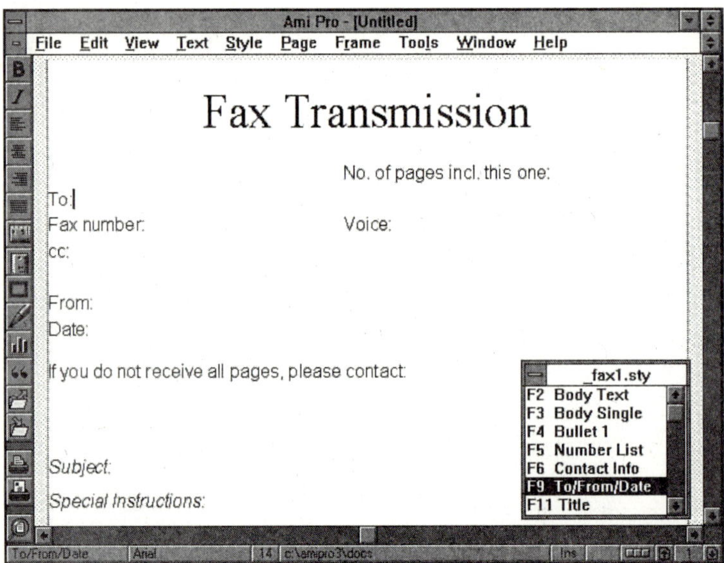

Fig. A.10
_FAX1.STY

_FAX2.STY

For a more professional-looking fax cover sheet, _FAX2.STY style sheet provides a frame containing reversed text for your company's name when you choose **W**ith Contents. A table enables you to easily enter information such as To, From, Company, Date, Time, and so on. If you choose Run **M**acro, both the Default and Optional Information dialog boxes appear. Another place is provided at the bottom of the style sheet for your address, fax, and voice numbers.

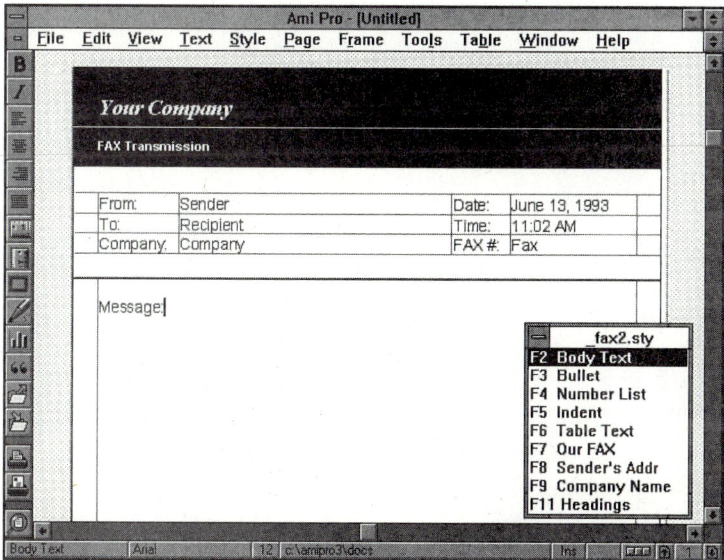

Fig. A.11
_FAX2.STY

_FAX3.STY

When you choose **W**ith Contents, this style sheet provides a table to organize the necessary information for your fax transmission. Choose Run **M**acro, and the Default and Optional Information dialog boxes appear.

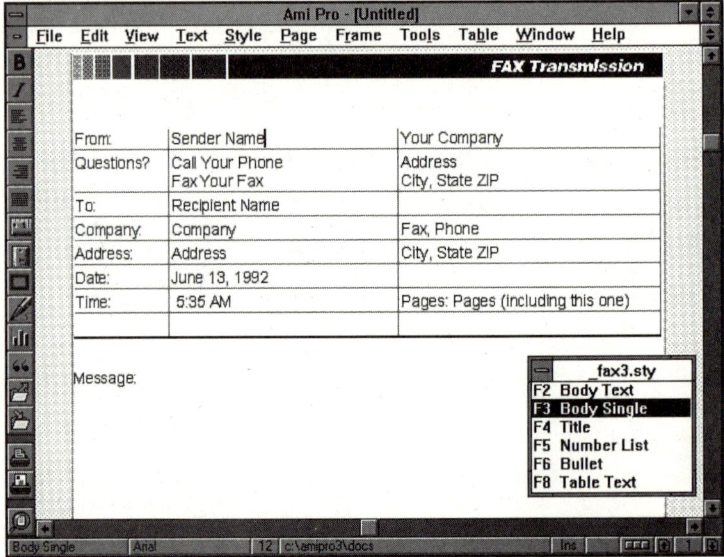

Fig. A.12
_FAX3.STY

_INDEX.STY

When you choose the **W**ith Contents option, this style sheet provides an index with a three-column format that includes the paragraph styles for primary and secondary entries, separator, letter, title, and so on. The Ami Pro master document feature automatically uses this style sheet when creating an index.

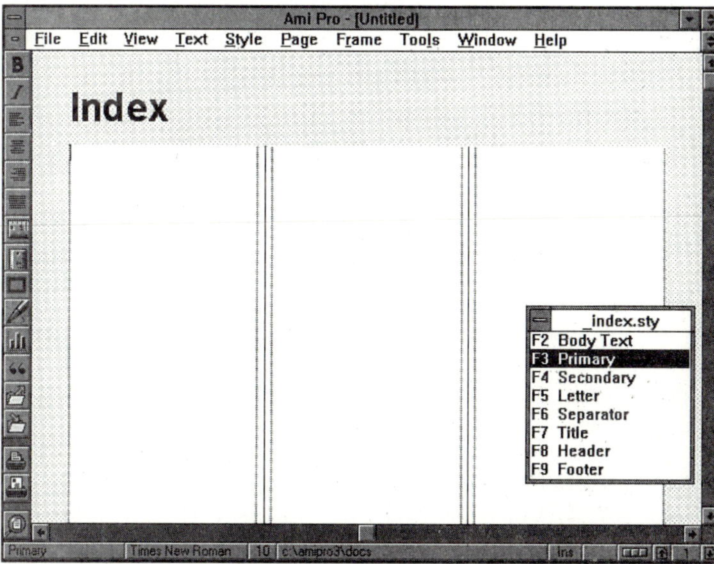

Fig. A.13
_INDEX.STY

_INVOICE.STY

Choose **W**ith Contents to use the invoice style sheet. This style sheet provides places for your information, your customer's information, dates, terms, description of services, rate, totals, and self-totaling columns. Choose Run **M**acro, and the Default and Optional Information dialog boxes appear.

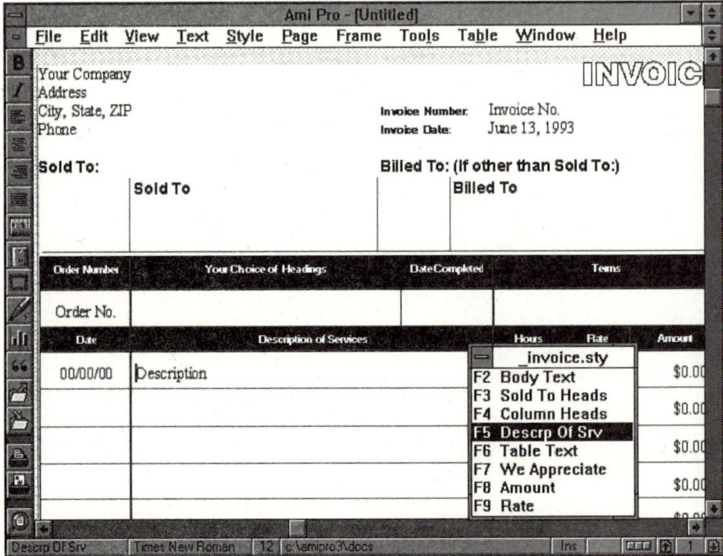

Fig. A.14
_INVOICE.STY

_LABEL.STY

The _LABEL.STY style sheet provides you with three paragraph styles—body text, heading, and small heading. This style sheet also includes a dialog box with over 40 label types and sizes from which to choose (choose Run **M**acro). Included are address, diskette, full sheet, name tags and badges, video cassette, and custom label sizes. This dialog box (as shown in fig. A.15) also enables you to merge text with the style sheet, enter text manually, and create custom labels.

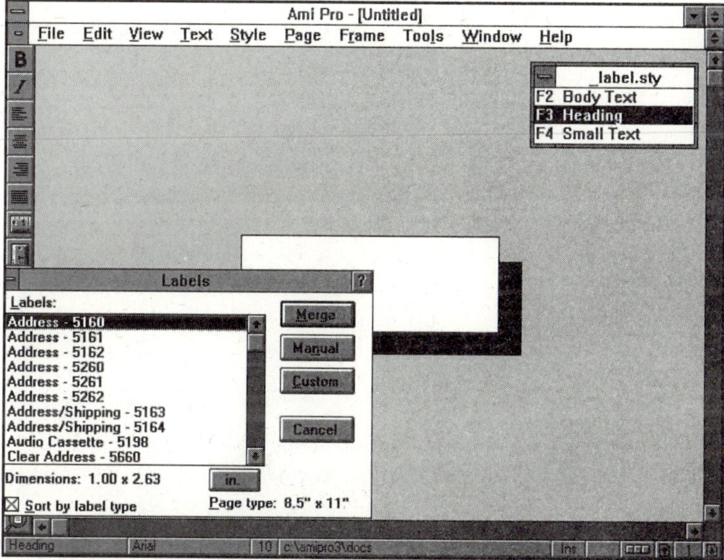

Fig. A.15
_LABEL.STY

_LETTER1.STY

Choosing **W**ith Contents in the business letter style sheet provides you with a logo, the current system date, and Default and Optional Information (choose Run **M**acro). The _LETTER1.STY is a basic style sheet but with several additional paragraph styles to enhance your letter, such as bullet text, numbered list, header, and footer.

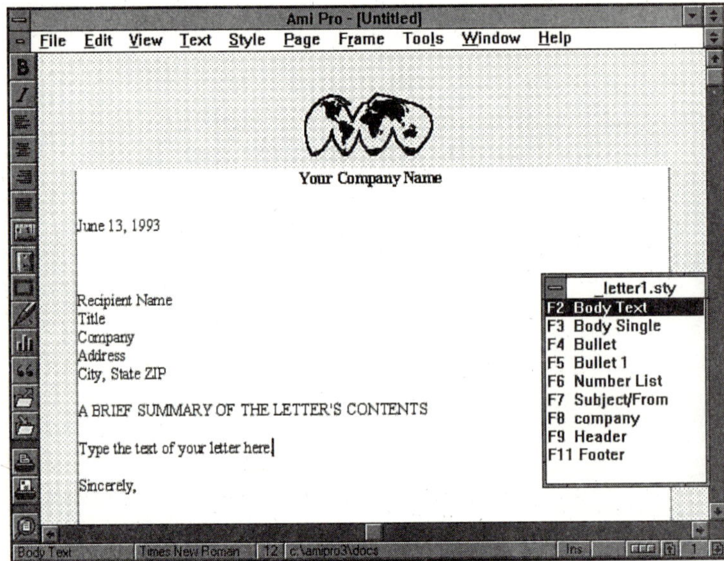

Fig. A.16
_LETTER1.STY

_LETTER2.STY

Choose **W**ith Contents, and the letter style sheet provides you with graphic rules and information, including name, address, notation, subject, and so on. Choose Run **M**acro, and the Default and Optional Information dialog boxes appear. You can choose from several extra paragraph styles, including the bullet and numbered list styles.

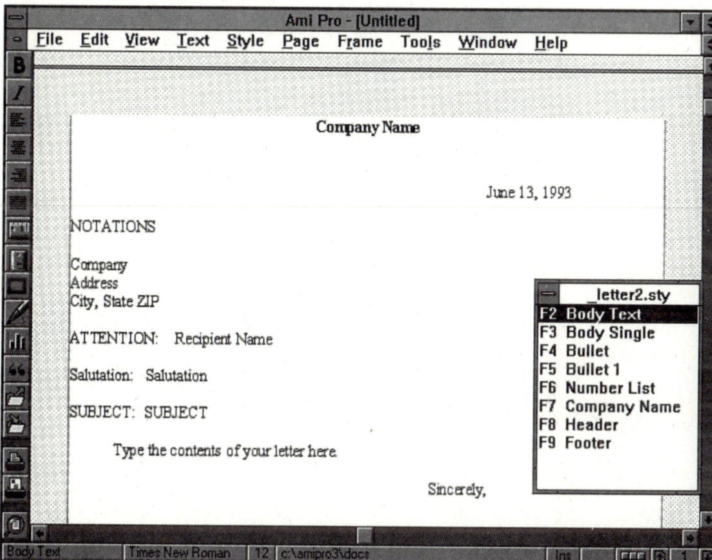

Fig. A.17
_LETTER2.STY

_LETTER3.STY

A somewhat more complicated layout exists in the _LETTER3.STY style sheet than in other letter style sheets. Similar to other letter styles, this style offers the same macros and **W**ith Contents text; however, a few extra paragraph styles are offered in this style sheet. In addition to the bullet and numbered list styles, this style sheet contains two indent styles and a title style that makes the longer business letter easier to format.

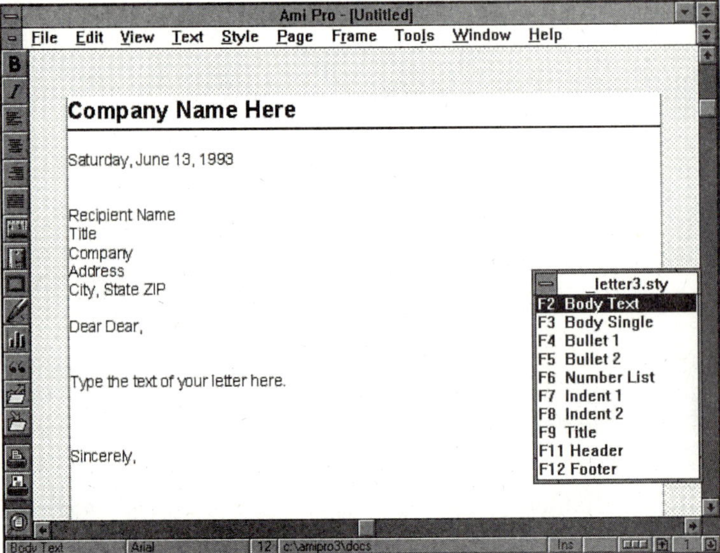

Fig. A.18
_LETTER3.STY

_LETTER4.STY

Almost identical to the _LETTER3.STY, _LETTER4.STY uses Times instead of Helvetica for the body text so you can produce a business letter. This style also contains the text and macros that _LETTER3.STY uses and most of the paragraph styles. _LETTER4.STY excludes header and footer styles from its list.

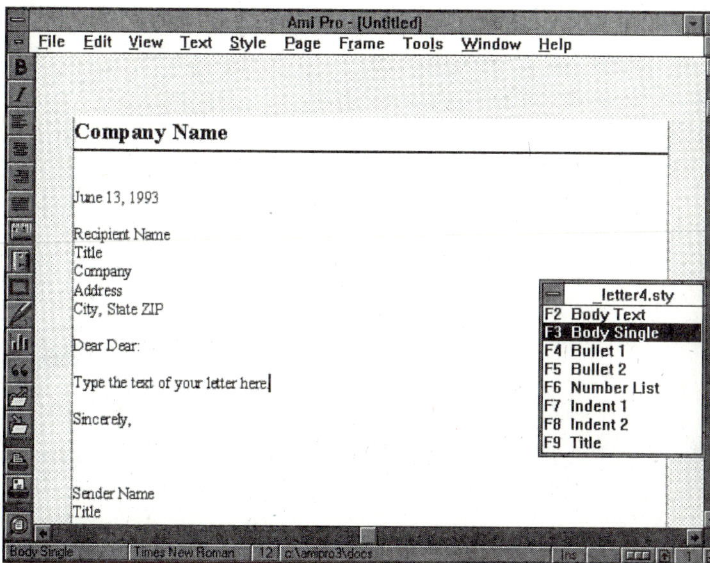

Fig. A.19
_LETTER4.STY

_MACRO.STY

Ami Pro includes a simple style for you to create macros; paragraph styles for Body Text, Body Single, and Function enable you to create, record, and save your macros for future reference.

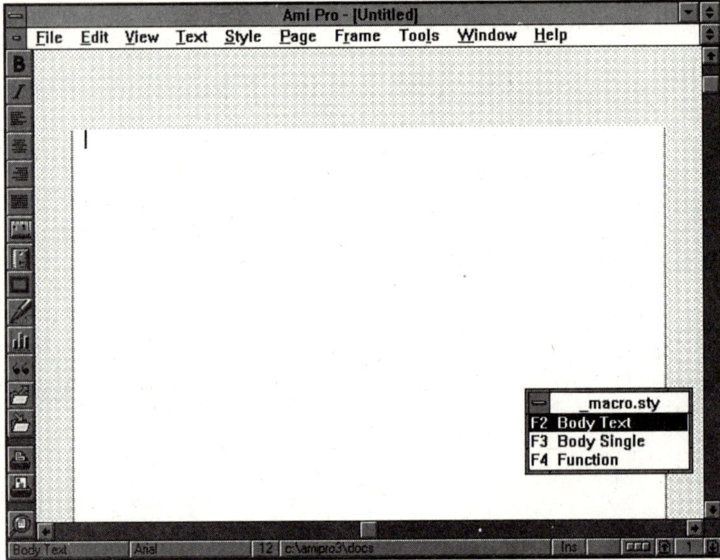

Fig. A.20
_MACRO.STY

_MEMO1.STY

When you choose **W**ith Contents, the memo style sheet supplies you with a double vertical rule and banner lines of text (To, From, Date, and Re). The macros attached to this style sheet are the Default and Optional Information dialog boxes. Many of the paragraph styles are similar to the style in the letter style sheets, including bullets, numbered lists, and indents.

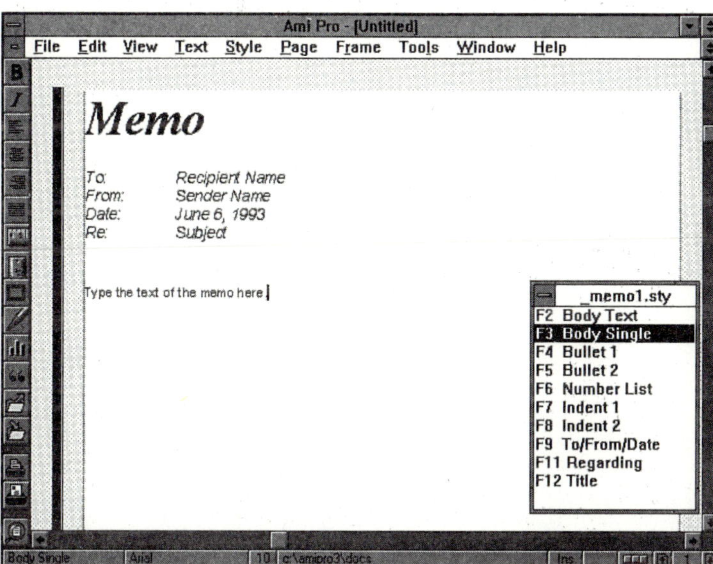

Fig. A.21
_MEMO1.STY

_MEMO2.STY

When you choose the **W**ith Contents option, this memo style sheet provides you with banner lines, a shadow box frame with the title "Memo," and a dividing line after the banner lines (To, From, Date, Subject). If you choose Run **M**acro, both the Default and Optional Information dialog boxes appear.

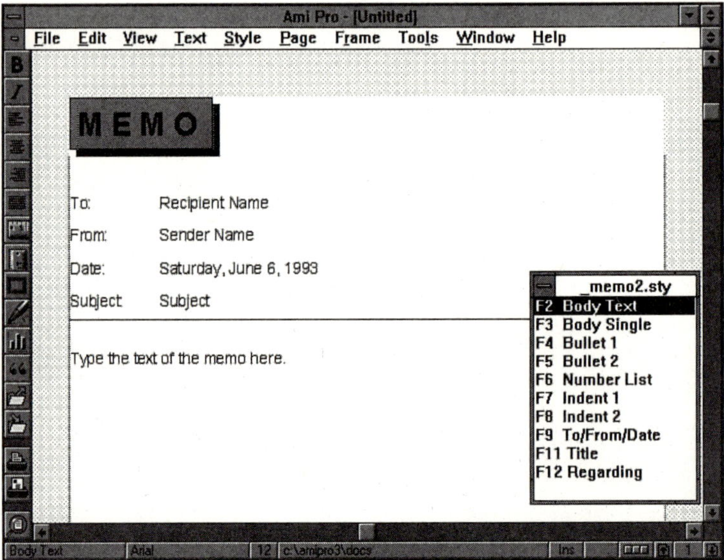

Fig. A.22
_MEMO2.STY

_MEMO3.STY

Using different graphic elements, _MEMO3.STY provides you with two horizontal lines bordering the word "Memorandum" and the normal banner lines of text to create a memo (choose **W**ith Contents). Paragraph styles are similar to the styles in the letter styles; the macros for Default and Optional Information are also included.

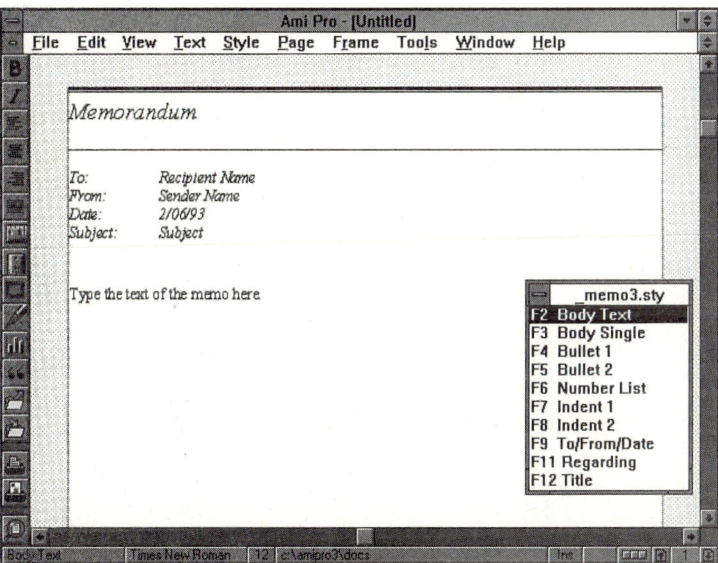

Fig. A.23
_MEMO3.STY

_MEMO4.STY

Another memo style, _MEMO4.STY, provides you with the same banner lines of text and a decorative line along the top bordering the title "Memorandum" if you choose **W**ith Contents. Choosing Run **M**acro provides you with Default and Optional Information dialog boxes.

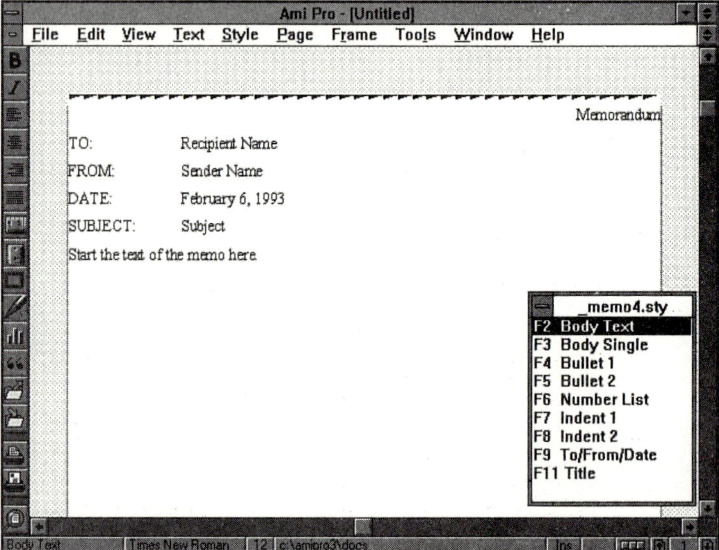

Fig. A.24
_MEMO4.STY

_MEMO5.STY

When you choose the **W**ith Contents option, this memo style sheet provides you with the title "Memo" in reversed type followed by a screened frame and common banner lines. If you choose Run **M**acro, Default and Optional Information dialog boxes appear. Paragraph styles are limited to body and bullets; however, you can add your own styles to any style sheet.

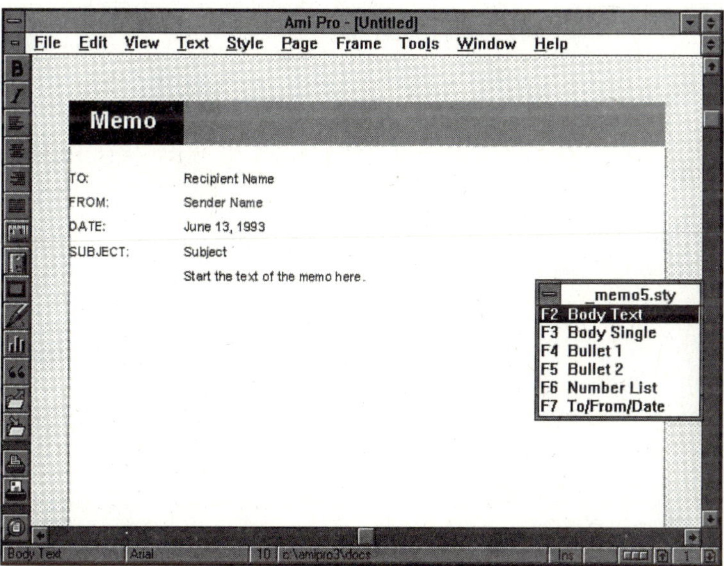

Fig. A.25
_MEMO5.STY

_MEMO6.STY

When you choose **W**ith Contents, this style sheet provides you with a decorative border, the title "Memorandum," and common banner lines. The Run **M**acro option provides both the Default and Optional Information. The paragraph styles include one bullet, one numbered list, and one indent style for a useful variety.

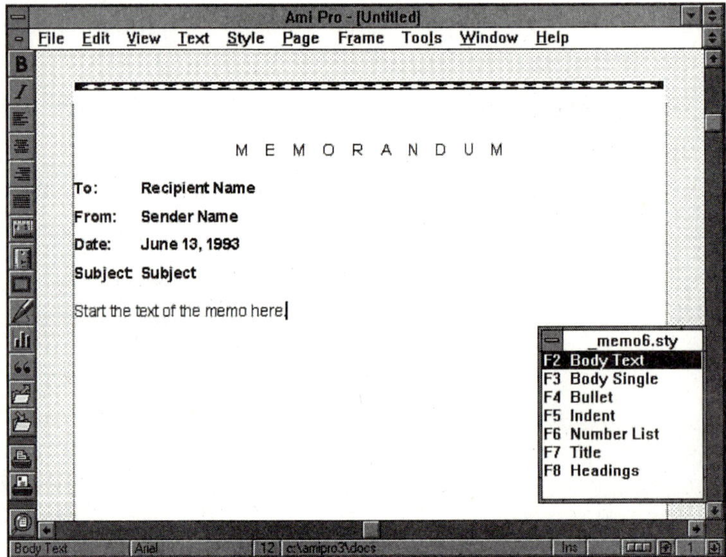

Fig. A.26
_MEMO6.STY

_MERGDAT.STY

Use this style to merge data files with field names and delimiters. The Run **M**acro feature is useful with this style sheet. The macro inserts a Data File dialog box on which you can enter your data. As shown in figure A.27, the dialog box looks like an index card. Other options are available in this dialog box, including adding, deleting, and updating records; beginning a new record; closing a record; field management; and sorting records. When you close the Data File dialog box, Ami Pro prompts you to save the current record; then Ami Pro prompts you to save the current document as a file. The paragraph styles include single, two bullet styles, body text, a numbered list, subhead, and a title.

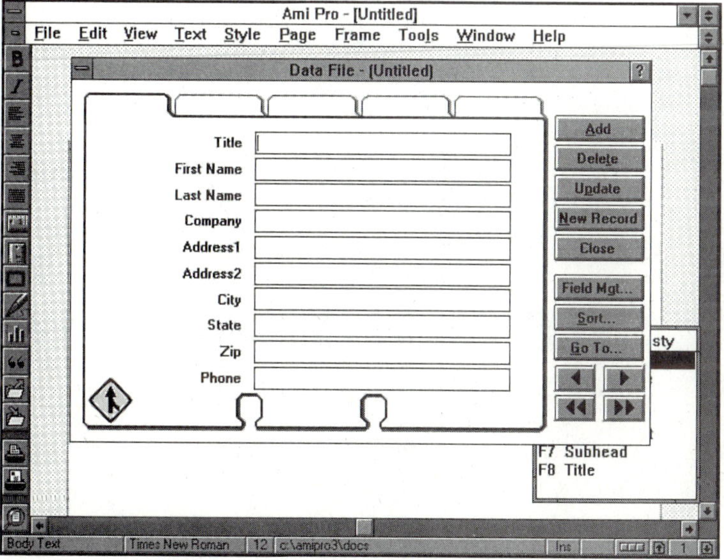

Fig. A.27
_MERGDAT.STY

_MERGLET.STY

Use the _MERGLET.STY in conjunction with the _MERGDAT.STY. This style sheet consists of the _LETTER1.STY but with merge fields, as shown in figure A.28. Choose Run **M**acro, and the style sheet provides you with the Default Information dialog box that fills in the merge fields.

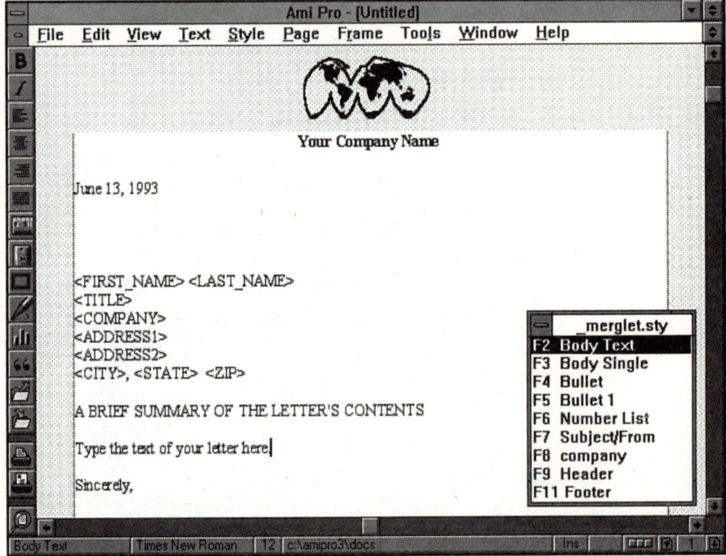

Fig. A.28
_MERGLET.STY

_NEWSLT1.STY

When you choose the **W**ith Contents option for this newsletter style, the style provides you with various frames plus instructions for their use. A nameplate frame (title) bordered with rules, a dateline frame (press), and two graphic frames are included. If you choose Run **M**acro with this style sheet, the Default Information dialog box asks for the title name and press information. The Optional Information dialog box asks for the issue number and date. If you choose one of the graphic frames, the Frame Options dialog box appears with a list of choices for you to insert (picture, table, chart, drawing, equation, text, or nothing).

The newsletter design consists of two columns, with paragraph styles for various headings and subtitles, bullets and numbered lists, and headers and footers.

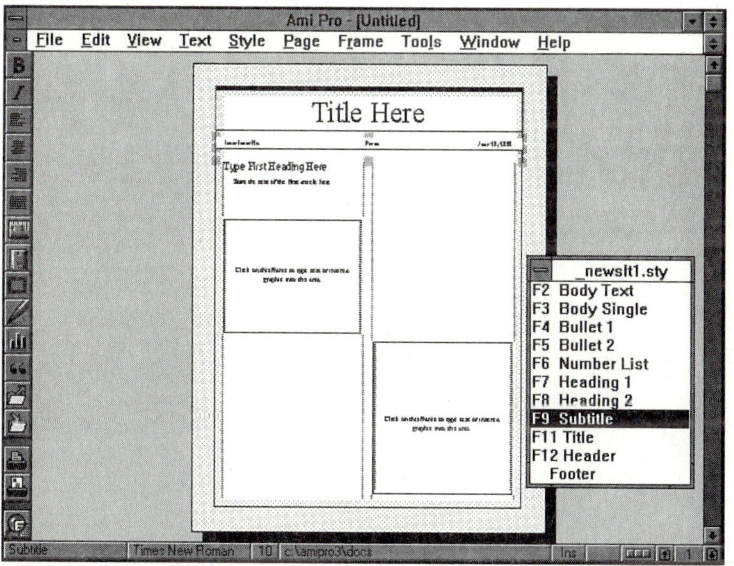

Fig. A.29 _NEWSLT1.STY in full page view.

_NEWSLT2.STY

When you choose the **W**ith Contents option, this newsletter style sheet provides you with a screened frame for the company name and title, placement for the date and volume number, and directions as to where to start your text. The macros include Default Information (title and company name) and Optional Information (volume number and date).

The design of this style sheet is one column with a graphic box containing the title of the newsletter. The paragraph styles include body text and body single, two bullets, two headings, a numbered list, subtitle, title, header, and footer.

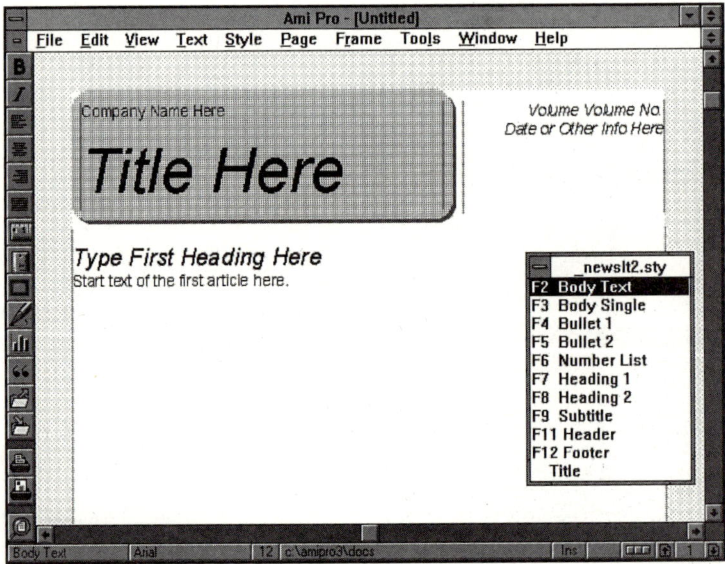

Fig. A.30
_NEWSLT2.STY

_NEWSLT3.STY

When you choose the **W**ith Contents option, this newsletter style sheet provides you with frames for the nameplate, dateline, and graphics. The Run **M**acro option supplies the name of the newsletter (title), the dateline information (press), and issue number. Selecting a frame for a graphic provides you with the Frame Options dialog box; choose to insert picture, table, chart, drawing, equation, text, or nothing.

The design is three columns with a frame between the second and third columns, providing an area for the text to wrap around. A variety of paragraph styles are available, including bullets, numbered lists, headings, subtitle, title, header, and footer.

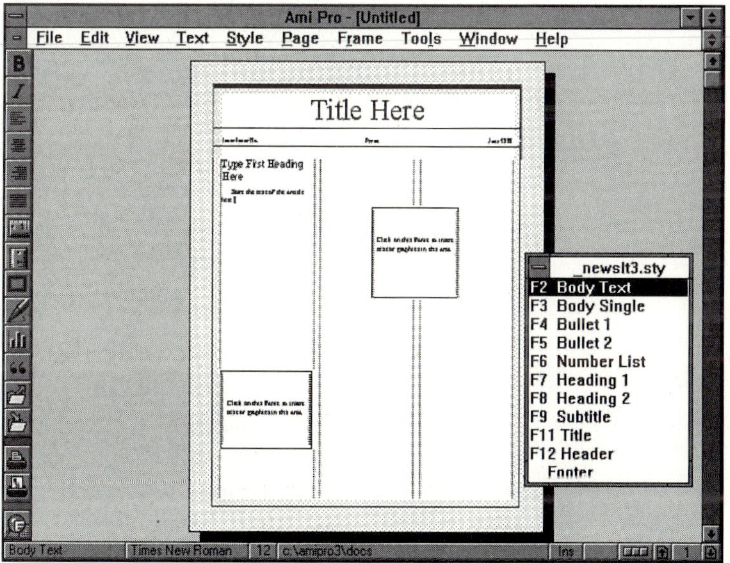

Fig. A.31
_NEWSLT3.STY in full page view.

_NEWSLT4.STY

Tip
If you use this design, add more gutter width between the columns of type for easier reading of the text.

If you choose **W**ith Contents, this newsletter style sheet provides you with many graphic elements, including a page border, vertical inter-column lines, dividing lines between the nameplate and dateline and between the dateline and text, plus a bordered frame for a picture. The style sheet also contains instructions for placing your information. The macros are similar to the other newsletter styles, fill-in title and subtitle information, volume numbers, and so on.

The design consists of a great many lines and borders, a black frame with reversed text, and additional frames and borders for other text.

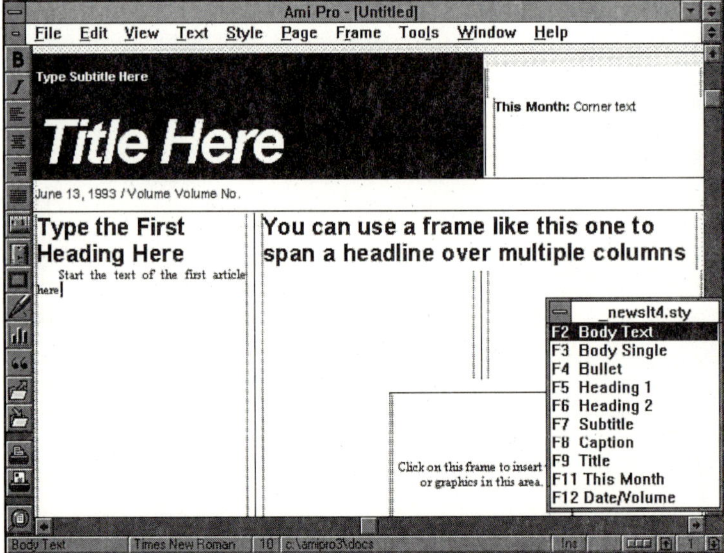

Fig. A.32
_NEWSLT4.STY

_NEWSLT5.STY

The last newsletter style provides you with a graphic, a few lines, and limited paragraph styles when you choose **W**ith Contents. The basic two-column design is simple, yet attractive. The Default and Optional Information dialog boxes (choose Run **M**acro) insert the title, volume number, and so on. Your address positions at the bottom of the page.

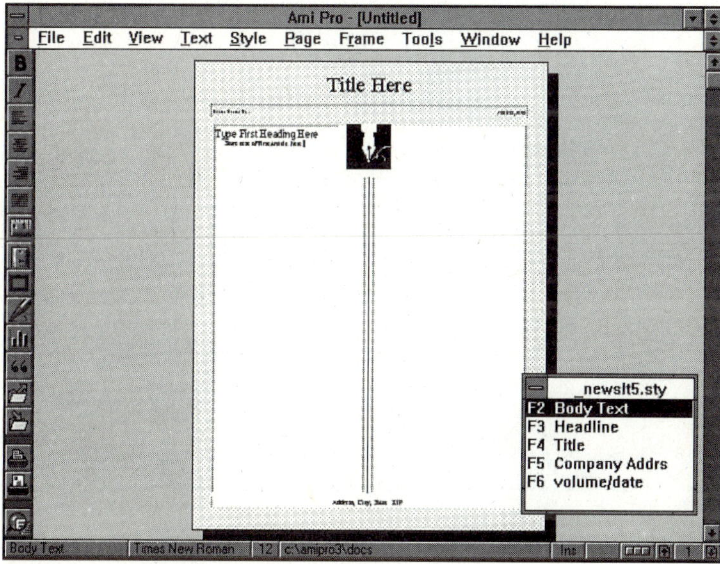

Fig. A.33 _NEWSLT5.STY in full page view.

_OUTLIN1.STY

Choosing **W**ith Contents in this style sheet gives you examples of some outline styles. The formatting for nine outline levels is included in the paragraph styles.

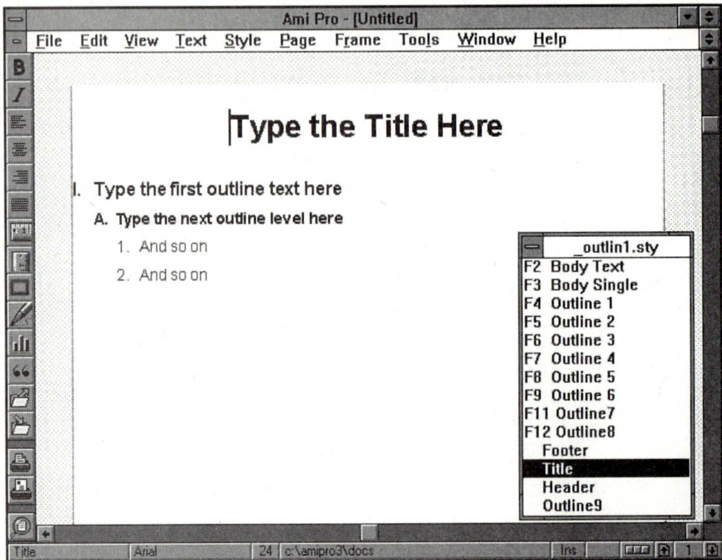

Fig. A.34
_OUTLIN1.STY

_OUTLIN2.STY

When you choose the **W**ith Contents option, this outline style sheet provides a frame in the left margin for a heading and an outline level sample to the right. The wide left margin is bordered on top by a thick line, and the actual page margin (on the right) is bordered on top by a thin line. This style sheet provides you with nine outline levels.

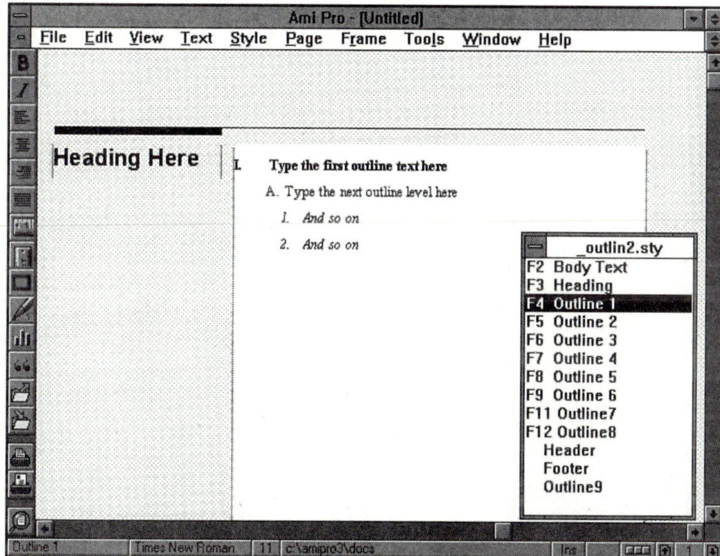

Fig. A.35
_OUTLIN2.STY

_OUTLIN3.STY

This outline style provides a frame in the wide left margin for entering text. The actual page margin contains the outline levels. Selecting **W**ith Contents provides sample text in the frame and on the page. This style includes nine outline levels.

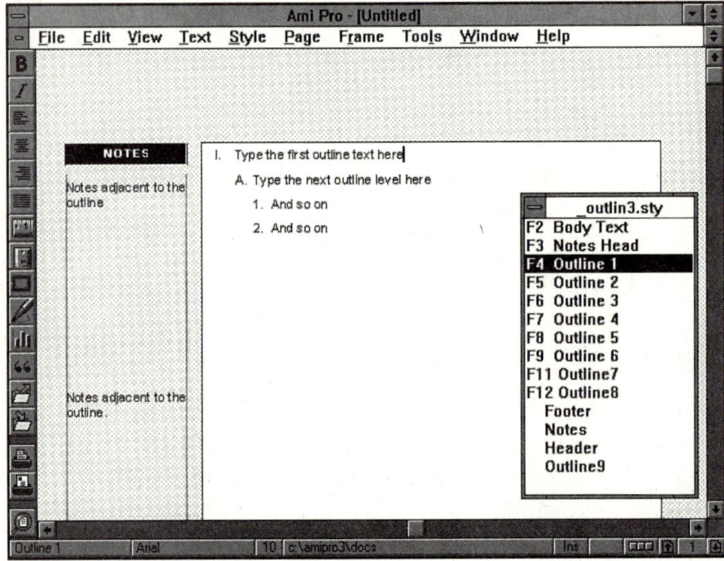

Fig. A.36
_OUTLIN3.STY

_OUTLINE.STY

In contrast to the more complex outline style sheets, _OUTLINE.STY uses a very basic design. Nine outline levels are included, as are paragraph styles for a header, footer, and body text.

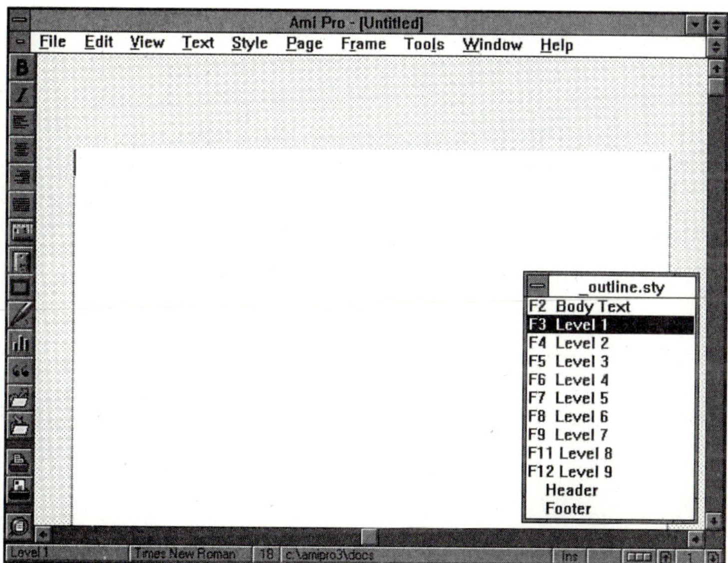

Fig. A.37
_OUTLINE.STY

_OVERHD1.STY

This style sheet provides an overhead projector format that includes a frame at the top of the page with a graphic and reversed text. This style also includes sample text when you choose **W**ith Contents. The paragraph styles include a headline, numbered list, bullet, header, and footer.

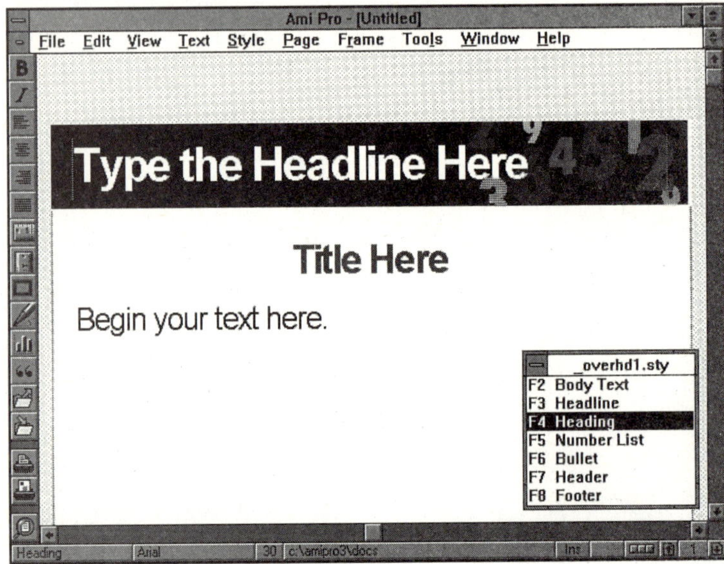

Fig. A.38
_OVERHD1.STY

Tip
This style sheet contains a note box that you can see if you choose **V**iew View **P**references **N**otes. It shows how to copy the frame containing the graphic to other pages.

_OVERHD2.STY

When you choose the **W**ith Contents option, this style sheet provides an overhead projector format including a frame that contains the graphic arrow. The style sheet also provides three lines of sample text, formatted as headline, heading, and body text, respectively. The design is landscape-oriented.

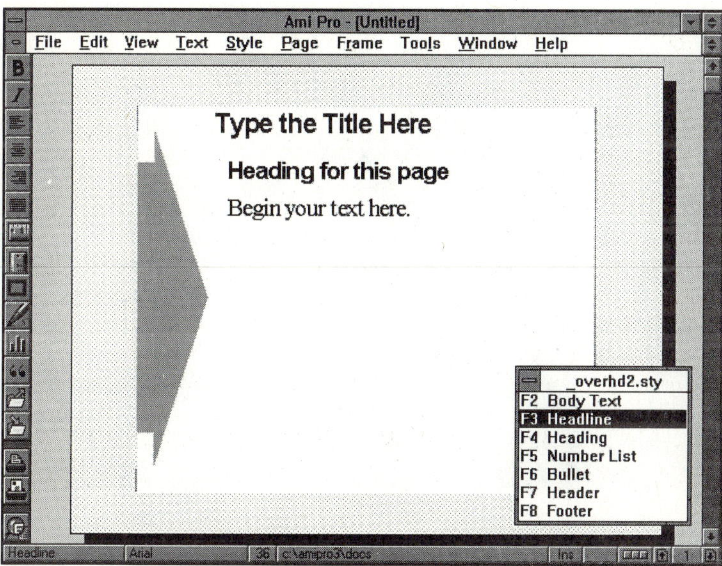

Fig. A.39 _OVERHD2.STY in full page view.

_OVERHD3.STY

When you choose the **W**ith Contents option, this style sheet provides an overhead projector format that includes a full page frame containing a graphic of a starburst. This starburst has an overlapping frame containing the sample text for the title and text.

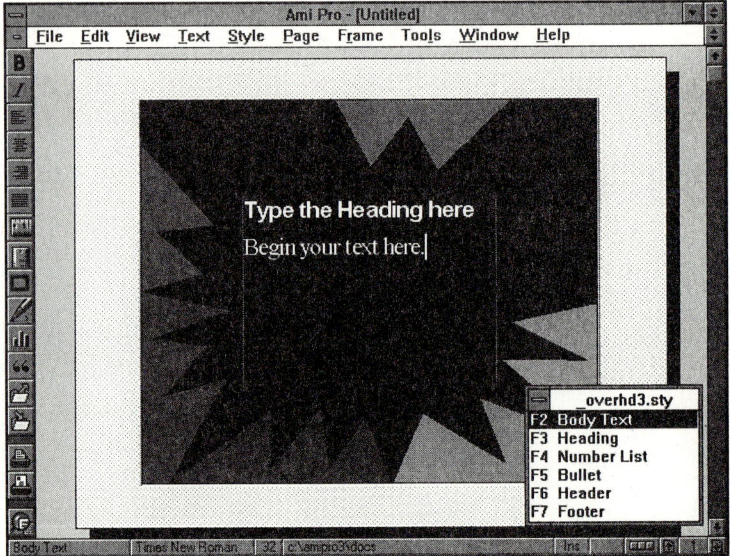

Fig. A.40
_OVERHD3.STY in full page view.

_OVERHD4.STY

This overhead style sheet includes a horizontal line from margin to margin. If you choose **W**ith Contents, the sample text appears as in figure A.41. Paragraph styles provided include bullets, headings, numbered lists, a title, and a header style.

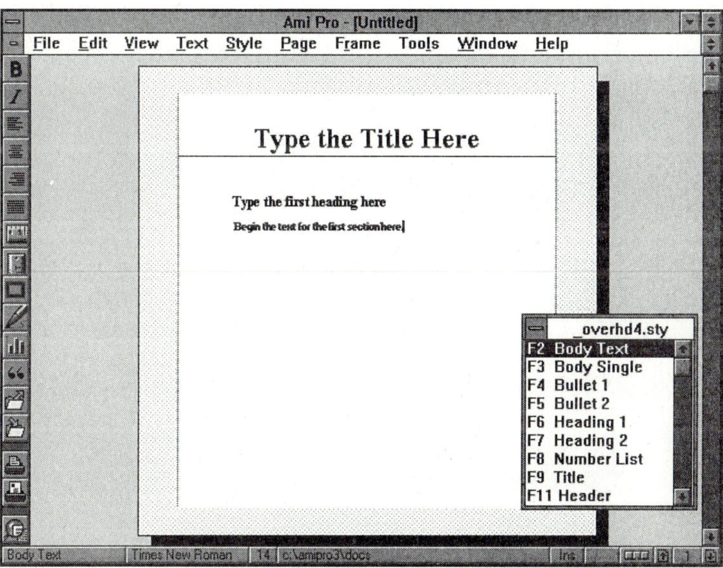

Fig. A.41
_OVERHD4.STY in full page view.

_OVERHD5.STY

When you choose the **W**ith Contents option, this overhead style sheet provides an overhead projector format that includes two lines at the top of the page (one above and one below the title) and sample text. Paragraph styles include bullets, headings, numbered list, title, header, and footer.

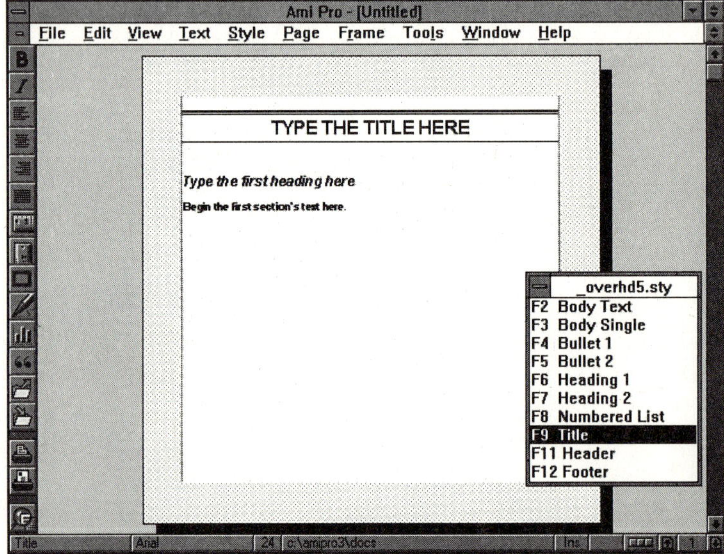

Fig. A.42
_OVERHD5.STY in full page view.

_PHONLST.STY

This style sheet provides you with two columns for listing names and phone numbers. The columns are divided by a vertical line. Merge fields are included when you open the style sheet, so you can merge a database file containing names and phone numbers.

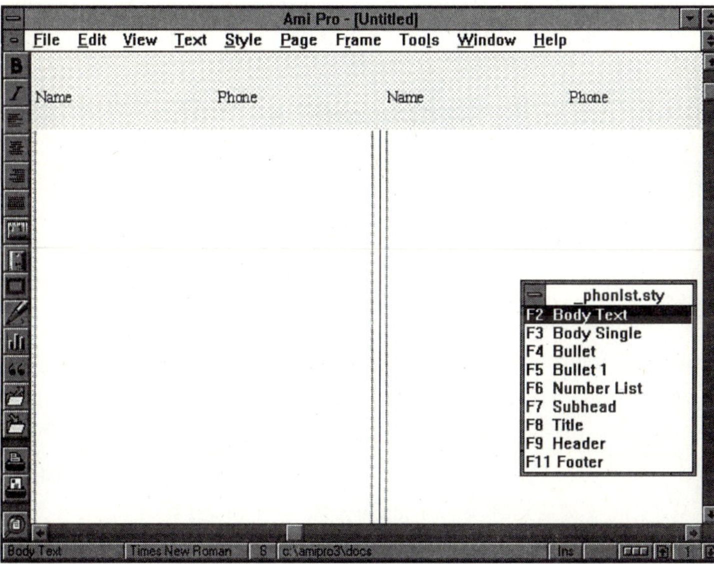

Fig. A.43
_PHONLST.STY

> **Note**
>
> This style sheet uses default tabs at 1/2 inch. Using the ruler, you can set a right leader tab at four inches to help organize your phone list. You also may want to add more tabs if you merge to a database. See Chapter 5, "Working with Page Layout," for information about using the current ruler.

_PRESS1.STY

When you choose **W**ith Contents, this press release style sheet provides you with thick, screened lines bordering the top and bottom of the title, company information, heads, and so on. Choose Run **M**acro, and the Default Information dialog box appears. Optional Information enables you to enter the headline, first heading, city, and state, as you want them to appear in the document. Several paragraph styles are included, such as bullets, headings, a header, and a footer.

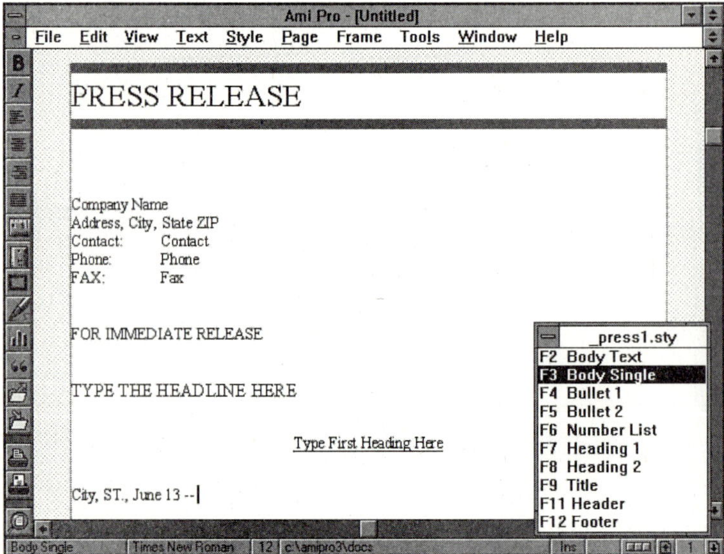

Fig. A.44
_PRESS1.STY

_PRESS2.STY

The second press release style sheet provides you with a horizontal line bordering the top of the page, a graphic heading (News Release) at the top of the page, and sample text when you choose **W**ith Contents. Select Run **M**acro. The Default Information dialog box prompts you for your company name, address, and so on. The Optional Information dialog box enables you to enter the headline, city, and state. This style sheet also includes a note box suggesting what to include in a three-part press release.

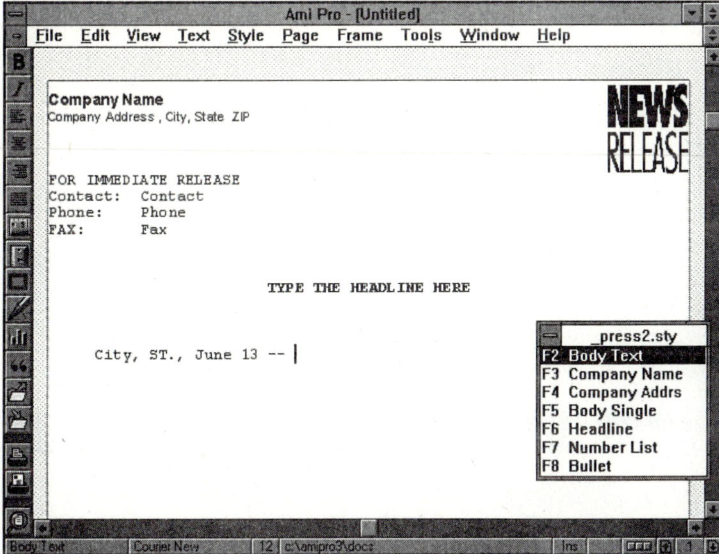

Fig. A.45
_PRESS2.STY

_PROPOS1.STY

This style sheet provides a format to create a proposal with two horizontal lines (one above and one below the title) and extra paragraph styles such as bullets, headings, numbered list, title, header, and footer. If you choose **W**ith Contents, sample text appears.

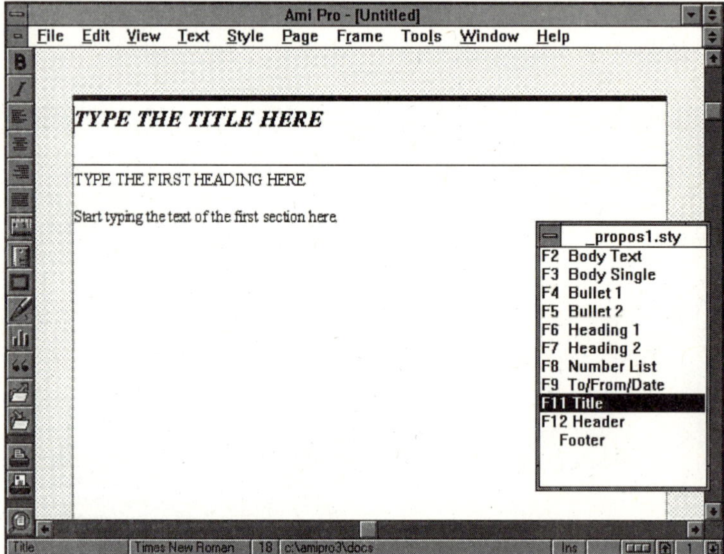

Fig. A.46
_PROPOS1.STY

_PROPOS2.STY

When you choose **W**ith Contents, this style sheet provides you with a format to create a proposal that includes a header with a place for the company name, page number, and current system date; four floating frames with sample headings (Introduction, Management, Project Profile, and Summary); and a note box. The note box gives you ideas of what to include in the proposal. Run **M**acro creates a Default Information dialog box that completes the header information automatically.

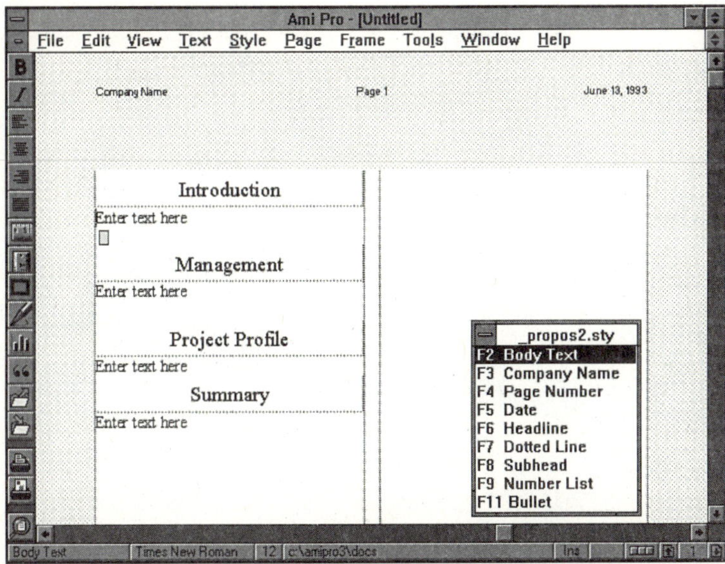

Fig. A.47
_PROPOS2.STY

_REPORT1.STY

This style sheet provides you with a report format that includes a horizontal line and common paragraph styles such as bullet, heading, numbered list, header, footer, and title.

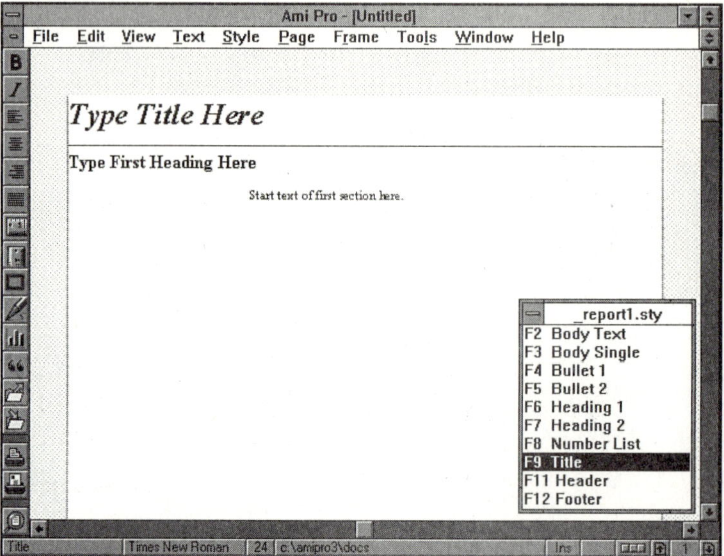

Fig. A.48
_REPORT1.STY

_REPORT2.STY

When you choose the **W**ith Contents option, this style sheet provides a two-column report format that includes shadowed title frames with the reversed sample text (Summary, Introduction, Report Title, and Recommendations). The format provides a place to enter text below each floating title frame.

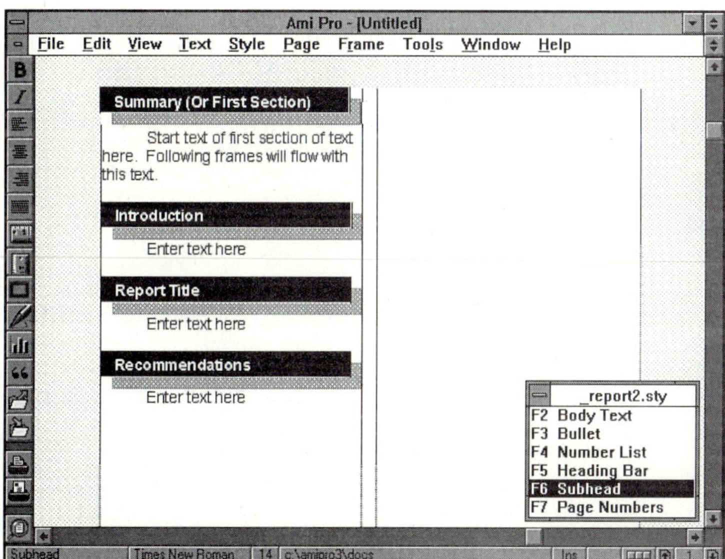

Fig. A.49
_REPORT2.STY

_REPORT3.STY

When you choose the **W**ith Contents option, this style sheet provides a two-column report format that includes a title frame spanning two columns. The paragraph styles include bullet, heading, numbered list, title, header, and footer.

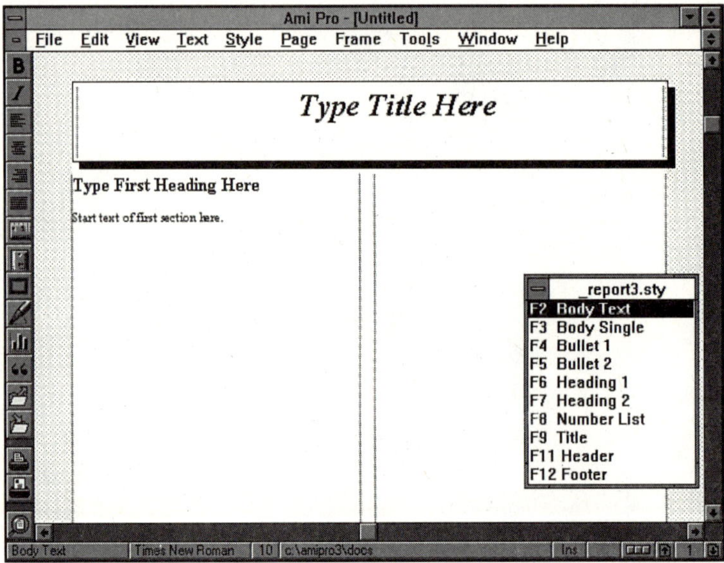

Fig. A.50
_REPORT3.STY

_REPORT4.STY

This report style sheet provides you with shadowed title frames with reversed sample text in a one-column format. Paragraph styles include body text, heading, subhead, numbered list, bullet, and page numbers.

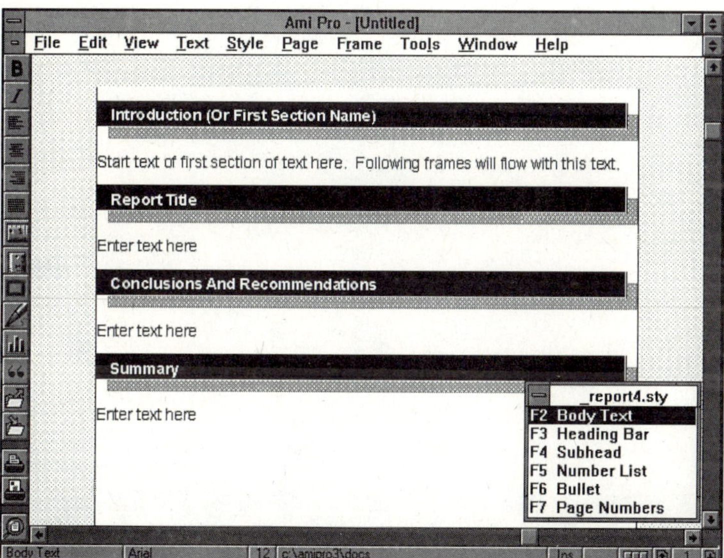

Fig. A.51
_REPORT4.STY

_TERMPPR.STY

The term paper style sheet provides you with a basic format and paragraph styles including bullets, subhead, title, numbered list, header, and footer.

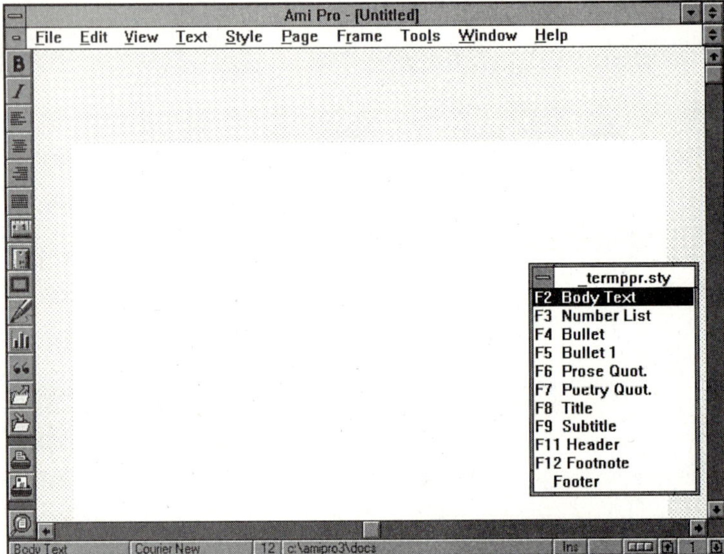

Fig. A.52
_TERMPPR.STY

_TITLE1.STY

When you choose the **W**ith Contents option, this style sheet provides a title page format with a full-page border; sample headings for the company, address, and so on; sample text, lines above and below the title; and a place for the current system date. The paragraph styles include body text, report title, and dotted line. This style also includes a macro for Default Information and Optional Information when you choose Run **M**acro.

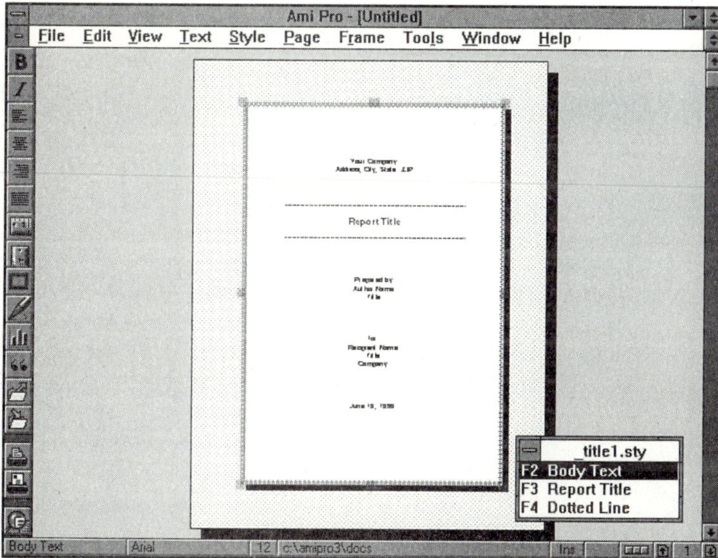

Fig. A.53
_TITLE1.STY in full page view.

_TITLE2.STY

When you choose the **W**ith Contents option, this title page style sheet provides you with a full page frame with a multiple-line border, another border with a thin line, sample text for a title, name of author, and name and address space at the bottom. Paragraph styles are limited to body text, title, and subtitle. This style also includes a macro (Run **M**acro) for Default Information and Optional Information.

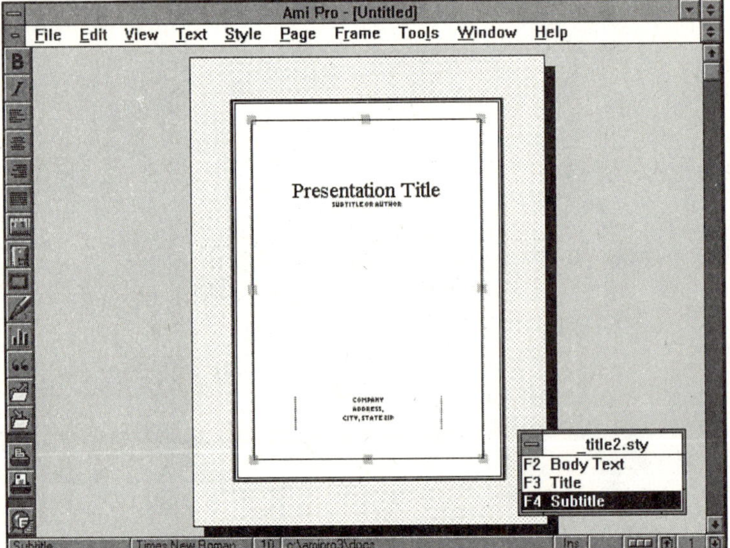

Fig. A.54
_TITLE2.STY in full page view.

_TITLE3.STY

This title page style sheet includes a full-page screened frame with a drop shadow; sample text for the company name; report title (with lines above and below); other sample text, such as author's name, recipient's name, and so on; and the current system date. This style also includes a macro (Run **M**acro) for Default Information and Optional Information.

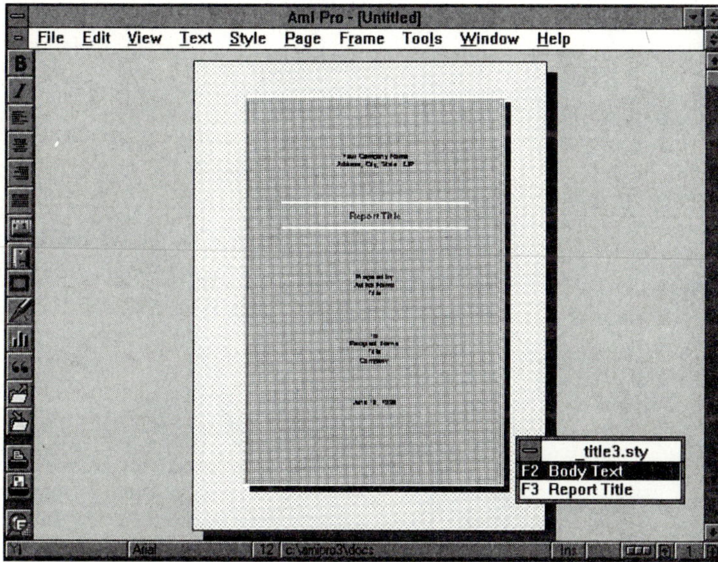

Fig. A.55
_TITLE3.STY

_TOC.STY

This style sheet provides the format that Ami Pro uses to generate a table of contents. The paragraph styles include nine contents levels, nine page number levels, table text, header, footer, and so on. The page layout provides for a wide left margin.

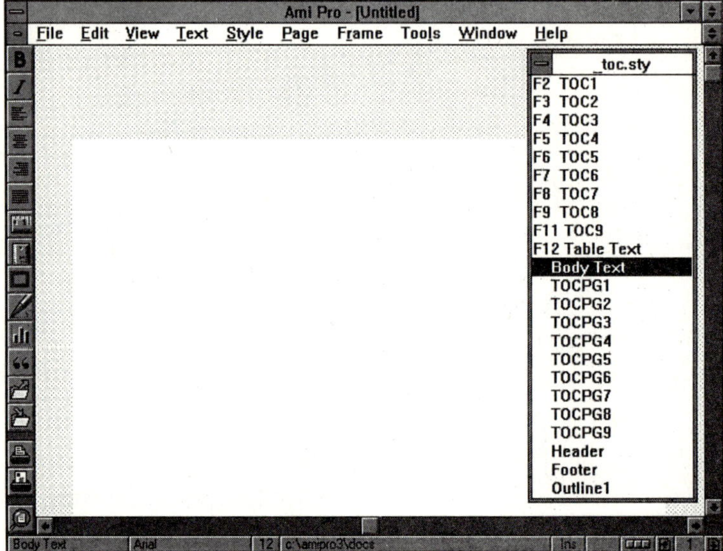

Fig. A.56
_TOC.STY in full page view.

Index

Symbols

A

D

F

G

H

I

J-K

L

M

N

Q

R

S

T

U

V

W-Z